Foreign Relations of the United States, 1955–1957

Volume XVI

Suez Crisis July 26– December 31, 1956

Editor in Chief   John P. Glennon

Editor   Nina J. Noring

United States Government Printing Office
Washington
1990

DEPARTMENT OF STATE PUBLICATION 9740

OFFICE OF THE HISTORIAN

BUREAU OF PUBLIC AFFAIRS

For sale by the Superintendent of Documents, U.S. Government Printing Office
Washington, D.C. 20402

Preface

The publication *Foreign Relations of the United States* constitutes the official record of the foreign policy of the United States. The importance of publishing the complete and comprehensive documentary record of U.S. diplomacy was set forth in an order by Secretary of State Frank B. Kellogg on March 26, 1925, and supplemented and revised by Department of State regulations in the *Foreign Affairs Manual*. (2 FAM 1350–1353)

The Office of the Historian, Bureau of Public Affairs, is directed by the *Foreign Affairs Manual* to collect, edit, and publish the authoritative diplomatic record, including papers from other concerned government agencies. (1 FAM 857) Official historians of the Department of State seek out relevant official foreign affairs documentation in other agencies and documentary repositories bearing on subjects documented in the volumes of the series. The topics to be documented are determined by the Editor in Chief of the series in concert with the compilers of individual volumes.

Secretary of State Kellogg's order, as codified in the *Foreign Affairs Manual*, remains the official guidance for editorial preparation of the series:

"The editing of the record is guided by the principles of historical objectivity. There may be no alteration of the text, no deletions without indicating the place in the text where the deletion is made, and no omission of facts which were of major importance in reaching a decision. Nothing may be omitted for the purpose of concealing or glossing over what might be regarded by some as a defect of policy." (2 FAM 1352)

Principles of Selection for Foreign Relations, 1955–1957, Volume XVI

The documentation in this particular volume was collected and selected by Dr. Nina J. Noring of the Office of the Historian from the Department of State's centralized and decentralized files and the records of the Dwight D. Eisenhower Presidential Library. Dr. Noring also examined selected records of the Joint Chiefs of Staff deposited at the National Archives and Records Administration and obtained a small amount of additional documentation from the

Department of Defense and the Central Intelligence Agency. For a complete listing of particular collections consulted, see the List of Sources.

Dr. Noring observed the following criteria in selecting documents for inclusion in this volume:

The U.S. decision-making process: The central focus of this volume is the process of U.S. foreign policy formulation and execution, as it serves to illuminate the key decisions made during the Suez Crisis and in regard to U.S. policy toward Egypt and Israel. To this end, documents have been included such as: memoranda of conversations held at the highest level of the U.S. Government; National Security Council and Department of State policy papers and memoranda discussing policy options; intelligence reports on which policy decisions were based; communications with foreign governments; and policy recommendations and analyses sent by U.S. missions abroad. In order to examine more fully the decision-making process, drafts of documents that were never formally executed and early drafts of key communications are also included.

Multilateral policy execution: Documents were selected to emphasize U.S. communications and interaction with Egypt, Israel, France, and the United Kingdom. U.S. interchanges with the Soviet Union over the Suez Crisis also receive full treatment, as do U.S. attendance at the First and Second Suez Conferences at London and deliberations at the United Nations. In addition, documentation is included that provides an overview of the U.S. diplomatic strategy that took into account the concerns of more than 20 other countries. Exchanges with these countries are frequently condensed in annotation or treated in summary form in the Special Suez Reports prepared by the Department of State's Executive Secretariat during the crisis.

Relations with Israel and Egypt: Documentation has been included to record the key issues under discussion between the United States and Israel, including the rise in tension between Israel and the surrounding Arab countries, during the period prior to the outbreak of hostilities on October 29. U.S. discussions with Egypt during this period were consumed by the Suez Canal question. Following the Arab-Israeli war, documentation is presented concerning U.S. interest in the Arab-Israeli peace process. Minimal coverage is given to developments within Egypt and Israel, as reported by U.S. Embassies, that do not bear directly on the crisis.

Crisis diplomacy: Detailed coverage has been given to the period of hostilities, October 29–November 7, 1956, in order to trace the U.S. response at times on a minute-by-minute basis. Again the main focus is on U.S. relations with Egypt, Israel, France, and Great Britain, but documentation is also included to indicate the multilateral nature of the crisis, the dangers of Soviet involvement, and the role such nations as Canada played in helping to resolve it.

Intelligence operations: A special effort was made to determine what intelligence information was available to the United States concerning the military intentions of Israel, Great Britain, and France. Special reports of the Watch Committee were obtained from the Central Intelligence Agency and these are printed together with reports from the U.S. Government's Intelligence Advisory Committee. Also printed is a detailed retrospective, prepared in the Department of State and reviewed by the Central Intelligence Agency, which examines the entire question of what information on this subject was available to the United States at the time. While Dr. Noring did not have access to the full range of documentation on U.S. intelligence operations and the diplomacy of the Suez Crisis, the available intelligence records allow for an extensive and balanced compilation on this aspect of the diplomacy of the crisis.

Editorial Methodology

The documents are presented chronologically according to Washington time. Incoming telegrams from U.S. missions are placed according to the time of receipt in the Department of State, rather than the time of transmission; memoranda of conversations are placed according to the time and date of the conversation, rather than the date the memorandum was drafted. When a source text does not indicate a particular date or time of day, the editors have used the President's and the Secretary of State's daily appointment records, internal and other documentary evidence, and at times the logic of events to determine, as closely as possible, the precise placement of the document. There are two major exceptions to the order of placement: documentation on the First and Second Suez Canal Conferences at London is arranged chronologically according to London time.

Editorial treatment of the documents published in the *Foreign Relations* series follows Office style guidelines, supplemented by guidance from the Editor in Chief and the Chief Technical Editor. The source text is reproduced as exactly as possible, including marginalia or other notations, which are described in footnotes. Obvious typographical errors are corrected, but other mistakes and omissions in the source text are corrected by bracketed insertions: a correction is set in italic type; an omission in roman type. Brackets are also used to indicate text that has been omitted by the compiler because it deals with an unrelated subject. Ellipses are inserted to replace material that remained classified after the declassification review process. Ellipses of three or four periods identify excisions of less than a paragraph; ellipses of seven periods spread across the

page identify excisions of an entire paragraph or more. All ellipses
and brackets that appear in the source text are so identified by
footnotes.

The first footnote to each document indicates the document's
source, original classification, distribution, drafting information, and,
in the case of telegrams, the time of receipt in the Department of
State. The source footnote also provides the background of important documents and policies, indicates if the President or Secretary of
State read the document, and records its ultimate disposition.

Editorial notes and additional annotation summarize pertinent
material not printed in this volume, indicate the location of additional documentary sources, describe diplomatic reportage and key
events, and provide summaries of and citations to public statements
that supplement and elucidate the printed documents. Information
derived from memoirs of participants and other first-hand accounts,
available when this volume was originally compiled in 1979, has
been used where possible to supplement the official record.

Declassification Review Procedures

Declassification review of the documents selected for publication is conducted by the Division of Historical Document Review in
the Bureau of Diplomatic Security, Department of State. The review
is made in accordance with the Freedom of Information Act, the
Privacy Act, and the criteria established in Executive Order 12356
regarding:

1) military plans, weapons, or operations;
2) the vulnerabilities or capabilities of systems, installations,
projects, or plans relating to the national security;
3) foreign government information;
4) intelligence activities (including special activities), or intelligence sources or methods;
5) foreign relations or foreign activities of the United States;
6) scientific, technological, or economic matters relating to the
national security;
7) U.S. Government programs for safeguarding nuclear materials
or facilities;
8) cryptology; and
9) a confidential source.

Declassification decisions entailed concurrence of the appropriate geographic and functional bureaus in the Department of State
and of other concerned agencies of the U.S. Government, and
communication with foreign governments regarding documents or
information of those governments. The principle of declassification
review is to release as much information as is consistent with
contemporary requirements of national security and sound foreign

relations; some documents or portions of documents are necessarily withheld.

Dr. Noring compiled this volume under the supervision of Editor in Chief John P. Glennon. M. Paul Claussen provided initial planning and direction. Lynn Chase and Bret D. Bellamy of the Historian's Office prepared the lists of sources, names, and abbreviations. Rita M. Baker, Chief of the Editing Division of the Historian's Office, performed the technical editing. Barbara Ann Bacon of the Publishing Services Division (Paul M. Washington, Chief) oversaw production of the volume. Do Mi Stauber prepared the index.

William Z. Slany
The Historian
Bureau of Public Affairs

Contents

Preface.. III

List of Sources.. XI

List of Abbreviations... XXI

List of Persons.. XXVII

Suez Crisis

United States response to Egyptian nationalization of the Suez Canal
    Company and related Arab-Israeli developments, July 27–October 29,
    1956:
  Initial U.S. reaction to Egyptian nationalization of the Suez Canal
    Company, July 27–July 28 1
  The London tripartite conversations, July 29–August 2 34
  Continued U.S. consideration of the Suez sitation; United States diplomatic
    activity prior to the Suez Canal Conference, August 3–15 128
  The Suez Canal Conference at London; inception of the Anderson mission
    to Saudi Arabia, August 16–23... 212
  U.S. involvement in the Suez Committee; the Anderson mission to Saudi
    Arabia; the Menzies mission to Egypt, August 24–September 9 284
  Secretary Dulles' proposal for a Suez Canal Users' Association,
    September 9–18... 448
  The Second Suez Canal Conference at London; continued consideration of
    the Users' Association proposal; increasing violence along the
    Israel–Jordan border; the Macmillan visit to Washington,
    September 19–October 4... 516
  U.N. Security Council debate on the Suez Canal question; the Iraqi
    proposal to move troops into Jordan; Anglo-American differences over
    SCUA; Israeli mobilization; and U.S. diplomatic activity prior to the
    outbreak of hostilities, October 5–29 638

United States diplomacy and the Sinai and Suez Campaigns,
    October 29–November 6, 1956:
  The Israeli invasion of Sinai and the Anglo-French ultimatum,
    October 29–30 821

Deadlock in the U.N. Security Council; convening of the first emergency
session of the U.N. General Assembly; the Anglo-French air
bombardment of Egyptian installations; creation of a U.N. Emergency
Force, October 30–November 5 881
Anglo-French assault on the Canal Zone; the threat of Soviet intervention;
acceptance of a cease-fire, November 5–6 984

United States efforts to obtain a British, French, and Israeli withdrawal from
occupied territory, November 7–December 31, 1956:
Referral of the Middle East item to the U.N. General Assembly; the
European oil supply problem and the activation of the Middle East
Emergency Committee's plan; Anglo-French decision to withdraw
forces from the Suez Canal Zone, November 7–December 4 1038
U.S. retrospection on the Anglo-French Israeli collusion; NATO summit
meeting at Paris; continued U.S. interest in General Assembly action
concerning the Palestine and Suez questions; agreement on financial
arrangements for clearing the Suez Canal, December 5–31 1249

Index 1345

List of Sources

Unpublished Sources

Department of State

1. *Indexed Central Files.* The main source of documentation for this volume and for other volumes on the Middle East in the 1955–1957 triennium of *Foreign Relations of the United States* was the Department of State's indexed central files. Documents in classes 200 (protection of interests), 400 (trade relations), 500 (cultural relations), 600 (international relations), 700 (internal political and national defense affairs), 800 (internal economic and social affairs), and 900 (communication, transportation, science) were searched for decimal combinations involving all countries in the Middle East (country nos. 74, 80, and 83 through 88) and for the Middle Eastern relationships of the United States (no. 11), Western Europe (no. 40), the United Kingdom (no. 41), France (no. 51), and the Soviet Union (no. 61), and Turkey (no. 82).

Other files and related subfiles searched for Middle East related materials include: 033 (official visits); 110.11–17 (Department of State senior officials files); 120.15 (special missions); 123 (Department of State personnel files); various files in class 300 (international organizations and conferences); and 601 (diplomatic representation). Other documents were located through pursuing cross-references and referenced telegrams.

More than 100 separate decimal designations from the Department of State Central Files are cited in this volume. Documentation on the major and some of the minor themes covered in this volume are located in the following files:

974.7301: Suez Canal question, main file
674.84A: Egyptian-Israeli relations
684A.86: Israeli-Arab relations, main file for Arab-Israeli war
684A.85: Israeli-Jordanian relations
103–XMB: U.S. Export-Import Bank, Israeli interest in loan
110.11–DU: Secretary of State John Foster Dulles, correspondence, travel, conversations
110.13–HE: Deputy Under Secretary of State Loy Henderson, involvement in Suez Committee
274.1122 and 280.1122: U.S. evacuation plans for the Middle East
280.4122 and 285.41: British evacuation plans for the Middle East
320: U.N. General Assembly, consideration of Middle East hostilities
320.5770 and 320.5780: U.N. Emergency Force and related U.N. peace efforts
330: U.N. Security Council, consideration of Suez question and Middle East hostilities
396.1–LO: Various Suez conferences at London
611.41, 611.51, 611.74, 611.80, 611.84A and subfiles: U.S. relations with the United Kingdom, France, Egypt, the Middle East, and Israel, respectively

641.74 and subfiles: Anglo-Egyptian relations; 641.74231 for blocked accounts
651.74: Franco-Egyptian relations
674.00: General Egyptian international relations
711.11–EI: President Dwight D. Eisenhower
711.56382: U.S. military bases in Turkey
740.5 and subfiles: North Atlantic Treaty Organization, interest in Suez Crisis and Middle East hostilities
741.5 and subfiles: United Kingdom national defense and military activity
751.5 and subfiles: French national defense and military activity
774.00: General internal political and military situation in Egypt
774.11: President Gamal Abdul Nasser
774.5, 774.5–MSP, 774.56: Egyptian national defense, military assistance and equipment
784A.00: General Israeli political situation
784A.5 through 784A.5622: Israeli National Defense, military assistance and supply; 784A.5622 for fighter aircraft
840.04 and 840.2553: Western Europe's interest in fuel and petroleum, respectively
841.10: United Kingdom financial matters
841.2553: United Kingdom interest in petroleum
884A.10: Israeli financial matters, especially interest in Export-Import Bank loan

2. *Lot Files.* Documents from the central files were supplemented by lot files of the Department, which are decentralized files created by operating areas. A list of the lot files used or consulted for this volume follows:

Conference Files: Lot 62 D 181

See entry under Washington National Records Center.

Current Economic Developments: Lot 70 D 467

See entry under Washington National Records Center.

Current Foreign Relations: Lot 64 D 189

Master set of the Department of State classified publication *Current Foreign Relations* for the years 1954–1962, as maintained by the Executive Secretariat of the Department of State.

Daily Press Conferences of the Department of State

See entry under National Archives and Records Administration.

Daily Summaries: Lot 60 D 530

Master set of the Department of State classified internal publication Daily Secret Summary and Daily Top Secret Summary for the years 1953–1958, as maintained by the Executive Secretariat of the Department of State.

INR–NIE Files

Files retained by the Bureau of Intelligence and Research.

INR Files: Lot 58 D 776

Miscellaneous files of the Bureau of Intelligence and Research for the years 1946–1957.

IO Files

Master files of the Reference and Documents Section of the Bureau of International Organization Affairs of the Department of State, comprising the official U.N. documentation and classified Department of State records on United States policy in the U.N. Security Council, Trusteeship Council, Economic and Social Council, and various special and ad hoc committees for the period from 1946 to currency.

IO Files: Lot 60 D 113

Consolidated files of the Assistant Secretary of State for International Organizations Affairs for the years 1955–1957.

IO Files: Lot 71 D 440

Master files of classified records and correspondence of United States delegations to sessions of the U.N. General Assembly for the years 1945–1965, as maintained by the Bureau of International Organization Affairs.

L/NEA Files: Lot 64 D 290

Miscellaneous country and subject files maintained by the Assistant Legal Adviser for Near Eastern, South Asian, and African Affairs for the years 1948–1961.

London Embassy Files: Lot 61 F 14

Files maintained by the Embassy in the United Kingdom for the years 1956-1958.

Luce Files: Lot 64 F 26

Records of Clare Boothe Luce as Ambassador to Italy, 1953–1956.

NEA Files: Lot 58 D 545

Contains country files for Egypt, Nepal, Libya, Pakistan, The Sudan, Syria, Tunisia, Cyprus, Turkey, and Yemen, and subject files for United Nations, Personnel, and the Baghdad Pact for the year 1956, as maintained by the Bureau of Near Eastern, South Asian, and African Affairs.

NEA Files: Lot 58 D 722

Files maintained by the Office of Near Eastern Affairs for the years 1954–1956, relating to the Middle East Watch.

NEA Files: Lot 59 D 518

Top Secret records pertaining to the Near East, and in particular to Project Alpha and the Anderson Mission, for the years 1954–1957, as maintained by the Office of Near Eastern Affairs of the Bureau of Near Eastern, South Asian, and African Affairs.

NEA Files: Lot 59 D 582

Files on Lebanon and Israel for the years 1953–1958, including reports, memoranda, and correspondence, as maintained by the Office of Near Eastern Affairs of the Bureau of Near Eastern, South Asian, and African Affairs.

NEA/IAI Files: Lot 70 D 229

Political and refugee files on the Middle East for the years 1950–1964, as maintained by the Office of Israel and Arab-Israel Affairs of the Bureau of Near Eastern, South Asian, and African Affairs.

NEA/IAI Files: Lot 72 D 438

Miscellaneous Top Secret records concerning the Middle East for the years 1955–1964, as maintained by the Office of Israel and Arab-Israel Affairs.

NEA/NE Files: Lot 58 D 398

Files on Israel and Lebanon for the years 1954–1956, as maintained by the Office of Near Eastern Affairs of the Bureau of Near Eastern, South Asian, and African Affairs.

NEA/NE Files: Lot 59 D 38

Files maintained by the Office of Near Eastern Affairs for the years 1956–1957, including documentation on Syria, Egypt, and the Sudan.

NEA/NE Files: Lot 60 D 48

Multi-topic subject files for Sudan, Syria, and Egypt for the years 1954–1957.

NEA/NE Files: Lot 61 D 59

Miscellaneous files maintained by the Office of Near Eastern Affairs for the years 1953–1960, including documentation on Syria, Egypt, and the United Arab Republic.

Phleger Files: Lot 58 D 517

Miscellaneous files of Herman Phleger, Legal Adviser of the Department of State, concerning the Middle East, Latin America, and the Far East for the years 1953–1957.

Presidential Correspondence: Lot 66 D 204

Exchanges of correspondence between the President and heads of foreign governments for the years 1953–1964, as maintained by the Executive Secretariat of the Department of State.

Presidential Memoranda of Conversation: Lot 66 D 149

Chronological record of memoranda of conversation with foreign visitors for the years 1956–1964, as maintained by the Executive Secretariat.

PPS Files: Lot 66 D 487

Subject files, country files, chronological files, documents, drafts, and related correspondence of the Policy Planning Staff for the year 1956.

Secretary's Memoranda of Conversation: Lot 64 D 199

Chronological collection of the Secretary of State's memoranda of conversation for the years 1953–1960, as maintained by the Executive Secretariat.

Secretary's Staff Meetings: Lot 63 D 75

Chronological collection of the minutes of the Secretary of State's Staff Meetings during the years 1952–1960, as maintained by the Executive Secretariat.

S/P Files: Lot 66 D 487

See PPS Files.

S/P–NSC Files: 61 D 167

Serial file of memoranda relating to National Security Council questions for the years 1950–1961, as maintained by the Policy Planning Staff.

S/S–NEA Files: Lot 61 D 417

See State–JCS Meetings.

S/S–NSC (Miscellaneous) Files: Lot 66 D 95

Administrative and miscellaneous National Security Council documentation, including NSC Records of Action, as maintained by the Executive Secretariat for the years 1947–1963.

S/S–NSC Files: Lot 66 D 148

Miscellaneous files concerning subjects considered by the National Security Council during the years 1949–1962, as maintained by the Executive Secretariat.

State–JCS Meetings: Lot 61 D 417

Top Secret records of meetings between the Joint Chiefs of Staff and representatives of the Department of State for the years 1951–1959 and selected problem files on the Middle East for the years 1954–1956, as maintained by the Executive Secretariat.

UNP Files: Lot 58 D 224

Miscellaneous country and subject files relating to political issues before the United Nations for the years 1943–1956, including the Collective Measures Committee, Palestine, and Suez, as retired by the Office of United Nations Political and Security Affairs.

United States Mission to the United Nations, New York

USUN Files

Files of the United States Mission to the United Nations, 1950 to date.

Central Intelligence Agency

CIA Files

Documents received by the Office of the Historian from the Central Intelligence Agency by request.

Department of Agriculture

See entry under National Archives and Records Administration.

Department of Defense

Joint Chiefs of Staff

JCS Files

> Documents received upon request by the Office of the Historian from the Historical Office of the Joint Chiefs of Staff.

> See also JCS Records under National Archives and Records Administration.

International Cooperation Administration

> See entry under Washington National Records Center.

Dwight D. Eisenhower Library, Abilene, Kansas

Dulles Papers

> Records of John Foster Dulles, 1952–1959, including General Memoranda of Conversation, Meetings with the President, General Telephone Conversations, White House Telephone Conversations, and files "Suez Problem", "Miscellaneous Papers–U.K.(Suez Crisis)", and "Israel Relations 1951–1957".

President's Daily Appointments Record

> Records of Dwight D. Eisenhower as President, Daily Appointments, 1953–1961.

Staff Secretary Records

> Records of the Office of the White House Staff Secretary, 1952–1961, including records of Paul T. Carroll, Andrew J. Goodpaster, L. Arthur Minnich, Jr., and Christopher H. Russell.

White House Central Files

> Records of Dwight D. Eisenhower as President, 1953–1961. Documents cited in this volume are from the confidential file, "Suez Canal Crisis."

Whitman File

> Papers of Dwight D. Eisenhower as President of the United States, 1953–1961, maintained by his personal secretary, Ann C. Whitman. The Whitman File includes the following elements: the Name Series, the Dulles–Herter Series, Eisenhower (DDE) Diaries, Ann Whitman (ACW) Diaries, National Security Council Records, Miscellaneous Records, Cabinet Papers, Legislative Meetings, International Meetings, the Administration Series, and the International File.

National Archives and Records Administration

Daily Press Conferences of the Department of State

> National Archives Record Group 59, Transcripts of daily news conferences of the Department of State, January 1946–December 1975.

JCS Records

> National Archives Record Group 218, Records of the United States Joint Chiefs of Staff and the Chairman of the Joint Chiefs of Staff.

Office of the Secretary of Agriculture Records

> National Archives Record Group 16, Records of the Office of the Secretary of Agriculture. Subject files of the Secretary of Agriculture for the years 1879–1972, containing reports, letters, memoranda, and other records arranged under topical headings.

Princeton University Library, Princeton, New Jersey

Dulles Papers, Dulles Daily Appointment Book

> Daily log of the meetings and appointments of Secretary of State John Foster Dulles for the years 1953–1959.

Washington National Records Center

Conference Files: FRC 59–83–0066

> Lot 62 D 181: Collection of documentation on official visits by heads of government and foreign ministers to the United States and on major international conferences attended by the Secretary of State for the years 1956–1958, as maintained by the Executive Secretariat.

Current Economic Developments: FRC 72 A 6248

> Lot 70 D 467: Master set of the Department of State classified internal publication *Current Economic Developments* for the years 1945–1969, as maintained in the Bureau of Economic Affairs.

ICA Director's Files: FRC 61 A 32

> Subject file of the Director of the International Cooperation Administration, containing correspondence, memoranda, reports, messages, and other material accumulated from 1955 to 1958.

Published Sources

U.S. Government Documentary Collections

U.S. Department of State. *American Foreign Policy: Current Documents, 1956* (Washington: U.S. Government Printing Office, 1959)
————. Department of State *Bulletin,* 1956, Vols. XXXIV and XXXV (Washington: U.S. Government Printing Office, 1956–1957)
————. *The Suez Canal Problem, July 26-September 22, 1956* (Washington: U.S. Government Printing Office, 1956)
————. *United States Policy in the Middle East, September 1956–June 1957* (Washington: U.S. Government Printing Office, 1957)
U.S. National Archives and Records Administration. *Public Papers of the Presidents of the United States: Dwight D. Eisenhower, 1956* (Washington: U.S. Government Printing Office, 1958)
U.S. Congress. Senate. *Executive Sessions of the Senate Foreign Relations Committee (Historical Series),* Vol. VIII, Eighty-fourth Congress, Second Session, 1956 (Washington: U.S. Government Printing Office, 1978)
————. *Joint Hearings before Subcommittees of the Committee on the Judiciary and the Committee on Interior and Insular Affairs, United States Senate, Eighty-fifth Congress, First Session, Parts 1–4* (Washington: U.S. Government Printing Office, 1957)

Memoirs

Note: The following memoirs which contain information on the Suez Crisis were consulted at the time this volume was prepared in 1979. The Department of State takes no responsibility for their accuracy nor endorses their interpretation of the events.

Adams, Sherman. *First Hand Report* (New York: Harper & Brothers, 1961)

Aldrich, Winthrop W., "The Suez Crisis: A Footnote to History," *Foreign Affairs*, April 1967, pp. 541–552

Ben Gurion, David. *Israel: A Personal History* (New York: Funk & Wagnalls, 1971)
————. *Israel: Years of Challenge* (New York: Holt, Rinehart and Winston, 1963)

Bohlen, Charles E. *Witness to History, 1929-1969* (New York: W.W. Norton & Company, 1973)

Bowie, Robert R. *Suez 1956* (London: Oxford University Press, 1974)

Burns, Lt. Gen. E.L.M. *Between Arab and Israeli* (New York: Obolensky, 1963)

Butler of Saffron Walden, Richard Austen Butler, Baron. *The Art of the Possible* (Boston: Gambit, 1972)

Cooper, Chester. *The Lion's Last Roar, Suez, 1956* (New York: Harper & Row, 1978)

Copeland, Miles. *The Game of Nations: The Amorality of Power Politics* (London: Wiedenfeld & Nicolson, 1969)

Dayan, Moshe. *Diary of the Sinai Campaign* (New York: Harper & Row, 1976)
————. *Moshe Dayan: Story of My Life* (New York: Morrow, 1976)

Eban, Abba. *Abba Eban: An Autobiography* (New York: Random House, 1977)

Eden, Sir Anthony, Earl of Avon. *Full Circle: The Memoirs of Anthony Eden* (Boston: Houghton Mifflin, 1960)

Eisenhower, Dwight D. *The White House Years. Waging Peace, 1956-1961* (Garden City, N.Y.: Doubleday and Company, 1965)

Eveland, Wilbur Crane. *Ropes of Sand: America's Failure in the Middle East* (New York and London: W.W. Norton & Company, 1980)

Ewald, William Bragg, Jr. *Eisenhower the President, Crucial Days: 1951–1960* (Englewood Cliffs, N.J.: Prentice-Hall, Inc., 1981)

Gallman, Waldemar J. *Iraq Under General Nuri: My Recollections of Nuri al-Said, 1954-1958* (Baltimore: Johns Hopkins Press, 1964)

Georges-Picot, Jacques. *The Real Suez Crisis: The End of a Great Nineteenth Century Work* (New York: Harcourt Brace Jovanovich, 1978)

Haykal, Muhammed Hasanayn. *The Cairo Documents: The Inside Story of Nasser and His Relationship With World Leaders, Rebels and Statesmen* (Garden City, N.Y.: Doubleday, 1973)

Hayter, Sir William. *The Kremlin and the Embassy* (London: Hodder & Stoughton, 1966)

Hughes, Emmet John. *The Ordeal of Power: A Political Memoir of the Eisenhower Years* (New York: Atheneum, 1963)

Hussein, King of Jordan. *Uneasy Lies the Head: An Autobiography* (London: Heinemann, 1962)

Khrushchev, Nikita S. *Khrushchev Remembers* (Boston: Little, Brown and Company, 1970)

Lloyd, Selwyn. *Suez/1956* (London: Jonathan Cape, 1978)

Lodge, Henry Cabot. *As It Was, An Inside View of Politics and Power in the 50's and 60's* (New York: W.W. Norton & Company, Inc., 1976)
————. *The Storm Has Many Eyes* (New York: W.W. Norton & Company, Inc., 1973)

Macmillan, Harold R. *Riding the Storm, 1956-1959* (New York: Harper & Row, 1971)

Meir, Golda. *My Life* (New York: G.P. Putnam's Sons, 1975)

Menzies, Sir Robert. *Afternoon Light, Some Memories of Men and Events* (London: Cassell, 1967)

Mollet, Guy. *Bilan et Perspectives Socialistes* (Paris: Librarie Plon, 1958)

Moncrieff, Anthony (ed.). *Suez, Ten Years After* (London: British Broadcasting Corporation, 1967)

Murphy, Robert. *Diplomat Among Warriors* (Garden City, N.Y.: Doubleday, 1964)

Nutting, Anthony. *No End to a Lesson* (London: Constable, 1967)

Pearson, Lester. *Mike. The Memoirs of the Right Honorable Lester B. Pearson.* Vol. 2, 1948-1957 (New York: Quadrangle, 1973)

Peres, Shimon. *David's Sling. The Arming of Israel* (London: Weidenfeld & Nicolson, 1970)

Pineau, Christian. *Suez/1956* (Paris: Robert Laffont, 1976)

Spaak, Paul Henri. *The Continuing Battle: Memoirs of a European, 1936-1966* (London: Wiedenfeld, 1971)

Trevelyan, Humphrey. *The Middle East in Revolution* (Boston: Gambit, Inc., 1970)

Urquhart, Brian. *Hammarskjold* (New York: Alfred A. Knopf, 1972)

List of Abbreviations

Editor's Note: This list does not include standard abbreviations in common usage; unusual abbreviations of rare occurrence which are clarified at appropriate points; and those abbreviations and contractions which, although uncommon, are understandable from the context.

A, airgram
AA, anti-aircraft
ACSP, Arab Collective Security Pact
AFSC, American Friends Service Committee
AKA, Attack Cargo Vessel
AL, Arab League or Arab Legion (Transjordan)
ALCSP, Arab League Collective Security Pact
ALO, series indicator for military telegrams
AmEmb, American Embassy
AMS, Agricultural Marketing Services, Department of Agriculture
AP, Associated Press; Atlantic Pact
ARA, Bureau of Inter-American Affairs, Department of State
ARAMCO, Arabian-American Oil Company
ARMATT, Army Attaché
ASRP, Arab Socialist Resurrectionist Party (Syrian)
AWD, Allen W. Dulles
B/D, barrels of oil per day
BG, David Ben Gurion
BIS, Bank of International Settlements
BJSM, British Joint Services Mission or British Joint Staff Mission
BMEO, British Middle East Office

BNA, Office of British Commonwealth and Northern European Affairs, Department of State
BSFMC, Bilateral San Francisco Memorandum of Conversation
CA, circular airgram
CARE, Cooperative for American Remittances to Everywhere
CASU, Cooperative Association of Suez Canal Users
CCS, Combined Chiefs of Staff
CF, Conference File
CHMAAG, Chief, Military Assistance Advisory Group
CIA, Central Intelligence Agency
CIA/LC, Central Intelligence Agency, Legislative Counsel
CINCARIB, Commander in Chief, Caribbean
CINCFE, Commander in Chief, Far East
CINCLANT, Commander in Chief, Armed Forces, Atlantic
CINCNELM, Commander in Chief, U.S. Naval Forces, Eastern Atlantic and Mediterranean
CINCPAC, Commander in Chief, Pacific
CINCSAC, Commander in Chief, Strategic Air Command
CINCUSAFE, Commander in Chief, United States Air Force, Europe
CINCUSAREUR, Commander in Chief, United States Army in Europe

circ, circular telegram

cirtel, circular telegram

COM, communications

comite, committee

CONAD, Continental Air Defense Command

CONADR, Continental Air Defense Command Regulation

ConGen, Consulate General

Contel, Consulate telegram

CRO, Commonwealth Relations Office

CS, Chief of Staff

CSA, Chief of Staff, U.S. Army

CSAFM, Chief of Staff, Air Force Memorandum

CSS, Commodity Stabilization Service, Department of Agriculture

CVA, Attack Aircraft Carrier

CVS, Anti-Submarine Warfare Aircraft Carrier

CX, Army telegram designator

CZ, Canal Zone

DA, Development Assistance

DCI, Director of Central Intelligence

DEFREPAMA, Defense Representative Army Attaché

Del, Delegation

Delga, series indicator for telegrams from the U.S. Delegation at the United Nations General Assembly; also used to refer to the U.S. Delegation at the United Nations General Assembly

Dento, series indicator for telegrams sent from the Denver White House

Depcirgram, Department of State circular airgram

Depcirtel, Department of State circular telegram

Deptel, Department of State telegram

desp, despatch

DIB, Defense Intelligence Briefing

DirGen, Director General

DL, Demarcation Line

DRN, Division of Research for the Near East, South Asia, and Africa, Department of State

DRS, Division of Research for the Soviet Union and Eastern Europe, Department of State

DRW, Division of Research for Western Europe, Department of State

Dulte, series indicator for telegrams from Secretary of State Dulles while away from Washington

DZ, Demilitarized Zone

E, Bureau of Economic Affairs, Department of State

EARIS, Egyptian-American Rural Improvement Service

ECA, Economic Cooperation Administration

E–I, Egyptian-Israeli

EIMAC, Egyptian-Israeli Mixed Armistice Commission

E.J., Eric Johnston

Embdesp, Embassy despatch

Embtel, Embassy telegram

ES, Emergency Session of the United Nations General Assembly

ES–I, First Emergency Session of the United Nations General Assembly

ESS, Egyptian-Syrian-Saudi Pact

ETW, Eden Talks, Washington

EUR, Bureau of European Affairs, Department of State

EUR/RA, Office of European Regional Affairs, Bureau of European Affairs, Department of State

EURATOM, European Atomic Energy Community

EXIM Bank/EX–IM, Export-Import Bank

FAF, French Air Force

FAO, Food and Agricultural Organization of the United Nations

FAS, Foreign Agricultural Service, Department of Agriculture

FBI, Federal Bureau of Investigation

FBIS, Foreign Broadcast Information Service

FE, Bureau of Far Eastern Affairs, Department of State

FinAtt, Financial Attaché

FLO, Foreign Liaison Office

FN, Division of Financial Affairs, Department of State

F.O., Foreign Office

FOA, Foreign Operations Administration

FonMin, Foreign Minister; Foreign Ministry

FonOff, Foreign Office

FPSC, Foreign Petroleum Supply Committee

FRC, Foreign Relations Committee of the U.S. Senate

FSD, Division of Fuels, Department of State

FTC, Federal Trade Commission

FY, fiscal year

FYI, for your information

G, Office of the Deputy Under Secretary of State

G–2, Army (or Marine) general staff section dealing with intelligence at the divisional level or higher

GA, United Nations General Assembly

GAA, General Armistice Agreement

Gadel, series indicator for telegrams to the U.S. Delegation at the United Nations General Assembly

GHQ, General Headquarters

GMT, Greenwich mean time

GOE, Government of Egypt

GOI, Government of Israel; Government of India

GOL, Government of Lebanon

GOS, Government of Syria

GSA, General Services Administration

H, Office of the Assistant Secretary of State for Congressional Relations, Department of State

HICOM, High Commission(er)

Histradut, General Federation of Jewish Labor in Israel

HJK, Hashemite Jordanian Kingdom

HJK–IMAC, Jordanian-Israeli Mixed Armistice Commission

HKJ, Hashemite Kingdom of Jordan

HM, His/Her Majesty

HMG, His/Her Majesty's Government

HQ, Headquarters

IAC, Intelligence Advisory Committee

IBRD, International Bank for Reconstruction and Development

IC, Division of International Conferences, Department of State

ICA, International Cooperation Administration

ICA/W, International Cooperation Administration, Washington

ICAO, International Civil Aviation Organization

ICJ, International Court of Justice

IDAB, International Development Advisory Board

IDF, Israeli Defense Forces

IDF–FLO, Israel Defense Forces–Foreign Liaison Office

I–E, Israeli-Egyptian

IEG, Imperial Ethiopian Government

IFC, International Finance Corporation

IG, Israeli Government

IIS, Israeli Intelligence Service

IMF, International Monetary Fund

INR, Bureau of Intelligence and Research, Department of State

INS, International News Service

IO, Bureau of International Organization Affairs, Department of State

IO/OES, Office of International Economic and Social Affairs, Department of State

IO/OIA, Office of International Administration, Department of State

IPC, Iraq Petroleum Company

IRD, International Resources Division, Department of State

ISA, Office of the Assistant Secretary of Defense for International Security Affairs or the Assistant Secretary of Defense for International Security Affairs; also Office of International Security Affairs, Department of Defense

ISMAC, Israeli-Syrian Mixed Armistice Commission

JCS, Joint Chiefs of Staff

Jlem, Jerusalem

JSPC, Joint Strategic Plans Committee of the Joint Chiefs of Staff

JSSC, Joint Strategic Survey Committee

Jugs, Yugoslavs

JVP, Jordan Valley Plan; Jordan Valley Proposal

K, kilometer

kw, kilowatt

L, Office of the Legal Adviser, Department of State

L/E, Office of the Assistant Legal Adviser for Economic Affairs, Department of State

L/NEA, Office of the Assistant Legal Adviser for Near Eastern, South Asian, and African Affairs, Department of State

LE, Egyptian pounds

Leb, Lebanon

Lon, London

MA, Military Attaché

MAAC, Mutual Assistance Advisory Committee

MAAG, Military Assistance Advisory Group

MAC, Mixed Armistice Commission
MAG, Military Advisory Group
Mapai, Israeli Labor Party
Mapam, Israeli United Workers' Party
MATS, Military Air Transport Service
MC, Memorandum of Conversation; Office of Munitions Control, Department of State
MCM, Milliard Cubic Meters
MDA, Mutual Defense Assistance
MDAP, Mutual Defense Assistance Program
ME, Middle East
MEEC, Middle East Emergency Committee
MEPPG, Middle East Policy Planning Group
MilAtt, Military Attaché
MinDef, Minister or Ministry of Defense
MinFonAff, Minister or Ministry of Foreign Affairs
MP, Member of Parliament (United Kingdom)
MSA, Mutual Security Agency/Act/ Assistance
MSP, Mutual Security Program
MSTS, Military Sea Transport Service
mytel, my telegram
NAC, North Atlantic Council; National Advisory Council
NATO, North Atlantic Treaty Organization
NE, Near East; Office of Near Eastern Affairs, Department of State
NEA, Near East and Africa; Bureau of Near Eastern, South Asian, and African Affairs, Department of State
NEACC, Near East Arms Coordinating Committee
NH, Note to Holders
Niact, communications indicator requiring attention by the recipient at any hour of the day or night
NIC, National Indications Center
NIE, National Intelligence Estimate
Noforn, not releasable to foreign nationals
NSC, National Security Council
NZ, New Zealand
O, Office of the Deputy Under Secretary of State for Administration
OCB, Operations Coordinating Board
ODM, Office of Defense Mobilization

OEEC, Organization for European Economic Cooperation
OFD, Office of Financial and Development Policy, Department of State
ONE, Office of National Estimates
ORM, Office of Refugee and Migration Affairs, Department of State
OSD, Office of the Secretary of Defense
OSP, Offshore Procurement
PAO, Public Affairs Officer
PCC, Palestine Conciliation Commission
PIO, Public Information Officer
PL, Public Law
PLG, Paris Liaison Group
PM, Prime Minister
PMCG (NY), preparations for the Meeting of the Chiefs of Government (New York)
POL, petroleum, oil, and lubricants
Polto, series indicator for telegrams from the Office of the United States Permanent Representative to the North Atlantic Council to the Department of State
POM (NY) MC, preparations for the October Meetings (of the Foreign Ministers) (New York), Memorandum of Conversation
PPS, Parti Populaire Syrien, Syrian National Party
PriMin, Prime Minister
PTS, proposed talks with the Soviets
R, Office of the Special Assistant for Intelligence, Department of State
R&D, Research and Development
RA, Office of European Regional Affairs, Department of State
RAF, Royal Air Force
RCC, Revolutionary Command Council of Egypt
RCT, Regimental Combat Team
reftel, reference telegram
Res, Resolution
RGT, Army Regimental Combat Team
RLG, Rome Liaison Group
RMA, Reimbursable Military Assistance
RO, Reports and Operations Staff of the Executive Secretariat, Department of State
S, Office of the Secretary of State
S/P, Policy Planning Staff, Department of State
S/PV, Security Council/Procès-Verbal

S/S, Executive Secretariat, Department of State

S/S–RO, Reports and Operations Staff, Executive Secretariat, Department of State

SA, Saudi Arabia

SAC, Strategic Air Command

SAG, Saudi Arabian Government

SC, United Nations Security Council

SCUA, Suez Canal Users Association

SEA, Southeast Asia

SEATO, South East Asia Treaty Organization

Sec, Secretary

Secto, series indicator for telegrams from the Secretary of State (or his delegation) at international conferences

Secy, Secretary

SFIO, Société Française de l'Internationale Ouvrière (French Society of International Socialists)

SHAPE, Supreme Headquarters, Allied Powers, Europe

SNIE, Special National Intelligence Estimate

SOCONY, Standard Oil Company of New York

SOSUS, Sound Surveillance Underwater System

SPC, Special Political Committee of the U.N. General Assembly

SPD, Sozialdemokratische Partei Deutschlands (German Social Democratic Party)

SS, submarine

SY, Division of Security, Department of State

SYG, Secretary-General

T/O & E, Table of Organization and Equipment

TAPLINE, Trans-Arabian Pipeline Company

TC, Truce Commission (in Palestine); United Nations Trusteeship Council

Tedul, series indicator for telegrams to Secretary of State Dulles while away from Washington

Toden, series indicator for telegrams sent to the Denver White House

Tosec, series indicator for telegrams from the Department of State to the Secretary of State (or his delegation) at international conferences

TS, Top Secret

TSO, Truce Supervisory Organization (United Nations)

TVA, Tennessee Valley Authority

TWA, Trans World Airlines

U, Office of the Under Secretary of State

U/MSA, Office of the Special Assistant for Mutual Security Affairs, Department of State

U/PR, Office of the Chief of Protocol, Department of State

UJA, United Jewish Appeal

UK, United Kingdom

UKG, United Kingdom Government

UN, United Nations

UNA, Office of United Nations Affairs, Department of State

UNGA, United Nations General Assembly

UNMIS, United Nations Mission

UNP, Office of United Nations Political and Security Affairs, Department of State

UNRRA, United Nations Relief and Rehabilitation Administration

UNRWA, United Nations Relief and Works Agency for Palestine and the Near East

UNSC, United Nations Security Council

UNSCOP, U.N. Special Committee on Palestine

UNTS, United Nations Truce Supervisor; United Nations Treaty Series

UNTSO, United Nations Truce Supervisory Organization

UNSYG, Secretary-General of the United Nations

UP, United Press

urtel, your telegram

USA, United States Army

USAF, United States Air Force

USAREUR, United States Army, Europe

USARMA, United States Army Attaché

USCINCEUR, United States Commander in Chief, Europe

USDel, U.S. delegation

USG, United States Government

USGADel, United States Delegation at the United Nations General Assembly

USIA, United States Information Agency

USIS, United States Information Service

USLO, United States Liaison Officer

USMC, United States Marine Corps

USNMR, United States National Military Representatiave to Supreme Headquarters, Allied Powers, Europe

USOM, United States Operations Mission

USRO, United States Mission to the North Atlantic Treaty Organization and European Regional Organizations

USSR, Union of Soviet Socialist Republics

USUN, United States Mission at the United Nations

Wafd, Egypt's principal political party

WE, Western Europe; Office of Western European Affairs, Bureau of European Affairs, Department of State

WFTU (WFTCU), World Federation of Trade Unions

WH, White House

ZI, Zone of Interior

List of Persons

Editor's Note: The identification of persons in this list is limited to circumstances and positions under reference in this volume. Historical personages alluded to in the volume and certain minor officials are not identified in this list. All titles and positions are American unless there is an indication to the contrary.

In this and in other editorial material throughout the volume (document headings, footnotes, and editorial notes), every effort has been made to provide recognizable and consistent transliterations of names of individuals from countries using non-Roman alphabets. The transliterations adopted for proper names were those commonly used by the Department of State at the time, or in documents or official publications of the countries concerned. (In the case of Arabic names, differences arise in the transliteration of vowels. The editors have generally rendered the definite article as al- rather than el-, and have omitted diacritical marks.)

Adams, Sherman, Assistant to the President

Adams, Ware, Director of the Office of United Nations Political and Security Affairs, Department of State, from September 1956

Aldrich, Winthrop W., Ambassador to the United Kingdom until February 1, 1957

Allen, George V., Assistant Secretary of State for Near Eastern, South Asian, and African Affairs, January 24, 1955–July 26, 1956; Ambassador to Greece, October 12, 1956–November 13, 1957; Director, United States Information Agency, from November 15, 1957

Alphand, Hervé, Permanent Representative of France at the United Nations until August 24, 1956; Ambassador to the United States from September 10, 1956

Amer, Gen. Abdel Hakim, Egyptian Commander in Chief of the Armed Forces; Minister of War and Marine; Chief Commander of the Egyptian-Syrian Joint Command from October 23, 1956

Anderson, Dillon, Special Assistant to the President for National Security Affairs, April 2, 1955–September 1, 1956; White House Consultant from June 29, 1957

Anderson, Robert B., Special Emissary for the President to the Middle East, January–March 1956, and again in August 1956; Secretary of the Treasury from July 29, 1957

Armstrong, W. Park, Special Assistant for Intelligence, Department of State, until June 16, 1957

Asbjornson, Mildred, Secretary of State Dulles' secretary

Bailey, Ronald W., First Secretary of the British Embassy in the United States until October 25, 1957

Barbour, Walworth, Minister-Counselor of the Embassy in the United Kingdom after February 23, 1956

Barco, James W., Counselor of the Mission to the United Nations from June 16, 1955; also Deputy Representative to the U.N. Security Council from April 12, 1956; also Counselor of the Delegation to the U.N. General Assembly at the 10th, 11th, and 12th Sessions

Beckett, John A., Assistant Secretary of the British Ministry of Fuel and Power

Beckner, Earl R., Associate Chief of the Fuels Division, Department of State, January 29–May 20, 1956; thereafter Chief

Beeley, Harold, British Ambassador to Saudi Arabia, May 1955-June 1956; thereafter Assistant Under Secretary in the British Foreign Office

Ben Gurion, David, Israeli Minister of Defense from February 17, 1955; also Prime Minister from November 3, 1955

Bennett, W. Tapley, Special Assistant to the Deputy Under Secretary of State, August 9, 1955–September 8, 1957

Berding, Andrew H., Assistant Director for Policies and Programs, United States Information Agency, until March 22, 1957; Assistant Secretary of State for Public Affairs from March 28, 1957

Bergus, Donald C., Officer in Charge of Israel-Jordan Affairs, Office of Near Eastern Affairs, Department of State

Bernau, Phyllis D., Secretary of State Dulles' Personal Assistant

Berry, J. Lampton, Special Assistant to the Deputy Under Secretary of State for Administration, October 21, 1955–August 30, 1956; thereafter Deputy Assistant Secretary of State for Near Eastern, South Asian, and African Affairs

Birgi, Nuri, Secretary General of the Turkish Ministry of Foreign Affairs until June 1957; Ambassador to the United Kingdom from June 1957

Black, Eugene, President of the International Bank for Reconstruction and Development

Blackiston, Slator C., Jr., Vice Consul at Jerusalem until February 9, 1956; Consul, February 9–April 8, 1956; Office of Near Eastern Affairs, Department of State, April 8, 1956–March 10, 1957; thereafter Attaché of the Embassy in Lebanon

Bliss, Don C., Bureau of Near Eastern, South Asian, and African Affairs, Department of State, February 13, 1955–June 22, 1957; thereafter Ambassador to Ethiopia

Boggs, Marion W., Coordinator, National Security Council Board of Assistants, until 1957; Director of the National Security Council Secretariat from 1957

Bohlen, Charles E., Ambassador to the Soviet Union until April 18, 1957; Ambassador to the Philippines from June 4, 1957

Boone, Adm. Walter F., USN, Commander in Chief, Naval Forces, Eastern Atlantic and Mediterranean, after May 1, 1956

Bourgès-Maunoury, Maurice, French Minister of Defense, January 31, 1956–June 11, 1957

Bowie, Robert R., Director, Policy Planning Staff, Department of State, until October 18, 1957; Assistant Secretary of State for Policy Planning, August 10, 1955–October 18, 1957; Department of State member of the National Security Council Planning Board, August 28, 1955–October 18, 1957

Brilej, Josa, Permanant Yugoslav Representative at the United Nations from June 1954

Brosio, Manlio, Italian Ambassador to the United States from February 3, 1955

Broustra, Vincent, Head of the French Delegation to the United Nations, 1956

Brownell, Herbert, Jr., Attorney General of the United States

Bulganin, Nikolai A., Soviet Minister of Defense until February 1955; Chairman, Council of Ministers, Presidium Member of the Soviet Communist Party, and Head of Government

Burdett, William C., Jr., Deputy Director, Office of Near Eastern Affairs, Department of State, October 9, 1955–October 7, 1956; Special Assistant to the Assistant Secretary of State for Near Eastern, South Asian, and African Affairs, October 7, 1956–August 11, 1957

Burgess, W. Randolph, Under Secretary of the Treasury for Monetary Affairs until July 1957; Permanent Representative to NATO with personal rank of Ambassador from July 3, 1957

Burke, Adm. Arleigh A., USN, Chief of Naval Operations and member of the Joint Chiefs of Staff from August 1955

Burns, Maj. Gen. Eedson L.M., Canadian Army Officer; Chief of Staff of the United Nations Truce Supervisory Organization until November 1956; Commander, United Nations Emergency Force, from November 1956

Butler, Richard A., British Lord Privy Seal and Leader of the House of Commons, December 1955–January 1957; thereafter Home Secretary

Byroade, Henry A., Ambassador to Egypt, March 10, 1955–September 10, 1956; Ambassador to the Union of South Africa from October 9, 1956

Cabell, Lt. Gen. C.P., USAF, Deputy Director of Intelligence, Central Intelligence Agency

Caccia, Sir Harold, Deputy Under Secretary in the British Foreign Office until November 1956; Ambassador to the United States from November 9, 1956

Carrigan, John W., Consul General at Dhahran, July 20, 1955–August 1957

Casey, Richard G., Australian Minister for External Affairs

Chamoun, Camille, President of Lebanon

Chauvel, Jean, French Ambassador to the United Kingdom

Chiperfield, Robert B., Democratic Congressman from Illinois and member of the House Foreign Affairs Committee

Comay, Michael S., Israeli Ambassador to Canada until April 1957

Connors, W. Bradley, Counselor for Public Affairs at the Embassy in the United Kingdom from July 29, 1955

Cornut-Gentille, Bernard, Permanent French Representative to the U.N. Security Council, August–December 1956

Coulson, Sir John E., Minister of the British Embassy in the United States from October 27, 1955

Crosthwaite, Ponsonby Moore, Deputy Permanent Representative of the United Kingdom at the U.N. Security Council; Alternate Representative at the General Assembly; Alternate Representative on the Disarmament Commission

Dale, William N., First Secretary and Consul of the Embassy in the United Kingdom until July 29, 1956; thereafter Officer in Charge of United Kingdom and Ireland Affairs, Office of British Commonwealth and Northern European Affairs, Department of State

Daridan, Jean Henri, Assistant Director of the Cabinet of the Minister, French Foreign Ministry, February–July 1956; Director General of Political and Economic Affairs from July 5, 1956

De Palma, Samuel, Deputy Director, Office of United Nations Political and Security Affairs, April 8, 1956–August 25, 1957

Dean, Sir Patrick Henry, Assistant Under Secretary of State, British Foreign Office, until August 29, 1956; thereafter Deputy Under Secretary of State

Dillon, C. Douglas, Ambassador to France until January 28, 1957

Dixon, Sir Pierson, Permanent Representative of the United Kingdom at the United Nations

Dulles, Allen W., Director of Central Intelligence

Dulles, John Foster, Secretary of State

Eagleton, William L., Second Secretary and Vice Consul of the Embassy in Iraq until September 14, 1956; thereafter Office of Near Eastern Affairs, Department of State

Eban, Abba, Israeli Ambassador to the United States and Permanent Representative at the United Nations

Eden, Rt. Hon. Sir Anthony, British Prime Minister and First Lord of the Treasury, April 6, 1955–January 10, 1957

Eisenhower, Dwight D., President of the United States

Elbrick, C. Burke, Deputy Assistant Secretary of State for European Affairs until February 14, 1957; thereafter Assistant Secretary of State for European Affairs

Engen, Hans, Permanent Representative of Norway at the United Nations

Faisal ibn al-Aziz ibn Abd al-Rahman al-Faisal al Saud, Saudi Arabian Foreign Minister

Faisal II, King of Iraq

Fawzi, Mahmoud, Egyptian Minister of Foreign Affairs; Chairman of the Egyptian Delegation at the United Nations and Representative at the General Assembly

Finn, Richard B., Special Assistant to the Deputy Under Secretary of State for Political Affairs after February 26, 1956

FitzGerald, Dennis A., Deputy Director for Operations, International Cooperation Administration

Flemming, Arthur S., Director, Office of Defense Mobilization, until February 1957

Foster, Andrew B., Counselor of the Embassy in the United Kingdom

Fulbright, J. William, Democratic Senator from Arkansas and member of the Senate Foreign Relations Committee

Gaitskell, Hugh, British Member of Parliament and Leader of the Labour Party since December 1955

George, Walter F., Democratic Senator from Georgia until January 3, 1957; Chairman, Senate Foreign Relations Committee, until January 3, 1957; Special Ambassador to NATO, January 3–August 4, 1957; died August 4, 1957

Gleason, S. Everett, Deputy Executive Secretary of the National Security Council

Glubb, Lt. Gen. Sir John Bagot, British Chief of the General Staff of the Arab Legion in Jordan until March 2, 1956

Goodpaster, Brig. Gen. Andrew J., USA, Staff Secretary and Defense Liaison Officer to the President; became Brigadier General on January 1, 1957

Gray, Gordon, Assistant Secretary of Defense for International Security Affairs, July 14, 1955–February 27, 1957

Green, Theodore F., Democratic Senator from Rhode Island; Chairman, Senate Foreign Relations Committee, from January 3, 1957

Greene, Joseph N., Jr., Deputy Dirdctor of the Executive Secretariat, Department of State, September 9, 1956–October 1957

Gruenther, Gen. Alfred M., USA, Supreme Allied Commander, NATO, until November 1956

Hagerty, James C., Press Secretary to the President

Hammarskjöld, Dag, Secretary-General of the United Nations

Hanes, John W., Jr., Special Assistant to the Secretary of State until April 1957

Hare, Raymond A., Ambassador to Egypt from September 25, 1956

Harlow, Bryce N., Administrative Assistant to the President
Hayter, Sir William Goodenough, British Ambassador to the Soviet Union until
January 1957
Heath, Donald B., Ambassador to Lebanon from March 9, 1955
Heeney, Arnold D.P., Canadian Ambassador to the United States until April 1957
Henderson, Loy W., Deputy Under Secretary of State for Administration from
January 26, 1955
Hollister, John B., Director of the International Cooperation Administration, July 1,
1955–September 15, 1957
Hoover, Herbert, Jr., Under Secretary of State until February 21, 1957
Howe, Fisher, Deputy Special Assistant for Intelligence, Department of State, until
March 12, 1956; thereafter Director of the Executive Secretariat
Humphrey, George M., Secretary of the Treasury
Hussein, Ahmad, Egyptian Ambassador to the United States
Hussein, King, King of Jordan

Jebb, Sir Hubert Miles Gladwyn, British Ambassador to France
Johnson, Lyndon B., Democratic Senator from Texas; Senate Majority Leader from
January 3, 1955
Johnston, Eric, Chairman of the International Development Advisory Board, Foreign
Operations Administration (after 1956, International Cooperation Administration)
Jones, G. Lewis, Jr., Minister-Counselor of the Embassy in Iran, November 9,
1955–July 27, 1956; Ambassador to Tunisia from October 4, 1956
Jones, John Wesley, Director, Office of Western European Affairs, Department of
State, until February 14, 1957
Joxe, Louis, Secretary General of the French Foreign Ministry from July 5, 1956

Kalijarvi, Thorsten V., Deputy Assistant Secretary of State for Economic Affairs
until March 14, 1957; Assistant Secretary of State for Economic Affairs, March
15–September 26, 1957
Khrushchev, Nikita S., First Secretary of the Central Commitee of the Soviet
Communist Party
Kidron, Mordecai R., Israeli Deputy Representative to the United Nations
Kirk, Roger, Reports and Operations Staff, Executive Secretariat, Department of
State, until May 5, 1957
Kirkpatrick, Ivone A., British Permanent Under Secretary of State for Foreign
Affairs
Kiselev, Yevgeniy Dmitrievich, Soviet Ambassador to Egypt from February 13, 1956
Knowland, William F., Republican Senator from California; Senate Minority Leader
and member of the Senate Foreign Relations Committee

Laboulaye, François de, Second Counselor of the French Embassy in the United
States
Lall, Arthur S., Permanent Representative of India to the United Nations
Lange, Halvard, Norwegian Minister of Foreign Affairs
Laskey, Denis S., Head of the Economic Relations Department, British Foreign
Office, from May 9, 1955; Counselor of the Foreign Office; Private Secretary to
the Foreign Secretary from 1956
Lawson, Edward B., Ambassador to Israel
Lay, James S., Jr., Executive Secretary of the National Security Council
Lister, Ernest A., Deputy Director of the Office of British Commonwealth and
Northern European Affairs, Department of State, May 6, 1956–August 25, 1957
Lloyd, Selwyn, British Secretary of State for Foreign Affairs from December 12,
1955

Lodge, Henry Cabot, Jr., Permanent Representative at the United Nations

Loutfi, Omar, Permanent Representative of Egypt at the United Nations

Luce, Clare Boothe, Ambassador to Italy until December 27, 1956

Lucet, Charles E., Minister-Counselor of the French Embassy in the United States from June 1955

Ludlow, James M., Office of United Nations Political and Security Affairs, Department of State, until November 4, 1956; thereafter Acting United Nations Adviser, Bureau of Near Eastern, South Asian, and African Affairs

McAfee, William, Psychological Intelligence and Research Staff, Department of State, until winter 1956; Office of the Special Assistant for Intelligence, winter 1956–October 1957

MacArthur, Douglas, II, Counselor of the Department of State until November 24, 1956; Ambassador to Japan from February 25, 1957

McAuliffe, Eugene V., Reports and Operations Staff, Executive Secretariat, Department of State, until April 7, 1957; thereafter Director

McCardle, Carl W., Assistant Secretary of State for Public Affairs until March 1, 1957

MacDonald, Thomas L., New Zealand Minister of External Affairs

Macmillan, Harold M., British Chancellor of the Exchequer, December 20, 1955–January 10, 1957; thereafter Prime Minister and First Lord of the Treasury

Macomber, William B., Special Assistant to the Secretary of State, November 16, 1955–August 15, 1957

Makins, Sir Roger M., British Ambassador to the United States until November 15, 1956

Malik, Charles, Permanent Representative of Lebanon at the United Nations, 1956–1957; Minister of Foreign Affairs and Minister of Education from November 19, 1956

Mansfield, Mike, Democratic Senator from Montana; member of the Senate Foreign Relations Committee; Senate Majority Whip from January 3, 1957

Mathews, Elbert G., Member of the Policy Planning Staff, Department of State, March 13, 1955–November 13, 1957

Meir, Golda, Israeli Minister of Labor until June 1956; Foreign Minister from June 18, 1956

Menon, V.K. Krishna, Permanent Representative of India at the United Nations and Representative on the Trusteeship Council; Minister without Portfolio, 1956; Minister of Defense, 1957

Menzies, Robert G., Australian Prime Minister

Merchant, Livingston T., Ambassador to Canada from May 23, 1956

Minnich, L. Arthur, Jr., Assistant Staff Secretary to the President

Mirza, Maj. Gen. Iskander, Governor General of Pakistan, August 7, 1955–March 23, 1956; thereafter President of Pakistan

Moline, Edwin G., Officer in Charge of Economic Organization Affairs, Office of European Regional Affairs, Department of State, from May 6, 1956

Mollet, Guy, Prime Minister of France, January 31, 1956–June 11, 1957

Monckton of Brenchley, 1st Viscount (Walter Turner Monckton), British Minister of Defense, December 1955–October 1956; Paymaster General, October 1956–January 1957

Morris, Willie, First Secretary of the British Embassy in the United States from August 1, 1955

Mossadeq, Mohammad, former Prime Minister and Defense Minister of Iran

Murphy, Robert D., Deputy Under Secretary of State for Political Affairs

Nasser (Nasr, Nassir), Gamal Abd'ul, Egyptian Head of Government; President and Head of State from June 24, 1956

Nehru, Jawaharlal, Indian Prime Minister and Minister for External Affairs; Head of the Department of Atomic Energy

Nixon, Richard M., Vice President of the United States

Noon, Malik Firoz Khan, Pakistani Foreign Minister, September 1956–September 1957

Ogburn, Charlton, Jr., Chief, Research Division for Near Eastern, South Asian, and African Affairs, Bureau of Intelligence and Research, Department of State, until spring 1957

Ordonneau, Pierre, Minister and Adviser for Security Council Affairs, Permanent French Delegation to the United Nations

Overby, Andrew N., Assistant Secretary of the Treasury until February 28, 1957

Pahlevi, Mohammed Reza, Shah of Iran

Pate, Gen. Randolph M., USMC, Assistant Commandant of the Marine Corps and Chief of Staff until January 1, 1956; thereafter Commandant

Pearson, Lester, Canadian Secretary of State for External Affairs until June 21, 1957; Representative to the 11th Session of the U.N. General Assembly, November 1956–March 1957

Perkins, George W., Permanent Representative on the Council of the North Atlantic Treaty Organization, March 15, 1955–October 12, 1957

Persons, Maj. Gen. Wilton B. (Jerry), USA, Deputy Assistant to the President

Phleger, Herman, Legal Adviser of the Department of State until April 1, 1957

Pineau, Christian, French Foreign Minister from February 1, 1956; Head of the French Delegations at the United Nations, 1956 and 1957

Popovic, Koca, Yugoslav Foreign Minister; Head of the Yugoslav Delegation to the 10th, 11th, and 12th Sessions of the U.N. General Assembly

Prochnow, Herbert V., Deputy Under Secretary of State for Economic Affairs, November 7, 1955–November 11, 1956

al-Quwatli (Quwaitli, Quwatly, Kuwatly), Shukri, President of Syria from August 18, 1955

Radford, Adm. Arthur W., USN, Chairman of the Joint Chiefs of Staff until August 14, 1957

Rayburn, Sam, Democratic Congressman from Texas; Speaker of the House of Representatives

Riad, Gen. Mahmoud, Egyptian Army; Egyptian Ambassador to Syria

Roberts, Randolph, Office of Near Eastern Affairs, Department of State, after January 29, 1956

Robertson, Reuben B., Jr., Deputy Secretary of Defense, August 5, 1955–April 25, 1957

Robertson, Walter S., Assistant Secretary of State for Far Eastern Affairs

Rockwell, Stuart W., Deputy Director, Office of Near Eastern Affairs, Department of State, July 1, 1956–August 11, 1957; thereafter Director

Rountree, William M., Deputy Assistant Secretary of State for Near Eastern, South Asian, and African Affairs, October 9, 1955–July 26, 1956; thereafter Assistant Secretary of State for Near Eastern, South Asian, and African Affairs

Rowan, Sir (Thomas) Leslie, British Second Secretary of the Treasury; Alternate Governor, Board of Governors, International Bank for Reconstruction and Development, and the International Finance Corporation

St. Laurent, Louis S., Canadian Prime Minister until June 21, 1957

Salisbury, Lord, Leader of the British House of Lords

Saud, ibn Abd al-Aziz, King of Saudi Arabia

Seaton, Fred A., Secretary of the Interior from June 8, 1956

Sharett, Moshe, Prime Minister of Israel until November 2, 1955; also Foreign Minister until June 16, 1956

Shaw, John F., Office of Near Eastern Affairs, Department of State, July 3, 1955–September 23, 1956; thereafter Officer in Charge of Economic Affairs

Shepilov, Dimitri T., Soviet Foreign Minister, June 1, 1956–February 15, 1957; Head of the Soviet Delegation at the United Nations, 1956

Sherwood, Robert K., Office of Near Eastern Affairs, Deparatment of State, until October 6, 1957

Shiloah, Reuven, Minister of the Israeli Embassy in the United States

Sisco, Joseph J., Officer in Charge of General Assembly and Security Council Affairs, Department of State, July 1, 1956–January 27, 1957; thereafter Officer in Charge of United Nations Political and Security Affairs

Smith, Gerard C., Special Assistant to the Secretary of State for Atomic Energy Matters, January 1, 1956–October 18, 1957

Smith, H. Alexander, Republican Senator from New Jersey; member, Senate Foreign Relations Committee

Sohm, Earl D., Special Assistant to the Under Secretary of State until March 1957

Spaak, Paul Henri, Belgian Minister of Foreign Affairs until May 11, 1957; Head of the Belgian Delegation to the 10th and 11th Sessions of the U.N. General Assembly

Spender, Sir Percy, Australian Ambassador to the United States

Stassen, Harold E., Special Assistant to the President from March 22, 1955; Representative on the United Nations Disarmament Commission from August 2, 1955

Stelle, Charles C., Deputy Assistant Secretary of State for Policy Planning, August 26, 1956–August 25, 1957

Stevenson, Adlai, Democratic candidate for President, 1952 and 1956

Suhrawardy, Husayn, Pakistani Prime Minister, September 12, 1956–October 17, 1957

Taylor, Gen. Maxwell D., USA, Chief of Staff, U.S. Army, from June 30, 1955

Timmons, Benson E.L., Director of the Office of European Regional Affairs, Department of State, from September 13, 1955

Trevelyan, Sir Humphrey, British Ambassador to Egypt from August 1955

Twining, Gen. Nathan F., USAF, Chief of Staff of the Air Force until June 30, 1957

Tyler, William R., Deputy Director, Office of Western European Affairs, Department of State, until February 14, 1957

Unden, Osten, Swedish Foreign Minister

Vallat, Francis A., Deputy Legal Adviser of the British Foreign Office and Alternate Representative of the United Kingdom at the United Nations

Vimont, Jacques, Minister-Counselor of the French Embassy in the United States until September 1957

Von Brentano, Heinrich, German Foreign Minister from June 6, 1955

Wadsworth, George E., Ambassador to Saudi Arabia

Wainhouse, David W., Acting Deputy Assistant of State for International Organization Affairs, July 20–October 7, 1956

Walmsley, Arnold R., British Consul at Jerusalem until April 27, 1956

Walmsley, Walter N., Jr., Deputy Assistant Secretary of State for International Organization Affairs after October 8, 1956

Waugh, Samuel C., President and Chairman of the Board of the Export-Import Bank from October 4, 1955

Weeks, Sinclair, Secretary of Commerce

Wentworth, Brig. Gen. Richard D., USAF, Secretary to the Joint Chiefs of Staff from summer 1956

White, Gen. Thomas D., USAF, Vice Chief of Staff of the Air Force until June 1957

Whitman, Ann, President Eisenhower's personal secretary

Wilcox, Francis O., Assistant Secretary of State for International Organization Affairs after September 6, 1955

Wiley, Alexander, Republican Senator from Wisconsin; member of the Senate Foreign Relations Committee and the Senate Judiciary Commitee; ranking Republican member of those Committees

Wilkins, Fraser, Director of the Office of Near Eastern Affairs, Department of State, July 3, 1955–September 1957

Wilson, Charles E., Secretary of Defense until October 8, 1957

Wilson, Evan M., First Secretary and Consul General of the Embassy in the United Kingdom until September 1957

Wormser, Felix E., Assistant Secretary of the Interior for Mineral Resources

Yassin (Yasin), Shaikh Yusuf, Saudi Royal Counselor; Deputy Minister of Foreign Affairs; Secretary to King Saud

Suez Crisis

United States Response to Egyptian Nationalization of the Suez Canal Company and Related Arab-Israeli Developments, July 27–October 29, 1956 [1]

INITIAL U.S. REACTION TO EGYPTIAN NATIONALIZATION OF THE SUEZ CANAL COMPANY, JULY 27–JULY 28

1. Editorial Note

On July 26, 1956, during a broadcast address delivered from Alexandria, Egyptian President Gamal Abdel Nasser announced that he had signed into law a presidential decree nationalizing the *Compagnie Universelle du Canal Maritime de Suez* (henceforth referred to as the Suez Canal Company), effective immediately, and that while he spoke, Egyptian officials were taking over the administration and management of the Company. The decree, which Nasser read, explained that an autonomous Egyptian agency, under the Ministry of Commerce, would operate the Canal, stipulated that all employees, under penalty of imprisonment, must continue to discharge their duties, and promised that all shareholders would be compensated according to the value of shares indicated at the close of business the previous day on the Paris Bourse. Nasser led up to this announcement by giving a long review of "imperialistic efforts [to] thwart Egyptian independence", and he particularly condemned past British actions and the United States refusal to finance the Aswan High Dam. Revenue gained from the Canal Company nationalization, Nasser explained, would enable Egypt to build the High Dam without American aid. An English translation of the Nationalization Decree, contained in despatch 188 from Cairo, September 5 (Department of State Central Files, 974.7301/9–556), and an extract from Nasser's speech, taken from an English translation of the complete text contained in despatch 97 from Cairo, July 31 (*ibid.*, 774.00/

---

[1] For previous documentation on this subject, see volumes XIV and XV.

7–3156) are reprinted in *The Suez Canal Problem, July 26–September 22, 1956* (Washington: Government Printing Office, 1956), pages 25–32. The Embassy in Cairo forwarded news of the nationalization to the Department of State on July 26 in telegram 146, printed in volume XV, page 906.

Arrangements made by the Egyptian Government with French engineer Ferdinand de Lessups during the nineteenth century provided the legal basis for the Company's existence as an Egyptian joint stock company. The original concession for the construction and operation of the Suez Maritime Canal, dated November 30, 1854, and signed by the Viceroy of Egypt, Mohammed Said Pasha, authorized de Lessups to form a financing company for the construction and operation of the Suez Canal. The definitive concession, signed by the Viceroy of Egypt on January 5, 1856 (which superseded the Concession of 1854), authorized the establishment, in the form of a corporation, of the Universal Company of the Suez Maritime Canal, listed the company's obligations and the concessions conferred upon it, authorized the cutting of the Canal, and provided that 15 percent of the profits would revert to the Egyptian Government. Article 16 of the definitive concession fixed the life of the company at 99 years, "counting from the completion of the work and the opening of the maritime canal to large vessels." At the expiration of that period, the Egyptian Government could either resume possession of the Canal with fair value compensation paid to the company or it could extend the company concession for successive periods of 99 years with an increase in the percent of levy. (The Canal was eventually opened to traffic in 1869, which set the concession's expiration date for 1968.) A subsequent convention between the Egyptian Government and the Suez Canal Company, signed by the Viceroy of Egypt Ismail Pasha and de Lessups on February 22, 1866 and sanctioned by the Imperial Firman on March 19, 1866, incorporated the 1854 and 1856 concessions by reference, delineated the relationship between the Egyptian Government and the Company, and established Egyptian jurisdiction over the Company and the Egyptian nationality of the Company. (The texts of these three documents respectively are printed in *British and Foreign State Papers, 1864–1865,* volume 55 (1870), pages 970–973 and 976–981 and volume 56 (1870), pages 277-283; and in *The Suez Canal Problem, July 26–September 22, 1956,* pages 1–20.)

As for the Canal itself, the Constantinople Convention of 1888 as well as the definitive concession affirmed its international character. The definitive concession guaranteed that the Canal and its ports "shall be open forever, as neutral passages, to every merchant vessel crossing from one sea to the other". Infringements of that guarantee, the desire to regulate the passage of warships, and other historical circumstances, caused the Governments of Great Britain, Austria-Hungary, France, Germany, Italy, the Netherlands, Russia, Spain and Turkey (Egypt being legally part of the Ottoman Empire) to sign a Convention at Constantinople on October 29, 1888 respecting the free navigation of the Suez Maritime Canal. Article I of that Convention provided: "The Suez Maritime Canal shall always be free and open, in time of war as in time of peace, to every vessel of commerce or of war, without distinction of flag. The Canal shall never be subject to the exercise of the right of blockade." (The text of the Constantinople Convention of 1888 is printed in *British and Foreign State Papers, 1887–1888*, volume 79, pages 18–22, and in *The Suez Canal Problem, July 26–September 22, 1956*, pages 16–20.)

---

2.   Telegram From the Embassy in the United Kingdom to the Department of State [1]

London, July 27, 1956—5 a.m.

481. Lima pass Secretary. [2] Cairo and Paris eyes only Ambassadors. Reference my telephone call to Acting Secretary Hoover. [3] Eden sent for me at eleven o'clock tonight, within a few minutes after the news from Cairo reached here, and I found myself attending a two-hour emergency meeting of the Cabinet attended also by the British Chiefs of Staff and the French Ambassador to discuss Nasser's action in nationalizing the Suez Canal. [4]

---

[1] Source: Department of State, Central Files, 974.7301/7–2756. Top Secret; Niact. Received at 3:38 a.m. Repeated to Lima, Cairo, and Paris.

[2] Dulles arrived in Lima, Peru, on July 27 to attend the inauguration of Peruvian President-elect Dr. Manuel Prado y Ugarteche on July 28.

[3] No account of this telephone conversation has been found in Department of State files.

[4] Sir Anthony Eden recalled in his memoirs that on the night of July 26 he received news of the nationalization while dining with King Faisal of Iraq, Nuri el-Said, Selwyn Lloyd, and other Iraqi and British officials. After the Iraqis had left, Eden, Lloyd, and Lord Salisbury met with British Lord Chancellor Viscount David Patrick Kilmuir and the British Chiefs of Staff and decided to invite to their meeting French Ambassador Chauvel and the American Chargé, Andrew Foster. (The Earl of Avon, *The Memoirs of Anthony Eden: Full Circle,* (Boston: Houghton Mifflin Company, 1960), pp. 472–473) The U.S. Ambassador, Winthrop Aldrich, had left London earlier in the day for a short vacation. (Winthrop W. Aldrich, "The Suez Crisis, A Footnote to History," *Foreign Affairs,* April 1967, p. 541)

Cabinet takes an extremely grave view of situation and very strong feelings were expressed, especially by Eden, to effect that Nasser must not be allowed to get away with it.

As to legal aspect, consensus of Cabinet discussion was that although Nasser had certainly breached the Canal company's concession it was not clear that his act of expropriation itself violated the convention of 1888. Such violation would presumably occur, however, if practical effect of expropriation impaired maintenance and operation of Canal.

Cabinet agreed that recourse to United Nations Security Council ran too great risk of matter becoming "hopelessly bogged down". Regardless of international legal aspects, interested Western governments must consider possible economic, political, and military measures against Egypt to ensure maintenance Canal, freedom of transit through it, and reasonable tolls.

The question confronting Cabinet tonight was of course extent to which United States would go in supporting and participating in firm position vis-à-vis Nasser in terms of economic sanctions and, beyond that if necessary, military action. I said that the United States would certainly also consider the situation a most serious one and that I would try to obtain on the most urgent basis at least a preliminary indication of our position. It is arranged that I shall see Eden and Lloyd at five o'clock this (Friday) afternoon by which time they hope Department will have given me some word for them.

Tentatively I expressed that United States, France and United Kingdom should continue discussions for the moment and that other interested friendly governments, e.g., the Commonwealth members and such leading users of the Canal as Norway, should join in later and broader consultation. List of signatories of 1888 convention not considered much use in this connection. Eden said Washington, London, or Paris equally agreeable to him. He evidently has in mind that a United States–United Kingdom–French meeting at the ministerial level may be called for in the very near future.

Cabinet had before it a telegram from British Ambassador at Cairo,[5] asking what to tell Canal Company which had asked his advice concerning Nasser's decree that company personnel would not be allowed to resign and would be punished if they failed to continue work. Eden strongly of view that HMG would not advise personnel to continue work under expropriation, even though this meant they might go to prison and Canal might have to close down. To advise them to continue work meant conceding Nasser's position and giving in to his blackmail. Decision on this held over, however, until today.

---

[5] Sir Humphrey Trevelyan.

Cabinet decided to have chiefs alert British Commanders in Mediterranean to situation. Chiefs were instructed to produce soonest a study of what forces would be required to seize Canal and how they would be disposed if military action became necessary.

Cabinet decided upon statement to be issued by HMG at eleven o'clock this morning, London time, along following lines:

"The unilateral decision of the Egyptian Government to expropriate the Suez Canal Company, without notice and in breach of the concessions, affects the rights and interests of many nations. HMG are consulting other governments immediately concerned with regard to the serious situation created; both in respect of the effect of the decision upon the operation of the Suez Canal and also of the wider questions raised by this arbitrary action."

Eden expressed the strong hope that United States and French Governments would issue similar statements today. French Ambassador left meeting and returned to say he had phoned Paris which agreed issue comparable statement.

As meeting broke up Lloyd told me he himself was moving towards conclusion that only solution lay in a Western consortium taking over and operating the Canal, establishing itself if need be by military force.

Please telegraph soonest concerning possible public statement by United States as well as what I can tell Eden and Lloyd today concerning United States position.

Foster

---

3.   **Memorandum of a Conference With the President, White House, Washington, July 27, 1956, 8:30 a.m.** [1]

OTHERS PRESENT

Acting Secretary Hoover
Mr. Allen Dulles
Colonel Goodpaster

The meeting was concerned with Nasser's seizure of the Suez Canal, and his speech yesterday relating to this. The President read

---

[1] Source: Eisenhower Library, Whitman File, Eisenhower Diaries. Secret. Drafted by Goodpaster.

State Department message from London No. 481 [2] reporting reaction in the British government.

In the discussion which followed, the President said this action is not the same as nationalizing oil wells, since the latter exhausts a nation's resources and the Canal is more like a public utility, building them up. He asked if this action was a violation of international agreements, and Mr. Hoover said it violates the concession (which was not a treaty) and may result in interference with the use of the Canal, which is the subject of a treaty (to which Egypt is not, however, a party).

Mr. Hoover said it will be necessary to make a statement this morning, and thought it should be in terms of "viewing with grave concern", not giving details. The President endorsed this view, commenting that we should give no hint of what we are likely to do. [3]

Mr. Hoover then said the basic problem is that the British will want to move very drastically in this matter, having in mind the worldwide impact on their position, including their relations with other countries. The President said that no nation is likely to allow its nationals to be held in what amounts to slavery, that operations of the Canal may suffer, and that we and many others have a concern over its operations (Secretary Hoover commented that two-thirds of the Middle Eastern oil passes through the Canal.)

Mr. Hoover said that Nasser's speech is a sustained invective in the most violent terms against the United States and its officials containing many inaccuracies. The President thought we must challenge these inaccuracies, including in the statement a comment that the speech is full of inaccuracies about the United States. It should also make clear our great interest in the Canal since the commerce of the West with the East passes through it. In response to a question by the President, Mr. Hoover pointed out that Nasser had taken control of the Canal Company at the time of his speech. The President asked Secretary Hoover to prepare a statement, the shorter the better, discuss it with Secretary Dulles by phone, and then bring it to him. He was sure the British would want action in this matter in view of the large block of stock they hold and the importance to them of shipping through the Canal.

---

[2] *Supra.*

[3] At 10:59 that morning the Department of State received a telegram from Secretary Dulles which reads: "Suggest the Department or I here might make following comment: 'The reckless attempt to confiscate a great international investment already in Egypt confirms that conditions are not propitious for embarking large amounts of foreign capital on another great development such as the Aswan Dam.'" (Dulte 6 from Lima, July 27; Department of State, Central Files, 874.2614/7–2756)

Mr. Hoover said he was considering whether NATO discussion of the matter might not be advantageous inasmuch as the Western European countries are deeply involved. The President said he saw a good deal in this idea. He went on to say that Nasser must be counting on support in the UN or from Russia. Mr. Hoover said, however, that Nasser's actions are not based on reasoning but are irrational and emotional. Mr. Dulles said there is a note of desperation in Nasser's action, relating to the Aswan Dam, and failure of the Russians to offer help when the United States turned the proposition down.

The President thought the statement should bring out that we regard the matter with utmost seriousness and are consulting with others affected. There should be one sentence making clear that Nasser's speech was full of misstatement regarding the United States. [4]

Mr. Allen Dulles said that a quick check should be made to see if there are Americans who would be involved in Nasser's statement that all employees must remain on duty, and the others agreed.

G

Colonel, CE, US Army

---

[4] At noon on July 27, the Department of State issued press release No. 413 which reads: "The announcement by the Egyptian Government on July 26 with respect to the seizure of the installations of the Suez Canal Company carries far-reaching implications. It affects the nations whose economies depend upon the products which move through this international waterway and the maritime countries as well as the owners of the Company itself. The United States Government is consulting urgently with other governments concerned." (Department of State *Bulletin,* August 6, 1956, pp. 221–222)

---

4.   Telegram From the Embassy in France to the Department of State [1]

Paris, July 27, 1956—5 p.m.

469. London eyes only Ambassador. Rome eyes only Secretary Thomas. [2] Lima eyes only Secretary. Pineau sent for me this afternoon to give me French Government views regarding Egyptian

---

[1] Source: Department of State, Central Files, 974.7301/7–2756. Top Secret; Niact; Limit Distribution. Received at 2:51 p.m. Repeated to Lima, London, and Rome.

[2] Secretary of the Navy, Charles Sparks Thomas.

seizure of Suez Canal. Pineau said that French Government takes most serious view of the affair and likens it to seizure of Rhineland by Hitler. Pineau said that French Government felt it was essential to react strongly so as to prevent Nasser from getting away with this outrage. Without such action Pineau said that inevitable result would be that all of Middle Eastern pipelines would be seized and nationalized within the next three months and Europe would find itself totally dependent on the goodwill of the Arab powers. This was obviously unacceptable situation.

Pineau said that he was going to London on Sunday[3] for the meeting with Eden which had been previously scheduled for Monday. At that time he hoped that British and French would be able to take firm decision as to action required. French Government feels it is vital that US position be fully known by that time and request earliest possible indication of US thinking. Pineau said that British and French Governments hope that Secretary would be able to attend the meeting on Monday but realized that he was very far away and that it might be impossible.

As to immediate action Pineau said he hoped the British Government would freeze Egyptian assets in London and he said that Suez Canal Company this morning had instructed all of its employees to refuse to work for Egyptian Government. This Pineau said would undoubtedly lead to arrests and imprisonments which would further aggravate the situation.

Pineau also said that French and British were jointly studying the military problem involved in the reoccupation of the canal zone. He said that their preliminary views were that this would not be too difficult an undertaking and that his opinion was that Soviet Union would not be prepared to take any effective counter action to protect Egypt.

As an immediate step the French Government has instructed French Embassy Washington to request immediate approval by NEACC of authority for French to send 24 more Mystere 4 aircraft to Israel immediately. Pineau said French hope for approval of this demand within 24 hours so they can make announcement before or during the course of this weekend and he asked me to request US Government to take any special steps necessary to expedite favorable action on this request. Pineau said that French Government had also made strong representations to Canadian Government urging them

---

[3] July 29.

to agree to immediate sale of F–86 aircraft to Israel in view of new French decision to send additional Mysteres. [4]

Dillon

[4] From Lima, Secretary Dulles cabled as follows:
"Have just read Paris 469 to Department. Re last paragraph my initial reaction is that we should go slow about mixing up canal problem with Israel-Arab problem." (Dulte 8 from Lima, July 27; Department of State, Central Files, 974.7301/7–2756)

---

5.   Message From Prime Minister Eden to President Eisenhower [1]

London, July 27, 1956.

DEAR FRIEND: You will have had by now a report of the talk which I had last night with your Chargé d'Affaires about the Suez Canal. This morning I have reviewed the whole position with my Cabinet colleagues and Chiefs of Staff. We are all agreed that we cannot afford to allow Nasser to seize control of the Canal in this way, in defiance of international agreements. If we take a firm stand over this now, we shall have the support of all the maritime powers. If we do not, our influence and yours throughout the Middle East will, we are convinced, be irretrievably undermined.

2. The immediate threat is to the oil supplies to Western Europe, a great part of which flows through the Canal. We have reserves in the United Kingdom which would last us for six weeks; and the countries in Western Europe have stocks, rather smaller as we believe, on which they could draw for a time. We are, however, at once considering means of limiting current consumption so as to conserve our supplies; and if the Canal were closed we should have to ask you to help us by reducing the amount which you draw from the pipeline terminals in the Eastern Mediterranean and possibly by sending us supplementary supplies for a time from your side of the world.

[1] Source: Eisenhower Library, Whitman File, International File. Secret. British Ambassador Makins forwarded this message to Eisenhower and sent a copy to Hoover. (Department of State, Presidential Correspondence: Lot 66 D 204, Eden to Eisenhower Correspondence 1955-1956 Vol I) The Department of State transmitted the text to Dulles in Lima in Tedul 18, July 27, and to London in telegram 546, July 27. (Both *ibid.*, Central Files, 974.7301/7–2656)

3. It is, however, the outlook for the longer term which is more threatening. The Canal is an international asset and facility, which is vital to the free world. The maritime powers cannot afford to allow Egypt to expropriate it and to exploit it by using the revenues for her own internal purposes irrespective of the interests of the Canal and of the Canal users. Apart from the Egyptians' complete lack of technical qualifications, their past behaviour gives no confidence that they can be trusted to manage it with any sense of international obligation. Nor are they capable of providing the capital which will soon be needed to widen and deepen it so that it may be capable of handling the increased volume of traffic which it must carry in the years to come. We should, I am convinced, take this opportunity to put its management on a firm and lasting basis as an international trust.

4. We should not allow ourselves to become involved in legal quibbles about the rights of the Egyptian Government to nationalise what is technically an Egyptian company, or in financial arguments about their capacity to pay the compensation which they have offered. I feel sure that we should take issue with Nasser on the broader international grounds summarised in the preceding paragraph.

5. As we see it we are unlikely to attain our objective by economic pressures alone. I gather that Egypt is not due to receive any further aid from you. No large payments from her sterling balances here are due before January. We ought in the first instance to bring the maximum political pressure to bear on Egypt. For this, apart from our own action, we should invoke the support of all the interested powers. My colleagues and I are convinced that we must be ready, in the last resort, to use force to bring Nasser to his senses. For our part we are prepared to do so. I have this morning instructed our Chiefs of Staff to prepare a military plan accordingly.

6. However, the first step must be for you and us and France to exchange views, align our policies and concert together how we can best bring the maximum pressure to bear on the Egyptian Government. This we cannot easily do by correspondence. A tripartite meeting will, I am sure, be required at the earliest date. It should be at a high level. So far as we are concerned, it could be held either here or in Washington. But, as it happens, Pineau was due to come over here for talks with Selwyn and will be arriving on Sunday next, July 29. Could you possibly arrange to send someone over at once who could join in discussions, not later than Monday of next week with Selwyn and Pineau. We should, of course, be delighted to see Foster, if that were practicable.

7. Meanwhile we are in close touch with the French and with the Commonwealth Governments. The High Commissioners here

have all expressed their readiness to meet me to discuss the situation this evening. Some or all of them might be glad to join in the tripartite discussions. They are deeply interested, financially and otherwise.

Yours ever,

Anthony [2]

---

[2] Printed from a copy that bears this typed signature.

---

6.   Memorandum of a Conference With the President, White House, Washington, July 27, 1956, 5 p.m. [1]

OTHERS PRESENT

    Secretary Hoover
    Colonel Goodpaster

The President had just received a message from Sir Anthony Eden, [2] and had asked Mr. Hoover to come over to discuss the Suez situation. The message had requested a U.S. representative at discussions in London and indicated they would be happy to have Secretary Dulles come. It had also spoken of readiness to use force in the situation created by Egyptian seizure of the Canal Company.

On the first point, after discussion, the President decided to notify Eden that Deputy Under Secretary Murphy would go to London immediately, arriving on Sunday. He told Mr. Hoover that Secretary Dulles, on arriving from South America, could decide whether he felt he should join the conference. Regarding the possible use of force, unless the United States limited itself to providing arms, it would be necessary to call Congress back into session. Mr. Hoover said that if the United Kingdom intervenes with force, the appearance would be simply protecting its 400,000 shares of stock. On the other hand, if the British or the French were to pull out their pilots, insurance companies would not then cover ships in passage through the Canal; the result would be a halt in operations. If they tried to seize or hold the pilots, the UK would undoubtedly use force, and would undoubtedly be justified in the eyes of the world. (Later information indicated that the insurance

---

[1] Source: Eisenhower Library, Whitman File, Eisenhower Diaries. Top Secret. Drafted by Goodpaster on July 30.
[2] *Supra.*

companies would not cancel coverage if the European pilots were to leave.) Secretary Hoover said he felt we must be very cautious and reserved about thinking of going in with forces to carry out the broad objectives Eden had indicated. Before we come to that, there are several steps to be gone through.

The President said he doubted if we would use force unless they attacked our people. Secretary Hoover said, however, that it is his feeling, in which Secretary Humphrey agrees, that we must move strongly in the Middle East—otherwise the whole Western position will be quickly challenged.

After further discussion, the President asked Mr. Hoover to notify the top leaders of both parties in Congress on a most secret and confidential basis that the situation might get so serious that they might have to be called back into session. They could be told that this development has the most serious implications for the Western world. If the movement of oil were interfered with, or if the pipelines were cut, we would be faced with a critical situation. The President phoned the Vice President [3] and asked him to convey the above to Senators Johnson and Knowland. He asked Secretary Hoover to talk to them too, and also to call Mr. Rayburn and Mr. Martin.

The President asked Mr. Hoover to bring the Joint Chiefs of Staff up to date on the matter. Mr. Hoover indicated he was keeping Arthur Flemming informed, and the President indicated that this action was correct.

The President dictated a brief note to Eden, which was quickly put into final form and transmitted. (I phoned it to Secretary Hoover's office for dispatch.) [4]

G

Colonel, CE, US Army

---

[3] A summary memorandum of this telephone conversation between Eisenhower and Richard Nixon is in Eisenhower Library, Whitman File, Eisenhower Diaries.

[4] The response to Eden, telephoned by the White House to the State Department at 5:30 p.m. for transmittal to London, reads as follows:

"Your cable just received. To meet immediate situation we are sending Robert Murphy to London to arrive there Sunday or very early Monday. In view of Foster's long trip, I doubt that he will be able to join in these talks, particularly since he could scarcely reach there Monday in any event.

"I shall not take time in this cable to outline for you the trend of our own thinking. While we agree with much that you have to say, we rather think there are one or two additional steps that you and we might profitably consider. Murphy will be prepared to talk these over with Selwyn Lloyd.

"We are of the earnest opinion that the maximum number of maritime nations affected by the Nasser action should be consulted quickly in the hope of obtaining an agreed basis of understanding. DE" (*Ibid.*, International File) The message was transmitted in telegram 545 to London, July 27. (Department of State, Central Files, 974.7301/7–2756) It was delivered to Eden on the morning of July 28. (Telegram 513 from London, July 28; *ibid.*, 974.7301/7–2856)

7.   **Telegram From the Embassy in the United Kingdom to the Department of State** [1]

London, July 27, 1956—8 p.m.

510. Cairo and Paris eyes only Ambassador. Department pass Secretary. For the Acting Secretary. Ref: Embtel 481. [2] Immediately after my telephone conversation this afternoon with the Acting Secretary [3] I met with Lloyd and Ambassador Chauvel at the Foreign Office and we discussed the Canal problem for an hour. I mentioned the points conveyed to me by the Acting Secretary, namely that he had consulted with the President and by telephone at Lima with the Secretary; [3] that the United States also took a very serious view of the situation created by Nasser; that the Department was about to issue a statement comparable to that issued by the British and French Governments this morning; that the United States favored consultation, at first on a tripartite basis and perhaps broader later, for example conceivably NATO; that the United States agreed the United Nations did not offer a useful forum at this stage; that the United States would prefer London or Paris for a tripartite meeting; that the Secretary did not consider it appropriate at this stage to attend such a meeting even if other engagements permitted but that the Dept. would send a high ranking officer soonest if desired; that the United States would at present prefer to have a look at proposals for action, economic, political or otherwise, now under consideration by United Kingdom and French rather than make proposals of its own; that nothing in the foregoing should be construed as any carte blanche approval of such proposals as might now be under consideration; and finally the Department's preliminary view of legal aspect was that Nasser's expropriation of Canal Company very different from the expropriation of such an institution as an oil company, there being possibility here of legal foundation for action.

Foregoing received with appreciation by Lloyd, particularly bearing in mind speed with which it was made available by Washington.

Chauvel summarized French position as of this evening under eight points which he said would be conveyed by French Embassy

---

[1] Source: Department of State, Central Files, 974.7301/7–2756. Top Secret; Niact. Received at 8:31 p.m. Repeated to Paris and Cairo. The Department repeated the telegram Niact to Lima for Dulles as Tedul 21 and to Rome for Thomas as telegram 370, both on July 28. (*Ibid.*)

[2] Document 2.

[3] No account of this telephone conversation has been found in Department of State files.

Washington to Department. [4] In brief (1) freeze Canal Company's assets abroad, 2) French Government disposed to give favorable consideration to Mysteres for Israel, 3) French had made protest to Egyptians this morning in Paris, 4) France wondered what U.K. might do about freezing Egyptian sterling balances, 5) French recommended early tripartite meeting, 6) French wondered what thoughts British might have on possible military action, 7) French Government taking steps protect French interests and nationals in Canal Company, and 8) French believed closest solidarity among Western governments indispensable in this matter.

Lloyd strongly argued against French point (2) and said HMG thought it imperative to keep Israel out of the situation, as much in Israel's interests as anyone's. Added regarding French point (4) that U.K. already has about one hundred million pounds sterling blocked and there was possibly ten million to twenty million pounds additional not now blocked that might be withheld by one means or another from Egyptians.

Lloyd then said there were several U.K. points worth mentioning. First and most important was that HMG considered it was "No good starting any measures unless we are prepared to take military measures in the end and if they should become necessary". He considered political and economic measures would not succeed, they would not be enough, and therefore success of Western effort would depend on acceptance necessity take military measures in the last resort. British chiefs of staff now working on study of possible military measures.

HMG felt, Lloyd continued, it essential to freeze Company's monies abroad. Understood shipowners now pay their tolls roughly 55 percent in London, 10 percent in Paris, and 35 percent in Egypt. British shipowners being told pay as usual. As to Company's resources abroad, Britain would try to freeze them here as French were doing in Paris. Understood about one million dollars held by Morgan's [5] in New York as trustee for Company and wondered whether United States could block this asset. I said I had no knowledge of this fund or of possible basis on which U.S. could freeze it.

Lloyd referred to question of status of Canal Company's personnel under Nasser's decree (seventh paragraph Embtel 481). HMG considered that Company should make decision and personnel should take Company's orders. Chauvel said French Government agreed and had so informed Company. Company had in fact in-

---

[4] The message has not been found in Department of State files.
[5] Reference is to J.P. Morgan and Company.

formed personnel that "whole subject is under consideration and meantime you should carry out your normal duties".

Lloyd said message from Eden to President had gone forward today, that it outlined general views expressed at last night's meeting (and contained Embtel 481), and that it urged a tripartite meeting in the near future which it was hoped the Secretary could attend. Lloyd added that visit of Pineau to London commencing Sunday offered an ideal opportunity for a high level tripartite discussion. After what I had told him he realized Secretary probably could not come but he urgently hoped United States would send a high-ranking officer of the Department to London to reach here in time for a first meeting on Sunday evening, with further discussions to follow Monday. I said I had no idea whether a high-ranking officer of the Department could come here as fast as that but I would certainly convey Lloyd's request as a matter of priority.

Lloyd said he envisaged that these tripartite discussions might result in the formulation of a tripartite note to the Egyptian Government making it clear that the three Western powers consider it necessary to ensure the full international status of the Canal, its security, free transit, etc. Note would continue that the three governments could not accept Nasser's expropriation of the Company and would suggest that their objectives could be fulfilled by the establishment of some kind of an international consortium, perhaps as a specialized agency of the United Nations. Lloyd remarked the United Nations aspect would appeal to India. If Nasser refused to go along with this proposal, the three governments, together with any other friendly powers which might join with them, would then take strong action. This would, incidentally, solve the 1968 problem in 1956. Lloyd emphasized that this thesis was not to be taken as a definitive recommendation for the tripartite group but rather as an indication of HMG's present general thinking.

Chauvel asked whether governments should send military advisors to tripartite meeting. Lloyd said he thought not and I ventured personal opinion United States would probably agree with Lloyd. (I later told Caccia not in Chauvel's presence that Admiral Boone CINCNELM was of course in London and I thought might possibly be made available if governments decided military advisors should be present.)

Lloyd mentioned that there had been a meeting this morning in London with all the Commonwealth High Commissioners. It was necessarily a preliminary sort of meeting but it seemed to him clear that all the HICOMs were in agreement that Nasser's action had created a very serious situation.

Finally, Lloyd emphasized in strongest terms the importance of keeping secret the fact that the United States, United Kingdom and

French Governments had under consideration the possibility of military action.

Please inform me most urgently whether a high-ranking officer of the Department could reach London on Sunday for tripartite discussions. Would also appreciate information on Morgan Trust Fund (above) and whether there is any means whereby United States could freeze it.

Foster

---

8.   **Memorandum by the Assistant Legal Adviser for United Nations Affairs (Meeker)** [1]

Washington, July 27, 1956.

EGYPTIAN NATIONALIZATION OF THE SUEZ CANAL COMPANY

According to information compiled in the Department several years ago, the Universal Suez Maritime Canal Company is a company established and registered under Egyptian law. The concession agreement relating to the Suez Canal appears to be an agreement between the Government of Egypt and the Company. There is evidently no international agreement of governments regarding the concession. The most recent revision of the concession agreement was concluded in 1949. The nationalization decree provides for compensation to bondholders and stockholders. The amount of the compensation is stated to be the market value of these securities just prior to the date of the nationalization decree. The decree does not fix any definite date for the payment of compensation, nor does it specify the form in which compensation shall be made. The decree provides: "Payment of this compensation shall take place after completion of the hand-over to the State of all the funds and property of the nationalized Company." This implies that compensation may not be paid unless and until Egypt has acquired control of all Company assets, including assets located outside of Egypt.

---

[1] Source: Department of State, NEA Files: Lot 59 D 518, Background Material London Conference on Suez Canal, Book I. Official Use Only. Transmitted under cover of a July 27 memorandum from Acting Deputy Legal Adviser Raymond to Murphy, under the subject heading "Legal Implications of Suez Canal Company Situation."

Article III of the Egyptian decree purports to "freeze" all "funds and rights" of the Company in the Republic of Egypt and abroad. "Banks, bodies, and individuals are forbidden to dispose of these funds in any way or to spend any sums or to settle any claims or liabilities except by a decision of the body provided for in Article II." Egypt is competent to give effect to the provisions of Article III within its own territory. Other countries are not bound to concede effectiveness to the Egyptian nationalization decree so far as Company assets abroad are concerned. In the United States, it is a matter for judicial decision, according to the public policy of the forum, whether recognition will be accorded to a purported foreign seizure of assets in this country. The Department of State has on some occasions intervened in judicial proceedings to support or attack the application to assets in the United States of foreign decrees purporting to transfer title thereto to the foreign government, depending on the circumstances. The United States has not adopted a policy of opposing the recognition of such foreign decrees in every case. In the present situation, the Department might be guided in its future attitude by the question of how promptly, adequately, and effectively the promised compensation is paid by the Egyptian Government. The answer to this question may not become apparent in the immediate future. Meanwhile, if asked by banks or others in this country what attitude they should adopt toward the Egyptian nationalization decree, the Department of State might wish to advise them to wait and see until the picture became clearer regarding the payment of compensation. Ultimately, the issue of the effect to be given in this country to the nationalization of the Suez Canal Company will have to be determined by courts in the United States.

While most of the securities of the Company are in British or French ownership, there are small American interests, privately held. No precise information is presently available in the Department as to the amount or character of the Suez Canal Company assets in this country, but it appears that the Company has substantial assets here, totalling perhaps five million dollars or more in value. These would probably be more than adequate to satisfy American claims if the assets should ultimately be needed for this purpose in the absence of proper compensation from Egypt.

Article IV of the Egyptian decree requires present officials, employees and workmen of the Company to continue carrying out their duties. Imprisonment is provided by Article V as a punishment for anyone violating the provisions of Article IV. There is at least one American citizen employed by the Company in Egypt, as a Canal pilot. There may be other Americans employed in the administrative services of the Canal in Egypt. Their number is probably not large. Articles IV and V of the nationalization decree provide for a form of involuntary servitude, and on their face furnish a basis of protest. In the event that any American national in Egypt should leave his position with the Company and be subjected to criminal penalties by the Egyptian Government, the United States would have a clear basis for diplomatic action.

A reading of the Egyptian decree nationalizing the Suez Canal Company does not indicate any design to impinge on obligations and rights under the Suez Canal Convention of 1888. The decree does not purport to affect traffic through the Canal.

Similarly, the decree does not appear to contravene the British-Egyptian Agreement of October 19, 1954 concerning the Suez Canal base. [2] Nor does the decree appear to give rise to any fresh rights on the part of the United Kingdom as against Egypt under that Agreement.

----

[2] For text of this agreement, taken from Cmd. 9586, see *The Suez Canal Problem, July 26–September 22, 1956,* pp. 20–23.

----

9.   Memorandum by Warren E. Hewitt of the Office of the Assistant Legal Adviser for United Nations Affairs [1]

Washington, July 27, 1956.

UNITED STATES RIGHTS UNDER THE SUEZ CANAL CONVENTION

The Suez Canal Convention, signed in 1888, entered into force in 1904, and is still in force. The Convention was signed and ratified by nine states, who declared in the Preamble that they wished "to establish, by a conventional Act, a definite system destined to guarantee at all times, and for all powers, the free use of the Suez Maritime Canal . . . " [2]

The intent of the treaty parties to confer rights upon third states may be inferred, both from the language of the treaty and the conduct of the parties subsequent to its entry into force. Although the United States is not a party to the Convention, the United States may as a third-party beneficiary claim rights under it, rights which

----

[1] Source: Department of State, NEA Files: Lot 59 D 518, Background Material London Conference on Suez Canal, Book I. Official Use Only. Attached to Raymond's memorandum of July 27; see footnote 1, *supra.*

[2] Ellipsis in the source text.

cannot be lost without its consent. The right of the United States to "make use of" the Suez Canal was acknowledged by the Egyptian Government in a note of June 28, 1948, in which it was stated:

"The Egyptian Government has never put in doubt the right of the vessels of all the Powers, whether or not they be signatories to the Constantinople Convention of October 29, 1888, to make use of the Suez Canal, on a basis of perfect equality, whilst conforming to the stipulations of said Convention. The United States has always exercised this right in respect of both its commercial and war vessels."

Under the Convention the United States may claim a right of transit through the Canal for all United States vessels of commerce or of war, in time of war as in time of peace. The Egyptian Government is charged with taking "necessary measures for insuring the execution of" the treaty and is permitted to take measures necessary for the defense of Egypt and the maintenance of public order. However, it is provided that such measures "shall not interfere with the free use of the canal."

Unlike the situation with respect to the Suez Canal, which is regulated by a general convention under which non-parties may claim rights, the possibility of third-party beneficiaries claiming rights with respect to the Panama Canal does not arise. No general convention has been concluded with respect to the Panama Canal. The Parties (United States and Great Britain) to the Hay–Pauncefote Treaty [3] clearly did not intend to confer rights under this treaty upon third parties.

It should be noted, however, that certain legal authorities deny the right of a state to acquire any "rights" under a treaty to which it is not a party. Nevertheless it is believed the position outlined above is probably justified in the situation under consideration.

---

[3] The Hay–Pauncefote Treaty was signed in Washington on November 18, 1901. Under its provisions, the United States and the United Kingdom agreed to remove any existing objections to the construction of a ship canal to connect the Atlantic and Pacific Oceans under the auspices of the United States. Their agreement did not impair the general principle of neutralization. For text, see 12 Bevans 258–260.

10.   Telegram From the Embassy in Jordan to the Department of State [1]

Amman, July 27, 1956—11 p.m.

67. As instructed Deptel 88 July 27 [26] [2] requested audience with King Hussein who received me 1130 today. Reviewed border situation with him including information Jerusalem's 21 July 26 [3] that wounding UN observer and Jordanian officer investigating exchange fire near Kastel July 25 now definitely established as work Jordanian villagers. Then went over with him in detail points made Deptel 88 including USG concern at continuing incidents, apparent lack well-disciplined Jordanian efforts maintain order and our support strongest cooperation with MAC and UNTSO. Emphasized as especially deplorable wounding UNTSO observer, importance to Jordan affording maximum protection UN observer personnel and urged HKJ take all possible measures end present bloody cycle.

King's reply on which he allowed me take notes as follows:

In my opinion Jews trying their best picture Israeli-Jordan border as highly unstable. They using their wide-spread propaganda organization to put Jordanians in wrong and swing public opinion to Israeli side in order justify possible aggressive action in not too distant future. In past Jordan has done all it could prevent anyone crossing demarcation line and efforts this direction being strengthened all the time.

Incident in which observers injured near Mount Scopus not fault Jordan but clear proof Israelis violating armistice agreement and storing munitions various types on that mountain. We regret injuring of UN personnel that area but do not feel responsible. As to Kastel Beit Surik incident we do not yet know how shooting started. We do know Arab villages fired on with rifles, machine guns and substantial number mortar shells. After firing continued many hours Jordan replied but only with small arms. We look to UN to obtain complete and accurate story this incident and will cooperate with them. Regret very much having to shoot but when attacked must defend ourselves.

As you know we have very severe law against infiltrators and have issued orders shoot infiltrators regardless direction they going, but there more than one kind infiltration. Consider for instance

---

[1] Source: Department of State, Central Files, 684A.85/7–2756. Confidential; Niact. Received at 6:43 p.m. Repeated to Baghdad, Beirut, Cairo, Damascus, Jerusalem, London, Paris, Moscow, Tel Aviv, and USUN.

[2] Vol. xv, p. 904.

[3] Reference should be telegram 29 from Jerusalem, July 26, not printed. (Department of State, Central Files, 684A.85/7–2656)

Israeli tactics of sending explosives to persons inside Arab countries. This particularly dangerous form action which appears to me to be aggression.

Please inform your government Jordan regrets deeply wounding of UN observer near Kastel July 25. We have in past done everything possible protect UN observers and shall continue do so. Do not forget however inhabitants of many frontier villages living under tension for years. When this tension heightened by shelling it is regrettable but not surprising villagers may lose judgment and shoot innocent bystanders. We are taking strongest measures against those responsible, but all I can say at moment is repeat my regrets and assure you we too deeply interested bringing present cycle incidents to immediate end.

Sanger

---

11.   Editorial Note

On July 27, the Joint Chiefs of Staff directed the Joint Strategic Plans Committee (JSPC) to prepare a study detailing the arguments for and against the following courses of action: (1) participation by U.S. forces with British forces in direct military action to seize control of the Suez Canal; (2) United States support of British military action without direct participation by U.S. forces; and (3) United States support of British military action limited to diplomatic and economic measures. The study, which was submitted the following day, offered no recommendations but concluded that the United States should take only diplomatic and economic measures in support of any British military action. The JSPC study found the first and second courses of action undesirable in that they would alienate the Arab states and involve the risk of limiting U.S. ability to meet commitments in other theaters. (Memorandum for the Joint Chiefs of Staff from Director of the Joint Staff Vice Admiral B.L. Austin with enclosure, DM–33–56, July 28; JCS Records, CCS 092 Egypt (7–28–56)) The staff study, however, generated strong criticism from Admiral Burke, General Twining, and General Taylor, who in separate memoranda on July 29 and 30 argued that the study did not sufficiently emphasize how militarily unacceptable the Egyptian action was to the United States. (Memorandum from General Twining to the Joint Chiefs of Staff, CSAFM 236–56, July 29;

memorandum from Admiral Burke to the Joint Chiefs of Staff, July 30; memorandum from General Taylor to the Joint Chiefs of Staff, July 30; all *ibid.*) Consequently, on July 31 the Joint Chiefs of Staff approved a revised study on "Nationalization of the Suez Maritime Canal Company by the Egyptian Government" and a memorandum for the Secretary of Defense, printed as the Enclosure to Document 50. (J.C.S. 2105/38, July 31; *ibid.*)

---

12.   Telegram From the Embassy in Israel to the Department of State [1]

Tel Aviv, July 27, 1956—7 p.m.

97. Reference: Deptel 71. [2] Because Ben Gurion was in Tel Aviv this afternoon, I was able to take up substance Department's message with him here within a few hours of its receipt. I placed particular stress on our hopes for restraint by the Government of Israel, and expressed concern over Israel's apparent preoccupation with "right of retaliation" as alluded to in press and elsewhere.

He appeared somewhat flushed and under pressure of some sort when I arrived. Although at beginning of my conversation he appeared disturbed and I anticipated some rather explosive reaction, he listened carefully and replied only briefly with the firmly expressed assurance that US "has no ground for worry that we will do anything to disturb peace".

He pointedly implied prospects on other side of frontiers were not so reassuring. He read from a letter from Hammarskjold dated July 24 in which SYG apparently quoted Nuwar as saying measures had been taken which should help substantially to restore quiet; and, re his visit to Egypt, that Nasser was "sincerely working to bring disturbances to an end." He said he did not know which Egypt it was that Hammarskjold had visited. "SYG was obviously very intelligent man but there was something wrong in his reactions and appreciation. There had been incidents just before he arrived, while he was here, and immediately after he left Middle East." It was obvious to me Ben Gurion had in mind that at same time Nasser

---

[1] Source: Department of State, Central Files, 684A.85/7–2756. Confidential; Priority. Received at 8:16 a.m., July 29. Repeated to Amman, London, Paris, Moscow, Jerusalem, Cairo, and USUN.
[2] Vol. XV, p. 903.

was reassuring Hammarskjold he had taken measures to bring disturbances to an end, he must have been contemplating his attack on US in his speech July 26.

He expressed personal distress over injuries suffered by UNTSO personnel and said he had just written to Burns on this subject.

After our discussion of border problems he asked following two questions:

(1) Could I find out for him when he might expect decision on their Export-Import Bank loan application (Department please inform) and
(2) Was there now any possibility of US supplying defensive arms?

To first question I replied I would cable Washington; to second, that I had nothing new to report.

Following my conversation with Ben Gurion, I talked briefly with Yaacov Herzog, Director US Division, Foreign Ministry, who said Prime Minister had had a second letter on July 26 from Hammarskjold in which SYG said he was returning to New York and might summon Security Council, presumably to discuss deteriorating situation Israel/Jordan border.

Lawson

---

13.   **Editorial Note**

On July 27 Canadian Foreign Minister Lester Pearson informed Ambassador Livingston Merchant that Canada would announce its decision to grant to Israel export permits for 12 F–86's and to consider an Israeli request for 12 additional jets. This would be done as soon as the fact became public that the United States was granting to Israel export licenses for helicopters and scout cars. Merchant reminded Pearson that the United States wished to avoid all publicity, but Pearson insisted that the U.S. action must be mentioned when the Canadian decision was reported to Parliament. Pearson added that eventual release of the second dozen jets would be virtually automatic and that he intended to inform Israeli Ambassador Michael Comay in confidence about this decision. (Telegram 57 from Ottawa, July 27; Department of State, Central Files, 784A.5622/7–2756) The Department of State responded in telegram 42 to Ottawa, July 27, that the Suez Canal situation "renders it inadvisable this juncture implement plan outlined Embtel 57. Particularly coming at this time, public knowledge that US shipping significant military items Israel would add fuel to intensified Egyptian propaganda that recent US action in Egypt result of pro-Israel and anti-Arab policies. Shipments by US and Canada might be assumed widely to be in retaliation for nationalization Suez Canal and indicative open support for Israel in its dispute with Arab states. Settlement Suez issue would then become more difficult." Telegram 42 also expressed the hope that the Canadians would defer action on the F–86's and it instructed Merchant to ask Pearson not to inform the Israeli Ambassador of the Canadian decision, if Pearson had not already done so. (*Ibid.*) At the same time the Department cabled Ambassador Dillon: "We urge French reconsider their proposal deliver 24 additional Mysteres Israel at this time. Announcement as proposed by French would add to Arab claim recent actions of West including Aswan Dam decision motivated by pro-Israel policies, and would further complicate settlement of grave Suez Canal problem. Until situation clarifies and other elements possible Western measures re Egypt determined, believe it wise delay decision re further significant arms shipments to Israel. You requested approach French along these lines." (Telegram 382 to Paris, July 27; *ibid.*)

---

14.   Telegram From the Department of State to the Secretary of State, at Lima [1]

Washington, July 28, 1956—12:43 a.m.

Tedul 20. Eyes only Secretary from Acting Secretary. Following are salient events on Suez situation since our noon telephone call: [2]

1. Eden made strong plea to President for concerted action against Nasser, based upon broad principles of international interest, with stated willingness to back up with military force. (Eden message rpt Lima Tedul 18, July 27). [3] At conference with President this afternoon I pointed out grave dangers of engaging in military intervention on grounds outlined by Eden and that while strong position should be taken to preserve Western status in Middle East, I did not

---

[1] Source: Department of State, Central Files, 974.7301/7–2856. Top Secret; Niact.
[2] No account of this telephone conversation has been found in Department of State files.
[3] Document 5.

believe confiscation of company was in itself sufficient reason for military invasion. Some other overt act would be necessary before we would be justified in adopting such measures. Otherwise our entire posture would be compromised. President agreed. (President's reply to Eden rpt Lima Tedul 17, July 27) [4]

2. In view forthcoming Eden–Pineau meeting on Sunday, we decided to have Murphy go London arriving there Sunday noon. We are much concerned at reports from London and Paris re inclination toward military measures, and fear that unless we can introduce an element of restraint Eden and Pineau will tend to move much too rapidly and without really adequate cause for armed intervention.

3. Our preliminary thinking is along following lines: (a) Egyptian order that foreign technical personnel (such as pilots) must remain on job under duress of imprisonment may provoke incidents, including possible stoppage of transit, which would provide better basis of intervention; (b) action in name of NATO might be more effective than operation in UN and also more suitable than tripartite measures; (c) firm and positive position by US, UK, France and other interested countries is necessary to prevent loss of other Western assets such as air bases, oil concessions and pipelines.

4. French and Canadians both now appear eager to support Israelis with considerable armament. We believe this could be most dangerous and therefore making every effort have them hold off deals for Mysteres and F–86's. We are also postponing announcement Operation Stockpile.

5. President has followed events with keen interest and is looking forward to your return early Sunday morning. He fully concurs in our view that we must adopt a firm policy but at same time not jeopardize our long-term posture by precipitate action.

Hoover

---

[4] See footnote 4, Document 6.

15.   Memorandum of a Conversation With the President, White House, Washington, July 28, 1956, 10 a.m. [1]

Principal points developed in the discussion of Acting Secretary Hoover and Deputy Under Secretary Murphy with the President this morning are set out below.

Mr. Hoover said that in talking to Secretary Dulles this morning [2] he had suggested a general line of holding down developments for the present, discouraging French and British suggestions of early armed action, and that he understood Secretary Dulles tended to agree. The President referred to British worries over possible loss of international position through other Mid-Eastern countries challenging British interests.

In discussion of a report that the French favored arming the Israelis, there was agreement that for the present it is desirable not to mix the present problem with the Israeli question.

The President did not think the means that would be required for Western countries to go in and operate the Canal would be very great at the present time, but said it is a question whether there is a basis for such action in terms of world opinion. The problem arises that, lacking intervention now, the Canal operations may gradually deteriorate without giving a specific occasion for intervention at any later time. This has been a deliberate, unilateral seizure, and people around the world are expecting some reaction now. Of course, if there were seizure of the nationals of Western countries, that would give a basis for action later.

There was agreement on the importance of keeping this Government clear of any precipitate action with the French and the British, which might later tie our hands. The President thought that if any sweeping action is taken, it should be not on just a tri-partite basis, but should involve all the maritime powers. He saw considerable merit in having Perkins lay the matter before NATO. Mr. Hoover thought that Mr. Murphy might take up with the French and the British the question of bringing NATO into the problem.

In discussion the President developed an idea that the French and the British might make a statement that they do not recognize the validity of the Egyptian action, that they will continue to operate the Canal, putting the matter before the World Court for determination, and putting tolls in escrow until that determination is

---

[1] Source: Eisenhower Library, Whitman File, Eisenhower Diaries. Top Secret. Drafted by Goodpaster.

[2] No account of this telephone conversation has been found in Department of State files. According to Dulles' Appointment Book, it began at 8:35 a.m., Lima time. (Princeton University Library, Dulles Papers)

made. We might join in such a statement; also the NATO countries might join in it. Basically they would say they would operate as before, and that if Egypt was to bring in the use of force, they would meet it with force of their own. Such a line of action would probably be justified before world opinion. The President thought that if such an announcement were made it would satisfy the requirement for action in the Mid-East to prevent other countries from challenging the West, and would show that the countries having maritime interests are trying to put the matter before an impartial tribunal. He did not consider that the Western world could sit and do nothing, waiting to see whether the operation of the Canal deteriorates. He referred to the provision in the Convention [3] providing for the placing of warships by each maritime power at each end of the Canal, and spoke of using them to escort traffic through the Canal.

Mr. Hoover also mentioned his thinking concerning starting a movement of some of the U.S. nationals out of Egypt. He also mentioned Egyptian failure to respond regarding Mr. Hare's assignment to Egypt. [4]

G

Colonel, CE, U S Army

[3] Reference is presumably to the Constantinople Convention of 1888.
[4] See telegram 61, July 12, vol. XV, p. 822.

---

16.   Memorandum of a Conversation With the President, White House, Washington, July 28, 1956, 10 a.m. [1]

SUPPLEMENTARY NOTE

Mr. Hoover referred to the possibility of freezing Egyptian funds in the United States. He thought it would be better to have the old Suez Canal Company sue and freeze the funds, rather than have the United States Government intervene, and the President indicated general agreement.

The President thought it was not too desirable to take action on a tri-partite basis—he thought action should be with all of the

[1] Source: Eisenhower Library, Whitman File, Eisenhower Diaries. Top Secret. Drafted by Goodpaster on July 30.

maritime powers affected. Also, he had some reservation about a proposal to shift our payment of tolls to the old company offices in the United Kingdom. This would be made to look like a boycott, and would give the Egyptians a basis for interfering with passage through the Canal. Mr. Murphy said the United Kingdom is proposing a UN consortium, when Mr. Hoover referred to Eden's note in which they seemed to be assuming a termination of movement through the Canal and asking us to rearrange our oil movement patterns.

Secretary Murphy said Egypt has acknowledged that it is bound by the provisions of the 1888 Convention. Mr. Hoover said that Admiral Burke had said that piloting through the Canal is not difficult, as had been earlier reported, and that insurance would not be cancelled if the European pilots were to leave. The President asked about tolls, and Mr. Hoover said the Egyptians are free to raise them if they so decided.

During further discussion the President said he felt it was very clear that the Soviet Union was not going to get into a major war over a question of this kind. Mr. Murphy pointed out that they may, however, give financial, moral and political support in the UN to the Egyptians. In discussion of the legal position, the President said that it seemed to him State was taking the stand that Egypt was within its rights, and that until its operation of the Canal was proven incompetent, unjust, etc. there was nothing to do. Mr. Hoover said he did feel that action must be taken since otherwise the Western position in the Middle East would be cut down.

Later in the discussion Secretary Hoover said he would call Ambassador Hussein in and give him a very strong oral statement regarding the inadmissability of Nasser's intemperate and inaccurate statements. [2]

G
Colonel, CE, US Army

---

[2] At 4:45 p.m., the Department of State issued press release No. 414 which announced that the U.S. objections to Nasser's remarks had been discussed with Ambassador Hussein. For text, see Department of State *Bulletin,* August 6, 1956, p. 222; or *The Suez Canal Problem, July 26–September 22, 1956,* p. 33. No other account of Hoover's conversation with Hussein has been found in Department of State files. Telegram 190, July 28, transmitted to the Embassy in Cairo the contents of this press release and added: "In giving press foregoing Department Press Office stated: 'The Egyptian Ambassador informed Mr. Hoover that he had not received the texts of President Nasser's statements. He further said that he could not accept the protest.' Embassy instructed make representations along lines Acting Secretary's statement." (Department of State, Central Files, 611.74/7–2856)

17.   Telegram From the Embassy in the United Kingdom to the Department of State [1]

London, July 28, 1956—2 p.m.

516. Cairo eyes only Ambassador. Paris eyes only Ambassador. Department pass Secretary. For the Acting Secretary.

1. Reference Embtels 481 and 510. [2] Caccia (Acting Head of Foreign Office in Kirkpatrick's absence on holiday) sent for French Ambassador and met this morning to review latest developments on Canal problem.

2. Chauvel informed us that he had just had word from Paris that France could make available certain naval units if they were needed. He said the details were being communicated to the Department through the French Embassy at Washington. [3]

3. Caccia said that, as we had seen in the newspapers, HMG had issued orders last night freezing the Canal Company's assets in the United Kingdom. Details to be communicated to Department through British Embassy Washington. [4]

4. Caccia said masters of British vessels had been instructed pay Canal tolls on the spot if Egyptian authorities insisted, since HMG considers it essential keep Canal traffic moving.

5. We discussed Canal Company's present orders to its personnel in Egypt which are in substance that (1) they should consider themselves as remaining under the orders of the original company and not of the Egyptians, (2) they should avoid anything which [may] be construed as sabatoge of transit of the Canal, and (3) if they have to follow orders given by the Egyptian authorities, they should do so under protest.

6. Caccia said that he had seen the Italian Ambassador this morning and had been surprised over latter's apparent unawareness gravity situation. He had taken opportunity to impress upon the

---

[1] Source: Department of State, Central Files, 974.7301/7–2856. Top Secret; Niact. Received at 3:18 p.m. Repeated to Cairo and Paris.

[2] Documents 2 and 7.

[3] Not found in Department of State files.

[4] On July 28, the Counselor of the British Embassy, Ronald Bailey, telephoned the Department of State to explain that the British Government had that day effectively blocked all Egyptian sterling assets by these measures: "(1) Regulation 2.A has been used to block the whole of the Suez Canal Company's assets in the United Kingdom. Sterling balances, sterling security, etc. (2) Steps have been taken to exclude Egypt from transferable account arrangements thus making her a 'bilateral' country. (3) No payments to or from Egyptian accounts are being allowed with the exception of authorized payments from the sterling area to Egypt." (Copy of an unsigned typewritten memorandum; Department of State, L/NEA Files: Lot 64 D 290, Suez Canal 1947–1959) In parentheses below the quoted message is the typed inscription: "In other words, payments are allowed under license."

Ambassador the very serious consequences—not least for Italy—which might flow from Nasser's seizure of the Canal.

7. Caccia said that as result Cabinet meeting last night HMG was now even more firmly of the view that in the last resort the West would have to take military measures to maintain the Canal as a free international waterway (fifth para Embtel 510).

8. Caccia and Chauvel said that their Governments feel it essential broaden basis consultation soonest at tripartite meeting and reached its conclusions [sic]. I said I had received indication Washington agreed. Caccia added it was now necessary and urgent that three Governments should compile list of those to be brought into consultation. His preliminary view was that list of signatories 1888 Convention no use nor was list of mail users of Canal.

9. As to forthcoming tripartite meeting, I said that Murphy had been designated and would arrive Sunday evening or Monday morning. I also mentioned Minister Barbour's [5] return Monday morning. Caccia expressed strong hope that Murphy might possibly take a plane tonight so as to be in London in time for meetings to start Sunday evening (eighth para Embtel 510). I promised phone Murphy immediately but said I doubted he could start for London before Sunday since I assumed he would need at least minimum time for briefing before departure.

10. Chauvel said Pineau, who arrives Sunday, had planned to stay through Monday but he thought could remain here Tuesday if necessary; feared Pineau would have to return to Paris not later than Wednesday morning.

11. Caccia said HMG now considered that attendance military advisors at tripartite discussion might be desirable after all though HMG had not reached definite decision on this (tenth para Embtel 510). (I have alerted Admiral Boone to possibility he may be needed here and he has cancelled trip which he planned to take to the Mediterranean starting Monday. I have also given him full background on developments to date. My own view Admiral Boone could be substantial assistance to Murphy even if military advisors do not formally attend discussions.)

12. Finally, would recall that Randolph Burgess on holiday in England and had planned to stay here till August 10. In view several financial aspects Canal problem Murphy might find his advice and assistance valuable. I have not been in touch with Burgess about Canal problem but could easily do so if Department and Treasury desire. He is presently visiting in East Anglia.

Foster

---

[5] Deputy Chief of Mission in London, Walworth Barbour.

18.   Telegram From the Embassy in France to the Department of State [1]

Paris, July 28, 1956—7 p.m.

492. London eyes only for Ambassador. Reference Deptel 382. [2] Since Pineau had asked me to keep in close touch with Joxe regarding Suez, I saw latter this afternoon in accordance instructions reftel.

I commenced interview by repeating U.S. position as given in paragraph one of London 510 to Department, [3] saying that I wished to confirm information which had already been given Chauvel by our Chargé in London. I then told Joxe that I had specific message re the 24 Mysteres which Pineau had mentioned to me yesterday. I said that while U.S. understood French feelings in the matter, we considered it most important to act in such a way as to isolate Nasser to the greatest extent possible. Therefore we felt that any action which might tend to confuse the Canal problem with the Arab–Israel quarrel would be most undesirable as it would only serve to rally the other Arab countries to Nasser's side, and would thus further complicate settlement of Suez Canal problem.

Joxe replied that he could well understand the importance of keeping the two issues separate. In fact French felt that Western action should be directed as much as possible against Nasser as an irresponsible individual dangerous to his own people as well as to the rest of the world. The West should make a real effort to differentiate Nasser from Egypt and from the Egyptian people. On the other hand Joxe said that the French were particularly susceptible to the sort of action Nasser had taken not only because of their previous troubles with him over Algeria but also because of their memories of Hitler. Therefore, the French took an extremely grave view of the present situation and felt that it was essential that some positive action be taken promptly. If it should not be possible for Western powers to agree rapidly on concrete action of some sort, there would inevitably be a strong movement in public opinion and in governmental circles to induce Israel to go to war with Egypt in order to put an end to Nasser by this indirect means.

Joxe said that re the Mysteres the French would of course take no action that was not approved by the three powers in NEACC, and he said that the matter could be discussed further on Monday in

---

[1] Source: Department of State, Central Files, 974.7301/7–2856. Top Secret; Niact; Limit Distribution. Received at 5:18 p.m. Repeated priority to London.

[2] See Document 13.

[3] Document 7.

London. The French have clearly calmed down about the need to send Mysteres to Israel immediately but unless some alternative concrete means can be found to take action against Nasser I feel that subject of Mysteres for Israel will continue to be brought up with greater insistence by the French.

Joxe said that he had heard that Murphy would be in London Monday morning and inquired if there was really no possibility of the Secretary's coming. I repeated that the Secretary would in any event not reach Washington until Sunday afternoon and that as indicated by our Chargé in London the Secretary did not think it would be advisable or appropriate for him to come immediately to London. Joxe said that he regretted this decision because meeting in London would lose some of its importance and Nasser would be apt to feel that U.S. did not place importance on issue equal to that placed by French and British. In spite of assurances that I had given him earlier that U.S. took very serious view of situation, he wondered whether U.S. fully realized the gravity with which the French and British Governments regarded the affair. I again reassured him that we considered the situation to be very serious and were giving it our entire attention.

Dillon

---

19.   Editorial Note

At 7 p.m. on July 28, British Ambassador Makins handed to Under Secretary Hoover a note from the British Embassy entitled "Suez Canal: Oil Supplies", which made the following points:

(1) joint planning by the governments and oil industries of the United States and the United Kingdom was an urgent necessity and should concentrate on formulating plans to ensure a steady supply of oil, if the Suez Canal were closed and the pipeline supplies interrupted;

(2) both government and industry should be engaged in the joint planning process; and

(3) the British Government was prepared to obtain the assistance of British industry through the government's Oil Supplies Advisory Committee; and wished that the United States Government would put comparable procedures in motion. (Department of State, Central Files, 974.7301/7–2856)

Attached to the file copy of the British note is a note from Kirk to MacArthur that reads: "It was agreed at the meeting in the Secretary's house on Sunday [July 29] that the US should take urgent action on the problems discussed in the attached note. Mr. Rountree said he would be in touch with you on this matter." Regarding the meeting, see Document 23.

20.   Editorial Note

Between July 29 and August 2, representatives of the Governments of the United States, France, and the United Kingdom met in London to discuss the Suez situation. Under Secretary Murphy headed the United States Delegation until the arrival of Secretary Dulles on August 1; Foreign Minister Pineau headed the French Delegation; and Foreign Secretary Lloyd served as chief British spokesman. During this period, there were eight formal tripartite meetings and several informal bipartite meetings. The British Foreign Office prepared summary records of the eight formal meetings and at least one of the bipartite meetings. Department of State Conference Files: Lot 62 D 181, contain copies of British documents entitled "Record of Meeting . . . " (hereafter referred to as "Record"), copies of Department of State telegrams sent to and from the United States Delegation at London, and other records, including chronologies, kept by the United States Delegation. Additional documentation is *ibid.,* Central Files 396.1–LO and 974.7301.

Following his return to Washington on August 3, Secretary Dulles requested that the Department prepare an American record of the Conference and the task was assigned, under the general supervision of Burdett, to the Department's Historical Division. In preparing the American record, the Historical Division made use of: (1) telegraphic reports from the United States representatives in London; (2) memoranda prepared by members of the United States Delegation; (3) papers circulated among the delegations; and (4) the British records of the eight formal tripartite meetings and one bipartite meeting. A copy of the study entitled, "The London Tripartite Conversations on the Suez Canal, July 29–August 2, 1956" (hereafter referred to as "London Tripartite Conversations"), is *ibid.,* Conference Files: Lot 62 D 181, CF 724. The introduction to the study states that "supplemental British material has been checked by officials of the Department in attendance at the London meetings." The introduction also contains the caveat that "the lists of participants given for respective meetings are in many cases incomplete for the British and French Delegations."

21.   Telegram From the Embassy in the United Kingdom to the Department of State [1]

London, July 29, 1956—6 p.m.

517. For the Secretary and Under Secretary from Murphy. Paris eyes only Ambassador. At the first tripartite meeting starting at six o'clock tonight, I shall begin with the following statement:

"We are most happy to participate in this exploratory discussion with our British and French colleagues. Secretary Dulles would have been personally most happy to be here and was unfortunately prevented from coming because of his absence on a South American tour. I want to assure you that the gravity of the Suez Canal question is fully appreciated by President Eisenhower and Secretary Dulles and both are giving it their urgent attention.

"We are of course eager to have the benefit of your thinking and to listen to whatever proposals you may have formulated. I would like to take this opportunity to outline briefly one or two thoughts that have occurred to us. We deplore the violent and even reckless language employed by President Nasser in announcing unilaterally and without any consultation an arbitrary action which has far-reaching consequences affecting all nations whose products move through the Canal and all maritime powers, including the United States. We believe that there is in some respects a distinction to be made, perhaps, between British and French interests and American interests, as respects the equities of the Suez Canal Company. We understand that you likewise do not place major emphasis on this factor.

"We frankly do not wish to be put in the public posture of merely defending the legitimate interests of the shareholders of this Company as important as that may be. We do not believe that our action should relate principally to the question of the legal right of Egypt to effect a nationalization of this Company. The American interest relates rather to the right freely to use an essential international waterway, the free access to which is guaranteed by the Constantinople Convention of 1888. I refer particularly to the language in Article 1 of that Convention. Thus the essential question would seem to relate, in our view, to the maintenance and the operation of the Canal as it affects our shipping. We hope these talks will clarify the issues involved and enable all of us to arrive at a more satisfactory evaluation of the essential facts and whatever action should follow.

"We believe that whatever action is decided should be taken only after a sober estimate of the facts and that the decision should take fully into account the effect of such action on world public opinion. We desire to have the closest affiliation possible with the United Kingdom and France but we believe that whatever action is taken should, if possible, have a broader basis than the interests,

---

[1] Source: Department of State, Central Files, 396.1–LO/7–2956. Top Secret; Niact. Received at 3:15 p.m. Repeated to Paris.

however important, of those three powers. The interest of other nations, especially maritime and trading nations, is important and their association and support, it seems to us, is essential. We should have a clear notion of where we are going, in order to encourage such association. We should not overlook, it seems to us, the possibility that the North Atlantic Treaty Organization could be useful. The support of friendly Mediterranean countries as well as those lying to the east of Suez should be ensured. We should carefully consider, it seems to us, the eventual utility of the International Court of Justice and examine carefully what action, if any, might be undertaken by the United Nations.

"The question of eventual military intervention does not seem to arise. It would depend on developments. For the present we believe it should be relegated to the background. We feel equally strongly that the Arab-Israel question should be segregated from the present issue.

"As you undoubtedly know, yesterday the Acting Secretary of State, Mr. Hoover, called in the Egyptian Ambassador in Washington and told him that entirely apart from the question of the seizure by Egypt of the installation of the Suez Canal concerning which the Department of State had made a public statement on July 27, the United States Government was shocked by the many intemperate, inaccurate, and misleading statements regarding the United States made by the President of Egypt during the past few days and particularly in his Alexandria speech delivered on July 26. The Egyptian Ambassador was told that such statements are entirely inconsistent with the friendly relations between the two nations. Under the circumstances, the United States had no alternative but to protest vigorously the tone and content of these statements.

"We are also fully conscious of the factor of Western prestige in the Middle East. We believe that if our handling of the present situation is not adequate, there could be a sequence of other events which would be further damaging both to our prestige and interests. We believe that whatever posture is taken and whatever statements are made should have the broadest possible base and carry with them the benefit of an affirmative world opinion. Any announcement made should set the requirement for action in the Middle East to prevent other countries from challenging the West and show that the countries having maritime interests are trying to put the matter before an impartial tribunal. We agree the Western world should not sit still and do nothing, waiting to see whether the operation of the Canal deteriorates. The provisions of the Convention of 1888 should be studied carefully and invoked wherever possible in the furtherance of our interests.

"We are also alert to the question of the protection of American nationals in the area, and no doubt you are also concerned over the problem of your nationals."

Foster

22.   **Telegram From the Embassy in the United Kingdom to the Department of State** [1]

London, July 29, 1956—7 p.m.

520. For Secretary and Under Secretary from Murphy. Paris eyes only Ambassador. Re Embtel 518. [2] At lunch today I thought Caccia showed a welcome moderation of tone particularly in regard to the problem of possible military intervention. He accepted my proposed statement (Embtel 517 [3]) that consideration of such intervention should be "relegated to the background". Moreover, he volunteered that our big problem at the moment will be to restrain Pineau from giving public impression that three governments are making military plans and considering military intervention. Caccia suggested that such an impression would of course seriously jeopardize the initial position which the US and UK may decide to take and which we agree includes the major element that other interested and friendly governments should be persuaded to join soonest.

Caccia stated French had offered supply certain navy units for possible military action. He thought they would wish start tripartite military planning. We expressed misgivings re tripartite military discussions this stage.

On the other hand, Caccia did emphasize several different times that the interested governments should be clear among themselves that (as Lloyd said at meeting with Chauvel and Foster on July 27, Embtel 510, fifth paragraph) it was no good starting any political and economic measures unless governments were prepared if necessary in the last eventuality to take military measures.

Caccia inquired regarding Egyptian assets in US and hopes even though the amount of Suez Company assets might be relatively

---

[1] Source: Department of State, Central Files, 396.1–LO/7–2956. Top Secret; Niact. Received at 4:03 p.m. Repeated to Paris.

[2] Telegram 518 from London, July 29, reported that Caccia, during a luncheon with Foster, Burdett, and Murphy, handed to Murphy the following outline of the "initial British position": "1. The Suez Canal is an international waterway of vital importance and an essential factor in the world economy. 2. It is therefore essential that all countries concerned should have confidence that it will be so operated. 3. Our objectives today are: (A) to establish operating arrangements under international control guaranteeing free navigation, reasonable dues and continuity of efficient administration; (B) to establish the international control in a form which will secure the support of as many countries as possible, and particularly of the 'neutrals'. Such support is most likely to be forthcoming if the international control is established under the auspices of the United Nations; (C) to ensure that the Suez Canal Company is fairly treated and (D) to ensure full respect for the legitimate interests of Egypt, including a fair financial return from the operation of the Canal." (*Ibid.*, 974.7301/7–2956)

[3] *Supra.*

insignificant that we might take some Treasury action to show our sympathy for British and French action in this respect.

Caccia told us that UK Delegation at first Tripartite meeting, six o'clock this evening, will be headed by Lloyd and include Caccia, Ross (Shuckburgh's successor), Vallat (Legal Adviser), Rowan (Treasury), and possibly Proctor (Transport). Agreed no military advisers should attend (though I am in close touch Admiral Boone).

Foster

23. Memorandum of a Telephone Conversation Between the President in Gettysburg, Pennsylvania, and the Secretary of State in Washington, July 29, 1956, 5:40 p.m. [1]

I said to the President that since my return about noon I had been working actively on the Suez Canal matter. There was a conference at the moment going on at my house with Mr. Hoover, Mr. Allen Dulles, Mr. Phleger, Mr. Rountree, Mr. Elbrick, etc. [2] I said that while I had not yet completed my review of the case, I had come to the conclusion first that I should not go at this time to London to participate in the meeting with the British and French Foreign Ministers [3] and secondly that I thought that we were right in playing down the use of force, particularly at this juncture. I said that the latest cable from Murphy [4] indicated that the British were taking a somewhat calmer view.

---

[1] Source: Department of State, Central Files, 974.7301/7–2956. Secret. Drafted by Dulles.

[2] According to Dulles' Appointment Book, the Secretary arrived at Washington from Lima at 12:10 p.m., July 29. Hoover and Phleger met the Secretary and accompanied him to Dulles' home, where a meeting began at 3 p.m. "re Suez". Present at the meeting, in addition to the above, were Rountree, Elbrick, Allen Dulles, Copeland, Bowie, Allen, Russell, McCardle, and Kirk. (Princeton University Library, Dulles Papers) No account of this meeting has been found in Department of State files.

[3] On July 28, the French Embassy delivered to the Department of State a message to Secretary Dulles from Foreign Minister Pineau that pleaded for Dulles' attendance at the London meeting scheduled for July 30. (Department of State, Central Files, 110.11–DU/7–2856) Dulles received the message while in transit to Washington from Lima. (Tedul 23 to Lima, July 28; ibid., 396.1–LO/7–2856) Following this conversation with Eisenhower, Dulles sent to Pineau through the Embassy in London a cable stating his regret that he could not attend. (Telegram 570 to London, July 29; ibid., 974.7301/7–2956)

[4] Supra.

I said that as far as the seizure of the stock company was concerned, the United States did not have a very strong case because there were only insignificant U.S. holdings of the stock. On the other hand, the operation of the Canal was another matter. I thought we should be prepared, if necessary, to use force to keep the Canal going. I hoped that a broad international basis for this could be developed.

The President said he concurred in my not going to London, and also in general of the non-use of force at this juncture. However, he pointed out that there was danger of developing inefficiency in the operation of the Canal and that there might be a progressive decline and that it would be difficult to pick a particular point at which to take forcible action. I said I recognized this danger and said we would take it into account in our deliberations.

[Here follows discussion of unrelated subjects.]

---

24. **Telegram From the Embassy in the United Kingdom to the Department of State** [1]

London, July 29, 1956—11 p.m.

521. Dept eyes only Secretary and Under Secretary from Murphy. Paris eyes only Ambassador. British and French positions as presented by Selwyn Lloyd and Pineau during first part tonight's meeting [2] summarized below. Both requested urgently USG views on matters set forth at end this message.

UK. Whole Western position in Middle East will be jeopardized if Nasser gets away with his action. NATO, Western Europe and other parts of world will be at mercy of man who has shown himself irresponsible and faithless. We should be careful to place matter in correct perspective. (British tabled paper submitted Dept Embtel 518 [3] and subsequently amended point 3(C) to read "To

[1] Source: Department of State, Central Files, 974.7301/7–2956. Top Secret; Niact. Received at 7:14 p.m. Repeated to Paris.

[2] Reference is to the first tripartite meeting, which began at 6 p.m. Other accounts of the meeting are in British Foreign Office, "Record of Meeting Held at 1, Carlton Gardens at 6 p.m. on Sunday, July 29, 1956," and "London Tripartite Conversations," pp. 3–12. (Both *ibid.,* Conference Files: Lot 62 D 181, CF 724) According to the latter document, the following attended the meeting: Murphy, Foster, Connors, and Burdett for the United States; Lloyd, Caccia, and Ross for the United Kingdom; and Pineau, Chauvel, and Daridan for France.

[3] See footnote 2, Document 22.

insure that the Suez Canal Company and its employees are fairly treated".) [4]

Political and economic pressures unlikely have desired effect unless Nasser knows military sanctions are in background. (Pineau later agreed this position.) Preparations for military action should start immediately. At any moment Nasser might deny passage to ships or take unacceptable action regarding foreign nationals. HMG has taken decision to arrange to have it within its power to use force. We may come rather quickly to point where decision must be made to act. We are not suggesting today decision to use force but to prepare for use of force if necessary. [5]

Arab-Israel conflict entirely separate problem.

Next step should be conference of affected nations preferably in London to convene August 1 or 2. Tripartite powers could send Egypt note or issue communiqué making points given British paper. Alternatively could wait and ask conference to endorse this position. Conferees could be selected on basis of: tonnage transiting Canal; combined shipping and trade interests; geographical representation; or membership in international chamber of shipping. Foreign Office inclined favor latter. British hoped to have indication of US position within 24 hours. UK would be gravely disappointed if US would not participate in conference although of course invitation could be issued by France and UK.

French position. We are not confronted with juridical question but political one. Decision taken by Nasser was direct consequence of US withdrawal Aswan Dam offer. If Nasser succeeds supported

---

[4] The British Foreign Office "Record" indicates that this addition was made at French initiative.

[5] On military preparations, the British Foreign Office "Record" contains the following account:

"In reply to a question from Mr. Murphy, the Secretary of State [*Foreign Secretary*], explained that we were only proposing military preparations in order to enable us to ensure by force, as a last resort, the free transit of vessels through the Canal. We had to ensure that the Canal remained an international waterway. It was not intended to make any military ultimatum to Nasser at the present stage. We must however be ready in case he were to occupy the base or take action against our ships.

"M. Pineau agreed with the Foreign Secretary. Mr. Murphy pointed out that United States public opinion was not yet prepared for the idea of using force.

"The Foreign Secretary said that a situation might arise where it would be impossible to go on paying dues to Egypt, if Nasser did not accept an international convention. He stressed the point that Nasser had already threatened employees of the Company with imprisonment. M. Pineau also emphasized that we were talking only about preparations at this stage.

"The Foreign Secretary stated that Her Majesty's Government had decided to be ready to use force if necessary. Mr. Murphy said that the United States Government had not taken such a decision. M. Pineau said that the French Government had taken this decision. They were prepared to do whatever was necessary and considered that it was more important than anything else to check Nasser."

by USSR will affect entire Western position Middle East. We have precedence Hitler's actions before World War II.

France attaches greatest importance to effect on North Africa. If Nasser succeeds completely useless to continue fight there. This is one more reason why France prepared to give its full support for whatever is decided upon to bring Nasser to order.

France agrees with British paper.

French Government has taken decision to prepare now for military action if necessary. 400,000 troops deployed in North Africa which could be used. We should have joint force under common command ready to strike if Nasser interrupts traffic through Canal or threatens foreign nationals. If US will not participate military plans should be worked out between France and UK. French thinking of occupation of Suez Canal zone.

After present conference tripartite powers should send common note to Nasser. Next step would be conference of users of Canal. Conference should not be allowed delay other measures.

US position. I presented statement quoted Embtel 517 [6] and then through series questions endeavored ascertain exactly what British and French had in mind. Made clear USG had not yet taken decision with respect to military preparations, tripartite note to Egypt or conference. Emphasized necessity for mobilizing public opinion and that talk of military action without adequate public preparation highly dangerous.

Department's views needed on:

1. General objective as set forth British paper (Embtel 518 [7]).
2. Participation by U.S. in tripartite planning for possible military action.
3. Note to Nasser by tripartite powers at this stage, perhaps setting forth objectives as given British paper.
4. Larger conference and criteria for selecting participants. (Regarding proposed larger conference there would arise questions whether USSR and Egypt should be invited. Also if it takes place it would perhaps be best for invitations to be issued by UK and not tripartite.) [8]

Foster

---

[6] Document 21.

[7] See footnote 2, Document 22.

[8] At 12:21 a.m., July 30, the Department of State sent the following preliminary comments to Murphy: "1. We could make no commitments re use of force without Congressional action, which extremely problematical under existing conditions; 2. Believe action to be taken might best be in form conference called by three or more signatory powers under provisions Article 8 of 1888 Convention. In addition signatory nations, limited number powers, including U.S., which are beneficiaries of treaty would be invited." (Telegram 571 to London, July 30; Department of State, Central Files, 396.1–LO/7–2956) The telegram was drafted by Rountree and cleared in substance by Dulles, Hoover, and Phleger.

25.   Telegram From the Embassy in the United Kingdom to the Department of State [1]

London, July 30, 1956—11 a.m.

525. For Secretary and Undersecretary from Murphy. Paris eyes only Ambassador. At evening meeting 9:30 to 11 pm, [2] it was consensus that the Arab-Israel problem should remain separate from the Canal issue. [3]

Pineau stressed urgency of arms for Israel. He thought that orders already placed should be filled but without publicity. Selwyn Lloyd indicated the British also intended to ship certain existing orders especially anti-aircraft material. I said that U.S. felt strongly that there should be no public reference at this stage to supplying of military equipment to Israel and this was agreed.

Pineau cautioned that we could not predict what the Russians would do and he felt that the longer we delayed action the stronger the Soviet reaction would be. He noted Egypt–USSR coordination foreign policy had not yet been completed but might be effected when Nasser visited Moscow. We noted that Nasser is reported as meeting with Kiselev July 29. Lloyd mentioned that during the B and K visit here [4] he had tried to convince them of the dangers of Arab-Israel conflict, emphasizing this could start a world war. Russians, he said, initially seemed unconscious of this danger but he thought he had made a dent on them. Lloyd wondered if we should not indicate to the Soviets that they should play part in any UN specialized agency for operation of Canal but he questioned whether they should participate in suggested conference.

Pineau and I agreed our governments might not welcome their participation conference but there might be tactical advantages in invitation to Soviet Union and Egypt. I pointed out Russians are users of Canal and signatory 1888 Convention. Lloyd added we

---

[1] Source: Department of State, Central Files, 974.7301/7–3056. Top Secret; Niact. Received at 9:27 a.m. Repeated to Paris.

[2] Reference is to the second tripartite meeting. Other accounts are in British Foreign Office, "Record of Meeting Held at 1, Carlton Gardens at 9:30 p.m. on July 29, 1956" and "London Tripartite Conversations", pp. 13–22. (Both *ibid.,* Conference Files: Lot 62 D 181, CF 725 and 724, respectively) The latter document indicates the following attended: Murphy, Foster, Connors, Burdett, and Mak for the United States; Lloyd, Caccia, Ross, and Vallat for the United Kingdom; and Pineau, Chauvel, and Daridan for France.

[3] According to the British Foreign Office "Record", Pineau stated on this point that "Israel would have to play a part if we had to take drastic measures in the future. The Arab-Israel problem should be kept separate from the immediate considerations, but the Israeli factor would inevitably arise later."

[4] Reference is to the visit of Soviet leaders Bulganin and Khrushchev to Great Britain in April 1956.

would not want give Soviets another platform for appeal to Arab world. I brought up question whether Egyptians should be included in proposed Canal consortium. Lloyd said yes but he doubted UK would wish invite Egyptians participate in proposed conference. I said it likely Egypt would refuse invitation, but there might be at least tactical advantage extending invitation to Egypt in any larger conference regarding future of Canal. [5]

Lloyd brought up attitude of Commonwealth members. Canada, and he thought South Africa, also would prefer some sort of UN solution. He would seek meeting of Baghdad pact ambassadors, including Pakistan, to ascertain their attitude. India was very disturbed over situation and Nehru appeared shocked by Nasser's action. Ceylon Prime Minister [6] likewise disturbed in view 80 percent trade was via Suez.

Lloyd then brought up question of freezing Canal Company assets outside Egypt. UK and France have issued orders controlling Company assets. Treasury official stated UK does not accept Egyptian nationalization law and Egyptian right control Company's assets which are in UK and under UK control. Egypt has proven herself unreliable user of sterling and it difficult for UK allow Egypt use sterling to detriment UK. UK legal adviser said Egypt has no right exercise control over assets of company which are not physically in Egypt. I said U.S. had developed no position on freezing Egyptian assets. Lloyd urged that regardless of volume of Company assets in U.S. we should have position of solidarity with UK and France.

Lloyd referred to Egyptian order that all transit dues must be paid to Egypt's account rather than Company's. Question arose whether UK should advise shipowners make dues payable to Company accounts. In fact UK has not issued any instructions to owners re payment of dues. I asked whether advice by UK to shipowners that masters should use their judgment re paying tolls to Egypt would constitute legal acceptance validity of nationalization. Foreign Office legal adviser replied that if sterling is licensed for payment of dues by particular ship for specific passage this would tend to constitute acceptance. A course of conduct with knowledge of the circumstances would tend towards recognition. If general license given releasing certain amount of sterling to shipping companies without specifying purpose, this would not have such effect.

---

[5] At this point, the British Foreign Office "Record" indicates: "M. Pineau mentioned that Nasser was expected to visit Moscow on August 12. The Foreign Secretary said that we should give further consideration to playing the Russians along and should not take action which would force them into Nasser's camp from the beginning. Mr. Murphy, speaking personally, thought this was the view of his Government."

[6] S.W.R.D. Bandaranaike.

Lloyd said he thought tolls question of prime importance. In reply my question he said he did not know attitude of Dutch and other Canal users. Pineau suggested that if we do decide to pay tolls to Egypt, we should do so "without prejudice".[7]

Pineau raised question advisability boycotting Canal and/or Egypt. He said complete blockade of Egypt would be very serious as would boycotting Suez Canal. Pineau said it appeared impractical blockade though we could boycott it. Lloyd said if we believe situation will become serious enough to take any such actions, it would be advisable to get as much oil as possible through Canal in meantime.[8] I asked whether economic blockade might be tantamount to act of war. Caccia said he thought Egypt could exist under economic blockade. Lloyd added he felt blockade would be subsidiary and would follow if military measures were taken.

Pineau raised question of personnel of Canal Company in Egypt and stated it difficult to advise such personnel disobey Egypt's orders. Personnel could of course apply for permission to leave country, which Egypt would probably refuse. Lloyd asked if this would not in effect result in hindering operation of Canal and therefore constitute violation of Convention. Governments should not issue such orders to personnel though Company might do so. Company, he said, has told employees that if they continue work they should do so under protest. I asked if non-Egyptian pilots are as essential to operation of Canal as some thought. Lloyd said operation of Canal could probably go on without them as masters were generally capable of navigating Canal without pilots. However, this was contrary rules of Company and there was question whether

---

[7] On the "payment of dues" question, the British Foreign Office "Record" reads:

"The Foreign Secretary said that the Suez Canal Company had protected their own legal position by issuing orders that any payments should be made to their account. After a general discussion the Foreign Secretary said there appeared to be three alternatives: (a) Shipping to be redirected around the Cape of Good Hope. (b) Shipping to be kept waiting at both ends of the Canal. (c) Payment to be made without prejudice. No instructions had yet been given the United Kingdom ship owners.

"Mr. Murphy said that United States ship owners normally paid their dues in Egypt. The United States authorities would probably be most reluctant to alter this practice, which was continuing up to this moment. He could not say whether it would be possible to attach any reservation to these payments. The Foreign Secretary said this was the most immediate decision which had to be taken. He would like to know whether the United States Government had accepted the legality of expropriation. Her Majesty's Government had not accepted it as far as foreign assets were concerned. There were indications that other maritime nations were reserving their position. M. Pineau said that if dues were paid to the Egyptians, in order to keep traffic moving, they must be paid without prejudice. Sir Leslie Rowan stressed that we had a full legal right to give our ship owners any instructions we wished."

[8] At this point, the British Foreign Office "Record" reads: "*It was agreed* that we did not yet wish to divert traffic round the Cape."

insurance companies would insure vessels under these circumstances. [9]

I asked if "dumping" cotton by U.S. would constitute useful economic action against Egypt. Lloyd felt such action inadvisable and mentioned it would be particularly resented by Sudan, Pakistan, and certain British colonies. I added Mexico and Peru would not be pleased either.

We agreed on press guidance (Embtel 522 [10]) and adjourned.

Barbour

---

[9] The British Foreign Office "Record" adds: "*It was finally agreed* that Working Parties should be set up to: (i) Submit ideas about a draft communiqué to be issued after the talks. (ii) To draft an invitation to a possible Conference of powers primarily interested in maintaining the freedom of navigation through the Canal. (iii) To consider further which countries should be invited to such a Conference. *It was also agreed* that the following subjects required further consideration: (i) The question of payment of dues. (ii) Whether fresh instructions should be sent to the employees of the Suez Canal Company."

[10] Dated July 30, not printed. (Department of State, Central Files, 974.7301/10–3056)

---

26.   Editorial Note

At the third tripartite meeting, which began at noon (London time) on July 30, the delegates began consideration of a draft communiqué, prepared by a working group. The draft reaffirmed the principles stated in the 1888 Constantinople Convention, pointed to the need for operating arrangements under international control, stated a preference for United Nations involvement in this control, asserted that the legitimate interests of Egypt, including a fair financial return, would be fully respected, and invited specified governments to "participate in a conference to be held in London in the immediate future to consider what steps should be taken in order to reach the above objective." At this meeting, the delegates also discussed possible criteria for selecting the nations to be invited to the conference and the question of the payment of Canal dues to Egypt. Accounts of this meeting are in British Foreign Office, "Record of Meeting Held in Council Chamber, Foreign Office at Noon on July 30, 1956," and "London Tripartite Conversations," pages 23–31. (Both in Department of State, Conference Files: Lot 62 D 181, CF 724)

Later that afternoon, but before he had received telegram 574 (Document 28), Murphy forwarded to the Department of State a report containing the verbatim text of the draft communiqué and an account of the major points and differences raised at the meeting. Murphy noted that the British and French wished the United States to join with them in sponsoring the proposed conference, while the United States was willing to state that it would attend a conference convoked by three or more signatories of the 1888 Convention. Also, the British and French delegates suggested that the conference should consist of the full membership of the International Chamber of Shipping, while Murphy offered a formula which included all signatories of the 1888 Convention (except for Austria–Bohemia–Hungary) and the nine principal countries whose products moved through the Canal. In addition, Murphy requested the Department's views on the communiqué, on a French–British suggestion that a tripartite note condemning the nationalization be sent to Egypt, on the manner in which dues should be paid, and on the possibility of evacuating Americans from Egypt. (Telegram 532 from London, July 30; Department of State, Central Files, 396.1–LO/7–3056) The telegram was sent at 4 p.m., London time, and was received in the Department at 1:57 p.m.

---

27.   Memorandum of Telephone Conversations Between the President and the Secretary of State, Washington, July 30, 1956 [1]

TELEPHONE CALL FROM THE PRESIDENT

11:29 a.m.

The Pres. asked how the Sec. is feeling about it, and the Sec. said all right. He is having a cable typed out and will call back in 10 minutes to read it to the Pres.

---

[1] Source: Eisenhower Library, Dulles Papers, White House Telephone Conversations. Transcribed by Bernau. During the morning of July 30, Dulles held a series of meetings with Department of State officials regarding the Suez situation and the instructions to be sent to Murphy. At 10:34 a.m. a meeting began, attended by Dulles, Hoover, Phleger, Prochnow, MacArthur, Aldrich, Rountree, Bliss, Bowie and Elbrick. Eisenhower's call came during this meeting. (Dulles' Appointment Book; Princeton University Library, Dulles Papers)

11:44 a.m.

The Sec. called and said it looks as though the impression we got from Murphy at noontime [2] that they were more moderate has given way to a stronger line they want to take. The Sec. read the cable of instructions to Murphy. [3] The Pres. said that is our stand. We should not be indifferent to the rights of people who are invested in this. Egypt should operate the Canal efficiently and carry out its promise to those affected—show we are not indifferent but are not going to war over it. Say we are moderate but firm but not going to be hysterical and rush into it. The Sec. said the British and French want to use force not really because of the Canal situation primarily but because they feel this act should be knocked down or have grave repercussions in North Africa and the British position in other countries. The Sec. said if we called a special session of Congress with nothing to go on except what we have now it would be picked up as an effort to back French colonialism in North Africa etc. and the Democrats would make a political issue of it and would be a mess. The Pres. said he said when he had his meetings day before yesterday [4] we have to find a way of using the Canal and efficiently. Notice should be served this is going to operate or else. We have to act right to nationalize (?) [5]—the Pres. recalled that Britain did it on steel. [6] The Sec. said the concession to the Canal Company runs out in 1968 and the Treaty itself says rights go on irrespective of the lapse of the concession. The Pres. said he thinks the Sec. is right—insist on proper operation of the Canal and we must get a broader base for operating in the future—now we are in the position of just protecting someone's private property.

---

[2] Reference is to telegram 520 from London, Document 22.

[3] Reference is presumably to telegram 574 to London, *infra.*

[4] Reference is presumably to Eisenhower's meeting with Hoover and Murphy; see Documents 15 and 16.

[5] The question mark appears on the source text.

[6] Reference is to the law adopted by the British Labour Government in 1949, under which the iron and steel industry was brought under public ownership.

28.   Telegram From the Department of State to the Embassy in the United Kingdom [1]

Washington, July 30, 1956—12:59 p.m.

574. For Deputy Under Secretary Murphy from the Secretary. Re Embtel 521. [2] It is our basic view Nasser should not now be presented with, in effect, an ultimatum requiring him to reverse his nationalization action under threat of force. We believe it is most unlikely he would back down and that war would accordingly become inevitable.

In this connection it must be borne in mind that, under existing circumstances, our President has no authority to commit United States to military action. This would require Congressional authorization. Congress has now recessed to enable the members to engage in political activities incident to the forthcoming campaign and to attend forthcoming political conventions. Congress, if called in special session, would probably grant requested authority only under most compelling circumstances. Unless and until there is clearer evidence that Nasser's action will actually impede vital traffic through Canal and unless this danger is recognized more broadly than by a tripartite decision, we doubt Congress would give the authority.

We believe we should proceed on a more moderate though firm basis designed to bring about a stable and technically adequate administration of Canal and to bring this about through pressures other than an Anglo-French ultimatum which could be misinterpreted as being motivated by factors other than the Canal problem itself.

Accordingly, we believe that best procedure would be promptly for three or more subsisting signatories of the 1888 Treaty to call for a meeting of the subsisting signatories, together with selected additional states having major interests in traffic through Canal, with view to bringing about regime of administration which will be dependable.

We recognize that Soviet Union as a signatory would have to be present, but we believe the conference would be overwhelmingly in favor of a stable administration having some international elements.

If Egyptian Government defies such a conference by refusing to attend or, if having attended, it rejects reasonable proposals, then there would be a broader basis than now exists for other affirmative action, free of the imputation, however false in fact, that we were

---

[1] Source: Department of State, Central Files, 974.7301/7–3056. Top Secret; Niact; Limit Distribution. Drafted and approved by Dulles and signed by Rountree.
[2] Document 24.

backing French and British for purposes not directly related to operation of Canal. Only under such circumstances would it be feasible ever to consider reconvening Congress in special session and expecting favorable action.

We greatly doubt that conference suggested could be prepared for and held by August 1 or 2, as there should be fully adequate diplomatic preparation. Perhaps it could be held within two weeks. We suggest that it might be called by Britain and France and at least one other signatory power (Spain, Netherlands, or Italy would appear most logical. Also, Geneva might be suitable meeting place. London, Paris, or Cairo would seem out of question.)

Selection of about 12 non-signatory powers might be based upon combined criteria (a) nations with greatest tonnage flag vessels transiting Canal and (b) those with largest amount trade transiting Canal, with assurance selection would provide adequate geographical representation. Formula should not be such that Egypt could plausibly abstain on ground conference artificially weighted against it. Under provisions Article VIII of Treaty, Egypt would be expected to attend. Conference would be designed assure open, secure and efficient operation of Canal as international waterway as contemplated by Treaty. With this definition Egypt's refusal attend could be considered as breach of the Treaty or, attending in defiant mood, Egypt would place itself in extremely bad light before world opinion.

Procedure we suggest is designed to avoid reference to United Nations Security Council or General Assembly which we consider would surely bog down our efforts for indefinite time.

FYI. Also, we must consider our own position in Panama Canal which depends upon a treaty, and we would be unwilling to be party to procedure which assumed that United Nations had authority in such matters which could override treaty rights. End FYI. From U.S. standpoint, we consider it of utmost importance to conform broadly, even if not literally, to treaty procedures, particularly as Suez Treaty seems adequate to cover present contingency.

We fully agree that Suez Canal Company, its shareholders and employees should be fairly treated but this does not affect broad policy considerations involved above.

This cable is to guide your oral presentation and not for textual transmission.

We are by separate cable making comments on British draft of principles (Embtel 519). [4]

Dulles

---

[4] Reference should be to telegram 518; see footnote 2, Document 22. Telegram 575, July 30, transmitted the Department's comments on the British draft. It reads:

"Following revisions British paper quoted Embtel 518 would seem necessary to conform basic considerations contained Deptel 574: (a) In para 2, delete phrase 'that all countries concerned should have confidence.' (b) Revise para 3(a) to read 'To ensure free navigation, reasonable dues and continuity of efficient administration.' (c) Revise para 3(b) to read 'To marshal international support for this position, to be backed, if need be, by international force.' (d) Revise para 3(c) to read 'To seek that, etc.' " (Department of State, Central Files, 974.7301/7–2956) The telegram was drafted by Rountree and approved by Dulles.

---

29.   Memorandum of a Conversation, Department of State, Washington, July 30, 1956 [1]

SUBJECT

Current Developments in the Near East

PARTICIPANTS

Abba Eban, Ambassador of Israel
Reuven Shiloah, Minister, Embassy of Israel
NEA—George V. Allen
NE—Slator C. Blackiston

Ambassador Eban called to discuss current Near Eastern developments:

Canadian F–86s for Israel.

Ambassador Eban said that he had been informed of the desire of Canada to bring the matter of the sale of F–86s to a favorable conclusion provided the U.S. fulfilled certain modest Israel arms requests.

Mr. Allen said that he was glad things had proceeded to this point and he commended Ambassador Eban on his tenacity in pursuing the matter. However, said Mr. Allen, the Suez Canal nationalization has complicated the situation, and we do not wish to give the impression that our supply of arms to Israel is in any way

---

[1] Source: Department of State, Central Files, 784A.56/7–3056. Secret. Drafted by Blackiston.

connected with Suez events. It would be most unfortunate if Nasser was placed in a position to say that Western action against him was the result of a pro-Israel, anti-Arab policy. Therefore, we must delay for the present our anticipated action designed to result in Israel's acquiring Canadian jets.

Both the Ambassador and Mr. Shiloah expressed distress at learning that Israel's quest for F–86s had been brought to the verge of success only to find that other developments had barred completion of the transaction. Mr. Shiloah asked whether preliminary details preparatory to the release of the aircraft and other arms could not be worked out now even though delivery was held in abeyance "for a few days". Israel, he said, did not desire a propaganda victory and was not interested in publicity. Mr. Allen replied that this was one of the problems since the Canadians wished the U.S. to publicize its sales to Israel. While we could not state when the U.S. would be in a position to proceed with our proposed arms sales to Israel, it was not likely that Nasser, already preoccupied with the Suez affair would be inclined to launch an attack on Israel in the near future. Results of the London talks on Suez, now going on, may clarify our position.

Export-Import Bank Loan to Israel [2]

Ambassador Eban said during his last meeting with the Secretary he had been advised to discuss Israel's pending application for a $75 million Export-Import Bank loan with Mr. Hoover. Since this meeting he had seen Ambassador Eric Johnston who had suggested that he postpone his meeting with the Under Secretary until after he (Mr. Johnston) had spoken to Mr. Hoover. Since Ambassador Eban had not received any new information he asked whether he should not now ask for an appointment with Mr. Hoover. Mr. Allen suggested that he do so.

Seizure of the Installations of the Suez Canal Company

Mr. Eban said that Nasser's action was, of course, a momentous development. As Israel had earlier prophesied, Nasser's purchase of Soviet arms was only the beginning of a long series of pro-Communist and anti-Western moves on his part. Nationalization of the Suez Canal Company is another indication that Nasser considers himself the sole judge of Egypt's international obligations.

There followed a discussion of the Constantinople Convention of 1888 governing the rights of passage through the Suez Canal and the restrictions placed in the way of Israel shipping by the Egyp-

---

[2] Additional documentation on this subject is *ibid.*, 884A.10 and 103–XMB.

tians. The Security Council resolutions of 1951 and 1953 on this subject were also discussed. [3]

The Ambassador suggested that if Security Council action was contemplated by the Western Powers there was no need for submitting a resolution charging Egyptian failure to observe the provisions of the 1888 Convention since the SC resolution of 1951 had already established this point.

Mr. Allen replied that the present thinking did not tend toward SC action. However, the issue can best be handled if it is fought out on the basis of the effect that the seizure has on all maritime nations, permitting Israel to reap the benefit of a solution, rather than on the ground that Israel ships have failed to pass through the Canal.

Mr. Shiloah hoped there was no intention of coming to terms with Nasser which would acquiesce in the status quo ante with the restrictions which this situation imposed on Israel shipping.

Alternatives to the Suez Canal

Ambassador Eban suggested that thought be given to alternatives to the Suez Canal and he made the following proposals:

1) A canal from the Gulf of Aqaba through Israel to the Mediterranean. Mr. Allen asked whether he had in mind a canal following the Wadi Araba to the Dead Sea and thence westward to the Mediterranean. Mr. Shiloah answered that a more direct canal route was envisaged although the route via the Dead Sea had been suggested by a Captain Allen, an Englishman, some 100 years ago in a book entitled "Dead Sea—New Route to India." The Ambassador said public knowledge that such a project was being discussed might have a salutary effect upon Nasser. Mr. Allen felt that talk about an alternative canal at this time might lead Nasser to believe that the West contemplated accepting his seizure of the Suez installations.

2) An oil pipe line from Eilat across Israel to the Mediterranean. Mr. Allen said that this project appealed to him in view of the possibility that the Lebanese and Syrians might nationalize the pipe lines in their countries. He suggested that the Israel Government take this project up with one of the oil companies.

---

[3] On September 1, 1951, the U.N. Security Council adopted a resolution calling upon Egypt to terminate restrictions on the passage of goods bound for Israel. (U.N. doc. S/Res/95 (51)) On March 19, 1954, New Zealand introduced a draft resolution reaffirming this position; the resolution was vetoed by the Soviet Union. (U.N. doc. S/3188/Corr. 1) For text of the 1951 resolution, see *Foreign Relations*, 1951, vol. v, p. 848; or *American Foreign Policy: Basic Documents, 1950–1955*, vol. II, pp. 2251–2254. The U.N. Security Council did not consider the question during 1953.

Israel's Position in the Event of a Western Clash with Egypt over the Suez Dispute

Mr. Shiloah opined that what comes out of the Suez controversy may cause Israel to reappraise its military thinking. He said that the danger of a world conflagration still confronts Israel. Should the West take military action against Egypt bases might be needed in Israel. Discussions on this subject took place during the world crisis in 1951 and might once again be advisable.

---

30. Memorandum of a Conversation, Department of State, Washington, July 30, 1956, 4:45 p.m. [1]

SUBJECT

Economic Aspects of Suez Situation

PARTICIPANTS

Department of State	*Interior*
The Secretary	Secretary Seaton
The Under Secretary	Mr. Wormser
Mr. Prochnow	
Mr. Rountree	*Defense*
Mr. Elbrick	Asst. Secretary Gray
Mr. Bliss	Admiral Burke
Mr. Kirk	
	ODM—Dr. Flemming
Treasury	
Secretary Humphrey	CIA—Mr. Allen Dulles
Mr. Overby	
	ICA—Mr. Hollister
Commerce	
Secretary Weeks	

It was agreed that ODM and Interior should ask a few selected oil companies to meet with Government representatives to initiate planning of emergency measures to assure continued supply of oil to Western Europe in event the Suez Canal is closed. [2] Messrs. Flem-

---

[1] Source: Department of State, Central Files, 974.7301/7–3056. Top Secret. Drafted by Kirk. A marginal notation by Kirk indicates that Hoover approved the memorandum on July 31. For additional documentation on petroleum planning and the Suez Canal, see volume X.

[2] Subsequent to this conversation, Hugh Stewart, Director of the Office of Oil and Gas of the Department of the Interior, acting in his capacity as Chairman of the Foreign Petroleum Supply Committee (FPSC) met with the industry representatives on

ming and Seaton said they would request Mr. Brownell's clearance for this action. They will also request a waiver of the requirement that ten days notice be given prior to initiation of such planning. This group will give urgent attention to the desired procedure for coordinating our planning with the UK. No publicity will be given to this planning for the present. The Department of State and ODM will consult if they feel, at some future time, that publicity might be desirable.

Mr. Hoover requested all Departments and agencies represented to take the necessary measures to be ready to take instant action against Egyptian interests in their own spheres of responsibility. He said we were not planning any action at the present time but that we wished to be able to move very rapidly if necessary.

Secretary Weeks said that the Department of Commerce would not grant any licenses for shipment of goods to Egypt without first examining them very carefully and conferring with the Department of State. He said the Department of Commerce would make a rapid study of measures the US could take to put economic pressure on Egypt. He said this study should be ready July 31.

Mr. Hollister said that ICA would make no further commitments for the payment of freight charges for goods shipped to Egypt under the CARE Program. He said that shipments under PL–480 were already stopped and would remain so. Mr. Hollister said ICA would make a study of the exact status of shipments under our aid program for Egypt. This study will include an estimate of what shipments could be held up without undue publicity.

Mr. Gray said that there were some $339,000 of items under the military aid program for Egypt which had not yet been shipped. He said delivery of these items had been suspended.

It was agreed that Commerce and Defense would set up a task force to study the status of tanker construction under NSC Directives. The task force will prepare a report on the number of tankers which have been built, which are presently under construction, and which we have plans to construct. The report will analyze the optimum size for such tankers and will make recommendations on the possibility of constructing a number of super tankers.

---

the committee. At this meeting, the FPSC prepared a plan of action which called for the establishment of a Middle East Emergency Committee, composed of representatives of American petroleum companies engaged in foreign operations. In February 1957, the United States Senate held hearings on government and industry participation in emergency oil planning before and during the Suez Crisis. For additional information, see U.S. Congress, Senate, *Joint Hearings before Subcommittees of the Committee on the Judiciary and the Committee on Interior and Insular Affairs, United States Senate, Eighty-Fifth Congress, First Session,* Parts 1–4.

31.   Telegram From the Embassy in Egypt to the Department of State [1]

Cairo, July 30, 1956—6 p.m.

176. Nasser called for me come see him in first hour that I returned to office. He said he extremely eager see me so that there might be better understanding of his position in view of apparent excitement and concern over his action reference Suez Canal.

He stated he had taken action after Western turn-down because it was only safe course he could see before him in order to fulfill his pledge to Egyptian people that High Dam would be constructed. He reminded me that he had long ago given me his preferred priority list as regards High Dam. 1st choice was through World Bank and United States and UK, 2nd was with Western consortium, 3rd with Russian help and 4th Egypt attempting project by herself. He reminded me that he had also told me many times of Soviet offer which had in past been officially made twice although he and Soviets had never discussed details. He had not rejected Russian offer as he thought that would be "silly" without knowledge of what future developments might be. Last week he had received another confirmation of Russian offer. In spite of that he had decided not to discuss at this time any details of Russian assistance of any type. Any such discussion would take place during his trip to Moscow.

As far as High Dam concerned however Egypt had made decision to adopt course 4 and try to do it themselves. (I questioned him closely on this and obtained clear impression that his present thinking is that any assistance from Russia would be for other projects and as for present at least he thinking keeping Russians out of Dam project). He said he did not know the Russians from actual experience very well as yet and he did not know what would come after their loans. Stated he really had no definite plans at this time as to what type Russian economic assistance he might accept.

He said he had read in certain newspapers that nationalization of Suez Canal probably had been worked out with Russians. He wanted me to know at earliest possible moment that this was not true and that they did not have any advance information of his action.

Nasser said British and French reaction had been stronger than he had imagined. Said problems divided themselves into two categories. 1st was question between Company and Egyptian Government.

[1] Source: Department of State, Central Files, 974.7301/7–3056. Secret; Priority. Received at 9:17 p.m. Repeated Priority to London, Moscow, and Paris.

His main point was that Company was Egyptian and he perfectly within his rights to nationalize it provided there be just compensation. This was his plan and he stated Egypt could afford compensation. 2nd aspect was question of use of Canal emanating for the most part from Convention of 1888. He had said repeatedly that Canal would remain open and be efficiently operated and wanted me to report this as official statement from him.

Told Nasser that I thought he had again made very serious mistake. In my opinion problem far exceeded the inevitable arguments, legal and otherwise, that would obviously grow out of act of nationalization. Leaving legal arguments aside (which I not qualified discuss) real problem undoubtedly was concern of Western world that Canal would remain as an efficient waterway open to international use. He must realize this quite a different problem than question Britain's right to nationalize her own steel industry (to which he had referred).

He might as well face fact Egypt was looked upon by many with lack of trust and of confidence that things would work out as he promised. He had proven himself to be man of quick action and he should be able understand that there would be concern that at some future time, as an act of retaliation, he might interfere with traffic other nations. He countered by saying that he himself had already committed Egypt on this point in the 1954 agreement with Br and had stated in his recent declarations his intentions in this regard. Told him nevertheless this obviously the most important aspect of situation and problem was his and I could at this time at least offer no advice.

Told him I not yet informed as to attitude of US Government on any of these questions. Lectured him however on the inadvisability of a repeated series of moves which gave impression Egypt was ready and willing to challenge practically entire world. He might attempt to justify such acts as a measure of Egypt's true independence but he could not ignore, as he seemed prone to do, the international implications of some of his moves. He said he knew he was fighting with his back to the wall and he was ready for almost anything. He however plans no further moves and is wondering what big Western powers may do. He had yesterday overruled suggestions put to him for counteraction in the question of freezing assets. He however considered he had taken a step fully within his rights and would do anything he would have to do to resist to Egypt's capability any move against their sovereignty or right to take the action he had taken.

I referred in connection with this discussion to his unjust and inaccurate statements as regards the US as instructed in Deptel 190. [2] He at first told me to make protest to Fawzi. I replied that I was not making written protest and that I wished orally point out to him the implications of a number of his quotations. He discovered some errors in translation of copy of his speeches which I using but on whole discussion was unsatisfactory as he quite bitter about his negotiations on both High Dam and military equipment. He resents deeply public references to state of Egypt's economy which he felt placed him in a position of having to take case to Egyptian people. I told him his choice of words and manner of presentation of facts had undoubtedly made seizure more serious in Western world.

It developed from conversation this action was not as hurried as we have thought. He informed me that he had told Hussein that he would take this act if West backed out on offer. Hussein had attempted dissuade him but he had told him to "keep your nerves and it will turn out all right". Hussein had attempted convince him that aid from West still possible but he had told Hussein that he felt there was really no chance. I gather therefore that Hussein's return to Washington to make final effort was as much a personal desire on his part to salvage situation as it was instructions by Nasser to make such attempt.

Told Nasser I would report what he had said but unable carry discussion further at this time. In order that he might personally understand US action on High Dam I read to him (with only minor omission to protect Hussein) entire memorandum of conversation between Secretary and Hussein on July 19 [3] hoping this excellent presentation would remove somewhat sting he still feels from our public announcement. He listened intently and I believe felt a little better.

Nasser gave impression in discussion that he rather hoped US at least (not being directly involved in Company) would not be critical of his action when it was understood that he had made move as alternative to accepting Russian assistance on Dam. Knowing that he is accused of being pro Soviet and anti Western believe he may think that we should look upon move as proof of his desire remain truly independent from outside influence, which would include Russia. There was however no specific discussion along foregoing lines and I gave no indication of accepting his logic.

We have no specific recommendations at this time. I would be grateful however if we could be kept fully informed during this rather delicate period both from viewpoint of Embassy responsibility

---

[2] See footnote 2, Document 16.
[3] See vol. XV, p. 867.

in event trouble and as we might be able to furnish possible reactions here to various alternative courses of action Department may be considering.

Byroade

---

32.   Editorial Note

The fourth tripartite meeting convened at 6 p.m. (London time) July 30, and discussed a revised draft communiqué prepared prior to the meeting. Murphy informed the other representatives that he had not yet received Departmental instructions regarding the communiqué and, therefore, was not in a position to give United States approval to the document. Britain and France reluctantly agreed to postpone publication of the communiqué. After discussions, in which Murphy participated, the draft communiqué was again revised. The new version retained most of the provisions of the initial draft except that: (1) the reference to a fair financial return was deleted from the clause asserting that Egypt's legitimate interests would be protected; (2) all reference to a forthcoming conference was deleted; and (3) a new paragraph strongly condemning the particulars of the Egyptian action was added. The text, entitled "First Redraft of Communiqué", reads:

"(I) The Governments of France, the United Kingdom and the United States regard the Suez Canal as an international waterway of vital importance which is an essential factor in the whole world economy, and consider that it should continue to be operated in accordance with the principles laid down in the Convention of October 29, 1888.

"(II) The three Governments note with grave concern that the Egyptian Government in proclaiming that they were acting in a spirit of retaliation, have given a political character to their action of July 26, 1956, and have, by that action, arbitrarily and unilaterally, purported to abolish a system which afforded all the guarantees necessary to ensure the respect of the principles. They deplore the fact that the Egyptian Government have had recourse to what amounts to a denial of fundamental human rights by compelling foreign employees of the Suez Canal Company to continue work under threat of imprisonment.

"(III) In order that all countries concerned may have confidence that the principles embodied in the Convention of 1888 will be respected, it is necessary to establish operating arrangements under international control, guaranteeing free navigation and open use of the Suez Canal and continuity of efficient administration.

"(IV) Such arrangements should preferably be associated with the United Nations.

"(V) The legitimate interests of Egypt would be fully respected."

At this meeting, the delegates also continued their discussion of the Canal dues question and the criteria for selecting conference participants. Accounts of this meeting are in British Foreign Office, "Record of a Meeting Held in the Council Chamber, Foreign Office, at 6 p.m. on July 30, 1956," and "London Tripartite Conversations," pages 32–43. (Both in Department of State, Conference Files: Lot 62 D 181, CF 724)

Telegram 593 to London, July 30, written in response to Murphy's report on the third tripartite meeting that morning, arrived in London too late to provide guidance for the 6 p.m. meeting. In telegram 593 the Department forwarded its own version of a draft communiqué for Murphy's guidance. It reads as follows:

"(1) The Governments of France, the United Kingdom and the United States regard the Suez Canal as an international waterway of vital importance and an essential factor in the whole world economy and consider that it should continue to be operated in accordance with the Convention of October 29, 1888.

"(2) They consider that the action taken by the Government of Egypt to nationalize the Universal Suez Canal Company threatens the use of the Canal as contemplated by the Convention and that it is necessary that steps be taken to assure that the signatories of the Convention and all of the other powers entitled to enjoy the benefits of the Convention shall in fact secure such benefits.

"(3) Accordingly, they propose that a conference should be held of the signatories of the Convention and of the principal users of the Canal to consider what steps should be taken to assure the continued operation of the Canal in accordance with the Convention of October 29, 1888. Such arrangements would in any event respect the legitimate interests of Egypt, including a fair financial return from the operation of the Canal.

"The invitation to the conference will be made by governments signatory thereto and the United States of America has indicated that it is prepared to take part in such a conference."

Telegram 593 also informed Murphy that, in regard to evacuation, the Embassy in Cairo had advised against taking special precautionary measures at that time, as it would tend to exaggerate tensions. (Ibid., Central Files, 974.7301/7–3056)

In response to telegram 593, Murphy forwarded to the Department the text of the "First Redraft of Communiqué", developed at the 6 p.m. meeting, with the comment that it represented "whittling down of more aggressive draft by UK and France" and that Murphy had agreed to recommend its approval to the Department. Murphy noted that the Department's proposed revisions, contained in telegram 593, would require the deletion of the reference to operating arrangements "under international control" in paragraph 3 of the revised draft communiqué and that both Lloyd and Pineau had stressed that they considered this provision to be the key feature. Murphy, however, believed that the Department's other proposed revisions would be acceptable to the British and French. (Telegram 547 from London, July 30; *ibid.*, 396.1–LO/7–3056) This telegram was sent from London at 11 p.m., July 30, and received in the Department at 8:16 p.m., July 30.

Later that evening Murphy reported to the Department on the major developments at the 6 p.m. meeting. The delegates had agreed that the Western powers should not submit the matter to the United Nations at this stage; but the British and French still held firmly to their position that attendance at the conference should be based on membership in the International Chamber of Shipping. When Murphy persisted in his earlier position on attendance, Lloyd suggested that the United Kingdom alone might issue the invitations to the conference, thereby relieving the United States of responsibility for choosing participants. Lloyd also suggested that the conference be held between August 7 and 9 and he urged that a quick consensus be reached on how Canal dues would be paid. The British Prime Minister then raised the possibility that the three nations might make a public statement affirming that its ships were paying dues to Egypt only under protest. (Telegram 551 from London, July 30, and telegram 549 from London, July 30; both *ibid.*, 396.1–LO/7–3156)

---

33.   Telegram From the Embassy in the United Kingdom to the Department of State [1]

London, July 31, 1956—2 a.m.

550. Eyes only for Secretary and Under Secretary from Murphy. Today and this evening Barbour and I have had private separate and lengthy talks with Eden and Macmillan. These will be recounted in greater detail in other messages [2] but I want to segregate one urgent

---

[1] Source: Department of State, Central Files, 674.84A/7–3156. Top Secret; Niact; No Other Distribution. Received at 10:17 p.m., July 30.

[2] No other messages relating to Murphy's private talks with Eden and Macmillan on July 30 have been found in Department of State files. "London Tripartite Conversations", (p. 31a) indicates that an Anglo-American meeting between Murphy

note both men struck which they requested be communicated in utter secrecy to you and the President. They said British Government has decided to drive Nasser out of Egypt. The decision they declared is firm. They expressed simple conviction military action is necessary and inevitable. In separate conversations each said in substance they ardently hoped US would be with them in this determination, but if we could not they would understand and our friendship would be unimpaired. If we were with them from beginning chances of World War III would be far less than if we delayed. They seem convinced USSR will not intervene but they assert that risk must be taken. Macmillan repeated over and over in language similar to that employed by Eden that Government had taken the decision and that Parliament and British people are with them. They both repeated wish that the President clearly understand decision is firm and has been arrived at calmly without emotion. They see no alternative. Macmillan in referring to our close wartime association in French North Africa emphasized several times his belief that as a former adviser and member of President's wartime staff he felt he could assure the President that Britain had no intention of submitting to Nasser's dictation, that British stake in ME is vital, that a demonstration of force provided only solution. Macmillan described some of the military planning which contemplates he said the landing of three British divisions in Egypt in an operation which would take six weeks to mount. The British estimate of importance of Egyptian resistance is low. Macmillan talked about costs. He said this operation would cost four to five hundred million pounds which they couldn't afford but they would pay. All British shipping would be allocated to it except the two Queens. [3]

During these conversations I advanced I believe all of the considerations which you and the President as well as the Under Secretary have raised. Eden, Macmillan and Lloyd showed throughout unexpected calm and no hysteria. They act as though they really have taken a decision after profound reflection. They are flexible on procedures leading up to showdown but insist over and over again that whatever conferences, arrangements, public postures and maneuvers might be necessary, at the end they are determined to use force. They hope we will be with them and believe French are with them.

---

and Eden took place at 5 p.m. on July 30, but notes that "the substantive record of this meeting is filed in the Office of the Secretary of State." (*Ibid.*, Conference Files: Lot 62 D 181, CF 724) Such a "substantive record" has not been found in Department of State files.

[3] Presumably reference is to the British passenger liners the *Queen Mary* and the *Queen Elizabeth*.

Macmillan indulged in much graphic dissertation on British past history and stressed that if they had to go down now the Government and he believed British people would rather do so on this issue and become perhaps another Netherlands. To do another Munich leading to progressive deterioration of ME position and in end the inevitable disaster is he said something he Eden and his colleagues in Government are simply not prepared to do. At dinner [4] Macmillan and Field Marshal Alexander (Harold Caccia only other person present) urged repeatedly that President as their former C in C fully appreciate finality of British decision. Macmillan several times expressed wish he could explain all this orally to President.

I apologize for length of this message but I am persuaded that flavor of these calm and very serious statements should be conveyed urgently as they request to the President.

Barbour

---

[4] Murphy gives an account of this dinner conversation in his memoirs (*Diplomat Among Warriors* (London: Collins, 1964), pp. 462–464), but he describes it taking place on Sunday evening (i.e., July 29).

---

34.   Memorandum of a Conference With the President, White House, Washington, July 31, 1956, 9:45 a.m. [1]

OTHERS PRESENT

Secretary Dulles
Under Secretary Hoover
Mr. Phleger
Deputy Secretary Robertson
Assistant Secretary Gordon Gray
Admiral Burke
Secretary Humphrey
Mr. Allen Dulles
Colonel Goodpaster

Secretary Dulles, Mr. Hoover and Mr. Phleger had been with the President about fifteen minutes when the larger group came in. They and the President had read a message (London 550) [2] which the President then had handed to the others to read. In essence it

---

[1] Source: Eisenhower Library, Whitman File, Eisenhower Diaries. Top Secret. Drafted by Goodpaster.
[2] *Supra.*

stated that the British had taken a firm, considered decision to "break Nasser" and to initiate hostilities at an early date for this purpose (estimating six weeks to be required for setting up the operation).

In opening the discussion, the President said he considered this to be a very unwise decision on their part. Military support from us would require Congressional action, and a request for such action on the basis of the British decision would not be well received. He felt that the British were out of date in thinking of this as a mode of action in the present circumstances. To take such action without having made a "counterproposal" to the Egyptian action would be an extremely serious matter for us. The Middle East oil would undoubtedly dry up, and Western hemisphere oil would have to be diverted to Europe, thus requiring controls to be instituted in the United States. He thought Secretary Dulles had better go to London at once and make clear how impossible it would be to obtain Congressional authorization for participation by the United States in these circumstances. (We must recognize that our participation would be essential if order and access to oil were to be restored).

The President asked Allen Dulles what he estimated the reaction to a British action of this kind would be in the Arab world. Mr. Dulles said that if the move were made now, i.e., without a conference or a counterproposal, the whole Arab world would unite in opposition in all likelihood. If, however, a conference were held, the situation might be considerably different, and the opposition be much less widespread and intense. Today action would arouse the whole Arab world. The President enlarged this to the whole Moslem world.

Secretary Dulles said that he thought there was better than an even chance that, if a conference were held by calling in all of the countries involved, unanimous backing for an international regime to operate the Canal could be obtained. If a proposal of this kind were made to the Arabs with world backing (including Asian backing which seems reasonable to expect) it would then be possible to take armed action if it became necessary with a good chance of retaining a large measure of world support. The British seem to have dropped the idea of a conference in favor of an ultimatum, and want us to join in a communiqué, which is designed to cause a breach. Mr. Allen Dulles suggested that Nasser might not come to the conference, but Secretary Dulles thought that if the conference is one of signatories to the Treaty he probably would come.

Secretary Humphrey asked, with regard to the British proposal, what end was in sight—what the final situation might be toward which they would be working. Secretary Dulles said it could only be a return to the situation in the Canal Zone that had existed a few years ago in which terrorist attacks by the Egyptians were unceasing, with nearly 90,000 British troops present there. Secretary Humphrey said it looked as though they were simply trying to reverse the trend away from colonialism, and turn the clock back fifty years. It did not seem that the action could lead to a solution in the area.

Secretary Dulles referred to the proposed communiqué for the meetings currently in progress in London and stressed the lack of any mention of a conference in the British draft. [3] It appeared that they wished to associate the United States with the first phase of their operations, with the result of tending to commit us to their whole course of action or leave us in the position of letting them down. He thought that unless the British are ready to have a genuine conference, we should not take the first step with them, i.e., joining in the communiqué they propose. He read off the U.S. proposed text for the communiqué. [4]

In response to a question, Admiral Burke said the JCS are of the view that Nasser must be broken. They thought this should be accomplished with economic and political means. If, however, these are tried and prove insufficient, the United Kingdom should then used armed force, and we should declare ourselves in support of their action. (He did not indicate the U.S. should participate with armed force.) The President felt that it was wrong to give undue stress to Nasser himself. He felt Nasser embodies the emotional demands of the people of the area for independence and for "slapping the white Man down." He said we must consider what the end could be. It might well be to array the world from Dakar to the Philippine Islands against us. Admiral Burke said the suggestion is to search for and try to develop means of splitting off Egypt from other Arab and Moslem groups. If Nasser retains power, he will spread his influence progressively, to the detriment of the West through the Middle East. The President recalled that we have been trying to find means of doing just this for several months.

Secretary Dulles thought we could make Nasser disgorge what he has seized, and agree to internationalize the Canal. He recognized that this action would not serve the French and British interests in the Middle East and Africa so dramatically, and understood why, in their circumstances, they felt a bolder action was necessary. Such did not necessarily represent our interest, however. Secretary Humphrey cited, as a danger in negotiation, that we might be pressed into the position of agreeing to finance the building of the Aswan Dam in return for Nasser's giving up the Canal. Such action could only build up his prestige. Secretary Dulles said he would not agree to such a

---

[3] Reference is to "First Redraft of Communiqué"; see Document 32.
[4] See *ibid.*

proposition. Nasser must be made to disgorge his theft. Mr. Humphrey said all the rest of the world would press us to build the dam. Secretary Dulles said such action would simply be one of rewarding theft.

The President said that Nasser has an exaggerated idea of the income from the Canal. In the discussion that followed, Secretary Dulles brought out that he can pay off the shareholders very largely with accumulated reserves, and would then have somewhere between $30 and 50 million a year clear. We must try to make him disgorge by international means—not by force. After such a try, if it is then necessary to act, world opinion would give greater support.

Secretary Dulles brought out that if Middle Eastern oil were lost to the West, rationing of oil in the United States would be an immediate result, with curtailment of automobile production, and a severe blow to the United States economy. Secretary Humphrey said there would be great anger against the UK on the part of the people of the United States if such a result came from unilateral British action.

Secretary Dulles said the British action would be likely to provoke Israeli attack on Jordan, with the result of inflaming the whole Arab world. He recalled that the British went into World War I and World War II without the United States, on the calculation that we would be bound to come in. They are now thinking they might start again and we would have to come in again. Mr. Allen Dulles said that initial military opposition by the Egyptians would be light, but that the problem of pacifying the area would be extremely difficult.

The President said we must let the British know how gravely we view this matter, what an error we think their decision is, and how this course of action would antagonize the American people despite all that could be done by the top officials of the Government. He felt it was essential to try other measures. Mr. Allen Dulles said that public opinion has flared up strongly in Britain. There is a demand for more than "calling a conference" on Eden's part. Secretary Humphrey reported that there had been wild cheers for Eden at his mention of using the British Navy. The British people are extremely worked up over this situation.

The President said that, thinking of our situation in Panama, we must not let Nasser get away with this action. Secretary Dulles said we want to base whatever is done on this Treaty. [5] The President added, "and on the operation of the Canal." Mr. Dulles said that we want to stick to the Treaty since, if we ever get away from it, we might be pried away from our status in Panama. Mr. Allen Dulles

---

[5] Reference is presumably to the Constantinople Convention of 1888.

said we should consider what might have to be done to protect Persian Gulf oil—sources in Kuwait, Saudi Arabia, etc. In response to a question, Admiral Burke said the Navy has four destroyers on station in the Persian Gulf or immediately available to it.

Secretary Dulles turned to subsidiary problems of an economic and financial nature, such as keeping hold of Egyptian assets in the United States for at least another forty-eight hours. By doing so we would be able to have added effect with the British and French. Press reports say that the Egyptians have subjected United States funds to license in Egypt. Mr. Humphrey said we could freeze the Egyptian funds and subject them to license. He said there are about $60 million worth of Egyptian government funds in the U.S. (Mr. Hoover said there are also perhaps $50 million in private Egyptian funds here) and the Egyptians are trying this morning to move some $10 million in treasury bills. Mr. Humphrey said he had issued instructions to catch this operation and hold it up for the moment. Secretary Dulles thought that freezing and licensing would have value, indicating that ordinary commercial transactions could go forward. We would thus keep some cards to play. Secretary Humphrey said that yesterday he had not wanted to do this, but in light of the British message he was not inclined to think we should freeze these funds and then soften the controls. Mr. Allen Dulles said that the repercussions in Egypt and throughout the world would be very severe. Secretary Dulles said we could be careful not to interfere with normal transactions, and asked what the Egyptians have done about American assets in Egypt. Mr. Allen Dulles thought they might retaliate by seizing all American assets in Egypt.

Secretary Dulles said he had suggested Byroade forward his views regarding commencing evacuation of American nationals, and Byroade had advised against that action. [6] Secretary Dulles thought that the Egyptians if inflamed would attack Americans along with Europeans. He thought we should quietly move to get women and children out of the country. Mr. Hoover said that the first stage as planned has been to encourage personnel to volunteer for evacuation, with the U.S. paying the way. Byroade had agreed that planning for this action should go forward. Secretary Dulles asked how many private citizens and their families are in Egypt, and Mr.

---

[6] In telegram 191 to Cairo, July 28, the Department suggested certain precautionary measures be put into effect for personnel and dependents. (Department of State, Central Files, 274.1122/7–2856) Byroade responded in telegram 170, July 30, that "issuance warnings to staff and public would immediately become known Egyptians and would tend exaggerate tension, possibly to serious degree." (*Ibid.*, 974.7301/7–3056) At 10:11 p.m., July 31, the Department instructed the Embassy in Cairo to abide by the precautionary measures and noted that the British Government had instructed its Embassy in Cairo likewise. (Telegram 219 to Cairo; *ibid.*)

Hoover said that there were not many. Mr. Allen Dulles said in response to a question that the British have made no move thus far to remove their people. Secretary Dulles summed up by saying that we should get ready to move our people at once.

Secretary Humphrey thought that with regard to both the freeze and the evacuation, it might be better to wait until Secretary Dulles has talked to the British. Mr. Hoover thought that a formula on the freeze might be "since Egypt is freezing U.S. funds, we are freezing theirs while the matter is considered." Mr. Humphrey thought that such action will start money movements throughout the world, to Switzerland, for example, and telegraph that something extremely serious is developing. The President pointed out that the French and British have already frozen funds. Mr. Humphrey commented that British funds were already blocked, so that the effect was not so great. Mr. Hoover brought out that the British had in effect prohibited the use of sterling in Egyptian trading. The President thought an announcement indicating that the situation is cloudy and that we are holding matters in the status quo while investigations are going on, but that normal commercial transactions could continue, might be considered. He thought the language of the announcement itself might serve to allay repercussions.

Mr. Dulles said that if he goes to London that action telegraphs that something serious is on. The President said that if Mr. Dulles can't persuade the British from their course, the news of the rift would come out right away. Secretary Dulles said that if separate communiqués were issued, indicating a rift, the effect would be spectacular.

The President commented that the British apparently believe the pipelines from the Middle East would continue to run. Secretary Dulles recalled that they are reportedly extensively mined and that the Syrians could blow them immediately. The President thought the British should be told that we regard this as startling, that Secretary Dulles is coming over to explain how thoroughly and in what ways we disagree. He recognized the intensity of British feeling—specifically their feeling that they have been going down and down in the Middle East and that they have now reached a point where they must strike back. Mr. Allen Dulles said that British comment is full of references to Hitler's occupation of the Rhineland. A number of differences were cited.

Secretary Humphrey asked what the repercussions would be if Secretary Dulles comes back with an obvious split of views between us and the British. The President said such an event would be extremely serious, but not as serious as letting a war start and not trying to stop it. Secretary Dulles said the situation would be almost as serious if we were simply to have Murphy disassociate himself from the communiqué; in that case we would be criticized for not having the Secretary of State go over to work the matter out. He said he thought there is a chance—just a chance—that he can dissuade them, perhaps a bit at a time, gradually deflecting their course of action. The President noted that the British have not yet taken the matter up with Parliament.

The President then said he wanted "not a whisper about this outside this room."

Mr. Hoover recalled that the British had mentioned needing six weeks to mount the offensive they had in mind.

Mr. Humphrey said he would like to study how to carry out a freeze—how to frame the announcement in the best possible way. [7]

Secretary Dulles said he would plan to leave for London in two or three hours, and would call to ask that they keep the conference going until he got there.

The President said he would write immediately to Anthony Eden.

G

Colonel, CE, U S Army

---

[7] Later that day the U.S. Treasury issued the following statement:

"The Treasury announced today that it had temporarily placed under licensing procedure the assets in this country of the Suez Canal Company and the Egyptian Government pending determination of the ownership of these assets and clarification of the existing situation. All transactions with respect to such assets will be subject to Treasury license. This action does not in any way affect private Egyptian funds." (Text of announcement is in telegram 218 to Cairo, July 31; *ibid.*, 974.7301/7–3156)

Subsequently on August 3 the Treasury issued a general license for all new transactions made after July 31. This license was issued on the condition that transactions involving the payment of Canal tolls by ship owners or operators, who were subject to the jurisdiction of the U.S. Government, be accompanied by a statement that payment was being made "under protest and without prejudice to all rights of recovery or otherwise." Under this new licensing procedure, the assets of the Suez Canal Company and the Egyptian Government, on hand in the United States as of July 31, continued to be blocked. (The Treasury license was transmitted in telegram 260 to Cairo, August 3; *ibid.*, 974.7301/8–356.) Telegram 582 to Paris, August 12, explains that "Decision unblock current transactions taken highest level to avoid exacerbating situation vis-à-vis Egypt and maintain free transit Canal pending Conference." (*Ibid.*, 611.74231/8–1256)

35.   **Letter From President Eisenhower to Prime Minister Eden** [1]

Washington, July 31, 1956.

DEAR ANTHONY: From the moment that Nasser announced nationalization of the Suez Canal Company, my thoughts have been constantly with you. Grave problems are placed before both our governments, although for each of us they naturally differ in type and character. Until this morning, I was happy to feel that we were approaching decisions as to applicable procedures somewhat along parallel lines, even though there were, as would be expected, important differences as to detail. But early this morning I received the messages, communicated to me through Murphy from you and Harold Macmillan, telling me on a most secret basis of your decision to employ force without delay or attempting any intermediate and less drastic steps. [2]

We recognize the transcendent worth of the Canal to the free world and the possibility that eventually the use of force might become necessary in order to protect international rights. But we have been hopeful that through a Conference in which would be represented the signatories to the Convention of 1888, as well as

[1] Source: Eisenhower Library, Whitman File, International File. Top Secret. The source text bears the following typewritten notation: "1 copy only retained. This." A series of telephone conversations between Eisenhower and Dulles on July 31 preceded the dispatch of this letter. At 12:55 p.m. Eisenhower telephoned Dulles to convey the substance of the letter and to ask whether it should be cabled to London or hand delivered by Dulles. The Secretary responded that it would be more effective for him to carry it. Eisenhower said that the note was to be seen only by the Secretary and the Under Secretary and that at the White House only Colonel Goodpaster had seen it and only one copy would be retained in the files. (Memoranda of telephone conversations, July 31; *ibid.*, Eisenhower Diaries and *ibid.*, Dulles Papers, White House Telephone Conversations)

At 1 p.m. Dulles telephoned Eisenhower and suggested that the President not comment on the Suez situation at his press conference the next day. Eisenhower said that he would refer to the situation as serious and say that negotiations were going on and that he had sent Dulles there. (*Ibid.*) At 1:05 p.m. the President telephoned Dulles and said that "he feared his first version of page two intimated too strongly possibility of calling special session of Congress. He dictated revised page two to me [Ann Whitman], which was sent over barely in time for Secretary to make his scheduled departure." (Notes by Ann Whitman; *ibid.*, Whitman File, Eisenhower Diaries) No copy of the original version of p. 2 has been found in either the Eisenhower Library or Department of State files. Dulles' Appointment Book indicates that the Secretary was airborne for London at 2 p.m., July 31. (Princeton University Library, Dulles Papers)

[2] Dulles wrote a covering note to this letter which he handed to Eden along with Eisenhower's letter on August 1. It reads in part: "I think that the sentence at the end of the first paragraph refers not to the going through the motions of having an intermediate conference but to the use of intermediate steps as a genuine and sincere effort to settle the problem and avoid the use of force." (Eisenhower Library, Dulles Papers, Miscellaneous Papers—U.K. (Suez Crisis)).

other maritime nations, there would be brought about such pressures on the Egyptian government that the efficient operation of the Canal could be assured for the future.

For my part, I cannot over-emphasize the strength of my conviction that some such method must be attempted before action such as you contemplate should be undertaken. If unfortunately the situation can finally be resolved only by drastic means, there should be no grounds for belief anywhere that corrective measures were undertaken merely to protect national or individual investors, or the legal rights of a sovereign nation were ruthlessly flouted. A conference, at the very least, should have a great educational effect throughout the world. Public opinion here and, I am convinced, in most of the world, would be outraged should there be a failure to make such efforts. Moreover, initial military successes might be easy, but the eventual price might become far too heavy.

I have given you my personal conviction, as well as that of my associates, as to the unwisdom even of contemplating the use of military force at this moment. Assuming, however, that the whole situation continued to deteriorate to the point where such action would seem the only recourse, there are certain political facts to remember. As you realize employment of United States forces is possible only through positive action on the part of the Congress, which is now adjourned but can be reconvened on my call for special reasons. If those reasons should involve the issue of employing United States military strength abroad, there would have to be a showing that every peaceful means of resolving the difficulty had previously been exhausted. Without such a showing, there would be a reaction that could very seriously affect our peoples' feeling toward our Western Allies. I do not want to exaggerate, but I assure you that this could grow to such an intensity as to have the most far-reaching consequences.

I realize that the messages from both you and Harold stressed that the decision taken was already approved by the government and was firm and irrevocable. But I personally feel sure that the American reaction would be severe and that the great areas of the world would share that reaction. On the other hand, I believe we can marshal that opinion in support of a reasonable and conciliatory, but absolutely firm, position. So I hope that you will consent to reviewing this matter once more in its broadest aspects. It is for this reason that I have asked Foster to leave this afternoon to meet with your people tomorrow in London.

I have given you here only a few highlights in the chain of reasoning that compels us to conclude that the step you contemplate should not be undertaken until every peaceful means of protecting the rights and the livelihood of great portions of the world had been thoroughly explored and exhausted. Should these means fail, and I think it is erroneous to assume in advance that they needs must fail, then world opinion would understand how earnestly all of us had attempted to be just, fair and considerate, but that we simply could not accept a situation that would in the long run prove disastrous to the prosperity and living standards of every nation whose economy depends directly or indirectly upon East-West shipping.

With warm personal regard—and with earnest assurances of my continuing respect and friendship,

As ever

D.E. [3]

---

[3] Printed from a copy that bears these typed initials.

---

36.   Editorial Note

While Dulles was attending the 9:45 a.m. meeting at the White House, Murphy and other United States officials in London contacted Rountree and Howe at the State Department via teletype. During the exchange, Rountree and Howe said that the Secretary particularly wanted Murphy's evaluation as to whether the international conference would be a "rubber stamp operation". Murphy responded that he believed that France and the United Kingdom desired a broad-based conference but "with a minimum of risk to the proposition that some form of international control of the Canal must be established". Murphy continued:

"British and French do want a representative conference with a built in guarantee of favorable action. In that sense the rubber stamp element is certainly present. Their main fear is Soviet participation in the first stage. Mind you we are talking really in terms of two conferences. The British and French want the Soviets out of the first meeting. I have told both that I personally do not share their apprehensions about Soviet participation. The latter may refuse the invitation. In that case we are in good public posture. If they accept they would be in the minority, I believe, if they oppose some form of international control. I believe British fear is that USSR will insist on participating in whatever international Canal control authority may be established. British and French want conference essentially to endorse action they are prepared I believe to take anyway." (Telecons between London and Washington, beginning at 2 p.m. from London and 9:30 a.m. from Washington, July 31; Department of State, Conference Files: Lot 62 D 181, CF 725. The copy of the outgoing message is incorrectly identified as between Washington and Paris.)

---

37.   Telegram From the Embassy in the United Kingdom to the Department of State [1]

London, July 31, 1956—7 p.m.

579. For Acting Secretary from Murphy. Paris eyes only Ambassador from Murphy. At restricted session July 31. [2] I informed Lloyd and Pineau that Secretary planned arrive London tomorrow. Both expressed pleasure. We agreed to state in reply to press queries that possibility Secretary's joining meeting always contemplated; his trip did not mark any dramatic new development.

Remainder meeting devoted to discussion communiqué transmitted Deptel 593. [3] Both Pineau and Lloyd expressed vigorous opposition.

Pineau stated he had shown previous draft, Embtel 547, [4] to Coty and Mollet yesterday. Both thought it weak. Dept's text even weaker, and he believed French Government would not wish ascribe [subscribe] to it. Pineau declared numbered paragraph 2 failed condemn Egypt's action vigorously enough. Regarding conference, he said that if US Government suggestion of basing it upon Convention 1888 adopted, it would be necessary, in opinion French legal experts, to invite both East and West Germany. Successive [Successor] powers to Austria/Hungary would include Czechoslovakia, Rumania, Poland and Hungary in addition to Austria. Conference with these participants could not be expected to agree to satisfactory international operation of Canal. France realized USSR might propose meeting

---

[1] Source: Department of State, Central Files, 396.1–LO/7–3156. Top Secret; Priority. Received at 5:22 p.m. Repeated to Paris.

[2] The fifth tripartite meeting began at 4 p.m. (London time) July 31 and, while in plenary session, dealt primarily with the Canal dues and evacuation questions. Murphy explained that he had not yet received detailed instructions from Washington on these subjects. Following this discussion, Lloyd, Pineau, and Murphy held a restricted session. Other accounts of the fifth meeting are in British Foreign Office, "Record of Meeting Held in the Council Chamber, Foreign Office, at 4:00 p.m. on Tuesday, July 31, 1956" and "London Tripartite Conversations," pp. 44–52 (both *ibid.*, Conference Files: Lot 62 D 181, CF 724); and telegrams 578 and 574 from London, July 31 (both *ibid.*, Central Files, 974.7301/7–3156).

[3] Not printed; for text of the Department's proposed communiqué, see Document 32.

[4] Not printed; for text of the "First Redraft of Communiqué," see *ibid.*

with even less desirable participants. US Government is suggesting that UK and France issue invitations while it prescribes who should attend, time and place. France would much prefer single inviting country, namely UK, which would select other participants. Conference would be expected to draw agreement for operation of Canal which could then be submitted to second, larger meeting.

Selwyn Lloyd said he largely shared Pineau's views. Regarding basing conference on Convention of 1888 he mentioned difficulty determining successor states. If conference broadened as suggested by US to include certain trading and maritime nations, it would be almost impossible to draw line and matter would probably end up in General Assembly. Draft communiqué discussed yesterday purposely spoke only of principles of Convention 1888, since, in British view, Convention itself out of date. London preferred as site for conference. Intent was not to place Canal problem before some form of international tribunal but to mobilize responsible body of international opinion behind concept of international arrangements for operation of Canal. Regarding numbered paragraph 2 of US draft, condemnation of Egypt not as strong as desired. Also, British attach greatest importance to unequivocal statement regarding international control. While US wording does not exclude this possibility, it is not specifically provided for.

I replied in substance as follows:

US, of course, does not recognize East Germany and we do not believe that possibility attendance by East Germany represents serious danger. USSR would be included but might well decide not to attend if East Germany not invited. This would be all to the good. We doubt that question of successor states to Austria/Hungary raises serious problem. We would include only Austria. We see many advantages in insisting upon continued validity 1888 Convention. Not logical to argue that only principles still valid while Convention itself no longer in force. We question whether stronger language in a communiqué is desirable. Present text makes clear our views on Egypt's actions without resort to emotional language. While wording of numbered paragraph 2 does not specifically provide for international operation of Canal, we believe it adequately meets British views on this point. Purport of paragraph is that present situation unacceptable and that some other arrangement must be made. Regarding participants, US is suggesting not only signatories but other main users of Canal. We fail to see any special magic in International Chamber of Shipping. In concluding, I agreed bring British and French views to Secretary's attention prior next meeting.

Barbour

38.   Telegram From the Embassy in France to the Department of State [1]

Paris, July 31, 1956—8 p.m.

549. Dept for Acting Secretary. London for Secretary and Murphy. Mollet asked me to come to see him on an urgent basis this afternoon and I remained with him for some 45 minutes. I found him quiet but obviously in a highly emotional state. He said that he was very disturbed at the apparent lack of unity between Britain and France on the one hand, and the US on the other in regard to Nasser. He said he felt that the present moment was equally as critical as the beginning of the Berlin blockade and invasion of Korea. He was convinced that if Nasser is successful all Western positions in the Middle East and North Africa will be lost within the next 12 months. He said that French intelligence was positive in its view that Nasser was acting in close accord with the Soviet Union, and he noted that Nasser had advanced the date of his trip to Moscow so as to be there before Aug 12. He said he was convinced that US did not realize full gravity of the situation. Therefore, he had sent a letter this morning to the President. [2] He gave me formal text of the letter which he said had been telegraphed to the French Embassy for delivery today in Washington.

After reading the letter I told Mollet that I had seen all of Murphy's reports to the Dept from London and that I had not received any impression of disunity comparable to what he was describing. Mollet said that on the contrary there had been real disunity and both the French and the British had been very much disappointed at Murphy's attitude which had been to say continually (1) he had no instructions, (2) must refer all questions back to Washington, (3) US not convinced of Soviet influence behind affair, (4) US is in period of elections and therefore cannot take any important action, and (5) continued effort water down the communiqué so that it will in effect be triumph for Nasser. Mollet then

---

[1] Source: Department of State, Central Files, 974.7301/7–3156. Top Secret; Niact. Received at 10:23 p.m. Repeated Niact to London.

[2] Mollet's letter to Eisenhower, written "in view of the attitude of the United States delegation at the London discussions", conveyed the French Government's fears and concerns on the situation in the Middle East. Mollet warned that the position of the Free World in that area was endangered and he proposed "a rapid and energetic riposte" which would provide a powerful and effective demonstration of Western solidarity. "Only such a positive action," he noted, "can forestall the rapid deterioration of the situation and prevent the Soviet Union from exercising shortly a determining influence in the region concerned." (A copy of the official translation is *ibid.*, Presidential Correspondence: Lot 62 D 204, DeGaulle, Mollet, Gaillard exchange of corres. with pres/sec, 2/53 thru 1/61; a copy of an unofficial translation is in the Eisenhower Library, Whitman File, International File.)

observed that it would be catastrophe for the Free World if US, because of the approach of elections, allowed the whole of the Middle East to fall under Soviet control.

Mollet affirmed several times that the question was not a local one and that France agreed entirely with the US that they should not be put in position of defending the shareholders of Suez Canal Co. or of any outdated colonial rights. The real question was that Nasser's unilateral action could not be accepted as Suez was an international problem and secondly Nasser should not be allowed to impose conditions of slave labor on the foreign employees of the Suez Canal Co. in Egypt who now had the choice of working on Nasser's terms or going to jail. Mollet repeated again that the importance of the matter lay in its influence on the other countries in the Middle East and North Africa and not just on its effects in Egypt.

Mollet said that French opinion was particularly disturbed because they had the feeling that they were being abandoned by the US after the US had started the whole affair by their withdrawal of aid for Aswan Dam. Mollet said the French fully approved of this action by the US but felt that the US should also accept the consequences.

Mollet then said that the French had been somewhat shocked by their military study of the situation when they realized that Egypt had a modern bomber force piloted by Polish and Czech pilots, which was far and away superior to any bomber force possessed by France. This situation had developed according to Mollet, because of France's loyalty to NATO, and the fact that France had accepted the division of effort in NATO where France was asked to concentrate on a fighter airforce and leave the bombing job to the US and to Britain.

Finally, Mollet said that there had been frequent comparisons between Nasser and Hitler and he hesitated to make the comparison because it might seem banal. However, he had to admit that the parallel was extremely close. Nasser's deal with the Soviets for arms is the parallel to the Hitler Stalin Pact of 1939. While Nasser is head of a country far weaker than Hitler's Germany, the Soviet Union is now far stronger than in 1939. He then picked up a copy of Nasser's book "The Philosophy of Revolution" which he had on his desk and said that he felt that all leading officials in the Dept of State should read this book promptly if they had not done so already. He considered it a perfect parallel to "Mein Kampf". He predicted that Nasser would now attempt to digest the seizure of the Suez Canal and would fill this period of digestion with all sorts of appeasing and innocent sounding noises, thus closely paralleling the Hitler technique of always talking peace after each aggression.

At this point I again said to Mollet that I was not aware of any concrete proposition which had been made by the British and French at London to which the US had taken strong objection. Mollet promptly interrupted me and said that the US had objected strongly to any sort of military action. I said that I had not realized that military action was being contemplated at the moment but rather that a proposal was being prepared for the international control of the Canal. Mollet agreed that this was correct and said that if Nasser should accept such a proposal there would be no need whatsoever for military action. However, if he should refuse to accept it as Mollet considered inevitable then Mollet felt it was imperative that the West be united in taking whatever military action was necessary to make Nasser back down.

I then inquired as to whether France wished the US to join with her and Britain in such military action as they might consider necessary and whether they had made any such request to Murphy in London. Mollet replied that he did desire US agreement partici- pate in military action should it be decided that such action was necessary. I then pointed out to Mollet the great constitutional difficulties involved for the US and the fact that we could not initiate military action without Congressional approval, and I ex- pressed some surprise as to why the French and British felt that US military participation would be necessary. Mollet then said that actual participation might not be necessary and that it would be satisfactory if the US would make a declaration showing that they were in full agreement with British and French. With such a US statement he felt that the British and French could carry out any military action required by themselves.

Mollet then said that what he feared was that the US was leaning towards the strategy of continental defense and was losing interest in the defense of Europe and the Middle East. He felt that the US was embarking on the same course of error by appeasement that had been followed toward Hitler in the 1930's. He said he considered the situation so serious that he was prepared to take an airplane to Washington and see the President if that would be acceptable to US Govt. He said he had never been so disturbed and worried for the future and was certain that if we did not take action to stop Nasser now we would be faced with the same problem 3, 6 or 9 months hence, only the Western position by that time would have greatly deteriorated.

As I got up to leave Mollet said he wished to tell me one more thing in greatest confidence which he had not mentioned previously. He said that it was made clear to him by the Soviet leaders when he was in Moscow that they were prepared, in concert with Nasser, to agree to bring about peace in Algeria on a basis acceptable to his government provided he would agree to come part way to meet their views on European matters. They did not ask that France make any dramatic moves, such as the abandonment of NATO, but only that she be less faithful to the West and become in effect semi-neutralist. Mollet said I must realize the temptation that such an offer regarding Algeria offered to any French statesman. He hoped that I would understand when he said that he felt that his firm rejection of this Soviet offer gave him the right now to speak frankly of his fears for the Western position and to request a sympathetic hearing by the US Govt.

Dillon

---

39.   Message From President Eisenhower to Prime Minister Mollet [1]

Washington, July 31, 1956.

DEAR MR. PRESIDENT: I have received your letter of July thirty-first [2] regarding the Suez Canal situation which at this moment is being studied and discussed by representatives of our Governments in London. I am glad to have this frank expression of your thoughts on a matter which we all view with grave concern. As you are already aware, I have today asked Secretary Dulles to fly to London to confer with the French and British representatives there.

While I recognize that events may ultimately make forceful action necessary, I feel that the present situation demands that we act moderately, but firmly, to bring about a dependable administration of the Canal. I feel that the utmost calm is required in charting the course of the Western nations at this time and it is for this reason that we propose that a meeting of interested states be held promptly. I believe that our efforts now should be directed toward

---

[1] Source: Department of State, Presidential Correspondence: Lot 66 D 204, The Pres. and Sec. exchanges of Corres. with DeGaulle, Mollet, Gaillard, 7/56–1/61. Secret. The text of this message was transmitted to Paris in Niact telegram 418, August 1. (*Ibid.*, Central Files, 974.7301/8–156) Chargé Cecil B. Lyon delivered the message to Mollet at 9:50 a.m., August 2. (Telegram 576 from Paris, August 2; *ibid.*, 711.11–El/8–256) Ambassador Dillon had joined Dulles in London. Howe transmitted a draft of this message, a copy of telegram 549 (*supra*), and a copy of an August 1 *New York Times* article by Harold Callender to Goodpaster on August 1. (Covering memorandum dated August 1; *ibid.*, 974.7301/7–3156)

[2] See footnote 2, *supra*.

the holding of such an international conference which would have an educational effect on public opinion throughout the world. If the Egyptian Government defies such a conference, or rejects reasonable proposals, then there should result a broader basis than now exists for other affirmative action.

I am convinced that the Western nations must show the world that every effective peaceful means to resolve this difficulty has been exhausted and I sincerely hope that precipitate action can be avoided.

With assurances of my highest esteem.

Sincerely,

Dwight D. Eisenhower

40.   Special National Intelligence Estimate [1]

SNIE 30–3–56   Washington, July 31, 1956.

NASSER AND THE MIDDLE EAST SITUATION [2]

The Problem

To assess the implications of Egyptian nationalization of the

---

[1] Source: Department of State, INR–NIE Files. Secret. Special National Intelligence Estimates (SNIEs) were high-level interdepartmental reports presenting authoritative appraisals of vital foreign policy problems on an immediate crisis basis. SNIEs were drafted by officers from those agencies represented on the Intelligence Advisory Committee (IAC), discussed and revised by interdepartmental working groups coordinated by the Office of National Estimates of the Central Intelligence Agency (CIA), approved by the IAC, and circulated under the aegis of the CIA to the President, appropriate officers of cabinet level, and the National Security Council. The Department of State provided all political and some economic sections of SNIEs.

[2] According to a note on the cover sheet, "The following intelligence organizations participated in the preparation of this estimate: The Central Intelligence Agency and the intelligence organizations of the Department of State, the Army, the Navy, the Air Force, and The Joint Staff." This estimate was concurred in by the Intelligence Advisory Committee on July 31, 1956. "Concurring were the Special Assistant, Intelligence, Department of State; the Assistant Chief of Staff, Intelligence, Department of the Army; the Director of Naval Intelligence; the Director of Intelligence, USAF; and the Deputy Director for Intelligence, The Joint Staff. The Atomic Energy Commission Representative to the IAC, and the Assistant Director, Federal Bureau of Investigation, abstained, the subject being outside of their jurisdiction.'

Suez Canal Company and probable developments in the resultant situation. [3]

Conclusions

1. By nationalization of the Suez Canal Company, President Nasser has for the time being greatly strengthened his position, not only as leader of Egypt, but also as the spokesman and symbol of Arab nationalism throughout the Middle East. He has won wild acclaim from the Egyptian population, warm support from the greater part of the Arab world, and approval from the USSR. This has happened, moreover, just as his policies had appeared to have suffered a humiliating reversal through the unexpected refusal of the US and UK, and seemingly of the USSR as well, to finance the Aswan High Dam project.

2. It is not impossible for the Egyptians to run the canal with reasonable competence, although Nasser would almost certainly come to use control of the canal to advance his own policies. The primary significance of Nasser's move lies in its political and psychological aspects rather than in the threat it poses to canal operations. Nasser's action has strengthened anti-Western, anticolonial, and nationalist trends throughout the area, and if successful, will encourage future moves toward early nationalization or other action against foreign-owned oil pipelines and petroleum facilities.

3. The courses of action open to the West in this situation range from acquiescence with as good grace as possible, though recourse to diplomatic representations, legal action in international or other tribunals, appeals to the United Nations, and economic sanctions, to military operations against Egypt. The UK has already adopted drastic economic measures, freezing the blocked Egyptian sterling

---

[3] A memorandum from Allen Dulles to Acting Secretary Hoover, August 1, regarding the "Egyptian Situation" notes that a preliminary draft of this estimate was handed to Secretary Dulles before he left. The memorandum continues: "Last night late, I sent a confirmatory cable regarding the general approval of this estimate by the entire Intelligence community, and then added a supplement regarding the Soviet action with regard to Western military action which read as follows: 'In the event of Western military action against Nasser, we believe that the USSR would make every effort to avoid direct involvement, but short of that would intensify its efforts to give aid to Nasser, including possible covert introduction of military advisors and specialists and would capitalize on this situation in the UN and in the Arab and Neutralist world.'

"I now have confirmation that both this cable and the cable based upon my talk with Howard Page were delivered to the Secretary at 10:00 a.m. this morning." (Department of State, Central Files, 684A.86/8–156) Copies of the cables are *ibid.,* Conference Files: Lot 62 D 181, CF 725A. Concerning his talk with Howard Page, a director of Standard Oil of New Jersey, Allen Dulles had reported the decision of the Executive Committee of Standard Oil of New Jersey to proceed immediately with finding alternate pipeline routes, if the Suez Canal were not placed under international control.

balances (about 110 million pounds) and all other Egyptian financial assets in the sterling area. These actions may seriously curtail Egyptian trade with the West, since nearly all of it is conducted in sterling. France has fully supported the UK.

4. The courses of action open to Nasser in countering Western measures short of military action include seizure of British and other Western assets in Egypt, harassment of shipping in the canal by delays and hindrances, or full closure of the canal to Western shipping. Major interference with canal shipping would not only reduce the canal revenues accruing to Egypt but would probably also arouse the active disfavor of a wide range of nations, including some of neutralist and anticolonialist feeling. It would also provide justification for possible forceful Western action to keep the canal open. Accordingly, Nasser is likely to avoid such interference except as an extreme measure in retaliation for Western actions.

5. Both the UK and France on the one hand, and Nasser on the other, have already taken positions from which they are unlikely to retreat in the near future. The prospect is for a prolonged period of crisis, during which existing nationalist and anti-Western sentiment in the Arab states, and probably among neutralist anticolonial peoples, will probably be intensified.

6. The recent developments are markedly to the Soviet interest, opening as they do a wider gulf between Egypt and the West, between the Arab world and the West, and possibly among Western nations themselves as they try to agree on concerted countermeasures. The USSR will probably participate in any negotiated solution of the canal crisis, and thereby will expand its influence in the Middle East. The USSR will probably give Nasser support, both political and economic, in his resistance to Western pressures. Nasser would welcome such support. Although at the present time his interests appear to run parallel to those of the USSR, we still believe that Nasser intends to avoid Soviet domination and to refrain from a firm and permanent alignment with either side in the East-West struggle.

7. In the event of Western military action against Nasser, we believe that the USSR would make every effort to avoid direct involvement, but short of that would intensify its efforts to give aid to Nasser, including possible covert introduction of military advisers and specialists, and would also capitalize on this situation in the UN and in the Arab and neutralist countries.

8. Israel will view with satisfaction the widened rift between its principal Arab antagonist and the major Western Powers. It will probably appeal for greatly increased shipments of arms; such shipments would almost certainly lead to violent anti-Western reactions throughout the Arab world. We do not believe, however, that Israel

will attack Egypt, at least during the early phases of this crisis. Nasser will probably feel it necessary to avoid conflict with Israel while he is engaged in his contest with greater powers. However, if Nasser emerges as the victor in the present crisis, he is likely to take an increasingly stiff attitude toward Israel.

9. It is possible that an international conference of the signatories to the 1888 Convention and other interested parties might produce a formula recognizing nationalization of the Canal Company but protecting the rights of international transit, which would be acceptable to the West, the USSR, and other interested user countries. There would be many obstacles to achieving Egyptian adherence to any *new* accord involving international control, particularly in the light of Nasser's position that he would refuse to accept any measure of such control. However, it would be difficult for him to reject a solution if the Western Powers, the USSR, the Colombo Powers, and the major shipping powers agreed in urging it upon him, particularly if it fell within the framework of the 1888 Convention.

Discussion

I. The Nationalization of the Suez Canal

10. President Nasser's nationalization of the Suez Canal Company represents—for the moment at least—a highly effective move to extricate himself from what appeared to be a humiliating setback in an otherwise extremely successful foreign policy. By accepting arms from the Soviet Bloc in September 1955, Nasser at one stroke elevated himself to a position of extraordinary prestige throughout the Arab world as well as at home. This, and a series of other moves, alienated the US and UK from Egypt without completely severing connections; and they signified that Nasser had accepted the support of the USSR without subjecting Egypt to Soviet domination. Subsequently it appeared to many in the world, and it must have appeared to Nasser himself, that the USSR and the Western Powers were bidding against each other for his friendship. As the token of this competitive bidding, Nasser secured an offer from the US and UK to finance the Aswan High Dam project, and he either obtained, or at least gave the impression that he had obtained, a corresponding offer from the USSR. Thus he seemingly demonstrated the advantages to be gained for his own primarily Arab interests from playing both sides in the East-West conflict, and he caused some allies of the West to wonder if they had chosen the most profitable course.

11. As things developed, however, the estrangement between Nasser and the Western Powers grew until the US, followed by the

UK, withdrew its offer of aid for the High Dam. At the same time it appeared that the USSR either had never clearly made an acceptable offer, or if it had done so had also withdrawn it. The project had been so publicized by Nasser abroad as to become a symbol of his prestige in the area; its abandonment would have been a severe blow to his position. To this situation he responded by a speech vigorously attacking the US and especially the UK as exponents of imperialism, and he announced the nationalizing of the Suez Canal Company, promising that the revenues from that enterprise would be used to finance the High Dam, and would be sufficient for that purpose. Nasser's announcement was greeted with enthusiasm in Egypt and throughout the Arab world. At least for the time being it has strengthened his position not only as leader of Egypt, but also as the spokesman and symbol of Arab nationalism throughout the Middle East.

12. We believe that the nationalization decision was taken on short notice. Although the Egyptian government had long been planning for eventual assumption of control over the canal when the company's concession expired in 1968, Nasser had given no prior indication of desire to take over the canal ahead of time, and in fact had specifically stated that he did not wish to do so. After the US–UK announcements, the Egyptians showed every sign of expecting that the USSR, which had certainly displayed interest in financing the dam, would come to the rescue when the possibility of Western assistance disappeared.

13. In view of the Canal Company's status as a private organization incorporated within Egypt and operating within Egyptian territory and Nasser's proposal to recompense shareholders on the basis of Paris Bourse quotations just prior to his announcement, it must have appeared to the Egyptian government that seizure would be difficult to upset on legal grounds. Moreover, if Egypt should fulfill its international obligations in operating the canal, there would be little basis for legal action by the using powers. Although most of the liquid assets of the Canal Company are now outside Egyptian control, Nasser has already threatened to hold up compensation of shareholders unless these assets are made available to him. He has additional leverage by virtue of the fact that the British, who are principal shareholders, are also the principal users of the canal and thus have a strong interest in keeping it in operation. Now that British troops are no longer stationed in the canal zone—the last contingents left only a few weeks ago—the British cannot undertake military action to regain control of the canal except through outright invasion of Egyptian soil.

14. Meanwhile, nationalization could bring Nasser important advantages. Net annual revenues will probably remain far below the

$100 million cited by Nasser in his 26 July speech, even if he takes advantage of the leeway for an increase in tolls provided by the present operating agreements. Nevertheless, net revenues of $40 or $50 million would ease Egypt's financial position, and some work on the Aswan Dam might be undertaken. More importantly the psychological initiative temporarily lost by Nasser at the time of the US–UK announcements on the Aswan Dam has for the moment been triumphantly restored, both in Egypt and in the surrounding Arab states. The fact that he has been able to strike back on his own, without acceptance of Bloc assistance, further enhances his appeal.

15. Nationalization of the Canal Company has brought an angry reaction from the UK and France, both of whom have formally protested the move; there have also been expressions of concern from other Western nations. The UK has already retaliated by stopping arms shipments to Egypt, and by freezing all Egyptian private and public assets under its control (including about 110 million pounds in sterling balances). France is cooperating in the Canal Company's refusal to release its French-held liquid assets to Egypt.

16. British and French opposition arises in part from their status as owners of the Canal Company (the British government owns about 45 percent of the stock and French private investors practically all the remainder) and as major users of the canal itself or of products transported through it. The most important of these is oil, which in 1955 accounted for 63 percent of the tonnage through the canal; more than 60 percent of Middle East oil shipments, which now furnish about 90 percent of Western European requirements and are major revenue producers for the UK in particular, now go by the canal rather than by pipeline. In particular, oil from Kuwait and Qatar, which is least likely to be affected by oil nationalization moves, is wholly dependent on tankers for lifting.

17. Even if the Egyptians were to recompense the stockholders and operate the canal in good faith, their seizure of the canal would pose a number of dangers for shippers and those dependent on products transported through the canal. It is uncertain whether Egypt will be able to run the canal efficiently or whether an Egyptian administration will expend the amount on canal improvements which the increasingly heavy traffic burden is making necessary. Egypt could raise tolls to something like twice their present level without violating present agreements binding the company. Direct administration of the canal, moreover, will facilitate Egyptian use of it as a political weapon. Egypt's control of the canal approaches has already enabled it to do this, as its prohibition of Israeli ships and its restriction of shipments to Israel have demonstrated. With actual control of the administrative machinery, Egypt

will be in a position to impose delays and harassments against the ships of unfriendly or uncooperative powers of a sort difficult to present for action by the UN or the World Court.

18. The political and psychological impact of Egypt's move weighs far more heavily in British and French thinking than concern for the company's revenues or even the risks of interference with traffic. The British and French see nationalization of the Suez Canal Company as but another, and probably the gravest, in a long series of attacks on Western interests in the area—the most notable being Iran's nationalization of the oil industry and Egypt's unilateral "abrogation" of the 1936 treaty with the UK in 1951. They are almost certainly convinced that if Nasser's move goes unchecked it will be followed by similar actions throughout the Middle East, and the position of Western oil interests, which the British in particular consider vital to their own survival, will be gravely jeopardized. Moreover, they recognize that successful nationalization of the canal will greatly increase Nasser's influence in the other Arab states and is thus likely to lead to a further erosion of Western prestige and an increased willingness on the part of these states to follow Egypt's lead in relations with the Bloc and the West. It is primarily for these reasons that the British and French are likely to demand the strongest measures, to prevent Nasser from "getting away with it."

19. Reactions from other nations thus far have been less intense. The nationalization announcement was generally hailed throughout the Arab world, including Iraq. In Asia, the acceptance of Egypt's right to nationalize has been mingled with some expression of concern over the abruptness of the move and the possibility of adverse effects on trade links with the West; Ceylon's prime minister has suggested the possibility of a meeting of the Colombo Powers to discuss the matter. Early Bloc reactions have been favorable.

II. Possible Egyptian Courses of Action

20. The immediate outlook is for an extremely critical period in which Egyptian moves will depend in great part on what actions are taken by interested outside powers—including the UK, France, and the US, as well as the USSR and even Israel. Nasser is, however, not likely to make any major concessions because of Western diplomatic persuasion or Western efforts to secure legal redress through international law. Indeed, to defy such limited Western efforts would probably at least temporarily strengthen his position, since his actions could be made to appear as a struggle against Western imperialist conspiracy. By the same token, he is not likely to make major concessions because of Western economic sanctions against

Egypt, a boycott of the canal, or the impounding of the Egyptian sterling assets in the UK, even though such moves would create critical problems for Egypt—which is already short of foreign exchange and confronted with difficulties in selling its cotton. He probably believes he could count on assistance from the Bloc and the Saudis in such a situation.

21. If the UK and other Western Powers should attempt to enforce their demands by occupation or blockade, Nasser would probably attempt such military resistance as he could, meanwhile appealing to the UN. Although he himself would realize the hopelessness of military action by Egypt alone, he would feel compelled to make the gesture, hoping for assistance from the Bloc, and counting on the revulsion of Arab and neutralist opinion against the West to bring him further aid.

22. It is possible that an international conference of the signatories to the 1888 Convention and other interested parties might produce a formula recognizing nationalization of the Canal Company but protecting the rights of international transit, which would be acceptable to the West, the USSR, and other interested user countries. There would be many obstacles to achieving Egyptian adherence to any *new* accord involving international control, particularly in the light of Nasser's position that he would refuse to accept any measure of such control. However, it would be difficult for him to reject a solution if the Western Powers, the USSR, the Colombo Powers, and the major shipping powers agreed in urging it upon him, particularly if it fell within the framework of the 1888 Convention.

Egyptian Operation of the Canal

23. Nasser initially reacted to the UK's freezing of Egyptian assets by threatening to close the canal to British shipping. At present, he is emphasizing Egypt's intention to operate the canal efficiently and to maintain it in good condition. However, he would probably take measures to prevent the passage of ships involved if he were confronted with a persistent refusal on the part of major users of the canal to pay tolls to Egypt.

24. If the West decides to accept Egyptian control of the canal, or makes only ineffective protests, Nasser is probably prepared to abide for some time by current rules and practices with respect to level of charges, freedom of transit, and the like. Having taken the big gamble in seizing control, he would probably prefer to avoid harassing measures against Western shipping interests, at least in the near future, lest such actions should serve as the final provocation calling forth violent countermeasures by the West. Moreover, he will

be anxious to demonstrate the legitimacy of his action to other nations, particularly the neutralist states of south and southeast Asia.

25. In time, however, if he felt his control of the canal to be secure, the temptation to exploit his position to gain increased revenue would probably become irresistible. Eventually, moreover, Nasser might come to use control of the canal for political purposes; for example, as part of a campaign against British interests in the Middle East.

Actions With Respect to Other Western Interests Within Egypt

26. Whatever the outcome of the Suez controversy itself, the tensions engendered by that affair can only increase Nasser's already strong hostility toward Western influence in the Middle East. In almost any event, his campaign against Western interests in the area will be continued. The actions already taken by the British and French indicate that an intensified struggle is virtually certain to occur.

27. Nasser may move to take over private Western interests in Egypt. Such action would be particularly likely as a form of reprisal in the event that sanctions by the Western Powers resulted in a form of economic warfare between the latter and Egypt.

Other Egyptian Actions

28. Nasser has for some time been clearly committed to the broad goal of undermining Western influence in the Middle East and Africa. The Nasser regime's active propaganda against the West, both within Egypt and in other areas of the Arab world and Africa, is virtually certain to continue. The Suez issue may increase its appeal among anti-Western and neutralist elements, especially if Western reaction to the canal seizure enables Nasser to appear either as a martyr to imperialism or as one who has successfully defied the West.

29. One important target of the Egyptian anti-Western campaign will continue to be Western oil interests in the Arab states. Nasser would probably like to see a nationalization of the oil industry throughout the Arab world, and in the longer run may be expected to encourage such a development. In the short run, however, a more promising opportunity for undermining the Western oil position would be to promote action by oil transit states aimed at weakening or terminating Western control over the oil pipelines from Iraq and Saudi Arabia to the Mediterranean. Such action might be particularly appealing to Nasser since the unsettled situation in the Suez Canal increases the importance to the West of these pipelines. If Egypt seeks to bring about such action, its chief hope would be in Syria, where Egyptian influence is strong among impor-

tant factions in the anti-Western and unstable government. Egypt also seeks to weaken the Western oil companies in the Middle East by promoting labor unrest and nationalist-led organizations among employees of the companies.

30. Other Egyptian action against Western interests in the Arab states will continue to include political support for anti-Western nationalists in Syria and Jordan, and encouragement of Saudi Arabia in its already prohibitive demands on the US as the price of renewal of the Dhahran Airfield. Nasser will continue his efforts to diminish US and UK influence in Libya and his campaign against France in North Africa. Nasser will also increase efforts to extend Egyptian influence in the Sudan. There is nothing new in this pattern of Egyptian action, which has been going on since Nasser emerged as the spokesman for nationalism in the area. The chief danger in the present situation, however, is that existing nationalist and anti-Western sentiment in these states may be intensified by sympathy for the Egyptian leader in his struggle over the canal issue. In such an event, Nasser's influence over other Arab governments may increase.

31. *Actions toward Israel.* Nasser's hostility toward Israel will not be lessened by his current conflict with the Western Powers, and the Egyptian regime will continue to exploit the Israeli issue as an effective means of gaining sympathy and support in the Arab world. At least in the immediate crisis over the canal, Nasser will probably be anxious to avoid serious trouble with Israel, and is not likely to go out of his way to provide the Israelis with an excuse for military action against Egypt. However, if Nasser emerges as the victor in the present crisis, he is likely to take an increasingly stiff attitude toward Israel.

III. The Role of the USSR

32. The Soviet role in recent developments is obscure. There is strong evidence that the USSR did in fact offer to finance the foreign exchange requirements of the High Aswan Dam some months ago and that—possibly with Soviet acquiescence—Egypt took no action on the offer in the expectation of getting the money from the West. Since the unexpected withdrawal of the US–UK aid offer, the record has been ambiguous, with statements by Soviet officials in Egypt and Egyptian officials that the aid offer still stood being matched by statements of Foreign Minister Shepilov and others that the USSR was willing to support other development projects, leaving the implication that it was not prepared to help finance the dam.

33. It is possible that Nasser's decision to nationalize the Suez Canal Company was taken in collusion with the USSR. We consider this unlikely, though we believe that Nasser made his decision with confidence that he would receive Soviet approval and support.

34. The USSR will probably help Nasser in his political and economic difficulties with the West by such methods as diplomatic support in the UN and elsewhere and economic assistance to alleviate the effects of Western economic sanctions. It will almost certainly continue to provide military aid and help for industrial projects and other enterprises of economic development, probably including some assistance toward launching the High Dam project if Nasser requests it.

35. In the event of Western military action against Nasser, we believe that the USSR would make every effort to avoid direct involvement, but short of that would intensify its efforts to give aid to Nasser, including possible covert introduction of military advisers and specialists, and would also capitalize on this situation in the UN and in the Arab and neutralist countries.

36. The USSR has recently made some efforts to cultivate better relations with Israel and certain Baghdad Pact members. Although it will almost certainly take advantage of opportunities for widening the breach between Egypt and the West at little cost to itself, it probably considers that rapid consolidation of an especially close and exclusive relationship with Egypt is not only unnecessary but actually undesirable at this time in view of the probable adverse effects on its freedom of maneuver. It will probably continue to avoid full endorsement of the Arab position on Palestine.

37. Nasser himself, unless involved in hostilities, will probably continue to place important limitations on the political commitments he would willingly give to the Bloc. He probably believes that he can pursue indefinitely an "independent foreign policy" and that the present necessity of accepting heavy economic commitments to the Bloc is a temporary proposition which can be brought back into proper focus at a later date if he takes reasonable precautions. In so doing, Nasser probably overestimates his own unaided ability to retain genuine freedom of action. Should the situation so worsen as materially to increase his already great economic dependence on the Bloc he might find himself trapped. However, we believe that at least for some time to come Egypt and the Bloc will be linked by a substantial though by no means complete community of interest with respect to Middle East questions rather than by any more binding ties, and that both sides will continue to have important reservations about their mutual relationship.

38. The canal crisis has clearly opened to the USSR the opportunity of further expanding its influence in the Middle East, since a

negotiated resolution of the crisis is likely to involve the approval
and perhaps the participation of the USSR.

IV. Reactions in Pro-Egyptian and Uncommitted Arab States

39. The initial public reaction to Nasser's action in the pro-
Egyptian and uncommitted Arab states has been highly favorable.
His dramatic act of defiance has raised his standing in the Arab
world to new heights. At least in the short run, the action will have
an intoxicating effect on Arab nationalist sentiment similar to that
engendered by the original Egyptian arms deal with the Soviet Bloc.
In addition, certain Arab states may be encouraged, both by example
and persuasion, to take similar anti-Western actions in proportion as
Nasser's action appears to have been a profitable move. While Arab
nationalists will generally approve Nasser's action, the degree of
concrete support they will be prepared to offer Egypt will probably
depend on the strength of Western and general world reaction.
Moreover, the ultimate effect in both the uncommitted and in the
pro-Egyptian Arab states will depend on whether Nasser can carry
through the action successfully without incurring severe Western
penalties.

40. *Saudi Arabia.* [4] Nasser's decision comes at a particularly unfortunate time so far as Western relations with Saudi Arabia are
concerned. While fundamentally opposed to Communism and professing to the West a desire to maintain friendly relations with the
US and UK, King Saud is using his diplomatic influence and
considerable financial resources to stir up trouble for the UK, the
Hashimite dynasties of Iraq and Jordan, and the Baghdad Pact; he
seeks to stiffen Arab opposition to Israel and actively supports the
North African nationalists. King Saud has set a high price for
renewal of the agreement covering use of the US air base at
Dhahran, and in the wake of Nasser's defiance of the Western
Powers, it is unlikely that Saud will come down enough to meet
present US terms. Failure to reach agreement concerning the air base
would cause Saud seriously to consider obtaining Bloc arms, although he would prefer to obtain arms from the US or some other
non-Soviet source. Meanwhile, Saudi Arabia (and Yemen) will be
encouraged by Nasser's action to press territorial claims against the
British and the British-supported sheikhdoms even more strongly.

41. At the same time, the Saudis will remain anxious to avoid
such a deterioration in their relations with the US as would endanger their vital oil revenues from the Arabian American Oil Company
(ARAMCO). While the Egyptian action in taking over the Canal

---

[4] See NIE 36.6–56, "The Outlook for Saudi Arabia," 24 April 1956. [Footnote in
the source text. NIE 36.6–56 is not printed.]

Company will provide a powerful fillip to Arab inclinations to nationalize foreign-owned assets, the Saudis are aware from the Iranian experience of the great difficulties of attempting to operate an oil industry in the face of concerted Western commercial opposition. Nationalization of the TAPLINE facilities (and raising rates) may be considered, but would probably not be undertaken if ARAMCO threatened to retaliate by cutting production. While an attempt to nationalize the oil industry as a whole in the next several years appears unlikely, the Egyptian action might encourage the Saudis to raise their royalty demands against the company. Even here they will probably proceed cautiously, however, and may counsel moderation should the Egyptians threaten to raise canal tolls to such an extent as to interfere with the flow of oil.

42 *Syria, Jordan, and Lebanon.* Egypt's ally Syria will support Nasser's action. Under Nasser's influence, Syria might be encouraged to undertake nationalization of the oil pipelines traversing the country or, at least, seek to obtain larger revenues from the operating companies. Syria's actions will be determined in considerable measure by the orientation of its government. Conservative elements appear in recent weeks to have regained some strength, especially within the army. However, Nasser's coup is more likely to strengthen pro-Egyptian elements who would be inclined toward anti-Western moves. On balance, unless the Egyptians receive a setback at Western hands, the chances of eventual actions against Western pipelines and other interests appear to be better than even.

43. The present weak Jordanian government is probably unwilling to jeopardize its British support and subsidy, but will temporize for fear of the public reaction to any pro-Western stand. It will be subject to strong internal pressures to give Egypt maximum diplomatic and propaganda support. Jordan will nevertheless probably continue seeking to avoid Egyptian domination. Should the Egyptians decide to oust the US economic aid mission, they might well urge other Arab states having such programs to follow a similar course. In such a case, Nasser's greatest chance of success would be in Jordan, where US aid has already been subject to severe nationalist attacks.

44. The Lebanese government will probably adopt a noncommittal attitude until it ascertains the degree of Egypt's success in defying the West. While presently engaged in a dispute with the Iraq Petroleum Company concerning its share of the pipeline revenues, Lebanon would prefer to avoid drastic actions against Western interests because of its own economic self-interest as a trading and financial center in the area. Lebanon will, however, find it increasingly difficult to resist being swept along in any general wave of

anti-Western sentiment and activities which may follow Nasser's action.

45. *Reactions to Western Retaliatory Measures.* The reaction in the pro-Egyptian and uncommitted Arab states to strong measures against Nasser by the Western Powers would probably be sharp. Imposition of economic sanctions would probably arouse sympathy for Egypt and give further impetus to demands for anti-Western retaliatory measures. The likelihood of such effects would be increased in the event of intervention by Western military forces or a substantial increase in Western arms shipments to Israel, and widespread attacks on Western lives and property might take place. Should Nasser be forced to make compromises in order to reach a settlement there would at best be a grumbling acceptance by pro-Egyptian elements. Persons and groups friendly to the West would, however, be encouraged to assert themselves more openly. The Western position would accordingly be strengthened, but further actions to bolster the position of friendly nations would probably be required if the gains were not to be lost.

V. Reaction of Turkey, Iraq, and the Persian Gulf Principalities

46. The reaction in Turkey to Nasser's action has been unfavorable. Relations between the two countries have not been good in recent years and the present Turkish government would in all probability favor strong Western retaliatory measures against the Nasser regime. While there appears to be little the Turks can do to influence the situation directly, they would give moral support to Western countermeasures. On the other hand, Western failure to act would tend further to weaken Turkish faith in the UK—already somewhat under a cloud because of the Cyprus issue—as a firm partner in the Baghdad Pact.

47. The situation in Iraq is more complicated. The Iraqi press and public has responded favorably to Nasser's action but the Iraqi government has so far acted with greater reserve. In addition, some popular pressures may be generated for nationalization of the British dominated Iraq Petroleum Company. The opposition is virtually impotent to force the pro-Western ruling group's hand, however, and in any case the pressures in this direction are not likely to be significantly greater than when Iran nationalized its oil industry, and hence should be containable. In the event Nasser successfully establishes his control of the canal, however, the anti-Western pressure on the ruling group in Iraq will be greatly increased.

48. Meanwhile, the Iraqi government will try to turn the West's attitude toward Nasser to its own advantage by privately urging increased Western pressure on Egypt and more sympathetic consider-

ation of Iraqi arms needs. The government would regard strong Western measures against Nasser as a sign that their membership in the Baghdad Pact was not a mistake; Western inaction would further disillusion them. Considering the difficulties which they would face in effecting a physical take over in Syria, the Iraqis would probably not seek to carry out this long-time ambition unless the Syrians threatened to take action with respect to the IPC pipeline which would jeopardize Iraqi oil revenues. The possibility of a British-inspired Iraqi move against Syria designed both to divert attention from Nasser and to fulfill Iraqi ambitions should not be entirely excluded.

49. There will probably be little immediate reaction to the moves involving Egypt in the oil producing sheikhdoms of Kuwait, Bahrein, and the smaller Persian Gulf entities which are under British protection. Nationalist elements will sympathize with Nasser, but anti-British actions—except possibly on Bahrein—will not immediately develop.

VI. Reactions of Other Asian States

50. In Iran, reactions to the Nasser government's moves and to possible Western countermeasures will be mixed. As a member of the Baghdad Pact and on the basis of its own experience with oil nationalization, the Iranian government is apt to be skeptical of Nasser's move. It will furthermore be concerned over the possible effect on oil shipments through the canal. Nationalist elements which have long opposed the British will sympathize with Egypt.

51. India, Pakistan, and Ceylon will probably all feel some concern over the future status of the canal and the possible effect on their economies of higher tolls which the Nasser regime might seek to levy. At the same time, these three Commonwealth members will tend to share the feeling that Nasser has a right to take such action in Egypt's interest, however much some of them may disapprove his abrupt methods. The press and vocal public in these countries have already expressed sympathy for Egypt's position. Such Southeast Asian countries as Burma and Indonesia can be expected to give Egypt moral support as a member of the Bandung grouping. Their involvement will, however, be less direct. On the other hand, Japan, which relies heavily on overseas trade, is concerned over the effect on its commerce of a possible increase in canal tolls or any slow-down or closing of the waterway, and might support Western efforts to correct the situation.

VII. Israeli Reaction to the Situation

52. The predominant reaction of Israel to recent events has been one of satisfaction over the clear and sharp conflict which has emerged between the Western Powers and Israel's principal Arab enemy. Despite some concern lest Nasser increase his power by another success against the West (and thereby also achieve the power permanently to block Israeli access to the Suez Canal), Israel almost certainly counts on being able to achieve a net benefit from the situation.

53. In general, Israel may be expected to pursue the line that the more trouble the Western Powers have with the Arab states, the greater should be their support for Israel. The most immediate objective of the Israelis will be to secure arms from the West, hoping that the Western Powers' resentment and disillusion with Nasser will cause them to revise their previous policies against arming Israel. Israel also probably feels that the opportunity has come to focus attention on its own transit rights in Suez and the Gulf of Aqaba, which Egypt has always denied it (with minor exceptions in the case of vessels of other nations carrying Israeli cargoes). Israel will probably seek to associate itself with any multilateral international action taken against Nasser on the canal issue, and will also press in the UN and with the Western Powers for implementation of the 1951 UN Security Council resolution calling on Egypt to permit the transit of Israeli shipping through the canal.

54. Israel would probably welcome Western military action in response to Nasser's seizure of the canal. The Israelis would probably estimate that determined Western military action would not only lead to Nasser's downfall, but would also very likely strike a severe blow at the potential for action of militantly anti-Israeli elements in Syria and Jordan. We believe that the chances are against Israel itself deliberately initiating war with Egypt, at least during the early phases of the present crisis. The danger of such action might materially increase if the Western Powers undertook military action—in which case Israel might seek to join them; or if Western relations with Egypt deteriorated so drastically that Israel could feel reasonably confident of avoiding severe Western punitive measures as a result of attacking Egypt—presumably with the aim of destroying the Egyptian forces and toppling Nasser. Short of such situations, Israel's military policy toward Egypt and its other Arab neighbors is likely to remain confined to a tough one of retaliation for border harassments and readiness to fight if border incidents expand into war.

41.   Memorandum of a Conversation, British Foreign Office, London, August 1, 1956, noon [1]

SUBJECT

Suez Canal

PARTICIPANTS

Great Britain: Mr. Selwyn Lloyd, Sir Harold Caccia, Messrs. Ross and
Fitzmaurice
United States:
Secretary Dulles
Ambassador Aldrich
Mr. Carl W. McCardle (P)
Mr. Herman Phleger (L)
Mr. Robert Murphy (G)

Secretary Dulles met at noon today with Selwyn Lloyd at the British Foreign Office. Mr. Lloyd began with a reference to Nasser as a paranoiac like Hitler but without the power that Hitler had back of him. He said in essence that the British people feel they cannot let Nasser get away with his action on the Suez Canal. He talked about the strong feeling in Parliament and the unanimous support of the Conservatives enjoyed by the Government and discussed the question of oil shipments which might have to be routed around the Cape. Mr. Lloyd said naturally Britain wants to arrange matters peaceably, but there is universal feeling that there must be resolution to see this through. He said they wished to be reasonable regarding any measures necessary to arrive at a peaceful solution but that he did not quite fully understand American views regarding a larger conference. He raised questions regarding the idea of applying Article 8 of the Convention of 1888 which would contemplate an invitation by three of the signatory powers. He raised questions regarding states successors to the signatories of the Convention.

Secretary Dulles said the real question seemed to be what the Conference is for; that once that was decided he thought the composition of the Conference would not be too difficult. He said

---

[1] Source: Department of State, Central Files, 974.7301/7–3156. Top Secret. Drafted by Murphy. The source text is erroneously dated July 31. Other accounts of this meeting are in British Foreign Office, "Record of a Meeting Held in the Foreign Secretary's Room, Foreign Office, at 12 noon on Wednesday, August 1, 1956"; "London Tripartite Conversations," pp. 53–60 (both *ibid.,* Conference Files: Lot 62 D 181, CF 724; and Secto 7 from London, August 1 (*ibid.,* CF 726).

Dulles arrived in London at 9 a.m. He spent the morning at the Embassy where he conferred first with Aldrich, McCardle, Phleger, Murphy, Barbour, and Foster, and then later with Caccia, Aldrich, and Murphy. No accounts of these conversations have been found in Department of State files. (Memorandum of Secretary's Engagements, August 1; *ibid.,* CF 728)

that what we needed to decide is where we come out. It would be intolerable that an international waterway should be under the domination of one country without international control and supervision. The whole concept of the Suez Canal from the beginning is international—its construction, its financing, its management. In reply to Lloyd's question whether that point of view would affect Panama, Secretary Dulles replied in the negative saying that the only bearing Panama has on the present question is the importance we attach to sticking to the treaty which governs. Panama was built as a U.S. waterway and the treaty with the U.K. gives the latter certain privileges. Panama was not built as an international waterway but in effect on American soil for our interests so that we would not need two navies. We obtained in Panama what amounts to sovereign rights, and international interest is really limited to the tolls agreement with the U.K.

The Secretary said the U.S. does not want to get into the position that any waterway is automatically an international waterway. In the case of Suez, however, a powerful case can be made for it as an international waterway; that does not apply to Panama. We feel no embarrassment about Panama as long as we stick to the treaty. Otherwise, we would have grave difficulties dealing with the Suez problem. The U.S. must proceed in accordance with the treaty. We could agree that it would be unacceptable to have any one nation dominate Suez, especially if it would be the dictatorship of a fanatical person who openly avowed an intention to use the Canal for the purpose of exploiting it for national purposes and ambitions. We are in entire agreement, the Secretary said, that a way must be found to make Nasser disgorge. We believe, however, that force is the last method to be tried. We do not exclude it if all other means fail, but if it is used we believe that it must be backed by world opinion. We must be aware of effects in other Moslem countries and remember that even if the Soviet Union does not openly intervene it could operate by more subtle means. Without adequate preparation of public opinion, we could not associate ourselves in a military undertaking. The Secretary pointed out that for that we would require Congressional authorization, which under present circumstances would be most difficult to obtain. We believe that Nasser can be forced to disgorge by means other than military. Some form of organized effort to create a favorable world opinion is required. [2]

---

[2] Dulles' remarks on the use of force were transcribed in the British Foreign Office "Record" as follows: "Mr Dulles continued by saying that while it was unacceptable that any one nation should dominate the Canal, it was far more unacceptable when this one nation was Egypt. Egypt was under the dictatorship of a man who had avowed that the use of the Canal was not for the benefit of the nations of the world but for the satisfaction of his own national ambitions. A way had to be

There might be, the Secretary said, a difference between the U.S. and the U.K. in respect of preliminary efforts as these seem to be regarded by the U.K. as pro forma, whereas we think bona fide and substantial effort should be made. We think that if we proceed on the basis of a treaty to which the Soviet Union is a signatory we do not see how we can exclude the Soviet Union and we are not sure under the circumstances that their influence would be totally evil. The Secretary said it was quite possible that the Russians have been playing a careful game to disguise their support of Nasser but that he, the Secretary, could not believe that the Russians are very happy over Nasser's announcement last week that the military supplies received are from the Soviet Union and not from Czechoslovakia. The Secretary referred to the fact that Molotov at San Francisco made a big point that the arms transaction was a commercial one with Czechoslovakia.

The Secretary said that in any event the conference should be so organized as to insulate the Russians. He referred to the procedures we had worked out in connection with the Japanese Peace Treaty. There we had agreed among ourselves where we would come out and then we went into a conference with agreed rules of procedure. Thus the Russians and satellites were boxed in and the treaty was signed according to plan. Lloyd inquired how long it took to set up that Conference, and the Secretary agreed that in the present instance we would have to move faster.

Lloyd admitted that they had in mind an arbitrary list of countries for the purpose of getting unanimous endorsement and said that after that it would have to be put in some way to include

---

found to make Nasser disgorge what he was attempting to swallow. Force was the last method to be tried to accomplish this, but the United States Government did not exclude the use of force if all other methods failed. However, the use of force, if not backed by world opinion, would have disastrous results. It would involve the loss of Western influence in all the Moslem countries, unless it were intended to take the whole of the Middle East by force. Such action would be highly dangerous and even if the Soviets did not openly intervene they would activate resistance, send 'volunteers' and supply weapons. During his visit to the Middle East in 1953 he had observed the military difficulties of operating against the Egyptians. Since then the Egyptians' potential for resistance had increased, because of the military supplies and technicians obtained from the U.S.S.R. He doubted if the United States Government would be able to associate themselves with an operation involving force, which had not been preceded by genuine efforts to reach a satisfactory solution by negotiation. In such a case it would not be possible to get the necessary legislation through Congress.

"Mr. Dulles thought that there was a fair chance that Nasser could be brought to give up what he had seized. Failing that it should be possible to create a world public opinion so adverse to Nasser that he would be isolated. Then, if a military operation had to be undertaken, it would be more apt to succeed and have less grave repercussions than if it had been undertaken precipitately. He therefore strongly urged that a genuine effort should be made to bring world opinion to favour the international operation of the Canal, before force were used."

the Egyptians. He said that they had not thought out the procedure in precise detail and their thinking had run along the lines of a rapidly summoned conference of shipowning countries.

The Secretary referred to the fact that the U.S. yesterday took rather drastic action[3] which had been approved by our Treasury people only reluctantly. We had learned that Egypt had been planning to take out perhaps $10 million from its credits in the U.S. today. We know that our action will draw down upon us serious reaction against us in Egypt. Nevertheless we took the action as public notice of the gravity we attached to the present situation. Lloyd expressed the deep appreciation of the British Government.

There was discussion regarding advance combination of lists of countries to be invited to an eventual conference.[4] The meeting which lasted forty-five minutes was adjourned for the Secretary's luncheon with Eden. Lloyd jocularly made the parting remark that he would go along with us if we could guarantee a three-day conference with a satisfactory resolution, plus our agreement to join a military action. The Secretary commented that we believed that we would have to have a two-thirds majority lined up with us in the conference.

---

[3] Reference is to the Treasury announcement on July 31; see footnote 7, Document 34.

[4] According to the British Foreign Office "Record", Dulles proposed that the following countries be invited to the Conference: on the basis of the 1888 Convention—the United Kingdom, France, Egypt, the Netherlands, Italy, Turkey, Spain, and the U.S.S.R.; on the basis of ownership of tonnage—Norway, Sweden, Federal Republic of Germany, United States, and Denmark; on the basis of vital interests in trade—India, Australia, Pakistan, Japan, possibly Iran, and possibly Saudi Arabia. According to the British "Record", Dulles then noted: "A slightly greater tonnage of products from Saudi Arabia passed through the Canal than from Iran, but on the other hand Iran, as a Baghdad Pact Power, would be more acceptable. It might therefore be necessary to leave out Iran to avoid giving offense to Saudi Arabia. A group comprising the Powers mentioned above would overwhelmingly want international control of the Canal." The "Record" then notes that the addition of Ceylon and New Zealand was discussed.

42.   Memorandum of a Conversation Between Prime Minister Eden and Secretary of State Dulles, 10 Downing Street, London, August 1, 1956, 12:45 p.m. [1]

This conversation took place partly between the two of us, partly with the participation of Lord Salisbury and partly with the participation of Ambassador Aldrich and Foreign Minister Selwyn Lloyd.

Sir Anthony referred to the letter from President Eisenhower. [2] I explained that the President had asked me to say that he had dictated this letter quite hastily and that it was perhaps not as polished as it would have been had he had more time, but that the President felt that there was no doubt that the letter adequately expressed his basic thinking on the subject. (I said this for the purpose of making it clear to Eden that this letter was a spontaneous one of the President's and not something that somebody else had drafted and the President had merely signed.) Eden expressed his appreciation of the letter and the great importance he and his Government would attach to it, and said that it would be answered in due course.

He then went on to express his Government's view that prompt forcible action was necessary. He said that if Nasser "got away with it", it would mean disaster for British interests in the whole Middle East, and France felt the same way with respect to their interests in North Africa.

Eden said that while, of course, they would like to have the United States take part militarily in the Suez operation with them, they did not count on this. They did want our moral support and economic support in terms of petroleum products diverted from our side, and would want us to neutralize any open participation by the Soviet Union. If we could keep Russia out of open intervention, by the assurance that if Russia came in we would be in, they and the French could and would take care of the rest.

I said that I agreed that Nasser should not "get away with it", but the question was how his course should be reversed and he could be brought to "disgorge". I said that United States public opinion was not ready to back a military venture by Britain and France which, at this stage, could be plausibly portrayed as motivat-

---

[1] Source: Department of State, Central Files, 971.7301/8–156. Top Secret. Drafted by Dulles. The time of the meeting is from "London Tripartite Conversations", p. 60a. "London Tripartite Conversations" contains no account of this meeting but notes: "The substantive record of this meeting is filed in the Office of the Secretary of State." (*Ibid.,* Conference Files: Lot 62 D 181, CF 724) Presumably the memorandum of conversation printed here is the "substantive record" indicated.

[2] Document 35.

ed by imperialist and colonialist ambitions in the general area, going beyond the Canal operation itself, which was still open. I felt that for the British and French to undertake such an operation without at least the moral support of the United States would be a great disaster because it opened the way for many future evil consequences. I also pointed out that whereas the initial Egyptian resistance to a military operation might not be considerable, the long-term opposition would be very great. I recalled the position of the British at the Suez Base in 1953 when I was there, and that 88,000 U.K. troops had difficulty in defending themselves against the infiltration and assassination tactics of the Egyptians. Now the situation would be much worse. Egypt was much stronger militarily, and was getting moral and material support from the Soviet Union and Egypt's prestige and influence in the Arab world was much greater. I said they would have to count not merely on Egyptian reaction but on Egyptian reaction backed by assistance from the Soviet Union at least in the form of military weapons and supplies, and perhaps "volunteers". All the Arab, and parts of the Moslem world would be arrayed against the United Kingdom and France. Also they would be in trouble in the United Nations. I could not see the end of such an operation and the consequences throughout the Middle East would be very grave and would jeopardize British interests, particularly in the production and transportation of oil even more than the present action of Nasser. I felt that it was indispensable to make a very genuine effort to settle this affair peacefully and mobilize world opinion which might be effective.

After considerable discussion, pro and con, along these lines, Eden said they would be willing to give a try to the conference method, if it could be pushed ahead quickly and not be a procedure which would involve de facto acquiescence in the existing situation.

I referred to the Japanese Peace Treaty Conference as indicating a procedure whereby quick action could be achieved if there could be early informal agreement among the principally interested powers and if then rules of procedure for the conference were adopted which would prevent a filibuster. Eden said this was an interesting precedent, to be looked into.

Eden expressed strong opposition to the presence of the Soviet Union at any conference. I said I did not like their presence anywhere, but that I did not see how we could get away from the fact that Russia was a signatory party to the 1888 Treaty. We ourselves could not accept getting away from that Treaty. Our own position in Panama was dependent upon a treaty and if we accepted the view that merely because a waterway had international use the world generally was able to deal with it and control it, we would be cut away from our moorings in Panama.

At about this point, the French arrived for luncheon and our private conversation broke up. [3]

JFD

---

[3] Present at the luncheon meeting were: Eden, Lloyd, Salisbury, Caccia, Pineau, Chauvel, Dulles, Aldrich, Dillon, and Murphy. In a memorandum of conversation, Murphy recorded the following points, among others, as being raised at this meeting. Eden "made it clear that the British hoped that if eventually the worst developed and military action happened in the Mediterranean, the U.K. and France would see it through as far as Arab forces are concerned 'if the U.S. would take care of the Bear.' " Dulles, in turn, "repeatedly emphasized the importance of mobilizing world public opinion favorable to international control of the Canal and the need that the U.S. public understand the problem." (Memorandum of conversation by Murphy, August 1; Department of State, Central Files, 974.7301/8–156).

After the meeting, Dulles sent the following message to President Eisenhower: "Have had extended talk with Eden and Lloyd and some discussion with Salisbury. Matters are not going badly." (Dulte 1 from London, August 1; ibid., 110.11–DU/ 8–156) On receipt of this message, Hoover read its contents to Eisenhower over the telephone at 2:15 p.m., and commented, "one interesting thing is the leaks, particularly out of the French, on preparing to use force." He continued, "Dulles seems to be having luck on top, but may have troubles at the bottom level." (Memorandum of telephone conversation; Eisenhower Library, Whitman File, Eisenhower Diaries)

---

43.   Telegram From the Embassy in the United Kingdom to the Department of State [1]

London, August 2, 1956—1 a.m.

Secto 6. Secretary accompanied by Murphy and Dillon met with Pineau at latter's hotel. [2] Pineau was accompanied by Chauvel.

Secretary outlined US position on seizure of Suez Canal. Stated Nasser's action coming after previous unfriendly actions, including attacks on French and British, creates a very serious situation. US feels that Nasser must be forced to reverse his position. The question is how to achieve this end. The US does not feel military action is appropriate at present time. This because situation is not clear to world opinion, much of which remains favorable to Nasser. This even true of large segments of public opinion in United States which are not at all conscious of Nasser's faults.

---

[1] Source: Department of State, Central Files, 396.1–LO/8–256. Top Secret; Niact; Limit Distribution. Received at 8:55 p.m., August 1. Repeated to Paris.

[2] "London Tripartite Conversations" (pp. 64–67) contains an account of this conversation, which began at 4 p.m. (Ibid., Conference Files: Lot 62 D 181, CF 724)

Therefore US feels strong and sincere effort must be made to repose question on the basis of detailed plan for international operation of the Canal. Such a plan should be agreed in detail by US, France and Britain and then taken up with friendly countries who are large users of Canal or are dependent on trade moving through Canal or are signatories of 1888 Treaty and who will be eventual members of conference to be called to consider problem.

Secretary indicated that this should be completed rapidly in order keep momentum and he mentioned ten days as goal for completion this step. Then should follow conference of signatories 1888 Treaty except for Germany and Austria-Hungary where problems of successor states arise. Conference also would include large users and those who depend on Canal traffic for their trade. Federal Republic would be included as large user.

If Nasser should accept an arrangement for international control endorsed by conference all would be settled. World opinion mobilized by conference would bring great pressure on Nasser to accept. If Nasser refused to accept their arrangement for international control recommended by conference, world opinion, and in particular US opinion, would be clarified and it would then become possible to consider stronger action if it should appear necessary. In conclusion Secretary emphasized importance of mobilizing world opinion and in particular US opinion and of taking no strong action until such opinion fully mobilized.

Pineau then stated French position as follows: Nasser, by his unilateral and unjust act, has caused great excitement and disturbance in Near East and throughout North Africa. Under no circumstances can Nasser be allowed to keep control of Canal. Our basic principle must be that Nasser gives up operation and control of Canal to an international body. If this does not occur and Nasser succeeds in maintaining his position, Bourguiba in Tunisia and Sultan in Morocco [3] would be overwhelmed by extremist elements favorable to Nasser and all North Africa would be lost. French would have no reason to continue fighting in Algeria under such circumstances. Therefore, if it should be necessary France is prepared take military action against Nasser, acting alone if necessary. However, British have different reasons for identical views as French, and so military action, if it should come, will probably be joint Anglo-French action.

French perfectly willing to agree proposal for international operation provided it very clear that operation would be by international organization which would force Nasser to give up his nationalization. If Nasser should accept such an arrangement there would be no

---

[3] Mohammed V.

need for military action and French would be very pleased. However, if Nasser refuses, military action would be needed and during next 30 days France intends make necessary military preparations. Pineau said that if Nasser conscious that military preparations are under way he would be more likely to find a way to agree to international control of Suez which would make military action unnecessary.

Pineau said that if military action becomes necessary because of refusal by Nasser to accept internationalization, France would hope for US moral support and US indication to Soviets that they must leave matter alone as US would be forced to counter any Soviet action. This would be very important help to Britain and France.

The Secretary said he felt there seemed to be general agreement on principles but that it was most important to work fast to develop the formula for the international regime. He emphasized that this would be a difficult job. Secretary then pointed out great difficulty for constitutional reasons of obtaining US military action even in the event Nasser should refuse conference proposal for internationalization. Secretary emphasized the importance of having full support of US public opinion for any action which might be taken by Britain and France. He re-emphasized that this could only be obtained if a fair formula for international operation was presented to Egypt with the backing of a large number of interested countries. In conclusion he again stated US fully agreed that Nasser should be made to give up unilateral control of Canal.

Dulles

---

44.   **Telegram From the Embassy in the United Kingdom to the Department of State** [1]

London, August 2, 1956—1 a.m.

Secto 8. Paris eyes only Ambassador. I have had useful talks with Eden, Pineau, Lloyd and Macmillan which will be covered

---

[1] Source: Department of State, Central Files, 396.1–LO/8–256. Top Secret; Niact; Limit Distribution. Received at 10:04 p.m., August 1. Repeated to Paris. The outgoing copy of the telegram, *ibid.,* Conference Files: Lot 62 D 181, indicates Burdett as the drafting officer.

separately. There follows account of formal tripartite meeting [2] held
five p.m. London time August first at FonOff with Lloyd presiding.

Payment of transit tolls. Pineau stated French Govt had taken
decision to pay tolls in escrow to bank in neutral country and that if
Egypt refused accept such payment to divert French shipping around
Cape. French delegate reported that today's meeting International
Chamber of Shipping had agreed unanimously to recommend that all
tolls be paid in escrow in neutral country. I commented that we
were not disposed to agree but instead thought payments should be
made under protest. [3] Lloyd said it would be unfortunate if only one
of three powers ordered diversion of shipping. No definite conclusions reached and matter will be discussed again tomorrow.

Foreign nationals employed by Suez Canal Company. Lloyd and
Pineau reported that Suez Canal Company wished to order its
employees in Egypt to give immediate notice and prepare to leave
between now and August fifteenth. Company proposed to say
governments concerned approved its action and to promise employees leave with full pay for one to three years depending upon
seniority. Pineau read telegram received from Company's chief agent
in Cairo stating employees not prepared work for new Company and
preparing to leave with families. Agent asserted that if British and
foreign pilots ceased work, others would probably follow suit and it
would then become impossible to handle large volume of ships.
Pineau thought employees who would be facing prison should be
advised of government's support for their action. Lloyd had misgivings regarding Company's proposed action. I pointed out problem
insignificant for US since only two Americans employed by Company but that it would be great mistake for breakdown in operation of
Canal to appear to occur as result of action by Western governments. Pineau said French Govt could not disapprove Company's
proposed action but might refrain from any specific approval stating
only that if French nationals wished to leave Egypt, they would
receive support. I said French nationals clearly had right of choice;
that any coercion would be improper and would provide good case

[2] Other accounts of this, the sixth tripartite meeting, one in British Foreign
Office, "Record of the 6th Meeting Held in the Council Chamber, Foreign Office, on
Wednesday, August 1, 1956 at 5:00 p.m." and "London Tripartite Conversations," pp.
68–78. (Both *ibid.*, CF 724) According to the latter document, the following attended
the meeting: Dulles, Murphy, Phleger, McCardle, Aldrich, Dillon, and Burdett for the
United States; Lloyd, Caccia, Ross, and Vallat for the United Kingdom; Pineau,
Chauvel, and Daridan for France.

[3] In Secto 9, August 2, the Embassy in London informed the Department:
"Secretary stated at tripartite meeting August 1 that he thought all U.S. government
controlled ships transitting Suez Canal which subject to tolls should pay Egyptian
authority only under protest, and if payment under protest not accepted and transit
blocked, then they might pay under coercion to be noted in ship's log." (*Ibid.*, Central
Files, 396.1–LO/8–256)

for government action. I pointed out our whole position based on concept Suez Canal is public utility of concern to entire world and not catspaw of any one nation. If breakdown of operation resulted from action by one of three governments, it would incur same blame as Egypt. No final decision reached and matter will be discussed tomorrow.

Communiqué. Lloyd said he hoped we could agree to issue communiqué soon covering disapproval of Nasser's action, support for principle of some type of international arrangement for operation of Canal, and indication conference would be held but not necessarily specifying participants. He wished to avoid appearance of inactivity.

I read draft submitted Embtel Secto 5, [4] both Lloyd and Pineau indicated general approval subject to careful study. Lloyd thought international control should be mentioned more specifically.

Conference. Lloyd said UK would be reluctant to include USSR in Conference but was prepared to accept US views regarding composition of Conference if US would work for early Conference and adoption resolution providing for international operation Canal.

UK then suggested following countries as participants: all signatories of 1888 Conference except Germany and Austria which would be omitted to avoid disagreements over successor powers; five leading countries on basis flag tonnage transitting Canal—Norway, Germany, Denmark, Sweden, and US (each had tonnage in excess of two million tons); other countries with vital trade interests in Canal—Australia, New Zealand, India, Pakistan, Ceylon, Japan. Pineau agreed to list and I stated it appeared acceptable.

I said that we attached considerable importance to having invitations issued by three signatories of Convention of 1888, using article 8 for purpose. If this was agreed to, US would associate itself with inviting countries. British legal advisor presented history of article 8 alleging article long considered "dead letter". Lloyd urged that US/UK/France issue invitations. I promised answer tomorrow.

Lloyd also pressed for London as site stating that because crises could occur suddenly it necessary to be in close touch with governments. I agreed consider matter.

With respect to timing I suggested latter part of August, stating I would be elsewhere engaged for four days beginning August 17. Pineau and Lloyd both thought that postponement of such duration would be difficult to explain publicly and would risk initiative by USSR perhaps in conjunction with Egypt. Lloyd urged August 13 as starting date. No definite conclusions reached.

---

[4] See footnote 3, Document 49.

I stressed that we attached high importance to prior tripartite agreement on objectives of conference. Britain said that their legal advisor preparing plan which we agreed to discuss later in evening.

I did not advance idea at meeting, but our preliminary thought is that conference should seek agreement on some treaty arrangement succeeding and incorporating principles of Convention of 1888. Treaty would be open to accession by interested powers and would provide for internationalization of Company nationalized by Egypt. Adequate rights would be granted by Egypt to permit efficient operation of Canal as international public utility. We envisage international board of directors to take possession of assets of previous Company. Stockholders would be paid for shares held. Egypt would be assured of adequate financial return on basis her territorial interest. Proposal would be presented as "heads of agreement" avoiding specific details which might be subject to attack, and consisting instead of series of broad principles designed to appear eminently fair to all concerned. Egyptian adherence to treaty would be sought. Proposal would be difficult for Egypt to reject and would place Western powers in good public relations position. We would not advance above as US plan but would endeavor to induce UK and France to incorporate ideas in their plan.

Dulles

---

45. Telegram From the Embassy in Egypt to the Embassy in the United Kingdom [1]

Cairo, August 1, 1956—noon.

39. London for Secretary. Department for Hoover. This message may miss its mark as I do not know agenda or trend of discussions in London. Implications of news tickers are such however that I want to feel certain you have all possible views and facts before you. In what follows please do not assume I underestimate gravity of situation, nor of ill effect Nasser's action may have on other holdings in area.

---

[1] Source: Department of State, Central Files, 396.1–LO/8–156. Secret; Niact. Received in the Department of State at 11:38 a.m. The source text is the copy sent to Washington.

First of all I hope you will accept Nasser's statement to me contained in Embtel 36 [2] to London that he will do anything he has to do to justify this act before world opinion and will resist to fullest extent of Egypt's capability any moves against her sovereignty or designed to undermine action he has taken. I cannot over-emphasize popularity of Canal Company nationalization within Egypt, even among Nasser's enemies (if challenged at present time on this issue he would be supported in almost anything he does and this support I fear would range far beyond Egypt.) In my opinion Nasser will now never accept a superimposed form of international authority and reported discussion as to composition of such group seems academic here, even if sponsored by other than Western powers.

If lawyers here, including oil company, are correct, we do not have case against the act of nationalization itself. This leaves the question of international use and it seems to us Nasser's statement of yesterday, [3] with copy to United Nations, pledging Egypt to live up to its international commitments must be borne in mind.

Would it not be wise to let things calm down while preparing the way for action if and when Egypt violates these international commitments? This is a time of high emotion and if a move is made now involving force in face of two points above it would merely be moving against sovereign right and pledged word of Egypt rather than proven act (such as stoppage of shipping) detrimental to our vital interests. Under these circumstances, I fear Nasser would have masses behind him and certainly would further consolidate his emotional hold over Middle East (which I would guess would include Iraq). While there are no forces here which it is not in our power to over-throw, we would I fear in this day and age, live with the after effects for many years to come.

While hoping present conference in London may be able to think [4] of safe ways that had not occurred to us here, [to] meet this danger to Western interests and which would be more quickly effective, it seems to us that possibly we should only plan for future moves if and when Egypt violates its international commitments and put Nasser on notice that we would not tolerate such violations.

---

[2] Printed as telegram 176 from Cairo, Document 31.

[3] On August 1, the Embassy in Cairo transmitted to the Department of State the text of a statement released on behalf of Nasser. The statement affirmed that the Egyptian Government was determined to honor all of its international obligations, including the Convention of 1888 and the assurance concerning it given in the Anglo-Egyptian agreement of 1954. (Telegram 190 from Cairo, Department of State, Central Files, 974.7301/8–156).

[4] A garble at this point in the source text has been corrected on the basis of a copy of this telegram *ibid.*, NEA Files: Lot 59 D 518, Omega—Memos, etc. for July 1 to August 31, 1956.

Realize this may be meager results for public opinion and present domestic political difficulties of varying degrees in the three capitals, but it might be wisest course from a foreign policy point of view.

In drafting this message, Mossadeq case [5] is clearly in my mind. Nasser may by this act have finished himself in the end—but this is not necessarily so as the use of a vital facility has not been discontinued and believe implications clear enough to him that if left alone he will most carefully avoid violation international agreements. Point is however we could not with success move against Mossadeq at height of his prestige and I believe same applies here, with added factor that support for Nasser and Egypt will spread across much larger area than the relatively politically isolated state of Iran could muster. In considering countermoves hope it will be borne in mind that we believe that potentialities exist in this issue which could cause type of situation existing in Algeria to spread across to the Persian Gulf, with ill side effects down through South Asia.

Byroade

---

[5] Reference is to the circumstances surrounding the fall from power of former Iranian Prime Minister Dr. Mohammad Mosadeq. For documentation concerning Mosadeq's downfall, see *Foreign Relations,* 1952–1954, volume X.

46.   Memorandum of a Conversation, 11 Downing Street, London, August 1, 1956, 6:30 p.m. [1]

SUBJECT

Suez Canal

PARTICIPANTS

Great Britain
Chancellor of the Exchequer Harold Macmillan
United States:
Secretary of State John Foster Dulles
Ambassador Winthrop W. Aldrich
Deputy Under Secretary of State Robert Murphy

Mr. Macmillan said that the position taken by the British Cabinet, in response to the expropriation of the stock of the Suez Canal Company by Egypt was brought about by the realization of the fact that if this action were not met by the utmost firmness a chain reaction would be started which would ultimately lead to the loss of the entire British position in the Middle East and that the final result might be that even the oil reserves in Kuwait might be lost. The cumulative effect of the successive nationalization of pipe lines and concessions by one Middle Eastern country after another would be disastrous not only to the economy of Great Britain but to Europe as well. He said that if the final result was to be the destruction of Great Britain as a first-class power and its reduction to a status similar to that of Holland, the danger should be met now and that even "If we should be destroyed by Russian bombs now that would be better than to be reduced to impotence by the disintegration of its entire position abroad." He also said that this was the feeling not only of the Cabinet, but of both parties in Parliament and of the British people. No one wanted to see another Munich. They would rather die fighting than slowly bleed to a state of impotence.

He went on to say that if the present crisis were successfully met and if Nasser were obliged to abandon his present course he (Macmillan) felt that the road would have been made more easy for a settlement between Israel and Egypt along the lines developed

---

[1] Source: Department of State, Central Files, 974.7301/8–156. Top Secret. Drafted by Aldrich. 11 Downing Street was Macmillan's residence. A typewritten note at the end of the memorandum indicates: "Foregoing was drafted by Ambassador Aldrich en route from London to Washington and handed by him to Deputy Under Secretary Murphy for the record." Murphy wrote a briefer memorandum of this meeting which contained many of the same points as Aldrich's version. (Memorandum of conversation by Murphy, August 1; *ibid.,* 974.7301/8–156)

during the Alpha negotiations. [2] In this connection he spoke of the two triangles which had been considered as a means of giving Egypt a corridor to Jordan and said that once Nasser had been brought under control perhaps a larger triangle could be provided for Egypt.

It was not specifically stated by Macmillan that the British had been planning to use force immediately, but that they were planning to use it if necessary. He spoke of a three-division operation. Ambassador Aldrich said that President Eisenhower had said this would take some weeks. Macmillan said that they could move more rapidly.

The Secretary briefly went over the position of the United States, namely that the expropriation of the shares, if proper compensation was given, was within the sovereign power of Egypt but that the international status and management of the Canal must be maintained under the treaty of 1888, and pointed out the necessity of having a conference of the signatories of the treaty and the other nations interested in the operations of the Canal to mobilize world opinion in case Egypt should be unwilling to agree to international control before further action could be decided upon. The Secretary said he realized the necessity of the holding of this conference as soon as possible and of its being organized in such manner as to reach a prompt conclusion.

Macmillan was obviously deeply impressed by the Secretary's exposition of the position and Ambassador Aldrich felt very clearly would support the U.S. position in future discussion in the Cabinet.

The atmosphere of the entire discussion was most informal, intimate and cordial and Ambassador Aldrich felt that it must have had very great influence in bringing about the reversal of the attitude of the British Government which took place during the two days of the Secretary's visit.

---

[2] For documentation on the Alpha negotiations, see volume XV.

47.   Telegram From the Department of State to the Secretary of State, at London [1]

Washington, August 1, 1956—3:08 p.m.

Tedul 6. Eyes only for the Secretary. You will recall that in commenting upon possible repercussions UK–French military action against Egypt, Rountree mentioned likelihood Israeli would embark upon military campaign thus associating in Arab mind Western intervention with Israeli objectives. You might be interested know in conversation yesterday with Russell, Shiloah [2] volunteered that if Western powers take any military measures in connection Suez, Israel would insist on participating in them.

Hoover

---

[1] Source: Department of State, Central Files, 974.7301/8–156. Top Secret; Niact. Drafted by Rountree and approved and signed by Hoover.

[2] The memorandum of this conversation by Russell, dated August 1, is *ibid.*, NEA Files: Lot 59 D 518, Omega—Memos etc. July 1 to August 31, 1956.

---

48.   Message From the Secretary of State to the President [1]

London, August 2, 1956.

DEAR MR. PRESIDENT: We are working here most intensively. I have talked privately with Eden, Salisbury, Macmillan and Pineau. There is little doubt in my mind but what the present determination of both the British and French is to move into the Canal area with force unless Nasser renounces his determination to operate the Canal on a national basis and accepts international control. I am not sure from their standpoint they can be blamed as they feel, probably with reason, that if Nasser gets away with his action, this will stimulate comparable action throughout the area which will end British and French positions in Middle East and North Africa, respectively. I believe I have persuaded them that it would be reckless to take this step unless and until they have made a genuine

---

[1] Source: Department of State, Central Files, 684A.86/8–256. Secret. Transmitted Priority and eyes only for Hoover to the Department of State in Dulte 2 from London, August 2, 2 p.m., which is the source text. It was received at 9:57 a.m. Hoover forwarded the telegram to the White House; a copy is in the Eisenhower Library, Whitman File, Dulles–Herter Series.

effort to mobilize world opinion in favor of an international solution of the Canal problem. However, when it comes to the details of applying this principle they are inclined to procedures which I fear will in fact alienate world opinion.

I am trying to hold up instructions from the Canal Company to its employees to quit at once which would automatically disrupt traffic. I pointed out that if the disruption of traffic comes about through British and French action, then there would be little sympathy in US for sacrifices to make good the resulting deficit of petroleum in Europe. I am trying to have the conference broadly based and not loaded in favor of the Western powers. Also I am trying to get enough time so that there can be reasonable diplomatic preparation for the conference. It is hard going in all of these respects and at noon today I cannot foresee the result in detail. We shall probably have to compromise in some respects but I hope for a result which will provide the time and a setting favorable to counsels of moderation and a maximum chance for a peaceful international solution.

I hope to start back sometime tonight.

Faithfully yours,

Foster [2]

---

[2] Dulte 2 bears this typed signature.

Eisenhower's response was transmitted in Tedul 9 to London, August 2: "Many thanks for your message. You are proceeding exactly in accordance with my convictions, and we can all hope that you will achieve a program that can marshal world opinion behind it. With warm regard. DE" (Department of State, Conference Files: Lot 62 D 181, CF 727; copy also in Eisenhower Library, Whitman File, Dulles–Herter Series)

---

49.   Telegram From the Embassy in United Kingdom to the Department of State [1]

London, August 2, 1956—8 p.m.

Secto 11. Paris eyes only Ambassador. Account follows of formal tripartite meeting held 10 a.m. London time August 2 at

---

[1] Source: Department of State, Central Files, 396.1–LO/8–256. Top Secret; Niact; Limited Distribution. Received at 6:05 p.m. Repeated to Paris.

Foreign Office with Lloyd presiding. [2] We are meeting again at 4:15 p.m. after participation by Lloyd in House of Commons foreign affairs debates.

Conference: [3] I said that because of importance of advance diplomatic preparations I did not see how conference could be held in less than three weeks. Our entire purpose was to hold conference of such character that rejection of results would isolate Egypt in world public opinion. This would not happen if other free countries judged that we had not made genuine effort but had only gone through the motions so we could later use force. First, tripartite powers would have to agree among themselves on nature of international organization they had in mind and then explain matter to others. It was necessary to get 2/3 of participants committed before conference. I said I was highly skeptical that this could be done in two weeks.

Pineau pressed for earliest possible date. He thought three weeks too long. If August 13 not possible he would accept August 16 or 17. Lloyd commented that August 16 or 17 was about maximum which British could take. He wished to consult Eden and suggested that in communiqué we might use phrase "as soon as practicable" instead of specifying date.

With respect to place, I said we should not select capital of one of parties most directly concerned. US would prefer Geneva or Rome. Pineau favored London. He mentioned possibility of Brussels, but Selwyn Lloyd pointed out Belgium not on list of participants.

Lloyd asked who would issue invitations, saying US draft of communiqué indicated France and UK would do so. I said we had no special views on whether one or both issued invitations. If London is site of conference UK should probably be inviting power. Pineau supported UK as inviting power and London as site with statement

---

[2] Other accounts of this, the seventh tripartite meeting, are in British Foreign Office, "Record of the 7th Meeting Held at 10 a.m. on Thursday August 2, 1956, in the Council Chamber, Foreign Office" and "London Tripartite Conversations", pp. 82–100. (Both *ibid.*, Conference Files: Lot 62 D 181, CF 728 and 724, respectively) According to the latter document, the following attended the meeting: Dulles, Murphy, Phleger, McCardle, Aldrich, and Burdett for the United States; Lloyd, Caccia, Fitzmaurice, Ross, Watkinson, and Proctor for the United Kingdom; and Pineau, Chauvel, and Daridan for France.

[3] The meeting began with a discussion of the U.S. draft communiqué during which several textual changes were made subject to final agreement. These were reported to the Department in Secto 10, August 2. (*Ibid.*, Central Files, 396.1–LO/8–256) The changes included several stylistic revisions and the substitution of new texts for paragraphs 4 and 5. The original paragraphs 4 and 5 contained in the U.S. draft (Secto 5, August 2; *ibid.*) had provided for the possibility of associating the proposed conference with the United Nations. For text of the final communiqué, see Document 53.

in communiqué that France and US would participate. I replied this appeared satisfactory if London selected as site.

Lloyd said UK had great difficulty in swallowing USSR as participant. He urged that to avoid any misunderstanding we agree clearly that (1) conference would last only few days; (2) every sort of pressure would be applied to obtain positive results. If not, the West would suffer major diplomatic defeat. At same time, UK anxious that conference not appear to be bogus exercise. If it fails, UK would use force. Force is only alternative open if Egypt does not accept results. He added if conference not held force would still be used, but under less favorable circumstances. [4]

Conference adjourned while Lloyd consulted Prime Minister. Upon his return he said Eden agreed tripartite powers should reach complete agreement before issuing communiqué and therefore would not read it during debate in Commons today. Eden accepted August 16 as starting date for conference and for practical reasons preferred London as site. He would be glad for UK to serve as invitor.

I suggested adding Saudi Arabia and Iran to list of participants transmitted Secto 8 [5] pointing out that economies of both dependent upon Canal and their omission would appear to be arbitrary act. Pineau commented that their addition would not make achievement 2/3 majority any easier. Lloyd said omission Iraq would then be difficult. I suggested including Iraq. Pineau mentioned adding Ethiopia. After considerable discussion, both Pineau and Lloyd said they preferred list submitted Secto 8. Lloyd stated UK as inviting power would like to say both US and France had approved list. It could add UK could not conceive of conference excluding Commonwealth countries whose lifeline under discussion. I said I was concerned principally over creating general impression that we have arbitrarily and artificially isolated Egypt from its friends by not including other countries largely dependent on Canal. I doubted Egypt would come if conference held in London and therefore did not want to give Egyptians excuse for saying conference packed. No definite conclu-

---

[4] On this point, the British Foreign Office "Record" reads: "The Foreign Secretary said that Her Majesty's Government were equally anxious that the conference should not appear to be a bogus exercise. If the conference failed the United Kingdom would use force. He would much prefer to settle the problem without the use of force by bringing, through the conference, such pressure to bear on the Egyptians that they would accept the conference's resolution. M. Pineau said he had understood Mr. Dulles' view to be that if the Egyptians did not accept the result of the conference they would be placed in an impossible situation vis-à-vis world opinion. He thought himself that we must be careful that the resolution of the conference was not too easy for the Egyptians to accept. It might even be that Egypt could accept the resolution of the conference and win a victory."

[5] Document 44.

sion reached and working group established to provide additional statistics on use of Canal for consideration at afternoon meeting.

Nature of international organization: British tabled draft prepared by legal advisor.[6] Pineau said it went too much into detail and French Delegation submitted short paper.[7] Pineau suggested number of questions submitted to proposed conference should be kept to minimum. Details should be considered later to avoid embarrassing discussions over small points with consequent increased risks of abstentions. It was important to speak only of compensating Suez Canal Company and not about any possible future role for it in order to avoid appearance that object of conference is to reestablish Company.

Rough summary translation French paper follows:

Purposes of international authority shall be: Take charge of Canal; assure its functioning; compensate Suez Canal Company; provide Egypt equitable return. International organization shall be headed by administrative council designated by powers most interested in navigation and maritime commerce and by necessary technical and administrative organs. Powers of authority should include: approval and modification of tolls, carrying out necessary works, financing, control of technical organs.

Pineau said he would propose asking conference: Are you for Nasser system or for international system? If for latter what should be powers of controlling body?

I expressed general sympathy for Pineau's idea. Nasser has decreed national control of Canal. We want international regime to prevail. If issues kept simple any rejection by Nasser will be attacked by world opinion. We should seek agreement on principles with details to be worked out later. It inadvisable to raise details that could divide conference. I suggested adding to French draft provision for arbitration. Egypt would be asked whether it accepts principles embodied in conference resolution. If it does, we have won our victory and details may then be worked out. If Egypt refuses, there is no need to go into detail.

Selwyn Lloyd asserted that if Egypt rejected conference resolution and then stopped ships from transiting which paid to old Company [sic] we would be free to take whatever action appeared appropriate. I replied that I supposed if Egypt rejected proposals all would feel free to do what they considered appropriate.

---

[6] Not printed. The document is entitled "International Operation and Control of the Suez Canal," and is attached as Annex A to British Foreign Office, "Record of the 7th Meeting".

[7] Not printed. The document is entitled "Projet d'invitation: questions posées," and is attached as Annex B to British Foreign Office, "Record of the 7th Meeting".

Memorandum of agreement: Pineau suggested tripartite powers agree to memorandum setting forth their understanding of results of present meetings and course to be followed. Selwyn Lloyd said he thought suggestion important. I did not comment.

Lloyd left meeting at this point to attend foreign affairs debate in Commons.

Foreign nationals employed by Suez Canal Company: British delegation reported upon intention of Suez Canal Company to order its employees to leave Egypt, as described in Secto 8. British said they had sent two messages to British Director of Company ordering him to insure instructions not sent out as currently drafted, since present conference considering matter.

FYI: British Director of Suez Canal Company informed US delegation privately that Company wished act quickly because it understood Egyptians planning request employees to sign undertaking to go on serving and Company thought many would gladly sign in absence firm instructions and inducements to leave. He also said prior Company message already sent instructing French personnel to apply for repatriation personally approved by Pineau. End FYI.

Pineau argued that Company had perfect right to send any instructions of this nature to its employees which it wished. Employees had perfect right to follow such instructions and France, and he understood UK, was prepared absolutely to protect rights of their nationals in this respect. Caccia replied HMG had not reached decision. He pointed out that whether or not governments actually approved message, public would assume it had their approval. He thought message exposed Western powers to charge that they were interrupting operations of Canal. UK confronted with special difficulty since it only govt with large shareholding. Public would suppose that action of Company would not have been taken against wishes largest shareholder. British thoroughly agreed with Pineau on right of employees to do as individuals what they considered right in conformity with their contracts but question became political matter if Suez Canal Company took measures leading to interruption of transit. Caccia specifically reserved position of UK Govt.

I said proposed message was grave matter. If operation of Canal discontinued as result instructions appearing to have approval of French Govt and if, as consequence, flow of oil disrupted, US would have difficulty in taking measures to compensate for disruption. Instruction to Suez Company employees to quit and offer of financial inducements to do so would make it appear that Canal's operations disrupted by UK and France. US, of course, agreed employees should not be forced to work against their will. Discussion this subject continued at afternoon meeting. [8]

Dulles

---

[8] Also at the seventh tripartite meeting, the tripartite working party presented a summary of the Canal tolls situation. An account of that presentation is in telegram 631 from London, August 2, not printed. (Department of State, Central Files, 974.7301/8–256)

---

50.   Memorandum From the Acting Secretary of Defense (Robertson) to the Executive Secretary of the National Security Council (Lay) [1]

Washington, August 2, 1956.

SUBJECT

Nationalization of the Suez Maritime Canal Company by the Egyptian
Government

1. Forwarded herewith are the views of the Joint Chiefs of Staff with respect to the above subject, which I should like to make available for the information of the members of the National Security Council.

2. I fully concur in the gravity of the implications of the recent Egyptian nationalization of the Suez Maritime Canal Company, as outlined by the JCS, and I feel that the points raised by them in their memorandum merit the most careful analysis and consideration. In this connection I believe that all feasible political and economic measures should be taken before a decision is made to resort to the use of military force. I recommend that the members of the NSC be prepared to discuss these issues at such time as the Suez Canal situation may be brought before the Council.

Reuben B. Robertson, Jr. [2]

---

[1] Source: Department of State, S/S–NSC (Miscellaneous) Files: Lot 66 D 95, Suez Canal Situation. Top Secret. Lay transmitted the memorandum and its enclosure to members of the National Security Council for their information under cover of a memorandum dated August 3. (*Ibid.*, S/S–NSC Files: Lot 66 D 95)

[2] Printed from a copy that bears this typed signature.

[Enclosure]

**Memorandum From the Joint Chiefs of Staff to the
Secretary of Defense (Wilson)** [3]

Washington, July 31, 1956.

SUBJECT

Nationalization of the Suez Maritime Canal Company by the Egyptian
Government

1. The Joint Chiefs of Staff are seriously concerned with the implications of the recent Egyptian nationalization of the Suez Maritime Canal Company. They consider this Egyptian action to be militarily detrimental to the United States and its Allies. Among the military implications of this action are those affecting the continued United States control of military bases and facilities in the general area; the future of the Baghdad Pact Organization; the economic and military strength of European nations and therefore of NATO; the French position in North Africa; the free flow of shipping through the Suez Canal; and those affecting the United States security interests if Nasser's arbitrary action is tolerated and a further precedent for such arbitrary action thereby established.

2. The Joint Chiefs of Staff consider this Egyptian action, with its attendant implications, to be of such importance as to require action by the United States and its Allies which can reasonably be expected to result in placing the Suez Canal under a friendly and responsible authority at the earliest practicable date. Furthermore, they believe that, if action short of the use of military force cannot reasonably be expected to achieve this result, the United States should consider the desirability of taking military action in support of the U.K., France and others as appropriate. They are aware that the matter is receiving full consideration by other governmental Departments, but would emphasize their conviction that promptness in reaching an early decision and of taking definite and appropriate action is particularly important in this instance.

3. In view of the foregoing, the Joint Chiefs of Staff strongly recommend that the Secretary of Defense request the National Security Council (NSC), as a matter of urgency, to formulate and

---

[3] Top Secret. Bowie forwarded a copy of this memorandum to Dulles on August 3 under cover of a memorandum which reads: "I think you should read the attached JCS memorandum on nationalization of the Suez Canal. It recommends that the NSC discuss the matter. Would you want this put on the agenda for the meeting on Thursday, August 9?" (Department of State, S/P–NSC Files: Lot 61 D 167, Near East) Dulles initialed his approval.

direct the early implementation of appropriate courses of action designed to assure that the Suez Canal comes under the control of a friendly and responsible authority and that the danger of future actions elsewhere, of the nature of Egypt's expropriation of the canal is minimized. In this connection, the Joint Chiefs of Staff believe that there is an urgent requirement for the NSC to determine whether the western world can reasonably expect to obtain the necessary results without recourse to military action by any western power. Concurrently the NSC should appraise the desirability of a U.S. guarantee to give political and economic support to military action by the U.K., whether taken alone or in concert with France, while abstaining, ourselves, from direct military participation; and of a public commitment to prompt direct military participation by U.S. forces in the event that third parties intervene militarily on behalf of the Egyptians.

4. If there is reasonable assurance that non-military actions will achieve the necessary results promptly, it is preferable to avoid military action by any of the nations concerned. However, timely U.S. action in this situation is believed to be so vital that, pending the outcome of the NSC study, the Joint Chiefs of Staff are conducting further military studies on:

a. The implications of this situation to the United States from the military point of view.

b. The extent and nature of measures required to support U.K. (or U.K.-French) military action without commitment of U.S. forces.

c. What U.S. military forces will be required if the United States participates in combined direct military action.

d. The military forces required if the United States is forced to take unilateral military action to protect U.S. nationals.

5. The Joint Chiefs of Staff desire to point out that Israel may be tempted to capitalize on the situation by taking unilateral action inimical to U.S. interests. Any such unilateral action should be prevented.

6. The Chairman, Joint Chiefs of Staff, did not participate in the action of the Joint Chiefs of Staff outlined in this memorandum.

For the Joint Chiefs of Staff:
Maxwell D. Taylor [4]
General, United States Army
Chief of Staff

---

[4] Printed from a copy that bears this typed signature.

51.   Telegram From the Embassy in the United Kingdom to the Department of State [1]

London, August 3, 1956—2 a.m.

654. Paris eyes only Ambassador. Following account plenary tripartite meeting afternoon August 2 [2] submitted after departure Secretary. [3]

Statement

Meeting agreed to statement transmitted separately [4] for distribution to press at 9 pm London time with 10 pm release time.

Proposed Basis for the International Conference.

Tripartite working group tabled draft telegraphed separately. [5] Sec commented text appeared excellent but wanted day or so to study. Lloyd said it should not be referred to in statement but might be used in initial explanation of conference purposes to participating govts. Sec thought it should be used where would do most good and not automatically transmitted to everyone. Meeting agreed draft would be studied and comments submitted through diplomatic channels by August 5. Pineau said he would wish give substance to

---

[1] Source: Department of State, Central Files, 396.1–LO/8–356. Top Secret; Niact. Received at 11:16 p.m. Repeated to Paris.

[2] Other accounts of this, the eighth tripartite meeting, which began at 4:15 p.m. (London time), August 2, are in British Foreign Office, "Record of the Eighth Meeting in the Council Chamber, Foreign Office, at 4:15 p.m. on Thursday, August 2, 1956," and "London Tripartite Conversations," pp. 101–128. (*Ibid.,* Conference Files: Lot 62 D 181, CF 728 and 724 respectively) The latter document indicates that the following attended the meeting: Dulles, Murphy, Phleger, Aldrich, Dillon, McCardle, Barbour, Connors, and Burdett for the United States; Lloyd, Caccia, Fitzmaurice, Vallat, Ross, Rowan, and Proctor for the United Kingdom; and Pineau, Chauvel, and Daridan for France.

[3] Dulles, Murphy, McCardle, Aldrich, Phleger, and their staff departed by air at 10 p.m. for Washington. Before boarding the plane, Dulles cabled Eisenhower: "Dear Mr. President: I appreciate your message of August 2. We have just now concluded and I am on my way to the airplane and will be seeing you tomorrow morning. I think we have introduced a valuable stopgap into a dangerous situation and while the danger is still there we have perhaps made it more remote and more manageable. I hope so. Faithfully, Foster." (Dulte 4 from London, August 2; *ibid.,* Central Files, 110.11–DU/8–256) For the August 2 message, see footnote 2, Document 48.

[4] Document 53.

[5] The tripartite working group draft, entitled "Proposed Basis for the International Conference," was transmitted to the Department of State in telegram 647 from London, August 2. (Department of State, Central Files, 396.1–LO/8–256) Subsequent revisions to the draft paper are in telegram 719 to London, August 3, and telegram 696 from London, August 4; *ibid.,* 974.7301/8–356 and 974.7301/8–456 respectively. The final text, entitled "Proposal for the Establishment of an International Authority for the Suez Canal," is printed as part of circular telegram 90, Document 63, and in *The Suez Canal Problem, July 26–September 22, 1956,* p. 44.

French Parliament. Lloyd suggested and meeting agreed substance could be conveyed August 6 to certain countries as indication tripartite thinking.

Participants at Conference

Tripartite working group presented tables [6] re foreign trade passing through Canal of following countries: Australia, Iran, Iraq, Saudi Arabia, Ethiopia, India, Indonesia, New Zealand, Pakistan, Ceylon, Sudan, Philippines, Burma, Thailand. Figures showed both value of exports and imports transitting Canal and percentage of total trade using Canal. Sec asked working party to include statistics on Philippines, Burma and Thailand and to examine map carefully to be certain no country was inadvertently omitted. Conference in general agreement that eight signatories 1888 Convention plus eight largest users of Canal on basis of ownership tonnage should be invited. Considerable discussion ensured regarding final eight users to be selected on basis of pattern of trade.

Sec stated US base negotiations in Saudi Arabia in critical stage and exclusion Saudi Arabia could cost US its base rights. Lloyd informed conference Prime Minister Nuri then in FonOff and instructed member delegation to ascertain Nuri's views regarding invitation to Iraq. Subsequently Lloyd reported he hopes Iraq will not be invited. [7] Sec expressed doubts regarding issuing list of participants as annex to statement since time needed to prepare countries omitted through diplomatic channels. He mentioned Greece in particular. Caccia suggested issuing list and explaining basis for selections. Pineau thought list should accompany statement, otherwise competition would occur for place at conference.

List agreed upon transmitted Embtel 644. [8] Sec thought it would result in heavy majority for proposed action. He anticipated three negative votes—USSR, Egypt, Indonesia; and four doubtful—Iran, India, Spain, Ceylon. Meeting agreed that appropriate press guid-

---

[6] Not attached to either British Foreign Office, "Record" or "London Tripartite Conversations".

[7] At this point the British Foreign Office "Record" indicates that further consideration was then given to the "Proposed Basis for the International Conference." During this discussion, Foreign Secretary Lloyd "suggested it should be agreed to send this document to certain friendly countries as a proposition, to give them an idea of how our minds were working. This would be initially sent for information and then a firm proposition should be sent on August 6. It was not the intention to show the document in advance to Iraq and Saudi Arabia. He suggested it might be sent in advance to all Commonwealth and NATO countries and possibly Sweden. Mr. Dulles suggested sending it through the Permanent Council of NATO. The Foreign Secretary pointed out that it would be necessary to take diplomatic action quickly with those friendly countries which it was not intended to invite. He was thinking particularly of Belgium and Portugal."

[8] See footnote 1, Document 53.

ance [9] would be issued to make clear reasoning behind selection and fact that list had tripartite approval. At Sec's suggestion signatories of 1888 Convention listed separately so that reason for inclusion of USSR would be obvious.

Procedure Regarding Invitations

Meeting agreed UK should dispatch invitations immediately. [10] Sec stressed necessity flexibility in informing countries of purpose of conference and that matter might be discussed with friendlier nations in more detail first. For example, UK might talk with Commonwealth members. Pineau thought Egypt should not be left in position of being able to claim it kept less well informed than others. Lloyd questioned whether any response would be received in less than one week. Sec commented Italy appeared quite disturbed over not having been more fully consulted and said would be necessary watch situation there carefully.

Caccia thought Indonesia, Egypt and USSR should be consulted before conference and that US should assume responsibility in Indonesia. Pineau questioned whether USSR should be consulted. Lloyd thought Soviets should be approached shortly after friendly countries to avoid their taking offense. Lloyd agreed that UK would inform Belgium, Canada and South Africa who not on list of participants. Sec said he would speak to Menzies if still in US. [11]

Sec stressed need for steps shortly with respect to NATO; problem might be handled in NATO Council.

US, UK and France each agreed assume primary responsibility for approaches to countries specified below. Each would say acting with support of other two. France—Western Germany, Italy, Netherlands, Ethiopia. UK—Commonwealth (Australia, Ceylon, India, New Zealand, Pakistan), Scandinavian countries (Denmark, Norway, Sweden), and Portugal. US—Iran, Japan, Greece, Spain, Turkey. At suggestion of Sec meeting agreed defer until initial reaction received decision re approach to USSR, Egypt and Indonesia.

Meeting subsequently agreed to establishment of small committee in London consisting of US and French Ambs plus representative of FonOff poll information on reactions [sic]. It would make recom-

---

[9] Following the eighth tripartite meeting, at 8:30 p.m., Dulles held a background press briefing for American correspondents. Telegram 651 from London, August 3, contains a transcript of the briefing. (Department of State, Central Files, 974.7301/8–356)

[10] The text of the invitation was transmitted in telegram 650 from London, August 2. (*Ibid.*, 974.7301/8–256) It is printed in *The Suez Canal Problem, July 26–September 22, 1956*, p. 42.

[11] Subsequently, Dulles spoke with Menzies on August 4 at 4 p.m. A memorandum of their conversation is in Department of State, Central Files, 974.7301/8–456.

mendations regarding which of three powers should approach USSR, Egypt, Indonesia and also on timing.

Statements of Position

Pineau tabled suggested protocol Embtel 652 [12] and sought agreement from US and UK. Lloyd explained that protocol would be kept strictly secret and was equivalent to "heads of agreement" between three govts. Commenting on protocol Sec said that he viewed proposed conference as being for purpose of ascertaining views of participants upon whether they accepted or not seizure by Nasser of Suez Canal. He did not wish to place himself in position of being bound by unexpected result. He might wish to put proposal to Egypt in any case. Lloyd agreed three powers did not wish to bind themselves not to put proposition to Egypt in event adverse vote at conference. Sec said he was in accord with proposal to expedite conference and he thought first phase should not last more than one week. If Egypt agreed technical matters could then be discussed. Pineau maintained language in last para of French protocol based upon statement by Sec previous day. Sec commented he did not wish his statement to be interpreted as meaning that if one of three powers was prepared to take action another thought ill-advised others would be barred from expressing their views. Lloyd concurred in necessity retaining liberty of action. Sec declared that business of being "free" is illusory concept. If US decided to take no action in face of Egyptian reaction, UK and France would endeavor to persuade it otherwise. If US thought action contemplated by UK or France would precipitate world war it would try to dissuade them. While he agreed with spirit of last para French protocol he did not think three powers should be barred from talking matters over together. Lloyd said that if Egypt refused there was no commitment either with respect to taking any particular action or refraining from action.

Sec read to meeting text of US statement transmitted Embtel 649. [12] He observed that he could not agree to a protocol which would constitute a secret agreement. US would incorporate statement in minutes. Other countries could make similar statements. Pineau urged that UK and US both join in French protocol arguing that otherwise there would be no real tripartite agreement. Lloyd stated that he recognized weight of "secret agreement" problem. He thought UK could note US statement and express appreciation, Pineau said France could note US statement, but French Govt could not say that it was in accord with exact terms. Pineau then advanced various objections to US draft. Sec reiterated he did not consider it

---

[12] See the editorial note, *infra.*

wise to try to obtain paper to which all three could agree. He said in statement he had tried to express US view of rationale behind Conference. If Egyptians were morally isolated, measures required would involve much less danger. Statement set forth US philosophy. He hoped France and UK would concur in its spirit if not express wording. He realized that there were nuances of meaning and was not seeking agreed paper. Lloyd and Pineau then read Brit and French Govts' statements transmitted Embtel 649. [13]

Foreign nationals employed by Suez Canal Company

Lloyd referred to discussion in morning meeting regarding Canal Company employees and said UK Government could not agree to anything tonight. Cabinet would consider problem August 3. Steps taken this matter could alter entire position. Question especially difficult for UK since it Company stockholder. Secretary thought three powers should try to keep traffic moving. Lloyd said nothing would be more unfortunate than for Suez Canal Company to publish its proposed message and for UK to have to say it not in agreement. He asked only for 24 hour delay. Pineau described first message sent by Company and said he did not know whether second message of instructions (reported Secto 8 [14]) had been despatched. He said he could do nothing further until after meeting of French Government August 3. Lloyd replied he would communicate with French after cabinet meeting through usual channels.

Payment of Transit Tolls

Pineau said only argument he could see for changing French position (reported Secto 8) would be in order to take same stand as UK. Lloyd asserted he understood US vessels were paying new unlawful owners. Phleger pointed out that private US shippers had not asked for government advice and were only continuing past practice. Secretary said only navy ships had asked and we instructed them to pay under protest. If they were refused transit on this basis

---

[13] The U.K. statement, as contained in telegram 649 from London, reads as follows:

"H.M.G. welcome Mr. Dulles' statement. They share his view that the Conference should reach a speedy decision. They would not, however, consider themselves bound by any decision of the Conference adverse to the idea of the internationalization of the Suez Canal. They understand that this is also the position of the U.S. and French Governments."

The French statement, as contained in telegram 649, reads as follows:

"The French Government take note of the statement of Mr. Dulles. They will participate in the Conference with a sincere desire to bring it to a speedy conclusion and to obtain Egyptian acceptance of the internationalization of the Canal. But they reserve the right, in the event of an Egyptian refusal, to take any measures which they judge appropriate." (Department of State, Central Files, 396.1–LO/8–356)

[14] Document 44.

they would pay under coercion and enter details in ship's log. Lloyd said UK would continue consultations with France and expected to adhere to practice now adopted at least until British ship actually refused passage.

Miscellaneous Agreements Reached

UK to prepare first draft of rules of procedure for conference using Japanese Treaty Conference as model. London accepted as site of conference. Secretary remarked he overruled by 2/3 majority. Conference should be held at Foreign Minister level.

Concluding Statements

Lloyd—We have done lot of good work on short notice.

Secretary—Yes, we have launched something here and we must make it a success. We have done good work but we have much more hard work if we are to make it successful. We have done good work at this conference and it is a good omen for the future.

Pineau—If we had acted this way in 1936 there might not have been World War II.

Barbour

---

52.   Editorial Note

At the plenary tripartite meeting held on the afternoon of August 2 (see *supra*) French Foreign Minister Pineau tabled a suggested protocol. A rough translation of its text, transmitted to the Department of State, reads as follows:

"1. As the result of their discussions the Foreign Ministers of the United States, France and the United Kingdom have decided that the Conference which will be convened on the — August, 1956 to consider the future of the Suez Canal will be required to: (A) discover whether the majority of its members accept the seizure by Egypt of the Canal or whether, on the contrary they intend to place this international waterway under the control of an international management for an indefinite period; (B) if, as seems probable, the Conference decides to place the Canal under the control of an international management, to draw up the general framework by which such management would be put into effect.

"2. The Foreign Ministers have decided that if the results of the Conference are positive Egypt will be required to accept the proposals that will be put to her.

"3. The Foreign Ministers have similarly agreed, if Egypt accepts these proposals, to invite the governments participating in the Conference to take note of her agreement and to undertake without delay the detailed study of the modalities of the international organization which has been agreed in principle.

"4. Finally, the Foreign Ministers are agreed that, if Egypt should refuse the proposal which will be put to her, each of the three Governments should be free to take whatever action it judges appropriate." (Telegram 649 from London; Department of State, Central Files, 396.1–LO/8–356)

During the discussion that followed, Secretary Dulles read the following statement:

"The United States joins in the program outlined in the communiqué (tripartite statement) on the assumption that it represents, and will be implemented as, a genuine effort to enable relevant free world opinion to express its views on the subject of international operation of the Suez Canal as required, under the circumstances, to give assured effect to the internationalizing Convention of 1888. We believe that if such opinion impressively calls for such international operation, then the Egyptian Government would either accept such a solution or, in rejecting it, be morally isolated.

"This procedure requires, on the part of the three powers meeting here, a respect for the opinions of the governments of other free world nations that are themselves deeply concerned. Therefore, these others should have a reasonable opportunity to formulate and express their views. This should preferably be done through diplomatic channels prior to the Conference, so that the Conference itself will not be prolonged and controversial. We hope, and think it desirable, that the Conference be concluded within a week. With this in mind, we would cooperate to secure advance agreement of appropriate rules of procedure.

"The United States will also cooperate with France and the UK to make clear that it favors the international solution here outlined which protects those who use and depend on the Canal and which is fair to Egypt.

"We hope and will seek that the Conference will assure an acceptable solution. But if, unfortunately, the results of the program here agreed to are negative, that would create a new situation, to be dealt with in the light of the then circumstances without prior commitment." (Telegram 652 from London; *ibid.*)

53.   Tripartite Statement Issued at London, August 2, 1956 [1]

The Governments of France, the United Kingdom and the United States join in the following statement:

1. They have taken note of the recent action of the Government of Egypt whereby its attempts to nationalise and take over the assets and the responsibilities of the Universal Suez Canal Company. This company was organised in Egypt in 1856 under a franchise to build the Suez Canal and operate it until 1968. The Universal Suez Canal Company has always had an international character in terms of its shareholders, directors and operating personnel and in terms of its responsibility to assure the efficient functioning as an international waterway of the Suez Canal. In 1888 all the great powers then principally concerned with the international character of the Canal and its free, open and secure use without discrimination joined in the Treaty and Convention of Constantinople. This provided for the benefit of all the world that the international character of the Canal would be perpetuated for all time, irrespective of the expiration of the concession of the Universal Suez Canal Company. Egypt as recently as October 1954 recognised that the Suez Canal is "a waterway economically, commercially and strategically of international importance", and renewed its determination to uphold the Convention of 1888.

2. They do not question the right of Egypt to enjoy and exercise all the powers of a fully sovereign and independent nation, including the generally recognised right, under appropriate conditions, to nationalise assets, not impressed with an international interest, which are subject to its political authority. But the present action involves far more than a simple act of nationalisation. It involves the arbitrary and unilateral seizure by one nation of an international agency which has the responsibility to maintain and to operate the Suez Canal so that all the signatories to, and beneficiaries of, the Treaty of 1888 can effectively enjoy the use of an international waterway upon which the economy, commerce, and security of much of the world depends. This seizure is the more serious in its implications because it avowedly was made for the purpose of enabling the Government of Egypt to make the Canal serve the purely national purposes of the Egyptian Government, rather than the international purpose established by the Convention of 1888.

---

[1] Source: Department of State, Central Files, 974.7301/8–256. Transmitted to the Department of State in telegram 644, August 2. The text is attached to the U.K. invitation to other governments to attend the Suez Canal Conference in London. See *The Suez Canal Problem, July 26–September 22, 1956*, pp. 34–35, 42.

Furthermore, they deplore the fact that as an incident to its seizure the Egyptian Government has had recourse to what amounts to a denial of fundamental human rights by compelling employees of the Suez Canal Company to continue to work under threat of imprisonment.

3. They consider that the action taken by the Government of Egypt, having regard to all the attendant circumstances, threatens the freedom and security of the Canal as guaranteed by the Convention of 1888. This makes it necessary that steps be taken to assure that the parties to that Convention and all other nations entitled to enjoy its benefits shall, in fact, be assured of such benefits.

4. They consider that steps should be taken to establish operating arrangements under an international system designed to assure the continuity of operation of the Canal as guaranteed by the Convention of October 29, 1888, consistently with legitimate Egyptian interests.

5. To this end they propose that a conference should promptly be held of parties to the Convention and other nations largely concerned with the use of the Canal. The invitations to such a conference, to be held in London, on August 16, 1956, will be extended by the Government of the United Kingdom to the Governments named in the Annex to this Statement. The Governments of France and the United States are ready to take part in the conference.

[Annex]

PARTIES TO THE CONVENTION OF 1888

Egypt	Italy	Spain	United Kingdom
France	The Netherlands	Turkey	U.S.S.R.

Other Nations largely concerned in the use of the Canal either through ownership of tonnage or pattern of trade.

Australia	Federal Republic	Indonesia	Norway
Ceylon	of Germany	Iran	Pakistan
Denmark	Greece	Japan	Portugal
Ethiopia	India	New Zealand	Sweden
			United States

CONTINUED U.S. CONSIDERATION OF THE SUEZ SITUATION; UNITED
STATES DIPLOMATIC ACTIVITY PRIOR TO THE SUEZ CANAL
CONFERENCE, AUGUST 3–15

54.   Editorial Note

Between August 3 and 15, tripartite planning for the forthcoming Suez Canal Conference was conducted primarily in London. Walworth Barbour and other officials from the Embassy, guided by instructions from the Department of State, represented the United States in these discussions, until the return to London of Secretary Dulles on August 15. In Washington, various departments and agencies of the United States Government continued to discuss the ramifications of the Suez situation, while officials of the Department of State began to prepare position papers for the forthcoming Suez Canal Conference. At the same time, Secretary Dulles sought to explain and gain support for the American position, through diplomatic correspondence with foreign leaders, and through numerous conversations with the representatives of foreign governments directly or indirectly involved in the Suez situation.

In addition to the documents printed here, Department of State Central File 974.7301 constitutes the main collection of Suez-related material for this period. The file includes, among other items of interest, reports and instructions passing between the Department of State and the Embassy in London, documentation concerning meetings of the State Department's Suez Economic Task Force, diplomatic correspondence, and memoranda of conversation with foreign diplomats. Department of State Central File 396.1–LO also contains Suez-related correspondence and memoranda of conversation. Conference Files: Lot 62 D 181 contains the United States position papers for the Suez Canal Conference, most of which were prepared during the period August 3–15. Reports concerning the Anglo-French military buildup in the eastern Mediterranean are primarily in Central File 974.7301, but additional material can be found in Central Files 396.1–LO, 741.5–MSP, 740.5, and 751.5.

55.   Memorandum of a Conversation, Department of State, Washington, August 3, 1956 [1]

PARTICIPANTS

The Acting Secretary
Ambassador Makins
C. Burke Elbrick, EUR
Mr. R. W. Bailey, Counselor, British Embassy

The Ambassador called to present a note inviting the United States Government to take part in an international conference on the Suez Canal to be held in London on August 16. [2]

He also gave the Acting Secretary a note regarding bilateral petroleum planning. [3] The Ambassador said that the United Kingdom would like to begin on government-to-government planning on this very important matter to be followed by industry planning. He understood that planning in this field presented problems for the United States, particularly when it came to such measures as rationing. The United Kingdom hoped that this question of rationing would not arise, except as a last resort, and felt that advance planning might even obviate the necessity of invoking such drastic measures. Mr. Hoover commented that if the pie to be cut up is only so big, no amount of advance planning can make it any bigger. In any event, U.S. planning in this field would not take much time since the Foreign Advisory Committee for petroleum problems, which is now being reactivated, [4] has dealt with such matters ever

---

[1] Source: Department of State, Central Files, 974.7301/8–356. Top Secret. Drafted by Elbrick. This conversation evidently took place prior to Secretary Dulles' return to the Department of State at 12:20 p.m., August 3. (Dulles' Appointment Book; Princeton University Library, Dulles Papers)

[2] The British note of invitation, dated August 3, and the U.S. note accepting the invitation, dated August 4, are *ibid.*, 396.1–LO/8–356. Their texts are printed in *The Suez Canal Problem, July 26–September 22, 1956,* pp. 42–43.

[3] The aide-mémoire from the British Embassy, entitled "Suez Canal and Oil Supplies", stated that the British Government regarded it as a matter of the greatest urgency to begin effective joint petroleum planning with the United States. It predicted that a closure of the Suez Canal accompanied by an interruption of the pipeline flow would cut Western Europe's oil imports by approximately one-half and would have a catastrophic effect on Europe's economy. The aide-mémoire recalled previous exchanges the previous spring between the two governments on the subject, and urged that such discussions resume immediately at both government and industry levels. (Department of State, Central Files, 974.7301/8–356)

On August 2 in London, Caccia had handed to Dulles a note regarding petroleum planning almost identical in substance to the British aide-mémoire of August 3. The Embassy in London had transmitted a summary of the note to the Department in Secto 12 on August 3 with the comment: "Question is subject of great anxiety here." The Embassy in London transmitted the complete text of the August 2 note to the Department in despatch 358, August 3. (Both *ibid.*, 974.7301/8–356)

[4] See footnote 2, Document 30.

since the second World War. There is no problem with the major oil companies but there are several independent companies on this Committee and at the present time it was felt best not to invite the independents to take part since they might leak the news to the public. Mr. Hoover informed the Ambassador that on the U.S. side the whole matter of petroleum planning is in train.

On the general question of planning the Acting Secretary said that a great deal would depend on whether the oil pipelines would be closed concurrently with the closing of the Canal. In other words, the alternatives to be considered are extreme denial (in the event the pipelines are also closed) or merely taking up the slack (in the event that only the Canal is closed) by rerouting tankers.

In connection with the payment of Canal tolls the Acting Secretary emphasized the importance of refraining from any action which could provoke the closure of the Canal and which could be blamed upon the Western powers. In other words, if the Canal is to be closed it should be closed by unilateral Egyptian action and not as a result of actions by the West. Only in this way could we expect to have public opinion behind us. Sir Roger said that on the question of tolls he was still waiting for final views from London. The Acting Secretary informed the Ambassador that Secretary Dulles had recommended from London that United States Government ships transiting the Canal protest any payment of tolls to the Egyptian Government and only make payment under coercion, entering this fact in the ship's log. Instructions to this effect had been sent to Government ships but no advice as yet has been given to merchant vessel owners.

---

56.   Editorial Note

During the evening of August 3, the Department of State delivered to the British Embassy the Department's response to the Embassy's note of July 28 on petroleum planning. Regarding the British note, see Document 19. The text of the Department's response reads as follows:

"The Department of State agrees with the point made in the British Embassy's note of July 28, 1956 'Suez Canal: Oil Supplies' that the expert knowledge and practical assistance of U.S. and UK oil industry experts are indispensable to the preparation of effective plans of action to cope with the oil supply problem which closure of the Suez Canal would create. The Department sees no obstacle to effective participation of such experts in U.S. or joint planning on the problem.

"Currently the U.S. Government is consulting, through the medium of a reconstituted Foreign Petroleum Supply Committee, certain U.S. companies concerned in international oil matters. It believes similar consultation between the UK Government and British oil companies through the Oil Supplies Advisory Committee, mentioned in paragraph 3 of the British Embassy's note, would be useful and a necessary prelude to such joint planning as might be appropriate.

"It is the Department's view that no publicity should be given to the fact of the planning which is being undertaken or which may be undertaken, or to the conclusions reached, and that special attention should be given to this point in view of the number of individuals necessarily concerned with it."

This response was drafted by the Officer in Charge of Economic Organization Affairs in the Bureau of European Affairs, Edwin G. Moline, and forwarded to Acting Secretary Hoover on August 1, under cover of a memorandum by Don C. Bliss of the Office of the Deputy Under Secretary for Economic Affairs. The text of the response is attached to the August 1 memorandum by Bliss, which is the Department's file copy and which is stamped August 3 at the bottom of the page. (Department of State, Central Files, 974.7301/ 8–156) A memorandum from Lister (BNA) to Dale (BNA), dated August 6, indicates that Lister handed the original of the note to Morris of the British Embassy, Friday evening, August 3. (*Ibid.*, 986B.7301/8–656)

---

57.   Editorial Note

According to Dulles' Appointment Book, the Secretary arrived outside Washington at noon, August 3, and proceeded immediately to the State Department where he discussed the Suez situation over lunch with Hoover, Murphy, and Phleger. (Princeton University Library, Dulles Papers) No account of this conversation has been found in Department of State files. At 2:15 p.m., the Secretary telephoned Allen Dulles. Their conversation, as transcribed by Bernau, went as follows:

"AWD said congratulations. They agreed it was tough. The Sec. said the fellows there are steamed up. They agreed the job is not done yet—just a cooling-off period. They agreed there should be a meeting at the Sec's house to pull together the next steps. The following will be present: AWD, K. Roosevelt, someone from Defense and the JCS which Mr. Hoover will arrange, G. Humphrey?, Hoover?, Phleger, Murphy, Elbrick, Rountree." (Eisenhower Library, Dulles Papers, General Memoranda of Conversation)

At approximately 2:30 p.m., Dulles and Hoover met with President Eisenhower at the White House. (Dulles' Appointment Book; Princeton University Library, Dulles Papers) Presumably at this meeting, Dulles, Hoover, and Eisenhower reviewed the Suez situation; but no account of the discussion has been found in either Department of State files or the Eisenhower Library. Later that evening, Secretary Dulles delivered a televised report to the nation on the Suez situation. A transcript of this report is in Department of State, Conference Files: Lot 62 D 181, CF 728, and is printed in Department of State *Bulletin,* August 13, 1956, pages 259–261; and in *The Suez Canal Problem, July 26–September 22, 1956,* pages 37–42.

On Saturday, August 4, at 11:15 a.m. at Dulles' home, a meeting was held on the Suez situation. According to the Secretary's Appointment Book, those present at the meeting were: Allen Dulles, Kermit Roosevelt, Gordon Gray, Arthur Flemming, George Humphrey, Herbert Hoover, Jr., Herman Phleger, Robert Murphy, C. Burke Elbrick, William Rountree, Eugene McAuliffe, and John B. Hollister. (Princeton University Library, Dulles Papers) No account of this conversation has been found in Department of State files.

***

58.   **Editorial Note**

On August 3, the Department of State advised the Embassy in Moscow of the difficulty encountered in convincing Great Britain and France to include the Soviet Union on the list of invitees to the Suez Conference and instructed the Embassy to ascertain as soon as possible what the attitude of the Soviet Union would be to the invitation that the British Government would be delivering to the Soviet Government perhaps on August 6. The telegram, drafted and approved by Murphy who signed for Dulles, indicated: "What I think Russians should know is that we have had very difficult time restraining our friends from quick direct action in defense of what they consider their urgent and basic rights and their standing in Middle East and North Africa. Russians will certainly understand dangers inherent in such a course which is still not excluded." (Telegram 131 to Moscow, August 3; Department of State, Central Files, 974.7301/8–356)

The following day in response to these instructions, Ambassador Charles Bohlen reported that the British Government had already delivered the invitation to the Soviet Government the previous day so that he was unable to convey the United States perspective prior to Soviet receipt of the invitation. Bohlen added that he seriously questioned the approach contained in telegram 131 "which could only confirm to Soviets fact of serious division in Western camp over courses of action, and I believe would tend to stiffen Soviet opposition" to the terms of reference and composition of the conference. Instead, Bohlen proposed that he be authorized to tell Soviet officials that "rejection of Conference proposal by Egypt or the Soviet Union would cause situation to revert to one of extreme danger, to indicate that U.S. in such event would be disposed to back its friends in more direct action." (Telegram 279 from Moscow, August 4; *ibid.*, 974.7301/8–456)

---

59.   Telegram From the Embassy in Egypt to the Department of State [1]

Cairo, August 4, 1956—4 a.m.

240. Am aware that Department would wish me to take no initiative with Nasser at present time in absence instructions and without background of London talks. However Nasser asked me to come see him evening August 3 and there seemed no alternative but to comply.

Nasser was relaxed and friendly. As a sidelight on the nature of this man he had spent the day in Alexandria with his children on the beach and went to a movie to "clear his mind".

Nasser seemed reluctant turn conversation to business but when he finally did he made following points (which he stressed were his preliminary and tentative views):

[1] Source: Department of State, Central Files, 974.7301/8–456. Secret; Niact. Received at 5:43 a.m. Repeated Niact to London and Priority to Paris. In a later telegram, Byroade cautioned the Department: "Hope extraordinary precautions will be taken to see that contents niact 240 do not get in hands of press. This would tend to make more cautious our best source of political intelligence, i.e. Nasser, in delicate period and perhaps freeze him into unfavorable position when we are still not entirely without influence to guide him if this later desired." (Telegram 241 from Cairo, August 4; *ibid.*)

1. He could not accept international control. This would mean that by formal agreement he was accepting not merely return of the form of colonialism exemplified by "a French company" but a permanent subordination to "nearly everybody". Everything he stood for and for which he had pledged himself to the people of Egypt was against this.

2. He did not see how he could accept participation in the proposed conference. He had been placed in the position of attending under threat of invasion and starvation (in case of latter he referring to freezing of assets). Surely we could understand his feelings at least re former and he could not help wondering whether British were not deliberately making it impossible for him to be represented. Not only was the agenda already fixed but final decision as well. Egypt would stand alone or perhaps with only Russia by her side. This latter point worried both him and Fawzi as great propaganda against Egypt would be made if this turned out to be the case.

3. He thought the choice of nations was very strange and composed for the large part of "satellites" of the Big Three. How for instance he wondered was Ethiopia chosen. The combination of Commonwealth and close friends and allies of the United States left little doubt that conference would be pro forma. British would put in "paper" and great majority of the others would quickly agree with very little discussion or consideration of Egypt's case.

4. He was still groping as to what to do but felt his best recourse was to go to the United Nations without delay. In UN Egypt would not be "so alone" as regards friends and choice of participating nations. He has therefore instructed Fawzi and others give fullest study tactics this end. Pending their report he uncertain grounds and forum but implied he was not at moment giving much consideration to claiming "threat to peace" or reference to Security Council. He implied however Egypt would probably refer matter to UN prior August 16. For the present he plans not reply invitation.

5. He was ready to sign new international agreement "with anyone" guaranteeing freedom of passage and uninterrupted use of Suez Canal facilities. This could be a bringing up to date of 1888 convention and agreement with a new group of signatories if this appeared wise or some other measure.

6. He was obviously pleased there had been no incident as regards Canal traffic and stated that there would be none. He said he did not intend that Egypt should "indulge itself with minor troubles" in this connection.

7. He did not know Russian position except on question of internationalization itself. He had asked Soviet Ambassador [2] this morning but Ambassador said he did not know. He informed Soviet Ambassador that he felt he should postpone his Moscow trip. No new date was set.

I had opened session by informing Nasser that since tripartite meeting in London had been chaired by British who had also issued invitations, British Ambassador here would no doubt be representa-

---

[2] Yevgeniy Kiselev.

tive with whom he should discuss any aspect of meeting. I informed him categorically US Government fully supported principle international control of operation of Suez Canal. He said he understood that this was our position. Obviously he was seeking advice. I refrained however from giving any as am without specific guidance and believe Department would probably not wish me offer advice at this stage. However I did counsel him in one respect. He stated that if case was taken to UN he felt that Egypt should take the position that all waterways of international importance should be discussed. He could then take the position he would accept any form of international control that was accepted by others. He mentioned most of principal canal arteries in world including Panama Canal. I told him I thought he was treading on dangerous ground indeed in any reference to Panama Canal. If as he predicted Egypt and Russia might end up side by side in an effort to place international control over all restricted waterways, including the Panama Canal, he would have the wrath of all America against him. Believe I dissuaded him from this course but cannot be sure. I had hoped this meeting would be private as am aware British and others will wonder what we talked about. Nasser has however chosen to let press know of meeting. In any event will brief Trevelyan as soon as possible.

Byroade

**60.   Memorandum From the Secretary of State's Special
Assistant (Russell) to the Secretary of State** [1]

Washington, August 4, 1956.

SUBJECT

Robert Anderson's Meeting with Ambassador Eban and Reuven Shiloah

Mr. Robert Anderson gave me the following account of his
luncheon meeting yesterday with Eban and Shiloah, Ambassador and
Minister, respectively, of the Israel Embassy:

Eban had a much more relaxed attitude than at any previous
meeting with Anderson. His general attitude was one of "I told you
so", although he did not push it.

Eban said he had left his meeting with the Secretary in March
following the Anderson visit to the Middle East with the following
impressions:

1. As a result of the Anderson mission and other developments
the U.S. felt it had to make a reappraisal with respect to the
reliability and objectives of Col. Nasser and that such a reappraisal
was underway;
2. The reappraisal would be evolutionary and not precipitous
and would become most apparent in connection with the ultimate
decision on the Aswan Dam;
3. The U.S. was convinced that Israel's arms strength should be
increased but it was preferable that the arms should be provided by
other nations than the U.S.

This impression of the Secretary's thinking had been an important factor in guiding the Israel Government since March. With
respect to the third point, however, Ben Gurion had been extremely
skeptical about the requirement that Israel should obtain its arms
from non-U.S. sources. He felt we were being naive and that there

---

[1] Source: Department of State, NEA files: Lot 59 D 518, Omega—Memos, etc. for
July 1 to August 31, 1956. Top Secret—Omega. A covering memorandum from
Russell to Dulles, dated August 6, which notes that Shiloah had asked for another
secret meeting, reads in part:

"It can be assumed that they wish to raise, in addition to the Suez Canal
problem, the line they developed with Robert Anderson (attached memorandum of
conversation.)

"It is already obvious that the Israel Government will attempt to exploit the
present situation in the Eastern Mediterranean to achieve as many as possible of its
own objectives. It seems equally clear that any general fusion of the Palestine issue
with the Canal issue at this time would only operate to further complicate both
questions. This latter comment is, of course, without prejudice to the possibility that
the necessities of dealing with Nasser might later require coordination of measures by
the Western powers and by Israel." Russell recommended that Dulles see Eban and
Shiloah and give them his view "as to the position Israel can most usefully take at the
present time." The memorandum indicates that Dulles approved the meeting with the
Israelis; see Document 75.

was more benefit for Israel and the U.S. if the arms could come directly from the U.S. This skepticism has now reached a point of crisis. The IG was being told that as a result of the U.S. decision on the Aswan Dam and the Suez Canal crisis, matters were improving for the IG. As a matter of fact, however, things were not improving. Canada was being asked to delay on providing the F–86's. A favorable action of which the IG had felt sure was now in doubt. They understood our theory that the providing of arms to Israel should not appear to the Arab world to be in retaliation to Nasser's actions but they were apprehensive that the delay might become prolonged.

Eban said the IG felt that developments in the Middle East had vindicated them in their analysis and this vindication should have a historical significance and lesson both with respect to future U.S. policy toward Egypt and U.S. cooperation with Israel.

Eban said the IG applauds the London decision to hold a conference on the Suez but it is important to understand that the calling of the conference is not an achievement in itself. The important thing is what comes out of it. It will, in fact, turn out to be a retrogressive step if there is any slackening in the West's attitude toward Nasser or if anything is done to help Nasser save face.

Eban said that while it might logically be assumed that Nasser did not intend to attack Israel in the near future, Nasser had proven to be a most illogical person and that since he is illogical, Israel has to assume that he might decide to attack at any time. There should, therefore, be no further delay in the receipt of planes by Israel from Canada and France.

Eban believed that it would help in achieving success at the forthcoming London conference and would help to diminish Nasser's standing if there were to be official conversations and even public discussion about the possibility of a link through Israel between the Mediterranean and the Red Sea. The IG has made studies of the engineering feasibility and the cost of such a canal through Israel. It would cost less than the Aswan Dam. Eban will have those studies within the next week and will furnish them to Anderson. An alternative to a canal would be a pipeline through the Negev. Anderson told Eban he thought the matter should be carefully thought out before anything was said about it as a possibility. If it turned out to be utterly impractical, the proposal would be a propaganda boomerang.

Eban said that the IG had received assurances from "the powers" that if an international authority were set up pursuant to the London meetings, the IG would be guaranteed right of passage. Anderson queried Eban particularly on this and Eban reiterated that the IG had been given such assurances though he did not specify where, when or by whom.

Eban's final point, which he emphasized especially, was that recent developments ought to bring the U.S. to a realization that the whole cold war battlefront is in the Middle East; that we cannot rely on Nasser, on the North African complex, on Cyprus, or on Syria. The only country upon which the West can rely is Israel. Because of our recent policies toward Israel, it is not now in a position to be of much help if we should find we had to place primary reliance on them. It is time for highly secret discussions between the U.S. and the IG with respect to what the West needs and what Israel could provide in the way of making it the Western stronghold that it should be. The U.S. should, therefore, take immediate steps to put Israel in a position to be a bastion of strength. Eban said that the IG had made similar proposals in 1950–51 to Secretary Marshall. He assumed that these proposals were in the Department's files [2] and suggested Anderson might like to have them gotten out and take a look at them.

Eban said that the IG was making a serious study of the pattern of the Egyptian Government and was coming to the conclusion that it was closely following the Soviet model. There was a striking resemblance in the reduction of the group holding power from eleven to three, in the type of leading personalities, and otherwise.

Mr. Anderson expressed his gratification that the IG had remained quiet during the furor over the Suez and said he thought it would be greatly to Israel's advantage to keep quiet during the coming period. Eban said that this had been a policy decision on the part of the IG and that if Anderson had no objection, he would like to transmit to Ben Gurion Anderson's expression of approval. Anderson said he would have no objection providing it was made clear that he was speaking purely as a private citizen.

---

[2] Reference is presumably to a memorandum from Israeli Foreign Minister Sharett to Secretary of Defense George C. Marshall, transmitted under cover of a letter dated December 23, 1950 (see *Foreign Relations, 1950*, vol. V, p. 1077). In this memorandum the Israeli Government stressed the potential contribution which Israel could make to American security in the Near East and used this rationale as a basis for additional requests for arms and matériel. Israeli officials continued to discuss this matter with U.S. officials during 1951. See *ibid.*, 1951, vol. V, pp. 913 ff.

61.   Telegram From the Department of State to the Embassy in France [1]

Washington, August 4, 1956—2 p.m.

489. Please inform Pineau that after his return from London Secretary is more impressed than ever with importance that French and British should not take action which might place upon them responsibility for interruption to Canal transit. He therefore believes it would be unwise for instructions to be dispatched to Canal Company employees that they should leave Egypt. This of course does not imply that employees should be subject to coercion by Egyptian Government.

London should advise Lloyd of foregoing message to Pineau adding that Secretary hopes he will agree Company or governments should not instruct Canal employees to return. If individual employees should decide on their own volition to resign there could, of course, be no objection. That, however, would be quite different from resignations resulting from instructions to leave which would include attractive offers re continuation salary payments and generous retirement benefits. [2]

Dulles

---

[1] Source: Department of State, Central Files, 974.7301/8–456. Top Secret; Niact. Drafted by Rountree; cleared by Murphy; and approved by Rountree who signed for Dulles. Repeated Niact to London.

[2] On August 5, the Embassy in Paris reported that the French Government supported the recently-stated position of the Suez Canal Company and believed that it met U.S. wishes. On August 4, the directors of the Canal Company had requested the French Government to transmit through diplomatic channels a message to Company employees in Egypt indicating that the Company believed its employees should not work for the new Egyptian company except under duress. (Telegram 626 from Paris, August 5; *ibid.*, 974.7301/8–556)

62.   Paper by the Secretary of State's Special Assistant (Russell) [1]

Washington, August 4, 1956.

U.S. POLICIES TOWARD NASSER

Problem:

What should be U.S. policy toward Nasser in view of his July 26 speech at Alexandria, his seizure of the Suez Canal and his basic objectives as revealed by these and other recent actions?

Discussion:

Up to the present time there has been room for divergence of opinion as to whether Nasser is: (a) a progressive military dictator attempting to modernize Egypt's political, economic and social conditions and promote its leadership in the Arab world; (b) a symbol and leader of several centuries of accumulated Arab frustration, resentment and bitterness; or (c) an aspirant for power on a large scale, utilizing without scruple and without regard to the interests of his own or other peoples the tensions, resentments and capacities for trouble that exist in the Middle East and Africa. At different times during the past four years the balance of evidence has pointed to first one and then another of these possibilities. Developments of the past few weeks, however, point clearly to the conclusion that Nasser is an international political adventurer of considerable skill with clearly defined objectives that seriously threaten the Western world, though probably with no definitely planned tactics or timetable.

---

[1] Source: Department of State, NEA Files: Lot 59 D 518, Omega—Memos, etc. fr July 1 to August 31, 1956. Top Secret—Omega. Forwarded to Dulles under cover of a memorandum by Russell, dated August 6, which reads: "As a result of discussion at a recent meeting of the Middle East Policy Planning Group, I undertook to prepare the attached paper on U.S. policies toward Nasser. I have discussed the general ideas included in the paper with Messrs. Rountree, Hare, and Bowie and CIA representatives who expressed no dissent. I am circulating it to them and calling a meeting of the Middle East Policy Planning Group to discuss it. I am handing you a copy at this time as I thought you might be interested in some of the material at an early date in view of the urgent nature of the Suez problem." This covering memorandum bears the marginal inscription by Bernau, "Sec Saw." No documentation has been found in Department of State files of the Secretary's response, if any, to this paper and its recommendations.

At its August 1 meeting, the Middle East Policy Planning Group agreed that Russell, Mathews, and Fritzlan would prepare a paper on Nasser's goals and strategy and the best means of combating them and reducing his power. (Memorandum of conversation, August 1; *ibid.*, Omega—Meetings of MEPPG (Agenda, memos of conv., etc.) 4/9/56 to 6/30/56) The MEPPG discussed and approved Russell's paper during a meeting on August 7. (Memorandum of conversation, August 7; *ibid.*)

In May, 1953, Nasser appeared as the author of a small book called "The Philosophy of the Revolution". Some of the actual writing was done by a journalist friend, Mohammed Heikel, after a weekend which he spent with Nasser, but there is no doubt that the ideas and the final form of the statements are Nasser's. Attached ("A") [2] are excerpts from the book which throw a sharp light on developments of the past year. Briefly, they make clear that Nasser intends to make full use of the resources of the Arab world, notably the Suez Canal and the oil, the resources and turmoil of the entire African continent, and the support of Muslims in Indonesia, China, Malaya, Siam, Burma and elsewhere, "to wield a power without limit".

In retrospect it is apparent that Nasser's efforts to build a solidarity of the Arab countries, especially Egypt, Saudi Arabia and Syria, even at the expense of economic progress in Egypt; his rage at Iraq's participation in the Baghdad Pact; his lip service in private talks to a Palestine settlement while exacerbating the problem in public speeches; his firm insistence upon obtaining the entire Negev; his skill, for a period at least, in playing off the Soviet bloc against the West; his shrewdness in attacking at one time Britain and at another time the U.S. but rarely the two at the same time; his public dispatch of Ambassador Hussein to accept the U.S. offer to assist on the Aswan Dam, after having shown no interest for six months, at a time when he was aware that the Secretary of State was no longer in a position to make firm arrangements; and, finally, using the "turn-down" as a pretext for seizing the Canal and thus, if successful, putting Egypt in a position to affect the economy of Western Europe, the countries of South Asia and elsewhere—all fit into the pattern elucidated in "The Philosophy of the Revolution".

If this is a correct analysis, it must be assumed that Nasser considers that he has only made a beginning and that his action, to the extent possible, will be guided by the objective of building as much personal power as possible upon the exploitation of the tensions and resources of all of the Middle East and all of Africa. It must be concluded that Nasser is not a leader with whom it will be possible to enter into friendly arrangements of cooperation or with whom it would even be possible to make any feasible accommodations.

It would follow from this analysis that Nasser does not wish to become a stooge of the Kremlin. His role is a more ambitious one. He undoubtedly sees himself as a "third force", able to do business on equal terms with both the West and the East. He would, however, be a "third force" whose objectives, although of a different

[2] Not printed.

kind, would be as inimical to the interests of the West as those of the Kremlin. His movement would not have the elaborate ideology or skillful long-term planning of the Communists but it would be motivated by ancient, deep and powerful hatreds that are directed primarily against the West and not against the Soviet bloc.

While the hatreds, frustrations and resentments of the people of the Middle East and Africa certainly exist and there is no easy way of dealing with the problems which they create, it is to the interest of the West that they be dealt with as nearly separately as possible and that no leader of the Hitlerian type be permitted to merge the emotions and resources of the entire Middle East and Africa into a single onslaught against Western civilization.

On the basis of the foregoing, and regardless of the outcome of the London conference on the Suez Canal, the U.S. and the U.K. should lose no time in implementing policies designed to reduce . . . Nasser as a force in the Middle East and Africa. To the extent possible, this should be done in such a way as to incur a minimum of resentment on the part of the Arab world and the "uncommitted" nations generally. . . .

Conclusions:

The following conclusions emerge from the foregoing:

1. The possibility of our establishing a cooperative relationship with Nasser no longer exists.

2. While Nasser may regard himself as neutral between the Soviet and Free Worlds, it is only because he believes that through such a posture he can best promote his objective of creating a "third force" dominated by himself that would inevitably threaten the Free World.

3. It is in U.S. interests to take action to reduce Nasser's power. . . .

4. The U.S. should act in agreement with the U.K. and as far as possible with France and other countries who can be brought to pursue the foregoing objectives.

Recommendations:

1. *Political:*

a. . . .
b. . . .
c. We should step up our efforts to strengthen the Baghdad Pact and specifically Iraq. Provided Israel can be induced not to react violently and provided it would not appreciably increase the extent of our current difficulties with the Saudis, we should consider making an announcement of our intention to adhere to the Pact.

d. We should seek every practical opportunity to convince Jordan and Lebanon of our desire to assist them with economic aid and small amounts of military aid.

e. . . . We should take steps to try to effect a relaxation and tension between King Saud and the Hashemite Houses of Iraq and Jordan.

f. . . .

g. Should our efforts to negotiate a renewal of the Dhahran Airfield agreement fail, we should assess Saudi requirements in terms of internal security needs only and agree to sell arms on that basis.

h. The U.S. should continue its present attitude on development of the Nile, using suitable opportunities to secure agreement of all states concerned in an integrated Nile Valley development scheme and offering to help on the technical side and in the matter of securing loans.

i. We should prevent Israel from being overtly associated with the Western powers in any action which might be taken against Egypt.

2. *Economic:* [3]

a. . . .

b. The U.S. and the U.K. should cut off completely the spare parts for Egypt's military equipment (which is still a substantial part of its total) as well as of aircraft and endeavor to get other friendly nations to take similar action.

c. If the situation in Egypt in relation to the Soviet bloc warrants such course, the U.S. should apply Battle Act provisions [4] to international trade with Egypt.

d. The U.S. should refuse to extend any Export-Import Bank loans to Egyptian companies.

e. The U.S. and the U.K. should discourage tourist traffic to Egypt and thus deprive Egypt of substantial foreign exchange earnings.

3. . . .

4. . . .

---

[3] A Department of State position paper entitled "Economic Sanctions," dated August 9 and prepared in the Office of International Trade and Resources, recommended that the United States support the use of economic sanctions only if the Egyptian Government impeded navigation through the Canal, if economic sanctions were the only means of avoiding military action against Egypt by Great Britain and France, and if a sufficient number of countries intended to cooperate with the sanctions, thereby making them effective. If any of these criteria were lacking, the paper argued that the use of sanctions could be counterproductive in that it might alienate a large number of non-Western governments and could possibly lead to such retaliatory action as Egypt blocking navigation of the Canal or the Arab states hampering the flow of oil. (Department of State, NEA Files: Lot 59 D 518, Omega—Background)

[4] Reference is to the Mutual Defense Assistance Control Act of 1951, which provided for the control by the United States and cooperating foreign nations of exports to any nation or combination of nations threatening the security of the United States. (65 Stat. 575)

63.   Circular Telegram From the Department of State to Certain Diplomatic Missions [1]

Washington, August 5, 1956—3:26 p.m.

90. US–UK–France have agreed that principles set forth below would be good framework for discussions at August 16 London conference on Suez Canal. In order to facilitate work of conference it was also agreed seek, prior to conference, as wide agreement as possible among participating nations as to basis upon which deliberations would rest. [2] Three countries each agreed assume primary responsibility for approaches to nations specified below. Each will say acting with support of other two:

France: West Germany, Italy, Netherlands, Ethiopia.
UK: Australia, Ceylon, India, New Zealand, Pakistan, Denmark, Norway, Sweden, Portugal.
US: Iran, Japan, Greece, Spain, Turkey.

As matter of high priority and major importance missions in countries designated as US responsibility are requested make approaches on August 6 and to endeavor to obtain agreement or acquiescence of Governments concerned that below principles shall serve as basis from which conference will approach Suez problem. You should also make use of Secretary's radio speech of August 3 [3] (see USIA wireless file August 3) and as case may be of messages from Secretary to certain heads of government or Foreign Ministers. You should underline thought behind sentence in Secretary's letter which read: "I cannot overestimate the importance of this Conference or the dangerous consequences which might follow if there were a breakdown of peaceful processes in dealing with the future of the Canal operation." [4]

Missions in countries designated as UK or French responsibility should support representations made by UK and French officials.

US missions should approach Indonesia and Egypt. US should consult with UK and France and make consecutive approach to

---

[1] Source: Department of State, Central Files, 974.7301/8–556. Secret; Niact. Drafted by Rockwell and Wilkins; cleared with Dulles in substance and with Murphy; and approved by Wilkins. Rountree signed for Dulles. Sent to Ankara, Addis Ababa, Athens, Bonn, Cairo, Canberra, Colombo, Copenhagen, Djakarta, Karachi, Lisbon, Madrid, Moscow, New Delhi, Oslo, Rome, Stockholm, Tehran, The Hague, Tokyo, Wellington, London, and Paris.

[2] Documentation on the discussions preceding this agreement is *ibid.,* 974.7301.

[3] For text, see Department of State *Bulletin,* August 13, 1956, p. 259.

[4] This sentence was included in a message, sent over Dulles' signature, to the heads of government or foreign ministers of various countries invited to the first Suez Conference. The messages were transmitted telegraphically between August 3 and 5. Copies are in Department of State, Central Files 396.1–LO and 974.7301.

USSR starting with UK approach as host. Action in Indonesia, Egypt and USSR should be taken on August 7.

"Proposal for the Establishment of an International Authority for the Suez Canal. [5]

I. France, the UK and the US are in agreement that at the Conference a resolution shall be tabled for setting up an International Authority for the Suez Canal on the following lines:

II. The purposes and functions of this International Authority would be:

(i) to take over the operation of the Canal;

(ii) to ensure its efficient functioning as a free, open and secure international waterway in accordance with the principles of the Suez Canal Convention of 1888;

(iii) to arrange for the payment of fair compensation to the Suez Canal Company;

(iv) to ensure to Egypt an equitable return which will take into account all legitimate Egyptian rights and interests.

Failing agreement with the Company or with Egypt on either of the last two points, the matter would be referred to an Arbitral Commission of three members to be appointed by the International Court of Justice.

III. The constituent organs of the International Authority would be:

(i) A Council of Administration the members of which would be nominated by the powers chiefly interested in navigation and sea-borne trade through the Canal,

(ii) the necessary technical, working and administrative organs.

IV. The powers of the International Authority would, in particular, include:

(i) the carrying out of all necessary works;

(ii) the determination of the tolls, dues and other charges on a just and equitable basis;

(iii) all questions of finance;

(iv) general powers of administration and control." [6]

Repeat reactions to Embassy London.

---

[5] Regarding earlier drafts of this document, see footnote 5, Document 51.

[6] The Department of State also forwarded the text of these principles for background information and "for use in stimulating public expressions of support for Conference on these grounds" to the following diplomatic missions: Amman, Baghdad, Bangkok, Beirut, Buenos Aires, Caracas, Damascus, Jidda, Lima, Manila, Mexico City, Ottawa, Panama, Pretoria, Rabat, Rangoon, Rio de Janeiro, Saigon, Santiago, Tel Aviv, Tripoli, Tunis, Khartoum, and Taipei; and by pouch to: Guatemala, San Salvador, Tegucigalpa, San José, Managua, Habana, Port-au-Prince, Ciudad Trujillo, Quito, Bogota, Asuncion, Montevideo, and La Paz. (Circular telegram 111, August 9; Department of State, Central Files, 974.7301/8–956)

FYI We found in London that the situation was far more critical and danger of hostilities more immediate than had been believed. Solution here offered is only one safeguarding peace and therefore in interest of Government to which you are accredited. [7]

Dulles

---

[7] On August 6, Byroade cautioned the Department against presenting the Egyptian Government with a verbatim account of the principles as it would result in "flat rejection" by the Egyptian Government. Byroade proposed instead that reference to the principles be made only in very general terms. (Telegram 265 from Cairo; *ibid.*, 974.7301/8–656) Dulles approved this proposal in telegram 287 to Cairo, August 6. (*Ibid.*)

---

64.   Message From Prime Minister Eden to President Eisenhower [1]

London, August 5, 1956.

DEAR FRIEND: Thank you for the message which you sent me via Foster. [2]

In the light of our long friendship I will not conceal from you that the present situation causes me the deepest concern. I was grateful to you for sending Foster over and for his help. It has enabled us to reach firm and rapid conclusions and to display to Nasser and to the world the spectacle of a United Front between our two countries and the French. We have however gone to the very limits of the concessions which we can make.

I do not think that we disagree about our primary objective. As it seems to me, this is to undo what Nasser has done and to set up an International Regime for the Canal. The purpose of this regime will be to ensure the freedom and security of transit through the Canal, without discrimination, and the efficiency and economy of its operation.

But this is not all. Nasser has embarked on a course which is unpleasantly familiar. His seizure of the Canal was undoubtedly

---

[1] Source: Eisenhower Library, Whitman File, International File. Secret. The British Embassy transmitted this message to the White House under cover of a note from Makins to President Eisenhower which reads: "The Prime Minister has asked me to send you the enclosed personal message about the Suez Canal problem." Bailey signed for Makins and initialed the source text.

[2] Document 35.

designed to impress opinion not only in Egypt but in the Arab world and in all Africa too. By this assertion of his power he seeks to further his ambitions from Morocco to the Persian Gulf. In this connection you have no doubt seen Nasser's own speech at Aboukir on August 1, in which he said "We are very strong because we constitute a limitless strength extending from the Atlantic Ocean to the Arab Gulf".

I know that Nasser is active wherever Muslims can be found, even as far as Nigeria. The Egyptians tried to get one of the Nigerian Amirs who was on his way through Cairo to sign a message endorsing Nasser's deeds. The man tore it up, but, if Nasser keeps his loot, how long can such loyalty last? At the other end of the line, the Sheik of Kuwait [3] has spoken to us stoutly of his views of Nasser. But all these men and millions of others are watching and waiting now.

I have never thought Nasser a Hitler; he has no warlike people behind him. But the parallel with Mussolini is close. Neither of us can forget the lives and treasure he cost us before he was finally dealt with.

The removal of Nasser, and the installation in Egypt of a regime less hostile to the West, must therefore also rank high among our objectives. We must hope, as you say in your message, that the forthcoming conference will bring such pressures upon Nasser that the efficient operation of the Canal can be assured for the future. If so, everyone will be relieved and there will be no need of force. Moreover, if Nasser is compelled to disgorge his spoils, it is improbable that he will be able to maintain his internal position. We should thus have achieved our secondary objective.

Nevertheless I am sure you will agree that we must prepare to meet the eventuality that Nasser will refuse to accept the outcome of the conference; or, no less dangerous, that he, supported by the Russians, will seek by strategems and wiles to divide us so that the conference produces no clear result in the sense we both seek. We and the French Government could not possibly acquiesce in such a situation. I really believe that the consequences of doing so would be catastrophic, and that the whole position in the Middle East would thereby be lost beyond recall. But by all means let us first see what the conference can do—on the assumption that Nasser commits no further folly meanwhile.

You know us better than anyone, and so I need not tell you that our people here are neither excited nor eager to use force. They are, however, grimly determined that Nasser shall not get away with

---

[3] Sheikh Abdullah al-Salim al-Sahah.

it this time, because they are convinced that if he does their existence will be at his mercy. So am I.

I am infinitely grateful for your patience and understanding of our feelings. I cannot tell you how much they mean to us in this time of anxiety.

It is splendid news to hear of your growing strength.

We will do our best not to add to the strain.

Yours ever,

Anthony [4]

---

[4] Printed from a copy that bears this typed signature.

---

65.   Memorandum of a Telephone Conversation Between the President's Special Assistant for National Security Affairs (Anderson) and the Secretary of State, Washington, August 6, 1956, 10:23 a.m. [1]

TELEPHONE CALL FROM DILLON ANDERSON

The Sec. returned the call, and A. said he talked with the Pres. re NSC discussion on the ME. The Sec. said he understood it would be brought up Thursday. [2] The Sec. is seeing the Pres. at 3 and DA will be prepared to join for that portion of the mtg. They agreed Defense is anxious to have a meeting to present their point of view. The Sec. said he does not take particular exception to their views as expressed. The Sec. thinks they feel left out though we have tried to get them in meetings but many are absent. A. said the Pres. seemed to have in mind that necessary studies in various departments should be underway on an urgent basis. He did not contemplate any decisions. The Sec. does not think any are called for unless it develops some papers are obsolete. A. will have Lay run a check on that. The Sec. said if for any reason this conf. breaks down, the situation will be grave and he thinks the British and French will move in with force. They agreed all lines cross Syria [3] and will probably be blown up.

---

[1] Source: Eisenhower Library, Dulles Papers, White House Telephone Conversations. Transcribed by Bernau.

[2] August 9.

[3] Reference is to the fact that oil pipelines from both Iraq and Saudi Arabia passed through Syria.

66.   Telegram From the Department of State to the Embassy in the Soviet Union [1]

Washington, August 6, 1956—1:10 p.m.

144. For Ambassador From Secretary. Your 279. [2] Our 131 was on the assumption based on prior messages from you that you could develop a quite informal confidential approach to high level Soviet officials and at that time express informal views, ostensibly personal but which would be understood by the high authorities as in fact being authoritative.

We still see no reason why we should attempt to disguise the fact, generally known, that the British and French have favored immediate strong military action and that we have been the protagonists of the conference method. Just as we have exerted influence in that direction with our friends, so the Soviet Union if it wants peace should exert comparable influence with those governments with which it feels it has any special influence.

Of course, this divergence of initial approach between us and the British and French does not by any means imply that we will not be solidly with them if the conference method breaks down. It would be a grave delusion if the Soviets thought that we would stay divided upon further measures which might be taken and we cannot imagine that they are so deluded. Experience in the First and Second World Wars should have taught them that whatever may be initial divergencies, the U.S. has become inevitably involved when the chips are down.

With this further background, we reaffirm our belief, unless you see strong objection that you should try to find an appropriate informal way of chatting about this situation with the highest available Soviet authorities without in any way formalizing the matter.

It is my personal belief that this matter is of the utmost seriousness and that unless the conference which has been called is

---

[1] Source: Department of State, Central Files, 974.7301/8–456. Secret; Niact; Limit Distribution. Drafted and approved by Dulles. At 8:32 that morning, the Department of State received telegram 288 from Moscow. In it, Bohlen advised that the British and French Ambassadors in Moscow (Hayter and Dejean) agreed with Bohlen that it would be suitable to discuss the Suez situation with Bulganin when Bohlen delivered a recent message from Eisenhower to Bulganin concerning disarmament. Bohlen proposed that his comments to Bulganin be based upon circular telegram 90 (Document 63) and upon telegram 131 (see Document 58). Telegram 288 from Moscow is in Department of State, Central Files, 974.7301/8–656. Eisenhower's message to Bulganin concerning disarmament, dated August 4, was written in response to a message from Bulganin of June 6. Both are printed in Department of State *Bulletin*, August 20, 1956, pp. 299–301.

[2] Not printed. (Department of State, Central Files, 974.7301/8–456)

held and its result is substantially accepted by Egypt, the result will be forcible action with grave risk of its becoming enlarged.

The Soviet leaders have from the beginning pretended to treat their action in the Near East as not having a grave international consequence, although we have pointed out the contrary from the beginning. See in this connection the President's message to Bulganin of October 11. [3] It is now demonstrable that they have started a chain of events, which we foresaw, which may lead to hostilities of unpredictable proportions unless they reverse their course.

We are advising the British and French of substance President's personal message to Bulganin [4] but this cable and any action thereunder are secret.

Dulles

---

[3] Vol. XIV, p. 576.

[4] The text of the message, as transmitted in telegram 141 to Moscow, August 6, reads as follows:

"Dear Mr. Chairman: I understand that Ambassador Bohlen may be seeing you within the next few hours to deliver my reply to your letter of June 6 on disarmament. I have asked Ambassador Bohlen in this connection to let you know personally how seriously I regard the situation precipitated by the Egyptian Government's effort to seize the operations of the Suez Canal. The United States is strongly exerting itself in favor of a solution by the peaceful conference method, as has been proposed, and I hope that you will do the same. I also greatly hope that the Egyptian Government will not reject this approach.

"The prospect of any good progress in the field of disarmament would indeed be dimmed unless those primarily concerned with the Suez international waterway can meet, as proposed, to seek peacefully an acceptable solution. With assurances of my best wishes, Sincerely, Dwight D. Eisenhower." (Department of State, Central Files, 974.7301/8–656)

The message was drafted by Dulles. The President added the phrase, "with assurances of my best wishes" and approved the text of the message. (Telephone call from the President, 11:16 a.m., August 6; Eisenhower Library, Dulles Papers, White House Telephone Conversations and ibid., Whitman File, International File)

67.   Memorandum for the Record of a Conversation Held in the President's Office, White House, Washington, August 6, 1956, 3 p.m. [1]

RE

Egypt—Suez

PRESENT

The President, The Secretary of State, and Dillon Anderson

As I entered the President's office, Mr. Dulles was saying that he felt, in view of the critical conditions now obtaining in the area, the U.S. course did not lend itself so much to Council action as it did to decisions day by day by the President to meet developments and rapidly emerging problems; that an effort to chart a course by a Council paper might unduly freeze our position and thus destroy needed flexibility. The President apparently agreed with this view.

I called attention to a memorandum of July 31 from the Joint Chiefs to the Secretary of Defense, forwarded to the National Security Council by a letter of transmittal dated August 2, 1956, from the Acting Secretary of Defense. [2] I raised the question of Council consideration of these and related matters at the meeting on Thursday, August 9th. With reference to the recommendation at the top of page 2 of the JCS memorandum that the NSC

"determine whether the western world can reasonably expect to obtain the necessary results without recourse to military action by any western power",

the Secretary expressed doubt that this was the type of issue which could, at this juncture, be resolved in the Council.

The President, while appearing to agree with this conclusion, nevertheless indicated that he felt this would not be an inappropriate subject for discussion in the Council. He also agreed that other aspects of the Suez crisis be considered at the upcoming NSC meeting. In this connection, he said he would like for the Secretary of State to introduce the subject by advising the Council of the status of the situation at the Thursday meeting, including last minute developments.

I gathered that the President felt that formal NSC action at this time would not be appropriate on the recommendations contained in

---

[1] Source: Eisenhower Library, Whitman File, Eisenhower Diaries. Top Secret; Eyes Only. Drafted by Anderson. The time of the meeting is from the record of the President's Daily Appointments, which also indicates that Anderson joined the meeting at 3:17 p.m. Dulles left at 3:42 p.m., and Anderson left 5 minutes after that. (*Ibid.*)

[2] Document 50.

the first and second sentences of paragraph three of the Joint Chiefs memorandum.

There was no discussion while I was present of the recommendation contained in the third sentence of paragraph three of the JCS paper—namely, that

"the NSC should appraise the desirability of a U.S. guarantee to give political and economic support to military action by the U.K., whether taken alone or in concert with France, while abstaining, ourselves, from direct military participation; and of a public commitment to prompt direct military participation by U.S. forces in the event that third parties intervene militarily on behalf of the Egyptians."

However, in another connection, the President did express the view, with the Secretary concurring, that (1) we should in no event indicate what our military course would be should other nations intervene militarily, at least not until after we had seen the results of the call for a 24 nation conference; (2) that our position then should be that no affirmative U.S. military course of action would be determined except with concurrences of the Congress. On this subject the Secretary observed that in two world wars and in Korea a clearer indication of our position and our intentions might have operated as a deterrent to the outbreak of hostilities. He agreed however that in the instant situation there should be no suggestion of U.S. military support pending the outcome of the conference.

I called the President's attention to the four subjects now being studied by the Joint Chiefs (paragraph 4, a, b, c, d, of JCS memo), and he stated that he would like to have the Defense representatives present at the Council meeting on August 9 [make] a brief statement as to the progress made on these studies, and such tentative conclusions as are now possible as a result thereof.

He said here that the discussion of these and other recommendations made by the Joint Chiefs should be confined to a severely limited group, and in this, the Secretary strongly concurred, adverting to the dangerous consequences of any possible leaks as to areas of military planning.

The President also indicated he would like a report from Dr. Flemming on the status of the studies now being made by the U.S. oil companies, as to the continuity of petroleum supplies in the event the Middle East sources are impaired.

I am advising Defense and Dr. Flemming of the President's wishes in regard to their presentations.

Dillon Anderson

P.S. In the same meeting, the Secretary advised the President of some recent communications intelligence on the attitude and intentions of Spain and Syria. This part of the discussion is omitted for obvious reasons.

---

68.   Memorandum From the Secretary of Defense (Wilson) to the Executive Secretary of the National Security Council (Lay) [1]

Washington, August 7, 1956.

SUBJECT

> Nationalization of the Suez Canal; Consequences and Possible Related
> Reactions

REFERENCE

> Memo for the Executive Secretary, NSC, from the Deputy Secretary of
> Defense, subject: "Nationalization of the Suez Maritime Canal
> Company by the Egyptian Government", dated 2 August 1956 [2]

1. Forwarded herewith for the information of the members of the National Security Council are certain views of the Joint Chiefs of Staff regarding the above subject additional to those transmitted by the reference memorandum. I believe these views can be helpful in connection with the discussion of the item at the Council meeting on Thursday, 9 August 1956.

2. I am requesting the Chairman of the Joint Chiefs of Staff to be prepared to give the Council on Thursday the benefit of any additional information which may be developed by that time as a result of the study being made by the JCS, as indicated in paragraph 6 of their memorandum.

C.E. Wilson [3]

---

[1] Source: Department of State, S/S–NSC (Miscellaneous) Files: Lot 66 D 95, Suez Canal Situation. Top Secret. Lay transmitted the memorandum and its attachment to members of the National Security Council for their information under cover of a memorandum dated August 7, not printed. (*Ibid.*)

[2] Document 50.

[3] Printed from a copy that bears this typed signature.

[Attachment]

Memorandum From the Joint Chiefs of Staff to the Secretary of Defense (Wilson) [4]

Washington, August 3, 1956.

SUBJECT

Nationalization of the Suez Canal; Consequences and Possible Related Reactions

1. In furtherance of the views expressed by the Joint Chiefs of Staff in their memorandum for you dated 31 July 1956 concerning the expropriation of the Suez Canal by Nasser, the Joint Chiefs of Staff are becoming increasingly concerned about the possible future consequences to the United States should Nasser's venture be successful.

2. At first examination the nationalization of the Suez Canal might appear to be a matter of primary and vital importance to the United Kingdom and France, but only of secondary and indirect importance to the United States. However, in the opinion of the Joint Chiefs of Staff, if Nasser's expropriation and nationalization of the Suez Canal are permitted to stand, related reactions may well develop which will jeopardize U.S. military, political and economic interests throughout the world.

3. The following are among the possibilities which can be anticipated:

a. That Nasser would become so strong a spokesman and symbol of Arab nationalism that he would be able completely to unite and dominate the Arab world from Morocco to Iraq.

b. Nasser's influence as leader of the Arab world, if unchecked, could react in a manner inimical to U.S. interests in all Moslem countries and in neutralist and under-developed countries throughout the world.

c. Nasser would be in an improved position to play off the West against the USSR, and in so doing probably could not avoid

---

[4] Top Secret. On August 8, during a telephone conversation between Dillon Anderson and Secretary Dulles, the following exchange took place regarding this memorandum:

"A. said in briefing the Pres. for tomorrow he brought in the JCS letter of the 3rd which Gray showed the Sec. Saturday [August 4]. The Sec. thought it was the same as the other. A. said it goes into political considerations—and would not be so, he does not think, if Radford were here. A. told the Pres. it seemed to go far. The Pres. said in the Council he welcomes any thought anybody has, but in the main he looks to the Sec. for judgment in political matters and to the military for various consequences." (Memorandum of telephone conversation by Bernau, 10:27 a.m., August 8; Eisenhower Library, Dulles Papers, White House Telephone Conversations)

entering into relationships with the Soviet Union which would substantially enhance the position of the USSR in the Middle East, Asia, and Africa. An ancillary result of these developments would be to increase the likelihood of open Arab-Israeli hostilities.

d. As Nasser's influence spreads it may be anticipated that other Arab States initially, and subsequently other nations, will use his successful act of nationalization as justification for themselves expropriating and nationalizing U.S. and Western enterprises, with little fear of the possible consequences of their acts. Additional steps in the field of nationalization/expropriation may include the following, each of which could have major military implications:

(1) Syria, Lebanon, Jordan—pipelines.
(2) Iraq, Saudi Arabia—all POL facilities.
(3) Persian Gulf and Trucial Coast States—all POL facilities.
(4) Persian Gulf and Trucial Coast States—complete rejection (and ejection) of U.K. control, guidance and influence.

In connection with above, it should be noted that concessions to the USSR on the part of the nations concerned would be a *logical* corollary to the acts of expropriation. Were these granted, the result would be an acceleration of Soviet expansion and a consolidation of Soviet power throughout the Middle East.

4. The resultant decrease in Western prestige, should the foregoing occur, could result in the loss of U.S. bases in the Middle East and North Africa and ultimately in other areas such as Iceland, the Phillipine Republic, Spain, and the Azores.

5. Without at this time suggesting a specific solution to the problem posed above, the Joint Chiefs of Staff wish to bring to the attention of the Secretary of Defense the possible and even probable repercussions which could result from permitting the ascendancy of Nasser as a "champion of Arab nationalism". The Joint Chiefs of Staff also desire to point out that if Nasser's action is profitable to him or to Egypt and if subsequent events of similar nature occur, the United States will find it necessary to take active steps to change the course of events. By such time the cumulative problem could be vastly greater than today.

6. The Joint Chiefs of Staff are presently making a study of the problems arising from the nationalization of the Suez Maritime Canal Company. This study will include an analysis of possible military courses of action and their consequences in the event that political and economic measures fail to achieve a timely and acceptable solution. Although a copy of this study will be forwarded to the Secretary of Defense upon completion, this memorandum is considered of sufficient importance to warrant prior submission.

7. The Chairman, Joint Chiefs of Staff, did not participate in the action of the Joint Chiefs of Staff outlined in this memorandum.

For the Joint Chiefs of Staff:
Maxwell D. Taylor [5]
General, United States Army
Chief of Staff

---

[5] Printed from a copy that bears this typed signature.

---

69.   Telegram From the Embassy in the Soviet Union to the Department of State [1]

Moscow, August 7, 1956—4 p.m.

302. For Secretary. After having delivered President's reply to Bulganin's letter June 6 to Bulganin, [2] I told Bulganin that I had another communication received only this morning from the President. I then gave him letter (Deptel 141) [3] which was translated into Russian. Bulganin listened very attentively and said that he appreciated very much the President writing him on this subject. I then said, as indicated in the letter, I had a number of other comments to make on the subject.

I said I thought the President's letter in itself showed the deep concern with which he and the U.S. Government view the situation created in regard to the Suez Canal by the action of the Egyptian Government; that the U.S. had strongly supported the principle that this situation should be settled by negotiation and on a basis that would be fair and equitable to all concerned; that at the London conference, as might be expected, other and more direct measures of dealing with this situation had been considered but in large measure due to U.S. position these more direct courses of action had not been adopted and that the three Western powers had agreed on an attempt to settle this question fairly through peaceful negotiations, and to this end had proposed a conference to which his government had received an invitation last week. I said that the U.S., having made every effort, and successfully, to obtain acceptance of the

---

[1] Source: Department of State, Central Files, 674.84A/8–756. Secret; Niact; Limited Distribution; Presidential Handling. Received at 2:44 p.m.

[2] See footnote 1, Document 66.

[3] The text of the letter is printed in footnote 4, *ibid.*

principle of peaceful solution this problem felt that it was of the most vital importance that the proposal for peaceful solution should not fail and, in particular, should not be rejected by the Egyptian Government. In such an event the situation created by the Egyptian action would revert to a most dangerous stage and that more direct measures which had been considered and rejected by London conference might well become inevitable.

I added that as a personal opinion, but one based on information I had received, that it would be extremely difficult for the U.S. to argue in favor of solution by negotiation if this proposal met with no satisfactory response.

I added that having heard many times since I had been here statements from Soviet leaders that all international disputes and differences should be settled by negotiation, we had every right to expect support of the Soviet Union for the principle which had been adopted in regard to the Suez Canal by the three Western powers and expressed the hope that Soviet influence would be used to that end with other countries.

Bulganin listened very carefully to my statement and said that in general the position of the Soviet Government had been set forth in Khrushchev's speech at the Lenin Stadium, [4] that they had not yet reached a final decision as to the reply to the British invitation, but he expected the reply to be given either today or tomorrow. He said, however, Soviet Government had been giving careful consideration to the matter and he would like first of all to say that there seemed to be between the United States and the Soviet Union a common position in that both felt this matter must be settled by peaceful means. As to the conference itself, after repeating that no final decision had been made, he said nevertheless that they had doubts 1) as to the aim of the conference and 2) as to composition. In regard to the aim of the conference he mentioned that he had already seen the proposed resolution which the British Ambassador had given that morning to Shepilov, and from this it would appear that the purpose of the international authority was to undo the act of nationalization of the Egyptian Government, that the view of Soviet Government on this point had been clearly stated by Khrushchev and they felt that Egypt was entirely within her rights in so doing and that any attempt to undo this legitimate act would in effect be interference in Egypt's internal affairs. As a result, he said, the purpose of the conference had aroused "doubts" and even invoked a "negative" reaction from Soviet Government.

[4] A summary of Khrushchev's speech of August 1 is in telegram 258 from Moscow, August 1. (Department of State, Central Files, 974.7301/8–156)

He felt that the composition of the conference was "tendentious", a word which he was not using idly, since he felt that the list had been carefully drawn up in order to include nations favorable to Western powers. For example, he said, even the criteria for participants had not been observed since neither Austria nor other successor states of Austria-Hungary who was original signatory, for example Czechoslovakia, Hungary, Yugoslavia were not invited. As to other criterion of interest in navigation why, for example, had Ethiopia been included while Poland and the Arab countries, to say nothing of China, who had great interest in navigation Suez Canal, had not been included. Another question that had arisen was why had London and not Cairo been selected. He concluded by repeating that Soviet Government fully shared views U.S. Government as to necessity peaceful solution but felt that actual conference proposed raised doubts he had referred to.

With reference to his comments on nationalization, which of course follow standard Soviet line, I told him I thought if he read carefully declaration of the three powers he would see nationalization was not chief issue, but rather whether international agreements such as the Convention of 1888 could be violated with impunity by one country under the pretext of nationalization and that navigation Suez Canal, which was international question could not be left to the unilateral control and arbitrary will of any one country. I then said I did not believe that Soviet Government supported principle of unilateral abrogation international agreements, which we had already seen in pre-war period when Hitler's action produced dangerous anarchy in international relations. Bulganin, at my reference to Hitler, first and only time during conversation showed signs of irritation and said that comparison between "legitimate" action of Nasser and Egyptian Government could not be compared to Hitler and he felt this comparison was inappropriate and could not accept it. I replied that it was he and not I who mentioned Egyptian Government and Nasser, I was merely citing fact of history and a principle which U.S. strongly supports. Bulganin then repeated that Soviet Government supported principle of peaceful solution this matter through negotiation but in any attempt to undo legitimate action Egyptian Government, which he felt proposal for international authority was designed to achieve, would be interference in Egypt's internal affairs which Soviet Union could not support.

I then said to Bulganin that I wished to get the attitude of his government as clearly as possible so I could report accurately to the President. Was I correct in interpreting his statement that any international action in regard to the Suez Canal would constitute interference in Egyptian internal affairs, to which he initially said yes that was the Soviet position. I then said from that it would appear that Soviet Government was taking position that navigation Suez Canal was solely matter for Egypt to decide, that other countries had no rights in this connection and that entire matter, therefore, was not one for any form of international action or discussion. I said I wished to be entirely clear on that point because it was cardinal to the whole subject. Bulganin (who is not as fast on his feet as Molotov) saw the awkwardness of this position and backed away from his original statement, saying that other countries had an interest, including the Soviet Union, in the free navigation through the Canal and that, therefore, that aspect was legitimately a subject for negotiation, and even said that he "did not see why UN was being bypassed in this matter." I asked him under what article of the charter and to what body he felt a question of this kind could be submitted, to which he had no clear reply. I pointed out to him that in 1954 Security Council (Deptel 145)[5] Vishinsky had taken line that matters of Suez Canal were no concern of UN but only for signatories 1888 Convention. Bulganin merely said he was not familiar with this statement "former Comrade Vishinsky."

At least five times I emphasized to him the seriousness of the situation which would be created if the attempt at peaceful solution which the U.S. had been instrumental in having accepted was rebuffed by Egypt or other interested powers, and left him in no doubt, without stating explicitly, as to what U.S. position might well be in that event. Bulganin at one point criticized Britain and France for use of threats, pressures and military measures such as movement of ships, which he said hardly creates atmosphere for peaceful solution. I told him that the official position of British and French was that set forth in the proposal for a conference and the measures he complained about were merely elementary precautionary measures in face of a very dangerous situation brought on by action Egyptian Government, and that only way to make sure more serious developments did not occur in regard to this question would be to support principle of peaceful international negotiation proposed by three powers.

In conclusion, Bulganin repeated his appreciation President's letter which would be given "most serious consideration" by Soviet Government.

---

[5] In telegram 145 to Moscow, August 6, the Department of State sent the following report to the Embassy for background information: "The Soviet Union on March 29, 1956, at 664th mtg. Security Council, in course of debate on Israeli complaint re Egyptian restrictions ships passing through Canal in trade with Israel, referred to itself as successor to Russian signature to Constantinople Convention of 1888. Referring to Article 36 of UN Charter USSR objected to Security Council consideration of questions arising under Convention citing absence of certain parties to Convention and stated such questions should be dealt with in direct negotiations between signatory states." (Ibid., 974.7301/8–656)

Comment: Although as can be seen conversation with Bulganin was not satisfactory, and he stuck to Soviet line supporting Egypt in nationalization action and resistance to any international authority over Canal, it is not possible from conversation alone to judge effect of President's letters and my comments Soviet position. I did, however, have impression that Soviet Government along general lines has reached its decision concerning reply to conference invitation which, as anticipated (Embtel 272), [6] will probably support principle of negotiation but reject terms of reference, composition and probably date and place of conference. Bulganin's reference to it may have been fortuitous, on the other hand may be indication line Soviet counterproposal. Whatever effect today's discussion may have on Soviet position it has certainly left them no doubt as to seriousness with which US would view complete rejection by Egypt or Soviet Government conference.

Since I had no information as to how absolute terms of reference and membership were I did not attempt to discuss these aspects with Bulganin. [7]

Bohlen

---

[6] Not printed. (*Ibid.*, 974.7301/8–356)

[7] On August 9, the Government of the Soviet Union issued a declaration containing its reply to the invitation to attend the Suez Canal Conference. In the declaration, the Soviet Government stated that it would attend the Conference, but it also expressed a series of reservations and objections to the proposed Conference and the manner in which it was called. On August 10, the Embassy in Moscow, in telegram 341, summarized the "most important statements" made in the Soviet declaration as follows: "(1) that Egypt's right as sovereign state and nationalization of Suez Company 'cannot be called in question by any international conference' and (2) 'Soviet govt considers that this conference neither by composition of its participants nor by its character and aims can be in any way regarded as an international gathering competent to take any decisions in regard to the Suez Canal' and (3) that insofar as Soviet attendance is concerned 'Soviet govt does not consider that there is incumbent on Soviet Union any limitations or obligations arising out of either those principles which were declared by the three powers in joint declaration August 2 or which might be damaging to the sovereign rights and dignity of Egypt'." (*Ibid.*, 974.7301/8–1056) The text of the Soviet declaration and the note from the Soviet Ministry of Foreign Affairs, in which the Soviet declaration was transmitted to the Embassy, are in despatch 74 from Moscow, August 10. (*Ibid.*)

70.   Telegram From the Embassy in Egypt to the Department of State [1]

Cairo, August 7, 1956—10 p.m.

292. Suez Canal. As could foresee no possibility Nasser's acceptance of proposal contained in circular 90, [2] thought it best use Fawzi as buffer to avoid immediate and flat turndown. Saw Fawzi evening August 7.

I had carefully worked out oral presentation (see following message) [3] containing all essential points tripartite proposal, but presenting its main elements more diplomatically and avoiding appearance of cold or exclusive agenda form transmitted circular 90. I presented this to Fawzi along with explanation that tripartite powers now in process consultations with invited nations in order obtain as wide agreement and understanding as possible before conference began. "In interests accuracy" Fawzi asked for copy. Since GOE would soon receive it from other sources it seemed to me I had no alternative but to provide him with text of proposal as set forth circular 90 as well.

Fawzi asked if I had come to receive Egyptian reply to invitation. I stated this not the case as actual invitation had been extended by British Government; purpose my call was to urge consideration of principles I had outlined. Fawzi said in any case invitation still under consideration. GOE still in process obtaining information and was studying matter most carefully and in consultation with others. He

---

[1] Source: Department of State, Central Files, 974.7301/8–756. Secret; Niact; Limit Distribution. Received at 9:44 p.m. Repeated Niact to London and Paris.

[2] Document 63.

[3] In telegram 293, August 7, Byroade summarized his intended presentation to Fawzi as follows:

"My government has joined Governments of United Kingdom and France in seeking exchange views, with countries invited August 16 London conference, as to the principles which should govern discussions of the application of an international system to Suez Canal. Objective would be to insure through an international authority the efficient functioning and operation of the canal as free and open international waterway in accordance with principles convention 1888, to insure Egypt an equitable return which will take into account all legitimate Egyptian rights and interests, and to arrange for payment fair compensation to shareholders original Suez Canal Company. With respect to latter two points, we envision settlement disputes which may arise by an arbitral commission.

"The international authority consisting of a Council of Administration and other necessary technical, working and administrative organs would have competence in questions of finance, works, and the determination of rates and dues.

"It is present thought of three powers that a resolution embodying above principles might serve as a useful framework for August 16 conference." (Department of State, Central Files, 974.7301/8–756)

In telegram 294, August 7, Byroade explained that this summary of the tripartite proposal had been "carefully worked out with British". (*Ibid.*)

would prefer not discuss proposal because question attendance still not finally determined. GOE however would now look at proposal as another factor in helping them decide one way or the other.

Fawzi said that since I had already heard President's views he would not repeat them. He stressed Egypt fully realized vital importance this matter and whatever decision would be reached it would be a responsible one resulting from considered thinking. He said every effort would be made to see that Egypt's objectivity would not be impaired by her natural feelings at being invited to a conference held in atmosphere of pressure and threats, where issue already prejudged, and in respect which they had been treated as "Ceylon" or any other invitee in that they had not been consulted as to date, place, invitees, or anything else.

Fawzi went on to say Egypt was convinced whole approach of three powers, and of UK and France particularly, was "imperialistic, anti-charter, and destructive of peace and security". He believes Egypt's stand will not merely belong to its present government and present generation, but will have much deeper significance as it will encompass very fundamental issues concerning imperialism and domination of others. He stated Egypt's friends in rest of world could feel certain of following two things: (1) Egypt's full determination cooperate with rest of world on basis freedom, mutual respect, and recognition sovereign rights and (2) Egypt's full determination defend "up to the last shreds of our land" what Egyptians honestly believe to be their own rights.

If objective West was really to be certain freedom of navigation would be maintained, this could certainly be achieved without atmosphere or processes of proposed London conference. If objectives on other hand were to secure imperialism and domination then he thought atmosphere and proposed processes of London conference were quite logical.

Fawzi spoke at great length about Egypt's intention give every consideration to needs of users canal so they would not feel insecure or uncertain regarding its future use, or fear being mistreated, delayed or over-charged, as this would first of all hurt Egypt. Egypt determined maintain and obtain best possible employees, Egyptian or foreign, and GOE would devote itself to preserving what was good canal operation and improving it wherever possible. If Egypt allowed carry out its determination this respect, he completely unable find any justification for hostilities or disturbance of any kind. On other hand if Egypt were not allowed carry out this plan he virtually certain great disturbance in area would result. He emphasized this was not threat but was what the picture showed as he saw it.

In reply my query Fawzi said he thought it would not be helpful at this time forecast timing and nature of Egyptian response to invitation or of counterproposals they might make.

I told Fawzi that in my opinion US is as firmly committed as UK and France to some type of international control and stressed our concern as to possible consequences (without defining them) which might result from negative action by Egypt at this time. Fawzi is meeting with Nasser and colleagues tonight when tripartite proposal undoubtedly will be discussed.

Byroade

---

71.   Memorandum of a Conversation Between the President and the Secretary of State, White House, Washington, August 8, 1956, 11:30 a.m. [1]

(1) The President spoke of his press conference. [2] He said it had not been a very satisfactory one. He had had the impression that most of the questions were tricky ones with some political motivation, designed to trap him into indiscretions rather than to elicit light. He recapitulated briefly what he had said about the Suez matter.

(2) I reported to the President on the status of acceptances of the invitations to the London Conference, indicating that the acceptances had mounted to a point where it seemed as if the Conference would be held as planned. [3] I said we still did not know about Egypt, although it was almost surely a negative, or about the Soviet Union and Indonesia.

(3) I mentioned to the President that there was some indication that Panama was getting into contact with Egypt. The President indicated considerable annoyance and stated that if we left the Panama Zone we would take the locks with us. He again reverted to

---

[1] Source: Eisenhower Library, Dulles Papers, Meetings With the President. Secret; Personal and Private. Drafted by Dulles.

[2] For an extract from the transcript of the White House news conference, held on August 8, see *The Suez Canal Problem, July 26–September 22, 1956*, pp. 45–46. For the complete text, see *Public Papers of the Presidents of the United States: Dwight D. Eisenhower, 1956*, pp. 660–671.

[3] During a telephone conversation between Dulles and Eisenhower which began at 8:54 that morning, the Secretary noted that 18 countries had accepted the conference invitation. (Eisenhower Library, Whitman File, Eisenhower Diaries)

a suggestion that he had made once or twice before that we should consider the desirability of building an alternative route in Nicaragua so that we would not be subject to blackmail.

(4) I said I expected to be in New York on Friday to lunch with Hammarskjold and talk to him about the Arab-Israel business and also Suez. [4]

(5) I said I had given a great deal of thought to some possible personal role for the President in this Suez situation. The President had greater prestige throughout the world than any single man had ever had before. This was something which on the one hand should not be dissipated; on the other hand it should, if necessary, be used. However, the problem of using it was a very difficult one. I recalled how Wilson had dissipated his prestige at the Paris Peace Conference. The President said that he felt clearly that the forthcoming Conference was no place for him, particularly as I had indicated that Nehru would probably not be there personally, but only Krishna Menon. I said there might develop a situation after the Conference where some personal intervention by the President might be required. The President acknowledged that possibility. We agreed it would have to be studied very carefully.

(6) I discussed with the President possible Congressional participation in terms of Senators Mansfield and Alex Smith going with me and possibly having Knowland and Lyndon Johnson, if available, come to Washington in advance for consultation with me or perhaps with the President. The President concurred in this plan and thought that Mansfield and Smith would make a good couple.

[Here follows discussion of the Cyprus question.]

(8) I referred to the President's message from Eden, which I pointed out was a reply to the President's prior message to Eden. [5] I thought that all it required was a cordial acknowledgment. The President agreed. [6]

---

[4] A memorandum by Dulles of this conversation with Hammarskjöld which took place in New York on August 10, is in Department of State, Central Files, 680.84A/8–1056.

[5] Documents 64 and 35.

[6] At 6 p.m. that day, Dulles forwarded to the White House a suggested reply to Eden's letter, which reads:

"Dear Anthony: I have read very carefully, and with a great deal of sympathy, your response to my message dated July 31, 1956, which Foster left with you in London last week. It was extremely good of you to send me so promptly your thinking on this subject.

"What you say is very much in our thoughts and we are devoting the major part of our time to this important problem.

"I was glad to hear from Foster that you are looking so well. With warm personal regard, Sincerely, DE." (Eisenhower Library, Dulles Papers, White House Memoranda)

The message was transmitted to London in telegram 845 on August 9, and delivered to Eden on August 10. Department of State, Central Files, 611.41/8–956 and

[Here follows discussion of thermonuclear weapons.]

JFD

Eisenhower Library, Whitman File, International File) The telegram indicates Dulles as
the drafting officer.

---

72.   **Memorandum of Discussion at the 292d Meeting of the
National Security Council, Washington, August 9, 1956,
9–11:33 a.m.** [1]

[Here follow a paragraph listing the participants at the meeting
and agenda items 1–3.]

4. Significant World Developments Affecting U.S. Security

[Here follows a report by Allen Dulles on unrelated subjects.]

Mr. [Allen] Dulles said he would conclude his remarks with
some background on the Suez Canal situation, which was the subject
of the next item on the agenda. The proposal for the London
Conference had been accepted by all those invited except the USSR,
Egypt, Indonesia, Greece and Spain. Egypt would probably not
attend, but the others invited, including the USSR, would probably
accept. He expected that eleven countries would be firm supporters
of the US-UK-French position, and that the USSR, with Indian
support, would spearhead Egypt's case. The Egyptian case might
receive support from Greece because of Cyprus, and from Spain
because of Gibraltar. Pakistan, Ceylon, Ethiopia and other countries
would probably play a waiting role.

Mr. Dulles then noted a report that Ben-Gurion had told Nasser
that Israel would not take advantage of the present situation to
attack Egypt. Reports had also been received of plans for sabotage in
the area in general and of the Canal in particular, in the event of
hostilities.

Mr. Dulles said that the Canal had never been under organized
political international control. The Canal Company had performed
housekeeping functions only, with no authority over who used the
waterway. In the Russo-Japanese War, the Russian fleet used the

---

[1] Source: Eisenhower Library, Whitman File, NSC Records. Top Secret; Eyes
Only. Prepared by Marion W. Boggs on August 10. The time of the meeting is from
the record of the President's Daily Appointments. (*Ibid.*)

Canal, although Britain was an ally of Japan. In the Spanish-American War, the Spanish fleet entered the Canal, but had to turn back when it could not replenish its fuel supplies because the American Consul had bought all the bunkering coal available in the area. The Canal was open to Italy during the Ethiopian War, in spite of the League of Nations. The U.K. closed the Canal to its enemies both in World War I and World War II. The President said that in World War II, Germany had in effect closed the Canal to the Allies because capture of Crete and El Alamein had enabled German forces to take a heavy toll of shipping.

The National Security Council:

Noted and discussed an oral briefing by the Director of Central Intelligence on the subject, with specific reference to the situations regarding Laos, the Burmese-Chinese Communist border, and the Suez Canal.

5. *The Suez Canal Situation* (Memo for NSC from Executive Secretary, subject: "Nationalization of the Suez Maritime Canal Company by the Egyptian Government", dated August 3, 1956; [2] Memo for NSC from Executive Secretary, subject: "Nationalization of the Suez Canal; Consequences and Possible Related Reactions", dated August 7, 1956 [3])

Mr. Anderson said that the final item on the agenda was a discussion of the Suez Canal situation. In accordance with the directions of the President, the discussion would be based on the following reports: (1) A report by the Secretary of State on the status of the Egyptian-Suez situation, including the latest developments. (2) A report by the Department of Defense on progress being made on the military studies referred to in paragraph 4 of the Joint Chiefs of Staff memorandum dated July 31 (transmitted by the reference memorandum of August 3), together with such tentative conclusions as may have resulted from the studies to date. Mr. Anderson noted that the Joint Chiefs had made a further comment, which had been circulated to the Council by the reference memorandum of August 7. (3) A report by the Director, Office of Defense Mobilization, on studies being made by U.S. oil companies as to the means of continuing petroleum supplies in the event that Middle East sources are impaired. Mr. Anderson then called on the Secretary of State for the first of these reports.

---

[2] This memorandum transmitted the JCS memorandum of July 31 to the NSC; see Document 50.

[3] This memorandum transmitted the JCS memorandum of August 3 to the NSC; see Document 68.

Secretary Dulles said that it is well known that the United States regards the Suez situation very seriously. The Suez Canal has long been called the life-line of the British Empire, and this is truer today than ever before because of the growing dependence of Western Europe on the oil of the Middle East, with the Canal as the primary artery for its transportation. Pipelines could not be considered dependable alternate means for the transit of oil because the same political factors which can disrupt Canal traffic can also disrupt pipelines.

Secretary Dulles then turned to the challenge by Nasser, which he felt was not an erratic or an isolated action but an integral part of a long-term program. He recalled that Nasser's book, *Revolution,* published in 1952, had developed at some length Nasser's ambitions for Egypt and for the Arab world, and had described the sources of power available to the Arabs—Arab unity, Arab control of important crossroads in the world, of lines of communication and transportation, and of great oil resources. Secretary Dulles said that in connection with oil, Nasser's book made the statement that without Middle Eastern oil the machinery of Western Europe would grind to a stop. Secretary Dulles felt that Nasser was dreaming of a great buildup of Arab power and a corresponding diminution in the power of the West. The Canal seizure was one of a series of steps to this end, and had accordingly raised basic questions involving the balance of power and the future of Western Europe.

Secretary Dulles reported that the Suez situation had been discussed fully in London last week. In these conversations both the British and French, with some support from their neighbors, had indicated that they were prepared to take action to repossess the Canal by force. We expressed the view that such action would be precipitate and would not be completely understood in the United States, especially since the use of force would be portrayed in some quarters as an aggression if it took place without prior efforts at peaceful settlement, to which the British and French were pledged under the UN Charter. Action by the British and French without the understanding and sympathy of the United States would thus open fissures between the United States and its allies. In deference to this view, Secretary Dulles continued, the British and French were attempting to secure world support for their case through the mechanism of the Conference scheduled to meet on August 16.

Secretary Dulles said there had been question as to whether the Conference on the Suez situation would meet, but it now seems likely that it will be held—due partly to U.S. effort—even though Egypt probably will not be there. A solid majority of the states attending—as many as two-thirds on some issues—would favor the Western position. The goal of the Conference would be the peaceful achievement of international operation and financing of the Canal. There had never been an international authority in charge of the Canal; the 1888 arrangements had placed operations in the hands of a private company with an international composition, but had not set up a public international organization. At the forthcoming Conference an effort would be made, not to reinstate the company, but to establish a public international authority to operate the Canal in accordance with the Treaty of 1888. Such an authority would have control of Canal finances and would set up an operating body. Egypt would be fully represented in both organizations, but would control neither. In addition, Egypt would participate generously in Canal revenues.

Secretary Dulles said the acceptance of this program was open to serious question. If the only issues were Egypt's income from the Canal, or how much voice Egypt should have in its technical operation, the problem would be simple. But the issues were more fundamental: Nasser's action was part of a series of actions designed to reduce Western Europe to subservience to Arab control. Anything less than full Egyptian control of the Canal might be interpreted by Nasser as a step backward in the fulfillment of his grandiose ambitions. Some alternatives to European dependence on Middle Eastern oil coming through the Canal would be pointed out by Dr. Flemming, but Secretary Dulles felt that these alternatives were unsatisfactory in the long run. He said he wished to repeat the basic facts that the transit of oil through the Canal and the pipelines constituted the life-line of Western Europe, and that the British and French were unwilling to accept domination of the life-line by the Arabs.

Secretary Dulles said he felt that the United States could not ask the British and French, or Western Europe, to accept subservient dependence on fanatical Egyptian control of the waterways. Such a surrender would reduce Europe to a dependency and jeopardize the objectives we sought in the Marshall Plan.

Secretary Dulles said there was some hope of a solution being reached, since the situation was more tractable than it had been a week ago; but still it was difficult to see how the two sides to this basic conflict could be reconciled. At the Conference, however, he anticipated some covert support for the US-UK-French position from the USSR and India. He had received information that an effort was being made in the Arab League to get the Arab countries to stop oil production in sympathy with Egypt. [4] However, this move was not

---

[4] On August 6, Nuri Said told Ambassador Waldemar Gallman that Syria under Egyptian prodding would introduce a resolution at a meeting of the Political Committee of the Arab League that called for a complete stoppage of either oil production or

favored by all the Arab countries, some of which have mental reservations on the whole situation while ostensibly cheering Nasser on.

Secretary Dulles then raised the question of what the United States should do if the Conference fails to agree or if its proposals are rejected by Nasser. In this situation the British and French would be disposed to take forcible action. Should the United States put pressure on the British and French not to take such action? And, if so, how strong should this pressure be? Or should the United States support British and French action, or at least acquiesce in it? Secretary Dulles said he had discovered in London that the British and French would want from the United States (1) moral support, (2) economic support in the form of more oil and the financing of oil shipments from the Western Hemisphere, and (3) an indication of U.S. determination to keep the USSR out—that is, the United States would exercise a deterrent by making it clear that if the hostilities were enlarged by the overt participation of the USSR, we would move in in full force. (Secretary Dulles said parenthetically that the covert participation of the USSR in any hostilities that may occur was to be expected, including pressure on Iran.) Secretary Dulles felt that these matters should be studied carefully, since the United States might have to make important decisions in the next ten days or two weeks.

Secretary Dulles then reported that he hoped to confer on Sunday with a fairly representative group of Congressional leaders, including Senators Johnson, George, Mansfield, Knowland, Wiley, and Smith. Consultation would be harder on the House side; possibly Speaker Rayburn would be consulted. Secretary Dulles felt that consultation with the Congress was necessary, and that even a special session of Congress might be required. He was not happy about precipitating great issues at this time, but the issues were so grave that it was necessary to move ahead without regard to the political situation.

The Vice President, noting that the Democratic Platform Committee was about to meet, asked whether it would be advisable to try to ensure that the platform did not take a position which would

at least pipeline operations. Nuri also mentioned reliable reports of probable sabotage in Jordan and Syria. He expressed his hope that the United States would use its influence to dissuade Saudi Arabia from any rash action. (Telegram 162 from Baghdad, August 6; Department of State, Central Files, 786.00/8–656) In a subsequent conversation, Yusuf Yasin left Ambassador Wadsworth with the strong impression that Saudi Arabia would not support the stoppage of oil shipments. (Telegram 62 from Jidda, August 9; *ibid.*, 786.00/8–956) On August 12 the Arab League Council adopted a resolution endorsing Egypt's nationalization of the Canal Company and proclaiming unity of sentiment with Egypt. Additional documentation relating to diplomacy preceding the meeting is *ibid.*, 786.00.

be embarrassing to our negotiations on the Suez situation. Secretary Dulles said he was trying to accomplish this by indirection, and was keeping in close touch with Senator Mansfield, who seemed sympathetic. [5] The Vice President said that there was some chance that the Democratic platform would recommend arms for Israel, and this might have an impact on the Near East. Secretary Dulles said the impact would not be great.

However, Secretary Dulles said that the attitude of Israel did complicate the Suez problem. The United States had planned, in line with the August statement of the President, to be prepared to give military assistance to the victim of an aggression in the Near East. If the British and French move into the Suez Canal and are attacked by Egypt, and if Israel then attacks Egypt, what is the situation? In any case, U.S. ability to exert an influence on the Arab-Israeli situation is diminishing. Secretary Dulles reported that the French feel that the Israelis should be armed rapidly, and are prepared to ship 24 additional jets. However, Secretary Dulles felt that while many Arab states are uneasy over Nasser's bold course, any action which would put the Israelis out in front in the Suez situation would solidify the Arab world. Also, he felt that the Democratic platform would not materially affect Arab attitudes, since the Arabs take it for granted that if the Democrats win, the United States will back the Israelis.

The Vice President said he understood that financial considerations were not particularly important to Egypt. The Philippine situation had once been confused by nationalistic attitudes on sovereignty, and we had made a deal recognizing Philippine sovereignty and our use of Philippine bases. Perhaps something similar could be worked out in the case of the Canal if old concepts were re-examined. Management contracts were needed providing for Egyptian sovereignty and Western management.

Secretary Humphrey said perhaps a settlement could be reached along the lines of the settlement with Iran. Mr. Allen Dulles said the Suez problem was different; it was a question of who could close the Canal. Secretary Humphrey said there were two things to keep in mind: (1) The real difference was that Europe was dependent on a single source of oil supply—Secretary Dulles, interrupting, asked whether the presentations should not be finished before the general discussion began, and the President agreed. Mr. Anderson then called upon Admiral Radford to report on the military studies.

Admiral Radford said he agreed with the JCS papers that had already been circulated. He said that the problem was broader than

---

[5] Dulles discussed the Suez situation with Mansfield on August 6. A memorandum by Dulles of that conversation, not printed, is in the Eisenhower Library, Dulles Papers, General Memoranda of Conversations.

the Canal, and that the Canal seizure might be only the first step in a chain of Arab action. He added that he had just read a cable from General Gruenther [6] which came as a revelation. This cable reported that there was no question but that the British Chiefs of Staff would recommend military action. Information from French sources, such as General Ely, indicated that the French were also determined. However, Admiral Radford said he was puzzled by one thing: The British and French must think they can end the military action quickly, for if they did not they would be dependent on our support.

Secretary Dulles said the British and French think the initial Egyptian resistance could be overcome very quickly, even though mop-up operations might last for years. He recalled that in the spring of 1953 the British had 88,000 troops ready to move against Cairo and Alexandria. The situation now was similar, only worse. Secretary Dulles then said that Mr. Macmillan had stated that the British realized they were starting something that might lead to an atomic war, but that they would rather die in that way than sink. . . .

Secretary Wilson said if the British felt so strongly about the Suez Canal, they should not have left it in the first place.

The President said that Prime Minister Eden, in a letter to him, had advanced the view that the pipelines would continue to function in the event of trouble. The President felt that this was a vain hope. Eden also asked us to provide the U.K. with oil from Venezuela. Mr. Allen Dulles said the pipelines would be cut in the event of war. Admiral Radford said all oil would be stopped before reaching the Mediterranean. The President pointed out, on the other hand, that the United States and the West are the markets for all this oil. Mr. Anderson then called upon the Director, Office of Defense Mobilization, for a report on the oil situation.

Dr. Flemming said that the Foreign Supply Petroleum Committee, consisting of oil company officials, had met Tuesday in New York and had developed a plan of action for the use of oil facilities, the rate of production, and so forth. The draft plan was now being studied by the Attorney General. Dr. Flemming said he hoped that the plan could be put into effect tomorrow or Saturday. [7]

Dr. Flemming said that if the Suez Canal were closed, it would be necessary for the United States to step up oil production by 800,000–900,000 barrels a day. The oil companies think this step-up can be accomplished. Demolition of the pipelines, with the Canal remaining open, would require the United States to step up produc-

---

[6] Telegram ALO 917, 081350Z Aug 56, from USNMR Paris to the Secretary of State, not printed. (JCS Files)

[7] See footnote 2, Document 30.

tion by 500,000–600,000 barrels a day. These figures, Dr. Flemming added, assume U.S. assistance to the U.K. and France, and no rationing in the United States. However, rationing might become necessary in the United States if the British were for a long period of time denied access both to the Canal and to the pipelines. In any case, a step-up in production would result in a serious problem in the transportation of oil.

The President asked about the prospects of increasing Free World refining capacity. He had been told, for instance, that with a small investment, Mexican refining capacity could be increased from 200,000 barrels a day to one million barrels a day.

Dr. Flemming said he thought it would require six months to get an additional 100,000 barrels a day. However, he said he would look into the situation.

The Vice President said he believed the President's information was correct.

. . . .

Secretary Dulles said that, in time, Venezuelan production could be stepped up.

Admiral Strauss asked how much U.S. production could be increased if the existing restrictions on production were lifted. Mr. Anderson replied that production could reach one million barrels a day in thirty to sixty days.

Secretary Wilson said he thought that possibly the United States should, as a gesture, fill the storage tanks now and immediately lift the restraints on production.

The Vice President agreed with Secretary Wilson, adding that the Arabs feel they have us by the throat and that it might therefore be advisable to indicate that we have more room for maneuver than they suppose.

Secretary Dulles pointed out that if we create the impression that Middle Eastern oil is not vital, we will knock the props from under the British case.

Secretary Humphrey said that Middle Eastern oil was vital in the long run. The Vice President said we could covertly indicate to the Arabs that we have maneuverability. Secretary Humphrey said that there was only one solution: To eliminate dependence on a single source of supply. He wondered about the possibility of pipelines through Turkey and Israel.

The President thought that even if there was a pipeline through Israel, the Arab oil-producing countries could always stop production.

Secretary Humphrey said these countries must produce for Western markets. Moreover, if they have any brains they must know that Nasser will be able to dominate them by control of the Canal. . . . Secretary Humphrey said that in any case, there must eventually be a petroleum transit route that could not be cut.

Admiral Radford said that a pipeline through Israel could be cut. He was very dubious about the idea of parallel pipelines. Mr. Allen Dulles added that the Arabs also control the Gulf of Aqaba. . . .

Secretary Humphrey thought the producing countries would have to produce in order to get money. Mr. Allen Dulles pointed out that they could get money from the USSR. Secretary Dulles agreed that the USSR would buy the oil and sell it to Western Europe.

Secretary Humphrey said Western Europe had a strong position as a market if the United States could assist it through the present crisis. He thought Nasser would probably "shake down" the other Arab countries next. The President said the possibility of a "shake-down" should be especially apparent to Nehru, who is dependent on the Canal for more than oil. The President understood that six million tons of India's imports went through the Canal. Secretary Dulles said Nehru would accept Egyptian management of the Canal. Secretary Humphrey said that as long as Nasser had possession of the sole route of transit for oil, he would control the situation, regardless of the Canal management, unless the West had troops in the area.

Secretary Wilson said the collapse of colonialism had been too rapid, and was having as much effect on the world as the rise of Communism. We should try to make the world see that the Western powers are not embarking on a new colonialism policy. The problem was not so much what Nasser has done, as what he threatens to do.

Secretary Humphrey said that, ostensibly, Nasser wants to build a dam. Perhaps an Iran-type settlement would enable him to get the money to build the dam. The President said this solution would make Canal tolls too high. He understood there was a limit to the tolls that could be charged if the Canal was going to be used. Secretary Humphrey thought a cash settlement might be possible. Secretary Wilson asked whether the Canal and dam questions should be merged. Secretary Humphrey said Nasser wanted to use the Canal to buy the dam.

Secretary Dulles feared the problem was not that simple. If we had built the dam, the Canal seizure would have occurred anyhow.

Secretary Humphrey inquired about the 86,000-ton tankers, and Mr. Allen Dulles said they would not be completed for three years.

Dr. Flemming said we must plan on losing the pipelines, which might be denied longer than the Canal. After all, the British and French could open the Canal.

The President said the Departments of State and Defense should have a staff committee, including military officers, constantly at work to prepare factual statements of what the situation would be under each of the various possible contingencies relating to the Suez.

Secretary Dulles agreed that a study was needed of the various policy alternatives and policy questions that would arise if the Suez Conference breaks down. Should we try to stop use of force by the British and French? He did not favor this course, but it should be considered. How much help should we give the British and French? He felt the United States must make it clear that we would be in the hostilities if the Soviets came in.

Secretary Wilson wondered whether we ought not restrain our allies from drastic action.

The President said Egypt had gone too far. He asked how Europe could be expected to remain at the mercy of the whim of a dictator. Admiral Radford said Nasser was trying to be another Hitler. The President added that Nasser's prestige would be so high, if he got away with the Canal seizure, that all the Arabs would listen to him. The Vice President felt the Arabs would probably not adopt a reasonable view of the situation. The President said the Arabs did not wish a quick settlement. If Nasser is successful, there will be chaos in the Middle East for a long time.

Secretary Wilson said Egypt had once owned a percentage of the Canal, but had sold it. The President said harems were expensive. Mr. Allen Dulles thought the West might well forget the history of the Canal.

The Vice President felt that the British and French preferred the use of the Canal to saving face. He wondered whether concessions could be made to Egyptian sovereignty in order to reopen the Canal. Secretary Wilson said Egypt has sovereignty now. The Vice President said Nasser must save face, secure more money, and ostensibly obtain more control.

Secretary Dulles said the British and French were unwilling to let him have all the things mentioned by the Vice President.

Secretary Wilson wondered whether the British and French, if they moved into the Canal area, would establish arrangements similar to those in Gibraltar. Mr. Allen Dulles pointed out that the Treaty of 1888 recognized the Canal as an integral part of Egypt.

Secretary Wilson said nationalization was too familiar to cause excitement. The British had engaged in nationalization. Secretary Dulles said the cases were not parallel.

Dr. Flemming said he would like to develop action programs relating to oil supply, to go along with the alternative courses of action being studied by the State-Defense Committee. Admiral Radford said the Middle East Committee was at work now. The President remarked that he had not realized this Committee was dealing with the Suez situation.

Secretary Dulles thought that no new mechanism was required. However, the military implications of a statement on our part that we would intervene if the USSR does, must be studied and must be available to the Council on short notice. The Secretary added that the visit of a Russian fleet to the Suez area on August 15 was a possibility. Should we also send a fleet? The President said every possible outcome of the situation must be studied.

Mr. Peaslee asked whether consideration had been given to requesting an advisory opinion from the International Court of Justice. Secretary Dulles said that this action had been considered, but that Egypt was unwilling to accept the jurisdiction of the Court.

Secretary Dulles then turned to the question of the UN role in the Suez situation. He reported that he was lunching with Hammarskjöld tomorrow to discuss this question. He added that the British and French feel that UN action would be too slow to be effective. However, the American Republics feel the UN should take action. In connection with the slowness of UN action, Secretary Dulles felt that long acquiescence in the Egyptian seizure of the Canal would be virtually tantamount to de facto acceptance of Nasser's action. He added that the British and French were thinking in terms of prestige and power, and not solely in terms of transit through the Canal.

The National Security Council: [8]

a. Discussed the subject in the light of:

(1) A briefing by the Secretary of State on the status of developments and possible future contingencies.

(2) The views of the Acting Secretary of Defense and the Joint Chiefs of Staff contained in the enclosures to the reference memoranda of August 3 and 7.

(3) A report by the Director, Office of Defense Mobilization, on the status of studies as to possible contingencies affecting oil supplies from the Middle East.

b. Noted the President's directive that, in order to provide the basis for decisions which may be required in the future, the Departments of State and Defense should be jointly studying all possible contingencies which might develop out of the present crisis in Egypt,

---

[8] The following paragraphs constitute NSC Action No. 1593, approved by the President on August 10. (Department of State, S/S–NSC (Miscellaneous) Files: Lot 66 D 95, Records of Action by the National Security Council, 1956)

what courses of action the United States might have to take under each of these contingencies, and the military as well as the diplomatic implications of each such course; advising the Director, Office of Defense Mobilization, as such studies progress, in order that planning in reference to oil supplies might be coordinated with such State–Defense studies.

Note: The action in b above, as approved by the President, subsequently transmitted to the Secretaries of State and Defense and the Director, ODM. [9]

Marion W. Boggs

---

[9] On August 10, Lay transmitted NSC Action No. 1593–b to the Secretaries of State and Defense. (*Ibid.*, Suez Canal Situation) Subsequently, Dulles and Wilson decided that the existing planning group for the Middle East (MEPPG), including State, Defense, and CIA representatives, should undertake the preparation of contingency studies, as directed in the NSC Action. (*Ibid.*, S/P Files: Lot 66 D 487, Egypt, and S/S–NSC Files: Lot 66 D 148, Suez NSC Action No. 1593b, contain drafts and final versions of the seven papers written in response to this request as well as memoranda of discussions held during the relevant MEPPG meetings and other pertinent memoranda.)

---

73.   Memorandum of a Telephone Conversation Between the Secretary of State and the Assistant Secretary of Defense for International Security Affairs (Gray), Washington, August 9, 1956, 2:41 p.m. [1]

TELEPHONE CALL FROM GORDON GRAY

The Sec. returned the call, and G. said he has a problem which seems inconsequential but it could have important ramifications. They have a request from the British to allow the Expeditionary Forces to take some MDA equipment—in this case radio electronic equipment. G. stopped it because he thinks the British know what they are doing and if we specifically approve it—he does not want to compromise the Sec.'s ultimate position. If we specifically approve it there may be other requests and we may be in the position of endorsing the Expedition. And if we don't, it may appear we are not giving them the proper support. If the Sec. thinks it is trivial, we will approve it. The Sec. read from a cable from London making

---

[1] Eisenhower Library, Dulles Papers, General Telephone Conversations. Transcribed by Bernau.

some requests. [2] G. does not have it. The Sec. would agree to the above request because of its relative unimportance but put in a caveat so it won't establish a precedent. They agreed we will have to face up to this.

The Sec. said he spoke to Wilson re Gray's going to London. G. will.

---

[2] Reference presumably is to telegram 764 from London, August 8, which relayed a request from the British War Office to purchase under reimbursable aid 106MM recoilless rifles and ammunition from USAREUR stocks, the material being urgently required to equip troops being redeployed in connection with the Suez situation. The Embassy in London commented that this might be the first of several requests for weapons and equipment under reimbursable aid for the same purpose. (Department of State, Central Files, 974.7301/8–856)

---

74.   Editorial Note

In response to the British War Office request to purchase recoilless rifles and ammunition conveyed in telegram 764 (see footnote 2, *supra*), the Department of State on the evening of August 9 forwarded to London and Paris a telegram, approved by Dulles, which reads:

"As a matter of policy and within framework normal reimbursable aid procedures, Washington agencies prepared receive and handle on emergency basis British reimbursable requests which may be submitted as indicated reference telegram [telegram 764]. Decisions on specific requests will of course have to be taken in light individual supply situations, whether diversion from U.S. forces involved and similar factors. You should particularly make clear that recoilless rifles and ammo present particularly difficult problem, as these items in extremely short supply.

"In present circumstances, foregoing conditional upon arrangements to assure no publicity. We particularly would insist upon assurances of no indication that requests related to NE crisis." (Telegram 860 to London, repeated to Paris; Department of State, Central Files, 974.7301/8–856)

On August 9 and 10, Dillon conveyed to the Department separate accounts of a conversation with French Defense Minister Bourgès-Maunoury in which the latter had discussed joint Franco-British military planning in regard to the Suez situation. Bourgès-Maunoury told Dillon that the current plan contemplated the French sending 120 fighter aircraft to Cyprus, including 90 F84F's, and he asked for top priority assistance in obtaining necessary spare parts for this type of aircraft. (The file copy of telegram 708 from Paris is a corrected copy dated August 12; *ibid.,* 974.7301/8–956; also telegram 717 from Paris, August 10; *ibid.,* 974.7301/8–1056)

On August 12 the Department responded to the French request in telegram 583 to Paris, as follows:

"You are authorized to confirm to French that U.S. is prepared in principle to supply France with items mentioned reftel [telegram 717 from Paris]. Question of whether items will be supplied on grant or reimbursable aid basis can be determined only after French have given MAAG list of specific items requested. In conveying foregoing to French you should make clear that conditions contained last paragraph Deptel 860 to London, rptd Paris Topol 208, apply." (*Ibid.*)

---

75.   Memorandum of a Conversation, Department of State, Washington, August 9, 1956, 3:40 p.m. [1]

SUBJECT

Suez Canal, Canadian Jets for Israel, Export-Import Bank Loan

PARTICIPANTS

Abba Eban, Ambassador of Israel
Reuven Shiloah, Minister Plenipotentiary
The Secretary
NE—Slator C. Blackiston, Jr.

1. *Suez Canal:* Ambassador Eban remarked that Israel was the only state discriminated against by Egypt in the matter of passage through the Suez Canal. However, the Security Council resolution of 1951 does not specifically refer to Israel shipping but to the right of free passage of all vessels of all nations to all ports wherever bound. Israel supports the London statement confirming the right of all nations to passage through the Canal. Although Israel has no financial interest in the Suez Canal Company, it is naturally interested in the preservation of international contracts. The discrimination by Egypt against Israeli shipping began while the British were still in control of the Suez base and the Canal Company in the "plentitude" of its rights.

---

[1] Source: Department of State, Central Files, 974.7301/8–956. Secret. Drafted by Blackiston. The time of the meeting is from Dulles' Appointment Book. (Princeton University Library, Dulles Papers)

Ambassador Eban said Selwyn Lloyd had explained the failure to invite Israel to the Conference on the grounds that were Israel to attend, Egypt might refuse. Assuming that Egypt does not attend, could not an invitation to Israel be reconsidered? [2]

The Secretary said that invitations to countries in the third (pattern of trade) category were based on a mathematical formula. Thus, in this category only nations 50% or more of whose trade passed through the Canal were invited. The Government of Israel intends to seek assurances from the 24 nations invited to the forthcoming conference that they support the 1951 Security Council resolution. These assurances were being sought in a confidential manner but public expressions of support would be appreciated. Ambassador Eban stated that he was confident of the U.S. position and had therefore informed his Government of United States support of the resolution.

An assurance from the U.K. has already been obtained. The Secretary asked whether memorandum on this subject would be submitted since we wished to know how the question was formulated before giving a definitive reply. Our Panama Canal relationship has to be considered. The Ambassador replied that a note would be forthcoming. [3]

Ambassador Eban expressed the opinion that if Nasser was able to get away with his seizure of the Suez Canal, he would seek new worlds to conquer. Control of the oil resources of the ME and the elimination of Israel were his goals. Whether or not the present crisis is overcome, it has become obvious that the strength of the Western

---

[2] During a conversation with Assistant Secretary Allen on August 4, Shiloah requested, on instructions from the Israeli Government, that Israel be invited to the forthcoming Suez Conference. Shiloah said that similar representations were being made in Paris and London. Allen said that he would repeat the request to Secretary Dulles, but advised that it was not in the interest of the United States or Israel that the Palestine dispute be interjected into the Suez affair. (Memorandum of conversation by Blackiston, August 4; Department of State, Central Files, 974.7301/8–456)

[3] On August 13, the Israeli Embassy forwarded to the Department of State a note which contained the Government of Israel's position concerning Israel's right to transit the Suez Canal. In paragraph 10 of the note, the Government of Israel noted the verbal assurances given by Secretary Dulles on August 9 that the United States would continue to uphold the right of free passage through the Canal by ships of all nations wherever bound, and stated its assumption that the United States would insist on ensuring free passage for Israeli shipping. In paragraph 11, the Government of Israel expressed the confident hope that during the forthcoming Conference in London, the U.S. representative "will demand the abolition of the present restrictions against Israeli shipping and will seek the inclusion in any arrangement of the future operation of the Canal of effective guarantees to avert the recurrence of any discrimination against Israel shipping and against the shipping of other nations bound to and from Israel." (Ibid., 974.7301/8–1356) On August 16, the Israeli Embassy forwarded to the Department of State a supplementary note, which quoted several U.S. statements made before the Security Council in support of the Israeli position. (Ibid., 974.7301/8–1656)

world is dependent upon the whim of one man who controls the lifeline of the Suez. Means to lessen this degree of dependence should be explored. Suggested projects to this end include:

(1) Increased experimentation in the field of nuclear reactors to replace the need for oil as a fuel.

(2) Larger tankers for use on the Cape of Good Hope route.

(3) An alternate canal through Israel to lessen the bargaining power of Egypt. Whether or not the need is sufficiently great to justify the enormous expense of construction is the principal question.

(4) A pipeline from the Gulf of Aqaba through Israel to the Mediterranean with an extension to Haifa to permit the refining capacity located there to be utilized. A pipeline had been considered by the Anglo-Iranian Oil Company some years ago. A somewhat prophetic report on this project was prepared in which it was stated that the continued security of the Suez route for the future was not assured and that a pipeline through Israel would be beneficial in negotiations with the Arab states through which the present pipelines pass. The report estimated that the Israel pipeline could be completed in one year and would cost £20 million. A present obstacle in the pipeline is Egypt's control of the islands at the mouth of the Straits of Tiran. It can be assumed that a tanker with oil bound for the Israel terminus of the pipeline would be fired upon by Egyptian batteries. Such resort to force would not be sustained by public opinion and resistance to the assault would be justified.

A discussion of the legality of Egyptian control of the Straits of Tiran ensued. The Secretary wondered whether the three mile limit did not constitute a legal basis for Egyptian control. Ambassador Eban held that the Corfu ruling [4] sustained the freedom of navigation of such restricted seas. Ambassador Eban said that Israel hoped for a peaceful solution to the Suez problem but that failure of the conference might result in Western military action. The West would therefore be placed in need of bases from which to operate. It was inferred that such bases would be available in Israel.

To speculate that Israel will not be attacked by Egypt would not be wise, said the Ambassador, since Nasser was reckless and had displayed his recklessness in nationalization of the Canal.

According to the Secretary excessive dependence on Suez has been a problem which has bothered the State Department for a long time. Any situation which jeopardizes the Canal is likely to jeopardize the pipelines as well and thus far, we have no alternatives. The Western world can get over the loss of Arab oil on a short-term basis. However, the long-term effect would be critical. Although the West is dependent on oil, the Arab countries are likewise dependent on oil royalties. A possibility of alternatives to the Canal is however,

---

[4] Reference is to the Corfu Channel Case decided by the International Court of Justice in 1949.

very important. History has shown that when a monopolist attempts extortion alternatives to the product of the monopolist are found. It is a good idea to permit it to be known that other Canal routes and new pipelines are being considered.

2. *Canadian Jets for Israel*: The Israel Ambassador expressed the opinion that the implementation of the "agreement" between the U.S. and Canada to permit Canadian jets to be supplied to Israel should go forward in secret with the U.S. supplying the arms which would justify Canadian action. If this could be done, Israel would inform Canada that the U.S. had fulfilled its commitment and would seek to convince the Canadians to sell F-86s without publicity.

The Secretary replied that we still felt that it would not be prudent to seem to be expediting planes to Israel lest it appear as a retaliatory move against Nasser. The Suez situation is not improved if it takes on the aspect of an Israel-Arab dispute. Despite public pronouncements to the contrary, there is a genuine feeling among certain influential groups in Arab nations that Nasser's attitude gives rise to fears of his ultimate intentions. We do not wish any action on our part with respect to Israel to cause this opposition to Nasser to change to support. [5]

3. *Export Import Bank Loan*: The Ambassador stated that, according to his information, the Export Import Bank had completed its report on Israel's loan application. Israel would appreciate being able to bring this matter to a satisfactory conclusion. The Ambassador hoped to be able to see Under Secretary Hoover on this subject after Mr. Hoover returns from his vacation.

---

[5] On August 10 Eban forwarded to Dulles a letter which among other points asked that the United States: (1) clarify to the Governments of France and Canada that the postponement sought by the United States affected publication of specific arms shipments to Israel, not the actual measures toward shipment; and (2) issue normal export permits for the arms requested without publication. (*Ibid.,* 611.84A/8–1056)

76.   Memorandum of a Conversation Between Secretary of State Dulles and Secretary-General Hammarskjöld, Waldorf Towers, New York, August 10, 1956, 1 p.m. [1]

Present also were Ambassadors Lodge and Wadsworth

Mr. Hammarskjold spoke about his impressions of the Arab-Israeli problem. He spoke particularly of his talks with Prime Minister Ben-Gurion [2] and of his sense that Ben-Gurion was very much isolated. Despite the framework of democratic processes, Ben-Gurion was almost a solitary dictator. This has some advantages, but also some risks. Mr. H thought that Israel would probably play a quiet role in the situation now created by the Suez crisis, and would probably not attempt to take overt action.

Mr H. felt that on the concrete issues which he had discussed Israel was almost totally in the wrong. He spoke of his (H's) efforts to get Ben-Gurion to give up the principle of "retaliation" as both immoral and inexpedient. He also spoke of five concrete issues, e.g., militarizing the demilitarized areas, facilities to the UN Truce Supervision Organization, physical delimitation of frontiers, etc., where nothing had been done to carry out what H. thought were the agreements he had arrived at on his first mission. H. showed us a draft of a letter which he was writing to Ben-Gurion [3] in this respect and also a copy of a letter to the Head of the Israeli Mission in New York [4] with respect to one aspect of the matter. He said he felt he would have to bring this matter to the attention of the Security Council unless there was some positive action by Israel, although of course the timing of that would have to be carefully chosen.

I referred to our "Stockpile" Operation and said that we were holding up any announcement. I said that since the issues out there had become triangular rather than bilateral, it was harder to find ways to exert deterrent pressure.

Mr. H. then turned to the Suez matter. He expressed regret that so far the UN had been ignored. He felt that there were dangers that the handling of the matter would develop a Europe v. Asia complexion, although he was sure there were many Asians who at heart did not approve of Nasser's conduct.

I explained the problem we had confronted in getting any conference at all and the principles which had underlain the selec-

---

[1] Source: Eisenhower Library, Dulles Papers, General Memoranda of Conversation. Secret; Personal and Private. Drafted by Dulles.

[2] Hammarskjöld visited Egypt, Israel, and Jordan July 19–22. See vol. XV, pp. 882 ff.

[3] A copy of an unsigned draft letter to Ben Gurion, dated August 10, is in Department of State, NEA Files: Lot 58 D 722, UN in the Arab-Israel Dispute.

[4] Not found in Department of State files.

tion of invitees. I pointed out that at least eight non-Western Asiatics were invited and that it was not going to be a "rubber stamp" conference. I said that some discussion had been given to the matter of identifying a future Canal authority with the UN, but time had not permitted of agreeing on that formulation, but that I did not anticipate serious difficulty in bringing that about if the principle of an authority were accepted.

H. said he could not see how the British and French could possibly justify the use of force. This would strain Article 51 beyond all recognition. He thought possibly force might have been understood as an immediate "hot blood" reaction, but that after delay and deliberation it could never be invoked.

I said that I certainly thought the more delay there was the less likelihood there was it would be invoked. That was one reason why I advocated the conference. I spoke of the "prestige" issues involved, affecting the British throughout the Middle East and the French throughout North Africa, and on the other side Nasser throughout the Arab and Moslem world. This, I felt, created a real difficulty.

I went on to explain the big issue was one of extreme nationalism v. interdependence. I referred to the present dependence of Western Europe upon the oil and the means of transportation through the Middle East. I also spoke of the dependence of the Arab world upon the revenues from the oil and its transportation. I said that while the Arabian countries could seriously embarrass the West, the result of attempting to do so would be to develop alternatives to Middle East Oil for Western Europe. There were other oil supplies that could be developed, new means of transportation could be created such as big tankers, and atomic energy might in time supplant oil as oil has largely supplanted coal. Whenever a person, believing he had a monopoly, tried to use that monopoly oppressively, he found that new alternatives sprang into being. Thus, the long-range result of Nasser's action unless it was corrected by agreement—or by force, which I would deplore—might be the ruination of the Arab world.

Mr. H. said he agreed with this analysis.

JFD

77.   Telegram From the Embassy in Lebanon to the Department of State [1]

Beirut, August 10, 1956—7 p.m.

310. Eyes only for the Secretary. Charles Malik suddenly asked to see me this afternoon. This noon Egyptian Ambassador [2] had brought him personal message from Nasser. Nasser asked him urgently transmit to Secretary of State following message:

(1) He, Nasser, cannot assent any solution of Suez problem that would impair Egypt sovereignty or dignity;
(2) Egypt therefore cannot accept international operation canal when other canals and waterways are not subject such control;
(3) He, Nasser, would be willing give most explicit guarantees efficiency of operation, reservation of revenues for necessary expansion canal, and freedom of transit;
(4) He would be ready explore with other countries problem maintaining and increasing efficiency canal operations;
(5) In larger conference he would be glad negotiate new international convention regarding canal based 1888 convention.

Egyptian Ambassador in transmitting this message to Malik for re-transmittal to Secretary added that he thought Malik should know that [in] case force were resorted to, Egyptians would resist to end and would destroy installations of canal and western pipelines in other Arab countries would be destroyed. Egyptian Ambassador said he did not know precisely what was message British Ambassador had brought Chamoun from Eden this week but he understood there was phrase in there about "fair international operation of canal". Egyptian Ambassador thought exploration that phrase might lead to mutually satisfactory compromise.

Malik says he told Egyptian Ambassador he would transmit message to Secretary but made no commitment as to his recommending its consideration. He did say to Egyptian Ambassador that he advised Nasser that if he was going take this line in his speech on August 12 he explain Egypt's attitude in words of humility and sober simplicity, and without attacks on west.

Malik then asked me to transmit to Secretary following message and recommendation. Although he personally liked Nasser and understood reasons for some of his actions and applauded some of his reforms, it was not in interest of peace or western civilization that

---

[1] Source: Department of States, Central Files, 974.7301/8–1056. Top Secret; Priority. Received at 6:38 a.m., August 11. Repeated Priority to London.
[2] Abdelhamid Ghaleb.

Nasser's government should remain in control of Egypt. This was his profound conviction and recommendation to the Secretary. [3]

Heath

---

[3] In telegram 177 to Beirut, August 11, drafted by Wilkins and approved by Rountree, the Department responded: "You may inform Charles Malik we appreciate his conveying message from Egyptian Ambassador and thank Malik for giving us benefit his own views." (Department of State, Central Files, 974.7301/8–1156)

---

78.   Memorandum of a Conversation, White House, Washington, August 12, 1956, 10:15 a.m. [1]

SUBJECT

> Suez Canal Situation—Presidential Meeting 10:30–11:00 a.m. (Preliminary to Noon Meeting with Congressional Bipartisan Leaders) Sunday, August 12, 1956

ATTENDANCE

> The President
> Secretary John Foster Dulles
> Admiral Arthur W. Radford
> Honorable Arthur S. Flemming
> Honorable Wilton B. Persons
> *Part-Time*:
> General Alfred M. Gruenther
> Honorable Allen Dulles
> Honorable Gordon Gray
> Honorable Dillon Anderson

[Here follows discussion concerning the attendance of Senatorial leaders at the forthcoming Suez Conference.]

2. In opening the discussion on the Suez Canal the President stated that he was troubled by the position in which the Western world would find itself if Nasser continued to insist on the fact that he was going to keep the canal open and if he made very firm promises relative to the way in which he was going to operate the

---

[1] Source: Eisenhower Library, Whitman File, Eisenhower Diaries. Secret. Prepared in the White House, but no drafting information is given on the source text. The time of the meeting is from the record of the President's Daily Appointments, which indicates that Allen Dulles joined the meeting at 10:30 a.m., Gray at 10:55 a.m., and Dillon Anderson at 11:15 a.m. (*Ibid.*) Anderson drafted a separate memorandum of the conversation, which primarily covered items discussed after the conversation recorded here on Suez. (*Ibid.*, Whitman File, Eisenhower Diaries)

canal from the standpoint of protecting the interests of other nations. Nasser could then point up the reasonableness of his position by stating that in 12 years, under the provisions of the treaty, he would have complete title to the canal anyhow and at that time it would not be necessary for him to make the kind of payments to the stockholders that he was offering to make at the present time.

Secretary Dulles in his comments pointed out that although Egypt would have complete title to the canal in 12 years, those portions of the treaty guaranteeing the international status of the canal remained in effect indefinitely. He pointed out that Nasser in both his writings and in his speeches had indicated a very clear intention of using the canal in a manner that would run contrary to the guarantees of its international status that are contained in the treaty. He stated that it was this threat to impair the international status of the canal that provided the British and the French with a solid foundation for possible action.

Admiral Radford pointed out that under the provisions of the treaty the Egyptian Government would be required at the end of the 12-year period to compensate the present owners.

The President stated that the discussion that had taken place put the question of the treaty in a different light. He said that he felt it was very important that a careful analysis be made of the provisions of the treaty so that there would be a thorough understanding of the basis for our dealings with the Egyptian Government.

3. General Persons suggested that at the Conference with the legislative leaders the question might very well be raised as to what policy we intended to follow if the London Conference should fail to accomplish the purposes that we have in mind for it.

Secretary Dulles stated that this was a question that had to be handled very carefully. He pointed out that it is necessary for us to convey to Egypt and the other Arab nations our own convictions relative to the impossibility of the Western World tolerating the kind of a situation that confronts us as a result of Nasser's action. At the same time he feels that we must not lead the British and the French to believe that we are willing to support any kind of precipitous action they may take. As a result, he believes that we must indicate that our next step will be governed to a considerable degree by the attitudes taken by the various nations at the London Conference. If the London Conference does present a reasonable proposal to Nasser and he rejects it and the British and French then feel that it is necessary to act in order to protect their interests, it would seem to be clear that the United States should give them moral and economic support. On the other hand, if the British and French adopt an unreasonable position at the London Conference, the desirability of our giving them support in their dealings with Nasser would not be as clear.

Secretary Dulles said that he would point out to the legislative leaders that the British and French have said that they can handle the type of military operation they contemplate and that they would not expect the United States to commit any of its armed forces. The British and French would, however, expect us to provide them with economic assistance and with assistance in dealing with a basic problem such as the petroleum problem. Also, they would hope that we would neutralize Soviet Russia by indicating very clearly to Russia that if it should enter the conflict openly, the United States would enter it on the side of Britain and France.

4. Secretary Gray indicated that the British had requested certain types of arms with the understanding we were to be reimbursed. The President felt that we should respond affirmatively to requests of this kind. General Gruenther also underlined the desirability of our following a policy of this kind. (This is covered in more detail in Gordon Gray's memorandum for the record. [2])

---

[2] Attached as Annex A to the memorandum of conversation by Anderson.

79.   Memorandum of a Conversation, Washington, August 12, 1956, noon–1:25 p.m. [1]

NOTES ON PRESIDENTIAL-BIPARTISAN CONGRESSIONAL LEADERSHIP MEETING

The following were present:

The President

The Vice President	Mr. Dillon Anderson
The Secretary of State	Gen. Persons
The Chairman of the Joint Chiefs	Mr. Jack Martin
of Staff	Mr. Harlow
Asst. Sec. of Defense Gordon Gray	Mr. Murray Snyder
Dr. Arthur Flemming	Mr. Chesney
Honorable Allen Dulles	
Mr. Herman Phleger	
Senator Lyndon Johnson	Senator Wm. F. Knowland
Senator Earle C. Clements	Senator Styles Bridges
Senator Walter F. George	Senator Eugene D. Millikin
Senator Theodore Francis Green	Senator Leverett Saltonstall
Senator Richard B. Russell	Senator Alexander Wiley
	Senator H. Alexander Smith
Speaker Sam Rayburn	Rep. Joseph W. Martin, Jr.
Rep. Carl Albert	Rep. Charles Halleck
Rep. Thomas E. Morgan	Rep. Leslie C. Arends
Rep. A.S.J. Carnahan	Rep. Leo Allen
	Rep. Robert B. Chiperfield
	Rep. John M. Vorys
	Rep. Dewey Short

After expressing thanks to the group for interrupting their activities to attend this meeting, the President said that things were not going so well as to give "unbounded hope" for a peaceful solution. He noted the latest advice that Egypt probably would not attend the London Conference. [2] He then stressed the importance of

---

[1] Source: Eisenhower Library, Whitman File, Legislative Meetings. Top Secret. Drafted by Minnich.

[2] That same day during a press conference which began at 5 p.m. Nasser delivered a statement in which he affirmed that the "proposed conference has no right whatsoever to discuss any matter falling within the jurisdiction of Egypt or relating to its sovereignty over any part of its territory. The invitation to it cannot, therefore, be accepted by Egypt." The complete text of Nasser's statement was transmitted in despatch 127 from Cairo, August 13. (Department of State, Central Files, 974.7301/8–156) It is printed in *The Suez Canal Problem, July 26–September 22, 1956,* pp. 47–52. Reports from the Embassy in Cairo are in Department of State, Central File 974.7301.

oil and indicated that Dr. Flemming would develop this subject more fully.

The President expressed his hope that one Senator from each Party would accompany Sec. Dulles to London since the outcome may be in treaty form, and it would also be well to have the Senators there so that the Secretary might draw on them for advice. He anticipated no secret agreements.

Sec. Dulles reviewed recent events involving the Suez, made reference to the Treaty of 1888, and characterized Nasser's act as far more than a domestic nationalization issue. He cited Nasser's public statements about the need for money for the Aswan Dam and the elimination of Western imperialism. He referred to a desire on the part of Nasser to unite the Arab world and if possible the Moslem world, and to use Mid-East oil and the Suez Canal as weapons against the West.

Sec. Dulles stated that the immediate reaction of France and England was to use force and that those countries had sent us messages on their readiness to use force, and requesting US support. As a result, the Secretary said, he went to London and stated the opinion that the immediate use of force would alienate world opinion since France and England had not yet made their case. He had expressed to the French and British the view there that the United States would regard immediate resort to force as a violation of French and British undertakings in regard to the United Nations and other such efforts for world peace, all of which would be wrecked if they moved violently at this time. Sec. Dulles thought that such action by the French and British then would have alienated the United States and would have given the Soviet unbounded opportunities in the diplomatic sphere. He had therefore proposed the calling of a conference for the purpose of establishing international assurances—within the limits of legitimate Egyptian interests—that the Canal would be properly operated. He then explained the basis for the twenty-four invitations, and he reported that twenty-two nations had accepted or indicated their intention to accept. He believed that Greece and Egypt would not accept.

The Secretary believed that the conference would provide a forum which would determine whether or not it is possible to obtain a solution in accord with the 1888 Treaty and taking into account legitimate Egyptian interests. He believed such a solution possible but not easy to be achieved. He believed that the British and French will resort to force if such a solution cannot be obtained. He thought the United States could not be unsympathetic to the British and French views in the light of Nasser's ambitions. He warned that fulfillment of Nasser's ambitions would result in reducing Western

Europe literally to a state of dependency and Europe as a whole would become insignificant. He explained this in terms of availability of oil and in terms of the far-reaching interests of the French and British in Africa. He said that Britain and France cannot let Nasser have a strangle-hold on the Canal.

Sen. Knowland asked whether Egypt had signed the 1888 Treaty. Sec. Dulles explained why Turkey had signed and added that Egypt in its 1954 Treaty recognized the binding nature of the 1888 agreement.

Sec. Dulles said that the United States will have to play an important, perhaps decisive role in seeking a fair solution—perhaps to the extent of indicating that if there is no fair solution we will in our future conduct place much importance on who was responsible for the failure of the conference.

Sen. Russell asked if it was contemplated having an international authority to own the Canal. The Secretary said international ownership was not contemplated and added that it was primarily a matter of overseeing those who operate the Canal and the methods of operation. He stressed the view that Egypt should not be solely responsible; that nevertheless there remained a serious question as to whether the British and French would accept this type of solution. Sen. Lyndon Johnson pursued the matter by asking if it would not be a conceivable solution to have some international authority acquire title. The Secretary replied that he did not think it feasible or necessary to acquire title. He drew the analogy of public utilities and regulatory commissions, and he believed such an arrangement would be easier to effect than attempting to take title away from Egypt. The Secretary went on to add that he was not saying it was theoretically impossible to have operation of the Canal by Egypt compatible with the 1888 Treaty but he did feel that such an operation could not reasonably be expected in the light of Nasser's professions. He explained that by manipulations in the administration of any set of rules the Egyptians could use the Canal for unacceptable national and political purposes.

(Sen. Knowland began a question, then broke it off.)

Sec. Dulles added that in the long run it is almost intolerable to Western Europe to feel that it cannot rely on access to the oil of the Middle East and that this is almost a life and death issue for Britain and France. He pointed out that two-thirds of the vital oil supplies to Western Europe travel through the Canal while one-third goes through pipelines; that the two transit methods being cut off together and at the same time posed an intolerable threat to Europe that oil might be cut off entirely. He thought that the views of those two countries can be reduced to reasonable proportions and that an international authority of small dependable countries can be established, but this will not be easy since national prestige is at stake.

Sen. Knowland asked what the relationship of such action would be to the Panama Canal in light of our treaty with Britain and potential Russian propaganda. Sec. Dulles pointed out important differences, such as the fact that Panama has never been fully internationalized, that Britain only has a treaty right to equal tolls, that we alone built the Canal and that all operating rights are ours. More important, he thought, was the consideration that the United States was not threatening the free use of the Canal by others, and he said there might well be reason for action to internationalize the Panama Canal if the United States threatened to halt use by others. He pointed out that such facilities do develop international characteristics through usage and growing dependence on them of the trade of nations, irrespective of title and initial control. He referred again to Nasser's bullying tactics. Sen. Green ascertained that Nasser's statements were made in the immediate Suez situation rather than at some indefinite time in the past.

Sen. Russell questioned the grounds for thinking Nasser might agree to a fair solution when it seemed he would not even attend the conference. Sec. Dulles, after a pause, commented on his feeling that others such as India, Ceylon and Pakistan can exert sufficient pressure on Nasser. Sen. Russell noted that Nasser seemed determined to dominate the situation. The President cited the importance of the Western market for oil, and Western control of marketing outlets on which income from production depends. He adverted to the damage Arab nations would suffer if their income should be cut off. He thought Nasser would begin to lose his prestige if he were responsible for cutting off oil income of other countries. The Secretary added that there is some evidence (not open) that some of the Arab countries think Nasser is going too fast. He said that the Arab States realize that alternative supplies can be developed, though at the cost of some austerity in Europe.

Rep. Vorys asked about other economic measures that might be taken since Egypt belongs to the Sterling Bloc. The President noted that no heavy British payments to Egypt fall due until next January. The President went on to quote from Nasser's speech and to stress the heavy investment the United States has made in strengthening Western Europe, a big stake for us beyond the immediate considerations involving oil.

Rep. Halleck cited the big problem that would arise if the British and French "move in" as respects the UN Charter and our relationship to it. The President replied in terms of the many complexities that would be involved at that point. He re-emphasized the need for exploring every peaceful means for settlement and world awareness of the effort. Mr. Halleck asked if the matter could properly be put before the United Nations. Sec. Dulles said it could be brought before the Security Council but that Britain and France have veto power. He said the General Assembly could be called into emergency session but that it could only make recommendations which would involve long, inconclusive debate and lead to acquiescences amounting to a de facto recognition of what Nasser has done.

Sen. Green thought the London Conference might give consideration to laying down general principles for all waterways. Sec. Dulles thought it undesirable to interject other waterways since it would tend to drop the Suez matter out of sight. Sen. Green thought a beginning might well be made. Sec. Dulles doubted that the United States would want to interject the Panama Canal. Sen. Green said that if everybody took that position no progress would ever be made. Sec. Dulles replied that many treaties are involved and he asked if Sen. Green really meant to scrap all the pertinent treaties. Sen. Green commented that times and conditions have changed much.

Sen. Knowland asked if it were not really a question of an overt act, such as closing the Canal. He also asked what the case might be if Nasser promised to adhere to the 1888 Treaty and prevented any overt act violating the Treaty. In that case, he thought, Nasser might take to the United Nations any threat of forceful action by Britain and France The President recalled Nasser's aggressive statements which seemed much like Hitler's in "Mein Kampf", a book no one believed. The President agreed that many embarrassing questions could be posed but that the main thing was the economy of Europe.

Sen. Smith asked whether any change of leadership in Egypt might bring in a person even worse than Nasser. Sec. Dulles replied that Nasser was the worst we have had so far. The Secretary referred again to Nasser's book and his "Hitler-ite" personality. He emphasized again our stake in Western Europe. Sen. Smith noted divisions within the Arab world that had been apparent at the United Nations. Sec. Dulles elaborated on Iraq's position but concluded that Iraq cannot make an open stand against Nasser.

Rep. Short commented about Nasser playing the old Hitler game. Sen. Bridges interjected that Nasser had to be stopped before he really got started. Sec. Dulles recalled all our efforts to work with him until we finally became convinced that he is an extremely dangerous fanatic. He expressed the view that if Nasser gets by with this action, the British and French are probably right in their appraisal of the consequences.

Dr. Flemming reported the work done with the committee of American oil companies engaged in overseas operations. At our request the committee prepared a plan of action for pooling resources, and this plan has been cleared by the Attorney General and the FTC. Dr. Flemming said he approved the plan last Friday night.

Dr. Flemming noted that an emergency Middle East Oil Committee is being set up to check on the statistics currently available. He stressed that all of the statistics he would present were not so firm as he desired.

Dr. Flemming said that 1.5 million barrels per day went through the Suez, of which 1.2 million went to Britain and Western Europe. Should the Suez be closed, Gulf Coast and Caribbean production could be increased fairly soon by 800,000 to 900,000 barrels per day to meet US and European requirements. Similarly, should the pipelines be lost but the Canal remain open, an increase here of 400,000 to 500,000 barrels per day would meet the situation. Finally, should both the pipelines and the Canal be lost, the situation might be met by rationing oil in Britain and Western Europe (saving 20%) and by increasing production here by 1.3 million barrels per day. The Committee will develop a program designed to deal with this.

Sen. Bridges asked about the destination of the 2.3 million barrels shipped daily through the pipelines and Canal. Dr. Flemming indicated that 300,000 came to the United States and 1.9 million to Britain and Western Europe. A question by Sen. Bridges as to the amount of this used by the American fleet and NATO remained unanswered.

Dr. Flemming stressed the "dollar drain" of an additional $400 million or $500 million per year that would result should the Canal be closed. Should both the pipeline and the Canal be closed, the additional dollar drain would be perhaps $600 million or $700 million.

Sen. Knowland asked whether oil would be shipped from the Middle East around Cape Horn. Dr. Flemming indicated that the figures he previously gave assumed some to be shipped around the Cape. Rep. Vorys asked how soon the million barrel per day increase could be accomplished. Dr. Flemming replied "in a very short period", and inventories can be drawn upon in the interval. Sen. Saltonstall asked if an acute tanker shortage would not appear very soon. Dr. Flemming said that at first look there seemed to be sufficient tankers to accomplish the programs outlined. He believed firmer figures will be available in a week.

Sen. Russell thought this whole subject of an oil program might be an over-simplification of the problem, for the real question would hang upon the United States having to support the European countries financially. The President agreed that this is a serious problem and added that we were talking in the first instance about sheer existence.

Speaker Rayburn asked if Nasser had definitely said he will close the Canal. The President and the Secretary of State replied that he had not. The Secretary added that the French and British view is that his words cannot be trusted. Speaker Rayburn inquired if an income was the only real objective of Nasser's action. Sec. Dulles said that a treaty can assure him the income. Sen. Smith asked who would determine the level of tolls. The Secretary said that in the final analysis an international tribunal might determine. Mr. Vorys asked about the collection of tolls during this period of controversy, and Sec. Dulles explained the approaches of the United States, Britain and France with regard to "payment under protest" or "payment under coercion". He added that the Egyptians seemed to be trying to appear thoroughly reasonable in this respect. Mr. Vorys asked how great is the income from the Canal. The President replied that Egypt gets $17 million per year and that another $31 million profit is had by the Company and used for set-asides, etc. The Vice President thought the question was a larger one than the money involved.

Sen. Saltonstall saw a need for clarifying the relationship of the matter to the United Nations and pointed to the danger that if the UN failed in this matter its prestige and acceptance would be greatly undermined. Sec. Dulles reported on his talk with the Secretary General who seemed greatly concerned about the UN role. It appears that the British and French haven't given the UN quite enough attention. He thought that any international board that might be created might be related to the UN but he felt that answers were lacking with respect to possible developments should no peaceful solution be obtained. He commented that other nations are not so intent on going to the UN when that body does not seem to offer any practicable solution.

Sen. Wiley noted British and French troop movements and asked where we go should those countries attempt to take over by force. Sec. Dulles replied that the two countries had promised to avoid use of force pending the conference and that we have at least ten days' time to work for a solution. Sen. Wiley then asked if the Soviets were stirring up the situation in order to get control of Middle East oil. The President replied that there shouldn't be much doubt but what the Soviet will fish in troubled waters. Sen. Wiley repeated his question on US actions should the British, French or Egyptians resort to force. Sec. Dulles replied he could not today say what the US reaction would be, that much depended on developments of an evolving situation. He restated his earlier comments on the US attitude toward those responsible for obstructing a settlement.

Speaker Rayburn questioned the Secretary's earlier comment about Egypt having a legal right to take the action taken. Sec. Dulles believed his earlier comment somewhat different from what Speaker Rayburn had repeated, and went on to say that he meant that the Canal is located on Egyptian soil. He added that Nasser's actions do, however, violate the earlier Treaty. Speaker Rayburn noted that traffic is now flowing through the Suez and he asked as to what the situation would have to develop for the British and French to say that they must "act". Sec. Dulles replied that the French and British maintain the situation has already occurred but that they are holding back because of the conference. He reported their belief that Nasser is a wild man brandishing an axe and that they do not have to wait for the blow to fall. Speaker Rayburn asked the Secretary's estimate of the result should the British and French act. The Secretary thought it would start a long and involved affair whose end was difficult to see, particularly in light of the difficulties Britain previously had in Suez even with many troops there. He referred to the bad situation in Libya also. Speaker Rayburn asked whether the Secretary thought the situation had gotten beyond the point of reason. Sec. Dulles thought not.

Sen. Johnson asked if we had not had enough experience with this type of situation to realize that we can't deal with this Colonel, and shouldn't we face up to it and say so to our allies. He went on to the effect that they expect us to help and we seem to be sympathetic to their case, hence should we not face up to it. Sec. Dulles commented that he did not believe they had yet made their case. With regard to what aid might be expected, he reported the belief of the French and British that they can handle the situation so long as the Soviet does not enter. Personally, he believed they might be a bit over optimistic. Sen. Bridges asked if it were not clear that if we allow Nasser to get away with this, we would encourage others to act likewise. Sen. Bridges said he agreed with Lyndon, that we can't look the other way, can't put our tail between our legs, can't run away. Sen. Johnson said he had given much thought to this subject and there seemed only two alternatives: (1) to use all peaceful means to solve the problem (hence he had suggested exploring the possibility of an international authority to acquire title); (2) the only other course would be to tell our allies that we *are* their ally and to support them. He felt in this case that we can't underwrite them financially forever and that we should tell them they have our moral support and that they should go on in. The President told Lyndon he seemed perfectly right in one respect, that we can't accept an inconclusive outcome leaving Nasser in control; that on the other hand we can't resign ourselves to underwriting the European economy permanently.

Rep. Vorys asked about any specific plan for the use of force. Sec. Dulles believed the British and French intended to reoccupy the former base and station troops along the Canal. Adm. Radford commented that the initial plan would be to restore the World War II situation, using four to six divisions. The President noted how such an action would get to be a long and tedious one, allowing the other fellow to hit and run. Sen. Knowland noted that this plan involved an assumption that the action could be limited to that amount. Adm. Radford identified the plan as an *initial* one and noted that the British and French do not expect too much opposition from Egypt alone. Sen. Saltonstall recalled the favorable public attitude toward dropping the Aswan project. He believed Nasser should not be allowed to play both ends against the middle. He thought it might therefore be desirable to take the same firm approach now as was done in regard to the Aswan Dam. The President wanted everyone to understand clearly that we do not intend to stand by helplessly and let this one man get away with what he is trying to do. He stated that the reason the presentation at this meeting was not projected further into the future was that we do not know now what future developments will be. He again reassured the group that the US will look to its interests.

Speaker Rayburn commented that English thinking on the subject seems muddy. The President reviewed some of the indications of English thinking at the beginning of the crisis and wound up by noting Mr. Gaitskell's attitude and the opinion expressed in the *London Economist* just out. [3]

Sen. Russell noted that Nasser had already backed up somewhat. Sec. Dulles read a note just handed him stating that Nasser had announced he would call a conference to handle the matter.

The President remarked on the confidential nature of the material presented, particularly in regard to statistics and the attitudes of the allies. A few minutes later he repeated this caution with particular regard to the military plan.

[Here follows discussion concerning the press release to be issued after the meeting; for text, see Department of State *Bulletin*, August 20, 1956, page 314, or *The Suez Canal Problem, July 26–September 22, 1956*, page 52.]

---

[3] Reference is presumably to the August 11 issue of the *London Economist*.

80.   Memorandum From the Deputy Assistant Secretary of State for Near Eastern, South Asian, and African Affairs (Rountree) to the Assistant Secretary of State for Near Eastern, South Asian, and African Affairs (Allen) [1]

Washington, August 13, 1956.

SUBJECT

Ambassador Eban's Request for Arms

The Secretary spoke to us again this morning regarding Israel's request for helicopters, half tracks and machine guns from the United States. The Israelis contemplate that these American shipments will enable the Canadians to supply F–86s and the French the Mysteres.

I had endeavored to have the meeting put off until after your return today but was unable to do so because of the Secretary's tight schedule prior to his departure for London. During the several discussions with the Secretary I recited your views, [2] making it clear that you thought arrangements for American shipments might be made whose effects would not be too great.

The Secretary agreed it would be wise to separate the American shipments from the Canadian and French shipments. He did not believe that we should hold up the American shipments, but that we should stagger them over a period of time. He also thought that we might again look into the question of jet training for Israeli pilots in France and Italy. The Secretary directed that we discuss the general question orally with Ambassador Eban.

There is attached a talking paper [3] which outlines the substance of the oral response which the Secretary thought you might make to Ambassador Eban. He thought we should make our agreement to release any American shipments contingent on Israeli assurances

---

[1] Source: Department of State, Central Files, 784A.56/8–1356. Confidential. Drafted by Wilkins.

[2] According to a memorandum by Howe of August 9, Allen told Dulles that although there were many reasons for holding up arms shipments to Israel, several considerations in favor of supplying the arms included: (1) sending Nasser a message that "both sides can play at the armaments game;" (2) offsetting the British and French suspicion that the United States was favorable to Nasser because it opposed the use of force over Suez; and (3) rectifying the contradictory signals sent to Canada on the question. Allen also noted that Nasser's refusal to attend the London Conference would be a good psychological time to announce the release of at least the helicopters. (*Ibid.*, 784A.56/8–956)

[3] Not printed.

there would be no publicity or any reference to American shipments by Canada if it should decide to ship F–86s to Israel. [4]

---

[4] On August 15, the Department instructed the Embassy in Ottawa to inform the Canadian Government of the decision to approve the arms sales to Israel on the specific conditions that: (1) the Israeli Government agree to make every effort to prevent publicity concerning the sales and (2) neither France nor Canada refer publicly to U.S. arms shipments to justify their own sale of arms to Israel. (Telegram 83 to Ottawa; *ibid.,* 784A.5622/8–1556) On August 17, Murphy and Allen informed Eban of the Department's decision and the conditions attached thereto. (Memorandum of conversation by Wilkins, August 21; *ibid.,* 784A.56/8–1756) Subsequently, Eban conveyed the assurances that every effort would be made on the part of the Israeli Government to avoid publicity, and U.S. officials made clear to Israel that they planned to move forward on the orders. (Memorandum of conversation by Wilkins, August 22; and Tedul 24 to London, August 22; both *ibid.,* 784A.56/8–2256) On August 28, Foreign Minister Pearson provided assurances that the Canadian Government would not, in its announcement concerning release of the F-86s, link its decision to U.S. actions. (Telegram 111 from Ottawa, August 28; *ibid.,* 784A.5622/8–2856)

---

81.   Memorandum of a Conversation Between the President and the Secretary of State, White House, Washington, August 14, 1956, 10:30 a.m. [1]

[Here follow items 1 and 2 concerning unrelated subjects.]

3. I showed the President the letter reporting on the status of Congressional representation at the London Conference. [2] He read the letter and said he thought that it adequately and satisfactorily reflected the situation. I said that, as mentioned in the letter, Senator George would be closely watching the situation and seeing the normal cables and perhaps, if the President and Mr. Hoover felt it appropriate, my personal message to the President.

[Here follow items 4 and 5 concerning unrelated subjects.]

6. We then went on to discuss in detail the forthcoming Suez Conference. I said that I felt that the decisive issue would be whether or not Egypt alone should have the right to hire and fire in terms of Canal employees and also would have alone the right to fix

---

[1] Source: Eisenhower Library, Dulles Papers, Meetings with the President. Secret; Personal and Private. Drafted by Dulles. The time of the meeting is from the record of the President's Daily Appointments. (*Ibid.*)

[2] Attached to the source text, but not printed. The letter from Dulles to Eisenhower, August 12, summarized the unsuccessful efforts on the part of Dulles to obtain Democratic senatorial representation at the Suez Conference. It also noted that as no Democratic senator could attend, Republican Senator Alex Smith, who had held himself in readiness, would also not attend.

the Canal tolls. I indicated that I felt it essential that there be an international voice in these matters and that they should not be wholly under Egypt's political control. The President said he was disposed to agree, but asked how we would meet the situation that might arise if we were asked to accept the same control with reference to the Panama Canal. He said that he recognized that it was a treaty basis far different but that the broad equities might be the same. I said that in the first place there was not nearly the same degree of dependence on the Panama Canal as there was upon the Suez Canal which decisively affected the very livelihood of almost a score of nations. Also that the United States was not professing to use the Canal to further some grandiose plan of aggrandizement. If there was a comparable dependence and comparable political use of the Panama Canal, then indeed other nations might in equity claim some voice even though there was no treaty basis for it as was the case in the Suez Canal.

The President suggested there should be some kind of a supervisory board of say five persons designated by such countries as Egypt, Britain, France, India and Sweden, who would have a voice in the selection of a general manager who would be in charge of Canal operations. Also that there should be some right of arbitration on the question of tolls. I said this was in line with my thinking and that it might even be necessary to minimize the role of Britain and France, assuming dependable alternatives could be found. I said that one of our problems was that the Asian countries were not in the main dependable since their policies were apt to be swayed by political slogans such as "colonialism", "imperialism", "Asia for the Asians", etc.

I hoped that we could get the problem onto a practical basis such as the basis on which the President and I were discussing the matter. Then if that could be brought about there was a good chance of an acceptable solution.

The President said he recognized how difficult the task was, but that he had confidence and wished me well. [3]

JFD

---

[3] By 2:20 that afternoon, Dulles and his party were airborne. Accompanying the Secretary on the plane were Mrs. Dulles, Gray, Phleger, Bowie, McCardle, Rountree, Macomber, and three others. (Dulles' Appointment Book, August 14; Princeton University Library, Dulles Papers)

82.   Telegram From the Joint Chiefs of Staff to the
       Commander in Chief, Eastern Atlantic and Mediterranean
       (Boone) [1]

Washington, August 15, 1956.

The JCS are concerned in regard to possible developments in the event that negotiations starting in London 16 August fail to produce satisfactory resolution of the Suez Canal problem. In view of the above and with due consideration of delicate public relations aspects involved, you should do all practicable to insure optimum readiness to undertake on short notice tasks related to protection U.S. interests and evacuation measures from Egypt and other Arab countries in the Middle East. In the latter category, JCS feel that U.S. ground forces up to one RCT might possibly be called upon to protect oil fields and installations in vicinity of Dhahran. Augmentation of present air lift capability in Europe to extent this can be done without adverse public reaction will be made subject of separate message [2] to CINC-USAFE, info other addressees.

---

[1] Source: JCS Records, CCS.092 Egypt (7–28–56). Top Secret. Transmitted as JCS 908488, also sent to USCINCEUR, CINCUSAREUR, and CINCUSAFE. The source text is enclosure "A" to a note from the Joint Secretariat of the JCS to the Joint Chiefs of Staff. The note indicates that the Joint Chiefs at their meeting on August 15 agreed to dispatch the message printed here and a second message (enclosure B, not printed) to U.S. commanders in chief throughout the world which would personally alert them to the possibility that the Middle East situation could deteriorate rapidly if the London Conference failed to resolve the Canal problem.

[2] To be dispatched by Chief of Staff, U.S. Air Force. [Footnote in the source text.]

---

83.   Telegram From the Embassy in Egypt to the Department
       of State [1]

Cairo, August 15, 1956—3 p.m.

379. London for USDel. For Secretary State. Fawzi asked that I call this morning (he seeing all chiefs of mission participating London conference, as reported Embtel 371 repeated London 91 [2]).

---

[1] Source: Department of State, Central Files, 974.7301/8–1556. Secret; Limited Distribution—Suez Canal. Received at 4:14 p.m. Repeated to London and Paris.

[2] Dated August 14, not printed. (*Ibid.*, 974.7301/8–1456)

His discussion with me much like that described above reference telegram and previous discussions already reported.

He said Egypt willing to consider any even half-way reasonable proposal that did not violate Egypt's sovereignty, emphasizing not only Egypt's willingness but desire formalize some sort of consultative body representing users of canal. In such forum there could be full consultation on questions of interest to users such as tolls, services, etc. Assurances through such framework could be problem to users on such technical questions for reasonable lengths of time. Egypt would be willing to volunteer complete information to such group and group could take initiative with Egypt to make suggestions for improved service. Egypt appreciated seriousness of concern of shipping countries and had no intention trying ignore now or in future weight of opinion of so many nations as long as Egypt treated as equal sovereign state. He felt that such machinery, together with existing arbitration mechanisms applicable disagreements on commercial items, and the United Nations forum for possible broader issues arising in future, should be sufficient.

Fawzi then launched into serious discussion re possibility of hostilities, admitting there some emotion in this feeling. He said Egypt not unconscious of huge responsibility which Egypt, and all others in this dispute, bear towards future of world peace. We would all be doing something unpardonable if we allowed spark of war to set off chain of events [end of which] could not be foreseen. If Egypt attacked there would be fighting not only in Egypt but elsewhere. He said that everyone including the West would say that they were only taking steps to defend themselves, recalling how Japan said she defending Japan through whole process of taking Manchuria. What Soviets would do he did not know but felt there would be some action (perhaps in Iran) also on basis they defending their own position. This process of self-defense could go on until whole thing blew up. He was thinking not only in terms of the millions of lives involved but moral values without which world would not be worth much anyway. Also he wondered if world could allow a new precedent in this day and age of people being subjected to force and whether Egypt really had right to give in.

Fawzi said we would now be subjected to efforts create misunderstanding between us all, as nations tried by every means to protect their own self interests, but Egypt would do its best to try to base its decision on solid facts. He said Egypt doesn't necessarily want London conference to fail but does not consider that conference has right to make final decisions affecting Egypt. He felt however there is something in between which could be achieved and hoped effort would be made to face problem in this light. [3]

Fawzi concerned at efforts British and French, and perhaps others to create trouble at Canal, etc. He said 10 out of 11 of French, British pilots yesterday were reported out sick. He wondered what kind of excuse for use of force British and French might be trying to set up, and hoped world opinion would not condone such tactics.

Fawzi said he available at any time for any suggestions we might have. Told Fawzi I not in position to make suggestions but would be in touch with him promptly if my government thought discussion of any particular aspect useful. In closing asked about strike scheduled for tonight [4] and was assured that things would not get out of control. Told him I more concerned as regards certain other Arab States. He said he could not of course assure me in that regard but that Egypt had asked all Arab States to do their best to avoid incidents in connection with strike.

Embassy concerned about efforts re walk-out of pilots and other personnel as mentioned above by Fawzi. Our assessment leads us conclude that as Egypt willing to make attractive offers to Canal employees, things would probably go along all right except for outside interference. Furthermore it seems to us that this type of effort on part British or French is too transparent and carries with it real danger Egypt might be forced rely upon Iron Curtain pilots and technicians in order keep Canal in operation. We believe this would be short-sighted indeed.

Byroade

---

[3] A marginal handwritten notation on the source text by Fraser Wilkins reads: "I wonder if Fawzi thought of some of these things when the Canal Co. was taken over and even when they bought arms for [*from*] Russia. FW"

[4] Beginning at midnight, August 15/16 (Cairo time), a general strike to protest the London Conference took place in Egypt and other parts of the Arab world.

84.   Telegram From the Embassy in the United Kingdom to the Department of State [1]

London, August 16, 1956—2 a.m.

Secto 5. I. Following is report of noon meeting between Secretary and Lloyd [2] attended by number of others on both sides. Lloyd had just received Shepilov and commented latter seemed recognize need some new plan meet Suez situation, appeared to accept Lloyd's statement that control Canal could not be placed under one man such as Nasser. Shepilov had not said what solution he might have in mind.

Secretary said he disturbed by news story speculating on difference between US and British-French positions. Secretary said he had put out statement denying this. [3] Suggested misleading story might have been attributable Indian Embassy Washington. Lloyd expressed satisfaction Secretary's statement and said in his broadcast had assumed US and UK stood together. Secretary commented that while he had not had opportunity review Lloyd's broadcast carefully, his impression from quick reading was that it very good. Referring to mention in Lloyd broadcast to United Nations, Secretary said this element should be included in tripartite statement of principles governing solution Suez problem. Believed it important however not bring UN into matter too early in view delays which would be involved. Suggested, and Lloyd agreed, that Phleger get together with French and British representatives to arrive at agreement upon paper setting forth principles. Re wording of agenda, [4] Lloyd agreed

---

[1] Source: Department of State, Central Files, 974.7301/8–1656. Top Secret; Priority; Limited Distribution. Drafted by Macomber. Received at 12:10 a.m.

[2] A memorandum by Rountree of this conversation, which took place on August 15 at the British Foreign Office, is *ibid.,* Conference Files: Lot 62 D 181, CF 745. Present at the meeting were: Dulles, Phleger, Bowie, McCardle, Barbour, and Rountree for the United States; and Lloyd, Caccia, Fitzmaurice, Ross, and other Foreign Office officials for the United Kingdom.

[3] During a Department of State press briefing on August 13, Department press officer Joseph Reap, in response to a question, noted that during the London tripartite conversations "the United States found itself in complete agreement with France and the United Kingdom that there should be international means to insure the practical and efficient functioning of the Canal as a free, open and secure international waterway in accordance with the Convention of 1888. The United States has not altered its view in this respect and is not aware of any difference in this matter between the British and French Governments and itself." (Department of State, *Daily News Conferences,* 1956)

[4] On August 13, the Embassy in London transmitted to the Department of State the texts of the rules of procedure and the agenda in telegram 865. (*Ibid.,* Central Files, 974.7301/8–1356) The text of the agenda reads as follows: "To decide whether, and if so what, steps should be taken to establish operating arrangements under an international system designed to assure the continuity of operation of the Suez Canal, as guaranteed by the convention of October 29, 1888, consistently with legitimate

with Secretary's suggestion that conference should "consider" a solution rather than "decide" upon a solution. Secretary believed that otherwise impression would be of imposing a solution upon Egypt without discussing with the latter. [5]

Lloyd raised question of chairmanship of Conference. Secretary believed would be wise to have permanent chairman other than Lloyd and give following reasons: 1) UK was looked upon with French as nation most deeply involved in controversies; 2) would be helpful if Lloyd would sit with British Delegation beside Secretary in order to discuss policy and tactics on continuing basis; 3) UK could express itself more strongly from floor as Lloyd as Foreign Minister could do this better than anyone else. Secretary thought Menzies might be best chairman. Lloyd stated that permanent chairman would not be elected before Friday and therefore still had further time to consider matter.

II. Secretary and Aldrich then met with Eden and Lloyd. [6] Eden assured Secretary that British do not intend move armor to Libya. [7] Present intention bring British forces in Libya up to strength by moving troops out of Malta, thus making room for further reinforcements there. Eden also said British have no intention taking military action against Egypt through Libya. Eden believed French may contemplate such action but would be impossible to do so.

Eden now thinking of utilizing economic sanctions against Nasser. Important thing would be deny Nasser revenues from Suez Canal. If such revenues could be put in outside bank and thus effectively denied to Nasser British believe his position would become untenable. Eden also said further economic sanctions being explored.

Re eventual use of force should that become necessary, British envision two possibilities: 1) convoying through the Canal; or 2) renouncing '54 Base Agreement and moving into base again.

Egyptian interests, and to deal with any necessary financial and other ancillary measures."

[5] On this point, the memorandum of conversation by Rountree reads: "The Secretary thought we would find strong sentiment that, in the absence of Egypt, the Conference could not 'decide' upon a solution, but could do no more than 'consider' one. The present terminology would make it appear that the Conference would be imposing a solution upon Egypt without discussion with the latter. He suggested that a way be found to avoid this, and thus perhaps preclude substantial opposition to the proposed rules and agenda."

[6] A memorandum of this conversation, which began at 12:30 p.m. August 15, by Aldrich, is in Department of State, Conference Files: Lot 62 D 181, CF 745.

[7] On August 9 Barbour reported to the Department that he had received the impression from various conversations with British officials that Libya was being given an important place in British military planning and might actually be envisaged as a principal point of departure if action against Egypt were undertaken. (Telegram 768 from London; *ibid.,* Central Files, 684A.86/8–956)

British reported Krishna Menon had urged that Lloyd be chairman of Conference and that India was prepared to endeavor to persuade Soviets accept Lloyd chairmanship. Queried on this, Secretary agreed US would support Lloyd candidacy, on understanding there would also be Executive Vice President to preside and enable Lloyd speak from floor.[8]

III. Immediately following this meeting, Secretary and Aldrich had lunch with Eden, Lloyd, Pineau and Chauvel.[9] During course of luncheon it was decided that US would speak first and table tripartite resolution. Copy will be cabled.

Secretary said he had been considering necessity of adopting new philosophy on nationalization of resources which are of concern to economies of number of countries. Believed a concessionary contract between sovereign state and private interest should entail same abridgement of sovereignty as is involved in contractual treaty between sovereign states when the resource covered by the concession is of major international economic concern. Secretary indicated he might develop this concept in course of present conference.

Dulles

---

[8] According to the memorandum of conversation by Aldrich, "Mr. Lloyd made clear that he had a strong desire to be President of the Conference so as to be able to take firm decisions. Secretary Dulles said of course he would go along with this, if after reflection it continued to be Mr. Lloyd's wish."

[9] A memorandum of this conversation, which began at 1 p.m., August 15, at 10 Downing Street, is in Department of State, Conference Files: Lot 62 D 181, CF 725. The document was prepared by the U.S. Delegation at the Suez Canal Conference, but it does not indicate a drafting officer.

85.   Telegram From the Embassy in the United Kingdom to the Department of State [1]

London, August 16, 1956—3 a.m.

Secto 6. Following uncleared summary Bohlen memo Secretary–Shepilov conversation 3:45 p.m., August 15, in Embassy. [2] Pouching cleared text.

After exchange amenities, Shepilov said he wished speak frankly to Secretary concerning difficult task they face this Conference. Secretary replied he welcomed frankness, since he considered that, although there were many difficulties between U.S. and U.S.S.R., he believed they agreed importance avoiding outbreak hostilities in Mid-East or any part of world, since full consequence of armed conflict could not be foreseen.

Shepilov said he agreed entirely on necessity peaceful negotiations. He added Soviet Union came to this Conference with no special interest, having no concessions of economic or other nature in Far [3] East and no intention of seeking any. He did not intend argue correctness or incorrectness Egypt's action or those U.K. and France assessing responsibility for present situation; important thing was to recognize that such situation exists. He said that recent U.S. statements led him believe U.S. had shared view that task here was to decrease tension and find peaceful settlement.

Shepilov stated his government view that under international law and historic precedent Egypt had right to nationalize Canal. He said he was not speaking here as to whether method had been proper or whether a more flexible form could not have been adopted.

The Secretary inquired whether Shepilov meant nationalization of Canal, itself, or of Company. Shepilov said he had Company in mind; that is, its privately-owned stock, assets, equipment, etc. He said denial Egypt's right nationalize Canal would be interference Egyptian internal affairs and would thereby aggravate situation, since it would arouse resentment not only in Egypt but other countries.

---

[1] Source: Department of State, Central Files, 974.7301/8–1656. Secret; Limit Distribution. Received at 12:47 a.m.

[2] The complete text of the memorandum of conversation by Bohlen is *ibid.*, Conference Files: Lot 62 D 181, CF 745. Present at the meeting, which began at 3:45 p.m., August 15, at the U.S. Embassy, were Dulles and Bohlen for the United States and Shepilov and his interpreter Oleg A. Troianovskii for the Soviet Union.

[3] The word "far" is omitted from this sentence in Bohlen's memorandum of conversation.

Shepilov said freedom of negotiation [*navigation*] of Canal was the problem for negotiation. Soviet Government realizes special UK and French interest in Canal. However, Soviet Union also uses Canal and expects increased use. Soviet Government believes economic sanctions, trends military preparations undertaken by UK and France not warranted and would not create necessary atmosphere for sober resolution matter. Some more flexible form must be sought based on reconciling rights Egypt and interests other countries in freedom Canal investigation [*navigation?*].

Shepilov said Soviets had already set forth disagreement with methods and composition this Conference. They felt composition did not abide by principles concerning signatories 1888 Convention or countries using Canal. He pointed out that without debating merits Egyptian attendance effect was that neither Egypt nor 24 other users of Canal represented London. Soviet Government had serious doubts whether it should come to such Conference, he repeated that task here was not to complicate work of even non-representative Conference but to find proper approach and added that even with present composition Conference could be useful.

Shepilov opined there seemed to be some common ground between US and USSR but certain differences between French and US positions. He said he did not raise this to attempt drive wedge between US, UK and France but that if this opinion true US and USSR together might find way out of this crisis.

Shepilov said that London Conference site not welcomed in East. Further report that UK might preside over talks might under present circumstances complicate situation. He asked if chairman from another country such as India might not have better effect among Eastern nations.

Shepilov said draft proposed procedures [4] seemed to him very strict and might have bad reception in certain areas of the world. He concluded by saying that Soviet Delegation would use all efforts to obtain fruitful discussion in calm atmosphere and felt that US was in position also to take calm objective approach. He said he would appreciate Secretary's views on tasks before Conference.

Secretary said he pleased Soviets had decided to attend Conference, that all his friends and associates did not agree with him and might be surprised to hear him say this. He said Minister had spoken of fact that Soviet Union had come to Conference with no special degree of self-interest. The US had some interests in the area and in the question at issue, if only for reason that U.S.-owned ships were second-largest category using Canal; and that they,

---

[4] Text in telegram 865 from London, August 13, not printed. (Department of State, Central Files, 974.7301/8–1356)

therefore, had interests in right of free navigation; however, U.S. did not have same dependency on Canal as U.K. or France and this enabled US to take somewhat calmer view. In this respect, there was to certain degree analogy between U.S. and U.S.S.R. attitudes. He stated that only purpose U.S. was to contribute to solution which while respecting reasonable rights and dignity Egypt as sovereign country would also assure to others exercise free navigation as indicated in 1888 Convention and to that purpose an efficient and fair operation of Canal.

He added that in U.S. there was large degree sympathy for U.K. and French positions, as well as strong feeling that every effort be made to promote peaceful solution, but that if fair and reasonable attempt this direction were rejected U.K. and France would have moral support of U.S. He added that honest people could differ as to what constituted reasonable and just proposal.

Secretary said that right of Egypt to cancel Suez Company concession 12 years before expiration raised serious doubts in U.S., but, as U.S. reserved position this point, he did not believe it profitable now to debate juridical aspects this matter. Secretary stated US purpose here was to find possible reasonable solution respecting rights and interests of both Egypt and U.K./France. He felt this agreed in principle with Shepilov's statement, namely, the need to reconcile rights of Egypt as sovereign state and interests of other countries vitally concerned in freedom navigation through Canal.

Secretary said that proposal circulated by three Western powers [5] was sufficiently flexible to encompass acceptable solution. He added that perhaps the word "authority" sounded worse than it really was (in Russian there is no comparable word for "authority" used in this sense). He said that he believed there could be no universal confidence in Egypt's ability alone to administer Canal operation. On details of how other participants could share administrative responsibility U.S. had open mind.

Secretary said U.S. completely agreed with U.K. and France they should not be forced rely only on Egyptian promises, which could be circumvented by methods very difficult to rectify by any international body. He did not think that Egypt had demonstrated that operation of Canal would be uninfluenced by its national considerations. He said most difficult aspect of problem was that some countries considered they could rely on Egyptian good will, others could not be expected to place much confidence in what perhaps best described as "ill will".

---

[5] Reference is to the "Proposal for the Establishment of an International Authority for the Suez Canal" transmitted in circular telegram 90, Document 63.

Secretary said attempt had been made to make Conference participation both representative and sufficiently limited so as to avoid interminable debate. Secretary outlined three principles on which participating countries had been invited. Secretary expanded explanation basis their invitations. He said that he did not mean to suggest formula perfect. But he wished to assure Minister that it had not been selected arbitrarily or without careful consideration.

As to the work and organization of the conference and, in particular, to Shepilov's remark re UK Chairman, Secretary said he thought it normal for host government to chair. He added he was aware of the considerations which Shepilov raised and could tell him in strictest confidence that he had taken up matter with UK today but as yet did not know their reply. He added that if UK Foreign Minister felt that normal precedent must be followed US would not oppose nor seek any different result. Shepilov agreed it impolite to question views of inviting country and added that if UK wished chairmanship Soviet Delegation did not intend officially to raise question.

Secretary said he appreciated Shepilov's point of view and agreed with him on "discourtesy". Shepilov added that event UK did not wish the chair they might discuss suitable chairman since in many ways he would prefer experienced UK chairman instead of "chudak" (roughly Russian equivalent of "screwball"). If UK did not take chair he suggested Krishna Menon might be suitable. Secretary agreed that if there was to be consideration of chairman other than UK, country and individual should be subject of US–USSR consultation.

In closing, Secretary observed it would be interesting experience to attend Conference at which US and USSR were not principal powers in dispute. He thanked Shepilov for frank presentation and clear outline his views and said that he had tried to be equally frank. Shepilov said he hoped during this conference it would be possible to have additional meetings this nature, to which Secretary agreed.

Dulles

86.   Message From the Secretary of State to the President [1]

London, August 16, 1956.

DEAR MR. PRESIDENT: I have had a busy first day. [2] I met with Selwyn Lloyd at the Foreign Office and then had lunch with Anthony and Pineau at 10 Downing Street. The atmosphere on the whole is much more composed than two weeks ago. There is I think a growing realization of the magnitude of the task of military intervention and of the inadequacies of their military establishments to take on a real fighting job of this size. Ambassador Dillon, who is here, tells me that the French are beginning to be quite sobered by their military inadequacy. [3] I do not mean to imply that they may not take the plunge if things go badly here, but they are much less apt to do so than two weeks ago. Also the domestic opposition has been growing.

After lunch I met successively with Foreign Minister Martino of Italy, Foreign Minister Artajo of Spain, Foreign Minister Shepilov of the Soviet Union and Krishna Menon of India. [4] I had good talks with the first three. Menon was unusually vague and little emerged except his desire to act as intermediary between the Western powers and Egypt.

Both Martino and Artajo are prepared to take a much less measure [*sic*] of international participation in operations than seems to the British, French and ourselves to be essential if there is to be any really effective assurance of efficient and impartial operation.

The talk with Shepilov was the most interesting. He made a very frank and orderly presentation of the problem and of his country's position. It was the best statement I have ever received

---

[1] Source: Department of State, Central Files, 684A.86/8–1556. Secret. Transmitted to the Department of State in Dulte 1 from Paris, 1 a.m., which is the source text, with the instruction "Eyes only Acting Secretary for President from Secretary". Dulte 1 was received at 11:15 p.m. A copy is in the Eisenhower Library, Whitman File, Dulles–Herter Series.

[2] August 15.

[3] In telegram 771 from Paris, August 13, Ambassador Dillon informed the Department of State that during a conversation, French Defense Minister Bourgès-Maunoury had stressed the difficulty of the military problem faced by the French and British. The Defense Minister had noted that the British had not yet decided whether the objective of the campaign should be to seize the Canal or to occupy Egypt. He added that the British had no aircraft capable of operating over Egypt from Cyprus modern enough to challenge Soviet MIGs. (Department of State, Central Files, 974.7301/8–1356)

[4] Secto 3 from London, August 16, contains an account of Dulles' separate conversations with Martino and Artajo. (*Ibid.*, 974.7301/8–1656) Secto 2 from London, August 16, contains a brief account of Dulles' conversation with Menon. (*Ibid.*) Separate memoranda of the three conversations are *ibid.*, Conference Files: Lot 62 D 181, CF 745.

from any Soviet Foreign Minister. He made clear that his government was disposed to support the Egyptian view that there could not be any active international role in operations, but he indicated that he would like to try to work with US for some positive solution. A summary of our talk is being cabled to the Department and the full text is being pouched. Either or both might be worth your looking at. [5]

The Conference proper starts tomorrow. Probably Selwyn Lloyd will be permanent chairman because he seems desperately to want it and because no one wants to seem discourteous in opposing it. Probably we shall have considerable trouble over the rules of procedure which are a bit on the tight side. We may thus not get down to the merits until Friday [6]—where the lines will be rather sharply drawn between those who are willing to rely upon Egyptian promises with some theoretical right of appeal to an international body, perhaps the UN, and the US–UK–French view that there should be actual international operation of the Canal so as to assure it will be non-political in character. At the moment it looks as though the former view has the majority, but it is too soon to forecast with any confidence.

Faithfully yours,

Foster [7]

---

[5] A copy of Secto 6 from London, *supra*, is in the Eisenhower Library, Whitman File, Dulles–Herter Series; but it bears no indication as to whether Eisenhower read it.
[6] August 17.
[7] Dulte 1 bears this typed signature.

87.   Editorial Note

The Suez Canal Conference (also known as the 22-Power London Conference) met in London August 16-23. Of the 24 nations invited by the United Kingdom to the Conference only Egypt and Greece declined the invitation. The 22 nations which sent representatives to the Conference were: Australia, Ceylon, Denmark, Ethiopia, the Federal Republic of Germany, France, India, Indonesia, Iran, Italy, Japan, the Netherlands, New Zealand, Norway, Pakistan, Portugal, Spain, Sweden, Turkey, the United Kingdom, the Union of Soviet Socialist Republics, and the United States. While the Government of Egypt refused to participate formally in the Conference, the Chief of Nasser's Political Cabinet, Ali Sabri, was in London August 19–22, acting as an unofficial observer. An unsigned memorandum, dated August 23, contains a brief summary of Sabri's activities, the summary having been forwarded to the Department of State by the CIA. According to the memorandum, Sabri spent most of his time attempting to influence other delegations, especially those from Asian countries. (Department of State, State–JCS Meetings: Lot 61 D 417, Omega #10) No indication has been found in Department of State files that Sabri spoke with United States officials while he was in London.

The membership of the United States Delegation to the Suez Canal Conference was as follows: United States Representative— John Foster Dulles; Special Assistant to the Representative—John W. Hanes; Coordinator of the delegation—William B. Macomber; Senior Advisers—Winthrop W. Aldrich, Herman Phleger, Gordon Gray, Carl W. McCardle, Robert R. Bowie, Charles E. Bohlen, C. Douglas Dillon, William M. Rountree, and Walworth Barbour; Advisers— Andrew H. Berding, Don C. Bliss, William C. Burdett, Jr., W. Bradley Connors, Andrew B. Foster, Dayton S. Mak, Stanley D. Metzger, Edwin G. Moline, Arthur R. Ringwalt, William R. Tyler, and Evan M. Wilson; Special Assistant to the Coordinator—J. Steward Cottman; Assistants—Roger Kirk and Frank E. Maestrone. For a list of the chief delegates at the Conference, see *The Suez Canal Problem, July 26–September 22, 1956,* pages xii–xiii.

The papers of the United States Delegation are contained in Department of State, Conference Files: Lot 61 D 181. Included are daily chronologies and schedules; position papers; verbatim minutes of the eight plenary sessions prepared by the United States Delegation; memoranda of conversations and other numbered documents prepared by the United States Delegation; copies of Secto, Tosec, Dulte, and Tedul telegrams sent between London and the Department of State; administrative papers; and miscellaneous papers. This collection also contains copies of records kept by the Conference's International Secretariat, including a verbatim record of the eight plenary sessions. An edited version of the verbatim record prepared by the International Secretariat, which contains all of the substantive statements made during the eight plenary sessions, as well as supporting documents, is printed in *The Suez Canal Problem, July 26–September 22, 1956,* pages 255–293.

---

88.   Telegram From the Delegation at the Suez Canal Conference to the Department of State [1]

London, August 16, 1956—8 p.m.

Secto 10. First session opened 11:10 am, Wednesday, August 16, with Eden greeting. UK Foreign Secretary Lloyd then took chair and Sweden proposed him as chairman. Iran seconded proposal. Soviet Union said it had "no basis for formal objection" to proposal but if for any reason UK reluctant, suggested India would seem appropriate choice. India supported nomination Lloyd and Pakistan also extended support.

Lloyd as chairman then suggested Conference not approve formal set rules procedure, but abide by procedures governing sessions main UN committees, in which the chairman's rulings subject challenge and vote. [2] Secretary observed that under UN procedures chairman's ruling stands unless overruled by majority.

India expressed general agreement but made clear could not agree accept majority vote substantive issues and that chair's decisions must apply exclusively to procedural and not substantive

[1] Source: Department of State, Central Files, 974.7301/8–1656. Secret. Drafted by Tyler. Received at 5:40 p.m.

[2] That same day, the Embassy in London informed the Department in Secto 12 that: "As a result of the negative attitude of the delegations, especially the Scandinavians, Lloyd called the Secretary before the 11:00 o'clock first plenary session this morning to say that they had decided not to press for the adoption of the draft rules of procedure (Secto 5). Instead, they proposed merely to operate on the general basis of ruling by the chairman guided by the practice in the United Nations committees. This was the position stated by Lloyd at the 11:00 o'clock first plenary session and adopted after a limited discussion." (*Ibid.,* 974.7301/8–1656) Secto 5 is printed as Document 84.

issues. Following question by UK whether this meant that Conference could not come to any decision, Soviet Union developed lengthy propaganda.

Criticisms irregularity and arbitrary character Conference and process selection membership, concluding with professed intention be helpful find approach peaceful settlement problem. Said Conference should reach agreed opinion on question holding another international Conference, or some other agreed process for solution Suez problem. Lloyd rejected Soviet criticisms in tone moderation. Indonesia expressed support Indian position. France then reviewed and defended circumstances summoning Conference and explicitly justified presence Federal Government Germany. Said object Conference not condemn Egypt or undertake military measures against any country. Asked India consider agreeing vote on any substantive issue which might seem appropriate to purpose Conference.

Italy supported Indian position regarding voting and said Conference should choose means of approach to peaceful solution problem. Ceylon also supported Indian position and said that Conference should not begin work on basis of decision that vote would have to be taken, asking what purpose holding vote if outcome not to be binding.

Chairman agreed no one would be bound by majority vote and suggested Conference proceed with its work and "See how things go".

India reiterated position and opposition to voting in absence Egypt. Soviet Union did same and said purpose Conference work toward creation united opinion. Chairman said he had submitted no proposal to Conference but only wanted to get rid procedural matters and pass on to substance, and then asked whether Conference needed agenda at all. India suggested no agenda and this view was supported Secretary Dulles. Conference agreed adjourn and meet again 1500 hours Thursday, and Friday and Saturday afternoon sessions only from 2:45 to 4:45 and from 5:15 to 7:15 pm.

Dulles

89.   Message From the Secretary of State to the President[1]

London, August 16, 1956.

DEAR MR. PRESIDENT: We have just completed the first day of the Conference other than a formal dinner tonight.

The morning was spent in getting over procedural hurdles. This afternoon we started on the substance of the matter, and I made the initial presentation of the US position.[2] This was the only full-scale speech of the day, and it apparently made a good impression, at least in some quarters, although I have no doubt that the reception in the Arab world will be bad. Von Brentano said, "We should have voted right after your speech and then we could all have gone home."

Foreign Minister Unden of Sweden spoke briefly supporting generally our tripartite position. Other brief speakers were Portugal, Italy and Indonesia. The Indonesian Foreign Minister[3] spoke in favor of the abrogation of international agreements on the ground that most of them did not adequately recognize human aspirations. I imagine that he was prompted more by Indonesia's abrogation of its agreements with the Netherlands than by the Canal situation itself.[4]

I think we have gotten off to a reasonably good start although the Soviet and Indian delegations have not shown their hand, and their position will give a clue to whether there is a fair chance of getting an agreement with Egypt which could be accepted. There is increasing evidence that the British and French, as they study the

---

[1] Source: Department of State, Central Files, 396.1–LO/8–1656. Secret. Transmitted to the Department of State Priority as Dulte 4 from London, August 16, 6 p.m., which is the source text, with the instruction: "Eyes only Acting Secretary for President from Secretary." The telegram was received at 3:36 p.m. A copy is in the Eisenhower Library, Whitman File, Dulles–Herter Series.

[2] Reference is to the statement made by Dulles at the second plenary session, which began at approximately 3 p.m., August 16. The text of Dulles' statement was transmitted to the Department of State in Secto 8 from London, August 16. (Department of State, Central Files, 974.7301/8–1656) A report on the remainder of the second session was transmitted in Secto 11 from London, August 16. (*Ibid.*) Dulles' statement is printed in Department of State *Bulletin,* August 27, 1956, pp. 335–339.

[3] Roeslan Abdulgani.

[4] In February 1956, Indonesia abrogated portions of the 1949 Round Table Agreements (relating to Indonesia independence), signed by the Indonesian and Dutch Governments. On August 4, 1956, the Indonesian Government announced the repudiation of its debts to the Netherlands, which Indonesia had assumed under these agreements.

logistics of their planned operation, are feeling the need for time for preparation.

Faithfully yours,

Foster Dulles [5]

---

[5] Dulte 4 bears this typed signature.

90.　Telegram From the Delegation at the Suez Canal Conference to the Department of State [1]

London, August 17, 1956—9 p.m.

Secto 15. Secretary met this morning with Menzies, Pineau, Eden and Lloyd [2] to discuss general tactics. Understood that Pineau will speak this afternoon's plenary session. Shepilov also indicated to Eden that he would wish speak today. Consensus was that general debate should if possible be completed Saturday, understood that Menzies would endeavor to be last speaker so that he can draw general summary and be in position respond particularly to speeches by USSR, India, Indonesia and Ceylon. Lloyd plans principal speech for UK in course Saturday session.

Secretary said he had been giving considerable thought to type of declaration or resolution which should be submitted to Conference. [3] He wanted to have ample time to discuss paper. He was thinking of declaration in terms so couched as to get maximum number of subscribers, consistent with basic principles for settlement included in his August 16 speech. He wondered whether best procedure might then be to seek the designation of committee which would be charged with negotiations with Egypt pursuant to general

---

[1] Source: Department of State, Central Files, 974.7301/8–1756. Secret; Priority. Drafted by Rountree. Received at 5:55 p.m.

[2] According to the schedule for August 17, prepared by the U.S. Delegation, the Secretary's calls on Eden, Pineau and Menzies, and Lloyd began at 12:15 p.m. The chronology, prepared by the U.S. Delegation for that date, indicated Secto 15 is the only account of these conversations. (*Ibid.*, Conference Files: Lot 62 D 181, CF 753)

[3] Draft proposals were discussed at meetings of the British-French-American working group on August 14 and 16. For accounts of the discussion, see memorandum by First Secretary of the Embassy in London Evan Wilson, August 14 (*ibid.*, Central Files, 974.7301/8–1556) and USDel/MC/17, August 16 (*ibid.*, Conference Files: Lot 62 D 181, CF 745).

declaration, suspending present Conference to give committee time to negotiate.

Consensus appeared favor this general procedure. Arrangements made for staff level and then high-level US–UK–France–Australian meeting tomorrow to go over draft declaration which Secretary undertook provide. Pineau suggested that declaration should not be too weak. He said that immediately after general debate Secretary might table paper Saturday evening in order provide opportunity delegates to study it over weekend and discuss it Monday. Secretary questioned advisability US taking sole responsibility for tabling "tough text" which inevitably would be watered-down. This would place US in awkward position since any subsequent modification would appear represent defeat. Moreover he had been talking with several delegates (this morning with Iranian and Pakistani) [4] who were anxious to be helpful but who had domestic political preoccupations which must be met without sacrificing basic principles. He did not want to ride "rough-shod" over their objections to a strong line. Papers should take reasonably into account their views in order to rally as much support as possible from the outset and avoid subsequent softening process.

Menzies observed that it is frequently dangerous to endeavor too much of a definition, but that inclusion in proposal of certain points of definition might improve prospects for general acceptance. He had in mind questions of who would arrange for payment to Suez Canal Company and who would arrange financing future development of Suez Canal. Answer to these questions, he said might turn attitude of several countries like Pakistan and India to support proposal. If international body could assume responsibility, advantages to Egypt would appear very great and it obviously in Egypt's interest to accept. He strongly favored this approach in lieu any indication of harsh proposition to be forced upon Egypt.

Secretary thought question of payments to Suez Canal Company and investments in development Canal itself were primarily matters for negotiation by committee with GOE and Canal Company. He felt however that international board should have responsibility for both matters. Menzies agreed and felt this would offer advantages to GOE that government could not refuse. Plan should make it clear that international board would be non-profit and that arrangements would be made by international board for compensation to Company and future of Canal.

---

[4] The conversation between Dulles and Pakistani Foreign Minister Choudhury began at 10:30 a.m., and the one with Iranian Foreign Minister Ardalan at 11:30 a.m., both on August 17. Memoranda of these conversations, prepared by the U.S. Delegation, are *ibid.*, CF 753.

Secretary observed that financing future development of Canal, including parallel Canal, might be quite feasible if Canal users could have confidence in its operation. He thought oil companies and other users might be prepared put up considerable capital to be amortized out of proceeds. On other hand if responsibility for operation should continue rest with Egypt countries would in common prudence seek alternatives to Canal which eventually would be by-passed for most part and become wasting asset.

Responding Lloyd's comment that offer should not be too attractive so that it would appear that Egypt had greatly benefited by her rash action, Eden observed that no one would think that if international control were injected. Secretary agreed saying that acceptance international control by Nasser would represent major political defeat for him.

Pineau observed that in addition other important questions, was that of who would be responsible for policing of Canal under arrangements now being thought about. He said that treaty might have clause to effect that any interruption in transit of Canal would be considered act of aggression as defined in UN Charter, and thus provide basis for protection.

Dulles

---

91.   Message From the Secretary of State to the President [1]

London, August 17, 1956.

DEAR MR. PRESIDENT: The principal feature of today's meeting [2] was the presentation by the Soviet Foreign Minister. It contained no surprises, being generally along the lines of the Soviet statement issued at the time they announced acceptance of the invitation to come here. There was, however, unmistakable emphasis upon features designed to appeal to the Asian countries, namely, right of

---

[1] Source: Department of State, Central Files, 396.1–LO/8–1756. Secret. Transmitted to the Department of State in Dulte 7 from London, August 17, 9 p.m., which is the source text, with the instruction "Eyes only Acting Secretary for President from Secretary". The telegram was received at 5:11 p.m.

[2] Reference is to the third plenary session, which convened at approximately 3 p.m., August 17. Summary accounts of this two-part session are in Sectos 16 and 17 from London, August 17 and 18, respectively. (*Ibid.*, 974.7301/8–1756 and 974.7301/8–1856, respectively)

nationalization, sanctity of sovereignty, elimination of the remnants of colonialism, etc.

The other speakers were favorable to our position, and the New Zealand and Turkish Foreign Ministers [3] made particularly strong and able presentations. Japan was non-committal, and Spain put in a proposal designed to be a compromise between our position and the expected Egyptian position as regards external participation in management.

We shall probably conclude the debate tomorrow, and at its close I shall be ready to put in a US paper which we are concerting with the British and the French. Also Menzies is taking an active part, as Eden has asked him to be available to serve on the negotiating committee with Egypt, assuming one is created, in lieu of the UK itself serving.

It looks as though, of the twenty-two participating countries, twelve can be counted on to back proposals along the lines we have in mind, six will almost surely be against and four are on the fence. The danger is that the ultimate line-up will be almost entirely the West on one side and Asia on the other side with the Soviet Union on the Asian side. The governments of Iran and Pakistan are friendly, but popular sentiment is so much with Egypt that the governments hesitate to seem to commit themselves to a course which seems anti-Egyptian. This is not what we would like, but also it is not unexpected.

Next week will probably be the pay-off, and before it is over there will be some smoke-filled rooms like Chicago and San Francisco.

Faithfully yours,

Foster [4]

---

[3] Thomas L. Macdonald and Nuri Birgi, respectively.
[4] Dulte 7 bears this typed signature.

92.   Telegram From the Department of State to the Secretary of State, at London [1]

Washington, August 17, 1956—8:14 p.m.

Tedul 8. Eyes only Secretary from Acting Secretary.

1. The President has followed your messages from London with the greatest interest and has asked me to express to you his confidence and appreciation. I will take your Dulte 7, [2] which has just arrived, to the White House tomorrow morning.

2. I discussed the proposed Saudi visit with the President last evening and he concurred on the advisability of having Bob Anderson go out as soon as possible. [3] He would, of course, welcome a Saudi visit after his return to Washington, but he did not want to have it going on during your London conference. Bob advises that he can probably leave on short notice and will give me a final answer tomorrow morning. We have a plane standing by.

3. Today I got word through Azzam Pasha that the King was extremely unhappy about Nasser, but was hesitant to oppose him openly at this time. This situation may ultimately prove to be the break we have been looking for.

[Here follows discussion of unrelated matters.]

Hoover

---

[1] Source: Department of State, Central Files, 974.7301/8–1756. Top Secret. Drafted and approved by Hoover who initialed the telegram.

[2] Dulte 7 transmitted the message *supra.*

[3] On August 16, Saudi Arabian Ambassador Sheikh Abdullah al-Khayyal informed Acting Secretary Hoover that King Saud wanted to convey certain observations in view of the grave situation in the Middle East and wished to know if a Saudi Arabian delegation headed by a Saudi prince might visit the United States immediately to convey them. The Saudi Ambassador added that the King was principally concerned about Suez and wished to cooperate with the United States. Hoover offered his personal thought that a visit by a Saudi delegation to the United States at this moment would cause great press speculation and wondered whether a visit to Saudi Arabia by a U.S. representative might be preferable. (Telegram 102 to Jidda, August 16; *ibid.*, 974.7301/8–1656) Subsequently, Dulles indicated his agreement. (Secto 14 from London, August 17; *ibid.*, 974.7301/8–1756)

93.   Memorandum of a Conversation, Soviet Embassy,
London, August 18, 1956, 11 a.m. [1]

USDel/MC/34

PARTICIPANTS

The United States	*Soviet Union*
The Secretary of State	Mr. Shepilov
Mr. Bohlen	Mr. Troyanovski

SUBJECTS DISCUSSED

Suez Conference

After an exchange of amenities the Secretary inquired what was Mr. Shepilov's opinion concerning the Conference.

Mr. Shepilov replied that it was difficult at the present time to come to any real evaluation, the first moves had been made and now the question was how to conclude the Conference with some result. He felt a great deal depended on Mr. Dulles and he ventured to conclude from Mr. Dulles' speech that the United States took a flexible approach which he felt marked some difference from the three-power statement of August 2 [2] in that he felt that the United States approach was less categorical in regard to an International Body to run the Canal. But there had been some points in the United States position which were not clear to him. For example, he did not understand what was meant by a non-political body and wondered if this meant an association of ship owners. Also the form of relationship with the United Nations was not clear. He had noted with great satisfaction, however, Mr. Dulles' statement that any solution must be just and acceptable to all. He felt that this was correct and gave hope for a positive result of the Conference. He said he was ready to discuss with Mr. Dulles the work of the Conference and to answer any questions concerning the Soviet attitude.

The Secretary said Mr. Shepilov was correct in understanding that our attitude was flexible to a considerable degree. He wished, however, to make clear that on one substantive aspect our attitude was not flexible and that was that the Canal could not be left under the exclusive control and operation of Egypt. He had not wished in any speech at the Conference to say anything which might reflect on Egypt, but that our sentiments had been well expressed by the New

---

[1] Source: Department of State, Conference Files: Lot 62 D 181, CF 754. Secret. Prepared by the U.S. Delegation at the Suez Canal Conference, but the source text does not indicate a drafting officer. Approved by Dulles on August 18.

[2] Document 53.

Zealand representative when he said that there could be no confidence in the political stability of Egypt, or that its Government was sufficiently removed from political passions and ambitions as to assure that under exclusive Egyptian control the Canal would not be used as an instrument of Egyptian policy. Even today ships carrying food to Israel encounter great difficulties in going through the Canal and similar discrimination could be employed against the ships of any country in the future if Egypt had exclusive control over the Canal. It was necessary to find means to insure that the Canal would not be used as an instrument of Egyptian national policy or of the national policy of any country. Any nation in complete control could find ways of discrimination which would be impossible to prevent or rectify through any board of appeal or similar advisory body. He mentioned that at the present time there seemed to be a high degree of illness among British and French pilots on the Canal. In reply to Mr. Shepilov's observation that this was not Egypt's fault, the Secretary said he had cited it as an example of the type of possibility which must be guarded against. If it were British and French pilots at the present time, under Egyptian control it could be Egyptian pilots, and it would be hardly feasible to call a session of the General Assembly to determine whether these pilots were really sick. As another illustration he outlined the operation of an airfield under which the person in the control tower, particularly in bad weather, could by innumerable, undetectable means discriminate against one airplane in favor of another. Similar undetectable discriminations could be employed in the operation of the Canal. He went on to say that none of us could with confidence state that Col. Nasser was not ambitious and could be counted on not to use the Canal to further his ambitions, and in any event, if not Nasser, there could be no guarantee concerning the actions of future Egyptian leaders. Therefore he felt that an international highway, upon which the economic life of so many nations literally depended, placed upon those at this Conference a duty to insulate the Canal from international politics. It is possible that in the past there had been too much Western political influence, but it would hardly be an improvement if it were made an instrument of Egyptian politics. In regard to Mr. Shepilov's question he could say that by "non-political body" he did not mean a private body of ship owners, but operation under the direction of countries divorced from political interest in the area but which did have an interest and confidence in shipping matters, such as, for example, Sweden. In regard to connection with the United Nations he had thought that, for example, the General Assembly might select the countries responsible for the operation of the Canal under a Treaty which would lay down the guiding principles such as equitable geographic representation and absence of political motivation in the area. It should be made clear that there would be no interference with Egyptian sovereignty but that this body would deal only with the technical side. He then referred to the sentence in Mr. Shepilov's speech of yesterday which referred to international cooperation in safe-guarding the operation of the Canal and said that he felt that within the spirit and language of that paragraph a bridge might be built by the United States and Soviet positions which would be a good thing not only for this Conference but for the future of the world. At this Conference, as he had said before, for the first time the United States and the USSR were not the principal antagonists and if they could reach an agreement it would be a very good sign. In conclusion he said that this was a situation which would not remain static and if the Conference could not find an agreed solution, it would become chaotic. He said other questions upon which agreement had not been possible had not been of this nature, and while their failure had been unfortunate there was at least a status quo which could be maintained without chaos resulting from the failure to agree. He did not wish to suggest that armed force would be used since he felt that it was never useful to confront nations or conferences with the threat of force and United States influence has been and continues to be in the direction of peaceful solution. But he did not believe that our two countries either separately or jointly could guarantee that passions and clashes might not arise in the area in the event that the Conference came to nothing. There was one other question also which had been submerged by the Suez strife but which should never be forgotten, and that was the Israeli-Arab conflict. Incidents had begun to flare up again and could easily touch off hostilities since one side or the other might try to seek advantage for itself during the present crisis.

He said the possibility of hostilities was the worst aspect of the situation and the United States was devoting all its efforts to preventing such an occurrence. But even if hostilities were avoided the situation would not be good and there would remain grave tensions and uncertainties. He mentioned that if the economic blood stream of so many nations was poisoned, they would be forced to seek alternate means of satisfying their vital economic needs. For example, the United States could produce without difficulty and speedily a great deal more oil (about 1 million barrels a day), as could Western Canada, but that this increased production would interfere with the pattern of world economic life and would furthermore tend to separate East and West when all efforts should be in the opposite direction. He concluded by saying that he had given a full and frank exposition of the problem as he saw it.

Mr. Shepilov said he appreciated very much Mr. Dulles' confidence and frankness and he would also be candid. He did not exclude the possibility of a rapprochement between the positions of the US and the USSR, and that such a rapprochement would have a positive effect on the whole situation. He also agreed that a bridge between them would be a happy possibility leading to a revival of the spirit of Geneva which they had all welcomed. It would be an unforgivable mistake to neglect the opportunity afforded at this conference not only for the relations between their two countries, but for the whole cause of world peace.

He felt they were witnessing a favorable evolution of British and French thinking on the Suez problem which he felt resulted from two factors: 1) the influence of world opinion including opinion in Britain and France; and, 2) the restraining, in the good sense of the word, influence of the United States. He found evidence of this evolution in the recognition not only of public opinion but in responsible British officials that the use of force would be disastrous and that a settlement by peaceful means was necessary. He found further evidence in the fact that there seemed to be no longer any question of the restoration of the old regime for the Canal nor of questioning the Egyptian act of nationalization. He felt that the British were exercising common sense. The current question was what should the conference do next, and as he saw it the chief problem was that of guarantees concerning the functioning of the Canal. And, he felt many here were showing goodwill and desire to meet Egypt halfway, but they were likewise interested in the question of what guarantees could be obtained. He felt this aspect could not be ignored. This was even more so since the Egyptian Government and Colonel Nasser had obviously been influenced by passion, had shown intemperance, and had even made mistakes. While he could understand the feelings of the Arabs towards the Jews, he felt that some of their actions, and in particular, the prohibition of the passage of Israeli ships through the Canal, had aroused mistrust which could have been avoided had Egypt shown greater political maturity. Mr. Dulles is quite right in saying that the question does not relate only to Colonel Nasser's personal qualifications since the settlement they should seek here would obtain for scores of years. The question, therefore, is how to safeguard the interests of other countries in the free navigation of the Canal and not encroach on Egypt's sovereign rights. It would be useful to keep in mind clearly on what basis guarantees had rested in the past. A private company based on a concession operated the Canal but it was the Convention of 1888 which dealt with the guarantee of free navigation. However, the 1888 Convention did not envisage nor provide any mechanism for sanctions. It was the instrument of guarantee since the private company could not deal with this question. Therefore, he felt they should seek to devise a more perfect instrument of guarantee than the 1888 Convention, either through amendment or a new Convention. He said he wished to make a few general observations which he hoped Mr. Dulles would note carefully. He had twice been in Egypt and in other Arab countries during the past year and he wished to tell Mr. Dulles of his deep conviction of the strength of the upsurge of national feelings in those countries. Anything that appeared to disregard their national feelings or to smack of colonialism was greeted with great sensitivity. He knew that the United States, with no colonial heritage in the area, could take a more objective view of the situation. This aspect of the problem was very important for the solution of the problem of the Suez Canal. He was deeply convinced that if at this conference or any other the position is taken for the international operation of the Canal, Egypt and other countries in the area would view that as an attempt to restore the old colonial system and far from producing tranquility in the area we should contribute to a deepening of the contradictions and bring about an increase of troubles. Therefore, instead of international operation with Egyptian participation he felt a better formula would be Egyptian operation with participation of countries concerned in order to guarantee their interests and the proper use of the Canal. This abstract formula could be filled in with different concrete proposals, but he felt the task was to give it content which would be just and acceptable to all concerned. He felt there were two organizational questions: 1) the drawing up of a new Convention which would have no trace of colonialism but would be based on the principle of free navigation and guarantees to insure this with respect for the sovereign rights of Egypt; 2) a mechanism for operating the Canal on the basis of the formula of Egyptian operation with the participation of other interested countries. He could not go into detail and felt that at the present stage to seek to work out all the provisions without the participation of Egypt would not be possible, but the principle of Egyptian operation with participation of other countries for the purpose of guaranteeing the free and efficient functioning of the Canal was the correct line. He said he would support also the idea of some relationship with the UN. He felt also there was a possibility of finding common ground between the US and Soviet positions.

As to Israel, he continued, he felt this situation was not hopeless and that when the atmosphere became calmer it might be something that could be discussed. But he felt there were no insuperable obstacles to a future settlement. He concluded by saying that he now understood what the Secretary meant by non-political operation which could be discussed when they came to consider mechanisms. He then inquired how Mr. Dulles envisaged bringing to an end the work of the conference.

The Secretary said first of all he would like to comment on some of Mr. Shepilov's observations before coming to that question. He agreed there had been an important evolution in British and French thinking; that two or three weeks ago when he was here they had been prepared to take precipitate action but that now calmer views were prevailing. In fact, it had been his hope that the present conference, which had not been immediately acceptable to his associates, would produce just that result. He felt, however, that it would be a mistake to conclude that if this conference found no solution or, more accurately, envisaged no prospect of solution, the danger had entirely passed. It should also be recognized that even though the US might disagree with certain views of the British and French, should those countries become engaged in the long run they could count on US moral support and possibly more than moral support. Mr. Shepilov had correctly pointed out that the Convention of 1888 does not in itself provide mechanism for enforcing its guarantees. In the past the entire system had rested on three elements: 1) the Convention of 1888; 2) the Suez Company; and 3) the actual presence of Great Britain in Egypt and subsequently in the Canal Zone. Two of these elements have disappeared and he agreed that the Convention of 1888 needed to be supplemented or replaced. He also agreed that what they should do in this regard should be of a lasting nature since they could not continue to have recurring crises since this placed too great a strain on the fabric of peace. Mr. Shepilov then inquired what was Mr. Dulles' attitude in regard to the formula of Egyptian operation with the participation of other countries.

The Secretary replied he would wish to think about this; that it has possibilities but it would be premature for him to express an opinion. It was a serious suggestion and he would give it serious attention. As to the end of the conference, he said it was the present purpose of the United States delegation to formulate today and tomorrow for possible submission to the conference on Monday a document which would endeavor to reflect the views expressed in his speech with such adaptations as might be suitable taking into account the views and suggestions made by other members of the conference including those of Mr. Shepilov. He said this would lead to further discussion at the conference leading towards the initiation of negotiation with Egypt on behalf of those countries who accepted these principles, but not on behalf, of course, of those who did not.

The Secretary concluded that he felt it might be useful over this weekend to maintain contact, with which Mr. Shepilov expressed complete agreement.

94.   Message From the Secretary of State to the President [1]

London, August 18, 1956.

DEAR MR. PRESIDENT: We have finished the "General Debate" today [2] except for Menon, who refused to speak although there was ample time because he wants to do something special apart from the rest, and we will probably hear from him on Monday.

In the meantime we have finally worked out with the British and the French a draft of concrete proposal which we will be quietly circulating to the other delegations tonight and on Sunday. [3] We expect to introduce it formally sometime Monday afternoon. It will go in as a U.S. paper and not a tripartite paper as I felt it wiser to have the control of the situation which goes with its being a U.S. paper. Also I believe it will be more acceptable as such. This is also the view of our British and French friends.

More important than the formal proceedings today was the talk of an hour and a half which I had with Shepilov [4] this morning. It was a frank and businesslike talk on both sides, or at least I know it was on my side, and it seemed to be so on his side. I feel that the Soviets would be open to making some kind of an arrangement with us and perhaps join to impose it upon Egypt if on the one hand it were couched in a way which would not gravely prejudice the Soviet Union with the Arab world and if on the other hand we would more or less make it a two-party affair with some downgrading of the British and the French. I doubt whether Soviet agreement is worth having at that price but I shall do everything possible short of disloyalty to the British and the French to get Soviet agreement.

We have no meeting tomorrow, and while I have plenty to do, I hope at least to get to church and to have lunch in the country.

Faithfully yours,

Foster [5]

---

[1] Source: Department of State, Central Files, 396.1–LO/8–1856. Secret. Transmitted to the Department of State in Dulte 10 from London, August 18, 9 p.m., which is the source text, with the instruction "Eyes only Acting Secretary for President from Secretary". The telegram was received at 6:14 p.m. A copy is in the Eisenhower Library, Whitman File, Dulles–Herter Series.

[2] Reference is to the fourth plenary session which convened at 2:45 p.m., August 18. A summary account of the meeting is in Secto 19 from London, August 18. (Department of State, Central Files, 974.7301/8–1856)

[3] See Secto 20, *infra.*

[4] See the memorandum of conversation, *supra.*

[5] Dulte 10 bears this typed signature.

95.   Telegram From the Delegation at the Suez Canal Conference to the Department of State [1]

London, August 18, 1956—11 p.m.

Secto 20. Secretary today reached agreement with UK and French Foreign Ministers on following text draft USA Declaration. Copies this Declaration being discreetly circulated tonight to delegation heads all participating nations. Secretary now plans formally submit declaration at fifth plenary Monday afternoon as US paper.

Selected officers assigned liaison task personally to follow up with other delegations Sunday.

Begin text:

London Conference on the Suez Canal
U.S.A. Proposal for a Declaration
The govts approving this Declaration, being participants in the London conference on the Suez Canal;

Concerned by the grave situation regarding the Suez Canal;

Determined to seek a peaceful solution in conformity with the purposes and principles of the United Nations; and recognizing that an adequate solution must, on the one hand, respect the sovereignty and rights of Egypt and, on the other hand, safeguard the Suez Canal as an international waterway in accordance with the Suez Canal Convention of October 29, 1888; join in this Declaration:

1. They reaffirm the purpose stated in the preamble of the Convention of 1888, to establish "A definite system destined to guarantee at all times, and for all the powers, the free use of the Suez Maritime Canal".

2. Such system must assure:

A. Efficient and dependable operation, maintenance and development of the Canal as a free, open and secure international waterway in accordance with the principles of the Convention of 1888.

B. Insulation of the operation of the Canal from the influence of politics of any nation.

C. Respect for the sovereignty of Egypt.

D. An equitable and fair return to Egypt for the use of the Suez Canal as an international waterway on Egyptian territory.

E. Payment to the Universal Suez Canal Company of such sums as may be found its due by way of fair compensation.

F. Canal tolls as low as is consistent with the foregoing requirements, and otherwise without profit.

---

[1] Department of State, Central Files, 974.7301/8–1356. Secret; Niact; Limit Distribution. Drafted by Cottman. Received at 7:45 p.m.

3. To achieve these results on a permanent and reliable basis there should be established by treaty:

A. Institutional arrangements for cooperation between Egypt and other interested nations in the operation, maintenance and development of the Canal and for harmonizing and safeguarding their respective interests in the Canal. To this end there should be an international board for operating, maintaining and developing the Canal and enlarging it so as to increase the volume of traffic in the interest of the world trade and of Egypt as a participant in the benefits of the Canal. Egypt would grant this board all rights and facilities appropriate to its functioning as here outlined.

The members of the board, in addition to Egypt, would be other states chosen in a manner to be agreed upon from among the states parties to the treaty, with due regard to equitable geographical distribution in relation to the Canal and its use and to assuring that the proposition of the board would be such as to assure that its responsibilities would be discharged solely with the view to achieving the best possible operating results without political motivation in favor of, or in prejudice against, any user of the Canal.

The board would make periodic reports to the United Nations.

B. An arbitral commission to settle any disputes as to the equitable return to Egypt or fair compensation to the Universal Suez Canal Company or other matters arising in the operation of the Canal.

C. Effective sanctions for any violation of the treaty, including provisions for treating any use or threat of force to interfere with the use or operation of the Canal as a threat to the peace and a violation of the purposes and principles of the United Nations Charter.

D. Provisions for appropriate association with the United Nations and for review as may be necessary.

End text.

Dulles

96.   Telegram From the Department of State to the Secretary of State, at London [1]

Washington, August 18, 1956—7:14 p.m.

Tedul 11. Eyes only Secretary from Acting Secretary.

1. This morning I advised the President that Bob Anderson had agreed to undertake the Saudi mission and would be ready to leave Monday afternoon if the invitation comes through. In such event he will stop over for an hour or so in London Tuesday morning, and I am suggesting to Rountree and Page that they talk with him at the airport.

2. The President was most interested in the overnight cables from London and wrote out his note of appreciation to you in longhand. [2]

3. In commenting on the cables the President said he fully agreed with you that we should not allow the British and French to insist on too rough a line with Nasser, even though we might thoroughly sympathize with their viewpoint. To do so would be counterproductive under present circumstances.

4. The President said he had been thinking over possible solutions, and believed we could accept almost any of them so long as we are assured of "international supervision". The word "supervision" seemed much better to him than "control". He thought that a commission of smaller countries was an excellent concept. He had been thinking along the following lines: Such a commission, upon which Egypt would be represented, should have the right to (a) appoint a general manager, (b) fix tolls, and (c) lay out and execute plans for maintenance, expansion and financing of the canal. Any actions of the commission could be appealed by (1) Egypt, (2) other commission members, or (3) users of the canal, to the World Court or other suitable body. He did not exclude other possibilities. I told him that I thought your ideas ran very much parallel, but that the immediate problem was to get Egypt up to the trough.

5. I still plan to leave for San Francisco, Sunday, Noon, August

---

[1] Source: Department of State, Central Files, 974.7301/8–1856. Top Secret; Priority. Drafted by Hoover and approved by Sherwood.

[2] The note was transmitted in Tedul 9 to London, August 19. It reads: "Dear Foster: From all reports you seem to be surpassing even your own unique capacity for bringing some order and sanity to confused situations. We here follow with great confidence and interest your cables and the news through collateral sources. Good luck and warm regards. DE" (*Ibid.*, 110.11–DU/8–1856)

19, but it is not yet firm that Cabinet members will participate in the proceedings. [3] If they do not, of course, I will not go.

Hoover

---

[3] Reference is to the national convention of the Republican Party, held at the Cow Palace in San Francisco August 20–24.

---

97.   Message From the Secretary of State to the President [1]

London, August 19, 1956.

DEAR MR. PRESIDENT: Harold MacMillan dined with us last night. He reaffirmed most soberly, yet strongly, the view that Britain was finished unless Nasser could be brought to accept in some form an effective international participation in the practical operation of the Suez Canal. He said, "there are only three choices: (1) Nasser voluntarily takes a proposal along lines of US paper; or (2) we compel Egypt to take it; (3) we accept Nasser's refusal. In the last event, Britain is finished and so far as I am concerned, I will have no part in it and will resign."

It seems as though domestic support for a strong line has dwindled to a point where if Nasser rejects, the Macmillan policy can scarcely be carried through and that some form of a governmental crisis may result. The attitude of the Labor Party [2] is a hard blow for the government at this juncture when bi-partisan unity would give Britain the best chance of retrieving its position without actually having to use force. I have no doubt that Nasser is fully aware of

---

[1] Source: Department of State, Central Files, 684A.86/8–1956. Secret. Transmitted to the Department of State in Dulte 12 from London, August 19, 1 p.m., which is the source text, with the instruction "Eyes only Acting Secretary for President from Secretary". The telegram was received at 9:12 a.m. A copy is in the Eisenhower Library, Whitman File, Dulles–Herter Series.

[2] On August 13, the shadow cabinet of the Labour Party issued a statement which, according to the Embassy in London, contained these main points: "1. Nasser's nationalization of Canal was not wrong in itself except arbitrary manner in which it was done caused great anxiety. 2. Armed forces in settling dispute could not be justified except in accordance with obligations and pledges under UN Charter. 3. Apart from continued stoppage of Israel ships Nasser has not done anything so far which would justify use of armed force against Egypt. 4. Government should make plain military measures taken in last ten days are purely precautionary and solely for defence against possible aggression. 5. Recall of Parliament upon conclusion of Conference." (Telegram 870 from London, August 14, Department of State, Central Files, 974.7301/8–1456)

the situation and may calculate that if he stands firm the result will be not solid strength against him but perhaps a Labor government which would be softer.

Faithfully yours,

Foster[3]

---

[3] Dulte 12 bears this typed signature.

---

98.   Message From the President to the Secretary of State[1]

Washington, August 19, 1956.

DEAR FOSTER: I have just received your personal telegram to me, dispatched last evening,[2] and your cabled copy of the text of the agreement.[3] I should think that if Nasser has any disposition whatsoever to negotiate this difficulty, you will find your paper fairly acceptable except possibly for that part in 3A which prescribes the duties of the Board. The paper apparently contemplates that the Board shall do the actual "operating, maintaining and developing of the Canal." Nasser may find it impossible to swallow the whole of this as now specified. On the other hand, I realize that you may have already written into the draft the minimum position that our British and French friends feel they can take.

So far as we are concerned, I see no objection to agreeing to a Board with supervisory rather than operating authority. Of course the authority for supervision would have to be clear, and the contention could be made, therefore, that there is no real difference between the two concepts. I think, however, that if we should get something like one of our corporate board of directors, with operating responsibility residing in some one appointed by Nasser, subject to Board approval, we should be establishing an organization which could achieve the ends we seek.

---

[1] Source: Department of State, Central Files, 974.7301/8–1956. Secret. Transmitted to London in Tedul 13, August 19, 2:21 p.m., which is the source text, with the notation: "Eyes only Secretary from Murphy Acting. President sends following message, dated August 19. References mentioned first paragraph are Dulte 10 and Secto 20. Latter passed to President at request Mr. Hoover."

[2] Document 94.

[3] Secto 20, Document 95.

Under such a system I realize that your "Arbitral Commission" might become very busy in settling disputes between Nasser and the Board, but as long as the Canal operated effectively this would be a detail.

Other than expressing the hope that the results of the conference will not be wrecked on the rigidity of the positions of the two sides on this particular point, I have no other comments to submit. Your document looks extraordinarily good to me.

With warm regard,

As ever,

DE [4]

---

[4] Tedul 13 bears these typed initials.

---

99.   Memorandum of a Conversation, Ambassador's Residence, London, August 19, 1956, 10 p.m. [1]

USDel/MC/49

PARTICIPANTS

The United States	*The United Kingdom*
Secretary Dulles	Sir Anthony Eden
Ambassador Aldrich	Rt. Hon. Selwyn Lloyd
Ambassador Dillon	
Mr. Phleger	Later joined by Prime Minister
	Menzies

SUBJECTS DISCUSSED

Suez Canal Problem and the Conference

After dinner at Ambassador Aldrich's the above (excepting Menzies), joined in a discussion of the Suez problem.

Eden and Selwyn Lloyd joined in a request that the United States act to stop further Canal payments to Egypt. They said the British and Dutch would join in this, with the result that Nasser would be faced with the alternative of permitting free passage through the Canal or closing it up. If he permitted free transit, his position would be unstable. If he stopped the transits the U.K. would then be in a position to act.

---

[1] Source: Department of State, Conference Files: Lot 62 D 181, CF 755. Secret. Prepared by the U.S. Delegation, but no drafting officer is indicated.

The Secretary replied that the U.S. had frozen more than fifty million dollars of Egyptian Government funds, which is more than adequate to cover any tolls now being paid at the Canal, and that he did not see how the U.S. could issue orders to private companies not to continue payment in their accustomed way. He further suggested that refusal to pay the tolls, followed by refusal by Nasser to permit transit, might well be taken by the public to be a closure justified by the refusal of users to pay dues.

Selwyn Lloyd and Eden then pressed the Secretary for his views as to what would happen next at the Conference. The Secretary said that he thought the Conference should proceed to formulate its views on the problem and obtain a consensus. These views could then be presented for [to] Egypt to ascertain if it would agree to a negotiation for a Treaty to give them effect. If Nasser should reject this suggestion, the matter would then be remitted to the Governments for their consideration of future action. He did not believe that matter to be one for the Conference. If on the other hand Nasser agreed to negotiate, then the Conference might be recessed until the results of the negotiation were ready for its consideration. The Secretary stressed that the views of the Conference should not be presented to Nasser as an ultimatum but as an expression of views to form the basis of a negotiated settlement.

There was then discussion of possible economic sanctions in the event Egypt refused to agree to negotiations. Eden pointed out various measures that could be taken. The Secretary observed that economic measures might not be successful because USSR or other Arab countries might come to the assistance of Egypt.

Premier Menzies then joined the group.

Eden and Selwyn Lloyd stressed the importance from the U.K. standpoint of bringing the matter to a speedy conclusion, either by Nasser's acceptance of the Convention's views or by his rejection of them. Delay would be fatal. Eden said he has suspended military preparations during the pendency of the Conference but further action could not be long delayed.

The Secretary said that he had encountered a general feeling that the British public would not support the use of force and that Shepilov had also expressed this view. Eden and Selwyn Lloyd said this view was incorrect. The British public, except the Left-Wing Labor element, was strongly behind the Government; that a recent Gallup poll had shown that two-thirds approved the way in which the Government was conducting this matter. Eden said he had refrained from building up public sentiment for the use of force, but he was absolutely confident that when the chips were down, the Government would have the full backing of the public in any military operation. He said that Gaitskell was in favor of Britain fighting to protect Israel. He felt the British public would be much more unanimous in fighting to protect Britain.

In this connection, Eden at the end of the meeting drew Ambassador Aldrich aside and asked him to assure the Secretary that he (Eden) was completely satisfied that Gaitskell would stand with the Government in the use of force if that should appear to be necessary. This was the second time Eden had made this statement privately to Ambassador Aldrich and asked him to reassure the Secretary.

The Secretary pointed out that public opinion in Britain on that question was of vital importance and in addition world opinion and opinion in the United States must be taken into consideration; that as to the latter, there was certainly at present no opinion that would support the use of force.

There was then further discussion regarding procedure at the Conference. Menzies expressed opinions similar to Secretary Dulles' regarding the formulation of the Conference's views and their presentation to Nasser. This should be done so as to avoid the appearance of an ultimatum, but should be designed to bring about a prompt response. He thought a Committee should be named to do this. He, though reluctant, would be glad to serve on it.

There was then discussion regarding a composition of a Committee. Eden and Selwyn Lloyd strongly pressed the Secretary to act on such a Committee. The Secretary said that while he would give the matter consideration, he would not make any commitment on it at this time.

There was some discussion regarding the importance of pilotage in the Canal, Eden expressing the view that the Canal could not be operated without the present pilots. The Secretary said there was some question about this, and inquired whether the hazards of Canal operation were being reflected in increased insurance rates. Eden said he did not know but would look into this.

The meeting broke up about midnight after further general discussion regarding further procedure. Selwyn Lloyd said he felt sure the Indians would put in a proposal on Monday, and that Menon would make a long speech. He then urged the Secretary to introduce his paper on Monday. The Secretary said he was inclined to do this, and would accompany it by an explanatory speech. He also indicated that he might make changes in the draft to accommodate the views of the other Delegations whose views he had asked.

100.   Message From the Secretary of State to the President [1]

London, August 20, 1956.

DEAR MR. PRESIDENT: I have your message of August 19, [2] suggesting the concept of "supervisory authority" rather than "operating authority". As you say, the real difference is not in the name, which can be adjusted to meet Nasser's sensibilities, but in what are in fact the responsibilities. It is felt very strongly here by most of the countries that if all of the hiring and firing of pilots, traffic directors and other technicians and engineers is made by the Egyptians with only some right of appeal, then in fact Egypt will be able to use the Canal as an instrument of its national policy.

It would be very difficult, and perhaps impossible from the standpoint of the British and French, to get agreement now to take a position which would seem to involve abandonment of this principle.

It is to be borne in mind that we are not here negotiating with Egypt for Egypt is not present, and I doubt whether we should make at this stage concessions which we might be willing to make as a matter of last resort in order to obtain Egypt's concurrence.

Perhaps something along the lines you suggest may have to be accepted ultimately and may become acceptable, but neither is clear today.

It may be possible to soften up somewhat the sentence to which you refer, but with your approval I shall at this stage defer use of your suggestion.

Faithfully yours,

Foster [3]

---

[1] Source: Department of State, Central Files, 684A.86/8–2056. Secret. Transmitted to the Department of State in Dulte 13 from London, August 20, 9 a.m., which is the source text, with the instruction "Eyes only Acting Secretary for President from Secretary". The telegram was received at 6:56 a.m. A copy is in the Eisenhower Library, Whitman File, Dulles–Herter Series.

[2] Document 98.

[3] Dulte 13 bears this typed signature.

101.   Message From the Secretary of State to the President [1]

London, August 20, 1956.

DEAR MR. PRESIDENT: Eden and Selwyn Lloyd dined with us last night and later on toward midnight we were joined by Menzies. [2] We mostly discussed procedure from here on and how to deal with the Egyptians. There will probably be some committee established and the question will be up as to who should be on the committee.

I can see that I may be subjected to very strong pressure to carry forward the negotiation with Nasser. I am disinclined to do so as this might engage me for a considerable time. Also, while the US has played a dominant role in the conference so far, I think it is preferable that we should become less conspicuous if this can be done without jeopardizing the whole affair.

I shall greatly appreciate your reaction on this problem.

Faithfully yours,

Foster [3]

---

[1] Source: Department of State, Central Files, 684A.86/8–2056. Secret. Transmitted to the Department of State in Dulte 14 from London, August 20, 9 a.m., which is the source text, with the instruction "Eyes only Acting Secretary for President from Secretary". The telegram was received at 6:55 a.m. A copy is in the Eisenhower Library, Whitman File, Dulles–Herter Series.

[2] See Document 99.

[3] Dulte 14 bears this typed signature.

---

102.   Memorandum of a Conversation, U.S. Embassy, London, August 20, 1956, 12:15 p.m. [1]

USDel/MC/52

PARTICIPANTS

The United States	*USSR*
The Secretary	Mr. Shepilov
Mr. Bohlen	Mr. Troyanovski

---

[1] Source: Department of State, Conference Files; Lot 62 D 181, CF 746. Secret. Prepared by the U.S. Delegation, but the source text does not indicate a drafting officer.

SUBJECT

US and USSR views on the Suez problem

Mr. Shepilov expressed his appreciation for Mr. Dulles' kindness in sending him a preliminary draft of his proposed resolution [2] which he had received on Saturday.

The Secretary said he hoped that this draft would obtain Soviet agreement.

Mr. Shepilov replied no, he could not say that.

The Secretary said speaking seriously he did not think the differences should be too great.

Mr. Shepilov replied that unfortunately the differences were serious. He wished to recall the statement in Mr. Dulles' original speech [3] concerning the necessity of finding a solution which would be acceptable to all. After their conversation on Saturday [4] he had thought it might be possible to find an acceptable compromise and that instead of the more rigid and one-sided formula of international operation with Egyptian participation, there might be substituted the formula of Egyptian operation with foreign participation. Unfortunately he felt that Mr. Dulles' draft was disappointing in that it did not provide a basis for a compromise. The main reason was that while containing certain general references to Egyptian sovereignty, a question along with that of the right of nationalization which had been accepted by all, it made plain who would operate the Canal. On this point Mr. Dulles' draft provides for an international board to operate and maintain and develop the Canal and the Egyptian Government was called upon to grant this board all facilities. This meant that Egypt would not run the Canal and other members of the board apart from Egypt would have chief responsibility assigning to Egypt a secondary role. While he could not be sure he felt that this would not be acceptable to the Egyptian people and would be regarded as an attempt on an unequal basis to impose a colonial form. He continued that from their previous conversation he had been encouraged by the Secretary's views that a bridge might be built between their positions on the Suez Canal question which might have wider implications. He wished to ask Mr. Dulles if this was his final position and what was the reason for its rigidity.

(At this point Mr. Dulles excused himself for a few minutes to speak on the telephone with Mr. Selwyn Lloyd.)

The Secretary said that the United States had a problem in regard to the Canal which was somewhat different from that of the

---

[2] Presumably that contained in Secto 20, Document 95.

[3] Reference is to the statement made by Secretary Dulles before the second plenary session on August 16; see footnote 2, Document 89.

[4] See Document 93.

Soviet Union and also from that of the Western European countries. We had a practical rather than a political problem in so far as the future operation of the Canal was concerned. Many private people throughout the world would be affected in their willingness to invest money in industry, in transferring from coal to oil by their confidence in the future operation of the Canal. They would not invest in these enterprises unless they were confident that the Canal would be run efficiently and fairly; it made no difference what he thought but what was important is how these thousands of private investors would think. He had to attempt to judge their reactions but if he made a mistake it would have an adverse effect on the economic life of many countries.

It was his opinion, confirmed by the governments familiar with the problem, that an operation which in fact gave the Egyptian Government control in perpetuity over the Canal would not give that necessary confidence; that Egyptian political control over the selection of technicians, pilots, those charged with dredging the Canal would not be regarded as providing adequate insurance of efficient operation and other means to live would have to be found. He continued that there were many ways of expressing this factor as the Minister himself had said on Saturday revolving around the formula of foreign management with Egyptian participation or Egyptian management with foreign participation. He had no pride in the way this aspect was expressed in the draft and he would be prepared to meet Egyptian sensitivities in expression and to that extent his position was flexible. He said in absence of direct contact it was difficult to speculate on what would or would not be acceptable to Egypt when we have no way, due to Egypt's absence from this Conference, of obtaining an authoritative opinion. He assumed Mr. Shepilov had no mandate to speak for Egypt (Mr. Shepilov promptly signified he had no such mandate) but that if he had he would be happy to discuss with him concrete measures. In the absence of Egypt there was no way of finding out the Egyptian attitude and it was therefore better not to speculate on what might or might not be acceptable to them but rather to set forth in straight forward fashion our own views and then later to have negotiations begin with Egypt during which account could be taken of the Egyptian views and possibly consideration of a new formula.

Mr. Shepilov said that he felt that there was also the question of public opinion and that the formula set forth in Mr. Dulles' draft looked like the application of the principle of a state within a state. It was true that without Egypt it was difficult to settle a question in which Egypt was so directly concerned, but since they should take cognizance of world public opinion in the nature of the approach and avoid any appearance of inequality or laying down in advance as did this draft a formula which envisaged international control in the form of a concession, which could only be regarded as inimical to Egyptian sovereignty.

The Secretary pointed out that the US had a number of arrangements with other countries, and for example the St. Lawrence, involved an element of Canadian control but we did not feel that we [it] reflected on our sovereignty or dignity.

Mr. Shepilov said it was impossible to reflect on US dignity since it was a great power. Egypt on the other hand had only recently thrown off colonial rule.

The Secretary mentioned that we had done the same 150 years ago. He stated that we were not willing to subscribe to a paper which seemed to abandon the principle that the technical operation of the Canal be within the purview of non-Egyptian personnel. There could be latitude in the form of expression but in substance the issue was one of responsibility for operation and we felt that the composition of the board should not bring politics into its operation. There was just not enough confidence in Egypt or its future to give it sole responsibility. If Egypt should demand that the situation would be very serious. He said he felt the first thing was to find out what our views at this Conference were and then consider means for conveying these views to Egypt and obtaining an authoritative response. As to appearances, he on behalf of the US was prepared to go on taking cognizance of Egyptian feelings. He understood these feelings were stronger than in countries who had never or at least not recently been colonies. He then inquired if Mr. Shepilov agreed that they should try here as soon as possible to get some expression of views from this Conference which would then permit them to move on to the next stage of negotiations with Egypt.

Mr. Shepilov agreed that this should be the purpose of the Conference.

The Secretary then inquired whether Mr. Shepilov intended to submit any proposal today.

Mr. Shepilov said not today and he expected to listen and not even to speak unless it became necessary. In reply to the Secretary's question, Mr. Shepilov said he had heard that India might have something to present.

103.   Message From the President to the Secretary of State [1]

Washington, August 20, 1956.

DEAR FOSTER: I have just received both your personal cables to me dispatched this morning. [2]

With respect to the suggestion I made to you yesterday, [3] I tried to make clear in my original message that I understood the difficult position you were probably in, and I was merely expressing the hope that we would not permit negotiations to come to an eventual point of collapse over the details of the operating arrangement proposed. As a minimum, I am sure that any international Board should have the unquestioned right to appoint the general manager of the operation, or at least, to have a veto over the appointment of anyone unsatisfactory to the Board. If that authority should include also the dismissal of a general manager who proved incapable of handling the affairs of the Canal, I believe that the hiring and firing of all lesser officials would tend to become an administrative detail. I repeat, however, that I understand the box you are in.

With respect to your second message, I have to give you my opinion under the handicap of ignorance respecting your own confidence in anybody of another nationality who might do the job in your stead. In addition, I am unaware of the timing and duration of the negotiations visualized with Nasser.

By no means should you become involved in a long wearisome negotiation, especially with an anticipated probability of negative results in the end. On the other hand, if there were some advance evidence that Nasser might prove reasonable and agreement as to principle could be achieved in a very short time, I could see certain advantages of your doing the thing personally. In this way, there would be no chance for erroneous interpretation of our intentions and understanding, and I cannot help but believe that there would be more chance of success with you in a situation where you deal with Nasser than if some lesser individual should undertake the work.

Our Government has expressed the opinion that in this problem, the peaceful processes of negotiation should prove equal to the

---

[1] Source: Department of State, Centrals Files, 974.7301/8-2056. Secret. The source text is a memorandum from Goodpaster at the White House to the Department of State Secretariat. A note at the top reads: "Please dispatch the following message from the President to Secretary Dulles". Transmitted to London in Tedul 15, August 20 at 3:13 p.m. with the instruction: "Eyes only Secretary from Murphy, Acting." Preceding the message printed here, the telegram notes: "Following message from the President refers in its first paragraph to Dulte eyes only 13 and Dulte eyes only 14."

[2] Documents 100 and 101.

[3] Document 98.

development of a satisfactory solution. We cannot afford to do less than our best to assure success, and yet I repeat that it would be worse than embarrassing if you should get tied into drawn-out conversations which would in the long run prove unsuccessful.

I realize that this is very little help in your present problem, but I am a long ways from the individuals who are primarily concerned and the only feel I have of their temper and attitudes is as you have described to me in your cables.

I need scarcely add that I will approve your decision and support you in whatever action you finally decide you must take.

As ever,

DE [4]

---

[4] Printed from a copy that bears these typed initials.

---

104.   Telegram From the Delegation at the Suez Canal Conference to the Department of State [1]

London, August 20, 1956—9 p.m.

Secto 25. Suez Conference: Fifth Session August 20—Summary.

Session, 3:30 to 5, included one hour ten minutes Krishna Menon, who tabled Indian draft of principles and proposals [2] followed by Secretary Dulles who during 15 minutes gave speech formally introducing United States proposed declaration (Secto 24). [3]

Texts Indian draft and Secretary's speech being telegraphed separately.

Menon's speech, delivered from notes, rambling and repetitive. Canal very important to Indian economy and she approaches prob-

---

[1] Source: Department of State, Central Files, 974.7301/8-2056. Official Use Only; Priority. Drafted by Foster. Received at 7:16 p.m.

[2] The Embassy in London transmitted the Indian draft principles and proposals to the Department of State in Secto 26, August 20, not printed. (*Ibid.*) The text is printed in *The Suez Canal Problem, July 26–September 22, 1956*, pp. 288–289.

[3] Dated August 20, not printed. (Department of State, Central Files, 974.7301/8-2056) Secto 24 transmitted the proposed declaration introduced by Dulles at the fifth plenary session. (*The Suez Canal Problem, July 26–September 22, 1956*, pp. 289–290) This text is the same as in Secto 20, Document 95, except for minor stylistic changes; the addition of the phrase "including its rights to just, fair compensation for the use of the Canal", to the last paragraph of the preamble following the phrase, "respect the sovereign rights of Egypt"; and the deletion of the words "equitable and fair" in paragraph 2.

lem with full sense of all the realities including economic. Present situation critical and alternatives "very grim indeed". India regrets absence Egypt without whom no final solutions possible. Conference has met amidst great tensions, suspicion, and fear, particularly in Arab world. Egypt's nationalization Canal wholly within her sovereign rights has created much alarm and military movements. India fears that unless peaceful settlement there will be conflict extending far beyond Suez area. Conference must confine itself to two main questions: First, how can proper functioning Canal be assured; second, how can fear be allayed.

Company not an international organization but a concessionaire from Egyptian Government. Moreover Company should not be confused with Canal itself, which does have an international character. Role of Company is to operate and it hasn't done this too well. It was Egyptian state that enabled Company to function and latter has always been under Egyptian law.

Nevertheless, signatories of 1888 do have rights outside and beyond Company. Fact that nationalization carried out by Egypt in manner disturbing some people should not obscure Egypt's sovereign right nationalize. Anyone concerned should seek arbitration in UN or ICJ.

Menon then enumerated what he called the five major problems: First, freedom navigation, which ensured by 1888. Second, security of ships transiting Canal, which can only be provided by Egyptian Government. Third, tolls. Menon acknowledged Nasser's Aswan proposition created alarm and said there should be no "mulcting of the international community" but added India understood Egypt wouldn't impose unreasonable tolls. Fourth, Company personnel, there should be provision in international agreement against discrimination. Fifth, efficiency of operation and improvements, answer is these have been effected by old Company (apparent inference new Egyptian Company will continue them).

Old Company would have ended in any case 1968 and meanwhile everyone including old Company knows no Egyptian Government would have been willing extend concession.

As to original tripartite proposals, the internationalization proposed is merely of the Company, i.e., a new Company is proposed. Effect would be to repeal Egypt's nationalization. New agency could not guarantee 1888 rights any better than old. Only party that can do so is Egypt. Egypt agreed as far back as 1856 to guarantee free navigation. There should be no trouble fixing tolls "by agreement" (not specified by and with whom). No doubt Egypt will honor her obligations meantime and improve Canal.

As to UN, there is nothing in Charter which gives UN any authority whatever to impose itself here. Might consider a specialized UN agency but this could be achieved only by imposing on Egyptian sovereignty.

Egypt on record as far back as 1880 as opposed to institution of an international authority to operate Canal. This illustrated when Khedive told de Lesseps Egypt could not admit to principle of selling Canal to European powers or suffering international authority in Egypt.

Not purpose present Conference examine problem world's waterways but would recall Western Powers opposed their being internationalized.

Remedy is to "refurbish" 1888 "so as to remove all doubt from these matters". He recited Article 8 of 1888 which has been "dormant" but which could be initiated. Will Egypt honor 1888 obligations? Yes, Egypt has said so.

Let's reexamine 1888 and include assurances on the above problems regarding freedom navigation, security transit, tolls, personnel, operations and improvements. 1888 would be registered with UN and any breach would be a violation UN charter. Whole world can assist in operation Canal if there's less crisis atmosphere. Can user interest be related new Company? Can't answer this because Egypt isn't represented London conference. How can new Company be put under international management? Can't do it except by imposing on Egyptian sovereignty. So let's hope Egypt will subscribe to principles 1888.

At this point Menon tabled Indian paper text of which transmitted immediately following telegram. Added that its principles are common ground and that its proposals would have sanction of international law and UN. India does not suggest a second conference but doesn't exclude it.

Eastern nations alarmed and don't say others aren't. India convinced a compromise settlement is possible. If Canal was closed India would lose. Finally, "I plead with you to adopt the part of conciliation—not dictation".

Conference adjourned until Tuesday afternoon.

For your information. Pakistan Delegate proposed adjournment after consultation many Western and friendly Asian countries in order provide time for coordination position Turkey, Iran, Pakistan, Ceylon, Indonesia and Ethiopia. First three of these Asian countries appear taking strong initiative to [under] Turk leadership to provide basis upon which all of them could support Secretary's proposal. Their idea is to introduce certain amendments which would be agreed in advance with US, UK, France, which would not change substance, but only form of document. If this possible they believe added "Asian flavor" would render the statement easier for certain borderline countries particularly Ceylon and Indonesia to go along.

Consultations among them and between them and US Delegation taking place this evening and tomorrow.

Dulles

---

105.   Message From the Secretary of State to the President [1]

London, August 20, 1956.

DEAR MR. PRESIDENT: I had my third meeting with Shepilov this noon [2] when he came to see me about our US paper. Nothing of great significance transpired except that he expressed his "disappointment" that our paper might not prove acceptable to the Soviet Union.

At our session this afternoon Menon made a long speech and introduced his proposals which were all right as generalities but which could be accepted by Nasser without there being any assurance whatsoever that the Canal could not be one hundred percent operated purely in the political interests of Egypt and as an instrument of its national policy. There are references to international bodies but they are pure scenery.

I put in the US paper as a Conference document and just got it under the wire ahead of Menon's so that ours will presumably be the first to be considered. Several of the Asian countries, primarily under Turkish initiative, are meeting to try to devise some relatively minor amendments to our proposal which will enable them to accept it. [3] We are doing all we can to encourage this, but the Soviet Union and India are exerting strong political pressure to break up the group. Also Pakistan faces a difficult political problem at home.

We adjourned early to permit of further study and inter-delegation consultation.

Shepilov is giving a dinner for all of the Arab ambassadors here in London on Thursday night so he is presumably not expecting the

---

[1] Source: Department of State, Central Files, 684A.86/8–2056. Secret. Transmitted to the Department of State in Dulte 17 from London, August 20, 8 p.m., which is the source text, with the instruction "Eyes only Acting Secretary for President from Secretary". The telegram was received at 4:15 p.m. A copy is in the Eisenhower Library, Whitman File, Dulles–Herter Series.

[2] See Document 102.

[3] Dulles discussed the subject with Turkish Foreign Minister Birgi at 9:45 that morning. The memorandum of conversation is in Department of State, Conference Files: Lot 62 D 181, CF 756.

Conference to come to an early end. I myself had hoped of getting back to Washington by Thursday to partake at least by TV in your acceptance speech. [4] From the draft I saw I know it will be the speech of a great man worthy of a great occasion.

Faithfully yours,

Foster Dulles [5]

---

[4] On August 22, the National Convention of the Republican Party unanimously renominated Dwight Eisenhower as its candidate for President of the United States. Eisenhower delivered his acceptance speech to the Convention on August 23.

[5] Dulte 17 bears this typed signature.

---

106.   Editorial Note

On August 20, while en route to have lunch with King Saud, Ambassador Wadsworth was met at the Riyadh airport by Saudi Deputy Minister for Foreign Affairs Yusuf Yasin, who proceeded to brief Wadsworth on Saud's reaction to the Suez situation. Yasin emphasized that the King was gravely concerned, as only the Soviet Union had so far benefited from the crisis and would gain from its continuance. The King believed that the United States and Saudi Arabia could profitably exchange views and contribute toward a peaceful settlement of the crisis. According to Yasin, Saudi interests in speaking with the Americans were three-fold:

(1) to lend all appropriate support to its sister Arab country, Egypt;
(2) to protect Saudi interests by maintaining oil exports and food imports; and
(3) to do all that was possible to counter the threat to peace in the area. (Telegram 69 from Dhahran, August 20; Department of State, Central Files, 974.7301/8–2056)

Shortly thereafter Wadsworth met with King Saud and received direct confirmation that Saud would welcome Robert Anderson as President Eisenhower's emissary. Wadsworth then suggested that, to ensure secrecy, arrangements could be made through Terry Duce, Vice President of Aramco, so that Anderson would appear as a distinguished American traveling as a guest of Aramco. Saud agreed to the arrangements. Also during the discussion, the King informed Wadsworth that Saud's "aim and purpose [in approaching the Americans] was that our two friendly countries cooperate in contributing to a solution of the problem, the outcome of which none knows but God. We have wanted to find an effective solution, and we wanted our friend, the United States Government, to show a willingness on its part to reach an effective solution. This was my aim when proposing to send a special delegation to Washington with a special message for President Eisenhower." (Memorandum of audience with His Majesty, King Saud; *ibid.*, NEA Files: Lot 59 D 518, Report of Special Mission to Saudi Arabia August 20–27, 1956. The folder entitled "Report of Special Mission to Saudi Arabia" constitutes the most complete collection of documentation on the Anderson Mission to Saudi Arabia found in Department of State files. It includes a chronology, summary report, list of members of the official party, memoranda of conversation, telegrams sent by the official party, and other related documents.)

That same day, at 4 p.m., Anderson left New York by plane. On August 21, he was in London where he discussed the Suez situation with Dulles and reviewed petroleum problems with Howard Page, Director of Standard Oil of New Jersey. No accounts of these conversations have been found in Department of State files. On August 22, Anderson stopped in Rome and from there proceeded to Dhahran, Saudi Arabia, where he arrived early in the morning of August 23. (Telegram 48 to Dhahran, August 20; *ibid.*, Central Files, 974.7301/8–2056; and Chronology of Special Mission to King Saud; *ibid.*, Conference Files: Lot 59 D 518, Report of Special Mission to Saudi Arabia August 20–27, 1956)

107.   Memorandum of a Conversation Between the Ambassador to France (Dillon) and Foreign Minister Pineau, 10 Downing Street, London, August 20, 1956, 11 p.m. [1]

USDel/MC/59

SUBJECT DISCUSSED

Possible use of force in Suez dispute

M. Pineau took me aside at the reception last night and said he was convinced that military action would be inevitable in the Suez dispute and that he considered that it would be most important to have arrangements completed ahead of time so that an international conference could be called within a few days after the initiation of military action to consider the future international status of the canal.

_____

[1] Source: Department of State, Conference Files: Lot 62 D 181, CF 746. Drafted by Dillon. The conversation took place at a reception given by Prime Minister and Lady Eden.

_____

108.   Memorandum of a Conversation Between Secretary of State Dulles and Foreign Minister Macmillan, 10 Downing Street, London, August 21, 1956 [1]

As I was leaving Sir Anthony Eden's Reception last night, Harold Macmillan said he would like to speak to me privately. We went into one of the private rooms. Macmillan asked first of all whether I planned to stay on as Secretary of State. He said that he was thinking of perhaps going back to take over the Foreign Office in the reasonably near future and that his decision in this matter would be influenced by whether I would be his vis-à-vis in the United States. He spoke of the very happy relations we had together when we were both Foreign Ministers and that he would very much like to renew this.

I said I had no definite plans but that it was a pretty gruelling job and that I did not expect to stay on indefinitely. Probably if

_____

[1] Source: Eisenhower Library, Dulles Papers, General Memoranda of Conversation. Drafted by Dulles. Confidential; Personal and Private.

President Eisenhower were re-elected as anticipated, there would be no immediate change.

Macmillan then urged me most strongly to take on the negotiation with Nasser. He said he did not have confidence that anybody else could pull it off. He was particularly concerned with the idea of their going to Cairo. He would have no fear if I should go to Cairo, but he felt that the atmosphere would almost surely influence others to weaken unduly.

JFD [2]

---

[2] Hanes initialed for Dulles.

---

109.   Memorandum From Carl W. McCardle of the Senior Staff of Advisers in the Delegation at the Suez Canal Conference to the Secretary of State [1]

London, August 21, 1956.

At the Reception at 10 Downing Street last night, Prime Minister Eden went out of his way to tell me "what a wonderful job Foster has done here". He repeated that if the Suez crisis is settled, it will "be due to the job that Foster has done."

A few minutes later Harold Macmillan reiterated to me Sir Anthony's praise of your efforts. But he quite plainly had another point that he wanted to make and as a matter of fact urged me to help persuade you to do it. That was, as Macmillan sees it, the first stage of the battle has been won with the way you have handled the Suez Conference. The next stage is the one that worries him. In his opinion the only one who stands a chance of negotiation with Nasser is yourself. Macmillan says that you are the only one Nasser will pay any attention to. He said that it would be all right to have a Committee of Norway, Iran and Australia, but if we were to get any place with Nasser it would have to be you in charge of the negotiation. He went so far as to say that you were the "only hope". He said that whatever success the London Conference achieved, it would be lost unless you undertook the negotiation with Nasser. I knew that Macmillan had already mentioned this to you, so I merely

---

[1] Source: Department of State, Central Files, 974.7301/8–2156. Top Secret. Sent through Macomber. A marginal notation reads: "Sec Saw".

said I would confirm to you the strength of his feeling about the matter. I know the arguments against your getting involved personally in the negotiation with Nasser—the commitment of and possible jeopardy of your personal prestige, the fact that in order to bring the negotiation off effectively you might have to undergo a certain amount of diplomatic retreating, and finally the possibility that even with your conducting the negotiation, Nasser being the irrational type he is, it might fail. My own inclination is that for all these reasons, it is a thing you should stay out of. But I am bound to say that I have a strong feeling that if there is to be any successful negotiation with Nasser, you are the only one who can accomplish it.

Ivone Kirkpatrick in a conversation at the Reception was, as usual, quite blustery. He said in effect that we would, as he put it, "have to have a row" with Nasser. He said we might as well have it early as late. He compared Nasser to Hitler and the Rhineland and said it was just a question of how long all of us would have to go along appeasing Nasser "before we had the inevitable row". I do not know to what extent Ivone was speaking in the official British view; but if he was, then the British like the French, as conveyed by Ambassador Dillon's memorandum, [2] feel sure that force is the only answer. I did say to Ivone that I did not believe that public opinion in the United States, or for that matter in Great Britain, would support a resort to force at this time. He snapped back that he did not care about public opinion, that it was the business of informed leaders to lead their countries in what they thought was the right course of action and not merely to "follow public opinion".

CWMc

---

[2] Document 107.

---

110.   Editorial Note

At the sixth plenary session, which convened at 2:45 p.m., August 21, the Pakistani Representative acting on behalf of his country, Ethiopia, Iran, and Turkey presented several amendments to the United States draft proposal. The text of the proposal as revised was then circulated by the Conference Secretariat to all delegations. In the Secretariat's document, the amendments proposed by Ethiopia,

Iran, Pakistan, and Turkey were underlined and the parts omitted from the United States proposal were shown in brackets. The text reads as follows with italics substituted for the underlining:

"Proposal by the Delegates of Ethiopia, Iran, Pakistan and Turkey

"The Governments approving this Statement, being participants in the London Conference on the Suez Canal:

"Concerned by the grave situation regarding the Suez Canal:

"Seeking a peaceful solution in conformity with the purposes and principles of the United Nations; and

"Recognizing that an adequate solution must, on the one hand, respect the sovereign rights of Egypt, including its rights to just and fair compensation for the use of the Canal, and, on the other hand, safeguard the Suez Canal as an international water way in accordance with the Suez Canal Convention of October 29, 1888;

"Assuming for the purposes of this statement that just and fair compensation will be paid to the Universal Company of the Suez Maritime Canal, and that the necessary arrangements for such compensation, including a provision for arbitration in the event of disagreement, will be covered by the final settlement contemplated below.

"Join in this expression of their views:

"1. They affirm that, as stated in the Preamble of the Convention of 1888, there should be established 'a definite system destined to guarantee at all times, and for all the Powers, the free use of the Suez Maritime Canal'.

"2. *Such a system which would be established with due regard to the sovereign rights of Egypt,* should assure:

"a. Efficient and dependable operation, maintenance and development of the Canal as a free, open and secure international waterway in accordance with the principles of the Convention of 1888.

"b. Insulation of the operation of the Canal from the influence of the politics of any nation.

"[c. Respect for the sovereignty of Egypt.]

"*c.* A return to Egypt for the use of the Suez Canal which will be fair and equitable and increasing with enlargements of its capacity and greater use.

"*d.* Canal tolls as low as is consistent with the foregoing requirements and, except for *c.* above, no profit.

"[e. Payment to the Universal Suez Canal Company of such sums as may be found its due by way of fair compensation.]

"3. To achieve these results on a permanent and reliable basis there should be established *by a Convention to be negotiated with Egypt.*

"a. Institutional arrangements for cooperation between Egypt and other interested nations in the operation, maintenance and development of the Canal and for harmonizing and safeguarding their respective interests in the Canal. To this end, operating, maintaining and developing the Canal and enlarging it so as to increase the volume of traffic in the interest of the world trade and of Egypt, would be the responsibility of a Suez Canal Board. Egypt would grant this Board all rights and facilities appropriate to its functioning as here outlined. *The status of the Board would be defined in the above-mentioned Convention.*

"The members of the Board, in addition to Egypt, would be other States chosen in a manner to be agreed upon from among the States parties to the Convention with due regard to use, pattern of trade and geographical distribution: the composition of the Board to be such as to assure that its responsibilities would be discharged solely with a view to achieving the best possible operating results without political motivation in favour of, or in prejudice against, any user of the Canal.

"The Board would make periodic reports to the United Nations.

"b. An Arbitral Commission to settle any disputes as to the equitable return to Egypt [or fair compensation to the Universal Suez Canal Company] or other matters arising in the operation of the Canal.

"c. Effective sanctions for any violation of the Convention by any party to it, or any other nation, including provisions for treating any use or threat of force to interfere with the use or operation of the Canal as a threat to the peace and a violation of the purposes and principles of the United Nations Charter.

"d. Provisions for appropriate association with the United Nations and for review as may be necessary." (Conference Secretariat doc. SUEZ/56/D/12; Department of State, Conference Files: Lot 62 D 181, CF 757)

This text, which received United States approval, was henceforth referred to as the Five-Nation (or Power) Proposal. The text of the Five-Power Proposal was forwarded to the Department of State in Secto 30 from London, August 21. (*Ibid.*, Central Files, 974.7301/8–2156)

Also at the sixth plenary session, the Spanish Delegate submitted an amendment to paragraph 3(a) of the United States proposal. The Spanish amendment provided for an Egyptian Board, having adequate representation of the community of nations using the Canal, to operate, maintain, and develop the Canal. (Conference Secretariat doc. SUEZ/56/D/13; *ibid.*, Conference Files: Lot 62 D 181, CF 757)

Summary accounts of the sixth plenary session, which was a two-part session, are in Sectos 31 and 32 from London, both dated August 21. (Both *ibid.*, 974.7301/8–2156)

111.   Message From the Secretary of State to the President [1]

London, August 21, 1956.

DEAR MR. PRESIDENT: Our session today [2] virtually completed the line-up of the twenty-two nations on our proposal. The big achievement was that we got four Asian-African countries—Ethiopia, Iran, Pakistan and Turkey—to introduce as their own the United States proposal with some very nominal amendments [3] so that they are now definitely committed to our program, and the program becomes not just a Western program but one with Asian and African support. This means we shall have 18 of the 22 countries (Spain having made a minor reservation) [3] with only four not joining, namely, the Soviet Union, India, Indonesia and Ceylon. This is a more impressive result than we had anticipated. Tomorrow we shall be completing the record in this respect and then I hope adopt a resolution designating a committee to present the plan to Egypt and find out whether they are willing to negotiate along the lines indicated.

We have had many back-stage talks about the constitution of this committee. I have been urged from many quarters to act, but I have decided that I ought not to engage myself personally as a negotiator with Egypt. We are now thinking tentatively of a committee of three, made up of Australia, Norway or Sweden and Pakistan.

The Scandinavians told me as a group that they would not serve unless the United States served, but I am not sure they will stick to that.

The disappointing aspect of the situation is that at the meeting today Shepilov made a very inflammatory speech [4] charging our plan as being a maneuver of colonialism and designed to reimpose Western rule upon Egypt. This statement will of course be widely circulated throughout the Arab world, and was I think deliberately calculated to make it difficult for Nasser now to accept our program unless it is heavily disguised.

I feel that this speech made when he realized that the conference itself was going overwhelmingly against him was a last-ditch

---

[1] Source: Department of State, Central Files, 684A.86/8–2156. Secret. Transmitted to the Department of State in Dulte 19 from London, August 21, 10 p.m., which is the source text, with the instruction "Eyes only Acting Secretary for President from Secretary". The telegram was received at 7:46 p.m. A copy is in the Eisenhower Library, Whitman File, Dulles–Herter Series.

[2] Reference is to the sixth plenary session

[3] See the editorial note, *supra.*

[4] For text, see *The Suez Canal Problem, July 26–September 22, 1956,* pp. 209–218.

maneuver which, however, I think clearly reveals that their purpose is to prevent a settlement and to become themselves dominant in the Arab world, by bribing it into a hostility toward the West which will make the Arabs ever more dependent upon the Soviet Union. Shepilov's speech makes a mockery of their protestation of their desire to achieve a relaxation of tension in this area.

At the close of the session at my suggestion, Menzies made a brief statement showing how absurd it was to charge that this project with its broad backing from many former colonial countries could be a maneuver of colonialism. I thought it better for Menzies to make that statement than for me to make it as that would have reproduced the customary clash between the United States and the USSR. I am not discouraged as to the final outcome but certainly the Russians have taken a step which makes a peaceful solution more difficult to achieve. On the other hand, we have more resources on our side than we had dared hope for.

Faithfully yours,

Foster [5]

---

[5] Dulte 19 bears this typed signature.

---

112.   Memorandum of a Conversation, U.S. Embassy, London, August 22, 1956, 11 a.m. [1]

USDel/MC/75

PARTICIPANTS

The United States	India
The Secretary of State	Mr. Krishna Menon
Mr. Rountree	

SUBJECT DISCUSSED

Future Procedures at the Conference

Mr. Menon asked urgently to see the Secretary on the morning of August 22nd, the day after the Five-Power Proposal was tabled and adhered to by 18 countries. In an atmosphere somewhat cooler

---

[1] Source: Department of State, Conference Files: Lot 62 D 181, CF 758. Secret. Prepared in the U.S. Delegation, but the source text does not indicate a drafting officer.

than usual, Mr. Menon reviewed essentially the Indian position as stated by him on previous occasions, including the speeches at the Conference. He emphasized his belief that the Egyptian Government could not and would not negotiate on the basis of the Five-Power Proposal, since they would consider it an infringement upon their sovereignty and contrary to their national interests. He extolled the virtues of his own plan and said that only a proposal along those lines would have any chance of success. He had reason to believe that the Egyptians would be willing to begin negotiations on that basis, and his idea was that such negotiations could develop the kind of satisfactory relationship between Egypt and the users of the Canal which would give confidence that the Canal would be operated properly.

In response, the Secretary again set forth his views as given in his various statements and in previous conversations with Mr. Menon. He said that he, and the other delegates who adhered to the plan, had fully in mind Egyptian sovereignty and rights and that the plan definitely would not be put to the Egyptians as an ultimatum. Certainly, however, it was necessary for the users of the Canal to agree among themselves on the type of arrangements which they would consider workable if they could be negotiated with the Egyptian Government. He dwelt upon the role of the United States in trying to bring about a peaceful solution to the problem, in a situation which, three weeks ago, and still today, is fraught with danger. The Secretary stressed that this is not the type of problem which could remain unsettled with assurance that no harm would come through delay. It was vital to peace in the area, he said, to find some satisfactory solution. He deplored the speech on August 21st of the Soviet delegate injecting into the discussions for propaganda purposes extraneous matters and allegations that the Five-Power Proposal represented an effort on the part of 18 states to impose some form of colonialism upon Egypt. The Soviets must know that statements of that sort were not conducive to the kind of atmosphere needed if a solution was to be found.

Mr. Menon inquired regarding the Secretary's views concerning other procedures to be considered by the Conference. The Secretary answered only in general terms along the lines that consideration should be given to the best way of communicating to the Egyptian Government the views of the Conference and to trying to arrange for fruitful negotiations. He said that the Indians could make a major contribution in this regard by the attitude which they assumed and the statements they made which might have a bearing upon Egypt's willingness to negotiate on a sound and reasonable basis.

While Mr. Rountree was accompanying Mr. Menon to his car, the latter reiterated in the strongest terms that the course being pursued by the 18 nations was not right. His parting words were: "I tell you, Mr. Rountree, that if this thing is pushed, it will lead to a holy war".

113.   Memorandum of a Conversation Between Secretary of State Dulles and Prime Minister Eden, 10 Downing Street, London, August 22, 1956, 1 p.m. [1]

USDel/MC/83

SUBJECT DISCUSSED

Negotiating Group

Shortly before 1:00 o'clock today Prime Minister Eden asked Secretary Dulles to come to see him. The request apparently was the result of a discussion which took place at a U.K. Cabinet Meeting. This meeting adjourned just as the Secretary arrived at 10 Downing Street.

At the meeting, the Prime Minister urged the Secretary to serve personally on the small group which would seek to ascertain whether Nasser was willing to negotiate on the basis of the 5-Nation statement. The Prime Minister stressed the importance, in his opinion, of the Secretary personally serving on this group. The Secretary made no commitment to Mr. Eden, but did say that he would consider the possibility of the U.S. participating in this group and of personally participating in the initial phase of its work following which, he would be replaced by a Deputy.

Mr. Eden then raised the matter of Mr. Menzies serving as Chairman of this group. He said he was planning, at Menzies' suggestion, to send a message to the latter's colleagues in Australia stressing the importance of this undertaking and ask that they acquiesce in Menzies' continued absence from his country in order to participate in it. The Prime Minister indicated he would like to say in his message that Menzies would be Chairman of the Group. He wanted to clear this with the Secretary, however, in view of his hope that the Secretary himself would also agree to serve on the

---

[1] Source: Department of State, Conference Files: Lot 62 D 181, CF 746. Confidential. Drafted by Macomber.

Committee. The Secretary replied that whether or not he ultimately served on the Committee, he felt that Menzies should be designated the Chairman. The Secretary gave two reasons for this. First was that Menzies was a Head of Government, and the second was that the Secretary's participation on the Committee (if he should accept) would be of a temporary nature.

The conversation then turned to a discussion of Shepilov's speech at yesterday's session of the Conference. Mr. Eden agreed with the Secretary that this was designed to continue tension in the Middle East.

The conversation ended with Eden strongly complimenting the Secretary on his masterly performance at the Conference. Mr. Eden said that he was very pleased at the large number of delegates who had subscribed to the five-nation statement, and indicated that before the Conference opened, he had not thought that so large a number could be obtained. Mr. Eden also said that he was surprised that the Conference had moved along as quickly as it had. He had thought before the Conference began it would take much longer to complete than now appeared to be the case. He indicated that both accomplishments were largely due to the Secretary's work.

---

114.   Telegram From the Department of State to the Secretary of State, at London [1]

Washington, August 22, 1956—5:04 p.m.

Tedul 20. Eyes only Secretary from Under Secretary.

1. This morning the President discussed with me your Dulte 19. [2] The Soviet tactics to stir up tension are certainly disappointing although not unexpected. The wide support that you have gained for a moderate Western position has been most impressive. It lays the foundation for a sound outcome and gives a strong position upon which to negotiate.

---

[1] Source: Department of State, Central Files, 974.7301/8–2256. Secret. Drafted and approved by Hoover and signed for Murphy by Howe. Murphy served as Acting Secretary in the absence of Secretary Dulles and Under Secretary Hoover, who was then attending the Republic National Convention in San Francisco. An attached handwritten note, initialed by Howe, indicates that the message and handling instructions were read over the White House phone from San Francisco and sent to Hoover's office in Washington.

[2] Dulte 19 contained Dulles' August 21 message to Eisenhower, Document 111.

2. The President wondered if the Indian position in London was so intransigent that a direct appeal from him to Nehru might do any good. He recalled that the August 10 message to him from Nehru [3] closed with the following paragraph:

"I need not tell you how anxious we have been about the recent developments in regard to the Suez Canal. I earnestly hope that the great influence of the United States will help in arriving at a peaceful settlement of this difficult and intricate problem. It would be disastrous if the efforts to solve this problem peacefully failed and conflict resulted."

The President said he would be guided entirely by your advice on the scene. In the event you desire such a message I suggest that draft of text be forwarded to Washington for relay to San Francisco by telephone.

3. The President expressly asked me to send you his "most personal felicitations".

4. Progress in San Francisco has been excellent. The platform was adopted without argument and Thruston Morton [4] has won wide recognition for his handling of the foreign policy phase. Your message was very well received on the floor and it went out over the TV networks just before they switched to the President's arrival at the airport. His reception here last night and again during this morning was extraordinarily enthusiastic.

5. Everyone sends you messages of confidence and appreciation. It is a matter of deep regret to all of us that you could not be here to receive their expressions of support and acclaim in person.

6. I expect to be back in the Department early Friday morning [5] unless some unforeseen development necessitates my earlier return.

Murphy

---

[3] A copy of the message is in Department of State, Presidential Correspondence: Lot 66 D 204, Prime Minister Nehru's Correspondence with Eisenhower/Dulles, 1953–1961. In it, Nehru discussed the possibility of visiting the United States.

[4] Subcommittee Chairman for Foreign Policy on the Republican Platform Committee.

[5] August 24.

115. Telegram From the Secretary of State to the Department of State [1]

London, August 22, 1956—5 p.m.

Dulte 21. For Hoover. Will decide later today on composition of small negotiating group to approach Nasser on basis of five nation statement put forward yesterday's meeting.

There is much pressure here to have US and me personally serve on this group. While I have reached no decision on this am considering possibility of serving at initial meeting London to fix committee procedure and then be replaced by deputy. Re identity of latter am thinking of Phleger, Murphy, Henderson or Rountree. Would like your views re these and any other names you wish to suggest.

Menzies, in view his position head of government and my temporary participation only, would probably serve as negotiating group chairman. [2]

Dulles

---

[1] Source: Department of State, Central Files, 684A.86/8–2256. Secret; Niact. Received at 1:03 p.m.

[2] Later that day the Department of State forwarded to Secretary Dulles a message from Hoover which had been transmitted over the White House phone from San Francisco. The message reads: "This afternoon I had opportunity to show Dulte 21 to the President. I said that all things considered I thought Phleger would be the best choice on the negotiating group. The President fully concurred. Menzies would seem to be a most excellent choice as Chairman of the group." (Tedul 23 to London, August 22; *ibid.,* 974.7301/8–2256)

---

116. Editorial Note

At the seventh plenary session which convened at 2:45 p.m. on August 22, Spanish Foreign Minister Artajo modified his previous decision and announced that Spain would support the plan to submit the Five-Nation Proposal to Egypt as a basis for negotiations. Artajo also requested that, if agreement was not reached with Egypt on the basis of this proposal, negotiations proceed on the basis of the Spanish proposal made the previous day. (See Document 110) The United States Delegation prepared summary accounts of this two-part meeting, which were transmitted to the Department of State in Sectos 37 and 38 from London, August 22. (Department of

State, Central Files, 974.7301/8–2256) The text of Artajo's statement is in Secto 35 from London, August 22. (*Ibid.*)

Dulles had met with the ranking Spanish Representative at the Conference, the Marquis de Santa Cruz de Inguanzo, at 10:20 a.m. on August 22. The memorandum of that conversation reads in part: "The Secretary said to the Marquis of Santa Cruz that it would certainly come as a shock and surprise to American public opinion if, in the final count, Spain sided with the Soviet Union, India and the other two countries which had followed the Communist line, instead of with the United States and other powers. Spain had always been considered hitherto a strong pillar of anti-communism and such a development would undoubtedly produce an unfavorable impression on the Congress of the United States, which had frequently had the occasion to manifest its confidence in Spain. The Secretary said that our two countries had enjoyed close and friendly relations. He added that the United States had been making efforts and that it was our hope that Spain would one day become a member of NATO. It would be difficult for us to be persuasive in Spain's behalf in this direction, if she were to part with us and the other countries on the present issue." The memorandum of conversation records that later in the discussion Santa Cruz said that he had "good hope" that he would be able to work out a formula, which both Secretary Dulles and Foreign Minister Artajo could accept. (*Ibid.*, Conference Files: Lot 62 D 181, CF 758)

A memorandum for the record, drafted by Tyler on August 22, indicates that following the meeting with Dulles, Santa Cruz prepared a text of a statement for Artajo which was shown to Dulles shortly before the seventh plenary session convened. Dulles approved it, but when Artajo arrived, the Spaniard rejected the statement. Consequently, Santa Cruz presented another draft text, which was acceptable to Dulles. Artajo asked through intermediaries that Dulles speak with him during the recess, but the Secretary sent back word that Artajo should make his statement before the recess. Artajo hesitated but finally managed to catch the eye of the Chairman just as he was about to adjourn and read his statement. (*Ibid.*, Central Files, 396.1–LO/8–1456)

117.   Message From the Secretary of State to the President [1]

London, August 22, 1956.

DEAR MR. PRESIDENT: It seems that our conference is drawing to a close. We should have finished today but Shepilov and Menon fought for delay and it seemed expedient to give it to them. If, however, our lines hold solid, we shall conclude tomorrow (Thursday).

This morning Spain altered its position sufficiently [2] to be included with our group rather than with the Soviet-Indian group. I pointed out to Foreign Minister Artajo [3] that it would be a great shock to American public opinion which had counted so much upon Spain's stout anti-Communist position to find that at this first major international conference where Spain participated it was aligned with the Soviet Union, India, Ceylon and Indonesia. Artajo seemed to get the point, and although they always want to follow an Arab policy different from that of the French, they altered their position so that today they joined the separate meeting of 18 [4] which concerted tactics in support of our common position.

When our common position emerged clearly after the intermission, the Soviets and the Indians seemed quite taken by surprise and at a loss. They played for time and for the reason I indicated we finally gave in.

I have been under very strong pressure to act personally in the development of this matter but have decided against it. There was a proposal before our 18-nation meeting that I alone should carry on the negotiations on behalf of them all, but I said I could not do that because of my broader responsibilities. I would have for the most part to act by a deputy. The group tentatively agreed upon is Australia, Ethiopia, Iran, Sweden and the USA. [5] We could not make

---

[1] Source: Department of State, Central Files, 684A.86/8–2256. Secret. Transmitted to the Department of State in Dulte 22 from London, August 22, 9 p.m., which is the source text, with the instruction "Eyes only Acting Secretary for President from Secretary". The telegram was received at 8:26 p.m. A copy is in the Eisenhower Library, Whitman File, Dulles–Herter Series.

[2] See the editorial note, *supra.*

[3] The schedules and chronologies prepared by the U.S. Delegation contain no reference to a Dulles–Artajo conversation on either August 21 or 22, but see the editorial note, *supra.*

[4] The schedule and chronology, prepared by the U.S. Delegation for August 22, contains no reference to an 18-power meeting for that day. No memorandum of that meeting has been found in Department of State files.

[5] During the seventh plenary session, New Zealand Foreign Minister MacDonald submitted a proposal which envisioned that several governments would be selected from among the 18 supporters of the proposal and asked to approach the Government of Egypt to submit the Eighteen-Power Proposal, to explain its purposes and objec-

it definitive because some of the representatives want to clear with their governments.

If this business is completed tomorrow, I shall probably stay over here Friday in order to have a first meeting of the committee to lay out our plan for approach to Egypt. Then much will depend upon whether Egypt will be willing to deal with the committee which will then be speaking for 18 nations representing over 95 percent of the Suez tonnage. If Nasser refuses to let his government even deal with this committee, then there will be a serious crisis. If meetings and exchanges of views take place, then the chance of a peaceful settlement will, I think, be considerable.

Much will, I think, depend upon the propaganda from the Soviet Union and India, particularly the former. Shepilov spoke much more calmly today but Moscow radio is still of a character making it hard for the Egyptian Government to do anything but give a complete rejection.

My thoughts are much with you tonight when the second nomination is to come to you. I am deeply grateful that you have the sense of duty not only to your country but also to the world which leads you to accept this great but essential responsibility.

Faithfully yours,

Foster [6]

---

tives, and to ascertain whether Egypt would agree to negotiate a Convention on the basis of it.

[6] Dulte 22 bears this typed signature.

118.   **Memorandum From the Acting Executive Secretary of the National Security Council (Boggs) to the National Security Council** [1]

Washington, August 22, 1956.

SUBJECT

Nationalization of the Suez Canal; Consequences and Possible Related Reactions

REFERENCES

A. Memo for NSC from Executive Secretary, subject: "Nationalization of the Suez Maritime Canal Company by the Egyptian Government", dated August 3, 1956 [2]
B. Memo for NSC from Executive Secretary, same subject, dated August 7, 1956 [3]
C. NSC Action No. 1593 [4]

At the request of the Deputy Secretary of Defense, the enclosed views of the Joint Chiefs of Staff on the subject, additional to those transmitted by the reference memoranda, are transmitted herewith for the information of the National Security Council in connection with the studies being developed pursuant to NSC Action No. 1593–b.

The enclosed JCS views are being given a special limited distribution, and it is requested that special security precautions be observed in their handling.

Marion W. Boggs

---

[1] Source: Department of State, S/S–NSC (Miscellaneous) Files: Lot 66 D 95, Suez Canal Situation. Top Secret.

[2] This memorandum transmitted the JCS memorandum of July 31 to the NSC; see Document 50.

[3] This memorandum transmitted the JCS memorandum of August 3 to the NSC; see Document 68.

[4] Regarding NSC Action No. 1593, see footnote 8, Document 72.

Enclosure

CONCLUSIONS REGARDING EXPROPRIATION OF THE SUEZ
    MARITIME CANAL COMPANY BY THE EGYPTIAN
    GOVERNMENT [5]

A. General Conclusions:

1. Britain and France are convinced that they cannot accept the consequences of a further rise in Nasser's power and prestige and can be expected to take any action they consider necessary, including military action, to safeguard their interests.

2. Although Arab League nations generally have expressed themselves as being in favor of the expropriation of the Suez Canal Company, they are not uniformly in favor of increasing further the stature of President Nasser.

3. While the Near East members of the Baghdad Pact were not expected to officially support the abrupt action of President Nasser, the action of Iraq in hailing President Nasser's seizure may adversely affect the Iranian and Pakistani views on this subject.

4. Israel will view with satisfaction any action which will discredit Egypt in the eyes of the Western World. Israel will probably contend that the abrupt action of Egypt provides justification for increased shipment of arms to Israel.

5. The USSR has publicly applauded Nasser's action and may have influenced his decision. It is to the USSR's advantage to upset the West's equilibrium in any way possible. It is within the realm of possibility that the USSR and Egypt will announce a mutual defense or mutual security pact within the next few days.

6. Unsuccessful U.S. military action would be most damaging and must not be permitted to occur. Accordingly, the United States must be prepared to commit whatever forces may be required to bring its military intervention to a successful conclusion.

B. Conclusions on the Implication of this Situation to the United States from the
    Military Point of View are as Follows:

7. The war-making potential of the NATO powers would be seriously affected by the interruption of the movement of vital raw

---

[5] On August 8, the Joint Chiefs of Staff forwarded to the Secretary of Defense the text of the conclusions printed here under cover of a memorandum by General Twining, which indicated that the studies referred to in paragraph 4 of the JCS memorandum of July 31 (see Document 50) had been completed and formed the basis of the conclusions. Also attached to the JCS memorandum of August 8 was a 23-page paper entitled "Expropriation of the Suez Maritime Canal Company by the Egyptian Government", which contained a discussion of the problem. (JCS Records, CCS.092 Egypt (7–28–56))

materials through the Canal. It is militarily unacceptable to the United States and NATO for this movement to be controlled by a power which is hostile or potentially hostile to the Western Powers.

8. If Egypt closes the canal, the movement through the Suez Canal of raw materials for Western use will have to be rerouted with resultant delays, increased shipping costs, and a demand for ocean freighters and tankers which exceeds the current availability.

9. If the Suez Canal, the Trans-Arabian pipelines and Iraq Petroleum Company pipelines were closed, but crude oil from the Persian Gulf continues to be available, it would have the following implications to the Western Powers:

a. Necessity for the introduction of national and international controls on petroleum consumption.

b. Crude oil production would have to be increased in the United States and Canada by 1.3 million B/D, the Caribbean by 200,000 B/D, and the Persian Gulf by 500,000 B/D to maintain Western Europe's present demand.

c. The United States and Caribbean could meet the increased crude oil production for the first 90 days; beyond that point doubt exists if this increased production could be maintained for an extended period. In any case, serious depletion of Western Hemisphere oil reserves would result.

10. If the Suez Canal, Trans-Arabian pipeline and Iraq Petroleum pipelines were closed and no crude oil was available from the Persian Gulf there would be an immediate shortage of approximately 3.1 million B/D to the Free World, particularly Western Europe, which can be met only partially by rationing and additional production from other sources.

11. Military action by either the United Kingdom, France, or United States will probably require a withdrawal of forces from NATO commitment and thus temporarily weaken the military posture in Western Europe. However, this is considered of small consequence when compared to the long-term economic effect on NATO and the loss of Western prestige and influence in the Middle East.

12. If Nasser emerges as the apparent victor in his contest with the West, the following consequences may be anticipated:

a. The resultant decrease in Western prestige could result in the loss of U.S. bases in the Middle East and North Africa and ultimately in other areas such as Iceland, the Philippine Republic, Spain and the Azores.

b. The rebellion against the French in North Africa will gain new impetus.

c. The governments and leaders of Middle East countries who have identified themselves with U.S. policies will be seriously weakened.

d. Other Moslem governments would come under increasing pressure to expropriate Western investments in oil fields and pipelines. Concessions to the USSR on the part of the nations concerned would be a logical corollary to such acts of expropriation. Were these granted, the result would be an acceleration of Soviet expansion and a consolidation of Soviet power throughout the Middle East.

e. The likelihood of Arab military action against Israel would be considerably increased and vice versa.

f. Iraqi participation in the Baghdad Pact might become so slight that the Pact would be seriously weakened.

C. *Conclusions on the Extent and Nature of Measures Required to Support U.K. (or U.K.-French) Military Action without Commitment of U.S. Forces are as Follows:*

13. United States could lend support by public endorsement of United Kingdom/French military action in the Suez and by an unqualified commitment to intervene militarily in case third parties come to the assistance of the Egyptians.

14. United States could provide certain needed critical raw materials to the United Kingdom-French for the period of time that the Suez Canal is closed by hostile action.

15. United States could provide increased economic support and financial aid to the United Kingdom and France.

16. United States could provide military supplies and equipment as required by the United Kingdom and France to guarantee the successful seizure and holding of the canal area.

17. United States could eliminate economic aid to Egypt and freeze all additional Egyptian assets which are in the United States.

18. United States could provide more active support to the Baghdad Pact, including adherence, to counter the rise of Arab nationalism. Steps might include: (a) prompt and resolute U.S. adherence to the Pact; (b) a substantial increase in military assistance to the Pact countries; and (c) stepped-up economic aid.

D. *Conclusions on United States Participation in Combined Direct Military Action:*

19. Assuming that third parties do not intervene militarily on behalf of Egypt, the U.S. contribution toward combined military forces might be on the order of:

a. *Army*—1 Division Reinforced.
b. *Navy*—1 Fast Carrier Task Force
       1 Amphibious Task Group including a Marine Regimental Landing Team and supporting Air Component
c. *Air Force*—Air Div Hq
       1 Fighter Bomber Wing
       1 Tactical Reconnaissance Sqdn Airlift as required and as practicable

E. Conclusions on United States Unilateral Action to Protect U.S. Nationals.

20. The forces required would be as follows:

a. *Army*—Army Regimental Combat Team (RCT)
Service support units as necessary
b. *Navy*—Present Sixth Fleet forces (plus augmentation from WESTLANT)
Persian Gulf–Red Sea Forces
1 Air Transport Detachment
MSTS and amphibious shipping for Army Units, if necessary.
c. *Air Force*—1 Fighter-Bomb Squadron alerted in Europe
1 Reconnaissance Flight (6 A/C alerted in Europe)
Airlift for above Army units, if ordered
6 C–119's, if required

---

119. Memorandum of a Conversation, U.S. Embassy, London, August 23, 1956, 11:45 a.m. [1]

USDel/MC/84

PARTICIPANTS

The United States	*Indonesia*
The Secretary	Mr. Abdulgani
Mr. Bowie	

SUBJECTS DISCUSSED

Proposal Procedure

Abdulgani called at his request to discuss the procedural situation. He said he felt that if the New Zealand proposal [2] was pushed, Indonesia would be eliminated from the Conference, which was contrary to its desire. They had come as the result of a special message to [*from?*] Sukarno [3] even though the Cabinet did not fully favor it and had later given certain limiting instructions. He said that the Secretary knew Indonesia's viewpoint. They were not against the principles of the United States proposal but questioned the manner of presenting it. They had made this clear to Egypt and to India

---

[1] Source: Department of State, Conference Files: Lot 62 D 181, CF 759. Secret. Prepared in the U.S. Delegation, but the source text does not indicate a drafting officer.
[2] See footnote 5, Document 117.
[3] Dr. Achmed Sukarno, President of the Republic of Indonesia.

which had included paragraph 3 of its proposal[4] in response to Indonesian pressure. Under his instructions he could go no further and might have to withdraw if the New Zealand procedure was forced to an issue.

The Secretary said he hoped the Conference would end today to which Abdulgani agreed. The Secretary said he felt that the Conference had already contributed to peace, especially by the broad participation including the assurance and the atmosphere of conciliation. The others could hardly expect the eighteen nations not to promote their view in the negotiations, but he agreed that the Conference should not be asked to act on the New Zealand proposal but should merely be informed about the action of the eighteen. In that case Indonesia would not need to take a position and the only Conference action would be the transmittal of the Conference record, presumably by the Chairman.

Abdulgani said he expected the Soviets to put forward some proposal this afternoon for submission of both the five-power and the Indian statements to Egypt. He recognized that this would be unacceptable because it gave Egypt the means to lay aside the eighteen-nation proposal. As a way out he had worked up a draft communiqué (attached).[5] On his way back he said that he intended to go through Cairo with the hope of persuading Nasser to negotiate.

The Secretary said that if Egypt had handled the matter wisely, it could gain a great victory even under the proposals of the eighteen. It would receive far greater revenues, foreign money could be attracted to expand the Canal, and Egypt might be able to finance the Aswan Dam itself from revenues. This would be far better than

---

[4] The third paragraph of the Indian proposals reads as follows: "That consideration be given, without prejudice to Egyptian ownership and operation, to the association of international user interests with 'The Egyptian Corporation for the Suez Canal'." The text of the principles and proposals, introduced by India on August 20, is printed in *The Suez Canal Problem, July 26–September 22, 1956*, pp. 288–289.

[5] The text of the Indonesian draft communiqué, which is attached to the source text, reads as follows:

"The London Conference participated in by the Governments of [blank] in its assembly from [blank] to [blank], after frank and fruitful exchange of views, expressing their concern about the gravity of the Suez Canal problem,

"Realizing the legitimate interest in the Suez Canal as a waterway of international importance

"Recognizing the respect for Egyptian sovereignty and dignity

"Calls upon all Government participants of this Conference to feel the urgency to approach the Government of Egypt and to convey to the said Government the purposes and objectives of the Conference.

"For this purpose a Committee will be set up of six Government participants.

"The verbatim record of the Conference will be sent to the Government of Egypt.

"The participants of the Conference are given freedom to work out their respective proposals as they deem necessary to arrive at an agreeable and lasting solution."

foreign financing which would only involve friction over the requisite austerity within Egypt. He explained that this had been our real reason for refusing to go forward with the Dam. Even under the eighteen-nation proposal the Secretary stressed that in his view the international participation would be primarily technical and mainly by nations with no political ambitions in the region. Thus the plan would end any British or French combination through the Canal and reduce foreign influence in Egyptian affairs. The present proposal was the minimum the French and British would accept and it had been sold to them only as a result of great efforts by the United States. Since many in France and Britain wanted to see a major defeat for Nasser, the Secretary anticipated that the United States would be very unpopular in those countries if Nasser accepts. If he rejects, then we will be back to a worse situation than two weeks ago.

The Secretary said that the Indonesian draft had some interesting ideas but stressed that the sentence calling for a committee was wholly unacceptable. Otherwise it would be possible to use the Indonesian draft if it should later be decided to have a communiqué. He said he would study it further.

---

120. Telegram From the Delegation at the Suez Canal Conference to the Department of State [1]

London, August 23, 1956—8 p.m.

Secto 50. Suez Conference: Eighth session August 23—summary. [2]

Lloyd opened by saying Conference decisions cannot be made binding on all; majority cannot bind minority; full record of proceedings should be sent Cairo.

New Zealand: MacDonald stated that after discussion with other govts he wished substitute "statement" for "proposal" he had made at previous day's meeting. This was a statement of what 18 of the govts proposed to do. He then tabled statement (text in separate telegram). [3]

---

[1] Source: Department of State, Central Files, 974.7301/8–2356. Official Use Only; Priority. Drafted by Foster and Ringwalt. Received at 6:42 p.m.

[2] The session convened at 2:45 p.m., August 23.

[3] Secto 48 from London, August 23, not printed. (Department of State, Central Files, 974.7301.8–2356) For text of the New Zealand statement, see Document 128.

Shepilov asserted new statement of NZ Delegate did not change substance of previous day's proposal. New situation has arisen whereby certain group attempting cancel out all efforts made at conference, with nations splitting into two groups and no effort reconcile various viewpoints. It is UK purpose discriminate against nations opposed to Dulles plan which flagrant violation of Egyptian sovereignty. Minority views ignored. Present group of powers does not properly represent views of users of Canal. Dulles plan is couched in language of ultimatum. Obvious UK and France wish impose colonial procedures on Egypt, thus providing pretext denounce Egypt as intransigent. There have been amendments to Dulles plan, majority emphasizing negotiations and absence of pressure. Egypt has agreed negotiate only on basis of equality, and there is no basis for negotiations in Dulles plan. He thereupon offered draft resolution to following effect:

It is agreed settlement should be achieved by peaceful means through negotiation on basis of sovereign rights of Egypt, freedom of navigation of Canal according to Convention of 1888, taking into account changed circumstances. Members of Conference gave preliminary consideration to drafts of India, US and Spain, and considered modifications suggested by other powers. They agreed all proposals and other records of conference could be subject to discussion with Egypt so that draft agreement acceptable to all nations could be prepared in course of negotiations. Representatives of six countries (USSR, UK, France, US, India and Indonesia) should be authorized establish contact with Egypt in order discuss with Egypt aforesaid records and determine what further steps were required.

Pineau in effort clarify situation offered short proposal as follows: "The conference, taking note of the declarations and communications made during its work by the representatives of the 22 member countries, asks its chairman to communicate the full record of its proceedings to the Egyptian Govt." Luns supported French proposal.

Martino lectured Shepilov on his curious ideas of democracy. If 18 of 22 nations had reached common position it should be expressed in a way representing the collective will. He had heard much from Soviet Union about democracy in quite new phraseology. He ridiculed idea that large population of Soviet Union and India should override majority vote on conference. This is a democratic system and not a democratic system. Vote of each sovereign govt is equal. He supported French proposal.

Choudhury like others before him stressed impossibility conference to draft communiqué, because inability arrive at general consensus.

Menon feared Conference would lose itself in procedural wrangle. Obvious Conference not democratic assembly of users of Canal but nations arbitrarily chosen by chairman. He argued at length in favor of a communiqué which would include more points of agreement. He recommended appointment of drafting committee of three or five representing differing views of delegates in order find areas of agreement. He suggested both US and Indian proposals be sent to Cairo. If any nation or group of nations wished present Egypt with their proposal they were free to do so. Egypt might accept one which could be made basis further negotiations.

Lange noted opinions have crystallized around two points of view, that chairman had agreed transmit complete records, including views of 18 and views of 4. Group of 17 govts has decided send delegation explain their viewpoint to Cairo to find out whether they can be accepted as basis for negotiations.

Von Brentano in short statement agreed with French proposal. He felt unnecessary have joint communiqué. He noted statements of various delegations had been made public and it unnecessary and impossible agree on text of communiqué.

Corea in confused speech suggested that there might be less opposition in Egypt, if Indian proposal were sent along with that of NZ. If 18 nation proposal were to be considered Conference statement, Ceylon could not agree.

Pineau again suggested Conference take note of all statements by various delegates and groups and have chairman transmit them to Egypt.

Abdulgani reiterated views other minority delegates and insisted on communiqué giving consensus of all delegates. He urged complete document containing text all proposals. He circulated draft communiqué (text of which sent in separate telegram). [4]

Cunha then spoke briefly in favor of French proposal suggesting complete verbatim record be sent Egypt and various delegates or groups of delegates could approach Egypt as they wished. Anything else would be waste of time.

Lloyd urged conference not end in procedural wrangle. He noted no agreement for Soviet or Indian proposals. He asked whether it was Conference's wish that French suggestion be adopted.

After a forty-five minute interval a revised Indonesian proposal was circulated (text in separate telegram). [5] Lloyd asked whether it

---

[4] Secto 47 from London, August 23, contains the text of the Indonesian proposal. It is the same as that printed in footnote 5, *supra*, with a few stylistic revisions. (Department of State, Central Files, 974.7301/8–2356)

[5] Secto 49 from London, August 23 contains the text of the revised Indonesian proposal, which reads as follows:

"The London conference on the Suez Canal, participated in by the governments

acceptable Conference. Turkey said acceptable. Lloyd noted it included Pineau proposal. Pineau said it added "decorative" element but okay with him. Lloyd asked whether everyone now agreed. Menon said he hoped grammar would be corrected before Indonesian proposal published. (Laughter)

Shepilov said Indonesian proposal gave rise all sorts of questions, omitted points of actual agreement such as desire for peaceful settlement by negotiation, and contained ambiguities such as "gravity of the problem" which meant different things to different govts. Suggested return to Pineau proposal. Questioned New Zealand statement in terms of it containing references to conference documents; if it was statement of eighteen it should have no reference Conference.

Pineau suggested view questions concerning Indonesian proposal, return Pineau proposal. As to New Zealand statement, it was in fact a part of Conference and discussed by Conference. Shepilov said if Conference agreed on Pineau suggestion he'd like to suggest an amendment to delete phrase in middle so Pineau proposal would read simply "the Conference asks its chairman to communicate the full record of its proceedings to the Egyptian Government".

Lloyd said he understood USSR opposed. Would Shepilov please confirm. Shepilov said yes, USSR was opposed Indonesian draft and again suggested taking French proposal and deleting "a couple of words".

Secretary said chairman had said he'd transmit Conference record and documents to Egyptian Govt so there seemed nothing more for Conference to do. Lloyd agreed and asked whether any purpose in prolonging Conference further. Thereupon gave thanks to staff and to all delegations for their attendance.

Menon gave thanks to UK for its hospitality and also to Lloyd for manner in which he had conducted Conference. Hoped spirit of friendship and tolerance characterizing Conference would continue in future.

Pakistan also gave thanks to staff and to Lloyd. Menzies said he did not wish remark included in record but he desired say he would

---

of (blank) in its assembly from August 16 to August 23 after a frank and fruitful exchange of views in which all took part;

"Expressing concern about the gravity of the Suez Canal problem; expressing the hope that the participating countries will endeavor to promote an acceptable settlement of this problem;

"Requests the chairman of this conference to transmit to the government of Egypt the verbatim record of the proceedings of the conference in order thereby to convey to the said government an understanding of the spirit and the purposes and objectives of the conference.

"The participants of the conference, now terminating its work, are recognized as having freedom to carry forward their respective proposals as they deem necessary in their search for an acceptable and lasting solution." (Ibid., 974.7301/8–2356)

discharge his task as chairman of the group appointed by the eighteen to the best of his abilities and "in behalf of all of you". Conference ended five p.m.

Dulles

---

121.   Telegram From the Consulate General at Dhahran to the Department of State [1]

Dhahran, August 23, 1956—10 p.m.

77. From Anderson. [2] In an initial interview August 23 [3] King stated he believed situation critical because of public opinion in area favoring nationalism and the talk on both sides of using force which creates a condition under which peaceful settlement is difficult. He appreciates US opposition to use force and believes US and Saudi Arabia have many aspects of the problem in common and that we have a common objective to find a solution that will preserve the peace of the area. He believes our positions toward working out such an arrangement are not far apart. He earnestly desires find solution and intended send mission to review situation and seek solution. He appreciates my mission and believes it makes Saudi mission unnecessary for moment.

Stressing Egypt has right to do as it wishes toward domestic enterprise provided rights to users are preserved, he emphasized that Egypt had recognized international aspects of Canal and had promised to meet responsibilities of operations and maintenance. He seemed quite prepared accept such promises himself and believes they should be acceptable to other nations.

Pointing out SA committed under treaty to go to defense Egypt in event attack, he said any attack on Egypt would be attack on

---

[1] Source: Department of State, Central Files, 974.7301/8–2356. Top Secret; Niact. Received at 9:46 p.m. Repeated Niact to London and pouched to Jidda.

[2] Anderson arrived in Dhahran early in the morning of August 23. He reviewed the situation with Ambassador Wadsworth and discussed the Aramco viewpoint with Fred Davies, Chairman of the Board of Aramco, before proceeding to Riyadh. Other members of the party accompanying Anderson to Riyadh were David D. Newsom of the Department of State, Wilbur Eveland of the Central Intelligence Agency, Ambassador Wadsworth, Alfred Jenkins of the Embassy, Embassy Consultant Mohamed Massoud, and personal attendant Naim Nakkad. (Chronology of Special Mission to King Saud; *ibid.*, NEA Files: Lot 59 D 518, Report of Special Mission to Saudi Arabia August 20–27, 1956)

[3] An unsigned memorandum of this conversation is *ibid.*

whole Arab world. He proposed England and France withdraw forces sent Mediterranean and Egypt similarly reduce mobilization as first step to reestablishment of friendly relations, needed prior conditions to peaceful solution.

Most dangerous aspect in King's mind is fact Communists have gained as result threat to use force and actual use would give Communists further opportunity intervene. He stressed neither Saudis nor US wished this. He opposed internationalization any waterway because it would make Communists "partners". He stated that if Suez was internationalized with Russia a willing or unwilling participant the world could demand similar internationalization all waterways such as Panama, Dardanelles, with result we would have them as undesirable partners in all world waterways.

He stressed several times Egypt would not agree to any infringment its sovereignty over Canal but believes Egypt willing take steps restore confidence through negotiations of a new convention. King would be willing to help arrange such convention.

To my point Nasser's breaking contract and strong words created lack of confidence the King said that was "thing of past". Egypt in his opinion was bidding to carry out international user right to Canal and willing accept international advisory board if agreement "not dictated".

Prince Faisal who participated with Yusuf Yasin and Jamal Husseini in meeting asked why world should anticipate breaches of contract by Nasser when free passage has not yet been denied.

In my general reply to Saudi positions, I placed heavy emphasis on proposal approved by 17 nations at London and their desire respect sovereignty of Egypt and at same time insulate by a control board daily operations of the Canal from politics of any nation. This is to high interests private users as well as nations. King said however he frankly doubted Egypt would ever agree to this arrangement.

I further emphasized that any solution must preserve peace and at same time restore continuing confidence in Canal operations. I suggested Western world would in event confidence in Canal is not restored seek alternative methods shipment, alternative source petroleum and be forced by necessity, "mother of invention" produce new sources energy. I told King that obviously this was detrimental to his intent and not in Egypt's interest which desired maintain revenue from Canal. With that he agreed. Emphasizing we have so many common interests with Saudi Arabia in production and use of petro I stressed we did not wish for such situation to arise and would be pleased work with Saudi Arabia in seeking means of avoiding these contingencies.

First impression is that King and his advisors are seriously worried and greatly fear that a solution unacceptable to Egypt would jeopardize peace in the area and promote Communist interests.

However, he has not yet put forward any specific suggestions as an alternative to our London proposals, other than general statement that Egypt would agree to supervision that did not impinge on her sovereignty. While he appreciates that any obstacles to traffic through the Canal would be to his detriment, he has not yet expressed any feeling that his interests are diverse from Nasser's.

This represents summary preliminary exchange in friendly two hour audience. Meeting with Faisal this afternoon to discuss London proposal in detail and hope for private audience after dining with King this evening. [4]

Carrigan

---

[4] Also during this meeting, Anderson gave to King Saud the text of the Five-Nation Proposal and presented a personal message from President Eisenhower. See the editorial note, *infra*.

---

122.   Editorial Note

During Anderson's conversation with King Saud on August 23 (see the memorandum of conversation, *supra*), Anderson handed the King a personal message from President Eisenhower. It reads as follows:

"Your Majesty:

"I have learned from Acting Secretary of State Herbert Hoover, Jr., of Your Majesty's desire to send a delegation headed by a member of your family to discuss with representatives of the United States Government the present situation in the Near East.

"In view of my expected absence from Washington this week and the presence of Secretary Dulles in London, I have taken the liberty of suggesting through Ambassador Wadsworth that Your Majesty agree to receive from me a personal and confidential emissary for preliminary discussions. I am very pleased that you have agreed to this proposal, and I am sending to you the Honorable Robert Anderson, a distinguished United States citizen and a former Deputy Secretary of Defense, who enjoys my complete confidence. Mr. Anderson has worked closely with me for a long time and I believe Your Majesty will find that he enjoys a very extensive knowledge of the problems which are of mutual interest. I have every confidence in his wisdom and discretion.

"I feel strongly that consultation and collaboration between Your Majesty and the United States Government has in the past contributed greatly to peace and stability in the Near East. In these unsettled times the importance of such consultation and collaboration is even greater. Your Majesty may be confident that Mr. Anderson will faithfully report to me your views regarding the state of affairs in the Near East, and I believe his discussions with you will be most useful in any subsequent conversations we may consider desirable.

"May God have Your Majesty in His safekeeping.

"Your sincere friend, Dwight D. Eisenhower" (A copy of the message is in Department of State, Presidential Correspondence: Lot 66 D 204, King Saud–Eisenhower Vol. I)

---

123.   Memorandum of a Conversation, Lancaster House, London, August 23, 1956, 5–5:50 p.m. [1]

USDel/MC/82

PARTICIPANTS

The United States	*Great Britain*
The Secretary and Advisors	Mr. Lloyd and Advisors
	France
	M. Pineau and Advisors

SUBJECTS DISCUSSED

Economic Aspects of the Suez Canal

The Secretary reported that a meeting of the Committee of five to consult with Nasser had been called for 11 o'clock tomorrow which would permit Mr. Loy Henderson who was to act for the United States [2] to meet with the others. He said he also planned to attend this meeting himself.

---

[1] Source: Department of State, Conference Files: Lot 62 D 181, CF 759. Secret. Prepared in the U.S. Delegation, but the source text does not indicate a drafting officer. According to the schedule and chronology prepared by the U.S. Delegation for August 23, this tripartite Foreign Ministers meeting took place at 11 a.m. at the Foreign Office. The editors have been unable to reconcile the discrepancy.

[2] At 10 a.m. on August 23, the Embassy in London forwarded to the Department of State the following message from Dulles to Hoover: "On reflection, feel Henderson would be best choice as handling at this stage is profoundly affected by Middle East politics. Please advise promptest whether he could come, as I need this information today soonest." (Dulte 23 from London; *ibid.*, Central Files, 110.13–HE/8–2356) An unnumbered service message from London, sent later on August 23, indicates that Hanes contacted Hoover in San Francisco by telephone at 11:25 a.m. London time and received Hoover's concurrence to the Secretary's proposal. (*Ibid.*) Loy Henderson

Mr. Lloyd said that it was desirable to consult together about what should be done if Egypt turned down the proposals for negotiation. He said there were two aspects, but which should be done and what other nations should be consulted.

Turning to the subject of the meeting, Mr. Lloyd and his advisors reported on the result of their talks with insurance companies regarding the situation of the Canal. Their conclusion was that there was no immediate pressure regarding insurance.

The discussion then turned to the British paper on economic measures which might be taken to put pressure on Egypt.[3] Mr. Pineau began the discussion on payment of the Canal dues. He felt they should be paid into a special fund (paragraph 1.b.). The Secretary was not sure how the United States could do this under its law. We could freeze payments in Egyptian dollar accounts but would have no control over payments outside. The United Kingdom also recognized the existence of such a limitation but hoped to be able to persuade shipping companies to adopt this practice by offering to indemnify them against future liability.

Mr. Lloyd said there were really several questions. First, policy of depriving Nasser of revenue if he rejects the offer; second, how to carry it out; and third, what to do if he refuses passage without payment. The Secretary said this last question was the crucial one; Nasser will hardly allow passage indefinitely without payment. He agreed with the idea of putting pressure on Egypt if he refuses to negotiate but wished to be sure that the methods would put more pressure on Egypt than on the users. The question was if United States tankers go around the Cape, would Nasser or Europe suffer more in view of the resulting shortage of oil and increased costs?

Mr. Lloyd said there were other means of pressure to be considered. They might shut down their base which yielded Nasser

---

arrived in London at 8:16 a.m., August 24. (Secto 52 from London, August 24; *ibid.*, 110.13–HE/8–2456)

[3] Not attached to the source text. Reference is to a "UK Paper" entitled "Measures Which May be Required if Colonel Nasser Rejects the Invitation to Negotiate", dated August 22. This paper listed six possible courses of action to be taken if Nasser turned down proposals for negotiation: (1) denial of Canal dues to Egypt, with payment being made (a) to the Suez Maritime Canal Company either in London or in Paris, or (b) into special accounts set up by each participating government, or (c) into an account held by an interim Suez Canal Board; (2) other forms of economic pressure such as control of all transactions on Egyptian accounts in participating countries; (3) persuading the current Canal staff to remain at work, subject to (a) the attitude of the Egyptian authority toward the staff, and (b) individual willingness to stay; (4) routing of ships round the Cape (a measure which would do more harm to the countries adopting it than to Egypt, but which might become necessary if the operation of the Canal declined in efficiency); (5) establishing machinery to prepare measures to counter a reduction in the flow of oil to Europe; and (6) policies with respect to assets and bank balances of the Suez Canal Company outside of Egypt. (*Ibid.*, Conference Files: Lot 62 D 181, CF 747A)

four or five million pounds in local spending but the effects would be slow. Another pressure might be to induce the Canal employees to quit, but uncertain who would be hurt most. Mr. Lloyd then asked whether the United States would be willing to block current dollar approvals to Egypt. The Secretary said again that the basic issue was the effect of non-use of the Canal which might result from some of these pressures. The United States would actually benefit from the added demand for United States oil. It was for the United Kingdom and Europe to decide whether they wanted to see the tankers go around the Cape with the attendant rationing and dollar cost of oil. On the issue of blocking of Egyptian capital funds, our only ground has been possible mingling of Canal assets with other assets. If Canal tolls were put into a separate fund it would be hard to block all Egypt's funds except as explicit economic warfare. The United States again stressed, nevertheless, that this was a strong method of pressure.

M. Pineau said that the French had studied the question of the burdens of going by way of the Cape and were prepared to take the consequences.

The British experts then reviewed other popular measures stressing that many of them would be very much more effective if adopted generally. They then discussed the following possibilities: (1) embargo of imports or exports between the U.K. and Egypt; (2) forbidding U.K. nationals to trade with Egypt outside the U.K.; (3) embargoing wheat from Western sources for shutting off oil to Egypt. Obviously the latter two would require cooperation from others.

The Secretary then mentioned cotton as another field, but the U.K. felt that efforts to disrupt the Egyptian cotton market would seriously hurt others. He felt there were two aspects of the problem; first, the policy decision whether economic pressure should be attempted and, second, the balancing of relative damage to Egypt and to ourselves from specific economic measures. Public support would be required for any such policy and was now lacking in the United States. So far, the political conventions reduced the educational effect of this Conference. If Egypt defies the eighteen nations, opinion would begin to be roused. On specific measures, expert study is needed at once. The United States is prepared to move as rapidly as possible toward study and acting together.

The U.K. again repeated that it would be feasible to bring Egypt's trade to a stand-still (except for that with the Bloc) by blocking all its current balances.

At the end of the meeting it was suggested, though not finally settled, that some organized tripartite study should be carried on. [4]

---

[4] August 28, 1956—The Secretary has indicated that he does not wish to set up at this time any such Committee as that discussed in the last paragraph of this memorandum of conversation. However, he does wish that appropriate offices in E be informed of this conversation. E.V. McAuliffe S/S–RO [Footnote in the source text.]

---

124.   Memorandum of a Conversation Between Secretary of State Dulles and Foreign Secretary Lloyd, London, August 23, 1956 [1]

Following the Tripartite Meeting, Lloyd said he wanted to speak to me alone. He then said that the British Chiefs of Staff had received a request from the Pentagon to be informed as to what were the British "war plans" in the Middle East. He said this was an embarrassing request which seemed to him to have serious political implications, and he wanted to know whether the request came from the United States Government or was merely from the Joint Chiefs.

I said that my impression was that there was some anxiety on the part of our military people that the UK-French plans might unexpectedly throw heavy responsibilities upon our naval and air-craft in the area for evacuation and like purposes, and I thought that was doubtless the motivation of the request. I said I recognized it had political implications and suggested he withhold a reply until he heard from me further.

John Foster Dulles [2]

---

[1] Source: Eisenhower Library, Dulles Papers, General Memoranda of Conversation. Secret; Personal and Private. Drafted by Dulles on August 24. The source text bears a handwritten marginal inscription that reads: "MacArthur, Rountree has seen."

[2] Printed from a copy that bears this typed signature.

125.   **Message From the Secretary of State to the President** [1]

London, August 23, 1956.

DEAR MR. PRESIDENT: The conference is now history. We adjourned an hour ago after wrangling for several hours about whether there should be a communiqué, and if so, what it should say. In this maneuvering we gained ground with Indonesia, India and Ceylon. They wanted a communiqué, and we were able to agree with them on a text and get the agreement of all of our friends. In the end Shepilov stood alone to reject it, and thus while we did not get these three Asian countries to go along one hundred percent with us, at least they ended on a note of discord with the Soviet Union and not in the Soviet camp.

I note your suggestion of a possible message to Nehru. [2] I think this is a good idea, and I am suggesting a text by separate cable. [3]

I have asked Loy Henderson to act as my deputy on the Committee of Five, [4] which will handle the next stage of approaching Nasser on behalf of the eighteen countries. We expect to have our first meeting tomorrow. Bob Menzies will head it up. [5] Then I expect to get back, leaving tomorrow evening and possibly stopping at Bermuda for a swim before getting back to the heat which will no

---

[1] Source: Department of State, Central Files, 684A.86/8–2356. Secret. Transmitted to the Department of State in Dulte 26 from London, August 23, 9 p.m., which is the source text, with the instruction "Eyes only Acting Secretary for President from Secretary". The telegram was received at 8:20 p.m. A copy is in the Eisenhower Library, Whitman File, Dulles–Herter Series.

[2] The suggestion was contained in Tedul 20, Document 114.

[3] The proposed text is substantively the same as that sent to Nehru on August 25, not printed. (Dulte 30 from London, August 23, and telegram 523 to New Delhi, August 25; *ibid.*, 684A.86/8–2456 and 974.7301/8–2556, respectively)

[4] Reference is to the Suez Committee, composed of representatives of Australia, Ethiopia, Iran, Sweden and the United States. See Document 128.

[5] Menzies recalled in his memoirs that he was awakened at 2 a.m. on August 22 by a phone call from Ambassador Aldrich, who asked Menzies to come immediately to Aldrich's residence for a meeting with Dulles and Lloyd. When Menzies arrived, Dulles and Lloyd stated their strong desire that Menzies should be the chairman or chief spokesman of the committee which would present the Five-Nation Proposal to Nasser. Menzies replied that he would have to consult his government. The following day both Eden and Dulles sent messages to Australian Deputy Prime Minister Sir Arthur Fadden, which urged that Menzies be allowed to accept the chairmanship. According to Menzies, Fadden agreed to the request within 12 hours of the receipt of these messages. (Sir Robert Gordon Menzies, *Afternoon Light, Some Memories of Men and Events*, London: Cassell, 1967, pp. 156–158) Dulles' message to Fadden was transmitted to Canberra in telegram 13 from London, August 22, and repeated to the Department of State as Secto 36. (Department of State, Central Files, 974.7301/8–2256)

doubt be generated by the political campaign. I hope you will get a few days of good rest in Southern California.

Faithfully yours,

Foster Dulles[6]

---

[6] Dulte 26 bears this typed signature.

---

126. Memorandum of a Conversation Between Secretary of State Dulles and Foreign Secretary Lloyd, London, August 23, 1956[1]

Following dinner Mr. Lloyd and I sat apart and he expressed to me his very great preoccupation with the plans of his Government for military action. He said that no doubt Sir Anthony would talk to me about this when I saw him the next day. However, he could say that the plans were such that in effect there would be a button pushed early in September and after that everything would happen automatically and be irrevocable. He thought I was the only person who could alter these plans. He said he was gravely concerned because they did not take any account of UN pledges nor did they "set the stage" so that the military action would have a justifiable basis and not be "open aggression", which was not in keeping with the times.

During this conversation Mr. Lloyd showed obvious emotional strain.

John Foster Dulles[2]

---

[1] Source: Eisenhower Library, Dulles Papers, General Memoranda of Conversation. Top Secret; Personal and Private. Drafted by Dulles on August 24. The source text bears a handwritten marginal inscription that reads: "MacArthur, Rountree has seen."

[2] Printed from a copy that bears this typed signature.

127.   Telegram From the Consulate General at Dhahran to the Department of State [1]

Dhahran, August 24, 1956—4 p.m.

78. From Anderson. In meeting with Faisal August 25 [23] [2] I had opportunity to fully outline US efforts to secure settlement without resort to force and to urge acceptance by Saudi Arabia of London proposals in ultimate best interests of area and to present facts concerning future requirements of canal, need for international capital to expand facilities, problems of creating alternative methods shipment and the peculiar problems that would face Saudi Arabia in event canal became involved and confidence in its use was not restored.

While Faisal continued stress his "personal belief" conference as composed was not way to approach problem, proposal not in accord with Egyptian sovereignty, it was obvious he had not studied matter and was simply following agreed line. Faisal wished to make two points (A) Situation must be cleared of any threat of use of force by both parties; otherwise anything emerging from conference would appear dictated and (B) No country should be asked to negotiate on basis of "stipulated" proposal. He expressed Egypt would negotiate directly with US on this type proposal, but would likely not agree consider conference proposal which he says had the appearance of being presented under threat of use of force.

We pointed out Dulles statement at conference August 20, [3] and Faisal and counselors impressed. Yusuf Yasin told me this was first time he knew US had made clear we would support no ultimatum. This he said was good.

Following meeting, however, decision apparently taken study US proposal further. Private audience with King scheduled same

---

[1] Source: Department of State, Central Files, 974.7301/8–2456. Top Secret; Priority. Received at 3:23 p.m. Repeated Priority to London and to Jidda and Cairo.

[2] A memorandum of this conversation, dated August 23, is *ibid.*, NEA Files: Lot 59 D 518, Report of Special Mission to Saudi Arabia August 20–27, 1956.

[3] See footnote 3, Document 104.

evening cancelled, apparently because King was conferring with advisers on this problem. I am meeting Faisal morning August 24 and hope have further audience with King prior departure afternoon August 24.

While the Counselors continue to stress need for settlement and hope we will do "more", they are vague as to what may be done other than to make proposal more palatable to Egypt. I consider their apparent decision actually study proposal may be beneficial.

Carrigan

128. Editorial Note

On August 23, during the eighth and final plenary session of the Suez Canal Conference, the head of the New Zealand Delegation tabled the following statement, which announced the establishment of the Five-Nation Committee (also known as the Suez Committee):

"I am authorised by the Governments of Australia, Denmark, Ethiopia, France, the Federal Republic of Germany, Iran, Italy, Japan, the Netherlands, New Zealand, Norway, Pakistan, Portugal, Sweden, Turkey, the United Kingdom and the United States of America, to state that they have requested Representatives of the Governments of Australia, Ethiopia, Iran, Sweden and the United States of America, with Mr. Menzies, the Prime Minister of Australia, as their Chairman, to approach on their behalf the Government of Egypt to place the statement recorded as Conference Document No. 12 before that Government, to explain its purposes and objectives to the said Government, and to find out if Egypt would agree to negotiate a Convention on the basis thereof. If Egypt expresses its willingness to enter into such negotiations, further arrangements, in consultation with Egypt, will be made to proceed with negotiations.

"The position of Spain is, I understand, as set forth by its Delegation yesterday in Conference Document No. 18. " *(The Suez Canal Problem, July 26–September 22, 1956,* page 293)

In the statement above, Conference Document 12 refers to the Five-Nation Proposal, also known as the Eighteen-Power Proposal; for text, see Document 110. For a summary of the Spanish position as set forth in Conference Document 18, see Document 116.

Following adjournment of the Conference, the Suez Committee remained in London to prepare for its mission. Secretary Dulles was the titular head of the United States Delegation to the Suez Committee, but after his departure for Washington on August 24, Loy Henderson served as the chief United States representative on the Committee. Other members of the Delegation were: Don C. Bliss, William C. Burdett, Jr., Stanley D. Metzger, Edwin G. Moline, and Virgil L. Moore of the Office of International Conferences in the Department of State.

At its first meeting on August 24, the Suez Committee accepted Secretary Dulles' suggestion that the Committee's first approach to Nasser should be a formal communication sent through the Egyptian Ambassador in London, Aboul Fetouh. (Secto 55 from London, August 24; Department of State, Central Files, 974.7301/8–1456) That evening, Prime Minister Menzies delivered to the Egyptian

Embassy the message to Nasser, which transmitted the Committee's request to meet with the Egyptian President and to place before him and explain the views of the 18 Powers regarding the Suez Canal. (The text of Menzies' message is printed in *The Suez Canal Problem, July 26–September 22, 1956*, page 303.) On August 28, President Nasser agreed to meet with the Committee in Cairo, and subsequently the Committee visited Cairo between September 3–9. The Suez Committee formally disbanded following its return to London from Egypt on September 10.

Department of State, Conference Files: Lot 62 D 181, contains the records kept by the United States Delegation to the Suez Committee, including summary minutes of meetings, administrative documents, memoranda of conversation, miscellaneous documents, and the numbered documents issued by the Suez Committee. Department of State Central File 974.7301 contains copies of the telegrams sent between Henderson and the Department of State. Menzies describes this mission to Cairo in his memoirs, *Afternoon Light*, pages 160–172.

---

129. Memorandum of a Conversation Between Secretary of State Dulles and Prime Minister Eden, 10 Downing Street, August 24, 1956, 11 a.m. [1]

The two of us were alone. I said to Eden that I felt that the point of view put forward by President Eisenhower in his letter which I had brought with me three weeks ago [2] was as relevant today as then in its reference to the dangers of a military action. Eden said we are very much "on the spot". We do not feel that Nasser can be allowed to get away with this, and if he does, it is disastrous for Great Britain. For example, the situation in Kuwait is still in hand, but it would not stay so long if Nasser defies the eighteen countries and nothing happens. The same goes for Iraq. We have to take military preparations, and it is very difficult to keep them in suspense. We have requested merchant ships and the like, but we cannot keep them indefinitely on a standby basis. The present plans are to move in a week or ten days unless the situation definitely clears up. Eden said he was going to try if possible to have

---

[1] Source: Eisenhower Library, Dulles Papers, Misc. Papers—U.K. (Suez Crisis). Top Secret. Drafted by Dulles.
[2] Document 35.

that delay period somewhat prolonged and that he would be discussing it with the Cabinet today. They could not hold in suspense indefinitely.

I then raised the question of their posture vis-à-vis the United Nations and urged that this be taken into account, and if possible a situation created so that if force had to be used, the primary responsibility could be put upon Egypt through their perhaps using force to prevent transit through the Canal. He said he thought this should be studied. We also considered possible action before the United Nations Security Council to get some sort of an "injunction" against Egypt.

I mentioned that I was seeing Gaitskell.[3] I said I would indicate to Gaitskell that it seemed to me at a time like this a show of national unity was important and made more possible, rather than less possible, a peaceful solution. Eden indicated satisfaction that I would reflect that point of view.

Eden spoke to me about the request of the Pentagon for information about their military plans, and said that this was somewhat embarrassing as if they told us their plans, we might then feel we had to raise objections or else be a party to what might seem to be an improper use of force. I said that I told Selwyn Lloyd to hold the request in abeyance and to forget it unless I advised otherwise after meeting with President Eisenhower next Monday.[4]

. . . .

At this point, we were joined by others.[5]

John Foster Dulles [6]

---

[3] The memorandum of conversation between Dulles and Labour Party leader Hugh Gaitskell, which took place at 3 p.m. on August 24, is not printed. (Department of State, Conference Files: Lot 62 D 181, CF 760)

[4] August 27.

[5] Dulles and his party left London for Washington at 6:46 p.m., August 24. (Secto 56 from London, August 24; Department of State, Central Files, 974.7301/8–2456) After stopping in the Azores, they arrived outside Washington at 6:15 p.m., August 25. (Dulles' Appointment Book; Princeton University Library, Dulles Papers)

[6] Printed from a copy that bears this typed signature.

130.   Memorandum of a Conversation, Riyadh, August 24, 1956 [1]

PARTICIPANTS

His Royal Highness, Prince Faisal, Prime Minister and Foreign Minister

Yusuf Yasin, Deputy Foreign Minister

Jemal Bey Houseini, Royal Counselor

Mr. Robert B. Anderson, Presidential Envoy

Ambassador George Wadsworth

David D. Newsom, Department of State

William Eveland, OCB

Alfred le S. Jenkins, Counselor of Embassy

Interpreter: Abdul Aziz

[Here follows discussion of unrelated subjects.]

And: Has Your Highness had the opportunity to hear the latest news from the London Conference?

Fai: Yes, last night the broadcast said the Conference had terminated.

And: The Ambassador might give you a bit more.

Amb: The Conference terminated with the decision on the part of the 17 powers that five of their members would form a committee which, on behalf of all 17, would discuss with Nasser. The Chairman is the Minister for Foreign Affairs of Australia. The other four are Iran, Ethiopia, Sweden and the United States.

Loy Henderson is on the way from Washington to London to get instructions to be the American representative on the committee. We were old crusaders together in the battle for Palestine.

Fai: Sometimes a crusade is not always successful.

Amb: Loy and I fought at the time for what we considered to be the best interests of the United States. We were both promoted to be Ambassadors, in order to get us as far away as possible from Palestine!

It would be nice to see Loy—to go to Cairo in this connection.

We have been wondering, Your Highness, how far you could go in lubricating the way in connection with the Suez problem. The committee is going to Egypt with every desire to find agreement on a convention. There is a systematic presentation in this proposal. If parts are encouraging to Your Highness, or if there are parts which Your Highness believes would be offensive to Arab sensibilities— just how can we lubricate the way?

---

[1] Source: Department of State, NEA Files: Lot 59 D 518, Report of Special Mission to Saudi Arabia August 20–27, 1956. Top Secret. The source text does not indicate a drafting officer.

Fai: According to what I have heard from the radio, those measures and tendencies revealed will contribute to an amelioration, since it is not a definite resolution on the part of the Conference itself but is left to individual countries or groups of countries to work out by themselves the approach.

Only yesterday I expressed the view that submitting the proposal as coming from the Conference proper *as a resolution* might involve difficulty. At any rate, this is a good step, showing wisdom on the part of the Conference.

And: We have heard by radio that India is not objecting to the submission of the proposal, for the reason we have been discussing: it is not in the form of a resolution.

Fai: Yes, India did not object specifically, but rather agreed to submit the entire records of the Conference to Nasser. This has been agreed.

And: His Majesty and His Highness have emphasized the common aim of the United States and Saudi Arabia: settlement of the crisis without the use of force. I am very encouraged this morning that Your Highness feels a step forward has been made by the submission of the proposal as from individual nations.

It seems to me that the most important thing is that these suggestions be calmly and judiciously studied by Egypt; and the essence of the next step is that Egypt agree to sit down and negotiate in an atmosphere of friendliness. The purpose of this group of nations is not to intimidate, but to inform Egypt of their thinking. We hope Your Highness might exercise the good offices of your Government, which is so influential—perhaps the most influential agent in this part of the world, to urge this kind of acceptance, in order to achieve an atmosphere and spirit of friendship which His Majesty and Your Highness have emphasized in these discussions.

Fai: I agree with you. The next step should be the abolition of all military and economic measures which have been taken. An atmosphere of friendliness and quietness is imperative.

And: I want to be quite clear on this point. Your Highness feels you can and will exercise good offices to the end that Nasser and the Egyptian Government may agree to negotiate, but you feel that there should be a mutual reduction of forces on both sides, in order to create an atmosphere for final settlement of the issue.

Fai: I think it quite necessary and imperative that all military and economic measures be abolished once and for all, in order that those concerned may think quietly.

And: The reason I make the point is because the information we have by radio indicates that the committee will shortly call on Nasser. Hence it is very important that Egypt not take a hasty judgment in declining to meet, but a considered judgment in agreeing to negotiate.

All of us recognize, too, that this is an important matter; but it might not be accomplished as quickly as Egypt might wish.

Fai: In fact, I am thinking of sending an emissary to Egypt to explain the viewpoint after our present discussions. He would explain to the Egyptian Government the attempts and tendencies of the United States Government in this connection—if you have no objection, of course.

And: Of course the viewpoint of the United States is the viewpoint expressed by the Secretary of State. Any efforts we may make are in furtherance of the efforts of the Secretary of State—on which we will keep Your Highness informed.

Fai: This is undoubtedly so, but we must express to the Egyptian Government the different stages which have been passed, and explain the dangers which have been avoided through the efforts of the United States. This is necessary so that the Egyptian Government might know fully the position of the United States Government as it is.

Yus: Some of the measures taken by the United States Government itself seem to be a hindrance to progress. For instance, the stoppage of the sale of railroad equipment. Also, French and British actions in hindering navigation in the Canal, in exhorting pilots to quit. This is bound to affect the operation of the Canal. Afterwards they will ascribe this to negligence and incompetence of the Egyptian Government. These acts are bound to affect the general atmosphere.

Amb: Prince Faisal often says if we agree in principle, we can clear up the details afterwards. There are so many details in this, let us get at the principle—get people to talking in the right spirit and atmosphere—without trying to repaint the whole picture.

Fai: We do not want to repaint the picture, but we do not want others to scrape it off, through jeopardizing the situation you want to create. These examples are slight, and should be so viewed by the other party, who should desist in them. Again I should like to look at the main issue.

Amb: The main issue being peaceful settlement.

Fai: Yes. To make this situation possible we should create the necessary atmosphere, and not try to spoil it by small things. As I said yesterday, how do you expect to say to the two parties they should have an understanding, while each party is carrying a gun in his hand.

Amb: You have done it all through history in your wars in the desert, if Philby's accounts [2] are right. Rarely has peace been made without guns in the hands of both sides.

Fai: If this is the idea of Philby, he is still ignorant of the Desert.

Amb: I read him because he writes good English.

And: I should like to make two or three points, for clarity. We talked about the creation of the right atmosphere in which we could arrive at a peaceful conclusion. I am sure Your Highness realizes the cancellation of recent military and economic measures taken on both sides would be extremely complicated, because they are related not only to this matter, but to the Baghdad Pact, to Palestine, to Cyprus, etc. I should not like to leave the impression that any of these could be accomplished simply and easily.

Fai: These measure[s] of which I speak have not been taken with respect to other issues—they were in the picture long ago. These are actions taken subsequent to Suez. Economic sanctions against Egypt have nothing to do with the Baghdad Pact.

And: I only wanted to point out the complications.

I want to be clear that Your Highness knows the circumstances under which our Secretary of State joined and participated in the London Conference, and the efforts directed to avoid the use of force. I do not want to leave the impression with His Majesty or Your Highness, or in your subsequent discussions with Egypt, that we are participating in two separate negotiations. We support the efforts of the Secretary of State to achieve a settlement on the basis of facts and of the viewpoints of all nations involved. In other words we are not negotiating through Saudi Arabia with the Egyptian Government. We respect His Majesty's desire to discuss the matter fully.

Fai: I have not said we are carrying on separate negotiations, but that we are exchanging ideas as to the best way to follow in treating the question.

And: Another thing I wish to emphasize. It is very important we not regard a willingness to negotiate on either side as accomplishing the final result we want to achieve. Each side must enter in a spirit which will make it possible seriously and honestly to strive to reach a lasting convention. Only thus will we achieve what we seek here. Unless there is this spirit, there is no point in entering into negotiations.

---

[2] Reference is to Harry St. John Bridger Philby, author of *Sa'udi Arabia*, and other books on Arabia.

Fai: For more than one year we have been carrying on negotiations with Britain, but without results. [3]

Amb: May I see your reply to the British? Have you written a good one? I should like to talk with Yusuf about it. I see an opportunity just now to get down to negotiating about Buraimi.

And: Has Your Highness given further study to the language of the proposals? [4]

Fai: Of course we have not contacted Egypt, so we do not know its ideas, but we have some comments about points which may not be acceptable to Egypt.

For example, Paragraph B on insulation from political influence. In appearance it is not offensive, but we do not know what is behind this. Exactly what is intended?

In Paragraph C, concerning returns to Egypt from the revenue. This is alright, but—connected with item D about fees being as low as possible—this seems to me it will not be acceptable to Egypt because it is unmasked intervention in the sovereignty of Egypt, in trying to define or restrict the tolls Egypt could prescribe.

And: On this point I do not find myself in entire agreement. I point out there is provision in paragraph C that there should be a fair return to Egypt. If there should be disagreement, there is provided on the next page, paragraph B, that an arbitral committee should settle it. This would be a committee jointly established by Egypt.

If, in addition to a fair return, any exorbitant amount could be charged, it might be possible that the oil of His Majesty's Kingdom could not be sold in Western Europe. The market would turn to others.

Fai: I do not mean that Egypt would prescribe exorbitant tolls; it would not be in the interest of Egypt itself to do so. My meaning is that so to restrict Egypt is a restriction on its own sovereignty. The airfield here has the right to fix the fees for landing. If someone should say we could not do this, I should reject it—it would be interference with sovereign rights. We might, however, come to an agreement to fix a ceiling price—a maximum, for so many years.

And: Your Highness has anticipated what I was going to say. Correct. This is not an ultimatum to Egypt. It is not a dictated statement. This is merely a basis for our thinking.

I wish to emphasize more strongly than anything else, when these points are being negotiated, that act in itself is the highest act of sovereignty which can be performed.

---

[3] Reference is to negotiations between Saudi Arabia and the United Kingdom on the Buraimi question. For documentation on this subject, see volume XIII.

[4] Reference is to the Five-Nation Proposal; see Document 110.

Fai: Yes. I am only pointing out what I think Egypt may object to in the proposals.

And: Your Highness is doing us a great service. Our exchange of thought is not argumentative. It is simply an exchange of ideas between friends trying to get other friends to agree.

Fai: The word "operation" bothers me. This could be considered as intervention. Egypt might not accept it.

And: We are talking here of the kinds of things laborers do—skilled labor, yes. For example, Your Highness does not feel that sovereignty is impaired if, in the operation of a petroleum company, the company with whom you have made an agreement hires and fires its personnel. You are interested in the barrels of oil going through the plant, and in its efficiency. You do not feel that the day to day operation is the sort of thing Your Majesty's Government wants to participate in. Likewise, we want to get all the ships possible through the Canal. These things which skilled people have to do are apart from political decisions, in order to make it work.

Fai: There is need of technical and skilled labor, of course. But Egypt has constituted a Board for the operation of the Canal. And Egypt is protesting that others want to take away some of these people whom Egypt wants to work.

And: The comparison is probably not a good one, except as applied to technical skills, because even Egypt admits the Suez Canal is possessed of international characteristics. It must be a question of all ships. If all ships are to use it, it must be a question of confidence.

Fai: Before nationalization, were other countries represented?

Amb: Yes, shareholders.

Fai: Most Directors of the Board were French.

And: I want to make this point. This does not mean that we simply substitute one political group for another group; but in day to day operation, it would be free from all political groups. It must be used for the trade of the world, and developed as far as it can be developed, so it can carry more ships. Again, this is the work of technical experts. Above all else there must be the confidence of the users.

This is an attempt to achieve all these objectives.

Fai: Is this lack of confidence restricted to certain nations?

And: I should not say it is circumscribed by any particular nations.

Fai: In our opinion, nothing has changed. The staff and operation remains as it was. As for freedom of navigation, all are agreed the Canal should be used as in the past.

And: Confidence involves the matter of intention. Not everyone arrives at an area of confidence by the same process. Whether rightly or wrongly, the facts are that the users do not have long-term confidence. This being the case, to avoid some of the bad consequences I described yesterday, it is not enough to say one should believe—should have confidence. The question is, is this the way, or does someone have a better way?

The United States is trying to view objectively. There are two questions: 1) what are the facts? and 2) what is the solution?

Fai: Everyone has his own idea about the question of confidence. Our own is that there has not been anything which would warrant lack of confidence. We admit we in the East lack technical skills. But we do not consider Egypt inferior to the West in the assumption of responsibility.

And: Let me make this very clear. We not only have the highest respect and regard for His Majesty's Government, but we also regard other nations of the world without reference to race, creed, etc. There is no difference. If Suez were under the political influence of any Western country, there would be fear that decisions would be made on the basis of political aspirations of that given country. We are trying to say that this is not the place for political decisions. It is a place for work—to get the maximum number of ships through the Canal.

Fai: It seems our discussions have two aspects: 1) operation and 2) authority and politics. They must be treated separately.

And: Operation is separate from political aspects. That is the purpose of the declaration—that day to day work be isolated. But both points are still subject to negotiation with Egypt.

Fai: So now we put aside the question of sovereignty. It is recognized.

And: Your Highness has put his finger exactly on the point. I am glad you recognize the difference between operation of the Canal and . . . [5]

Fai: According to the proposal you are insulating operation from the question of sovereignty. But this proposal as it is, at the same time jeopardizes sovereignty.

And: The important thing, if Your Highness agrees with us that the important thing is the question of operation is separate from sovereignty, I am not so concerned with the words as with the principle. You negotiate on principle, then settle on words.

Fai: From the beginning the Canal has been separated from the question of sovereignty and politics. We do not want the question of operation to interfere with the question of sovereignty.

And: That is the very reason it is stated in paragraph 2 "with due regard for the sovereign rights of Egypt".

---

[5] Ellipsis in the source text.

Fai: We want this to coincide with the foregoing.

And: They must all coincide.

Fai: Even if operation of the Canal is separate and independent, the mere fact of putting foreign states on this Board I believe would be considered intervention in the affairs of Egypt.

So my thinking—I do not speak for Egypt—is that perhaps for example a consultative committee might achieve results without infringing on sovereignty. The Board would be technical, and would advise in the proper carrying on of the Canal.

And: A consultative group idea is the basis of proposals made by India at the Conference. Most nations at the Conference elected to make the proposal the basis—a Board with multilateral composition.

I come back to the point Your Highness does not consider a [our] proposal a breach of sovereignty. I do hope the Egyptian Government and His Majesty's Government can be brought to feel the view of most of the nations, agreement in negotiations with Egypt.

---

131.   Message From King Saud to President Eisenhower [1]

Riyadh, August 24, 1956.

YOUR EXCELLENCY: When I contemplated sending a delegation to Your Excellency to review certain aspects of the present situation in this part of the world, I was motivated by the traditional policy which has characterised, for a long time, the relations between our two countries.

It is natural for friends to consult each other on certain questions which are of mutual interest to them, seeking an adequate solution which would realize security, tranquility, and welfare.

It is primarily of Your Excellency's concern, as well as of ours, to endeavor to remove the causes of tension which stand in the way

[1] Source: Eisenhower Library, Whitman File, International File. During the farewell visit between King Saud and Robert Anderson on August 24, with other members of the U.S. official party present, Saud gave Anderson this message written in reply to Eisenhower's letter of August 20; see Document 122. A memorandum of the farewell conversation, by Newsom, and a copy of Saud's message are in Department of State, NEA Files: Lot 59 D 518, Report of Special Mission to Saudi Arabia August 20–27, 1956.

of promoting international relations and to solve disputes through pacific means.

Your Excellency has taken the initiative in preceding us by sending to us your personal emissary, the Honorable Robert Anderson, whom we were pleased to receive, and whom we found possesses high merits and extensive knowledge of the problems of this area.

We have received from him, with great appreciation and consideration, your message dated August 20, 1956, which included expressions of friendship and cordiality, happily existing between us and tying our two countries and nations.

We, and members of our government, have talked and exchanged views with His Excellency, your personal Envoy concerning matters which absorb, in the present circumstances, our great concern, and explained to him our viewpoint with respect thereto. He, as well, explained, on his side, the sincere efforts which Your Excellency and members of your government are exerting in order to reduce the gravity of tension and restore the situation to normal after removing the causes of disturbance which is troubling to all.

We are confident that Your Excellency, being greatly interested in removing the causes of tension, is exerting your faithful efforts to stop the economic and military measures. I, for my part, am working with Egypt to negotiate; thus we are seeking solutions which would realize, for all states, the actual and legitimate interest of guaranteeing the free navigation in the Suez Canal, and would maintain, for Egypt, the rights of its full sovereignty. Through this means, it can be possible to avoid this crisis which, if left to itself, would have developed to unforseen results.

In praying God to help in the success of your and our efforts, I avail myself of this opportunity to renew, to Your Excellency, the assurances of my highest cordiality. [2]

---

[2] Printed from an unsigned copy.

132.   Telegram From the Embassy in Saudi Arabia to the Department of State [1]

Jidda, August 24, 1956—9 p.m.

97. From Anderson. In subsequent conversations August 24 with Yusuf Yasin, we have learned King considered possibility sending special emissary to US on Suez issue prior latest Arab League political committee meeting. [2] When suggestion made in political committee meeting Saudi Arabia approach US in endeavor discuss issue, Yusuf, knowing King's thoughts, endorsed idea. Yusuf, without giving further details, said Nasser consequently aware Saudi request that President receive emissary. Yusuf says, however, Nasser knows nothing of further developments, including my mission.

Yusuf later informed me he had been named by King to proceed immediately as emissary to Cairo which proposal mentioned my previous message. Yusuf affirms he wishes be in best possible position to influence Nasser to follow US leadership and, to this end, believes it most desirable he be able inform Nasser that, in response Saudi suggestion for emissary and in view President's absence, US demonstrated keen interest this problem by sending special mission bearing letter from President. He further wishes report my presentation and explanation US objectives and US London proposal. He gave us his assurance my name would not, in any event, be used.

He also asked our suggestion on what might be told Nasser about substance my mission. We prepared following suggested Saudi statement (to be used privately with Nasser only) and gave informally to King and Yusuf today. At airport Yusuf said he was willing use statement as written with Nasser, provided King agreed.

"We have been in touch through our own channels with US Government who are genuinely working toward solution this crisis in order preserve peace of area.

---

[1] Source: Department of State, Central Files, 974.7301/8–2456. Top Secret; Niact. Received at 9:40 p.m. Repeated Niact to London and Priority to Cairo.

[2] On August 23, Byroade forwarded to the Department of State the following: "Departing Iraqi Ambassador [Syd Neguib el-Rawi] revealed to me today background behind King Saud's desire send personal representative to President. He stated that in restricted meeting of recent Arab League Political Committee meeting here, delegates requested Yusuf Yasin relay their request to Saud that he send representative to President. Purpose of mission was for Saud to use his special position with United States to persuade U.S. to work for a solution of Suez controversy that could be accepted by Egypt as consistent with its sensitivity over sovereign rights. El Rawi said suggestion came not from Egypt but from Syrians and Lebanese." Byroade added that he could not speculate as to what the Saudi position would be in talks with the United States, but he did not doubt the accuracy of El Rawi's information. (Telegram 447 from Cairo, repeated to London and Jidda; *ibid.*, 974.7301/8–2356)

"They have persuaded us that efforts of Secretary of State, from beginning, have been based on this objective and that proposals put forward in London and joined in by other nations represent honest effort of US toward seeking of peaceful solution in light of all conditions that exist. They make special point that US entered into London conference at crucial time in what they believed to best interest of Egypt, area, and world and had put forth their views and proposals at that conference openly and in best of faith and cannot undertake any other activities except in support of efforts of Secretary of State.

"They have urged that gravity of situation be fully realized by all nations and that best possible efforts be made toward achieving workable and satisfactory solution. And we, for our part, would hope that Government of Egypt would receive and negotiate in good faith with representatives of five nations."

I informed Yusuf I could not agree to mention my mission to Nasser as he suggested and emphasized that the US had gone to London at crucial time in good faith and I could not enter into any other efforts save those conducted by the Secretary of State at London and related thereto. In view his belief that fuller explanation would create better atmosphere for his talks with Nasser and increase possibility Nasser's acceptance our viewpoint, in view fact Nasser knows original Saudi intention, I agreed ask Department on most urgent basis for the decision as to whether or not to permit Yusuf to mention mission, without my name, in private talks with Nasser. Department may, in view nature my mission, wish also consult President. Whatever Department decides, reply should be cabled urgently Wadsworth Jidda and Byroade Cairo. Yusuf may wait in Jidda for answer, or proceed to Cairo and wait, depending on King's instructions. [3]

Wadsworth

---

[3] On August 25, Hoover replied to Anderson's report as follows: "Saudi support for five power proposal might have extreme beneficial effect on Nasser at this particular moment. It seems to us Saudi approach to Nasser would be more effective if it were made entirely at Saudi initiative and on grounds that Saudis themselves had concluded five power proposal should be examined by Egypt.

"We would have no objection if Saudis said they had consulted U.S. through diplomatic channels but would not wish them to go further in mentioning your mission or by presenting proposed statement mentioned in Embtel 97. Nasser might look on mission and statement as indirect approach by U.S. behind back of Suez committee and draw erroneous conclusion.

"We most encouraged by your reports and look forward to your return with much anticipation." (Telegram 133 to Jidda, repeated to Cairo and London; *ibid.*, 974.7301/8–2456)

133.   Telegram From the Embassy in the United Kingdom to the Department of State [1]

London, August 25, 1956—1 p.m.

1078. Suez from Henderson. As aftermath discussion between Secretary, Lloyd and Pineau reported USDel/MC/82 [2] meeting held August 24 in UK Treasury [3] discuss economic sanctions in event Egypt refuses meet with Suez committee and situation becomes critical. British representatives included Treasury, FonOff, both Min-Transport and MinFuel and Power. [4] French represented by Wormser, Marjolin and FinAtt. [5]

British wished exchange views on question economic sanctions and possible effects on Egypt and probable consequences applying sanctions as basis for paper to be presented Ministers next week.

Sanctions discussed under four headings.

1) Denial Canal dues to Egypt.
2) Wider blocking Egyptian accounts.
3) Control exports to Egypt.
4) Refusal purchase Egyptian cotton.

Five questions specifically directed US.

1) What can be said concerning US preparedness help finance increased requirements for dollar oil [sic] if Canal traffic stopped as result denying Canal tolls.

2) Are there technical or legal obstacles to US instructing or advising owners not pay Canal tolls into unblocked account Egyptian Government?

3) If UK refuses license sterling payments for crude oil delivered Shell refinery in Egypt would US companies refrain from supplying crude?

4) Are there technical or legal difficulties in way US controlling exports to Egypt?

5) What does US export to Egypt?

---

[1] Source: Department of State, Central Files, 974.7301/8–2556. Secret; Priority. Received at 9:36 a.m.

[2] Document 123.

[3] Minutes of this meeting, prepared by the Delegation in London, are in Department of State, Conference Files: Lot 62 D 181, CF 765. A separate memorandum of this same conversation, evidently prepared by the British Foreign Office, is *ibid.*, CF 747A. The minutes and memorandum indicate that the meeting began at 10:30 a.m., August 24.

[4] Minister of Transport and Civil Aviation Harold Watkinson and Minister of Fuel and Power Aubrey Jones.

[5] Olivier B. Wormser, Assistant Director-General for Economic and Financial Affairs in the French Foreign Ministry; Robert Marjolin, Technical Counselor to the Cabinet of the French Foreign Minister; and presumably Paul Leroy Beaulieu, Financial Attaché in the French Embassy in London.

Believe have sufficient information deal with most aspects questions raised but would appreciate any additional views or advice on general question application sanctions prior next meeting now scheduled August 28.

Barbour

---

134.   Telegram From the Embassy in Saudi Arabia to the Embassy in Egypt [1]

Jidda, August 26, 1956—2 a.m.

24. For Ambassador Byroade from Ambassador Wadsworth. London for Henderson. Department telegram 133, repeated information Cairo 496, London 1345. [2]

(1) Reference telegram was delivered to me at midnight one hour after Yusuf Yasin had left my house. He is flying Cairo 6 a.m., I will get word to him at airplane to see you before seeing Nasser.

(2) Yusuf said he had conveyed Anderson's message to King Saud who had given him following instructions:

He was not to mention Anderson mission except with approval USG conveyed to him by me or you.

If he should arrive Cairo and find you had no answer from USG, he was to tell Nasser why King had not sent special emissary to Washington, i.e., because of President's absence in San Francisco, and then say that in lieu thereof King had conveyed special message his grave concern and had received in reply special message highly reassuring as to USG effort achieve peaceful settlement. In latter connection he was to speak substantially along lines proposed statement Embassy telegram 97 [3] and "to urge and endeavor persuade Nasser to work with US".

He was then to use his discretion, as changing circumstances might dictate, in endeavoring ascertain how far Nasser willing go to meet 5-power proposal and, after consulting Henderson, in assisting in lessening tensions. In latter connection he was especially to endeavor persuade Nasser to stop his radio and other propaganda attacks against Western powers.

---

[1] Source: Department of State, Central Files, 974.7301/8–2856. Top Secret; Niact. Repeated Priority to London and to the Department of State, where it was received at 4:29 a.m. The source text is the copy sent to Washington.

[2] See footnote 3, Document 132.

[3] Document 132.

(3) Apparently reflecting considerations which had prompted these instructions, Yusuf said: "We should face facts frankly; any international system will be refused by Nasser; so we must find some other way to attain same end". His first task, therefore, would be to endeavor gain Nasser's confidence by convincing him King Saud truly wished assist in finding solution.

Wadsworth

---

135.   Telegram From the Department of State to the Embassy in the United Kingdom [1]

Washington, August 27, 1956—3:22 p.m.

1366. For Henderson. Herewith Department comments on questions Embtel 1078. [2]

1) Nothing can be said at this time.

2) Advising shipowners not pay canal tolls into unblocked account would be inconsistent with existing general license. However such license could be amended to require that such payments be made into blocked account.

3) Suppliers most likely to furnish crude could refrain from supplying, and probably would if U.S. Government asked them. No guarantee could be given that some U.S. firm would not however supply if it chose to do so, unless such sales were prohibited by new U.S. Treasury regulations.

4) No technical or legal difficulties.

5) Figures contained in paper with Bliss, but may be summarized as follows: Total—$78.5 million of which: machinery and vehicles 27.7; relief goods (mostly food) 21.3; tobacco 6.3; chemicals and pharmaceuticals 4.9; foodstuffs 3.6; non-metallic minerals 3.3; metals and manufactures 3.2; other 8.2. Breakdown of figure for machinery and vehicles is: industrial machinery $11.9 million; autos, trucks and parts 11.0; electrical machinery 2.5; tractors and parts 1.5; other machinery 0.8.

---

[1] Source: Department of State, Central Files, 974.7301/8–2556. Secret; Priority. Drafted and approved by Armstrong; cleared by Roberts (NE), Mathews (S/P), Nehmer (IRD), Carre (FN), Beckner (FSD), and Maurer (L/E); and signed by Armstrong for Dulles.

[2] Document 133.

Department would consider any comprehensive program of sanctions inadvisable at this time, and would think it unprofitable to seek definition now of kind of contingency in which a comprehensive program of sanctions would be desirable. It is also highly important to consider whether a sanctions program would gain enough support to be genuinely effective. Sanctions invoked by two or three countries, such as U.S., U.K., France would probably be ineffective and hence counterproductive. [3]

Dulles

---

[3] In telegram 1138 from London, August 29, Henderson reported that Bliss had presented the U.S. position outlined in telegram 1366 to the tripartite working group. (Department of State, Central Files, 974.7301/8–2956) A note of this tripartite meeting, presumably prepared by the British Foreign Office, is *ibid.*, Conference Files: Lot 62 D 181, CF 766.

---

136.   Editorial Note

Robert Anderson returned to Washington on August 27 and at 3:46 p.m. that afternoon met with Secretary Dulles for 2 hours. (Dulles' Appointment Book; Princeton University Library, Dulles Papers) Evidently at this meeting, Anderson reported on his mission to Saudi Arabia. Although no memorandum of this conversation has been found in Department of State files, Anderson presumably either discussed orally or presented to Dulles a memorandum, dated August 26, which contained a summary of the important points raised by King Saud and Prince Faisal concerning the Five-Power Proposals. That memorandum reads as follows:

"Introduction:

"The following is a summary of the important points raised by HM King Saud and HRH Prince Faisal during discussions of the 'Five Power Proposal' to the London Conference. This summary concerns itself only with remarks made by the Saudi Arabian participants in the discussions without reference to explanations and replies submitted by representatives of the U.S. Government.

"Justification for the London Conference:

"The Saudi Arabian participants contended that:

"(1) The Conference was arranged by one party and its participants selected by that party. The 'Five-Power Proposal' is submitted as a proposal of a conference to which Egypt has never agreed. Egypt will not accept this proposal from the Conference, nor can Egypt accept negotiation within the confines of a predetermined proposal.

"(2) Egypt might be willing to negotiate on the basis of proposals submitted by the United States or another friendly nation.

"Prerequisites to Negotiations with Egypt:

"As measures necessary to ensure the proper atmosphere for negotiations with Egypt the Saudis propose:

"(1) Both England and France should withdraw the forces sent to the Mediterranean and Egypt should scale down the mobilization which it has started. (The withdrawal of U.K. and French forces was defined as the withdrawal of those forces mobilized and sent to the area after the nationalization of Suez.)

"(2) The cancellation of all economic sanctions imposed against and by Egypt following the nationalization of Suez. In this connection, specific mention was made of the U.S. action in withholding the shipment of locomotives to Egypt.

"Egypt's Right to Nationalize the Canal:

"(1) The Canal is Egyptian. This was true from the [time the ?] Canal was opened until the British occupied Egypt in 1882. The Convention of 1888 was held at the request of other nations who feared complete British control of the Canal.

"(2) Nationalization was consistent with the sovereignty of Egypt. A distinction must be made between ownership of the Company and the question of freedom of navigation.

"(3) Egypt has given adequate assurance of its willingness to allow free passage through the canal in accordance with the 1888 Convention. Until such time as Egypt refuses to live up to these assurances, there is no need for international control or for a board to ensure efficient operation of the Canal.

"(4) It is Egypt's own interest to ensure maximum operation of the Canal. The Egyptians are fully aware that an increase in tolls or failure to maintain the Canal would be detrimental to Egyptian interests.

"Egypt's Ability Efficiently to Operate the Canal:

"(1) Provided efforts are not made to encourage the withdrawal of foreign technicians, the Egyptians are capable of continuing operations at the same technical level.

"(2) Egypt has constituted a Board for the operation of the Canal. Given free access to foreign technical help there should be no difficulty in continuing efficient operations.

"Specific Comments on the 'Five-Power' Proposal:

"(1) Paragraph 3 A: The use of the words 'institutional arrangements' implies unmasked intervention into the sovereignty of Egypt.

"(2) Paragraph 2 C: Egypt must have the right to determine the Canal tolls. It is believed that Egypt would agree to the stipulation of a maximum fee. Egypt could not agree to 'fees as low as possible'.

"(3) Paragraph 3 B: There is [no?] mention of the composition of the 'arbitral commission' and to the means to be employed in enforcing its decisions.

"(4) Paragraph 2 B: The proposal for 'insulation' of the operation of the Canal brings into question the problem of sovereignty. Sovereignty must be accepted and the question of operations must not conflict with Egypt's ownership of the Canal. The mere fact that foreign states are members of the Board to ensure operations is in conflict with Egyptian sovereignty.

"The Role of the United States in London:

"Throughout the conversations the Saudi representatives spoke with deep appreciation of the role of the U.S. in preventing the use of force and in working for a peaceful solution of the problem." (The memorandum does not indicate a drafting officer; Department of State, NEA Files: Lot 59 D 518, Report of Special Mission to Saudi Arabia August 20–27, 1956)

That evening at 7:02 p.m., the Department of State sent to Jidda in telegram 136 and to Cairo in telegram 507, these instructions: "Following conference with Anderson, Department now believes it desirable further assist Yusuf Yasin in his mission by giving US agreement to his mentioning privately to Nasser US special emissary. Department intended to indicate in its earlier cable [telegram 133 to Jidda; see footnote 3, Document 132] that it had no objection to substance suggested statement given Yasin, but would not wish any paper passed to Nasser under impression US was acting independently of London conference or that such statement represented joint US-Saudi position. Believe it would be helpful if Yusuf Yasin developed thought with Nasser along lines suggested in statement. (Jidda's 97)" (Department of State, Central Files, 974.7301/8–2656) This telegram was drafted by Newsom and approved by Rountree.

On August 28, the Department directed Henderson to keep in "close touch" with Yusuf Yasin while Henderson was in Cairo. (Telegram 1401 to London; *ibid.*)

137.   Message From Prime Minister Eden to President Eisenhower [1]

London, August 27, 1956.

DEAR FRIEND: This is a message to thank you for all the help Foster has given. Though I could not be at the Conference myself, I heard praise on all sides for the outstanding quality of his speeches and his constructive leadership. He will tell you how things have gone. It was, I think, a remarkable achievement to unite eighteen nations on an agreed statement of this clarity and force.

Before he left, Foster spoke to me of the destructive efforts of the Russians at the Conference. I have been giving some thought to this and I would like to give you my conclusions.

I have no doubt that the bear [2] is using Nasser, with or without his knowledge, to further his immediate aims. These are, I think, first to dislodge the West from the Middle East, and second to get a foothold in Africa so as to dominate that continent in turn. In this connection I have seen a reliable report from someone who was present at the lunch which Shepilov gave for the Arab Ambassadors. There the Soviet claim was that they "only wanted to see Arab unity in Asia and Africa and the abolition of all foreign bases and exploitation. An agreed, unified Arab nation must take its rightful place in the world".

This policy is clearly aimed at Wheelus Field and Habbaniya, [3] as well as at our Middle East oil supplies. Meanwhile the Communist bloc continue their economic and political blandishments towards the African countries which are already independent. Soon they will have a wider field for subversion as our colonies, particularly in the West, achieve self-government. All this makes me more than ever sure that Nasser must not be allowed to get away with it this time. We have many friends in the Middle East and in Africa and others who are shrewd enough to know where the plans of a Nasser or a Mossadeq would lead them. But they will not be strong enough to stand against the power of the mobs if Nasser wins again. The firmer the front we show together, the greater the chance that Nasser will give way without the need for any resort to force. That is why we were grateful for your policy and Foster's expression of it

---

[1] Source: Eisenhower Library, Whitman File, International File. Top Secret. Delivered to the White House on August 27 under cover of a note from the Minister of the British Embassy, J. E. Coulson, which reads: "I have been asked by the Prime Minister to convey to you the enclosed message about the Suez Canal."

[2] Reference is to the Soviet Union.

[3] Reference is to the U.S. military base in Libya and the British military base in Iraq, respectively.

at the Conference. It is also one of the reasons why we have to continue our military preparations in conjunction with our French Allies.

We have been examining what other action could be taken if Nasser refuses to negotiate on the basis of the London Conference. There is the question of the dues. The Dutch and the Germans have already indicated that they will give support in this respect. The Dutch may even be taking action in the next few days. Then there is the question of currency and economic action. We are studying these with your people and the French in London and will be sending our comments soon. It looks as though we shall have a few days until Nasser gives Menzies his final reply. After that we should be in a position to act swiftly. Selwyn Lloyd is telegraphing to Foster about tactics particularly in relation to United Nations.

Meanwhile I thought I should set out some of our reflections on the dangerous situation which still confronts us. It is certainly the most hazardous that our country has known since 1940. I was so glad to see such excellent photographic testimony of your growing health and abounding energy. That is the very best news for us all.

With kindest regards,

Yours ever,

Anthony [4]

---

[4] Printed from a copy that bears this typed signature.

---

138.   Editorial Note

At noon in London, August 28, the Egyptian Ambassador in the United Kingdom, Samy Aboul-Fetouh, delivered to Prime Minister Menzies a note from President Nasser, in which the Egyptian President acknowledged receipt of Menzies' message of August 24 and agreed to the proposed meeting as requested by the Committee. (Suez Committee doc. No. SC/D/4; Department of State, Conference Files: Lot 62 D 181, CF 762) The text of Nasser's response was transmitted to the Department of State in telegram 1113, August 28. (*Ibid.*, Central Files, 974.7301/8–2856) Telegram 1113 was received in the Department of State at 8:59 a.m.

The Suez Committee then met at 2:45 p.m. in London that day and agreed that Menzies would see the Egyptian Ambassador as soon as possible and ask him to inform Nasser via telephone that the Committee preferred to meet in a place not directly involved, such as Geneva, but would go to Egypt if Nasser could not meet at a place outside his country. Also, the Committee proposed to leave London on August 31 with a view to commencing talks with Nasser as soon as possible thereafter. (Telegram 1117, August 28; *ibid.*, 974.7301/8–2856) Following the meeting, Menzies formally notified Aboul-Fetouh of the Committee's wishes. (Suez Committee doc. No SC/D/11; *ibid.*, Conference Files: Lot 62 D 181, CF 762)

At 7 p.m., August 29, Aboul-Fetouh delivered to Menzies a letter which conveyed Nasser's proposal to meet with the Committee in Cairo on Monday, September 3. (Suez Committee doc. No. SC/D/17; *ibid.*) Menzies responded in a letter to Aboul-Fetouh, written on August 29 and delivered on August 30, that the Committee of Five Powers was happy to concur in Nasser's proposal. (Suez Committee doc. No. SC/D/17; *ibid.*)

For texts of the four notes that passed between the Committee of Five Nations and the Egyptian Government, see *The Suez Canal Problem, July 26–September 22, 1956*, pages 303–306.

---

139.   Telegram From the Embassy in the United Kingdom to the Department of State [1]

London, August 28, 1956—2 p.m.

1114. Suez—From Henderson. For the Secretary.

1. Since your departure we have had two meetings Suez Committee [2] and I have had talks with French Ambassador, [3] Selwyn Lloyd, [4] Menzies, [5] and various other interested persons. It might be useful give you in this telegram brief description atmosphere and developments.

---

[1] Source: Department of State, Central Files, 974.7301/8–2856. Secret; Priority; Limit Distribution. Received at 12:10 p.m.

[2] The first meeting convened in London at 11 a.m., and the second at 4:40 p.m., August 27. Summary reports of these meetings were transmitted in telegrams 1104 and 1105, August 27. (*Ibid.*, 974.7301/8–2756)

[3] This conversation took place on August 27; reported in telegram 1102, August 27, not printed. (*Ibid.*)

[4] This conversation took place on August 27; reported in telegram 1103, August 27, not printed. (*Ibid.*)

[5] No account of a conversation between Henderson and Menzies has been found in Department of State files.

2. I am far from impressed re competence Committee. Menzies agreeable, intelligent and articulate but has not yet provided firm leadership. He has not presented any plan his own for approaching Egyptians but has welcomed most of suggestions we have made. Iranians and Ethiopians have thus far contributed little. Their role has been to sit and listen and to express agreement or disagreement—mostly agreement—with various suggestions offered. I recognize importance maintaining their support. Swedish Ambassador who represents Unden highly intelligent and although somewhat protocolaire is being constructively helpful and offers from time to time what seems to us to be excellent suggestions and advice.

3. At meeting Committee on morning August 27 Menzies announced no reply yet received from Egyptians; suggested we try depart Thursday morning August 30 if answer should come during course day; and suggested we adjourn until afternoon. I suggested that we take advantage meeting to begin discussing various points of our terms of reference and that we attempt find meeting of minds with regard kind of approach we should make to Nasser from point of view both procedure and contents. Menzies agreed and we spent remainder of morning in quite useful discussion. It was decided that our basic task would to be to obtain from Nasser agreement to enter into International Convention supplementary to that of 1888 and that we should try work with him Heads of Agreement for use during negotiation such Convention. While discussing what Heads Agreement should embrace, we ventured suggest Committee make analysis of "Operations of Canal", endeavor break down these operations into various component parts with purpose ascertaining what aspects of operations might be left to Egyptian handling without threat to non-political and efficient management of Canal. Swedish Ambassador suggested that British shipping people might be able give us useful information re various problems connected with operation and number of them were invited to afternoon session.

4. Our discussions re various phases operations during morning meeting were of general character. We hoped we could become more specific after we had talked with British shipping representatives. This hope did not materialize since representatives in afternoon confessed ignorance of operational activities of Canal and since we had no opportunity for discussion after having quizzed them. They devoted their remarks for most part to stressing superiority of European pilots and personnel over Egyptian and to complaining of increasing difficulties which Canal authorities and ship suppliers in Canal area had been encountering from Egyptians even before nationalization. Their assertions of superiority of Europeans clearly did not make good impression upon Iranians and Ethiopians. Neverthe-

less latter remained placid and continued try to be helpful. Our next meeting will be this afternoon and we hope then make more progress in direction working out projects for Heads of Agreement.

5. Early yesterday afternoon I called on French Ambassador. During course conversation he displayed rigidity which not at all in keeping, in my opinion, with realities. In brief his idea seemed to be that Committee was expected to adhere strictly to terms of reference. Although he did not go so far as to say it should not even illustratively indicate to Nasser how it would be possible for international board to control basic operations of Canal without real derogation Egyptian sovereignty, he nevertheless stressed that no details re relations international manager with Egyptian Govt had been worked out as far as he aware and thought Committee should therefore be extremely careful not to give illustrations to which France might not be able to agree during course subsequent negotiations.

6. I was somewhat surprised at attitude of Selwyn Lloyd. In previous encounters which I had with Lloyd he had appeared relaxed and cordial. On this occasion I found him apparently in state of tension. There was touch of asperity in his voice. Without bothering about amenities he commenced firing rather sharp questions: "What will you do if Nasser says no, but—" "Will you accept qualified reply?"; "How soon will you have answer for us? Menzies has promised answer by Friday." "If your committee is to be of any use to us we must have answer without delay and answer must be clear-cut." I refused to be ruffled by his abruptness and he gradually became a little more friendly. Nevertheless it seemed to us he not happy re Committee, had little hope that Committee would be able to bring kind of answer which would satisfy him, and in fact was somewhat suspicious of Committee. He like French Ambassador made clear he expected Committee would keep strictly within terms of reference and would not be too imaginative in advancing illustrations showing their flexibility.

7. Later in afternoon I touched on these conversations with Menzies. He took position that we should approach Egyptians in a spirit of conciliation; that while adhering firmly to position that Canal should be under international management to extent necessary for guaranteeing that it would operate effectively and not become political instrument of any power, we should try to convince Nasser (A) that this was possible without infringing on Egyptian sovereignty and (B) that if Nasser agreed to negotiations on basis of our terms of reference, he would find that they had high degree flexibility.

Barbour

140.   Memorandum From the Deputy Under Secretary of State for Political Affairs (Murphy) to the Secretary of State [1]

Washington, August 28, 1956.

SUBJECT

NATO Consultation on Suez

UK Minister Coulson called on me today to say that he had been instructed by Selwyn Lloyd to inform the Department that the UK considers that the next step in the Suez matter should be to consult with the North Atlantic Council. Lloyd believes that such a consultation would be in accord with the general desire to extend the consultative process in NATO. The purpose of the consultation would be to tell the other NATO representatives "how our minds are working" and get their views. Lloyd suggests that a UK representative brief their permanent NATO representative on the 18 nation decision at London and that a U.S. representative brief George Perkins on the work of the 5 nation committee; in this way our permanent representatives would be better able to lead the discussion in the NAC. Lloyd also asks whether we think Iceland and Greece should be included in the NAC consultation and expressed the view that probably Greece should be invited to take part. Coulson also advised me that a similar approach is being made to the French Government by the UK and that Lord Ismay is being asked for his views on the desirability of NAC consultation. The UK also desires to consult with the Western European Union Council [2] on Suez.

The two questions on which Lloyd, therefore, desires your position are whether you agree that consultation in the NAC should be held forthwith and, if so, whether the U.S. will send a representative to brief George Perkins on the work of the 5 nation committee. The second question is whether we think Iceland or Greece should be excluded from NAC consultation.

---

[1] Source: Department of State, Central Files, 740.5/8–2856. Confidential. A handwritten marginal notation by Murphy on the source text reads: "8/28 Sec saw. & Geo Perkins read this. Agreed to early meeting & report by UK reps of London Conferences results. Sec believed premature discuss work of committee of five. Saw no objection attendance of Iceland & Greece under these [?] circumstances. RM. Mr. Coulson informed 1830–8/28. RM."

[2] The membership of the Western European Union Council consisted of the Foreign Ministers or their representatives of the following countries: Belgium, the Federal Republic of Germany, France, Italy, Luxembourg, the Netherlands, and the United Kingdom.

141.   Telegram From the Embassy in Egypt to the Department of State [1]

Cairo, August 28, 1956—4 p.m.

488. Position conveyed Department's telegram 507 to Cairo [2] given Yusif Yasin today. He said most grateful and thought would strengthen his position.

Yasin spoke freely about his long talk with Nasser. Said he believed he had accomplished following:

1. Instilled more confidence on part of Nasser in attitude King Saud. Felt this important as "some parties" had been at work to undermine such confidence.

2. Managed to convince Nasser United States really stood for peaceful settlement.

3. Told Nasser King did not really stand for international control of Canal. In making this point clear, at same time made two points (A) King's strong feeling that Five Power mission should be received with "broad mind and heart" and search on Nasser's part for acceptable compromise; (B) King's equally strong feeling that Nasser should do everything possible reduce tension and particularly see that press and radio drop attacks against West.

As regards latter, he said Nasser spoke of United States, and particularly, British press with some bitterness. He, however, promised that there would be a gradual tone down on part of Egypt. Yasin hopes if this happens there will be similar response Western press.

He said Nasser seemed willing and eager solve question amicably and is searching for compromise. He felt both sides should be willing compromise and that United States must know that Egypt could not accept true international control. He personally thought a satisfactory compromise could be found but that much depended upon United States efforts to reduce military and economic measures in order to create climate for compromise. He said that Anderson said this was most difficult, but that he felt time was now if we were to open door for real discussions.

Yasin said he had stressed upon Nasser King's desire that there be better relations between Egypt and United States which seemed vital for interests Saudi Arabia as well. He said Nasser seemed willing to do what he could but obviously retained bitterness over manner in which High Dam, arms, et cetera had been handled.

---

[1] Source: Department of State, Central Files, 974.7301/8–2856. Top Secret; Priority. Received at 7:12 p.m. Repeated Priority to London and Cairo.

[2] See Document 136.

Yasin said he had also seen General Hakim Amer and thought he had convinced him that United States was truly against use of force and sought amicable solution.

Yasin said Nasser had asked him to stay Cairo for period of talks and he had wired King for this authority. I was surprised he thought Five Power group might get here as late as Saturday and talks start next Monday.

Yasin said Saudi Arabia attitude governed by three wider points.

1. Egyptian question is now really Arab question. As far as Arabia concerned there was also question of alliances and treaties with Egypt.
2. Freedom of navigation as important to Saudi Arabia as anyone else, including British.
3. Overall danger of Russia and advantage she was getting out of present situation.

He ended statement, however, that come what may, Arabia could not afford to be enemy of Egypt.

All of above without interruption my part. Did not wish comment on substance in any event as not aware in sufficient detail what Anderson conveyed and do not wish to cross lines with what Henderson's mission may be. However as flat statement of King's position on international control seemed contrary to statement (Jidda 97) [3] asked his understanding of United States position conveyed by Anderson. He felt we stood for international control and really believed in our plan as being best solution. He under impression however, as far as we concerned, [it] is something that could be "talked about". I told him that United States felt some form international control necessary to reinstill lost confidence.

We promised to keep each other informed of upcoming developments. [4]

Byroade

---

[3] Document 132.

[4] On August 29, Yasin visited Byroade to make a special plea that the United States lift its economic restrictions against Egypt and use its influence with others to do likewise. He said that Nasser felt strongly that he should not negotiate under military and economic duress. Also, Yasin thought that Nasser wanted to delay the opening of talks with the 5-power group until September 3 if possible, but this only meant that Nasser and his advisers were busy preparing for the talks. (Telegram 508 from Cairo, August 29; Department of State, Central Files, 974.7301/8–2956)

142.   Telegram From the Embassy in the United Kingdom to the Department of State [1]

London, August 28, 1956—9 p.m.

1131. Suez—From Henderson. At PriMin's request I saw him this afternoon at six o'clock. He obviously worried and perplexed. He said he glad that Committee was finally leaving Thursday (August 30). [2] When I told him we had decided to depart Friday morning he clasped his head and groaned "Oh these delays. They are working against us. Every day's postponement is to Nasser's gain and our loss." I explained Committee's reasons for leaving Friday. He admitted they sound but still found them exasperating.

He asked re size mission, expressed concern when I told him possibly 40 persons would be involved. He said he failed understand why it so large since it his understanding there would be no negotiations. I pointed out our terms of reference called for explanations and preparation of explanations sometimes required considerable staff. He asked how long our conversations in Cairo would last. I said difficult give accurate answer. They might last only two hours, they might last two or more days. He said he would not mind two hours or even two days but protracted negotiations could be disastrous. Their very length might frustrate purpose of Committee. I told him I thought members of Committee understood urgency their mission and had no intention remain in Cairo indefinitely. It was my hope and I thought hope other members of Committee it would not require protracted period to extract answer from Nasser sufficiently clear to justify termination of mission.

PriMin said Suez problem vital to Great Britain. He hoped it could be settled peaceably. He could tell me confidentially, as he had already told Mr. Dulles, consideration being given to presentation matter to Security Council if Nasser should reply in negative. It therefore important that reply be clear and prompt.

I said that if this matter submitted to Security Council it might be dragged out almost indefinitely. Resolutions might be presented by members such as Yugoslavia calling upon both parties exercise restraint. There could be many debates. Sov Representative would veto. PriMin said he recognized danger but it would be advantageous to UK to show world that it had exhausted all peaceable methods before resorting to other methods. It was clear Soviet Union

---

[1] Source: Department of State, Central Files, 974.7301/8–2856. Secret; Limit Distribution. Received at 9:53 p.m.

[2] Reference is to the planned departure of the Menzies mission to Egypt; see Document 138.

would undoubtedly veto any kind of constructive resolution Security Council. Such veto however, would give UK needed freedom of action.

I said I recoiled at idea use of force. Forceful methods might release chain of events which could be disastrous to whole world. I had some concern for instance lest Soviet Union might move into Iran in case Great Britain and France should become involved in armed struggle with Egypt. I had no grounds for this concern other than feelings derived from my experiences re Soviet Union and Iran. Prime Minister said he realized that employment of force would involve risks. On other hand if UK and France should capitulate to Nasser there were other serious risks. I admitted that if Nasser should "get away with" his nationalization actions re Canal there could also follow chain events disastrous to free world.

Eden indicated, although he did not use precise words to that effect, that if UK was to meet disaster it preferable it should come as result action rather than inaction.

In final words to me before my departure, Eden again said that he was depending on Committee to bring back with minimum amount of delay clear-cut answer from Nasser.

Barbour

---

143.   Memorandum from the Chairman of the Joint Chiefs of Staff (Radford) to the Secretary of Defense (Wilson) [1]

Washington, August 28, 1956.

SUBJECT

Military Capabilities of Israel and the Arab States

1. In a memorandum for you, dated 25 April 1956, [2] subject: "Arms for Israel", the Joint Chiefs of Staff informed you that if Israel initiated hostilities before mid-summer 1956 she could, in less than a month, defeat the Egyptian army in the Sinai and contain the ground forces of the other Arab States. It was further estimated that after mid-summer, the balance of ground force superiority would

---

[1] Source: Department of State, Central Files, 784A.5/9–656. Top Secret. A copy was forwarded to the Department of State under cover of a letter, dated September 6, from Gordon Gray to Hoover.

[2] Forwarded to the Department of State on May 4; for text, see vol. XV, p. 610.

begin to shift to the Arabs and a stand-off position in the air would be reached.

2. The Joint Chiefs of Staff now consider that Israel has a degree of military superiority, which it will retain for about the next three months. At the end of this period and until about April 1957, the military power of the two sides will be roughly in balance. After the spring of 1957, a margin of Arab military superiority will become manifest and, if present trends continue, will gradually increase.

For the Joint Chiefs of Staff:
Arthur Radford [3]

---

[3] Printed from a copy that bears this typed signature.

---

144.   Memorandum of a Conversation Between the President and the Secretary of State, White House, Washington, August 29, 1956, 9:30 a.m. [1]

(1) Suez. I outlined to the President my talks with the British, particularly those with Eden, Macmillan, Salisbury, and Lloyd, indicating the British were determined to move militarily unless there was a clear acceptance of the 18-Power plan by Nasser by around the 10th of September. I said that Eden had indicated that their military planning would have to take a definite and irrevocable status by about that time and could not be left appreciably longer in a state of indecision.

The President raised the question of the attitude of the Labor Party and I said that this did involve a question mark. I said I felt that Gaitskell's open opposition to the Government policy was not in the interest of the peaceful solution because it was apt to encourage Nasser to feel that he could reject with impunity, and there then might come incidents or action which would in fact precipitate hostilities which the Labor Party could not prevent.

---

[1] Source: Eisenhower Library, Dulles Papers, Meetings with the President. Secret; Personal and Private. Drafted by Dulles. Following the Republican Convention, President Eisenhower remained in California for several days. He returned to Washington at 8:30 p.m. on August 28. (Record of the President's Daily Appointments; Eisenhower Library)

I referred to the contrast in the British position from our position in relation to Taiwan, where there had been virtual unanimity.

I said that my own belief was that it would be very difficult to disengage the talks with Nasser in accordance with Eden's timetable, and that in fact the British might be drawn into a situation where they would have to accept a result which, while reasonably safeguarding the Canal, would not give the blow to Nasser's prestige which the British and French felt indispensable because of their positions in the Middle East and North Africa respectively.

I said that the British were also thinking in terms of possible Security Council action and that again might get them into a situation from which they could not readily disengage for the purposes of hostilities.

The President raised the question as to whether there was anything we could do to help bring about acceptance of the 18-Power proposal by Nasser. I said I thought it might be a good idea if he would issue a statement indicating, with his personal authority, support for the 18-Power proposal. The President agreed with this and I then dictated the draft of such a statement. By the time it was typed out, Admiral Radford joined us and a copy was shown to him. A few suggestions were made and the statement then agreed upon with the understanding that I would read it to the press and television. [2]

(2) We discussed Eden's letter received on August 27, [3] and it was agreed that I would draft a suggested reply.

[Here follows discussion relating to China, Panama, and personnel matters. For text of the discussion on Panama, see volume VII, page 302.]

(7) I referred to the confidential trip of Bob Anderson to Saudi Arabia and said I thought the President would find it both interesting and instructive to hear a report from him.

[Here follows discussion of Yugoslavia and Germany.]

JFD

---

[2] Eisenhower's statement was issued as a White House press release later that day. For text, see *Public Papers of the Presidents of the United States: Dwight D. Eisenhower, 1956*, pp. 716–717; or Department of State *Bulletin*, September 10, 1956, p. 405.

[3] Document 137.

145.   Telegram From the Embassy in the United Kingdom to the Department of State [1]

London, August 29, 1956—2 p.m.

1147 Suez—From Henderson.

1. We are sure Dept realizes after reading our various telegrams that one of perplexing problems which Suez Committee facing and which USDel in particular facing is interpretation of phrase contained proposition New Zealand [2] authorizing Committee in presenting 18 Power statement to "explain its purposes and objectives". It seems clear that at least British and French Govts, if not various other European govts, take position that Committee has no power "to negotiate" and therefore its discussions with Nasser should be strictly within framework 18 Power statement. These govts apparently fear that if Committee ventures illustrate to Nasser how he could agree to principles set forth in statement without losing too much face, or endeavors through illustrations to impress upon him high degree flexibility in negotiations he will retain even after agreeing to these principles, Committee may advance ideas which would not be acceptable to UK and France and that UK and France might have difficulty in opposing such ideas during negotiations if Nasser should point out that they originated with Suez Committee. It furthermore apparent that UK and France do not believe that Committee has facts and experts at its disposal which would enable it to hold its own in case Nasser should endeavor convert explanations into preliminary negotiations. UK and France are particularly concerned lest explanations should lead to discussions which would be drawn out to considerable length or which may lead to obscuring what seems to them to be clear cut issues. They expect Committee to obtain flat yes or no answer from Nasser quickly with minimum amount of "explanation".

2. Although Menzies has asserted that Committee should be prepared to give Nasser illustrations as to how principles in statement [3] could be applied in manner which would really be to advantage of Egypt as well as to users of Canal, he has thus far made no concrete move in direction of formulating illustrations or asking any member Committee to do so.

3. Members U.S. Delegation staff have nevertheless been devoting considerable time in endeavoring formulate certain illustrations

---

[1] Source: Department of State, Central Files, 974.7301/8–2956. Secret; Niact. Received at 11:02 a.m.

[2] For text of the New Zealand statement, see Document 128.

[3] Reference is to Five-Nation Proposal, also known as the Eighteen-Power Proposal; see Document 110.

and in fact we have drawn up tentative outlines of plans for operation of Canal in accordance with principles contained in statement. During course of today one such possible outline is being sent to Dept for comment.[4] We believe this outline close to British thinking, as disclosed their memo handed U.S. Del early London Conference, but British and French may correctly fear this would be first position to be bargained down.

4. Unless we hear otherwise from Dept we shall assume that it desires USDel and Committee not to hesitate in discussion with Nasser to present various suggestions illustrating flexibility which he would have negotiating on basis of principles contained in statement provided he given clearly to understand such illustrations should not be regarded as binding in initial stages upon 18 Powers which Committee represents. We recognize of course that Nasser would nevertheless not hesitate to so use them if suited his advantage.

5. If after discussions Committee finds that Nasser is prepared to cooperate in drawing up "heads of agreement", Committee will be almost sure to face problem as to whether contents of this document should be limited strictly to principles contained in 18 Power statement or whether it could also include certain details which would no longer be considered as merely illustrative. We doubt Nasser would be prepared approve any "heads of agreement" limited to generalized statement principles of 18-Nation statement. Thus we see little alternative to working out with Nasser at some stage fairly detailed "heads of agreement", including outline of system, if we are to have any real chance of obtaining agreement from him to move on to formal negotiation on predetermined basis.

Any views which Dept might be able to give us in this regard would be appreciated.

Barbour

---

[4] Telegram 1144 from London, August 29, not printed. (Department of State, Central Files, 974.7301/8–1956)

146.   Telegram From the Department of State to the Embassy in the United Kingdom [1]

Washington, August 29, 1956—2:24 p.m.

1439. For Henderson. The Suez Committee seems to have made a good start with your valuable assistance. I am gratified that Menzies' attitude as reported your 1114 [2] remains consistent with views which I expressed in putting forth to Suez Conference my proposals. I made clear my belief that the proposals should not take the form of an ultimatum to Nasser, and that there should be an element of flexibility in working out details, although the arrangements agreed upon should be in accordance with the basic principles which the 18 nations considered essential to give assurance that the Canal will be operated on an efficient and non-political basis.

Following my talk with the President this morning he issued statement which is being cabled you separately. The purpose was to give maximum support to your Committee. On the other hand it was not designed to subtract in any way the actual element of flexibility which we believe should be present in the negotiations as more fully expounded in my press conference of yesterday. [3]

Dulles

---

[1] Source: Department of State, Central Files, 974.7301/8–2856. Secret; Priority; Limit Distribution—Suez. Drafted by Rountree; cleared, approved, and signed by Dulles.

[2] Document 139.

[3] The transcript of Dulles' press conference on August 28 is printed in Department of State *Bulletin*, September 10, 1956, pp. 406–411; excerpts pertaining to the Suez Canal situation are in *The Suez Canal Problem, July 26–September 22, 1956,* pp. 295–301.

147.   Note From the British Minister (Coulson) to the Secretary of State [1]

Washington, August 29, 1956.

MY DEAR SECRETARY OF STATE: I enclose the text of a message which Mr. Selwyn Lloyd has asked me to communicate to you. As you will understand he is extremely anxious that no idea of its contents should become known.

I should be grateful for an opportunity to discuss this question with you as soon as you have had time to consider the message. There are also one or two questions arising out of the studies now proceeding in London which I should like to raise with you at the same time.

Yours sincerely,

J.E. Coulson

[Attachment]

Message From Foreign Secretary Lloyd to Secretary of State Dulles [2]

London, August 28, 1956.

As you know, it is our intention to proceed with our plans unless Nasser can be seen clearly and decisively to have given in. I have therefore been considering what our next step should be, if he rejects the proposals endorsed by the eighteen countries. I think that there is on balance much to be said for raising the Suez problem in the Security Council immediately we have his reply if it is negative. This course would have the advantage that it might affect his further attitude to our proposals. It would also put us in a better posture if we are obliged to take action against him.

---

[1] Source: Department of State, Central Files, 974.7301/8–3056. Top Secret. Attached to the source text is a memorandum from Howe to Rountree, dated August 30, which among other points noted that although further information was expected from the British, Wilcox in coordination with Rountree would prepare a preliminary draft reply for Dulles recognizing that Dulles "may wish himself to draft or to hold up any reply until further word from the British." Howe also noted that the attached message from Lloyd "must be handled with the greatest care."

Dulles directed that copies of Coulson's note and Lloyd's message be forwarded to the White House for the information of President Eisenhower. The copies are in the Eisenhower Library, Whitman File, International File. A marginal notation by Eisenhower on the first page of Lloyd's message reads: "Secret Files/D.E."

[2] Top Secret.

2. I realize the risks involved. All sorts of things might be suggested. For example, a call to the parties to settle their differences by discussion, a call to the London Conference to resume, a reference to the International Court or the appointment of a Committee of the Security Council. There might be a desire to refer the matter to the General Assembly or even to despatch a peace observation commission to the area. I realize that it would be impossible to get from the Security Council a resolution justifying the use of force without further reference to the United Nations. Nor would it be possible to get even if we wanted it a resolution in favour of economic sanctions passed by a satisfactory majority.

3. On the other hand, the concentration of our forces in the Mediterranean is bound to result in someone raising the matter in the Security Council. It might be the Soviet Union, Yugoslavia or even Iran under pressure from the Arab states. This last possibility would be most unfortunate.

4. Therefore I think that the balance of advantage lies in our taking the initiative in raising the matter in the Security Council immediately after a negative reply from Nasser. The following points of procedure arise:—

(a) *Calling the Meeting*
This could be done either by the United Kingdom alone, or by the United Kingdom and France or by the five members of the Security Council who supported the Eighteen Power Declaration with the possible addition of Belgium.

(b) *Representation at the Meeting*
So far as possible this should be at Foreign Minister level. Pineau and I should represent France and the United Kingdom. It is my hope that you will be able to come yourself. We should try to get Spaak to represent Belgium. His views are particularly robust.

(c) *A Resolution*
A resolution should be tabled emphasizing the seriousness of the situation and recommending the Eighteen Power solution and perhaps expressing regret at Egypt's rejection of it.

5. The essence of the matter would be to infuse an atmosphere of urgency into the debate, making it clear that we want an expression of opinion from the Security Council within one week. And that we were not prepared to embark on a lengthy procedural discussion. The presence of Foreign Ministers would make it easier to attain such an atmosphere. If the proceedings become bogged down in procedural wrangles and interminable amendments, the Foreign Ministers would endeavour to wind up the debate, saying that the proceedings were futile and that the United Nations had shown itself incapable of dealing with the matter.

6. I cannot emphasize too strongly that your active help is essential to the success of this plan. The plan might pay a dividend

with regard to Nasser's reactions but the main object of the exercise would be to put us in the best possible posture internationally in relation to the action which we may be obliged to take. I think that moderate opinion would be shocked at forcible action by us without any reference at all to the United Nations. In view of the great issues at stake I venture to suggest that it is of the greatest importance to the United States that our action should be shown to be reasonable, that is to say that we had tried the Conference of twenty-two under Article 33 and then we had gone to the Security Council under Article 35, that neither of these courses had produced any result so we were bound to take police action to procure an international solution.

7. I know that to go to the Security Council is full of risks because of its dilatoriness but I believe that *not* to do so would be certain to have consequences of greater gravity. I had a brief talk with Pineau whilst the Conference was sitting along these lines. He did not dissent. I should welcome your views very urgently. If we could tackle the Security Council as a combined operation in the way in which we managed the London Conference I think that we could derive considerable benefit. After all the composition is not too bad. There are five signatories of the Eighteen Power Declaration together with Belgium, whose Government feels most strongly. In addition there are two friendly Latin Americans and the possibility of Nationalist Chinese support. It is not a bad membership and under your leadership I believe that we could pull off another success.

8. I cannot tell you how grateful we all are to you for your masterly handling of our case here during the Conference. [3]

---

[3] Printed from an unsigned copy.

148.   Memorandum of a Conversation, Department of State, Washington, August 29, 1956, 5:30 p.m. [1]

SUBJECT

Suez Canal

PARTICIPANTS

The Secretary	Mr. J. E. Coulson, Minister, British
Mr. Hoover	Embassy
Mr. Wilcox	Mr. Ronald Bailey, Counselor,
Mr. Rountree	British Embassy

The Secretary referred to Mr. Lloyd's message of August 28 [2] to him and said the suggestions concerning United Nations Security Council action had raised several problems in our minds. He pointed out that if the Suez issue was raised as a dispute, the parties at interest must refrain from voting. In this event, even with a lenient interpretation of who were the parties at interest, it was not at all certain that a proposed resolution could receive as many as seven votes. The wording of Mr. Lloyd's letter indicated that the London conference had been held pursuant to Article 33 of the Charter, [3] and the implication of this was that the matter would be raised as a dispute. Mr. Coulson said he had not realized the wording "dispute" appeared in Article 33. Clearly the intention of the British Government was to raise the matter as a situation and he wished to get on record at once that intention in order to avoid the problems which would arise if it were presented as a dispute. The Secretary said that the British were not, of course, bound to say that what was done at London was technically under Article 33. A more difficult question was, however, that if the matter was called a "situation," it was doubtful that the Security Council would have power to make substantive recommendations, its action in this case presumably being limited to procedural suggestions only. Mr. Coulson expressed as his own view the idea that what would be sought from the Security Council would in fact be procedural, in that no decision would be asked upon the substance of the controversy.

---

[1] Source: Department of State, Central Files, 974.7301/8–2956. Secret. Drafted by Rountree. The time of the meeting is from Dulles' Appointment Book. (Princeton University Library, Dulles Papers)

[2] Attached to Coulson's note, *supra.*

[3] The text of Article 33 (Chapter VI), of the U.N. Charter reads:

"1. The parties to any dispute, the continuance of which is likely to endanger the maintenance of international peace and security, shall, first of all, seek a solution by negotiation, enquiry, mediation, conciliation, arbitration, judicial settlement, resort to regional agencies or arrangements, or other peaceful means of their own choice.

"2. The Security Council shall, when it deems necessary, call upon the parties to settle their dispute by such means." (3 Bevans 1161–1162)

In discussing the possible voting of the Security Council on this matter, it was mentioned that Cuba, Peru and Nationalist China probably could be counted upon to vote in favor of the United Kingdom position. Those definitely opposed would be the Soviet Union and Yugoslavia, and Iran's delicate position rendered it doubtful that that country could definitely be counted upon.

The Secretary said that his initial reaction to Mr. Lloyd's letter was that he would like further British views upon the question of whether the matter would be raised as a situation or a dispute. He wondered whether, in light of the interpretation of the Charter and previous practices, it would be possible to make a recommendation on substance rather than on procedure. Also, he asked whether it would not be difficult to exclude the appearance before the Security Council of at least those countries represented at the London conference who might want to be heard. Mr. Coulson observed that India might not wish to come, and that it should be possible to prevail upon members of the 18-nation group not to insist upon being heard.

The Secretary said that if any of the countries felt that the U.N. action was setting the stage for "police measures" they might wish to inject themselves into the matter. The general concept inherent in the British position of excluding direct military action until there had been recourses to the United Nations was sound. He observed that Mr. Lloyd's letter had referred to United States public opinion in this regard, but he assumed that the Foreign Minister also had in mind, to some extent at least, public opinion in the United Kingdom.

Continuing, the Secretary said that the London conference was completed in just over one week, but we were able to accomplish that only because of simplified procedures and the fact that only simultaneous translation was provided. The procedural complications in the Security Council and the successive translation would require over three weeks to do the same amount of work. Mr. Coulson responded that the Foreign Office had that in mind in suggesting that representation at the Security Council be at the Foreign Minister level. Officials of that category could not engage too much of their time in the meeting.

Mr. Coulson said he wished to mention the studies which were now going on in London with regard to (1) the possibility of denying to the Government of Egypt Canal dues and (2) financial and economic measures which might be imposed as economic sanctions against Egypt. He said that Nasser was now getting only 40 percent of the Canal dues—the remainder being paid to the company in England and France. The British Government hoped that if Nasser should decline the 18-nation proposals, we could get as many countries as possible to refuse payments to Egypt but to place them in some special account. That, he felt, would "bring matters to a head very quickly." The British Government also felt that if Nasser should reject the proposals, as many countries as possible should agree to take economic action against Egypt similar to that taken by the United Kingdom and France. He noted that the United States had blocked only those balances existing at the time the freezing order was put into effect. It would seem desirable for the United States, as well as other countries, to block current Egyptian accruals.

The Secretary and Mr. Hoover pointed out that, with regard to tolls, the British and French were essentially following past practices in making payments in London and Paris. United States ships were likewise following past practices in that most of the tolls for such vessels continued to be paid in Egypt at the time of the passage of the ships. It would be far more difficult for us to require payment under some other arrangement. While United States governmental influence might be brought to bear, it was doubtful that we had at this time legal power to stop ships from making payments in Egypt. It was also pointed out to Mr. Coulson that the freezing of current Egyptian accruals of funds in the United States would be far more difficult than the action taken several weeks ago in freezing balances current at that time. Mr. Coulson concluded the discussion of this matter by saying that the problems which he had raised were now being studied jointly in London but that he merely wished to emphasize the British interest in them.

Before departing, Mr. Coulson read a short telegram from Mr. Lloyd to the effect that the latter planned to attend the September 5 meeting of the NATO Council in order to give, in his capacity as Chairman of the Suez Conference, a personal account of what transpired. His own attendance should not be taken as indicating that he felt the meeting should be attended at the ministerial level.

---

149.   Memorandum of Discussion at the 295th Meeting of the National Security Council, Washington, August 30, 1956, 9 a.m. [1]

[Here follows a paragraph listing the participants at the meeting.]

---

[1] Source: Eisenhower Library, Whitman File, NSC Records. Top Secret. Prepared by Gleason on August 31. The time of the meeting is from the record of the President's Daily Appointments. (*Ibid.*)

1. The Suez Canal Situation (Memo for NSC from Executive Secretary, subject: "Nationalization of the Suez Maritime Canal Company by the Egyptian Government", dated August 3, 1956; [2] Memos for NSC from Executive Secretary, subject: "Nationalization of the Suez Canal; Consequences and Possible Related Reactions", dated August 7 [3] and 22, [4] 1956; NSC Action No. 1593)

Mr. Anderson informed the Council that the Secretary of State would make a brief report on the London conference on the Suez Canal problem. He also reminded the Council of the views of the Joint Chiefs of Staff on this problem, and pointed out that Admiral Radford would probably wish to make some remarks when Secretary Dulles had concluded his.

Secretary Dulles first recalled the circumstances which led up to the London conference, emphasizing his own anxiety to avoid resort to military force against Egypt at least until such time as world public opinion had been mobilized and tested. He then indicated the basis of the invitations which had been issued to 24 nations to meet at London. 22 of the 24 nations invited had finally accepted. Egypt itself did not accept, perhaps, thought Secretary Dulles, because of the strong personal attack on President Nasser by Sir Anthony Eden just prior to the opening of the meeting. Greece had likewise refused to attend, because of the Cyprus affair. Secretary Dulles said that we had informed the Greeks that we perfectly understood the reason for their failure to attend.

Secretary Dulles went on to explain that the London conference concluded with approval by 18 of the 22 nations of his proposal to settle the Suez problem. This proposal involved the association of Egypt and certain foreign powers in the administration of the Suez Canal. Secretary Dulles thought it important that Turkey, Iran, Pakistan and Ethiopia had been among the nations approving the plan, since he was particularly anxious that there should be no clear-cut division between the Western powers and the Moslem states on the Suez issue. Much credit for winning the allegiance of the aforesaid countries went to the Turkish Foreign Minister. The latter had not had an easy task, in view of the wrought-up state of public opinion, particularly in Iran and Pakistan. Ethiopia's adherence to the U.S. plan Secretary Dulles attributed entirely to the cordiality of the U.S. relations with Ethiopia.

---

[2] The memorandum transmitted the JCS memorandum of July 31 to the NSC; see Document 50.

[3] The memorandum transmitted the JCS memorandum of August 3 to the NSC; see Document 68.

[4] Document 118.

The other main plan for settling the Canal problem was offered by India. The Indian plan emphasized that the connection of any foreign powers with the Suez Canal should be solely consultative in character, and that no nation except Egypt should have a voice in the actual control of shipping through the Suez Canal. Secretary Dulles said that the Indian plan was accordingly not satisfactory to France or Britain, for both of which countries the Suez Canal constituted a lifeline.

The main objective of the U.S. plan was to take the Suez Canal out of politics. Secretary Dulles speculated that perhaps in past years the French and British had been guilty of involving the Canal too much in politics. In any event, the U.S. plan envisaged that foreign association with the new Suez Canal operation should not be confined to the powerful Western nations, but that prominence should be given to neutral states who had not had in the past any special political interest in the Suez Canal.

The Indian plan was, of course, backed by the USSR. The Soviets did not particularly like the Indian plan, but did not wish to be completely isolated. The Indian plan was also supported by Indonesia and Ceylon, both of which countries were undoubtedly sincere in their desire to find a solution to this crisis. Secretary Dulles added that Krishna Menon was largely responsible for preventing the Indian delegation from accepting the U.S. plan, because Menon was anxious to bring the USSR and the Western powers into agreement and believed that he was capable of doing so.

In point of fact, of course, the Soviet Union obviously did not wish to find any solution to the Suez crisis, in which respect its attitude differed fundamentally from that of India, Indonesia and Ceylon. The Soviet Union had done everything possible to make it difficult for Nasser to accept the U.S. proposal for a settlement of the Suez Canal crisis.

Secretary Dulles commented that the British and French had gone along with the U.S. plan very reluctantly and in obvious hope that Nasser would not ultimately accept the plan. They calculated that his refusal to accept the plan would permit them to resort to military force with better grace. In the first instance the British and French were concerned with the Canal issue itself because the Canal was vital to the economic health of Western Europe in general and to the United Kingdom in particular. For this reason the British were wholly unwilling to permit the Canal to be subject to the whims of Egyptian politics, realizing full well the depths of Nasser's hatred for Britain. On the other hand, both the British and the French looked at this crisis in broader terms than the Suez Canal itself. These two countries were greatly concerned about Nasser's growing stature in the Middle East, and the resultant jeopardy to their whole position in the Middle East and North Africa. Secretary Dulles admitted that the U.S. plan could be made to appear to be a victory for Nasser, or at least so the British and French argued. They therefore felt that they must come out of the crisis with some action that would cut Nasser down to size. Otherwise they felt that they would lose their entire positions in the Middle East and North Africa. These sentiments explained the hope and expectation of the British and French that Nasser would reject our London proposal.

After the acceptance of the London proposal by the 18 nations, the conference proceeded to create a committee charged with going to Nasser to explain the agreed plan. Initially they had wanted Secretary Dulles along to present the plan to Nasser. Secretary Dulles, however, had resisted this suggestion, and accordingly a committee of five nations was selected, headed by Prime Minister Menzies of Australia. Actually, said Secretary Dulles, he would have preferred that the United States not be represented at all on the five-nation committee, but the other four nations had all insisted on U.S. membership if they themselves were to agree to serve on the committee. The indications were that this committee would have very rough going in presenting the plan to Nasser, and Secretary Dulles believed that Nasser would end by rejecting the proposal. Secretary Dulles pointed out that the USSR had been playing a very reckless game in its effort to induce Nasser to reject the plan; unless, of course, the Soviet Union was actually hopeful that war would break out. Indeed, at the very time that Secretary Dulles was personally trying to gain the cooperation of Foreign Minister Shepilov at London, the Soviet radio was viciously attacking the U.S. plan as an example of Western imperialism and colonialism. Such attacks had continued without interruption ever since.

Secretary Dulles pointed out that there existed some division of opinion within the five-nation committee as to the committee's mandate for its forthcoming dealings with President Nasser. The British and French were insistent that the committee make no effort to try to sell the plan to Nasser, and that the committee should avoid any negotiating role. The majority of the nations, however, took the view of the United States, that an effort at least should be made to explain to Nasser the basis of the plan that was being proposed to him. The final attitude of the committee in its dealings with Nasser would depend fundamentally on the view of Prime Minister Menzies.

Meanwhile, said Secretary Dulles, both the British and the French were continuing their military preparations to deal with the Suez crisis. They seemed to be extremely serious in their intention to resort to military force if no other acceptable solution is found. At this juncture, thought Secretary Dulles, the strongest elements in the

British Cabinet were Macmillan and Lord Salisbury. Sir Anthony Eden had shown himself to be somewhat vacillating. Even so, Eden had informed Secretary Dulles that on or about the 10th of September, the British Government would have to make decisions with respect to the resort to force which, once made, would be irrevocable. Moreover, the Secretary of State said, he had word from London yesterday that in order to prepare British public opinion, the British Government proposed to take the Canal issue to the United Nations the moment that Nasser rejected the plan. The general British objective appeared to be to secure a UN Security Council resolution backing the British and French point of view. Of course, the British realized that such a resolution would be vetoed in the Security Council by the USSR. Nevertheless, the British believed that the backing they would gain in the Security Council (despite the Soviet veto) would provide a better basis on which to proceed with the invocation of force against Egypt. In any event, such a procedure would free Britain and France from the charge of having resorted to war without paying any attention to the United Nations.

Secretary Dulles stated that French public opinion was, if anything, more wrought-up and more united over the Canal issue than was British public opinion. After all, the French were already fighting in Algeria. They argued that it was more or less hopeless to fight in Algeria if Nasser was simultaneously to win a great victory in Egypt on the Canal issue. In short, they would rather fight at the center of the trouble—namely, Egypt—than fight around the periphery of the difficulty—namely, Algeria. Moreover, they would have the advantage of fighting Egypt with British assistance. Accordingly, with the exception of the Communist Party the French were united in favor of military action against Egypt.

The situation was not quite so solid in Great Britain. While initially the Labour Party had supported the Government's insistence on the validity of resorting to force, they had lately had second thoughts on the subject, and were now opposed to invoking force to solve the problem. Gaitskell had informed Secretary Dulles that there was very great doubt whether Great Britain would be in a position to go to war against Egypt if the Labour Party opposed this plan of action. The Labour Party was also very strong in its belief and conviction that Britain could not afford to ignore the UN in the existing circumstances.

Summing up, Secretary Dulles said that the foregoing was approximately the way the situation stood at the present time. The issue, he said, was very grave, and he himself found it extremely difficult to take a strong stand against the British and French views since, after all, the British and French would be finished as first-rate powers if they didn't somehow manage to check Nasser and nullify his schemes. Indeed, they had told Secretary Dulles that failure to do this would reduce them to the rank of third- or fourth-rate powers. Both Salisbury and Macmillan were strong-minded people, thoroughly imbued with the tradition of British greatness. They would rather go down fighting than to accept an accomplished fact from President Nasser. Admittedly, they are not clear as to how they could successfully carry through a war against Egypt, with which view Secretary Dulles agreed. The whole Arab world would be pitted against them, and obviously it would be easier to start such a war than to finish it. In order to achieve their objectives, they might even have to try to re-establish colonial rule over the whole area of the Middle East. All of this constituted a morass from which it was hard for Secretary Dulles to see how the British and French could ever hope successfully to extricate themselves. Needless to say, continued Secretary Dulles, the British and French hope that we will be fighting along with them if it comes to war against Egypt.

At the conclusion of Secretary Dulles' remarks, Mr. Anderson asked Admiral Radford if he had anything he wished to add.

Admiral Radford first referred to the several papers prepared by the Joint Chiefs of Staff for the Council, analyzing some eight possible military courses of action. These JCS reports had been turned over to the so-called State–Defense study group, as the President had recently directed. [5] The general conclusion reached by the Joint Chiefs of Staff was that the most desirable course of action for the United States would be strong public, political and logistic support for Great Britain and France, without direct military intervention by the United States in support of these countries against Egypt unless a third party intervened in the hostilities. Such a course of action, Admiral Radford believed, would be most likely to prevent a war over Suez from spreading. [6]

---

[5] On August 23, pursuant to NSC Action No. 1593 (see footnotes 8 and 9, Document 72), the Joint Chiefs of Staff forwarded to the Secretary of Defense an "Analysis of U.S. Military Courses of Action with Respect to the Expropriation of the Suez Maritime Canal Company" under cover of a memorandum by Radford which recommended that a copy be forwarded to the Defense member of the State–Defense study group formed in response to Eisenhower's directive. The analysis was based upon the assumption that the British and French could seize the Canal without direct U.S. participation and that political and economic actions already taken by Western governments had not produced acceptable results. (JCS Records, CCS.092 Egypt (7–28–56))

[6] In addition, the JCS viewed as militarily acceptable the following courses of action: (1) to guarantee publicly that the United States would take appropriate action, including direct military action by U.S. forces as necessary, in the event of significant military intervention by third parties which threatened to expand the conflict; (2) to publicly endorse and politically, economically, and logistically support British-French military action without direct participation of U.S. forces; and (3) to participate from the outset in combined military action with Britain and France. (Memorandum from the Joint Chiefs of Staff to the Secretary of Defense, August 23; ibid.)

Admiral Radford went on to point out that although the U.S. military have not taken part in the development of UK-French plans for the use of force against Egypt, we do know in a general way what the British and French intend to do and the character of the forces they are mobilizing for possible use against Egypt. The British and French have informed us that they would be ready to undertake military operations against Egypt some time in the period between August 29 and September 5. As far as Admiral Radford knew, the British and French were proceeding on this schedule, and are presumably nearly ready to take military action if the decision to do so is made.

The studies by the Joint Chiefs of Staff, continued Admiral Radford, indicate in general the Chiefs' feeling, from the military point of view, of sympathy for the British and French analysis of the Suez dilemma. They agree that if the Suez crisis is not handled decisively the result will be grave long-term repercussions. Admiral Radford also predicted that if the British and French go to war against Egypt, the United States would have to provide them at least with logistic support. This, of course, would identify us with the British and French in the eyes of the world. Admiral Radford concluded by pointing out that in any event the United States should do all that is possible to do to avoid committing U.S. land forces in action against Egypt.

At the conclusion of Admiral Radford's comments, the President inquired whether any members of the Council had any questions he wished to put. There being no questions, the President added his own view that the Suez situation was so grave that it must be watched hourly. It seemed to the President, he said, that the limit of what we can consider doing now is to take the necessary steps to prevent the enlargement of the war if it actually breaks out. This immediately raised in his mind the question as to whether it would be necessary to consult with the Congress. He asked Secretary Dulles for his view on that question.

Secretary Dulles replied that in his opinion such a U.S. course of action would require consultation with Congress, since the area of hostilities was not covered by any treaty to which the United States was a party. Secretary Dulles went on to state that up to now we have all tended to consider the Suez crisis as likely to result in either (1) a great victory for President Nasser or (2) a very serious war. Nevertheless, Secretary Dulles thought it at least possible to entertain an intermediate point of view—namely, we might be able, if we maneuvered correctly, to deny to Nasser the full fruits of victory. Secretary Dulles pointed out that the leaders of several Arab countries were concerned with the growing preeminence of President Nasser in the Moslem world. These leaders would be very happy indeed to find an issue that could be used to deflate Nasser's prestige. Unfortunately, they do not consider the Suez Canal issue a suitable weapon for deflating Nasser. In any event, all of this suggested the possibility of an intermediate situation which would not mean a total success for Nasser, who might subsequently be successfully deflated.

Acting Secretary of the Treasury Burgess informed the Council that he had been in London at the time that the conference opened, and wished to pay a tribute to Secretary Dulles. He said that after two days of the meeting in London, Secretary Dulles had succeeded in changing the entire direction of British public opinion. The President agreed that Secretary Dulles' accomplishment was impressive, but pointed out that the present situation with respect to British public opinion might be even worse. A country in which public opinion was divided, as in the case of Britain, could give aid and comfort to Nasser, who might now calculate that he could get away with practically anything without the risk that Britain would resort to military force. Secretary Dulles expressed agreement with the President's view, and said that he was by no means sure that Gaitskell's performance was wholly to the good.

Governor Stassen inquired whether any thought had been given to various other courses of action which might be pursued to resolve the Canal crisis. For example, had any thought been given to the possibility that the Israelis might defeat Egypt, or that some other Arab country or countries might take up arms against the Nasser government? Secretary Dulles replied that such courses of action had been explored and had been found wanting . . . .

The President intervened to say that as quickly as that happened the United States would find all the Arab countries of the world united against us.

Secretary Dulles agreed with this view of the President, and then said that he had just received a memorandum from officials of the State Department pointing out that we may presently have to take steps for the evacuation of U.S. citizens from Egypt. The British and French are already doing this, and we may soon be compelled to do it under forced draft. This will throw some heavy responsibilities on the Defense Department, because we will probably have to use military facilities to evacuate civilians, which will mean that these military facilities will not be initially available for military purposes.

Admiral Radford pointed out that a plan for the evacuation of U.S. civilians from Egypt had been developed. The great concern of the military at present was how to obtain advance warning in sufficient time to evacuate our civilians prior to the outbreak of military action. Also, he added, we are very greatly concerned to be assured of continued access to Saudi Arabian oil.

The President inquired as to the character of the U.S. civilians in Egypt. Were they mainly commercial people? Secretary Dulles replied that they were largely so, and went on to point out the serious repercussions, from a political point of view, of any public notice that the United States was evacuating American citizens from Egypt.

Dr. Flemming assured the National Security Council that we were moving ahead with our plans for dealing with the oil situation in the event of trouble in the Suez Canal. We are also talking with the British,[7] who have provided us with a preliminary study of what the closure of the Canal would do to their dollar position. Secretary Dulles turned to Secretary Burgess and said that he had better have his checkbook ready.

The National Security Council:[8]

a. Noted and discussed a report by the Secretary of State on the status of developments and future contingencies, based on the recent Conference in London.

b. Noted and discussed the views of the Joint Chiefs of Staff on the subject, transmitted by the reference memorandum of August 22.

c. Noted a statement by the Director, Office of Defense Mobilization, on the status of oil studies pertaining to the Suez Canal situation.

[Here follow agenda items 2 and 3. Agenda item 3, "U.S. Policy in Mainland Southeast Asia," is printed in volume XXI, page 241.]

S. Everett Gleason

---

[7] Documentation relating to Anglo-American discussions concerning the oil situation is in Department of State, Central Files 840.2553 and 974.7301 and in Conference Files: Lot 62 D 181, CF 748–749.

[8] The following paragraphs constitute NSC Action No. 1597, approved by the President on September 5. (*Ibid.*, S/S–NSC (Miscellaneous) Files: Lot 66 D 95, Records of Action by the National Security Council, 1956)

150.   Memorandum of a Conversation, Department of State, Washington, August 30, 1956, 2:35 p.m. [1]

SUBJECT

Call on the Secretary by the Egyptian Ambassador

PARTICIPANTS

Dr. Ahmed Hussein, Ambassador of Egypt
The Secretary
The Under Secretary
NEA—William M. Rountree

The Egyptian Ambassador, who had requested an urgent appointment explaining that he had a message from President Nasser, said that Nasser had been concerned at the use by President Eisenhower in his public statement on August 29, [2] of the word, "internationalized" in describing the Suez Canal. He said that the 1888 Convention and subsequent agreements all recognized the sovereignty of Egypt over the Suez Canal. The purpose of the Convention was to assure the users of the Canal that their ships could pass freely and without obstruction. The Egyptian Government had noted that the Secretary also had described the Canal as having been internationalized and felt that the expression of this concept by the American leaders would create confusion in the minds of many people throughout the world.

The Secretary responded to the effect that he did not quarrel with the Ambassador's statement regarding the status of the Canal. In referring to it as an international waterway, we had in mind the use of the Canal pursuant to the Convention by vessels of all nations and not the actual ownership or sovereignty question.

The Ambassador expressed appreciation for this clarification and asked the Secretary whether he might find it possible to make a public statement which would correct any misunderstandings which might have resulted from the previous use of the term "internationalized". The Secretary thought it would be possible for him to clarify the term as applying to the use of the Canal.

There was some discussion as to what the Egyptian Ambassador would say to the press upon his departure. At the conclusion of the

---

[1] Source: Department of State, Secretary's Memoranda of Conversation: Lot 64 D 199. Confidential. Drafted by Rountree. The time of the meeting is from Dulles' Appointment Book. (Princeton University Library, Dulles Papers)
[2] See footnote 2, Document 144.

meeting, however, the Secretary suggested that the Ambassador use his own discretion as to what he should say. [3]

---

[3] That same day in Cairo, Nasser summoned Ambassador Byroade and informed him that he would be issuing a statement in response to Eisenhower's statement of August 29. Nasser explained that Eisenhower's statement had been a great disappointment and that he had erroneously referred to the Suez Canal as "this waterway internationalized by the Treaty of 1888". The Egyptian President then read to Byroade most of the statement that he would issue. Byroade reported that Nasser's statement contained no attack or personal reference to President Eisenhower apart from expressing Egypt's disappointment that the President had used the phrase mentioned above. (Telegram 521, August 30; Department of State, Central Files, 974.7301/8–3056) The text of Nasser's statement of August 30 was forwarded to the Department of State in telegram 522, August 30. (Ibid.)

---

151.   Memorandum of a Conversation Between the President and the Secretary of State, White House, Washington, August 30, 1956, 4:30 p.m. [1]

I said I wanted to be sure that my mind was working along with that of the President on the basic issues of the Suez matter. I said I had come to the conclusion that, regrettable as it might be to see Nasser's prestige enhanced even temporarily, I did not believe the situation was one which should be resolved by force. I could not see any end to the situation that might be created if the British and the French occupied the Canal and parts of Egypt. They would make bitter enemies of the entire population of the Middle East and much of Africa. Everywhere they would be compelled to maintain themselves by force and in the end their own economy would be weakened virtually beyond repair and the influence of the West in the Middle East and most of Africa lost for a generation, if not a century. The Soviet Union would reap the benefit of a greatly weakened Western Europe and would move into a position of predominant influence in the Middle East and Africa. No doubt it was for this reason that the Soviets were seeking to prevent a peaceful adjustment of the Suez problem.

The President said he entirely agreed with me in this basic analysis. He realized how tough it was for the British and French but that this was not the issue upon which to try to downgrade Nasser. Every reasonable effort should be made to get an acceptable

---

[1] Source: Eisenhower Library, Dulles Papers, Meetings with the President. Secret; Personal and Private. Drafted by Dulles.

practical solution of the Suez dispute, but that this issue and the question of Nasser and prestige in the Middle East and North Africa could not wisely be confused.

I reported to the President on my meeting with the Latin American Ambassadors [2] and the sentiment I felt there in favor of UN action. The President felt that it would probably not be possible to have the kind of action which the British wanted but that if the negotiations broke down, there should be some appeal to the UN. He said he might mention this in his press conference tomorrow.

[Here follows discussion concerning a canal through Nicaragua, (printed in volume VII, page 303), the possibility of inviting some people from behind the Iron Curtain to observe the United States election, and Yugoslavia.]

JFD [3]

---

[2] According to Dulles' Appointment Book, the Secretary met with the Latin American Ambassadors at 3:30 p.m., August 30. (Princeton Library, Dulles Papers) An account of this conversation is in circular telegram 164, August 31. (Department of State, Central Files, 974.7301/8–3156)

[3] Macomber initialed for Dulles.

---

152.   Memorandum of a Conversation, Department of State, Washington, August 30, 1956, 5:35 p.m. [1]

SUBJECT

Call by the British Minister; Suez Question

PARTICIPANTS

The Secretary
Under Secretary
Mr. J.E. Coulson, Minister, British Embassy
Miss Barbara Salt, Counselor, British Embassy
Mr. Francis O. Wilcox, IO
Mr. David W. Wainhouse, IO
Mr. William M. Rountree, NEA
Mr. Fraser Wilkins, NE

Minister Coulson and Miss Barbara Salt of the British Embassy joined the Secretary and his colleagues at a meeting this afternoon

---

[1] Source: Department of State, Central Files, 974.7301/8–3056. Drafted by Wilkins. The time of the meeting is from Dulles' Appointment Book. (Princeton University Library, Dulles Papers)

on the subject of several questions arising from letters addressed to the President by Prime Minister Eden and to the Secretary by the British Foreign Secretary.[2] In the latter communication the possibility of consideration by the Security Council of the United Nations of the Suez question in the event of a failure of the work of the Suez Committee was discussed.

Minister Coulson said that following his conversation with the Secretary yesterday he had been in touch with London and had received a number of replies which he had been requested to communicate to the Secretary orally. Minister Coulson said that as a result of the observations made by the Secretary, the British Foreign Office now believed that if it were necessary to refer the Suez question to the Security Council it should be taken up under Article 39 of Chapter VII, rather than Article 35 of Chapter VI. He handed the Secretary a British draft of the proposed Security Council resolution (Tab A).[3]

Minister Coulson continued that Selwyn Lloyd had made a number of additional observations: (1) It was important that there be a group of five countries which would be able to block diversionary tactics in the Security Council. The British believe this group might consist of the UK, France, Belgium, Iran and the United States. The British felt certain that France and Belgium would be in accord with the British view. They also believed that Iran would support their position because Nasser's continued success would inevitably lead to an undermining of the pro-Western Iran Government and its collapse. The British Foreign Secretary hoped the United States would support the British position. The British Foreign Minister continued that Egypt would undoubtedly be heard by the Security Council but that additional countries might be excluded by the group on the grounds that the question is now a dispute rather than a situation.

The Secretary read the British draft of the proposed Security Council resolution and observed that the shift from Article 35 to Article 39 was an extremely important one; that it would now represent a consideration of a dispute rather than a situation and that the resolution had teeth in it. He said that he and his colleagues would like to study the resolution and would be in touch with the British concerning it. He observed there were a number of points; for example, the reference to the Security Council Resolution of 1951 would bring the Arab-Israel question into the Suez matter.

---

[2] For Eden's message to Eisenhower of August 27, see Document 137; for Lloyd's message to Dulles, see the attachment to Document 147.

[3] Not printed. Tab A is substantively similar to the text of the draft Security Council resolution sent by Lloyd to Dulles on September 7; see Document 184.

The Secretary said that he had been studying Selwyn Lloyd's letter and wondered whether Minister Coulson would want a reply in writing. Minister Coulson said that as events were taking place so rapidly it would perhaps not be necessary. The Secretary continued that Selwyn Lloyd's letter and Minister Coulson's further remarks, together with the British draft of the proposed Security Council resolution, carried implications regarding use of force in the Suez situation to which the United States would not want to be committed.

The Secretary added that if the activities of the Suez Committee should break down he believed that the Suez question should be considered in the Security Council rather than the General Assembly. He noted that during a discussion with the various Latin American Ambassadors in Washington today he had found a strong feeling among them regarding Suez that it would be quite impossible wholly to by-pass the United Nations in the event of adverse developments.

The Secretary went on to remark that by thus discussing contingencies and plans following a possible failure of the work of the Suez Committee, we did not in any way intend to imply that the Committee would fail or that we believed its normal functions should be cut short.

The Secretary added that if it were necessary for the Security Council to consider the question he would appear for the principal presentation of the United States position and that Ambassador Lodge would present other aspects of the United States position. Minister Coulson said that Selwyn Lloyd would ask the Iranian Foreign Minister to be present at Security Council deliberations.

The Secretary emphasized that study of Selwyn Lloyd's letter, Minister Coulson's remarks and the British draft of the proposed Security Council resolution would be made, and that we would be in touch with the British.

Minister Coulson then read one or two additional observations by Selwyn Lloyd. He said that consideration of the question of some initiative in the Security Council was dependent on a clear answer from Nasser. If Nasser should spin out the discussion with the Suez Committee there might be no time to refer the Suez dispute to the Security Council. Minister Coulson also said that the British were only prepared to take the course of reference to the Security Council on the understanding that there would be United States support for that course.

The Secretary replied to these observations that the United States would give its support to British action not as an exercise but as an honest means to bring pressure to bear upon President Nasser.

The U.S. would, in other words, give its support in an honest effort peacefully to settle the Suez dispute.

---

153.   Telegram From the Department of State to the Embassy in the United Kingdom [1]

Washington, August 30, 1956—10 p.m.

1513. Suez for Henderson. Embtels 1144,[2] 1147,[3] 1170[4] and Cairo's 496,[5] August 29. Suggestions made in Urtel 1147 are heartily approved. Support indicated by Menzies, Unden and Aklilou is encouraging. We are also encouraged by Cairo's 496 which indicates, on basis of confidential sources, that GOE will be prepared go considerably further in effort reassure users and that GOE is thinking in terms of counter proposals for possible presentation to Committee.

We fully appreciate difficult position Committee may find itself if Nasser attempts turn explanations into negotiations but feel Committee, as representative 18 countries, should not hesitate make suggestions, using illustrative approach much possible.

While UK, France may react adversely later do not feel this possibility should influence USDel, Committee's best judgments manner explanation to Nasser. We agree Menzies' suggestion in urtel 1170 that Committee could give Nasser written statement that its illustrative suggestions only tentative.

We also believe it would be useful to recast 5-nation proposals for purpose of exchange notes as you suggested in 1170. [6]

---

[1] Source: Department of State, Central Files, 974.7301/8–2956. Secret; Priority. Drafted by Wilkins and Rice; cleared by Ludlow, Armstrong, and Raymond; approved by Rountree who signed for Dulles.

[2] Telegram 1144, August 29, contained a series of ideas, prepared by the U.S. Delegation, as to how the principles contained in the Eighteen-Power Proposal might be implemented. (*Ibid.*)

[3] Document 145.

[4] Dated August 29, telegram 1170 contained a summary report of a meeting of the Suez Committee held during the afternoon of August 29. (Department of State, Central Files, 974.7301/8–2956)

[5] Dated August 29, not printed. (*Ibid.*)

[6] In telegram 1170, Henderson described his exchange with Menzies on this subject as follows: "I then asked whether committee should use Five-Power Proposal as actual 'Heads of Agreement' to be agreed with Egypt or whether we should have five nation proposals recast in form which could be embodied in an exchange of notes signifying willingness of both sides to enter into negotiations on basis of principles outlined therein. Menzies suggested this might also be considered by experts of

We will send separately shortly several suggestions [7] on details of ideas outlined in urtel 1144.

Dulles

---

committee but thought my latter suggestion be recast heads of agreement might be preferable."

[7] The suggestions were forwarded in telegram 1548 to London, August 31 (*ibid.*) and in telegram 657 to Cairo, September 5 (*ibid.*, 974.7301/9–156). Neither is printed.

---

154.   Telegram From the Department of State to the Embassy in the United Kingdom [1]

Washington, August 30, 1956—10 p.m.

1514. London pass Henderson. Paris for USRO, Embassy. Department distributed British announcement North Atlantic Council meeting next week "consider" Suez situation, which carries implication NATO will be seized with problem.

You should speak soonest with Selwyn Lloyd along following lines: With delicate discussions between Committee of Five and Nasser about to start, we sure British agree it essential NATO per se should not appear become involved in deciding future courses of action re Suez. One of remarkable achievements London Conference was avoidance East-West split, and we fear solidarity 18 nations might be jeopardized if it were appear NATO as such directing Suez policy.

Further, crystalization of Arab sentiment and further unity among Arab states might well result from providing whipping boy of anti-NATO (anti-white, anti-colonial) rallying point which Arab propaganda could exploit.

Thus most important that world public opinion not gain erroneous conception purpose forthcoming meeting. It should be made clear to press and public that Suez is not NATO problem, and that

---

[1] Source: Department of State, Central Files, 974.7301/8–3056. Secret; Priority; Limit Distribution—Suez Canal. Drafted by Timmons and Wolf (EUR/RA); cleared by Beam (EUR), Lister (BNA), and Ambassador Perkins; and approved by Rountree who signed for Dulles. Repeated Priority to Paris.

essential purpose of meeting is to hear report on London Conference. [2]

Dulles

---

[2] In response to telegram 1514, Barbour reported on August 31 as follows: "In absence Lloyd until Monday [September 3], Kirkpatrick assures that British concept NATO 'consideration' Suez situation does not involve NATO being seized with problem or in fact doing more than hearing report on London conference, although British might expect other NATO nonparticipants conference to express views. Kirkpatrick explained that British use word 'consider' in announcement was designed meet long standing NATO sensitivity regarding ex post facto report to NATO Council." (Telegram 1231, August 31; *ibid.*, 974.7301/8–3156)

---

155.   Memorandum of Telephone Conversations Between the President and the Secretary of State, Washington, August 31, 1956 [1]

TELEPHONE CALL TO THE PRESIDENT

8:35 a.m.

The Sec. commented [that] the Pres. had perhaps seen in the press the big fuss the Egyptians were making over internationalization in line with the Treaty of 1888. [2] The Sec. termed it a silly performance. It appeared to him that the Egyptians were getting jittery. The Secretary read to the President a statement (draft) stating

---

[1] Source: Eisenhower Library, Dulles Papers, White House Telephone Memoranda. Transcribed by Asbjornson. Between 8:15 and 8:59 a.m. on August 31, Robert Anderson met with President Eisenhower at the White House. (*Ibid.*, President's Daily Appointments) No memorandum of this conversation has been found in the Eisenhower Library. A memorandum of August 31 by Newsom who was not present at the meeting, indicates that on August 31 Anderson reported to Eisenhower on the substance of his conversations with Saudi officials. Anderson later reported that the President expressed his satisfaction with the mission and urged that it be followed up as necessary and that particularly sensitive details be closely held. (Department of State, NEA Files: Lot 59 D 518, Report of Special Mission to Saudi Arabia August 20–27, 1956)

During the meeting between Eisenhower and Anderson, the two telephone conversations recorded here occurred. Less detailed accounts of the conversations, transcribed by Whitman at the White House are in the Eisenhower Library, Whitman File, Eisenhower Diaries.

[2] Reference is to Egyptian criticism of Eisenhower's statement of August 29; see Document 150. Later on August 31, Dulles telephoned Eisenhower and read him a message from Byroade reporting Nasser's démarche on this subject. (Eisenhower Library, Whitman File, Eisenhower Diaries) Byroade's message is summarized in footnote 3, Document 150.

we were at cross purposes, etc.[3] The President said he was going to say something along the same lines—something to the effect that as a facility it had been internationalized and its use was given to all the nations of the world. No one, he said, had ever questioned the sovereignty of Egypt over the area. He said he had made a formal statement the day before yesterday. This solution, while respecting the sovereignty of Egypt, did provide an answer. The President said for this reason, he could show he had already said that.

The Secretary likened the situation to an easement—where someone owned the property but a great many people could cross the property. The Secretary said it was amazing that Nasser should have made that great a fuss. The President said that he had not said "protest" but "regret".

8:50 a.m.

The Sec. called the President back. The Pres. said Bob Anderson had with him a paper which he had never read which had to be translated. This paper had been slipped into his hands.[4] The President wanted to know if there was any significance to this? The Sec. couldn't quite recall it. The Pres. said he had given a photostat copy to Loy Henderson. The Pres. said it purported to be the "bad boy's"[5] (I think he said) minimum terms. The President asked that a copy (translation) be sent to him on a secret basis. (Bob Anderson to have one too)

The Sec. said he was sending to Pres. a statement on Suez Canal. I think it a highly technical legal question.

[Here follows discussion concerning Nicaragua.]

---

[3] Dulles subsequently forwarded the text of the statement to Eisenhower with the comment: "I would suggest sticking fairly close to this, as highly technical international law problems are involved." The statement reads as follows: "We are, I think, at cross purposes. I referred to the Suez Canal as a waterway internationalized by the Treaty of 1888. That Treaty gives many nations rights in and to the Canal in perpetuity. Of course that does not mean that these nations own the Canal. It does mean that, under the Treaty, Egypt cannot now, or in the future, jeopardize those rights of other nations. Therefore, in the sense of usage of the Canal, it is 'internationalized'. In my statement of two days ago, expressing the hope that the 18-nation proposal would prove acceptable to all concerned, I noted that the proposal fully respected the sovereignty of Egypt." (Eisenhower Library, Whitman File, Dulles–Herter Series)

At the press conference which began at 10:30 a.m., Eisenhower read the statement with a few stylistic changes. A transcript of the press conference is in *Public Papers of the Presidents of the United States: Dwight D. Eisenhower, 1956*, pp. 719–727.

[4] Not printed. Later on August 31, Dulles forwarded to Eisenhower a copy of the translation under cover of a note which reads: "Here is a copy of the paper of which Bob Anderson spoke and of which you spoke to me over the telephone. I do not think it is particularly significant, being substantially a re-statement of the position which Egypt has officially taken." (Eisenhower Library, Whitman File, Dulles–Herter Series)

[5] Reference is to Nasser.

156.   Memorandum of Discussion at a Department of State–Joint Chiefs of Staff Meeting, Pentagon, Washington, August 31, 1956, 11:30 a.m. [1]

[Here follows a list of 25 persons present, including Admiral Radford, General Taylor, Admiral Burke, and General White, and Murphy, Robertson, Stelle, Bennett, Wilkins, and Compton for the Department of State. The first item discussed was "French Military Effort in Viet Nam"; see volume I, page 736.]

2. The Suez Situation

At Mr. Murphy's request Mr. Wilkins presented the latest information on the Suez situation. He mentioned that the Five Nation Committee appointed from the London Conference was scheduled to present the majority plan [2] resulting from the London Conference to President Nasser on September 3. He stressed that the committee's action would be for information rather than negotiation and remarked that it seemed clear from the Secretary's recent talks in London that the British are presently determined to move militarily unless Nasser accepts the London majority's suggestions by September 10. He reviewed several steps which were involved in the current situation:

a. The NATO Advisory Council is scheduled to meet on September 5 in Paris. The British have tried to make it seem that this is a special meeting although it is actually a regular NAC session.

b. British diplomatic missions throughout the Middle East area have been instructed to persuade British subjects to leave the area.

c. The British are making plans to submit the issue to the Security Council of the United Nations, but at the same time plans for military action go on uninterruptedly.

d. The Suez Canal Company has instructed its pilots to stay on only until September 15.

e. There are defense preparations everywhere in Egypt, with considerable apprehension evident, and tension has increased generally in the area.

Mr. Murphy pointed out with respect to the third item that it is a highly sensitive matter and expressed the personal view that the British talk of submitting the problem to the Security Council is primarily a smoke screen, designed to cover them against charges of neglecting the United Nations.

---

[1] Source: Department of State, State–JCS Meetings: Lot 61 D 417. Top Secret. Drafted by W. Tapley Bennett. An note on the title page reads: "State Draft. Not cleared by any of the participants."

[2] Reference is to the Eighteen-Power Proposal.

General White inquired relative to Israel and its position. Mr. Wilkins responded that Israel is very quiet at the moment and is expected to remain so. Admiral Radford said there had been some discussion as to whether the United Kingdom might at an appropriate time from her standpoint urge Israel to attack Egypt but that he personally thinks Israel will not do so, at least for the present. Mr. Murphy added he received the impression during his recent London talks that the United Kingdom had the Israelis very much in mind in various moves it is making.

Admiral Radford said that the JCS is, of course, interested in what they may be called upon to do in the event of hostilities. He pointed out that action to evacuate Americans, particularly if it occurred simultaneously with a landing by the UK-French forces, would cause grave problems and might well give the appearance that the United States was intervening militarily along with the UK and France. He said he realized the difficulty for the Department in the situation and the desire of our government not to cause undue alarm in the area or complications in the situation by premature announcements regarding evacuation. However, he warned that if no instructions are made public before military action should start, he very much fears that it would not be possible to get all Americans out. Mr. Murphy mentioned a discussion he had with Secretary Dulles regarding the timing of an evacuation announcement. He pointed out that the Five Nation Committee would be arriving in Cairo on Monday, September 3, and that this would give us some days in which to get a more definitive estimate of the situation. He thought that decisions regarding evacuation might be required early during the week beginning September 3. Admiral Radford again stressed the danger of waiting until too late to make our decision and give it adequate publicity.

Admiral Radford then mentioned that in the event of hostilities the JCS had certain plans for air-lifting some ground forces non-stop from Wiesbaden to Dhahran for the purpose of assisting in the defense of oil installations. He pointed out that the oil for our Far East activities comes largely from the Persian Gulf area. Mr. Murphy inquired regarding the magnitude of the forces in mind. Admiral Radford was not particularly forthcoming as to numbers, but discussion brought out the fact that the force would be approximately the size of a regimental combat team. . . . Admiral Radford said that the above information should be held very closely but declared that the JCS are ready to put their plans into motion if so directed. He said he had informed both the President and the Secretary of State of the state of readiness. He went on to say that it would be helpful to have as much advance notice as possible of UK-French future intentions.

General White mentioned the NATO exercise planned for mid-September in Turkey, with particular reference to the fact that there would be a sizeable air movement from this country to Turkey at that time. He wondered whether such movements in the present situation might not give the wrong impression. It was pointed out that this exercise had been planned for a long time and was well known, but Mr. Murphy said that we might give it another look in view of the Suez situation and consider it again early in the week of September 3.

[Here follows discussion of item 3, "MAAG Advisers on the Chinese Off-Shore Islands"; item 4, "Japanese Labor Relationships of U.S. Armed Forces"; item 5, "Austrian Force Levels"; and item 6, "Plane Incident off the China Coast". For text of items 3 and 6, see Volume III, pages 425–426.]

---

157.   Telegram From the Department of State to Certain Diplomatic Missions [1]

Washington, August 31, 1956—8:35 p.m.

Paris for USRO and Embassy.

1. FYI British Embassy approached Dept August 28 [2] suggesting that Suez situation be discussed at North Atlantic Council Meeting next week, at which UK would report results London Conference and US would report work Committee of Five. Dept informed British we agreed that NAC meeting should hear report from UK on London Conference, but that we believed any report on work Committee of Five premature.

2. Subsequently British FonOff announced publicly NAC meeting next week to "consider" Suez and that FonMin Lloyd will represent UK. End FYI. Dept disturbed at this announcement, which carries implication NATO will be seized with problem. Embassy London has been instructed [3] see Lloyd soonest and say we certain British agree it essential NATO per se should not appear become involved in making decisions re Suez, stressing [that] we fear this

---

[1] Source: Department of State, Central Files, 740.5/8–3156. Secret; Limited Distribution—Suez. Drafted by Timmons, cleared by Rountree, and approved by Beam. Sent Priority to Ankara, Athens, Bonn, Brussels, Copenhagen, Lisbon, Luxembourg, Oslo, Ottawa, Paris, Rome, and The Hague. Repeated to London and Reykjavik.

[2] See Document 140.

[3] In telegram 1514 to London, Document 154.

would have extremely adverse effect on solidarity eighteen nation group and on work Committee of Five. London also pointing out danger promoting further unity Arab states by providing anti-NATO rallying point.

3. Action addressees this message should approach FonMin or other appropriate senior official and make following points (drawing on foregoing as appropriate) re September 5 NAC meeting which will discuss Suez:

a) We of course recognize that UK report may well be followed by discussion. However, in view fact talks between Committee of Five and Nasser will be beginning appears in best interests all concerned such discussion in Sept 5 meeting NAC stop short of consideration future courses of action in event Nasser rejects proposals or attempts spin out talks. FYI We fear British and French will attempt portray meeting as approving at least by implication Anglo-French military preparations. End FYI. If NAC discussion were to give rise to action suggestions this would inevitably become known publicly, with possible results referred to para 2 above. We must also bear in mind security problem re Iceland, which will be at meeting.

b) We hope that line taken by all NATO govts will be that September 5 meeting simply for purpose receiving report on London Conference, as part normal regular process whereby Council informed developments affecting NATO. UK is making report in its capacity host to London Conference. Helpful if this line stressed both before and after meeting. FYI Present Dept thinking is that no communiqué should be issued at end of meeting; prefer instead that International Staff spokesman (preferably Ismay) make background statement to press adhering strictly to above line. End FYI.

c) We strongly hope govt to which you accredited shares these views and that its representative at Sept. 5 meeting will be appropriately instructed accordingly.

4. FYI London and USRO advise following FonMins may attend meeting in addition Lloyd: Pineau, Martino, Pearson, Spaak, Bech. [4] End FYI.

5. USRO comment to Dept soonest re last sentence para 3 b). [5]

Dulles [6]

[4] Joseph Bech, Prime Minister and Minister of Foreign Affairs of Luxembourg.

[5] In Polto 432 from Paris, September 1, the U.S. Mission to NATO supported the issuance of a brief communiqué that would describe the NAC discussion of the Suez situation in the terms used by the Department, but noted that if the Department preferred that the matter be handled on a background basis, then Ismay should do it in view of the presence of the Foreign Ministers. (Department of State, Central Files, 974.7301/9–156)

[6] Dulles left the Department of State at 10:41 a.m., August 31, for his home on Duck Island on Lake Ontario for a short vacation. He returned on September 4. (Dulles' Appointment Book; Princeton University Library, Dulles Papers)

158.   Telegram From the Embassy in the United Kingdom to the Department of State [1]

London, September 1, 1956—noon.

1249. With Committee of Five scheduled initiate discussions with Nasser Monday [2] attitude top Brit Govt officials continues to be one of skepticism whether Nasser can be persuaded to accept arrangement which will adequately ensure effective international operation of Canal and make clear to world that Nasser has not "gotten away with" his Canal seizure. Their thinking is still to effect that military action will be necessary and they are not prepared appreciably to delay forcing issue. Their reasoning as heretofore seems to be along two lines. On one hand they reiterate negative arguments previously set forth as to disastrous effect upon Western and particularly Brit position in Middle East if Nasser is not effectively checked at this time. On other hand they seem increasingly to have convinced themselves that military operations could be confined to narrow area of Egypt and could be swiftly successful at small cost in men and treasure. On this assumption they foresee military defeat Nasser as restoring Brit position and prestige Middle East permitting favorable solution Brit problems with Saudi Arabia, Jordan, Syria, etc. as well as Egypt. They also seem confident that Govts of Tunisia, Libya, Lebanon, Saudi Arabia and Iraq would all welcome use of force against Nasser. Although admitting its certainty they tend to minimize contrary public reaction throughout Arab world and are relatively unimpressed when it is pointed out that history of French military action Algeria, Morocco, etc. argues against likelihood rapid local success of operations in Egypt.

Same govt circles are aware that Brit public opinion of various shades is increasingly opposed to use of military force but tend to ignore strength of such opinion apparently in genuine belief that current situation is historic turning point for Britain and govt has traditional responsibility take forceful course regardless consequences.

Barbour

[1] Source: Department of State, Central Files, 974.7301/9–156. Top Secret; Limit Distribution—Suez Canal. Received at 9:44 a.m. Repeated to Paris. A copy of this telegram is in the Eisenhower Library, Whitman File, Dulles–Herter Series.
[2] September 3.

159.   Memorandum of a Conversation, Department of State, Washington, September 1, 1956 [1]

SUBJECT

Representations from King Saud on Suez

PARTICIPANTS

Sheikh Abdullah Al-Khayyal, Ambassador of Saudi Arabia
Azzam Pasha, Representative of Saudi Arabia
Mr. William M. Rountree, Assistant Secretary, NEA
Mr. Fraser Wilkins, Director, NE

The Saudi Arabian Ambassador called on Mr. Rountree this afternoon accompanied by Azzam Pasha. The Ambassador said that he had a private and special message from King Saud for the United States Government. In response to Mr. Rountree's question, the Ambassador said that the message was for the President and other U.S. Government officials. He handed Mr. Rountree a copy of the message, which is attached.

After reading the message, Mr. Rountree said that we understood that Yusuf Yassin was presently in Cairo and had had conversations with President Nasser and was urging a peaceful solution. Mr. Rountree continued that the President and the Secretary had, from the beginning, urged that the Suez dispute be settled peacefully. The Committee of Five, on which the U.S. was represented, was presently in Cairo and we were much encouraged by its progress. We understood that discussions between President Nasser and the Committee of Five would commence on September 3.

Mr. Rountree then turned to King Saud's message and said he wished to make a few preliminary comments. He said that the military steps which had been taken by the U.K. and France were on their own initiative and that the U.S. had not been consulted in advance.

Azzam said that in addition to the Ambassador's comments he had been instructed by the King to go into this question with the U.S. Government. Azzam pointed out that in addition to the British and French measures, the United States had blocked assets of the Suez Canal Company and the Government of Egypt. He believed that the British and French measures were completely unjustified in that the British and French held funds far in excess of possible compensation to the stockholders of the Suez Canal Company. He said that the U.K. had the equivalent of $300 million and the equivalent of $150 million in excess. Since these funds were avail-

---

[1] Source: Department of State, NEA Files: Lot 58 D 722, Saudi Arabia—General. Confidential. Drafted by Wilkins on September 5.

able for compensation, why had it been necessary for the U.S. to take action?

Mr. Rountree explained that the question should be looked at in proper perspective. On July 26 President Nasser had made a speech regarding the Suez Canal in which he had said that nationalization was retaliation. The U.S. licensing had been undertaken against this background. The situation was confused and we wished to be certain that funds were paid to the proper persons or companies. The British and French were saying that the steps which they had taken were precautionary. It was Mr. Rountree's personal view that there was little if anything the U.S. could do to halt these steps. There would in any event be no possibility on grounds of time because the discussions between the Committee of Five and the Government of Egypt were beginning the week of September 3.

Mr. Rountree said that he would immediately convey King Saud's message to the Acting Secretary who would pass it to the President. It would be given the most careful consideration. He would be in touch with him regarding the response of the U.S. Government.

Azzam then turned to the question of funds of the Egyptian National Bank which were blocked in the United States. He said that these funds totalled $30 million, of which $15 million were now needed by the Egyptian depositors. Azzam thought that if the U.S. Government was able to release the $15 million that it would improve the atmosphere.

Mr. Rountree replied that it had been necessary to place the assets of the Suez Canal Company and the Government of Egypt under license until the situation had been clarified. These assets were substantial. We had many legal and monetary problems regarding them. The question arose as to who owned them. It was for these reasons only that the balances had been placed under licensing until the situation had been clarified. Mr. Rountree noted, however, that current transactions could take place under general license.

Azzam pressed that the United States release all funds which had been blocked. He said that because Nasser made a mistake on July 26, there was no reason for the United States to make a mistake by blocking. He said that the U.S. had no connection with the Suez Canal Company and that in any event the British had twice as many funds as they needed for compensation. Furthermore, it was King Saud's opinion that the release of funds in the United States would help.

Mr. Rountree commented on Azzam's statement regarding U.S. licensing, that our action was not in the same category as Nasser's nationalization of the Suez Canal Company. Our action had been precautionary pending clarification of the situation. Mr. Rountree continued that the U.S. placed great value on the views of King Saud and would give them the most careful consideration. Mr. Rountree hoped to be in touch with the Ambassador and Azzam shortly.

[Attachment]

Message From King Saud to President Eisenhower

The United States Government is aware that our efforts have been devoted to work out a peaceful settlement in the dispute over the Suez Canal.

We believe that the United State is adopting the same policy to achieve such a settlement. We fully realize the difficulties that we all must face in order to accomplish this; but our good intentions and willingness, equally shared by the United States, will no doubt enable us to overcome all the difficulties involved.

We asked the American representatives who visited us here lately whether the United States could use every possible effort to end the military and economic measures taken against Egypt; they in turn assured us that they would use their best endeavours to bring this about.

Our own efforts have contributed greatly in bringing about the decision of the Egyptian Government to meet the Menzies Committee; and to a certain extent succeeded in appeasing press and radio publications.

We hope that the United States will be able to take the necessary steps to release frozen Egyptian assets and at the same time continue working out its peaceful solution. Such an action, if taken under present circumstances will no doubt have its favorable effect in the Arab World as well as paving the way for negotiations to reach a peaceful solution.

We hope that the American Government will make every possible effort to stop such economic and military measures in order to create the necessary peaceful atmosphere during negotiations.

160.   Telegram From the Department of State to Certain Diplomatic Missions [1]

Washington, September 2, 1956—12:39 a.m.

Eyes only Chief of Mission and Henderson. We view with deepest concern reports and evaluations from Embassies London and Paris [2] on attitudes and apparent intentions of UK and French governments regarding plans for direct military intervention in Egypt. Furthermore, reports from U.S. Missions Cairo and Amman [3] regarding evacuation British and French nationals add greatly to critical nature of situation. U.S. press is giving widest coverage to these developments.

U.S. is committed to endeavoring find peaceful solution to Suez issue and is doing all in its power to prevent outbreak of hostilities consequences of which might be incalculable. We believe discussions in Cairo of Five Nation Committee scheduled commence September 3 must be given every opportunity for success. If nevertheless these discussions are not successful we intend pursue efforts toward peaceful solution.

While we have been aware certain military measures [4] undertaken by British and French as "precautionary steps", we deeply concerned that intensified preparations on eve of Cairo discussions are anything but helpful in the mobilization of world opinion behind

---

[1] Source: Department of State, Central Files, 684A.86/9-256. Top Secret; Niact. Drafted and approved by Hoover. Sent to London, Paris, Cairo, Rome, Amman, Baghdad, Damascus, Jidda, Beirut, and Tel Aviv. It was separately repeated to Moscow on September 2. (*Ibid.*, 974.7301/9–256) A copy in the Eisenhower Library, Whitman File, International File, is initialed by Eisenhower with the comment: "Sent at my direction. D. ~~File with~~ Make cross reference on this file to my letter to Eden. D" The letter to Eden is Document 163.

[2] See telegram 1249 from London, Document 158. In telegram 1047 from Paris, September 1, the Embassy reported: "Even if decision eventually employ force not yet taken by Cabinet (as we believe) there is every evidence of growing feeling in France, and apparently unanimous sentiment in Cabinet, that military measures may very well come to pass." (Department of State, Central Files, 974.7301/9–156)

[3] Telegram 544 from Cairo, September 1, reported that the British Embassy had recently announced publicly that it had been instructed to reduce Embassy functions and to recommend evacuation of dependents. The telegram also noted that the French Embassy had received similar instructions, but had made no public announcements. (*Ibid.*) Telegram 155 from Amman, August 30, reported that the British Embassy had been instructed to take immediate steps to induce as many British subjects as possible to leave Jordan. (*Ibid.*, 285.11/8-3056)

[4] On August 29, the British Foreign Office issued the following statement: "The French Government have informed Her Majesty's Government that, in view of developments in Egypt and in the canal zone, they wish to be in a position to ensure, in case of need, the protection of French nationals and their interests in the eastern Mediterranean. For this purpose the French Government have asked and Her Majesty's Government have agreed, that a contingent of French troops should be temporarily stationed in Cyprus." (*The London Times*, August 30, 1956)

the Western position and will not enhance chances success of Committee. Of great concern in this regard is the widely publicized evacuation at this stage of British and French nationals particularly from Egypt and Jordan (Cairo's 544 to Department, repeated to other addressees). In a sense these measures more disturbing than troop movements which may be described as precautionary. Not only local populace but wide segments world opinion interpret such action, in absence clear indication that local security situations have deteriorated to point where security of foreigners placed in jeopardy, as evidence that UK and France contemplate military intervention even while Committee is discussing peaceful settlement.

Dillon and Barbour should meet soonest with high level officials French and British Foreign Offices, preferably Ministers, and speak along foregoing lines. They should express serious concern re circumstances surrounding evacuation, and obtain information as to why British and French nationals being evacuated on large scale in absence any indication deteriorating security in Arab countries.

FYI only. Pending clarification British and French positions and in absence reports from Arab capitals indicating worsening local situations Department does not perceive necessity of wisdom of going beyond Phase I in U.S. evacuation plans in those countries for which that phase now applicable. End FYI.

Hoover

---

161.   Memorandum by the Secretary of State [1]

Duck Island, Lake Ontario, September 2, 1956.

It seems to me, as I reflect in semi-retirement, that we are somewhat hynotized by the pattern of the Concession and do not enough rely on the Treaty itself. [2]

---

[1] Source: Department of State, Conference Files: Lot 62 D 181, CF 772. Top Secret. The source text, which contains Dulles' first thoughts on creating an association of Suez Canal users, was initialed by Dulles and bears his handwritten revisions. A retyped copy is *ibid.*, Central Files, 974.7301/9–256.

According to Dulles' Appointment Book, on September 2 the Secretary met with Fraser Wilkins "re Suez" between 9:30 and 11 a.m. at Duck Island. (Princeton University Library, Dulles Papers) Presumably, Wilkins conveyed the contents of the memorandum back to the Department of State and discussed the proposed response to Lloyd. See Document 163.

[2] Reference is to the Egyptian Concession to the Universal Suez Maritime Canal Company and the Treaty of 1888. See Document 1.

Unfortunately, I do not have a copy of the Treaty, but as I recall it gives the right to pass "freely" through the Canal. Does this not mean free of any charges and impediments that Egypt may impose in its national interest?

It is true that the Concession involved an arrangement, somewhat inconsistent with the Treaty, in that it provided that both Egypt and the Company and its shareholders, largely British and French, would get a profit and, because this was modest, it was generally acquiesced in. But Egypt has called that off. Did she not thereby call off her right to profit and the Canal automatically revert to a "non-profit" status?

As to pilots, why do the ships have to hire pilots through Egypt? Why cannot the British, French or any others supply pilots? There are some physical problems, but could not these be handled, if need be, through the Naval craft authorized to be stationed at each end of the Canal?

Then there is the question of keeping the Canal physically free from fill-ins and obstructions. This, it seems to me, is a matter of common interest and not a means of discrimination. If Egypt cannot or does not do this, then I believe that the Parties to the 1888 Treaty have the right to keep the Canal "free" in this physical sense. A charge could be made to create a fund to defray this cost.

Then there is the question of "traffic pattern". I see no reason why Egypt has any right to direct this. I do not, however, know enough about the physical set-up to suggest a solution, but there should be one. Probably 98 percent of the traffic would voluntarily follow non-Egyptian guidance.

We could agree that some of the functions could be directed by an agent appointed by the Security Council.

Would not a program along these lines, announced as an alternative to the 18 Nation proposal, "deflate" Nasser and be a better alternative than force? It rests squarely on the 1888 Treaty, and if Nasser uses force to obstruct this program he would be violating the Charter and its "renunciation of force" Covenant.[3]

JFD

---

[3] Dulles handed this memorandum to the President on September 4; see Document 168.

162.   Telegram From the Embassy in France to the Department of State [1]

Paris, September 2, 1956—2 p.m.

1050. Eyes only Chief of Mission London. Reference: Deptel 826, repeated London 1590, Cairo 617, Rome 954, Amman 223, Baghdad 312, Damascus 386, Jidda 165, Beirut 706, Tel Aviv 187. [2] Pineau, as well as Mollet, is out of town and highest Foreign Office official immediately available was Daridan. We presented Department's views to him and he promised to convey them to Joxe and, as soon as possible, to Foreign Minister and Prime Minister.

Daridan was not surprised at our démarche. He said French themselves had been disturbed at publicity surrounding military preparations. Announcement regarding dispatch French troops to Cyprus had been made only because stationing foreign troops on British territory required Queen's proclamation which had to be made public.

Concerning evacuation French nationals from Egypt and Jordan, Daridan insisted this is not psychological warfare but is motivated by genuine anxiety for safety French women and children. If hostilities or disorders should occur they might arise so rapidly that necessary transport for evacuation could not be provided. In view extreme excitability and ruthlessness Arab mobs, French Government felt it could not take responsibility for failing to issue timely warnings. They may well have to extend warning to Syria and Lebanon as British have done.

Concerning basic policies and future plans, Daridan said that, as far as he knows, no decision has been taken to use military force and indeed French Government is most anxious avoid use of force if possible. French do not wish to prejudice work of committee of five and intend take no action until committee has completed its work and reported. At that time they will certainly consult at once with United States and United Kingdom and perhaps with all seventeen which had approved London proposals.

On the other hand, the French are firmly determined that Nasser shall not be allowed "to get away with it." They understood committee of five discussions would not be dragged out and consider it necessary to be prepared for all eventualities thereafter. They continue to hope for peaceful solution and indeed believe their

---

[1] Source: Department of State, Central Files, 974.7301/9–256. Top Secret; Niact. Received at 2:52 p.m. Repeated Priority to London, Cairo, Rome, Amman, Baghdad, Damascus, Jidda, Beirut, and Tel Aviv. A copy in the Eisenhower Library, Whitman File, Dulles–Herter Series is initialed by Eisenhower.

[2] Document 160.

precautionary measures will help to convince Nasser that the game is up and he will have to give way. He will not be convinced by sweet reason. French have evidence Russian arms are continuing to reach Egypt in substantial quantities. There must be no doubt in Nasser's mind that resort to force on his part would produce immediate and effective riposte.

Comment: We went over Department's views several times with Daridan and made sure he fully understands extreme seriousness with which we regard situation. If Daridan accurately reflects French thinking, and we believe he does, French position could be summarized as follows:

1. Nasser must be made to yield and to yield in such way as not to save his face, at least to any substantial degree;
2. Best way to induce him to yield is by demonstration absolute Anglo-French determination to carry through, including demonstrated intention to use military force if necessary.
3. These tactics will probably succeed and peaceful solution is likely, but force must be used if other means do not succeed.

We shall follow up tomorrow to make certain our views have reached highest quarters.

Dillon

163.   Message From President Eisenhower to Prime Minister Eden [1]

Washington, September 2, 1956.

DEAR ANTHONY: I am grateful for your recent letter, and especially for your kind words on the role of the United States during the London Conference on the Suez Canal. I share your satisfaction at the large number of nations which thought as we do about the future operation of the Canal. In achieving this result we have set in motion a force which I feel will be very useful to us— the united and clearly expressed opinion of the majority users of the Suez waterway and of those nations most dependent upon it. This will exert a pressure which Nasser can scarcely ignore. From Foster I know that this accomplishment is due in no small measure to the expert leadership exhibited by Selwyn Lloyd as Chairman of the Conference, and to the guidance which he received from you.

As for the Russians, it is clear that they sought, at London, to impede the consolidation of a majority point of view, and to generate an atmosphere in the Near East which would make it impossible for Nasser to accept our proposals. I entirely agree with you that the underlying purpose of their policy in this problem is to undermine the Western position in the Near East and Africa, and to weaken the Western nations at home. We must never lose sight of this point.

Now that the London Conference is over, our efforts must be concentrated on the successful outcome of the conversations with Nasser. This delicate situation is going to require the highest skill, not only on the part of the five-nation Committee but also on the

---

[1] Source: Eisenhower Library, Whitman File, International File. Top Secret. Transmitted Priority to London in telegram 1593, September 2, 5:37 p.m., which is the source text. At President Eisenhower's request, copies were also sent on September 2 for background purposes to Ambassador Dillon (telegram 827 to Paris; Department of State, Central Files, 711.11–EI/9–256) and to Henderson (telegram 623 to Cairo; *ibid.*, 974.7301/9–256). Barbour reported that the message was delivered at 12:15 p.m., London time, September 3. (Telegram 1266 from London, September 3; Eisenhower Library, Whitman File)

Late in the afternoon of August 31, Hoover forwarded to President Eisenhower a suggested reply to Eden, which Dulles apparently had drafted while en route to Duck Island. (Note from Hoover to Eisenhower with attachments; Department of State, Central Files, 974.7301/8–3156 and Eisenhower Library, Whitman File, Dulles–Herter Series) Eisenhower made, in his own hand, extensive changes on this draft reply. (*Ibid.*) A clean version of the text, which incorporated Eisenhower's revisions, was typed on September 1. (Department of State, Central Files, 974.7301/8–3156 and Eisenhower Library, Whitman File, International File) After that, Dulles and Hoover made a few additional changes, which were added by hand to both copies of the September 1 draft. The major revisions, which Eisenhower made to Dulles' original draft, are indicated in footnotes below.

part of our Governments. I share your view that it is important that Nasser be under no misapprehension as to the firm interest of the nations primarily concerned with the Canal in safeguarding their rights in that waterway.

As to the possibility of later appeal to the United Nations, we can envisage a situation which would require UN consideration and of course there should be no thought of military action before the influences of the UN are fully explored. However, and most important, we believe that, before going to the UN, the Suez Committee of Five should first be given full opportunity to carry out the course of action agreed upon in London, and to gauge Nasser's intentions.

If the diplomatic front we present is united and is backed by the overwhelming sentiment of our several peoples, the chances should be greater that Nasser will give way without the need for any resort to force. This belief explains our policy at the Conference and also explains the statement which I gave out through Foster after I got back from San Francisco and had a chance to talk fully with him. [2]

[3] I am afraid, Anthony, that from this point onward our views on this situation diverge. As to the use of force or the threat of force at this juncture, I continue to feel as I expressed myself in the letter Foster carried to you some weeks ago. Even now military preparations and civilian evacuation exposed to public view seem to be solidifying support for Nasser which has been shaky in many important quarters. I regard it as indispensable that if we are to proceed solidly together to the solution of this problem, public opinion in our several countries must be overwhelming in its support. I must tell you frankly that American public opinion flatly rejects the thought of using force, particularly when it does not seem that every possible peaceful means of protecting our vital interests has been exhausted without result. Moreover, I gravely doubt we could here secure Congressional authority even for the lesser support measures for which you might have to look to us.

---

[2] For text of Eisenhower's statement of August 29, see *Public Papers of the Presidents of the United States: Dwight D. Eisenhower, 1956*, pp. 716–717.

[3] At this point, Eisenhower deleted the following sentence in Dulles' original draft: "Although I can see that this thesis provides, as you say, a reason to continue your military preparations in conjunction with the French, the actual use of force is another matter." In its place, Eisenhower inserted the paragraph printed here. A few changes were made subsequently, including the addition of the first sentence, "I am afraid, Anthony, that from this point onward our views on this situation diverge." Also, the fifth sentence in the text printed here originally read in Eisenhower's draft: "I must tell you frankly that American public opinion flatly rejects the thought of using force until every possible peaceful means of protecting our vital interests has been exhausted without result."

I really do not see how a successful result could be achieved by forcible means. The use of force would, it seems to me, vastly increase the area of jeopardy. I do not see how the economy of Western Europe can long survive the burden of prolonged military operations, as well as the denial of Near East oil. Also the peoples of the Near East and of North Africa and, to some extent, of all of Asia and all of Africa, would be consolidated against the West to a degree which, I fear, could not be overcome in a generation and, perhaps, not even in a century particularly having in mind the capacity of the Russians to make mischief. [4] Before such action were undertaken, all our peoples should unitedly understand that there were no other means available to protect our vital rights and interests.

We have two problems, the first of which is the assurance of permanent and efficient operation of the Suez Canal with justice to all concerned. The second is to see that Nasser shall not grow as a menace to the peace and vital interests of the West. In my view, these two problems need not and possibly cannot be solved simultaneously and by the same methods, although we are exploring further means to this end. The first is the most important for the moment and must be solved in such a way as not to make the second more difficult. Above all, there must be no grounds for our several peoples to believe that anyone is using the Canal difficulty as an excuse to proceed forcibly against Nasser. And we have friends in the Middle East who tell us they would like to see Nasser's deflation brought about. But they seem unanimous in feeling that the Suez is not the issue on which to attempt to do this by force. Under those circumstances, because of the temper of their populations, they say they would have to support Nasser even against their better judgment.

Seldom, I think, have we been faced by so grave a problem. For the time being we must, I think, put our faith in the processes already at work to bring Nasser peacefully to accept the solution along the lines of the 18-nation proposal. I believe that even though this procedure may fail to give the setback to Nasser that he so much deserves, we can better retrieve our position subsequently than if military force were hastily invoked. [5]

---

[4] At this point, Dulles' original draft reads: "I quite agree that Nasser definitely needs deflating. And we also have friends in the Middle East who tell us they would like to see this brought about. But they seem unanimous in feeling that the Suez is not the issue on which to attempt to do this by force. Under those circumstances, they say they would have to support Nasser even against their better judgment." Eisenhower inserted instead the remainder of the paragraph printed here and the entirety of the next one with one minor subsequent change. In Eisenhower's original draft the third sentence read: "In my view, these two problems need not and possibly cannot be solved simultaneously and by the same means."

[5] In Dulles' original draft, this sentence reads: "I believe that even though this procedure may seem to give Nasser a partial victory, we can better retrieve our

Of course, our departments are looking into the implications of all future developments. In this they will keep in close touch with appropriate officials of your Government, as is my wish.

With warm regard,

As ever,

D.E. [6]

---

position subsequently than if military force is invoked." Eisenhower's version is that which appears in text printed here.

[6] Telegram 1593 bears these typed initials.

---

164. Telegram From the Embassy in France to the Department of State [1]

Paris, September 3, 1956—2 p.m.

1054. Eyes only Chief of Mission. Reference: Embtel 1050; repeated London 157, Cairo 31, Rome 62, Amman 5, Baghdad 1, Damascus 6, Jidda 1, Beirut 11, Tel Aviv 15. [2] Joxe and Daridan informed us this morning that they had presented our views on Suez developments to Pineau and that he had endorsed comments which Daridan had made to us yesterday.

They repeated evacuation their nationals from Egypt, Jordan and elsewhere is not designed to exacerbate situation, but insisted that, while French Government has given no orders for evacuation, it could not fail under circumstances to issue timely and serious warning.

Comment: We do not believe French are disposed to alter their policy on evacuation though they may proceed a little more slowly than they would have done had we not raised question.

Concerning basic issue, Joxe and Daridan reaffirmed (1) French wish to facilitate and in no way to jeopardize work of committee of 5; (2) French desire to avoid military action; (3) French determination that Nasser shall accept international administration of canal and shall not even appear to emerge triumphant from present crisis.

---

[1] Source: Department of State, Central Files, 974.7301/9–356. Top Secret; Priority. Received at 11:37 a.m. Repeated Priority to London, Cairo, Rome, Amman, Baghdad, Damascus, Jidda, Beirut, and Tel Aviv. A copy in the Eisenhower Library, Whitman File, Dulles–Herter Series is initialed by Eisenhower.

[2] Document 162.

Joxe was not optimistic that Nasser in discussions with committee of 5 would accept solution which would be satisfactory to French and British.

Comment: While this conversation revealed no avowed shift in French line, we had definite impression our démarche had been taken very seriously and that henceforth French may proceed with more caution. However, it will be extremely difficult for them to back away from unyielding position which French leaders have repeatedly taken in public statements and which press continues to reflect with undiminished fervor.

Dillon

---

165. Telegram From the Embassy in the United Kingdom to the Department of State [1]

London, September 3, 1956—5 p.m.

1270. Eyes only Chief of Mission and Henderson. I saw Selwyn Lloyd this afternoon and gave him Department's views (Deptel 1590) [2] emphasizing US serious concern developments with particular reference evacuation nationals and inquiring why large-scale evacuation taking place under present security conditions.

Lloyd explained evacuation as precautionary measure in line other military steps and necessitated solely by magnitude evacuation problem. He said there are 6,000 UK nationals in Egypt out of 13,000 British and some 2,500 in Jordan, figures with which it would be impossible to cope expeditiously if hostilities broke out. He claimed to be conscious of psychological effect being created by evacuation measures and said that for that reason British are minimizing evacuation to maximum extent possible. No evacuation being undertaken in the Persian Gulf, Iraq or the Lebanon (despite French report to contrary contained Paris telegram 1051). [3]

---

[1] Source: Department of State, Central Files, 974.7301/9–356. Top Secret; Priority. Received at 5 p.m. Repeated to Paris, Amman, Jidda, Cairo, Baghdad, Beirut, Rome, Damascus, and Tel Aviv. A copy in the Eisenhower Library, Whitman File, Dulles–Herter Series is initialed by Eisenhower.

[2] Document 160.

[3] The reference is evidently in error. Telegram 1051 from Paris concerns an unrelated matter.

Re intensified military preparations on eve Cairo discussions, Lloyd said preparations essential for British to be in position accomplish military intervention if such becomes necessary. Response my comment that preparations not helpful mobilizing world opinion behind Western position, he stated British conviction that preparations should have salutary effect on Nasser. His reports from Egypt indicate Nasser betting ten to one against military intervention and Lloyd said he would prefer if Nasser thought odds 50–50.

Lloyd concerned at ten days delay which has preceded talks in Cairo and stressed urgency concluding Menzies mission and proceeding to next steps. He acknowledged understanding that US committed to endeavoring find peaceful solution and that US intends pursue efforts towards such peaceful solution, even if Menzies mission not successful. He stated British have "not pushed any buttons yet" and gave impression further peaceful steps could be taken in absence successful Menzies mission. However, he noted if mission did not produce results in approximately a week, such further steps would have to be considered immediately and he also remarked that if military measures are to be taken they cannot be postponed indefinitely.

Barbour

---

166.   Editorial Note

According to notes taken at the meeting, the following exchange took place at the Secretary's Staff Meeting which began at 9:15 a.m. on September 4 prior to Secretary Dulles' return to Washington:

"Mr. Rountree said that, in accordance with the Secretary's wishes, L, IO, and NEA had prepared comments on the next step to be taken in the Suez crisis and he wanted those comments to reflect the Under Secretary's views before being presented to the Secretary. The Under Secretary said that he would discuss this matter with Mr. Rountree before the Secretary's arrival." (Department of State, Secretary's Staff Meetings: Lot 63 D 75)

The comments mentioned by Rountree were presumably those contained in the memorandum from Rountree to Dulles, *infra*. No account of the subsequent discussion between Hoover and Rountree has been found.

167.   **Memorandum From the Assistant Secretary of State for Near Eastern, South Asian, and African Affairs (Rountree) to the Secretary of State** [1]

Washington, September 4, 1956.

SUBJECT

New Proposal for the Suez Canal [2]

In collaboration with L, E and IO, we have examined your new proposal from several angles as follows:

Legal Considerations

Article 1 of the 1888 Treaty provides that the Canal "shall always be free and open, in time of war as in time of peace, to every vessel of commerce or of war, without distinction of flag." There are several other articles which refer to "free passage" of the Canal. It is not believed, however, that the word "free" as used in this text is to be construed as meaning "without charge". The 1888 Convention was written with the knowledge of the 1856 Concession to the Canal company, Article 17 of which specifically provided: "In order to indemnify the company for expenses of construction, maintenance and management . . . we authorize [the company] . . . [3] to establish and collect for the right of passing through the canals and the ports belonging, navigation, all pilotage, towage, or anchorage dues, according to tariffs to be modified by the company at all times." Nothing in the Convention of 1888 modified this provision for charging dues to meet the costs of construction, maintenance and management. Such charges have continuously been imposed and paid without objection. All of this negates any thought that the Convention of 1888 provided for passage without charge.

It should also be noted that the Hay–Pauncefote Treaty relating to the Panama Canal [4] adopted in Article 3 "the following rules substantially as embodied in the Convention of Constantinople, signed the 28th October 1888, for the free navigation of the Suez Canal . . . (1) the Canal should be free and open to the vessels of commerce and war of all nations . . . on terms of entire equality so that there should be no discrimination . . . in respect of the condi-

---

[1] Source: Department of State, NEA Files: Lot 58 D 545, Egypt. Top Secret. The source text also indicates Raymond, Armstrong, Ludlow, and Wilkins as drafting officers. No indication has been found that the memorandum was forwarded to Dulles.

[2] Reference is presumably to Dulles' memorandum of September 2, Document 161.

[3] All ellipses and brackets in this document are in the source text.

[4] For text, see 12 Bevans 258–260.

tions or charges of traffic, or otherwise". It would seem clear that the expression "free and open" was used in the same sense in both cases, but in both cases contemplating appropriate charges.

"Free" should be construed as meaning "without impediment". Such impediment might be physical, operational, or even created by excess charges over and above what would be fair and reasonable to meet the expenses of construction, maintenance and management.

Should there be an impediment to the free passage of the Suez Canal, in the sense just described, by operational failure through lack of pilots, there would seem to be no legal objection to alternative arrangements being provided by the interested parties to assure a supply of pilots.

Practical Considerations

There is raised the question of "traffic pattern" and the suggestion is made that there is no reason why Egypt has any right to direct this. Without going into the question of who has the right to direct it, the chief point is that the Canal is physically the type of facility which on practical grounds must have centralized direction and control, and authority over the movement of ships within it, if it is not to become completely jammed as a result of uncontrolled voluntary actions. The Canal is not wide enough for a steady flow of ships to pass each other at all times and at all places. There are places where ships can pass each other, but control must be exercised to see that ships do not encounter each other at other places. A voluntarily organized control over ship movements, not based on Egyptian soil or operating under Egyptian authority, might well obtain compliance from the great majority of the ships operating through the Canal, but could certainly not enforce its will on Egyptian ships or on ships of other nations which did not choose to cooperate, such as the Soviet Union. The failure of a single ship to cooperate could block the entire facility.

In the short term, the problem of physical obstructions arising from sand storms, cave-in of banks, or silting up is probably not urgent. Nevertheless, over the longer term, work to correct any hydrographical deficiencies would have to be related to and coordinated with whatever centralized control over traffic was in effect, simply because important dredging or earthmoving work could not be undertaken while ships were passing the spot where the work was being done. Furthermore, if there were a "voluntary" control authority over ship movements (not under Egyptian control) and if there were need for dredging or work on the banks, the question of sovereignty would arise if the external "voluntary" authority sought to put personnel and equipment on the shore, which is Egyptian territory.

Opinions differ on pilotage. Presumably, experienced pilots could be assembled to pilot ships through the Canal without being subject to the jurisdiction of the Egyptian Government, but this does not mean a resolution of the problem of centralized control of the facility covered in the first paragraph above. Pilots are not legally responsible for the movement of the ships on which they are stationed but the masters of the ships must, for practical reasons, be subject to some central traffic authority. A set of pilots operated by an external "voluntary" organization might well give one set of instructions to masters at a time when masters were receiving contrary instructions from the Egyptian Government authority which would still be trying to run the Canal. This leads to the conclusion that from a practical standpoint, the operation of the Canal by any kind of duality in authority or without the assent of the Egyptian Government is an impossibility.

Political Considerations

At the present time, 18 nations support the 5-power proposal. If the work of the Committee of 5, which is discussing this proposal with Nasser, reaches no conclusion, it is possible that some of the 18 nations would support the new proposal. It would appear to them to be an alternative to more forceful action which the British and French would almost certainly be advocating. It is believed, however, that most of the 18 nations would immediately make the point that steps taken to implement the new proposal would probably result in the threat of an aggressive Egyptian response or an incident itself. Security Council consideration would undoubtedly follow because of the Egyptian threat or action. Most of the 18 nations might therefore prefer to proceed to the Security Council directly following a breakdown of the work of the Committee of 5 than to take an intervening step which seemed certain to result in an incident. They would argue that direct reference to the Security Council might avoid hostilities entirely.

An announcement of the new proposal, based on the Treaty of 1888, would have the psychological effect of deflating Nasser momentarily. As previously indicated, it would not have been possible to implement the proposal which would have been referred to the Security Council. Nasser would claim that those favoring the new proposal were infringing upon Egyptian sovereignty and that he would be forced to respond to protect Egyptian interests. During the ensuing Security Council consideration, Nasser's popularity would be restored and he would be depicted as the defender of the Arabs against the West. Mossadeq did not lose his position of popularity and support throughout the years of the Iranian dispute preceding his deposal.

Conclusions

The legal, practical and political considerations set forth above would indicate there is substantial doubt that the proposal could in fact be implemented over Egyptian opposition, particularly if there were not virtual unanimity among all users of the Suez Canal and unless the action was sanctioned by some recognized authority such as the United Nations.

There may, however, be advantages from the psychological viewpoint to an announcement or some other indication that the users of the Canal were considering an alternative of this nature if satisfactory arrangements with the Government of Egypt could not otherwise be achieved.

If it were decided to pursue this course, an announcement of a proposal for a voluntary international association to operate the Suez Canal containing the following points might be made:

1. The actual operation of the Canal presently being a matter of dispute and the status of the concession of the Canal Company yet to be settled, the nations which constitute the majority users of the Suez Canal have taken cognizance of the fact that the Egyptian Government has asserted that it will continue to respect the Constantinople Convention. They expect the Government of Egypt to continue to abide by this pronouncement. For their part, they are determined to ensure that their rights under the Convention shall be maintained and fully exercised.

2. To this end they have agreed that they will establish an international shipping control association for the purpose of transitting the Canal. The association will be set up with headquarters to be determined. It will employ pilots who will be fully qualified to effect passage through the Suez Canal. It will establish a traffic and convoy system for those ships using its facilities so that the Canal shall continue to be operated with maximum efficiency. It will collect tolls from ships using the association for the sole purpose of a) paying the pilots; b) paying operational and administrative expenses of the association and c) establishing a fund to be used whenever it is determined that construction and repair work should be undertaken on the Canal.

3. The services and facilities of the association will be unqualifiedly available to ships of any nation at all times.

4. The association will stand ready at all times to cooperate with the Egyptian authorities and ensure that the Canal remains free and unobstructed to shipping.

If it should be necessary to go to the Security Council, Mr. Wilcox' memorandum of September 3 [5] sets forth a possible course of action under article 40.

---

[5] Not printed. (Department of State, UNP Files: Lot 58 D 244, Suez–1956)

---

168.   Editorial Note

During the morning of September 4, Secretary Dulles returned from Duck Island, arriving outside Washington at 11:10 a.m. He proceeded immediately to the Department of State where, among other activities, he discussed the Suez situation with Hoover, Rountree, other Department officials, and at one point with representatives of the Esso Shipping Company. No accounts of these conversations have been found in Department of State files. At 3 p.m. Dulles, accompanied by Hoover, met with President Eisenhower at the White House. (Dulles Appointment Book; Princeton University Library, Dulles Papers) During this meeting with Eisenhower, Dulles handed to the President his memorandum of September 2 (Document 161), which contained the Secretary's first thoughts on creating an association of Suez Canal users. A copy of the memorandum of September 2 in the Eisenhower Library, Dulles Papers, Meetings with the President, bears a handwritten notation "Sec. took to W.H. 9/4/56". Another copy of the paper is *ibid.*, Whitman File, Dulles–Herter Series. No memorandum of the conversation between Eisenhower and Dulles has been found. Eisenhower later appended to his memoirs a discussion of how he and Dulles viewed the users association proposal at the time. (*Waging Peace*, pages 672–675)

According to Dulles' Appointment Book, the Secretary met with Coulson at 7:36 p.m. that evening. Although no memorandum of this conversation has been found, a memorandum of a subsequent conversation with Coulson (Document 172) indicates that at the September 4 meeting Dulles outlined the users association proposal.

169.   Report Prepared in the Executive Secretariat of the Department of State [1]

Washington, September 4, 1956.

SUMMARY OF DEVELOPMENTS IN SUEZ SITUATION

Suez Committee

Prior to the movement of the Suez Committee to Cairo, a series of exchanges took place between the Department and Under Secretary Henderson regarding the US positions. Henderson stated the Committee's understanding that it was not called upon to negotiate on the question of compensation to the Suez Canal Company. [2] In reply, we told Henderson [3] that the Secretary has said, although there is a close relationship between the disposition of the company's assets and the proposed final settlement by convention, we should not at this time attempt to take a final decision on this aspect of the problem.

We responded to Henderson's suggestions for practical implementation of the five-power proposals by recommending changes and comments. Most of these related to our thinking with regard to

---

[1] Source: Eisenhower Library, Whitman File, International File. Top Secret; Eyes Only for Designated Recipient. The source text is initialed "DE."

On September 4, Hoover forwarded this report to Goodpaster under cover of a memorandum which reads: "I thought it would be helpful for you to have each day for use with the President a brief summary of the most important cables received and despatched on the Suez situation. I also plan to send such summaries on an 'Eyes Only' basis to the following: Treasury—Secretary Humphrey; Defense—Secretary Wilson; White House—Mr. William Jackson; JCS—Admiral Radford; ODM—Dr. Flemming; CIA—General Cabell. A copy of the first of these summaries is enclosed. Subsequent summaries should be shorter than this first summary which covers the cable traffic over the holiday weekend [Labor Day, September 1–3]." (Department of State, Central Files, 974.7301/9–456)

Between September 4 and November 1, 41 of these reports, all entitled "Summary of Developments in Suez Situation" were forwarded to the White House for Goodpaster's use in briefing President Eisenhower. Copies of the report were also sent to the individuals mentioned above. The series was officially discontinued as of November 5 "in view of the changed Middle East situation." (Memorandum from Howe to William Jackson, November 5; *ibid.*, 974.7301/11–556) The reports were prepared by the Reports and Operations Staff of the Executive Secretariat of the Department of State. They are filed in the Eisenhower Library, Whitman File, International File under a covering sheet entitled "Special Suez Summary".

[2] Reported in telegram 1243 from London, August 31, not printed. (Department of State, Central Files, 974.7301/8–3156)

[3] The Department's response was sent to Henderson in Cairo in telegram 607. (*Ibid.*) In a letter dated August 22, Foreign Minister Pineau queried Secretary Dulles as to the U.S. position on the compensation question. (Letter from Pineau to Dulles; *ibid.*, 974.7301/8–2256) Dulles responded on August 29 along the lines indicated here. (Letter from Dulles to Pineau; *ibid.*, Phleger Files: Lot 58 D 517, Suez Canal—Special File of Papers Mar–Oct 1956 (H. Phleger)) None of these documents is printed.

the operation of the canal system by a new Suez Canal Board, but we also suggested a strengthening of the section relating to sanctions which may be taken against any party which interferes with the use or operation of the canal. [4] We hold it important that immediate resort to the UN can be taken in such an instance, even in the face of a Soviet veto.

The Committee traveled to Cairo over the week-end and had its initial meetings with President Nasser yesterday. Henderson reported [5] that the meeting, which was devoted only to procedural matters, was cordial and apparently successful in creating a good atmosphere for the talks.

At the first meeting, Menzies gave Nasser an aide-mémoire [6] which was intended to set forth the atmosphere of the London Conference on Suez and of the Committee discussions since that time. Attached to the aide-mémoire was the 18-power statement.

Menzies expressed the thought to Nasser that the Committee's viewpoint, and that of the Egyptian Government, might be presented at successive meetings. He stressed, however, that while a vigorous exchange of views might ensue after Nasser had given the Egyptian position, the Committee would speak always in a friendly spirit. Menzies mentioned that at a later stage the Committee might work out with Egypt an agreed document, perhaps in the form of heads of agreement. He said that the Committee was not empowered to negotiate but only to report back to its principals Nasser's ideas on the proposals it would advance.

Henderson states that Nasser, while obviously nervous and ill-at-ease, successfully reciprocated the friendly approach by Menzies. Nasser spoke very briefly, saying that no "hostile arguments" would be advanced from the Egyptian side. He suggested that meetings be flexible without prior determination of the exact course to be followed after the initial presentations. Nasser also stated his preference for one meeting a day at the Committee's convenience, remarking that he was occupied by other matters with Egypt being obliged

---

[4] Henderson forwarded to the Department of State a list of ideas on how the Eighteen-Power Proposal might be implemented in telegram 1144 from London, August 29. (*Ibid.*, Central Files, 974.7301/8–2956) The Department transmitted its comments on these ideas to Henderson in telegram 1548 to London, August 31 (*ibid.*), and in telegram 657 to Cairo, September 5 (*Ibid.*, 974.7301/9–156).

[5] Henderson reported on the Suez Committee's initial meeting with Nasser, which began at noon September 3, in telegram 570 from Cairo, September 3. (*Ibid.*, 974.7301/9–356)

[6] The text of the aide-mémoire was transmitted to the Department of State in telegram 569 from Cairo, September 3 (*ibid.*) and is printed in *The Suez Canal Problem, July 26–September 22, 1956*, pp. 306–309. Exchanges between Henderson and the Department of State concerning the drafting of the document are in Department of State, Central File 974.7301.

to "overcome economic sanctions" and "keep an hourly watch on military preparations in the Mediterranean".

On Monday evening, the Committee's first substantive meeting with Nasser took place.[7] The informal friendly atmosphere was maintained during the course of the one-hour meeting, which was taken up almost entirely by Menzies in explaining the Committee's proposals. Henderson indicates that Menzies presentation was admirable and that he showed consummate tact in presenting the more unpalatable passages.

Menzies advanced the International Bank as the illustration of the type of "institutional arrangement" which might be resorted to in operating the canal. While emphasizing the respect of the user nations for Egypt's sovereignty, Menzies stated that they also had a stake in the canal, which he was sure Egypt would not wish to ignore. With all due respect to Egypt, Menzies said there would be a diminution in international confidence if any subsequent government of Egypt could use the institutional arrangement for the operation of the canal as a political instrument.

Following the meeting Menzies met alone with Nasser for about 15 minutes.[8] He informed Committee members later that he wished to clarify certain points and in particular he thought that Nasser should know that the London Conference did not consider the use of armed force. The purpose of this Committee, Menzies told Nasser, was also to seek a peaceful solution.

British and French Positions

[Here follow a summary of the special instructions sent at the direction of President Eisenhower on September 2 to London, Paris, and other diplomatic missions, Document 160; the responses received

---

[7] The meeting took place at 7 p.m. in Cairo September 3. Henderson's report is in telegram 575, September 3. (*Ibid.*, 974.7301/9–356) A copy of this telegram in the Eisenhower Library, Whitman File, Dulles–Herter Series, is initialed by Eisenhower.

[8] Henderson conveyed Menzies' account of the private meeting in telegram 575 from Cairo, September 3, as follows: "Stories had been circulating that one of chief results of London Conference was removal of danger of resort to armed force in obtaining solution of Canal problem. He thought it only fair to let Nasser know that Conference did not consider matter use armed force. Purpose of Conference had been to try to find peaceful solution. Although this committee did not represent Conference, it represented eighteen powers present at Conference and its purpose also was to seek peaceful solution. In certain countries which had major interest in Canal, particularly in Great Britain and France, feeling still very high. Although it was devoutly to be hoped that peaceful solution could be found, nevertheless it was impossible to give assurances that failing peaceful solution no force would be applied. If he were representing the British and French Governments, he could not make such statement without giving impression that he engaging in threats. He wished it understood no threat was implied. It was purpose of committee to indicate what might happen if peaceful solution could not be found." (Department of State, Central Files, 974.7301/9–356)

from Paris in telegrams 1050 and 1054, Documents 162 and 164; and the response received from London in telegram 1270, Document 165.]

Operation of Canal

An Egyptian Exchange Control Circular issued on August 30 requires that Suez Canal dues be paid in Egypt in Egyptian pounds and that the shipping companies establish accounts for this purpose. To feed these accounts, the Exchange Control Office has authorized for the time being the purchase of local currency against blocked sterling or francs. As sterling or franc disbursements from blocked accounts will be credited to the Egyptian Government in London or Paris, the effect of this action is to deprive the Suez Canal Company of the canal fees.

The Department has informed Paris, London and Cairo [9] that there have been virtually no inquiries from US citizens interested in jobs as Suez pilots. We plan to stress the uncertainties of employment conditions and the state of tension prevailing in the area if such inquiries are forthcoming. However, because of our desire to avoid any accusation that the US is contributing to the breakdown of Canal operations, and our preference that any new pilots be hired from the West rather than Iron Curtain countries, we do not plan to take any official action against individuals who might wish to accept Suez jobs.

---

[9] In telegram 825 to Paris, September 1, repeated to London and Cairo. (*Ibid.*)

---

170.   Telegram From the Department of State to the Embassy in Egypt [1]

Washington, September 4, 1956—8:47 p.m.

640. Suez for Henderson. We have been giving careful thought to steps which might be taken if Nasser should reject Five Power proposal. As you know from recent messages, we have reiterated our belief that every effort should be made to find peaceful solution to problem. We attach utmost importance to avoiding application of

---

[1] Source: Department of State, Central Files, 974.7301/9–456. Top Secret; Niact. Drafted by Rountree; cleared in draft by Dulles, Hoover, Wilcox, and Raymond; approved by Rountree who signed for Dulles. Repeated Niact to London.

force in any circumstances in which it would not be abundantly clear that this was last resort and that Egyptians were responsible for creation of situation which brought about hostilities.

We of course hope result of Five Power Committee's work will be to bring about area of agreement and atmosphere conducive to negotiation of new treaty along lines 18-Nation proposal. If, however, this should not be possible believe you should know while you are in Cairo general lines of our thinking re next steps. British are contemplating bringing matter before SC, although we as yet unconvinced they are thinking along lines which give promise that SC would in fact be able to contribute materially to a solution. On the contrary British intention appears to be quick consideration by SC more as an "exercise" which must be gone through before moving to more drastic measures. Our feeling is that if matter is to be brought to SC it must be for purpose sincerely seeking action which would contribute to peaceful solution. We recognize, however, that resolution meeting minimum position of Canal users not likely be adopted by SC due to Soviet veto, and that procedural difficulties would require considerably more time for SC consideration than British have in mind. Added difficulty is that during this time it possible or probable that incidents in Canal would precipitate showdown.

Alternative which appears to us to have substantial merit is based upon thought that perhaps if and when Nasser rejects 18-Nation proposal, we should concentrate more upon guarantees provided by 1888 Treaty and measures which users of Canal might legally and morally take to assure that rights guaranteed to them under Treaty are not impaired. Although we have offered to negotiate a new treaty with Egypt, that should in no way indicate that we are not determined to utilize rights under existing treaty.

We know of no way to impose a new Canal treaty upon Egypt. Egypt's resistance to the principles developed by the 18 powers is not a proper basis for action against her. Our case is legally weak so long as it rests on Egypt's refusal to accept the 18 power proposal because this depends upon Egypt voluntarily agreeing to a new treaty. The rights accorded under the 1888 Treaty constitute a perpetual easement to use freely the Canal and insistence on the right so to use the Canal places us on the best possible ground. For the users of the Canal to form, through an agreement, an association to exercise the right of user is in no way dependent upon Egyptian consent nor inconsistent with the 1888 Convention which indeed by Article 8 [2] contemplates some such possibility. Should the Egyptians

---

[2] For text of the Convention Respecting the Free Navigation of the Suez Maritime Canal, Constantinople, October 29, 1888, see *British and Foreign State Papers, 1887–1888*, vol. 79, pp. 18–22; or *The Suez Canal Problem, July 26–September 22, 1956*, pp. 16–20.

seek to obstruct the use of the Canal under these circumstances, she would then in the eyes of the world be the party who has violated the Treaty of 1888. In these circumstances the Canal users would be in a far better position to bring case to the Security Council if they had to, or take such other action as might then be required.

Vast majority of shipping passing through Canal at present is owned by no more than half dozen nations. Over 90 percent such shipping is owned by 18 nations which Committee represents. Most if not all of those nations might agree to concerting among themselves and with other Canal users to effect arrangements for transit of Canal which do not depend upon any new agreement with Egypt. If it decided to pursue this course an announcement of a proposal for voluntary international association to operate the Canal, containing the following points, might be made:

1. Actual operation of Canal presently being matter of dispute with imminent possibility of difficulties in transit, and status of concession of Canal Company yet to be settled, nations which constitute majority users have taken cognizance of fact that Egyptian Government has asserted that it will continue to respect Constantinople Convention. They expect Government of Egypt to continue abide by this pronouncement. For their part, they are determined to ensure that their rights under Convention shall be maintained and fully exercised.

2. To this end they have agreed that they will establish an international shipping control association for purpose of transitting Canal. Association will be set up with headquarters to be determined. It will employ pilots who are fully qualified to effect passage. It will establish traffic and convoy system for those ships using its facilities so that Canal shall continue to be operated with maximum efficiency. It will prorate the cost of operation to ships using the Canal and the proceeds would be used for sole purposes of a) paying pilots; b) paying operation and administrative expenses of association and c) establishing a fund to be used whenever it is determined that construction and repair work should be undertaken on Canal.

3. Services and facilities of association will be available to ships of any nation at all times.

4. Association will stand ready at all times to cooperate with Egyptian authorities and ensure that Canal remains free and unobstructed to shipping.

It will be noted that foregoing does not provide for payment to Egypt, although Egypt would acquire profits under 18-nation proposal, as Suez Canal Company. Since the concession has been cancelled there is no existing agreement under which Egypt could claim "profits". Any claim for rental or other compensation for use of her property would be matter for future negotiation but not a matter of Egypt's right.

A main problem would be question of scheduling of traffic. A voluntarily organized scheduling of ship movements, not based on Egyptian soil nor operating under Egyptian authority could, we believe, effectively meet requirements in this regard although there would be many difficulties involved. An obvious point is that full compliance with traffic pattern established by the scheduling agency would be required of all vessels, including Egyptian vessels, since failure of a single ship to cooperate could, as today, block the entire facility. Users, however, would take cognizance this difficulty, and, through its standing offer, take all possible steps to cooperate in keeping Canal free and unobstructed. Onus for obstruction legally and in public eye would be on Egypt or non-cooperating users.

Regarding pilots, there would appear to be no legal or insuperable practical reasons why pilots would have to be hired through Egypt. These might be provided for the most part directly by the nations using the Canal for their own ships, and some might be provided in a central pool to be operated by scheduling agency. Such pilots provided locally might be stationed upon ships at either end of the Canal pursuant to Article 7 of the Treaty.

It would, of course, be necessary to carry on certain maintenance operations, such as dredging and maintenance of buoys and other navigational guides. If Egyptian Government were willing to undertake this maintenance and did so efficiently (for which it would be paid by the control authority), there would be no reason to interfere. If it failed to do so, it would correspondingly be impeding the free use of the Canal and the users would then be entitled to take necessary measures themselves.

Our thought is that if it appears that your discussions with Nasser are not going well, it might be greatly beneficial for him to learn that proposition along the foregoing lines is being given serious consideration. First, however, we believe it necessary to have reaction interested parties. I am urgently consulting with British Chargé here to set forth general outline of thinking. I would appreciate receiving soonest your own reaction and any suggestions which you might have. In this connection, unless you perceive objection, I suggest you discuss matter on strictly secret basis with Menzies omitting of course reference to British intentions re SC action. If these various reactions favorable, we would plan discuss with other members of 18 power group.

Dulles

171.   Editorial Note

At 9:05 a.m. on September 5, White House Press Secretary Hagerty telephoned Secretary Dulles to discuss suggested responses for President Eisenhower's press conference scheduled for 10:30 that morning. The portion of their conversation on the Suez situation, as transcribed by Bernau, went as follows: "Hagerty suggested he [the President] just reiterate U.S. position of settling question by peaceful means. Hagerty asked if we were keeping President informed of Henderson's reports. The Sec said yes but we had only received parts of Henderson's most recent cable." (Eisenhower Library, Dulles Papers, White House Telephone Conversations)

The Henderson report to which Dulles referred was telegram 596 from Cairo, September 5 (Department of State, Central Files, 974.7301/9–556), which is summarized in Document 173. The last section of telegram 596 was not received in the Department of State until 8:51 a.m. that morning.

During the press conference that began at 10:30 a.m. Eisenhower was asked whether the United States would support Great Britain and France if they insisted on nothing less than the Eighteen-Power Proposal. The President responded: "Well, I am not going to comment on the contents of that proposal while it is being discussed in Cairo. I will repeat what I have said, I think, each week here before this body; the United States is committed to a peaceful solution of this problem, and one that will insure to all nations the free use of the canal for the shipping of the world, whether in peace or in war, as contemplated by the 1888 convention." (*Public Papers of the Presidents of the United States: Dwight D. Eisenhower, 1956*, page 737)

172.   Memorandum of a Conversation Between the British Chargé (Coulson) and the Assistant Secretary of State for Near Eastern, South Asian, and African Affairs (Rountree), Department of State, Washington, September 5, 1956 [1]

SUBJECT

> (1) New Approach to Suez Canal Problem; (2) Visit Between the Kings of Iraq and Saudi Arabia

1) Mr. Coulson called on Mr. Rountree at the former's request to obtain more information on the Secretary's new suggestion for an approach to the Suez Canal problem. Mr. Rountree gave the British Chargé the substance of the message the Secretary sent to Mr. Henderson yesterday [2] on this matter, explaining that the Secretary, when he discussed the subject with Mr. Coulson yesterday, had only given the general lines of his idea since he did not wish to create the impression that all the details had been worked out. It would, of course, be necessary to give the most careful scrutiny to these details should the general idea be found to have merit.

After Mr. Rountree had finished summarizing the telegram under reference, Mr. Coulson commented that one very important point had been cleared up for him—the question of whether the new approach would be carried out by the signatories of the 1888 Convention or by the majority users of the Canal. He thought that the idea of a proclamation by the users would be very helpful. Mr. Rountree said that if you could get the relatively few nations who control 95% of the shipping going through the Canal to agree to a new international arrangement for passage through Suez, a very heavy onus would fall upon those powers representing the minority users who might choose not to go along with the new system.

Mr. Coulson then raised the question of whether force would be required to set up the new arrangement. Mr. Rountree replied that essentially the new idea was a fall-back position of the type which people sometimes have to have but hope they will not be required to use. If, however, you formulate a fall-back position you have to be ready to carry it out if necessary. The Secretary's idea was that what was proposed was within the rights of the users of the Canal under the 1888 Treaty, and opposition to it would place Egypt in the position of going against the Treaty.

---

[1] Source: Department of State, Central Files, 974.7301/9–556. Top Secret. Drafted by Stuart W. Rockwell, Deputy Director of the Office of Near Eastern Affairs, on September 6 and Rountree on September 8.

[2] Reference is to telegram 640, Document 170.

The British Chargé then said that one of the difficulties would be that it would be hard to carry out the new approach in time, in view of the likelihood that the Five-Nation Committee would probably soon end its work in Cairo. In this connection Mr. Rountree commented that Nasser's response to the initial presentation by Mr. Menzies had not been good.

Mr. Coulson said that the Foreign Office had acknowledged the receipt of his message sent after talking with the Secretary yesterday. It had commented that the proposal was very interesting and that it was seeking the reaction of the various Government entities concerned with this problem. Further comment would shortly be sent.

[Here follows discussion of unrelated subjects.]

---

173. Report Prepared in the Executive Secretariat of the Department of State [1]

Summary No. 2   *Washington, September 5, 1956.*

SUMMARY OF DEVELOPMENTS IN SUEZ SITUATION

Cairo Negotiations

The Committee's third session with Nasser took place on Tuesday evening [2] with Nasser replying to Menzies' presentation of the previous day. He said that Egypt's sole international obligation with regard to the canal was the Convention of 1888 which Egypt had not violated and to which it continued to adhere. Egypt had only exercised its sovereign rights in nationalizing the Suez Canal Company.

He stressed that, in making arrangements for cooperation between Egypt and other nations in operating, maintaining and developing the canal, there was a distinct difference between cooperation and domination. The proposals he had heard envisaged the seizure of the canal by an international board, which would certainly be considered by the Egyptian people as "collective colonialism in

---

[1] Source: Eisenhower Library, Whitman File, International File. Top Secret; Eyes Only for Designated Recipient. At the top of the source text Eisenhower wrote: "File/ D".

[2] This session began at 7 p.m. in Cairo, September 5. Henderson's report is in telegram 596 from Cairo, September 5. (Department of State, Central Files, 974.7301/ 9–556)

regulated form". Nasser indicated that an institutional arrangement such as that of the International Bank, to which Menzies had referred, would be unacceptable.

He turned to the phrase "insulation of operation of the canal from the influence of politics of any nation." He said that it was impossible to disassociate the canal from Egyptian politics, flowing as it does through Egyptian territory and employing Egyptian nationals.

An international board could not safeguard the canal, said Nasser. It was not the intention of Egypt to close the canal to the traffic of any country. Nevertheless, if she should decide to do so, no institution of the type suggested could stop her; nor could any Egyptian Government give the canal its necessary protection if the control of the canal were taken out of her hands.

When Nasser finished, Menzies reiterated the intention of the 18-nations to find a friendly solution which would be satisfactory to the Egyptian people and to their own people. However, the canal represented a life line to many people. In particular, the people of Great Britain and France considered the Egyptian action as a dangerous threat to their welfare.

Nasser commented here with asperity: if Menzies was trying to convey the idea that rejection of these proposals would lead to trouble, he was quite prepared to let it come at once. Egypt would not give up its sovereignty because it feared trouble. Menzies replied that Nasser had misinterpreted his meaning; he certainly did not intend to make direct or implied threats; he was trying to point out that the international tension would continue to exist until satisfactory arrangements for the future of the canal could be concluded.

Alternative Solutions

In the event of Nasser's rejection of the 18-nation proposal, we question the value of bringing the matter before the Security Council. However, the British are considering this as an "exercise" which must be gone through before more drastic measures are undertaken. We believe that, if the matter is brought to the SC, it must be for the purpose of sincerely seeking a peaceful solution, but we recognize that a resolution meeting the minimum demands of the canal users is not likely to be adopted by the SC because of the Soviet veto. Further, incidents in the canal would probably precipitate a showdown while the matter was under consideration in the SC.

(Nevertheless, Hammarskjold told our UN delegation yesterday, [3] and is so informing Selwyn Lloyd, that he will feel himself

---

[3] Hammarskjöld met with Lodge and other members of the U.S. Delegation during the morning of September 4 in New York.

obliged to bring the matter to the SC under Article 99 if the Cairo
negotiations are unsuccessful and if the parties to the negotiations
fail to bring the matter before the SC under Article 37.)

We have told Henderson[4] that, if Nasser rejects the 18-nation
proposal, we should concentrate more upon the guarantees provided
by the 1888 treaty and the measures which users of the canal might
legally and morally take to assure that the rights so guaranteed are
not impaired. We know of no way to impose a new canal treaty on
Egypt. However, the guarantees of the 1888 treaty constitute a
perpetual easement for the free use of the canal, and insistence on
this right to use the canal places us on the best possible ground. For
the users of the canal to exercise their guaranteed rights by forming
an "international shipping control association" is in no way dependent upon Egyptian consent, nor is it inconsistent with the 1888
Convention.

Evacuation Plans

Embassy Amman reports[5] that the drift of British nationals
from Jordan, Syria and Egypt, coupled with the continuing British
and French military buildup, is causing growing bitterness among
Jordanians—who question the necessity of such preparations if the
UK is sincerely trying to reach an agreement in Cairo. Both Jordanians and Europeans have commented that the fact that all Americans
are remaining has had a reassuring influence and has strengthened
the belief in the sincerity of US efforts to obtain a peaceful settlement. Henderson says[6] he is unable to comment on the question of
safety of Americans in the area until the course of the Cairo
discussions becomes clearer.

Canal Pilots

Embassies London and Paris have been instructed[7] to raise
urgently with the UK and French Governments a report that the
Suez Canal Company plans to encourage pilots to serve notice today
that they are leaving within 24 hours. Such a move would obviously
seriously prejudice the Cairo talks. If the report is true, we hope the
UK and French Governments will seek to persuade the Company not
to take this step. Meanwhile, Embassy Cairo reports[8] that, although

---

[4] See telegram 640, Document 170.

[5] In telegram 174 from Amman, September 4, not printed. (Department of State,
Central Files, 684A.86/9–456)

[6] In telegram 578 from Cairo, September 4, not printed. (*Ibid.*, 974.7301/9–456)

[7] In telegram 1628 to London, September 4, also sent to Paris as telegram 845, not
printed. (*Ibid.*)

[8] In telegram 592 from Cairo, September 4, not printed. This telegram also
reported that the morale of the American community in the region was good, that

European pilots have never been treated more solicitously, they are working extremely long hours and their morale is low.

---

there was no backlog of ships awaiting canal clearance, that no action had yet been taken to ensure compliance with the new order requiring toll payments in Egyptian currency, and that it was generally expected in the region that force would be used if the talks failed. (*Ibid.*)

---

174.   Annex to Watch Committee Report No. 318 [1]

SC 05194/56   *Washington, September 5, 1956.*

CONCLUSIONS ON BRITISH-FRENCH INTENTIONS TO EMPLOY FORCE AGAINST EGYPT

1. Military action by UK-French forces will almost certainly not be launched while discussions are under way in Cairo.

2. The UK and France are likely to launch military action against Egypt if they decide that their objectives are not obtainable within a reasonable time by negotiations or by other non-military means.

I. [2] *In reaching its conclusions, The Watch Committee considered that:*

A. British and French forces now in the Middle East are sufficient for an attack against the Suez Canal Zone, although

---

[1] Source: CIA Files. Top Secret; Noforn; Limited Distribution. The Watch Committee was composed of senior representatives from the Department of State, the Department of the Army, the Department of the Navy, the Department of the Air Force, the Joint Intelligence Group, the Central Intelligence Agency, the Atomic Energy Commission, and the Federal Bureau of Investigation. The Watch Committee of the Intelligence Advisory Committee was chaired by the Deputy Director of the CIA and met regularly on Wednesday of each week as well as being on call for emergency sessions. Its mission was to provide the United States Government with the earliest possible warning of hostile action on the part of the Soviet Union and its allies. The Watch Committee analyzed and evaluated information and intelligence, furnished by agencies represented on the IAC, relating to the imminence of hostilities and developed conclusions concerning Soviet/Communist intentions to initiate hostilities and other developments susceptible to direct exploitation by Communist countries that would jeopardize the security of the United States. A more detailed description of the Watch Committee is in CA–7918, May 14, 1955; Department of State, Central Files, 101.2/5–1455.

This is the first of several annexes dealing with the Suez Canal situation attached to the regular Watch Committee Report.

[2] The Special Assistant for Intelligence, Department of State, considers that this section should be deleted because it goes beyond the task assigned by the IAC to the Watch Committee. [Footnote in the source text.]

additional ground forces would be required to seize and occupy more than the Canal area; such additional deployments could be accomplished in a short period of time.

B. The UK and France appear determined to attain their objectives vis-à-vis the Suez by one means or another; there is little likelihood that they will accept the humiliation of backing down.

C. British and French statements have provided strong indications of an intent to employ force if a satisfactory solution is not reached by negotiation.

D. Although it cannot be determined what time limit the British and French may set on negotiations, they have revealed a reluctance to permit discussions to be dragged out.

E. Any provocative act by Nasser could serve to precipitate hostilities.

F. The UK and France are apparently convinced that the USSR will not intervene directly and that indirect Soviet assistance to Egypt would be ineffective.

II. List of Possible Significant Indications Bearing on British and French Intentions to Employ Force Against Egypt

A. British and French Statements

1. A US Embassy, London, report that top British Government officials consider that Nasser cannot be persuaded to accept international operation of the Canal and that military action will be necessary.

2. An alleged statement by a British military attaché in Damascus that the British plan military occupation of the Suez Canal Zone should Nasser refuse to accept the terms of the five-nation committee.

3. Reports that the British Embassy in Cairo at a secret meeting hinted to British correspondents that resort to military action would be made in a short time.

4. Statements by Prime Minister Eden (a) implying that if the United Kingdom is to meet disaster as a result of a possible Soviet reaction to its policy on Suez, he preferred that such disaster come about as a result of British action rather than inaction; and (b) indicating that an appeal might be made to the Security Council, in expectation of a Soviet veto, prior to recourse to military action.

5. Reports that there is a growing feeling in France, and apparently unanimous sentiment in the French Cabinet, that the use of force may be necessary; also a firm belief in official French circles that the USSR would not intervene if the British and French used force.

6. A statement by the French Army Attaché in Cairo that the British and French are bent on getting rid of Nasser and will use all pressures possible to force him to accept the full British and French position; also a report that France would be prepared for military action by 10 September and that there will be no crisis before 15 September.

7. An expressed belief by French officials that France would have less trouble in Algeria if Nasser were removed.

8. A statement by a British official to a reliable American source that British timing concerning possible joint British and French military action against Egypt had not been set, and would not be, pending the outcome of the negotiations in Cairo.

B. Military Preparations

1. *British*

a. Alert of British Armed Forces for emergency operations in the Middle East.

b. Authorization to call up all organized reserves, numbering more than 500,000.

c. Operational plans including preparations for amphibious assaults known to be under way in the British War Office in early August.

d. Recent rehearsals by two British parachute battalions of the 16th Airborne Brigade now in Cyprus for a special drop in the Suez Canal area along with French paratroopers; the readiness of the British 16th Airborne Brigade for immediate operations; and the appointment of Lt General Sir Hugh Stockwell to command operations against the Suez Canal.

e. Movement of 8,100 British troops to Malta and Cyprus between 1 August and 5 September. Forces available in the Mediterranean for employment in Egypt now total 25,000 troops.

f. The completion of equipment loading of the British 3d Infantry Division in England which is reportedly being held there pending the outcome of the five-nation committee negotiations with Nasser.

g. The reported alerting of the British 2d Infantry Division in Germany for the apparent replacement of the 3d Infantry Division in the UK but possibly for use in the Middle East.

h. Reinforcement of the British Mediterranean Fleet, particularly in landing craft and minesweepers.

i. Augmentation of land-based aircraft strengths in the Mediterranean area to 149 fighters, 40 jet light bombers and possibly 16 jet medium bombers.

j. Increase of British naval aircraft strength in the Mediterranean to at least 70 fighters.

k. Reported scheduling for Mediterranean deployment of other land-based fighter and light bomber units and one more carrier with 28 fighter aircraft.

l. Authorization for extension of expiring enlistments in British naval and ground units.

2. *French*

a. Assembly of major elements of the French Mediterranean Fleet at Toulon for possible employment in the Mediterranean area.

b. Establishment of the French Air Force Middle East Command and the reported departure of some elements from their bases in France.

c. The reported arrival in Cyprus about 30 August of the advance party of French Army units which will total about 12,500 men consisting of the 7th Rapid Mechanized Division and the 10th Airborne Division, actually estimated to be a regimental combat team.

d. The reported presence at Algiers on 24 August of a French planning staff for Suez operations under command of Maj General Beaufre.

e. French notification to NATO that some French units committed to NATO may be withdrawn because of the Suez crisis.

C. Other Indications

1. An unconfirmed report that the British are planning the overthrow of Nasser and the capture of Cairo, Alexandria and the Canal Zone, regardless of the outcome of the London Conference.

2. Evacuation of British and French nationals from Egypt and reported plans to evacuate British nationals from Syria and Jordan.

3. Reported French Government concern over the problem of its available foreign exchange in the event that the Suez Canal is closed and the oil pipelines cease to operate.

175.   Special National Intelligence Estimate [1]

SNIE 30–4–56   *Washington, September 5, 1956.*

PROBABLE REPERCUSSIONS OF BRITISH-FRENCH MILITARY ACTION IN THE SUEZ CRISIS [2]

The Problem

To estimate the probable repercussions, in the Middle East and elsewhere, of a British-French move to resolve the Suez crisis by military action against Egypt.

The Estimate

Introduction

1. Assuming that the British and French use military force against Egypt, it will probably be after they are confronted by another direct and major Egyptian challenge—such as Egyptian denial of their transit rights through the canal or violence against their nationals. They would consider that such an action would improve their chances of justifying the use of force before world opinion.

2. We do not estimate in this paper the repercussions in the Middle East of a British-French acceptance of a peaceful settlement. The UK and French governments, however, have almost certainly estimated that a compromise with Nasser on the principle of international control of the canal would greatly weaken their position in the Middle East and Africa. They may believe that use of force would produce less undesirable consequences than would such a compromise. Therefore, even without further provocation, they might resort to force if convinced that negotiations were not going to produce a prompt settlement satisfactory to them. In these circumstances, they would attempt to document Nasser's refusal to

---

[1] Source: Department of State, INR–NIE Files. Top Secret. According to a note on the cover sheet, "The following intelligence organizations participated in the preparation of this estimate: The Central Intelligence Agency and the intelligence organizations of the Departments of State, the Army, the Navy, the Air Force, and The Joint Staff." This estimate was concurred in by the Intelligence Advisory Committee on September 5, 1956. "Concurring were the Special Assistant, Intelligence, Department of State; the Assistant Chief of Staff, Intelligence, Department of the Army; the Director of Naval Intelligence; the Director of Intelligence, USAF; and the Deputy Director for Intelligence, the Joint Staff. The Atomic Energy Commission Representative to the IAC, and the Assistant Director, Federal Bureau of Investigation, abstained, the subject being outside of their jurisdiction."

[2] This estimate does not consider the question of whether the British and French will take military action against Egypt. Indications that they may do so, however, are sufficient to warrant this estimate of the probable repercussions of the action if it should occur. [Footnote in the source text.]

negotiate such a settlement, and to dramatize it before world opinion as justification for the use of force.

The Impact Within Egypt of British-French Military Action

3. Barring the unlikely prior entry of substantial numbers of Soviet personnel for combat duty, British and French forces now in the Eastern Mediterranean could probably attain their purely military objectives in Egypt within a very few days. Within 24 hours, they could probably seize key points along the Suez Canal by amphibious landings in the Port Said area and airborne landings near Ismailia and possibly elsewhere. However, it would probably be about a week before military control of the canal could be assured, and in any case Egyptian execution of prepared demolitions and other blocking operations in the canal could not be prevented. The time required to remove obstructions from the canal cannot be foreseen.

4. If the bulk of Egyptian forces remains concentrated along the Israeli border, British-French forces could quickly capture Cairo and other main centers in northern Egypt, and organized Egyptian military opposition could probably be overcome within three or four days after the initial assault. If there had been redeployment of Egyptian forces from the Sinai, the operation might take about a week to 10 days.

5. Nasser might put poorly organized and obviously ineffective forces into the battle, and attempt also to organize civilians for passive resistance on a large scale, in order to dramatize the plight of Egypt, and to stir up additional world indignation against the British-French action.

6. Despite the probable early cessation of regular military operations, rioting and destruction of property would probably occur in Cairo, Alexandria, and other cities. There would probably also be substantial guerrilla activity by elements of the regular armed forces and by Nasser's "Army of Liberation." Most of this activity would probably be suppressed within a few weeks and essential order maintained throughout most of Egypt. Nevertheless, small-scale but widespread acts of sabotage and terrorism would almost certainly continue, and Egyptian restiveness under military occupation would be manifest to the world. Nasser would probably seek to dramatize this resistance and to furnish a basis for UN or other international action by establishing a government-in-exile in one of the other Arab or Asian states.

7. Even if effective security were established, the British-French occupation would almost certainly have to be prolonged. It would be extremely difficult, although probably not impossible, to find Egyp-

tians willing to assume the responsibilities of government under foreign auspices and to meet British-French terms on the canal issue. Moreover, it is almost certain that a government thus established could not long continue in office once British and French troops had been withdrawn.

Arab World Reaction

8. Anglo-French military action against Egypt would provoke a violent anti-Western popular reaction throughout most of the Arab world. Anti-Western demonstrations and riots, affecting US installations and personnel, would be likely in most major population centers. The local authorities would probably be unable or unwilling to restore immediate order, though this might be less true in Saudi Arabia and Iraq, where security controls are relatively strong. Rioting would probably be most serious in West Jordan, Amman, and Damascus, where anti-Western feeling is already high and security controls tenuous.

9. Such anti-Western manifestations would be vigorously encouraged by the USSR and local Communists and by Nasser as long as his radio and other propaganda facilities were functioning. Egyptian agents, assisted to some extent by local nationalists, would also attempt widespread sabotage of Western installations. Those attempts would probably be most successful along the pipelines and in the pipeline terminal areas of Syria, Jordan, and Lebanon, with the main efforts being directed initially against the Iraq Petroleum Company lines. Some damage might also be done to oil installations in Iraq, Saudi Arabia, the Persian Gulf, and Aden, despite the efforts of the local authorities to prevent it.

10. Virtually all the Arab governments would make gestures of solidarity with Egypt and would publicly protest the violation of Egyptian sovereignty and independence. Syria, for example, might shut down the IPC pipeline. In this initial period the chances would be about even that Nuri would feel compelled to withdraw Iraq from the Baghdad Pact. Regardless of their personal feelings, all Arab leaders would feel it necessary to make such gestures to avoid having popular emotion on the Suez issue turned against them. Moreover, while most of the leaders of other existing Arab governments would probably be privately glad to see the end of Nasser, this feeling would be offset by their concern over the reoccupation of an Arab state by Anglo-French military force. Notwithstanding Arab League or other agreements, however, the other Arab governments would almost certainly not commit their regular military forces in support of Egypt and indeed would not be able to do so to any significant extent.

11. How far the Arab governments would go toward a serious break with the West would probably depend on how successful Nasser and his supporters were in maintaining and dramatizing resistance to the British and French. If, contrary to our estimate, the organized military resistance of the Egyptians were prolonged for a considerable period, the popular rioting and demonstrations taking place in other Arab countries would probably remain at a high pitch. The governments of most of these countries would probably countenance, and perhaps organize, acts against Western personnel and installations and lend assistance to the Egyptian cause. The governments of Jordan, Libya, and Iraq would almost certainly renounce their treaty relations with the UK if they had not already done so. The situation in some of these countries might become so disastrous for Western interests as eventually to require Western military intervention to restore and maintain order.

12. On the other hand, if as we estimate, Nasser's organized resistance collapsed in a matter of days, we believe that while the Arab leaders would continue vociferously to condemn the Western action and to proclaim their support of Egypt, a number of factors would incline them as a matter of expediency to refrain from acts seriously damaging to Western interests. Political leaders in the oil producing states of Saudi Arabia and Iraq, and to a lesser extent the pipeline states of Jordan, Syria, and Lebanon, would be aware of the danger of losing their oil revenues. The leaders in Jordan would probably be somewhat constrained by the Israeli threat to their country, and by their dependence on Western subsidies. In addition, with the passage of time there would be some decline throughout the Arab world in the position of those elements which had relied on Egyptian encouragement, example, or subsidy, and an increase in the relative strength of their local rivals. Thus some of the elements of the opposition to the Nuri regime in Iraq would be eliminated, and Egyptian-supported forces in Lebanon would be weakened. In Jordan, the latent strength of the refugee-Palestinian elements and the internal divisions in the military establishment would continue to endanger the government, but the threat of a coup by pro-Egyptian antimonarchial extremists would probably recede. Over the course of time the violent manifestations of popular emotionalism would gradually subside, and the danger of new riots and demonstrations would lessen. Nevertheless, popular anti-British and anti-Western feelings throughout the area would remain at a high pitch for a protracted period, and the danger of assassination or other acts of individual terrorism against those suspected of undue partiality for the West would continue almost indefinitely.

13. While the various Arab governments would probably adjust themselves to the changed alignment of forces in the area, neither

they nor the Arab people would be reconciled to the occupation of Egypt or to the occupation of any other Arab country should such become necessary. Basic anticolonial and anti-Western tendencies would be greatly reinforced and resentment of the continued presence of Western power elements in the Middle East would be intensified, even though violent manifestations were temporarily subdued.

14. During the crisis most Arabs would increasingly regard the USSR as the friend of Arab nationalism, the enemy of imperialism and colonialism, and a righteous opponent of the use of armed force against weaker nations. The political and moral appeal of the USSR, already strong in some elements of the Arab world, would almost certainly increase greatly. We believe that this increase would only be offset to a slight degree by the demonstration that Soviet arms and political support did not save Egypt from foreign occupation. On the whole, the Arabs would become more susceptible to Soviet influence.

15. *Effects of a Possible Coup in Syria.* In Syria, the possibility exists of an attempted coup by conservative and pro-Iraqi forces, perhaps with British encouragement, or conversely of an attempted coup by leftist Egypt-oriented military elements and the Arab Socialist Resurrectionist Party. Action by either wing would touch off counteraction by the other. The outcome of such a conflict would depend heavily on its timing:

a. Under present circumstances in Syria, if the conflict took place prior to the British-French military action, a conservative move would have backing by Iraq and Turkey, probably including the use of Iraqi military forces now deployed within striking distance of Damascus. In the latter case the move would have a substantial chance of success. Regardless of its outcome, an attempted pro-Iraqi coup would widen the split within the Arab world. If successful, it would be a blow to Nasser's prestige, and might consequently provoke an Egyptian reaction which would incite or be used to justify British-French military action against Egypt.

b. However, at the time of and shortly after British-French military action against Egypt, anti-Western feeling would probably be too strong for a conservative pro-Iraqi coup to succeed except possibly as the result of outright military action by Iraq. The Iraqi government might wish to launch such action, but popular feeling in Iraq would regard it as exploiting Egypt's difficulties, and in the face of such sentiment the Iraqi government would be unlikely to go ahead.

The Role of Israel

16. We consider it highly unlikely that the Israeli government would take advantage of a British-French military operation against Egypt to launch unprovoked major attacks on the Egyptian forces in

Sinai or against any of the other Arab states. Despite probable demands for action on the part of Israeli extremists, Israeli government leaders would probably feel that, with the most serious military threat to them already being taken care of by others, the possible gains of military aggression would be considerably outweighed by the political risks involved. In particular, the Israeli government almost certainly recognizes that the Western powers could not let it get away with such an attack if the West wished to preserve any standing with the other Arab states.

17. However, if there should be a serious breakdown of internal control in Syria or Jordan, we believe the Israelis would probably take the opportunity to seize the demilitarized areas and to achieve some minor rectification of boundaries. We do not believe it likely that they would make major seizures of territory. In any event, Israel would maintain a strong military posture along its borders and would probably respond promptly to any provocation.

Soviet Reaction

18. The USSR would take vigorous action both directly and in the UN to exploit the adverse reactions in the Arab-Asian world to the Western action and to make capital of its support of the Arab cause. It would seek to organize collective moral, political, and economic support of Egypt and might dramatize the issue by covertly inciting civil disturbances in colonial areas. It would probably offer with greater expectation of success further aid to other Arab nations now dependent upon Western sources of income. By intensive agitation of the issue of Western "aggression" it would endeavor to make it costly for any Asian-African leader to identify himself with the West. It would also exploit opportunities for causing friction among the Western allies, particularly between the British and French on the one hand, and West Germany and the smaller NATO countries on the other.

19. Although the USSR, either directly or through its Satellites, would probably be prepared to furnish matériel and possibly additional specialists and technicians to Egypt, its opportunities for doing so would be limited if the British and French achieved a quick military victory. If the military action in Egypt should be prolonged the USSR or its Satellites might make statements and military redeployments calculated to alarm European or other countries; we do not believe, however, that these would go to the length of actual attacks, even on a small scale. We believe that the USSR would not directly participate in the fighting in Egypt. However, the situation could develop in such a way that the Soviets would become more closely involved: for example, through the stopping or seizure by the

British or French of Soviet shipping in Egyptian waters, or the capture of Soviet personnel in Egypt.

Effects on the North African and Cyprus Situations

20. A successful demonstration of British and French military power in Egypt would, at least for a time, considerably bolster the strength and prestige of the British and French governments at home and their power position in the Mediterranean. The morale of the rebels in Algeria and Cyprus would be lowered, and Egyptian political and material support for the Algerian rebels would be ended. Thus, the British and French might gain an opportunity to move towards settlements in these areas on terms they would presently regard as meeting their minimum conditions. In other countries—Morocco, Tunisia, Libya—the basic situation would probably not be substantially affected, though for a time there would probably be difficulties in relations between these countries and Western nations.

General Free World and UN Reactions

21. British-French military action against Egypt would provoke strong adverse reactions within the Afro-Asian area and in many other portions of the world as well. We believe that the bulk of Afro-Asian opinion would overwhelmingly consider mere Egyptian refusal to accept international supervision or control of the canal as an inadequate justification for Western military intervention. Moreover, it is possible that many Afro-Asian countries might condone some Egyptian interference with Western shipping through the canal if clearly undertaken in retaliation against Western economic harassment. Although the adverse reactions in the Afro-Asian world would be considerably reduced if Nasser without provocation had demonstrably interrupted the flow of canal traffic, few of the Afro-Asian leaders could publicly condone the use of force, which would be widely interpreted as a reimposition of "colonialism" on Egypt. India in particular would almost certainly take the lead in moves for condemnation of the Western action.

22. The reaction of Western European nations would be mixed. Although most would probably be relieved to see the canal removed from Nasser's unilateral control, those with economic interests in the Arab-Asian world would wish to avoid too close an association with the action for fear of jeopardizing their economic and political position in that area. There would be considerable concern lest the British-French move lead to increasing Soviet involvement and hence to a dangerous rise in East-West tensions.

23. In the probable event of appeal to the UN General Assembly by the USSR, India, and others, we believe that Egypt's partisans would obtain support from the Soviet Bloc and almost all Arab-Asian countries. The attitude of Latin American countries and of many Western European countries would be influenced heavily by the nature of provocation prior to the British-French action. If Egypt had merely rejected the London Conference proposals, enough of these countries would probably vote against the British-French position so as to produce a GA majority, at least for condemnation. Even if Egypt had impaired operation of the canal or if violence had taken place against Western nationals, the British-French action would be attacked vigorously in the UN.

Effect on the US Position

24. A decision by the British and French to go ahead with military operations against Egypt would pose serious problems for the US regardless of what position it took. Should the US openly throw in its lot with the British and French, even without committing troops, it would thereby incur most if not all the risks and drawbacks involved in a resort to force. Throughout the Arab-Asian world it would be attacked as the ally of "colonialism" and "imperialism" and charged with having been hypocritical in its initial espousal of moderation in the Suez crisis. In addition, the dangers of violence against US installations and personnel would be enhanced, with TAPLINE probably becoming a major target. King Saud would almost certainly act to prevent violence and sabotage against AR-AMCO installations and personnel and by virtue of his dependence on oil revenues would probably seek to avoid a break with the oil company. Thus he would probably not interrupt oil operations. However, he would be under some compulsion to show disapproval and might demand immediate withdrawal of the US Air Force from Dhahran.

25. A US effort to disassociate itself would provide some opportunities for efforts at conciliation and localization of the conflict. However, serious problems would also ensue:

a. The British and French might reconcile themselves to US refusal formally to associate itself with the venture, but they would expect US sympathy and diplomatic support in what they considered to be a defense of vital Western interests. Moreover, it would be extremely difficult for the US to avoid an open indication of approval or disapproval during UN deliberations.

b. If the US came out sharply against the UK and France, a considerable strain would be imposed, at least temporarily, on US relations with its principal allies. Moreover, such US opposition, unless it extended, for example, to a vote of condemnation in the UN, would be unconvincing to large segments of public and official opinion, particularly in the Arab-Asian world. Some might even believe that US noninvolvement was a pose resulting from a secret agreement with the UK and France and that the US could have prevented the British-French military action if it had really wished to do so. Among those who accepted US noninvolvement as a fact, a large and possibly a majority element in the Arab-Asian world would probably attribute the US unwillingness to support the British and French to lack of resolution or election year expediency rather than to any real sympathy and understanding for the rights and aspirations of the ex-colonial nations.

c. Finally, though threats to US installations, personnel, and interests would probably be somewhat reduced, they would still be substantial since much of the Arab popular reaction would be indiscriminately anti-Western. Despite its efforts to remain aloof, the US would thereby be forced to consider the diplomatically delicate question of direct military intervention to safeguard US lives and property.

Longer Range Implications for the West [3]

26. Even though the more violent of the manifestations of Arab-Asian emotionalism over a British-French military move against Egypt would sooner or later subside, the Western action would be so deeply resented that fundamental nationalist and anti-Western feelings would be magnified for years to come. This is not to say that the use of military force against Egypt would of itself fatally weaken the Western position in the Arab-Asian area. Much would depend on the length, severity, and mode of termination of the occupation of Egypt. Much would also depend on Western success, under the circumstances, in finding leaders willing and able to cooperate with the West. Use of military force against Nasser would remove the chief organizer of nationalist pressures against the West in the Middle East, and it might temporarily check the erosion—inevitable in the long run—of the Western position of special privilege in the area. However, it would also probably cause the nationalist attack on this special position to rebound later with increased vigor, and by reviving Arab-Asian fears of colonialist domination, would make more difficult the establishment, over the long run, of a normal and mutually advantageous relation with the Arab-Asian states.

27. Throughout the underdeveloped areas of the world, this deepened suspicion and resentment of the West would provide new opportunities for the Communist powers, which have already had substantial success in convincing the Arab-Asian nations that they are willing to extend friendship and support on a basis of full equality. The Sino-Soviet Bloc would almost certainly take full

---

[3] As noted in paragraph 2 above, it is beyond the scope of this estimate to weigh the consequences of *not* using military force against Egypt, i.e., of making a compromise settlement with Nasser. [Footnote in the source text.]

advantage of these opportunities to extend its economic penetration of the area, to increase its diplomatic and cultural ties with the Arab-Asian nations, and to spread the concept that the interests of the underdeveloped nations lie more with the Communist powers than with the West. [4]

[4] On September 6, Acting Director of Central Intelligence Cabell read a condensation of this document during the 296th meeting of the National Security Council. After the reading, Secretary Dulles inquired whether it was Cabell's view that a resort to force by Great Britain and France in the Suez crisis would result in increased Soviet pressure on Iran. General Cabell responded that increased pressure on Iran would probably result. (Memorandum of discussion at the 296th Meeting of the National Security Council, September 6; Eisenhower Library, Whitman File, NSC Records)

176.   Telegram From the Office of the Permanent Representative to the North Atlantic Treaty Organization to the Department of State [1]

Paris, September 5, 1956—8 p.m.

Polto 461. Suez. As indicated in reporting telegram on N.A.C. meeting on Suez this afternoon, [2] U.S. did not participate in discussion except to endorse communiqué proposed by Secretary-General.

After meeting Lloyd protested somewhat to me at our failure to participate. . . .

. . . .

I did not feel I could say anything except to endorse the Dulles plan now being discussed by five in Cairo, and that U.S. endorsement of Dulles plan was unnecessary and superfluous. If I had spoken and said no more, the implication of failure to support British and French positions might have been worse than keeping quiet. It was also difficult to take the floor and not respond to some of the statements made . . . . It seemed to me that to initiate any such argument was quite undesirable at this time, ran the risk of publicity about disputes in N.A.T.O. and might have encouraged participation by others and led the discussion much further than

[1] Source: Department of State, Central Files, 974.7301/9–556. Secret; Limit Distribution. Received at 6:13 p.m. Repeated to London.
[2] Polto 462, September 5, not printed. (*Ibid.*, 740.5/9–556)

U.S. wanted it to go. It should be [noted] that no other permanent representative participated in any point.

Perkins

---

177.   **Memorandum of a Conversation Among the President, the Secretary of State, and the Under Secretary of State (Hoover), White House, Washington, September 6, 1956** [1]

[Here follows discussion concerning Cyprus.]

We then discussed the Suez situation. I read Loy Henderson's last cable [2] indicating there was no possibility of agreement on the basis of the 18-Power proposal but that Egypt insisted upon the sole right to manage and operate the Canal. The President then raised the question as to where we stood. He indicated that he thought we should take something less than the 18-Power proposal along the lines of the suggestion he had made to me in London with respect to "supervision". [3] He recalled that at the time I had said that it would not be acceptable to the British and the French. He asked what the attitude was today. I said I thought the passage of time was working in favor of some compromise and that they might take today what they would not have taken a month ago or a week ago. I referred to Dillon's cable regarding French sentiment [4] and the recent article in *The Observer*. I referred again to my suggestion as to a position based squarely on the rights under the Treaty of 1888 as giving us a much better negotiating position than any we now had where the alterna-

---

[1] Source: Eisenhower Library, Dulles Papers, Meetings with the President. Secret; Personal and Private. The source text indicates the meeting took place after the September 6 NSC meeting.

[2] Reference is to telegram 613 from Cairo, September 5, received at 11:36 p.m., not printed. (Department of State, Central Files, 974.7301/9–556)

[3] See Document 98.

[4] Reference is presumably to telegram 1075 from Paris, September 5, which reported the results of a recent survey of French opinion on the Suez affair, made by the French Ministry of Interior. The conclusions of this survey, as told to the Embassy in Paris by a highly-placed official in the Ministry of Interior, were: (1) outside of Paris there was very little interest in the crisis and a general antipathy to forceful measures; (2) in Paris, one school of thought maintained that military measures would result in the quick crushing of the Egyptian Army, thus putting the Arab world in its place and helping the French cause in North Africa; (3) a second school of thought in Paris, however, maintained that forceful measures were danger-ous beyond all proportion. (Department of State, Central Files, 974.7301/9–556) A copy of telegram 1075 in the Eisenhower Library, Whitman File, Dulles–Herter Series is initialed by Eisenhower.

tive was either to ask Egypt for a treaty which Egypt clearly had the right to reject, or else to use force to try to impose such an arrangement. The President recognized the bargaining value of such a position but expressed doubt as to whether it was practically workable. Mr. Hoover agreed that it might not work practically as a permanent arrangement but that it immensely improved our bargaining and negotiating position.

I said that one of the problems we faced was whether we should put such pressure on the British and French that they could pass the blame to us for the subsequent losses they might incur in the Middle East and Africa as a result of Nasser's "getting away with it". I said if this happened, it could have a serious effect for some time upon good relations between our countries and certainly the existing British and French Governments would have a tendency to try to find an alibi for themselves in our action.

JFD [5]

[5] Macomber initialed for Dulles.

---

178.   Report Prepared in the Executive Secretariat of the Department of State [1]

Summary No. 3   *Washington, September 6, 1956.*

SUMMARY OF DEVELOPMENTS IN SUEZ SITUATION

Cairo Negotiations

In last night's meeting with the Suez Committee, [2] Nasser made it completely clear that Egypt would not accept any institutional arrangement which would provide for the operation of the Canal by an international body. Nasser stated, however, that he was prepared to enter into international conventions to dispel the justified uneasiness of user powers, e.g., to regulate tolls. Nasser also emphasized Egypt's willingness to discuss international arrangements for the

[1] Source: Eisenhower Library, Whitman File, International File. Top Secret; Eyes Only for Designated Recipient. The source text bears Eisenhower's initials.
[2] This meeting with Nasser took place in Cairo from 7 to 8:45 p.m., September 5. Henderson reported on the highlights of the meeting in telegram 613, September 5. (Department of State, Central Files, 974.7301/9–556) His full report is in telegram 614, September 6. (*Ibid.*, 974.7301/9–656) Neither telegram is printed.

regulation of the canal. Henderson took this to mean that Egypt would be prepared to give an undertaking not to misuse its operational power by discriminating in such matters as the order in which vessels of various nations would enter the canal.

Nasser said that Egypt would be prepared to submit to the International Court of Justice any claims that it was violating the Convention of 1888. He indicated agreement, although he did not give a definite undertaking, that the violation of any supplementary international agreements regarding tolls and so forth would also go to the International Court.

Henderson comments that, clearly, the Committee will not now be able to obtain Egypt's agreement to the 18-nation proposals. The Committee is meeting this morning to decide on its next step. Although he infers that Menzies wishes the mission to terminate its work almost immediately in a friendly atmosphere and return to London to make its report, Henderson agrees with the Iranian and Swedish belief that the Committee should have more conversations before returning.

Canal Pilots

In response to our query, our Embassies in London and Paris have both reported [3] their understanding that the Suez Canal Company is not encouraging its pilots to leave at this time. The company's decision to ask the pilots to stay at work at least until the conclusion of the Suez Committee's discussions apparently still stands.

Nevertheless the pilots' present state of low morale and physical exhaustion has created a critical situation. The French Foreign Office pointed out that, although it is impossible to control absolutely the actions of either the Suez Company or of the pilots, it would be very helpful if Menzies could communicate directly with the pilots, expressing his appreciation for their continued services under present difficult conditions and urging them to be patient.

---

[3] In telegram 1299 from London, September 5, and telegram 1090 from Paris, September 5, neither printed. (Both *ibid.*, 974.7301/9–556)

King Saud's Comments on Suez Situation

King Saud has told an Embassy Jidda representative [4] that, if he had not sent Yusuf Yasin to Cairo, Nasser would have refused to talk with the Suez Committee, and that Nasser had stopped the radio attacks on the US on his advice. While Nasser would not accept international control or authority over the canal, Saud thought a satisfactory compromise could be found and said he would continue to use his influence with Nasser. He suggested the US could assist by lifting its economic controls and persuading its friends to stop their military mobilization and economic sanctions. [5] He said he understood Menon was working along these lines and that the UK has asked Nehru to mediate with Egypt to find a mutually acceptable compromise.

---

[4] Telegram 118 from Jidda, September 4, reported that on September 1 Ambassador Wadsworth had sent a Saudi consultant employed by the Embassy, Mohamed Massoud, secretly to Riyadh to deliver a copy of a message from Eisenhower to Saud. That evening the King met secretly with Massoud and conveyed to him the views contained in this summary report. The following morning the King's formal reply to the President's message was handed to Massoud. Saud's message once again requested the United States to issue orders that would annul the economic measures taken against Egypt and to convince other states to terminate military mobilizations and economic and financial controls, as these impeded the attainment of a peaceful solution. (*Ibid.*, 974.7301/9–456) A copy of telegram 118 in the Eisenhower Library, Whitman File, International File bears Goodpaster's handwritten notation: "Noted by President 5 Sept 56. G."

[5] On September 6, Deputy Assistant Secretary of State Berry informed the Saudi Arabian Ambassador that President Eisenhower and Secretary Dulles had received King Saud's message of September 1 (attachment to Document 159) and were most appreciative of the continued exchanges with the King on this issue. Berry explained that the provisions for control of Egyptian assets were a product of unusual circumstances, but that adequate provision had been made so that funds could be released. Berry emphasized that the funds were not irrevocably frozen; but in the present circumstances the United States did not feel that it could completely remove the freezing order. The United States still hoped for satisfactory results from the Cairo talks and for a peaceful solution that would make current regulations regarding Egyptian funds unnecessary. Berry also explained that private Egyptian funds had not been blocked and that funds were being made available for normal Egyptian Government operations in the United States. (Memorandum of conversation by Newsom, September 7; Department of State, NEA Files: Lot 58 D 722, Saudi Arabia—General)

179.   Memorandum of a Conversation, Department of State, Washington, September 6, 1956, 2:30 p.m. [1]

SUBJECT

Congressional Consultation on Cairo Meeting re Suez

PARTICIPANTS

The Secretary

Senator Hubert H. Humphrey	Representative James P. Richards
Senator Mike Mansfield	Representative A. S. J. Carnahan
Senator William Langer	(Also Carl Marcy and Boyd Crawford [2])

The Secretary welcomed the Congressional leaders explaining that since he had learned that there were a number of important members of the Senate Foreign Relations and House Foreign Affairs Committees present in Washington, he thought it was worth while to meet with them and bring them up-to-date on the Suez situation. He described the background of events leading to the London Conference and outlined the positions taken at that Conference. He then described in general terms the so-called "Dulles proposal".

The Secretary said that the initial reports, including the ones of the Menzies committee meeting last night with Nasser, were not encouraging. The Egyptians showed no compromise on the fundamental issue of international control. The problem now was what next to do. The British and French have felt from the beginning that military operations would be necessary to curb Nasser. The British feel that if Nasser gets away with it, it will start a chain of events in the Near East that will reduce the U.K. to another Netherlands or Portugal in a very few years. The French feel that they are already at war in North Africa and that they might as well carry that war to the real heart of the opposition, namely Cairo. The Secretary said we now must find further steps to postpone the U.K. and French use of force. We are, with the U.K., exploring possible steps in the U.N.

The Secretary said that he and the President were strongly discouraging the U.K. and France on the use of force. The Secretary described the problems that the U.K. would face in any use of force in the area. The initial advantage would be more than offset in the long run. The Secretary doubted British assurances that they would be able to take care of the situation without U.S. help provided the Soviets stayed out. Therefore we felt in the long run that it is

---

[1] Source: Eisenhower Library, Dulles Papers. Top Secret; Personal and Private. Drafted by Deputy Assistant Secretary of State for Congressional Relations O'Connor.

[2] Staff administrator and committee clerk of the House Foreign Affairs Committee.

disastrous for the French and the U.K. militarily to intervene at this point. On the other hand we cannot oppose too strongly their taking steps which they feel to be in their own national interest; otherwise responsibility shifts to us.

Senator Mansfield reiterated suggestions which he said he had publicly made before: All necessary steps should be taken and publicly announced for expanding shipment of oil to Europe by means other than via the Suez. All U.S. tankers should be taken out of the mothball fleet. A program of construction of 70 to 100 thousand ton tankers should be started at once. All alternative methods of shipping oil to be thoroughly explored so as to minimize Western dependence on the Suez. Senator Mansfield praised the Secretary for an outstanding job in moderating the British and French positions. He described the over-all situation as an effort for the West to buy sufficient time in the Middle East to allow the Western nations to switch from an oil economy to an atomic energy economy. He said that regardless of the political situation in the Middle East, it was clear that the world's oil supply was not inexhaustible and such a switch must come sooner or later.

Senator Humphrey also praised the Secretary and hoped that we could at the proper time take a strong lead in the U.N. Senator Humphrey strongly supported Senator Mansfield's idea of creating alternatives to Western dependency on the Suez. The Secretary said that the Soviets have been playing an "evil game" in this situation and that they were actively seeking to bar any settlement, realizing that they themselves would be the only victors if war broke out in the area. The Secretary pointed out that many of the Arab Governments were very worried by Nasser's actions but felt powerless to interfere with him in view of his great popularity with the peoples of their own country. The Secretary stressed that our problem in the long run was how to guide the new nations from colonialism to independence in an orderly way. We must have evolution, not revolution. In this effort the United States is destined to play a mediating role between the powers of Western Europe and the new nations of Asia and Africa; a most unpopular position but one essential to orderly transition. The Congressmen appeared to agree with this analysis of the situation.

Senator Langer asked if we were bound to assist the British and the French if they used force in the area. The Secretary said not legally but that in a similar situation in 1st and 2nd World Wars we had ultimately intervened in order to save our Allies. As to whether that might happen again, the Secretary said the Congressmen were in a better position to judge than he was—that it was Congress who declared war.

398   Foreign Relations, 1955–1957, Volume XVI

The Secretary was asked as to the Israeli role in the present crisis. He said they were keeping quiet, undoubtedly on the calculation that whatever happened in the area would be helpful to them in one way or another. The Secretary indicated that the Israelis have finally rejected all of Hammarskjold's suggestions for strengthening the armistice and that Hammarskjold feels he can do nothing more with them. The Secretary was asked what form action in the U.N. might take. He said we had not reached any final decision as yet but that we would probably go to the Security Council and seek some kind of resolution calling upon the parties to renounce the use of force and to accept some form of international regulations over operations of the Canal.

The meeting throughout was most cordial and friendly in tone. There was no partisanship injected and the Secretary was not criticized at any point. The conversation was exceedingly frank and candid and there is no doubt that the Congressmen present were fully aware of the gravity of the situation but also understood that the next moves in the situation were up to the British and French. There is no doubt that they quite thoroughly approved the Secretary's role in attempting to moderate the British and French positions.

180.   Telegram From the Embassy in Egypt to the Department of State [1]

Cairo, September 6, 1956—5 p.m.

623. Suez—From Henderson.

1. We have carefully studied suggestions contained in Deptel 640, September 4, [2] which because technical difficulties received only last evening. British Ambassador meantime received description these suggestions and mentioned them to Byroade. Apparently British Ambassador considered suggestions as ingenious but impracticable.

2. We inclined believe in view attitude Egyptian Government and people attempt put suggestions this kind in practice would lead to many complications and to constant difficulties and friction. Such

---

[1] Source: Department of State, Central Files, 974.7301/9–656. Top Secret; Niact. Received at 11:57 p.m. Repeated to London.

[2] Document 170.

institutional arrangements in our opinion would be even more un-palatable to Egypt than 18-nation proposals which Nasser is reject-ing. Egypt considers canal is and always has been integral part of Egyptian territory and that responsibility for its operations, safe-guarding and protection rests on Egypt. There is no doubt that Egypt would refuse permit pilots employed by association of users formed without Egypt's consent to enter what is considered as Egyptian territory. Furthermore Egypt would ignore any decisions taken uni-laterally by such association for setting up traffic and convey sys-tems and would certainly insist that tolls be paid to it-not to an association residing abroad. It difficult see how repair and construc-tion work could be carried on without consent and cooperation Egyptian Government.

3. In our opinion attempt users of canal put suggestions into effect would serve merely increase international tension and danger resort to force. We doubt whether united front user nations could be maintained during tortuous course negotiations to carry out these suggestions and whether we would have good case in Security Council if we should complain that Egypt would not accept deci-sions of a users association formed without reference to it.

4. In any event I am convinced Menzies and other members our committee would not look with favor on suggestion and would oppose our making any hints to Nasser that his refusal accept 18-power proposal might lead to an association this kind. Nasser in our opinion would react vigorously to such hint as an imperialistic attempt to impose foreign control on canal in utter disregard Egypt's sovereignty.

5. As it is I am beginning encounter certain difficulties with Menzies. Tireless campaign Egyptian press that U.S. does not really have its heart in proposals of committee is commencing to have effect both on Menzies and other members committee.

Egyptian press has not hesitated interpret statements made by President and Secretary to mean U.S. no longer fully backs these proposals and is looking for other solutions more acceptable to Egypt. Menzies was really concerned this morning when I objected to his suggestons that: (A) We send Nasser's document presenting our proposals his stated objections thereto and our replies to his objections. (B) We accept Nasser's reply as rejection 18-nation proposals. (C) We refrain from discussing any counter-proposals from Nasser or transmitting them to 18 nations.

In my view we should provide Nasser in writing with careful unprovocative résumé of committee's presentation; we should obtain further details from Nasser regarding his counter-proposals; and we should transmit such counter-proposals as part of committee's report to 18 nations.

Byroade

---

181.   Message From Prime Minister Eden to President Eisenhower [1]

London, September 6, 1956.

DEAR FRIEND: Thank you for your message [2] and for writing thus frankly. There is no doubt as to where we are agreed and have been agreed from the very beginning namely that we should do everything we can to get a peaceful settlement. It is in this spirit that we favoured calling the twenty-two power Conference and that we have worked in the closest cooperation with you about this business ever since. There has never been any question of our suddenly or without further provocation resorting to arms while these processes were at work. In any event as your own wide knowledge would confirm we could not have done this without extensive preparation lasting several weeks.

This question of precautions has troubled me considerably and still does. I have not forgotten the riots and murders in Cairo in 1952, for I was in charge here at the time when Winston was on the high seas on his way back from the United States.

We are both agreed that we must give the Suez Committee every chance to fulfil their mission. This is our firm resolve. If the Committee and subsequent negotiations succeed in getting Nasser's agreement to the London proposals of the Eighteen powers there will be no call for force. But if the Committee fails we must have some immediate alternative which will show that Nasser is not going to get his way. In this connection we are attracted by Foster's suggestion if I understand it rightly for the running of the Canal by the users in virtue of their rights under the 1888 Convention. We heard

---

[1] Source: Eisenhower Library, Whitman File, International File. Secret. Delivered to the White House on September 6 under cover of a note from Coulson to President Eisenhower which reads: "I have been asked by the Prime Minister to convey to you the enclosed message about the Suez Canal." Coulson also delivered a copy of the message to the Department of State on September 6. (Department of State, Presidential Correspondence: Lot 66 D 204, Eden to Eisenhower Correspondence 1955–1956 Vol. I)

[2] Document 163.

about this from our Embassy in Washington yesterday. I think that we could go along with this provided that the intention was made clear by both of us immediately the Menzies Mission finishes its work. But unless we can proceed with this or something very like it what should the next step be?

You suggest that this is where we diverge. If that is so I think that the divergence springs from a difference in our assessment of Nasser's plans and intentions. May I set out our view of the position. In the 1930's Hitler established his position by a series of carefully planned movements. These began with the occupation of the Rhineland and were followed by successive acts of aggression against Austria, Czechoslovakia, Poland and the West. His actions were tolerated and excused by the majority of the population of Western Europe. It was argued either that Hitler had committed no act of aggression against anyone or that he was entitled to do what he liked in his own territory or that it was impossible to prove that he had any ulterior designs or that the covenant of the League of Nations did not entitle us to use force and that it would be wiser to wait until he did commit an act of aggression.

In more recent years Russia has attempted similar tactics. The blockade of Berlin was to have been the opening move in a campaign designed at least to deprive the Western powers of their whole position in Germany. On this occasion we fortunately reacted at once with the result that the Russian design was never unfolded. But I am sure that you would agree that it would be wrong to infer from this circumstance that no Russian design existed. Similarly the seizure of the Suez Canal is, we are convinced, the opening gambit in a planned campaign designed by Nasser to expel all Western influence and interests from Arab countries. He believes that if he can get away with this and if he can successfully defy eighteen nations his prestige in Arabia will be so great that he will be able to mount revolutions of young officers in Saudi Arabia, Jordan, Syria and Iraq. (We know from our joint sources that he is already preparing a revolution in Iraq which is the most stable and progressive.) These new Governments will in effect be Egyptian satellites if not Russian ones. They will have to place their united oil resources under the control of a united Arabia led by Egypt and under Russian influence. When that moment comes Nasser can deny oil to Western Europe and we here shall all be at his mercy.

There are some who doubt whether Saudi Arabia, Iraq and Kuwait will be prepared even for a time to sacrifice their oil revenues for the sake of Nasser's ambitions. But if we place ourselves in their position I think the dangers are clear. If Nasser says to them, "I have nationalised the Suez Canal. I have successfully defied eighteen powerful nations, including the United States, I have defied the whole of the United Nations in the matter of the Israel blockade, I have expropriated all Western property. Trust me and withhold oil from Western Europe. Within six months or a year the continent of Europe will be on its knees before you". Will the Arabs not be prepared to follow this lead? Can we rely on them to be more sensible than were the Germans? Even if the Arabs eventually fall apart again as they did after the early Caliphs, the damage will have been done meanwhile. In short we are convinced that if Nasser is allowed to defy the eighteen nations it will be a matter of months before revolution breaks out in the oil bearing countries and the West is wholly deprived of Middle Eastern oil. In this belief we are fortified by the advice of friendly leaders in the Middle East.

The Iraqis are the most insistent in their warnings; both Nuri and the Crown Prince[3] have spoken to us several times of the consequences of Nasser succeeding in his grab. They would be swept away. Other warnings have been given by the Shah[4] to our Ambassador when he said that he gave getting rid of Nasser a very high priority. The Libyan Ambassador[5] here, who was formerly Prime Minister, said that wise men must see the danger of Nasser succeeding. King Saud of whose advice you will know more than we do also spoke in apprehension to Prince Zaid of Iraq when he was there the other day. He said that it would be bad if Nasser emerged triumphant for he agreed that Nasser's ambition was to become the Napoleon of the Arabs and if he succeeded the regimes in Iraq and Saudi Arabia would be swept away.

The difference which separates us today appears to be a difference of assessment of Nasser's plans and intentions and of the consequences in the Middle East of military action against him.

You may feel that even if we are right it would be better to wait until Nasser has unmistakeably unveiled his intentions. But this was the argument which prevailed in 1936 and which we both rejected in 1948. Admittedly there are risks in the use of force against Egypt now. It is however clear that military intervention designed to reverse Nasser's revolutions in the whole continent would be a much more costly and difficult undertaking. I am very troubled as it is that if we do not reach a conclusion either way about the Canal very soon one or other of these Eastern lands may be toppled at any moment by Nasser's revolutionary movements.

I agree with you that prolonged military operations as well as the denial of Middle East oil would place an immense strain on the economy of Western Europe. I can assure you that we are conscious

---

[3] The Amir Abdullah.
[4] Mohamed Reza Pahlavi, Shah of Iran.
[5] Mahmud Muntasser.

of the burdens and perils attending military intervention. But if our assessment is correct and if the only alternative is to allow Nasser's plans quietly to develop until this country and all Western Europe are held to ransom by Egypt acting at Russia's behest it seems to us that our duty is plain. We have many times led Europe in the fight for freedom. It would be an ignoble end to our long history if we tamely accepted to perish by degrees.

With kindest regards,

Yours ever,

Anthony[6]

---

[6] Printed from a copy that bears this typed signature.

---

182.   Memorandum of a Telephone Conversation Between the President and the Secretary of State, Washington, September 7, 1956, 8:40 a.m. [1]

TELEPHONE CALL TO THE PRESIDENT

The Secretary mentioned the most recent communication from Eden[2] which was received late last night. The Sec. said he did not think the note was very well thought out. Eden talks about the elimination of Western influence. The Sec. did not think you could go to war to preserve influence. He mentioned territorial rights, which was what Hitler had violated. The Sec. said some of his statements in the note were somewhat intemperate and the concepts not thought through. He mentioned the moral and persuasive tone at the end of the note. The President said that the last paragraph about the British having reached the end of the road was strongly reminiscent of Churchill and reminded him of Churchill's arguments during the war. He said he felt as though "here is where I came in."

The President said that the British had gotten themselves into a box in the Middle East. They have been choosing the wrong places in which to get tough. He mentioned Buraimi where they had only

---

[1] Source: Eisenhower Library, Dulles Papers, White House Telephone Conversations. Transcribed by Asbjornson. Another memorandum of this conversation, transcribed at the White House presumably by Whitman, is ibid., Whitman File, Eisenhower Diaries. The two memoranda differ in detail. The memorandum printed here appears to contain a more complete version of the conversation.

[2] Supra.

succeeded in incurring the hatred of the Saudis. The Pres. said it was pretty hard to attack Egypt so long as Egypt doesn't get in the way of running the Canal. Nasser is apparently trying to pull the pilots out. Pres. said he did not know what the answer was. We were in an unfortunate position because we could not really take a stand. The Pres. said we did not want to alienate our friends and we did want to keep NATO strong but we can't agree with these people in their extreme attitude.

The Secretary said he expected to hear further from Eden on the Secretary's alternate proposal. Henderson had cabled they had doubts about the proposal. [3]

The Secretary mentioned his talk with the Congressmen on yesterday. [4] The Sec. said they were all eager for us to sell oil and close up the Canal. The Pres. wanted to know where we would end up if we did this. Pres. asked what Richards said and Sec. said very little. Mansfield mentioned developing alternatives to Canal—building tankers, developing more oil, etc., but the Sec. said all this took time. Sec. said this was good long-range thinking but this all took time—3 or 4 years. Mansfield mentioned tankers in mothballs. President said we had a few old ones. He would talk to Defense about this to see if there was anything we could do. Sec. said we may have to do something like this. Pres. said he had read something by a Scripps-Howard writer about the Canal no longer being as useful as it once was and in a sense belittling it. The Sec. said he thought the Canal more a lifeline now than it had ever been before.

---

[3] See telegram 623, Document 180.
[4] See Document 179.

183.   Memorandum of a Telephone Conversation Between the President and the Secretary of State, Washington, September 7, 1956, 9:40 a.m. [1]

TELEPHONE CALL FROM THE PRESIDENT

The Pres. asked why it wouldn't be possible for the big nations to buy up all the stock of the Suez Company and give 49% to Egypt and say that is our solution. The Egyptians would get ½ the revenue and have on the Board 3 out of 5 or 4 out of 9 or something like that. We would get all we wanted and they would be in a better position than they were today. The Secretary said he would like to think about this—it was not anything you could give a telephone answer on. The President said in this way the Egyptians would get the Aswan Dam, which is what Nasser wants. The President said he did not know if this was a serious proposal but Tom Stephens had been in and asked why the Company could not be reorganized. [2] Nasser might accept this as a face-saving measure. The Secretary said that technically the Suez Canal Company was non-existent at the present time under the Egyptian decree.

---

[1] Source: Eisenhower Library, Dulles Papers, White House Telephone Conversations. Transcribed by Asbjornson. Another memorandum of this conversation, transcribed at the White House presumably by Whitman, is *ibid.*, Whitman File, Eisenhower Diaries. The two memoranda differ in detail. The memorandum printed here appears to contain a more complete version of the conversation.

[2] The memorandum of this telephone conversation, prepared at the White House, indicates that the President said that the idea to give Egypt 49 percent of the Canal Company stock originated with former Presidential Appointments Secretary Thomas E. Stephens. Eisenhower spoke with Stephens between 8:17 and 8:30 a.m., September 6. (Record of the President's Daily Appointments; *ibid.*)

184.   Messages From Foreign Secretary Lloyd to Secretary of State Dulles [1]

London, September 7, 1956.

[Message 1]

MESSAGE FOR MR. DULLES

Our messages from Cairo are depressing. It looks as though Nasser is not prepared to budge at all and therefore the probability is that by the week-end Menzies will have to announce that his mission is a failure.

On that assumption it seems to me most urgent that we should concert together our next steps. These seem to me to fall under two heads:

(a) Recourse to the Security Council.
(b) Action with regard to the dues would, I hope, be coupled with the setting up of some kind of International User Agency such as you suggest.

Although I agree that these two matters are inter-related, for convenience I deal with them in separate messages.

[Message 2]

Recourse to the Security Council.

I feel that the state of public opinion in the United Kingdom and indeed in the United States and elsewhere makes it necessary that we should, having explored the possibilities under Article 33 of the Charter, now go to the Security Council preferably under Chapter 7, as you suggest. I discussed this matter with the French Prime Minister and Foreign Secretary in Paris yesterday. They are reluctant to take this course, but are prepared to acquiesce. They do, however, feel and I agree that we should have agreed among ourselves a common approach before we embark upon this course which is obviously full of pitfalls.

---

[1] Source: Department of State, Presidential Correspondence: Lot 66 D 204, UK official corres. with Secretary Dulles/Herter 7/54 thru 3/57 Vol I. Secret. The six messages printed here were delivered to the Department of State under cover of a note from British Chargé Coulson to Secretary Dulles which reads: "I have been asked to deliver to you the enclosed six messages from Mr. Selwyn Lloyd." This note is dated September 6; but the memorandum of conversation with Coulson, *infra*, indicates that these messages were delivered on the morning of September 7.

2. I readily give you the assurance that any recourse by us to the Security Council will be genuinely directed towards a peaceful settlement. We have no idea of using the Security Council proceedings as a cover for military operations. We would regard them as another effort to using international pressure to bear upon Colonel Nasser to make him conform to the kind of solution which you so admirably expounded at the London Conference. At the same time I take it that we are agreed not to countenance any resolution or wrecking amendment which would tend to limit our respective freedom of action in the last resort if Colonel Nasser continued to be obdurate.

3. The item which we would propose to inscribe would be something along these lines:

"The situation created by the unilateral action of the Egyptian Government in bringing to an end the system of international operation of the Suez Canal which was confirmed and completed by the Suez Canal Convention of 1888."

4. The resolution which we have in mind (without prejudice for the moment as to the time at which it would be tabled) is contained in my immediately following message. I obtained from the French Prime Minister and Foreign Minister yesterday agreement to the deletion of any reference to the passage of Israeli ships. That I am sure is an improvement.

5. Would you like to join with the French and ourselves in calling for the meeting and/or sponsoring this resolution? I have no doubt that we are agreed that our resolution should advocate the London plan and that we should all of us agree not to put forward or support in the Security Council any resolution or amendment involving any significant modification of it.

[Message 3]

Following is text of the Draft Security Council Resolution:

"Recognising that the unilateral action of the Government of Egypt in relation to the operation of the Suez Canal has disturbed the status quo and, by bringing to an end the system of international operation of the Suez Canal, which was confirmed and completed by the Suez Canal Convention of 1888, has created a situation which may endanger the free and open passage of shipping through the Canal, without distinction of flag, as laid down by that Convention, and has thus given rise to a threat to the peace;

Noting that a Conference to discuss this situation was called in London on August 16, 1956, and that eighteen of the twenty-two states attending that Conference, who between them represent over ninety-five percent of the user interest in the Canal, put forward proposals to the Egyptian Government;

Regretting the refusal of the Egyptian Government to negotiate on the basis of the above-mentioned proposals, which offer a just and equitable solution;

Considering that such refusal constitutes an aggravation of the situation;

1. Finds that a threat to the peace exists;

2. Reaffirms the principle of the freedom of navigation of the Suez Canal in accordance with the Suez Canal Convention of 1888;

3. Requests the Government of Egypt to negotiate on the basis of the Eighteen Power Proposals with a view to reaching a just and equitable arrangement for the international operation of the Suez Canal."

[Message 4]

Following is the text of the letter which Sir P. Dixon would send to the President of the Security Council asking him to call the Meeting:

"In accordance with instructions received from Her Majesty's Government in the United Kingdom, I have the honour to request you in your capacity as President of the Security Council for this month to call an emergency meeting of the Council for —. The purpose of this meeting would be to consider the following item:

'Situation created by the unilateral action of the Egyptian Government in bringing to an end the system of international operation of the Suez Canal which was confirmed and completed by the Suez Canal Convention of 1888'

"Since the action of the Egyptian Government created a situation which may endanger the free and open passage of shipping through the Canal without distinction of Flag, as laid down by the above-mentioned Convention, a Conference was called in London on August 16, 1956, of the twenty two States attending that Conference. Eighteen, representing between them over 95% of the user interest in the Canal, put forward proposals to the Egyptian Government for the future operation of the Canal. The Egyptian Government have, however, refused to negotiate on the basis of the above-mentioned proposals which, in the opinion of Her Majesty's Government, offer means for a just and equitable solution. Her Majesty's Government consider that this refusal constitutes an aggravation of the situation which, if allowed to continue, would constitute a manifest danger to peace and security."

[Message 5]

Nasser's rejection of the proposals put forward by Menzies constitutes a major rebuff to the eighteen powers. We know that Nasser wants to string us along and meanwhile to strengthen his hold on the Canal. To this extent we are playing his game if we go to the Security Council. There is the danger that whilst we are engaged on discussions there the situation will deteriorate and the pro-Western regimes in the Middle East will be fatally weakened. To avert this it is essential that we should all make it publicly clear that Nasser is not [by?] pending discussion going to benefit from his act of unilateral expropriation. I should regard our action in going to the Security Council as fraught with even more than the obvious dangers if we have not beforehand reached some agreement with regard to payment of the dues.

2. Therefore I propose that we should ask all the major user friendly governments to make a statement as early as possible and on the lines suggested by M. Spaak in N.A.T.O. yesterday to the following effect:—

(A) We do not recognise the nationalisation of the Canal;
(B) We shall take steps to deny the transit dues to the Egyptian Government or the new Egyptian Board;
(C) We are advising our ship owners accordingly.

3. Your wider scheme for a users agency seems to us to have distinct advantages but I think it unlikely that it will be formulated in time for us to take action as urgently as we think is necessary. The above proposals would however be a first step towards it.

4. In a following message I deal with your proposal in greater detail.

[Message 6]

Your proposal for a users agency, if I have understood it correctly, is entirely in line with the plan approved by the eighteen in London, and its adoption would have the great merit of showing our determination to implement it as far as we could in the absense of Egyptian participation. In the absence of Egyptian consent, there will of course be limitations to the authority which such an agency can effectively exercise. But I assume that your plan would be to establish an interim authority with its headquarters outside Egypt and to invite the widest possible cooperation with this authority by the users of the Canal. As a minimum this cooperation would take the form of payment of transit dues to the interim international authority, which would thus become the agent for the policy which in an earlier message I have suggested adopting in the immediate future.

2. Your suggestions as to the juridical basis for the proposed agency are being studied by my legal advisers. Meanwhile it seems to me that the preamble of the 1888 Convention, which shows that the intention of its signatories was to complete the system under which the navigation of the Canal had been placed by the concessions previously granted to the Company, would provide firm ground for our action. We could argue that because the concessions and convention are linked in this way, the unilateral abrogation of the concessions automatically brings into question whether the rights assured under the Convention are any longer effectively guaranteed.

3. I take it that your plan would be to take rapid action to bring an agency of this kind into existence. I should be grateful for your thoughts on ways and means. I assume we should want to leave the door open for future Egyptian membership and to organise the agency in such a way that it could eventually take over all functions envisaged for the International Board in the London proposals.

185.   **Memorandum of a Conversation, Department of State, Washington, September 7, 1956, 11:30 a.m.** [1]

SUBJECT

British and French Proposal on the Suez Question

PARTICIPANTS

The Secretary
Mr. J. E. Coulson, Chargé, British Embassy
Miss Barbara Salt, Counselor, British Embassy
Mr. Jacques Vimont, Chargé, French Embassy
Mr. Francis O. Wilcox, IO
Mr. John M. Raymond, L
Mr. William M. Rountree, NEA
Mr. Fraser Wilkins, NE

The British Chargé said that he had been instructed to concert his present approach to the Secretary with the French Chargé. They wished to ascertain the Secretary's views regarding the various papers on Suez which the British Chargé had sent to the Secretary earlier that morning. [2] Mr. Coulson's telegram from London indicated the British wished to make an early announcement that they intended to refer the Suez question to the Security Council. London hoped that the US, UK and France would be able to reach agreement before going to the SC. Mr. Coulson thought there might be some difference of views.

The Secretary said that he had just received the papers which the British Chargé had forwarded to him. He had had no opportunity to exchange views with his associates. He would, however, be willing to give his initial reaction. He believed that under the steps proposed in the British papers they were moving too rapidly to the SC, that a case had not been prepared, that there were elements in the situation which urged speed but that there was no point in going to the SC without an adequate case. One might have the votes in the SC to force the issue but we were reluctant so to act.

The Secretary said that the parties to the Convention of 1888 had rights which he believed Egypt was prepared to challenge. The first step was to formulate those rights which we could legitimately claim and to exercise those rights. If Egypt should challenge those rights there would be a basis on which we could go to the SC. As of today we have by presenting the 5-power proposal to Egypt merely requested it to make a new treaty. We recognize that the new treaty

---

[1] Source: Department of State, Central Files, 974.7301/9–756. Secret. Drafted by Wilkins. The time of the meeting is from Dulles' Appointment Book. (Princeton University Library, Dulles Papers)

[2] *Supra.*

involves an alteration of the present situation but we said that no ultimatum was being given to Egypt and that it was free to accept or reject the new treaty. It appeared that Egypt was going to reject it. We should then seek to exercise our rights in two ways: 1) We should arrange for pilots of our own choosing qualified to take ships through the Suez Canal; 2) there was no provision for the payment of profits to Egypt which was a matter for negotiation. The concept did not mean that we should not reimburse Egypt but there was no basis under the treaty of 1888 for reimbursement. If there were a right to make a profit it was not established by the treaty. If Egypt should insist upon a profit we would have a violation of the treaty of 1888. The Secretary added there were perhaps other rights under the treaty of 1888 as follows: There was a right to make a pattern of traffic; there was a right to keep the Canal open. It seemed to the Secretary that we could challenge Egypt on the right to choose pilots and on the right not to pay profits to Egypt on reasonably sound grounds. It was important that we develop a real case otherwise we would, in effect, be using the SC to impose on Egypt a new treaty in the form of the 18-power proposal. The Secretary was concerned regarding a concept under which a certain number of nations could use the SC for such purposes. If it were accepted a certain number of nations might go to the SC and attempt to impose a treaty on the U.S. with respect to the Panama Canal. This was, he said, a novel concept.

The British Chargé interjected that the proposed British draft of a SC resolution was not worded to this effect. The Secretary thought the resolution was pretty close and Mr. Coulson accepted the Secretary's point.

The Secretary also raised the question of whether or not the Egyptian nationalization of the Suez Canal Company represented a threat to the peace or whether it was this action in the context of other events. He believed most people would say the threat to the peace arose from the military preparations of other governments. Mr. Coulson replied that the UK was concerned that some other country would refer the Suez dispute to the SC. Pearson of Canada and Spaak of Belgium had said in the North Atlantic Council meeting that it should be referred to the SC. The Secretary noted that the Secretary-General of the UN also might refer it to the SC but perhaps not in a way we would approve. Mr. Coulson stressed that the UK wished to retain the initiative if the talks in Cairo broke down. Mr. Rountree said that we did not yet have definite word that the talks had broken down and that there probably would be another meeting in Cairo.

The Secretary said that he did not wish to speak hastily in this matter; he wanted to give the question careful thought. However, it would be difficult to go along with the British and French proposal.

Mr. Wilcox said that there seemed to be two courses in the SC, either action with respect to a threat to the peace or with regard to negotiation. It seemed to him that neither would be a move in Egypt's direction. Mr. Coulson thought that the essence of the British-French proposal would be to stand fast. He asked the Secretary whether they could count on U.S. co-sponsorship or support.

The Secretary said that perhaps he had spoken too soon. He had not had an opportunity to give his considered judgment to the British-French proposal. He had had no chance to talk with his associates. He could say, however, that his initial reaction was that there should be appreciable changes in the proposal before he could say we would co-sponsor or support it. He thought we would be in trouble in the SC unless we could demonstrate we had rights which were threatened by Egypt. We either had rights or we did not. If we wished to impose a new treaty it was a weak case. If we had rights what were they? Do we agree we can go through the Canal with pilots of our own choosing? Do we agree that we can collect tolls? On the other hand, if Egypt had these rights why were we debating the matter? The Secretary thought that we did have these rights and that if we formulated them Egypt would probably defy them. During the London Conference we had proceeded on the theory that Nasser would negotiate but it now appeared that Egypt was turning us down. A new situation would thus be created under the 1888 treaty. Egypt had in effect thrown away its chance to a profit which was not stipulated under the treaty of 1888.

The Secretary believed that our next step was to clarify our own thinking which had thus far not been concerted in any way. If we now went to the SC we would be in an awkward position. We should have some regard for public opinion and prepare a strong case. We might technically have votes but we needed a meritorious case which, the Secretary believed, could be developed. Time was, of course, needed and he asked how much we had.

Mr. Coulson said that Egypt might take the Suez dispute to the SC on Monday, September 10. The Secretary said unless there were evidence to this effect he doubted Egypt would do it. Mr. Wilcox said there had been a report that Egypt might do so. Mr. Coulson thought that the uncertainty of the matter was the dilemma we faced. He asked how we should conclude the present discussion. Could he say the Secretary had misgivings regarding the British-French proposal. The Secretary said he would not want his reaction expressed more strongly than that. He said he would immediately study the British papers and would meet with the British and French Chargés later that afternoon for more considered views.

The French Chargé said that the French Ambassador-designate, Herve Alphand, was arriving today. The Secretary said that although he had not presented his credentials he would be pleased to receive him.

The British Chargé said he had another question which he wished to raise. It was the question of payment of transit dues. The British proposed that a number of countries concert their action to deny transit dues to Egypt. Until now most countries had been able to make payment in London or Paris or in fact anywhere they pleased, including Egypt. The British would like general agreement to deny payment to Egypt before referring the Suez dispute to the SC. The Secretary said he supposed this action would lead to Egyptian denial of passage through the Suez Canal which in turn would lead to a stringency of oil in the UK and Western Europe. Mr. Coulson said the British had some slack in oil stocks in UK and in Western Europe. There would be some delay in stopping all oil shipments from the Near East.

The Secretary said that we could take measures to increase oil production in the US but we needed some notice. We could not turn the oil production on and off. Mr. Coulson said that notice had been given in the sense that various committees consisting of British and American members had been discussing this subject. Mr. Rountree said it had been discussed at a technical level.

The Secretary agreed that thought had been given to transport of oil by tankers around the Cape and through Near Eastern pipelines. There was a possibility of additional production. However, one could not go into such developments lightly without planning. Mr. Coulson agreed that it would be a long-term plan. The Secretary said that as he had indicated in London the economic consequences of oil denial would hit the UK first and France next. In addition, the financial implications were great. He said that he wanted to be sure that the British and French accepted the economic consequences which might flow from initiating the proposed action, starting with denial of payment of transit dues.

Mr. Coulson replied that the economic consequences to which the Secretary referred were another reason why users of the Canal should band together to make certain that the oil tankers could go through the Canal.

The Secretary observed that it would be preferable to place transit dues in a separate fund for the Canal itself and for Egypt. Mr. Coulson thought that was the proposal but he had no details. The Secretary recalled that while in London it had been desired to go on paying to the old Company. If this procedure were now changed it would open up the question of the freezing of the assets of the Government of Egypt. If we changed the licensing procedure in the U.S. it would weaken our case concerning the assets frozen which total approximately $100 million of which $48 million were in the name of the Canal Company and approximately $60 million in the name of the Government of Egypt.

Mr. Rountree observed that if we changed the present arrangement the basic elements of the British plan would be affected. He believed that it would be preferable to enumerate our rights rather than to come out against nationalization. We would have to say what we were going to do with the payment of transit dues. Mr. Coulson said he would see whether he had more technical information on this subject.

The Secretary thought we needed more information. Did we know whether Soviet pilots would be employed by Egypt? We should adhere to our rights under the treaty of 1888. Those rights did not belong to Egypt. What in effect was the legal situation? It did not seem to him that we had given any thought or reached any agreement on the present situation. In such circumstances he thought it reckless for us to go to the SC. Nasser himself had said that the users of the Canal were protected by the 1888 treaty. This was an admission by him of the rights to which we should adhere.

---

186. Report Prepared in the Executive Secretariat of the Department of State [1]

Summary No. 4   *Washington, September 7, 1956.*

SUMMARY OF DEVELOPMENTS IN SUEZ SITUATION

Cairo Negotiations [2]

Nasser has made it clear that he is irrevocably opposed to any international authority with control and management functions; such matters must be in the hands of Egypt. He has only proposed an agreement on certain matters such as tolls.

---

[1] Source: Eisenhower Library, Whitman File, International File. Top Secret; Eyes Only for Designated Recipient.

[2] Reference is to the meeting between the Five-Nation Committee and Nasser on the evening of September 5. Henderson reported on this meeting and on the meeting of the Five-Nation Committee that follow in telegram 618, September 6, not printed. (Department of State, Central Files, 974.7301/9–656)

As, therefore, the central feature of the 18-nation proposal is unacceptable, Menzies considers there is no need for further discussions. He urges the submission to Nasser of a memorandum rehearsing with great care the 18-nation proposal, arguments supporting it, and Nasser's answers thereto. Such a document would probably elicit a written reply from Nasser, which Menzies considers the Committee should accept as Nasser's rejection of the 18-nation proposal. But Menzies does not feel the Committee should discuss Nasser's counter-proposals with him nor transmit them to the 18 nations.

Henderson's view is that details of Nasser's counter-proposals should be transmitted as part of the Committee's report to the 18 nations. However, Henderson reports[3] that he is commencing to encounter difficulties with Menzies and the other committee members as a consequence of the tireless Egyptian press campaign to the effect that the US does not really support the proposals of the Committee and is looking for other solutions more acceptable to Egypt.

US Proposal

Henderson considers[4] that our suggestion for institutional control through an international "association of users" would lead to constant difficulties and friction, and would be even more unpalatable to Egypt than the 18-nation proposal. He is convinced that Menzies and the other committee members would not look with favor on such a suggestion, which the British Ambassador has already rejected in talks with Byroade.

UK Views

The British position was reviewed at length by Eden and Lloyd in a talk yesterday with Senator George, Barbour and Holmes.[5] Eden stressed that he cannot permit the situation to remain static. Lloyd advocates announcing within two or three days after the end of the Cairo talks that the principal users of the canal will, in the future, pay tolls only to the old company or to an account in escrow outside of Egypt. He envisages the effect of such an announcement will be that Nasser might refuse to permit ships to transit the canal, in which case he would be in clear violation of the 1888 Convention.

---

[3] In telegram 623, Document 180.

[4] In telegram 623.

[5] Barbour reported on this conversation in telegram 1335 from London, September 6, not printed. (Department of State, Central Files, 974.7301/9–656) Julius C. Holmes, the Secretary of State's Special Assistant, evidently accompanied Senator George on his trip.

Although Barbour pointed out that such an action would probably *not* put Nasser in the wrong in so far as American opinion was concerned, Eden said that the Arabs will interpret any other course short of military intervention as a sign of weakness. With such an announcement, the British position in the Arab world can be maintained while other steps towards a peaceful solution are taken.

Eden also acknowledged his understanding of the US position. Although reiterating a determination to intervene militarily if all else fails, he indicated that he is disposed to take the matter to the UN in the first instance. He was extremely skeptical that any useful result could be expected from UN action, but said that in any event the British are not prepared to take military steps yet and, in fact, that he has slowed down the military build-up.

French Views

The close liaison between the UK and French on the Suez question is clearly evident. Foreign Office officials have discussed very tentatively with our Embassy in Paris[6] possible economic sanctions and the reference of the problem to the UN. They view as the only effective economic sanction that of refusing to pay tolls to the new company, or making payment outside of Egypt to be held in escrow pending eventual settlement. In the case of the UN, they would strongly oppose calling a special session of the General Assembly but would probably go along with a reference to the Security Council—although having no faith in its utility.

Emergency and Evacuation Plans

Embassy London reports[7] that a Cabinet decision on British plans for Middle East evacuation is possible this week-end. The Foreign Office wishes to advise UK nationals in Egypt, Jordan, and Syria to leave as soon as possible, but does not plan evacuations in any other countries in the area for the time being.

Embassy Amman reports[8] that the "drift" of British civilians from Jordan is continuing. King Hussein has expressed real satisfaction to our Chargé at the absence of a similar American movement.

Byroade emphasizes[9] that, in the event of UK-French armed action against Egypt, the Embassy would require several days' advance notice to carry out evacuation by air. Lacking such notice, no

---

[6] Reported in telegrams 1092, September 5, and 1115, September 6, both from Paris, neither printed. (Both *ibid.*, 974.7301/9–556 and 974.7301/9–656)

[7] In telegram 1334 from London, September 6, not printed. (*Ibid.*, 280.4122/9–656)

[8] In telegram 185 from Amman, September 6, not printed. (*Ibid.*, 785.41/9–656)

[9] In telegram 626 from Cairo, September 6, not printed. (*Ibid.*, 974.7301/9–656)

evacuation would be possible and the Embassy would find itself in a "state of siege".

Tappin, meanwhile, points up [10] the danger of flash action by Egyptian-organized mobs in Tripoli if hostilities develop over Suez. He has no confidence that the Government would provide protection for Westerners in Tripoli, although law and order should be maintained in Benghazi. Nuri plans to declare martial law in Iraq [11] if the Suez talks break down, not as military action, he told Gallman, "but as insurance against Communist-inspired actions".

(Summary closed 11:30 a.m., September 7)

---

[10] In telegram 145 from Tripoli, September 6, not printed. (*Ibid.*)
[11] Reported in telegram 376 from Baghdad, September 6, not printed. (*Ibid.*)

---

187.   Memorandum of a Telephone Conversation Between the President and the Secretary of State, Washington, September 7, 1956, 3:40 p.m. [1]

TELEPHONE CALL FROM THE PRESIDENT

The President called and said he had been thinking some more of the plan about reorganizing the Canal which he had mentioned to the Secretary this morning. [2] He had in mind sending someone like Bob Anderson over to talk with Nasser, explaining how the reorganization would work. The Pres. admitted the idea did not have everything which Nasser wanted but at least it was so much different than anything else that had been offered that it might work and it did not constitute complete surrender. The Sec. said this would require Nasser to cancel his nationalization decree, which the Sec. said was a much tougher thing for him to do than the proposals we had made.

The President said that Nasser had started the whole business by wanting to build the Aswan Dam. The Secretary said he would rather have the rights than the money and he did not think Nasser

---

[1] Source: Eisenhower Library, Dulles Papers, White House Telephone Conversations. Transcribed by Asbjornson. Another memorandum of this conversation, transcribed at the White House presumably by Whitman, is *ibid.*, Whitman File, Eisenhower Diaries. The two memoranda differ in detail. The memorandum printed here appears to contain a more complete version of the conversation.
[2] Reference is to the telephone conversation between Eisenhower and Dulles that morning; see Document 183.

could be bribed. The Sec. said one trouble was we are working with the Committee and representing the 18 nations and he did not know how we could go off on our own and negotiate.

The Sec. mentioned the British proposal for action on the Security Council and that the British and French were coming in again at 5:00 today for further discussion. They want to bring action saying that the Egyptians are threatening the peace because they haven't accepted the proposals. The Sec. considered this a very extravagant idea. The Sec. thought it maybe was all right to get it into the Security Council in some way. Undoubtedly there would be a race on Monday in the Security Council to see which one—the Egyptians or the British and French—would bring charges against the other first.

The Sec. said the British liked the second plan [3] but felt there was not time to work it out. They say they have to be prepared to move.

Going back to Bob Anderson, [4] the Sec. said he had been used so much he wondered about the advisability of choosing him. The Pres. wondered about Eric Johnston. He had been identified with another plan and maybe that would work out. The Pres. said he was just trying to think of some solution "this fellow" [5] would accept. The Sec. said the British were getting awfully sensitive because they feel we are not working with them. The Sec. said Menzies was giving Henderson trouble, accusing Henderson of playing a separate game.

---

[3] Reference presumably is to Dulles' idea for a Suez Canal Users Association.

[4] The version of this conversation, transcribed in the White House, at this point reads as follows:

"Dulles said: I would like to have some channel of private negotiation. I have a notion this could be worked out if we were in a position to do it. But we are part of a committee representing 18 nations—could not go off and negotiate ourselves. President agreed it would have to be done secretly and delicately, by someone outside of government. Thought also of Eric Johnston. Dulles said we're under pressure of time. He would of course like to have someone out there, but without double-crossing British & French."

[5] Reference is to Nasser.

188.   Memorandum of a Conversation, Department of State, Washington, September 7, 1956, 5:05 p.m. [1]

SUBJECT

British and French Proposals on the Suez Question

PARTICIPANTS

Mr. Herve Alphand, French Ambassador-Designate
Mr. Charles Lucet, Minister, French Embassy
Mr. Francois de Laboulaye, Counselor, French Embassy
Mr. J. E. Coulson, Chargé, British Embassy
Miss Barbara Salt, Counselor, British Embassy

The Secretary
NEA—William M. Rountree
NE—Fraser Wilkins
L—John M. Raymond
IO—Francis O. Wilcox

The French Ambassador-Designate said that when the British Chargé had presented the British-French views that morning the French representative had been an observer and had not been able to make known French views. Mr. Alphand therefore wished to state the French position. The French were not, he said, especially in favor of a Security Council meeting. French public opinion would consider it an alibi to do nothing, a legalistic way of avoiding a solution. However, Selwyn Lloyd had spoken with Pineau in Paris. Pineau had accepted the idea because of the special arguments of British friends. Pineau had asked Alphand to ascertain U.S. views. Pineau wished to avoid any misunderstanding which might later cause bad feelings. The French wished U.S. views regarding two points: 1) Will the U.S. agree not to accept any formula which would be short of the Five-Power Proposal and 2) if a counter proposal were put forward from the other side by which it would try to limit our right to act, would we agree not to accept that counter proposal?

The Secretary said that if the Suez dispute were taken to the Security Council we would assume that it would include an effort to bring about an acceptance of the London proposals. We would not

---

[1] Source: Department of State, Central Files, 974.7301/9–756. Secret. Drafted by Wilkins. The time of the meeting is from Dulles' Appointment Book. (Princeton University Library, Dulles Papers) Tabs A–G are attached to the source text. Tabs A–E, printed below, are a series of papers containing the U.S. response to the messages delivered by Lloyd, Document 184. In composing their response, State Department officials treated Lloyd's first message as an introductory statement. Hence, references to Paper I indicate Lloyd's second message, etc. Tab F is a copy of the instructions received that day by the British Embassy from the Foreign Office; it is summarized in footnote 5 below. Tab G, identified as "Recourse to the Security Council", is the message from Lloyd printed as Message 2 in Document 184.

expect the Security Council to modify or depart from the London proposals by amendments, nor did we feel at all confident that the Security Council could be confined to seeking to impose the London proposals on Egypt. It was the primary function of the Security Council under Chapter VII to maintain and restore international peace and security. It would be difficult to contend that the only way to do so would be to require Egypt to accept these proposals. It would be difficult to exclude reference to the maintenance of international peace and security and to the renunciation of the use of force. Article 2 of the UN Charter was pertinent. Mr. Alphand had asked two questions which the Secretary wished to answer as follows: We would agree to stand by the London proposals but we could not guarantee the results. We would not want to be bound by developments we could not foresee.

Mr. Alphand interpreted the Secretary's remarks to indicate that he accepted Alphand's first point, but did not accept his second point. Mr. Coulson observed that it was this latter question that concerned the U.K. The Secretary suggested that if we went through the written paper which he had prepared, he would be able further to explain his views.

The Secretary commenced reading comments on Paper I . . . [2] "Recourse to Security Council". He read the following paragraph (Tab A—page 2, paragraph 1):

"It would, we suppose, be very difficult to assure that a Security Council resolution would not call on the parties 'to maintain international peace and security' and to 'refrain from the threat or use of force', as this is a basic function of the Security Council acting under Chapter VII."

Mr. Alphand asked if the U.S. would vote for such a formula. The Secretary said that we would not want to feel bound to vote against it. We might want to abstain. Mr. Alphand said that his instructions were to ascertain the U.S. position on this point. Selwyn Lloyd had pointed out that "we are agreed not to countenance any resolution or wrecking amendment which would tend to limit our respective freedom of action in the last resort if Colonel Nasser continued to be obdurate". (Tab G—"Recourse to the Security Council"—paragraph numbered 2) [3] Mr. Wilcox pointed out that other portions of a resolution before the Security Council might be sufficiently favorable to justify acceptance even if there were limiting amendments.

Mr. Alphand said that they might want to proceed with the use of force where their vital interests were involved. Mr. Coulson

---

[2] Ellipsis in the source text.
[3] See footnote 1 above.

observed that this was precisely what the U.K. wished to know. The Secretary thought his answer would be somewhat hypothetical. If the resolution called upon both Egypt and the parties, it might be satisfactory. He said that he would give further thought to the matter and would endeavor to be more precise. He observed, however, that we could not agree in advance to vote against a resolution which called upon the parties not to resort to force. Mr. Alphand observed that seven votes would be needed for the passage of the resolution. There was some discussion regarding adoption and rejection of resolutions in the Security Council.

The Secretary continued reading comments on Paper I. He read "We comment later on the formal resolution. We agree that it is preferable to delete the reference on passage of Israeli ships". (Tab A, page 2, paragraph numbered 4)

Mr. Alphand said that France preferred to refer to the 1951 resolution. [4] He noted that the USSR had abstained on this resolution at that time. Mr. Coulson said that the UK would accept it either way. The Secretary said that we did not feel very strongly about it. He believed, in general, that discussion of the Arab-Israeli dispute might complicate discussions of the Suez dispute. He noted that there were some who did not strongly support Nasser but who were silent for the time being. If the Arab-Israeli dispute were now debated, these other Arabs would feel obliged to come forward. For this reason he thought it preferable to omit reference to the 1951 resolution. On technical ground he could see that it was juridically important. Mr. Alphand suggested that reference to the 1951 resolution might be made in speeches before the Council and not in the resolution itself. The Secretary and Mr. Coulson thought well of this suggestion.

The Secretary continued reading comments on Papers I, II, III and IV (Tabs A–D). He asked if the British and French had any precise formulation of how they proposed to handle the matter of transit dues (Tab D—Paper IV, page 2, paragraph 2). Mr. Coulson said that each country should have a separate account to which dues would be paid and which would be frozen. The Secretary saw complications in this suggestion. The pilots had been hired by the old company and also by the new Suez Board. They had been paid out of dues received. If dues were handled by each country there would be no funds for payment. Mr. Coulson said he hoped to have further instructions by the end of the present meeting.

The Secretary completed reading comments on Paper V (Tab E).

---

[4] Reference is to the U.N. Security Council Resolution of September 1, 1951 (U.N. doc. 5/2322), which affirmed the right of shipping to and from Israel to transit the Suez Canal.

The Secretary said that we may have acted hastily in responding to the British-French proposals, but because of the need for speed we had done the best we could.

Mr. Alphand referred again to the point regarding freedom of action as made by Pineau and Selwyn Lloyd. He said that if the U.S. response did not appear satisfactory he would be in further touch with the Secretary. He thought that the Secretary had spoken with wisdom and that a Security Council Resolution would be dangerous if it did not prove Egypt had violated the Charter. What, he asked, could be done? If we do not go to the Security Council, Egypt might do so. It was for this reason that France adopted the same position as his British colleagues.

The Secretary said that we had not as yet had an opportunity fully to explore the question of reference of the Suez dispute to the Security Council in the course of events as he anticipated them. The Secretary thought that the question might be put on the agenda but not brought up until a later date. He recalled that Quemoy and Matsu had been placed upon the agenda and had had priority but had not been subsequently discussed. The Secretary asked if the British and French had explored this possibility. It might represent a means of gaining some advantage by referring the Suez dispute to the Security Council before Egypt did.

Mr. Coulson said that unless the Secretary had further remarks he wished again to refer to the question of Canal dues. He had just received telegraphic instructions from London which he would like to read. Mr. Coulson then read the attached telegram (Tab F). [5] The Secretary said that as he had remarked that morning, the question of Canal dues had two facets: 1) practical and 2) legal. He thought that denial of payment would probably lead to refusal to allow ships to pass through the Canal and to a period of economic stringency in the U.K. and Europe. The Secretary assumed that the British and the French were prepared to face these eventualities and without concerting with the U.S. Mr. Coulson said that the British were prepared to face these eventualities. They had been concerting with the

---

[5] Not printed. This telegram instructed the British Embassy in Washington to communicate to the U.S. Government the following views of Her Majesty's Government: Reports from Cairo indicated that Nasser was not prepared to negotiate on the basis of the 18-Power Proposals; and this rejection would constitute a major rebuff to the 18 Powers. In order to offset this and to prevent Nasser from stringing the 18 Powers along while he strengthened his hold over the Canal, the British Government considered it essential that as many governments as possible make clear publicly that Nasser would not be allowed to benefit from his act of unilateral expropriation. Therefore, the governments concerned should issue statements forthwith indicating that they did not recognize either the validity of the nationalization decree or the new canal authority and that they were taking steps to deny transit dues to the Egyptian Government and were advising their shipowners and charterers accordingly. The government confidently expected that the U.S. Government would act in this sense.

U.S., although there had been no agreement. He thought that the materials resulting from these discussions would be available in a week's time. The Secretary said this might well be the case but what to do about it was important. From the U.S. standpoint some pretty serious policy considerations would be involved. More domestic oil production would be necessary. Mr. Coulson noted that transport of oil was also a major matter. Mr. Alphand inquired who was on the Committee. Mr. Coulson said that it had not been meeting in Washington but in New York. Mr. Alphand observed that questions of finance and currency would arise. The Secretary again said that denial of payment of transit dues involves a decision to face up to practical economic problems.

The Secretary said that as to his second point he was not sure that he agreed with Mr. Coulson's legal reasoning. He said that the maritime nations had the benefit of easement across Egypt in the form of the Suez Canal. Egypt would be entitled to be reimbursed for services. The maritime nations had a right to expect to take services from Egypt. We should try to place operation of the Canal on a cost basis. We ought not to acquiesce in Egypt's taking over our rights. If Egypt did so and employed Soviet pilots, would we be willing to accept Soviet pilots on our ships? It is against this background that the Secretary was not sure he agreed with Mr. Coulson's legal reasoning. He said that he would wish to study the question further.

Mr. Rountree observed that politically the British concept seemed to challenge Egyptian nationalization and for that reason the proposal was not desirable. The Secretary agreed and said that it seemed far-fetched to make an argument which would perpetuate the concession. Mr. Raymond added there were a number of legal questions involved. Mr. Alphand said that if the concession were broken, the Convention[6] would be violated as well. He noted that Egypt had not published the preamble of the Convention. The Secretary thought that Article 14 of the Convention would be applicable, which said that engagements resulting from the present treaty shall not be limited by the duration of the acts of the concession. The Convention, he said, stood on its own feet.

Mr. Alphand asked when it would be desirable to refer the Suez dispute to the Security Council. Mr. Coulson replied that the British wished to make an announcement very soon.

The Secretary cautioned that the substance of today's discussions was secret and requested that it be maintained.

---

[6] Reference is to the Convention of 1888.

Note: Following the discussion with the British and French this afternoon, the Secretary spoke with the President [7] regarding the request made by the British Chargé and the French Ambassador-Designate for the U.S. attitude regarding amendments to a Security Council resolution containing the Five-Power Proposal on Suez. The British and French were particularly interested in an amendment which would call upon the parties not to resort to force. The Secretary authorized Mr. Rountree to inform the British and the French that further thought had been given to the question of amendments in the Security Council and that he would not like to go further than the statement made in Comments on Paper I, page 2, paragraph numbered (5) (Tab A). Mr. Rountree so informed the British Chargé and the French Ambassador-Designate late in the afternoon of September 7.

[Tab A]

September 7, 1956.

COMMENTS ON PAPER I—"RECOURSE TO SECURITY COUNCIL" [8]

(1) We did not intend to suggest Chapter VII action at the present time although we did point out difficulties in acting under Chapter VI. We are not sure that Egypt has as yet committed any action which would be held to be a "threat to the peace, breach of the peace, or act of aggression". We doubt whether this situation will develop until the parties to or beneficiaries of the Treaty of 1888 have agreed on the scope of their rights and given evidence of their intention to exercise them. At that point there may occur the action or threat of action on the part of Egypt which would bring the situation under Chapter VII.

(2) We welcome assurance that any recourse by you to the Security Council will be genuinely directed toward peaceful settlement.

We doubt that we could be confident that Security Council action would be limited to seeding to impose upon Egypt the 18-Power solution. This was frankly recognized to be an invitation to Egypt to make a new treaty. At the same time we recognized the right of Egypt not to make such a treaty. It seems to us that Security Council action should be designed to provide effectively for the

[7] See *infra*.

[8] Secret. The reference to Paper I indicates Message 2 in Document 184.

rights contemplated by the 1888 Treaty, but it might not be possible to confine the action to the precise solution contemplated by the 18 powers which, as I say, was dependent upon Egypt's voluntary acceptance thereof.

It would, we suppose, be very difficult to assure that a Security Council resolution would not call on the parties "to maintain international peace and security" and to "refrain from the threat or use of force", as this is a basic function of the Security Council acting under Chapter VII.

(3) We believe that the formulation of the item to be inscribed is adequate, although it does not clearly bring the item under Chapter VII. Superficially at least the item as formulated seems more the subject for Chapter VI.

(4) We comment later on the formal resolution. We agree that it is preferable to delete the reference on passage of Israeli ships.

(5) We do not now feel disposed to join with you and the French in calling for the meeting and/or sponsoring the resolution in the form submitted. While we would expect to support and not to modify the London plan, we would not want to feel bound in advance not to advocate a Resolution containing something besides this plan. (See (2) above.)

The function of the Security Council acting under Chapter VII is to make recommendations or decide what measures shall be taken to maintain or restore international peace and security. This is quite a different purpose from that of the London proposal which was an invitation to Egypt to make a new treaty in exercise of her sovereignty.

We doubt that it could plausibly be urged that Egyptian acceptance of the London proposal is the only formulation which permits of maintaining international peace and security.

It seems to us that the basis for Security Council action under Chapter VII is that certain nations possess rights of a vital character under the 1888 Treaty; but Egypt has taken or threatens action to interfere with those rights thus creating a threat to the peace.

It seems to us that the basis for Security Council action should be found in some existing treaty rights rather than upon Egyptian refusal to make a new treaty granting other rights than those now possessed.

[Tab B]

September 7, 1956.

COMMENTS ON PAPER II—"TEXT OF DRAFT SECURITY COUNCIL RESOLUTION" [9]

We have reservations to the formal resolution which are indicated by our comment on the first Paper. [10] We doubt that there is yet any adequate evidence of Egypt's endangering the free and open passage of shipping through the Canal as laid down by the 1888 Convention. Egypt has consistently reaffirmed its purpose to abide by the 1888 Convention and while Egypt's interpretation of that Convention doubtless differs from ours, the fact is that we do not yet have any agreed position as between ourselves as to what is the correct interpretation. Nor do we have any evidence so far that rights under that Treaty have been violated by Egypt, except as regards the ships and cargoes for Israel.

Also we do not see where the proposed resolution would get us, assuming it were passed. Of course, it may be justifiable to gamble that the Soviet Union will veto the resolution so that it will never pass. But we think it must also be considered where we would be if the Soviet Union does not exercise a veto power. The only operative paragraph is a request to the Government of Egypt to negotiate on the basis of the 18-Power proposal. If the resolution is passed, Egypt could conduct such a negotiation and prolong it and finally break it off and them we would be precisely where we are today.

Furthermore, the form of resolution leaves unanswered the question as to whom Egypt is supposed to negotiate with. Thus, Egypt in response to this request might call a conference of the 46 user nations for the purpose of the negotiation, as she has indicated a willingness to do.

[Tab C]

September 7, 1956.

COMMENTS ON PAPER III [11]

We do not, as of today, know whether the Egyptian Government has "refused to negotiate".

---

[9] Secret. The reference to Paper II indicates Message 3 in Document 184.
[10] See Tab A above.
[11] Secret. The reference to Paper III indicates Message 4 in Document 184.

We are not clear that a situation "which may" endanger the free and open passage of the Canal constitutes a threat to peace in the face of the repeated Egyptian Government affirmations of its intention not to interfere with the free and open passage of the ships. This again seems to us to emphasize the basic weakness of our position. So long as we do not specify what are our rights of the 1888 Treaty we cannot prove that Egypt threatens, or acts, to violate these rights.

The concluding sentence of the paper, which speaks about a "situation which, if allowed to continue, would constitute manifest danger to peace and security" closely paraphrases Article 33, [12] falling under Chapter VI and not Chapter VII.

We greatly doubt that a refusal to negotiate—which was in reality merely a refusal to accept—certain proposals, constitutes "a manifest danger to peace and security".

[Tab D]

September 7, 1956.

COMMENTS ON PAPER IV [13]

We are, as you know, sympathetic to the idea of the principal users of the Canal agreeing upon their rights under the 1888 Treaty and taking concerted action to exercise their rights. This action, in our opinion, should comprehend the development of a uniform system for handling the dues to be paid by ships passing through the Canal. Also, we believe it should deal with the question of pilots and perhaps some other matters such as arranging the pattern of traffic and the system of signals and aids to navigation, perhaps also the dredging of the Canal. It seems to us that the Treaty of 1888 creates a sort of an international easement and that those entitled to benefit therefrom have the right, and perhaps the obligation, to maintain and operate their easement.

It does not seem to us that we should acquiesce in the exercise by Egypt of functions which are more properly those of users than of the sovereign through whose territory the easement passes. Obviously, all this would take time. Also, it might lead to a clash with Egypt which, while it would provide a clearer basis for Security Council action, would also entail major economic consequences.

---

[12] See footnote 3, Document 148.
[13] Secret. The reference to Paper IV indicates Message 5 in Document 184.

I do not feel at all confident that we are prepared for those economic consequences. It may take as much time to make preparations for these as it will to achieve some program of concerted action by the users.

Have you any precise formulation of how you propose to handle the matter of transit dues?

[Tab E]

September 7, 1956.

COMMENTS ON PAPER V [14]

Our suggestion for a users agency is, we would say, an effort to implement the 1888 Treaty rather than to implement the London proposal of eighteen.

That proposal frankly sought a new treaty with Egypt. It gave Egypt rights and advantages which Egypt could not demand under the 1888 Treaty. On the other hand, the users would gain greatly by thus obtaining Egyptian cooperation.

It may not be practical in the long run to use the Canal without Egyptian cooperation, but it seems to us that since our basic rights flow from the 1888 Treaty, we should not assume that Egypt can and will nullify those rights or that there are no alternatives other than to accept Egyptian terms or to seek by force to impose our own.

It does not seem to us that it carries much conviction to say that we have rights under the 1888 Treaty unless we try in good faith and reasonably to use those rights. If we do try to use them and Egypt takes forcible action to prevent such use, then, and perhaps only then, will Egypt be an aggressor or guilty of a threat to peace.

Theoretically, of course, each nation having rights to use the Canal could attempt to use these rights without concerting its action with others. As a practical matter this would lead to confusion and breakdown of the Canal operation which could be attributed to the users rather than to Egypt. Therefore, we should act as though we had rights and, having them, concert for their effective use.

You speak of "future Egyptian membership". We think of our proposal for a concert of users as a provisional arrangement and not a substitute in the long run for another arrangement which would involve Egyptian participation. But this, when it came about, would

---

[14] Secret. The reference to Paper V indicates Message 6 in Document 184.

probably be something quite different than the interim user agency which might now be adopted as a makeshift.

As previously indicated, it is our thought that the user agency would be set up to perform functions broader than the mere collection of dues.

---

189. Memorandum of a Telephone Conversation Between the President and the Secretary of State, Washington, September 7, 1956, 6:37 p.m. [1]

TELEPHONE CALL TO THE PRESIDENT

The Secretary said he had just finished a couple of hours with the British and French going over papers which relate to possible Security Council action. The particular matter they are concerned about is say supposing that an amendment is introduced which calls upon the parties to refrain from the use of force, would we stand with them to oppose the amendment in question. The Secretary had told them he did not think we could agree now to oppose a proposition that the parties should refrain from the use of force, which is the language of the Charter. They said that would restrict freedom of action. The Secretary said he did not know if they had that. The Secretary said in the matter if we would abstain if such an amendment was proposed, he was inclined not to give them assurances on either one.

The President said he had been trying a draft on the latest note from Eden on the Suez and indicated he had said that he was convinced that not only would they consolidate Arab force if they resorted to force before they exhausted every possibility and got a favorable word from the UN, if they insisted on using force that would weaken and probably destroy the UN. The Secretary said he did not believe we should connive with them on that proposition. The President said it was important "not to make any mistakes in a hurry". The British and French were trying to make a mistake from which there was no recall. The President stressed how important it was to go slowly. If we are right that that fellow can't run the Canal, there is bound to be a breakdown in the Canal or he (Nasser) will commit aggression. The Secretary agreed about going slowly and

---

[1] Source: Eisenhower Library, Dulles Papers, White House Telephone Conversations. Transcribed by Asbjornson.

said if we could work it out they would have to unmount and the President said, "Let them unmount". The Secretary said he believed we had plenty of user rights. If we organize to carry these out and if the Egyptians obstruct us then we have a case. The President said he was sorry he hadn't finished the draft to Eden. [2] The Secretary said it was not necessary to get it out today. (Sec. saw President on Saturday 6:30 p.m. and carried with him Sec's revised version of draft which President sent the Sec. on Saturday morning.)

---

[2] *Infra.*

---

190. Draft Message From President Eisenhower to Prime Minister Eden [1]

Washington, September 8, 1956.

DEAR ANTHONY: Whenever, on any international question, I find myself differing even slightly from you, I feel a deep compulsion to re-examine my position instantly and carefully. But permit me to suggest that when you use phrases in connection with the Suez affair, like "ignoble end to long history" in describing the possible future of your great country, you are making of Nasser a much more important figure than he is.

We have a grave problem confronting us in Nasser's reckless adventure with the Canal, and I do not, repeat not, differ from you in your estimate of his intentions and purposes. The place where we apparently do not agree is on the probable effects in the Arab world of the various possible reactions by the Western world.

You seem to believe that any long, drawn-out controversy either in the ad hoc twenty-two nations' committee or in the United Nations will inevitably make Nasser an Arab hero and seriously damage the prestige of Western Europe and the United Kingdom and including the United States. Further you apparently believe that

---

[1] Source: Eisenhower Library, Dulles Papers, Misc. Papers—U.K. (Suez Crisis. Secret. On September 8, President Eisenhower forwarded this draft to Secretary Dulles under cover of a note which reads: "Dear Foster: Here is a draft in reply to Anthony's letter [Document 181] that I have been preparing. The only usefulness it might have is in its attempt to destroy Anthony's apparent fixation that delay or long drawn out negotiations might result in catastrophe for Great Britain and the West.

"I am not even sure that it is worth while sending the document, but won't you look it over and send it back to me with any comments you may care to make? As ever, DE."

there would soon result an upheaval in the Arab nations out of which Nasser would emerge as the acknowledged leader of Islam. This, I think, is a picture too dark and is severely distorted.

It took your nation some eighteen years to put the original Napoleon in his proper place, but you did it. You have dealt more rapidly with his modern imitators.

I shall try to give you a somewhat different appraisal of the situation. First, let me say that my own conclusions are based to some degree upon an understanding of current Arab feeling that differs somewhat from yours. I believe that as this quarrel now stands before the world, we can expect the Arabs to rally firmly to Nasser's support in either of two eventualities. The first of these is that there should be a resort to force without thoroughly exploring and exhausting every possible peaceful means of settling the issue, regardless of the time consumed.

The second is that we should act forcibly when there is no evidence before the world that Nasser intends to do more than to nationalize the Canal Company. Unless it can be shown to the world that he is an actual aggressor, then I think all Arabs would be forced to support him, even though some of the ruling monarchs might very much like to see him toppled.

The matter might become even more serious than this. I venture the thought that if any large nation should attempt to settle by force an argument with a small one, without first having exhausted all of the peaceful avenues open to it, the United Nations organization would be badly weakened and possibly destroyed.

It is for reasons such as these that we have viewed with some misgivings your preparations for mounting a military expedition against Egypt. We believe that Nasser may try to go before the United Nations claiming that these actions imply a rejection of the peaceful machinery of settling the dispute, and therefore may ask the United Nations to brand these operations as aggression.

I think the beliefs I have just expressed are shared by the vast bulk of the American people, including most of those in official life.

At the same time, we want to stand very firmly with you in assuring permanent free and effective use of the Suez waterway under the terms of the 1888 Treaty. Assuming the breakdown of the present conversations with Nasser, I think we must strive to the utmost of our ability to convince the United Nations that the eighteen-nation stand in this affair was just and fair. Possibly we may fail to do that because of the veto privilege. Nevertheless, as time goes on in these arguments, one of two things must surely happen *if we are correct in our belief that the Egyptians cannot, and possibly even do not intend to, operate the Canal for the benefit of all nations and without prejudice to any.*

The first thing that might likely happen would be the complete or partial breakdown of operations. If this came about, I would suspect that no nation in the world would object to a physical penetration of the area by the principal users for the purpose of getting their shipping through the waterway. If Egypt should use force to prevent this, we would have to evaluate the event at that moment. They would then be the aggressor and under those circumstances we might gain almost universal approval for restoring order and effective operation, and this approval might even include the other Arab countries.

The other likely possibility during long negotiations would be that Nasser's impatience might lead him to some kind of drastic action that would be aggressive in character and which could again bring to our side world opinion, including the Arabs.

Whatever time might elapse between now and the occurrence of some such incident as I have indicated, the Canal would presumably be operating efficiently, and during that period there should be some opportunity for cementing our relationships with other Arab countries who would be damaged by the closing of the Canal, and in which countries the governments could be doing something to educate public opinion. Gradually, it seems to me, we could isolate Nasser and gain a victory which would not only be bloodless, but would be more far-reaching in its ultimate consequences than could be anything brought about by force of arms. In addition, it would be less costly both now and in the future.

I assure you we are not blind to the fact that eventually there may be no escape from the use of force. The Canal must operate under conditions in which all users can have confidence. But to resort to military action when the world believes there are other means available for resolving the dispute would set in motion forces that could lead, in the years to come, to the most distressing results.

I know, of course, that in our general philosophy we are as one. These letters are confined to the discussion of differing methods and for me, at least, serve the purpose of clarifying the confusing and conflicting considerations that obviously apply to this problem. As it now stands, our main difference seems to be largely the result of differing conclusions as to the probable reaction of the Arab world to the various lines of action open to us.

With warmest regard,

As ever, your friend, [2]

---

[2] Printed from an unsigned copy.

191.   Memorandum of a Conversation Between the President and Secretary of State, White House, Washington, September 8, 1956, 6:30 p.m. [1]

I met with the President in the Oval Room at the Mansion. I told him that I had spent some time studying his draft of the reply to Eden [2] and that I had suggested some changes, particularly designed to give the British and the French a stronger case for not resorting to force. I felt that after they had gone as far as they had and were now rebuffed by Nasser, they could not merely bring their troops home and say they would wait to see whether Nasser was as bad as they feared. Therefore, I suggested holding out the prospect of an organization of the users which would be designed in effect to carry on the momentum of the London Conference; the use by the users' organization of their own pilots and their collection of the fees with allocation to Egypt on a cost basis; the putting into effect or the announcing of alternatives to the use of the Canal so far as oil was concerned, and the continuance of some economic measures taken against Egypt.

The President went over my draft [3] and indicated his approval of it, although he expressed the view that he felt that world opinion inclined to side with Nasser on the proposition that since the Canal went through their territory, he was entitled to direct the operations. The President said that even though as a matter of law those who enjoyed an easement were entitled to organize themselves for its use, the public was not yet educated to accept this legal point of view, and that we would still have a job to do in public relations.

I questioned the paragraph about Napoleon and his successors on the ground that they had been dealt with by force and it might be inappropriate to suggest that analogy. The President laughed and said he guessed I was right and struck out the paragraph.

After the President had finalized the text he sent it to Mrs. Whitman to retype so that I would have it to deliver that evening to the British Ambassador.

While the typing was going on, I showed the President the draft outline of a plan for a users' association. [4] The President went through this and said he thought it was interesting but was not sure

---

[1] Source: Eisenhower Library, Dulles Papers, Meetings With the President. Secret; Personal and Private. Drafted by Dulles.

[2] *Supra.*

[3] Attached to the source text. The text of the message as delivered to the British Embassy is printed *infra.*

[4] Attached to the source text, but not printed. The document is entitled "Outline of Proposal for a Voluntary Association of Suez Canal Users". The first page indicates that it was drafted by Dulles and that this paper was draft no. 2, dated September 8.

that it would work. I said I was not sure either but that I felt we had to keep the initiative and to keep probing along various lines, particularly since there was no chance of getting the British and the French not to use force unless they had some alternatives that seemed to have in them some strength of purpose and some initiative.

The President expressed again his deep concern that military measures should not be taken.

At this point the message to Eden was brought back, the President initialed it and gave it to me to deliver to the British Ambassador. [5]

JFD

A handwritten marginal notation reads: "Taken by Sec. to show to Pres 9/8/56". A subsequent draft (no. 4), dated September 9, is Document 198.

[5] *Infra.*

---

192.   Message From President Eisenhower to Prime Minister Eden [1]

Washington, September 8, 1956.

DEAR ANTHONY: Whenever, on any international question, I find myself differing even slightly from you, I feel a deep compulsion to reexamine my position instantly and carefully. But permit me to suggest that when you use phrases in connection with the Suez affair, like "ignoble end to our long history" in describing the possible future of your great country, you are making of Nasser a much more important figure than he is.

We have a grave problem confronting us in Nasser's reckless adventure with the Canal, and I do *not* differ from you in your estimate of his intentions and purposes. The place where we apparently do not agree is on the probable effects in the Arab world of the various possible reactions by the Western world.

[1] Source: Eisenhower Library, Whitman File, International File. Secret. A copy of this message in Department of State, Presidential Correspondence: Lot 66 D 204, Eden to Eisenhower Correspondence 1955–1956 Vol I, bears this marginal notation: "Given to Makins by Secy Sat. evening 9/8/56". Eisenhower's original draft of this message is Document 190. The text printed here, which was the one sent to Eden, reflects Dulles' subsequent revisions.

You seem to believe that any long, drawn-out controversy either within the 18-nation group or in the United Nations will inevitably make Nasser an Arab hero and perilously damage the prestige of Western Europe, including the United Kingdom, and that of the United States. Further you apparently believe that there would soon result an upheaval in the Arab nations out of which Nasser would emerge as the acknowledged leader of Islam. This, I think, is a picture too dark and is severely distorted.

I shall try to give you a somewhat different appraisal of the situation. First, let me say that my own conclusions are based to some degree upon an understanding of current Arab feeling that differs somewhat from yours. I believe that as this quarrel now stands before the world, we can expect the Arabs to rally firmly to Nasser's support in either of two eventualities.

The first of these is that there should be a resort to force without thoroughly exploring and exhausting every possible peaceful means of settling the issue, regardless of the time consumed, and when there is no evidence before the world that Nasser intends to do more that to nationalize the Canal Company. Unless it can be shown to the world that he is an actual aggressor, then I think all Arabs would be forced to support him, even though some of the ruling monarchs might very much like to see him toppled.

The second would be what seemed like a capitulation to Nasser and complete acceptance of his rule of the Canal traffic.

The use of military force against Egypt under present circumstances might have consequences even more serious than causing the Arabs to support Nasser. It might cause a serious misunderstanding between our two countries because I must say frankly that there is as yet no public opinion in this country which is prepared to support such a move, and the most significant public opinion that there is seems to think that the United Nations was formed to prevent this very thing.

It is for reasons such as these that we have viewed with some misgivings your preparations for mounting a military expedition against Egypt. We believe that Nasser may try to go before the United Nations claiming these actions imply a rejection of the peaceful machinery of settling the dispute, and therefore may ask the United Nations to brand these operations as aggression.

At the same time, we do not want any capitulation to Nasser. We want to stand firmly with you to deflate the ambitious pretensions of Nasser and to assure permanent free and effective use of the Suez waterway under the terms of the 1888 Treaty.

It seems to Foster and to me that the result that you and I both want can best be assured by slower and less dramatic processes than military force. These are many areas of endeavor which are not yet fully explored because exploration takes time.

We can, for example, promote a semi-permanent organization of the user governments to take over the greatest practical amount of the technical problems of the Canal, such as pilotage, the organization of the traffic pattern, and the collection of dues to cover actual expenses. This organization would be on the spot and in constant contact with Egypt and might work out a de facto "coexistence" which would give the users the rights which we want.

There are economic pressures which, if continued, will cause distress in Egypt.

There are Arab rivalries to be exploited and which can be exploited if we do not make Nasser an Arab hero.

There are alternatives to the present dependence upon the Canal and pipelines which should be developed perhaps by more tankers, a possible new pipeline to Turkey and some possible rerouting of oil, including perhaps more from this hemisphere, particularly to European countries which can afford to pay for it in dollars.

Nasser thrives on drama. If we let some of the drama go out of the situation and concentrate upon the task of deflating him through slower but sure processes such as I described, I believe the desired results can more probably be obtained.

Gradually it seems to me we could isolate Nasser and gain a victory which would not only be bloodless, but would be more far-reaching in its ultimate consequences than could be anything brought about by force of arms. In addition, it would be less costly both now and in the future.

Of course, if during this process Nasser himself resorts to violence in clear disregard of the 1888 Treaty, then that would create a new situation and one in which he and not we would be violating the United Nations Charter.

I assure you we are not blind to the fact that eventually there may be no escape from the use of force. Our resolute purpose must be to create conditions of operation in which all users can have confidence. But to resort to military action when the world believes there are other means available for resolving the dispute would set in motion forces that could lead, in the years to come, to the most distressing results.

Obviously there are large areas of agreement between us. But in these exchanges directed toward differing methods I gain some clarification of the confusing and conflicting considerations that apply to this problem.

With warmest regard,

As ever, your friend,

D.D.E.

---

193.   Memorandum of a Conversation, Department of State, Washington, September 8, 1956, 9 p.m. [1]

SUBJECT

Suez Canal

PARTICIPANTS

Sir Roger Makins, British Ambassador
Mr. J. E. Coulson, Minister, British Embassy
The Secretary
NEA—William M. Rountree

The Ambassador called at 9 p.m. Saturday evening to discuss with the Secretary possible next steps in connection with the Suez crisis. He said that Messrs. Mollet and Pineau planned to come to London on Monday at Prime Minister Eden's request. London felt, he said, that we might be drifting apart in our attitude toward steps which should be taken. The UK had made two proposals upon which the US was disposed to throw cold water. Assuming that Nasser would reject the eighteen nations' proposal, the British felt that effective and positive action should be taken immediately. Otherwise, Nasser would strengthen his hold on the Canal; it would appear as though he were getting away with a substantial victory; and many Arabs who were now hoping for a defeat for Nasser would get progressively more worried. If we were not in a position early next week to take quick steps, the consequences might be bad. On the other hand, the British felt that force should be used only as the last resort. As an alternative to the use of force, the British were quite attracted to the proposals made by the Secretary regarding an association of Canal users. They would like to know whether Mr. Dulles' thoughts in this connection had been reduced to a plan of action or whether his ideas were still of a general character. Regard-

---

[1] Source: Department of State, Central Files, 974.7301/9–856. Secret. Drafted by Rountree.

ing the United Nations, the Ambassador recalled that the UK had prepared a draft of a letter to the Security Council, asking for Council action and enclosing a proposed resolution. [2] In view of the comments which the Secretary had made earlier, [3] however, the British were prepared as an alternative simply to write a letter to the Security Council informing it of the situation but requesting no action at this stage. The Ambassador observed that this appeared to be in line with the Secretary's proposal.

Responding first to the UN aspect, the Secretary said that he had not intended to propose the letter as an alternative, but that he had merely suggested that this might be explored as an alternative if it should be decided by the British for the reasons he had given not to proceed along the lines of their earlier draft communication and resolution. He had thought it might be a means of informing the Council and of getting priority for Council consideration on the basis of a British request, if the Egyptians should subsequently decide to bring the matter themselves before the Council. (He recalled the New Zealand letter to the Council in connection with the Quemoy and Matsu affair.) While he had no desire to assume a negative attitude in connection with the earlier British suggestion, he had pointed out the difficulties inherent in that program, which difficulties he considered to be very real. He observed that while it might be wise to go to the Council to get redress if treaty rights were violated or if force was threatened, it would be an entirely different matter to try to get the Council to force a country to negotiate a new treaty. At this point the Secretary handed to the Ambassador a classified communication. [4] The Ambassador, after reading the document, observed that it answered some of the questions which he had been asked to put to the Secretary.

The Secretary said he considered it essential to determine a course of action which would be in between the extremes of employing force and of giving in to Nasser. He felt that if the users of the Canal could be organized, capitalizing upon the momentum gained at the London Conference, it should be possible to work together upon a plan which would give promise of success. He believed that we had rights which were very substantial. These rights should not be given up. Apart from that, we had means of employing economic pressures, and we had the possibility of alternatives to the Suez Canal which, if effectively employed, could obtain the desired results. Force, he said, was hard to justify under

---

[2] Reference is to the tabs to Document 184. The draft letter to the Security Council is Message 4; the proposed Security Council resolution is Message 3.

[3] Reference is to Dulles' meeting with Coulson and Alphand on September 7 and the papers containing the U.S. response to Lloyd's messages. See Document 188.

[4] Presumably the message from Eisenhower to Eden, *supra.*

the UN Charter and, in any event, it would be very difficult to say where military action would end. The President was very deeply concerned by the situation and where it would lead. He did not see any end through the course of moving in with military force, since that might set East against West to a degree which had never before existed. There would not be enough forces to send troops to put out all the fires which might start once hostilities in Egypt began.

The Secretary realized vividly that we could not let Nasser win a victory, but he thought the way to avoid this lay through longer range projects than through too hasty action. He recognized that the British and French military preparations were expensive and he appreciated the importance attached by those Governments to keeping the forces in a state of readiness. This naturally created a hardship and expenses which, he understood, led the British and French to desire some quick action. However, if the next steps to be taken were determined on the basis of a few days or a week's time limit, the possibilities for the most helpful measure might correspondingly be limited.

The Ambassador said that he understood fully the merits of the Secretary's comments. On the other hand, London had its problems. Parliament was to convene on September 12 and the British Government would be asked what would be done in this critical situation. The Prime Minister would feel compelled to say something of a definite character. Perhaps a statement of the Government's intentions regarding the UN would be helpful. Mr. Dixon had been asked to draft a letter for Makins to show to the Secretary which would report the situation to the Security Council without asking for specific action. The Ambassador showed a copy of the letter to the Secretary [5] who made certain minor suggestions but thought the letter otherwise satisfactory.

At this point the Secretary showed the Ambassador a draft of the outline of his plan for a users association. [6] Sir Roger said that he was tremendously impressed with the plan and stated he thought it would be extremely useful if he could have a paper to send to the British Government. He felt this would give to them a much more concrete idea of what the Secretary had in mind and might be very influential in connection with their consideration of measures to be taken.

The Secretary said he wished to work on the document further, but that on the following day (Sunday) he would give a copy to the Ambassador for transmittal to the British Government. He made it

---

[5] At 12:30 p.m. on September 10, Makins presented the draft letter to Dulles. See Document 206.

[6] A subsequent draft of this outline is printed as Document 198.

clear, however, that it should be considered to be an illustrative plan only and should not be regarded as a US Governmental document since he had not had an opportunity to discuss it with the other interested agencies.

While accompanying the Ambassador to his car, the Secretary mentioned his concern that the British had brought the French into discussions of the Canal users proposal. He pointed out that in giving his idea to Mr. Coulson he had said that he did not intend at this stage to take it up with the French. He understood, of course, the explanation which had been given that Mr. Lloyd had not understood this qualification which was set forth in the British Embassy's telegram to the Foreign Office when he had raised the matter with Mr. Pineau. He also understood the British-French relationship in this whole affair, but said we were concerned about maintaining complete secrecy in connection with this matter. Ambassador Makins replied that he saw the Secretary's point.

194.   Editorial Note

On September 7 in Cairo, the Five-Nation Committee agreed to the text of an aide-mémoire explaining the purposes and rationale of the Eighteen-Power Proposal, which was to be delivered to Nasser that evening. Henderson reported that all members of the Committee had contributed substantively to the process of revising Menzies' original draft, but that the majority of changes had been suggested by the United States and to some extent by Iran. Henderson noted that the United States Delegation was not completely satisfied with the final text of the aide-mémoire, but he believed it to be the best obtainable without creating friction within the Committee, especially in view of "Menzies' sensitivities". (Telegram 643 from Cairo, September 7; Department of State, Central Files, 974.7301/9–456) The text of the aide-mémoire was transmitted to the Department of State in telegram 645 from Cairo, September 7. (*Ibid.*) Also on September 7, Menzies forwarded to Nasser a proposal from the Spanish Delegation with a covering note in which Menzies explained that at the Suez Conference the Spanish Delegation had requested the Committee to bring to Nasser's attention its proposal, if the Committee proved unable to reach agreement with Egypt on an international board for operating the Suez Canal. The Spanish proposal, as forwarded to Nasser, called for the establishment, by Convention, of institutional arrangements for cooperation between Egypt and other nations interested in the operation, development, and maintenance of the Canal. The Spanish proposed that this be achieved through adequate international representation on the Egyptian Board which operated, maintained, and developed the Canal. The text of the Spanish proposal and Menzies' covering note were forwarded to the Department of State in telegram 679 from Cairo, September 9. (*Ibid.*)

Nasser's response was delivered to Menzies at 12:45 p.m., September 9. In it, the Egyptian President reaffirmed his government's right to nationalize the Suez Canal Company, Egypt's commitment to adhere to the Convention of 1888 guaranteeing freedom of passage through the Canal, and Egypt's readiness to give full and equitable compensation to shareholders of the Company. Nasser maintained that a crisis atmosphere had been created by threats to use force, mobilization of troops, and other hostile measures. He reiterated his willingness to negotiate a peaceful solution which respected the rights of Egyptian sovereignty and ownership, safeguarded freedom of passage through the Canal, and ensured dependable and efficient operation and development of the Canal; but he also maintained that the proposals presented by the Committee were unacceptable and served to undermine these very objectives. The text of Nasser's reply was forwarded to the Department of State in telegram 681 from Cairo, September 9. (*Ibid.*)

Also on September 9, the Five-Nation Committee agreed to the text of a final report, containing a summation of its activities, and decided to release to the press upon returning to London the texts of the following documents: the Committee's aide-mémoire to Nasser of September 3; the Committee's letter to Nasser of September 7; the Committee's letter to Nasser of September 7 enclosing the Spanish proposal; and Nasser's reply to the Committee of September 9. (Reported to the Department of State in telegrams 677 and 685 from Cairo, September 9; *ibid.*) The text of the Committee's report is in telegram 687 from Cairo, September 9. (*Ibid.*)

At 7 p.m., September 9, the Committee paid a farewell call on Nasser. Henderson reported that the meeting did not concern itself with substance. Menzies thanked Nasser for courtesies extended to the Committee and cooperation on procedural matters. Nasser spoke only briefly, expressing his appreciation for the manner in which the Committee had discharged its mission. Nasser and the Committee then agreed upon the text of a final communiqué, which acknowledged that discussions had taken place, that the Committee had presented and explained the Eighteen-Power Proposal, and that the Committee had received the views of the Egyptian Government on the proposals.

Henderson reported that Nasser appeared preoccupied and almost somber during this meeting. (Telegram 693 from Cairo, September 9; *ibid*.) The text of the agreed communiqué is in telegram 691 from Cairo, September 9. (*Ibid*.) Later that evening the Committee returned to London where the above-mentioned documents were released to the press. On the following day the Department of State made the documents public in Press Release No. 474. (Department of State *Bulletin*, September 24, 1956, pages 467–475) These documents and the Committee's final report are printed in *The Suez Canal Problem, July 26–September 22, 1856*, pages 303–326.

---

195.   Draft Telegram From the Embassy in the United Kingdom to the Department of State [1]

London, September 9, 1956.

Suez from Henderson. For Secretary.

1. We deeply regret failure of mission. Menzies and other members in my opinion did all possible in framework terms of reference to find common meeting ground with Nasser. Although he courteous and correct throughout our stay he never wavered from the position which he had apparently adopted prior our arrival—that Egypt could never agree to entrust any phase of operations of canal to body over which Egypt would not have unquestioned control. We were unsuccessful in our efforts during our discussions to get away from phrases which might be offensive to Egyptian nationalism and to concentrate on specific aspects of operations in hope that piece by piece we could erect institutional structure in framework our proposals which could be acceptable to Egypt. Nasser clearly unwilling abandon his general position that he unprepared consider any plan

---

[1] Source: Department of State, Central Files, 974.7301/9–1156. Secret. Forwarded to Dulles on September 11 under cover of a memorandum by Henderson which reads: "Attached hereto is a draft of a telegram partly prepared in Cairo and party enroute in which we summarized some of the views which we shared as we left Cairo.

"We planned to send the telegram from London, but when it was decided for me to proceed direct to Washington it seemed preferable for me to take it with me. We thought that it might make a useful addition to the reports which we submitted from Cairo.

"In preparing this report we realized of course that the unwillingness of Nasser to accept one or other plan for maintaining Canal as efficiently operated waterway open to the vessels of all nations would be merely one of various factors to be considered by the U.S. in determining what its policies should be with regard to the Canal." This covering note is marked "Sec saw".

whatsoever which would permit non-Egyptian nationals not taking orders from Egypt to have executive powers over canal operations. We do not believe from our observations here that our Committee could have achieved success regardless degree of ingenuity and persuasiveness displayed. In our opinion Nasser had become an almost hypnotic prisoner of his own propaganda and ideology long before our arrival. He had already practically tied his own hands in the presence of Egyptian nationalism, international communism, and evangelical neutralism, particularly that brand found among certain members Bandung bloc. Not only would it have been almost impossible for him change his attitude re substantive matters during period our stay in Egypt, but it would have been even more difficult for him to make concessions to Committee representing powers which did not include nations that had been giving him sympathetic support.

2. Although, in our opinion, Nasser could not, without feeling that he was abandoning Egyptian nationalism and deserting his foreign supporters, accept our proposals or in fact treat us as representatives of all of users of canal, he nevertheless had sufficient respect for collective power and influence of 18 nations which we represented not to assume towards us attitude calculated to give offense. During our stay in Egypt, Egyptian press and radio continued to disseminate propaganda criticizing and ridiculing West. This campaign aimed particularly at UK and France and was somewhat restrained re US. Nasser personally, however, exercised extreme care in showing us every courtesy, consideration and facility. Without making counter-offers he made it clear that he recognized that users of canal had legitimate interest in manner in which canal was to be operated and should be given appropriate assurances that it would remain as waterway open without discrimination to vessels all nations. He indicated during our conversations that Egypt was prepared to enter into one or more conventions supplementary to convention of 1888, which should satisfy users. He at least hinted at willingness to consider devising some scheme whereby users could seek remedies in case they should believe Egypt guilty of violating such conventions. He expressed desire make use of most competent technicians available and of foreign technical advice. He was, however, rather vague in outlining what he had in mind. It difficult for us believe that he will not in almost immediate future make public in some way or other in more specific and detailed form what Egypt willing to do.

3. Although object of mission has not been achieved, we consider it has served useful purpose in that through the arguments which Committee has presented orally it has helped to cause Nasser to realize that interests of users in canal are so real and important that

he cannot afford to ignore them. We believe that in spite of his refusal recognize London conference or 18 nations as accredited spokesman for users of canal, he was impressed by his study of the proceedings of the conference and by earnest, sincere, and yet friendly manner in which Committee presented and explained proposals of 18 powers. In our opinion the menacing gestures of UK and France have not been helpful to the work of our Committee, although success could not have been achieved in any event. We believe that those who think that threats of use of armed force can make Nasser and his associates more reasonable fail to understand psychology of current Egyptian nationalism buttressed as it is with the support of international communism and nationalism of Asian-African countries recently released from Western control.

4. Since our delegation was integral part of Committee and since each move and even every facial expression of our members were watched by Egyptians and others with idea detecting differences of opinion in Committee, we were not free to engage in type of exploration in which members of diplomatic group on other kind of mission might engage. We, therefore, not able as result firsthand probing, gauge with any degree assurance just how far Nasser might be willing go in efforts pacify at least some of users of canal. We believe, however, we safe in saying he would not accept, regardless threats of military action or extent application economic pressure, any arrangement which would take operations of canal out of Egyptian hands. He might at present be prepared undertake commitments which would give users of canal considerable voice in making decisions with regard to certain operational policies affecting canal and perhaps even to limited extent with regard to regulation of traffic through canal. For instance, he might agree not raise tolls without users' consent and not make enlargements or other alterations canal without approval of users. He might be willing undertake commitments much more far-reaching and clear than convention of 1888 not to discriminate against any user. He might be willing agree to establishment some kind of international body representing all interested users of canal which could observe operations and examine policies re canal and which could serve as instrument for expression views users with respect thereto. He would not, we believe, work with any such body which had been established without previous consultation with Egypt or set up in atmosphere of pressure on Egypt. He might agree that such body could make suggestions re qualifications certain employees of canal, etc. He would not, we are confident, tolerate injection such body into operations. In order to give assurance to users of his good faith, he might be willing agree that differences re interpretations or violations of such conventions could be submitted to arbitral Commission

to be established under such conventions or, in case flouting of decisions of such Commission, to ICJ.

5. In reading our speculations in paragraph 4 above, it should be borne in mind that what Nasser might be willing to do today he might not be willing do tomorrow. If conditions alter so that he would lose face in doing later what he considers himself able voluntarily to do now, his attitude would certainly harden. If, for instance, Western pilots should be withdrawn under undisguised encouragement their governments, if Western powers would concert in endeavor deprive Egypt of receipt of tolls, if display willingness on his part make concessions to users should be greeted by West as sign weakness, he might by further irresponsible acts widen and make more difficult of bridging present gulf between Egypt and West.

---

196.   Telegram From the Embassy in Egypt to the Department of State [1]

Cairo, September 9, 1956—10 a.m.

674. Suez from Henderson. Eyes only for Secretary. Menzies has been ill and for most part in bed for last two days. His illness has aggravated his disappointment at failure Mission which he undertook with optimism. Failure particularly painful to him since he has been under sharp criticism Australia for accepting Mission and has been hoping success would be best answer critics.

Although he restrained in his comments I understand he believes announcements from Washington greatly increased difficulties his Mission. [2] His idea in accepting Mission apparently was that Nasser should be given understand that West would determine from his decision re proposals whether there any possibility cooperation with him in future. He sincerely believes, therefore, that announcements other proposals might be put forward if his Mission should fail seriously weakened Committees position and gave Nasser impression there was lack of unity among great Western powers. Although he was uncritical and friendly when I explained motivation these statements he nevertheless clearly continues to be deeply

---

[1] Source: Department of State, Central Files, 974.7301/9–956. Secret. Received at 12:08 p.m.
[2] See Document 171.

hurt. During recent years he has been one most loyal friends and best supporter of US among Commonwealth heads of government. It would be unfortunate if his friendliness should cool as result these developments. I hope, therefore, President or you can on appropriate occasion during next few days make public statement praising his devotion to world peace in accepting Mission and his manner conduct of Mission. [3]

Byroade

---

[3] In telegram 722 to Cairo, September 9, Dulles informed Henderson that his report "greatly distresses me" and asked that he deliver the following personal message to Menzies: "Dear Bob: I deeply appreciate the able way in which you have conducted the tremendously important task which you undertook for the 18 nations. Although the immediate result is negative, I am confident that your mission constituted a vital element in this unfolding drama of worldwide significance and that your part in it will prove historic. With best regards, Foster." Dulles also told Henderson that he frankly did not understand the reference to "announcement that other proposals might be put forward if his mission should fail." Dulles maintained that although alternatives to the use of force had been considered, he was "not conscious of any announcements of the kind you suggest." (*Ibid.*)

On September 10, Dulles issued a statement extending "particular thanks" to Prime Minister Menzies. See *The Suez Canal Problem, July 26–September 22, 1956*, p. 327; or Department of State *Bulletin*, September 24, 1956, p. 469.

197. **Memorandum of a Conversation, Secretary Dulles'
Residence, Washington, September 9, 1956, 5:45 p.m.** [1]

SUBJECT

Suez Canal

PARTICIPANTS:

Sir Roger Makins, British Ambassador
Mr. J. E. Coulson, Minister, British Embassy
Mr. Arthur S. Flemming, Director, Office of Defense Mobilization
The Secretary
NEA—William M. Rountree

The Ambassador called on the Secretary at the latter's home on
Sunday afternoon to receive a copy of the Secretary's outline of a
proposal for a Suez Canal users association. [2] After reading the
paper, the Ambassador described it as an intensely interesting and
constructive document. The Secretary and the Ambassador then
discussed, for the purpose of clarification, various aspects of the
outline. Ambassador Makins said that the British Government had
been very interested at Mr. Dulles' thinking on this matter, and had
raised certain legal questions which seemed clearly set forth in the
document so that he did not have to discuss them further.

The Ambassador inquired as to what conditions he should set
forth regarding the paper when he telegraphed it to London. The
Secretary replied that he thought secrecy should be maintained and
that, for the time being until we had agreed upon this point, it
should not be given to the French. The Secretary said that in
considering how we might proceed to implement the plan, he
thought it most important to assume the most effective posture vis-
à-vis Nasser. We might recall the latter's failure to cooperate in
achieving a solution to the problem and state that in the absence of
such cooperation we had decided to organize our efforts to utilize
our rights under the Treaty. It might be stated, moreover, because of
our inability to rely on the conduct of Egypt, we had considered
alternative arrangements to the use of the Canal. If we could disclose
in some appropriate way that we were prepared to reroute tankers,
build new pipelines, construct large tankers, etc., that would show
Nasser that he did not have a strangle-hold on the countries whose

---

[1] Source: Department of State, Central Files, 974.7301/9–956. Secret. Drafted by
Rountree.
[2] *Infra.*

448

traffic moves through the Canal, and thus destroy his philosophy as set forth in his book. The Secretary thought that steps seeking alternatives to the use of the Canal would require cutting down the production of oil in certain Arab countries, which could not fail to understand that their consequent loss of revenue was the result of Nasser's folly. He thought it important, however, that reductions in production should not be allowed to affect Iran or Iraq. If the other producing countries income was reduced, they would become even less enthusiastic regarding Nasser. At this point the Secretary gave Ambassador Makins a copy of the memorandum prepared by Mr. Flemming[3] which set forth the oil supply position within the context of movements through the Suez Canal.

The Secretary said our basic purpose was to show that there were alternatives to capitulation to Nasser on the one hand and to the use of force on the other. We could set up the user organization, we could maintain economic pressures, we could seek alternatives to the Suez Canal and take other steps which would have an appreciable effect on the situation. The diversion of tankers could either take place as a deliberate act on the part of the Western countries to demonstrate to Nasser that we had no dependency upon the Canal, or as a result of denial by Nasser of passage through the Canal. However, either would bring about great economic consequences which the British and French should consider carefully and be prepared to meet.

The Secretary observed that the various things that we could do short of employment of military force could be presented in a way to carry a tremendous sense of restrained power. He earnestly hoped that the British would agree that this was a far better alternative than the use of force.

The Ambassador said he entirely agreed, and had already clearly represented his views in this respect to London. He inquired whether some United States Government order would be needed to enable the oil companies to undertake a program which would be required to meet European requirements if tankers did not transit the Canal. Mr. Flemming responded that authority for this already existed. The planning work which was now being done was under that authority. The Petroleum Authority would have authority to proceed if need be. If it were deemed necessary to proceed, the companies would be informed and the consent of the Attorney General would be obtained. Mr. Flemming said that he was going tomorrow to New York to meet with the oil committee[4] and he hoped to have them put us

---

[3] Not found in Department of State files.

[4] Reference is to the Middle East Emergency Committee, composed of representatives from certain U.S. oil corporations.

in a position very soon to make a public announcement if circumstances should render it necessary to proceed with the plan. The Secretary said he had told Mr. Flemming that we might want to say something about our ability to meet any contingency after Mr. Eden's speech on Tuesday or Wednesday. The Ambassador agreed that it was extremely important to be ready to implement the plan. London, however, would want to look carefully at the financial aspects before deciding when the plan should be implemented.

The Secretary observed that the UK had pressed for action which would have had great economic consequences and he had asked whether the British were prepared for the consequences incident to their plan. As yet, he had no answer to that important question. It must be recognized that the economic consequences of bringing about hostilities would be infinitely greater than the consequences merely of a diversion of shipping from the Canal.

The Ambassador said that he was in some difficulty in his relations with the French. Mr. Alphand had been extremely anxious to see him to talk about the Canal users plan but he had not felt free to do so since the United States had not yet discussed the matter with the French. Moreover, the French Prime Minister and Foreign Minister were expected in London tomorrow and would want to go into the matter. He inquired what he should do.

The Secretary said that of course the French, as a result of Mr. Lloyd's discussions with Mr. Pineau in Paris, knew in a general way of the plan. He thought that the Ambassador might provide the French with a paraphrase of the Secretary's paper which might be better than giving them our own text.

Ambassador Makins said he was sure the French would raise the question of compensation of shareholders. The users plan did not cover compensation, and he assumed that that would have to be worked out separately. The Secretary agreed.

The Ambassador recalled that the Canal pilots had been asked to stay on until after the conclusion of the Menzies mission. The Company now contemplated saying soon that the injunction had now been lifted and the pilots were free agents and could either stay or leave as they wished. The Secretary said that an extremely important element of our new plan was that the pilots would be employed by the association. He felt it vitally important to keep them together until the association was organized. The Ambassador replied that London thought the pilots would be available for the new plan. Mr. Rountree inquired whether the two matters should not be coordinated. It would seem to him that the pilots should not leave Egypt until after the plan was ready for implementation. The Ambassador said he agreed and would make the point again to

London and suggest that the pilots be held until the users plan had been worked out.

---

198.   Paper Prepared by the Secretary of State [1]

Washington, September 9, 1956.

OUTLINE OF PROPOSAL FOR A VOLUNTARY ASSOCIATION OF SUEZ CANAL USERS

I.

The need for user cooperation

The Convention of 1888 provided that the Canal "shall always be free and open" and gave "every vessel of commerce or of war, without distinction of flag" a right of use of the waterway. All parties agreed "not in any way to interfere with the free use of the Canal" (Article 1). Moreover, the parties agreed to respect the plant, establishments, buildings, and works of the Maritime Canal (Article 3). The agents of the signatory powers were charged to watch over its execution (Article 8), and Egypt, which was then a part of the Ottoman Empire and on whose behalf the Treaty was signed by Turkey, was bound to take (shall take) the necessary measures for insuring the execution of the Convention (Article 9).

The rights thus accorded under the Convention of 1888 constitute a perpetual easement to use the Canal freely.

It is obvious that the users' rights can best be exercised by cooperation as among the users, and as between the users and Egypt through whose territory the Canal passes. Such cooperation was deemed assured at least until 1968 by the concession to the Universal Suez Canal Company which is referred to in the Treaty of 1888. However, the Government of Egypt acted unilaterally to annul that concession, and while the legality of that action is open to serious question, the Government of Egypt itself treats the concession as annulled and the cooperative arrangement evidenced thereby as terminated.

---

[1] Source: Department of State, Conference Files: Lot 62 D 181, CF 722. Secret. The source text indicates that this paper was the fourth draft and that it was drafted by Dulles. It also bears the handwritten marginal notation: "cc—UK. 9/9 Phleger. cc—French 9/10".

In the face of this situation the seven nations which constitute the only indisputable survivors of the signatories to the 1888 Treaty, together with eight other nations which, with the foregoing, represent over 90 percent of the ownership of shipping through the Canal, together with seven other nations whose pattern of foreign trade shows distinctive dependence on the Canal, met at London to consider the situation. 18 of the 22, including nations of Europe, Asia, Africa, America and Australia, agreed on proposals for cooperation with Egypt which gave Egypt the maximum participation which they deemed compatible with their own rights under the 1888 Convention. These 18-power proposals were carried to Egypt by a Committee of Five and explained to the Government of Egypt. The Government of Egypt rejected these proposals and did not suggest any alternative proposal for cooperation.

Under the circumstances it has become both appropriate and necessary that the governments of the users should organize as among themselves for the most effective possible enjoyment of the right of passage given by the 1888 Convention. Of course, each user could exercise that right independently. But the requirements for pilotage and for a coordinated pattern of traffic are such as to make user cooperation a practical necessity.

Accordingly, in order effectively to carry out the stated purpose of the Convention of 1888 to guarantee at all times and for all the powers the free use of the Suez Maritime Canal, the governments subscribing hereto have agreed to create and join a voluntary Cooperative Association of Suez Canal Users (CASU).

II.

Basic Purposes of CASU

The Association (CASU) will function according to the following principles:

(1) To organize the use of the Canal by member controlled vessels so as to promote safe, orderly, efficient and economical transit, and

(2) To assure that such use will, as among member controlled vessels, be impartial and uninfluenced for or against any ship or cargo by reason of the policies of any government;

(3) To cooperate with Egypt in the discharge by Egypt of its obligation to take the necessary measures for insuring the execution of the 1888 Convention;

(4) To coordinate generally, on behalf of the members, the rights of users granted by the 1888 Convention, with scrupulous regard for the sovereign rights of Egypt in consonance with the 1888 Convention.

III.

The Form of Organization

Membership in the Association

The Association shall consist of the governments subscribing hereto and it shall remain open to all nations, whose nationals or ships of registry have been users to the extent of —— gross tons or more of the Canal or whose foreign trade has, to the extent of —— percent or more passed through the Canal, on the basis of the last calendar year's figures available, and the governments of which accept the principles above set forth.

Other governments which desire to obtain the benefit of the facilities of CASU may become affiliates on a basis of equality by indicating such desire and by subscribing to the principles above set forth in Section II.

Organization

The headquarters of the Association will be established at Rome.

The nations members of the Association will create an Executive Group consisting of 5 nations which shall be chosen from among their members with due regard to use, pattern of trade, and geographical distribution; the composition of the Executive Group to be such as to assure that its responsibilities will be discharged solely with a view to achieving the best possible operating results without political motivation in favor of, or in prejudice against, any user of the Canal.

The term of office of the members of the Executive Group shall be one year, with eligibility for reelection.

The Executive Group would make periodic reports to the United Nations and would be authorized to develop such further relations with the United Nations as may be agreed upon by the Association and the United Nations.

The Executive Group will be responsible for giving general policy guidance to the Administrator, hereafter referred to, in carrying out the objectives of the Association. It shall be responsible for approving the scale of salaries and wages of the employees and shall prepare the annual budget, for approval by the Association, on the basis of which will be calculated the fees payable by ships using the facilities of the Association.

Members of the Association will advance to the Executive Group a working fund of $—— to be reimbursed out of fees collected from ships using the facilities of the Association.

The ship-scheduling points, unless otherwise determined by the Executive Group, shall be designated vessels of one or more of the member governments stationed in the ports of access of Port Said and Suez as expressly authorized by Article 7 of the Convention of 1888.

The Association shall, upon the recommendation of the Executive Group, designate an individual Administrator to administer the operations of the Association and the members will give such assistance to the Administrator as may be useful for the effective operation of the Association.

The Administrator, subject to the authority of the Executive Group, shall have the following powers:

To establish and control the scheduling for ships using the facilities of the Association;

To allocate pilots to the masters of such ships;

To employ the personnel necessary for the operation of the Association, including the hiring and training of pilots;

To make such rules and regulations for ships using the facilities of the Association as in his opinion will best insure free and unobstructed transit of the Canal;

To take the steps necessary, under the direction of the Executive Group, to insure the maintenance and repair of the Canal, and the facilities incidental thereto, and to remove obstructions from the Canal should they occur;

To collect fees from ships using the facilities of the Association, which the Executive Group shall establish as equitable and necessary to defray the costs of the operations of the Association, without profit to any member;

To make available the services and facilities of the Association to ships of any nation at all times. (Ships of members or affiliates of the Association, however, shall, whenever necessary, have priority in the use of the services and facilities of the Association.)

IV.

The Association's Relations with Egypt

The Association will cooperate with the Egyptian Government to insure that the Canal remains free and unobstructed to shipping. The Administrator, under the guidance of the Executive Group, will maintain such relations with the Egyptian Government as may be acceptable to the Egyptian Government and necessary to effect such cooperation. It will reimburse the Government of Egypt for any expenses reasonably incurred by it in connection with the performance by Egypt of the measures to which Egypt is obligated, by the Convention of 1888, to assure the free and open use of the Canal.

V.

Settlement of Disputes

Disputes arising between members of the Association relating to their rights and obligations as members of the Association, or as users of the Canal shall be settled by the Executive Group.

VI.

Meetings of the Association

The Association shall act by meetings of its members. Affirmative action will require a vote which represents both a majority of the members and a majority in terms of the registry of member tonnage through the Canal during the last calendar year for which statistics are available. If the nation of ship registry is not a member of the Association, then the tonnage shall be credited to the member nation whose nationals possess ownership of such tonnage.

VII.

Withdrawal of Members or Affiliates

Members of the Association or affiliates may withdraw from the Organization at any time by giving notice to the Executive Group.

---

199.   Memorandum of a Conversation Between the French Ambassador-Designate (Alphand) and the Secretary of State, Secretary Dulles' Residence, Washington, September 9, 1956, 9 p.m. [1]

SUBJECT

Suez Canal

Ambassador Designate Alphand called on the Secretary on Sunday evening at the latter's home after requesting an urgent appointment to discuss the Suez situation. Mr. Alphand said Messrs. Mollet and Pineau were probably going to London tomorrow (September 10). He said the French Government felt that the Secretary's idea of

---

[1] Source: Department of State, Central Files, 974.7301/9–956. Secret. Drafted by Rountree.

informing the Security Council of the Suez situation, rather than asking Security Council action and proposing a resolution, was a good one. The British had prepared a draft letter and his impression was that the French would accept the draft with perhaps some minor changes. He thought both the French and the British would sign it. Mr. Alphand commented that Secretary Dulles' ideas concerning the manner in which the item should be brought to the attention of the Security Council were very good and constructive.

Continuing, Mr. Alphand said that he must cable tonight to Paris further information concerning the Secretary's plan for a "shadow authority" to handle transit of the Canal. He said the French Government was favorably impressed with the general idea and wished a further elaboration of it.

The Secretary commented that we should not assume that because Egypt had nationalized the Suez Canal Company all rights of the company would go back to Egypt. It seemed to him that the rights would revert to the users of the Canal. He saw no reason why the pilots employed by the Canal Company should be lost since we would have the right to use them ourselves. Egypt could not with justification say that the pilots were not qualified since they have been taking ships through the Canal for many years. If we proceed along the lines suggested for an association of Canal users and offer to provide pilots to take our ships through, Egypt would be the offender if it should object.

Mr. Alphand inquired as to how far the Secretary had gone in preparing the details of a plan. The Secretary responded that we had given considerable thought to the matter and had made some progress in outlining details of how the plan might operate. He could not provide an outline at the time but said he would endeavor to hand one to Mr. Alphand the following day.

Mr. Alphand observed that there would be an interim between the rejection by Egypt of the 18-Nation proposal and the establishment of the "shadow authority". If we should do nothing immediately following the Egyptian rejection of negotiations, it would appear throughout the world that the Western Powers had suffered a defeat. He inquired what could be done as an interim measure. He understood that it would take perhaps two weeks to put the new plan into operation. He wondered whether we could not soon make a statement regarding the "shadow authority" and also take immediate action to deny payments to Egypt of ships' tolls. Emphasizing that his views with regard to these measures were personal, he inquired whether he could say that the Secretary agreed with them.

The Secretary said that in considering the denial to Egypt at this time of tolls, we must take into full account the implications. We have had studies made by oil experts who have come to the conclusion that it would be possible, if necessary, to eliminate all tanker traffic through the Canal and still meet European requirements by sending tankers around the Cape and supplementing Middle Eastern shipments with oil from the Western Hemisphere. However, this would create economic burdens for most of the European countries, although the principal burden would fall upon the British because of their foreign exchange condition. We would have to be prepared to face up to that situation. However, if an announcement were made 1) conveying our intention to create the user association, 2) making clear that this would involve payments of fees to this authority (while reimbursing Egypt for any out-of-pocket expenses which that country might incur in connection with services to the association) and 3) stating that we are prepared if need be to meet any resulting situation by not sending tankers through the Canal but by meeting European needs in other ways, this might be fully adequate for the situation. This would demonstrate that the Egyptians do not have a strangle-hold on the users of the Canal. In considering any action now taken which might cause a denial of the Canal to our ships, however, we must be certain that we appreciate fully the economic considerations.

Mr. Alphand said that the French foreign exchange position was, as in the case of the British, serious and wondered whether the French could not pay for Western Hemisphere oil with francs. The Secretary replied that the payment itself was of course a commercial matter and that any United States governmental relief would require an act of Congress, which was not now in session.

Mr. Alphand repeated his concern lest something be announced quickly if a bad impression throughout the world was to be avoided. The Secretary agreed and observed that Mr. Eden must say something to Parliament on Wednesday.

Mr. Alphand asked again whether we should not immediately boycott the Canal. The Secretary replied that that was mainly for the French and the British to decide. So far as we were concerned, we were prepared to cooperate in a new oil program if that should become necessary either as a result of Nasser's action or as a means of bringing pressure upon Nasser. However, the British and French must decide whether they were prepared to accept the economic consequences.

Continuing, the Secretary discussed the extreme difficulties involved in military action, pointing out that the inauguration of hostilities might bring about a hopeless proposition. He realized the need to fight in certain circumstances as a last resort, but he thought that we must explore all alternatives. He fully agreed, however, that we could not afford to do nothing.

Upon his departure, Mr. Alphand commented privately to the Secretary that the latter's position was greatly misunderstood in France, where they had the impression that the Secretary did not wish to take any positive action because of the effect which it might have upon the forthcoming elections. The Secretary responded that in considering what should or should not be done in connection with this critical issue, he had never given any thought to the effect upon the elections. The position of the United States was to seek the solution which would be most effective in the circumstances.

---

200.   Memorandum of a Conversation, Department of State, Washington, September 10, 1956, 11:02 a.m. [1]

PARTICIPANTS

Ambassador Herve Alphand
The Secretary
John F. Simmons, U/PR [2]
William M. Rountree, NEA
C. Burke Elbrick, EUR

In the course of the call of the new French Ambassador this morning to present to the Secretary a copy of the credentials which will later be presented to President Eisenhower, a discussion took place of the latest developments on the Suez problem.

The Secretary read to the Ambassador a draft statement [3] which he felt was called for by Nasser's rejection of the 18 nation proposals. He then referred to this morning's Homer Bigart article in the *New York Times* which he characterized as entirely inaccurate. He said, for example, that contrary to Bigart's assertion the United States has given no thought to the Spanish "compromise plan". The Ambassador agreed that the Bigart article was "very bad". The Ambassador said that such articles as the Bigart article were widely disseminated in France and obviously produced a bad impression. He was entirely in agreement that something must be done to redress the situation. The Secretary said that he had thought of having the Department

---

[1] Source: Department of State, Central Files, 974.7301/9–1056. Secret. Drafted by Elbrick. The time of the meeting is from Dulles' Appointment Book. (Princeton University Library, Dulles Papers)
[2] Chief of Protocol.
[3] Presumably the statement is the same as that issued by Dulles on September 10; see footnote 3, Document 196.

spokesman issue a denial and he hoped that it would be effective although a denial of this sort never commands the same attention as the original story.

Ambassador Alphand said that he assumed that Nasser's proposal for a new conference does not change plans under discussion with the Secretary regarding future action. After reading the text of the Nasser statement [4] which the Ambassador had taken from the Agence France Presse ticker, the Secretary said that he did not think this development would make any change in the situation, although he would like to see an official text before making any definitive comment. The Ambassador felt that this new proposal by Nasser was another effort at "foot dragging" and was merely designed to gain time. He felt that the action we contemplate taking should not be delayed.

The Secretary remarked that the new Nasser proposal seems to differ somewhat from the previous Soviet proposal for a 46 nation meeting in that it proposes a meeting of the "other signatories" of the 1888 Convention. Presumably East Germany and the Balkan States as successors to the Austro-Hungarian Empire would be invited. Nasser says that he wants differing opinions on the Suez problem to be represented at such a conference. The Secretary said that he has already been made aware of the opinion of the states responsible for over 90 per cent of Canal traffic.

The Secretary said that he wanted to clarify the point made yesterday regarding the non-payment of Canal tolls. Either one or both of two conditions must exist before the plan for refusing to pay tolls to the Egyptian company can be put into effect. We must be prepared to route shipping around the Cape of Good Hope, and/ or we must be prepared to go forward with the plan for the association of Canal users. The Ambassador said that he thought that the Secretary had agreed yesterday that it would take approximately two weeks to organize such an association of users and that meanwhile we would make payments only to a blocked account. The Secretary said that if we stopped payments now it is obvious

---

[4] On September 10, the Egyptian Government issued a statement, in which it proposed that "as an immediate step, a negotiating body should be formed which would be representative of the different views held among the states using the Suez Canal and that discussions should take place forthwith to settle the composition, the venue and the date of the meeting of such a body. To it may also be entrusted the task of reviewing the Constantinople Convention of 1888." The Egyptian Government also affirmed its belief that solutions could be found for questions relating to: (1) the freedom and safety of navigation in the Canal; (2) the development of the Canal to meet the future requirements of navigation; and (3) the establishment of just and equitable tolls and charges. The Egyptian Embassy forwarded the text of the statement in a memorandum to the Department of State. (Department of State, Central Files, 974.7301/9–1056) The complete text of the statement is printed in *The Suez Canal Problem, July 26–September 22, 1956*, pp. 327–330.

that the ships will not get through since we would not "fight" them through the Canal but would route them around the Cape. The Ambassador observed that only strong action would be effective now and that otherwise the "Bigarts" around the world would think that we are weak and ineffectual. At the present time the French and British are paying tolls in the UK and France and the United States is paying tolls in Egypt. The Secretary reiterated that the United States is not prepared to take action to stop paying tolls in Egypt unless the French and the British are willing to accept the consequences of routing ships around Africa. Certainly it would be highly impolitic to provoke a situation which the French and British are not prepared to accept economically. The Ambassador acknowledged the validity of this point and said he would inquire of his Government.

The Ambassador said that it is proposed that Eden make a statement on Wednesday in the House of Commons and that the French Government do the same and that the United States Government thereupon indicate its support of these two statements. The statements would include: (1) an announcement of an agreement to create, on the basis of the 1888 Convention, an interim authority of users of the Canal; (2) a description of the rights and duties of this authority; and (3) an announcement that either tankers for the supply of Europe are being rerouted or a statement to the effect that if Nasser interrupts traffic as a result of this decision we are ready to face the situation. The Secretary thought that there was some virtue in demonstrating some flexibility on our side in indicating that we are prepared to face up to a possible blockade by Egypt by routing ships around Africa. This, he felt, might make it easier to bring about "de facto" what we want to accomplish "de jure". The offer of the users association to pay Egypt "out-of-pocket" expenses provided an intermediate position which Egypt might well accept. The discontinuance of the use of the Canal by the Western nations would cut traffic through the Canal to the point where Canal tolls would have to be raised to meet operating expenses and this in turn would impose additional burdens on the Arab and Asian countries.

The Secretary said that we are willing to consider playing this either way the British and French want. If it is only a matter of paying tolls into a blocked account he wished to make it clear that the United States was not prepared to fight its way through the Canal and would reroute ships around the Cape if they were denied passage through the Canal. Our allies must be prepared to face up to the economic implications of our decision. The Ambassador commented that the French foreign exchange position was extremely tight, and wondered whether the Secretary felt it would be possible for the French to pay francs for Western Hemisphere oil if it should become necessary to obtain it from that source as a result of the Canal closure. The Secretary said that this raised a difficult question, and that United States governmental assistance in this regard might require Congressional action. As the Ambassador knew, Congress is not now in session.

In reply to the Ambassador's question the Secretary repeated that he did not think that Nasser's action in calling for a new conference changed the position which we had previously established. The Ambassador proposed that he come with Sir Roger Makins to see the Secretary as soon as possible to show him the draft statements to be made in Paris and London this week, for which he hoped to obtain U.S. support. [5]

[5] At 3 p.m. on September 10, Ambassador Alphand presented his credentials to President Eisenhower. The two discussed, among other topics, the Suez situation. A memorandum of this conversation is in the Eisenhower Library, Whitman File, International File and in Department of State, Central Files, 601.5111/9-1056.

201.   Telegram From the Embassy in France to the Department of State [1]

Paris, September 10, 1956—1 p.m.

1158. Eyes only Barbour and Henderson. I have just had very disturbing interview with Pineau. He is very much upset at what he considers lack of definite policy in Washington. French Government feels that it is now imperative to take some action which they hope would be in the economic field, in particular Pineau mentioned agreement regarding non-payment of tolls to Egyptian authorities. Pineau said that during course of last week Department had turned down all positive suggestions for action of this nature on one excuse or another. He said the effect of this attitude by Department was to leave only one out for France and Great Britain, namely, war. He said he realized that policy of US was to exhaust every possible means for peaceful settlement, but he said in actual effect US through its inability to agree on any positive program of economic sanctions was actually bringing about very result it sought most to avoid, namely use of military force.

Pineau said that French and British prestige were now totally committed not only with their own public opinion but throughout Middle East and Africa. Therefore, there should not be slightest doubt in our minds that if no other solution could be found France

[1] Source: Department of State, Central Files, 974.7301/9-1056. Top Secret; Niact; Limit Distribution—Suez. Received at 11:45 a.m. Repeated Niact to London.

and Great Britain would resort to arms. Pineau said that he had felt up until the last four or five days that use of military force was most unlikely and some sort of a peaceful solution would be found. Now for the first time he was beginning to fear there might be no way out save use of military force. The one possibility would be prompt agreement by US, UK, France and other important shipping countries on a positive program of economic sanctions, including non-payment of tolls to Egyptian authorities. Pineau asked me to underline the gravity of the situation to Washington and to stress the fact that there was absolutely no time to be lost as present situation could not be allowed to continue.

During the course of his talk Pineau mentioned that he could no longer request French personnel, including French pilots to stay on in their jobs against their will. He said the French Government had made a tremendous effort in this regard up until now but there no longer was any excuse for asking the pilots to continue work and the decision would now be left up to them. He felt it probable that the majority of them would leave some time this week. [2]

Dillon

---

[2] In a follow-up message, Dillon reported that he had never seen Pineau as upset as during this conversation. The French Foreign Minister had given examples of two contradictory reports on the U.S. position, which he had received from the French Embassy in Washington, and had commented that he could not help but feel that there was no United States policy on Suez and that there did not seem to be a means available in the Department of State for arriving at one in the short time required. Pineau had asked Dillon, because of the implied criticism of the workings of the Department of State, not to report this part of the conversation. Dillon commented to the Department that: "I personally feel that unless there has been a change in heart in British government of which I am unaware, or unless the United States within course of the week can agree to a definite program of economic sanctions, chances of avoiding military action will be slim." (Telegram 1160 from Paris, September 10; *ibid.*)

---

202.   Editorial Note

At 1:53 p.m., September 10, Secretary Dulles telephoned President Eisenhower. Their conversation, as transcribed by Bernau, went as follows: "The Sec said the French Amb was in and repeated the suggestion which he made yesterday that if they had to reroute ships and buy oil here, would we help them get the dollars. The British are in a worse position than the French but are not holding out their hands. The Sec wondered re his reaction. The Pres said

Congress would have to do it. The Sec said that was the line he took—we could help the British by letting them off on the payment of interest on the amortization of the loan. The Sec does not know re the French. The Pres and the Sec do not think there is money in ICA for this. The Pres said they [presumably the French] are encouraging pilots to quit. The Sec said they [the pilots] are likely to quit en masse this week. The Sec is inclined to think from the talks he had with the Br and Fr Ambs that they will follow our lines rather than resort to force. The Pres said he might get just a small amount of money without going to Congress. The Sec referred to the Pres's transfer authority. The Pres said he would not encourage it without a session of Congress. They agreed if Congress were called back and were mad, there would be trouble." (Eisenhower Library, Dulles Papers, White House Telephone Conversations)

At 5:06 p.m. that day, President Eisenhower telephoned Secretary Dulles. Their conversation on Suez, as transcribed by Whitman, went as follows:

"In reading daily Suez reports [telegram 1158, *supra*], President finds Pineau is upset because of our decision, backing and filling, etc. President thought we had taken a pretty plain attitude on this from the start, & does not know exactly what he means.

"Dulles saw it—has no explanation except things we read in the press. He thinks the sort of things that upset them are stories such as Homer Bigart's in N.Y. *Times* this morning, which says we never thought the 18-nation plan would go through, & have another plan up our sleeves along the lines of the Spanish amendment. But there's no feeling on the part of diplomatic people here. President said Amb. Alphand seemed to understand where we stood.

"Mr. Dulles thought, too, perhaps they misinterpreted President's last press conference [September 5] statement as turning toward appeasement. President does not know what he said, but added that he always said the same thing as far as he understood language." (Eisenhower Library, Whitman File, Eisenhower Diaries. A separate memorandum of this telephone conversation, transcribed by Bernau, is *ibid.*, Dulles Papers, White House Telephone Conversations.)

203.   Report Prepared in the Executive Secretariat of the Department of State [1]

Summary No. 5   *Washington, September 10, 1956.*

SUMMARY OF DEVELOPMENTS IN SUEZ SITUATION

[Here follows a brief account of recent developments concerning the Five-Nation Committee. See Document 194.]

Present US Position

With regard to the reference of the problem to the UN, Secretary Dulles has now agreed with the British and French proposal that they should write to Secretary General Hammarskjold, "reporting" on the Suez situation but *not* asking for action at this time. This will establish a "priority" in case the Egyptians raise the question but is contrary to the earlier UK/French intention to take the problem to the UN for consideration and action.

We are not prepared to announce our unwillingness to pay tolls to Egypt as requested by the British and French, at least not until there has been a thorough study of the consequences which would result from the diversion of shipping from the Suez following such action, and an indication by the British and French that they are prepared to accept such consequences.

The Secretary has given informally to the British and communicated orally in summary to the French as a "think-piece" his Outline of Proposal for a Voluntary Association of Suez Users, designed to ensure the most effective possible enjoyment of the right of passage given by the Convention of 1888. It recommends that the governments of the users should organize a Cooperative Association of Suez Canal Users (CASU) to function through a 5-nation Executive Group chosen from among the members; said Executive Group to designate an Administrator who will manage the operations of the canal and will maintain relations and cooperate with the Egyptian Government to ensure that the canal remains free and unobstructed.

Dillon has indicated that, when talking with him, Pineau had not yet seen the report from the French Embassy in Washington of the Secretary's meeting with Alphand and the British Chargé on Sunday.

[Here follow a report that the Greek Government intended to inform the Egyptian Government that United States proposals on

---

[1] Source: Eisenhower Library, Whitman File, International File. Top Secret; Eyes Only for Designated Recipient. A marginal notation on the source text reads: "Pres has seen".

Suez offered a way to an honorable solution (reported in telegram 866 from Athens, September 10; Department of State, Central Files, 974.7301/9–1056) and an update on emergency and evacuation plans.]

---

204.   Memorandum of a Conversation, Department of State, Washington, September 10, 1956, 3:39 p.m. [1]

SUBJECT

    Suez Canal; Canadian Jets for Israel; Israel's Security; Export-Import Bank Loan to Israel

PARTICIPANTS

    The Secretary
    The Ambassador of Israel, Mr. Abba Eban
    Mr. Reuven Shiloah, Minister, Israel Embassy
    Mr. Slator C. Blackiston, ME

Suez Canal

    Ambassador Eban opened the conversation by saying that he had read the Secretary's statement [2] on the failure of the 5-nation Mission on Suez and that Israel shared U.S. regrets that the Mission had proved unsuccessful. Egypt's out of hand rejection of the committee's very reasonable proposals had prompted Israel to draw the following conclusions: 1) the Egyptian action is but another in a long series of anti-Western moves by Nasser; 2) the world should look carefully at the consequences of a Nasser victory coming out of this issue. Increased prestige would cause Nasser to look for new worlds to conquer such as the oil of the Near East, and Israel; 3) Nasser is not invincible, his difficulties are very great. Although Nasser may have caused great difficulties to others, he is also in trouble himself. These difficulties can be exploited. 4) It is not certain that SC action on the Suez case would be helpful. It is

---

[1] Source: Department of State, NEA Files: Lot 58 D 722, Israel—Aid & Assistance, 1954–1956. Confidential. Drafted by Blackiston. The time of the meeting is from Dulles' Appointment Book. (Princeton University Library, Dulles Papers) Three separate memoranda of this conversation cover different topics: "Suez Canal" (*ibid.*, Central Files, 974.7301/9–1056), "Israel's Defense Needs" (*ibid.*, 784A.5/9–1056), and "Israel's Economic Problems" (*ibid.*, 884A.00/9–1056). A briefing memorandum for Dulles by Rountree prior to this conversation is *ibid.*, 974.7301/9–1056.

[2] See footnote 3, Document 196.

believed a majority favoring international control of the Canal could be obtained in the SC but it is questionable whether Nasser would take any greater cognizance of SC action than he has of the proposals of the 5-nation committee. The Ambassador indicated Israel is most interested in not doing anything which would jeopardize its position with respect to the Canal which is so important to it. He sought continued consultation with the Department on the Suez problem in order that Israel might receive the benefit of our advice on this matter.

Israel still seeks written assurances from the U.S. that we support the right of Israel shipping to unfettered use of the Canal. The receipt of such assurances would encourage other nations which Israel has approached on this matter, to give similar statements of support.

The Secretary replied that he shared the Ambassador's views that Nasser's action showed a certain lack of responsiveness to world opinion. Nasser is probably more responsive to Arab views than he is to those of other nations of the world. Nasser was actually less responsive to the approach of the 5-nation committee than he had believed. We continue to feel that force should not be used against Nasser since it would set into motion forces and events the end of which could not be seen. We realize that he has many internal problems and that those problems can be exploited to his disadvantage. We have not been sympathetic to the British and French proposals with regard to steps to be taken in the UN against Egypt since we think that these steps would lead to difficulties for the West and might prove a two-edged sword. There is a question whether the SC has the authority to do more than make suggestions for procedural steps rather than substantive recommendations. It is doubtful whether the SC has the authority to force Egypt to make a new treaty along the lines of the 1888 Constantinople Convention. It is, however, quite possible that the British and French may write a letter to the SYG calling his attention to the situation and asking that the matter be put on the agenda of the SC without pressing for early consideration. This step would have certain procedural advantages and very few disadvantages. Israel is one of the countries which should be kept advised of developments and it is hoped that the Israel Embassy will keep in touch with an appropriate person in NE for this purpose. In pressing for a solution to the Suez problem Israel can be confident that the U.S. will endeavor to reach an agreement which will be of benefit to Israel. Ambassador Eban suggested that a tanker either of the U.S., U.K., France or other flag be sent through the Canal with a consignment of oil for Israel in order to test Nasser's reaction. The Secretary asked Mr. Blackiston to bring this suggestion to the attention of Mr. Rountree. [3]

Canadian Jets for Israel

The Ambassador expressed his appreciation for U.S. efforts to clarify in Ottawa our position with regard to the supply of Canadian F-86 jets to Israel. The problem now was narrowed down to the Canadian requirement, imposed by a commitment to Parliament, to make a public statement regarding the release of the planes. [4] The return of Lester Pearson was being awaited in connection with this matter. Israel would be happy if no statement were made; however, if the Canadian Government feels that a statement is required, Israel feels that now is the appropriate time for the announcement to be made. The Suez affair is for the moment relatively dormant—the Menzies committee has left Cairo and no other meetings are presently scheduled. The Israel Ambassador to Canada broached this subject to the Canadian FonOff this morning. The Secretary asked Mr. Blackiston to look into this matter. [5]

Israel's Security

The Ambassador said the mobilizations which have been going on in the Near East are causes of concern to Israel—especially the British and French troop movements to Cyprus and the more recently announced Parliamentary decision of Iran giving the government emergency powers. He noted numerous U.S. statements concerning U.S. determination to support the State of Israel in the event of aggression. The Ambassador asked whether the U.S. could now advise Israel of what steps the U.S. contemplated should aggression occur. The Secretary stated that the U.S. had planned to make a statement on the subject of plans to counter an aggressor in the Near East but Nasser's nationalization action occurred before the announcement could be made, and since then events have precluded

---

[3] Attached to the source text but not printed is a memorandum from Wilkins to Rountree, informing the Assistant Secretary of this aspect of the conversation.

[4] On September 4, the Embassy in Ottawa informed the Department of State that the Canadian Cabinet had decided to defer action on the release of the F-86's to Israel until the return of Foreign Minister Pearson during the latter part of September. The Embassy noted that "principal anxiety was avoidance rocking Suez boat during Menzies–Nasser negotiations." (Telegram 119; Department of State, Central Files, 784A.5622/9–456)

[5] In telegram 107 to Ottawa, September 11, the Department requested the Embassy to ascertain what the Canadian reaction had been to the Israeli approach concerning the F-86's. The telegram noted that Eban had sought United States support in this démarche, but that no commitment had been made to him. (Ibid., 784A.5622/9–1156) On September 13, the Embassy in Ottawa reported that the Canadian Cabinet at next week's meeting would decide to release the airplanes without waiting for Pearson's return. (Telegram 132; ibid., 784A.5622/9–1356)

the issuance of the announcement. The Secretary took the opportunity to express his disappointment that the Israel Government had failed to implement the proposals for reduction of tension on the Armistice Lines proposed by the SYG. Ambassador Eban said that in the opinion of the Israel Government those measures are not effective. The Secretary said that he and SYG Hammarskjold felt that Israel was utilizing the present Suez crisis as a means of avoiding taking action on those proposals. The Ambassador stated that Ben Gurion wished for some reciprocity from Egypt, such as releasing of Israel shipping, prior to unilaterally undertaking the steps proposed by the SYG.

Export-Import Loan

The Ambassador said that he understood the Bank had completed its study of Israel's loan application and that it was in a position to grant the loan if encouraged to do so by the Department. Israel was willing to accept any mission needed to investigate any aspects of the loan.

The Secretary explained that his preoccupation with the Suez matter had precluded his study of a paper[6] which he understood had been prepared in the Department on the matter. Asked by Mr. Eban whether he continued to favor the loan in principle the Secretary said that he wished to investigate the matter before giving a definitive answer. Ambassador Eban explained that the Israel Minister of Finance[7] was due in the U.S. this week and he hoped to be able to give him some definite news while he was here.

Socony–Vacuum Operations in Israel

There followed a discussion of the Socony-Vacuum decision to terminate its operations in Israel. The Ambassador said it came at a very bad time in view of the Suez crisis. He sought U.S. intervention with Saudi Arabia to halt the Saudi Arabian pressure which had prompted the Socony-Vacuum decision.

Alternative Pipe Line

There was a discussion of an alternative pipeline through Israel and the Ambassador stated that the Israel Government had been in touch with American companies on this matter. The Secretary commented that presumably representatives of these companies would

---

[6] Reference is presumably to a memorandum from Prochnow (E) and Rountree to Dulles, dated September 6, on the subject of "Israel Application for Export-Import Bank Loan". (*Ibid.*, 884A.10/9–656) There is no indication whether Dulles actually saw it.

[7] Levi Eshkol.

call in the Department to discuss this matter. The Ambassador asked whether Israel officials could be put in touch with a U.S. committee which, he understood, was studying problems which would arise should the Canal be closed and the pipelines cut. He hoped that Israel's views and proposals could be made known to this committee. The Secretary explained that the committee to which the Ambassador referred was concerned with long-range aspects of the problem and that, therefore, he doubted whether Israel officials would benefit from talking to the committee members.

---

205.   Memorandum of a Conversation, Department of State, Washington, September 10, 1956, 5:26 p.m. [1]

SUBJECT

Suez Canal

PARTICIPANTS

Sir Roger Makins, British Ambassador
J.E. Coulson, Minister, British Embassy
The Secretary
Herman Phleger, Legal Adviser—L
William M. Rountree, NEA

Ambassador Makins began by saying that in the messages which he had just received the British Government had expressed its gratitude for the Secretary's efforts. He handed to the Secretary a letter dated September 10 [2] setting forth several messages from London. He said that, in brief, London agreed with the Secretary's proposal for the Canal users organization but was up against an extremely tight time schedule because of the meeting of Parliament.

The Ambassador said that importance was attached to the proposed letter informing the President of the Security Council of the Suez situation, but the British Government regarded that as a compliment to announcing the users association. They hoped the letter would be signed by the United States, as well as by the British and French, and the Ambassador said he would communicate later with the Secretary on this point.

[1] Source: Department of State, Central Files, 974.7301/9–1056. Secret; Suez Distribution. Drafted by Rountree. The time of the meeting is from Dulles' Appointment Book. (Princeton University Library, Dulles Papers)
[2] Infra.

Regarding the detailed users association plan, the Ambassador said he assumed that there was no question that the proposal would not be negotiated with Egypt but that the latter would merely be informed. Also, the British Government assumed the adoption of the plan would not involve recognition of the validity of the Egyptian nationalization decree. The Secretary said that he concurred and pointed out that the latter point had been made clear in the preamble of his paper setting forth the plan.

The Ambassador said the British Government would like the composition of the proposed Executive Committee to be the same as the Five-Man negotiating committee which was recently in Cairo, with the addition of the United Kingdom and France. Continuing, he said the British assumed that the users association would be a legal entity, that it would be organized as soon as possible and that it would have a bank account. The Secretary said that his own plan contained a provision for a bank account. Regarding the question of the legal basis of the organization, he wondered whether the international status would not be lost if the association were incorporated. The act of incorporation must be under the laws of some state, and it would seem to him that there were real disadvantages to doing that inasmuch as to have maximum power, the group should act as nations and not as a mere corporate body. Mr. Phleger observed that the organization might be considered to be in the form of an international partnership. The Secretary felt we should avoid giving the organization the role of private citizen. In any event, it could act as an entity and the Administrator could carry out appropriate functions including depositing and drawing out funds established in an account at his disposal.

The Secretary said he had met earlier this morning with the French Ambassador and had emphasized to him that when the plan went into effect and the Canal tolls were denied to the Egyptian Government, it was possible that ships would be denied passage. In this event, there would be substantial economic consequences. Ambassador Makins observed that if ships were denied passage, it would be the intent to take the matter to the Security Council and, under the circumstances, he assumed the United States would stand by the British and French. He asked the Secretary to confirm his understanding. The Secretary said that certainly in principle the United States would stand in back of them but, of course, we would not know what relief they would seek. The action requested of the Security Council was, of course, an important consideration.

The Ambassador reverted to the fact that the British were acting under time pressures. If they avoided taking the matter to the Security Council and adopted the alternative proposal of the users association, the Prime Minister felt that to hold his position he would have to say something along the lines set forth in the letter of September 10 which the Ambassador had just handed to the Secretary. He inquired whether the Secretary approved the substance of that statement. The Secretary said that the wording of the statement was not clear in certain respects. It might be implied from one point that the United States, in agreeing to the wording, would also agree to joining in military action. Of course, we would not want any misunderstanding in that regard. The Ambassador thought the Secretary would question that portion of the statement, and said that he himself did not know exactly what was meant. Mr. Phleger observed that it seemed to imply that the US, UK and France had decided physically to take over the Canal by any means.

The Secretary thought the statement might also be more clear regarding payments which might be made to Egypt. He felt that Egypt should, as a minimum, be reimbursed for out-of-pocket expenses.

The Secretary said that before giving the Ambassador his considered reaction to the statement suggested by the Prime Minister, he would like to talk with the President. He would try to do so as soon as possible so that he could give an early reply to the Ambassador. The Ambassador said that if he could have his observations by noon the following day, adequate time should be provided to communicate to Mr. Eden.

The Secretary stated that the Ambassador had earlier made the remark which he wished again to comment upon. We had never opposed going to the United Nations; although we had pointed out what we thought were serious impediments to bringing the matter before that body in the form which had been suggested by the British. He had also pointed out that we could not agree in advance to oppose any appeal which might be made by other countries in the United Nations not to resort to force. He thought the decision not to take the matter to the Security Council was entirely one for the British to make, although he thought it incumbent upon him as a friend to state his reaction to the British proposal.

Ambassador Makins said that it would be dangerous to go to the United Nations unless the British had complete American support in all circumstances. Since the Secretary had been unable to give this assurance, his Government felt that the alternative which the Secretary had put forward should be adopted.

The Ambassador stated that the Foreign Office had informed him that the Canal pilots were at the end of their rope and the British Government did not think it was possible to hold them against their will. They thought the best way of keeping the pilots was to make an announcement regarding the users association as soon as possible, and it was believed the pilots would be available for employment with that agency.

The Secretary inquired whether the Ambassador had heard from London regarding the British position on the question which he had raised about possible economic consequences of denying Canal tolls to Egypt or diverting tankers from passage through the Suez Canal. He pointed out that the users association program involved the British and the French facing up to this problem. The Ambassador said he had as yet received no answer to his communications in this subject. He hoped to receive further elucidations before meeting with the Secretary the following morning. [3]

---

[3] At 7 p.m. September 10, Dulles telephoned President Eisenhower. Their conversation on Suez, as transcribed by Asbjornson, went as follows: "The Sec telephoned the President and said he had just seen Makins, who had left a letter with him [infra] and which the Secretary said he would send to the President this evening. (This was done.) It relates to the position Eden wants to take when he addresses Parliament on Wednesday [September 12]. On the whole, it is encouraging and is along the lines suggested in your letter [Document 192]. The Sec said that on the whole what he wants to say goes somewhat too far. The Sec said he would be working tonight on some alternative suggestions. The Sec said he had a meeting set up with the President for 10:45 tomorrow morning saying he had promised Makins a reply by noon tomorrow. The British had to make some pretty critical decisions. The Sec said he thought Makins would want to turn these things in the letter over in his mind." (Eisenhower Library, Dulles Papers, White House Telephone Conversations)

---

206.   Letter From the British Ambassador (Makins) to the Secretary of State [1]

Washington, September 10, 1956.

MY DEAR SECRETARY OF STATE: I reported our conversation of yesterday about the proposed Voluntary Association of Suez Canal Users, and I have now heard how the position is seen in London.

2. On Wednesday, September 12 at 2:30 p.m., the Prime Minister has to make a speech in the House of Commons announcing the policy of the United Kingdom Government on the situation caused by Colonel Nasser's summary rejection of the 18 power proposals. This summary rejection will be a second blow to Western influence

---

[1] Source: Department of State, Central Files, 974.7301/9–1056. Top Secret. Handed by Makins to Secretary Dulles during the conversation which began at 5:26 p.m.; see *supra.* A copy is also in the Eisenhower Library, Whitman File, Dulles–Herter Series.

in the Middle East unless it is followed at once by a statement of a clear and decisive Western policy in the light of it.

3. Our initial reaction to Nasser's action on July 26 was to make military preparations which, failing an agreed settlement satisfactory to us, would enable us to resume physical control of the Canal. We readily co-operated with the United States Government in promoting the London Conference and seeking a peaceful settlement. That effort has failed. Therefore our original plan of resuming physical control of the Canal would appear to be the next logical step.

4. It was at one time our understanding that the United States Administration considered that, in the event of the talks with Nasser failing, recourse should be had to the United Nations. That is indeed our view, and discussions have been taking place between us as to how to frame our request to the President of the Security Council for a meeting and a subsequent resolution. Her Majesty's Government have made it clear that such action would be extremely dangerous unless they had complete assurance of United States support; it now seems that they cannot count on this in all circumstances.

5. Her Majesty's Government have now received the alternative proposition of a Users' Club. For that to be a practical alternative to going to the Security Council, it would be necessary for the Prime Minister to announce on Wednesday Anglo-American agreement upon this course. He would have to be able to say that the Users' Organisation was to be set up forthwith with British, American and French participation at least; that all dues payable to the Users' ships would forthwith be paid to the new organisation; that the new organisation propose to exercise the rights of members under the 1888 Convention; that pilots would be provided for its ships; and that it would call upon the Egyptian Government to provide the necessary co-operation to enable the organisation to function. It would have to be stated that if the Egyptian Government sought to interfere with the operations of the organisation or refused to extend the necessary co-operation on land, then the Egyptian Government would be regarded as being in breach of the Convention of 1888, and users could take such steps as seemed fit to them to enforce their rights. Anything short of that would not be regarded as an indication that we meant business.

Yours sincerely,

Roger Makins

207.   Report Prepared in the Executive Secretariat of the Department of State [1]

Summary No. 6   *Washington, September 11, 1956.*

SUMMARY OF DEVELOPMENTS IN SUEZ SITUATION

British Views

Kirkpatrick told Barbour yesterday that the British have been encouraged by the President's message and the Secretary's conversations with British Embassy representatives in Washington. [2] They now feel that there is a large measure of identity of views between us.

Barbour comments on the significance of Kirkpatrick's now envisaging the application of such relatively long-range measures as economic sanctions. This is in contrast with the views expressed by Eden at his luncheon for Senator George on Thursday [3] when the Prime Minister contended that such measures would not be effective with sufficient rapidity to maintain the British position with the other Arab states. Barbour also noted that action toward the establishment of a canal users organization such as the Secretary has suggested will be sufficient to maintain pro-Western sentiment in the other Arab countries.

Embassy London has been informed [4] that a White Paper on Suez will be presented at the opening of the special session of Parliament tomorrow. Eden will then lead off the debate. The Embassy also reports that leading Conservative MP's consider that a firm decision has been taken to bring the Suez matter to the UN, but that it has not yet been determined whether the Security Council or a special session of the General Assembly should be used. Nevertheless, the Tory MP's continue to back Eden and the Government firmly in a decision to use force if and when the Prime Minister finds it necessary.

British Labour Party Position

Gaitskell suggested to Senator George and Holmes yesterday [5]

---

[1] Source: Eisenhower Library, Whitman File, International File. Top Secret; Eyes Only for Designated Recipient. A marginal notation on the source text reads: "File/ DE".

[2] Reported in telegram 1366 from London, September 10, not printed. (Department of State, Central Files, 684A.86/9–1056)

[3] Reported in telegram 1335 from London, September 6, not printed. (*Ibid.*, 974.7301/9–656)

[4] Reported in telegram 1383 from London, September 10, not printed. (*Ibid.*, 974.7301/9–1056)

[5] Reported in telegram 1368 from London, September 10, not printed. (*Ibid.*)

that a compromise over Suez might be reached by recognizing that Egypt should handle the "daily operation" of the canal while leaving to an international council specific matters such as freedom of passage, tolls, development, and possibly the larger question of investments in Egypt. Gaitskell commented, as have other Labour Party leaders, that he would welcome UN consideration of the canal dispute.

[Here follows a report of Pineau's conversation with Dillon of September 10. See telegram 1158, Document 201.]

Emergency and Evacuation Plans

Although Byroade has reported substantially increased tension,[6] Henderson says[7] the security situation appears good at present. He notes that Nasser seems to have both the desire and the capability to maintain security and avoid incidents, but that this situation could change under severe Anglo-French pressure or armed attack. If Americans begin to leave Egypt, other foreign communities would probably become panicky, and the Egyptians themselves would become angry and frightened. Consequently, Henderson advises against evacuation unless Anglo-French armed action is imminent.

The first contingent of British Embassy dependents has already left Cairo, and a special French evacuation ship is expected by the end of the week. In Syria, the French Embassy has been ordered to reduce its staff and evacuate dependents; in Jordan, dependents of British troops have been advised to leave.

Embassy Jidda states that it expects the Saudis to try to protect Americans even if war comes. And we have received assurances from President Chamoun that security will be maintained in Lebanon. So far we have no plans for going beyond the Phase I stage which has been instituted only in Egypt, Syria and Jordan.

(Summary closed 2:05 p.m., September 10, 1956)

---

[6] In telegram 668 from Cairo, September 8, not printed. (*Ibid.*, 974.7301/9–856)
[7] In telegram 671 from Cairo, September 8, not printed. (*Ibid.*, 274.1122/9–856)

208.   Memorandum of a Conversation, Department of State, Washington, September 11, 1956, 12:25 p.m. [1]

SUBJECT

Suez Canal

PARTICIPANTS

Sir Roger Makins, British Ambassador
Mr. J. E. Coulson, Minister, British Embassy
Secretary of the Treasury Humphrey
The Secretary
L—Mr. Phleger
EUR—Mr. Elbrick
NEA—William M. Rountree
(Mr. Flemming, Director, Office of Defense Mobilization, joined the
   group for the latter part of the discussion.)

Ambassador Makins said he had just received another important message from London. Mr. Lloyd had discussed with Messrs. Mollet and Pineau the Secretary's document setting forth the Canal users association plan. [2] They were all grateful to the Secretary for having provided this suggestion. They agreed in principle and were particularly anxious for American participation. They attached great importance to the payment of dues to the association by all participants, including the United States. On this basis they had decided not to bring the Suez matter before the Security Council. If the plan did not work, however, they would go to the Council without delay. They hoped the Secretary would agree to the statement which Mr. Eden proposed to make before Parliament and that he would say something along similar lines. The French proposed to make a statement comparable to Mr. Eden's. Mr. Pineau and Mr. Lloyd had expressed the hope that they could meet urgently with Mr. Dulles to work out details of the plan, including arrangements for the participation of other countries. Finally, the British and French Foreign Ministers asked if Mr. Dulles would authorize the United States representative at the UN to join with the British and French in sending an informative letter to the Security Council, the text of which had been amended in accordance with suggestions earlier made by the Secretary. [3]

---

[1] Source: Department of State, Central Files, 974.7301/9–1156. Secret; Suez Distribution. Drafted by Rountree. The time of the meeting is from Dulles' Appointment Book. (Princeton University Library, Dulles Papers)

[2] See Document 198.

[3] A copy of the draft letter to President of the Security Council is in Department of State, Central Files, 974.7301/9–1156. A handwritten notation on the copy reads: "Left w. Secretary, by Makins 9/11/56 12:25 p.m." The draft letter, to be circulated to members of the Security Council, affirmed among other points, that the British and

The Secretary said he wanted to make it clear that he had never opposed taking the matter before the Security Council. He had felt it his duty to point out certain hazards and told the British and French that we could not commit ourselves to oppose any amendment which might be proposed on the question of the use of force. He now understood that the British and French had decided not to take the matter to the Security Council. He assumed that was an action taken by them on the basis of their own judgment and not under the assumption that he opposed any such action. The Ambassador said there could be no misunderstanding in this regard. The Secretary's position had been set forth clearly in messages which he telegraphed to London yesterday.

The Secretary referred to the letter which Ambassador Makins handed him yesterday [4] setting forth the position which Mr. Eden intended to take in his speech on Wednesday. He said that he had discussed this matter with the President and was now prepared to give to the Ambassador a paper (copy attached) [5] on the American position which Mr. Eden might, if he liked, use in his speech. The Ambassador read the statement and said that it seemed to make the case clear. He was grateful for the Secretary's assistance.

The Secretary said he should point out the main departures from the British draft. First, his statement brought in the fact that when the association collected dues, some equitable portion would go to Egypt. Second, he phrased the proposal to indicate that the organization of the Canal users would be proposed by those of the 18-Nations which wished to do so. Third, he had indicated in the last sentence that action should be taken through the UN, which he assumed the British in any event would want to do in the first instance, and otherwise as may be deemed appropriate to the circumstances.

The Secretary said he would inform the Ambassador as soon as possible as to whether we would be prepared to join in the informative letter to the UN. As to making a statement on the users association following Mr. Eden's speech in Parliament, he said that

---

French Governments considered that the Egyptian Government's refusal to negotiate on the basis of the Eighteen-Power proposal "is an aggravation of the situation, which if allowed to continue, would constitute a manifest danger to peace and security."

[4] Document 206.

[5] According to the record of the President's Daily Appointments, Dulles met with Eisenhower at 10:32 the morning of September 10. (Eisenhower Library) The memorandum of their conversation prepared by Dulles, however, does not mention a discussion of the Suez situation. Attached to that memorandum of conversation is a memorandum, presumably by Dulles, which contains guidance on the Suez question, for use at the President's press conference. Also attached is a copy of the paper handed to Makins at the 12:25 meeting. A marginal notation on this copy of the paper reads: "Taken to WH by Sec 9/11/56 10:45 a.m. cc to Makins 9/11/56—12:25 p.m." (Ibid., Dulles Papers, Meetings with the President)

he was holding a press conference on Thursday[6] and thought that that would be an appropriate time to make his comments. The Ambassador agreed that this timing would be quite satisfactory. Regarding the proposed meeting with the British and French Foreign Ministers, the Secretary wished to consider the matter and said that he would let the Ambassador know later. He observed that one of the great dangers of the proposed association was that it might be entirely a Western organization, primarily in view of the fact that most of the vessels were owned by Western countries. He thought we should endeavor to bring in a few Asian countries. Perhaps the best approach would be to work for a nucleus of the organization consisting of the five nations on the Menzies Committee plus the British and French.

Regarding the payment of tolls to the association, the Secretary stated that we could undertake only to instruct vessels of US registry and not vessels owned by Americans but which flew foreign flags. He said he understood Secretary Humphrey would be prepared to amend the Treasury licensing procedure with respect to Egyptian assets in order to accomplish the objective of having American ships pay to the association. He would anticipate moving as rapidly as possible when the organization was established.

The Secretary said that the President had emphasized this morning that the broader aspects of the problem should be given urgent consideration. He thought we should think ahead in terms of achieving minimum dependency upon the Canal. However things might go, there was likely to be some stoppage in the Canal. If Nasser should accept the users association, all would be well, but that was perhaps over-optimistic. The Secretary thought there was an advantage in not formalizing things so that the plan would have to be accepted in a formal way by Nasser. By proceeding on a de facto basis, it might be conceivable that Nasser would allow the arrangements to proceed for a while. However, we must anticipate that Nasser will refuse to let the ships go through. The Secretary said that the President felt it important to avoid continuing dependency upon this single artery. Secretary Humphrey had observed that a cardinal rule of business was to avoid getting into a position where one is in a bottleneck with a hostile competitor's hand on the bottle.

The Secretary turned to the question of the economic consequences upon Great Britain and France of the denial of passage of ships through the Canal. He said he had asked Secretary Humphrey to discuss the financial situation in this regard. Secretary Humphrey said he thought it might be possible to help in financing dollar purchases of oil on a temporary basis. However, the only avenue

---

[6] September 13.

would appear to be the Export-Import Bank. Loans might be made to the UK and France for US purchases. He did not think other European countries would have urgent need for this type of dollar assistance. Such loans would probably be in the form of a line of credit. The terms of the loans and other details would have to be worked out.

The Secretary said he understood that Ambassador Makins was anxious at the moment to send telegrams to London. He thought it would be good if the Ambassador could meet later with Mr. Flemming to discuss the oil problem generally and possible long-term and short-term solutions. He emphasized his belief that we should have a program which would end once and for all our critical dependence upon the Suez Canal. It was arranged that Ambassador Makins and his colleagues would get together with Mr. Flemming later in the day.

[Attachment]

Draft Statement Prepared in the Department of State

Washington, September 10, 1956.

Since the Government of Egypt is unwilling to negotiate an accord regarding the use of the Canal in accordance with the 1888 Convention, as proposed by the 18 nations at London, the United States believes that it is appropriate that the governments which derive for their vessels the right to the free use of the Suez Canal should associate themselves together for the collective enjoyment and exercise by their vessels of their rights. We do not believe that these rights can be safeguarded if each nation, much less if each ship, fends for itself. We believe that, under the circumstances, practical cooperation on the part of Egypt can only be effectively achieved if the users are organized so that they can deal jointly with Egypt and Egypt deal with them jointly.

Accordingly, if the United Kingdom alone or in association with others should propose a users' association to be organized by the 18 sponsors of the London proposals, or such of them as were so disposed, and perhaps others, the United States would participate in such a users' organization.

We assume that the users' organization would exercise on behalf of the users the rights which are theirs under the 1888 Convention and seek such cooperation with Egypt as would achieve the results designed to be guaranteed by that Convention. In accordance with this principle the users' association would, among other things, provide qualified pilots for the users' ships; would receive the dues from ships passing through the Canal, which would be used to defray the expenses of the organization and to pay appropriate compensation to Egypt for its contribution to the maintenance of the Canal and the facilities of transit; and so far as practical arrange for the pattern of traffic of member vessels through the Canal.

It is our view that if the Egyptian Government sought to interfere with such operations of the users' organization or refused to take the necessary measures for insuring the execution of the Convention of 1888, that would be a breach by Egypt of the Convention. In this event the parties to or beneficiaries of the Convention would be free to take steps to assure their rights through the United Nations or through other action appropriate to the circumstances.

---

209.   Memorandum of a Conversation, Department of State, Washington, September 11, 1956, 2:50 p.m. [1]

SUBJECT

Suez Canal

PARTICIPANTS

Herve Alphand, French Ambassador
Jacques Vimont, Minister, French Embassy
The Secretary
William M. Rountree, NEA
Stuart W. Rockwell, NEA/NE

Ambassador Alphand said he was pleased to inform the Secretary that the French and British Governments had agreed reactions to several aspects of plans in connection with the Suez Canal. Within this context he had the following messages:

1. The French and British had agreed to the proposal for the international authority and the outline plan contained in the Secretary's paper;

2. The French and British assumed that the U.S. Government would give all support to the implementation of the plan. Mr.

---

[1] Source: Department of State, Central Files, 974.7301/9–1156. Secret; Suez Distribution. Drafted by Rountree. The time of the meeting is from Dulles' Appointment Book. (Princeton University Library, Dulles Papers)

Alphand said that if Mr. Eden made his statement tomorrow on the plan, the French would make one simultaneously. He hoped that the US would make some sort of statement on Thursday [2] and wondered if the Secretary agreed that this might be done. The Secretary said he planned to comment on the matter at his press conference Thursday. The Secretary gave Mr. Alphand a copy of a statement which he had earlier handed to the British Ambassador [3] setting forth, for use by Prime Minister Eden in connection with his speech, the American position with respect to the Canal users proposal; and,

3. The French and British Governments had decided not to bring the Suez matter before the Security Council for action, but would limit themselves to a letter merely informing the President of the Council of the situation.

Mr. Alphand said that if the Secretary agreed to points 2 and 3 above, the British and French Foreign Ministers would be ready to meet him in London, Paris or Washington to study the Canal users plan in detail and to consider arrangements for associating other countries with it.

The Ambassador added that he would send to the Secretary a note containing the text of what he had just stated under instructions from his Government.

The Secretary commented that he believed we had made progress. The French Ambassador said that this was due to Mr. Dulles' efforts. The Secretary added that he was not hopeful that Nasser would cooperate. If he did not, then we would come to the second point, the possible blocking of the Canal. We might need to send tankers around the Cape. He had talked with the Secretary of the Treasury this morning about the economic strictures which this would place upon the UK and France. Mr. Humphrey had been of the opinion that it might be possible to arrange an Export-Import Bank loan to finance exports of oil from the US to the UK and France. The Bank was going to look into this. This might take care of the situation for a time, said the Secretary, but it would not be a permanent solution. Unfortunately, we could not look ahead now more than a few weeks or a month or so at a time.

The Ambassador asked for the Secretary's comments on the meeting he had previously mentioned. He said he thought the French and British Governments were willing to send representatives to Washington. The Secretary said this was very good of the two Governments. He would think this over and would give his reply tomorrow.

The Ambassador then raised on a personal basis a matter on which he had not been instructed by his Government. According to news reports the Suez Canal Company had announced that its pilots

---

[2] September 13.
[3] See the memorandum of conversation, *supra.*

were free to do what they wished after September 15. Mr. Alphand thought this was very harmful. Of course, it was a decision of a private company, but it would be hard to demonstrate that the British and French Governments were not responsible. These Governments could press the Company to retain its employees but they might be criticized for this. The Secretary said in his view it was essential to keep the pilots on the job until they could be taken over in the new users' pool. The supply of pilots should not be allowed to be dissipated. The USSR might fill the vacancies, and we would have no pilots for the new association. The Secretary hoped that France and the UK could exert influence on the Company so that the pilots would remain at work. Mr. Rountree commented that the object of the new proposal was to protect the users' interests in the Canal. If Egypt blocked a ship with users' pilots aboard, then the blame for disruption of transit would fall squarely on Egypt. If, on the other hand, it appeared meanwhile that by encouraging their nationals to leave their jobs as pilots, the UK and France were responsible for impeding passage, this would have harmful effects on the plan.

The Ambassador asked if the Secretary would be willing to say the above to the two Governments. The Secretary replied in the affirmative directing that a telegram be sent to London and Paris expressing the hope that the UK and France would exert such influence as they could to keep their nationals on the job as pilots until the users' pool could take them over. The Secretary also said that he would appreciate it if Ambassador Alphand would similarly communicate with the French Government. The Ambassador agreed to cable at once to Paris.

Ambassador Alphand then asked how we would go about approaching the other 15 of the 18 nations we hoped might participate initially in the plan. The Secretary suggested we should start with the nucleus of the 5 members of the Menzies Committee, plus France and the UK. Mr. Alphand commented that the initial group should not get too big.

The Secretary said he had not thought much about invoking the meeting. It would be better to move on this on Thursday. If the general scheme met with British and French approval, we could divide the approach to the other nations. The US could take Iran. France perhaps together with the US could take Ethiopia. The UK could handle Sweden and Australia.

210. Memorandum of a Telephone Conversation Between the British Ambassador (Makins) and the Assistant Secretary of State for Near Eastern, South Asian, and African Affairs (Rountree), Washington, September 11, 1956, 3:30 p.m. [1]

SUBJECT

Suez Canal

I telephoned Sir Roger Makins at 3:30 p.m. September 11 and told him, at the Secretary's request, that we appreciate the opportunity courteously afforded us to go along (as a signatory) with the UK-French letter to the Secretary-General. However, we feel that it would be preferable for us not in this way and at this time to create an identity of interests which might prove somewhat of an embarrassing limitation on the UK and France in the future. (A copy of the UK-French letter is attached.) [2]

I told Ambassador Makins that the Secretary had given to French Ambassador Alphand [3] a copy of the statement of the US position on the Canal users plan which he had handed to Sir Roger this morning. Ambassador Makins said he was glad the Secretary had provided a copy to the French Ambassador. He had intended discussing the matter with Mr. Alphand later today.

I told Sir Roger of the Secretary's conversation today with Ambassador Alphand concerning ticker reports to the effect that the Suez Canal pilots had been told by the Suez Canal Company that they were at liberty to leave Egypt after September 15. I said the Secretary had asked Ambassador Alphand to communicate to the Foreign Office his view that the Canal Company should be requested not to encourage the pilots to leave at this time. It seemed to us that withdrawal of the pilots before inauguration of the users association might bring about a situation in which the Canal traffic would be stopped in circumstances where the British and French would receive the full blame. It was the object of the users association plan to create a situation in which either Canal traffic continued under satisfactory arrangements, or ships were impeded in their traffic clearly as a result of action on the part of the Egyptian Government. Premature withdrawal of the pilots would, in our

---

[1] Source: Department of State, Central Files, 974.7301/9–1156. Secret. Drafted by Rountree.

[2] See footnote 3, Document 208. On September 12, the French and U.K. Representatives forwarded this letter to the President of the Security Council with the request that its contents be brought to the notice of the Security Council. (U.N. doc. S/3645)

[3] See the memorandum of conversation, *supra.*

judgment, jeopardize the plan's chances of success. Moreover, the pilots constituted the most important single element in the plan, and they should not be withdrawn from Egypt until we had alternative arrangements clearly worked out whereby they would be employed immediately by the users association. I asked if Sir Roger would communicate our views to the Foreign Office and ask that the British Government use its influence to avoid precipitous action with respect to the pilots. Sir Roger recalled that he had mentioned to the Secretary the fact that the pilots were most unhappy and wanted to leave, and that the British felt that they, as free agents, should be permitted either to stay or leave as they wished. He said that he would, of course, communicate the Secretary's views to the Foreign Office. I recalled that the Secretary had always pointed out the vital importance of keeping hold of the pilots.

---

211.   Report Prepared in the Executive Secretariat of the Department of State [1]

Summary No. 7   *Washington, September 12, 1956.*

SUMMARY OF DEVELOPMENTS IN SUEZ SITUATION

UK Views

Lloyd has told Aldrich [2] that the UK Government is particularly pleased with the Secretary's plan for an association of canal users because it constitutes a "slap in the face" for Nasser, and that it will be popular in Parliament for that very reason. If the US will "join this club" and pay the canal tolls to the association, Eden will express approval of the plan in Parliament. Thereafter, the British Government will ask for Security Council action requiring Nasser to implement the 1888 Convention on the basis of this plan. With US support, the British hope that this action would be approved by the SC by a vote of 9 to 2.

Aldrich comments that Lloyd expects if, under these circumstances, Nasser should refuse the proposed plan, the UK and France

---

[1] Source: Eisenhower Library, Whitman File, International File. Top Secret; Eyes Only for Designated Recipient. A marginal notation by Goodpaster on the source text reads: "DE noted. G".

[2] Reported in telegram 1410 from London, September 11, not printed. (Department of State, Central Files, 684A.86/9–1156)

would be on as firm ground as possible in taking whatever measures might then seem to be desirable.

Canal Pilots

In the light of press reports on the Canal Company's action in authorizing the pilots to leave Egypt, we told Embassies London and Paris urgently to ask the British and French Governments [3] to exert such influence as they can to keep the pilots on the job until an agreement can be reached on the proposed users' association and the association can take over the pilots now working in Suez as a pool for future operations. The Embassies were to point out that, if the users of the canal do not do their best to keep their nationals on the job, the blame for disrupting traffic will fall on them and a major purpose of the users' association might be defeated.

In reply to our approach, Pineau has responded [4] that it is impossible for the French Government to take the action requested. However, he also said that the 60 pilots who have completed their vacations in Europe are being sent to Cyprus and will be immediately available for employment by the users' association, and the pilots now returning to France will be similarly available when their vacations are over.

Arab Support for Nasser's Counterproposal

Nuri has told Gallman [5] that Syria and Jordan have already replied favorably to the Egyptian approach. Iraq will turn down Nasser's request for support and is hoping to induce Saudi Arabia to take similar action. Lebanon still has the matter under consideration but, says Nuri, may be influenced also to turn down Egypt if Iraq and Saudi Arabia act together.

(Summary closed 11:25 a.m., September 12, 1956)

---

[3] Instructions were sent in telegram 1812 to London and telegram 935 to Paris, September 11, neither printed. (*Ibid.*, 974.7301/9–1156) The Canal Company notified its non-Egyptian employees on September 11. (Telegram 1185 from Paris, September 11; *ibid.*)

[4] Reported in telegram 1205 from Paris, September 12. (*Ibid.*, 974.7301/9–1256) On September 12, Aldrich discussed the Suez pilot situation with Lloyd. (Telegram 1425 from London, September 12; *ibid.*)

[5] Reported in telegram 421 from Baghdad, September 11, not printed. (*Ibid.*, 686A.87/9–1156)

212.   Editorial Note

On September 12, in a statement made to the British House of Commons, Prime Minister Eden announced that the British Government had decided, in agreement with France and the United States, to establish without delay an organization to enable the users of the Canal to exercise their rights. This users' association was to be provisional in character and was meant to prepare the way for a permanent system which could be established with the full agreement of all interested parties. According to Eden, the users' association would employ pilots, undertake responsibility for the coordination of traffic through the Canal, and, in general, act as a voluntary association for the exercise of the rights of Suez Canal users. The Egyptian authorities would be requested to cooperate in maintaining the maximum flow of traffic through the Canal, and Egypt would receive appropriate payment from the association in return for the facilities which it provided. Transit dues, however, would be paid to the users' association and not to the Egyptian Government. The membership of this association would consist of Great Britain, France, and the United States; other principal users of the Canal would also be invited to join. In addition, Eden made clear that if the Egyptian Government sought to interfere with the operations of the association or refused to cooperate with the association, then Her Majesty's Government and the others concerned would be free to take further steps, either through the United Nations or by other means, for the assertion of their rights. (House of Commons, *Parliamentary Debates*, 5th series, volume 558, columns 10–11. An edited version of Eden's remarks is printed in *The Suez Canal Problem, July 26–September 22, 1956*, pages 333–334.)

That same day at 5 p.m. in Washington, the Department of State issued the following statement: "If the United Kingdom alone or in association with others should propose a users' association to be organized by the 18 nations which sponsored the London proposals, or such of them as were so disposed, and perhaps others, the United States will participate in such a users' association. We assume that the users' association would exercise on behalf of the users the rights which are theirs under the 1888 Convention and seek such cooperation with Egypt as would achieve the results designed to be guaranteed by that Convention." (Reported in telegram 1833 to London, September 12; Department of State, Central Files, 974.7301/9–1256)

213.   Memorandum of a Telephone Conversation Between the British Ambassador (Makins) and the Secretary of State, Washington, September 12, 1956, 5:20 p.m. [1]

TELEPHONE CALL FROM SIR ROGER MAKINS

M. said he has a message from Lloyd—he says there is a lot of talk in the lobbies about attributing the plan to the Sec. and he wants M. to explain that they have done nothing to do that. They would like to give the Sec. all the credit for it but L. does not think the Sec. wants it. The Sec. said he does not. M. wanted to explain. L. said in his message that they are deeply grateful to the Sec. for all the work which he has done but their official line has been and will be that this is a plan jointly prepared. The Sec. said that is what he wants.

The Sec. said we have tried to reach a conclusion as to how we can meet their wishes about next week. [2] Hoover is going to be out for a while—the Sec. thought maybe he could but is afraid we may not be able to count on it. He is somewhat perplexed and may not be able to give an answer until tomorrow, but the Sec. thinks it is unlikely we will be able to have anyone there before Monday. [3] The Sec. does not think Paris is a good idea. The atmosphere is highly charged. The Sec. said he does not know if it will be he or Loy Henderson and Phleger. M. said they would be terribly pleased if the Sec. went. The Sec. said a great deal depends on whether we can get together a high-level group representing the 18. Most of the ambassadors are up to date on it. The Sec. said he does not think he can go but is considering it.

M. said if the Sec. can give him a reply tonight, he will wait for it but in the meantime he will send a message that the Sec. would prefer to have it the way L. said and on the other matter we can have no one in London before Monday and will let M. know as soon as we can.

---

[1] Source: Eisenhower Library, Dulles Papers, General Telephone Conversations. Transcribed by Bernau.

[2] At 12:15 p.m. on September 12, Makins telephoned Rountree to convey a message to Dulles from Lloyd, suggesting that an early high-level U.S., U.K., and French meeting be held to coordinate planning on the Canal users association plan. Lloyd suggested that the meeting be held in Paris on September 14–15; a larger meeting would then be convened on September 17 in London, attended by representatives of as many of the 18 nations as possible. Makins also conveyed Lloyd's hope that the Secretary would find it possible to join Lloyd and Pineau in Paris. (Memorandum of telephone conversation by Rountree; Department of State, Central Files, 974.7301/9–1256)

[3] September 17.

The Sec. said he is worried about the pilot situation. M. is too. The Sec. said that may precipitate things before we can carry out the other scheme. M. pointed it out and does not know how it got to this stage. The Sec. told of his giving out the two sentences from the paper he handed M. to the press. The Sec. mentioned a further paper to M. tomorrow.

---

214.   Annex to Watch Committee Report No. 319 [1]

SC 00358/56   *Washington, September 12, 1956.*

CONCLUSIONS ON BRITISH-FRENCH INTENTIONS TO EMPLOY FORCE AGAINST EGYPT

1. There are strong indications that the UK and France may launch military action against Egypt in the event that their minimum objectives cannot be obtained by non-military means. There are a number of indications that they do not expect to achieve these minimum objectives by non-military means. However, there is no firm evidence that they have as yet reached a final decision on this matter.

2. The likelihood of a British-French resort to force would increase in the event of provocation such as an interruption of the flow of traffic through the Suez Canal. An interruption might develop within the next few days as a result of the Suez Canal Company's action authorizing its pilots to resign.

In reaching its conclusions, the Watch Committee considered the following:

1. Nasser's rejection of the proposals of the Menzies mission, eliminating one more possible peaceful solution, and British and French failure to accept Nasser's counterproposal for another international conference.

2. British notification to the UN Security Council of the Suez problem, without requesting action.

3. British and French reiterations of their readiness to resort to force against Egypt if peaceful efforts to establish international control of the Canal fail; on 12 September Eden asked Commons to give him freedom to use whatever means are required to "restore"

---

[1] Source: CIA Files. Top Secret; Noforn; Limited Distribution.

the Suez Canal situation and declared that under no circumstances would the UK accept "abject appeasement" of Nasser.

4. Eden's sponsorship of a US proposal for an international association comprising users of the Canal to maintain traffic, hire pilots and receive tolls for transit. Egypt would be paid for the use of certain facilities. Eden warned that interference with operations of the users' association would force its members to take steps to assert their rights either through the UN or "by other means."

5. Further Soviet warnings that military action in the Canal situation would have serious international consequences which might not be localized in the area. There has been a studied Soviet avoidance of any commitments to Egypt of direct military support. There are unconfirmed reports, however, of additional Soviet military advisers arriving in Egypt as extra "crew members" on Soviet vessels. Soviet military matériel shipments to Egypt continue with 12 Soviet Bloc ships in the Alexandria port between 2 and 5 September.

6. Continued buildup of British and French forces in the Eastern Mediterranean; joint British-French amphibious exercises off Malta; readiness of the British 3d Division at Southampton, for possible use in the Eastern Mediterranean, and the departure of its engineer equipment for the Mediterranean; the reported plans to move the British 10th Armored Division in Libya forward to Tobruk. There is no information, however, that French forces in Algeria or British forces on Cyprus are actually loading or that the limited air and sea lift in the Eastern Mediterranean is being augmented.

7. Continuing tension in which incidents or provocations in Egypt could be used to justify UK-French armed action, such as interruptions to the flow of traffic through the Canal caused by the departure of British and French Canal pilots or incidents connected with the evacuation of British and French nationals from Egypt.

215.   Telegram From the Embassy in France to the Department of State [1]

Paris, September 13, 1956—1 p.m.

1217. Deliver immediately to the Secretary. I accompanied Senator George on courtesy visits this morning to both Pineau and Mollet. Substantive conversation at both meetings dealt solely with Suez. Both Pineau and Mollet expressed great satisfaction with present situation. Mollet said that he had been disturbed by lack of agreement with United States during course of four, five days preceding agreement on users association. Both men gave clear impression that they felt users association fully satisfied need for action on the part of France and Britain and contributed to avoiding danger of armed hostilities. Mollet clearly indicated that he felt establishment of users association had had beneficial first effect on Nasser and had been of importance in persuading him to make no objection to departure of non-Egyptian pilots. [2]

Talking about the future Mollet said it was essential to success of any negotiation that Nasser understand clearly that he could not get away with his grab: he said that establishment of users association adequately covered this point. There was certainly clear inference that once users establishment set up French would be willing to enter into serious negotiations with Nasser for permanent settlement which would naturally have to be along general lines of the 18 power proposal.

Pineau indicated clearly that he expected great majority of shipping to use Cape of Good Hope route. He said he understood United States was planning to advise United States controlled tankers to use this route and he expressed satisfaction with this decision. Pineau also said he felt there was now good possibility of avoiding hostilities unless Nasser committed further grave act. In further conversation regarding possibilities that Egyptians would make it impossible for users association vessels to pass through canal Pineau at no time indicated that he felt such interference with traffic, if

---

[1] Source: Department of State, Central Files, 974.7301/9–1356. Secret; Niact; Limit Distribution—Suez Canal. Received at 8:36 a.m. Repeated to London. A copy in the Eisenhower Library, Whitman File, Dulles–Herter Series, bears a handwritten marginal notation that reads: "Sent to President at Gettysburg 13 Sept 56".

[2] On September 13 in telegram 734, the Embassy in Cairo reported that the Egyptian Government had announced that it would place no obstacle in the way of the pilots' departure and that the Egyptian Government had taken several steps to facilitate their departure. (Department of State, Central Files, 974.7301/9–1256)

carried out peacefully, would be the type of grave action by Nasser which might bring on hostilities.

Dillon

---

216. **Memorandum of a Conversation Between the Egyptian Ambassador (Hussein) and the Secretary of State, Department of State, Washington, September 13, 1956, 11:05 a.m.** [1]

Ambassador Hussein had telephoned the Secretary a few minutes before he came in to say that he had received an urgent message from Cairo, which he wanted to communicate before the Secretary proceeded to his press conference scheduled for 11:00 a.m. The Secretary having agreed to receive him, the Ambassador arrived at 11:05 a.m.

Ambassador Hussein repeated that he had just received a communication which he wished to convey to the Secretary before the Secretary's press conference. He had not had time to type the message.

The substance of the message was as follows:

"The scheme which Prime Minister Eden wants to impose is an open and flagrant aggression on Egypt's sovereignty and its implementation means war.

"If the United States desires war, it may support the scheme, but if its desire is to work for a peaceful solution, the scheme has to be abandoned."

The Secretary said that Nasser's reaction seemed to be based on a misconception of Mr. Eden's proposals. He hoped that as a result of what he would have to say at his press conference, the Egyptian Government would see that the plan did not involve a violation of Egyptian sovereignty or anything else that should unduly disturb the Egyptian Government. They would see that we have made a sincere effort to work out a procedure designed in fact to avoid grave consequences. He said that if such efforts toward a peaceful solution had not been pursued on an urgent basis, the result in all probability would have been that a war would have already started.

In the course of the brief discussion, the Secretary asked whether the message meant that the Egyptians were considering war. Ambassador Hussein obviously was unprepared to interpret the meaning of the

---

[1] Source: Department of State, Central Files, 974.7301/9–1356. Secret. Drafted by Rountree.

message but said that he had been instructed only to deliver it as soon as possible.

Upon departing, the Ambassador asked for the Secretary's suggestion as to what he should say to the press. The Secretary said that he might wish to say that he had called under instruction to give to the Secretary the provisional reaction of the Egyptian Government to Mr. Eden's proposal.

(*Note*: The Ambassador reportedly told members of the press that the message he conveyed was to the effect that imposition of the Users' Association plan would mean war.) [2]

---

[2] During the subsequent press conference, Dulles affirmed U.S. support for the creation of a users' association along the lines described by Prime Minister Eden. Under questioning, however, Dulles acknowledged that if physical force should be used to prevent passage through the Suez Canal, "then, obviously, as far as the United States is concerned, the alternative for us at least would be to send our vessels around the Cape." When pressed further that what he was advocating was a boycott of the Canal, Secretary Dulles responded: "It is not a boycott of the Canal, as far as I know, to refrain from using force to get through the Canal. If force is interposed by Egypt, then I do not call it a boycott to avoid using force to shoot your way through. We do not intend to shoot our way through. It may be we have the right to do it, but we don't intend to do it as far as the United States is concerned." (The transcript is printed in Department of State *Bulletin*, September 24, 1956, pp. 476–483; excerpts are in *The Suez Canal Problem, July 26–September 22, 1956*, pp. 335–345.)

---

217.   Memorandum of a Conversation, Department of State, Washington, September 13, 1956, 6:25 p.m. [1]

SUBJECT

Suez Canal

PARTICIPANTS

Sir Roger Makins, British Ambassador
The Secretary
Herman Phleger, L
William M. Rountree, NEA

The Secretary said he had been giving thought to the British and French suggestion regarding a meeting at London [2] and was

---

[1] Source: Department of State, Central Files, 974.7301/9–1356. Secret. Drafted by Rountree.

[2] See footnote 2, Document 213. Also on the morning of September 13 Makins forwarded through Rountree to Dulles a message from Lloyd which reads: "I am sure we shall have many matters to discuss while C.A.S.U. is set up during the next few days. The Prime Minister and I would be very grateful if you found it possible to

prepared to give his reaction. He suggested the 18 Governments which shared in the proposals carried to Cairo by the Committee of Five should be asked to meet again at London on Wednesday, September 19. The purpose would be to discuss the report of the Committee of Five and consider what action should be taken in light thereof; to consider the Egyptian memorandum proposing the establishment of a negotiating group representing different views; [3] and to consider the suggestion for a Suez Canal users' association.

The Secretary suggested that Foreign Ministers be invited to attend wherever possible, and said that under these circumstances he would himself plan to attend. He assumed that the presence of the Foreign Ministers or their Deputies would not be required for more than two or three days. He felt it should be made clear that attendance by the 18 Nation group would not involve any commitments for any course of action in relation to the matters to be discussed.

The Ambassador said he was very pleased that the Secretary would go to London. He felt this would be an occasion on which his authority and persuasion could play an extremely important role.

The Secretary said he thought it important to emphasize the desirability of keeping cohesion among the group and to capitalize upon the spirit of cooperation which had been established. [4]

The Secretary observed that he could not help but feel that Egypt was beginning to worry about the responsibility which it had assumed. Nasser appeared to be acting in a highly nervous and emotional manner. The message which the Egyptian Ambassador had delivered to the effect that the users' plan meant war indicated a state of nervousness. The Ambassador agreed, saying that he was sure that putting forth the users' plan was the right thing to do. It would apply pressure upon the Egyptians without closing any doors. He mentioned that the Egyptians had indicated to the IMF that it wished to make a withdrawal from the fund. He said that the United States Treasury representative had been informed concerning Saad's [5] request and the latter's comment that "if there were not too much opposition among the IMF members, Egypt would keep

---

come over yourself. Monday [September 17] would suit us very well, and we should both be delighted to see you." (Letter from Makins to Dulles; Department of State, Presidential Correspondence: Lot 66 D 204, UK officials corres. with Secy Dulles/ Herter 7/54 thru 3/57 Vol I incoming)

[3] See footnote 4, Document 200.

[4] Subsequently on September 14, the British Government issued invitations to the governments of the 18 Powers to meet in London on September 19. Secretary Dulles sent a personal message to various Foreign Ministers in support of the invitation. (Circular telegram 206, September 14; Department of State, Central Files, 974.7301/ 9–1456)

[5] Dr. Ahmad Saad, Governor and President of the National Bank of Egypt.

quiet." The Ambassador could not elaborate upon the import of this comment.

---

218. Letter From the Representative at the United Nations (Lodge) to the Secretary of State [1]

New York, September 13, 1956.

DEAR FOSTER: In discussing the Suez Canal situation with you on Tuesday,[2] I raised with you the following two-point plan as a basis for a Security Council resolution, assuming that this matter gets into the Security Council and we must make a move of our own:

1. Egyptian sovereignty to be recognized, and Egypt to operate the Canal on the basis of keeping it open to all;
2. If stoppage of the Canal should occur, this would be regarded as a threat to the existence of the user nations, thus enabling them to apply sanctions as a matter of self-defense.

This is very rough and needs considerable refinement. It is perhaps a "working paper" idea on which a finished product could be based.

It seems to me that Nasser could hardly object—because how could he object to arrangements providing for punishment for doing something which he swears he will never do? If he did object he would lay himself open to the suspicion that he did in fact intend to block the Canal, since he would, under the provisions of my idea, be obtaining the two things that he says he wants most—sovereignty and the operation of the Canal as an adjunct to his sovereignty. The British and French, on the other hand, would get something they badly need—a moralistic basis for using force.

I believe you said that Nasser had already objected to a proposal of this kind. The question that arises in my mind is whether such a proposal was put to Nasser linked *with* a strong reaffirmation of Egyptian sovereignty. While Nasser may have objected to the threat of sanctions, would he do so if Egyptian sovereignty and operation

---

[1] Source: Department of State, Central Files, 974.7301/9–1356. Secret. A marginal notation by Bernau reads: "Sec saw".

[2] Reference is to a telephone conversation between Lodge and Secretary Dulles on September 11. A memorandum of conversation, transcribed at the Department of State by Bernau, is in the Eisenhower Library, Dulles Papers, General Telephone Conversations.

of the Canal were guaranteed? I raise this again with you in the thought that, should the matter come to the Security Council, this might provide the basis for a resolution which could be accepted all around. [3]

Faithfully yours,

Cabot L.

---

[3] In a letter of September 17, Dulles informed Lodge: "I believe that further careful thought should be given to what you propose, but, for the time being, I do not see how we could expect your proposal to meet adequately the fears of the users of the Canal, and thus attain British and French support in the Canal. Perhaps after the forthcoming London talks we will have a better idea of the likelihood and feasibility of successful UN consideration of this critical problem. For the present, it would appear that the chances of any fruitful Security Council action are limited, but it may be desirable to explore possible Council action under Article 40 of the Charter." (Drafted by Ludlow; Department of State, Central Files, 974.7301/9–1756)

---

219.   Report Prepared in the Executive Secretariat of the Department of State [1]

Summary No. 9   *Washington, September 14, 1956.*

SUMMARY OF DEVELOPMENTS IN SUEZ SITUATION

London Ministerial Conference on Suez

Consideration is being given to the suggestion that the 18 governments which shared in the proposals carried to Cairo by the Committee of Five should be asked to meet again in London on Wednesday, September 19. The purpose of the new conference would be to hear the report of the Committee of Five, to consider what action should be taken in the light thereof, to consider the Egyptian memorandum proposing the establishment of a negotiating group representing different views, and to consider the suggestion for a Suez Canal Users Association. The respective Foreign Ministers would be invited to attend the conference and Secretary Dulles would be present. It would be made clear that attendance would not involve any commitment to any course of action in relation to the problems to be discussed.

---

[1] Source: Eisenhower Library, Whitman File, International File. Top Secret; eyes Only for Designated Recipient. The source text is initialed by Eisenhower.

Bulganin Note to Eden and Mollet

Embassy London has been told by the Foreign Office that the Soviet note received yesterday contained a number of passages which are offensive to the British Government and is a "monument to hypocrisy"; the British Government's reply is expected to be curt. [2]

The French reply [3] is being prepared in accordance with suggestions by Pineau that: 1) the falsity of the Soviet claim that the USSR has consistently urged a peaceful solution should be exposed; and 2) it make clear that France judges its friends according to the stands they take on matters which France considers vital to its own interests.

Reaction to Users Association Plan

The initial reaction of French officials [4] was one of general satisfaction derived from the feeling that Western solidarity has been reestablished in support of a mutually acceptable course of action. Few, however, understand the full implications of the proposal— authorization of which is attributed to the US—and most anticipate that ships will soon be taking the Cape of Good Hope route.

The first reaction in London [5] was that of incredulity on both sides of the House and in the press gallery. This has now given way to strongly partisan support by the Government side in the House and press, and violent opposition from Labour and Liberal MP's and newspapers.

Aldrich reports [6] that the timing and substance of the Secretary's press conference yesterday was a decisive factor in determining the

---

[2] Reported in telegram 1453 from London, September 13. (*Ibid.*, 974.7301/9–1356) The Embassy in London also reported in this telegram that, according to its Foreign Office source, the Soviet note was largely a lecture on the dangers involved in the use of force and an appeal for a peaceful settlement of the Suez dispute according to the principles embodied in the U.N. Charter.

On September 20, Prime Minister Eden forwarded to President Eisenhower copies of Bulganin's note of September 11 and Eden's undated response to Bulganin. (Eisenhower Library, Whitman File, International File) Eden describes this exchange of correspondence with Bulganin in *Full Circle*, pp. 543–544.

[3] Reported in telegram 1229 from Paris, September 13. (Department of State, Central Files, 974.7301/9–1356). In this telegram, the Embassy in Paris also reported that, according to its source in the French Foreign Ministry, the Soviet note had urged the desirability of a peaceful settlement of the Suez problem without offering any specific proposal and had counseled against the use of force. According to the source, the letter also insinuated that the United States wished to replace the French in Algeria and gain ascendancy in the Middle East.

[4] Reported in telegram 1238 from Paris, September 13, not printed. (*Ibid.*, 974.7301/9–1356)

[5] Reported in telegram 1447 from London, September 13, not printed. (*Ibid.*)

[6] Reported in telegram 1472 from London, September 14, not printed. (*Ibid.*, 973.7301/9–1456)

course and outcome of the debate in the House. Gaitskell was enabled to prod Eden into giving assurances that the UK would take the Suez matter to the Security Council before using force, except in an emergency. This has greatly lessened tension not only in the opposition ranks but even among many Tories. There is now far wider approval of the nature and purpose of the canal users plan than heretofore existed.

The preliminary reaction from the Scandinavian Governments [7] was not encouraging; officials of all three expressed their surprise and confusion at US support for the projected association. We have asked our missions [8] to emphasize urgently to the Scandinavian Foreign Ministers that the US, UK and France regard the proposed association as a serious and practical step towards a peaceful solution of the Suez problem and that the US hopes to count on their cooperation.

Italian Foreign Minister Martino expressed to Dillon in Paris yesterday [9] his concern regarding the proposed users association. He did not see how such an arrangement could pass shipping through the canal and said that Italy, for geographic and financial reasons, could not route her shipping around the Cape of Good Hope. He advocated another conference of the 18 nations. Meanwhile in Rome the Foreign Office evinced sympathetic interest in the users association as explained by the British Chargé but said that Italy could not give a reply regarding possible membership until it knew more of the details.

Krishna Menon told our Chargé in New Delhi [10] of Nehru's sharp disappointment in the tenor of Eden's proposal and his deep hope that the US will throw its great weight on the side of solution by negotiation. The Government of India did not see how Egypt could accept the unilateral action envisaged under the plan and still maintain its position as a sovereign power.

(Summary closed 12:00 noon, September 13, 1956)

---

[7] Reported in telegrams 188 from Copenhagen, September 13; 311 from Oslo, September 13; and 299 from Stockholm, September 13, none printed. (All *ibid.*, 974.7301/9–1356)

[8] These instructions were sent on September 13 in telegrams 342 to Oslo, 218 to Copenhagen, and 329 to Stockholm, none printed. (All *ibid.*)

[9] Reported in telegram 1223 from Paris, September 13, not printed. (*Ibid.*)

[10] Reported in telegram 688 from New Delhi, September 13, not printed. (*Ibid.*)

220.   Memorandum by Arthur H. Dean [1]

New York, September 14, 1956.

Last Tuesday morning September 11 by invitation I had breakfast with Ambassador Eban and Minister Shiloah of Israel.

I brought up with them informally the suggestion that you had made to me over the telephone some time that "Things had been going very well lately" and that it might be possible to work out a statement that the question of arms for Israel was no longer an issue, etc. [2] Ambassador Eban said:

(1) That you had been exceptionally helpful in issuing the necessary instructions in the Department and in telephoning to the French and to Canada but that Ambassador Heeney of Canada had said that the Secretary for External Affairs, Lester Pearson, advised him that Prime Minister St. Laurent had agreed with the leaders in Parliament that they would not release further arms to Israel without notifying them and making a statement to that effect. Ambassador Eban said someone in the State Department had expressed the view to the Canadians that now was not the time for a public statement and that for a while the Canadians had interpreted that as meaning they should not release the arms, but that that conversation has now been cleared up but that they still had to work out some modus operandi with Prime Minister St. Laurent and Pearson about advising the Parliamentary leaders that the arms would have to be released. I suggested that this would have to be done in an informal conversation and Ambassador Eban said that they were exploring this with Ambassador Heeney.

(2) Minister Shiloah said that although you had issued the instructions, perhaps due to your and Mr. Rountree's absence at the Suez Parley the subordinates at the Department did not fully understand that they were to proceed with expedition because as late as last Monday the Military Attaché said the documents were not coming through from the Department. I said I would speak to you about this. Ambassador Eban said that they were very hopeful that they could work out the terms of the loan with the EXIM Bank for internal developments (not the Jordan developments) and that Sam Waugh had said he did not wish to make the loan until he had your approval. Ambassador Eban said he understood the papers were on

---

[1] Source: Eisenhower Library, Dulles Papers, Israeli Relations 1951–1957. A notation on the source text indicates that Secretary Dulles saw this memorandum.

[2] During a conversation with Dean on July 11, Eban advised that if prompt action could be taken on the arms question and something done on Israel's request for an Export-Import Bank loan, then he believed that he could get clearance to say to responsible people supporting the Israeli position within the United States that there were no essential points of difference between Israel and the United States. See Dean's letter to Dulles, vol. xv, p. 809. During a telephone conversation with Dean on August 27, Dulles referred to Dean's conversation with Eban of July 11 and commented, according to Bernau's transcript of the conversation: "Things have been going pretty well lately and sometime if D[ean] has the chance he might follow up on it." (Eisenhower Library, Dulles Papers, General Telephone Conversations)

your desk but that you had not yet had a chance to approve them. I again raised the question of whether if the Canadian matter could be cleared up and the procedural matters in the Department could be cleared up and the flow of arms to Israel could be cleared, they could not make some statement that the question of arms was no longer an issue.

(3) Minister Shiloah said he had attended recently a right-wing Zionist Committee meeting, who were apparently going to favor the Democratic plank on Israel and denounce the absence of one in the Republican platform and that he had withdrawn from the meeting on the ground that it was not within his province as a foreign minister; but that he had urged the leaders privately not to express a public opinion on this matter, and believed that he had been successful.

I asked Ambassador Eban what he thought the best method of making such a statement was and he thought when it could be worked out it might be well if someone could ask the Prime Minister a question about it in the Israel Parliament and he could then reply that there were no problems between Israel and the United States which could then be put on the press wires and taken up here. I said I thought the wording of that statement ought to be very carefully worked out; and he agreed.

They expressed themselves as being well pleased with the Suez negotiations in London and thought your ability to have gotten non-European nations to go along with you was a great tribute to your diplomatic ability. They expressed great interest in building a canal through Israel from the Red Sea to the Mediterranean and they gave me a copy of a report on this project prepared five years ago by the Anglo-Iranian Oil Company, Limited, Production Department, and they emphasized that some of the figures were out of date and the cost could be greatly reduced by bulldozing equipment and American earth movers, etc. I am enclosing a copy of this report. [3]

They said that they had recently had a conference with the new French Ambassador and he had commented that despatches from the *New York Times* to the French Foreign Office were often regarded as more authoritative than despatches from the French Embassy and that some of the despatches of the *New York Times* reported to have emanated from the State Department while you were in London were most unfortunate. They particularly commented on a despatch of Homer Bigart and Harold Callender from abroad.

They said they thought that your conversations on the Suez had been on such a high level and your views on the internationalization of the canal had been discussed on such a top level that they did not think that some of the younger men in the Department were fully

---

[3] Not attached to the source text.

au courant with your views and they knew of their own knowledge that several of the younger men in the Department theorized a good deal and speculated a good deal with newspaper men and that this was the basis of a number of the despatches which apparently indicated a view in the Department somewhat different from the one that you were expressing. Whether this is correct or not or has any substance I of course do not purport to know.

In leaving I again urged upon them to do everything they could to try to bring about the fairly immediate issuance of the statement that there were at present no major problems at issue between Israel and the Department and they said that they would, just as soon as they could clear up the matters with respect to the movement of arms mentioned above.

Jake Javits sent in word this afternoon that he feels that he is going to have a rather rough time on this issue in the coming election and that the President will also and wondered if something on this matter could be done. I told his emissary that I did not consider myself free to make any comment on this matter but that I was hopeful that something could be worked out in the near future which would be reasonably satisfactory to him.

Respectfully yours,

Arthur H. Dean

---

221.   Circular Telegram From the Department of State to Certain Diplomatic Missions [1]

Washington, September 14, 1956—8:49 p.m.

209. Circular 193 [2] and cirtel 201. [3] With regard to Egyptian

---

[1] Source: Department of State, Central Files, 974.7301/9–1456. Secret. Drafted by Wilkins and approved by Rountree. Sent to Canberra, Copenhagen, Addis Ababa, Paris, Bonn, Tehran, Rome, Tokyo, The Hague, Wellington, Oslo, Karachi, Lisbon, Madrid, Stockholm, Ankara, and London.

[2] In circular telegram 193, September 12, the Department of State instructed the Embassies to inform host governments that the United States was studying the Egyptian memorandum of September 10 (see footnote 4, Document 200) and that the United States believed it highly desirable that an exchange of views between the United States and other members of the Eighteen-Nation group take place before a reply was sent to Egypt. (Department of State, Central Files, 974.7301/9–1256)

[3] Circular telegram 201, dated September 13, contained a selection of public statements, made by U.S. officials, concerning the Egyptian memorandum of September 10 and the proposal for a Suez Canal users' association. (*Ibid.*, 974.7301/9–1356)

memorandum of September 10 setting forth proposal for negotiating body in connection Suez Canal, following are US views which you should immediately communicate orally to Government to which you are accredited:

1. USG has received memorandum of Embassy of Egypt dated September 10, 1956. This proposes that negotiating body be formed which would be representative of different views held among States using Suez Canal to consider solution of questions involving Canal and to review Constantinople Convention of 1888.

2. Also GOE recalls its proposal of August 12, 1956 that new conference, to which it is understood substantially all nations of world would be invited, be convened for substantially same purposes as was London Conference on Suez. This proposal is in all essentials similar to that advanced by representatives of USSR at London Conference. That proposal did not meet acceptance of members that Conference, which included States representing ownership of more than 95 percent of tonnage transiting Canal.

3. USG doubts it is practical to negotiate simultaneously with all countries which are parties to or beneficiaries of Suez Canal. Such group would embrace practically all nations of world and could not be effective negotiating body.

It also doubtful these nations will delegate discretionary negotiating authority to small group. Such delegation of authority not compatible with normal exercise of sovereign rights.

4. Procedure followed at London Conference of August 16 to August 23, 1956 represents, in our opinion, only practical procedure. That Conference drew together all indisputably surviving parties of 1888 Treaty, nations representing over 90% of traffic through Canal, and also nations whose pattern of foreign trade showed significant dependence upon Canal. Unfortunately GOE was not represented, but that was due to its own preference to be absent.

5. At this Conference there was found to be large measure of agreement to conditions necessary to assure that Canal would be operated in accordance with principles of 1888 Treaty. This judgment of 18 nations was carried to Egypt and carefully explained to GOE which, however, did not accept viewpoint thus expressed even as basis for negotiation.

6. It is believed views of 18 nations as presented and explained to GOE by five-nation Committee on September 3, 1956 furnish basis for further discussions and negotiations looking toward fair and equitable settlement of Suez Canal problem, and that convening of conference, as suggested by GOE, would not be helpful in solution of this difficult problem.

USG understands this matter is to be discussed in London at conference September 19 for which invitations issued by UKG and is looking forward to exchange of views there.

Action London and Paris should be only to inform UK and French Governments foregoing is being communicated to other members 18-Nation group.

Dulles

---

222.   Message From President Eisenhower to Prime Minister Nehru [1]

Washington, September 15, 1956.

DEAR MR. PRIME MINISTER: I have read with interest and appreciation your messages of September 8 and 11 [2] on the Suez Canal situation. I have also had the opportunity to study the text of the statement you made on September 13 in Lok Sabha.

I consider it a privilege to receive the benefit of your views on this important and difficult problem, satisfactory solution of which is so vital to the peace and well-being of the nations of the world. I am in complete agreement with you that a peaceful approach must be made to this issue, and I have so indicated in several public statements recently. You may be certain that the United States Government will not abandon its belief that, given good will and the realization of the vast implications of the matter, a peaceful solution can be achieved.

---

[1] Source: Department of State, Central Files, 974.7301/9–1556. Secret. Transmitted to New Delhi Priority in telegram 705, September 15, 11:53 a.m., which is the source text, with the instruction: "Deliver promptly following message from President to Nehru. Confirm time delivery. Signed original to follow." Telegram 705 indicates the message was drafted by Howe and cleared with Goodpaster.

[2] Neither printed. In the September 8 message, Nehru emphasized the need to establish a basis for negotiation which would bring Egypt into the discussions and he expressed the hope that the United States would use its great influence toward a peaceful approach and settlement of the Suez Canal problem and would discourage and deter all talk of solving the problem by force. In the September 11 message, Nehru spoke in behalf of the Egyptian proposal of September 10 (see footnote 4, Document 200), noting that it offered ways for a peaceful solution which should be explored. Copies of these and several other messages between Eisenhower and Nehru concerning the Suez situation are in the Eisenhower Library, Whitman File, International File and in Department of State, Presidential Correspondence: Lot 66 D 204.

I shall not conceal from you my deep disappointment that President Nasser saw fit to reject the proposals of the 18 nations which were so ably set before him by Prime Minister Menzies and the members of the 5-nation committee which went to Cairo. I believed, and continue to believe, that these proposals show the way to a peaceful and constructive arrangement which would benefit all parties concerned.

You have mentioned the Egyptian memorandum of September 10 setting forth a proposal for the formation of a negotiating body to consider the solution of questions involving the Canal and to review the Constantinople Convention of 1888. My preliminary reaction to this runs along the following lines:

It is doubtful that it would be practical to negotiate simultaneously with all countries which are parties to or beneficiaries of the Suez Canal. Such a group would embrace practically all nations of the world and, it seems to me, could not be an effective negotiating body. It is also doubtful that these nations would delegate discretionary negotiating authority to a small group, as such delegation of authority would not be compatible with the normal exercise of sovereign rights.

The procedure followed at the London Conference seems to me the only practical one. The conference drew together all indisputably surviving parties of the 1888 Convention, the nations representing over ninety percent of the traffic through the Canal and also those nations whose pattern of foreign trade has shown significant dependence upon the Canal. To my great regret the Government of Egypt was not represented, but that was entirely due to its own preference to be absent.

At the London Conference there was found to be a large measure of agreement with regard to the conditions necessary to assure that the Canal would be operated in accordance with the principles of the 1888 Convention. This judgment, shared by 18 nations, was carried to Cairo and carefully explained to the Government of Egypt which unfortunately did not accept the viewpoint thus expressed even as a basis for negotiation.

It is my belief at the moment that the views of the 18 nations as presented and explained to the Government of Egypt by the 5-nation Committee furnished the basis for further discussions and negotiations looking toward a fair and equitable settlement of the Suez Canal problem, and that the convening of a new conference on the basis suggested by the Government of Egypt would not be a development helpful in the solution of this difficult issue.

A conference is planned for September 19 in London to enable the 18 nations which joined in the proposals to President Nasser to discuss the Menzies report and various other matters relating to the

Suez question. It is planned that this group will discuss the response to the Egyptian memorandum. The final position of the United States on this particular point will not be determined until after the consultation afforded by the new London meeting.

Another subject which will be discussed at London is the proposed association of Canal users, to which the United States has given its support. This step, while it can only be an interim measure might, I think, if accepted by Egypt in the spirit in which we join in it, permit of some practical progress toward an acceptable operation of the Canal.

Please allow me to say how much I appreciate receiving your views. Your messages have given me a clear understanding of the position of the Indian Government, and convince me all the more that there is harmony of purpose in this matter between our two countries.

With kind regard,
Sincerely,

Dwight D. Eisenhower [3]

---

[3] Telegram 705 bears this typed signature.

---

223.   Memorandum for the Record by the Counselor of the Department of State (MacArthur) [1]

Washington, September 15, 1956.

The Secretary informed me last evening at 6:30 p.m. that he did not wish any action taken with the Canadians suggesting that the Canadians might delay action on the supply of certain F–86 aircraft to Israel. In Mr. Rountree's absence, I informed Mr. Wilkins of NEA this morning of the Secretary's wishes with respect to this problem. Mr. Wilkins told me that a telegram had gone out last evening to Ottawa instructing our Embassy to approach the Canadians about this problem. [2]

---

[1] Source: Department of State, Central Files, 784A.5622/9–1556. Top Secret.

[2] Reference is to telegram 115 to Ottawa, September 14. (*Ibid.*, 784A.5622/9–1356) The telegram, which was approved by Rountree, noted with great concern reports of recent Israeli attacks against Jordanian installations resulting in at least 40 Jordanian fatalities. In view of this situation, the Embassy was instructed to point out in confidence to the Canadian Foreign Office that an announcement of the sale of jets to

Accordingly and in the light of the Secretary's instructions of last evening, I telephoned to our Embassy in Ottawa this morning and spoke to Second Secretary Falkner, the Embassy duty officer. I instructed him to take no action on Deptel 115 to Ottawa and asked him to confirm that the telegram had been received and that no action had or would be taken on it unless the Embassy was further instructed by the Department. Mr. Falkner said he understood and would telephone me later this morning to confirm receipt of the telegram and the fact that action had been stopped. I told Mr. Falkner that I would send a confirming telegram to him canceling action.[3]

DMacA

Israel "would greatly inflate importance attached by Arab States and might be taken by Israelis as evidence their policy large scale retaliation does not adversely affect attitudes of others" and to suggest that the announcement be delayed.

[3] In telegram 116 to Ottawa, September 15, the Department instructed the Embassy: "Please take no action whatsoever on Deptel 115 unless further instructed." (*Ibid.*, 784.5622/9–1556) On September 20, the Embassy reported that the Canadian Cabinet had that day approved the release of 24 F–86 airplanes to Israel. (Telegram 143 from Ottawa; *ibid.*, 784.5622/9–2056)

---

224.   Memorandum of a Conversation Between the President and the Secretary of State, White House, Washington, September 17, 1956, 11:30 a.m. [1]

[Here follows discussion of unrelated matters.]

3. We then discussed the Suez Canal situation. I said that I thought that probably all of the 18 Governments would be represented at London, the only possible exception being Pakistan where a new Government was being installed. I said that despite the fact that the Users' Association proposal had gotten off to a bad start through Eden's presentation, it was now being better understood and I thought might be widely acceptable, although Spain was reluctant to go along and was always tempted to play with the Arabs and take a course somewhat opposed to that of France and the United Kingdom, with which it had considerable differences.

---

[1] Source: Eisenhower Library, Dulles Papers, Meetings with the President. Secret; Personal and Private. Drafted by Dulles.

I reviewed with the President the Egyptian course of conduct and indicated that it showed no single move of a conciliatory nature. The President remarked that with the arrival of Soviet pilots which I had long forecast there was really a close partnership between Egypt and the Soviet Union. I said this was so, but that I did not believe that any such partnership was durable. I pointed out that where countries were physically adjacent to the Soviet Union and where Soviet troops were there to sustain a pro-Soviet government, the people had little recourse. However, that was not the case where a country was not adjacent to the Soviet Union and where Soviet military power was not available to support the government. The President recalled, in this connection, Guatemala.

.   .   .   .

5. I then went over with the President the statement which I thought I might make after leaving him. The President read it and approved it and gave it to Mr. Hagerty to be mimeographed. (copy is attached) [2]

JFD [3]

---

[2] Dulles' statement, subsequently released at the White House, noted that President Eisenhower and Secretary Dulles had consulted on the Suez situation in advance of Dulles' departure for London and affirmed, among other points, that the United States was dedicated to seeking a solution through peaceful means which would protect the rights granted to Canal users by the 1888 Convention and that there must always be ways to assure the movement of vital supplies, particularly oil, to Western Europe. See *The Suez Canal Problem, July 26–September 22, 1956*, pp. 350–351.

[3] Macomber initialed for Dulles.

225. Memorandum of a Conversation, Department of State, Washington, September 17, 1956, 2 p.m. [1]

SUBJECT

Suez Canal

PARTICIPANTS

Mr. Herve Alphand, French Ambassador
Mr. Charles Lucet, Minister
Mr. Jacques Vimont, Minister

The Secretary
NEA—William M. Rountree
WE—William R. Tyler

The French Ambassador had asked urgently for an appointment with the Secretary and was received at 2:00 p.m. just prior to the Secretary's departure for the airport. The Ambassador said he had seen news reports of the Secretary's comments on Suez made at the White House [2] and he wished clarification of certain points. The Secretary had been quoted as saying that the United States did not intend to boycott the Suez Canal. He wondered how this might affect his understanding that, after the users' associations was set up, if Nasser should then refuse to permit transit of the Canal by vessels under association arrangements, we would reroute around the Cape. The Secretary responded by reading the text of what he had said at the White House.

The Ambassador inquired whether, if Nasser refused to let the vessels pass, in consequence of which they were rerouted around the Cape, the British, French and United States should not then bring the matter jointly before the Security Council. The Secretary responded that he could not say whether we would join in such action until he knew what Security Council action would be sought. He would not, however, exclude the possibility of the United States joining. The Secretary said that he was concerned by newspaper stories which had come out over the weekend to the effect that the United States had changed its views regarding the Suez matter and particularly the users' association. He stated there was no basis for these stories. The Ambassador was gratified to hear this. He observed that it would be extremely difficult to operate the proposed users' association without having personnel stationed on land. He

---

[1] Source: Department of State, Central Files, 974.7301/9–1756. Secret. Drafted by Rountree.

[2] See footnote 2, *supra.*

had discussed this with Mr. Hoover [3] and the latter had expressed his belief that the operation envisaged might be carried out from ships stationed at either end of the Canal.

The Secretary inquired whether the French thought they could obtain the pilots that would be necessary for the operation, to which the Ambassador replied he felt certain this would present no problem. He said one question which had concerned him was whether we should go forward with the users' association plan even though Nasser might demonstrate that the Canal operation could be carried out by pilots provided by Egypt. The Secretary said he thought this would not change the situation since it would not be enough for the Egyptians to prove that they could operate the Canal for a few days or a few weeks. What was necessary was a dependable system which could be counted upon. We could not place reliance upon any system run entirely by Egypt.

(The Secretary told Mr. Rountree during the meeting that he thought we should get out instructions to American ships not to accept Soviet pilots should they be provided by Egypt for transit through the Canal. He asked that this matter be looked into immediately to determine: a) what United States agency would have responsibility in this matter, b) whether there were existing laws or regulations which would permit an order to this effect, or whether it would have to be in the form of a request and c) how we should proceed. Later, while driving to the airport, [4] the Secretary reviewed the matter with Mr. Hoover and Mr. Rountree. He said he would discuss it with the British and French soon after his arrival in London, and would telegraph his views after such discussion. It was mentioned in this discussion that any instructions to our ships would undoubtedly become public knowledge and perhaps should therefore be preceded by a public announcement. One difficulty which was then not resolved was whether the public announcement should specify Soviet and satellite pilots or whether it should be couched in other terms which would provide a criterion excluding Soviet and satellite pilots, such as stating that no pilots would be accepted who had not a specified minimum number of years experience in the Suez.)

---

[3] Alphand and Hoover discussed the Suez situation on September 14. The memorandum of that conversation is in Department of State, Central Files, 974.7301/9–1456.

[4] According to the Secretary's Appointment Book, Dulles and his party, which included Henderson, Phleger, McCardle, Tyler, Berding, and several others, were airborne for London at 2:50 p.m., September 17. (Princeton University Library, Dulles Papers)

226.   Editorial Note

On September 17, Robert Bowie informed Secretary Dulles in a memorandum that papers on seven contingencies, prepared by the Middle East Policy Planning Group in response to President Eisenhower's directive of August 9 (NSC Action No. 1593; see footnotes 8 and 9, Document 72), had been completed and that copies of the papers had been forwarded to the Office of Defense Mobilization. Bowie added that although the papers had been reviewed by Assistant Secretary Rountree for the Department of State and by Gordon Gray for the Department of Defense, they were to be considered studies and not policy papers. (Department of State, S/P Files: Lot 66 D 487, Egypt)

The seven contingency papers were as follows:

1. "The Committee of the Majority of the London Conference on the Suez Canal Meets with the Government of Egypt". The paper envisioned the possibility that the Government of Egypt would reject the majority position, but would attempt to operate the Suez Canal satisfactorily. It recommended continued negotiations with Nasser accompanied by an intensive diplomatic effort to gain world support for the Western position and continuation of economic measures already in effect against Egypt.

2. "The Government of Egypt Refuses to Consider the Basic Principles of the Statement of the Majority of the London Conference on the Suez Canal." The paper envisioned that Nasser would reject the proposals and convoke a large international conference to discuss the Canal. It recommended that the United States oppose the holding of the Conference, but restrict its course of action to measures short of the use of military force. The latter included an enhanced diplomatic offensive coupled with increased economic and psychological measures.

3. "The Suez Canal Situation Is Referred to the UN in the Absence of Military Action." The paper recommended that the United States seek to avoid the introduction of a substantive resolution in the Security Council, which would probably be vetoed, and to urge instead the creation of a subcommittee of the Council to deal with the question or to provide for the intervention of the Secretary-General.

4. "UK and France Initiate Military Action against Egypt Despite US Objections." The paper recommended that the United States provide political and logistical support to the United Kingdom and France and to pledge United States intervention in response to other third party intervention. The paper rejected such options as

condemning Great Britain and France, remaining neutral, or engaging in direct military participation.

5. "The Government of Egypt Interferes with Free Passage through the Suez Canal." In this eventuality, the paper recommended that the United States use the full weight of its diplomatic influence to induce the greatest possible number of nations to protest the Egyptian action, that the United States impose maximum economic pressure upon Egypt, including the rerouting of ships around the Suez Canal and aiding the British and French to do likewise, and that the United States provide political and logistical support if Great Britain and France acted militarily.

6. "The USSR Makes New Military or Politico-Military Moves in the Near East." The paper noted that this would require a decision whether to risk World War III or to acquiesce in a British-French retreat before Soviet pressure. The paper maintained that such a decision lay beyond the competence of the Middle East Policy Planning Group.

7. "The Panama Canal Becomes Involved in the Suez Canal Situation". The paper recommended that the United States strongly resist any attempt to link the two questions.

A complete set of the final papers is *ibid.*, Conference Files: Lot 62 D 181, CF 772. Earlier drafts and the final versions of some of the seven papers, as well as memoranda of discussions held during the relevant MEPPG meetings and other pertinent memoranda are *ibid.*, S/P Files: Lot 66 D 487, Egypt and S/S–NSC Files: Lot 66 D 148, Suez NSC Action 1593b. Attached to Bowie's memorandum to Dulles of September 17 is a chit, dated September 24, from Macomber to Bowie, which reads: "The Secretary did not have a chance to read through the attached. On the plane ride to London, however, I did show it to Mr. Phleger who read through the papers fairly carefully."

227. Telegram From the Embassy in the United Kingdom to the Department of State [1]

London, September 18, 1956—11 p.m.

Secto 5. Secretary met with Lloyd and Pineau noon today [2] to discuss agenda for Conference. It agreed that item one (discussion Menzies' report [3]) would pose no problem, though there should be opportunity for questions, and that Henderson would attempt obtain agreement other members Menzies' Committee to invite Spender join other four members of Committee and to select spokesman for Committee at Conference.

Lloyd suggested item of agenda (response to be made to Egyptian note [4]) should follow discussion item three (formation users' association) as he feared item two might precipitate long discussion.

Pineau said he thought Egyptian note proposed second conference whereas Secretary and Lloyd thought note merely asked for discussions on how set up negotiation group. Secretary added he felt Egyptian proposal aimed at reviving Soviet idea of small negotiating group.

Secretary referred to Hammarskjold's memo [5] which had just received and Lloyd agreed his estimate that Hammarskjold proposal better than Egyptian, Pineau said he had not yet seen Hammarskjold's proposal. Secretary said while he hoped Conference would reject Egyptian initiative he felt Hammarskjold's proposal could be taken up at same time users' association was beginning function. He suggested Hammarskjold might in effect be intermediary to bring about acceptance of users' association by Egypt. He felt that when users' association was established it should be agreed take it imme-

---

[1] Source: Department of State, Central Files, 974.7301/9–1856. Secret. Drafted by Mak. Received at 9:24 p.m. Repeated to Paris.

[2] Dulles and his party arrived in London at 9:25 p.m., September 18. (Secto 1 from London, September 18; *ibid.*) A memorandum of the noon conversation, prepared by the Delegation to the Second Suez Canal Conference, is *ibid.*, Conference Files: Lot 62 D 181, CF 779. The conversation took place at the British Foreign Office.

[3] For text of the Menzies report, see *The Suez Canal Problem, July 26–September 22, 1956*, pp. 323–326.

[4] Reference is to an Egyptian memorandum forwarding the text of Nasser's September 10 statement to the Department of State. Regarding Nasser's statement, see footnote 4, Document 200.

[5] Reference is presumably to a paper which Hammarskjöld delivered to the U.S. Mission in New York at noon on September 14. In it, he proposed that the matter be brought before the Security Council under Article 37 of the U.N. Charter, with the aim of asking the Security Council to invite a restricted number of nations to set up a committee on the Suez question. The committee would then explore the ways and means to achieve the objectives mentioned in the Egyptian Declaration of September 10. (Telegram 212 from USUN, September 14; Department of State, Central Files, 974.7301/9–1456)

diately to Security Council and perhaps also obtain advisory opinion in World Court re our rights under 1888 Treaty. He added this represented his preliminary thinking. Lloyd said he wary of letting Hammarskjold moderate as free agent but all three agreed he could serve useful purpose if his operations were limited. Lloyd said he felt strongly users' association should be discussed first and we should state simultaneously that we would go to Security Council when users' association was set up. He felt such statement would help obtain greater support for users' association. Secretary expressed opinion agenda should remain as stated in British invitation but after some discussion it was agreed items three and two would be reversed provided the other countries agreed.

Secretary said he must leave Thursday [6] but would leave Phleger and Henderson behind to settle technical details of setting up users' association. Secretary then tabled preliminary draft reply to Egyptian note (Secto 6) [7] and it was agreed this draft would be circulated and discussed at afternoon Tripartite meeting.

Re chairmanship of Conference, it was agreed Pineau would nominate Lloyd and Secretary would second nominations.

Dulles

---

[6] September 20.

[7] In this draft reply, the U.S. Government acknowledged receipt of the Egyptian memorandum of September 10, but rejected its proposal for the formation of a negotiating body which would be representative of different views held among states using the Suez Canal. The U.S. Government noted that the members of the first Suez Canal Conference had rejected a similar proposal put forward by the Soviet Union and expressed its doubt as to the practicality of negotiating simultaneously with all countries which had an interest in the Canal. The reply closed with the assertion that the Eighteen-Power Proposals, and not the Egyptian proposal, furnished the basis for further discussions and negotiations looking toward fair and equitable settlement of the Suez Canal problem. (Secto 6 from London, September 18; Department of State, Central Files, 974.7301/9–1856)

228. Telegram From the Embassy in the United Kingdom to
the Department of State [1]

London, September 18, 1956—11 p.m.

Secto 7. Tripartite afternoon meeting Sept 18 convened 1545. [2]
Delegations headed by Lloyd, Pineau and Secretary.

Meeting agreed that Secretary in presenting to Conference proposal for cooperative association of Suez Canal users (CASU) would
mention that organization might be considered by Security Council
as provisional measure to prevent aggravation of situation but would
not suggest that proposal to form CASU be referred to Security
Council. Secretary said he wished to listen to comments of other
fifteen governments at Conference, but subject to this, if UK and
France agreed, US prepared to proceed with formation of CASU.

Meeting agreed with Pineau suggestion that draft CASU declaration and statute [3] should not be presented to Conference at start.
Secretary pointed out that during discussion ideas would be advanced which could well be incorporated and that nations attending
Conference would be given greater sense of participation if they
were not confronted with formal document at outset.

Secretary suggested discussion of two matters going to heart of
CASU plan: (1) whether ships of participating nations should be
required to use CASU exclusively; (2) should payments to Egypt be
made of sums collected by CASU; Lloyd added third question—
membership in CASU.

Use of CASU facilities: Pineau saw no way to avoid exerting
maximum pressure to assure that all ships use CASU services and
pay dues to CASU. Lloyd thought that unless this was done CASU
would not be of much use. Secretary said US could prohibit pay-

---

[1] Source: Department of State, Central Files, 974.7301/9–1856. Secret. Drafted by
Burdett. Received at 8:25 p.m. Repeated to Paris.

[2] A memorandum of this conversation, prepared by the Delegation to the Second
Suez Canal Conference, is *ibid.*, Conference Files: Lot 62 D 181, CF 779.

[3] On September 14, Willie Morris of the British Embassy delivered to the
Department of State two papers: a draft statute and a draft declaration for a
Cooperative Association of Suez Canal Users (CASU). Morris also stated that the
United Kingdom was making tentative arrangements for a meeting of experts in
London on September 17 and asked whether any American experts would be able to
attend. (Memorandum of conversation by Wilkins with attachments, September 14;
ibid., Central Files, 974.7301/9–1456) Subsequently, British, French, and U.S. experts
met on September 17 and again at 10 a.m. on September 18 to discuss and revise the
British draft declaration. (Memorandum of conversation, prepared by the U.S. Delegation to the Second Suez Canal Conference, September 17; *ibid.*, 974.7301/9–1756; Note
of a Tripartite Meeting, prepared by the British Foreign Office, September 18, 10 a.m.;
ibid., Conference Files: Lot 62 D 181, CF 772) At 5 p.m., September 18, the experts
met to consider the draft statute. (Note of a Tripartite Meeting, prepared by the
British Foreign Office, September 18, 5 p.m.; *ibid.*)

ment of dues directly to Egypt by amendment of Treasury regulations but had no right under existing legislation to direct US ships to pay CASU. He added practical effect of amendment of Treasury regulations would be payments to CASU. He said above applied only to US flag ships, not vessels under Panamanian or Liberian registry. He thought it might be possible to work out some voluntary agreement through shippers assn. Meeting concluded three countries would try to get all their ships to use CASU.

Payments to Egypt: Pineau said Egypt might be paid direct costs of any services rendered but should not be paid any "profit margin" derived from transit of vessels. Secretary pointed out practical difficulties arise in establishing costs. Lloyd inquired whether ships belonging to CASU members could use Egyptian services if CASU services unavailable.

Secretary emphasized that ability obtain cooperation from shippers would depend on policies followed by other major shipping nations. Shipping highly competitive business. If Nasser declined let ships pass in absence of payment, they would be obliged use Cape route, in which case competitors could offer cheaper services. Decision to withhold payments to Egypt should not be made lightly. Once decision taken it could not be reversed without severe loss of prestige and victory for Nasser. Secretary stressed need for allowing CASU great flexibility.

Lloyd suggested that in case CASU unable to provide needed services, it might be empowered make some arrangement with Egyptian Government. He agreed that administrator of CASU must have reasonable flexibility in determining how to get ships through Canal not excluding payments to Egypt. Secretary thought CASU might find it expedient make certain payments to Egypt. In principle it would pay Egypt as little as possible and would determine any payments made not by Egyptian demands but by its own interest. He thought serious problems would arise if all details debated at Conference. Participants would probably be divided. Difficulty could be overcome by giving flexibility to Executive Committee which would provide general guidance to Administrator.

Membership: Secretary pointed out supreme importance of composition Executive Committee. If membership in CASU opened to all comers, newcomers might obtain control of committee. Initial membership could consist of 18 nations attending Conference, thus including representatives from Asia, and in addition countries with specific interest in terms of tonnage or pattern of trade. Membership of the future would provide acceptable Executive Committee. Perhaps provision could be included prohibiting change in composition of Committee except by vote of majority both of members and users on basis of tonnage. Meeting agreed that statute setting up CASU should leave door open on question new members.

Secretary said he thought CASU could be set up effectively by executive action. Use of treaty form would require approval by US Congress, which not obtainable in time meet present emergency.

Lloyd raised matter of affiliates and Secretary suggested dropping concept. Lloyd said he had spoken to Spaak last week-end. He did not seem disturbed at omission of Belgium. Spaak stated he thought Belgium's role should be to support CASU proposal in Security Council.

Secretary said CASU services should be available to all countries in order avoid any charge of discrimination in violation of Convention of 1888.

Meeting agreed that working group of experts should complete draft of CASU declaration and statute in light of discussion for further consideration by Ministers. Pineau said he was in general agreement with proposed US reply to Egypt's note [4] discussed during morning meeting. Lloyd who apparently had not read draft made no comment.

Dulles

---

[4] See footnote 7, *supra.*

THE SECOND SUEZ CANAL CONFERENCE AT LONDON; CONTINUED
CONSIDERATION OF THE USERS ASSOCIATION PROPOSAL; INCREASING
VIOLENCE ALONG THE ISRAEL–JORDAN BORDER; THE MACMILLAN
VISIT TO WASHINGTON, SEPTEMBER 19–OCTOBER 4

229. Editorial Note

The Second Suez Canal Conference met in London September
19–21. All of the 18 nations invited by the United Kingdom to send
delegations to the Conference did so. They were: Australia, Denmark, Ethiopia, the Federal Republic of Germany, France, Iran, Italy,
Japan, the Netherlands, New Zealand, Norway, Pakistan, Portugal,
Spain, Sweden, Turkey, the United Kingdom, and the United States.

The membership of the United States Delegation to the Second
Suez Canal Conference was as follows: United States Representa-
tive—John Foster Dulles; Special Assistant to the Representative—
William B. Macomber; Senior Advisers—Winthrop W. Aldrich, C.
Douglas Dillon, Loy W. Henderson, Herman Phleger, Carl W.
McCardle, and Walworth Barbour; Advisers—Andrew H. Berding,
Winthrop G. Brown, William C. Burdett, Jr., W. Bradley Connors,
Norris B. Chipman, Andrew B. Foster, Stanley D. Metzger, Edwin G.
Moline, Arthur R. Ringwalt, William R. Tyler, and Evan Wilson. For
a list of the chief delegates to the Conference, see *The Suez Canal
Problem, July 26–September 22, 1956*, page xv.

The records kept by the Delegation are in Department of State,
Conference Files: Lot 62 D 181. They include position papers, daily
chronologies and schedules, memoranda of conversation, extracts of
verbatim minutes for the five plenary sessions, copies of Secto,
Tosec, Dulte, and Tedul telegrams sent between the Delegation at
London and the Department of State, and administrative and other
miscellaneous papers. The Conference Files also contain copies of the
verbatim record of the five plenary sessions and other documents
prepared by the Conference's International Secretariat.

230.   Memorandum of a Conversation, Lancaster House, London, September 19, 1956, 10:45 a.m. [1]

USDel/MC/9

PARTICIPANTS

The United States	*Spain*
The Secretary	Mr. Artajo, Foreign Minister
William R. Tyler	

SUBJECT DISCUSSED

C.A.S.U. and the Spanish position

The Spanish Foreign Minister urgently requested to talk with the Secretary, and a meeting took place shortly before the opening of the first session on September 19. Mr. Artajo showed the Secretary the text of a prepared statement which he intended making. The statement was of the following gist: the Spanish Government is interested in a "community" type association including Egypt, and raises a question as to the character and purpose proposed by the C.A.S.U. It feels that the Conference should consider Nasser's proposals for negotiation which were contained in the Egyptian statement released on September 9, [2] and to explore all possibilities of renewing negotiations with Egypt.

Mr. Artajo asked the Secretary for his comment. The Secretary said that he did not feel there was anything he wished to criticize in the Spanish statement and added that he hoped ways would be found ultimately to reach some sort of agreement with Egypt which would protect the legitimate rights of Canal users. Mr. Artajo said he was somewhat in the dark about the proposed C.A.S.U. and the Secretary outlined his ideas to him, stating that he did not agree with the British and French that membership in the C.A.S.U. should commit each country to use the C.A.S.U. exclusively. Such a decision, he said, should be up to each member country. The Secretary said he thought that after the establishment of the C.A.S.U. the next step might be an approach to the United Nations. Mr. Artajo voiced doubts as to the desirability of asking the UN to deal with the problem since there would be "pandemonium" among more than seventy countries, many of which are not concerned with the Suez Canal issue. The Secretary said the idea was that this organization might be considered by the Security Council as a provisional meas-

---

[1] Source: Department of State, Conference Files: Lot 62 D 181, CF 780. Secret. Drafted by Tyler, according to a copy of the memorandum *ibid.*, Central Files, 974.7301/9–1856.

[2] Presumably reference is to the Egyptian memorandum of September 10, which contained Nasser's proposals for negotiations; see footnote 4, Document 200.

ure to prevent deterioration of the situation, but not that it should be referred to it. He agreed that it was not desirable to refer the matter to the General Assembly. Mr. Artajo asked what the Secretary thought the Security Council could do, to which the Secretary replied the Council might provide a means to initiate further negotiations with the Egyptian Government on the basis of a solution of practical problems in operating the Canal. Mr. Artajo made no objections and suggested that the most appropriate body for such negotiations might be a "Mixed Commission" since this title would not contain the fateful word "international". The Secretary said he intended to develop his own ideas when he makes his statement and hoped that these ideas would prove of interest to Mr. Artajo.

---

231.   Memorandum of a Conversation, French Embassy, London, September 19, 1956 [1]

USDel/MC/7

PARTICIPANTS

The United States
The Secretary
Ambassador Aldrich
Ambassador Dillon (Reporting
    Officer)

France
Foreign Minister Pineau
Ambassador Chauvel
M. Daridan

SUBJECT DISCUSSED

Conversation re Suez

In a rather desultory conversation after luncheon at the French Embassy, Pineau expressed the view that his primary worry in the Suez problem was the question of timing. This was acute in Pineau's view because of what he characterized as the attempt of the Soviet Union to gain effective control of the operation of the Suez Canal. He said that if it were not for the actions of the Soviet Union there would be no hurry in reaching a settlement, and it would be perfectly all right to let the matter drag on for six months or so, at the end of which time Nasser might be overthrown because of economic pressures. However, he felt that the Soviet Union was very

---

[1] Source: Department of State, Conference Files: Lot 62 D 181, CF 780. Secret. Drafted by Dillon. A copy of this memorandum is *ibid.*, Central Files, 974.7301/ 9–1956.

rapidly moving to gain control of the Suez through sending numerous technicians to aid Egypt in the operation of the Canal. Therefore, he felt that a solution must be reached before the Soviet position in Egypt could be consolidated. To sum up, he felt that a solution must be reached within the next month or so or it might be too late.

There was some discussion of the procedure to be followed from now on in the Conference, and it was agreed that it would be advisable to set up a drafting committee later this afternoon to try to prepare a resolution setting up the Users' Association in view of Secretary Dulles' declaration, and such useful comments as might emerge from this afternoon's session. There was inconclusive discussion regarding the composition of such a drafting committee.

Mr. Pineau remarked that he thought Mr. Lloyd had made an error at this morning's session [2] in mentioning that a draft along these lines had already been prepared.

Mr. Pineau said that he felt that if Israel got the impression that the western powers were weakening, and that Nasser would emerge victorious, Israel herself would precipitate hostilities. He said the Israelis realized that they were Nasser's next target and would probably be attacked during the summer of 1957, and therefore they would wish to take action while the balance of power was still more in their favor. Pineau observed that the British Treaty with Egypt regarding the evacuation of the Suez would give Great Britain the right to reoccupy the Suez base in the event Israel initiated hostilities against the Arab countries.

There was some discussion regarding the procedure for taking the Suez question to the United Nations, and the French expressed opposition to the idea of merely establishing a negotiating body without any particular directives, such as seemed to have been suggested by the Swedish Foreign Minister this morning. It was agreed that the Swedish Foreign Minister's speech this morning had not been helpful.

The Secretary agreed that we should go to the U.N. with some sort of specific project. Pineau said that he intended to speak this afternoon on this subject indicating that recourse should be had to the U.N. on the basis of the 18-power proposal and the new Users' Association, but not on the basis of setting up a negotiating committee with an unlimited directive to negotiate. It was agreed that such a committee, if constituted, would in effect mean the adoption of a proposal closely approximating that made by Mr. Shepilov at the August Conference.

---

[2] See footnote 2, *infra*.

232.   Message From the Secretary of State to the President [1]

London, September 19, 1956.

DEAR MR. PRESIDENT: I have been here now a little over 24 hours, and we have just had the first formal meeting of the 18 this morning. [2] Yesterday was spent in conference with the British and the French, and I had private talks with Cunha of Portugal, [3] Martino of Italy [4] and Lange of Norway. [5] Also last night Harold Macmillan and Salisbury dined with us. At the meeting this morning there were a few desultory remarks, and then I made a prepared statement outlining my ideas of the Users' Association. [6] Thereupon there was a general request to recess so that my remarks could be carefully studied. We are meeting again at 4 this afternoon.

My general impression is that the British and the French have quite isolated themselves even from what are naturally their closest friends. The Norwegians, whom the British habitually count upon, are worried; and also Italy, which since the war had worked closely with France, is worried. The fact is that the United States is the only bridge between the British and the French and the rest of the countries here. I do not yet know whether that bridge is going to hold. The Egyptians are making an enormous effort to make it appear that the Users' Association is a device to lead the members down the path to war for which the British and the French are preparing, and Egyptian propaganda in this sense is having a definite impact. Doubt that we shall make as much or as rapid progress this week as the British and French have wanted, but we will know better by tomorrow.

---

[1] Source: Department of State, Central Files, 974.7301/9–1956. Secret. Transmitted Priority to the Department of State in Dulte 2 from London, 4 p.m., which is the source text, with the instruction: "Eyes only Acting Secretary for President from Secretary". Dulte 2 was received at 11:33 a.m. A copy is in the Eisenhower Library, Whitman File, Dulles–Herter Series.

[2] Reference is to the first plenary session of the Second Suez Canal Conference, which began at 11 a.m., September 19. A summary of the session was transmitted to the Department of State in Secto 10 from London, September 19. (Department of State, Central Files, 974.7301/9–1956)

[3] The memorandum of Dulles' conversation with Portuguese Foreign Minister Paolo A.V. Cunha is not printed. (*Ibid.*, Conference Files: Lot 62 D 181, CF 774)

[4] The memorandum of Dulles' conversation with Italian Foreign Minister Gaetano Martino is not printed. (*Ibid.*)

[5] The memorandum of Dulles' conversation with Norwegian Foreign Minister Halvard M. Lange is not printed. (*Ibid.*)

[6] The text of the Secretary's remarks was transmitted to the Department of State in Secto 11 from London, September 19. (*Ibid.*, Central Files, 974.7301/9–1956) The complete text is printed in *The Suez Canal Problem, July 26–September 22, 1956*, pp. 353–356; and in Department of State *Bulletin*, October 1, 1956, pp. 503–506.

Good luck in your speech tonight. [7]
Faithfully yours,

Foster [8]

---

[7] See footnote 3, Document 244.
[8] Dulte 2 bears this typed signature.

---

233. Memorandum From C. Douglas Dillon to the Secretary of State [1]

London, September 19, 1956.

SUBJECT

Estimate of Objectives Sought by Macmillan and Salisbury

1. As a result of conversation during your absence with Lange last night I feel that both Macmillan and Salisbury still regard military action as the only satisfactory solution to the Suez problem, and are desirous of undertaking such action as soon as politically feasible. In order to make such action politically feasible they probably feel it necessary to do two things: (1) dislocate Labor opposition, and (2) tie the U.S. in closer to them.

2. My feeling is based on the following remarks and attitudes:

(a) In reply to questions about what might happen when and if the Suez question was taken to the Security Council, both Macmillan and Salisbury at first showed great reluctance to speculate taking refuge in your remark that we should only take "one step at a time", and that present objective was to unite the 18, or as many of them as possible, in the Users Association.

(b) Nevertheless, when pressed a bit regarding the possibility of a Soviet veto in the Security Council, Macmillan remarked to me "I hope to God Russia does veto such an approach". Macmillan made clear that what he feared was a Russian amendment to a resolution from the Security Council to the effect that in no event should force be used to solve the Suez problem.

(c) In response to my inquiry as to what the effect of a Russian veto would be on the Labor opposition, both Salisbury and Macmillan with evident relish stated that such a result would undoubtedly fragment the Labor opposition and would satisfy a substantial part

---

[1] Source: Eisenhower Library, Dulles Papers, Misc. Papers—U.K. (Suez Crisis). Top Secret. An attached chit from Macomber to Howe, September 25, indicates that Dulles and Hoover read this memorandum.

of British liberal opinion which would have been shocked by the use of force without a prior appeal to the U.N.

(d) When Mr. Phleger mentioned the Hammarskjold memo [2] and indicated that this might lead to the creation of a negotiating body which might be able to reach a settlement with Nasser, both Macmillan and Salisbury reacted strongly against this suggestion, saying that it would be absolutely impossible to continue to drag this affair on for very long. Both of them said that a solution must be reached relatively soon.

3. Macmillan also repeated his very strong language of a month ago saying that a success by Nasser would mean the end of Great Britain and must be opposed at all costs. He was talking of this, however, in a financial context and said that England was prepared to sell all of her foreign assets, including all of her American securities if necessary to gain victory. He said the present affair was a case of all or nothing.

If the above estimate does truly represent the ideas of Macmillan and Salisbury, and if these views are shared by Eden, it would appear that the way might be prepared for action in about a month. Such action would, I assume, only take place as a result of a grave incident within Egypt. I also assume that it is not out of the question that such an incident could be arranged by the British without too much difficulty.

---

[2] See footnote 5, Document 227.

234.   Memorandum From the Chairman of the Joint Chiefs of Staff (Radford) to the Secretary of Defense (Wilson) [1]

Washington, September 19, 1956.

SUBJECT

Termination of Operation "Whiplash"

1. In late June 1956 Operation "Whiplash" was initiated to provide immediate arms assistance to the nation attacked in the event of an outbreak of hostilities in connection with the Arab/Israeli situation. The USS *Oglethorpe* was dispatched to the Mediterranean with a selected loading of weapons and ammunition for assignment to Egypt in the event of Israeli aggression. Similar arrangements were made to provide Israel with combat aircraft in the event of Arab aggression.

2. Recent developments in Egypt (the Suez Canal situation) indicate that it is now highly improbable that Operation "Whiplash" will be executed as planned in the near future. The present employment of the USS *Oglethorpe* constitutes a loss of one effective unit of the Amphibious Forces, Atlantic Fleet, and due to the highly selective nature of the *Oglethorpe's* cargo it is not readily adaptable to any other mission; however, certain portions of her cargo could be used to augment existing U.S. stocks in the European-Mediterranean area. Aircraft and equipment slated for augmentation of the Israeli Defense Force are maintained on 48 hours notice for movement by air from units now available in Europe.

3. In view of the above, the Joint Chiefs of Staff recommend that the Secretary of Defense initiate action to obtain governmental approval to terminate Operation "Whiplash". Upon release of the USS *Oglethorpe*, steps will be taken to redistribute the cargo to the

---

[1] Source: Department of State, Central Files, 784A.5622/9–2556. Top Secret; Limited Distribution; Eyes Only. Attached to a letter from Secretary Wilson to Dulles, dated September 25, which reads: "I am attaching a copy of the memorandum from the Chairman of the Joint Chiefs of Staff in which the Joint Chiefs of Staff recommend the termination of Operation "Whiplash". I concur in their recommendation and if you feel that the situation requires it I would be glad to take the matter up directly with the President, provided you agree to this action."

best advantage of the Services and reassign the ship as a unit of the Atlantic Fleet. [2]

For the Joint Chiefs of Staff:
Arthur Radford [3]

---

[2] According to a memorandum from Radford to Secretary Wilson dated January 18, 1957, only that portion of the plan pertaining to arms assistance to Egypt was terminated as a result of this memorandum. The remainder of the plan, which had provided for augmentation of the Israeli Defense Force with aircraft and equipment from USAF units currently in Europe was terminated in response to Radford's memorandum of January 18. (Memorandum from Radford to Wilson, January 18, 1957; Decision on J.C.S. 2105/49, January 18; and NH J.C.S. 2105/49, February 26; all in JCS Records, CCS 092 Egypt (7–28–56) sec 3)

[3] Printed from a copy that bears this stamped signature.

---

235.   Editorial Note

On September 19, after making several substantive changes, the Intelligence Advisory Committee concurred in Special National Intelligence Estimate 30–5–56, entitled "The Likelihood of a British-French Resort to Military Action Against Egypt in the Suez Crisis." The text of the SNIE as approved is printed *infra*; no copy of the earlier version has been found in Department of State files. According to the notes taken at the IAC meeting, the following discussion concerning SNIE 30–5–56 took place:

"There was considerable discussion on the statement of the problem. General Lewis requested clarification as to the exact period meant by the phrase 'during the next few weeks.' He expressed the view that the Estimate was valid if, by this phrase, one or two weeks was meant, but that if it meant any longer period, the Estimate would then not be reliable. Mr. Armstrong said he took it as meaning a period of less than a month and that for such a period the Estimate was valid. Mr. Smith indicated his view that even if no time angle were put in at all, the conclusions of the Estimate would be reliable. As a way out of the impasse, it was agreed that a footnote should be added indicating that the fluidity of the situation made precise estimation difficult.

"With respect to the conclusions, there was significant discussion on the second. General Lewis felt that, as drafted, this paragraph underplayed the likelihood of war. The Chairman noted the possibility that the policy people reading this paragraph might feel that it applied to a period beyond the few weeks covered by the Estimate. Mr. Armstrong suggested that a time angle be introduced into this conclusion to indicate that it applied only to the present stage of the crisis.

"Discussion on Conclusion 3 centered on use of the word 'provocations.' Mr. Armstrong pointed out that the Egyptians might consider certain acts as defense of their position rather than intentional provocation to the West. Mr. Armstrong also moved for the deletion of the last part of the Conclusion as it implied a U.S. course of action contrary to that which it has been publicly stated we will follow. Adjustments were made to meet Mr. Armstrong's objections." (Notes on IAC Meeting by McAfee, September 19; Department of State, INR Files: Lot 58 D 776)

---

236. Special National Intelligence Estimate [1]

SNIE 30–5–56   *Washington, September 19, 1956.*

THE LIKELIHOOD OF A BRITISH-FRENCH RESORT TO MILITARY ACTION AGAINST EGYPT IN THE SUEZ CRISIS

The Problem

To estimate the likelihood and probable circumstances of a British-French resort to military action against Egypt during the next few weeks.

Conclusions [2]

1. At least for the immediate future, the UK and France will almost certainly seek to keep the way open for the use of force. The temptation for the British and French governments to resort to

---

[1] Source: Department of State, INR–NIE Files. Top Secret. According to a note on the cover sheet, "the following intelligence organizations participated in the preparation of this estimate: The Central Intelligence Agency and the intelligence organizations of the Departments of State, the Army, the Navy, the Air Force, and The Joint Staff." This estimate was concurred in by the Intelligence Advisory Committee on September 19, 1956. "Concurring were the Special Assistant, Intelligence, Department of State; the Assistant Chief of Staff, Intelligence, Department of the Army; the Director of Naval Intelligence; the Director of Intelligence, USAF; and the Deputy Director for Intelligence, The Joint Staff. The Atomic Energy Commission Representative to the IAC, and the Assistant Director, Federal Bureau of Investigation, abstained, the subject being outside of their jurisdiction."

The text of this Special National Intelligence Estimate was transmitted to Dulles in London. (*Ibid.*, Conference Files: Lot 62 D 181, CF 772)

[2] The Suez situation has in the past two months undergone rapid changes, and is likely to do so again. Developments are, to an unusual degree, subject to influences which cannot be evaluated at this time. [Footnote in the source text.]

military action against Egypt will probably be great over the next few weeks, despite substantial opposition in the UK (and elsewhere) to the use of force.

2. On balance, at this stage of the crisis we believe that UK-French resort to military action is likely only in the event of some new and violent provocation—such as major violence to British and French nationals and property in Egypt—which would unite British public opinion behind such action. In such an event, the UK and France would probably use force against Egypt even without US support. We believe that Nasser realizes this, and will make every effort to prevent such violent provocation from occurring, though it is always possible that he may not be able to do so.

3. We do not believe that the nonviolent incidents which are likely to occur—interruption of shipping in the canal, refusal to admit ships with users' pilots, differences over tolls—will cause the UK and France to take military action against Egypt so long as the US continues to oppose the use of force. Should the situation develop so as to cause the US to sanction the use of force, there is at least an even chance that Prime Minister Eden would move despite the continued existence of public opposition to such a course.

4. Finally, it is possible, but we believe unlikely during the period of this estimate, that other situations of friction in the area—the Arab-Israeli conflict, or Iraqi-Syrian relations for example—might develop in such a way as to furnish an occasion for UK-French military intervention against Nasser.

5. The majority of the British cabinet, especially Prime Minister Eden, and virtually all the members of the French cabinet, are convinced that the elimination of Nasser is essential to the preservation of vital Western interests in the Middle East and North Africa. They are gravely concerned with the dangers of appeasement and probably believe that forceful action against Nasser offers the only real hope of arresting the decline of their positions. They have taken pains to emphasize that they remain prepared to use force if necessary. They are continuing their military buildup in the Mediterranean. They are now in a high state of military readiness and can initiate military action at any time.

6. Nevertheless, over the course of the Suez crisis, the British and to a lesser extent the French governments have come increasingly to recognize disadvantages to the use of force. Although they continue to believe that there would be no serious Soviet military reaction and appear to discount the likelihood of critical repercussions in the Arab states, they have been forced to recognize that a resort to military action would entail serious adverse reactions throughout the non-Communist world. In response to the pressure of domestic and world opinion, they have felt compelled to indicate

that they would use force only as a last resort, and the British government has reluctantly undertaken to take its grievances to the UN Security Council (except in case of emergency) before making any military move against Egypt.

7. The temptation to resort to military action against Egypt will be great over the next few weeks, particularly in view of the continuing Anglo-French military buildup and the unyielding stand of Nasser. As long as the USSR continues to support Egypt, it is highly unlikely that any diplomatic and economic pressures that can be brought to bear against Nasser will offer any early prospect that he will retreat from his refusal to accept a degree of international supervision or control of the canal which the UK and France would regard as effective. Having firmly rejected the plan to have ships transit the canal under "users' association" auspices, he will almost certainly deny passage to those ships which refuse to accept Egyptian-supplied pilots and may also bar those which refuse to pay tolls directly to Egypt in convertible funds. There are various technical means by which Nasser could prevent the passage of ships failing to meet Egypt's conditions, even without resort to military force.

8. Furthermore, to the extent that Western shipping continues to use the canal on Egypt's terms, it may encounter, at least in the early stages, accidents, delays, and obstructions arising from Egyptian failures of operation. The UK and France would view such incidents as further justification for forceful action against Nasser.

9. While these factors are thus likely to maintain the temptation to use force at a high level, the inhibitions to the use of force will probably also continue to be strong. Egypt and its Soviet and neutralist friends will probably continue to press Nasser's proposals for a new conference on the Suez situation, thus generating further worldwide pressure against the use of force. If the West refers the case to the UN (for example, on the grounds of denial of passage of Western shipping), this would provide further demonstration of British-French desire to exhaust all peaceful means of achieving their objectives. While the UK and France might then regard themselves to be in a better position to justify a resort to force, the appeal to the UN would almost certainly generate new demands for conciliation. It might even result in a resolution—politically difficult for the Western powers to oppose—specifically enjoining the parties to refrain from use of force. There will probably be a growing tendency on the part of many who had originally supported the use of force to feel that the opportune moment for such action had passed.

10. The attitude of the US will continue to be of very great importance. The UK and France fully recognize that a resort to military force against Nasser without at least implicit US support would involve risks which they would hesitate to assume alone. On

the other hand, there are limits to the US restraining influence. If a situation should develop in which British opinion generally was prepared to accept the use of force, the British government would probably resort to force even without US support.

11. It remains possible, though we believe unlikely during the period of this estimate, that if the UK and France are inhibited from using force over the Suez issue per se, they might eventually take military action against Nasser in connection with other possible crises in the area. It is possible that other situations of friction—the Arab-Israeli conflict or Iraqi-Syrian relations, for example—might develop in such a way as to furnish an occasion for UK-French military intervention against Nasser. [3]

---

[3] On September 25, the Intelligence Advisory Committee discussed SNIE 30–5–56 as follows:

"The Chairman asked if the developing situation had necessitated review of the recent SNIE. Mr. Armstrong expressed the view that developments subsequent to its issuance had diminished cause for concern over the time through which it would be valid. He noted that the move to take the matter to the United Nations had introduced certain fairly firm time factors, that the matter will first come up Wednesday for a decision concerning inscription on the agenda, that according to present indications neither side is anxious for discussion before next week, with October 3 apparently the earliest date for its consideration. He noted that a veto in the Security Council would by no means exhaust UN opportunity for consideration of this problem, and that if it goes to the General Assembly, it might well be mid-November before the pattern of UN action is known." (Notes on IAC Meeting by McAfee, September 25; Department of State, INR Files: Lot 58 D 776)

---

237.   Telegram From the Delegation at the Suez Canal Conference to the Department of State [1]

London, September 20, 1956—11 a.m.

Secto 13. Second session started Wednesday 4 p.m. [2] with Lloyd calling upon Spender of Australia. After tribute to colleagues of Menzies in Five Power Committee, Spender stressed need achieve peaceful solution Suez problem. Discussed legal basis 18 power position and stated Nasser had exceeded his right in taking over Canal. Asked that more attention be given legal aspects problem.

---

[1] Source: Department of State, Central Files, 974.7301/9–2056. Confidential; Priority. Received at 9:33 a.m. Drafted by Tyler, according to a copy of Secto 13 in the London Embassy File. (*Ibid.*, Conference Files: Lot 62 D 181, CF 775)

[2] Reference is to the second plenary session, which began at 4 p.m., September 19.

Referred to Paragraph 11 in Committee of Five Report. Stressed Nasser had absolutely refused basic principles proposals first conference. Said present conference must re-examine these principles, otherwise disaster. Pointed out Nasser's tactics since Cairo had objective divide 18 powers. Stressed importance powers remain united. Reaffirmed validity Article 33 UN Charter calling for negotiation between parties to a dispute before referring to UN. Said we must first organize our interests in manner suggested by Secretary before going to UN and make clear to world legal grounds on which our position rests since these had not been set forth adequately in public press. Said considered Secretary's proposal first step toward negotiations which might perhaps be protracted and that he reserved his rights make further specific comments on Secretary's proposal.

Italian Foreign Minister then spoke and expressed regret rejection proposals first conference by Egypt stating Egypt had shown lack good faith. Rejected Egypt's September 10 proposal which full political arguments. Stated that Nasser's nationalization Canal violated Convention 1888. Referring to regulations for operating Canal, questioned whether true, as Lloyd had said, that there is nothing which obliges 18 powers use pilots provided by Egyptian Canal Board. Pointed out they stipulated that freedom of navigation depends on observance of regulations, which provide that local Canal authorities shall supply pilots. He said it could be argued that since Egypt violated convention, use Egyptian pilots not mandatory, but while this may be valid legal argument, issue really political and in order to use Canal, we must have Egyptian agreement. Thus whatever legal situation, de facto situation is that we must have Egyptian agreement before Canal can be used. Approved Secretary statement that no question coercing Egypt and gratified Lloyd's statement that UK not thinking military measures but peaceful road solution. Commented that Iranian Foreign Minister had stated earlier that rerouting ships would gravely affect Asian countries economically, but that this equally true for Europe and particularly for Italy. Dulles proposal, he said, should be considered as step toward agreement and new base for negotiation. Approved idea CASU for defense legitimate rights under 1888 Convention and as contribution toward reaching agreement with Egypt. Said he had one or two doubts on specific points CASU proposal, such as necessity single administrator but felt that association should be established now. Did not agree with Spender that now no time for approach to UN since 18 powers have good basis for approach. UN good offices should be requested facilitate task negotiating convention with Egypt protecting rights users. Martino then tabled resolution of which text being cabled separately.[3] Martino concluded with reminder that right on side 18 powers and that they must be firm.

Followed by Norwegian Foreign Minister, who supported approach to UN with request for good offices and agreed with need for establishing CASU. Suggested terms of reference be broadened provide total coordination needs of powers in event passage through Canal prevented or delayed. Association should establish working relationship with local Canal authority and supply pilots to extent local authority unable handle traffic, plan rerouting and rebunkering needs taking into account financial factors. Also should be empowered deal with all problems arising from present situation pending final solution. Expressed general agreement with Martino resolution.

Netherlands Foreign Minister[4] stressed necessity uphold Menzies committee proposals and 18 power unity. Agreed particularly point six. Approved approach UN "in one way or the other" but recommending careful study on how and when. Said would study Martino resolution carefully and recommended need support not only decisions present conference but also conclusions previous conference.

Danish Foreign Minister[5] expressed regret Nasser turned down first conference proposal but stressed need avoid infringing Egyptian sovereignty. Recommended peaceful solution. Supported approach to UN and rejected Nasser's suggestion of Sept. 10. Said he understood CASU concept better since Secretary's statement but still had many questions in mind. Stated that for constitutional reasons Denmark unable now take final position CASU.

Pakistani Foreign Minister[6] said greatly reassured that everyone agreed on need peaceful means. Had felt that means previously employed by 18 power approach Nasser meant failure unavoidable because Menzies committee had no power negotiate and had merely presented proposals rigidly. While Egypt had nationalized Canal, he said, 18 power resolution tries internationalize it, thus both sides equally inflexible. Must not proceed again in this manner since waste time. Should carefully consider organization CASU. Then quoted from preamble UK draft resolution association, which, he said, also contained seeds failure. Referred to Pakistan solidarity with other Middle East countries to which bound by ties race and culture. Stated Egypt alone entitled under 1888 Convention ensure navigation Canal. Thus present draft proposal cannot be supported by Pakistan. Welcomed tone Dulles' statement and expressed hope

---

[3] Not printed. (Transmitted in Secto 14 from London, September 20; *ibid.*, Central Files, 974.7301/9–2056)

[4] Joseph Luns.

[5] Hans Christian S. Hansen.

[6] Malik Firoz Khan Noon.

might lead to fruitful negotiation with Egypt which should be tried first and then in event failure, approach UN. Reiterated need that any new approach negotiation with Egypt should be made on basis full negotiating powers.

French Foreign Minister then spoke listing two major objectives conference so far. Avoidance armed conflict and agreement Canal should not be subject to decisions single man or power. Said certain countries have been doing all they could encourage Nasser and prevent negotiation. Disagreed with Pakistani representative with regard role and tactics Menzies mission. Reaffirmed reasonable character proposals made to Cairo and said new negotiations undertaken on basis suggested by Pakistani, would give Nasser all trumps. Recommended payment dues be withheld from Egypt as inducement negotiate. Said so long Egypt feels if she turns down proposals she may expect more favorable ones, she will never agree negotiation. Supported CASU and recommended approach Security Council, which should be "seized" with problem on basis specific and detailed presentation. Concluded 18 power principles should be upheld and defended.

Hallstein spoke for Germany. Supported CASU and recommended present conference become permanent group with institutional arrangements. Approved practical and de facto character Secretary's proposal. Said we should prepare for future eventualities, such as rerouting and recourse to UN good offices. Followed by Japanese representative [7] who echoed position expressed by Japanese Foreign Minister at previous conference in favor peaceful solution. Raised several questions regarding character and role CASU which were later answered by Secretary in his statement cabled separately. Lloyd for UK then stressed CASU proposals complementary to and not substitute for proposals first conference. Disturbed by thought expressed by some delegates that 18 powers should abandon their idea of what is fair and reasonable simply because Nasser rejected proposals. This slippery path on road toward unconditional surrender. Rejected idea Nasser nationalization not breach legal obligations. Rejected view that rights formerly vested Suez Canal Company now vested Egyptian board which we not recognize as legal authority. Stated support CASU irrespective powers assigned and said functions should not be restricted immediate future Canal but for continuing problems. Stressed advantages cooperative body users Canal to safeguard rights threatened by possible covert and devious actions Egypt. Recommended establishment association now and regretted Denmark statement that could not join association at this time since important go ahead. Said dues should be paid CASU and held

---

[7] Haruhiko Nishi.

suspense pending final settlement with Egypt. UN matter should be dealt with later but at some stage problem should be placed before Security Council.

Australian Representative [8] then said he wished correct impression he opposed going to UN, and that merely felt important question was when and how, not whether recommended matter only be referred to UN after association had been organized. Followed by New Zealand Representative [9] who reaffirmed need for international control, unity and stressed legal rights. Felt should not approach UN prematurely since have not exhausted all possibilities [garble—to settle] matter by negotiation. Endorsed CASU. Swedish Foreign Minister [10] then said opinions within conference still divided on legal aspects and therefore suggested wiser not go into these too much. Session concluded with extemporaneous address by Secretary which cabled separately. [11] Third session scheduled 11 a.m. Thursday morning.

Dulles

---

[8] Sir Percy Spender.

[9] Sir Clifton Webb.

[10] Osten Undén.

[11] Dulles' extemporaneous comments were transmitted to the Department of State in Secto 12 from London, September 20. (Department of State, Central Files, 974.7301/9–2056) They are printed in Department of State *Bulletin*, October 1, 1956, p. 505; and in *The Suez Canal Problem, July 26–September 22, 1956*, pp. 356–364.

238.   Memorandum of a Conversation, British Foreign Office, London, September 20, 1956, 10 a.m. [1]

USDel/MC/10

PARTICIPANTS

The United States	*The United Kingdom*
The Secretary	Mr. Lloyd
Mr. Henderson	Mr. Fitzmaurice
Mr. Phleger	Mr. Beeley
Amb. Dillon	Mr. Ross
Mr. Brown	
Mr. Macomber	*France*
Mr. Metzger	
Mr. Burdett	Mr. Pineau
	Mr. Cheval
	Mr. Daridan

SUBJECT DISCUSSED

CASU

After Mr. Lloyd had opened the meeting, the Secretary said that he thought it was necessary to give the Conference something definite to consider in the form of a paper describing the proposed Users' Association. This procedure would serve to overcome the existing confusion. Apparently several of the delegations had instructions from their governments not to go along with the Users' Association. If an agreed paper could be worked out, they would be able on that basis to seek further instructions. Any strong moves made with respect to Egypt would have to be apart from the proposed association. In the case of the United States, at least, action in connection with the association would have to be such as not to require Congressional approval. The Secretary assumed that most other delegations were in a similar situation. If an association were set up which did not involve incurring formal obligations, less resistance would be encountered from the Conference. The Secretary concluded that he had planned to leave tonight but could stay over until Friday.

Mr. Lloyd said he hoped very strongly the Secretary would stay over so that some final decisions could be reached. Mr. Pineau observed that if the objective was to get agreement on Friday it would be impossible to work out a statute for the association.

[1] Source: Department of State, Conference Files: Lot 62 D 181, CF 774. Secret. Prepared by the U.S. Delegation, but the source text does not indicate a drafting officer.

Perhaps the proposed executive authority could be given the power to work out the statute.

At this point the United States drafts of a declaration and a statute for a Cooperative Association of Suez Canal Users (CASU) were distributed.[2]

The Secretary agreed to Mr. Pineau's proposal that the statute be omitted. Mr. Pineau thought that the executive group could set up some "internal regulations" which could serve in lieu of a statute. The Secretary commented that the executive group might be given the power to form its own rules. Mr. Phleger suggested language empowering the executive group to "direct and conduct the affairs of the association". Mr. Fitzmaurice expressed the view that the procedure adopted must depend upon whether it was intended that the governments should have specific obligations under the statute. If so, they would hardly delegate to the executive group authority to draw up the statute.

Mr. Fitzmaurice pointed out that the provisions of funds for the association was something that the governments participating would have to decide—it could not be left to the executive group as an "internal regulation". The Secretary doubted that an issue should be made of the source of funds. Two or three of the members could advance the money required and the contributions from the remainder could be nominal. Mr. Lloyd thought that a request for funds would frighten other potential participants. The Secretary suggested that the association have the power to borrow working funds from its members.

Mr. Lloyd said that an agreement with the Universal Suez Canal Company would be needed. Among other things it might lend the new association some of its staff. Mr. Fitzmaurice emphasized that CASU should do nothing which might prejudice the rights of the Universal Suez Canal Company. Mr. Beeley stressed that the Company was in a strong position. For example, its pilots would not agree to work for CASU on an individual basis. Therefore, relations with the Company were of fundamental importance. The Company would seek in the declaration some phrase protecting its position. Mr. Pineau added that there should be nothing in the statute which would tend to recognize the new Egyptian authority.

The Secretary stressed the importance of simplicity in the declaration. The meeting then went over the United States draft in detail and agreed upon the document [being] presented to the plenary

---

[2] Not attached to the source text. Copies of a U.S. draft statute and U.S. drafts, numbered 1–5, of a declaration are *ibid.* The first four of these declaration drafts are dated at various times on September 19; the fifth, which is dated September 20, is presumably the version which was distributed at this meeting.

meeting at 11:00 am. During the discussion, Mr. Lloyd said he was particularly worried over the fact that the declaration "funked" the question of whether dues should be paid to the association or not. The Secretary replied that the declaration would impose no obligation on any member; he saw no objection to mentioning the question of dues.

Mr. Henderson reported that he had just seen Foreign Minister Ardalan [3] who told him that Iran would not be able to adhere to the declaration unless an article was included providing that recourse would be had to the UN if Egypt refused to cooperate. Mr. Pineau said that it would not be the role of CASU to represent its members at the UN. He accepted the fact that the participating governments could go to the UN if Egypt did not agree. Mr. Lloyd concurred with Mr. Pineau. The meeting agreed to language suggested by Mr. Pineau to the effect that one of the purposes of the association would be "to facilitate the application of any provisional solution of the Suez problem which may be adopted by the UN".

Mr. Henderson said that he had had breakfast with the Pakistan Foreign Minister [4] who surprisingly had been most friendly. The Foreign Minister took pains to explain that the speech he made yesterday had been necessitated by the internal political situation in Pakistan. He thought he could persuade his Government upon his return to adhere to a declaration along the lines discussed if the declaration was held open for subsequent signature. Mr. Henderson said he had also talked with the Turkish delegate who thought it essential that Iran, Pakistan, Ethiopia and Turkey all sign simultaneously. Therefore, Mr. Birgi wished the declaration left open for signature for a few days. Mr. Birgi said that he was discussing the problem with the Ethiopians in order to obtain their adherence. The Japanese Ambassador [5] had informed Mr. Henderson that he was prepared to recommend participation to his Government, but that he would require a few days to get authorization to sign. The Secretary pointed out that the Scandinavian delegations also had to get additional instructions.

---

[3] Following the Conference, Henderson wrote a summary report entitled "Attitude Displayed During the Second Suez Canal Conference at London, September 19–21, 1956, by Dr. A.G. Ardalan, Iranian Minister for Foreign Affairs and Head of the Iranian Delegation to the Conference" containing a description of Henderson's conversations with Ardalan. The report is attached to a cover sheet of a memorandum of conversation between Henderson and Ardalan on September 19. (*Ibid.*)

[4] Henderson wrote a summary report containing a description of his conversations with Noon. The report is entitled, "Attitude Displayed During Second Suez Canal Conference at London, September 19–21, 1956, by Mr. Malik Feroz Khan Noon, Foreign Minister of Pakistan", and is attached to a cover sheet of a memorandum of conversation between Henderson and Noon at breakfast on September 20. (*Ibid.*)

[5] Haruhiko Nishi.

The Secretary suggested that the plenary session of the Conference be asked to designate technical or legal people to work on the draft further.

The meeting adjourned to permit attendance at the 11:00 o'clock session of the Conference.

---

239.   Telegram From the Delegation at the Suez Canal Conference to the Department of State [1]

London, September 20, 1956—3 p.m.

Secto 15. Conference—First session, September 20. [2] Lloyd convened session shortly after 11 a.m. Cunha (Portugal) opened by thanking UK for its "outstanding contribution" in preparing paper on legal position; [3] said issue however was local and political as well as legal and agreed with other delegates question of safeguarding unity of users was essential. Associated himself with an organization of users—"sort of union of all users that would give balanced solution". Users Association was not designed to pick a quarrel but rather to "act positively" and to show Egypt Europe did not wish to impose "European sovereignty" over Canal. There were many different means to attain this end but in general Portugal agreed with broad principles set forth by Secretary Dulles, especially in para six of his paper. [4] Association must have "real program" for substitution of Canal which may prove expensive and difficult to carry out; but he now saw Association plan was "practical step for working out provisional arrangement, a collective negotiating body". It could prepare long-term solution that could be presented to UN and could relieve Europe from "servitude" to Canal, an "extremely important task as a means of making Egypt 'fear' users of Canal". Although he reserved right to discuss "precise" proposals Portugal approved broad

---

[1] Source: Department of State, Central Files, 974.7301/9–2056. Confidential. Drafted by Chipman and Burdett. Received at 1:17 p.m. Repeated to Paris.

[2] Reference is to the third plenary session, which began at 11 a.m., September 20.

[3] Reference is to a British paper, entitled "Juridical Basis of the 'Users Scheme' ", which was circulated, at the request of the U.K. Delegation, to the other delegations attending the Conference. (Conference doc. Suez/II/56D/3; a copy is part of a documentary "Summary Record" of the Conference; Department of State, Central Files, 974.7301/9–2256)

[4] Reference presumably is to Dulles' statement at the first plenary session on September 19; see footnote 6, Document 232.

principles set forth at Conference for setting up association for maintaining unity of users.

Aklilou (Ethiopia) spoke briefly on excellent work and representational nature of Menzies' mission and regretted failure of Nasser to make counter proposals while mission was in Cairo. He then expressed pleasure original proposal for CASU had been "modified". Unfortunately proposal originally had been "accompanied by military preparations". Dulles' proposal was worthy of study and it would be useful to take it to UN. As for alternative of using Cape route he would associate himself with Italian colleague in saying Cape alternative was not even a good temporary solution.

Birgi (Turkey) thought yesterday's meetings had been useful and fruitful. He thanked UK for his legal paper, associated himself with "all points made by Lange" and said Dulles paper was a "reasonable basis for discussion". Also thanked Martino for Italian suggestions. He thought time had come to adjourn plenary session and get up a "Drafting Committee" of experts to prepare a paper setting forth conception of CASU and how issue could be brought to UN. Suggested Conference adjourn until 4 pm when experts' paper could be discussed. Birgi had been informed in confidence US had paper that could serve as basis for experts' consideration but did not state this.

Lange (Norway) said if nobody else wished to speak he would express thought that best way to proceed was now to prepare a "working paper". He wondered, however, whether paper could be ready by 4 pm, Birgi replied that if it could be done "so much the better".

Unden (Sweden) then got up and insisted on Sweden's "strong feeling for appeal to UN"; inviting govts had refused to take CASU to UN. Noted Sweden had given negative reply to Egypt's invitation to Conference. Happily idea for CASU had "changed from original proposal" and was now "a practical question" and in case of Nasser's refusal to pass ships they could go around Cape. Concluded he had no authority to commit his govt to CASU.

Lloyd then asked if delegates were agreed on adjournment and that "a working paper" should be prepared. Secretary Dulles explained that participation in Drafting Committee did not commit anyone to subscribe to paper and that US might not accept "all of it". He added "none of us can commit ourselves for or against".

Artajo (Spain) rose to say he had spoken yesterday prior to presentation of Dulles' proposal. He hoped Drafting Committee would consider a Spanish paper. He presented English text which summed up Spanish position as follows: "(1) That the correct course for a peaceful settlement of Suez Canal problem is a direct negotiation with Egypt, as in our view possibilities of agreement have by no means been exhausted, and other proposals should be used, which reconcile the interests and guarantees of the users with that of the country through which the Canal crosses. (2) That recourse to the United Nations is premature, because within spirit of its Charter, an arrangement should first be attempted by direct negotiation. (3) That the principal aim for an association of users should be to maintain unity of purpose and action among its members. (4) That simultaneously with conduct of negotiations, the association should in fact reach an understanding with the Egyptian authorities for the adoption of practical measures to ensure the efficiency of the technical services of the Canal."

Noon (Pakistan) said it was advisable to give each delegation right to join or not join Drafting Committee. Some delegations might not wish to join in work.

Chairman Lloyd said so-called Drafting Committee "not really a drafting committee" since idea was "to exchange views" on a paper "somebody" might propose after consultation. One had wrong impression to think of a formal drafting committee.

Birgi (Turkey) agreed his proposal would not prevent anybody from later clarifying ideas. There would merely be a "working paper".

Chairman Lloyd asked if experts could stay and work and whether 4 or 5 pm was agreeable. Martino rose to ask what "real aim" of group would be—"whether it would repeat what had already been said at Conference" or would make new proposals. Lloyd explained "a draft" had been prepared which committee could study and perhaps by 4 p.m. "a paper" could be produced.

Session adjourned at 12 noon. [5]

Dulles

---

[5] Following adjournment, a committee met at Lancaster House to consider the U.S. draft declaration and made several changes in the document. A summary record of the committee meeting, prepared by the Conference's International Secretariat, is in Department of State, Conference Files: Lot 62 D 181, CF 773. At 4:45 p.m., the fourth plenary session convened and the revised document, now entitled a "Resolution for a Cooperative Association of Suez Canal Users", was circulated to the delegates, who discussed the item paragraph by paragraph. A summary of the fourth session was transmitted to the Department of State in Secto 18 from London, September 20. (*Ibid.,* Central Files, 974.7301/9–2056) The text of the draft resolution as it stood at the close of the fourth session was sent to the Department in Secto 19, September 21. (*Ibid.,* 974.7301/9–2156)

240.   Editorial Note

At the 297th meeting of the National Security Council, September 20, Acting Director of Central Intelligence Cabell made the following comments in regard to the Arab-Israeli situation. Cabell "noted the sharp increase in Arab-Israeli tension and provided the Council with a summary of the latest incidents. He pointed out that the Israeli raids into the neighboring Arab states represented a firm application of the Israeli doctrine of prompt reprisal. The Israelis, he said, believed that such strong retaliatory actions would ultimately compel the Arab states to cease their raids into Israeli territory. Accordingly, while we must expect further Israeli reprisals, General Cabell believed that it was unlikely that Israel would initiate major hostilities against any Arab state at this time."

At the conclusion of General Cabell's briefing, Acting Secretary Hoover stated that he would like to comment on the Arab-Israeli situation. Hoover commented "that there were two major forces which tend to maintain the unity of the Arab states. The first of these was the threat of aggression from Great Britain and France, the second was the threat posed by Israel. If these two threats were not present, centrifugal forces would tend to have the upper hand in the Arab states. Accordingly, if the United States succeeds in checking the threat of aggression against the Arab states from the British and the French, as well as from Israel, we can be relatively optimistic as to the results. At the moment we are putting all possible pressure on the Israelis to restrain them. Nevertheless, we are not too optimistic that the Israelis will not continue their present tactics or otherwise take advantage of the grave Suez Canal situation.

"The President commented that the Israelis are of course well aware of how difficult it is for the United States to maintain its present policy of opposing aggression in the Middle East no matter which side commits it. What with the situation in Suez, the Israelis may feel that they have boxed the United States in." (Memorandum of discussion; Eisenhower Library, Whitman File, NSC Records)

241.   Report Prepared in the Executive Secretariat of the Department of State [1]

Summary No. 13   *Washington, September 20, 1956.*

SUMMARY OF DEVELOPMENTS IN SUEZ SITUATION

First Session of London Conference

Lloyd convened the first conference session yesterday morning and was chosen chairman. In declaring that the UK desired a peaceful solution to the dispute, Lloyd noted that the UK had proceeded to date under Article 33 of the UN Charter. It was realized that at some stage the dispute would have to be referred to the Security Council; the time and manner of such a move would be considered at the present conference.

It was agreed, after acceptance of the Menzies report, to combine agenda items 2 and 3: the formation of the users' association and the preparation of a response to the Egyptian memorandum. The Secretary then gave the US views on the current situation and described the users' proposal. The meeting adjourned until the afternoon so that representatives might study the Secretary's statement.

Second Session of London Conference

At the second session the Secretary spoke at length on the present stage of the dispute with particular comment on the relationship of the problem to possible UN action. He did not believe that the Security Council, much less the Assembly, had the authority to compel the conclusion of a new treaty which would redefine the rights of the parties and which would deal in perpetuity with the problem. The conference must first provide a setting which will permit of an actual solution by the UN within the competence of the Security Council. Speaking on the association proposal, he outlined the practical details of the plan and the minimum cooperation which would be necessary on the part of the Egyptian authorities.

Khrishna Menon's Activities

Embassy Cairo states [2] that the primary objective of the Khrishna Menon visit to Cairo is reported to have been to persuade Nasser

---

[1] Source: Eisenhower Library, Whitman File, International File. Top Secret; Eyes Only for Designated Recipient. A marginal notation by Goodpaster on the source text reads: "President informed of substance 20 Sept 56. G".

[2] Reported in telegram 808 from Cairo, September 19, not printed. (Department of State, Central Files, 974.7301/9–1956)

to adopt a more conciliatory attitude towards a Suez solution. At the same time Menon is reported to have expressed Nehru's view that the real British objective is to "get rid of Nasser", and to have conveyed Nehru's concern that the Saudi Arabian Government is in grave danger of a Communist coup if its oil revenues should be denied or substantially reduced.

Nasser's Talk with Ethiopian Ambassador

Ethiopian Ambassador Gebriehiwat has told Embassy Cairo [3] of his conversation yesterday with Nasser. The Egyptian Premier urged the defection of Ethiopia, among others, from the users' association plan so that the US might be persuaded to drop it. Gebriehiwat pointed out that small nations in the Red Sea area were completely at Egypt's mercy and felt uncomfortable. He also told Nasser that Ethiopia had not accepted Egypt's invitation to form a negotiating body because the invitation was not clear. The meeting would serve no purpose if it was to consist of the principal users of the canal for the views of this group were already known. If, on the other hand, it was intended to bring in countries who were not important users so that those who were might be outvoted, its purpose would not attract Ethiopia.

The Ethiopian Ambassador asked Nasser what he intended to do if users' association ships arrived in convoy for canal transit. Nasser replied that he would not shoot at them but would simply move another convoy into the canal. If blockage then occurred it would be the fault of the users' association which would be in the position of having acted without clearance with the Egyptian Canal authority.

Reply to Saud's Proposals

We have asked Wadsworth [4] to tell Saud that in our opinion his most constructive role would be to use his influence to persuade Egypt to negotiate realistically. We believe the 18-nation proposals provide the best basis for such negotiation and that a conference such as King Saud may have in mind would achieve no useful purpose in view of Nasser's inflexible attitude. We have also authorized Hare [5] to express to Yusuf Yassin, now in Cairo, our hope that Saud's influence may be used to bring about some Egyptian action to restore confidence in Nasser's government.

---

[3] Reported in telegram 815 from Cairo, September 19, not printed. (*Ibid.*) The Ethiopian Ambassador to Egypt was Balambaras Guebre-Hiot.

[4] Presumably reference is to telegram 195 to Jidda, September 18, not printed, in which the Department transmitted President Eisenhower's response to a recent message from Saud regarding the Suez situation. (*Ibid.*, 974.7301/9–1656)

[5] In telegram 836 from Cairo, September 19, not printed. (*Ibid.*, 974.7301/9–1856)

(Summary closed 12:15 p.m., September 20, 1956)

---

242.   Memorandum From the Assistant Secretary of State for Near Eastern, South Asian, and African Affairs (Rountree) to the Under Secretary of State (Hoover) [1]

Washington, September 20, 1956.

SUBJECT

Possibility that France has Delivered Additional Mystere Aircraft to Israel

The following may be of interest to you. [2]

It appears possible that Israel has 48 Mystere Aircraft rather than only 24 of these jet fighters as previously believed. Our information on this subject is as follows:

1. Reports have circulated in Israel that a number of Israel's Mysteres were sent to France to undergo a fifty-hour "overhaul". The French Ambassador to Israel has confirmed this report to our Ambassador, stating that this was a customary procedure in view of the availability of facilities in France. However, it now appears likely that eighteen Mysteres which were reported to have passed through Brindisi, Italy, were not in fact en route from Israel to France, but were actually proceeding in the reverse direction. A vague story in a Tel Aviv newspaper of August 29 stating that "a considerable number" of Mystere Aircraft had arrived in Israel "in due time" seems to bear this out.

---

[1] Source: Department of State, Central Files, 784A.5622/9–2056. Secret. Drafted by Blackiston. Initialed by both Rountree and Hoover.

[2] On September 5, the Embassy in Tel Aviv reported: "During the last half of August there were several reports, both of Israel and foreign origin, that some Israel Air Force Mysteres had been flown to France for overhaul or equipment modification. Since then, however, a theory has developed among foreign military attachés that the reported flight to Paris was an elaborate ruse fabricated to conceal delivery from France of a number of new Mysteres to the Israelis." The Embassy also recalled recent remarks of Ben Gurion to the Mapai Convention that "big things are now underway, which it is too early to speak out publicly". The Embassy admitted, however, that it had not yet arrived at any final conclusion regarding the status of the Mysteres. (Despatch 135 from Tel Aviv, September 5; *ibid.*, 784A.5622/9–556) Despatch 135 was received in the Department of State on September 14. The following day, a memorandum was drafted by Blackiston, to be sent to Dulles from Rountree, containing the same three paragraphs as are numbered 1, 2, and 3 in the memorandum printed here, as well as references to several statements made by Israeli officials. Evidently, the September 15 memorandum was not forwarded to Dulles. A copy of the memorandum is *ibid.*, NEA Files: Lot 58 D 398, Memos to the Secretary thru S/S Jan–June.

2. A report from our Air Attaché in Rome states that British sources in Rome feel that there have been secret dealings between Israel and France and that in fact Israel has received a total of forty-eight Mystere IVs from France.

3. At the beginning of the Suez crisis, the French proposed to NEACC the sale of twenty-four additional Mysteres to Israel. We advised the French that we felt that such shipment at this time would be undesirable. In the NEACC meeting which followed, the French representative stated that there was no need for discussion of the Mystere item although it had been inscribed on the agenda.

---

243.   Annex to Watch Committee Report No. 320 [1]

SC 05496/56   *Washington, September 20, 1956.*

CONCLUSIONS ON BRITISH-FRENCH INTENTIONS TO EMPLOY FORCE AGAINST EGYPT

There are no indications of imminent Anglo-French military action against Egypt; resort to force in the immediate future is unlikely unless Egypt should offer some serious provocation.

1. An apparent softening of the French position regarding the need to employ force against Egypt, revealed in a high level French statement that the establishment of the Association of Canal Users "fully satisfies the need for action," and that there is a good possibility of avoiding war provided Nasser does not commit a "grave act."

2. Apparent realization by the British Government that there is serious British internal, as well as world-wide, opposition to the use of force, and that all means short of war—including the imposition of further economic sanctions on Egypt and the reference of the problem to the UN Security Council—ought to be exhausted before a decision can be taken to resort to military action.

3. Continuing evidence that Nasser intends to maintain a "correct position" and will endeavor to prevent acts which could be regarded by the UK and France as serious provocations. There are indications, however, that the Egyptians, having reiterated their determination to defend their sovereignty over the Canal, and in-

---

[1] Source: CIA Files. Top Secret; Noforn; Limited Distribution.

creasingly confident of their ability to manage it, will not permit passage of a Users' Association ship.

4. Lack of evidence of a change in the British-French estimate that the USSR will not intervene militarily in the Middle East, in spite of repeated Soviet declarations of support for Egypt and warnings that the USSR "cannot stand aside" in situation which "threatens the security of the Soviet State."

5. Indications that the UK and France continue their preparations for the use of military force against Egypt if other methods fail.

a. The increase to a total of three British aircraft carriers in the Mediterranean, the deployment of a British light cruiser and destroyer from Malta to Cyprus, and the stationing of another British light cruiser and destroyer in the Red Sea within 24 hours' sailing time of the Suez Canal.

b. Some increase during the past week in British and French ground combat strength in the Mediterranean area and a continuing apparently urgent augmentation of medical, service, air, and unloading facilities on Cyprus, as well as additional preparations to move several divisional size combat units to the Eastern Mediterranean at some later date.

---

244.   Message From the Secretary of State to the President [1]

London, September 20, 1956.

DEAR MR. PRESIDENT: I am very grateful for your kind message. [2] You were good indeed to send it when you must have been so busy with your speech. [3] It was not fully reported here, but has been well received.

We made considerable progress today in getting agreement on the details for setting up the Users' Association. We have agreed

---

[1] Source: Department of State, Central Files, 110.11–DU/9–2056. Secret. Transmitted to the Department of State in Dulte 6 from London, 9 p.m., which is the source text, with the instruction: "Eyes only Acting Secretary for President from Secretary". Dulte 2 was received at 7:57 p.m. A copy is in the Eisenhower Library, Whitman File, Dulles–Herter Series.

[2] On September 19, Eisenhower sent Dulles a message thanking him for his cable of September 19 and commenting that the situation at the London Conference seemed confused and difficult. The message was transmitted in Tedul 10 to London, September 19. (Department of State, Central Files, 110.11–DU/9–1956)

[3] On September 19, President Eisenhower delivered a major address over radio and television to open his reelection campaign. For text, see *Public Papers of the Presidents of the United States: Dwight D. Eisenhower, 1956*, pp. 779–788.

that the governments here will have a week or ten days in which to make the ultimate political decision to join or not to join. We are hopeful that the Eastern Bloc of Turkey, Iran, Pakistan and Ethiopia can be brought along under Turkish leadership. However, this remains to be seen. The Egyptians are exerting the strongest kind of pressure against their joining. The Scandinavians are lukewarm, but may eventually come through under the influence of Norway. Spain continues equivocal. Yesterday afternoon [4] there were a series of very weak speeches which put all the emphasis upon the necessity for peace and no emphasis at all upon the need for what the United Nations Charter calls a settlement "in accordance with the principles of justice and international law". So at the close of the session I launched into a rather strong speech emphasizing that peace was only one side of the coin and that we must all exert as much effort for a just settlement as we would for peace or else all of our postwar structure would collapse. The general impression was that this talk of mine provided a useful tonic and bucked up the conference when it seemed to be sagging rather badly.

It seems almost certain that we will complete our work here tomorrow so that I can get off tomorrow night. Perhaps I shall stop at Bermuda Saturday morning for the swim I missed last time.

Faithfully yours,

Foster [5]

---

[4] Reference is to the second plenary session of the conference, which began at 4 p.m., September 19; see Document 237.

[5] Dulte 6 bears this typed signature.

---

245. Memorandum of a Conversation Between Prime Minister Eden and Secretary of State Dulles, London, September 20, 1956 [1]

Following the Selwyn Lloyd dinner last night, [2] I went into another room and talked alone with Anthony Eden for about half an hour. He expressed great appreciation for my efforts. He said they had now altered their military planning so that instead of having the

---

[1] Source: Eisenhower Library, Dulles Papers, Misc. Papers—U.K. (Suez Crisis). Top Secret. Drafted on September 21 by Dulles who initialed the source text.

[2] September 20.

fixed date, they were able to hold the military threat in status quo without any prohibitive expense. [Here followed matter not to be committed in writing.] [3] The French have been cooperative and discreet. Both they and the French remained determined that Nasser should not win a victory out of his action. Eden said that the British were unwilling to adapt themselves for any long period to the denial of the Canal route because it was too costly. When I pointed out that the military operation would be more costly, he said perhaps for a short time, but they had hopes that that phase would quickly be over. I said that military action might disrupt the pipelines as well as the Canal. Eden said he was not sure of this. In any event the interruption would be short-lived. I expressed some scepticism of his optimism.

I said that the United States fully agreed that Nasser should not come out ahead, and I thought that he would not. I reviewed his deteriorating economic situation and the increasing concern of other Arab countries. I felt that Nasser had already slipped. I said, however, I thought this could be promoted by closer cooperation between us. Perhaps we should set up a working party to work out plans in this respect. Eden seemed to think this would be a good idea, but no actual decision was taken.

JFD

---

[3] Brackets in the source text.

---

246.   Memorandum of a Conversation, U.S. Embassy, London, September 21, 1956, 10:45 a.m. [1]

USDel/MC/14

PARTICIPANTS

The United States	Spain
The Secretary	Foreign Minister Artajo
Mr. Tyler	Mr. Valls, First Secretary [2]

---

[1] Source: Department of State, Conference Files: Lot 62 D 181, CF 782. Secret. Drafted by Tyler.

[2] Aurelio Valls Carreras, First Secretary of the Spanish Embassy in the United Kingdom.

SUBJECT

Suez Canal Conference

The Spanish Foreign Minister said he thought it undesirable for the Declaration of the 18 powers to state merely that the 18 governments "do not consider that the proposal of the Egyptian Government of the 10th September to set up a negotiating body can be accepted". He said this would be bad for world opinion, and that it would diminish the chances of bringing about negotiations with Nasser. He pointed out that in his message to the UN, Nasser had mentioned the possibility of a negotiating body of nine members. The Spanish Foreign Minister said he thought that the declaration should state that the 18 governments will discuss or consider the Egyptian proposals, when the Association has been established.

The Secretary said that he had himself had in mind a text which would be somewhat more mild than the passage in the Swedish draft, but that nevertheless the Egyptian proposals were not acceptable as they have been presented. He pointed out that it was a very difficult matter to delegate to a small group of countries the authority to negotiate in behalf of others. They could not do this without specific terms of reference, since the other countries would naturally be apprehensive lest the smaller group might give away more than what the other countries considered to be their minimum position. The Minister repeated that he thought it would be a mistake at this stage solely to reject the Nasser proposals, and that it would place the 18 countries in a position of inferiority vis-à-vis world opinion.

The Minister then developed the thesis that Egypt's position was in fact growing stronger with the passage of time. He thought Egypt could stay put, maintain a passive attitude being in possession of the Canal, whereas the other countries had to do something and find ways of making some progress. He thought that a very poor country such as Egypt, could stand conditions of economic adversity better than richer countries, since the standard of living of Egypt is already so low that the Egyptians "would merely go on eating bread and onions and sit in the deserts". He said half-humorously that Spain had in recent years experienced the adverse effects of "the Truman blockade" which had denied it the benefits of the Marshall Plan, and that this had caused hardship by preventing the Spanish people from improving their standard of living and obtaining necessities they would otherwise have received. The Egyptian people, however, were already near rock bottom and could not go much lower.

The Secretary said that he did not share the Minister's theory that the Egyptian position would grow stronger as time passed. He pointed out that Egypt's prestige and international credit were much lower today than when Nasser had taken over the Canal. Apart from the question of receipts from the Canal, tourist trade had dried up and Egyptian industrial requirements could no longer be obtained from former sources. United States aid, which had been considerable and included supplies of wheat, had been stopped and Nasser's action had weakened Egypt's position in the eyes of the governments of several of the Arab states. He thought that on the contrary there would be an increasing inducement to Nasser to negotiate as time passed. The Minister did not attempt to argue the point further.

The Spanish Foreign Minister said he had talked on September 20 with the Egyptian Ambassador who had not had very much to say. He had, however, stated that the idea of the Association forming a unit with which it might be possible to negotiate was "not too bad". The Ambassador had referred to Nasser's proposal for a body of nine in his note to the UN, but had not pressed it unduly.

The Secretary said he had wondered why Nasser had been unwilling to make counterproposals and had merely rejected those made by the First Suez Conference without advancing any ideas himself. If he had done so, we might now have been already negotiating with him. The Minister said he thought it was important not to do anything at this stage which might diminish the chances of establishing an atmosphere favorable to negotiations later on.

---

247.   Memorandum of a Conversation, British Foreign Office, London, September 21, 1956, 11:30 a.m. [1]

USDel/MC/22

PARTICIPANTS

The United States	The United Kingdom
Secretary of State Dulles	Foreign Secretary Lloyd
Ambassador Aldrich	D. S. Laskey, Economic Relations Department, Foreign Office

---

[1] Source: Department of State, Conference Files: Lot 62 D 181, CF 782. Top Secret. Drafted by Aldrich on October 3. In his memoirs, Lloyd gives a lengthy account of a conversation with Dulles which, according to Lloyd, took place following the final plenary session on September 21. The schedule and chronology, prepared by the U.S. Delegation for September 21, indicate no other conversation between the two except this one at 11:30 a.m. Lloyd's account of the conversation differs from the U.S. account printed here. (*Suez 1956, A Personal Account* (London: Jonathon Cape, 1978), pp. 145–148)

SUBJECT

Suez—(1) Special Committee; (2) Security Council; (3) SCUA

After a short discussion with regard to the time of the Secretary's leaving, the Secretary said that in his private conversation with Sir Anthony last night [2] the question had been discussed of setting up a very secret working party here to consider continuously economic and political means of weakening and lessening the prestige of the regime of Colonel Nasser. The question was considered as to the make-up of such a committee, whether it should be formed by representatives of the Foreign Office and other branches of the British Government and representatives of the State Department and other branches of the United States Government. No final conclusion was reached, but Mr. Lloyd said that he would take the matter up immediately and Mr. Dulles said that he would also do so as soon as he returned to Washington, to bring about the formation and activities of such a committee.

Mr. Lloyd asked whether it would not be possible to take some action in the Security Council with regard to the Suez situation immediately and suggested that possibly an approach should be made to the Security Council to place the matter on the agenda for actual consideration ten days hence. The Secretary said that he felt strongly that the SCUA should actually be in existence before any move was made in the Security Council. He said that as soon as the governing board of SCUA had met he would be in accord that the matter should be taken to the Security Council at once.

Then Mr. Lloyd queried whether the Secretary did not think it would be possible to get an answer with regard to membership by next Thursday. The Secretary said that he thought that some of the countries would need at least ten days and that he felt that this would not lose any time because it would take at least that period to prepare the documents necessary to submit the matter to the Security Council. He said, however, that as soon as he returned to New York he would take the matter up with the US Delegation at the United Nations to see how soon such documents might be actually prepared and submitted. Mr. Lloyd was apparently convinced by the Secretary's statement that no time would be lost provided the governing board would meet by a week from next Tuesday.

Mr. Lloyd then raised the question of the payment of Canal dues to SCUA. The Secretary said that it was impossible for the US Government to compel any ship owner to pay the dues to SCUA. All it could do would be to forbid payment of the dues to the Egyptian operators, and he asked Mr. Lloyd what the British could

---

[2] See Document 245.

do. It then appeared that Great Britain was in precisely the same position as the US with regard to being able to compel ship owners to pay dues to SCUA, but Mr. Lloyd said he felt certain that it would be possible for the British Government to persuade the ship owners to pay the dues to SCUA.

He then asked whether it was not possible for the Secretary to make a statement today to the effect that the US Government would take such action as it could to bring about payment of the dues by American flag ships to SCUA instead of to the Egyptian Government. The Secretary pointed out that it would be impossible to persuade American ship owners to pay the dues to SCUA if any discrimination between American ships and other ships should result from such payment and that if such discrimination should occur the United States would have to re-examine the situation, but that, assuming no such discrimination would result, he felt sure that by Treasury action the ship owners would be prevented from paying the dues to Egypt.

At the close of the conference Mr. Lloyd pressed very hard for an assurance that a statement to this effect would be made today, and the Secretary finally said that he would make such statement as he could as a matter of law at the meeting this afternoon. Mr. Lloyd expressed great gratification at this statement.

In the midst of this conversation Mr. Henderson interrupted to state that he had just received word from Firoz Khan Noon that Noon had just received instructions from his Prime Minister [3] to denounce the formation of SCUA and that Mr. Henderson had been able to persuade Noon to tone down the original statement he was preparing to make at the session this afternoon so that it simply covered the inability of Pakistan to join in the organization. [4] Mr. Lloyd and the Secretary then joined in the drafting of a telegram to the British and American Ambassadors in Karachi, [5] telling them on an urgent basis to point out to the Prime Minister and the President the catastrophic effects the change in foreign policy of Pakistan would have, as evidenced by the position taken by the Prime Minister in his instructions to Noon.

---

[3] Husayn Suhrawardy.

[4] A memorandum of this conversation, which took place at noon on September 21, is in Department of State, Conference Files: Lot 62 D 181, CF 774.

[5] The telegram to Karachi has not been found in Department of State files. Later that day, Dulles sent to Foreign Minister Noon a letter expressing his concern and asking that Noon define his government's decision in a way that would allow further study before a definitive decision was announced. (Ibid., Central Files, 974.7301/9–2156)

248.   Memorandum From C. Douglas Dillon to the Secretary of State [1]

London, September 21, 1956.

SUBJECT

Deterioration of the Political Situation in France

1. It is apparent that during the last week, as a result of developments in the Suez crisis, there has been a marked deterioration of the political situation in France.

2. Daridan showed me an Eyes Only telegram from Mollet to Pineau describing the discussion on Suez in the Council of Ministers meeting on Wednesday. [2] This telegram has been seen so far only by Pineau, Daridan, and myself. The telegram, which was written before your speech Wednesday afternoon, stated that the Council of Ministers were greatly concerned by the lack of progress of the Suez negotiations. They expressed particular concern about the lack of support from "our American friends". They also felt that the British resolve was weakening, and expressed the fear that the situation seemed to be becoming entangled in interminable negotiations for which no good issue was in sight. They said that if that proved to be the case, the French Government would shortly have to make a public statement clearly placing the responsibility for the present situation, i.e., blaming the U.S. and Great Britain.

3. The increasing unsettlement in Parliamentary circles over Suez is indicated by the action of the Directing Committee of the Moderate Party (Conservatives, Pinay's party). This committee met and adopted a motion demanding debate on Suez immediately on the reconvening of Parliament on October 2nd. They also attacked the Government for failing to carry out the mandate of the Parliament, given prior to adjournment, to maintain its firm position.

4. I feel that your Wednesday afternoon speech will do much to help. Daridan said that Pineau was very appreciative of your important role at this Conference. Nevertheless, if things go bad, the French will be looking for a scapegoat, and a portion of the blame will inevitably be thrown on the U.S.

5. In my return to Paris I intend to try to see Mollet early next week to give him the personal flavor of happenings this week in London from the U.S. point of view, in an attempt to mitigate any public criticism of the U.S. by him. I also feel that from the point of

---

[1] Source: Eisenhower Library, Dulles Papers. Secret; Personal and Private. A marginal notation by Bernau on the source text reads: "Sec Saw".

[2] September 19.

view of our relations with the French a personal letter from the President to Mollet would be very helpful at this stage. The letter could reaffirm the determination of the U.S. not to allow Nasser to get away with his attempt to obtain sole control of Suez. The letter would not have to be for publication, as, for the moment, I think it is less important to directly impress public opinion in France than to avoid or mitigate, as far as possible, any attack on U.S. policies on the Suez crisis by Mollet on behalf of the French Government.

249.   Telegram From the Delegation at the Suez Canal Conference to the Department of State [1]

London, September 22, 1956—noon.

Secto 24. Fifth and final plenary session second Suez conference. Brussels for Tyler.

Today's session, twice postponed on account experts meeting [2] was eventually convened at 2:30 and spent three hours twenty minutes going over drafts of conference statement and annex (declaration on Users' Association) of which final texts being telegraphed separately. [3] Conference then spent forty minutes in general discussion before finally adjourning 6:30 p.m.

Following were principal points made during discussion of draft statement and declaration:

As objections raised to "CASU", "CASCU" and "ASCU" as conveying undesirable meaning in various languages it decided official abbreviation for Users' Association would be "SCUA".

Conference discussed criteria for membership in Users' Association with eventual decision leave it to original members to lay down criteria for any additional members (see paragraph of annex). Several representatives stressed need for making clear intent is not to exclude any country.

---

[1] Source: Department of State, Central Files, 974.7301/9–2256. Confidential; Priority. Drafted by Wilson. Received at 10:27 p.m., September 21. Repeated Priority to Brussels and to Paris.

[2] Reference is to the Committee Meeting held at Lancaster House 9:30 a.m.–12:15 p.m., September 21. A summary record of the meeting, prepared by the Conference's International Secretariat, is *ibid.*, Conference Files: Lot 62 D 181, CF 773.

[3] Reference is to Secto 25 from London, September 21, not printed. (*Ibid.*, Central Files 974.7301/9–2156) For the complete texts of the Declaration and Statement adopted by the Conference, see Documents 251 and 252.

It decided refer to annex as "declaration" rather than "resolution" but retain word "subscribe" rather than "adhere".

Discussions of Conference statement centered about (1) recourse to UN and (2) Egyptian memo of September 10. Re UN, considerable divergence of view developed between those countries such as Norway, Italy, Denmark, Japan and Ethiopia which thought conference should go on record as favoring immediate recourse to UN and others such as Australia, UK and France which thought Users' Association should be set up first. After considerable discussion Secretary proposed words "they (i.e. 18 governments) consider that recourse should be had to the UN whenever it seems that this will facilitate a settlement", which agreed. Secretary pointed out there various types of UN submission, i.e. whether to SC or GA and if to SC it important distinguish between measures under chapters six and seven.

During discussion this point Secretary said USG coming to conclusion we should probably move rather quickly in direction of taking Suez matter to UN. He did not want any thing he had said to be interpreted as meaning US wants any great delay. Said we first want to set up Users' Association, in next week or ten days. Immediately thereafter we might find it appropriate go to SC although Secretary unable commit USG definitely in this regard now. Lloyd expressed complete agreement and said this conformed exactly to view of UK. Pointed out UK had been criticized for not having consulted others regarding last week's announcement in Commons and wanted it clear there might not be time consult before taking matter to UN.

Re Egyptian memo, Pakistan representative [4] suggested it unwise condemn Egyptian proposals out of hand as they contained some points with which eighteen nations in agreement, e.g., support for 1888 convention. Japan, Ethiopia and Denmark urged deletion of any reference to Egyptian memo. Japan representative said if memo mentioned most he could agree was statement that memo discussed and "prevailing opinion in conference" was it not useful basis for discussion. After point had been discussed at length by various delegates, Secretary intervened to point out Egyptian memo so vaguely written as to raise question what it intended to propose. He suggested wording, which conference adopted, that Egyptian proposal "was placed before conference but was considered too imprecise to afford a useful basis for discussion". (See paragraph (3) conference statement.)

During foregoing discussion Lloyd stated it intention of UK to call another meeting October first to review progress made by then

---

[4] Malik Firoz Khan Noon.

on setting up Users' Association. Meeting would be at Ambassadorial, not Foreign Minister, level.

Beginning at 5:50 p.m. each representative in turn made statement of his government's position. All expressed appreciation to Lloyd for his work as chairman and for hospitality HMG. Pakistan representative, in brief statement, called attention to fact delegates were not being asked to "set their hand" to any document at this time, asserted users' proposal as it emerged from conference was quite different from that originally put forward in that it now stressed cooperation with Egypt, and pointed out he had already stated views of his government re proposal.

Danish representative [5] stated for constitutional reasons unable indicate acceptance of proposal at this time as matter must be referred to Parliament but expressed great interest this government in finding solution.

Ethiopian thought there general agreement on avoiding imposition of any formula on Egypt but he unable indicate position his government re users association in absence instructions.

Swedish representative said like Denmark unable state final attitude now but noted with satisfaction proposal changed considerably from original form.

Norway stated unable for constitutional reasons give general answer today but would strongly recommend acceptance.

Iran repeated view previously expressed that fresh approach should be made to Egypt, following which matter should be referred to UN. Commenting on British document on juridical aspects of users association he expressed doubt some parties to 1888 convention had right set up organization to safeguard their rights under convention when another party (Egypt) has stated such action would violate convention. Stressed Iran continued support 18 nation proposal.

Secretary then spoke, pointing out that as proposal had evolved it did not impose obligation on executive to submit it to Senate or to Congress. Said before leaving London this evening would give chairman written confirmation [6] of our willingness join association. Expressed opinion conference had been of great importance in preserving peace and developing solution in accordance with principles justice and international law. Stressed need for continuing unity between the 18.

France expressed willingness adhere to association while reserving right take appropriate measures if situation should arise contrary to its interests.

---

[5] Hans Christian S. Hansen.
[6] See *infra*.

Italy expressed formal adherence to association.

Japan expressed view conference had been constructive.

Turkish representative said Turkey would accept users association in principle although unable under his instructions signify formal adherence at this time.

German representative said would be happy recommend adherence to his government.

New Zealand representative said although definite instructions re adherence not yet received conference could take it for granted New Zealand firmly behind proposals.

Australia likewise stated that while proposals still must be formally submitted to government there no doubt whatever of their acceptance.

Netherlands representative said he would strongly recommend proposals to this government.

Spanish representative expressed hope Spain would adhere, while reserving his government's final position and repeating reservation made by Spain to original 18 nation proposal.

Portuguese representative expressed confidence his government would adhere.

Lloyd then thanked other representatives for their expressions of appreciation, said he regarded conference success, expressed regret concept of users association had originally been misunderstood and stated UK would adhere. Conference adjourned 6:30 p.m. [7]

Dulles

---

[7] Dulles and his party left London at 8:25 p.m. (Reported in Secto 28 from London, September 21; Department of State, Central Files, 974.7301/9–2156)

---

250.   Editorial Note

On September 21, Secretary Dulles sent to Foreign Secretary Lloyd a letter confirming that the United States would become a member of the Suez Canal Users Association. It reads as follows:

"The United States as a member of this Association will seek in cooperation with the other Members to assist the Association to achieve its intended purposes.

"Immediately upon my return steps will be taken with our Treasury officials and with the representatives of owners of American flag vessels which largely transit the Suez Canal with a view to perfecting this cooperation in terms of actual operating practices."

The text here quoted is the one attached to a circular memorandum by Harold L. Skean (S/S–RO), dated October 2, which indicates this text was the one actually delivered to Foreign Secretary Lloyd. (Department of State, Central Files, 974.7301/9–2156) The text forwarded to the Department of State in Secto 22 from London, September 21, was an earlier draft of the letter. (*Ibid.*)

---

251.   Statement Issued by the Second Suez Canal Conference at London, September 21, 1956 [1]

Representatives of the 18 Governments who joined in the proposals which were subsequently submitted to the Egyptian Government by the Five Nation Committee presided over by the Prime Minister of Australia, the Right Honorable Robert Menzies, as a basis for negotiating a settlement of the Suez Canal question, met in London from September 19 to 21, 1956. Their purpose was to consider the situation in the light of the report of that Committee and other developments since the first London Conference.

They noted with regret that the Egyptian Government did not accept these proposals and did not make any counter-proposals to the Five Nation Committee.

It is the view of the Conference that these proposals still offer a fair basis for a peaceful solution of the Suez Canal problem, taking into account the interests of the user nations as well as those of Egypt. The 18 Governments will continue their efforts to obtain such a settlement. The proposal made by the Egyptian Government on September 10 was placed before the Conference but it was considered too imprecise to afford a useful basis for discussion.

A Declaration was drawn up providing for the establishment of a Suez Canal Users Association. The text of this Declaration is annexed hereto. This Association is designed to facilitate any steps which may lead to a final or provisional solution of the Suez Canal problem. It will further cooperation between the Governments adhering to it, concerning the use of the Canal. For this purpose it will

---

[1] Source: Conference doc. SUEZ II/56/D/10; Department of State, Conference Files: Lot 62 D 181, CF 782. Also printed in *The Suez Canal Problem, July 26–September 22, 1956*, pp. 366–367.

seek the cooperation of the competent Egyptian authorities pending a solution of the larger issues. It will also deal with such problems as would arise if the traffic through the Canal were to diminish or cease. The Association will be established as a functioning entity at an early date after the delegates to this Conference have had an opportunity to consult in relation thereto with their respective Governments.

The Conference noted that on September 12, 1956, the Governments of the U.K. and France informed the Security Council of the United Nations of the situation, and that subsequently, on September 17, the Government of Egypt also made a communication to the Security Council. The Conference considers that recourse should be had to the United Nations whenever it seems that this would facilitate a settlement.

The representatives of the 18 Governments have found their cooperation at the Conference valuable and constructive. The 18 Governments will continue to consult together in order to maintain a common approach to the problems which may arise out of the Suez question in the future.

It is the conviction of the Conference that the course outlined in this statement is capable of producing by peaceful means a solution which is [in] conformity with the principles of justice and international law as declared in Article I of the Charter of the United Nations.

252.   **Declaration Issued by the Second Suez Canal Conference at London, September 21, 1956** [1]

I. The members of the Suez Canal Users Association (SCUA) shall be those nations which have participated in the second London Suez Conference and which subscribe to the present Declaration, and any other adhering nations which conform to criteria to be laid down hereafter by the Association.

II. SCUA shall have the following purposes:

(1) To facilitate any steps which may lead to a final or provisional solution of the Suez Canal problem and to assist the members in the exercise of their rights as users of the Suez Canal in conso-

---

[1] Source: Conference doc. SUEZ II/56/D/10; Department of State, Conference Files: Lot 62 D 181, CF 782. Also printed in *The Suez Canal Problem, July 26-September 22, 1956*, pp. 365–366.

nance with the 1888 Convention, with due regard for the rights of Egypt;

(2) To promote safe, orderly, efficient and economical transit of the Canal by vessels of any member nation desiring to avail themselves of the facilities of SCUA and to seek the cooperation of the competent Egyptian authorities for this purpose;

(3) To extend its facilities to vessels of non-member nations which desire to use them;

(4) To receive, hold and disburse the revenues accruing from dues and other sums which any user of the Canal may pay to SCUA, without prejudice to existing rights, pending a final settlement;

(5) To consider and report to members regarding any significant developments affecting the use or non-use of the Canal;

(6) To assist in dealing with any practical problems arising from the failure of the Suez Canal adequately to serve its customary and intended purpose and to study forthwith means that may render it feasible to reduce dependence on the Canal;

(7) To facilitate the execution of any provisional solution of the Suez problem that may be adopted by the United Nations.

III. To carry out the above mentioned purposes:

(1) The members shall consult together in a Council on which each member will be represented;

(2) The Council shall establish an Executive Group to which it may delegate such powers as it deems appropriate;

(3) An Administrator, who shall, inter alia, make the necessary arrangements with shipping interests, will be appointed to serve under the direction of the Council through the Executive Group.

IV. Membership may at any time be terminated by giving 60 days' notice.

**253.   Memorandum From the Secretary of State's Special
Assistant (Armstrong) to the Acting Secretary of State** [1]

Washington, September 21, 1956.

SUBJECT

Possibility that France has delivered additional Mystere aircraft to Israel

According to information currently available to U.S. Air Force
Intelligence, the total Israeli jet fighter strength at present is 87,
broken down as follows:

24 Mysteres Mark IV
36 Ouragans
15 Gloucester Meteors Mark VIII
6 Gloucester Meteors Mark IX
6 Gloucester Meteors Mark VII (trainers)

The U.S. Air Attaché, Tel Aviv, who was in Washington on
consultation in late August immediately after the reported "overhaul" flight to France, reported that at that time he had been able to
locate only 7 Mysteres in Israel in addition to those absent in France.
While it is entirely possible that the Israelis have purchased additional Mysteres since that time, it cannot be confirmed.

Air Force Intelligence considers that an additional 24 Mysteres
for the Israeli Air Force at this juncture would not materially affect
what is considered to be the present approximate balance of Air
Force capabilities between the two hostile sides, as represented by
Egyptian quantity of planes and Israeli quality of personnel and
matériel. It is believed that Israeli Air Force combat units cannot in
the immediate future absorb more than an additional 24 jet fighter
aircraft because of limitations imposed by training, ground facilities
and maintenance. These limitations also apply to the Egyptian Air
Force for a similar period. Air Force Intelligence stresses the very
great vulnerability of both sides and believes that under present
circumstances the attacker, whichever he might be, could in the first
five hours "win 50 percent of the air battle."

While the Israelis would undoubtedly wish to acquire more jet
fighter aircraft, these could not be added to combat strength in view
of the limitation referred to, but would have to be held in reserve.

We understand that the Canadian Government announced today
that it will make available to the Israelis 4 F-86's per month up to a
total of 24. Air Force Intelligence believes that the Israelis have a
five-to-one preference for the F-86 over the Mystere because of

---

[1] Source: Department of State, Central Files, 784A.56/9-2156. Secret. A handwritten marginal notation on the source text reads: "Mr. Hoover saw."

trouble experienced with the latter. The F-86 will therefore be used probably as a first-line combat aircraft, and any Mysteres received in the future will be held in reserve to replace combat losses. The Israelis may be expected to take the fullest psychological and propaganda advantage of F-86 deliveries.

---

254.   Memorandum of a Conversation, Department of State, Washington, September 22, 1956 [1]

SUBJECT

Reference of the Suez Dispute to the UN Security Council

PARTICIPANTS

Mr. John Coulson, Minister, British Embassy
Miss Barbara Salt, Counselor, British Embassy
William M. Rountree, Assistant Secretary, NEA
Fraser Wilkins, Director, NE

Mr. Coulson called this morning to say that the British wish to refer the Suez dispute to the Security Council today. He said that he had received instructions to speak with the Secretary on this subject but that, since the Secretary had not yet returned from London, he thought Mr. Rountree would wish to have the substance of these discussions as promptly as possible.

Following the Secretary's departure from London and after analyzing the whole situation relating to the question of the Suez Canal, the British had concluded, according to Mr. Coulson, that immediate action should be taken in the Security Council to place the Suez Canal question on the agenda of the Security Council. There were several important reasons for this conclusion:

1) There were indications, which the British believe were known to the United States also, that the Russians contemplated a similar move. The British believe that they could not accept the diplomatic defeat which would result from prior reference of the Suez question to the Security Council by the Russians.

2) The French were openly disturbed regarding the results of the recent London conference.

3) The British believe it important at this time to dispel the atmosphere of indecisiveness regarding reference of the Suez Canal

---

[1] Source: Department of State, Central Files, 974.7301/9–2256. Secret. Drafted by Wilkins.

question to the Security Council which had grown out of results of discussions during the recently concluded London meeting.

The British, therefore, propose that the President of the Security Council be asked to call a meeting for next Wednesday, September 26, for two purposes:

1) to place on the agenda an item regarding the question of the Suez Canal worded as follows: "situation created by the unilateral action of the Egyptian Government in bringing to an end the system of international operation of the Suez Canal which was confirmed and completed by the Suez Canal Convention of 1888" (Tab A); [2]

2) to arrange for a second meeting of the Security Council for October 2 which Egypt would be invited to attend.

Mr. Coulson added that the British thought that reference of the Suez Canal question to the Security Council would improve the prospects that countries like Sweden who wished reference of the matter to the United Nations would eventually participate in the Suez Canal users association.

Mr. Coulson said that the British Foreign Office planned to issue a statement regarding reference to the Security Council at 10 p.m. London time September 22 (5 p.m. Washington time).

Mr. Coulson said that a similar approach was being made to the French Government except that no reference was being made to possible Russian action because the British did not believe that the French were aware of this possibility.

Mr. Coulson said the French were being asked to associate themselves with the British approach to the Security Council, and it was hoped the Secretary would agree that the United States would also associate itself with this approach.

Mr. Coulson said that, immediately upon receipt of his instructions, he had telegraphed London that the Secretary was not likely to arrive in Washington much before 4 p.m. September 22 and that it might be physically impossible to obtain the Secretary's views prior to the presently scheduled release of the proposed British statement. Mr. Coulson had not as yet had a reply to this message.

Mr. Coulson also added that he had told the British Delegation to the United Nations in New York to prepare a letter addressed to the Security Council for delivery today. Meanwhile, the British Delegation should concert with its U.S. and French colleagues. They would thus be informed of the proposed British action.

Mr. Coulson said he himself planned to call at the French Embassy upon leaving the Department.

---

[2] Not printed; Tab A is the text of the letter to the President of the Security Council. The Representatives of the British and French Governments sent the letter with a few stylistic changes on September 23. (U.N. doc. S/3654)

Mr. Rountree said that he planned to be at the airport when the Secretary arrived at 3:08 p.m. September 22 and possibly there or immediately thereafter the Secretary could be consulted. Mr. Coulson said that he too would be at the airport and perhaps the Secretary's view could be ascertained.

Mr. Coulson subsequently telephoned Mr. Rountree to say that a further message had been received from London indicating that the French agreed with the British proposal and would go along with it. Mr. Rountree said that the Secretary would not arrive before 3 or 3:30, and it would be most unfortunate if the British and French made an announcement before there was an opportunity to consult with the Secretary. Mr. Coulson said he agreed and that he had already sent a message to this effect to London but would send another one asking London to delay an announcement until there had been an opportunity to consult with the Secretary.

Mr. Rountree raised the question of British Meteors for Israel which will be the subject of a separate memorandum.[3]

---

[3] Not printed. Rountree told Coulson that, in view of the forthcoming Canadian announcement concerning jets for Israel, he wondered whether it were wise for the United Kingdom to supply Israel with the planes at that time. Not only did a tense situation exist, but there were rumors that the United Kingdom and France were urging the Israelis to move against Jordan. Coulson stated his agreement that it would be unwise for the British to pursue the matter at that time and said that he would look into it. (Department of State, Central Files, 784A.56/9–2256)

---

255.   Telegram From the Department of State to the Embassy in Israel [1]

Washington, September 22, 1956—10:21 a.m.

233. At conclusion conversation with Rountree twenty-first on economic matters, Israel Ambassador referred to announcement Canadians would make 24 F-86's available Israel. Eban said GOI aware

---

[1] Source: Department of State, Central Files, 784A.5622/9–2256. Secret. Drafted by Bergus, cleared by Wilkins, and approved by Rountree. Repeated to Amman and Ottawa.

Secretary's deep interest this matter and appreciative his efforts. [2] Planned send letter to Secretary this effect.

Rountree said US pleased at result. In reply inquiries Department was stating US had been informed but that it had been Canadian decision. Rountree expressed hope Israel would exercise greatest restraint along borders so that Canadian announcement would not be associated with Israel policies which Arabs could denounce as aggressive. Eban said he understood point and referred to Israel assurances to Canadians planes would be used only for defense. More reassured Israel was on long term security situation easier for Israelis show restraint in short term security problems. Emphasized HKJ responsibility maintain order along borders. Rountree replied that while we did not dispute Jordan's responsibility, and were convinced King and HKJ leaders wished avoid trouble, realities of situation made it almost inevitable Jordan could not always prevent incidents.

Hoover

---

[2] On September 24, Arthur Dean telephoned Secretary Dulles. Their conversation, concerning the release of the F–86's, which was transcribed by Bernau, went as follows:

"AHD[ean] said he has had several meetings with Eban as the Sec. requested. He called Friday and said that they were delighted re the Canadian business and there would be a release by Ben-Gurion in the Sunday papers. He [Eban] wants to see AHD for breakfast tomorrow. AHD thinks if this is going to have the maximum effectiveness our press officer should say more than we have no objections. The Sec. said we can't play it from the political standpoint. The Sec. said if he has a press conf. he may be asked about it." (Eisenhower Library, Dulles Papers, General Telephone Conversations)

256.   Memorandum of a Conversation, Department of State, Washington, September 22, 1956, 3:58 p.m. [1]

SUBJECT

Security Council Action Regarding Suez Issue

PARTICIPANTS

Mr. J.E. Coulson—British Embassy
Miss Barbara Salt—British Embassy
The Secretary
Mr. Hoover
NEA—Mr. Rountree
IO—Mr. Wilcox

Mr. Coulson, in charge of the Embassy during Ambassador Makins' absence from the city, repeated the reasons which he had given Departmental officers earlier in the day for the UK proposal to request Security Council action on Suez. He said that they had information to the effect that the USSR planned to request a meeting of the Security Council at an early date. He also pointed out that after the London Conference a feeling had developed that the user countries ought to get into a better negotiating position with respect to Suez, and the UK believed strongly that it would be politically unwise to negotiate on this matter now except in a UN context.

Mr. Coulson pointed out that there were two objectives to the British move: (1) to get the Suez item on the agenda at an early date, and (2) to make arrangements for a meeting on October 2. He said that this would give the UK and other interested user countries an additional week to agree upon objectives and to prepare their tactics.

The Secretary said he thought it was sound to go to the United Nations. In this connection, he recalled a conversation he had had with Lloyd and Eden. The only difference, he said, was one of timing. The Secretary expressed the view then that it would be undesirable to rush to the Security Council because such action might serve to dissuade some states from joining the Users Association. Countries like Pakistan, Ethiopia and Iran might be disinclined to join if the matter is in the Security Council for that would serve as a good excuse. On the other hand, he agreed that it might work the other way and result in additional support for the Users Organization.

---

[1] Source: Department of State, Central Files, 974.7301/9–2256. Secret. Drafted by Wilcox. The time of the meeting is from Dulles' Appointment Book. (Princeton University Library, Dulles Papers) The Secretary arrived in Washington at 3:20 p.m., September 22, and proceeded immediately to the Department of State.

The Secretary observed that it would have been bad to file the notice today (Saturday) inasmuch as a good many representatives at the Conference would not have known about it and would have been annoyed because they were not notified prior to any such announcement. If the UK could wait until Monday it would be even better than delaying the announcement until Sunday. In the intervening time they could let the other members of the Conference know about it. Moreover in that event, it would look as though the decision to go to the Security Council was made after and not during the Conference.

Mr. Coulson pointed out again that the UK was very much concerned lest the Soviet Union beat them to the Security Council. They felt this would put them at a disadvantage from the point of view of public opinion and of tactics in the Council. The Secretary replied that we did not have any information about the Soviet Union's intention to call for a meeting of the Security Council.

Mr. Coulson then pointed out that the French had agreed to go along with the UK proposal and the British hoped that the US would be in a position to support their move. To this the Secretary replied that he thought it would be better for us not to go along with the UK—the US could be more helpful if the British and French would do it without our sponsorship, particularly since we did not know what the UK objectives in the Council would be.

In reply to a direct inquiry, Mr. Coulson said that he was not sure whether the UK planned to act under Chapter VI or Chapter VII of the Charter. [2] Moreover, he did not have any information from the Foreign Office as to the objectives the UK might seek to achieve in the Security Council.

---

[2] Chapter VI of the U.N. Charter pertains to the "Pacific Settlement of Disputes", Chapter VII to "Action With Respect to Threats to the Peace, Breaches of the Peace, and Acts of Aggression". See 3 Bevans 1161–1165.

257.   Memorandum of a Conversation Between the President and the Secretary of State, White House, Washington, September 22, 1956, 5 p.m. [1]

I called on the President at about 5:00 in the afternoon. We talked for about a half hour with reference to the Suez Canal matter. I reported to him the recent developments, thus supplementing my personal cables to him. The President expressed satisfaction at the outcome.

I referred to the private talk which I had had with Anthony Eden and to the possible military measures which he had outlined. [2] The President expressed some skepticism as to whether they would be decisive.

JFD [3]

---

[1] Source: Eisenhower Library, Dulles Papers, Meetings With the President. Secret; Personal and Private. Drafted by Dulles.

[2] See Document 245.

[3] Macomber initialed for Dulles.

---

258.   Telegram From the Department of State to the Embassy in Egypt [1]

Washington, September 22, 1956—5:47 p.m.

879. Embtel 840. [2] Department is repeating separately Secto 25 [3] which contains texts of declaration and statement issued final session second Suez Conference and Secto 26 [4] which contains transcript Secretary's background briefing of American correspondents at

---

[1] Source: Department of State, Central Files, 974.7301/9–2156. Confidential; Priority; Suez Canal—Limit Distribution. Drafted by Rockwell and Wilkins, cleared by Rountree, and approved by McCardle.

[2] In telegram 840 from Cairo, September 21, Hare requested the Department's guidance as to what general approach he should take if Nasser raised the Suez question. Hare also requested guidance as to what points he should make and what degree of initiative he should take if the Egyptian Government did not raise the question. (*Ibid.*)

[3] Dated September 21, not printed. (*Ibid.*, 974.7301/9–2256) For texts of the declaration and statement, see Documents 251 and 252.

[4] Dated September 21, not printed. (Department of State, Central Files, 974.7301/9–2256)

end of Suez Conference which is not for attribution to Secretary or U.S. officials.

Department suggests following points be stressed in your conversations with officials GOE if latter raise Suez issue. At moment would not appear desirable for you to take initiative on this.

1. US desires peaceful solution of problem but believes it should be fully consonant with rights of international community in Suez as well as rights of Egypt.

2. Eighteen-nation proposals provide basis for negotiations leading to such a solution.

3. Although major users of Canal, after reaching identity of views among themselves, approached Egypt in spirit of cooperation and conciliation, GOE did not respond to this initiative in its discussions with the Committee of Five.

4. In view attitude GOE and need of majority users protect their interests as a step leading toward permanent arrangement governing status Canal, users proceeding form users association in hope this will result in practical measures of cooperation at operating level with Egyptian personnel concerned with transit Canal. US hopeful such cooperation may lead to creation atmosphere conducive to establishment permanent arrangement.

5. US believes next move is up to Egypt. US desires that traditional friendship between Egypt and US shall be strengthened and is hopeful future attitude of GOE toward Suez problem will reflect conciliatory spirit and complete realization of deep importance which users attach to a permanent solution of problem which will ensure protection of their rights and interests in Suez.

Dulles

---

259.   Telegram From the Embassy in France to the Department of State [1]

Paris, September 24, 1956—1 p.m.

385. I accompanied Senator Mansfield during a half hour discussion of Suez with Pineau this morning. Pineau said the French were disappointed with outcome of London conference because they felt there was not adequately clear cut reaffirmation of the principles adopted by the 18 powers at the August meeting. Mansfield pressed Pineau fairly hard in an endeavor to find out what ultimate French

---

[1] Source: Department of State, Central Files, 974.7301/9–2456. Secret; Limit Distribution—Suez. Received at 10:44 a.m. Repeated to London.

policy was if appeal to the Security Council should end in failure as a result of Soviet veto and if Nasser should refuse Suez passage to S.C.U.A. vessels. Pineau said it would then be necessary to send shipping around Cape of Good Hope, and that he would hope that a substantial portion, if not all the shipping of the 18 powers would then refuse to use the Canal. He said that if there could be concerted economic pressure by all possible means on Nasser he felt that a successful result could be obtained.

If united economic pressure could not be brought to bear on Nasser Pineau said he feared the only alternative would be negotiation of a compromise. Such negotiation if it took place could only be along general lines suggested by Bulganin. The end result would be dictated by the Soviet Union. Such a result, Pineau felt, would be catastrophic as it would firmly implant the Soviet Union as the dominant power in the Middle East and Africa. Pineau said that the vital thing now was to make sure that U.S. vessels paid their dues only to S.C.U.A. thus indicating solidarity between the U.S. and Franco-British positions.

It was apparent throughout the discussion that Pineau did not feel confident of full U.S. support for all out economic pressure on Nasser.

Mansfield told Pineau that he thought the seizure of Universal Canal Company by Nasser was illegal and that Nasser was totally untrustworthy. Mansfield further said that he favored all out economic boycott of Nasser. He told Pineau he favored U.S. economic assistance to Western Europe in case it became necessary to use the Cape route and that in his view such a system should not take the form of Export-Import Bank loans but should be grant aid. He further told Pineau this was the general opinion of a group of senators and congressmen which the Secretary had consulted some two weeks ago.

Dillon

260.   Report Prepared in the Executive Secretariat of the Department of State [1]

Summary No. 15   *Washington, September 24, 1956.*

SUMMARY OF DEVELOPMENTS IN SUEZ SITUATION

Reasons for UK Referral of Suez Question to UN [2]

Dixon has told Lodge [3] that the UK took fast action on referring the Suez problem to the Security Council because: 1) the UK had an "indication" that the USSR might be intending to take the issue to the Council and, therefore, the British had moved quickly to avoid being put on the defensive; 2) public reaction in France over the results of the second London conference required some action to bring the French into line. According to the British plan, Dixon will probably state at the Council meeting on Wednesday that Lloyd and Pineau will "come out" to participate in the debate and Dixon will perhaps hint that Egyptian Foreign Minister Fawzi should do likewise. The British plan to make a big thing out of calling Egypt to the Security Council to answer for her behaviour.

Lodge observes that the British have moved so fast that they have not thought out what is to take place afterwards. Dixon speculated that his Government might regard the Council debate as letting off steam rather than pointing to anything constructive. Lodge, however, pointed out to him that the same logic impelling the British to take the initiative also impelled them to have a resolution at the outset; the USSR and other friends of Egypt were bound to put something in if the UK hesitated very long. While Dixon readily recognized the validity of this point he said he had nothing thus far to go on.

Pakistan's Probable Abstention from Users' Association

Hildreth reports [4] that the Deputy UK High Commissioner in Pakistan induced Prime Minister Suhrawardy to instruct Foreign Minister Noon not to denounce the users' association at the closing London meeting. However, when Hildreth thanked Suhrawardy for

---

[1] Source: Eisenhower Library, Whitman File, International File. Top Secret; Eyes Only for Designated Recipient.

[2] On September 23, Great Britain and France requested that the Security Council convene to consider the Suez situation. On September 24, Egypt requested an urgent meeting of the Council to consider the actions against Egypt, taken particularly by Great Britain and France. (U.N. docs. S/3654 and S/3655)

[3] Reported in telegram 242 from USUN, September 22, not printed. (Department of State, Central Files, 974.7301/9–2256)

[4] In telegram 840 from Karachi, September 22, not printed. (*Ibid.*)

his action and remarked that the final decision on the users' association would probably be made when Noon returned, the Prime Minister said that no further decision was needed; Pakistan was willing to concede to the West to the extent of not denouncing the association, but would not join it. Suhrawardy also remarked that the West had lost the first round in the Suez issue and that he would be willing to tell Nasser that he should be magnanimous in facilitating a reasonable settlement. In view of the mounting emotionalizing of the Suez issue in Pakistan, Hildreth comments that Suhrawardy, even if he were so inclined, would be running against public opinion if he tried to get Pakistan to join the users' association.

Hare to Discuss Suez with Nasser

Hare has cabled from Cairo [5] that, following the presentation of his credentials tomorrow, he expects Nasser will arrange a private substantive discussion. The Embassy has learned through an Egyptian source that Nasser's reaction to the users' association plan will largely be determined by his suspicion that a principal US–UK objective in the maneuvering has been to deny him funds with which he might build the High Dam. This issue dominates Nasser's thinking at present and, during the substantive discussions, he will try to ascertain whether US vessels will continue to pay Egyptian authorities for transits as they have since the nationalization of the canal. If the answer if affirmative, Nasser will probably look with greater sympathy upon the users' association which, according to the source, Egypt is considering as a possible nucleus for a negotiating group.

. . . Reports on Nasser's Views

. . . Cairo has been informed that: 1) as of his departure on Saturday noon, for the Big Three Arab meeting, Nasser was willing to meet Eden at Geneva or any other mutually agreeable spot to discuss any and all outstanding issues; [6] 2) Nasser has stated that Soviet bloc pilots would not be assigned to US vessels transiting the canal. [7]

(Summary closed 11:45 a.m., September 24, 1956)

---

[5] In telegram 854 from Cairo, September 22, not printed. (*Ibid.*)
[6] Reported in telegram 860 from Cairo, September 23, not printed. (*Ibid.*, 974.7301/9–2356)
[7] Reported in telegram 859 from Cairo, September 23, not printed. (*Ibid.*)

261.   Report Prepared in the Executive Secretariat of the Department of State [1]

Summary No. 16   *Washington, September 25, 1956.*

SUMMARY OF DEVELOPMENTS IN SUEZ SITUATION

Inauguration of SCUA

The UK has invited the 17 other nations who participated in the Second Suez Conference to attend a meeting in London on October 1 to inaugurate the Suez Canal Users' Association (SCUA). Matters to be dealt with at the meeting would include: 1) determination of the Executive Group; 2) decision on where the headquarters will be; 3) measures for the recruitment of staff, including the Administrator. The British Government stated its understanding that the governments would be represented at the meeting by their Ambassadors, supported by such experts as they might require. We have not yet replied formally to the British invitation.

In this regard, Aldrich reports [2] that Lloyd feels it is imperative that SCUA be set up as a functioning entity at the Ambassadors' meeting; it would be a severe diplomatic defeat if anything less resulted. Embassy London representatives are conferring with British officials today to get their ideas on the October 1 meeting. This is to be followed by a tripartite meeting with the French. It is probable that the representatives of all 18 nations will gather informally on Thursday or Friday to lay out the program of work for the Monday meeting.

Procedural Tactics for UN Meeting

Lodge, in discussing with the UK and French delegates the tactics for tomorrow's meeting of the Security Council on Suez, learned that they have no knowledge of plans for the future and expect the initiative to be taken by London and Paris. [3] Dixon and Cornut-Gentille stated firmly, however, that they wanted their item and the Egyptian item protesting UK and French actions to be completely separate. Dixon said that it might be feasible to allow the Egyptian item to be added to the agenda and then to organize its failure of adoption. The UK plans to suggest adjournment of the Wednesday meeting until next Tuesday before adoption of the

---

[1] Source: Eisenhower Library, Whitman File, International File. Top Secret; Eyes Only for Designated Recipient. Initialed by Eisenhower.

[2] In telegram 1649 from London, September 25, not printed. (Department of State, Central Files, 974.7301/9–2556)

[3] Reported in telegram 245 from USUN, September 24, not printed. (*Ibid.*, 974.7301/9–2456)

agenda so that the British and French Foreign Ministers may attend. According to Lodge, the UK is concerned that someone may suggest at the Wednesday meeting a resolution condemning force. It was agreed that this could be disposed of procedurally, but Lodge recalled that the Secretary had warned them that we might have to vote for such a resolution.

Italian Views

Ambassador Luce reports [4] that the Italians approve of the reference of the Suez problem to the Security Council. Martino has agreed with the British Ambassador in Rome that approval by a large Council majority—even if vetoed by the Soviets—would put pressure on Nasser to negotiate on the basis of the 18-nation proposal. Luce also says that the Italians have already indicated their intention to participate in the October 1 Ambassadorial meeting in London.

French Concern over SCUA

Mollet has told Dillon [5] that public opinion in France reacted violently to the Second Suez Conference and he had to fight to maintain government unity at a difficult cabinet meeting on Saturday. Mollet said that the French think it is illogical to include in SCUA nations such as Italy which would continue to pay dues to the association authorities. Mollet, with some diffidence, suggested that the President make a public statement that a final solution lay only in some form of international operation in accordance with the suggestions adopted by the 18 powers in August. Dillon favors such a statement or, if this is not possible, statements by the Secretary and other officials emphasizing the provisional aspects of SCUA and reiterating US support for a final settlement along the lines of the 18-power proposals.

Pakistan's Attitude Towards SCUA

According to Hildreth, [6] President Mirza indicated to UK Depu-

---

[4] In telegram 1328 from Rome, September 25, not printed. (*Ibid.*, 974.7301/9–2556)

[5] Reported in telegram 1408 from Paris, September 24, not printed. (*Ibid.*, 974.7301/9–2456) On September 25, Dulles forwarded to Eisenhower copies of telegrams 1408 and 1413 from Paris (September 25; *ibid.*), containing Dillon's recommendation that the President issue a public statement as suggested by Mollet, under cover of a letter containing the text of a proposed statement. (Eisenhower initialed Dulles' letter; Eisenhower Library, Whitman File, Dulles–Herter Series) For the transcript of Eisenhower's press conference of September 27, which does not include the proposed statement, see *Public Papers of the Presidents of the United States: Dwight D. Eisenhower, 1956*, pp. 806–818.

[6] Reported in telegram 841 from Karachi, September 22, not printed. (Department of State, Central Files, 974.7301/9–2256)

ty High Commissioner James on Saturday that he was reluctant to put pressure on Suhrawardy re Pakistan joing SCUA. Embassy London, however, has now been informed[7] by a Commonwealth Relations Office official that Mirza has assured James that he would see to it that Pakistan joined. Mirza indicated that he would threaten to resign unless Suhrawardy relented in his negative attitude towards the association.

On Sunday night in London,[8] Pakistan Foreign Minister Noon assured Aldrich that on his return to Pakistan he would urge Suhrawardy to join the association. Noon felt that, if continuous pressure was kept on Suhrawardy, Pakistan would ultimately join SCUA.

Bullock, the Australian High Commissioner in Pakistan, told Hildreth[9] yesterday that he had delivered to Suhrawardy a personal message from Menzies urging Pakistan to join the association. Suhrawardy told Bullock that he was still open-minded about joining. Bullock noted further that the Prime Minister was very much preoccupied with the legal status of the association under the treaty of 1888 and he thinks that another personal message from Menzies showing how the association is consistent with the treaty would not only please Suhrawardy's vanity but arouse his legal interest.

The Secretary has sent a personal message to Suhrawardy[10] thanking him for the participation of Pakistan at the Second Suez Conference and the cooperation of Foreign Minister Noon. After reviewing essential points about the Association, the Secretary expressed the hope that Pakistan would "continue to strengthen the unity of the 18 nations which have joined together to protect their common interests in the Suez matter."

(Summary closed 12:15 p.m. September 25, 1956)

---

[7] Reported in telegram 1640 from London, September 24, not printed. (*Ibid.*, 974.7301/9–2456)

[8] Reported in telegram 1626 from London, September 24, not printed. (*Ibid.*)

[9] Reported in telegram 849 from Karachi, September 24, not printed. (*Ibid.*)

[10] Transmitted to Karachi in telegram 701, September 24. (*Ibid.*, 974.7301/9–2256)

262.   Memorandum of a Conversation, Department of State, Washington, September 25, 1956, 3:02 p.m. [1]

SUBJECT

Suez Canal

PARTICIPANTS

The Secretary
Ambassador Herve Alphand
Mr. Charles Lucet, Minister, French Embassy
Mr. Francois de Laboulaye, Counselor, French Embassy
Mr. Phleger
Mr. Wilcox
Mr. Elbrick

The Ambassador said that while he had no instructions to do so he wished to raise two points which he thought required clarification. The first concerned the operation of the Canal Users' Association. He had originally understood that payment of canal tolls to this Association would be compulsory on the part of the vessels of the user states; now, he was given to understand that the payment of tolls to the Association would only be voluntary. He felt that under these circumstances the purpose of the Association had been greatly "watered down". He wished to inquire whether the United States has the authority and the intention to compel United States ship owners to make payments to SCUA. The Secretary thought that he had made our position clear on several occasions in London during the recent conference. He said that the United States does not have legal authority to require that U.S. flag vessels make payments to any designated person or entity but it does have the power to prevent payments to Egypt. This we can do under the Trading With the Enemy Act which, though it was designed for use in connection with the Korean war can be invoked for this purpose. He doubted that it could be made to extend to vessels of foreign registry even though owned by American companies or nationals. In the case of vessels flying the Panamanian and Liberian flags, for example, we might be confronted with a conflict of laws. In any event, he said, we cannot compel ship owners to make payments to SCUA.

The Secretary said that he had repeatedly urged the British and French to inform us whether they want us to take the required action in connection with the Users' Association, knowing that the possible result will be to detour ships around Africa. He said that

---

[1] Source: Department of State, Central Files, 974.7301/9–2556. Secret. Drafted by Elbrick. The time of the meeting is from Dulles' Appointment Book. (Princeton University Library, Dulles Papers)

this would be very costly to the Western European countries and he wanted to be sure that the British and French are prepared to accept the economic consequences. He said that it is quite probable that action on our part will touch off an Egyptian reaction and that ships will no longer be able to transit the Canal. Our position is unequivocal; we are willing and able to go through with this action but it must be at British and French request. The Ambassador said that he had informed his Foreign Office of the Secretary's views on this matter ten days ago but that he had had no reply. The Secretary repeated that we must have a clear answer to this question and that, with this in view, we are despatching memoranda to the British and French Governments at once. [2] He said that it should be understood that our action, in all probability, will not hurt Egypt but it will hurt the Western powers.

The Ambassador said that despite the fact that the United States does not have the power to require that payments be made to SCUA, the ship owners might still consider it wise to do so. The Secretary pointed out that some tankers are chartered by United States companies under foreign flags and the countries whose flags they fly may say that they—rather than the American companies— have the right to decide how payment will be made. Panama, for example, tends to side with Egypt in this crisis. Of the ships serving American companies U.S. flag vessels account for a relatively small part of the total tonnage (2.7 per cent in 1955) which transits the Canal. We cannot direct the routing of these vessels, but we can direct that no payments be made to Egypt and we can express the hope that the ships involved pay tolls to SCUA. If this action, in turn, means that the ships cannot go through the Canal they will then have to be routed elsewhere. The Secretary repeated that we would take this action only if the British and French wanted us to do so.

Ambassador Alphand then turned to the question of financing the increased costs which would result from the rerouting of ships and said that he had reported what the Secretary had told him about the possibility of utilizing Export-Import Bank funds for the time being to finance oil shipments from the United States. He said that this appeared to be in the nature of a temporary solution and he inquired concerning possible future Congressional action to meet this problem. The Secretary said that he could not predict the mood of Congress which has, in the recent past, shown some reluctance to give more aid to Western European countries and that he could make no commitment at this time.

---

[2] Transmitted to London in telegram 2248, also sent to Paris, Document 268.

The Ambassador said that he had been instructed to raise with the Secretary the question of the British and French approach to the Security Council on the Suez problem. He said that his Government fears that attempts will be made to amend the British-French proposal or to merge that proposal with the Egyptian proposal, and his Government would like assurances that the United States would oppose any such move. The Secretary said that in this matter of the British-French proposal to the United Nations we are "totally in the dark". While there had been some discussion of the matter in London, there had been no decision when the Secretary departed from London on Friday evening. It was only upon his arrival in Washington on Saturday that he was informed of the British and French action. He thought that this was an "extraordinary" performance. We are without information as to the purpose of the British and French approach to the Security Council; we do not know under what Article of the Charter the matter is to be considered; and we have not been informed of the procedure which France and the United Kingdom intend to follow. Under the circumstances it is extremely difficult for the United States to cooperate in this matter. The Ambassador said that the decision had not been made by the French Government and that it was his understanding that they had merely followed the British lead. He said that it was apparent that the British were very fearful that the Russians would move if such action were not taken. He said that the French Government hoped that the United States would oppose the "Egyptian complaint". The Secretary said that we cannot give piecemeal answers. The Cuban President of the Security Council had come to us for information regarding this matter and we were obliged to tell him that we knew nothing about it. This, as the Ambassador would understand, was embarrassing to the United States since the Cuban is apt to look to the United States from time to time for guidance.

The Ambassador said that he could only address himself to the question of procedures since he himself was not well informed as to substance. He asked whether the United States would be prepared to limit the participation in the Security Council debate on this subject to the Council members and Egypt. The Secretary replied in the negative, saying that it would be difficult to exclude Israel and perhaps others who will want to take part if Egypt participates. He repeated that we can't be expected to settle this kind of problem unless we know the real purpose of the exercise. Alphand said that he had received a draft resolution prepared in Paris which was being presented to the British Foreign Office for consideration. This draft resolution would invite Egypt to negotiate with the 18 powers on the basis of their proposal which had previously been presented to Nasser in Cairo. He said that urgent tripartite conversations are necessary and that it would be a serious matter if the three powers are not organized before the Security Council meets tomorrow. The Secretary interjected that it is a serious matter that the three powers were not organized before this question was introduced into the Security Council. The Secretary said that in any event it seemed the damage had been done and he feared that the introduction of the matter into the Security Council might offer to some countries a basis for hesitating to proceed with the formation of SCUA. It is possible that some may hang back and wait for the Security Council to pronounce itself before taking any further action.

The Ambassador said that he thought we should have talks on this subject before tomorrow's Security Council session and thought we should carry on these discussions in Washington this afternoon. The Secretary said that the British should take part in any such conversations and the Ambassador agreed.

---

263.   Memorandum of a Conversation, Department of State, Washington, September 25, 1956, 3:40 p.m. [1]

SUBJECT

Suez Canal

PARTICIPANTS

Sir Harold Macmillan, Chancellor of the Exchequer, UK
Sir Roger Makins, British Ambassador
The Secretary
Mr. Prochnow
Mr. Phleger
Mr. Wilcox
Mr. Elbrick

The Secretary said that he wished to make several points concerning the payment of Canal dues. He said that the United States was prepared to amend the Treasury license to make it unlawful for American flag vessels to pay Canal tolls directly to Egypt rather than to pay into a blocked account or into SCUA. The impact of this would be relatively slight since few U.S. flag vessels

---

[1] Source: Department of State, Central Files, 974.7301/2–556. Secret. Drafted by Elbrick. The time of the meeting is from Dulles' Appointment Book. (Princeton University Library, Dulles Papers) Macmillan visited the United States between September 20 and October 1. While in Washington, he attended a meeting of the International Monetary Fund.

regularly transit the Canal. In 1955, for example, U.S. flag vessels amounted to only 2.7 per cent of the total net tonnage. At present British and French vessels are allowed through the Canal on payment in blocked funds and action by the United States, as described above, might precipitate a change in that situation which would require British and French vessels to go around Africa. This in turn would mean a great economic loss to the two countries and the United States must know definitely, before it acts, whether the economic consequences of its action are understood and are acceptable to France and to the United Kingdom. He pointed out that if Nasser is prepared to take the offensive and to prevent ships from transiting the Canal unless payment is made to Egypt, the loss to Egypt would be minor but the loss to Europe would be very significant. It is important, therefore, that the French and British realize the possible consequences and that the fiscal and economic officials of their Governments are fully aware of the implications. Both the British and French Governments will receive an inquiry along these lines tomorrow morning. The Secretary pointed out that if we take the action indicated in connection with the payment of Canal dues the cost to the United States will not be very great, but he believed that the results would not be too agreeable for the United Kingdom. It had been estimated that it would cost between 500 and 600 million dollars to reroute tankers and to supplement the oil supply from the Western Hemisphere in the event the Canal was not used. The impact on cargoes other than oil had not been estimated. He was inclined to question the effectiveness of the action of rerouting ships and doubted that it was the best way to put pressure on Nasser. He pointed out that refusal to use the Canal will not be highly effective and that in time it is probable that many ships would change their registry in order that they might use the Canal.

Mr. Macmillan felt that the rerouting of ships around Africa is not an acceptable solution of the problem. He said that British economy cannot stand more borrowing on the scale envisaged. The Secretary said—with reference to the possibility of extending U.S. aid—that it is difficult to gauge what the attitude of Congress will be when it reconvenes next year and pointed to recent expressions of Congressional opinion against granting further aid to Western Europe. Mr. Macmillan said that it was apparent to him that the rerouting of ships around Africa would hurt the Western Powers more than it would hurt Nasser. He felt that something must be done to make Nasser lose face and he did not believe rerouting would accomplish this.

The Secretary said that it might be better to let the present situation continue but the French are violent on this subject and feel that such a course would provide a success for Nasser. If we take action to reroute ships and that action proves ineffective we would be faced with the humiliating prospect of backing down to permit ships again to move through the Canal. He questioned whether we should embark on such a problematical course and thought that other means of deflating Nasser should be explored. Nasser is now facing a difficult economic situation due to loss of trade and tourists and further action might be taken to accentuate this situation. While he believed that there were more effective ways than that now being proposed to handle this problem he wished to assure Mr. Macmillan that the United States is not going back on its promise to support the French and the British. He merely wished to assure himself that the British are aware of the possible consequences of the action contemplated.

Mr. Macmillan said that, while Nasser is undoubtedly becoming worried himself, he is in a much stronger position than the British. The Middle East is no longer the strategic area that it once was but the oil is vital to the economy of the United Kingdom. He felt strongly that if we manage to get through this crisis we must establish a more forward looking policy for the area which would help the countries dispose of their resources and employ the proceeds wisely.

Sir Roger Makins said there had been a stream of communications between London and New York on the subject of the approach to the Security Council on the Suez question. He understood that the French Government had produced a draft resolution (which he had not yet seen) which was to be discussed with his Government in London. (The Secretary said that Ambassador Alphand had mentioned the draft to him this afternoon "on a personal basis".) Makins said that the question of procedure is being discussed in New York by the French, British and U.S. representatives to the United Nations. The Secretary said that it was imperative that we seek an agreed position and mentioned particularly the question of the participation of other parties in the Security Council debate. He felt that it would be wise to carry on tripartite conversations in New York. He said that he did not know the exact purpose of the reference of this matter to the Security Council by the British and French and he wondered whether it was their intention to rush the matter through the Council. He said he thought that there should be a genuine effort to seek some solution and asked whether the United Kingdom would be willing to negotiate with Egypt under the aegis of the UN. Makins said that he had no indication that this was the case.

264.   Editorial Note

Before meeting with Secretary Dulles at the Department of State (see *supra*), Macmillan visited with President Eisenhower at the White House, but no formal memorandum of that conversation has been found. At 11:20 a.m., Dulles telephoned President Eisenhower to ask what Macmillan had said. According to the memorandum of telephone conversation prepared at the White House, the "President said that Mr. Macmillan talked very much more moderately (about the Suez) than he had anticipated. He cheerfully admitted that the issue was Nasser rather than the Canal (said if they had closed up the Shell Refinery, England would have been much worse off). President said they had had a 'nice chat'—had talked a little about the [Security Council] resolution Britain is drafting. Dulles said that the British were moving ahead without giving us an inkling of what is in their minds. He and the President agreed that probably the British didn't know exactly how they were proceeding themselves." The two then discussed the possibility that Senator Mansfield, who was then visiting Europe, was "playing politics" with the Suez situation. "Going back to conversation with Macmillan, President said that he had reported the loss in stock market, people selling short. Pointed out that the Users' Association might give opportunity for keeping the Canal open and thinking through to a solution. President said he thought that Macmillan rather thought the Users Association is a good thing—reiterated nothing was said that might cause Dulles concern. He said that Macmillan was far less bitter than he had been a few weeks ago." (Eisenhower Library, Whitman File, Eisenhower Diaries)

---

265.   Memorandum of a Conversation Between Secretary of State Dulles and Chancellor of the Exchequer Macmillan, Department of State, Washington, September 25, 1956 [1]

I had a private talk with Harold Macmillan. He expressed his great appreciation for my contribution in the Suez matter and particularly for the speech which I had made Wednesday night at the Conference. He referred to his pleasant talk with the President

---

[1] Source: Eisenhower Library, Dulles Papers, General Memoranda of Conversation. Top Secret; Personal and Private. Drafted by Dulles.

and his fine spirits. He said he hoped devoutly there was no question of his reelection.

I said that I hoped that nothing drastic would happen through British action which might diminish our chances. Macmillan said he recalled that we had been helpful in their election situation and he would bear that in mind. I said I felt that there was a basis for some reciprocity and he said he quite agreed.

We discussed the plans for diminishing Nasser's prestige and I expressed the view that this could be done by economic and political means more effectively than by military means. Mr. Macmillan said to me the same thing that Anthony Eden had said on Thursday [2] night, namely, that the present military situation was such that they could without undue expense hold action in abeyance. Their present military posture was not dependent on heavy shipping charges, as had originally been the case.

JFD

[2] September 20.

266.   Report Prepared in the Executive Secretariat of the Department of State [1]

Summary No. 17   *Washington, September 26, 1956.*

SUMMARY OF DEVELOPMENTS IN SUEZ SITUATION

Procedural Suggestions to Lodge [2]

The following procedural suggestions for the initial phase of the Suez debate in the UN have been furnished to Ambassador Lodge:

1) Following the adoption of the agenda, the next meeting should be not less than one week later so that SCUA may be established and agreement obtained on a firm UK-French-US course of action in the Security Council (SC);

2) Invitations to interested parties should be limited initially to Egypt;

[1] Source: Eisenhower Library, Whitman File, International File. Top Secret; Eyes Only for Designated Recipient.

[2] These suggestions were forwarded to USUN in telegram 110, September 25. (Department of State, Central Files, 974.7301/9–2556)

3) The Iranian representative, to whom France may have to yield its normal assumption of the Council Presidency in October, should be briefed on arguments to avoid having the case treated as a dispute, the chief of which is that there are so many potential parties the SC would be precluded from taking effective action;

4) We consider that the Egyptian complaint should be inscribed but as a separate item following that of the UK and France. We oppose making the UK-French and the Egyptian items into a single subject. Nevertheless, we would be prepared to have them listed as "A" and "B" under the general heading "The Question of Suez".

[Here follows discussion of Egypt's search for foreign credits (reported in telegrams 873 and 876 from Cairo and telegram 916 to Cairo, all September 25; all Department of State, Central Files, 611.74231/9–2256); Iran's position in the U.N. debate (reported in telegram 483 from Tehran, September 26; *ibid.*, 974.7301/9–2656); activities of the Users' Association (reported in telegram 2230 to London, September 25; *ibid.*, 974.7301/9–2556); and views of the British Commonwealth Relations Office (reported in telegram 1662 from London; *ibid.*).

(Summary closed 11:45 a.m., September 26, 1956)

---

267.   Memorandum of a Conversation, Department of State, Washington, September 26, 1956 [1]

SUBJECT

Security Council Consideration of Suez Issue

PARTICIPANTS

Mr. Zev Argaman, Minister Counselor, Embassy of Israel
Mr. Shimshon Arad, First Secretary, Embassy of Israel
Assistant Secretary Wilcox, IO
Mr. Ware Adams, UNP
Mr. Lincoln P. Bloomfield, IO

The Israelis called at their request to ascertain what will happen in the Security Council and what lay behind the timing of the British-French move.

Mr. Wilcox explained that after having exhausted attempts under Article 33 of the Charter, considerable sentiment developed at the second London meeting for some form of UN action. We had

---

[1] Source: Department of State, Central Files, 974.7301/9–2656. Confidential. Drafted by Bloomfield.

been somewhat taken by surprise by the timing of the British-French initiative, but while we cannot foresee in detail the outcome, our continued hope is for a peaceful settlement that will be satisfactory to the principal users of the canal.

In answer to Mr. Argaman's inquiry as to the possibility of fruitful Security Council action in the face of a probable Soviet veto, Mr. Wilcox mentioned the possibility of provisional measures under Articles 36, 37, or 40, as well as some procedural steps that might be possible.

Mr. Argaman then came to what was obviously his chief concern: the possibility that the Israeli shipping problem will be dealt with in the course of the Security Council discussion. Mr. Wilcox felt that undoubtedly this issue would be referred to in the course of the debate.

In answer to Mr. Wilcox's inquiry, Mr. Argaman confirmed that a request had already been made to the Secretary General for Israeli participation in the forthcoming debate. He did not expect this request to be taken up until next week. He did not agree that the main issue might be confused by the possibility that all the Arab states might now insist on their right to take part.

Mr. Wilcox expressed his keen disappointment with the Israeli action yesterday along the Jordanian border, [2] deploring not only the size and intensity of the Israeli raid, but its inevitable effect on Security Council action. Mr. Argaman replied that the timing was related to events along the border rather than events in New York. He did say that the Israeli Foreign Minister had just telephoned General Burns informing him of Israel's readiness to execute a cease-fire as soon as similar assurances are received from Jordan. He stated that for four months Israel has refrained from reacting to Jordanian attacks, and has suffered a number of casualties in this period. Mr. Wilcox stated that the Secretary General is becoming discouraged with the mounting breaches in the Armistice, and registered the hope that order will be restored quickly.

Mr. Bloomfield inquired as to whether the Israeli Government has any thoughts or predictions regarding Security Council action on the Suez matter. Mr. Argaman replied that they can foresee no constructive result at this time, but if SCUA can organize, and if Egypt then blocks a SCUA convoy, a sound case can then be taken to the Council.

FOW

---

[2] On the night of September 25, Israeli Defense Forces launched an attack against Jordanian military and police positions south of Jerusalem. See footnote 2, Document 279.

268.   Telegram From the Department of State to the Embassy in the United Kingdom [1]

Washington, September 26, 1956—6:42 p.m.

2248. Please present a memorandum in the following sense to the Government to which you are accredited.

Begin verbatim text.

The United States is prepared, if desired by both the British and the French Governments, to amend the present Treasury license so as to make it unlawful for American flag vessels to pay Canal duties directly to Egypt but permitting payment into SCUA as their agent with discretionary authority to SCUA to pay over to the Egyptian Government as it deems appropriate. This is in accord with my letter of September 21 to Foreign Secretary Lloyd. [2]

However, it should be borne in mind:

(a) The economic impact of this on Egypt will not be great because United States flag vessels transiting the Canal in 1955 amounted only to a little over 3 million net tons or about 2.7% of the total tonnage.

(b) It is understood that concurrently with United States action British and French regulations would be changed to eliminate payment to the old Suez Canal Company in favor of payments to SCUA. Thus, the course of action outlined might bring about a situation which will require the detouring of British, French, United States and some other flag vessels and throw upon the Western European, and indeed some Asian, countries a considerable economic burden.

The United States wants to be sure before it acts on tolls as above indicated that this is desired by UK and France despite the economic consequences which might result. Also we should like to know just what the new UK, French regulations would prescribe.

It is assumed that any Egyptian action to bar the Canal under the conditions above outlined would apply equally to all ships paying tolls to SCUA as above outlined. If there should be discrimination practiced by Egypt against United States vessels under these conditions, that would create a new situation.

The United States would encourage vessels controlled by United States citizens though not of United States registry to adopt the procedure above outlined. But we cannot guarantee a favorable response which, in any event, to be effective would require coopera-

---

[1] Source: Department of State, Central Files, 974.7301/9-2656. Secret; Priority. Drafted by Dulles; cleared by Phleger, Rountree, and Elbrick; and approved by Dulles. Also sent to Paris.

[2] See Document 250.

tion or acquiescence from the countries of registry, for example, Panama and Liberia, and such cooperation and acquiescence is dubious. *End verbatim text.*

FYI We yesterday orally presented the foregoing considerations to British Ambassador and Mr. Macmillan and also to French Ambassador, telling them that we would present them in London and Paris.

Please request a prompt written reply as we desire to be ready to act as soon as SCUA is organized to receive payments of dues.

Dulles

---

269.   Telegram From the Embassy in France to the Department of State [1]

Paris, September 26, 1956—7 p.m.

1450. London eyes only Ambassador; eyes only Secretary from Ambassador. Suez. During conversation with Jebb this morning regarding London Conference and prospects for UN debate, Jebb casually informed me that he had impression that Pineau, Bourges-Maunoury, and Mollet all felt that UN debate would be ineffective and that it would be terminated around the middle of October, at which time the way would be clear for military action against Egypt. I told Jebb that, as he knew, US had great fears regarding the eventual outcome of any military venture in Egypt in view of the feeling it would create throughout the entire Middle East. However, I told him, namely, that if hostilities should be initiated by France and Great Britain at any time between the 15th of October and the 6th of November such action would be most embarrassing and difficult for the Eisenhower Administration in the forthcoming election. I pointed out that military action would be bound to have the greatest possible effect on the election if it was initiated at such time.

Jebb said that he fully realized this and felt that if such action were to be undertaken it would be much better to put it off until later in November, or early December. I told him that I did not

---

[1] Source: Department of State, Central Files, 684A.86/9–2756. Secret. Received at 8:30 a.m., September 27. Repeated to London.

think that you [2] had mentioned this aspect of the situation to Lloyd or Eden while you were in London, but I felt that at an appropriate occasion during their visit here he should point this situation out to them.

I feel it will be most important for you personally to obtain agreement from Lloyd and Pineau, while they are in New York for the UN debate, on course of action to be followed upon conclusion of debate. There is some rather loose talk here originating with Mollet, which has been reported to me by two completely reliable sources, indicating that he feels that some sort of dramatic action should be taken shortly. What Mollet apparently has in mind is some form of economic sanctions outside the framework of SCUA which he considers to be an impotent organization. There has also been some talk by members of the French Cabinet regarding the construction of a new pipe line, and they may want to propose that plans for construction of such a pipe line be promptly announced. In any event, I feel that we will have to develop some sort of agreed concrete action in the economic field in order to ensure that military action does not follow an unsuccessful debate in the UN.

Dillon

---

[2] Reference is to Secretary Dulles.

---

270.   Telegram From the Embassy in Egypt to the Department of State [1]

Cairo, September 26, 1956—3 p.m.

891. Following is summary conversation with Nasser following presentation credentials (Embtel 878): [2]

He said realized this not occasion for substantive discussion but wanted give general idea his thinking. Burden of what followed was largely to effect that he had endeavored follow policy of frankness but apparently his efforts had only resulted in misunderstanding.

---

[1] Source: Department of State, Central Files, 674.00/9–2656. Secret. Received at 1:17 a.m., September 27. Repeated to London, Amman, Beirut, Baghdad, Damascus, and Jidda.

[2] In telegram 878 from Cairo, September 25, Hare reported that he had presented his letters of credence to Nasser at noon and that a summary of their conversation, which lasted one-half hour, would follow. (*Ibid.*, 123–Hare, Raymond A.)

However, impossible for him to operate in any other way since he did not have technique of politics and diplomacy at his command. Also his knowledge of English did not permit of nuances in expression.

One misunderstanding, he said, had been erroneous idea that he had ambition build up Egyptian empire over surrounding area. True he was interested in promoting cooperation and solidarity of area but that was far cry from seeking Egyptian domination. Thus, his ambassadors in Libya and Syria had been accused of improper activity but he had checked and found charges largely without foundation. He had been accused of stirring up trouble in Aden but first he knew of it was in press. Similarly groundless were charges of his causing difficulty in Bahrein.

However, such importance as he attached to Arab cooperation was in any event secondary to his principal purpose which was promoting welfare of Egyptian people. Here followed account of how he had struggled for and gained popular support which unnecessary repeat.

Second misunderstanding, Nasser maintained, was that he had tried play off Soviet against West. True that he had dealt with both but he had made no secret of it as evidenced by way he had kept Embassy informed regarding Soviet overtures on Aswan.

He felt there was also mutual misunderstanding by Egypt and United States regarding each others motives and actions. Egypt had impression United States sought reduce Egyptian position in Arab countries and was implementing this policy by certain lines of action, which led Egypt in turn to take counter-action. Trouble was this sort of thing led to a tit-for-tat sequence of events of which difficult see real purpose (what were we really driving at anyway?) or eventual outcome. Also he feared both we and they might sometimes be acting on basis of imperfect or erroneous information and this seemed compound difficulty.

Nasser then got on subject of nationalism in Near East which he maintained real driving and dominant force and necessary understand in assessing area problems. This in turn led to discussion Baghdad Pact which he felt had been major error. Reason was that weakness of Near East is internal and consequently building up of strength and stability should be from within not from without. He believed actually little danger Soviet military aggression in Near East for simple reason such action would touch off world war and great powers apparently in agreement rule that out. Consequently Baghdad Pact had earmarks of foreign intrusion which completely contrary to trend of indigenous nationalism. Egypt had considered carefully before deciding not to join and now in looking back he felt deterioration in Egyptian relations with United States traceable back to that event.

Regarding future, Nasser said he had no clear-cut plans but was largely acting on ad hoc basis. He hoped however misunderstandings could be removed and return made to normal relations with United States.

I said glad receive his views. We too had some serious misgivings which I looked forward to discussing when time and occasion permitted and I hoped in so doing it would be understood if I followed Nasser's example and spoke with complete frankness. It was also our desire to get back to traditionally friendly relations but there were serious problems to be resolved in order do so.

Realize foregoing is largely repetitive of conversations of others with Nasser and that it probably represents little more than preliminary warming up before real game begins. In circumstances, I feel would be premature attempt draw conclusions except to note that, in repeating previously expressed views, Nasser did not seem exactly exude confidence regarding road ahead. Also he gave no indication of animosity despite seriousness of problems which he outlined.

Incidentally, interesting no specific mention made either Canal question or Israel.

Hare

---

271.   Memorandum of a Conversation, Department of State, Washington, September 27, 1956, 11 a.m.[1]

SUBJECT

The Secretary's Briefing on Suez Situation with members of Senate Foreign Relations Committee

---

[1] Source: Department of State, Secretary's Memoranda of Conversation: Lot 64 D 199. Secret. No drafting information is given on the source text. The time of the meeting is from Dulles' Appointment Book. (Princeton University Library, Dulles Papers)

PARTICIPANTS

The Secretary	Senator Fulbright
The Under Secretary	Senator Mansfield
H—Mr. Hill	Senator H. A. Smith
H—Mr. O'Connor	Senator Langer

The Secretary opened the conversation by remarking that he was calling a "rump session" of the Senate Foreign Relations Committee to brief them on the Suez situation because he had heard that these members were in town. (These four Senators were the only members of the Senate Foreign Relations or House Foreign Affairs or the leadership of either House who were in town).

The Secretary described a little of the background of the first London meeting and of the Cairo meetings of the committee of five. He noted that at Cairo, Nasser had made no counter-proposals and had indicated no disposition to negotiate. After the Cairo meetings, a critical situation emerged because Eden had promised to convene Parliament in order to present to them a program of action if the Cairo meeting produced no results. Moreover, this date coincided with the date the British had set for the completion of their military preparations, i.e., September 15. It appeared that the U.K. had no alternative at this point, between a policy of force or surrender. It was at this point that the Secretary proposed to London and Paris his plan for a users' association. This proposal was adopted by Eden as a way out of his dilemma. Eden presented it to his Parliament in a far more bellicose manner than the Secretary had ever intended. Because of Eden's presentation, the Secretary thought it necessary in his press conference the day after to discuss the association with quite a different emphasis. This change has lead [led] to charges that we had "watered down" the original plan. The Secretary stressed that there had been no watering down from his original proposal but only from what had been Eden's version of it as presented to Parliament. It was only after the Secretary's presentation of the plan that we were able to obtain promises of attendance for the second London meeting; a number of nations had been reluctant to attend on the basis of Eden's original presentation.

At the second London meeting, the Secretary's proposals for the users' association were adopted substantially as originally proposed. Lange of Norway suggested that the association should coordinate the study of alternatives to the use of the Canal. This suggestion was adopted and the Secretary commented that it was in line with Senator Mansfield's suggestion on this point.

The Secretary described some of the problems involved in re-routing traffic around the Cape of Good Hope. The greatest burden would be in loss of dollar exchange because of the necessity of replacing Near Eastern oil with oil from this hemisphere. This would cost the U.K. $400 million and the French $100 million in exchange, assuming that the pipelines stayed open. The Secretary said the Export-Import Bank was ready to loan this money.

When the Secretary arrived in London, he found that the U.K.—particularly the Treasury people—were very worried about these costs and had become quite negative about any move which would result in re-routing traffic around the Cape. A further study made it clear that such re-routing would not appreciably hurt Egypt; regardless of the association's best efforts, much traffic would continue to go through the Canal. Moreover, the British would have very considerable sterling costs and all other countries would face additional expense. The more this matter was studied in London the more enthusiasm for re-routing started to wane. The Italians and Scandinavians, and the Asian countries were particularly opposed to the idea. It was finally agreed that re-routing should be a "next to last" resort. War is being regarded as the last resort.

The Secretary said that enough countries would join SCUA at the meeting on October 1 in London so that the organization could get started. He predicted that some countries of the original eighteen would hold back, waiting to see what happened at the U.N.

At London, there was considerable sentiment to go to the U.N.; however, the Secretary and a majority of others preferred to wait until SCUA was in operation, for two reasons: 1) feared that a number of nations would hold back from membership in SCUA pending U.N. action; 2) SCUA could provide the U.N. with a vehicle for provisional solution and thus allow the time for negotiations to develop, and for a thorough study of the legal rights involved. However, the U.K. and France decided to go ahead with an appeal to the U.N. and made their decision without consultation and while the Secretary was still in his plane returning from London. The Secretary was annoyed at this lack of coordination, but masked his annoyance for the sake of unity. He said that partially as a result of this action, Japan and Pakistan were holding back on joining SCUA and the Secretary feared that the SCUA meeting on October 1 might have only White Nations adhering. The U.K. apparently had been forced to move to the U.N. by domestic political pressures. The Labor Party had demanded such a move and some Conservative Party elements were pushing for U.N. action which would result in a Soviet veto and leave the U.K. free to use force. The Secretary felt the French and the British had moved in a hurry and had not thought through precisely what they hoped to achieve at the U.N. Moreover, it was not clear what their motivation was; there were certainly elements in both countries that hoped only to go through the motions at the

U.N., in order to be able to use force at a later date. We did not yet know what the British and French plans were, although hoped to get a draft of their proposed resolution today.

The Secretary said that the British Cabinet was sharply divided on the use of force. Salisbury and Macmillan favored it, and were very influential. The majority of the Cabinet opposed it, and Eden was thus in the middle. In talking with Salisbury and Macmillan, the Secretary observed that they clearly saw how to start the use of force, but did not see clearly how to end it. When SCUA is set up tentatively, the thinking is that U.S., U.K., and French tolls would be paid to the association rather than to Egypt. This action may set off the refusal of Egypt to let ships through the Canal and thus force the re-routing of shipping. However, before the U.S. takes this action, we will insist on firm commitments from the U.K. and the French that they want us to do so, that they are willing to do so themselves, and that they fully recognize the possible consequences thereof.

The Secretary said SCUA involved no legal obligations and therefore no Congressional action. It was an entirely voluntary organization, to which the United States expected to adhere by executive action at the London meeting on October 1.

The Secretary said there was some bitterness being generated against the U.S. in both the U.K. and France alleging that we had let them down. Such criticism was regrettable but inevitable in view of our moderating role.

The Secretary felt that events were working towards a settlement. The Egyptians were feeling the economic pinch, particularly in their balance of payments; also because of loss of tolls, tourists, business credit and markets for their cotton. We were receiving many indications that the Egyptians were ripening for a settlement. The Secretary was certain that the technical aspects of the problem could be worked out, but fearful that the prestige issues might make such settlement impossible. From a technical point of view, there were only two areas that needed protection against possible covert obstruction of Canal traffic by the Egyptians. These points were the allotment of pilots and the assignment of ships to the traffic pattern.

The Secretary felt that there was considerable danger that Israel might take advantage of the crisis by taking over the part of Jordan, west of the Jordan River. Under the circumstances, it would be almost impossible for the U.S. to implement the 1950 Declaration to protect Jordan against such Israeli action. The Israelis were being strongly tempted by this situation; however, the growing Israeli aggressiveness should produce some pressure on the Arabs and on Egypt for a settlement. The Saudi Arabians were not as close to

Nasser as would publicly appear, and seemed to be playing a helpful role in the situation.

Mansfield said that he would like to see the legal rights of the Suez Canal Company passed on by the International Court of Justice. He recognized that this was a lengthy process and did not offer an early solution, but felt that in the long run it was necessary to satisfy world opinion. He also felt this entire situation called for a speed up in the development of atomic power.

Mr. Hoover said that the Egyptian pilots thus far had been handling the job well, but that within a month or two would come the period of fog and sandstorms which would really test the ability to keep the Canal operating. In response to Senator Langer's question, re: "Sources of oil from Lignite and Shale," Mr. Hoover pointed out that technically the process was feasible, but that it was estimated to cost four to five times more than normal production to produce oil from this source. The present supply of oil reserves was nine years, but this did not include anticipated new discoveries.

At the conclusion of the meeting, Mr. Hill asked if the Senators had any suggestions as to being kept informed and as to whether they had heard any complaints from their colleagues as to lack of information. The only specific response was from Senator Fulbright that he had heard no complaints.

---

272.   Report Prepared in the Executive Secretariat of the Department of State [1]

Summary No. 18   *Washington, September 27, 1956.*

SUMMARY OF DEVELOPMENTS IN SUEZ SITUATION

Arab "Big Three" Conference at Riyadh [2]

Embassy Cairo has transmitted [3] a . . . report on the Arab "Big Three" discussions at Riyadh. Saud reaffirmed his support of the tripartite alliance but stated his genuine concern at Egypt's failure to undertake prior consultation before nationalizing the canal. Nasser

---

[1] Source: Eisenhower Library, Whitman File, International File. Top Secret; Eyes Only for Designated Recipient.

[2] On September 23, King Saud, President Nasser, and President Quwatly met at Riyadh.

[3] Reference is to telegram 892 from Cairo, September 26, not printed. (Department of State, Central Files, 786.00/9–2656)

replied that complete secrecy was necessary because the British and French might have "moved in" if they had had advance notice. He, however, agreed that Egypt would undertake prior consultation in the future on matters of comparable importance.

. . . Nasser went on to explain why the government of Egypt could not attend the first London conference and stated that with respect to the Menzies' mission there was no opportunity for counterproposals as that group had no authority to negotiate. With reference to SCUA, Nasser said that the prompt Egyptian action in rejecting this proposal stemmed from the threatening manner in which it was presented by Eden and was designed to discourage the US from adopting a similar role. He added that he preferred Saudi Arabia to India as a mediator.

Nehru's Attitude Towards Nasser

Embassy New Delhi reports [4] that Nehru, on the eve of his departure for Saudi Arabia, is apparently worried that Nasser will try to meet him and seek to associate India on an unqualified basis with Nasser's stand on Suez. Actually, while Nehru supports Egyptian independence and sovereignty, he does not want Egypt to have the power to stop ship transits through the canal. In this connection, the Indian Ministry of External Affairs has assured the Embassy that Nehru will not meet Nasser on his trip to Saudi Arabia. To the Embassy, the implication is that Nehru does not wish to be cast as the principal supporter of Nasser outside of the communist bloc.

[Here follow a report concerning the United States memorandum on the payment of Canal duties sent to London and Paris (see telegram 2248, Document 268); a report from London that the British Government's immediate objective was to get SCUA established with as many countries as possible (reported in telegram 1699 from London, September 26; Department of State, Central Files, 974.7301/9–2656); a report from Tokyo that the Japanese Government would not join SCUA immediately but might at a later date (reported in telegram 750 from Tokyo, September 27; *ibid.*, 974.7301/9–2756); and a report from Karachi that the Pakistani Government continued to refuse to join SCUA at that time (reported in telegram 878 from Karachi, September 26; *ibid.*, 974.7301/9–2656).]

(Summary closed 12:00 noon, September 27, 1956)

---

[4] In telegram 773 from New Delhi, September 25, not printed. (*Ibid.*, 791.00/9–2556)

273.   **Memorandum of Discussion at the 298th Meeting of the National Security Council, Washington, September 27, 1956, 2:30 p.m.** [1]

[Here follow a paragraph listing the participants at the meeting and agenda item 1.]

2. Significant World Developments Affecting U.S. Security

[Here follows discussion of unrelated subjects.]

Admiral Radford inquired whether General Cabell had anything new on the Arab-Israeli situation. General Cabell replied that tension had remained very high in the area since the recent large scale Israeli reprisal against Jordan. Jordan had taken refuge in diplomatic rather than military reaction to this Israeli attack and accordingly General Cabell believed that Jordan did not at this time wish to expand the incident into war with Israel. Furthermore, Nasser had indicated to the Jordan authorities his view that it was not advisable for Jordan to become embroiled at this time with Israel. General Cabell expressed the opinion that as long as Egypt remained so deeply involved in the Suez crisis, there was little likelihood that the Arab states would resort to war against Israel.

Secretary Dulles said that he would like to comment on General Cabell's estimate. He believed that we should clearly recognize the fact that the Suez Canal crisis has resulted in upsetting the balance of forces which had kept a precarious peace between Israel and her Arab neighbors. The deterrents to Israeli military action have in several instances already disappeared. There was growing evidence of a more belligerent Israeli mood. Accordingly, it would be extremely hazardous to speculate that Israel will continue to show restraint and will not, for example, try to take advantage of the situation to seize the Western Bank of the River Jordan.

The President commented that while Secretary Dulles was probably right, it seemed to him that if Nasser really wanted to unite the Arab states, it might seem to him a good move to try to provoke Israel. Secretary Dulles replied that he did not think Nasser was ready to run this risk at the present time.

Admiral Radford emphasized that the Joint Chiefs of Staff were very much concerned because of the temptation offered to Israel by the concentration of the armies of Jordan in a small area of Western Jordan. This concentration could enable the Israelis to wipe out or to

---

[1] Source: Eisenhower Library, Whitman File, NSC Records. Top Secret. Prepared by Gleason on September 28. The time of the meeting is from the record of the President's Daily Appointments. (*Ibid.*)

capture virtually the entire Jordan army. Admiral Radford added that the last Israeli reprisal was far from being a minor military action. Several thousand Israeli troops had been involved.

[Here follow the remainder of this item and the remaining agenda items.]

S. Everett Gleason

---

274.   Annex to Watch Committee Report No. 321 [1]

SC 05591/56   *Washington, September 27, 1956.*

CONCLUSIONS ON BRITISH-FRENCH INTENTIONS TO EMPLOY FORCE AGAINST EGYPT

Anglo-French military action against Egypt in the immediate future is unlikely unless Egypt should offer some extreme provocation.

The following are the more significant factors considered by the Watch Committee in reaching its conclusion:

1. The Anglo-French appeal to the UN that Egypt's "unilateral action" in the Canal Zone is an infringement of the Convention of 1888, and the Egyptian counter-appeal that "some nations, especially the United Kingdom and France," have committed action inconsistent with the UN Charter.

2. British and French statements that, while all efforts will be made to avoid war, the right to use force must be reserved.

3. French concern over the arrival of Soviet submarines in the Mediterranean; no information has been obtained on these submarines for the past ten days.

4. The status of British-French military forces:

a. The absence of major British and French military movements in the Mediterranean area during the past week; the continued stand-by status of the 3rd Infantry Division in England and the presence of the French 7th Rapid Mechanized and the 10th Airborne Divisions in Algeria and of the British 10th Armored Division in Libya.

b. The absence of a concentration of amphibious and airborne lift at Cyprus, and some evidence that the French build-up there has been halted.

---

[1] Source: CIA Files. Top Secret; Noforn; Limited Distribution.

5. Redeployment by mid-September from the Sinai to the Canal Zone and the Cairo area of all the Egyptian armor except one armored group and possibly one regiment of tanks: Although Egypt still has 34,000 men in the Sinai, these defensive moves against British-French attack have weakened Egyptian defenses in that area.

---

275.   Telegram From the Mission at the United Nations to the Department of State [1]

New York, September 27, 1956—7 p.m.

260. Suez in SC. At meeting this afternoon with Dixon (U.K.) and Ordonneau [2] (France) we discussed questions of: 1) Israeli request participate in SC meetings, and 2) Presidency of SC in October.

1) On Israeli request, Dixon felt would be highly prejudicial to orderly consideration of Suez question if Israelis were to participate. He feared it would confuse Suez with whole Palestine question and inevitably result in requests from all Arab states participate. As yet, there had been no decision by U.K. Foreign Office re how handle Israeli request, but trend of U.K. Delegation thinking was best solution would be have issue postponed, with statements in SC that it could be decided as debate developed when Israeli participation useful.

Ordonneau expressed general approval this proposal, although he had no instructions. He said if issue came to vote, he believed France would vote for Israeli's participation. Dixon felt, if it impossible avoid having Israelis participate, this should be limit and no others should be invited. He thought this applied equally to Arabs, India, and any others who might seek participate. He feared India would in fact request participate, and felt they should be turned down. Argument should be there were many states interested as users of Canal, and all of them obviously could not be invited. Israelis, on other hand, did have special standing inasmuch as SC had adopted resolution concerning their exclusion from Canal, and

---

[1] Source: Department of State, Central Files, 974.7301/9–2756. Confidential; Priority. Received at 7:51 p.m.

[2] Pierre Ordonneau, Adviser for Security Council Affairs on the French Delegation.

this could be used justify differentiation Israelis from others if invitation to Israelis could not in end be avoided.

My view is that best solution is find way postpone action by SC on Israeli request. British and French agreed that, if this is to be our joint position, we should try obtain informal agreement all SC members before next meeting to avoid debate in SC.

2) On SC Presidency in October, Ordonneau stated French Delegation had recommended to Paris that Pineau step down from Presidency and Nunez-Portuondo (Cuba) [3] be requested continue in chair. They recognized this was not in accordance SC rules of procedure (though SC could suspend rules by majority vote) which provide when interested party is in chair, he may pass Presidency to next month's chairman. If rules were followed, this would mean having Iranian take over which French thought not as desirable as continuing Nunez. They had discussed problem with Blanco (Cuba) [4] who stated Nunez would be happy continue. French Delegation did not yet have reaction from Foreign Office.

British raised question of having Ardalan (Iranian FonMin) come to SC meetings and take chair from French, having some feeling that departing from rules procedure might create bad impression and offend Iranians. They did not feel Abdoh would make good chairman because of his disposition consider himself Arab spokesman. They felt Ardalan would be much better in view of satisfactory attitude he showed in London. They recognized however superior ability Nunez. It was agreed we should all seek instructions on question having Nunez continue. It was also agreed that, if this our decision, effort should be made have matter settled informally outside SC before next meeting.

U.K. Delegation raised question whether it preferable take matter up with Abdoh in order have him take initiative step down, or to raise question directly with Iranian Foreign Office. Theory Abdoh and Iranian Government would have to follow in stepping aside would be they were interested party as member 18.

We all agreed that, if we reached common accord on how deal with Presidency and Israeli participation, a preliminary meeting of SC next week prior participation Foreign Ministers, should be held to dispose officially of these questions. Dixon felt strongly that, at their first meeting, FonMins should not have deal with these matters, even though agreement already reached informally and SC action pro forma.

---

[3] Dr. Emilio Nunez-Portuondo, Cuban Representative to the U.N. Security Council.

[4] Carlos Blanco, Alternate Representative of Cuba.

Continuing Nunez-Portuondo in chair seems to me be best solution to Presidency question. He is able chairman and can do much to aid us in reaching favorable outcome. He can be helpful in avoiding procedural pitfalls. Ordonneau said French Delegation had recommended French take initiative with Iranians and I suggest we assist U.K. and French this respect.

Re date SC meeting with FonMins, Dixon said he had asked latitude agree on either 10/4 or 10/5. If we are to have preliminary meeting, it should be called by Monday (10/1) and held on Wednesday (10/3).

Please instruct on:

(1) Postponement Israeli invitation;
(2) Invitations to any other would-be participants;
(3) What efforts we should make on Presidency (a) with Abdoh, (b) with other SC members;
(4) Whether have preliminary SC meeting on these questions;
(5) Date of SC meeting with FonMins (in this connection, Nunez-Portuondo has just requested all members state preference by tomorrow morning in view French request matter be determined in 24 hours). [5]

Lodge

---

[5] In telegram 121 to USUN, September 28, the Department indicated agreement that USUN should seek a temporary postponement of the vote on the Israeli invitation; that other interested states not be invited, even if Israel were invited at a later date; and that it was advisable to settle outstanding questions in a preliminary Security Council meeting to as to avoid a procedural wrangle when the foreign ministers were present. On the question of the Presidency, telegram 121 noted a preference to leave it to the French. It also noted that Dulles wished to defer the meeting to October 8, but doubted whether the other foreign ministers would be agreeable to wait that long and so would be available on October 5. (Department of State, Central Files, 974.7301/9–2756)

---

276.   **Memorandum of a Conversation Between the Secretary of State and the French Ambassador (Alphand), French Embassy, Washington, September 27, 1956** [1]

After dinner at the French Embassy last night, Mr. Alphand took me aside and discussed the Suez matter. He emphasized the

---

[1] Source: Department of State, UNP Files: Lot 58 D 244, Suez–1956. Secret. Drafted by Dulles on September 28. Copies were distributed to Hoover, Wilcox, Rountree, and Phleger. The source text is the copy sent to Wilcox.

importance that the US, UK, and France should be working together and that we should have plans in common. He said he thought the forthcoming visit of Pineau and Lloyd to the UN would provide an opportunity for this.

I said that the US would like it very much if our policies were concerted but that in fact we had been very much left out in the planning. I pointed out that the decision to go to the UN had been taken while I was in flight from London to Washington. Alphand indicated that the French too had been disconcerted by the rapidity of the British action in this matter. I asked what was the purpose? Was it to bring about a negotiation? Alphand indicated that he felt his Government was very strongly opposed to negotiation.

I said of course it was natural that the French should want to bring in the British in military action because in effect the French already had an Arab war on their hands and this would give them a powerful ally. Alphand said he did not think that was a primary motivation. They were more concerned lest there arise another dictator like Hitler and he should be dealt with at an early stage.

Alphand asked whether I could get together with Pineau and Lloyd when they were here, with a view to concerting a course of action not just for a week or two but the next year or even three years.

I said I would be glad to have such a meeting if the other two wanted it. He suggested Saturday or Sunday, October 6 or 7. I said I had a speaking engagement at Williams College on Saturday but that I could be available on Sunday. I said that the US accepted "in principle" the idea he suggested but I said laughingly that acceptance in principle did not mean much until the details had been worked out. He laughingly agreed.

Alphand said that he had been speaking in a "personal" capacity.

---

277.   Editorial Note

On September 27, Ambassador Gallman reported to the Department of State information received from Iraqi Prime Minister Nuri Said that, in the context of increasing border clashes with Israel, King Hussein had requested military assistance from the Iraqi Government, including the deployment of at least one Iraqi division into Jordan. Said told Gallman that Iraq was not in a position to supply

Jordan with arms and for the present had no intention of dispatching an Iraqi division into Jordan. He added, however, that the Iraqi Government was going to build up supplies within Jordan at Mafraq and would have to send a force of company or perhaps battalion strength to guard these supplies. According to Said, the force would be under orders not to become involved in border skirmishes. The Prime Minister then asked for assurances that the United States military assistance to Iraq would not be suspended, if the dispatching of an Iraqi force in strength into Jordan became necessary later in the defense of Jordan against aggression and in keeping with Iraq's treaty obligations to Jordan. "Iraq's aim," Said affirmed, "is to strengthen Jordan against Communism." Furthermore, Said requested the United States to explain to the Israeli Government that the sending of a small force to Mafraq was not an act of aggression but only a defensive move. He also asked whether the United States could supply through him a few thousand rifles and a few machine guns and army blankets for Jordan. (Telegram 513 from Baghdad, September 27; Department of State, Central Files, 684A.85/9–2756)

In response, the Department of State, in telegram 462, September 27, instructed Gallman to convey to Said the view that Iraqi agreement to the Jordanian request would be "ill-advised at this juncture." For text, see volume XIII, pages 52–53.

---

278.   Report Prepared in the Executive Secretariat of the Department of State [1]

Summary No. 19   *Washington, September 28, 1956.*

SUMMARY OF DEVELOPMENTS IN SUEZ SITUATION

British-French Draft Resolution

Miss Salt, Counselor of the British Embassy, gave to Mr. Wilcox yesterday the text of the British-French draft resolution to be proposed in the Security Council. [2] She said the draft was still under discussion by the Ministers in Paris and it had not been decided

---

[1] Source: Eisenhower Library, Whitman File, International File. Top Secret; Eyes Only for Designated Recipient.

[2] The memorandum of this conversation is not printed. (Department of State, Central Files, 330/9–2756) The British Foreign Office gave the Embassy in London a copy of the draft resolution on September 27. (Reported in telegram 1698 from London, September 26, not printed; *ibid.*, 974.7301/9–2656) The Embassy in Paris

whether the item would be regarded as coming under Chapter VI or VII, or be dealt with as a general matter not necessarily coming under either. She remarked that the British are quite happy about the handling of Egypt's complaint; they consider that the debate on the British-French item will become so all-embracing that there will be nothing much left to say about the Egyptian item when it is reached.

The draft UK-French resolution: 1) reaffirms the principle of freedom of navigation of the Canal under the 1888 Convention; 2) considers that Egypt should restore to all Canal users the rights and guarantees which they enjoyed under the system on which the Convention was based; 3) endorses the 18-nation proposal of August 22 as representing a just and equitable solution; and 4) calls on Egypt to cooperate by negotiation in working out, on the basis of these proposals, a system of operation to be applied to the Canal and, pending the outcome of such negotiations, to cooperate with SCUA.

French Position

Embassy Paris has just transmitted the French reply to our aide-mémoire [3] on France's forthcoming Security Council presentation. It states that the French Government expects the complete support of the US "to defend and to win acceptance from the Security Council of the principles defined in the proposals of the 18 powers, and to prevent any amendment or proposal advocating a formula which would be a retreat from the original proposals". The French Government also wishes prior consultations to be held between the US, UK and French delegations in New York on the procedures and tactics to be used in the Security Council.

Attendance at Security Council Meeting

So far, the following Foreign Ministers are expected to attend the Security Council discussions next week of the Suez situation: Lloyd (UK), Pineau (France), Spaak (Belgium), Shepilov (USSR), and Popovic (Yugoslavia). Egyptian Foreign Minister Fawzi is also expected to be present, accompanied by Ali Sabri.

---

received a copy from the French Government on September 28 and transmitted it to the Department of State in telegram 1490, September 28. (*Ibid.*, 974.7301/9–2856)

[3] The U.S. aide-mémoire was transmitted in telegram 2217 to London, September 25, not printed. The text of the French aide-mémoire was transmitted in telegram 1489 from Paris, September 28, not printed. (Department of State, Central Files, 974.7301/9–2556 and 974.7301/9–2856)

Anglo-French Talks

British Ambassador Jebb in Paris has told Dillon that Eden is very pleased with the results of the Anglo-French talks on the Suez crisis. [4] Eden was reported to have been highly impressed by Mollet but received a poor impression of Pineau whom he suspects is preparing an eventual attack on the British for having betrayed the French. Agreement was reached on maintaining a firm position, limited to the extent necessary by world and domestic opinion. Both the UK and France would maintain their forces in the Eastern Mediterranean but military action could not be resorted to unless canal traffic were almost totally interrupted or there were serious disturbances in Egypt.

The UK and France have agreed to accept the US offer to pay canal dues into SCUA. They also feel strongly that the US should use every effort to persuade American-controlled shipping under foreign registration to abide by the same practices which will be prescribed for American flag shipping.

SCUA Meeting

The Foreign Office has told Embassy London that the following countries have indicated they will attend the conference next Monday and join SCUA: US, UK, France, Netherlands, Denmark, Italy and Norway. [5] No country has yet refused the invitation to attend, but many have not yet replied. Ethiopia has agreed to attend the meeting, but on the specific condition that it not be bound to join the association. Warren has reported from Ankara [6] that Turkey will attend the conference and will support SCUA.

The British view is that the Ambassadors' meeting would itself constitute the Council of SCUA and that Lloyd in his opening remarks on Monday, after declaring SCUA to have come into existence, would then state that the Council as of now was constituted of representatives of adhering states. As all countries present on Monday will not yet have signified their intention to join SCUA, the British consider that the initial meeting should appoint the Executive Group provisionally for a period of, say, one month subject to reconfirmation by the expanded Council at a later meeting. Embassy London reports that the British wish the Executive

---

[4] Reported in telegram 1485 from Paris, September 27, not printed. (*Ibid.*, 974.7301/9–2756)

[5] In telegram 1724 from London, September 27, Aldrich reported on a meeting concerning SCUA, which was held among French, British, and American representatives, at the British Foreign Office. (*Ibid.*) Telegram 1709 from London, September 27, transmitted the text of a paper distributed at the meeting, which contained the British tentative thinking on the inaugural meeting of SCUA scheduled for October 1. (*Ibid.*)

[6] In telegram 706 from Ankara, September 27, not printed. (*Ibid.*, 974.7301/9–2756)

Group to have the broadest possible geographic representation. The UK will, however, insist on membership thereon. The British feel that the Executive Group should probably nominate someone for the Council to appoint as Administrator. (No alternate has yet been proposed to the British suggestion of the Norwegian Lars U. Svendsen.) The British consider the best alternatives for SCUA's headquarters as The Hague or Rome.

US Position

The Secretary and his advisers decided this morning that: 1) as the proposed resolution given to us by the UK has no chance of Council approval, we should try to work out a better resolution with the UK and France; 2) we should make very clear our position that payments for transit should be made from SCUA to the Egyptian Government; 3) it would be most desirable to defer voting on Israeli representation during the SC sessions. The Secretary has informed the French Ambassador that he will be available on Sunday for tripartite discussions.

(Summary closed 1:30 p.m., September 28, 1956)

---

279.   Memorandum of a Conversation, Department of State, Washington, September 28, 1956, 12:38 p.m. [1]

SUBJECT

    Israel Raids on Jordan; General Near East Situation

PARTICIPANTS

    The Ambassador of Jordan, Mr. Abdul Monem Rifa'i
    The Secretary
    Mr. Rountree, NEA
    Mr. Bergus, NE

The Secretary expressed his pleasure at the Ambassador's return to the United States.

The Ambassador referred to the magnitude of the last three Israel military operations into Jordan. [2] Military aircraft and heavy

---

[1] Source: Department of State, Central Files, 684A.85/9–2856. Secret. Drafted by Bergus. The time of the meeting is from Dulles' Appointment Book. (Princeton University Library, Dulles Papers)

[2] A "Chronology of Recent Jordan–Israel Border Incidents," prepared as part of the briefing material for a meeting between Secretary Dulles and Ambassador Eban

weapons had been used. In the September 25 raid, the Jordanians believed that two Israel battalions (2000 men) had been involved. The MAC had confirmed that at least one battalion had been used by the Israelis. Furthermore, the Israelis were now officially announcing and boasting about these raids. This meant that they represented Israel policy. Jordan had information that Israel intended to continue the raids.

This situation presented Jordan with three alternatives: first, to take the matter to the Security Council. Mr. Rifa'i had discussed this possibility in New York recently with the Secretary General and various delegations. He found that the consensus of opinion was that Jordan should avoid Security Council action in view of the fact that the Suez Canal matter was under discussion there. Mr. Rifa'i tended to agree with this thinking, as he did not like to see the Arabs in action on too many UN fronts, such as Suez, Algeria, and Arab-Israel, at one time. Furthermore, if Jordan did go to the Council they might succeed in getting a condemnation of Israel, but Israel has disregarded such condemnations in the past. Nevertheless, Jordan still might decide to take the matter to the Council. A second alternative was for Jordan to take military measures in connection with the other Arab states to prepare to protect itself from Israel. This might complicate the present situation and involve the whole area but Jordan might have no other course. A third alternative could be for the United States, perhaps in concert with Britain and France, to take economic and political measures against Israel—something more than diplomatic pressure—to make Israel stop these acts.

Mr. Rifa'i said he could not guarantee that Jordan could keep the frontier absolutely calm. Jordan was doing its very best. He could state privately that the Jordan Army was no longer under tight foreign control but in the hands of young Arab officers, some of whom were hot-headed. Israel was prone to provocative acts along its side of the border. This matter was so important that Mr. Rifa'i was bringing it to the Secretary personally to urge that something be done.

The Secretary said that first he wished Mr. Rifa'i to know that he deplored these large-scale outbreaks of violence. He had expressed this publicly on September 26 [3] and wished to repeat it

---

later on September 28 (see *infra*) listed eight violent exchanges resulting in fatalities along the Israeli-Jordanian border between August 21 and September 25, including Israeli cross-border raids on August 21, September 11, September 13, and September 25. (Attached to a memorandum from Rountree to Dulles, September 28; Department of State, Central Files, 601.84A11/9–2856)

[3] Dulles' remarks were made during a press conference. The transcript is printed in Department of State *Bulletin*, October 8, 1956, pp. 543–549. For excerpts pertaining

privately. Secondly, he was glad that the Jordanians felt that they could come to the United States as a friendly Government and talk over these matters frankly. The question of what to do was a very difficult one, largely because the delicate balance that had been maintained in the Near East had been disturbed by the seizure of the Suez Canal and the new forces thus released. Some of the things which we could have done to restrain Israel were now more difficult in the face of new issues such as anti-Western propaganda emanating from the Arabs. This had worried the Secretary, not only because of its direct consequences, and he had exerted himself to prevent a war over the Suez Canal. There were also interim consequences of upsetting the balance which had in the past restrained Israel. The Israelis might well feel that these other issues give them a protective shield behind which they can take strong measures. The Secretary hoped that the Jordan Government would realize this and exert its influence on Egypt to adopt a peaceful attitude in the Suez matter. He had been disappointed when the Egyptians simply rejected the proposals of the Committee of Five, rather than putting forward counter-proposals which could have been a basis for negotiation. He hoped that something constructive would come out of the Security Council handling of the matter. Those who did not wish Israel to take advantage of the present situation should do what they could to get the situation settled.

Mr. Rifa'i stated privately, off the record, that in the course of his sojourn in the Near East the King of Saudi Arabia had told him that he would give all reasonable support to Nasser but would not back him if he chose to challenge the West militarily or if he brought the Soviets into the area. Lebanon and Jordan had a similar attitude. He felt the British were going too far in describing Egypt's attitude. Both parties agreed to freedom of navigation. If it were a matter of lack of confidence in Egypt, the other Arab states were prepared to share the responsibility for free navigation. Mr. Rifa'i said he understood that Egyptian Foreign Minister Fawzi would be coming to New York prepared to "take an easy attitude" in negotiations in the corridor. Mr. Rifa'i wished to compliment the Secretary personally for what he had done to prevent war.

The Secretary pointed out that this Administration had gone much further than its predecessor in preventing Zionist elements from dictating our foreign policy. The tragic difficulty is that despite these efforts our relations with some Arab states, at least, have never been so bad. We were thus being told publicly that our policy had failed. Mr. Rifa'i did not think that US relations with the Arab

to the Middle East, see *United States Policy in the Middle East, September 1956–June 1957*, pp. 87–98.

states were so bad. The outstanding difficulties arose from acts committed during previous administrations.

As the Ambassador took his leave, the Secretary said that the United States valued its relations with Jordan and wished to be Jordan's friend. This was our desire, even though the present situation might make it hard for us to do everything which Jordan would like.

---

280.   Memorandum of a Conversation, Department of State, Washington, September 28, 1956, 3:14 p.m. [1]

Part I of II [2]

SUBJECT

Matters Relating to Suez

PARTICIPANTS

The Secretary
Mr. Abba Eban, Ambassador of Israel
Mr. Reuven Shiloah, Minister, Embassy of Israel
Mr. Fraser Wilkins, NE

At his own request the Israel Ambassador called on the Secretary this afternoon. He said that he had requested an appointment because he had planned to return to Jerusalem on consultation but that his consultation had been postponed because of developments relating to the Suez question. He now planned to leave the end of next week and wished to bring himself up to date regarding important developments.

First of all he wished to discuss the Suez Canal question. Israel had a real interest in this question and had a special interest in participating in Security Council consideration of the matter. Mr. Eban said that there had been no instance in which a country which applied to the Security Council to be heard had not been admitted. He said that in discussing this question with British representatives in New York some resistance to Israeli participation had been noted. Mr. Eban thought that if Israel were debarred from participation it

---

[1] Source: Department of State, Central Files, 974.7301/9–2856. Secret. Drafted by Wilkins. The time of the meeting is from Dulles' Appointment Book. (Princeton University Library, Dulles Papers)

[2] Part II is printed *infra.*

would be a momentous development in the history of the United Nations. He believed that Israel's British friends had not thought through the matter.

Ambassador Eban continued that the British had, in effect, said that the United Kingdom itself could bring charges against Egypt in the Security Council but that Egypt could not bring charges against the United Kingdom. Israel, for its part, had been glad to see the Egyptian reference placed on the agenda of the Security Council and Ambassador Eban hoped the United States would not resist Israel's appearance. Israel's participation would be limited to juridical aspects of the matter. Israel would refer neither to Egyptian nationalization of the Suez Canal Company, nor to possible use of force by the United Kingdom and France, nor to the Palestine question. Israel merely wished to place on the record its own experience regarding the passage of ships through the Suez Canal. Israel did not wish to speak at an early stage, but would be willing to speak after all others had spoken and would not present its case on emotional grounds but on juridical grounds.

The Secretary asked Ambassador Eban whether Israel wished to sit permanently. He said that if we accept the proposition that every interested country is entitled to sit and to participate in all phases of the proceedings, there would be a deluge of applicants.

Ambassador Eban said that no applicant had previously been refused. Israel merely wished to make its intervention and would then depart.

The Secretary continued that if the door were opened to all applicants the proceedings of the Security Council would become a mockery, and it was for this reason necessary to limit the number of participants. He noted that Panama, the Arab states, India, Pakistan, Ceylon and others had already manifested an interest in participating; consequently a real practical problem was created. He recognized that Israel in some respects had a better claim to be heard than the others. It was a matter of degree. One could not easily fix the quantum of interest. He would be glad further to study the matter.

Ambassador Eban said the second matter to which he wished to refer was the inclusion in any Security Council resolution on Suez of reference to its earlier action in 1951 regarding Israeli shipping. He said that Israel attached great importance to the Secretary's and to the President's public statements in which they had mentioned difficulties which Israel had experienced in passing through the Suez Canal. He said that they did not think the discussion could take place without reference to the 1951 action of the Security Council. Israel thought that this earlier action should be referred to in the new resolution.

The Secretary made no comment.

281.   Memorandum of a Conversation, Department of State, Washington, September 28, 1956, 3:14 p.m. [1]

Part II of II [2]

SUBJECT

Military and Economic Assistance to Israel

PARTICIPANTS

The Secretary
Mr. Abba Eban, Ambassador of Israel
Mr. Reuven Shiloah, Minister, Embassy of Israel
Mr. Fraser Wilkins, NE

Ambassador Eban said that his third matter related to the Canadian decision to supply Israel with Saber jets. The Israeli Foreign Minister had already been in touch with Ambassador Lawson in Tel Aviv and had expressed the gratification of the Israeli Government with respect to the Canadian action. He said that this action had improved the balance of forces in the Near East which would result in some deterrent to general conflict. Nevertheless, the general situation was one short of total settlement.

The Secretary said that he had been anxious that Israel receive some F–86 jets. For a time it had seemed problematical that Canada would take this step. Israel's retaliatory action against Jordan had almost prevented the step. The Secretary had felt, however, it important that Israel receive planes of this type and learn how to fly them. Experience with F–86 jets would open up another vista of assistance. He recalled that the President in March 1956 had stated publicly that assistance would be provided in the event of aggression.

Ambassador Eban said he understood the situation. In reply he wished first to refer to the past. He cited figures regarding the number of Israelis killed and wounded for the two years preceding March 1956 and for the period thereafter. These figures showed a substantial increase. Ambassador Eban continued that Israel had tried not to react. They had discussed the situation with General Burns and Secretary General Hammarskjold. There was no question in Israel's mind that the present state of affairs between Israel and Jordan had been initiated by Jordan. He added that Israel had had to

---

[1] Source: Department of State, Central Files, 784A.5–MSP/9–2856. Secret. Drafted by Wilkins. The time of the meeting is from Dulles' Appointment Book. (Princeton University Library, Dulles Papers)

[2] Part I is printed *supra*.

act, otherwise the Israeli people would not sustain the Israeli Government.

Ambassador Eban continued that with reference to the future, there was nothing farther from their mind than to cause general conflict. Israel was willing to agree on a cease-fire but believed it should be reciprocal. Israel had suggested to Secretary General Hammarskjold that King Hussein make a statement which would have an important effect in Jordan. Secretary General Hammarskjold had not been willing, but Israel would continue to urge the issuance of a statement by Jordan. Meanwhile, Israeli borders with Syria, Lebanon, and Egypt were tranquil.

Ambassador Eban said that his fourth point related to economic assistance. It was vital for Israel. Recently the economic burdens of security had increased greatly. In effect the USSR had caused all of the Near Eastern states to increase their security expenditures. At the present moment, however, Israel was concentrating upon its water development. Ambassador Eric Johnston had told him that his efforts were now bogging down, and that there was no prospect of his resuming the initiative in the immediate future. Ambassador Eban thought that the Export-Import Bank was the only way Israel could be assisted at this time and thus avoid complete paralysis within Israel. He said he understood the Export-Import Bank had reached an advanced stage of its discussions with the Department. He himself planned to discuss Israel's loan application with the Bank on October 3rd.

The Secretary said that the result of Israel's loan application to the Export-Import Bank was not as clear as Ambassador Eban and the Secretary had thought. The Export-Import Bank doubted whether the loan would be a good one. The Secretary asked if Israel had borrowed heavily from the Bank. [3]

Ambassador Eban and Minister Shiloah replied that $39 million had been repaid, leaving $105 million outstanding. They pointed out that the water development which would be undertaken under the loan would increase production out of which the loan could be repaid. The Secretary asked whether water would be taken from the Jordan at Jisr Banat Yacub. Ambassador Eban replied that no water would be taken from this source but only from within Israel.

The Secretary said that because of his preoccupation with Suez he had been unable to give the Israel loan application his personal attention. He said that Mr. Hoover had been working directly with

---

[3] On September 29, Eban forwarded to Dulles a letter which contained additional views of the Israeli Government on the question of its indebtedness to the Export-Import Bank and on other considerations pertinent to the Israeli loan applications. (Department of State, Central Files, 884A.10/9–2956)

the Export-Import Bank. The Secretary had thought that the matter was nearer conclusion and that the Bank planned to send out a technical group to Israel for further study, but that apparently the Export-Import Bank had had second thoughts regarding the merits and the total size of the loan. He hoped, however, that matters regarding the loan would move forward. Minister Shiloah urged that a decision in principle be reached at this time, leaving technical matters to a later date. The Secretary made no further comment.

Ambassador Eban said that his final point related to alternatives to the Suez Canal for transport of oil. He said that the possibility of a pipeline from the Gulf of Aqaba to the Eastern Mediterranean through Israel had been discussed with private interests in the United States. Although there were some differences of view, there seemed to be some support for this proposition. However the question of access had arisen. Ambassador Eban said that he would like to have the Secretary's opinion regarding the international right of innocent passage through the Straits of Tiran between the Gulf of Aqaba and the Red Sea. He said that Egypt had no legal right to obstruct passage through the Straits of Tiran by force. He would also like to be assured of a regular supply of oil at the source. This source would have to be outside of the states of the Arab League. It could come from Saudi Arabia but it might come from Kuwait or from Qatar.

The Secretary made no substantive comment, although he did remark that he had heard that the French Government was interested in the construction of a pipeline across Israel.

---

282.   Letter From the Secretary of State to the Deputy Secretary of Defense (Robertson) [1]

Washington, September 28, 1956.

DEAR REUBEN: I have received a letter from Secretary Wilson, dated September 25, [2] recommending the termination of that aspect of Operation "Whiplash" involving the USS *Oglethorpe*. I also note that the other aspect of Operation "Whiplash" involving the possi-

---

[1] Source: Department of State, Central Files, 784A.5622/9–2556. Top Secret. A marginal notation on the source text indicates that this letter was handed to Robertson on September 28, during a meeting in Secretary Dulles' office which began at 3:45 p.m.

[2] See Radford's memorandum to Wilson, Document 234, and footnote 1 thereto.

ble supplying of F–86 aircraft to Israel in the event of Arab aggression against that state will be maintained, and the aircraft and equipment in question could be moved on forty-eight hours' notice from units now available in Europe.

I agree with your recommendation that the USS *Oglethorpe* be released from its present mission and reassigned, and that its cargo be redistributed to the best advantage of the Services. The President concurs in this view. [3]

In the event that at some future date it should seem necessary or desirable to provide immediate arms assistance to an Arab nation which has been the victim of aggression, we could presumably arrange to supply certain types of equipment such as that contained in the USS *Oglethorpe*'s cargo from stocks which are available in Europe.

Sincerely yours,

John Foster Dulles [4]

---

[3] A memorandum from Dulles to President Eisenhower, dated September 28, reads as follows: "You will recall that following your Arab-Israel statement of last March, we had stockpiled equipment in the Mediterranean area, to be given to Israel or to the Arab States depending upon which was the victim of aggression. The equipment potentially designed for the Arab States is on a ship and the Defense Department feels that, in view of intervening events, it is in order to unload the ship and put it to other uses.

"I am inclined to agree that it is now unlikely that we should be giving military assistance to the Arabs and am disposed to agree that the Defense Department may discontinue this part of the operation. Do you agree?" (Eisenhower Library, Dulles Papers, White House Memoranda) A marginal notation in Eisenhower's hand reads: "OK/DE".

[4] Printed from a copy that bears this typed signature.

283.   Memorandum of a Conversation Between the French Ambassador (Alphand) and the Assistant Secretary of State for International Organization Affairs (Wilcox), Department of State, Washington, September 28, 1956 [1]

SUBJECT

Suez Canal

Ambassador Alphand called late this evening to report on a conversation he had on the preceding evening with the Secretary of State, [2] relating to the Suez canal, and the subsequent response he had received from the Foreign Office about it.

The Ambassador said that at a dinner party at the French Embassy on Thursday, the Secretary had asked him whether he had heard the rumors about the possibility of the Security Council setting up a negotiating committee to handle the Suez question. The Ambassador replied that he had heard such rumors and he wondered what the Secretary thought about them. According to the Ambassador, the Secretary replied that he was against such an idea. The Ambassador then commented that in his personal view he agreed that the idea was not a good one.

The Ambassador later reported the conversation with the Secretary to Paris and informed me that what he had expressed as a personal view was in fact the attitude of the French Government. He then went on to say that the French believed they could convince the UK that the concept of a negotiating committee was a bad one and that they should not press for such a development in the Security Council.

I replied to Ambassador Alphand that perhaps there had been some misunderstanding between him and the Secretary since I had never heard the Secretary comment adversely upon the idea of a negotiating committee. I said that I was not sure what the Secretary's views on this matter were but that I would discuss the question with him and contact the Ambassador later.

This I proceeded to do. The Secretary made it clear that he had not intended to take a position on the matter in his discussion with Ambassador Alphand. He had in fact replied in response to the Ambassador's inquiry in a non-committal way, saying that he did not know.

After ascertaining the Secretary's views, I immediately informed Ambassador Alphand and pointed out that there had in fact been a

---

[1] Source: Department of State, Central Files, 974.7301/9–2856. Confidential; Limited Distribution. Drafted by Wilcox.

[2] See Document 276.

misunderstanding; that the Secretary had not intended to take a position on the matter; that he had not studied the question in any detail, and that he believes it is something we ought to keep an open mind about.

I then asked the Ambassador whether his report to the French Government might have influenced the decision of the French. He replied that his Government had already taken a position before it had received his cable about the Secretary's views, and that in fact the report he had submitted had had no effect whatsoever upon the French decision.

In discussing the matter further with me, Ambassador Alphand stated that "It is my clear impression that the Secretary was not in favor of a negotiating committee—that he was against it." He went on to say that he himself felt it would be "very dangerous" and that the French were not in favor of giving any right to any committee to negotiate for the Council. "After having said what we did in London and Paris about the violation of rights", he commented, "if we now say we can accept a committee of the Security Council, we will be subject to ridicule."

---

284.   Memorandum of a Telephone Conversation Between the Secretary of State and the British Ambassador (Makins), Washington, September 28, 1956, 7:08 p.m. [1]

TELEPHONE CALL TO SIR ROGER MAKINS

The Sec. said he dined at the Fr. Emb. last night and after dinner had a chat re Suez [2] and in the course of conversation the possibility of negotiation coming out of this came up. A. [3] expressed himself very strongly against it, and asked if the Sec. did not agree. The Sec. said he did not know—it depends on how these things work out. Now we have a message from him saying he had informed his Govt of the Sec's opposition to any negotiation and that he had now been officially informed by his Govt that they agreed and we could persuade the Br. to drop the idea. The Sec. does not know what to do—he is embarrassed. The Sec. and M. said

---

[1] Source: Eisenhower Library, Dulles Papers, General Telephone Conversations. Transcribed by Bernau.

[2] See Document 276.

[3] Reference is to Ambassador Alphand.

they didn't believe in doing business at dinner like that. The Sec. said A. seems to read into his utterances what he wants to find. M. said he put him straight earlier on one thing. M. asked what the Sec. would like him to do. The Sec. does not know. He thought if the Fr. approach the Br. and say the above the Sec. wants them to know it is not his idea. The Sec. has not thought through on how it can work out etc.—the general concept of negotiating is one he favors. M. will send a personal message to Lloyd and said this has been a confusion and they better get it cleared here if the Fr. say anything. The Sec. said he was encouraged re the para. in M's memo. [4] It is a prospect we should keep open-minded on. The Sec. said Wilcox said while the implication was he communicated the conversation, it is not at all explicitly so said. The Sec. said it would be good if M. sent a message.

---

[4] Not further identified.

---

285.   Telegram From the Department of State to the Embassy in Israel [1]

Washington, September 29, 1956—3:57 p.m.

254. Tel Aviv's 295, [2] 296. [3] Department believes reftels have most disturbing implications. At earliest opportunity and in appropriate manner Lawson should point out to GOI multiplying dangers which would emerge if Israel should take military action on grounds of Iraqi-Jordanian moves, especially if latter clearly of defensive

---

[1] Source: Department of State, Central Files, 684A.85/9–2756. Top Secret; Priority. Drafted by Bergus and Rockwell and approved by Rountree who signed for Dulles. Also sent to Amman and repeated to Baghdad, Beirut, Cairo, Damascus, London, Paris, and Jerusalem.

[2] In telegram 295, September 28, the Embassy in Tel Aviv reported that the Director General of the Prime Minister's office, Teddy Kollek, had recently commented to an American official: "does the West realize that if Iraqi troops or the troops of other Arab States were to march into Jordan, Israel in self-defense would be compelled to occupy a portion of Jordanian territory?" The telegram also included several reasons why the possibility of Israeli action should be taken seriously. (*Ibid.*, 685.87/9–2756)

[3] Telegram 296 from Tel Aviv, September 27, responded to telegram 513 from Baghdad, September 27 (see Document 277). It noted that recent border incidents involved nothing more than a typical Israeli response to a series of incursions, that Israeli active duty strength was the lowest of any time during the past year, and that introduction of Iraqi forces into Jordan would increase pressure within Israel for a West Bank takeover. (Department of State, Central Files, 684A.85/9–2756)

nature. USG prepared take at face value Ben Gurion's declarations that Israel will not start a war. Israelis have expressed appreciation United States effort prevent Suez issue from developing into armed conflict. At some time, if present cycle events along armistice lines not halted trend toward more serious hostilities between Israel and Arab states seems inevitable. United States has continued urge Jordanians reinforce measures maintain order along armistice lines, and believes King and HKJ Government sincerely striving prevent incidents, although it can not be 100% effective. We feel Israel fully aware this fact and also aware that primary cause of Jordan efforts seek military support from other Arab states has been series of heavy Israel reprisals against Jordan. If GOI sincerely desirous of maintaining political status quo in Jordan, Israel should not adopt policies which make it unlikely HJK can achieve this objective.

We realize Jordan-caused incidents create grave problem to GOI view public reaction. Heavy Israel reprisal, however, has effect of weakening rather than strengthening Jordan efforts control situation. We feel most promising method of assuring Israel security includes: 1) full cooperation with efforts UNSYG and UNTSO, 2) increased vigilance on Israel side of line.

Mallory should seek audience with King and advise him we have urgently made clear to Israelis our view that their heavy reprisal operations should be stopped. At same time we urge Jordan take all possible steps prevent incidents along armistice lines caused by Jordanians or others. United States appreciates important factor represented by status Jordan public opinion after Israel raids, but at same time such HKJ efforts coupled with fullest cooperation with UNSYG and UNTSO would put Jordan in position obtain maximum support world public opinion. [4]

---

[4] In telegram 302 from Amman, October 2, Ambassador Mallory reported that he had delivered this message to Hussein. In response, the King said that he was making every effort to prevent incidents, as he always did, but especially at this time when Jordan faced Israel alone. Hussein offered his view that the recent strong attacks by Israel were substantially linked to the fact that Egypt was preoccupied with the Canal problem and to the possibility of catching Jordan off balance for all-out hostilities before winter set in. Hussein personally estimated that as a matter of national economy and national policy Israel would be obliged sooner or later to attempt to expand territorially into western Jordan. (*Ibid.*, 684A.85/10–256)

London should inform FonOff of this telegram and Department's 2283.[5]

Dulles

---

[5] Regarding telegram 2283 to London, sent for action to Baghdad as telegram 462, see Document 277.

In telegram 1783, October 1, the Embassy in London reported that it had conveyed the substance of these two telegrams to the British Foreign Office. In response, a Foreign Office official had mentioned two recent British démarches to Israel concerning the raids against Jordan. The Embassy also reported that the Foreign Office appeared firmly convinced that it would be unwise to discourage Nuri Said from sending Iraqi troops into Jordan for defensive purposes. On this point, the official had delivered a long list of arguments as to why such a troop movement would be desirable from the standpoint of Western interests in the Middle East and added that the British Embassy in Washington would be conveying the full extent of the Foreign Office's views on the subject. (Department of State, Central Files, 684A.85/10–156)

---

286.   Report Prepared in the Executive Secretariat of the Department of State [1]

Summary No. 20   *Washington, October 1, 1956.*

SUMMARY OF DEVELOPMENTS IN SUEZ SITUATION

SCUA Conference Opens Today

Embassy London reports[2] that the British Foreign Office has received acceptances from all 17 nations invited to attend today's meeting in London. Fifteen of the nations are immediately expected to signify their adherence to the Suez Canal Users' Association (SCUA), but Japan, Pakistan and Ethiopia have withheld any commitment.

We have authorized Aldrich[3] to participate as the US representative in the SCUA Council and Executive Group. We agree that Lloyd should announce the establishment of SCUA and its Council in his opening remarks, but beyond that we feel that today's agenda should be restricted to assigning the formulation of administrative arrangements to a working committee of the Council. The Executive

---

[1] Source: Eisenhower Library, Whitman File, International File. Top Secret; Eyes Only for Designated Recipient.

[2] In telegram 1757 from London, September 29, not printed. (Department of State, Central Files, 974.7301/9–2956)

[3] In telegram 2334 to London, September 29, not printed. (*Ibid.*, 974.7301/9–2756)

Group should not be selected until a later date but our present thinking is that the Executive Group (and the working committee of the Council) should consist of the five nations which composed the Menzies' Committee, plus the UK and France. If Australia, Sweden, Ethiopia or Iran are unwilling to participate, we propose the following alternates, in the same order: New Zealand, Norway or Denmark, Portugal, Turkey. We have stressed that any documentation must make it clear that SCUA has the authority to compensate Egypt for its maintenance of the canal transit facilities.

Selection of SCUA Administrator

Embassy London has been informed [4] that Svendsen is unwilling to serve as the Administrator of SCUA and can no longer be considered a candidate. The Embassy reports that the Germans and Dutch are supporting a Dutch candidate, Oyevaar, [5] who apparently has had experience in international organizations rather than in shipping. We have suggested that SCUA may also wish to consider Leif Hoegh, a Norwegian, [6] who has been proposed by US shipping and oil interests.

Change in French Attitude Towards US Policy

Embassy Paris reports [7] that the responsible French press and the French government have both now realized the gravity of the situation being produced by continual public attacks on the Suez policy of the US and have moderated their attitude. In confirmation of this change, Embassy Paris has just reported that, in a major foreign policy address yesterday, Mollet stated "I can affirm that international administration of the canal is the only solution acceptable to the US, UK and France." Mollet went on to associate himself fully with the Secretary's declaration at the second London conference wherein he emphasized the responsibility of seeking a solution in conformity with the law as well as the responsibility of preventing the use of force. "A Munich peace", said Mollet, "maintained without regard to justice, would be the negation of all efforts of international organization and of the United Nations themselves. Mollet said that indivisible British-French solidarity, and US agreement regarding the objectives to be obtained, gives confidence of success.

---

[4] Reported in telegram 1764 from London, September 30, not printed. (*Ibid.*, 974.7301/9–3056)

[5] Jan Johan Oyevaar, former Netherlands Director-General of Shipping.

[6] A Norwegian shipowner, member of the Executive Committee of the Norwegian Shipowners' Association, and Director of the Scandinavian Shipowners' Associations.

[7] In telegram 1516 from Paris, September 29, not printed. (Department of State, Central Files, 974.7301/9–2956)

Lodge Disapproves of UK-French Resolution

We have told our UN Mission [8] that we can support the UK-French draft resolution on Suez, but we have suggested several modifications designed to make the text of the resolution more acceptable. Lodge, however, thinks that the proposed UK-French draft resolution is non-conciliatory. [9] He believes that if a resolution of this type is pushed to a veto in the Security Council (SC), the resultant bad atmosphere could make it impossible to get any other resolution passed which would provide for peaceful negotiations on a basis which has a reasonable chance of success. This will then heighten the risk that the British and French might use force.

Attendance at Security Council Meeting

The following Foreign Ministers will attend the Security Council meeting on Suez this week: Lloyd (UK), Pineau (France), Spaak (Belgium), Shepilov (USSR), and Popovic (Yugoslavia). Egyptian Foreign Minister Fawzi will also be present, accompanied by Ali Sabri and Dr. Badawi, Director of the present canal authority. Embassy Cairo says that the inclusion of Sabri and Badawi indicates that Nasser wishes the delegation to be prepared to set the basis for negotiations if the opportunity arises.

(Summary closed 12:00 p.m., October 1, 1956)

---

[8] In telegram 123 to USUN, drafted by Wainhouse and De Palma; approved in substance by Dulles, Hoover, Phleger, and Rountree; and approved by Wilcox, September 29, not printed. (*Ibid.*)

[9] Reported in telegram 273 from USUN, September 30, not printed. (*Ibid.*, 974.7301/9–3056)

---

287.   Message From Prime Minister Eden to President Eisenhower [1]

London, October 1, 1956.

Harold has told me of his conversation with you. [2] I was

---

[1] Source: Eisenhower Library, Whitman File, International File. Top Secret. Delivered to the White House under cover of a note from Coulson to President Eisenhower which reads: "I have been asked to convey to you the enclosed personal message from the Prime Minister."

[2] Reference is to the conversation between Eisenhower and Macmillan on September 25, during the latter's visit to the United States. No copy of the memorandum

particularly delighted to hear from him that you were in such splendid form.

You can be sure that we are fully alive to the wider dangers of the Middle East situation. They can be summed up in one word—Russia.

I thought that you would like to see this further message from Bulganin to me.[3] I shall not reply for a day or two. There is no doubt in our minds that Nasser, whether he likes it or not, is now effectively in Russian hands, just as Mussolini was in Hitler's. It would be as ineffective to show weakness to Nasser now in order to placate him as it was to show weakness to Mussolini. The only result was and would be to bring the two together. No doubt your people will have told you of the accumulating evidence of Egyptian plots in Libya, Saudi-Arabia and Iraq. At any moment any of these may be touched off unless we can prove to the Middle East that Nasser is losing. That is why we are so concerned to do everything we can to make the Users' Club an effective instrument. If your ships under the Panamanian and Liberian flags would follow the example of those under your flag that would greatly help.

I feel sure that anything which you can say or do to show firmness to Nasser at this time will help the peace by giving the Russians pause.

As usual I send you my thoughts in this frank way.[4]

---

for that conversation has been found in the Eisenhower Library or Department of State files, but see Document 264.

[3] Attached to the source text but not printed. The letter is briefly described in *Full Circle*, p. 555.

[4] Printed from an unsigned copy. On October 9, Coulson handed Douglas MacArthur II a copy of Eden's response to Bulganin's letter, which had been sent to Bulganin on October 6. A copy of the memorandum of this conversation with the attached copy of Eden's message is in Department of State, Central Files, 641.74/ 10–956.

288.   Memorandum of a Conversation, Department of State, Washington, October 1, 1956 [1]

SUBJECT

Jordan's Request for Iraqi Troops

PARTICIPANTS

Mr. J.E. Coulson, Minister, British Embassy
Mr. W. Morris, First Secretary, British Embassy
Mr. Fraser Wilkins, Director, NE

Mr. Coulson called to discuss the question of Jordan's request for Iraqi troops. Mr. Coulson said that since Glubb left Jordan it had not been easy for the U.K. to maintain its influence in Jordan. The U.K. had encouraged fraternization between Jordan and Iraq but not much progress had been made. King Hussein frequently changes his mind. . . . Recently, however, there had been some improvement in relations between Iraq and Jordan. Jordan had not received much help from Egypt. Israel had attacked Jordan.

Mr. Coulson continued that Nuri had asked that the Jordanian request be brought to the attention of the U.K. and the U.S. The Foreign Office feared that unless Iraq met the Jordanian request, Jordan would fall into Egyptian hands. Mr. Coulson said the British Embassy had been instructed to approach the Department and say that the U.K. believed it could not prevent Iraq from sending troops into Jordan and that Iraq should under present circumstances cooperate with Jordan. Jordan was jittery regarding Israeli attacks and was doubtful that the U.K. would honor its obligations under the Anglo-Jordanian treaty. [2]

Mr. Coulson said that the U.K. realizes that the Israeli reaction would probably be sharp. The U.K. believes, however, that there is no justification for such reaction. The Iraqis would move only into Transjordan and not into West Jordan. Furthermore, Israeli aggression would bring the Anglo-Jordanian Treaty into play and also

---

[1] Source: Department of State, Central Files, 785.5/10–156. Secret. Drafted by Wilkins on October 2.

[2] Under Article 2 of the Anglo-Jordanian Treaty of Alliance, signed at Amman on March 15, 1948, the Governments of the United Kingdom and Transjordan agreed that should any dispute between either party and a third state produce a situation which would involve the risk of a rupture with that State, the parties would concert together with a view to the settlement of the said dispute by peaceful means in accordance with the provisions of the Charter of the United Nations and of any other international obligations which might be applicable to the case. Under Article 3 of that same treaty, the parties agreed that should either, notwithstanding the provisions of Article 2, become engaged in war, the other party would, subject always to the provisions of the U.N. Charter, immediately come to the aid of the party at war as a measure of collective defense. (77 UNTS 77)

action under the Tripartite Declaration. If it is decided that Iraqi troops shall be sent into Jordan, the U.K. plans to inform the Israeli Ambassador 24 hours in advance and to say that Jordan has requested Iraqi troops and that the U.K. believes it a wise move. Mr. Coulson said that if the U.K. should take this action and the U.S. should not, Israel might think we disapprove and might thus be encouraged to retaliate.

Mr. Coulson hoped that the U.S. would be prepared simultaneously to inform Israel we would say we would not consider the Iraqi action as justification for Israeli counter action; such counter action would have the gravest consequences and would bring the Tripartite Declaration into play. Mr. Coulson also said that when the U.K. approached the Israeli Ambassador he would be informed that Nuri had given the assurance that Iraqi troops would be sent to Jordan for defensive purposes only and would not be used except in the event of clear aggression.

Mr. Coulson added that the Jordanians were seriously apprehensive. The Jordanian Foreign Minister was presently in Baghdad and during the course of a meeting with the Iraqi and Jordanian officials the British Ambassador had given assurance that the U.K. intended to honor its Anglo-Jordanian Treaty obligations by providing air and naval support as planned. In addition, the U.K. would take action under the Tripartite Declaration and would call upon its co-signatories for action. Mr. Coulson explained that only air and naval forces would be used against Israel under such circumstances and no British Ground Troops would be sent to North Jordan or to the West Bank.

Mr. Coulson further said that he did not see how dispatch of Iraqi troops could be opposed. He thought the Israelis could be persuaded to accept it if they were informed in advance.

Mr. Coulson said that Ronald Bailey would supply the Department with further details of British plans tomorrow.

Mr. Wilkins said that the American Embassy in London had been told by the Foreign Office of the Jordanian request for Iraqi troops, but we had no detailed information. We therefore appreciated the information which Mr. Coulson supplied. Mr. Wilkins said that on the basis of the earlier report we thought movement of Iraqi troops to Jordan would have an unsettling effect and might be misunderstood not only by Israel but also by Egypt with serious repercussions. Mr. Wilkins noted that the Israelis were apprehensive because there was no Armistice Agreement between Israel and Iraq as there was between Israel and its immediate Arab neighbors. He also said that it might be anticipated that Egyptian Radio broadcasts might cause trouble in Jordan as they had in Jordan last winter.

Mr. Wilkins asked Mr. Coulson if Iraq had given Jordan any material assistance. Mr. Coulson said that he thought not and that

Iraq had rather hung back. Mr. Morris said that some might have been supplied to the Jordanian National Guard but very little.

Mr. Coulson concluded that Iraq would want to make its troop movement very soon and hoped that we could respond shortly. Mr. Wilkins said that he would inform Mr. Rountree and be in touch with Mr. Coulson.

289.   Editorial Note

In response to the instructions in telegram 254 to Tel Aviv, Document 285, Ambassador Lawson met with Prime Minister Ben Gurion on the evening of October 1. On the key question of Israel's response to a movement of token Iraqi troops into Jordan, Ben Gurion said: "If Iraq sends troops to other side of Jordan River, we will do nothing. If they send to our borders, that is different."

In discussing the proposed Iraqi troop movements with Ben Gurion, Lawson emphasized: (1) the stabilizing effect of the troops on the Jordanian Government, which in turn would help stabilize the Jordanian-Israeli border; (2) the non-aggressive character and purpose of the troops; (3) the remoteness of the troops from the Israeli border and the nonparticipation of the troops in border activities; and (4) the assumption that the troops would bear only light defensive arms. In addition, Lawson stressed U.S. confidence in Ben Gurion's earlier declaration that Israel would not start a war and the U.S. belief in the futility of reprisal raids, given the fact that Jordanian leaders were anxious to control the border and that the incursions were the result of forces beyond Jordanian control. In reply, Ben Gurion commented that many people doubted whether Jordan was viable. He added, however, that as long as Jordan existed and as long as it did not make war on Israel, Israel would leave it alone. Ben Gurion also noted that Iraqi movements provoked partic-ular concern in Israel as there was no armistice agreement with Iraq. In regard to reprisals, the Prime Minister acknowledged that they were no solution to the border problem, but maintained that they provided a deterrent and that border conditions would be worse without them. In conclusion, Ben Gurion inquired as to the status of the Export-Import Bank loan and expressed his personal interest in the matter. (Telegrams 91 from Jerusalem, October 1; Department of State, Central Files, 684A.85/10–156; and 306 from Tel Aviv, Octo-ber 2; *ibid.*, 684A.85/10–256)

290.   Report Prepared in the Executive Secretariat of the Department of State [1]

Summary No. 21   *Washington, October 2, 1956.*

SUMMARY OF DEVELOPMENTS IN SUEZ SITUATION

Inauguration of SCUA

At the inauguration of the Suez Canal Users' Association (SCUA) in London yesterday, [2] Lloyd was chosen as Chairman with Lord John Hope as his Deputy. Although Ethiopia, Japan and Pakistan did not immediately subscribe to the new organization, they accepted an invitation for their delegates to remain as observers. Working committees were formed to deal with organizational, finance, and shipping matters. Each delegation is represented on each working committee and the observers also attend the committee meetings.

Yesterday afternoon the working committee on organization reached tentative agreement on the sections in the draft "statute" of by-laws which related to membership, the component organs of the Association, and the Council. [3] Further meetings will consider the sections on the Executive Group, the Administrator, the headquarters, and the provisions for voting. Membership has not yet been discussed in the sense of future adherence to the organization, but our position is that additional members should be permitted to adhere on a two-thirds vote of the Council where the applicant shows sufficient dependence on or interest in the use of the Canal.

Aldrich notes that the British draft makes no mention of the receipt or disbursement of revenues accruing to SCUA from canal dues. However, he comments that, as the Council is specifically authorized to give directives to the Executive Group and Administrator, the result should be in accordance with our requirements. To avoid controversy, he thinks we should not insist on a specific reference to the dues question.

---

[1] Source: Eisenhower Library, Whitman File, International File. Top Secret; Eyes Only for Designated Recipient.

[2] The Embassy in London transmitted a report on the first meeting of SCUA in telegram 1784, October 1, not printed. (Department of State, Central Files, 974.7301/10–156)

[3] Reported in telegram 1785 from London, October 1, not printed. (*Ibid.*) The telegram also contained the complete text of the draft by-laws submitted by the British Delegation and tentatively accepted by the Committee as described in this report, and comments by Aldrich.

Selection of Administrator

Embassy London states [4] that, as the Scandinavians have now agreed that Norway should serve as their representative on the Executive Group, it will be more difficult to obtain a Norwegian as the Administrator. Further, although favorable reports have been received on Oyevaar, the Dutch Government has indicated some objection to his candidacy, probably because they are still campaigning actively for a place on the Executive Group. To forestall pressure by other delegations for the appointment of an American as Administrator—which we have been resisting—Aldrich asks if we have any other candidates to put forward.

Egyptian Willingness to Negotiate

Embassy Cairo has transmitted [5] a . . . report of a conversation in which Ali Sabri stated that Egypt hopes SC consideration of the Suez issue will lead to the creation of a negotiating body and that the Egyptians are convinced that a mutually satisfactory agreement can be reached through negotiation provided the UK basic objective is not to "get Nasser". Sabri also observed that Egypt, while opposed to international control, is willing to enter into international agreements providing for regulations which would be binding upon the Egyptian management and subject to review by the International Court or some other tribunal in the event of a dispute. He also indicated that Egypt would be satisfied if its revenues from the canal are based on the same percentage as was received by the original company. Finally, Sabri stated that the conference proposed by Egypt for October 10 was being held in abeyance as being unrealistic because of the unwillingness of the US, UK and France to participate.

French Views on Future Action

Dillon reports [6] that the French clearly intend to insist at the Security Council that Egypt must negotiate on the basis of the recommendations of the First London Conference and must accept international administration of the canal. Nevertheless, the French appear to have tacitly abandoned their intention to use force unless new provocation is offered. Dillon sees the danger of an unproductive French policy continuing to insist on a solution which could only be achieved by the employment of strong measures. He urges that we reach an agreement with Pineau and Lloyd on what the

---

[4] In telegram 1782 from London, October 1, not printed. (*Ibid.*)
[5] In telegram 955 from Cairo, October 1, not printed. (*Ibid.*)
[6] In telegram 1543 from Paris, October 1, not printed. (*Ibid.*)

three powers might realistically expect to achieve on the basis of the pressures—economic or otherwise—which they are prepared to undertake. If the three powers then publicly and unanimously state their firm adherence to this course of action, the US will not be repeatedly galled by what are made out by French spokesmen to be a constant series of retreats proposed by France's allies.

French Attitude on Canal Tolls

In a reply to our aide-mémoire on the payment of Suez Canal tolls, the French Government emphasized:[7] 1) its unwillingness to pay tolls to SCUA if only one or two other nations are prepared to conform to this practice; 2) its earnest hope that we will take steps to bring about the payment of tolls to SCUA by ships under Panamanian and Liberian registry belonging to US nationals. (In this latter regard, our Embassies in Monrovia and Panama have been told to convey to the Governments to which they are accredited the information that the US is prepared to sponsor their membership in SCUA should they so desire.)

(Summary closed 12:15 p.m., October 2, 1956)

---

[7] The text of the French aide-mémoire was transmitted to the Department in telegram 1529 from Paris, October 1, not printed. (Ibid.)

---

291.   Memorandum of a Conversation Between the President and the Secretary of State, White House, Washington, October 2, 1956, 2:20 p.m. [1]

SUBJECT

Suez Canal

We discussed the Suez Canal. I pointed out that we had rather bad relations with the British and the French, particularly the latter, because they did not feel we were backing them sufficiently and the governments were blaming their failure to get results on the fact that we were holding them back.

The President thought we should accept some solution which would, for example, assure that a general manager appointed by

---

[1] Source: Eisenhower Library, Dulles Papers, Meetings with the President. Secret; Personal and Private. The time of the meeting is from Dulles' Appointment Book. (Princeton University Library, Dulles Papers)

Egypt would be appointed subject to the approval of SCUA and only hold office as long as SCUA did not object. I said that I thought some solution along this line could be worked out. But the question was whether the British and French really wanted a peaceful solution. I referred to the various projects of the British seemingly in different directions—one favoring a settlement by negotiation; another favoring overthrow by economic pressures; another favoring overthrow by a covert operation and another favoring open use of military force. The President felt that we should have nothing to do with any project for a covert operation against Nasser personally. He felt we should exert strong pressure to get a settlement, but that we should not negotiate behind their backs or without their knowledge and acquiescence. In this connection, I gave the President the letter from Fanfani.[2] I expressed the view, in which the President concurred, that we had probably better not attempt to negotiate through him, although he could himself develop the subject as he thought appropriate.

I said that it looked as though the Egyptians were sending over a delegation which was itself qualified to negotiate and that it would probably be better to deal with them in this way if negotiation became the order of the day.

The President went on to express the view that he did not think that the Canal issue was the one on which to seek to undermine Nasser. He did feel that Nasser had indicated dangerous tendencies that needed to be curbed. He felt there was promise in developing Arab leadership elsewhere, and that this offered greater hope than a frontal attack on Nasser on the Canal issue.

The President felt that we had to maintain an independent position as regards the British and French until we knew definitely what they were up to.

---

[2] In a letter to Eisenhower of September 27, Political Secretary of the Italian Christian Democratic Party Amintore Fanfani proposed sending to Washington an emissary to report on high-level discussions regarding the Suez situation. (Eisenhower Library, Whitman File, International File) Fanfani later indicated that the Egyptians had told the Mayor of Florence that they wanted to use an Italian as intermediary between themselves and the United States on the Suez problem. Consequently, Fanfani sent an Italian Foreign Service officer, Raimondo Manzini, to Cairo and then to Washington, where he met with Dulles on September 30 and conveyed Nasser's assurances that he did not want the Soviet Union to take over Egypt. Dulles asked Manzini to find out exactly what Nasser was willing to do. Subsequently, Manzini visited Egypt twice during the week of September 30–October 7. Nasser gave Manzini the gist of a detailed plan for a permanent arrangement between the nationalized Canal Company and the Users Association and left Manzini with the impression that best results could be obtained by working through Ali Sabry. (Memorandum for the record by Collins, October 7; Department of State, Luce Files: Lot 64 F 26, Letters 1955–56; telegram 1492 from Rome, October 7; *ibid.*, Central Files, 974.7301/10–756)

We discussed briefly the possibility of the President going to New York to say a few words at the opening of the United Nations Security Council meeting. I said I would think this over and give the President my advice the next day. [3]

JFD

[3] Dulles discussed this matter again with Eisenhower on October 3. According to a memorandum of conversation by Dulles, "The President decided against it [going to the Security Council], feeling that it would overdramatize the situation and that the future program of the British and French was not sufficiently clear for him to commit his prestige. He thought that later on if a really critical situation developed which he could influence, he would be prepared to do so." (Eisenhower Library, Dulles Papers, Meetings with the President)

292. Memorandum of a Conversation Among the President, the Secretary of State, and the Secretary of the Treasury (Humphrey), October 3, 1956 [1]

Secretary Humphrey and I discussed with the President the matter of the Export-Import Bank loan to Israel for water development. Secretary Humphrey felt that this was very difficult to do because it did not involve the financing of US exports and it was almost ultra vires for the Bank to make this kind of loan. He added also that he thought the credit risk was excessive. [2]

[1] Source: Eisenhower Library, Dulles Papers, Meetings with the President. Secret; Personal and Private. Drafted by Dulles. According to the record of the President's Daily Appointments, Dulles and Humphrey accompanied the President to New York to attend a World Series baseball game. Presumably this conversation took place during the trip. (Ibid.)

[2] At a meeting with officials from the Department of State, the Department of the Treasury, and the International Cooperation Administration, President of the Export-Import Bank Samuel C. Waugh indicated that the Bank would not consider the proposed loan to Israel unless the Department of State asked for such consideration on the grounds of overwhelming political factors. Waugh informed the group confidentially that an independent audit of the Bank's accounts, arranged by the Chairman of the NAC, had raised serious doubts as to the wisdom of the Bank's earlier loans to Israel. While acknowledging that the Bank did not need to accept the audit in toto and that Israel had repaid part of its borrowing, Waugh also noted that Israel's indebtedness was very substantial. Israel had borrowed $135 million from the Bank in 1949 and 1950 and still had $120 million outstanding in principle. (A summary of the statements made by Waugh during the meeting is in a memorandum from Prochnow and Rountree to Dulles, October 2; Department of State, Central Files, 884A.10/9–656.)

He said that Israel had virtually no dollar earning power but depended almost always for dollars upon gifts from the US and US subscriptions to Israel bonds. He said that C.D. Jackson[3] had suggested that this loan be tied in with the proposal for Israel to pay off the refugees. If this element were added, it would merely make the credit risk greater.

The President felt nevertheless it was useful to continue to look into this matter. I suggested that before making a negative reply the Bank should send their technicians to Israel to satisfy themselves on the spot as to the feasibility of the project and its productivity. Secretary Humphrey thought this could be done.

[Here follows discussion of unrelated subjects.]

JFD[4]

---

[3] Former Special Assistant to the President.
[4] Macomber initialed for Dulles.

---

293.   Letter From the Assistant Secretary of Defense for International Security Affairs (Gray) to the Assistant Secretary of State for Near Eastern, South Asian, and African Affairs (Rountree)[1]

Washington, October 3, 1956.

DEAR BILL: This is to inform you that the Department of Defense concurs with Contingency Papers 1 through 7, inclusive, prepared pursuant to NSC Action 1593–b.[2]

While the implications of forays (or outright war) by Israel against Jordan are not dealt with in any of the Contingency Papers, I am sure you will agree that such actions could negate our efforts towards a peaceful solution to the Suez problem. These raids, which inherently carry the threat of all out Israel–Jordan hostilities, tend to unify the Arab and other Moslem States in their attitudes not only toward the Arab-Israeli dispute but also with regard to the Suez situation. I would therefore urge that in our representations to the Israeli authorities we point out to them the adverse effects their

---

[1] Source: Department of State, Central Files, 974.7301/10–356. Top Secret.
[2] See footnotes 8 and 9, Document 72, and Document 226.

hostile actions could have upon our efforts to bring about a timely and peaceful settlement of the Suez problem.

Sincerely yours,

Gordon Gray

---

294.   Annex to Watch Committee Report No. 322 [1]

SC 05674/56   *Washington, October 3, 1956.*

CONCLUSIONS ON BRITISH-FRENCH INTENTIONS TO EMPLOY FORCE AGAINST EGYPT

Anglo-French military action against Egypt in the immediate future is unlikely.

Note: In view of the preponderance of indications that the UK and France do not intend to resort to force at this time, the Watch Committee suspends publication of the Annex with this issue. The Watch Committee will continue to examine the Suez situation and will resume publication whenever events require.

The following are the more significant factors considered by the Watch Committee in reaching its conclusion:

1. The willingness of the UK and France to submit the Suez question for UN action, which is likely to be protracted, although they continue to reserve the right to an ultimate use of force.

2. The apparent release of the British 3rd Infantry Division from its standby alert and its return to home station; the division's equipment, however, remains loaded on board ship.

3. The absence of any further build-up of British-French air or ground strength on Cyprus.

4. The decreasing likelihood of Egyptian acts of violence against British or French persons or property which could provoke UK-French use of force.

5. The continuing efficient Egyptian operation of the Canal, diminishing the likelihood of a major interruption in traffic which could be used to justify UK-French military intervention.

---

[1] Source: CIA Files. Top Secret; Noforn; Limited Distribution.

6. The absence of any evidence of British-French intentions to act against Egypt through Israel, despite various reported rumors to the contrary.

---

295.   Telegram From the Department of State to the Embassy in Israel [1]

Washington, October 3, 1956—6:03 p.m.

266. You should inform Ben Gurion we take note of his assurance (Contel 91) [2] that if Iraqi troops remain east of Jordan Israel will take no action. You should add we are becoming increasingly concerned over anti-Western drift in Jordan and feel Jordan's request for Iraqi assistance in form of troops and limited equipment should be met, otherwise Jordan would look to Egypt or USSR for substantial amounts of aid. We understand Nuri plans send Iraqi troops to Jordan under Iraqi-Jordan Mutual Defense Treaty of 1947 [3] but that he would send only a small force which would remain east of Jordan River. Nuri has emphatically stated this force being sent purely for defensive purposes with ultimate objective helping Jordan resist Communism.

Prior making foregoing representations you should consult with your British colleague so your approach while separate from his will occur at approximately same time.

For Amman: Ambassador should state to Government we share its serious concern over security of country and we believe Iraqi assistance in form of troops and material would have salutary effect and provide element of strength against pressures from Communists and other extreme elements. We are expressing to Ben Gurion our understanding such Iraqi action is purely defensive in character. We believe plan to keep Iraqi forces east of Jordan is wise and that any move deploy them in West Jordan would invite serious Israeli counteraction. We continue feel most strongly that HKJ should take measures ensure that border incidents which might provoke Israeli retaliation are kept at minimum.

---

[1] Source: Department of State, Central Files, 684A.85/10–356. Secret; Niact. Drafted by Fritzlan and approved by Rountree who signed for Dulles. Repeated Niact to London, Amman, and Baghdad.

[2] See Document 289.

[3] This "Treaty of Brotherhood and Alliance" was signed at Baghdad on April 14, 1947. (23 UNTS 147)

For Baghdad: Ambassador should tell Nuri that in light deteriorating security situation in Jordan, together with information given us re size of force he contemplates sending to Jordan and its location east of Jordan, we see merit in his plan and have decided inform Ben Gurion we feel this step warranted. We shall stress to Ben Gurion increasing Communist and Egyptian influence in Jordan, and fact that Iraqi Government has assured us only small force will be sent for defensive purposes only and it will be kept east of Jordan. We are also informing HKJ of our support Nuri's project, emphasizing importance keeping border quiet in order avoid further retaliatory raids.

Important that neither Amman nor Baghdad disclose substance Ben Gurion's assurance.

British Embassy informed re foregoing but requested keep Ben Gurion's statement in strictest confidence.

Dulles

---

296.   Editorial Note

On October 3, the Israeli Foreign Ministry conveyed to Ambassador Lawson an oral message from Prime Minister Ben-Gurion containing his "additional views" on the proposed Iraqi troop movements. In the message, Ben Gurion sought to make clear that his previous comments on Iraqi troop movements (contained in telegram 91 from Jerusalem; see Document 289) referred only to the possibility of a token Iraqi force being sent to Jordan to help stabilize that country. The Prime Minister also sought assurances from the Department of State that this token force would be of a temporary character and bear no heavy armor; and he sought information concerning the size of the force and where it would be stationed. Ben Gurion emphasized that under no circumstances should the force come near Israel. Other points made by the Prime Minister, according to Lawson's report, were as follows:

"(A) He feels that there may be a definite plan on part of Washington, London, Baghdad to block any Egyptian penetration and possible take-over Jordan. He would like in strict confidence any details and comments on this and would like to discuss how Israel might fit into such a situation. . . .

"(B) Ben Gurion has heard with concern rumors of an intention to unite Jordan and Iraq and to grant political independence to west bank. Such a development would create new situation prejudicial to Israel and GOI has right to be consulted." (Telegram 310 from Tel Aviv, October 3; Department of State, Central Files, 684A.85/ 10–356)

Also on October 3, Foreign Minister Eban called at the Department of State and made similar points in a conversation with Rountree. The latter responded that the United States would advise Iraq not to send large forces into Jordan nor to put troops west of the Jordan River. Rountree added that the United States had the impression that the Iraqis had no intentions to do either or to equip their troops with heavy matériel. Eban also asked Rountree's views regarding an independent Arab state on the West bank of the Jordan River. Eban said that the present status quo in the Near East depended on the existence of the Armistice Agreements and the four Arab states which had signed them. If this situation were altered, and Jordan dismembered, Eban noted, "everybody, not only Arabs, would dream dreams." (Telegram 268 to Tel Aviv, October 4; *ibid.*, 684A.85/10–456)

---

297.   Memorandum of Discussion at the 299th Meeting of the National Security Council, Washington, October 4, 1956, 9 a.m. [1]

[Here follow a paragraph listing the participants at the meeting and agenda items 1 and 2.]

3. Significant World Developments Affecting U.S. Security

[Here follows discussion of unrelated subjects.]

At the conclusion of General Cabell's intelligence briefing Secretary Dulles said he wished to revert for a moment to the French situation. He said that the relations of the United States with France had lately become strained to a degree not paralleled for a very long time past. The French had apparently been eager to resort to the use of force in the Suez area on the ground that this course of action was vital to them in their own war in North Africa. They believed that they had had lined up the British behind this point of view but that we had pulled the British back. The tendency ever since in

---

[1] Source: Eisenhower Library, Whitman File, NSC Records. Top Secret. Prepared by Gleason on October 4. The time of the meeting is from the record of the President's Daily Appointments. (*Ibid.*)

France had been to blame the United States for not going along with French policy and with the French assumption that since France and the United States were allies in NATO, they must therefore be allies everywhere else in the world. Secretary Dulles remarked that even if we had accepted this French assumption, it would have been very difficult to provide appropriate support to the French because we really did not know what their plans were except that these plans involved the ultimate recourse to force in the Suez area if other means of settling the difficulty were unavailing. For example, said Secretary Dulles, he was not even privy to the British-French decision to take their case to the United Nations Security Council until after that decision had been made. We still did not really know whether this move to bring the case to the UN was designed to find a solution through negotiation, as the British insist, or whether taking the case to the UN was merely a cover for the ultimate use of force which seems to be the French position. Thus even the British and French did not seem to have coordinated their views as to the real purpose of the UN move. Never before in recent years, said Secretary Dulles, had we faced a situation where we had no clear idea of the intentions of our British and French allies. The repercussions of this situation with respect to public opinion in Britain and France were not good from the United States' point of view. These two governments tend to use the U.S. as a scapegoat for the popular disapproval of British and French policy.

Secretary Dulles indicated that he would be talking with the Foreign Ministers of France and Great Britain tomorrow morning in New York before the British-French case came up for action in the Security Council in the afternoon. He repeated that the situation was difficult for us because we were so much in the dark. He hoped to straighten matters out tomorrow morning but was doubtful of his success since neither Pineau nor Selwyn Lloyd could be regarded as strong men who spoke clearly for their governments. In any event all these things should of course have been ironed out before the British-French case was ever taken to the UN Security Council.

The President commented that he had recently read in the newspapers reports indicating that the Egyptians were in a mood for negotiation. Secretary Dulles replied that he believed that the Suez case could be negotiated if the British and French really wanted to follow such a course of action. The President concluded the discussion by stating with great emphasis that the United States would be dead wrong to join in any resort to force. We should instead hold out for honest negotiations with the Egyptians. Secretary Dulles expressed his agreement with the President's point.

[Here follow discussion of unrelated subjects and the remaining agenda items.]

S. Everett Gleason

---

298.   Telegram From the Department of State to the Embassy in France [1]

Washington October 4, 1956—8:03 p.m.

1261. Eyes only Dillon from Secretary. It is apparent that relations with French and perhaps to slightly lesser extent with British are at difficult stage. I know British and French want us to "stand with them". But we do not know where they stand nor are we consulted.

The decision to go to UN was taken overnight while I was flying back. We had been discussing that up to time I left London Friday evening and I had pointed to the many difficulties and possible adverse effect on SCUA membership if matter taken to UN prematurely. No decision had been reached and I had assumed there would be further discussion before any decision was reached. When I arrived Saturday I was confronted with decision already taken.

For weeks French and British have been hammering us to try to get US flagships to make toll payments to SCUA. Now that we would be ready to act jointly there is doubt as to what British and French themselves will do.

We have no real guidance as to what are purposes of British and French. British gave us a paper [2] which, I think, they also sent to Commonwealth countries, which said they were willing that UN move to initiate negotiations. But we cannot find out what kind of

---

[1] Source: Department of State, Central Files, 974.7301/10–456. Top Secret; Priority. Drafted by Dulles and Hoover; cleared by Phleger, Bowie, Rountree, and Elbrick; and approved by Dulles. Repeated to London Priority eyes only for Aldrich. On October 10, on instructions from Dulles, Fisher Howe sent Goodpaster copies of telegram 1261 and Dillon's and Aldrich's responses, Documents 306 and 316. (Eisenhower Library, Whitman File, Dulles–Herter Series)

[2] Reference is presumably to a paper containing instructions from the British Foreign Office to certain British diplomatic posts concerning the British position in the Security Council on the Suez situation. Barbara Salt of the British Embassy showed Dulles a copy of these instructions on September 27 and later that day gave a copy to Wilcox. (Attached to the memorandum of conversation among Salt, Wilcox, and others, September 27; Department of State, Central Files, 330/9–2756)

negotiation British have in mind and under what auspices. The French say they strongly oppose British position in this respect.

There are indications from some British and French quarters that UN move is genuinely designed to explore peaceful processes. But other such quarters represented move as designed quickly to put a Soviet veto "in their pocket", thereby giving them "liberty of action" which is politically expedient for meeting of British Conservative Party and French Parliamentary debate.

Both British and French Embassies seem to be completely in dark and we cannot get guidance from them.

We deplore the growing public sentiment in Britain and France that we are at fault because we are not showing solidarity. But their positions so far as we are aware are vague to point of non-existence. We do not know and cannot find out whether they want war or peace.

There is still not much American public opinion on this matter because of preoccupation with election (upon which World Series now superimposed). But we are convinced American public opinion would not favor giving British and French blank check in this matter and go along with British and French in measures the end purpose of which is concealed from us.

We are prepared to vote for British and French resolution, although we have made some minor suggestions which we think improve it from technical standpoint. However, our vote is not conditioned on acceptance of these changes. But as I told French with President's authority some weeks ago it would be very difficult for us to oppose an amendment calling for renunciation of force if couched in Charter language. [3] We note from Paris telegrams (1580 and 1586) [4] that French may insist that we oppose such amendments. But when they joined with British to go to UN they did so knowing our position.

I expect to see Lloyd and Pineau Friday morning and perhaps then some of these matters can be straightened out, although I am

---

[3] Reference is possibly to Dulles' conversation with Alphand on September 7; see Document 188.

[4] Telegram 1580 from Paris, October 3, reported French journalist and politician Maurice Schumann's concern about anti-NATO sentiment in the French Parliament and the necessity for a U.S. veto of any Security Council resolution barring the use of force. (Department of State, Central Files, 611.51/10–356)

In telegram 1586 from Paris, October 3, Dillon emphasized that U.S. failure to support the British-French position in the Security Council would seriously affect not only Franco-American relations but also the future of NATO. He noted a resurgence of French feeling that military measures were the only satisfactory way to resolve the Suez affair in a reasonable period of time and strongly recommended that the United States obtain a definite side agreement from Lloyd and Pineau regarding the course of Franco-British action immediately following the Security Council debate. (Ibid., 974.7301/10–356)

doubtful because neither seems to me to speak clearly for a united Cabinet.

This is background which you may use on your own responsibility. What follows is my thinking on a larger issue, expressed purely for your confidential information and to elicit your personal and confidential reaction.

I feel that this Suez issue points up some very basic factors.

The Western European nations have been preserving their political divisions which keep them weak, partly because they have felt that they could afford this luxury so long as they had more or less a blank check on the US for economic, military, and political support everywhere in the world. This Suez matter is bringing into the open the fact that they cannot count upon us outside the North Atlantic Treaty area automatically and without the exercise of our independent judgment. Under those circumstances they feel weak and frustrated.

I believe that their answer is to be found in increased European unity so that they will have together the strength which they need to be a powerful force in the world comparable to that of the Soviet Union and the United States, and more able to carry out their own policies. This unity movement is taking on new strength and is, I think, doing so largely because the European countries are increasingly aware that they cannot count unreservedly upon US support everywhere.

Unfortunately, it is the fact that great movements such as the federation of separate sovereignties rarely occur purely as a result of logic, but mainly as a result of emotion, largely generated by a sense of fear and of weakness. Western European unity will, I am afraid, not come about so long as each Western European country feels that it can in all respects count on US support because we are NATO "allies". The knowledge of such countries that they cannot count on such support irrespective of our independent judgment will naturally irritate them and create a measure of anti-United States feeling. But that may be the only atmosphere in which the momentous step of European union will be advanced.

Obviously we do not want anti-Americanism, but I do not think that we can, or indeed that we should, try to buy pro-American sentiment by leading the Western European countries to feel that we will blindly support them in any course which they may wish to pursue.

Of course the historical and cultural ties which bind the British, French and ourselves so deeply together shall of course always lead us to seek to work together and to regard any sharp difference as a grave misfortune. But I feel that this process would be easier with partners who were strong and self-reliant as would be the case if they had greater organic unity among themselves.

Dulles

U.N. SECURITY COUNCIL DEBATE ON THE SUEZ CANAL QUESTION;
THE IRAQI PROPOSAL TO MOVE TROOPS INTO JORDAN; ANGLO-
AMERICAN DIFFERENCES OVER SCUA; ISRAELI MOBILIZATION; AND
U.S. DIPLOMATIC ACTIVITY PRIOR TO THE OUTBREAK OF
HOSTILITIES, OCTOBER 5–29

299. Editorial Note

Between October 5 and 13, the United Nations Security Council
met on almost a daily basis to continue discussion of the Anglo-
French item, "Situation created by the unilateral action of the
Egyptian Government in bringing to an end the system of international operation of the Suez Canal, which was confirmed and completed by the Suez Canal Convention of 1888", this item having
originally been inscribed on the Security Council agenda on September 26. Of the eleven member nations of the Security Council, six of
them (Belgium, France, the Soviet Union, the United Kingdom, the
United States, and Yugoslavia) were represented by their Foreign
Ministers. Egyptian Foreign Minister Fawzi was also present for the
debate. Secretary Dulles was in New York for most of this period
and served as United States Representatives during the meetings.
Papers kept by the United States Delegation for this period are in
Department of State, Conference Files: Lot 62 D 181. They include
daily chronologies, memoranda of conversations, copies of telegrams
sent between the Mission in New York and the Department of State,
position papers, Security Council documents, and verbatim minutes
of the six open and three secret meetings of the Security Council
which were held during this period. The procès-verbaux of the open
meetings (735th, 736th, 737th, 738th, 742d, and 743d) are printed in
United Nations Security Council, *Official Records*, Eleventh Year.

At the 735th meeting of the Security Council on October 5, the
Representatives of France and the United Kingdom submitted to the
Security Council a draft resolution, the operative paragraphs of
which provided that the Security Council would: (1) reaffirm the
principle of freedom of navigation in accordance with the Convention of 1888; (2) affirm the necessity for safeguarding the rights and
guarantees that all users of the Canal enjoyed under the system
upon which the convention was based; (3) endorse the Eighteen-
Power Proposals for a settlement; (4) recommend that Egypt negotiate on the basis of these proposals; and (5) recommend to Egypt
that, in the interim, it cooperate with the Suez Canal Users Association. (U.N. doc. S/3666)

This draft resolution had undergone several revisions and reflected changes suggested by the United States. On September 29 in
telegram 123 to USUN, the Department of State had forwarded to

the Mission suggested modifications for the British-French draft resolution. (Department of State, Central Files, 974.7301/9–2956) On October 4 in telegram 304 from USUN, the Mission had sent to the Department a text of the revised draft, which incorporated certain of the changes. (*Ibid.*, 974.7301/10–456) On October 5, the Mission transmitted to the Department the text of the draft, containing additional revisions, which had been the basis of discussion at a meeting that morning with Lloyd and Pineau, and a summary report of that meeting, during which additional changes had been made. (Secto 1 and Secto 2; both *ibid.*, 974.7301/10–556) Later on October 5, the Mission informed the Department of last-minute changes in the text. (Telegram 309; *ibid.*, 330/10–556)

---

300.   Memorandum of a Conversation, Secretary Dulles' Suite, Waldorf Astoria, New York, October 5, 1956, 10:15 a.m. [1]

H.C. Lodge, Jr. notes on conversation between:

His Excellency Selwyn Lloyd, Foreign Minister of Britain
His Excellency Christian Pineau, Foreign Minister of France
The Honorable John Foster Dulles, Secretary of State

(These notes have been verified by Secretary Dulles and Mr. Phleger)

Dulles: I thought it was a good idea to have an intimate meeting to discuss the questions of substance. We can have a procedural talk later.

There is a need for clarification between us. In your countries there are those who don't understand American policy, and here are those who don't understand your policies. We feel somewhat out of touch with your thinking. I was so much surprised when I got out of the plane on my return from London to find that a decision to come to the United Nations had been taken overnight.

This raised a question as to your real purpose. Was it to be an attempt to find a peaceful settlement? Or was it to be an attempt to get the UN behind you to clear the way for a greater freedom of

---

[1] Source: Department of State, Central Files, 974.7301/10–556. Top Secret; Eyes Only. Drafted by Lodge. The time and place of the meeting are from a note attached to the source text from Macomber to Howe, dated October 6. According to Dulles' Appointment Book, Dulles and party (Phleger, McCardle, Wilcox, Bowie, Tyler, Ludlow, Macomber, Bernau, Asbjornson, and two others) left Washington by air at 7:55 a.m. and arrived in New York at 9:15 a.m., October 5.

action and stronger measures? We don't know whether the purpose is to promote a negotiation or do things that you think must be gone through with without hope or real desire for positive result.

Now, there must be real understanding as to what is planned. None of us can take for granted that the other will go along blindly. The issues are too momentous for that.

The United States believes in the principles of the 18-power resolution—not every detail necessarily, but that there must be some measure of international participation in the operation of the Canal. We think that resort to force is a desperate measure which is not to be considered until a genuine effort has been made to exhaust all other possibilities.

It is the military estimate of President Eisenhower, who assuredly is well qualified to have an opinion, that military measures would start a war which would be extremely difficult to bring to an end, and that before it was ended the sympathies of all the Middle East, Asian and African peoples would be irrevocably lost to the West— and lost to such an extent as to pose a very grave problem for the next generation. If we do not retain the sympathy of those people they will, in all probability, go over to the Soviet Union.

Elections in this country are not a factor, contrary to what has been said, in some quarters in your countries. We are doing precisely the same thing that we would advocate under other conditions. There are indeed some who think the re-election of President Eisenhower would be assured if there was a war. A prominent Democrat said the other night that a war would make the Democratic prospects absolutely hopeless and that if there was a question of a war President, there would be no choice but President Eisenhower. You can be assured that our policies are not swayed by political considerations.

We favor a peaceful settlement by all possible means. War would be a disaster for the interests of the West in Asia and Africa. We assume that you have invoked the United Nations in that spirit, but it would be helpful if you gave us a frank statement as to whether you agree or disagree with what I have said.

Lloyd: I take the full blame for the decision to come to the Security Council. I thought we had indicated in London that we would go to the UN at some time. The decision was taken Saturday[2] morning after you left London, and not while you were in the air. We felt that the impact of SCUA was less than was hoped for. We found that the Scandinavians would not come into SCUA without the UN having been invoked. The timing was due to a hint which we had received from an Indian source that the Russians were

---

[2] September 22.

talking about bringing the matter to the UN. We could not afford even the remote risk that the Soviet Union would beat us to it.

The British purpose is quite genuine. We do not want to "railroad through" our proposal. We have always realized that in coming here we expose ourselves to a period of negotiation. But we cannot be here more than 10 days. In other words, next week something must happen. The 18-power resolution is the best basis and we want Security Council endorsement of that. If there is a veto or nothing happens, we must consider what to do next.

We would favor economic pressure if it would show results within two weeks, but we do not believe that this is practical. Force has tremendous disadvantages: there is the question of how to get out once you get in? and how do you justify it? We think that if we were to resort to force we would denounce the 1954 agreement and would go back to the Suez Canal Zone on that basis.

We are very much moved by a feeling that there is a conspiracy afoot in the Middle East—to kill the King of Libya, and to upset the regime in Saudi Arabia. There is a young officer movement in Iraq. Nuri is losing ground. So, it may be, that the Menzies Mission having failed, and the UN having failed, force will be the lesser evil.

Pineau: The time has come to show our cards. French public opinion on this subject is clear. It is noteworthy that for the first time, the President of the National Assembly referred to a difference existing between France and England on the one hand, and the United States on the other. The whole question of the existence of NATO is raised. I assure you that I will never, as Foreign Minister, agree to give up NATO, but the state of European public opinion being what it is now (and what Adenauer said the other day shows it), these things must be faced. They are of extreme gravity and the destruction of the North Atlantic Alliance would be the greatest Soviet victory. We must, therefore, remove misunderstandings.

What is the great misunderstanding regarding Suez? We don't think the United States Government realizes the importance that France and the UK attach to Suez. It is not merely the Canal, but all the Middle East, Algeria, Morocco, and. Tunisia, that are involved. The Prince of Morocco told us recently that he cannot stay in power if Nasser wins. Communistic elements of Istiqlal [3] will come into power. In Tunisia, Bourguiba says the same thing. All of the top people in these countries say why have you not used force? The Turkish Foreign Minister said to the French Ambassador the other day: "We hesitate to go to the SCUA. Experience shows that it is better to be allied with Russia than it is to be allied with France, the

---

[3] The Istiqlal, or Independence Party, was the dominant political party in Morocco.

US and the UK." We risk much more than an economic difference over the Suez Canal. We are risking all of our influence in that part of the world. We do not desire to use force, but it is nonetheless true that the presence of the Franco-British troops on Cyprus account for such good treatment as we have had there. We are willing to do all in our power not to use force, but Nasser surely will go farther and farther. He will take over the French and British positions because they are nearest, but then he will go after the US positions. Russia is back of him. The chief of all navigation in the Canal Zone is now a Russian. We risk Russian domination of the whole area.

The temporizing tactics of the US alarm us. We will play the game in the Security Council but we will not get bogged down in procedure. SCUA is not very much, but let us try to negotiate on the basis of the 18-power policies, and if not, then give us our liberty of action.

Dulles: The U.S. would not want to say that circumstances might not arise where the only alternative would be the use of force. Sometimes one must use it without prospect of a satisfactory outcome, but force is not a measure which will improve our prospects in Asia and Africa, and it is a great illusion to think that it would.

I do not agree with your assessments of the results of the use of force or of the situation in the Near East.

The Pakistan Government is having a hard time to maintain its pro-Western orientation. If force is used, Pakistan, Ethiopia, and Iran will all go against us.

You had your choice in May of 1953 whether to stay or whether to get out of Suez. You decided not to stay, and I think rightly. Your position is much harder now. To try to turn the clock back creates a worse situation than that of 1953.

The use of force in violation of the Charter would destroy the United Nations. That is a grave responsibility. If you think the renunciation of force in the Charter was a mistake, it would be a great disillusionment to the United States.

I don't think the situation is deteriorating. Perhaps it is in Algeria, but there are many developments against Nasser in the Middle East. The situation in Jordan is clear. Egypt cannot help Jordan. Egypt has taken her troops out of the Negev and out of the Gaza Strip, which gives a chance for Iraq to move into Jordan. King Saud is seeking a rapprochement with Feisal. The situation in Syria can be improved. The whole situation is not deteriorating. It is true that economic pressures will not yield quick results. But what is the basic long-term trend? Nasser's prestige is beginning to decline and he is not getting the money he hoped for.

We need not decide here what the ultimate decision is going to be, but we must decide whether we will make a sound, sincere effort to obtain a just settlement in the UN. I agree with Mr. Pineau that you should keep your forces in being and it should be made clear that if good faith UN efforts fail, force may become a permissible alternative to be considered. I intend to re-affirm my London statement that peace and justice are two sides of the same coin.

If the UN can't do justice, the UN has failed. But there must be an honest and determined effort to get a settlement on the basis of the 18-power declaration. We are glad to note that in the UK memorandum there is a statement not ruling out the possibility of negotiation.

We need not, however, consider the ultimate decision now today, but we must consider the penultimate decision. If we are merely trying to clear the decks for the use of force, we will be condemned for having destroyed the UN, and that the US cannot agree to do.

Pineau: I cannot see that Nasser's prestige is any less. I am surprised that you cite Algeria as the one exception, since it is precisely there that we have the least trouble. The greatest difficulty is in the independent countries, that is, Morocco and Tunisia. Time is not working against Nasser.

The choice is not one to negotiate or to use force. The question is of negotiation on a proper basis. We would prefer to use the Security Council itself rather than a special negotiating body. It would be better to work in the whole Security Council rather than take 5 or 6 or 7 members. Then we would be taking Bulganin's proposal and there would be no end of it. If Egypt is willing to negotiate on the basis of the 18-power statement, fine. If not, and we negotiate on some other basis, we would be led to a capitulation to Nasser and that would be a catastrophe.

Lloyd: We have always said that we would not use force without going first to the UN, and we believe in doing all that we can to make the UN phase successful. But we can't get drawn into a long-term negotiation. I think that after the general exposition is finished there should be a private meeting, beginning Tuesday, then we could adjourn for two or three days, resume Friday, and if anything can come out of negotiation that should be enough time. We would prefer to negotiate on the basis of the 18-power declaration, but we will certainly look at any other basis for negotiation. We think that to take a week is not rushing.

Dulles: If you have ever argued in an Egyptian bazaar in Cairo you will know that they don't work that fast. There is merit in Mr. Lloyd's suggestion that after the general debate, in closed session, informal discussions be held to see if there is a possibility of serious negotiation. But we couldn't have 12 people in the informal negotiations. One secret meeting will be enough. Then, after that, three or four days with no formal proceedings at all. If Egypt will accept the heart of our proposal, that is, that the Canal be operated free from politics, then there are different ways of working it out. The U.S. has not encouraged any go-betweens and we have had no contacts with Egyptians. Is it your idea that we should talk to the Egyptians or others, if they wish, to ascertain what they are prepared to do?

Lloyd: Yes. We think you should have such contacts if there is an opportunity. I have talked in this way to Popovic and Shepilov. Shepilov says why not have a committee of six, including India? . . . Shepilov and Popovic appeared to agree with the idea of direct talks. We should fight off the idea of a negotiating subcommittee. If that happened, I would go home. Shepilov and Popovic agreed to try to conclude next week. I do not want to hurry, but I think that there should be a real sense of urgency about this.

Pineau: There seems to be some confusion concerning the negotiating body. As I see it, there is a first stage, to make Egypt admit that they will negotiate on the basis of the 18-power resolution. Then, if we get somewhere on this basis, we can set up a negotiating committee, but it should not be a committee of small countries—it should be a committee of principal powers.

Dulles: I agree that there should be some kind of negotiating body consisting of all the parties at interest.

Lloyd: I told Popovic it was no good talking of guarantees without defining them. What kind? Who would negotiate?

Dulles: I agree. We don't need new words, we have enough words now.

Pineau: What will we do after the general discussion?

Dulles: After the general discussion there will be one secret session of the Security Council, then recess for three or four days for informal contacts outside. Then we three meet again to decide whether any of our soundings hold any hope. Then the formal session is resumed and the resolution is acted on one way or the other. Then we decide what to do next.

Pineau: The secret meeting would come on Wednesday.

Lloyd: If we can eliminate consecutive translation for the set speeches, we could finish the general discussion Tuesday morning and have the first secret meeting Tuesday afternoon.

Dixon: summed up the conversation by saying that all had agreed that the objective was the endorsement of having negotiations on the basis of the 18-power declaration.

Dulles: That statement does not cover everything.

Lloyd: If we agree on procedural tactics there is an advantage in announcing them publicly as soon as possible.

Pineau: Let us fix Friday as the last day.

Lloyd: I suggest a secret session Tuesday afternoon.

Dulles: I plan to make a brief statement at the end of today's session that the U.S. stands on the 18-power statement.

Pineau: As President, [4] I plan today to recognize Dulles, then to read the Israeli-Arab letter, [5] then to recognize Lloyd, then recognize France, and then to recognize Dulles.

Lloyd: If the three days are fruitless, we can hear the Israelis then.

Dulles: We must hear Israel some time.

---

[4] The French Representative at the United Nations served as President of the Security Council during the month of October 1956. Following Pineau's return to France, Bernard Cornut-Gentille and Louis de Guiringaud served in the position.

[5] At the 735th meeting of the Security Council, which began at 3 p.m., October 5, the President of the Security Council noted that he had received a letter, dated October 3, from the Representative of Israel (U.N. doc. S/3663) requesting that the Israeli Representative appear before the Security Council to speak on the matter of free passage of Israeli vessels through the Suez Canal. The President of the Security Council also noted that he had received a letter, dated October 4, from the representatives of seven Arab States (U.N. doc. S/3664) requesting permission to participate in the discussion on the Suez situation. The Yugoslav Representative then proposed that the Council not make an immediate decision on either of these requests. The proposal was adopted without a vote. (U.N. doc. S/PV.735)

---

301.   Report Prepared in the Executive Secretariat of the Department of State [1]

Summary No. 24   *Washington, October 5, 1956.*

SUMMARY OF DEVELOPMENTS IN SUEZ SITUATION

Menon Seeking Compromise Solution

Our Chargé in New Delhi reports [2] that Khrishna Menon will be in Cairo today and tomorrow, will go to London Sunday [3] and stay until Tuesday to talk with Eden, and then possibly proceed to New York. Menon told our Chargé that his objective is to present a compromise plan to Nasser, attempt to secure his approval and then

---

[1] Source: Eisenhower Library, Whitman File, International File. Top Secret; Eyes Only for Designated Recipient.

[2] Reported by Frederic Bartlett, Minister-Counselor, in telegram 843 from New Delhi, October 4, not printed. (Department of State, Central Files, 974.7301/10–456)

[3] October 7.

raise it with the British. The plan, based upon the Indian Government's belief that Egypt "must not be unfettered" in the operation of the canal, is in three phases: 1) *Operation*—Egypt would set up a private corporation to run the canal with a link to some form of a users association; 2) *Supervision*—Egypt would associate itself with an international body to which complaints could be referred, and this body would carry out supervisory functions provided for in Article 8 of the 1888 agreement; 3) *Policy*—A high level international council would settle by agreement overall policy for canal transits including the establishment of tolls. In Menon's opinion the best procedure for the Security Council would be to merely request Egypt on the one hand and the UK and France on the other to attempt to negotiate the issue and report back to the Council. The parties could then request "good services" from whatever other countries they desired. Menon said that if he had an interview with Secretary Dulles, it could be misinterpreted that the Government of India was attempting to complicate US relations with the UK. Nevertheless, if the Secretary asked to see Menon, he would be glad to go to Washington.

SCUA Developments

The SCUA Council unanimously adopted yesterday the committee resolutions on organization and financing and referred the reports of the finance and shipping committees to the Executive Group.[4] In discussing the draft resolution on organization before its adoption, however, it was agreed that the question of new members (other than Ethiopia, Pakistan, and Japan) should be resolved at a later date. It was agreed informally that SCUA would continue to operate from London until a final decision on the headquarters site is taken by the Council. The task of choosing the Administrator was passed to the Executive Group, but the decision on the composition of the Group was deferred until today's session. With one exception, the entire Council accepted an Executive Group membership of the US, UK, France, Norway, Italy and Iran with one seat left open for Ethiopia, Pakistan or some other country east of the canal. France, however, was insisting on a prior commitment from Italy that the dues for the transits of Italian ships would be paid to SCUA.

---

[4] Reported in telegram 1871 from London, October 4, not printed. (Department of State, Central Files, 974.7301/10–456) For text of the resolutions adopted on October 4, see *United States Policy in the Middle East, September 1956–June 1957*, pp. 104–108. The Embassy in London transmitted the reports of the finance and shipping committees to the Department in despatch 846, October 5, not printed. (Department of State, Central Files, 974.7301/10–556)

Possible Secret SC Meeting on Suez

In a conversation with Lloyd, Dixon, Alphand and Cornut-Gentille,[5] Lodge stated he personally thought the chances of the British Security Council (SC) resolution receiving wider support would be enhanced if there were recourse to some conciliatory procedure before voting. He mentioned the possibility of bringing the Secretary General into the discussions, of creating a sub-committee of the SC, or of holding secret meetings of the SC. Both Lloyd and Alphand were opposed to the first two proposals. Lloyd said, however, he would be willing to have three or four days of secret meetings, but would rather not make a formal motion to that effect. Lodge pointed out that we should not let the initiative for any step of this kind slip to the USSR, with which the French indicated their agreement.

Egypt Rumored Seeking Private US Financing

Charles-Roux, President of the Suez Canal Company, has expressed concern to Dillon[6] over reports that Badawi, head of the Egyptian canal authority, is coming to the US to discuss with American oil companies a plan for financing the needs of the authority. Dillon told him he knew nothing of any such matter and doubted if it were true, but agreed to ask for further information. In this connection, Hare has previously reported that the Egyptian Finance Minister told an American newsman that Badawi was coming to seek the views of American oil and shipping companies on steps required to maintain and develop the Canal. Hare inferred that the Canal users would not be asked for financial support.

British Delay Decision on Canal Toll Payments

Although we told the UK and France on September 26 that we are prepared to effect payments by American-flag vessels of canal dues directly to SCUA by making it unlawful for them to pay to Egypt, the British have not yet made a decision on the regulations it would be willing to prescribe. However, the working level in the British Foreign Office has told our Embassy in London[7] that the British reply will probably be similar to that of the French, who have indicated their unwillingness to pay tolls to SCUA if it should appear that only one or two other nations were prepared to conform to this practice.

---

[5] Reported in telegram 299 from USUN, October 4, not printed. (*Ibid.*, 974.7301/10–456)

[6] Reported in telegram 1610 from Paris, October 4, not printed. (*Ibid.*)

[7] Reported in telegram 1870 from London, October 4, not printed. (*Ibid.*)

Canal Operation Difficulties Reported

Embassy Cairo has reported [8] three or four groundings of vessels transiting the canal and a six-hour delay yesterday morning in the departure of the south-bound convoy. These incidents are not exceptional and are probably due to the assignment of several newly-trained pilots and the appearance of the October fogs. Separately, Embassy Stockholm has reported [9] that many Swedish captains are so familiar with the canal that when they receive incorrect signals from shore, as is now happening, they disregard them and avoid accidents.

(Summary closed 12:15 p.m., October 5, 1956)

---

[8] In telegram 993 from Cairo, October 4, not printed. (*Ibid.*)
[9] In telegram 402 from Stockholm, October 4, not printed. (*Ibid.*)

---

302.   Message From the Secretary of State to the President [1]

New York, October 5, 1956.

DEAR MR. PRESIDENT: I have had a full day on what is now my fourth Suez Conference. It started with a "heart-to-heart" talk with Lloyd and Pineau. [2] I said that obviously there was not real understanding between us, and I pointed to a number of concrete illustrations. I said we could not get on this way and must at least know the purpose of their action in bringing the Suez to the United Nations. Was it for peace, or for war?

Both Pineau and Lloyd said in effect that they did not believe there was any peaceful way of solution and they argued that only the use of force against Nasser would restore Western prestige in Africa and the Middle East. I said I thought it would be just the contrary and cited the points you used in your prior letters to Eden. I concluded that all of Africa, the Middle East and Asia would be inflamed against the West and that Soviet Russia would have an easy time to pick up the pieces.

---

[1] Source: Department of State, Central Files, 974.7301/10–656. Top Secret. Transmitted to the Department of State in Dulte 1 from USUN, 11 p.m., which is the source text, with the instruction: "Eyes only Acting Secretary for President from Secretary". Dulte 1 was received at 12:26 a.m., October 6. A copy is in the Eisenhower Library, Whitman File, Dulles–Herter Series.
[2] See Document 300.

I do not think that either convinced the other, but I did say that if we cannot agree on the ultimate, let us at least try to agree on the penultimate, namely, the present proceedings in the United Nations. I said that so far as the United States was concerned, we were determined to make this an honest effort to reach a settlement and I hoped that they would do the same. The British agreed that they would do this, and Pineau grudgingly went along.

We then discussed procedure and tentatively agreed that after the general debate was over—perhaps Tuesday—we would have one restricted session of the Council and then recess for two or three days during which private talks would proceed and at the end of that time we would come together to agree on whether we thought that an acceptable formula could be found. If so, then a negotiating group would be organized to work out the details. It was understood that the United States would be free to play a role in the behind-the-scenes negotiation.

Then Spaak came in to see me,[3] and I found that he was strongly opposed to war and greatly worried at the French position. He said it would be disastrous not to give the United Nations a real chance and that the whole world would go against the British and the French if it was apparent they were to blame.

Then Shepilov came to see me.[4] He talked pleasantly about their desire to seek a settlement. I reminded him that when he had talked the same way in London, Soviet propaganda was doing its best to sabotage our effort by violent anti-Western propaganda. I said that while the United States was using its full influence to moderate the British and the French, the Soviet Union was merely trying to egg on the Egyptians to greater excesses. I said the measure of our respective efforts was to be found in the fact that I was today the most unpopular man in France and Britain and he was the most popular man in Egypt. Shepilov was obviously disconcerted but reaffirmed his real desire this time to try to accomplish a settlement. He talked about a negotiating group. I said there could be no negotiating group unless it was first ascertained that there was a real basis for negotiation so that the group would be working out details and not merely starting from scratch. The French and British, I said,

---

[3] A memorandum of this conversation, which began at 12:30 p.m. in the Secretary's suite at the Waldorf Astoria, is in Department of State, Conference Files: Lot 62 D 181, CF 788. A summary report of the conversation was transmitted to the Department in telegram 313 from USUN, October 5. (*Ibid.*, Central Files, 974.7301/10–556)

[4] A memorandum of this conversation, which began at 2 p.m. in the Secretary's suite, is *ibid.*, Conference Files: Lot 62 D 181, CF 788. A summary report of the conversation was transmitted to the Department in telegram 312 from USUN, October 5. (*Ibid.*, Central Files, 974.7301/10–556)

would not accept that. Shepilov indicated that they might go along with my procedure.

After our formal meeting,[5] Fawzi, the Egyptian Foreign Minister, came to see me.[6] He indicated a desire for settlement and emphasized particularly the importance of getting more money to develop the Canal and suggested that this might be the cover for some form of foreign participation in the Canal operations. I outlined the Conference procedure I had in mind and he indicated it would be agreeable. He also indicated that they would like to negotiate directly with us. I said of course we had no mandate to act for anybody else, but would be glad to exchange views. I suggested that their legal adviser who is quite an eminent international lawyer should work with Phleger. At this point Phleger came into the conversation,[7] and is planning to meet with the Egyptian lawyer tomorrow, Saturday.

It looks as though these next few days would "make or break" the situation. If we can put into it the spirit which seems to have animated the Dodgers in the game today, then there is a chance we can make it.

Faithfully yours,

Foster

---

[5] Reference is to the 735th meeting of the Security Council.

[6] A memorandum of this conversation by Dulles, which began at 5:30 p.m. in the Secretary's suite, is in Department of State, Central Files, 974.7301/10–556.

[7] Phleger drafted a memorandum of this second half of the conversation with Fawzi. It is attached to Dulles' memorandum, *ibid.*

---

303.   Memorandum of a Conference With the President, White House, Washington, October 6, 1956, 10:35 a.m.[1]

OTHERS PRESENT

Secretary Hoover
Colonel Goodpaster

Mr. Hoover handed the President a message from Secretary Dulles reporting on his Suez meetings in New York on October

---

[1] Source: Eisenhower Library, Whitman File, Eisenhower Diaries. Secret. Drafted by Goodpaster. The time of the meeting is from the record of the President's Daily Appointments. (*Ibid.*)

fifth. [2] Referring to the passage reporting the Secretary's discussion with Shepilov, the President said he was glad the Secretary had thrown Shepilov's words "into his teeth." Mr. Hoover left the message for the President.

Mr. Hoover next showed the President a copy of a note from Nehru to the Secretary giving his ideas how further action might proceed. Later, State Department sent over a copy of this note. [3]

In the course of discussion, the President said he thought Secretary Dulles can go along with the British so long as it is understood that what is being put forward now is simply a proposal, [4] and that we stand ready to take it into negotiation. The President felt there must be some kind of international participation in any acceptable solution, so that the whole power of control of the use of the Canal is not left to one little country. He did not feel that all the details could or should be spelled out in the treaty. He felt that a broad provision on the powers of a general manager might be of central importance—for example, the board (which would have international representation) might have authority to disapprove the actions of the manager by a majority vote, and fire him by a two-thirds vote. The manager must, however, have the operating authority subject to these controls.

Mr. Hoover next reported that the Egyptians seemed to be trying to split off the U.S. from the U.K. and France, using the American press in the process. The President indicated he might have himself fostered, at an early stage in this incident, one of the ideas they are now using—that of a private consortium. Mr. Hoover saw merit in a management group coming in to operate the Canal as had been done with the oil fields in Iran. The Egyptians appeared to be suggesting this in an effort to split us off from our allies. If something like this were done, it should be formalized in a treaty, in which our Allies would join. The President indicated that there might be merit in commercial users making a deal with Egypt

---

[2] *Supra.*

[3] Not printed. The message from Nehru was transmitted to the Department of State in a letter dated October 5 from the First Secretary of the Indian Embassy, B.K. Massand, to Secretary Dulles. In the message, Nehru informed Dulles that he had asked Krishna Menon to travel to Cairo and London, and then possibly to New York. He also noted that the Indian Government felt that the gap between the two sides on the Suez issue was "capable of being bridged" and that Menon's informal approaches to the parties involved might "yield better results than mere public assertion of rigid viewpoints in the Security Council." The Department of State transmitted a copy of this message to Dulles in New York in Tosec 3, October 5. (Department of State, Central Files, 974.7301/10–556) A copy of Tosec 3 in the Eisenhower Library, Whitman File, International File, bears a marginal inscription by Goodpaster: "Noted by President 6 Oct 56".

[4] Reference is to the draft U.K.-French resolution submitted to the Security Council on October 5. See Document 299.

(possibly including the deepening and improvement of the Canal) with the arrangement confirmed by the treaty. While there was some question whether the French would want a peaceful solution, the British might accept it.

The President saw the development of the matter in terms of our offering SCUA as our proposal, Egypt making a counterproposal, and then trying to reach agreement.

.   .   .   .

Summarizing, the President said he was highly pleased to have the Secretary's report. He thought we could go along with the U.K. and France in presenting the proposal. However, if there is any "give" on the other side, we should try to work for constructive negotiations.

Mr. Hoover reported that the studies of super-tanker development looked quite good. The optimum size might be 60,000–65,000 tons; these could transit the Canal empty and round the Cape when loaded. The key to this effort might be a statement by the Government guaranteeing to take the tankers off the shipbuilders' hands if they are unable to dispose of them otherwise.

G

Colonel, CE, US Army

---

304.   **Telegram From the Department of State to the Mission at the United Nations** [1]

Washington, October 6, 1956—2:43 p.m.

Tedul 3. Eyes only Secretary and Phleger from Acting Secretary. I showed your Dulte 1 to the President this morning and he was most appreciative. [2]

He was in full accord with your actions and particularly with the line you had taken with Shepilov.

After he finished your message he expressed the opinion that (a) the present proposal represented the views which we had been able to get the UK and France to go along with, and not necessarily

---

[1] Source: Department of State, Central Files, 974.7301/10–656. Top Secret. Drafted by Hoover, cleared by Goodpaster, and approved by Kirk who signed for Hoover.
[2] See *supra*. Dulte 1 transmitted Dulles' message to Eisenhower, Document 302.

the views of the US alone; (b) if Egypt, in the process of rejecting this proposal (which it probably will do), should indicate any "give" in its position, then we should press urgently for a negotiation and not allow the situation to deteriorate further. I gathered that you had had previous discussions with him along these lines and I made no comment.

The President said that he leaned very much toward an ultimate solution, when the appropriate time arrived, involving a private organization of commercial users of the canal, which would operate under contract with the Egyptian Government and which could finance necessary improvements to the canal. I pointed out that there were many hurdles to get over first, among them being an agreement and a treaty which would prevent the Egyptians from doing to a new entity what they had done to the old one. He went on to say, as he has on other occasions, that the general manager should have clear authority to conduct the operations without undue interference from the Egyptians. I believe he envisioned a council or board of directors on which user countries would have representation.

The President told me that he may have been partly responsible for the rash of stories started by Schmidt of the *NY Times* and Higgins of the *Herald Tribune* a few days ago. He said he had propounded his solution to several of his friends and it probably leaked out. I told him of our knowledge that the Egyptians had sent up a similar balloon.

                                                          Hoover

---

305.   Memorandum From the Acting Secretary of State to the Assistant Secretary of State for Near Eastern, South Asian, and African Affairs (Rountree) [1]

Washington, October 6, 1956.

General Cabell advised me this afternoon that a re-evaluation has been made by CIA and the Air Force of all available information concerning the number of Mystere Mark IV's in Israel. It is the combined intelligence estimate, which they consider to be reliable,

---

[1] Source: Department of State, Central Files, 784A.56/10–656. Top Secret. A marginal notation on the source text reads: "Mr. Rountree saw."

that there are in fact 60 Mark IV's now in Israel. The Israelis do not have any Mark II's and have expressed the opinion that they do not wish any in view of the difficulties of maintaining two different types.

At my request, General Cabell is going to forward this information to the Secretary in New York through his own communications system.

H.H. Jr.

---

306.   Telegram From the Embassy in France to the Department of State [1]

Paris, October 6, 1956—5 p.m.

1649. Eyes only Secretary from Dillon. Eyes only Aldrich. The following are my thoughts in response to Deptel 1261. [2]

I feel that French purposes in Suez picture are considerably clearer than those of British Government because of greater unity of French public opinion on subject. Basically French desire a settlement which will recognize principle of international control of the operation of the Suez Canal. French would much prefer reach solution by peaceful means, but if Nasser will not accept such a solution through negotiations the French Government has been and still is prepared to impose solution by military action. France, however, is not in a position to undertake military action alone and can only do so in alliance with Great Britain. Therefore, objectives of British Government become determining in this affair. If British Government has same basic objectives as outlined above for French Government and if Nasser continues to reject 18 nation proposals, then I would think that eventual use of force is likely.

I think some of the confusion regarding French intentions arises because, for very understandable reasons, French Government is not prepared to say to anyone that they intend to use military methods to reach a solution. I continue to feel that such methods will only be used if there is further provocation, probably of a violent nature from Egypt. I also believe, as I have stated before, that it is well

---

[1] Source: Department of State, Central Files, 974.7301/10–656. Top Secret; Priority. Received at 3:07 p.m. Repeated to London. A copy is in the Eisenhower Library, Whitman File, Dulles–Herter Series.

[2] Document 298.

within the power of the British and French to provoke such an incident should they so desire. Outbreak of Arab-Israeli hostilities giving British right to reenter Canal Zone remains another possible excuse for commencement military operations.

Regarding recourse to UN, French say this decision was primarily a British one with which they went along. French basic reasoning was that Eden was committed to take the matter to the UN before undertaking any further action and therefore it was advisable to get this precondition rapidly behind them so as to restore to them their "liberty of action". Naturally French will maintain publicly that they are going to UN in good faith in attempt to seek a solution but they will maintain equally strongly that only solution they can accept is along lines of that presented to Nasser by the Menzies committee.

What French ask of us is not military support, [but] acquiescence in such action should it be taken. They desire above all that US at this time give firm support to 18 nation proposal of international operation and indicate its concern at grave dangers which might arise if Egypt continues to reject such a solution. They feel that if US follows such a line there remains some chance that Nasser will agree rather than face the consequences of probable military action. In other words, they feel that policy of firmness at this stage may still cause Nasser to back down and is best way of avoiding war. Their judgment in this matter may not be good but that nevertheless is the general view here.

If United States does not hold firm in defense principle of international operation, and if war should then break out, French will inevitably attempt pin some portion of responsibility for war on us by saying that our attitude misled Nasser into believing he could successfully continue to defy the West. And if war should come after maintenance of firm position by US, responsibility would be thrown solely on Nasser and Soviets. French would then want us to refrain from condemning their actions and to assume a posture that would inhibit Soviet armed intervention.

Regarding SCUA French are thoroughly confused as to position of American controlled shipping operating under foreign flags. While they recognize that there are legal problems involved what they want to know is what will actually happen. They feel, rightly or wrongly, that US has means if it so desires to prevail upon great majority such ships to make payments into SCUA. If substantially all US owned shipping were to make payments to SCUA I feel certain there would be no doubt as to what French themselves would do. They would also be prepared to pay to SCUA. What they are worried about is possibility of situation arising where only a small percentage of American controlled shipping, namely, those ships flying American flag, would pay to SCUA and the rest would continue payments to Egypt.

Regarding your thinking on major issue of Western European union there is no doubt that development of Suez situation to date has given renewed impetus to concept of European unity in France. Unfortunately, however this impetus is based on a conception of European unity which would be fundamentally anti-American. While I have always been in favor of European unity as such, I have never conceived of it in terms of a union controlled by neutralist groups which would seek to make their own deal with the Soviet Union. Suez developments so far have tended to impair French confidence in NATO and to make them look seriously at possibilities of a strong grouping in Europe which would be able deal directly and on even terms with both US and USSR. Much as we favor principle of European unity I should think that we would view with grave concern the development of a European Union in which the leading foreign policy figures 2 or 3 years hence might well be Bevan for England, Daniel Mayer [3] for France, a member of the SPD for Germany and Nenni or one of his followers for Italy. Such a Western European union however is the type toward which French opinion is tending to veer as they continue to feel let down by US either in Suez or in Algeria.

Even if such a situation should eventuate historical and cultural ties to US would remain far stronger than to USSR. But situation would certainly be more favorable to USSR than anything we have previously thought of.

Dillon

---

[3] French journalist and politician, former Secretary-General of the SFIO.

---

307.   **Memorandum of a Conversation Between Secretary of State Dulles and Foreign Secretary Lloyd, Secretary Dulles' Suite, Waldorf Astoria, New York, October 7, 1956, 6:30 p.m.** [1]

I met alone with Selwyn Lloyd at his request prior to our more general meeting. He said he wanted to speak to me about his distress

---

[1] Source: Department of State, Conference Files: Lot 62 D 181, CF 794. Secret. Drafted by Dulles on October 8.

at persistent newspaper reports that the US and UK were divided on the Suez matter. He said that in fact there was an extraordinary degree of agreement, and that while we might not perhaps be in complete agreement as to what ultimately might happen, we were surely in agreement up to that point. He wondered what could be done to remedy the situation.

I said that I really did not know what could be done. The press constantly sought to give an impression of difference as this was newsworthy. I felt that merely to make statements protesting our agreement might be counterproductive on the theory that we "protest too much". The best thing, I thought, was to plug ahead instructing our press representatives to indicate agreement not just in terms of generalities but in terms of concrete steps that we were taking together. This, I thought, would be more convincing than general statements as to which the press would be skeptical.

I said that with respect to the actual measure of our agreement I thought that we had in fact achieved a remarkable amount of agreement and that even as regards the "ultimate" I did not disagree with the proposition that the possibility of force needed to be kept in the picture. If it wholly disappeared, then the chance of getting an acceptable settlement would also largely disappear.

John Foster Dulles [2]

---

[2] Printed from a copy that bears this typed signature.

308.   Memorandum of a Conversation, Secretary Dulles' Suite, Waldorf Astoria, New York, October 7, 1956, 7:15 p.m. [1]

SUBJECT

Arab-Israel Participation

PARTICIPANTS

The Secretary	Mr. Selwyn Lloyd
Ambassador Lodge	Sir Pierson Dixon
Mr. MacArthur	Mr. Coulson
Mr. Phleger	Sir George Young
Mr. Wilcox	Mr. P.M. Crosthwaite
Mr. Berding	Mr. Beeley
Mr. Tyler	Mr. D. S. Laskey
Mr. Macomber	Mr. Adam Watson
Mr. Ludlow	

Mr. Lloyd raised the question of whether the Israelis should be allowed to come before the Security Council.

The Secretary said that our position was that they should. Mr. Lloyd asked whether the Secretary had in mind their coming to the closed session, and the Secretary replied that he thought they should appear before the Security Council some time later on in the week at the end of the general debate. Mr. Lloyd said he had talked with Ambassador Eban and had tried to dissuade him from pressing the matter on the grounds that it might influence countries like Iraq toward lining up with Egypt. However, Eban had said that Israeli prestige was involved and that his government insisted that Israel should appear briefly and then leave, but not participate in the discussions. Mr. Lloyd said he understood that Pineau had it in mind to play a role in this matter and try to "keep the Arabs in order". Mr. Lloyd said he did not think this would be useful.

Mr. Lloyd queried whether the Arabs and Israelis could be restricted from the private session. He commented that Pineau, as President, was not really the best one to keep the Arabs in order on

---

[1] Source: Department of State, Central Files, 974.7301/10–756. Secret, Drafted by Ludlow. At 6:45 p.m., Dulles and Lloyd, who had been meeting alone (see *supra*), were joined by their advisers for a series of discussions. The U.S. record of these discussions was made according to the subjects discussed: NATO, the Suez Canal Users Association, Arab-Israeli participation in the Security Council debate on Suez, Cyprus, Libya, and Communist Chinese membership in the United Nations. Separate memoranda of these conversations are in Department of State, Conference Files: Lot 62 D 181, CF 788 and CF 794. The discussion on the Suez Canal Users Association is summarized in Document 314.

Also on October 7, Eban sent Dulles a letter, marked "Personal and Urgent", containing a summary of Eban's discussions with Pineau and Lloyd on Israeli participation at the Security Council session. (Department of State, Conference Files: Lot 62 D 181, CF 796)

their participation. Ambassador Lodge hoped the entire matter of Arab-Israeli participation could be put off until Friday. [2]

The Secretary and Lloyd agreed that it would be desirable to postpone. The Secretary went on to comment that it would be very difficult to oppose Israeli participation. He therefore suggested that it would be better to have the closed sessions and secret negotiations and then to take up the Arab-Israeli participation matter later. At that point, participation might be either academic or it might be desirable to inject the Israelis into the Suez matter. He pointed out that one of the strongest indictments of Nasser was his conduct vis-à-vis Israel.

Nasser had now withdrawn the major portion of his forces from the Israeli frontier because of his preoccupation with the Suez matter. Iraqi forces moving into Jordan might soon make an impression upon the other Arabs since the Palestine question and not Suez was their major interest. The stationing of some Iraqi forces in Jordan, if soon carried out, might undermine Nasser's position in Jordan, Syria, and Lebanon, and cause the Jordanians and other Arabs to turn more to Iraq in view of Nasser's action in giving priority to Suez over the Israeli question. It might actually therefore be of some advantage to us in the later stages of discussion if the matter did develop in the Security Council.

Mr. Lloyd indicated relief at our willingness to postpone the matter of participation. He said that Eban had indicated his desire to be heard on Tuesday [3] and that he thought this would present serious difficulties in debate.

The Secretary said he hoped that his speech would be a good wind-up of the Council debate on the matter at this stage prior to going into secret session, which he assumed we might anticipate Tuesday afternoon.

Mr. Lloyd inquired if the speakers in the Council debate had been lined up, and he expressed the hope that we would be able to get into private session on Tuesday.

---

[2] October 12.
[3] October 9.

309.   Report Prepared in the Executive Secretariat of the Department of State [1]

Summary No. 25   *Washington, October 8, 1956.*

SUMMARY OF DEVELOPMENTS IN SUEZ SITUATION

[Here follows a summary of Prime Minister Nehru's letter to Dulles; see footnote 3, Document 303.]

Secretary's Conversations at Security Council

At a meeting of the US, UK, and French delegations preceding Friday's [2] Security Council session, the Secretary agreed that the US would consult with the British and French on possible amendments to the two-power resolution if time permitted. He stated that the US would support the resolution but could not guarantee votes. In a private talk, Shepilov suggested to the Secretary [3] the establishment of a "mechanism" for possible negotiations with Egypt combining the protection of Egyptian sovereignty with the interests of the users. The Secretary replied that it is far better to ascertain first whether the basis for negotiation existed and then set up the mechanism. Shepilov asserted that he is more than ever convinced that any attempt to impose a rigid formula for international operation is bound to fail; he recommended instead Egyptian operation of the Canal with the international participation of all countries. Shepilov said that the Egyptian position is not irreconcilable and Egypt is prepared to search for some compromise as long as her sovereign rights are respected. In another conversation, Spaak voiced his deep concern to the Secretary over the premature recourse to the UN. [4] Spaak stated his conviction that a resort to force is impossible but he fears a UN crisis on top of the Suez problem.

[Here follows discussion of Italy's admission to SCUA executive group (reported in telegram 1884 from London, October 5; Department of State, Central Files, 974.7301/10–556); British stall on payment of tolls to SCUA (British memoranda transmitted in telegram 1888 from London, October 5; *ibid.*); Iran's reaction to the U.K.-French resolution (reported in telegram 541 to Tehran, October 8;

---

[1] Source: Eisenhower Library, Whitman File, International File, Top Secret; Eyes Only for Designated Recipient.

[2] Reference is to a meeting on October 5, a summary of which was transmitted to the Department in Secto 2 from USUN. (Department of State Central Files, 974.7301/10–556) At this meeting, the three delegations also discussed changes in the British-French draft resolution.

[3] See footnote 4, Document 302.

[4] See footnote 3, *ibid.*

ibid.); and possible adherence of Pakistan and Ethiopia to SCUA (reported in telegram 1883 from London, October 5; *ibid.*).]

(Summary closed 12:00 Noon October 8, 1956)

---

310.   Memorandum of a Telephone Conversation Between the President and the Acting Secretary of State, Washington, October 8, 1956, 4 p.m. [1]

The President called Herbert Hoover, said that he had been pondering what should be done in preparation for follow-up if no agreement was reached at the present meeting on the Suez Canal, being held in New York. He said it seemed to him that we should not fail to do something about it, possibly dramatic, possibly even drastic. He said he felt that the question of the Suez was probably #1 question in the minds of the American people. He said that we should tell the Council—"we come before you believing in the program of the first London Conference, but what other suggestions have you to offer?"

He said that there were all sorts of things to consider. The British and the French feel that they have got to cut off Nasser, but nothing would make him madder. President is sure we must do something more than talk.

Dulles has many things in mind, said Hoover. At the present time the Foreign Ministers are "sparring around."

President mentioned the fact that Shepilov tells Dulles one thing, then does another; Hoover said that was typical of the Russian technique.

President really thinks we should find some kind of mechanism to negotiate around. One thing suggested was to have the Security Council meetings in secret, not open to the public, to give a chance to talk in a more constructive way. President would hope that the UN would urge Nasser to confer directly with someone—maybe the Suez Canal Owners Association.

Hoover said that while the French were adamant still on this, the British seem to be taking a more constructive position. He said he was not despairing of the thing at all.

---

[1] Source: Eisenhower Library, Whitman File, Eisenhower Diaries. Prepared in the Office of the President.

President said he would call Dulles, but he never knew when he was free, and people chase him around if they know the President is calling. Hoover said Dulles would like to talk to him and President told him to arrange it at some time (he, the President, is always available). They did talk later in the evening. [2]

President said we ought to think of everything, including having Nehru negotiate—Hoover said if Menon were left out he would not mind—President said that he thought Menon's last suggestion had merit. [3]

---

[2] No account of this conversation has been found in the Eisenhower Library or in Department of State files.

[3] A summary of the plan, which reportedly Menon intended to present to the Egyptian and British Governments, is in the Executive Secretariat's Report for October 5, *supra*.

---

311.   Letter From the President to the Acting Secretary of State [1]

Washington, October 8, 1956.

DEAR HERBERT: As you could tell from my telephone conversation, [2] I have not any very definite views of what I might do either now or in the future in order to prevent the Suez business from getting out of hand. Some thoughts such as the following occur to me:

(a) Assuming that Foster finds the going very sticky at the UN, he might think it helpful if I should issue a White House statement outlining our position and detailing our step-by-step moves to keep the peace. The statement might also contain a frank warning that the United States will not support a war or warlike moves in the Suez area. It would insist that negotiations must be continued until a peaceful but just solution is reached—regardless of how long it takes.

(b) Without direct reference to the Suez, we might make public some of the results of studies conducted under the leadership of

---

[1] Source: Eisenhower Library, Dulles Papers, White House Memoranda. Secret. A marginal notation on the source text reads: "6:20 p.m." The source text, which is signed by Eisenhower, is attached to a covering note from Hoover to Dulles, dated October 8, which reads: "In connection with the attached letter, it occurs to me that as a result of the political situation the President may feel under some pressure to take a more direct part in the proceedings." A copy of Eisenhower's letter is in the Eisenhower Library, Whitman File, Dulles–Herter Series.

[2] See *supra*

ODM concerning the world's future need for big tankers. If we should conclude to go ahead with the construction of some of these (approximately sixty thousand tons) regardless of the Suez affair, the announcement of our intention might have calming effect.

(c) Of course the British and the French are bitterly against building up Nasser. This concern has been rather overtaken by events since he has already become, mostly as a result of this quarrel, a world figure. If therefore, we can think of any plan that we could accept, even though it falls somewhat short of the detailed requirements listed by Britain and France, we might through some clandestine means urge Nasser to make an appropriate public offer. Such action ought to start negotiations toward a peaceful settlement.

(d) Should we be any more specific in our communications with Nehru in the hope that he could influence Nasser into negotiations?

(e) Could the Organization of American States serve any useful purpose now or in the future—such as a joint resolution or the like?

(f) I assume that we are secretly keeping our communications with the oil-producing Arab States, in order to get their influence somewhat on our side.

(g) A more spectacular thing might be for me to invite a number of nations to a conference, including most of the eighteen who agreed upon the "London Plan" as well as India, Egypt, Israel and possibly Saudi Arabia.

As you know, I am immersed in the sum total of affairs necessitated by governmental and political work. None of the items on this list has been deeply studied; I send it to you more as a clear indication of my readiness to participate in any way in which I can be helpful than as a series of suggestions. However, if you see any virtue in any one of these possibilities, please have it studied, but only by your most trusted and reliable staff officers—those that surely will not leak. [3]

With warm regard,

DE

---

[3] On October 8, Hoover replied in a letter which reads: "I have your letter on the Suez situation, pursuant to our telephone conversation of this afternoon, and I am forwarding it to Secretary Dulles in the pouch this evening.

"When I talked with the Secretary later today, he felt somewhat more reassured about the outcome than previously. While nothing specific had taken place, he believed that the atmosphere was a good deal better.

"We will, of course, keep in close touch with you." (Eisenhower Library, Whitman File, Dulles–Herter Series) The letter was initialed by Eisenhower.

312.   Memorandum From Arthur H. Dean to the Secretary of State [1]

New York, October 8, 1956.

Following my conversation with you Friday evening [2] I relayed the information which you had given to me to Ambassador Eban Saturday morning, namely that the Exim Bank probably would not make the loan in the full amount requested but was studying the matter and would probably send a team of experts there shortly and would be making a public announcement to that effect in a few days.

Ambassador Eban appeared quite disappointed and said that plans were all in order for Prime Minister Ben Gurion to make his announcement in the Israeli Parliament on the 15th of October. He again urged that everything possible be done to expedite the paper work with respect to the release of arms in the United States; that everything possible be done to make sure that release of arms by other countries to Israel was going forward without any hitches and that every effort be made to expedite the Exim Bank decision.

As you know, I do not consider that it would be proper for me to recommend that you take any particular action in this matter. But if the United States Government officials have come to the conclusion, as I assume that they have, that they wish these other countries to release arms to Israel and that they wish to help the Israelis with an Exim loan on the internal water development, I would like to emphasize that the time is getting very short in which to work out all the details in order that the expected statement of the Prime Minister that there are no present differences of opinion between the Government of the United States and the Government of Israel on this question of arms can be made on October 15 so that it can be placed on all the wire services.

I noticed that both the Vice President and Senator Kefauver made speeches on this question before a Zionist Congress in Washington yesterday, and, although I did not hear it, I saw an announcement that there was to be a radio address on WRCA yesterday at 12:15 by a Bernard Katzen, sponsored by the Republican Committee, who was to discuss both "Dulles and Israel". Since I think it would

---

[1] Source: Eisenhower Library, Dulles Papers, Israeli Relations 1951–1957. Transmitted to Dulles under cover of a note from Dean which reads in part: "I enclose a memorandum with respect to my conversation with Ambassador Eban on Saturday morning [October 6], which I think is self-explanatory. If there is anything further that you want me to do on this matter, please let me know."

[2] October 5. No account of this conversation has been found in the Eisenhower Library or Department of State files.

not be feasible to do anything after about the middle of this week which Ambassador Eban could cable to his Government, if you are interested in having this announcement made, I would think it essential that all important decisions be arrived at just as soon as possible this week.

I have made it clear to Ambassador Eban that I am not making any recommendations in these matters and I am merely transmitting our discussions.

Respectfully submitted,

Arthur H. Dean

---

313.   Memorandum of a Conversation Between Secretary of State Dulles and Foreign Secretary Lloyd, Foreign Secretary Lloyd's Suite, Waldorf Astoria, New York, October 8, 1956, 10 p.m. [1]

I called on Selwyn Lloyd at his suggestion. He asked to see me alone. He seemed distraught and worried and said he had a press conference with British correspondents who had harassed him about differences with the United States. He had fruitlessly tried to reassure them that we were united.

He then turned to a long cable message which he had just received from Nutting, reporting a talk with Krishna Menon, and he had rather an elaborate outline of a plan which he had received from Menon. This followed with some elaboration the lines which had previously been reported to us [2] . . . . He asked me what I thought should be done with it. I said that that was pretty much up to him. He implied that he thought the outline might be acceptable, but that he did not like to negotiate through Menon.

John Foster Dulles [3]

---

[1] Source: Department of State, Conference Files: Lot 62 D 181, CF 795. Top Secret. Drafted by Dulles.

[2] On October 11, a member of the British Delegation handed Macomber a copy of the plan, which Krishna Menon had presented to the British upon his arrival in New York. The copy is *ibid.*, Central Files, 974.7301/10–1156.

[3] Printed from a copy that bears this typed signature.

314.   Report Prepared in the Executive Secretariat of the Department of State [1]

Summary No. 26   *Washington, October 9, 1956.*

SUMMARY OF DEVELOPMENTS IN SUEZ SITUATION

Secretary's Talk with Egyptian Foreign Minister

Egyptian Foreign Minister Fawzi told the Secretary on October 5 [2] that he foresaw no great difficulty in solving the problem with respect to the principle of "freedom of navigation", and arriving at a ceiling on Canal tolls. Fawzi continued that Egypt desired a peaceful solution and was prepared to recognize the rights of the user nations, and user participation to the extent compatible with Egypt's legitimate interests. Fawzi indicated that the international financing phase of the future operation of the Canal might be a desirable place to introduce the international interests into Canal affairs.

Badawi Sets Forth Egyptian Views

A suggestion made during the course of the Dulles-Fawzi conversation resulted in a meeting the following day between the Department's Legal Adviser, Mr. Phleger, and Helmi Badawi, head of the Egyptian Canal Authority. [3] Phleger and Badawi agreed on the desirability of establishing the principles under which a solution of the problem might be achieved; the details could be negotiated at a later date. Badawi said that Egypt proposed a "TVA" type of operation to run the Canal. He indicated that an international agreement which Egypt could contemplate undertaking might be encompassed in a treaty containing: 1) undertakings concerning Freedom of Navigation; 2) provision for consultation with an international users group regarding improvements to the Canal; 3) the division of tolls into two parts by agreement—one part for improvements and the other for operations and a monetary return. With regard to this latter point, Badawi stated that no tolls would be raised except after consultation, but he refused to agree that tolls would not be raised except by agreement with an international body. Phleger pointed out to Badawi that such a treaty would merely reaffirm treaty engagements which were already binding on Egypt; no practical measures for protecting the rights of the users had been

---

[1] Source: Eisenhower Library, Whitman File, International File. Top Secret; Eyes Only for Designated Recipient.

[2] The memorandum of the conversation, which began at 5:30 p.m., October 5, is in Department of State, Central Files, 974.7301/10–556.

[3] The memorandum of the conversation, which took place on October 6, is *ibid.*, 975.7301/10–656.

set forth. Badawi said that the primary assurance was that it was in Egypt's interest that the Canal be used to the maximum possible extent.

In commenting on his conversation, Phleger said that it was apparent Badawi was not in a position to negotiate. Further, Badawi's proposals may have been set forth to sound us out on the requirements of the situation.

US and UK Positions on Toll Payments

A conversation took place between the Secretary and Lloyd, with their advisers, on October 7. [4] The Secretary stressed that there should be an immediate attempt to change the method of the payment so that SCUA can receive the toll payments. Lloyd said that this was not possible until a contractual arrangement had been reached with the old Suez Canal Company. When the British indicated that it would be two weeks before the UK Government could tell British shippers that they should pay to SCUA, the Secretary said that this was too long. Lloyd said an effort would be made to shorten the period. Phleger indicated that the uncertainty over the French attitude in this connection was disturbing. There was general agreement that the French should also cooperate in making arrangements to pay the tolls to SCUA.

[Here follow sections entitled, "Early SCUA Agreement with Company Seen Essential" (reported in telegram 1923 from London, October 8; Department of State, Central Files, 974.7301/10–856); and "Swedish Allegations Believed Incorrect" (reported in telegram 64 from Port Said, October 6; *ibid.*, 974.7301/10–656).]

(Summary closed 12:45 p.m. October 9, 1956)

---

[4] The memorandum of conversation is *ibid.*, 974.7301/10–756. See footnote 1, Document 308, for a list of other topics discussed during this meeting.

315.   Memorandum of a Conversation, Waldorf Astoria, New York, October 9, 1956, 1:30–3 p.m. [1]

USDel/MC/16

SUBJECT

Suez Canal

PARTICIPANTS

U.S. Side:
Mr. William Rountree
. . .

Egyptian Side:
Mr. Ali Sabry

. . . Mr. Ali Sabry invited . . . us to lunch today in his rooms at the Waldorf-Astoria. The earlier part of the conversation was of a general character, relating mainly to my previous service in Cairo and the Middle East.

We then turned to current United States-Egyptian relations, and Mr. Sabry commented that the American Ambassador and other officials in Cairo had in recent months contacted Egyptian authorities very infrequently; in fact the only meetings which Ambassador Byroade had had with Nasser during the latter weeks of his mission were at the President's request. This reflected a highly unsatisfactory situation and lent credence to reports, now widely circulated, that the U.S. as well as Great Britain and France, had adopted a policy of bringing about the collapse of the Nasser regime. He said this widespread belief with regard to the policies of the Western governments made it extremely difficult for the Egyptian Government to foresee a solution of the Suez controversy, since obviously it could not accept a settlement which was designed in part to bring about its own collapse. He said the Egyptian Government had realized for some time that the British and French were actively seeking the downfall of the regime, but recent actions of the United States, particularly the withdrawal of the Aswan Dam offer and the manner in which it was accomplished, had raised serious questions as to our own intentions.

I spoke at some length on the question of American-Egyptian relations and reviewed the various policies and programs which were designed to help Egypt maintain its independence and progress economically. I went over the Aswan Dam negotiations and the

---

[1] Source: Department of State, Conference Files: Lot 62 D 181, CF 796. Secret. Drafted by Rountree. A marginal notation on the source text reads: "to give most limited distribution".

reasons for the withdrawal of our offer. I spoke particularly of the changes in the economic situation of Egypt which had come about after our offer was made, and alluded to the acutely unfriendly policies and pronouncements of the Egyptian government, which included vitriolic broadcasts, the recognition of Red China, and various other actions of this character. I emphasized that in withdrawing the offer for the Aswan Dam we had done so without recrimination, accompanied only by a perfectly objective and straightforward press announcement. I then pointed to Nasser's reaction, the tenor of his July 26 speech, and the act of nationalization in the explicit context of retaliation. I observed that the Egyptian Government surely must have recognized that such conduct could not but detract from the warm and friendly relations which our two countries had long maintained. Nevertheless, I asserted that we ourselves had by no means given up hope that good relations between the United States and Egypt could be restored and that the question of the Suez Canal, as well as other problems, could be worked out on a mutually advantageous and satisfactory basis. Our policies toward Egypt, moreover, were open and above-board, and the fears which Mr. Sabry had expressed concerning our desire to see the downfall of Nasser had no foundation.

This discussion served the useful purpose of producing a friendly and frank atmosphere and, I think, produced a feeling on the part of Sabry that he could usefully proceed to a more direct exploration of the Suez Canal situation.

Mr. Sabry said that Krishna Menon had formulated a proposal which he (Menon) claimed to have discussed, at least in general, with the British and which he had reason to believe would be accepted by them. Mr. Sabry claimed not to have seen a full presentation of the plan which, he said, had been drawn up in considerable detail. He said Mr. Menon was going to give a copy to Mr. Lloyd and Mr. Fawzi, but he did not know what further distribution would be made. Mr. Sabry did, however, mention various elements of the plan . . . .

Mr. Sabry seemed quite uncertain as to whether or not Mr. Menon would be successful in selling his plan to the Canal users. In reply to questions, he said he did not know how, when or to whom Mr. Menon would present the plan, but if his understanding of it were correct he thought it likely that the Egyptian Government would go along with it in general. He thought, however, that before committing itself, Egypt should have some assurance that the British and other interested governments would likewise find it acceptable.

At that point Mr. Sabry referred to various statements which had been made by the Secretary and others, to the effect that the Egyptians should come forward with a proposal of their own. He found this extremely difficult. In principle he had no objection, but he thought it would be impossible for Egypt to set forth the details of a plan since this would place the burden on Egypt of anticipating what the users required and fitting this into what the Egyptian government and people could accept. He felt that the details of an arrangement should be worked out by virtue of actual negotiations and not in advance of them.

He said that Egypt would be willing to negotiate with anyone with whom practical arrangements night be worked out. He would be perfectly happy to negotiate directly with the British alone, if that were feasible and were the way to bring about "the happy result." On the other hand, he thought the Russians would almost certainly insist upon participating in any negotiations in which the British and the French might be involved. He wondered if it might be possible for Egypt to negotiate with representatives of smaller countries, such as Sweden, India, Italy and Spain; although he recognized the difficulty inherent in this procedure, since these countries would really be negotiating on behalf of others vitally interested and who would be signatories to the treaty involved.

In summary, responding to questions put to him on this subject, Mr. Sabry said that he would be entirely willing to enter into negotiations at once with any group charged with the responsibility of representing the users of the Canal. As he saw it, one of the main difficulties lay in excluding the Soviet Union from such a group (although he definitely said Egypt would not insist upon Soviet participation). He did not have firm objections to putting up Egyptian proposals, although he appeared to be at a loss to know how this might usefully be done in advance of negotiations. He seemed to favor at least the general outline of Mr. Menon's proposals (while denying knowledge of their full content).

Upon leaving, Mr. Sabry said he very much hoped that the "whole problem" could be cleared up while he was in New York, one reason being that he wished to come to Washington to discuss, within the context of a settlement, the broader range of United States-Egyptian relations. I agreed upon the great importance of finding a solution as soon as possible, and said I would be glad to see Mr. Sabry in Washington if he should come down.

After I departed, Mr. Sabry informed . . . that Mr. Lloyd had asked to see Mr. Fawzi.

316.   Telegram From the Embassy in the United Kingdom to the Department of State [1]

London, October 9, 1956—5 p.m.

1932. Eyes only for Secretary. Paris eyes only for Ambassador. I agree that the Suez problem has strained US-British relations to an extent greater than any of the issues which have disturbed our alliance during my four years here and beyond the limits of divergencies which we might regard as generally normal between allies. I am making no comment on our relations with the French because I believe it is wiser to keep our thinking about Great Britain and France separate in contemplating our basic relationships.

It is clear that British thinking and action in regard to Suez have been considerably confused and indecisive, largely I think, because of the degree of emotionalism Nasser's action has aroused. However, although it is obviously an oversimplification, I believe that the basis of the British reaction as it was and still is can be summarized as a conviction that Nasser cannot be permitted "to get away with" nationalization. It is possible that in the face of increasing opposition from labor and other quarters in the UK, the Government's determination to administer Nasser a defeat at all costs has somewhat diminished. At the same time their conviction as to the catastrophic consequences for the Western position in the Middle East and Africa if Nasser is not brought to heel over this matter remains as firm as ever.

British confusion and US–UK divergencies over the methods by which our joint policies in the Middle East and particularly with regard to Nasser should be accomplished result, it seems to me, from a fundamental disagreement as to the time available to us. You will recall that last Spring the British were seriously concerned at the course events in the Middle East were taking and were so convinced that anti-Western developments would occur almost immediately as to suggest a number of immoderate and obviously impractical courses of Western counter-action. They still believe that various governments friendly to the West in the area are imminently threatened by Egyptian and Soviet instigated subversion. They fear violence or even assassination. This feeling is periodically fanned by intelligence reports to which they give credence. Their leaning toward the invocation of military measures is predicated to a considerable extent on these fears.

---

[1] Source: Department of State, Central Files, 974.7301/10–956. Top Secret; Priority. Received at 4:41 p.m. Repeated to Paris. A copy is in the Eisenhower Library, Whitman File, Dulles–Herter Series.

On the other hand, it appears to be our conviction that US–UK and other Western interests in the Middle East can be effectively safeguarded by measures short of war, despite the threat Nasser constitutes. The British are prepared to hope that such is the case and I believe will grasp at any concrete action that we have in mind involving specific measures of a political or economic nature which they believe will have a fair chance of achieving that result. They are floundering, however, since they believe that the various steps we have taken and have urged them to take do not point the way clearly to the results they feel are essential. At present they are clinging to your forthright espousal at the first London conference of the principle of internationalization for the Canal and your concept, expressed at the second London conference, that a solution must be obtained not only peacefully but in accordance with justice and international law. But they do not see how this is to be attained by any political or economic measures which have yet been put forward or espoused by the United States. Fundamentally also, as mentioned above, they remain firmly convinced that such political or economic measures will not take effect sufficiently rapidly to prevent Nasser from consolidating and expanding the psychological advantages his nationalization has so far obtained for him in the Arab World.

With regard to possible negotiations under the auspices of the United Nations, you know better than I what their present position is but up to the present time their position is that such negotiations must be within the framework of the principle of international operation of the Canal and with respect for justice and international law. They have been extremely skeptical that negotiation on this basis will be accepted by Nasser except after military action, but I feel certain that they would still be receptive to being shown what sort of action in the political and economic fields we believe would accomplish the desired end.

I think, for example, that if we were to put to them a policy based upon the concepts outlined in your background press conference of August 19,[2] namely,

1) Get on a basis of negotiation with Nasser to keep the Canal open with the best guarantees we can devise.
2) At the same time make it quite clear

a) that we are starting at once to make ourselves independent of the Canal by construction of tankers and pipelines;

---

[2] On August 19, during the first Suez Canal Conference at London, Dulles held a background briefing for selected American correspondents. The transcript of that briefing was transmitted to the Department of State in Secto 22 from London, August 19. (Department of State, Central Files, 974.7301/8–1956)

b) that we are doing this not in retaliation, or as an economic sanction, but simply because we have lost confidence in Egypt as a dependable partner for the future.

3) Refrain from military or economic sanctions in the short term, and also from additional aid.

a) thus we would show clearly to the world that irresponsible seizure of property doesn't pay;
b) that the West is not using force or economic warfare.

We have an illustration of the effectiveness of such a decision in the reaction of Lebanon to IPC's decision to put its new pipeline through Syria because of Lebanon's unreasonable insistence on high retroactive tax payments.

With regard to the larger issue which is pointed up by this Suez problem and on which you ask my personal and confidential reaction, I have for some time been pondering this question along the lines you set forth. The political divisions in Western Europe are of course fundamentally based on tradition and the proud nationalism of the various nations. The emotions involved go very deep and create barriers to integration which cannot be overcome easily or quickly. They are likely to persist in Europe for a long time regardless of what we do or what Europeans think we will do either in Europe or elsewhere.

The feeling of frustration among the nations of Europe, including Great Britain, is caused primarily by their economic weaknesses enhanced of course by the realization that although they are allied with us we do not see eye to eye on many major issues. Certainly the British do not feel that they have been able to count on our support "automatically and without the exercise of independent judgment" in connection with the problems of the Suez Canal base, with SEATO, with the problem of Communist China, or the questions of East-West trade, and I cannot imagine that anybody would think that we had not exercised our own independent judgment with respect to Cyprus.

[Here follow Aldrich's comments concerning the need for increased economic integration among European nations, including Great Britain, as a means of overcoming frustration and leading toward political integration.]

Aldrich

317.   **Memorandum of a Telephone Conversation Between the Secretary of State in New York and the Acting Secretary of State in Washington, October 9, 1956, 5:54 p.m.** [1]

TELEPHONE CALL FROM MR. HOOVER (one-sided)

The Sec. returned his call. The Sec. said he spoke today, [2] and he thinks it was well received. The British and French were pleased. This p.m. Spaak, Belaunde and the Iranian [3] asked pointed questions to Fawzi. F. made a statement which evaded the answers. Belaunde asked are you willing to deal on a provisional basis with ships going through etc. F. ducked that one. We are in trouble with the British about the Treasury regulation about paying dues because they are very anxious to get them paid to the Users Association and the Sec. thinks they will be willing to issue similar rules themselves—he does not know about the French. The crux is they want to start boats paying to SCUA before SCUA is organized to deal with Egypt. That is liable to precipitate a pretty sharp crisis. We were told today on behalf of Lloyd they would issue the requirement stopping payment to the old Company and require payment to SCUA. The Sec. thinks Picot [4] is in NY now.

The Sec. said he talked with the Pres. after talking with H. yesterday. [5] As far as time is concerned the Sec. sees no reason why he can't come back to Washington for a day or so. They are going into private negotiations. Menon is here with a plan which he is trying to sell. There is a certain reluctance to deal with him. Lloyd, Pineau and Fawzi are in consultation together under the auspices of Hammarskjold and are seeing about getting talks started. The Sec. thinks it is kind of an effort to bypass Menon. Menon has something he talked over with the Egyptians that has some merit in it. Rountree had lunch with Sabri [6] and thinks they are ready to negotiate. The problem is with whom and how. It has not quite crystallized yet. The next formal meeting [7] is secret—Thursday [8]—

---

[1] Source: Eisenhower Library, Dulles Papers, General Telephone Conversations. Transcribed by Bernau in New York.

[2] Reference is to Dulles' statement before the Security Council. For text, see Department of State *Bulletin*, October 22, 1956, pp. 611–615, or *United States Policy in the Middle East, September 1956–June 1957*, pp. 109–111.

[3] Presumably Iranian Representative Djalal Abdoh.

[4] Jacques Georges-Picot, Director-General of the Universal Suez Maritime Canal Company.

[5] No accounts of these conversations have been found in the Eisenhower Library or Department of State files.

[6] See Document 315.

[7] Reference is to a meeting of the Security Council.

[8] October 11.

3:30 and a plenary Friday. The Sec. said today at his suggestion they had a meeting of the representatives of the 18. [9] Did not do much but a good gesture and it gave the Turk [10] a chance to blow off steam—he has been upset. There is another such meeting at 2:30 Thursday. The Sec. said he could come down tomorrow if desirable without prejudice here. It is a little bit of a question of scenery. If you start to go back to confer with the Pres., it looks like a crisis. We don't have very secure telephone system here.

[9] A transcript of this meeting, held at U.N. Headquarters at 3 p.m., October 9, is in Department of State, Conference Files: Lot 62 D 181, CF 796.

[10] Turkish Representative Selim Sarper.

---

318.   Telegram From the Embassy in Israel to the Department of State [1]

Tel Aviv, October 9, 1956—8 p.m.

340. Reference: Embassy telegram 339. [2] Foreign Minister Meir told me this afternoon in serious and emphatic tones that even GOI's conditional consent to, or acquiescence in, movement Iraqi troops to Jordan is withdrawn until GOI understands and approves relationship of plan to (1) Nuri Said's reported statement that it time Israelis "forced" to accept 1947 partition plan (2) British Foreign Office spokesman's statement to effect British welcome Nuri's initiative and prepared to assist under terms Eden's Guildhall speech. [3]

She said situation completely changed since Ben Gurion gave qualified agreement to proposal. Now Israelis would have to know number of things at once. She made it crystal clear that Ben Gurion's cooperation even to extent indicated must now be consid-

[1] Source: Department of State, Central Files, 684A.85/10–956. Secret; Niact. Received at 12:56 a.m., October 10. Repeated Niact to London, Baghdad, and Amman.

[2] Telegram 339 from Tel Aviv, October 9 (*ibid.*) reported that the British Chargé had not yet spoken with Israeli officials concerning Iraqi troop movements, as he still had not heard that Iraq had made the actual decision to move. The Chargé's instructions were to inform Israel of the number of Iraqi troops, the date of their entry into Jordan, and Nuri Said's assurances that he had no aggressive intentions. He was also to remind Israel that the Anglo-Jordanian Treaty remained in effect. Consequently, Lawson requested authority to convey to Israel what Iraq had told the United States concerning its troop movements (reported in telegram 576 from Baghdad, October 6; *ibid.*, 684A.85/10–656).

[3] Reference is presumably to news reports in the *Times* of London on October 8 and 10.

ered as in abeyance until such time as he satisfactorily assured Iraqi troop movements are in no way connected with Iraqi-British program, objective of which is to force Israel into negotiations which would involve territorial concessions on her part or plan involving Iraqi-Jordan treaty if its invocation were for purposes detrimental to Israel's present boundaries or security (Embtel 330). [4] She asked if British were dreaming old dreams of merging not only Iraq and Jordan but also Syria?

Further details of conversation will be contained in following telegram. [5]

Lawson

---

[4] In telegram 330 from Tel Aviv, October 6 (Department of State, Central Files, 684A.85/10–656), Lawson confirmed that he had conveyed to Ben Gurion the views contained in telegrams 266 and 268 to Tel Aviv (see Documents 295 and 296). In reply, Ben Gurion requested specific information concerning the disposition of Iraqi troops in Jordan and requested clarifications from Washington on whether the movement was the first step in an agreed plan for Iraq to annex Jordan.

[5] Telegram 346 from Tel Aviv, October 10, contained an elaboration of points made by Meir which are summarized in telegram 340. Meir also asked for immediate full consultation with the United States and noted that Israel must know what Britain was about. (Department of State, Central Files, 684A.85/10–1056)

---

319.   Memorandum From the Representative at the United Nations (Lodge) to the Secretary of State [1]

New York, October 10, 1956.

Dixon handed me (for a "quick look") a copy of a telegram which Selwyn Lloyd sent to his Government last night giving his account of the meeting yesterday in Hammarskjold's office between Lloyd, Pineau, Fawzi and Hammarskjold. [2] What I remember of it is as follows:

---

[1] Source: Department of State, Central Files: Lot 62 D 181, CF 796. Secret.

[2] On October 10, Peter Ramsbotham, First Secretary of the British Delegation at the United Nations, gave Charles D. Cook, James Ludlow, and Norman Armour, Jr. of the U.S. Delegation an account of this meeting, based on Lloyd's report to London. (Memorandum of conversation by Ludlow, October 11; *ibid.*) A "Memorandum for the Files" by Cook, dated October 10, contains a more detailed account of Ramsbotham's presentation. (USUN Files, Unnumbered Files, Suez Canal) According to this memorandum, Ramsbotham reported that Fawzi, Lloyd, and Pineau met with Hammarskjöld on the morning of October 9 in the office of the President of the Security Council, for the purpose of establishing procedures for the afternoon secret session of the Security Council. Fawzi indicated that he would like to proceed into "private talks";

Fawzi said that he would accept any one of three alternatives to the Convention of '88: to leave it as it is, to change it, or to negotiate a new Convention.

He would agree on setting aside a definite percentage of the Canal revenues for development.

He would recognize the Suez Canal Users Association but he thought that Russia and India should be members. He appeared to agree with Lloyd's point that it was intolerable that a country like Yemen or Albania should have equal voting rights with England and France.

Fawzi appeared to favor a compromise between the international and the national viewpoints but was vague as to how the international viewpoint would be expressed. He said that he would agree to arbitral tribunal to settle complaints which might arise.

Fawzi said it was not impossible to use pilots employed by the SCUA.

He did not shut the door on using UN personnel.

He was vague on the question of paying dues to the Suez Canal Users Association.

He was also vague on the question of Israeli shipping.

---

subsequently, at Hammarskjöld's request, a meeting was held that afternoon in Hammarskjöld's office. See Document 326.

320.   Memorandum of a Conversation, New York, October 10, 1956, 11:30 a.m. [1]

USDel/MC/20

SUBJECT

Meeting with the Secretary-General on Suez Problems

PARTICIPATION

US Side:
The Secretary
Ambassador Lodge
Mr. Herman Phleger
Mr. Francis Wilcox
United Nations:
The Secretary-General

We met with the Secretary-General in his office at 11:30. The Secretary explained that he planned to go to Washington tonight and would see the President in the morning. He thought in making his report to the President he should have the benefit of the Secretary-General's ideas as to how things were proceeding.

The SYG expressed guarded optimism about the progress of discussions so far. He said he had talked with Dr. Fawzi after the first Security Council Meeting [2] and had gotten the impression that he (Fawzi) had a considerable margin within which to negotiate although he was not in a position to accept "this or that plan". He believed that the use of the term "system of cooperation" in Fawzi's speech was an indication of that fact. He interpreted these words to mean cooperation with the organized users of the canal. The Secretary pointed out that Fawzi drew away from any definition of this term in the speech during the secret Council meeting yesterday.

The SYG quoted Fawzi as saying that it was a pity Menon was coming to New York. He (Fawzi) could speak for the Egyptians himself. The SYG then commented upon his role in encouraging the British and French to establish direct contact with Egypt. He said he believed all along that the technique of secret meetings coupled with two or three days of private negotiations would prove most fruitful.

He then reported on the meeting he had had with the British, French and Egypt yesterday afternoon. [3] He said that Fawzi had suggested it might be helpful not to refer to the "national" or

---

[1] Source: Department of State, Central Files, 974.7301/10–1056. Secret. Drafted by Wilkins.

[2] Reference is presumably to the 735th meeting of the Security Council held on October 5.

[3] See supra.

"international" administration of the canal but to speak instead of "a system of cooperation". Moreover, Fawzi accepted the Secretary's principle that the canal should be insulated from the political influences of any country.

In general the SYG felt that there were sufficient constructive elements in Fawzi's position to give some notion of direction to the negotiations and to lend some degree of hope for a positive outcome. He said Fawzi seemed to be willing to accept the idea of an arbitrarial [sic] court, some kind of enforcement procedures, and that he would not say "no" to the idea of the users collecting fees, paying a portion of the fees to Egypt for services rendered. He also referred to some type of United Nations recruitment for certain high authorities in the canal system.

The Secretary reminded the SYG that Fawzi does not enjoy the confidence of Nasser and that Sabry was presumably in a better position to reflect Nasser's views. He expressed general approval of the three parties meeting with the SYG but suggested that the SYG's role was really not one of a chaperon (as the latter had suggested) because a chaperon is one whose function is to keep people apart and he thought the SYG's function in this case was that of bringing countries together. He said there was a great deal to be done within the next day and that something concrete ought to be put down in writing very soon. The time might come, he added, when the Secretary-General would want to play a more active role. He might, for example, set down the areas of agreement among the parties.

The Secretary added that the United States was anxious to see a peaceful solution of the situation. He said he was being prepared as a lamb for slaughter in England and in France but that was all right with him if a peaceful solution emerged. He also pointed out that our ability [to] moderate the United Kingdom and France position was pretty well exhausted since we had used our influence upon them from the time of the first London conference. He believed further that the situation had reached such a stage that Egypt should be expected to make the next contribution. She had made none so far.

The heart of the thing, said the Secretary, is that we must have a system which will reasonably protect the users of the canal against the capacity of Egypt to use the canal as an instrument of its own policy—to delay or to tie up or to obstruct the shipping of other countries. If the situation is such that when Egypt disagrees with another country on a matter of policy it would be in a position to interfere with shipping from that country, that would be bad. We need not concern ourselves so much about overt acts. Covert acts and acts of sabotage or deliberate delay are more to be feared. In this connection we were prepared to back the United Kingdom and

France. The job would be to get Egypt to accept their point of view in this regard.

The Secretary also pointed out that we must have efficient machinery which could act quickly with respect to any complaints filed by the users countries. Action by the World Court or the General Assembly would not be fast enough.

The Secretary said he wanted the Secretary-General to feel that the United States will stand ready to do anything we can although we would stand firm on this one point. He went on to add that our goodwill with France and Britain was not really exhausted and that we might be able to help in some way. He then referred to the French and British position in the Middle East pointing out that the French and British people do not want to get involved in hostilities. Even so, while the danger of war had abated, we could not overlook the possibility that conflict might break out. The canal problem itself is difficult enough but recent developments in North Africa make it much more complex. In addition, he said, the United Kingdom is afraid of losing its position in a number of the Arab countries.

If a plan can be evolved that makes sense and meets the major principle we have stated, said the Secretary, then it would be very difficult for any country not to take it.

Mr. Phleger pointed out that it is not a sufficient remedy for mistreatment of the users ships to be able to take such cases to arbitration. What is needed he said is a method of *preventing* difficulties from arising. You can't run a canal or a railroad by arbitration he said. The Secretary admitted that we would not be able to set up a system that would be 100% effective and he was not clear in his own mind what precise role the United Nations could play in such a system. The SYG commented that if there were two bodies cooperating with each other, with another body or agency above to which appeals might be taken, a workable system could perhaps be devised.

Mr. Wilcox inquired about the role of the United Nations in the appointment of officials in the Canal Company—whether Fawzi had suggested such appointments were to be made by the United Nations with the approval of Egypt or vice versa. The SYG replied that Fawzi had been unclear on this point and he did not know what the precise lines of authority would be. He thought that Fawzi had in mind more the possibility of securing officials from United Nations sources—presumably in the more technical aspects of canal administration. These would be on loan from the UN, but paid by Egypt and subject to its order, but they could quit if they thought matters were not being run properly. These would be selected by the UN Secretariat. It had provided UN personnel to Morocco and Tangier on this basis.

321.   Memorandum of a Conversation, New York, October 10, 1956, 12:30 p.m. [1]

USDel/MC/20c

SUBJECT

  Suez

PARTICIPANTS

  Selwyn Lloyd, Great Britain
  Christian Pineau, France
  The Secretary
  The US, French and British Ambassadors to the UN
  French Ambassador to Washington
  Mr. Phleger
  Mr. Rountree
  (Several additional British and French officials were also present during
    the meeting preceding the luncheon)

At 12:30 p.m., the Secretary and the British and French Foreign Ministers met with members of their staffs for an informal discussion just prior to a luncheon at 1:15 given by the French Ambassador to the UN. The pre-luncheon talks were held in small groups and it is therefore not possible to record the full scope of this meeting. The most significant aspect seemed to be an exchange between the French and British Foreign Ministers with the Secretary, in which they took the line that while an agreement with the Egyptians seemed otherwise practicable, it was very difficult to see how they could meet their respective political situations at home. They seemed to be considering the practical aspects of selling to public opinion a negotiated settlement.

At the luncheon the discussion also was fairly general, and toward the end turned to an effort to evaluate the seriousness of the Egyptians in their negotiations and the extent to which Foreign Minister Fawzi had authority to speak for President Nasser. There otherwise were no significant developments.

---

[1] Source: Department of State, Central Files, 974.7301/10–1056. Confidential. Drafted by Rountree.

322.   Memorandum of a Conversation, New York, October 10, 1956 [1]

USDel/MC/32

SUBJECT

Suez Canal

PARTICIPANTS

US Side
The Secretary
Mr. William Rountree
(The Secretary joined the conversation briefly at one point)
Israel
Ambassador Eban
Mr. Shiloah

Ambassador Eban said he had several matters to discuss with me. First was the proposed statement drafted by the Export-Import Bank in connection with the Israel application for a loan to finance water development work in Israel. [2] He said the statement as drafted gave no indication that the Bank had made a decision in principle to finance the project, and thus would probably do more harm than good. He earnestly hoped that wording could be added to the effect that, subject to the findings of the Mission, the Bank was prepared in principle to assist in financing the program. [3]

I told the Ambassador that the matter had been discussed earlier in the day with Mr. Waugh and that since the Bank had not made such an affirmative decision Mr. Waugh felt that the statement could not be amended as suggested. However, we hoped that it might be possible to add to the statement in some manner to make it more attractive from the Israeli viewpoint, but that the matter was one for decision by the Bank. I had understood that Mr. Waugh

---

[1] Source: Department of State, Central Files, 974.7301/10–1156. Secret. Drafted by Rountree. The source text is incorrectly dated October 11; the chronology prepared by the U.S. Delegation indicates that this conversation took place on October 10. (*Ibid.*, Conference Files: Lot 62 D 181, CF 797)

[2] The text of a proposed Export-Import Bank press release is attached to a memorandum from Joseph Palmer II to Hoover, dated October 9. The press release contains the announcement that the Export-Import Bank was planning to send a Mission to Israel about the end of October in conjunction with its study of an Israeli proposal to supplement and expand Israel's land development program. The press release also noted that an on-the-ground examination of existing projects and potential resources for further land development was a normal procedure for the Bank. (*Ibid.*, Central Files, 884A.10/9–2956)

[3] During a telephone conversation on October 11, Samuel Waugh informed Dulles that the Board of the Export-Import Bank refused to change the statement, as requested by Eban. (Memorandum of telephone conversation by Bernau, October 11; *ibid.*, 103–XMB/10–1156)

intended telephoning the Ambassador that afternoon to discuss alternative wording, and I suggested the Ambassador get in touch with Mr. Waugh to pursue the matter with him.

The Ambassador then referred to the Security Council consideration of the Suez Canal problem. He said he had read the Secretary's speech [4] with great interest and admiration. He had noted the emphasis which the Secretary had placed upon the necessity for insulating the control of the traffic from the politics of any one country. The Secretary had not, however, mentioned specifically the Egyptian refusal to permit transit of Israeli vessels. Because of the juridical background of this case and the fact that the denial of Israeli traffic was in fact the one concrete violation of the 1888 Convention, the Israeli Government would greatly appreciate it if the Secretary would seek an opportunity during the course of the Council deliberations to mention specifically the Israeli case. The Secretary joined the group at this point [5] and told the Ambassador that he would bear his request in mind and would try to make an appropriate statement if a satisfactory occasion presented itself, which he hoped it would.

The Secretary referred to previous conversations which he had had with the Ambassador concerning the Israeli request that their representative be heard by the Security Council. He had talked with Mr. Pineau, President of the Council, and had expressed the hope that the Israeli request could be met. The Secretary suggested that the Ambassador get in touch with Mr. Pineau to pursue the matter. (At this point the Secretary departed from the meeting.)

Ambassador Eban said that after the recent discussions in Tel Aviv and Washington concerning plans for Iraqi troops to be sent to Jordan, several disquieting events had occurred. First was the indication that the United Kingdom supported an Iraqi proposal that the Arab-Israel dispute be settled on the basis of a compromise which would be very much at Israel's expense. The proposal contemplated use of the 1947 UN Resolution, which would truncate Israel and would do serious damage to the only outpost of Western democracy in the Near East. The second development was an indication that the force would not be entirely temporary but would be the beginning of a movement for the annexation by Iraq of Jordan. He said that as a result of these developments Israel had considerable misgivings and wished to discuss the matter further before formalizing any agreement not to object to the movement of Iraqi troops. I told the Ambassador that on the basis of previous conversations which we

---

[4] See footnote 2, Document 317.
[5] According to Dulles' Appointment Book, the Secretary joined this conversation at 3:55 p.m. and left at 3:59 p.m. (Princeton University Library, Dulles Papers)

had had, some steps had already proceeded. I understood that conversations were going on in Tel Aviv between Ambassador Lawson and the Israeli Government, and also that the British Embassy was to discuss the matter with the Government. I would, of course, take note of his comments. I earnestly hoped that in view of the great importance of stability [in] the situation in Jordan, and of reducing Egyptian influence in that country, the Israel Government would agree to the wisdom of having Iraq move as planned within the limitations which had previously been set forth and which had been communicated to the Iraqi Government.

---

323.   Letter From the Acting Secretary of State to the President [1]

Washington, October 10, 1956.

DEAR MR. PRESIDENT: I have your letter of October 8 [2] raising a number of questions on the Suez situation.

The Secretary, I believe, would want to discuss personally with you three of your thoughts, namely, the possibilities of a White House statement, a plan wherein Nasser would make a public offer, and your calling another conference.

The other points contained in your letter were discussed by me with some of our senior officers and I am enclosing a memorandum covering them.

Faithfully yours,

Herb

[Attachment]

MEMORANDUM

1. *Question:* "Without direct reference to the Suez, we might make public some of the results of studies conducted under the leadership of ODM concerning the world's future need for big

---

[1] Source: Eisenhower Library, Whitman File, Dulles–Herter Series. Secret. Initialed by Eisenhower. A copy of this letter and the attachment are in Department of State, Central Files, 974.7301/10–1056.

[2] Document 311.

tankers. If we should conclude to go ahead with the construction of some of these (approximately sixty thousand tons) regardless of the Suez affair, the announcement of our intention might have a calming effect."

Answer: We are in close contact with Dr. Flemming and Governor Adams on the desirability of appointing an advisory group to study this matter.

2. *Question:* "Should we be any more specific in our communications with Nehru in the hope that he could influence Nasser into negotiations?"

Answer: We should not be any more specific in communications with Nehru than we have been. The President and the Secretary have already had several exchanges of views with Nehru. [3] During recent years India has tended to support the general course of Egyptian foreign policy; however, the Indian reaction to Nasser's nationalization of the former Suez Canal Company has been tempered by India's realization of its own dependence upon the Suez Canal. Nehru and his representative, Khrishna Menon, have been active in recent weeks, we believe, making suggestions to Nasser for a solution to the Suez Canal operations. The United States continues to support the principles contained in the 18-power proposal which provide for international participation in the Suez Canal operation. Nehru understands American flexibility within this framework. If we should now attempt to be more specific in communications to Nehru we might give an erroneous impression of willingness to compromise and thus undermine the general U.S.-U.K.-French discussions with the Egyptians in New York. As the United States now is in direct touch with the Egyptian officials in New York, it would be preferable to hold direct discussions with them. At the same time, it may be assumed that India will continue its own efforts to persuade Egypt to moderate its views.

3. *Question:* "Could the Organization of American States serve any useful purpose now or in the future—such as a joint resolution or the like?"

Answer: The Organization of American States could serve a more useful purpose in the future rather than at the present time. If there should be some agreement between Egypt and the Western powers, the OAS might be persuaded to adopt a joint resolution supporting the agreement. Effective action through the OAS at this stage would not be useful because: (a) Panamanian resentment over exclusion from the London conference; (b) some Latin American countries,

---

[3] This correspondence is in Department of State, Presidential Correspondence: Lot 66 D 204, Prime Minister Nehru's Correspondence with Eisenhower/Dulles 1953–1961.

such as Chile, are lukewarm regarding the U.S. position on the Suez Canal, although other Latin American countries, such as Brazil, Cuba and Venezuela, have been favorable; (c) the principle of nationalization has been popular in Latin America; (d) the involvement of the U.K. and France introduces an overtone of colonialism into the matter; and (e) it might precipitate debate about the status of the Panama Canal.

4. *Question:* "I assume that we are secretly keeping our communications [open] with the oil-producing Arab States, in order to get their influence somewhat on our side."

Answer: The United States has continued in close touch with the oil-producing Arab States, including especially Saudi Arabia, Iraq and Iran. In Saudi Arabia there have been a number of personal and confidential communications at a high level between King Saud and American officials regarding the Suez Canal. In Iraq we have endeavored to assist the Iraq Prime Minister on several important matters, including Iraq's relations with Saudi Arabia and with Jordan. In Iran we have continued consulting with the Shah and other Iranian officials on various aspects of Near Eastern matters, including the Baghdad Pact and SCUA.

---

324.   Telegram From the Department of State to the Embassy in Israel [1]

Washington, October 10, 1956—7:42 p.m.

287. Embtel 340. [2] Department continues to believe that entry Iraqi troops into Jordan will have effect of stabilizing situation there and recalls that Ben Gurion had no objection (Jerusalem 91) [3] provided Iraqi troops remained east of Jordan. BG's request for assurances this point and related matters were subsequently met. More detailed information re Iraqi troop movement which GOI has requested must necessarily come from Iraqi sources. We believe UK will shortly provide such information if Nuri agrees.

Our feeling that Iraqi move is in interest area stability, is in no way diminished by statements attributed in London *Times* to Nuri

---

[1] Source: Department of State, Central Files, 684A.85/10–956. Secret. Drafted by Wilkins and Bergus and approved by Wilkins who signed for Hoover. Repeated to London, Baghdad, Amman, and USUN.

[2] Document 318.

[3] See Document 289.

and by FonOff comment. We have discussed these statements with British Embassy and understand they represent reiteration earlier positions. Statement that USG knows of no plan for Iraqi annexation of Jordan and that we have noted Israel view that present status quo in NE (Deptel 278)[4] should be maintained should also prove reassuring on this point.

Department has renewed to British Embassy its belief that time has arrived for British Chargé Tel Aviv to make known to Govt Israel that UK favors Iraqi movement of troops to Jordan and that Nuri has reassured UK action was entirely defensive. Department also believed UK which is in touch with Nuri would be in better position to obtain Nuri's consent to supply information re troop movements to GOI. British Embassy reports that FonOff has said in response our earlier discussion with British (Embtel [Deptel] 284)[5] that there appeared be case for immediate British approach to GOI.

London has authorized British Chargé talk to Ben Gurion provided Nuri concurs. British Embassy Baghdad has been instructed report to Tel Aviv results its conversation with Nuri on this matter.

Substance of first two paragraphs should be conveyed to FonMin and if possible to BG, at earliest opportunity.

Hoover

---

[4] Telegram 278, October 8, transmitted to Tel Aviv a report on U.S. discussion with the British Embassy about the proposed Iraqi troop movements and Israeli concerns regarding the matter. (Department of State, Central Files, 684A.85/10–856)

[5] Telegram 284 to Tel Aviv, October 9, reported that the British Embassy in Washington had agreed to suggest urgently to the Foreign Office in London that the British Embassy in Tel Aviv immediately discuss the Iraqi troop movement with the Israeli Government. (Ibid., 684A.85/10–956)

325.   Telegram From the Department of State to the Embassy in Egypt [1]

Washington, October 10, 1956—7:53 p.m.

1107. Re Cirtel 106 [2] and 183. [3] Dept discussed with Defense [4] military operations plan for Middle East and status evacuation plans and action taken to date. Defense stressed 1) its over-all responsibilities in Europe and Middle East, 2) fact US does not have sufficient forces or equipment Europe and Middle East available meet simultaneous tactical and evacuation needs present number US nationals in area nor enough airlift cover entire area at one time and 3) fact normal commercial means cannot be depended upon if evacuation has to take place after start hostilities or serious trouble and inability military guarantee safe evacuation all US nationals this situation.

In view above Defense expressed concern its limited capability for evacuation all US nationals particularly if simultaneous action several countries necessary and requested Dept assure US official dependents and representatives American interests in area 1) understand that general situation in Middle East is such that hostilities or mob violence could commence suddenly and 2) are aware of limitations under which military would be operating if large-scale evacuation becomes necessary and impossibility evacuating all US nationals safely at such time.

---

[1] Source: Department of State, Central Files, 280.1122/10–1056. Top Secret; Limited Distribution. Drafted by Ryan (NEA/EX) and Wilkins; cleared with Berry and Murphy (G) and in draft with McQuaid (SCA), Henderson, MacArthur, and ISA in the Defense Department; approved by Murphy who signed for Hoover. Also sent to Amman and Damascus and repeated to Baghdad, Beirut, Tel Aviv, Jidda, Dhahran, Tripoli, Paris, Rome, Kuwait, and Jerusalem.

[2] Circular telegram 106, August 8, informed the Embassies in Amman, Baghdad, Beirut, Cairo, Damascus, Jidda, and the Consulates General at Dhahran and Jerusalem that it had ordered the adoption of Phase I of evacuation procedures in Egypt and that recipients should re-establish a 24-hour security watch, report any untoward developments, and discuss the situation with responsible leaders in the U.S. community. (*Ibid.*, 274.1122/8–856)

[3] Circular telegram 183, September 7, cautioned the Embassies in Amman, Baghdad, Beirut, Cairo, Damascus, Jidda, Tripoli, the Consulates General at Dhahran and Jerusalem, and the Consulate at Kuwait that tension might increase in the area following the termination of Menzies' talks in Cairo. As Arab action against oil installations was possible, recipients were instructed to advise U.S. companies to take all possible measures to guard against sabotage. (*Ibid.*, 774.00/9–756)

[4] Reference is to the Department of State–Joint Chiefs of Staff meeting held on September 28 at 11:30 a.m. at the Pentagon. A memorandum on the substance of the discussions is *ibid.*, State–JCS Meetings: Lot 61 D 417.

At the Secretary of State's 9:15 a.m. Staff Meeting on September 28, Rountree and MacArthur noted that the Department of Defense for several months had been writing extensively for the record concerning evacuation plans, in an effort to record their blamelessness, if difficulties arose. (Tentative Notes; *ibid.*, Secretary's Staff Meetings: Lot 63 D 75)

In connection general situation area Dept desires stress it has no information indicating hostilities or mob violence imminent any NEA country.

In discussions Dept pointed out 1) policy US Govt endeavor bring about peaceful settlement Suez problem and 2) relationship evacuation action to political situation including possibility large-scale withdrawal US nationals would be misinterpreted by other countries to mean US believed hostilities imminent and thereby precipitate type of action and repercussions US earnestly trying prevent.

For present Dept feels Phase I should be continued in Egypt, Syria and Jordan and general security coverage should be maintained in other NEA posts receiving this message for information. All posts addressed in further discussions situation with appropriate elements American community should, without arousing undue alarm, make sure these elements understand limitations of Defense if it should be called upon take evacuation action on short notice particularly if hostilities or mob action have already started.

Hoover

---

326. **Memorandum of a Conversation Between Secretary-General Hammarskjöld and the Representative at the United Nations (Lodge), Two Park Avenue, New York, October 10, 1956, 10 p.m.** [1]

USDel/MC/24a

SUBJECT

Suez in the Security Council

At 10:00 p.m. Wednesday, October 10, I called on Hammarskjold to get his account of the afternoon meeting with Pineau, Lloyd and Fawzi. [2] Hammarskjold's report was as follows:

---

[1] Source: Department of State, Conference Files: Lot 62 D 181, CF 797. Secret. Drafted by Lodge.

[2] At 8 a.m. the following morning the British Embassy in Washington delivered to the Department of State a copy of a report by Foreign Secretary Lloyd of the conversation among Lloyd, Pineau, and Fawzi, which took place in Hammarskjöld's office during the afternoon of October 10, and requested that the report be brought to the attention of Secretary Dulles. The report, not printed, is *ibid.*, Central Files, 974.7301/10–1056.

Pineau appeared to feel trapped. Lloyd was seriously looking for a way to make progress. In a skillful and consistent manner he put questions to Fawzi. Pineau got "greener and greener" at the picture of the split between him and Lloyd in the presence of Fawzi. He also didn't understand English so an interpreter had to be brought in.

Lloyd put questions to Fawzi that put him "right up against the wall and yet he did it in such a way as not to break any bridges".

Positive replies by Fawzi made Pineau feel that we were getting closer to a sensible solution, but, of course, a sensible solution is not what Prime Minister Mollet wants.

Hammarskjold said the real worry is what is Fawzi's power. He knows Fawzi well and says he is an extremely prudent man who has survived three changes of Government and that he is not binding himself. Moreover, Fawzi told Hammarskjold that he had "checked matters with his colleagues". When Lloyd got to the crucial points Fawzi replied honestly but preliminarily, and on the basis of referring it back to his Government. Fawzi was eager to get something on paper—not a record, but a summary of the stands that had been taken and he suggested that Hammarskjold do it. Hammarskjold said Nasser may let Fawzi down but Fawzi is not bluffing.

Lloyd was very constructive and able and Pineau was very worried.

There were two elements in the conversation.

The first was when Fawzi began by asking Hammarskjold: "Will you now give us the picture of where we stand?" Hammarskjold did this along the lines of the statement that he made to Dulles yesterday.[3] Lloyd and Fawzi agreed on Hammarskjold's summation but Pineau evinced no reaction.

Secondly, Lloyd directed his questions along the line: "What is Egypt's attitude toward SCUA?"

Pineau said: "Yesterday you told us you were willing to cooperate, now the press says you condemn it, how about it?"

Fawzi's answer was that the SCUA construction was none of Egypt's business—but it must be a serious and manageable organization and those who have ships and those who have cargo should be treated equitably. In the statute itself of SCUA there is an unacceptable provision, that is that the Users' Association should levy the tolls. That is something which must be negotiated.

Hammarskjold asked: "Does this mean that SCUA, if these adjustments are made till [will still] be acceptable?"

---

[3] See Document 320.

Fawzi: "Yes, but I don't want to put it that way. I prefer to talk about SCUA as it would be following an arrangement after the arrangement [*agreement*] was reached".

Fawzi also raised two further questions: (1) Will the Users' Association be entitled to pay tolls and charges from ships of nations which are not members?

Lloyd and Pineau said no—only for their own members. Lloyd added only to the extent that their own members agreed. In other words, the Users' Association has no monopolistic character.

(2) Fawzi said he wanted to raise a practical difficulty as follows: If a ship comes in, the officer must pay the toll. How is it paid?

Lloyd said the ship pays the tolls directly or the Captain gets it paid by an agent, it doesn't matter to you.

Fawzi said yes, the main thing is no discrimination. We will not raise legal difficulties as between the agent and the ship owner.

Pineau appeared very upset at this and said it was a crucial point of prestige.

Hammarskjold said that with what was already on the table— that is the Egyptian board, the Users' Association, the Administrative Tribunal, there was enough to make a pretty good piece of paper. He said that the plan was to meet tomorrow in the morning (this morning, October 11) to discuss guarantees, checks and controls, then to meet after the Security Council session Thursday afternoon and "sit until the end".

Lloyd said he would not make up his mind until the end as to whether or not he would press the resolution [4] to a vote in the Security Council.

Pineau said he wanted to raise in the secret meeting on Thursday [5] afternoon whether, on Friday, to hear Israel and one Arab state publicly.

Hammarskjold said this was unrealistic. You could not hear one Arab state, you had to hear them all. Moreover, he said, it was a very bad idea to have that whole performance out in public.

Lloyd said you couldn't decide the Friday meeting until later.

Hammarskjold thought Pineau had been very unwise with the press. He had said that there would be a short meeting tomorrow and he gave the press the impression that the talks had broken down, and notably in his statement that "Fawzi was more precise but did not change my opinion".

---

[4] Reference is to the U.K.-French resolution submitted on October 5; see Document 299.

[5] October 11.

The essence of it all is that Lloyd is working realistically for a practical arrangement with the Egyptians and Pineau feels he has been left in the lurch.

---

327.   Memorandum of a Conversation Among the President, the Secretary of State, and the Under Secretary of State (Hoover), White House, Washington, October 11, 1956, 9 a.m. [1]

We discussed at some length the Suez situation. I reported on the state of affairs at the United Nations, and my information as to the developments which had occurred at the meeting at Hammarskjold's office of Lloyd and Pineau with Fawzi. [2] It was, I thought, quite apparent that Lloyd was groping for some practical solution which would measurably give international assurance that the Canal would be safely and impartially operated, that Pineau was unsympathetic and that the Egyptians were somewhat evasively disposed to move toward what might be an acceptable solution.

The President mentioned that he had had a talk with Haley of *The London Times* [3] and had expressed to him the feeling that we should be satisfied with some form of international contact that would reasonably assure the operation of the Canal.

I outlined to the President the points which I had made in my speech before the Security Council [4] and the distinction between "principles" and "mechanisms" with which the President heartily agreed. He said he might make this point if the occasion offered at his forthcoming press conference. The President again expressed his view against military operations. I told him about my statement to

---

[1] Source: Eisenhower Library, Dulles Papers, Meetings with the President. Secret; Personal and Private. Dulles had returned to Washington on October 10 at 7 p.m. (Dulles' Appointment Book; Princeton University Library, Dulles Papers)

[2] At 8:45 a.m., October 11, Lodge briefed Dulles over the telephone regarding Hammarskjold's meeting with Lloyd, Pineau, and Fawzi on October 10 (see *supra*). (Memorandum of telephone conversation by Bernau, October 11; Eisenhower Library, Dulles Papers, General Telephone Conversations) No indication has been found that Dulles had received the British report of the meeting which had been delivered to the Department of State at 8 that morning (see footnote 2, *supra*).

[3] Sir William Haley, editor of *The Times* (London). Eisenhower met with him on October 10 at 2:30 p.m. (Record of the President's Daily Appointments; Eisenhower Library)

[4] See footnote 2, Document 317.

Lloyd at the Pineau luncheon [5] to the effect that the British had had their chance at a military solution when they were lawfully at the Suez Base with their 88,000 military personnel.

They then were lawfully there under a Treaty and with ample force and felt they could not stay without unduly extending themselves. I could not see why they should go back under more adverse conditions to a situation which they found intolerable under relatively favorable conditions.

The President spoke of various ideas he had had [6] and which I said we were studying. I thought some of them we were actually carrying out. I said that if things got into a real crisis, we might want to call on him to make some move.

I explained the present jealousy between Menon and Hammarskjold and their competition for the role as intermediary in the present situation.

I said it looked that the most hopeful prospect was there might be on the one side the Users' Association collecting dues and dealing with the Egyptian Canal Authority, that the Canal Code would be adopted to handle practical matters and that the Users' Association would have "sanctions" because they could cut off all or substantially all of the dues if there were a violation of the Code.

The President asked about the alleged "differences" between the British and ourselves, and I said I was not aware of any, and on the contrary had been assured by both Lloyd and earlier by Eden of their great appreciation of my sticking with them. The President said he might mention this at his press conference.

I showed the President a draft of acknowledgment of Eden's letter of October 1. [7] The President glanced over it, and said it seemed to him to be satisfactory and that he would write Eden along those lines.

---

[5] See Document 321.

[6] Reference is to Eisenhower's letter to Hoover, October 8, Document 311.

[7] See footnote 1, *infra.*

The President mentioned the tanker matter, and Mr. Hoover and I said that we were discussing this with Mr. Flemming. [8]

JFD

[8] Attached to the source text is a draft of a proposed memorandum from the President to Flemming. For the final version of the memorandum, sent to Flemming on October 12, see Department of State *Bulletin*, October 22, 1956, pp. 619–620. In the memorandum, the President directed Flemming to bring together members of the National Petroleum Council to meet with the heads of the State, Treasury, Defense, Interior, and Commerce Departments to consider plans that would help assure the efficiency and adequacy of distributing petroleum supplies in the Free World. The plans were to provide for building in U.S. shipyards a sufficient number of large tankers to help supplement existing means of distribution and, if necessary, to help serve as an alternative means of transportation of crude oil from the Middle East.

Dulles left for New York by air at 12:12 p.m. that afternoon.

---

328.   Message From President Eisenhower to Prime Minister Eden [1]

Washington, October 11, 1956.

DEAR ANTHONY: Let me acknowledge the note from you [2] which transmitted a copy of Bulganin's letter to you. Truly, this is a rather forbidding letter, and it is scarcely couched in the terms which one would expect in a communication from one Head of Government to another. Also, Foster tells me that Shepilov made a quite nasty speech at the United Nations Council last Monday.

It is clear that the Soviets are playing hard to gain a dominant position in the Near East area, and it is likely they have developed quite a hold on Nasser. This problem will probably remain with us whatever may be the results of the talks in New York. I know that Foster is working closely with Selwyn Lloyd, and I deeply deplore the suggestions of the press both here and abroad that you and we are at cross purposes.

[1] Source: Eisenhower Library, Whitman File, Dulles–Herter Series. Top Secret. A "Suggested Draft", attached to the source text, is presumably the one handed by Dulles to Eisenhower during their conversation that morning (see *supra*); it bears a few stylistic changes by Eisenhower. The revised draft, which Eisenhower initialed, corresponds to the text sent to Eden, except for the P.S. which was presumably added by the President shortly before transmission. The message was transmitted for immediate delivery to Eden in telegram 2628 to London, October 11, 7:02 p.m. (Department of State, Central Files, 974.7301/10–1156)

[2] Document 287.

With warm regard,
As ever

Ike E.

P.S. I got a chance, at this morning's Press Conference,[3] to say something on how much Britain & the British mean to us.

DE

---

[3] The transcript is printed in *Public Papers of the Presidents of the United States: Dwight D. Eisenhower, 1956*, pp. 880–894.

---

329.   Memorandum of a Conversation Between the Assistant Secretary of State for Near Eastern, South Asian, and African Affairs (Rountree) and Ambassador Hussein of the Egyptian Delegation to the United Nations, New York, October 11, 1956, 10:45 p.m.[1]

SUBJECT

Suez Canal

Ambassador Hussein telephoned me at my hotel room at 10:15 p.m. and began expressing his deep concern over the turn of events in the tripartite talks October 11 between the Egyptians on the one hand and the British and French on the other. I had with me at the time Ambassador Lall of India[2] and suggested to Ambassador Hussein that we might discuss the matter privately a bit later. He invited me to his suite at the hotel and I met with him at 10:45 p.m.

The Ambassador reviewed in some detail the progress of the talks to date and emphasized the desire of Egypt to find a compromise solution. He said that on all the major points the Egyptians had been willing to go as far as possible without actually bringing about a collapse of the Egyptian Government as a result of yielding too far, particularly on the question of "international control" of the Canal. He commented there were a number of reasons why the Egyptians wanted a settlement as quickly as possible. A primary one was that they were terribly concerned about the growth of Russian influence

---

[1] Source: Department of State, Central Files, 974.7301/10–1156. Secret. Drafted by Rountree.
[2] The memorandum of Rountree's conversation with Lall is *ibid.*

in Egypt and the long-term if not immediate effect which it would have upon Egyptian independence. Egypt was extremely anxious to avoid a situation in which the Soviets again became the champions of Egypt by virtue of a veto of the British-French resolution.

The Ambassador said Egypt was convinced of the objectivity of the United States and particularly of Secretary Dulles in this whole affair. He realized that the Secretary was playing a relatively inactive role at the present time, hoping that the parties more directly concerned could make progress toward an agreement. As a result of the events earlier in the day, however, Foreign Minister Fawzi and the Ambassador were hopeful that the Secretary could inject himself more directly into the situation in order to prevent the collapse of present discussions and the creation of a new difficult situation.

According to the Ambassador, the talks in the presence of Secretary-General Hammarskjold had been going remarkably well, particularly as between Fawzi and Lloyd. The latter seemed earnestly to be seeking a workable arrangement and pursued each point with apparent sincerity. On the other hand, Mr. Pineau had shown considerable reluctance, but the situation had become more acute during the course of the afternoon tripartite session.[3] At that time Mr. Pineau had taken the position, unrelated to any issue at that time under discussion, that he would insist upon calling a Security Council meeting in the immediate future and announce that the French would insist upon the 18-nation proposal and nothing else. He would then wind up the affair and return to Paris Saturday afternoon in order to attend meetings, his presence at which he attributed great importance. This attitude had been distressing to Fawzi and, the Egyptians believe, also to Lloyd.

At a subsequent meeting between Hammarskjold, Lloyd and Fawzi, the former two had stated that they would discuss the matter frankly with Secretary Dulles. It was not clear from what Ambassador Hussein said whether Hammarskjold and Lloyd had been critical of Pineau, and my efforts discreetly to draw him out on this point left me in some doubt, although Hussein was careful to avoid implying that there was an open breach between Pineau and Lloyd.

Emphasizing again that the Egyptians wanted a settlement, wanted to mend their relations with the Western world, and wanted to avoid if at all possible the further development of a situation in which the Soviets were the defenders of Egypt, Ambassador Hussein asked me to urge Secretary Dulles to do all that he could to prevent a breakdown of the talks and to persuade the French that it was in

---

[3] Reference is to the meeting among Hammarskjöld, Fawzi, Pineau, and Lloyd, during the afternoon of October 11. Hammarskjöld's account of this conversation is in the memorandum of conversation, *infra*.

their interest, as well as that of the whole world, to assume a conciliatory attitude. He said the Egyptians believed strongly that it would not be helpful in the present situation to have representatives of various other countries trying to become the "heroes" by pressing their own plans for a solution. He mentioned particularly Spaak and Krishna Menon in this connection and gave me the impression that he and his Egyptian colleagues were not at all enthusiastic over the Menon proposal or his efforts to inject himself into the situation.

During the course of the conversation, I responded only generally to Ambassador Hussein's comments and I was careful to make no commitments. I told him that I would report to the Secretary the substance of our conversation, and I was sure that the Secretary would continue to do all in his power to facilitate a peaceful solution to this question. I said that we had not heard from Lloyd and Hammarskjold following the private conversation which Ambassador Hussein had indicated they had had with Fawzi. But I assumed that they would be getting in touch with the Secretary. I said that I would, of course, report the matter fully to Mr. Dulles.

---

330.   Memorandum of a Conversation Between Secretary-General Hammarskjöld and the Counselor of the Delegation at the United Nations (Barco), New York, October 12, 1956 [1]

USDel/MC/31

SUBJECT

Suez: Lloyd, Pineau, Fawzi talks

Following Mr. Hammarskjold's meeting yesterday evening with Mr. Lloyd, Mr. Pineau and Mr. Fawzi, I met with him to learn the results of the talks.

Hammarskjold said that the afternoon's discussion had started extremely negatively. Mr. Pineau would discuss only the broadest generalities and no details. Hammarskjold said it could have been the end of the talks, except that none of the others was ready to end them. Pineau finally agreed that the questions had been reduced to ones of implementation and the latter half of the discussion had

---

[1] Source: Department of State, Central Files, 974.7301/10–1256. Secret. Drafted by Barco.

been very useful. He felt that there had been sufficient substance to make agreement possible between the United Kingdom and Egypt. Pineau's position, however, remained a question mark. Hammarskjold said that Pineau had the disadvantage of little experience in this forum, little or no knowledge of English, and apparent lack of understanding of the problems involved. He said he, Hammarskjold, could not tell at all what Pineau's position might become.

Hammarskjold said Fawzi had thrown out the suggestion that the points of substance which had been covered should be referred back to governments. Fawzi said he was prepared to continue the discussions as long as necessary but that if Mr. Pineau had to return to Paris, one way of ending this stage of discussions would be to refer these points to governments. Hammarskjold said no one really knew what ground had been covered on substance and he felt there should be a paper listing these points. He felt reasonably sure that both Fawzi and Lloyd would come to today's meeting with such a paper. Hammarskjold felt that to refer the points back to governments could lead to what might be a failure in the Security Council but he believed that if this were presented in the right way it could be accepted. The question would arise how long the Security Council could wait. He personally felt a maximum of two weeks should be allowed for government consideration but he had not checked this point with the others. He said that Pineau was not now ready to forego a vote on the Anglo-French Resolution but he thought that Lloyd might well be ready to do so twenty-four hours from now.

The Secretary-General said that as a result of the talks so far, he saw no difficulty over SCUA and its relationship to the operation of the Canal or to arrangements for "enforceability." He said the Egyptians were willing to accept recourse to a body to make findings of violations and to accept enforceability provisions.

With respect to Israel, the Secretary-General said he felt personally that the Western powers could not get away with the status quo. At the same time, the situation that had been allowed to go on for five years, he felt, could not be allowed to prevent agreement. He had told Fawzi that from his discussions with Egyptians in the past over Israeli transit rights, he felt that the problem then had been to find a proper setting for an arrangement with Israel. He had now told Fawzi that if a large settlement could be found he felt that the Egyptians would have to take agreement on Israel. He said Fawzi had smiled knowingly, without saying anything, but he interpreted his reaction to being one of agreement.

Hammarskjold said that the discussions would continue in his office today at 10:30, and again in the afternoon. He thought that a private meeting in the Security Council would either be very late today, or possibly Saturday morning. He was, I would say, generally optimistic that something would come out of the talks beyond a vetoed resolution or a breakdown.

---

331.   Telegram From the Mission at the United Nations to the Department of State [1]

New York, October 11, 1956—9 p.m.

335. Eyes only for Hoover. The following suggested statement which you might make to NSC: [2]

Security Council convened October 5, and after four public sessions arranged October 9 for subsequent meetings to be closed for time being as means stimulating more constructive discussion problem in effort reach basis of settlement. These closed sessions [3] have of themselves had limited utility but they have been brief and have been spaced so that a good bit of time of the Foreign Ministers primarily concerned could be devoted private conversations. There have been series talks among British, French and Egyptian Foreign Ministers in presence Secretary-General Hammarskjold. While nothing as yet has been reduced to writing there have been what may prove to be useful exchanges which give reason hope early agreement in principle is not out of question although success far from assured.

While Egyptians continue maintain they cannot in any circumstances accept "international control" of Canal, there are indications they may accept an arrangement providing for participation by Canal users to degree which might from technical viewpoint prove adequate to assure that interests of users can be safeguarded. They appear not to exclude direct collaboration with Users Association in achieving this objective, although neither they nor British and French visualize membership in Association as sine qua non to enjoyment by any country of facilities Canal. It thus appears possible that the SCUA can in fact be developed into mechanism of considerable importance in implementation of an arrangement agreed with Egypt.

---

[1] Source: Department of State, Central Files, 974.7301/10–1156. Secret; Niact. Received at 10:09 p.m. The outgoing copy of this telegram indicates Rountree as the drafting officer. (*Ibid.*, Conference Files: Lot 62 D 181, CF 786)

[2] See *infra.*

[3] The Security Council met in private at its 739th, 740th, and 741st meetings held on October 9, 11, and 12.

We have been encouraged by moderation shown by the British. They seem to favor compromise settlement but they deeply concerned at how they could square such a compromise with strong positions which their government has taken publicly. The French on other hand appear to adhere more closely to original position and show little give to date.

It is, of course, too early to judge whether these negotiations will in fact result in agreement. We cannot be sure of extent of authority with which Fawzi speaks, and he may in fact be repudiated in part or in whole by Nasser. Nor can we be certain whether apparently moderate approach now being pursued by British will be supported by the UK Government, or whether French can in the final analysis be brought along. Indeed, even assuming that they are all backed by their governments, there remains a very wide area which must yet be covered before an agreement, even in principle, is assured. Nevertheless, progress report at the moment is not discouraging.

Meanwhile, British, French and we agreed upon urgency completing arrangements so that SCUA can be put into operation. Delegations of the participating countries now working together London are having some difficulty perfecting plans and main problem at moment seems to be selecting administrator willing to serve and whose government willing to have him serve. When organization in position begin doing business, expected that US will issue appropriate regulations denying payment tolls Egypt by US flag vessels and encouraging payment by all US owned vessels to SCUA which would operate as agents shipowners. Our final decision this regard, however, will also depend upon agreement (which not yet been forthcoming from French but which we have with British) that three of us will be operating on the same basis. We would hope that other countries would immediately, or soon after follow suit. We attach considerable importance to activating SCUA, since if agreement in principle reached with Egyptians, latter could deal with SCUA pending completion detailed permanent arrangements. If no agreement in principle reached highly desirable for SCUA to be in position discharge multiple purposes for which created.

At Security Council secret session held afternoon of October 11, consideration again was given request Israel and seven Arab states to be heard. Council considered proposal special session be held for this purpose October 12 while Foreign Ministers UK, France and Egypt continuing their private talks. Permanent delegates those three countries would sit in lieu Foreign Ministers. Suggestion not accepted majority Council, however, and decided postpone until later decision upon appearance Israel and Arab states.

SC scheduled convene again closed session October 12, time to be set by President. Further public meetings to be preceded by private meeting to inform SC outcome private talks Foreign Ministers. Decision when next closed session will be held presumably depends upon degree progress made UK-France-Egypt talks. Although Pineau seems anxious end session soon as possible, appears British and other delegations contemplate possibility meetings going into next week. Meanwhile decision whether UK-France will press for vote their resolution in abeyance and will depend upon developments. If they in fact decide press for vote, it estimated resolution would receive minimum seven, with Soviet veto almost certain.

Lodge

---

332.   **Memorandum of Discussion at the 300th Meeting of the National Security Council, Washington, October 12, 1956, 9:15–9:40 a.m.** [1]

[Here follows a paragraph listing the participants at the meeting.]

1. The Suez Canal Situation

The President was delayed a few minutes. As he entered the Cabinet Room he remarked with a broad smile that he was sorry to be late but the Council must remember that he was a politician these days (laughter).

Mr. Jackson then explained that the order of Council consideration of this morning's agenda had been changed and that the first item would be the report by the Acting Secretary of State on recent developments in the Suez situation. He thereupon called on Secretary Hoover.

Secretary Hoover [2] informed the Council that he had in his hand

---

[1] Source: Eisenhower Library, Whitman File, NSC Records. Top Secret. Prepared by Gleason. The time of the meeting is from the record of the President's Daily Appointments. (*Ibid.*)

[2] In preparation for this meeting, the Bureaus of International Organization Affairs (IO) and Near Eastern, South Asian, and African Affairs (NEA) prepared briefing papers for Hoover. The IO paper, forwarded to Hoover on October 11, contained a summary of principal Security Council developments on the Suez situation. (Department of State, S/P–NSC Files: Lot 61 D 167, Near East) The NEA paper, forwarded to Hoover on October 11, was a talking paper on the non-U.N. aspects of

notes from Secretary Dulles from New York which he would like, if agreeable to the President, to read to the Council. The written report described the purpose of the closed sessions on the Suez problem currently being conducted in New York.[3] These closed meetings were brief in duration and spaced in such a way as to permit time in between for frequent meetings of the interested foreign ministers. Nothing in writing had yet come of any of these meetings but Secretary Dulles believed that early agreement in principle was a possibility. Nevertheless, many difficulties remained to be ironed out. This portion of the report was followed by statements indicating Secretary Dulles' view that SCUA could conceivably be developed as a means of implementing any future agreement which might be reached. According to Secretary Dulles' observation, the British were showing a marked disposition to compromise with the Egyptians. The French, on the other hand, were adhering rigorously to their original position. At this point Secretary Hoover said he would like to enlarge somewhat on Secretary Dulles' report. It was his own belief that the British and the Egyptians were now very close to agreement and that in fact the chief reason why no agreement has yet been reached is French opposition.

Resuming his reading of Secretary Dulles' notes, Secretary Hoover went on to state that it was still too early to say that an agreement would be reached. For example, the Egyptian Foreign Minister, Fawzi, might be repudiated by President Nasser or the U.K. Government might not support the moderate position now being taken by the British Foreign Minister. Finally, the French might prove unwilling to go along. Despite all these dangers, Secretary Dulles believed that for the moment at least, progress was not discouraging.

The concluding portions of Secretary Dulles' report dealt with the possibility of developing SCUA as a means of implementing any agreement which might be reached by the foreign ministers.

At the conclusion of Secretary Hoover's report, the President asked if there were any questions by members of the Council. There were none.

The National Security Council: [4]

Noted and discussed a report by the Secretary of State, as presented by the Under Secretary of State, on developments regard-

---

the Suez Canal situation and on other Near East developments. (*Ibid.*, S/S–NSC (Miscellaneous) Files: Lot 66 D 95, NSC–Misc Memos–1956)

[3] Transmitted in telegram 335, *supra.*

[4] The following paragraph constitutes NSC Action No. 1619, approved by the President on October 16. (Department of State, S/S–NSC (Miscellaneous) Files: Lot 66 D 95, Records of Action by the National Security Council, 1956)

ing the Suez Canal situation, particularly at the United Nations Security Council.

[Here follows agenda item 2.]

3. Significant World Developments Affecting U.S. Security

General Cabell stated that he would confine his briefing this morning to developments in the Middle East. He discussed briefly the Israeli attack across the border of Jordan on October 10 and stated that this attack had made still more precarious the stability of the Government of Jordan. He predicted that the forthcoming elections in Jordan were likely to go strongly in the direction desired by the Leftists, the ardent Nationalists, and the pro-Egyptian elements in Jordan. General Cabell went on to comment on the serious problem which had been raised by the proposal to permit Iraqi troops to be stationed in Jordan. Quite apart from the repercussions of such a move in Israel, it was also possible that the Syrians and the Egyptians would move forces into Jordan if Iraqi forces actually crossed the border. General Cabell concluded with a description of the Jordan attitude toward the proposal that Iraqi troops be stationed in Jordan and noted in closing that thanks to the acquisition by Israel of a number of French Mystère aircraft, Israel had once again secured air superiority over the Arab states. It seemed clear to General Cabell that any moves by the Arabs in Jordan which Israel deemed a threat to its security would certainly result in large-scale military action by Israel.

At the conclusion of the intelligence briefing the President reverted to Secretary Dulles' report on the developments in the Suez situation and stated that in essence he and Secretary Dulles were in agreement that if the United States could just keep the lid on a little longer, some kind of compromise plan could be worked out for a settlement of the Suez problem. Time and time alone will cure the disease; the only question was whether we could be sure of the time.

Secretary Hoover commented that no sovereign nation can ever admit it is in the wrong and British prestige was very heavily engaged in the Suez issue.

The President reminisced at this point on the invasion of North Africa. He stated that while he had much to quarrel with in President Roosevelt's policies, he did admire the manner in which Mr. Roosevelt had reacted to General Eisenhower's deal with Admiral Darlan. The storm both in Washington and in other allied capitals was terrific when news of the deal leaked out. General Eisenhower was fully prepared to be relieved of his command and believed that this was a small sacrifice for the advantages gained in the Darlan deal. Nevertheless, both Roosevelt and Churchill stood up firmly against the storm of protest and there was no talk of a replacement of General Eisenhower.

The National Security Council: [5]

Noted and discussed an oral report on the subject by the Acting Director of Central Intelligence with specific reference to the Arab-Israeli situation.

[Here follows agenda item 4.]

The President then inquired whether there were any further items on the agenda. On being informed that there was no other business, the President said jocosely that this had been a fine meeting of the National Security Council. Secretary Wilson observed that the brevity of the meeting was not a very good index of the actual troubles facing the United States (laughter).

S. Everett Gleason

---

[5] The following paragraph constitutes NSC Action No. 1621, approved by the President on October 16. (*Ibid.*)

---

333.   Editorial Note

On October 12, Acting Secretary Hoover returned to President Eisenhower an undated paper entitled "U.S. Opportunities in the Middle East".

The paper bears no indication as to its origin or authorship, nor does it bear a security classification. A marginal notation on the paper by President Eisenhower reads: "Mr. Hoover, Please return to my files. DE." The text of the paper reads as follows:

"1. All evidence points to the steady dissolution of Jordan.

. . . .

"3. Although the Israelis were willing to agree to the stationing of Iraqi troops without heavy armament in eastern Jordan to help bolster the country, they will never accept the complete absorption of Jordan by Iraq. Such a move would bring Iraq that has never signed an armistice agreement with Israel right up to her borders.

"4. If Iraq should try . . . to absorb Jordan, the overwhelming odds are that the Israel army would move to the Jordan River or even further.

"5. Moreover, Egypt would not remain passive to such a move since she could not afford to have Iraq gain that much. Egypt's probable response would be to seek an outright military alliance with Russia.

"6. This situation could conceivably be turned to a great victory for the West if the following could be accomplished:

. . . .

"b. An economic union between west Jordan and Israel. (This has been explored in the past.)

"c. An Iraq-Israel peace treaty . . . .

"d. The likelihood is that such a peace treaty would be quickly followed by additional peace treaties between Lebanon and Israel and Syria and Israel.

"e. Proceeding with the pipeline plan from Elath to Haifa which would reduce Nasser's opportunity to squeeze the West.

"f. With political tranquilization to move with the President's economic development plans for the area." (Eisenhower Library, Whitman File, Dulles–Herter Series)

---

334.   Memorandum of a Conversation, Secretary Dulles' Suite, Waldorf Astoria, New York, October 12, 1956, 2:30 p.m. [1]

USDel/MC/36

PARTICIPANTS

United States	United Kingdom
The Secretary	Foreign Secretary Selwyn Lloyd
Mr. Phleger	
Mr. Rountree	

SUBJECTS

(1) Hammarskjold's Understanding of Oral Agreement
(2) Organization of the SCUA
(3) Procedure and Tactics in the Security Council

Mr. Lloyd came to see me at his request. He had with him several pieces of paper, [2] one set of which represented Hammar-

---

[1] Source: Department of State, Conference Files: Lot 62 D 181, CF 788. Secret. Drafted by Dulles. The source text indicates Phleger and Rountree were not present for the full conversation.
[2] No copy of the papers, shown by Lloyd to Dulles, has been found in Department of State files.

skjold's understanding of what had been orally agreed to. [3] This was in three parts—one relating to "principles" of which there were six, the other relating to "mechanisms" and the other relating to "arbitration". There were also some pieces of paper prepared by Fawzi, which were quite vague.

The statement of principles in the Hammarskjold memorandum were [was] good, and included the proposition that the Canal should be insulated from the politics of any nation. The mechanisms included cooperation between the Users' Association and the Canal Authority with reference to such matters as tolls, non-discrimination, improvement of the Canal, etc. Provisions on arbitration were rather vague, and I got the impression that they were primarily for scenery.

Lloyd asked as to how we might proceed. He said that he could not wait around here indefinitely. On the other hand, he had to have something specific to take back to London. He said that Pineau had been somewhat less obstructive today, and he (Pineau) indicated that if he had something concrete, he might be willing to accept it and try to sell it to the French Government. Lloyd said that Eden stood ready to go to Paris to persuade Mollet, if this proved necessary.

I pointed out that it seemed to me that the heart of any arrangement was that the Users should be entitled to organize themselves as they saw fit and to handle the funds. I said that if they had a really effective organization and had control of the Canal's pocketbook, then they would really speak with authority. I said, however, that a Users' Association organized along Menon's lines, which could not speak except through 16 politically divided nations, would be utterly ineffective.

Lloyd said that Fawzi had indicated that the Users could organize themselves any way they wanted. Lloyd said he agreed about the importance of collecting the tolls, but felt that it was probably better to leave this implicit rather than explicit. I said I agreed with that approach provided it was clear that nothing was done to preclude the Users' Association from collecting the tolls as agent for the shippers which voluntarily used the Association, and then dealing for all of these with the Egyptian authority.

---

[3] On October 11, Hammarskjöld told Barco that there should be a paper listing the points of substance which Fawzi, Lloyd, and Pineau had covered during their secret discussions with Hammarskjöld. The Secretary-General also expressed the belief that Fawzi and Lloyd would bring such a paper to the meeting scheduled for October 12; see Document 330.

I also pointed out that there was need for some provisional measures. I said Spaak's plan [4] to perpetuate the present status quo was bad because the Users were not yet organized and not dealing with the Egyptian Canal Authority and the Egyptians had all they wanted and that all that they wanted was to preserve the status quo which under the Spaak formula they could do by merely prolonging negotiations ad infinitum. Lloyd said he recognized that this was an important aspect of the matter which had not been adequately dealt with. He hoped, however, that Belgium, Iran and Yugoslavia might perhaps come up with something acceptable along these lines.

Lloyd indicated that an effort would be made between now and 5 o'clock to get some greater precision on the second part of the Hammarskjold paper and then that Hammarskjold might report this to the Council at closed session at 5 o'clock. Egypt perhaps could not formally accept at that time, but might indicate that it would not object to the Security Council approving this paper as a basis for future proceedings and as a substitute for the Anglo-French Resolution.

I said that the Russians had still to show their hand. Lloyd said that Pineau had talked with Shepilov, and, according to Pineau's report, Shepilov had said that he thought there should be international rather than purely Egyptian operations and control of the Canal. I said this was hardly credible and that perhaps Pineau had misunderstood Shepilov. Mr. Lloyd admitted that that was a possibility.

Mr. Phleger joined us and then Mr. Rountree as we considered future procedures.

I asked Lloyd whether it was worth while my staying around. He said he thought it was vital and that what I said at 5 o'clock might be decisive. I asked him what he wanted me to say at 5 o'clock, but he indicated that he did not yet know. I said I would be sitting next to him and that if he wanted to tip me off, I would try to be responsive. Lloyd said that Pineau now indicated that he would be willing to stay over until Sunday, if the prospects were

---

[4] On October 11, Spaak handed Barco the text of a draft resolution to be delivered to Dulles. The draft resolution recommended the conclusion of an international convention, which would establish certain principles, provide certain guarantees for the users, and ensure close collaboration between the Egyptian Canal Authority and the users association. The final paragraph (3) of the draft resolution stipulated that the status quo would be maintained, pending entry into force of the convention. The memorandum of conversation by Barco and attached draft resolution are in Department of State, Conference Files: Lot 62 D 181, CF 788.

On October 12, Barco informed Spaak that Dulles believed that this matter should first be considered by France and the United Kingdom and was personally opposed to paragraph 3 of the draft resolution. Barco assured Spaak, however, that the Secretary still had the matter under consideration. (Memorandum of conversation by Armour, October 12; *ibid.*, Central Files, 974.7301/10–1256)

good, and the thought was that if we could get through the closed session with some indication of the acceptability to Egypt of the Hammarskjold memorandum, then there should be time taken to draft a substitute United Nations Security Council resolution and organize support for it with the idea that it might be adopted perhaps on late Saturday or on Sunday.

At this point, Mr. Lloyd left to join with Pineau and Fawzi at the Secretary-General's quarters.

John Foster Dulles [5]

---

[5] Printed from a copy that bears this typed signature.

---

335.   Editorial Note

On October 12, shortly after the British Chargé in Tel Aviv had discussed Iraqi troop movements with Foreign Minister Meir, Meir summoned Ambassador Lawson to convey her shock and alarm over the Chargé's presentation. She expressed special resentment at the Chargé's statement that a forcible Israeli reaction to a dispatch of Iraqi troops would bring the Anglo-Jordanian Treaty into play and the Chargé's refusal to respond to her questions concerning specifics of the Iraqi deployment, which Meir then readdressed to Lawson. (Telegram 365 from Tel Aviv, October 12; Department of State, Central Files, 684A.86/10–1256)

Meir then dispatched a letter to the Embassy which urged United States intervention to prevent the entry of Iraqi forces into Jordan. The letter, according to the Embassy in Tel Aviv, reviewed U.S.-Israeli discussions on the subject and statements made by Nuri Said and the British Foreign Office, and affirmed Israel's basic principle of maintaining the territorial status quo in the Middle East. It closed with the following plea:

"In view fact we have not received adequate assurances as to size of contemplated force, period of its stay in Jordan, its exact location, and particularly in view of light cast on entire operation by Nuri Said's statement as supported by British Foreign Office it is considered view of GOI that entry of Iraqi troops into Jordan represents grave infringement of status quo in area and serious threat to Israel. We feel it our duty to express our strongest opposition to contemplated action, and we request your government's urgent intervention to prevent it from taking place." (Telegram 366 from Tel Aviv, October 12; ibid.)

On October 14, the Department of State transmitted to Tel Aviv a response to the Israeli Government. The response recalled previous U.S.-Israeli exchanges on the subject, including Ben Gurion's assurances that Israel would do nothing if Iraqi troops remained east of the Jordan River, and noted that the United States had sought to be responsive to Israeli questions on the troop movement. But difficulties arose when Iraq and Great Britain reiterated policies first stated months and even years ago, compounded by Iraq's reluctance to release details of its troop movements. The Unites States had assured Israel that the Iraqi troop movement would be defensive in nature and limited to east of the Jordan River, and that Iraqi forces would be small and not carry heavy equipment. The British approach was meant to reassure Israel and there was no reason to believe that the reference to the Anglo-Jordanian Treaty was meant to be threatening. In light of this, the response requested that Israel give further consideration to the matter before reaching a conclusion. (Telegram 303 to Tel Aviv, October 14; *ibid.*)

---

336.   Memorandum of a Conversation, Waldorf Astoria, New York, October 12, 1956, 3:30 p.m. [1]

USDel/MC/37

PARTICIPANTS

Mr. Spaak (Belgium)
Mr. Robert Rothschild (Chief of Cabinet of Mr. Spaak)

U.S.
The Secretary
Ambassador Lodge
Mr. Phleger
Mr. William R. Tyler

The Secretary told Mr. Spaak he had heard that Mr. Pineau was in a rather better frame of mind. Mr. Spaak looked extremely dubious and said he was very much worried about Mr Pineau's attitude. The Secretary then said that the question now was what was going to happen this afternoon at the closed session of the Security Council at 5:00 o'clock. He said that the Secretary-General

---

[1] Source: Department of State, Central Files, 974.7301/10–1256. Secret. Drafted by Tyler.

of the United Nations would make a report to the Council and would state that agreement had been reached on six points of principle, and he would then mention four or five additional points concerning the operation and mechanism for provisional conservatory measures to keep the Canal going pending the working out of a final solution, which would probably take a considerable time. He thought it most important that agreement be reached today so that the Foreign Ministers should not disband without having made any progress.

It was also important to know what would happen after the meeting—what procedures would be followed as a framework for negotiation with Egypt, and what provisional or "conservatory" measures could be agreed to to ensure free and secure navigation in the Canal during the period of negotiation. He hoped that Mr. Spaak might be willing to stress the importance of agreement being reached on these subjects. If this were achieved, tomorrow morning might be spent in drafting a resolution which would then be approved in public session in the afternoon, and this would mean that the Anglo-French resolution would not have to come to a vote. Mr. Spaak observed that Mr. Pineau's position was very difficult vis-à-vis the French National Assembly, and that he must have something to go back with which his government could defend. The Secretary said it was tremendously important that the Egyptians should make a move. So far they had only spoken confidentially about points on which they might be willing to agree but had put nothing down on paper. Mr. Pineau would not be in a very happy position if he were to go back to France and only be able to say that some progress in the Egyptian position had been made orally, but that he had in fact nothing to show for it.

Mr Spaak said that there was also the question of what the Russians were going to do. Mr. Shepilov had kept very quiet so far and had not shown his hand; he thought that Mr. Shepilov would probably emerge to the surface again today and would speak. The Secretary said he thought that everything depended on whether the Egyptians were willing to move independently of the Russians if they really wanted an agreement. In answer to a question by Mr. Spaak, the Secretary said he thought that the Egyptians did want an agreement if they could in fact remain in control of the Canal.

Mr. Spaak then asked the Secretary what he thought would happen if no progress was made here in New York. The Secretary said that was the very question which we had been asking ourselves. Mr. Spaak said that he thought that in any case the British and the French would not have recourse to armed force. The Secretary said that he was perhaps not so sure about this. He referred to the overwhelming vote of the resolution at the Conservative Conference on October 11.[2] He said that right at the start the British had started building up their armed forces on a basis which suggested that they were in fact going to undertake military action, but that subsequently they had somewhat shifted the character of their build-up. However, he could not feel sure that all danger was past.

The Secretary went on to say that he did not feel it had been wise for the United Kingdom and France to go to the Security Council as they had. He had talked about this with Eden and Lloyd on his last day in London, and Eden had agreed that the manner and timing of the approach to the Security Council ought to be carefully considered and deliberated. The Secretary had hoped that SCUA would first be set up as an operating organization so as to strengthen the position of the 18 vis-à-vis the Egyptian Government and increase the chances of some provisional cooperation being worked out pending a final solution. However, hardly had his plane left the airport on his way back to Washington on Friday evening, September 21, when the British and the French decided to announce that they were going to the Security Council. Ambassador Lodge then gave an account of how he had been called by the British here in New York on that very evening and informed of the decision. He had not been given the opportunity to exert any influence to attempt to restrain the decision itself, but he had at least been able to persuade the British and the French not to announce the fact before the Secretary had had time to reach the State Department on Saturday morning.

The Secretary went on to say that he had reminded Mr. Lloyd here recently that in May 1953, the British were in the Suez Canal zone by right of Treaty, that they had 88,000 troops in the area, that they had started evacuating their women and children and that their plans involved taking Cairo and Alexandria. In actual fact, they were being so harassed by Egyptian guerrilla action and assassinations that they had decided to withdraw their troops and had concluded an agreement with Egypt in 1954. He had told Mr. Lloyd that he wondered how the British chances of military success could be better today than they were then. The trouble was that once you embarked on a military operation, it had a tendency to spread and you could never be sure where it would end.

The Secretary concluded by repeating his conviction that it was of great importance that some progress should be recorded here and now, and his hope that Mr. Spaak would see his way to participate

---

[2] On October 11, the British Conservative Party, during its annual conference, voted overwhelmingly in favor of an emergency resolution, endorsing the government's "resolute" policy throughout the Suez Crisis. (*The Times* (London), October 12, 1956)

in the debate and urge that agreement should be reached. Mr. Spaak sighed noncommittally and said he would be glad to see what he could do. He brightened up, however, as he said that Mr. Dulles was now a very popular person with "men of the left" in Europe. The Secretary observed that it was perhaps because of this that he was being called the "Rock and Roll" Secretary of State in the European press.

337.   Editorial Note

At the 741st meeting of the Security Council, which began at 5 p.m. on October 12, Secretary-General Hammarskjöld enumerated six principles and five modalities for implementing the principles concerning the Suez Canal. The principles were:

"1. There shall be free and open transit through the Canal without discrimination overt and covert. This covers both political and technical aspects.

"2. Egypt's sovereignty shall be respected.

"3. The operation of the Canal should be insulated from the politics of any country.

"4. The manner of fixing tolls and charges should be decided by agreement between Egypt and the users.

"5. A fair proportion of the dues should be allotted to development.

"6. In case of dispute, unresolved affairs between the Suez Canal Company and the Egyptian Government should be settled by arbitration with suitable terms of reference and suitable provisions for the payment of sums found to be due."

The modalities for implementing the principles included: 1) cooperation between the Egyptian Canal Authority and the users either individually or as a group, within the framework of specified conventions, codes, and regulations; 2) access to recourse for all parties to settle unresolved disputes or differences; 3) agreed arrangements on tolls and charges; 4) access to information and an "international element" in all branches of the Canal administration; and 5) an established relationship with the United Nations. (Telegram 345 from USUN, October 13; Department of State, Central Files, 974.7301/10–1356)

After the meeting, Secretary Dulles telephoned President Eisenhower at 7:30 p.m. The memorandum of their conversation, transcribed by Bernau, reads as follows:

"The Sec. said he just got back from a 2-hour meeting at the SC. The British, French and Egyptians have agreed on 6 basic principles and the rest of the Council have accepted them including the Russians. The Sec. read them. There is no agreement on provisional measures—how to pursue these negotiations—but the Sec. thinks enough has been said and done to make it virtually certain that the status quo will be preserved for quite a while and there will be no use of force. This may revive . . . The Israel thing is acute and may mean the Egyptians will send their forces back to the Neguib and the Gaza strip. You can't solve everything at once.

"The Sec. said between the two of them he does not think the British and French have done an awful good job here so far. The responsibility is entirely theirs which is the way it should be. This is the result of their talks with the Egyptians. They cannot outwardly at least place any blame on us if it works out badly. The Sec. said he had deliberately stayed out of it.

"The Pres. evidently asked re his press conference yesterday. The Sec. said he thought it was perfect—he has not had any . . . He did not get any adverse reaction here at all." (Eisenhower Library, Dulles Papers, White House Telephone Conversations. The ellipses appear in the text of the memorandum.)

---

338.   Editorial Note

On October 12, at the close of the Security Council session, the British Delegation gave to the U.S. Delegation an English translation of a draft resolution, originally in French. The draft resolution provided that the Security Council would: agree that any settlement of the Suez question must fulfill specified requirements (i.e., the six principles described by Hammarskjöld earlier that day; see *supra*); consider that the Eighteen-Power Proposals corresponding to the principles set forth were the most appropriate for bringing about a settlement; agree that the Egyptian Government had not yet formulated any proposal for the application of the principles set forth; invite the Egyptian Government to make known its proposals; and decide that pending the conclusion of an agreement: 1) the Government of Egypt should afford free passage through the Canal; 2) the Users' Association should be entitled to collect the dues payable by ships belonging to its members; and 3) the Users' Association and the Egyptian Suez Canal Authority should cooperate to ensure the satisfactory operation of the Canal according to the principles set forth above.

The Mission at the United Nations transmitted the text of this draft resolution to the Department of State in telegram 341, October

12. (Department of State, Central Files, 974.7301/10–1256) The telegram noted that the draft had not yet been seen by either Lloyd or Pineau. A memorandum of a brief conversation among Secretary Dulles, Foreign Secretary Lloyd, and other American and British officials at 10 a.m. on October 13 indicates that several changes in the text had already been made before British and French officials discussed the draft with United States officials on October 13. (Memorandum of conversation by Lodge, October 13; *ibid.*, Conference Files: Lot 62 D 181, CF 800)

---

339.   Memorandum of a Conversation, Secretary Dulles' Suite, Waldorf Astoria, New York, October 13, 1956, 10:30–12:30 a.m. [1]

USDel/MC/40

SUBJECT

> Minutes of the Tripartite US–UK–French Foreign Ministers Meeting

PARTICIPANTS

> *U.S. Side*
> The Secretary
> Ambassador Lodge
> Mr. Herman Phleger
> Mr. Francis Wilcox
> Mr. William Rountree
> Mr. J. Barco
> Mr. W.R. Tyler
> Mr. J. Ludlow
> Mr. W. Macomber
>
> *U.K. Side*
> Mr. Selwyn Lloyd, Foreign Minister
> Sir Pierson Dixon
> Sir Harold Beeley
> Sir Gerald Fitzmaurice
> Mr. Ramsbotham
> Mr. Adam Watson

---

[1] Source: Department of State, Central Files, 974.7301/10–1356. Secret. Drafted by Tyler.

France
Mr. Christian Pineau, Foreign Minister
Ambassador H. Alphand
Mr. Cornut-Gentille
Mr. Pierre Ordonneau
Mr. J. Roux
Mr. C. de Margerie

Sir Pierson Dixon said that the British wished to propose a revision in the text of the resolution,[2] by incorporating three paragraphs from the Preamble of the original UK-French Resolution.

The Secretary asked whether the UK and France had decided that the vote on the Resolution which they were introducing today should be taken paragraph by paragraph. Mr. Selwyn Lloyd felt that the pros and cons should be discussed, and the Secretary explained the disadvantage of a vote on a single resolution: this would run the risk of a veto which would apply also to the six principles on which unanimous agreement had already been reached. Sir Pierson Dixon said that the trouble with voting solely on the six principles was that we would be left with just the principles by themselves, "which would not be at all a good result". Sir Harold Beeley commented that the UK expected the Resolution to get nine votes, and that it would perhaps even not be vetoed. The Secretary said he thought that a veto was about as certain as anything would be. Mr. Lloyd said that the UK and French delegations planned vigorous action after the present meeting, to try to get the other members of the Council to accept their Resolution. The Secretary inquired whether this included the Russians, and Mr. Lloyd did not at the moment have a ready answer. Mr. Pineau observed that to get nine votes, it would be necessary to drop the three paragraphs which the British had just proposed to add to the text, and Mr. Lloyd agreed to do so.

There followed a long and detailed discussion on various paragraphs of the draft, particularly with regard to the paragraph on acceptance by Egypt of the principle of cooperation with SCUA, and the last paragraph of the text of the Resolution. During this discussion, both Mr. Pineau and Mr. Lloyd referred at various times to the political difficulties which beset them at home. Mr. Pineau said in particular that he could not accept anything in a resolution which resembled acceptance by him now of a specific negotiating procedure for the future, otherwise he would face a tempest in the National Assembly. He said that the Secretary General of the United Nations was fully aware of this and indeed had said to Dr. Fawzi in Mr. Pineau's presence that it was now up to him to make concrete suggestions on procedures for future negotiation. For his part, said

---

[2] See the editorial note, *supra.*

Mr. Pineau, any language relating to this would have been restricted to something like "pursuing exploratory exchanges of views".

After the revised text had been finalized, the Secretary asked Mr. Dixon and Mr. Pineau what they thought would happen if the Resolution were vetoed, as seemed probable. He said he wished to discuss a little more the question of a vote paragraph by paragraph. Mr. Pineau said that he was not in favor of this, because the Soviet Union would veto individual paragraphs and leave the rest. The Secretary observed that it would be a calamity, [if?] as a result of the way in which the Resolution were presented, we were to lose the benefit of the unanimous agreement on the six principles which had been achieved. Mr. Lloyd said he rather agreed with the Secretary, and that it would be better to make sure that the principles were voted, and then the proposals on implementation might be vetoed without affecting the principles. Mr. Pineau said he agreed and that a vote might be taken on paragraphs one through six of the text of the Resolution. The Secretary raised the possibility of dividing the text up into two parts, but Mr. Lloyd said he preferred sounding out the sentiment of the other members of the Council on the Resolution as a whole.

The Secretary said that support from some members, e.g. Iran and Peru would be more likely if they knew that if the Resolution were vetoed, there would be measures taken at least to salvage the principles.

In conclusion, Mr. Lloyd suggested that the three Foreign Ministers meet again at 4:00 p.m. to consider the results of the efforts of the UK and France to convince other delegations. The Secretary urged strongly that they should talk with Dr. Fawzi and the Secretary General of the United Nations, as a matter of courtesy. It was also agreed that there would be an 18 power meeting at 4:30 p.m. and that the public Council meeting should be at 5:00 p.m. instead of 3:00 p.m.

340.   Memorandum of a Conversation, New York, October 13, 1956, 4 p.m. [1]

SUBJECT

Suez

PARTICIPANTS

U.S.—The Secretary of State and members of the U.S. Staff
U.K.—Mr. Selwyn Lloyd and members of the U.K. Staff
France—Mr. Pineau and members of the French Staff

1. Prior to the meeting of the SC, the three Delegations met in the office of the President of the Council to hear reactions to the U.K.-French draft resolution and plans for the SC meeting.

2. Mr. Pineau said that the Secretary-General was not happy with the second part of the draft resolution, but that Peru and Cuba had indicated they were ready to vote for the entire resolution. Mr. Broustra of the French Delegation reported that Iran was ready to vote for the first part, but had suggestions for amending the second part. He objected to saying that Egypt had not made any proposals. Mr. Dulles said that the SYG had told him that, if the Egyptian Foreign Minister appealed to him he would have to say that the Egyptians had made proposals which were sufficiently precise.

There was further discussion of the draft resolution and some drafting changes were made. Mr. Pineau said that he did not think that the French Government would fall over this issue but feared that, unless the resolution was handled right, when the SYG called the Foreign Ministers of Egypt, France and the U.K. together for further talks, the French Government simply would not attend.

3. Mr. Pineau said, however, that if the Resolution were voted as a whole and it was vetoed, a second resolution should be introduced limited to the six principles with no additions and no proposals for negotiations. This would ease his position with the French Government, and the SYG would be able on his own to arrange further talks.

4. Mr. Dulles said it was clear that if this were the outcome, the SC would remain seized of the question. Mr. Pineau agreed, and said of course that was automatic. Mr. Dulles said that there had been a great gain in getting the U.S.S.R., as they had done in their speech to the SC, to endorse the talks that had taken place in New York. If that were not nailed down now, we might never again have the opportunity to keep the Soviets out of the talks. Mr. Dulles said he

---

[1] Source: Department of State, Conference Files: Lot 62 D 181, CF 800. Secret. Drafted by Barco on October 15. The time of the meeting is from the chronology prepared by the U.S. Delegation.

was sure that the Soviets would veto the second part of the resolution if it remained as drafted. Mr. Pineau reiterated that the French Government would refuse to attend any further talks if, after a veto of the second part, anything were included in the resolution on further talks. Mr. Pineau said his preference was to vote for the resolution as a whole, for which he expected nine votes, and then for a second resolution with the six points only. Mr. Dulles might, at that time, intervene and say that it was his understanding that the SYG and the three parties could still carry on negotiations.

5. During the following SC meeting, Ambassador Alphand asked if it was agreed that Mr. Dulles would make this intervention, and he was informed, with the Secretary's approval, that he agreed to do this.

---

341.   Editorial Note

During the 742d meeting of the Security Council, which convened at 5:30 p.m. on October 13, the British and French Representatives introduced the following draft resolution:

"The Security Council,

"Noting the declarations made before it and the accounts of the development of the exploratory conversations on the Suez question given by the Secretary-General of the United Nations and the Foreign Ministers of Egypt, France and the United Kingdom;
"Agrees that any settlement of the Suez question should meet the following requirements:

"(1) there should be free and open transit through the Canal without discrimination, overt or covert—this covers both political and technical aspects;
"(2) the sovereignty of Egypt should be respected;
"(3) the operation of the Canal should be insulated from the politics of any country;
"(4) the manner of fixing tolls and charges should be decided by agreement between Egypt and the users;
"(5) a fair proportion of the dues should be allotted to development;
"(6) in case of disputes, unresolved affairs between the Suez Canal Company and the Egyptian Government should be settled by arbitration with suitable terms of reference and suitable provisions for the payment of sums found to be due;

"*Considers* that the proposals of the Eighteen Powers correspond to the requirements set out above and are suitably designed to bring about a settlement of the Suez Canal question by peaceful means in conformity with justice;

"*Notes* that the Egyptian Government, while declaring its readiness in the exploratory conversations to accept the principle of organized collaboration between an Egyptian Authority and the users, has not yet formulated sufficiently precise proposals to meet the requirements set out above;

"*Invites* the Governments of Egypt, France and the United Kingdom to continue their interchanges and in this connexion *invites* the Egyptian Government to make known promptly its proposals for a system meeting the requirements set out above and providing guarantees to the users not less effective than those sought by the proposals of the Eighteen Powers;

"*Considers* that pending the conclusion of an agreement for the definitive settlement of the regime of the Suez Canal on the basis of the requirements set out above, the Suez Canal Users' Association, which has been qualified to receive the dues payable by ships belonging to its members, and the competent Egyptian authorities, should co-operate to ensure the satisfactory operation of the Canal and free and open transit through the Canal in accordance with the 1888 Convention." (U.N. doc. S/3671)

During the discussion which followed, Iranian Representative Abdoh proposed that certain changes be made in the second half of the draft resolution. The British and French Representatives accepted the Iranian proposals. The 742d meeting adjourned at 8:10 p.m., without a vote being taken. (U.N. doc. S/PV.742)

The Security Council continued its consideration of the British-French draft resolution at its 743d meeting, which convened at 9:30 p.m. that same evening. During the course of debate, Yugoslav Representative Popovic tabled an alternate draft resolution, which retained the first part of the British-French draft, but altered considerably the second half of the draft resolution. After further discussion, the British-French draft resolution was put to the vote in two parts. The first part, containing the preambular paragraph and the first operative paragraph, was adopted unanimously (S/3675); the second part, containing the last four operative paragraphs of the draft resolution, received a vote of nine in favor and two (the Soviet Union and Yugoslavia) opposed. Because of the Soviet veto, the second part of the draft resolution was not adopted. Subsequently, the Yugoslav Representative stated that he would not press for a vote on his draft resolution. (U.N. doc. S/PV.743)

For text of Dulles' closing statement at the 743d meeting, see Department of State *Bulletin*, October 22, 1956, pages 615–617; and *United States Policy in the Middle East, September 1956–June 1957*, pages 116–119.

342.   Editorial Note

During the evening meeting of the Security Council on October 13, a memorandum, which Sir Harold Beeley of the British Delegation had prepared for Foreign Secretary Lloyd, was handed to Secretary Dulles. The memorandum reads as follows:

"I have now had a further word with Mr. Phleger about dues for SCUA. He says that he thinks the misunderstanding can be cleared up. He suggests that the Secretary of State [Lloyd] should ask Mr. Dulles whether we can agree that dues should be paid to SCUA on the four following conditions:

"1. SCUA is organized and ready to operate (essentially appointment of an Administrator).
"2. The U.S. (as to U.S. flagships), the U.K. and France will all pay dues to it in the same way, and as many others as are willing.
"3. SCUA shall be enabled to pay out of these funds fair and proper compensation to Egypt as and when determined by SCUA, and any balance dealt with as determined by SCUA.
"4. The U.S. ships will receive the same treatment at the Canal in these circumstances as ships of the U.K. and France if not, a new situation arises.

"Mr. Phleger believes Mr. Dulles will confirm that this is the United States position. I think we could also accept it."

Later during the meeting, Dulles returned the British note to Lloyd along with a handwritten reply. Dulles' reply reads as follows:

"This, in substance, is O.K. I think it has been more accurately expressed in our prior communications, e.g., we cannot order payment to SCUA. We can forbid payments to Egypt except through SCUA. We can and will recommend payment to SCUA—also by U.S. owned ships not under U.S. flag." (Department of State, Presidential Correspondence: Lot 66 D 204, UK official corres. with Secy Dulles/Herter 7/54 thru 3/57 Vol I incoming)

343.   Memorandum of a Telephone Conversation Between the
President and the Secretary of State, Washington,
October 14, 1956, 12:30 p.m. [1]

I wished the President "happy birthday". He thanked me.

I then said that I thought matters had gone fairly well at the UN; that the "principles" had been adopted unanimously, and that negotiations would continue between the British, French and Egyptians under the auspices of the Secretary-General. I thought that talks would be resumed probably within about ten days and there might even be some further talks at the UN on Monday since the Secretary-General, Lloyd and Fawzi would all be there.

The President said he was relieved to hear this. He had listened to the radio news at 11:00 o'clock the night before and had been disturbed because the commentator had indicated that everything was in a state of collapse.

I said that he was probably referring to the prospective Soviet veto. I said, however, that was not an unmixed blessing and indeed the British and the French had wanted this. They had said that they could not live politically with a resolution which the Soviets would approve. I told the President that with some minor modifications we could have gotten a resolution, all of which probably would have been adopted unanimously, but that the British and the French deliberately rejected this.

I said that I felt that my statement at the closing about continuing the conversations was practically effective to assure this and that the moral effect of the adoption of the second part of the resolution by a vote of 9 to 2 was considerable.

[Here follows discussion of unrelated subjects.]

JFD [2]

---

[1] Source: Eisenhower Library, Dulles Papers, White House Telephone Conversations. Secret. Drafted by Dulles. Dulles and his party left New York at 10:40 a.m. and arrived in Washington at 11:50 a.m., October 14. (Dulles' Appointment Book; Princeton University Library, Dulles Papers)

[2] Macomber initialed for Dulles.

344.   Memorandum of a Conversation, Washington, October 15, 1956, 11 a.m. [1]

SUBJECT

Israeli Reaction to Iraqi Troops in Jordan

PARTICIPANTS

The President
The Secretary
The Under Secretary
William M. Rountree

The Secretary told the President that he was seeing the Israel Ambassador at 12:00 prior to the latter's departure for Tel Aviv where he and the Israeli Ambassadors to certain other countries had been called for discussions, presumably of the situation in Jordan. The Jordan situation had been deteriorating in recent weeks, in part as a result of Israel raids, three of which were on a large scale involving up to three battalions. [2]

The Secretary reviewed the chronology of our talks with Israel and other developments relating to the plan whereby Iraq would send limited numbers of troops in response to an appeal by Jordan. Whereas the Israeli had first agreed that it would be advisable for the Iraqi forces to come in under certain conditions, they had now taken a strong position in opposition to the move. The reasons given for this change were reviewed by the Secretary. He feared that Israel may use the matter as a pretext to move into Jordan themselves [sic]. In this connection, the U.K. was bound by a mutual defense treaty with Jordan, and British officials had pointed out the existence of this treaty in conversations which they had had with the Israel Government.

The Secretary said that Israel, in considering whether or not to move into Jordan, might consider that they should take advantage of the concatenation of several circumstances: (1) the virtual collapse of

---

[1] Source: Eisenhower Library, Dulles Papers, Meetings with the President. Secret; Personal and Private. Drafted by Rountree. Attached to the source text is a chit for Rountree dated 4:45 p.m., October 15, which reads: "Mr. Bergus just got a call from the Israel Embassy, pointing out how deeply they were impressed with the Secretary today. D[onald] B[ergus] asked that the message be passed along to you." For the memorandum of conversation between Dulles and Eban, see Document 346.

[2] On October 10, Israel launched a reprisal raid into Jordan, which the Embassy in Tel Aviv described as appearing to be the "heaviest Israel-Jordan military engagement since war of independence." The Embassy also reported that the Israelis were making use of their biggest artillery, mortars, machine guns, and, for the first time, tanks. (Telegram 352 from Tel Aviv, October 10; Department of State, Central Files, 684A.85/10–1056) The Embassy later reported that, according to Israeli sources, Israeli casualties included 9 dead and 12 wounded, and Jordanian dead and wounded numbered over 100. (Telegram 355 from Tel Aviv, October 11; ibid.)

Jordan; (2) the fact that Egypt had not sufficiently disengaged in the Suez matter to permit the movement of its troops into a position to help Jordan or to attack Israel; and (3) the elections in the United States, which Israel officials might calculate would prevent any American reaction against Israel. These factors might have been in the mind of Ben Gurion in undergoing what Eban described as "an evolution in his thinking" between the time he gave provisional approval to the Iraqi move and a few days ago when he declared his opposition to it.

In addition to the British-Jordan treaty which would presumably come into play if Israel should attack Jordan, we had, the Secretary said, the 1950 Tripartite Declaration [3] and the President's statement of last April [4] concerning the United States' attitude toward aggression in the area. We also were confronted with the fact that the United States had been instrumental in arranging for the provision to Israel by other countries of jet aircraft. There was some indication that Israel had in fact a good many more Mysteres than those which we had been informed had been delivered. There was some report, as yet unconfirmed, that Israel had used jet aircraft in the latest large scale attack on Jordan despite categorical assurances that planes provided would be used entirely for defensive purposes.

The Secretary observed that the Israel Government may be feeling "cockey" as a result of having acquired aircraft which at the present time placed them in a position of superiority to Egypt. Jordan and Iraq possessed limited air power.

The Secretary said he had wanted to review this question with the President in order to get the latter's views as to how strong he should be in his talk with the Israel Ambassador.

The President felt that Ambassador Eban should be told that while Israel might gain certain short-term advantages by attacking Jordan, we firmly believed that in the long run they stood to lose a great deal. In the face of such an Israeli aggression, the force of world opinion would be against them and in favor of the Arabs. It was possible under those circumstances that the Russians would provide large-scale assistance to the other side, and in so doing would be placed in the light of acting within the United Nations Charter. The United States' hands would be tied regarding assistance

---

[3] Under the Tripartite Declaration, which was made public on May 25, 1950, the United States, Great Britain, and France declared, among other points, their "unalterable opposition to the use of force or threat of force between any of the states in that area." For text, Department of State *Bulletin*, June 5, 1950, p. 886.

[4] In his April 9 statement, President Eisenhower affirmed U.S. support of Hammarskjöld's peace efforts in the Middle East, reiterated the U.S. commitment within constitutional means to oppose any aggression in the area, and expressed U.S. determination to support and assist any nation that might be subjected to such aggression. For text, see *ibid.*, April 23, 1956, p. 668.

to Israel if the latter should be responsible for bringing about an unjust war; for us to help it would place us in the position of violating the Charter ourselves.

The President emphasized that our position in this matter could not and should not be influenced by domestic political considerations. It would be a shame, he said, if the American leadership should make its decisions on any basis other than what was right and what was in our overall national interest. He would not under any circumstances permit the fact of the forthcoming elections to influence his judgment. If any votes were lost as a result of this attitude, that was a situation which would have to be confronted, but any other attitude would not permit us to live with our conscience.

---

345.   Memorandum for the Record by the President [1]

Washington, October 15, 1956.

The Secretary of State, accompanied by Mr. Hoover and Mr. Rountree of his office, came to see me about the deteriorating situation in the Israel-Jordan area. [2]

It seems to be taken internationally as a foregone conclusion that Jordan is breaking up, and of course all the surrounding countries will be anxious to get their share of the wreckage, including Israel. In fact, there is some suspicion that the recent savage blows of the Israel border armies against the strong points within Jordan territory are intended to hasten this process of dissolution.

On the other side of the picture, there is some indication that Britain is really serious in her announced intention of honoring her Pact with Jordan, [3] which requires her to help defend Jordan in the case of outside invasion.

Should this occur, we would have Britain in the curious position of helping to defend one of the Arab countries, while at the same time she is engaged in a quarrel—which sometimes threatens to break out into war—with Egypt over the Suez question.

---

[1] Source: Eisenhower Library, Whitman File, Eisenhower Diaries. Top Secret. Also printed in *Waging Peace*, pp. 676–677.

[2] See *supra*.

[3] Reference is to the Anglo-Jordanian Treaty of 1948.

All this brings to the fore one particular thing we must bear in mind. It is this: As of this moment we are dealing with the existing situation—that is, with Jordan enjoying the rights of a sovereign country. At the same time, in view of the possible disintegration of the Jordanian government, we must be ready to deal with the situation in which the people and territory of that country would be absorbed by others.

For the moment we can deal only with the first problem.

The Secretary of State is having a long conference with the Israeli Ambassador to this country, Mr. Eban. [4] The Ambassador is about to return to his own country and is visiting Foster to discuss some of the factors in the above problem.

I have told the Secretary of State that he should make very clear to the Israelis that they must stop these attacks against the borders of Jordan. If they continue them, and particularly if they carry them on to the point of trying to take over and hold the territory west of the Jordan River, they will certainly be condemned by the United Nations, and not only Arab opinion but all world opinion will be brought to bear against this little country. Moreover, should there be a United Nations Resolution condemning Israel, there will be no brake or deterrent possible against any Soviet move into the area to help the Arab countries. They could bring considerable forces in under the guise that they were carrying out a United Nations mandate, the ultimate effect of which would be to Sovietize the whole region, including Israel.

There has been some disposition to believe that Ben Gurion's obviously aggressive attitude is inspired, at this moment, by three things:

(a) His desire to take advantage of the gradual deterioration in Jordan and to be ready to occupy and lay claim to a goodly portion of the area of that nation;

(b) The preoccupation of Egypt and the Western powers in the Suez question, which would tend both to minimize the possibility that Egypt would enter a war against him promptly, while at the same time it would impede Britain's capability of reinforcing Jordan.

(c) His belief that the current political campaign in the United States will keep this government from taking a strong stand against any aggressive move he might make.

Secretary Dulles will warn the Ambassador that while, of course, we would hate to create misunderstandings and needless passion in this country over this question, at this moment he should inform his government that no considerations of partisan politics will keep this government from pursuing a course dictated by justice

----
[4] See *infra*.

and international decency in the circumstances, and that it will remain true to its pledges under the United Nations.

Ben Gurion should not make any grave mistakes based upon his belief that winning a domestic election is as important to us as preserving and protecting the interests of the United Nations and other nations of the free world in that region. The Secretary is to point out, moreover, that even if Ben Gurion, in an aggressive move, should get an immediate advantage in the region, that on a long term basis aggression on his part cannot fail to bring catastrophe and such friends as he would have left in the world, no matter how powerful, could not do anything about it.

Foster will make this attitude clear and unmistakeable to Mr. Eban.

At the same time I have Foster's promise to have ready a policy or plan that would guide our action in the event that the dissolution of Jordan would actually take place and thus create a new situation in the world. [5]

D.D.E. [6]

Appendix:

It is believed that one of the recent Israeli raids against Jordan involved two or three battalions of infantry, artillery, and jet airplanes. Incidentally, our high-flying reconnaissance planes have shown that Israel has obtained some 60 of the French Mystere pursuit planes, when there had been reported the transfer of only 24. Jordan has no aviation.

D.D.E. [6]

---

[5] No document corresponding to this description has been found in Department of State files.

[6] Printed from a copy that bears these typed initials.

346.   **Memorandum of a Conversation, Department of State, Washington, October 15, 1956, 12:07 p.m.** [1]

SUBJECT

Various Aspects of Near East Developments

PARTICIPANTS

Mr. Abba Eban, Ambassador of Israel
Mr. Reuven Shiloah, Minister, Embassy of Israel

The Secretary, John Foster Dulles
The Under Secretary, Herbert Hoover, Jr.
NEA—William M. Rountree
NE—Fraser Wilkins

The Israeli Ambassador called on the Secretary prior to his departure for Tel Aviv this afternoon to discuss various aspects of Near East developments. Mr. Eban thanked the Secretary for arrangements which had been made for the presentation of Israeli views regarding transit through the Suez Canal before the Security Council. He said these arrangements gave the matter greater status and greater public impact.

Mr. Eban said he wished to explain why the Israeli Government was agitated regarding the movement of Iraqi troops into Jordan. He recalled that Ambassador Lawson and Prime Minister Ben Gurion had discussed the question several weeks ago. [2] Israel greatly appreciated the content of Ambassador Lawson's remarks. Prime Minister Ben Gurion had responded in a similar vein. There had been no element of force majeure. There had, on the contrary, been a meeting of minds. Mr. Eban said his own conversations with Mr. Rountree had been of a similar character.

Mr. Eban continued that Ambassador Lawson and Mr. Rountree had both pointed out the greater role which the United Kingdom played in this matter. Mr. Eban said that since the matter was first discussed there had been a considerable change and the Israeli Government now had a contrary reaction. Mr. Ben Gurion had stipulated the Israeli Government wished information re the size of the Iraqi troop movement and regarding the temporary nature of its mission in Jordan as well as assurances that there would be no

---

[1] Source: Department of State, Central Files, 785.5/10–1556. Confidential. Drafted by Wilkins. The time of the meeting is from Dulles' Appointment Book. (Princeton University Library, Dulles Papers) Regarding the Israeli reaction to this conversation, see footnote 1, Document 344. A briefing memorandum from Rountree to Dulles, dated October 15, is in Department of State, Central Files, 601.84A11/10–1556. A marginal note indicates that Dulles saw the briefing memorandum.

[2] See Document 289.

annexation or territorial change. In subsequent conversations the United Kingdom had not been specific. There were reports that Iraq and Jordan were discussing the movement of an Iraqi division.

Two additional factors had now developed. The United Kingdom had referred to the Anglo-Jordan Treaty of 1948 and had warned or threatened Israel that if it moved against Jordan the British would respond under the Treaty. Mr. Eban said that some years ago following the inclusion of the west bank of Jordan into Jordan, the British had said that the Anglo-Jordan Treaty of 1948 did not apply to the west bank of Jordan. The British had also referred to the Tripartite Declaration of 1950 and the maintenance of the territorial status quo. Mr. Eban said that if there was to be a change in the territorial status quo, Israel had a right to think of taking part in this change. Israel was astonished and alarmed when the United Kingdom referred to the Treaty of 1948 and the Tripartite Declaration of 1950 and said it would use British forces if subsequent circumstances should so necessitate. The United Kingdom now seemed to be talking in the same way to Israel as it had to Egypt following the nationalization of the Suez Canal Company. The U.K. seemed to be taking advantage of the small countries of the Near East. Mr. Eban observed that the Declaration of 1950 was not a unilateral statement but was tripartite. He asked if the U.K. was speaking for the United States and France when they referred to possible action under the 1950 Declaration.

Mr. Eban said that recent Iraqi and British statements envisaged territorial change in the Middle East. It seemed strange that United Kingdom would pick this particular moment to reiterate its views regarding a compromise between the partition lines of 1947 and the armistice lines of 1948. Mr. Eban said that every statesman should be thankful that Israel prevented the continuity of the Arab world. The Secretary noted that under the Partition Resolution of 1947 the southern section of Palestine had been given to Israel.

Mr. Eban summarized Israeli views as follows: Iraqi troops of unknown numbers were entering Jordan. The U.K. now said that there were circumstances in which British forces would be used against Israel. The British had not said that if Jordan attacked Israel the British would defend Israel. Under present political and psychological conditions Israel felt that acquiescence in the Iraqi move as stated by Mr. Ben Gurion no longer prevailed. Mr. Eban hoped that the U.S. would at least disengage itself from the Iraqi move. He hoped there would be continuing discussions if it were not possible for the parties to change their attitudes.

The Secretary said that he thought the Anglo-Jordan Treaty had been extended to apply to the west bank of Jordan. Mr. Rountree said that was his understanding. Mr. Eban said he would check and would supply further details.

The Secretary said, with respect to Ambassador Eban's remarks regarding Iraqi movement of troops into Jordan that there were a number of fundamentals involved. The U.S. was not directly concerned. The U.S. had no treaty either with Iraq or Jordan whereas the U.K. had treaties with both countries. When we had first heard of the possible Iraqi move we had been struck with its favorable aspects. It seemed to serve the basic interests of the U.S. as well as what we thought were Israel's basic interests. It provided some substitute for the Arab Legion which now lacked the leadership of its former British officers. It would be desirable to preempt a position in Jordan in favor of Western interests rather than permit Egypt or possibly the Soviet Bloc to gain influence. We did not consider the Iraqi action as a move toward the fragmentation of Jordan but as a move to prevent fragmentation of that country. Because of developments relating to the Suez Canal, Egypt was not at the present moment in a position to react strongly. Mr. Ben Gurion's conversation with Ambassador Lawson indicated that Israel held similar views. There had been consultation in advance.

The Secretary continued that it was difficult to see how the fundamentals had changed in the situation unless Israel desired the fragmentation of Jordan and its annexation. He thought that the elements which had been set forth by Ambassador Eban on behalf of the Israel Government seemed superficial and not of such gravity as to upset the original calculations. It was no secret that Iraq had long held that the Partition Resolution of 1947 should provide a final basis for a solution to the Palestine question. Iraq had reiterated this position many times. Prime Minister Eden's statement of November 1955, [3] which was made without prior consultation with the United States, was also well known. The Secretary said he had been told that Selwyn Lloyd had stated that recent British Foreign Office comment on the Iraqi attitude was not to emphasize the territorial aspects but the peaceful aspects of the Iraqi statement. The Arabs had not during recent months referred to the possibility of a peaceful solution to the Palestine question because they felt more certain of Soviet support. The British explanation was not irrational. Neither the Iraqi nor the British statements seemed to alter fundamentally the situation as previously analyzed by the U.S. and Israel on which there had been agreement.

The Secretary noted, with respect to the Tripartite Declaration of 1950, that there had been no consultation between the U.S. and

---

[3] Reference is to a speech by Eden delivered at the Guildhall in London on November 9, 1955.

the U.K. prior to the latter's reference to this Declaration in its discussions with the Israel Government. We also understood that there had been no consultation between the U.K. and France. The Secretary said he did not wish to indicate it was not possible to take unilateral action under the Tripartite Declaration. He had not studied this aspect of the Declaration.

The Secretary also noted, with respect to the Anglo-Jordan Treaty, that it did not seem abnormal for the U.K. to refer to it. He could understand why Israel might be concerned. On the other hand some might interpret the matter differently. During recent Israeli actions there had been massive retaliatory raids against posts in Jordan which partook of the nature of acts of war. In the most recent incident three battalions carrying heavy weapons were reported as having been used. There were reports on the use of jet planes. (The Secretary asked Ambassador Eban for information re the use of jet planes.) These heavy blows by Israel were having the effect of weakening the Government of Jordan and hastening the fragmentation of that country. The Secretary drew a comparison between our mutual security arrangements and the Anglo-Jordanian treaty, observing that in both cases it was inherent in the treaty relationship for discussion to take place.

The Secretary continued that it would not be unnatural for Israel to believe that opportunities might arise in which it could acquire additional territory to augment its meager area. We were anxious, nevertheless, that there be a maintenance of the status quo and believed that the movement of Iraqi troops into Jordan would have a stabilizing effect. We understood that there might be some delay in executing the move during which Ambassador Eban would have an opportunity to question his Government and clarify some of the issues.

The Secretary said that we could not take responsibility in regard to the situation because there were factors in it which we do not control. There are other Governments which have other responsibilities under other treaties. These Governments have already taken certain steps and certain moves have already started. If Israel had been against the proposition in the beginning perhaps we could have exerted our influence to stop it. We still believe, however, the Iraqi move into Jordan should take place. We believe the Israeli objections do not go to the heart of the matter. We believe Israel should favor the Iraqi move if it wishes to maintain the status quo, to prevent the fragmentation of Jordan and to diminish the possibility of Egyptian, and possibly Soviet Bloc, influence in Jordan. The Secretary was not surprised that the Israeli Government might be distressed and anxious re the confused situation. He said that he had spoken with the President and wished to emphasize that in the long run it was important that the U.S. and Israel should find ways to work together and that it would be disastrous if the Israel Government took action which might seem to put it on the wrong side of the general armistice agreements between Israel and its Arab neighbors and of the United Nations Charter. If there were aggression the Soviet Union would have an excuse to come in as a defender of the United Nations Charter. We were concerned that the magnitude of recent retaliatory moves against Jordan would place Israel on the wrong side of the moral judgment of the American people. We were concerned that Israel might find it expedient to seek a temporary advantage and move against Jordan. The Secretary hoped Israel would continue to bear in mind the basic principles which govern U.S.-Israel relations. Ambassador Eban said that Israel continued to favor the maintenance of the status quo in the Near East, but that if there were a new deal in the Near East Israel should discuss and take part in it. There were many in Israel who were pressing for a change in the status quo because of Egypt's preoccupation with the Suez Canal, but the Israeli Government was resisting this advice. Ambassador Eban drew a distinction between retaliatory action and military efforts to change the status quo. He said the Israeli Government had changed its view regarding the Iraqi movement into Jordan because the psychological atmosphere in the Near East had altered.

The Secretary asked why Israel considered the Iraqi movement as doubtful today as the Iraqi force would be a small one and it would stabilize the situation in Jordan. Ambassador Eban replied that the British and the Iraqis had placed the matter in the context of the Arab-Israeli dispute and had made reference to the Tripartite Declaration of 1950. It was possible that the U.K. had given Israel the wrong impression. Israel believed British intentions were wider in scope.

The Secretary asked if Israel desired strong Egyptian influence in Jordan. Ambassador Eban said Israel did not and they had not reached final conclusions regarding the Iraqi move into Jordan. He said that the manner in which the U.K. had presented the matter to Israel had made it doubtful. He speculated that perhaps Israel had misunderstood the U.K. approach. The Secretary commented that although the British approach might have been awkward and "bad diplomacy", he would think that Israel would wish to adhere to the fundamentals in the situation.

Mr. Shiloah interjected to remark that according to Israeli information, discussions between Jordan and Iraq were much wider than had originally been understood. Iraq was now planning strongly to bolster Jordan. Not only was Jordan to be stabilized, but there were to be new territorial arrangements in the area.

The Secretary replied that we had the most categorical assurances that the purpose of the Iraq move into Jordan was to prevent the breakup of that country. Mr. Shiloah further noted that when American and Israeli officials had first discussed the question in Tel Aviv, the U.K. had not been in touch with us.

Ambassador Eban also said that there was a difference between Ambassador Lawson's discussions and the British discussions with the Israeli Government. Ambassador Lawson's remarks had had a most important effect. It was important that there now be a meeting of minds between Israel and the U.S.

The Secretary said he understood the U.K. was further discussing the question in Tel Aviv today and that the entry of Iraqi troops had been held up for a day or two. During the interval perhaps misunderstandings could be cleared up. He wished to make the U.S. attitude clear. The Iraqi troop movement was a small one. It was being made for defensive purposes at the request of the Government of Jordan and would not proceed to the other side of the Jordan River. The Secretary said that we would not regard this movement of Iraqi troops into Jordan as legal or moral justification for an Israeli move against Jordan. We could hardly take that position as the U.S. itself has troops abroad under Mutual Security treaties. The Treaty arrangement between Iraq and the U.K. seemed similar in this respect. Ambassador Eban said that he would convey this view to the Israel Government.

Mr. Shiloah interjected that when Ambassador Lawson had confidentially discussed the Iraqi move with the Israel Government, Israel had urged that if there were to be any territorial changes, the sooner Israel was consulted, the more effective Israel would be. The Secretary replied that he could say without any qualification or reservation that we were not privy to any conversation or arrangement for the fragmentation of Jordan. We had heard no talk from the U.K., Iraq or Jordan which included the liquidation of Jordan. Although it had not been expressed it was possible that this concept was entertained by some. He could give no guarantee as to what some might be thinking, but as far as we were concerned, we were not aware that this was a objective. It was not now an element in the situation as we saw it.

Ambassador Eban said he wished to raise another subject. The Israel Government interpreted the recent Security Council Resolution on Suez as juridically strengthening the freedom of passage of all ships through the Suez Canal.

The Secretary said that before Ambassador Eban left he wanted to make certain he had made clear U.S. concern regarding reports that Israel had used jet aircraft during recent Israeli attacks against Jordan. The Secretary noted that the U.S. has used its own influence not ineffectively to assist Israel in strengthening its armed forces and had been assured that Israel's new strength would be used for defensive purposes. Ambassador Eban replied that he had heard Jordanian reports Israel had used jet aircraft, but that he did not believe they were correct. Both Ambassador Eban and Mr. Shiloah said that they could assure the Secretary that none of the planes which they had recently obtained were used against Jordan. The Secretary said he would like to have definite word before his press conference on October 16 as he anticipated correspondents would question him on this point.

Ambassador Eban concluded the interview by thanking the Secretary for the recent press release from the Export-Import Bank regarding Israel's loan application for water development. [4] Ambassador Eban promised the Secretary a copy of a release from the Israel Embassy touching on this matter.

Ambassador Eban said that he would probably be questioned by the press on leaving the Department. Ambassador Eban, with the Secretary's agreement, said that he would merely indicate that they had had a general review during which they had touched on various aspects of the situation in the Near East, including the Suez Canal, Iraqi troops in Jordan, and other matters.

Note: Mr. Shiloah subsequently telephoned regarding jet planes and the Anglo-Jordanian Treaty. Mr. Shiloah said there was not the slightest doubt no jet planes had been used during recent Israel moves against Jordan. Mr. Shiloah said the Israeli statement that the Anglo-Jordanian treaty did not apply to the west bank of Jordan was not correct. Ambassador Eban and Mr. Shiloah had had an Israeli reservation to the extension by the British of the Treaty to the west bank. Mr. Shiloah asked me to correct the misleading impression which they had given the Secretary earlier today.

---

[4] On October 11, the Export-Import Bank announced its plans to send a team of experts to Israel in conjunction with Israel's pending request for a $75 million loan. At the same time, Samuel C. Waugh explained that an on-the-ground examination of existing projects and potential resources for further agricultural development was customary before any definite steps could be taken on proposals of this nature. (*The New York Times*, October 12, 1956)

347.   Letter From Secretary of State Dulles to Foreign Secretary Lloyd[1]

Washington, October 15, 1956.

DEAR SELWYN: In view of our talks in London about the Users' Association and the dues,[2] I should like to try to straighten the matter out or at least to make clear our point of view.

The Users' Association was designed to try to bring about practical cooperation with Egypt at the working level, and in a sense to replace in this respect the Universal Suez Canal Company.

At the time when I advised your Government and the French Government of our willingness to join the Association, I made this clear, in a memorandum of September 11, 1956, which was handed to Sir Roger Makins[3] and which I understand was at once transmitted to London and also to the French Embassy, Washington. This memorandum includes the following statement regarding the functions of the Users' Association including payment of dues to it, and payment therefrom of appropriate compensation to Egypt.

" . . . practical cooperation on the part of Egypt can only be effectively achieved if the users are organized so that they can deal jointly with Egypt and Egypt deal with them jointly . . . [the users' association] would receive the dues from ships passing through the Canal, which would be used to defray the expenses of the organization and to pay appropriate compensation to Egypt for its contribution to the maintenance of the Canal and the facilities of transit . . . "[4]

We were informed that this concept of SCUA was accepted by your Government, and Prime Minister Eden in his speech to Parliament the following day (September 12, 1956)[5] said in substance the same thing. With reference to payments to Egypt, he said:

---

[1] Source: Eisenhower Library, Dulles Papers, Misc. Papers—U.K. (Suez Crisis). Secret. Delivered to the British Delegation in New York on October 15 and transmitted to London in telegram 2753, October 16. (Department of State, Central Files, 974.7301/10–1556)

[2] The entry for October 13 in Dulles' Appointment Book indicates that Dulles met alone with Lloyd at 12:15 a.m., on Sunday, October 14. The two were later joined by Mrs. Dulles, Phleger, Dixon, and McCardle. (Princeton University Library, Dulles Papers) No account of this conversation has been found in either Department of State files or the Eisenhower Library. According to the account of the conversation in Lloyd's memoirs, Dulles told Lloyd that while the dues should be paid to SCUA, that organization would then pass on 90 percent of them to Nasser. Lloyd had told Dulles that he was horrified by this proposal which would give to Nasser a larger proportion than he was currently receiving. (*Suez 1956, A Personal Account*, p. 162)

[3] Attached to Document 208.

[4] Brackets and ellipses in the source text.

[5] For text of Eden's remarks, see House of Commons, *Parliamentary Debates*, 5th Series, vol. 558, cols. 10–11.

"It is contemplated that Egypt shall receive appropriate payment from the association in respect to the facilities provided by her, but the transit dues will be paid to the users' association and not to the Egyptian authorities."

At my press conference the day following the Prime Minister's speech (September 13, 1956), [6] I stated:

"We believe that, under present circumstances, practical cooperation with Egypt can be effectively achieved only if the users are organized so that they can deal jointly with Egypt and Egypt deal with them jointly.

"We are thus prepared to participate in a users' organization on the basis which I indicated. It is our thought that the users' association would, among other things, provide qualified pilots for the users' ships; would initially receive the dues from the ships of members of the association passing through the Canal, which sums would be used to defray the expenses of the organization and to pay appropriate compensation to Egypt for its contribution to the maintenance of the Canal and the facilities of transit; and so far as practical arrange for the pattern of traffic of the member vessels through the Canal.

"It is our hope that perhaps practical on-the-spot arrangements for cooperation can be achieved without prejudice to the rights of anyone. This may provide a provisional de facto working arrangement until formal agreements can be reached."

The United States has always made it clear that under our laws we could not actually direct that payments be made to SCUA, but that we could require that any payments to Egypt in connection with transit of the Canal be made only through SCUA. We thought this would have the practical effect of bringing about payments to SCUA as agent for the shippers.

We also pointed out that it was at least dubious whether we should attempt to impose our Treasury regulations upon ships of other than United States registry, but that we would try through persuasion to bring about a conformity of practice between United States registry ships and ships of United States ownership under foreign flags.

I dealt with these matters, you will recall, in my press conference of September 26, 1956, [7] when, in answer to a question, I stated:

"It is planned . . . [8] that we will take steps to amend the present Treasury license so as to preclude any direct payments to Egypt, and to permit such payments to Egypt only as they might

---

[6] For the transcript of Dulles' press conference, see Department of State *Bulletin*, September 24, 1956, pp. 476–483.

[7] For the transcript of Dulles' press conference, see *ibid.*, October 8, 1956, pp. 543–549.

[8] Ellipsis in the source text.

occur through payments to the Users' Association. Of course, you know the Users' Association, under its charter, is authorized to make certain payments over to the Government of Egypt, because we do not expect Egypt to help maintain the Canal entirely out of its own funds. And there could in that way be payments to Egypt through the Users' Association which would act, you might say, as an agent for the vessels. But outside of that, we would not expect that there would be any payments to Egypt by United States flag vessels. We do not have in mind extending that to vessels which are not of United States registry. That involves possible questions of conflict of laws and until we know more clearly what the views might be of the countries of registry, we do not expect, certainly initially, to impose a restriction upon those vessels. We would hope that they might find it desirable voluntarily, to conform to the same practice as United States flag vessels."

We always assumed that any action that we took in this respect would be taken also by the British and the French, with the result that we would have substantially similar Treasury regulations.

This I made clear in a memorandum handed to the United Kingdom and French Governments on September 27, 1956. [9] In this memorandum we asked whether the British and the French were willing to take similar action, and specifically what their regulations would prescribe. Only on October 5 did we receive a reply from your Government. On October 1 we had received a reply from the French Government, but in neither case was the reply fully responsive to our inquiry. [10]

There still seems to be a difference of opinion between us as to how the dues, if collected by SCUA, would be handled. It is apparently your view that the dues should be impounded with SCUA and no part of them paid over to Egypt. That is quite contrary to the ideas which we have had and expressed from the beginning, and, as I interpret it, differs from what Sir Anthony Eden said on September 12 pursuant to prior agreement with us that SCUA would seek a working arrangement with the Egyptian Canal authorities, in pursuance of which an appropriate portion of the tolls would be paid over to Egypt.

I gather that it is now your view that SCUA should serve as a means of exerting pressure on the Egyptian Government by withholding dues. Our idea, made clear from the beginning, is that it was to be a means of practical working cooperation with the Egyptian authorities, which would seek to establish de facto international participation in the operation of the Canal.

---

[9] See telegram 2248, Document 268.
[10] A summary of the French response is in Document 290. A summary of the British response is cited in Document 309.

If there is any misunderstanding between us in this respect, it cannot, I think, be due to any failure on our part to have made our views clear both before the idea of SCUA was announced, immediately afterwards, and continuously since then.

We believe that SCUA can be a valuable organization if it is organized and carried out in accordance with what I thought were our joint views.

In considering how it should operate in relation to Egypt and how much should be paid to Egypt, I think we must take account of the fact that:

(1) We do not want to create a situation where, due to differing past practices by ships of different registries, alteration in the method of paying dues would lead to the debarring only of United States ships. If this happened, it would face us with the alternative of altering our Treasury regulations, which would be a humiliating concession, or seeing United States ships alone forced to go around the Cape, which would be an intolerable discrimination unacceptable to our shippers and indeed to our nation.

(2) What would happen if, following the payment of dues to SCUA and their impounding, all our ships were denied access to the Canal? This is a contingency that we cannot ignore in our planning. I have made it perfectly clear that the United States does not intend to "shoot its way through the Canal". In these circumstances, and assuming that you share this view, we would have to face the economic consequences of going around the Cape. This we have discussed fully with you. So far as the United States is concerned, we can accept those consequences and help you to accept them by Exim Bank loans, but this situation, I understand, is not desired by your Government for quite understandable reasons.

I really believe that we need to make an effort to think together along these lines or otherwise there will be a growing impression that we are at cross-purposes, which is obviously undesirable.

Sincerely yours,

John Foster Dulles [11]

---

[11] Printed from a copy that bears this typed signature.

348.   Letter From Foreign Secretary Lloyd to Secretary of State Dulles [1]

London, October 15, 1956.

MY DEAR FOSTER: May I begin by saying how much I have appreciated your steady support in the Security Council proceedings. I feel that on balance we have come out of them well. Despite the veto, we have the moral support of all but the two Communist members of the Council for the affirmation that the 18 Power proposals conform to the agreed requirements, and for the view that it is now for the Egyptians to produce comprehensive and precise proposals. We have the same authority for the recognition of SCUA and the acknowledgment of its right to receive dues. At the same time we have avoided the risk we admittedly ran in going to the Council, namely that we might be faced with a demand for the reference of the issue to some wider negotiating committee or some process of mediation.

In this context your brief statement late on Saturday night, [2] to the effect that the Secretary-General still had authority to suggest further informal talks, was helpful. For my part, I am certainly willing to continue for a limited time the effort to find a basis for negotiation with Egypt.

But if we are to have any prospect of arriving at a settlement by negotiation, we must have at our disposal some means of pressure as a counterpoise to Egypt's physical possession of the Canal. Unless we can create a reasonable equilibrium of bargaining power, I do not see what incentive Nasser will have to make any substantial concessions. And of course such concessions are essential to agreement.

This brings me to SCUA, which seems to me to offer the best means of providing us with the necessary bargaining power. And here I must say at once that I have been deeply disappointed to find how far apart our conceptions of the purpose of the Users' Association now are.

I have looked again at the documents. I think you will agree that the original idea was that SCUA should organise itself to play a practical part in the transit of shipping through the Canal, by employing a body of pilots and through them cooperating with the shore services of the Egyptian Canal Authority. On that assumption,

---

[1] Source: Eisenhower Library, Dulles Papers, Misc. Papers—U.K. (Suez Crisis). A notation on the source text by Bernau reads: "Sec saw". Transmitted to London in telegram 2785, October 17, which indicates that this letter crossed Dulles' letter to Lloyd, *supra*. (Department of State, Central Files, 974.7301/10–1756)

[2] For text of Dulles' closing statement to the Security Council on October 13, see Department of State *Bulletin*, October 22, 1956, pp. 615–617.

the Association would have spent on its own activities an appreciable part of the dues received, and would have offered payment to Egypt for her contribution to the handling of Canal traffic.

For various reasons this conception of SCUA has had to be abandoned. It is not now conceived as an organization for operating, or playing a large part in operating, the Canal. In these circumstances I think we must seek guidance from the Declaration adopted in London on September 21.[3] In the course of its definition of the purposes of SCUA, this document states (Article II 4):

"To receive, hold and disburse the revenues accruing from dues and other sums which any user of the Canal may pay to SCUA, without prejudice to existing rights, pending a final settlement".

There is here no definition of the proportions in which revenue should be "held" or "disbursed". But there are two considerations which seem to me relevant to a decision on this point. In the first place we for our part do not admit Egypt's right to the Canal dues from July 26 onwards. We have not admitted the validity of the act of nationalisation, and in our view a decision as to the title to dues between July 26, 1956, and the date of the final settlement is a matter for future determination. We have already told the Suez Canal Company that in our opinion their request to be paid a proportion of these dues by SCUA cannot be accepted because it would prejudice the final settlement. And we must, it seems to me, take the same attitude towards any proposal that the bulk of the money should not be handed over to Egypt.

But the more important consideration, to which I return, is that SCUA was intended to strengthen our hand, not to weaken it. If we now decide to pay our dues to SCUA, only to see them passed on to Egypt, Nasser will be getting very much more money from the Canal than he is getting now, and our negotiating position will be much weakened. If I understood you correctly at our private talk early on Sunday morning,[4] it is your feeling that approximately 90% of the dues collected by SCUA should be offered to the Egyptian Canal Authority as payment for the services it renders. If we all agreed on this basis to pay our dues to SCUA, the effect would be that Nasser, while losing one-tenth of the 3% of Canal dues paid by American flag shipping, would at the same time gain nine-tenths of the 60% of Canal dues now denied to him by the ships of Britain, France and others who have followed our lead. This would be an altogether unacceptable result, and I cannot believe that it is what you really intend.

---

[3] For text, see Document 251.
[4] See footnote 2, *supra*.

We are both very conscious of the fact that this is a testing time for Anglo-American relations. I have done my utmost to prevent exaggeration of our differences of approach to the Suez Canal problem in recent weeks, and have emphasised the debt that we owe to your leadership. But we must face the fact that revelation of so grave a divergence between us on the purposes of SCUA would have serious repercussions in Britain.

I do rely on your statesmanship to resolve this difficulty before it becomes a serious factor in our relations. I am afraid that, if we cannot reach agreement, SCUA will prove to have been stillborn, and the prospects of a peaceful settlement with Egypt will be gravely diminished.

Yours ever,

Selwyn

---

349.   Memorandum of a Conversation, New York, October 17, 1956 [1]

SUBJECT

Suez

PARTICIPANTS

U.S.
Mr. Lodge
Mr. Barco
UN
Mr. Dag Hammarskjold, Secretary-General

At lunch today, Mr. Lodge told Mr. Hammarskjold that he had wanted to discuss with him as soon as possible the present situation on the Suez negotiations, and had asked him to lunch immediately upon Mr. Lodge's return from Detroit. Secretary Dulles was particularly anxious to have Mr. Hammarskjold's appraisal of the situation.

---

[1] Source: Department of state, Conference Files: Lot 62 D 181, CF 788. Secret. Drafted by Lodge and Barco. At 11:21 a.m., October 17, Dulles telephoned Barco to express his concern that there was "some evidence to suggest they [the British and French] are swinging to a tough, belligerent policy". He noted that he "would like to get what we can from Hammarskjold. When etc. The Sec. asked Barco to ask Lodge to let him know as soon as possible." (Memorandum of telephone conversation by Bernau, October 17; Eisenhower Library, Dulles Papers, General Telephone Conversations) Lodge was meeting with Hammarskjöld later that day; see *infra*.

Mr. Hammarskjold said that the outlook for negotiations was very favorable. He said that Dr. Fawzi, the Egyptian Foreign Minister, was ready and eager to begin discussions and had already gone over with Hammarskjold a draft paper setting forth the Egyptian position for the negotiations.

Hammarskjold said that, on the basis of their discussion, Fawzi was preparing a redraft. Fawzi planned to remain in New York until Friday [2] of this week and to have further discussions with Hammarskjold before his departure. He would take the paper which emerged from his discussions with Hammarskjold to Cairo and get it approved.

Fawzi had proposed that the talks begin on October 29th in Geneva, with Hammarskjold to issue an invitation to the French, British and Egyptians and to participate in the talks as he had done in New York. Hammarskjold would go to Geneva himself. Hammarskjold said that Lloyd, the U.K. Foreign Minister, was ready to enter into the talks, and he believed that Mr. Pineau, the French Foreign Minister, was ready likewise. Lloyd "would be happy with reasonable guarantees". Hammarskjold intended to arrange the specific date for the renewed discussions with the parties. [3]

In Hammarskjold's discussion with Lloyd, prior to Lloyd's departure for London, Lloyd had shown no particular enthusiasm for the idea of obtaining the agreement of the U.S. and other Users to begin at once paying tolls to SCUA. Hammarskjold said Lloyd had given the impression that this was something that was being urged upon Lloyd by his SCUA advisers, who believed that such pressure on Egypt would make them more amenable in negotiations. Hammarskjold had pointed out to Lloyd the dangers of creating a new set of circumstances at a time when negotiations were about to begin on the basis of the principles adopted by the SC, such circumstances being the existence of additional countries which would not pay tolls to Egypt. If "too much muddy water" was stirred up, none of the Foreign Ministers might come. Hammarskjold felt that Lloyd agreed with this. Pineau had told Hammarskjold that he thought things had gone very well in the SC, and appeared quite pleased with the outcome. Pineau had indicated that, before beginning new discussions, he wanted to get behind him the French Parliamentary debate.

---

[2] October 19.

[3] On October 19, Hammarskjöld suggested to the British, French, and Egyptian Governments that talks among representatives of the three resume in Geneva on October 29. He would issue invitations if all three governments were willing to continue the talks. Hammarskjöld gave Lodge a copy of this "confidential" message on October 19. (Department of State, Central Files, 974.7301/10–1956)

Hammarskjold said that the story by Tom Hamilton published in the *New York Times* on Monday [4] was Hamilton's own interpretation of events. Hammarskjold had asked Lloyd about it, who denied having said anything to Hamilton about using force if British ships were stopped by the Egyptians. Hammarskjold also said that Fawzi's letter to the President of the SC [5] complaining of Sir Anthony Eden's statement about using force as a last resort was Fawzi's way of avoiding a sharper reaction from Egypt. He did not feel that Fawzi was very concerned personally about Eden's statement but understood it in the context of British politics.

Hammarskjold said that, while he believed that the outlook for negotiations was good, he was still concerned that nothing should be done which would change the status of the Canal question from what it was when the SC passed its six principles. He believed that any steps to bring pressure upon Egypt by a shift in payment of tolls, for example, would be inconsistent with an honest desire to negotiate on the basis of the six principles, and would make it difficult—if not impossible—for the Egyptians to participate in negotiations. Hammarskjold said that this did not mean that he believed pressure should never be brought upon the Egyptians, but simply that this was not the time to do it. The situation might change and pressures might then become advisable, but this should be looked at in the light of the results of the next series of negotiations.

The gist of the above was telephoned to Mr. Dulles by Lodge. [6]

---

[4] October 15.
[5] Dated October 15. (U.N. doc. S/3679) Fawzi referred to remarks made by Eden on October 13.
[6] See *infra*.

---

350. Memorandum of a Telephone Conversation Between the Secretary of State in Washington and the Representative at the United Nations (Lodge) in New York, October 17, 1956, 3:25 p.m. [1]

Ambassador Lodge telephoned following his luncheon talk with Secretary General Hammarskjold. Hammarskjold had said that he

---

[1] Source: Eisenhower Library, Dulles Papers, General Telephone Conversations. Eyes Only. Drafted by Dulles. Another memorandum of this conversation by Bernau was attached.

felt that Egypt, France and the United Kingdom all wanted another meeting. They are thinking of the 29th of October at Geneva and Hammarskjold is prepared to invite them to meet with him at that time at the Geneva office of the United Nations. Hammarskjold was, however, worried about the possible results of imprudent and bellicose talks.

Fawzi is going to Cairo before coming to Geneva. He feels that doing that will add to his authority and put him in a better position to make a definitive proposal. Hammarskjold, however, is nervous lest the talking by the British and the French becomes so threatening in tone that Nasser will not let Fawzi go to Geneva. Also, Hammarskjold thinks that if the payment of dues is further disarrayed by further blockings through SCUA, then that might bring about a crisis and Fawzi may not come to Geneva.

Hammarskjold feels, as a result of his Monday talk with Lloyd, that Lloyd is in a good mood and wants to come to an agreement.

I mentioned to Lodge that the British and the French were trying very hard to get us and others to stop payments at the Canal and to pay into a blocked account with SCUA. Lodge said that Hammarskjold felt that if this happened it would blow things "sky high" and that if the British want an agreement they should not try to bring about this change in the tolls system.

Lodge added that Hammarskjold will not actually call the meeting until he has a further response knowing that all three will attend. In answer to an inquiry from me, Lodge said that Hammarskjold had had no word either from Lloyd or Pineau since they got home. Hammarskjold had added that he had a talk with Pineau before he left and that Pineau was "not unhappy".[2]

JFD [3]

---

[2] At 3:45 p.m., Dulles telephoned the President to give him the gist of this conversation: Hammarskjöld's belief that "things are on the track. Once we know we can make a positive statement, said the Pres., he would like to know. The Pres. asked can't we get word to the Egyptians not to believe all they read but go on and negotiate. The Sec. said we have to be careful not to undermine the British. The Pres. said he knows—but his idea was to tell them to keep their dispositions and get into this business." (*Ibid.*, White House Telephone Conversations)

[3] Macomber initialed for Dulles.

351.   Telegram From the Department of State to the Embassy in the United Kingdom [1]

Washington, October 17, 1956—10:27 p.m.

2786. Eyes only Aldrich and Dillon. Deptel 2785 to London 1411 to Paris contains text Lloyd's letter to Secretary October 15 [2] which crossed Secretary's letter to Lloyd same date delivered New York. [3] (Text latter contained Deptel 2753 London, Deptel 1394 Paris.) These communications point up substantial difference in view between UK and ourselves not only re tolls question per se but also re general concept SCUA. Recent conversations with French in New York and Washington disclosed similar differences. Following our provisional views on Lloyd's letter:

We are particularly disturbed at implication Lloyd's letter that original purposes SCUA have had to be abandoned, in lieu of which he conceives organization as an instrument of coercion. We had thought British and French resolution, which all of us supported at UN and which called upon SCUA and competent Egyptian authorities to cooperate to insure satisfactory operation of Canal, was necessarily based upon assumption that SCUA would operate earnestly as instrument to bring about de facto relationship with Egypt which would permit passage of ships through Canal pending final settlement. Obviously, no such satisfactory interim arrangement would succeed if purpose of SCUA was to impound tolls and deprive Egypt of reasonable portion thereof, thus giving no inducement on latter's part to provide "cooperation" called for. As Secretary stated his October 15 letter to Lloyd, he has consistently taken position that appropriate compensation should be paid by SCUA to Egypt but we have no preconceived idea what this should be in terms of percentage.

It is of course highly doubtful that many present members of SCUA would be willing participate in circumstances advocated by Lloyd. In any event, any such change in scope and purpose of SCUA should be dealt with at meeting SCUA members. New concept would have to be thought through carefully before presented as it very apt to face us with alternative of war or economic burdens which British have indicated would be unacceptable. Also thought must be given to impact of a significant change in the status quo upon pending negotiations. Under our concept SCUA would presum-

---

[1] Source: Department of State, Central Files, 974.7301/10–1856. Secret; Priority. Drafted by Rountree, cleared in draft by Dulles, and approved by Rountree who signed for Dulles. Also sent to Paris.

[2] Document 347.

[3] Document 348.

ably negotiate an acceptable provisional arrangement with Egypt for partition of tolls, but under the Lloyd concept an increasing amount of tolls would be arbitrarily denied Egypt pending final settlement.

Particularly disturbing in Lloyd's letter is statement that unless we accept his concept SCUA this will create divergencies between us which would have serious consequences on US–UK relations. Those relations have always been marked by an earnest desire to come to an agreement and willingness subordinate many considerations to achieve such agreement; but never has it been suggested that US would be expected to go along blindly with concept to which it has never agreed and import of which never explained but which seems involve danger of leading us into war or at least supporting a war which has been judged by President to be morally unjustifiable and practically imprudent.

Please let me know promptest your feeling as to a reply to Lloyd along foregoing lines. Also let me have your reaction as to what Government to which you accredited really wants. Is it trying to promote or collapse negotiations? What do you now guess to be its immediate and ultimate objectives?

Dulles

---

352. Editorial Note

At 10:09 a.m. on October 18, Secretary Dulles telephoned Allen Dulles. Their conversation, as transcribed by Bernau, went as follows: "The Sec. said he is quite worried about what may be going on in the Near East. He does not think we have really any clear picture as to what the British and French are up to there. He thinks they are deliberately keeping us in the dark. He wondered if AWD has any real feel of it. AWD said yes in Syria—Egypt fairly well. The Sec. wondered if it would be worth while to have some of his people and ours for meeting—11:30 tomorrow. AWD will bring [Kermit] Roosevelt and one other. The Sec. will have Armstrong and Rountree."

Dulles' Appointment Book for October 19 indicates that the Secretary attended a meeting on the Near East which began at 11:32 a.m. and which was attended by Armstrong, Rountree, Higgs, and Wilkins, who were later joined by Allen Dulles and Kermit Roosevelt. (Princeton University Library, Dulles Papers) No account of this meeting has been found in Department of State files or in the Eisenhower Library.

___

353.   Memorandum of a Conversation, Department of State, Washington, October 19, 1956 [1]

SUBJECT

    SCUA

PARTICIPANTS

    Mr. Anwar Niazi, Chargé, Egyptian Embassy

    NEA—William M. Rountree
    NE—Fraser Wilkins

Mr. Niazi called to say that the Egyptian Ambassador and the Egyptian Foreign Minister had both called him this morning regarding Drew Middleton's article in the *New York Times* of October 19, which stated that the United States was prepared to announce new measures of support for SCUA which would make it an instrument of pressure. Mr. Niazi said that the Egyptian Foreign Minister was quite concerned and that to turn SCUA into owners of the Suez Canal was morally, legally and technically wrong. Mr. Niazi also noted that the members of the Security Council during the recent discussions had requested that no step be taken to upset negotiations. He felt that the measures to which Drew Middleton referred would poison the atmosphere and torpedo the work which had thus far been accomplished. He was certain that the Secretary would appreciate these points and would agree that the chance of negotiations would be ruined. He said that Egyptian Foreign Minister Fawzi was in touch with the Secretary-General Hammarskjold regarding the talks scheduled to commence on October 29. [2]

___

[1] Source: Department of State, Central Files, 974.7301/10–1956. Confidential. A marginal notation on the source text in an unidentified hand reads: "Sec Saw".

[2] During a telephone conversation which began at 10:30 a.m. on October 19, Dulles informed Lodge that there was no basis whatsoever for the Middleton story and asked that Lodge inform Hammarskjöld. Lodge repeated the U.S. position as being that dues paid into SCUA would be transmitted to Egypt but would not be used as a pressure device. Lodge asked Dulles if the British understood this; the Secretary answered yes and added, according to Bernau's transcript, that "they [the British] use Middleton to put out what they would like our policy to be etc. etc." Dulles also told Lodge that he wanted Hammarskjöld to make clear the U.S. position to Fawzi. (Eisenhower Library, Dulles Papers, General Telephone Conversations)

Mr. Rountree said that he would convey the Egyptian Foreign Minister's message to the Secretary. Meanwhile, he wished to make several comments of his own. He said that he did not know what the origin of the *New York Times'* account had been, but wished to make clear that the position of the United States remained as stated by the Secretary on October 16. [3] He added that there were a number of misleading elements in the story. It mentioned reference to the American Embassy. Mr. Rountree said that he had checked with the Embassy in London and had ascertained that, in a discussion with Drew Middleton, they had only quoted from the Secretary's remarks to the press on October 16; therefore there obviously was nothing new in what they said. Mr. Rountree added that it had not been envisaged that SCUA was to engage in economic warfare against Egypt. It was our concept that SCUA, pursuant to its charter, was to become a means of cooperation among the member countries in relation to their common interests in the Suez, and in this connection it would endeavor to make arrangements with the Government of Egypt. Mr. Rountree recalled the Egyptian Foreign Minister himself had not excluded the possibility of a relationship between Egypt and the Users' Association even on a permanent basis. He hoped Mr. Niazi would reassure the Egyptian Foreign Minister that there had been no change in United States policy and that it remained as stated on October 16 by the Secretary.

Mr. Rountree further observed that it was the earnest desire of the United States that conversations between the British, the French and the Egyptians would be resumed and carried out in a favorable atmosphere. We urged that within the context of the six principles, on which there had already been agreement, the Egyptian Foreign Minister would make concrete proposals and suggestions. It was our hope that through this process we would see progress toward an agreement.

Mr. Rountree added that in making his observations regarding the article in the *New York Times*, he did not wish to imply in any way that we do not fully support SCUA. His point was that we did [not] envisage SCUA operating as had been stated in the press, but that we did support SCUA as stated, for example, by the Secretary in his press conference on October 16.

---

[3] On October 16 during a news conference, Dulles stated: "we believe that the organization [SCUA] should be set up to act as agent for the ships; that it should collect the dues from them as their agent, and be prepared to pay an appropriate share of those dues over to Egypt in order to recompense Egypt for its contribution to the passage through the Canal." For transcript of the press conference, see Department of State *Bulletin*, October 29, 1956, pp. 655–662. Excerpts relating to the Suez situation are printed in *United States Policy in the Middle East, September 1956–June 1957*, pp. 122–127.

Mr. Niazi subsequently telephoned to say that he had been in touch with Egyptian Foreign Minister Fawzi who was leaving New York today by plane and had conveyed to him the assurances given by Mr. Rountree. He said that Dr. Fawzi was glad to have the account of the conversation. Mr. Niazi also said that, in response to Mr. Rountree's suggestion regarding concrete proposals, it would not be possible to make them available prior to the talks now scheduled to begin on October 29, but that Dr. Fawzi would be ready with the proposals for negotiation at that time. Mr. Niazi implied that the Egyptians were looking forward to these talks during which they would present proposals for negotiation under each of the principles and wished to present them one by one. Mr. Niazi's main point seemed to be that the Egyptians did not wish to present their proposals in written form as a plan beforehand. [4]

---

[4] Information from the last three paragraphs was included in the Report prepared in the Executive Secretariat, October 23 (Summary No. 36, not printed). President Eisenhower initialed the copy of the report in the Eisenhower Library, Whitman File, International File.

---

354.   Report Prepared in the Executive Secretariat of the Department of State [1]

Summary No. 34   *Washington, October 19, 1956.*

SUMMARY OF DEVELOPMENTS IN SUEZ SITUATION

Resumption of Direct Negotiations Forecast

We have told Embassy Cairo [2] that, not withstanding the veto of the second portion of the resolution at the UN last week, continued exchanges between the foreign ministers of the UK, France and Egypt are being encouraged. The British and French have indicated their willingness to resume discussions with Fawzi, although the French have insisted upon a delay to avoid any implication that they are "too eager". In the absence of complications, we now expect the talks to resume by about October 29—probably at Geneva.

---

[1] Source: Eisenhower Library, Whitman File, International File. Top Secret; Eyes Only for Designated Recipient.
[2] In telegram 1188, October 18, not printed. (Department of State, Central Files, 974.7301/10–1856)

We have concluded that it is most important now to get the substantive discussions going again under Hammarskjold's auspices. In that connection, Egypt should make proposals to the UK and French which are sufficiently specific and which have such a realistic relationship to the six principles agreed upon at the UN and to the 18-nation proposals that negotiation to a conclusion is morally compelling. Such a development, if quickly begun, would prevent a further freezing of positions. We have suggested to Hare that he, in his discretion, put forward this general idea in his talks with Nasser and other appropriate Egyptian officials.

French View of SCUA's Role in Collecting Tolls

French Foreign Office officials have told Embassy Paris [3] that they understood the US believes 90% of the Canal tolls collected by SCUA should be paid to Egypt for the expenses of the Canal operation, whereas the French believe only about 10% should be paid to Egypt. The French consider that withholding as large a proportion of the tolls as possible will serve to stimulate Nasser to negotiate a settlement on the basis of the six principles adopted by the Security Council.

[Here follows discussion of the SCUA Council Meeting (reported in telegram 2137 from Paris, October 18; Department of State, Central Files, 974.7301/10–1856) and the appointment of the Danish Consul General in New York, Eyvind Bartels, as SCUA Administrator.]

(Summary closed 12:30 p.m., October 19, 1956)

---

[3] Reported in telegram 1816 from Paris, October 18, not printed. (*Ibid.*)

---

355.   **Memorandum of Discussion at a Department of State–Joint Chiefs of Staff Meeting, Pentagon, Washington, October 19, 1956, 3:30 p.m.** [1]

[Here follows a list of 25 persons present, including Admiral Radford, General Twining, General Taylor, Admiral Burke, and

---

[1] Source: Department of State, State–JCS Meetings: Lot 61 D 417. Top Secret. Drafted by W. Tapley Bennett. A note on the title page reads: "State Draft. Not cleared by any of the participants."

Lieutenant General Megee. The Department of State delegation included, among others, Murphy, MacArthur, and Phleger.]

1. The Suez Situation

At Mr. Murphy's request Mr. Phleger reviewed recent developments concerned with the Suez problem. He gave particular attention to the consideration of Suez by the U.N. Security Council and discussed the resolution which had been adopted by the Council. [2] Admiral Radford asked whether Egypt had taken part in the drafting of the final position, and Mr. Phleger explained that Egypt had participated in working out the six principles agreed on to govern a settlement. They had not, however, taken action with the others on the second part of the resolution favoring negotiations along the lines laid down in the earlier 18-nation proposals. Mr. Phleger explained that, in addition to their Security Council participation, the Egyptians had had intensive talks while in New York with oil and shipping authorities. It was his feeling that the Egyptians had had borne in on them the long range implications of an attitude of non-cooperation on their part with respect to operation of the Canal; in other words, they could now understand that, if they continued to insist on dominating the Canal and having everything their own way, alternatives to the present use of the Canal would undoubtedly be found by other nations which have too much at stake to submit to Egyptian dictation.

Admiral Radford declared that he was very interested from the military point of view in the problem caused for the British and the French by the expenditures which the two nations, especially the French, have gone to in building up their forces. He stressed the problem of keeping troops in a state of readiness over a long period. Mr. Phleger commented that the British now give the impression of being anxious to move ahead toward reasonable settlement of the Suez issue, whereas the French seem to be less anxious to compose the problem. General Taylor inquired as to the possible relationship between the Suez situation and Arab-Israeli tensions. Mr. Phleger commented briefly on Israeli fears over the Arab menace to their situation and said there are certain urgings on the part of the Israelis to take vigorous action vis-à-vis Jordan while Egypt is preoccupied with Suez. Mr. Phleger pointed out that it is often overlooked that under the 1954 Suez treaty between the United Kingdom and Egypt, the United Kingdom has the right to move back into its former bases in the Suez area in the event of aggression in the Middle East. Mr. Murphy called attention to the situation in Jordan and commented

---

[2] See Document 341.

that he was confident the British have the Jordanian situation and their bases there very much in mind at the present time.

[Here follows discussion of unrelated subjects.]

---

356.   Telegram From the Embassy in the United Kingdom to the Department of State [1]

London, October 19, 1956—8 p.m.

2170. Eyes only Secretary; Paris eyes only Ambassador. I called on Lloyd this morning with view to eliciting further information his thinking at time as to basic Brit position Suez problem and their real intentions (Deptel 2786). [2] Barbour accompanied me and Adam Watson was present with Lloyd. I opened conversation by professing to be confused divergence between US and UK positions revealed your correspondence with Lloyd re payment Canal tolls (Deptels 2753 and 2785). [3] I noted that I could not understand Brit concern over a reasonable portion of Canal toll receipts being paid by SCUA to Egypt, having in mind that SCUA's control over such receipts would not be prejudiced by such payment. I said I consequently would appreciate further exposition Brit reasoning in its opposition to such payment.

It developed that there is a clear demarcation in Brit thought between the role they envisage for SCUA in a final settlement and the means by which they intend to utilize SCUA in the interim to maintain pressure on Egypt to come to a final solution.

Lloyd believes there is no misunderstanding between the US and the UK that SCUA's purposes in connection with a final settlement will be to provide practical operative cooperation with Egypt and maintain the valuable, if not exclusive, sanction for Egypt's compliance with the final agreement, of control over financial payments to it. This seems basically to be an extension to permanency of the concept of SCUA as a provisional mechanism the US has had since the beginning. When such a final settlement is reached he would not be surprised to see 90 percent of the tolls go to Egypt through SCUA. The divergence seems clearly to relate to

---

[1] Source: Department of State, Central Files, 974.7301/10–1956. Top Secret; Priority. Received at 6:25 p.m. Repeated to Paris.

[2] Document 351.

[3] Telegrams 2753 and 2785 transmitted, respectively, Dulles' letter to Lloyd and Lloyd's letter to Dulles, Documents 347 and 348.

the interim period wherein the Brit and French anticipate negotiating directly with the Egyptians for a final settlement. Lloyd is optimistic that the Egyptians will come forward with something which will serve as a basis for further such negotiations within the next ten days or so. Meanwhile, and so long as the negotiations continue with Egypt. His concept is that pressure must be maintained on Egypt, and that that pressure means essentially that there must be no financial increase in Egyptian receipts. Aside from this negotiation concept, without which he believes it will be impossible to obtain Egyptian agreement to a satisfactory final solution, he regards it as impossible from the internal political standpoint for him to defend in Parliament the unblocking of presently frozen funds which would result in augmentation of Egyptian revenues from Canal dues above the 40 percent they are now receiving. The maximum he could envisage defending is around 10 percent although he might go to 20 percent. He was impervious to the suggestion that he could justify such an increase on the grounds that his government has simultaneously achieved the inauguration of SCUA as a practical instrument for maintaining control over Canal revenues. He was unresponsive to the comment that if we are agreed on the ultimate role SCUA should play, it would seem highly undesirable and unrealistic to ask it to take action on an interim basis which would be contrary to our ultimate aim and might not only postpone progress toward those purposes but involve provocations and risks of creating unacceptable consequences.

On basis this conversation and other evidence available here, I would consider it undesirable to respond further in writing to Lloyd's statement. I believe the situation is fundamentally less divergent than the two communications so far exchanged would suggest, at least in relation to the long term. As to the interim, I feel that flexibility exists and that the possibility of a further round of direct UK-French-Egyptian negotiations may make the resolution of this toll problem less urgent than would otherwise be the case. While, as I have indicated in recent messages, I do not believe that the depth of Brit determination in regard to the Suez problem as a whole has appreciably lessened, I do feel that the govt is disposed to try to promote a solution through negotiations rather than the contrary. Indeed, it would be unrealistic for them in their present internal political situation to expect to make political capital in the country out of a solution on any other basis.

In summary, the Brit ultimate objective is, according to their professions and I think realistically in the light of their internal situation, to achieve a settlement involving the Egyptian operation of the Canal under adequate safeguards against discrimination, etc., which would include machinery for the resolution of disputes by international arbitration and sanctions for Egyptian compliance with arbitral awards. Lloyd probably would not acknowledge such a conclusion at this point, but the trend of Brit thinking and other developments is obviously toward the acceptance of SCUA financial control over Canal moneys as the ultimate sole sanction. For the interim, pending agreement with Egypt, their objective can be succinctly stated to maintain maximum pressure on Egypt by any means available, and in any case to do nothing which lightens financial or other pressures under which Egypt now is. As far as Canal tolls are concerned, in this interim period, Brit thinking is that SCUA should function as a receiver of the assets for an estate under litigation, all or the maximum amount possible less minimum essential living expenses for the heirs being held in escrow pending final settlement. It would be the Brit intention to advise the Egyptians of the fact that this was being done which would minimize any provocative implications arising from arrangements. They do not conceive of this position as a change from the original SCUA concept and maintain that there was no such implication in Lloyd's letter of October 15. They do not demand that an increasing amount of tolls be arbitrarily denied to Egypt even in this interim negotiating period where they are looking for the maximum amount of leverage. They simply feel that in this same period it would be bad negotiating tactics and disastrous from their internal political situation to put Egypt in a better position than it is now by reason of the coming into operation of SCUA.

Aldrich

---

357.   Telegram From the Embassy in France to the Department of State [1]

Paris, October 19, 1956—7 p.m.

1839. Eyes only Secretary. Eyes only Ambassador Aldrich. I had luncheon alone today with Chaban-Delmas and during 90 minute conversation obtained clearest expression of official French views on Suez to date. I have been on a basis of personal friendship with Chaban-Delmas for over 3 years and as a result he talked freely and

---

[1] Source: Department of State, Central Files, 974.7301/10–1956. Top Secret; Priority. Received at 9:13 p.m. Repeated to London.

with great frankness. Chaban is a Minister of State in French Government ranking above Pineau, and as such, has been privy to closest held thinking in French Governmental circles.

Chaban-Delmas said that as he understood the problem the only difference between the French and United States position was one of time table. . . . as he understood the matter, the United States was prepared to view this as a rather long term operation which might take a number of years. For the United Kingdom Chaban said the time table was a question of months as the British could not allow the menace to their oil supplies represented by Nasser to continue over a period of years. For France the matter was a question of weeks because of the Algerian problem.

Chaban said that situation in Algeria was now greatly improved and it should be possible to move toward a settlement in the near future except for one thing. This one problem was the belief among Moslem masses that Nasser was winning his contest with Great Britain and France over Suez. Chaban said that in order to make possible a solution in Algeria it was absolutely necessary that Nasser lose face or go in the coming weeks. In this connection he mentioned Christmas as an outside date. In answer to my question regarding what would be a loss of face, Chaban said that we should remember that Nasser had seized the Suez Canal for express purpose of obtaining extra funds with which to build the Aswan Dam. If it could be clearly shown that he would not receive any excess funds from his seizure of the Canal this would be a loss of face such as Chaban had in mind.

In order to proceed Chaban said that we should now set up SCUA very rapidly and that practically all shipping should agree to pay dues to SCUA, in particular, all American controlled shipping, whether American flag or operating under Liberian and Panamanian registry. SCUA should also pay only a minimum percentage of its receipts to Egypt. This minimum percentage should be calculated to just cover the cost of operation and maintenance of the Canal. Chaban pointed out that these figures were readily available from the records of the Universal Suez Canal Company. In arriving at a percentage figure for SCUA payments to Egypt, account must be taken of those dues which are being paid directly to Egypt. The total receipts of Egypt, including both dues paid directly and payments from SCUA, should not be more than necessary to cover the operation and upkeep of the Canal. (I did not question Chaban regarding the profits which Egypt received from the Canal under the Suez Canal Company concession and it might be that French would agree that payments should be large enough to cover not only cost of maintenance and operation but also profits no larger than those received during the past years.) Chaban said that if this arrangement should prove acceptable to Egypt it would be possible for SCUA to allocate additional sums from time to time for specific improvement projects on the Canal. The fundamental point of this whole operation is that no extra funds would be available to Egypt for her own internal uses as a result of Nasser's seizure of the Suez Canal. This situation would continue in effect until such time as a permanent settlement had been negotiated in accordance with the principles approved by Security Council and by the 18 nations in London. Chaban made clear that there should be no negotiations with Egypt regarding these payments by SCUA but that SCUA should make a clear public explanation of the basis on which payments to Egypt were being made, i.e., payments would be adequate to cover operation and maintenance of the Canal and additional payments might be negotiated for specific improvement projects.

Chaban said that the institution of such a regime promptly seemed to him the only possible method of avoiding war. In this connection he felt the role of the United States was vital. He said that recently some members of French Government had become disturbed over the United States position and felt that differences between France and the United States might be more than a question of time table for replacement of Nasser. Some French had begun to feel that the United States might be succumbing anew to the temptation to give in to Nasser's blackmail, in other words to feel that United States should support Nasser in attempt to prevent domination of Egypt by Soviets. Chaban also mentioned at this time rumors that Egyptians were negotiating with Gulf Oil Company to in effect finance the Canal for them. While Pineau had mentioned this matter lightly in his speech to the National Assembly, Chaban said he wished to emphasize that any such action would be simply catastrophic as far as Franco-American relations were concerned.

I asked Chaban what would happen should Nasser decide that the percentage of dues to be offered him by SCUA was too small, and that therefore he would not let ships operating under SCUA use the Canal. He replied that in this event United States ships would go around the Cape, and France and the United Kingdom would take whatever action might be necessary to keep the Canal open.

In conclusion, Chaban said that he well understood that it was vital for the United States Government under the present circumstances to be absolutely sure that peace would be maintained through early November. France, on the other hand, could not allow the problem of Nasser to remain unsolved beyond Christmas at the latest. He said that France was fully prepared to meet the United States requirements for peace prior to early November but felt that the United States should then understand why France and the United Kingdom would be required to act after that date. He suggested that an announcement that SCUA would go into effect should be made around November 1 stating that payments to SCUA would actually begin on November 10. Chaban said that he had told Pineau to talk to you along these lines when he saw you in New York. He said that Pineau had raised some objection, saying he did not feel it was quite diplomatic to talk so frankly but Chaban said he had urged him to be fully frank.

Mindful of the fact that according to British Embassy sources here, as well as information received by our Embassy in London, Eden had been highly impressed by his talk with Chaban during his September visit to Paris, I asked Chaban what he thought of United Kingdom position as a result of his talks with British. Chaban answered that he had had a very frank talk alone with Eden in which he had told Eden it was obvious that Eden's whole future rested on the Suez problem. He had told Eden that there were two alternatives: first, that the United Kingdom Government would continue with its firm policy and achieve a victory in the Suez question which would thoroughly discredit the Labor opposition. The second alternative would be that nothing would be done and Nasser would in effect remain victorious. The result of this would inevitably be that Eden would be swept from power not only by the Labor Party but also as a result of dissatisfaction in Conservative circles. Chaban further told Eden that while he expressed this thought in personal terms it was more important than that because if Eden sincerely believed that his policy was the only one that was vital for the U.K. to follow, he would have to stay in power, as only in that way could his policy be carried out. According to Chaban, Eden told him he had no cause to worry and that it was Eden's intention to continue his firm policy no matter what the cost or how difficult. Chaban, incidentally, expressed a very poor personal opinion of Lloyd whom he felt had nowhere near the same clarity of views on the overall problem as Eden.

I told Chaban that I felt that his description of French position was exactly what I had assumed French position to be since August but I also told him that it had never been expressed with such clarity to U.S. officials. Chaban seemed surprised at this. He said that he assumed that Pineau had long ago made the same sort of exposition to the Secretary.

Comment: This information tallies closely with my earlier thinking except for the additional assurance that French do not contemplate any military action prior to approximately Nov. 10. Chaban insisted that French do not want military action and hope to avoid it. However, only means of avoiding it would be by successful operation of SCUA which would deprive Nasser of any benefits from nationalization. If this not acceptable to Nasser French are prepared to take military action. On other hand, from point of view of U.S. Chaban felt that we should give full support to SCUA as it would be only possible means of avoiding military action. If we did not give such support and SCUA operation such as he envisaged could not go into effect, Chaban indicated that there would be likelihood of disturbances taking place in Egypt of the sort that would necessitate military intervention by France and the UK. I feel that Chaban's views are accurate description of French Government policy in Suez affair as of today.

Next following telegram of lower classification gives Chaban's views of political effects in France of possible failure on Suez. [2]

Dillon

---

[2] Telegram 1840, October 20, reported Chaban's prediction that a prestige victory for Nasser would make it impossible for France to hold Algeria and would lead to a "Popular Front" government in France's and eventual French withdrawal from NATO. (*Ibid.*)

---

358.   Message From Secretary of State Dulles to Foreign Secretary Lloyd [1]

Washington, October 19, 1956.

DEAR SELWYN: I have your letter of October 15 which apparently crossed mine to you of the same date. I greatly appreciate what you say about the steady support which we gave you in the Security Council proceedings. I agree with your appraisal of the result. I think it particularly important that the discussions continue to be confined to the UK, France, and Egypt, with Hammarskjold assisting.

As regards SCUA I am disturbed by your apparent suggestion that the original idea of SCUA must now be abandoned in favor of some new and to me ill-defined concept. It has never occurred to me that the basic purpose of SCUA has been or should be changed. You seem now to envisage it primarily as an instrument of pressure. I conceive it as a collective effort by users to enable them better to

---

[1] Source: Department of State, Central Files, 974.7301/10–1956. Secret. Transmitted Priority to London in telegram 2851, October 19, 8:39 p.m., which is the source text, with the instruction: "Eyes only Aldrich and Dillon. Please deliver following message urgently to Lloyd from Secretary". Telegram 2851 was drafted by Dulles and repeated to Paris.

work out a satisfactory practical settlement with Egypt, because it represents the combined views and business of its member users.

I quite admit that the original concept has changed *quantitatively* in the sense that SCUA may not have to assume as heavy an operating burden, for pilots and the like, as it was first thought might need to be the case.

But I do not feel that this revolutionizes the character of SCUA. The basic purpose, as I have always conceived it, was to achieve an "on-the-spot" working arrangement with Egypt which would, in fact, amount to an international participation in the operation of the Canal under conditions which would protect the Canal users from covert discrimination and lead into a permanent satisfactory settlement. It would insulate the Canal operations from Egyptian policies designed to favor or hurt the shipping or cargoes of various nations and prevent making the Canal an instrument of Egyptian foreign policy.

This basic concept, it seems to me, remains sound. The purpose of SCUA, as set out in the basic Declaration creating it, is to *help* the member nations get through the Canal on an efficient and non-discriminatory basis. The same purpose was expressed in the public statement issued following the Second London Conference on September 21.

The Resolution which you and the French introduced at the UN, and which we were supporting, calls upon SCUA and the competent Egyptian authorities to "cooperate to insure the satisfactory operation of the Canal".

I cannot feel that the primary purpose of SCUA to cooperate with Egypt has changed. Certainly, I feel, no such change can be assumed unless the members of SCUA agree to it.

Of course, as you say, SCUA was intended to strengthen our collective hand, and not to weaken it. But would this not come from ability to represent locally the combined interests of the principal users so that the flow of revenue to Egypt could be stopped *if there were* discrimination? Thus there would come about a fair working arrangement, initially on a provisional basis, which could be the prototype of a permanent satisfactory arrangement. I believe this was the view of those who joined SCUA and that it is still their view.

That brings us to the question of dues. You calculate that Egypt is getting less than half of the dues because you and the French and others who follow your lead are now paying dues into the old Canal Company account.

As I see it, and as it has been reported to me from Egypt, the Government of Egypt views dues payments in London and Paris to the old Company as, in effect, payments to Egypt in the sense of diminishing to that extent Egypt's debt for compensation to that Company or its shareholders. Hence, Egypt views the present payments which you permit as payments to it, despite the fact that in form they are being paid to London and Paris accounts of the Company. Egypt will presumably accept the situation until it judges that accounts are even.

As to payments currently being made under protest by U.S. flag vessels in Egypt, you will recall that to pay in Egypt is only to continue the practice followed when the Canal was being operated by the Universal Company, and continuance of this practice furnishes the basis for freezing the more than $60 million of Egyptian funds in U.S. banks.

Nevertheless, I appreciate your feeling that payment of dues to SCUA should not result in larger immediate cash receipts by Egypt than it is now receiving, unless and until Egypt has come to an acceptable interim arrangement with SCUA for the operation of the Canal.

This would mean that the present method of paying dues would be continued until SCUA has reached such an arrangement, following which the dues would be paid to SCUA for disbursement in accordance therewith. Or, if it is considered to be desirable that payments of dues to SCUA begin at once, this can be done with SCUA handling the dues as now, pending an acceptable interim arrangement with SCUA; that is, the dues paid now to Egypt would be paid to Egypt through SCUA, and the dues not now paid would be impounded by SCUA pending such an arrangement.

We must have in mind that the U.S. Treasury regulations cannot compel payment of dues to SCUA. They can provide, and it is so proposed, that no Canal dues shall be paid to Egypt except through SCUA. As dues are paid by ships and not by governments, it is to be anticipated that payment will be made to SCUA only if the ships believe that such payment will discharge their obligation for tolls, and that, in fact, the ship will get through the Canal.

The new system which I think we envisage would require the management of SCUA to negotiate with the Egyptian Canal authorities for such practical "on-the-spot" cooperation as would assure the purpose of SCUA, namely, expeditious and impartial transit through the Canal. This arrangement would doubtless call for a payment to Egypt, as has been clearly contemplated from the beginning. The amount of this payment would, I suppose, in part be a matter of straight negotiation, but in general I suppose it would be designed roughly to compensate Egypt appropriately for its contribution to the maintenance of the Canal and the facilities of transit. The negotiation would determine what funds would be withheld for

Canal improvements and items other than the current costs and to pay off the old Company and its shareholders.

I do not know precisely what percentage of the dues received by SCUA would be paid to Egypt. I never intended to propose any specific percentage because I have no factual knowledge as to how much of the dues will correspond to a legitimate Egyptian share, since that, in turn, depends on the nature of the cooperative arrangements which will be established.

Perhaps I have misunderstood you and have wrongfully inferred that you felt that all, or virtually all, of the tolls should be impounded and Egypt faced with the alternative of letting the ships go through for the time being without any payment whatsoever or face the alternative of either force or a boycotting of the Canal.

This latter concept is, I feel, so different from the original one that it could not be adopted without reconsideration by the SCUA members as a whole. However, I hope and believe that we are still sticking to the original concept and that we merely face a misunderstanding as to how to apply it. Perhaps this letter will be helpful in clearing up the matter.

I do not comment on your observations on Anglo-American relations except to say that those relations, from our standpoint, rest on such a firm foundation that misunderstandings of this nature, if there are such, cannot disturb them.

Faithfully yours,

John Foster Dulles [2]

---

[2] Telegram 2851 bears this typed signature.

---

359.   Telegram From the Embassy in France to the Department of State [1]

Paris, October 20, 1956—2 p.m.

1853. Eyes only Ambassador Aldrich. Eyes only Secretary after conclusion of conversation at Quai d'Orsay with Maurice Faure [2] on

---

[1] Source: Department of State, Central Files, 684.86/10–2056. Secret. Received at 11:28 a.m. Repeated to London.

[2] French Secretary of State for Foreign Affairs and head of the French Delegation at the Common Market and EURATOM.

EURATOM problems reported separately, he raised Suez problem with me.

Faure said it was clear that Atlantic Alliance was now in the midst of its greatest crisis. He said that France considered Nasser to be a mortal danger to her existence and that she could not permit present situation to continue much longer. He said that it would be vital, immediately after American elections, to reach firm agreement on this problem.

Faure said he could well understand viewpoint prevalent in U.S. that French and British by their policies in former colonial areas were in effect promoting local nationalist movements which, for want of help elsewhere, were attempting to turn to Soviet Union. However, he said that French and British looked at present crisis differently and he was afraid that this was a case where the U.S. would have to decide which of her friends she preferred the most, the countries of Western Europe or the Bandung powers. Unless the U.S. clearly took her place with the Western powers when the showdown came he said that he felt the Atlantic Alliance was finished.

Comment: This point of view closely paralleling that of Chaban-Delmas, [3] and coming from a man belonging to a totally different political milieu, and who has always been strong supporter of NATO, is added confirmation of the gravity of present situation, not only from point of view of Franco-American relations but for the eventual position of Western Europe as a whole.

[Here follows a paragraph on an unrelated subject.]

Dillon

---

[3] See telegram 1839, Document 357.

360.   Note From the Assistant Secretary of State for Near Eastern, South Asian, and African Affairs (Rountree) to the Secretary of State [1]

Washington, October 20, 1956.

MR. SECRETARY: The attached telegram from Ambassador Aldrich has just come to my attention since it was not despatched Niact. [2] You will note his feeling that it is undesirable to respond further in writing to Mr. Lloyd. While, on the basis of the information which he presents, I do not see that we should rescind the instructions which went out last night to deliver your response to Mr. Lloyd, [3] I would appreciate your views.

There is also attached a telegram from Paris [4] which I find extremely interesting and which is, as you will see, extremely disturbing. Finally, I am enclosing a memo of conversation with the Egyptian Chargé, [5] the last paragraph of which contains information which I have not heretofore had an opportunity to convey to you.

I will be in my office all morning; I have a series of appointments including a 12 o'clock appointment with Coulson and a 1:00 o'clock meeting with Shiloah. I also plan to be in the office the first half of the afternoon at least. If you would like for me to come out at any time during the day, however, I will cancel whatever appointments are necessary. [6]

WR

---

[1] Source: Department of State, NEA Files: Lot 58 D 545, Egypt. A marginal notation on the source text reads: "Sec Saw".

[2] None of the documents mentioned in this note is attached. Reference is presumably to telegram 2170, Document 356.

[3] Reference is to telegram 2851, which transmitted Dulles' message to Lloyd, Document 358.

[4] Reference is presumably to telegram 1839, Document 357.

[5] Reference is presumably to Document 353.

[6] Dulles' Appointment Book does not indicate that the Secretary met with Rountree that day. (Princeton University Library, Dulles Papers)

361.   **Message From Prime Minister Ben Gurion to President Eisenhower** [1]

Jerusalem, October 20, 1956.

DEAR MR. PRESIDENT: On October 15, 1956, Secretary of State Dulles conveyed to the Government of Israel through Ambassador Eban your expression of hope for close friendship with Israel and his anxiety over certain developments and eventualities in the Middle East.

I warmly reciprocate your wish for growing friendship between our two countries. In the spirit of that friendship I feel bound to suggest urgently that you approach the appropriate capitals, in order to prevent the entry of Iraqi troops into Jordan.

I have given deep thought to this matter since Ambassador Lawson brought it to my attention on October 1st. I am now convinced that the proposed move which the British Government is actively promoting, would not increase stability in the Middle East, but would on the contrary have profoundly disturbing effects.

The entry of Iraqi forces into Jordan would be the first stage in the disruption of the status quo. It would evoke strongly conflicting passions within Jordan and would set in motion a chain of tension and increased instability within Jordan and throughout the other Arab countries. The Jordan-Israel frontier is in a state of high tension owing to continuing acts of murder and sabotage by infiltrators from Jordan. Iraq's army joined the other Arab armies in invading Israel eight years ago and still openly proclaims a "State of War against Israel". At the conclusion of the Arab invasion they refused to sign an armistice agreement with Israel. Israel could clearly not remain indifferent to a move which would bring Iraqi troops over their own frontier and closer to Israel.

In these circumstances the projected move of Iraqi troops would acutely aggravate the threat to Israel's security. I earnestly hope that you will find it possible to exert your eminent authority in the name of peace by urging the British Government, and others concerned, to desist from the implementation of this plan.

Very respectfully yours,

David Ben Gurion

---

[1] Source: Eisenhower Library, Whitman File, International File. Transmitted to the Department of State in a letter from Reuven Shiloah to Dulles, which asked that the message be transmitted to President Eisenhower.

362.   Memorandum of a Conversation Among the President, the Secretary of State, and the Under Secretary of State (Hoover), White House, Washington, October 21, 1956, 11 a.m. [1]

I reported on the Suez situation. I said that I was really baffled to know the real purposes of the British and the French. Perhaps they did not know themselves. I had the impression that they felt that our policy was merely for election purposes and that after election we might back them in a policy involving the use of force.

I pointed out that the French because of their war in North Africa understandably wanted the British in as fighting allies. The British position was equivocal. They seemed at times really to be seeking a peaceful settlement—and I thought a reasonable one was in sight—at other times they seemed to feel that any settlement would not eliminate Nasser fast enough and that they must have a more rapid time schedule.

We were working with them on long-term economic projects. But they seemed also to have in mind a number of other possible alternatives such as:

1. An inspired attempt against Nasser which probably would fail but in failing bring about violent anti-foreign demonstrations which would justify the introduction of military forces to save foreign life and property;
2. Claiming that the Suez Base Evacuation Treaty of 1954 had been violated by the Egyptians' violation of the 1888 treaty. Therefore, they had the right to go back to that basis [base?]; (At this point the President interjected that he thought it would be difficult for them to do so so belatedly.)
3. The introduction of troops into Jordan under cover of the Jordan Defense Treaty;
4. The introduction of troops into the area under cover of the 1950 Tripartite Declaration;
5. The cutting off of tolls to Egypt to a degree which would lead Egypt to stop passage through the Canal and then the use of force to get ships through the Canal.

I said I felt confident that the British and the French would not resort to any of these measures before election as they did not want to make it an election issue. I was more fearful as to what might happen after [the] election.

In this connection I said to the President that I had been thinking of the possibility of his inviting Eden and Mollet to come to Washington shortly after the election. I thought this invitation

---

[1] Source: Eisenhower Library, Dulles Papers, Meetings with the President. Secret; Personal and Private. Drafted by Dulles.

might have a stabilizing influence on the situation and that if accepted it would give an opportunity for a frank exchange of views at the highest level without danger that it would be interpreted as an election move. I said I had no firm recommendation to make, but I would like the President to be turning it over in his mind. The President said he would do so. I said, of course, I felt that the President ought to have some vacation immediately following the election but perhaps the latter part of November would be a suitable time.

[Here follows discussion of unrelated subjects.]

JFD

363.   Editorial Note

During a telephone conversation on October 22, Hammarskjöld informed Lodge that, according to Dixon, the British and French Governments would require something in writing from Egypt before a meeting among the three could take place. Dixon had also maintained that there must be "at least some delay" in replying to Hammarskjöld's message concerning a possible meeting of the three on October 29. Hammarskjöld commented to Lodge that he did not think the situation had gone to pieces, but that it had slowed down a little bit; the situation was not bad but it was not good either. (Memorandum of telephone conversation by Lodge, October 22; USUN Files, Unnumbered Files, Suez Canal)

At 4:44 p.m. on October 22, Lodge telephoned Dulles and repeated what Hammarskjöld had told him concerning Dixon and other subjects. According to Bernau's transcript, the conversation then proceeded as follows: "The Sec. said we have quite a bit of info from the Fr. They are willing to stall until after elections and then are not disposed to delay the use of force. L. said the Sec. has done a good job. The Sec. said it is not over. The Sec. does not think H. should be complacent. L. said he is not. The Sec. thinks the Br. and Fr. are trying to maneuver the Egyptians into the position of coming forth with a complete program. L. said H. agrees with that. The Sec. said it is contrary to trading instincts. They are willing to sit down and gradually work it out but to make a written proposal—the Sec. doubts they will do it. The negotiations have to proceed as in NY under H. H. told them that. The Sec. feels this delay is very bad. L.

said H. expects another reply tomorrow and L. will be in touch and L. will get word here." (Eisenhower Library, Dulles Papers, General Telephone Conversations)

---

364.   Telegram From the Department of State to the Embassy in France [1]

Washington, October 22, 1956—5:36 p.m.

1448. Eyes only Ambassador from Secretary. I have impression from your cables Nos. 1839 and 1853 [2] that French Government feels that our opposition to the use of force in connection with Suez results from an election situation and that we might not be as strongly opposed after election. I can assure you the views of the President and myself on this point are basic and fundamental and I do not see any likelihood of their being changed after election. I do not know whether anything needs to be said from our side with regard to this situation but we would not of course want French Government to feel that we had in any respect misled them.

Dulles

---

[1] Source: Department of State, Central Files, 974.7301/10–1956. Top Secret; Priority; No Distribution. Drafted by Dulles. Repeated to London eyes only for the Ambassador.

[2] Documents 357 and 359, respectively.

---

365.   Telegram From the Embassy in France to the Department of State [1]

Paris, October 23, 1956—noon.

1886. Eyes only Secretary and Ambassador Aldrich. Reference your 1448. [2] I do not feel that French Government considers that

---

[1] Source: Department of State, Central Files, 974.7301/10–2356. Top Secret; Priority. Received at 11:20 p.m. Repeated to London.

[2] *Supra.*

basic United States policy on Suez is dictated by electoral situation. They do feel, however, that electoral situation has influenced tone and frequency of public statements. More important they do not feel it appropriate or desirable push Franco-United States differences toward showdown prior to election. I consider it very likely that French shortly after election will push hard for their longstanding thesis that Atlantic Alliance cannot be limited in area but must involve world wide political agreement. Mollet in speech at farewell dinner to Gruenther last night brought this up saying "is it really possible to limit the North Atlantic Alliance to one area of the world? we do not think so . . . [3] Foreign policy, a world wide policy, must be a single whole (*un tout*)—solidarity is not divisible".

I continue to feel that key to future events in Suez lies in decision to be taken by Great Britain. French cannot undertake military action alone and will only act jointly with British. However, in joint United Kingdom-French meetings I think French Government will continue to favor forceful measures if solution along lines 18 power proposal not otherwise obtainable. Best method to counter French tendency toward action would appear to be Egyptian suggestions of such a concrete nature as to require renewal of United Kingdom-French-Egyptian negotiations.

Finally while French do not appear to be giving much thought to meeting of General Assembly, I would assume that once Assembly is in session it would supply strong moderating influence.

Dillon

---

[3] Ellipsis in the source text.

366.   Memorandum of a Conversation, Department of State, Washington, October 23, 1956 [1]

SUBJECT

Near East Situation

PARTICIPANTS

Mr. A. D. P. Heeney, Ambassador of Canada
Mr. S. S. Rae, Minister, Embassy of Canada
G—Mr. Robert Murphy
NE—Mr. Donald C. Bergus

The Canadian Ambassador reported that the contract for the sale of Canadian F–86 aircraft to Israel had been concluded. Payment had been effected for the eight aircraft to be supplied for the months of September and October. These planes were now Israel property. Four aircraft would be supplied monthly until the entire twenty-four had been delivered to Israel. The November quota of four might be added to the eight already paid for so that shipment of twelve planes could be made by sea before shipping on the St. Lawrence was halted by ice. Other arrangements might have to be made for the shipment of the remaining twelve aircraft. This was a matter of concern to the Israel Government, as the Canadians were transferring title to the planes in Canada. The Canadian Government had reserved the right to intervene to stop the transaction if political conditions so warranted.

The Canadian Government was not happy at what had developed along the Israel–Jordan border since the announcement of the Canadian sale of jets to Israel. The fact that the British had felt impelled to remind the Israelis of the Anglo-Jordan Treaty had also been disturbing. There had not been a substantial Arab reaction to the Canadians over this transaction, however. On balance the Canadian Government had decided to go ahead with the matter but would appreciate the views of the United States. Mr. Heeney inquired concerning the Department's assessment of the Jordan elections.

Mr. Murphy stated that we were not happy over the results of the election. Mr. Bergus mentioned that we had not yet received our Embassy's comment on the final result but there was some ground for belief that the results had not been quite so dire as some observers had predicted. [2] In reply to a question, Mr. Bergus men-

---

[1] Source: Department of State, Central Files, 784A.5622/10–2356. Drafted by Bergus.

[2] In the Parliamentary elections held in Jordan on October 21, three Communists were elected to the Jordanian Chamber of Deputies. According to a Department of

tioned that so far as we knew, Iraq troops were to remain stationed on Iraq territory near the Jordan border for the time being, although the matter was still under discussion in the Iraq Cabinet. Israel had taken a public position violently opposing the entry of Iraq troops into Jordan. The Ambassador asked if we intended to take any steps at the Security Council.[3] Mr. Murphy replied that the next step seemed to be the statement of the Israel representative. He understood that the possibility of asking General Burns to speak before the Council was being discussed in New York.

The Ambassador summarized by asking if the United States saw any reason why the Canadian transaction with Israel should not be completed. Mr. Murphy replied that he did not. So far as he was aware, the Secretary's position on the matter was unchanged.

In reply to a number of questions on the Suez Canal problem Mr. Murphy stated that no date had yet been set for the Geneva meeting. The United States felt that such a meeting should take place and the initiative now appeared to rest with Egypt. Perhaps each side was trying to outwait the other. Press accounts of differences between the United States and Britain on the question of the disposition of tolls had been greatly exaggerated and Mr. Murphy thought that such problems could be resolved. The United States was inclined to look upon SCUA primarily as a negotiating body.

State estimate, dated October 25, 19 of the total 40 members of the new Parliament were considered anti-Western and 9 of those elected were considered neutrals. Of this latter group, it was anticipated that some would be willing "to jump aboard a pro-Egyptian anti-Western band wagon." Moreover, the 12 pro-Westerners elected were considered weak. (Memorandum from Bergus to Wilkins, October 25; *ibid.*, 785.00/10–2556)

[3] On October 15, Jordan requested a Security Council meeting to consider the situation on the Jordan-Israel Armistice Demarcation Line (U.N. doc. S/3678); 2 days later, Israel asked the Council to consider persistent violations by Jordan of the Jordan–Israel General Armistice Agreement. (U.N. doc. S/3682). The matter was discussed by the Security Council at the 744th meeting on October 19 and at the 745th meeting on October 25. (U.N. docs. S/PV.744 and S/PV.745) The discussion was to be resumed on October 30, but was deferred because of the outbreak of the Hungary and Suez crises. Consideration of the Israel–Jordan question was not resumed during 1956.

367.   **Memorandum of a Telephone Conversation Between the Secretary of State in Washington and the Representative at the United Nations (Lodge) in New York, October 23, 1956, 5:17 p.m.** [1]

TELEPHONE CALL FROM AMB. LODGE

L. said Dixon took him aside at lunch and said he was worried re Suez (though not for the same reasons as we). Wednesday Hammarskjold asked him to come over and said the Egyptians had an overall proposal which they would not like but etc. Then something happened and it evaporated into nothing and he thought it was problemmatical there would be a meeting on the 29th. They must have something definite. He realized you could not expect that but thought some proposal should be made to get together on. L. said get in the room and then start questioning it. A failure to meet is not advancing anything. L. thinks he personally agreed but that is not the attitude of the govt. Dixon is worried about Anglo-American relations—their opinion of us. Then L. talked with Hammarskjold [2] and he said he would get in touch with them today and call L., but he has not as yet. L said H said to him he hoped the Sec. would bring his influence to bear. L. said he assumed the Sec. was and the Sec. said we have not done anything about it. The situation is such it is rather awkward for us to do it. They know how we feel. What has H done? L. said again re calling and putting them on the spot in front of the issue. The Sec. thinks H. may have to take almost public action here which maybe we could . . . . [3] Our position is quite awkward. We have used up about all our influence in this thing so far, and our relations have become strained on this matter and the Sec. thinks the Br and Fr are inclined to stall until after election and with the feeling that probably we will be more disposed to back the use of force. Of course we will not—the Pres feels strongly against it. Lodge asked and the Sec. replied he thinks it well to press the Egyptian(?) [4] when he sees him Thurs. The Sec. said it is hard to get American public opinion focused on it now. Two weeks is a long time to wait. The Sec. [said] word from Dillon is discouraging. They mentioned the latest No African incident as being bad etc. [5] The Sec. said unless they back down they will have lost all of

---

[1] Source: Eisenhower Library, Dulles Papers, General Telephone Conversations. Transcribed by Bernau.

[2] See *infra*.

[3] Ellipsis in the source text.

[4] The question mark appears on the source text.

[5] On October 22, French officials seized a Moroccan plane carrying leaders of the Algerian rebellion and placed them under arrest.

Africa in his opinion. L. asked what he should say to H. that we would do to back him up if he brings it to the open. The Sec. thinks we should concert it together carefully—what moves to make—it is unfortunate the election is on. The Sec. thinks it is dangerous to wait. L. said he will probably call tomorrow p.m.

---

368.   **Memorandum of Telephone Conversations Between the Secretary-General (Hammarskjöld) and the Representative at the United Nations (Lodge), New York, October 23 and 24, 1956** [1]

SUBJECT

Suez

I called Hammarskjold to express our concern with the bad state of affairs as regards the Anglo-French-Egyptian conversations over the Suez Canal.

Hammarskjold said he hoped the United States would bring its influence to bear and that he would call the French and U.K. Representatives.

At a lunch which I gave in honor of the next Brazilian Ambassador to Belgium, Sir Pierson Dixon (U.K.) took me to one side and told me the following: on last Thursday [2] night the SYG had told him that the Egyptians had an over-all proposal, some things in it that they liked and others that they didn't. "Then", he said, "something happened". Evidently there were adverse instructions from Nasser and the whole project was dropped. Now the British "must have something definite".

I said it would not be reasonable to expect the Egyptians to put in writing a final position before there had been any oral exchanges—which he agreed. But nevertheless, he said there had to be something more definite than now existed.

He said he was worried about the effect of all this on Anglo-American relations.

After talking to the Secretary, [3] I talked to Hammarskjold again

---

[1] Source: Department of State, Central Files, 974.7301/10–2356. Confidential. Drafted by Lodge. The last three paragraphs of the memorandum, which describe a conversation between Lodge and Cornut-Gentille, were evidently added at a later time. Norman Armour is indicated as codrafter with Lodge for this last section.

[2] October 18.

[3] See *supra*.

around 7:00 p.m. Tuesday [4] and said that we would do what we could, but we have used up a great deal of our influence and relations are rather strained. I added: "We think that you (Hammarskjold) may have to bring this into the open and if you do we will concert our own actions carefully with you."

Hammarskjold said: (paraphrase) I have tried to get both Cornut and Dixon together and was unable to do so. I have seen Cornut and he sees the situation exactly as I do. I described all the risks to him. I am seeing Dixon at 12 tomorrow, Wednesday, and will bring stronger pressure to bear on him.

I think it is quite true that as a matter of integrity this matter must be in public eventually. The time is not yet. I will bring up this possibility directly with Dixon. He and the French must both count on the possibility of my taking an open position when the time is ripe.

Wednesday morning Hammarskjold called me and said that he is very disturbed by the French and British meeting in London last night [5] which is seeking to build up the impression that there is nothing to decide here in the meeting on October 29. He added the following: (paraphrase) Having thought it over I have decided to write a letter to Fawzi summing up my understanding of what has been proposed, that is, the detailed provisions which would go under the six major headings which we agreed upon when the Foreign Ministers were in New York. I would set this all down and then ask Fawzi: am I right or am I wrong?

Inasmuch as the French and British think that the Egyptians have done nothing, I must once again be the midwife and have a baby on the table.

I shall talk over the draft of this letter with Dixon and Cornut and then send it to Egypt. I want them to know what I am doing.

In a subsequent conversation with Ambassador Cornut-Gentille, I asked him if he had anything more on the Suez Canal negotiations, specifically the October 29th meeting. Ambassador Cornut-Gentille replied that the French found themselves in a dilemma as they could not see how they could meet with the Egyptians when the latter had not provided any concrete suggestions. He did not see how they could sit down without a piece of paper in front of them.

---

[4] October 23.

[5] According to The New York Times for October 24, Pineau attended an emergency high-level meeting with Eden and Lloyd in London during the evening of October 23. Following the meeting, a spokesman for the British Foreign Office told the press that Pineau, Eden, and Lloyd had discussed the Suez Canal Users' Association proposal and the situation arising from the recent Security Council debate on the Suez Canal situation. Regarding Pineau's visit to London, see Document 373.

I said I did not see how the Egyptians could give the French and UK their final position as then it would make it impossible for the Egyptians to negotiate. I thought possibly they could sit down with the six principles of the Security Council resolution and use that as a paper for discussion. I pointed out that if the UK and France refuse to sit down with the Egyptians, they would be placed in a very bad position, vis-à-vis world public opinion. Whereas if they did sit down with the Egyptians they would be in a much better position, especially if the Egyptians remained adamant.

Mr. Ordonneau (France) pointed out that the seizure of the ship *Athos*, carrying arms from Alexandria to the rebels in Algeria, cast a whole new light on the problem. He pointed out the ship had originated in the military port of Alexandria and this was the fourth such ship which traveled between Egypt and the rebels in Algeria. He indicated the French would have to take this concrete proof of Egyptian collaboration with the rebels into consideration in dealing with the Suez problem.

369.   Editorial Note

The notes taken at the meeting of the Intelligence Advisory Committee, held on October 24, indicate the following discussion on Suez-related matters:

"After consideration of various factors bearing on the Suez and Arab-Israeli situation, it was agreed that at least for another week no revision of outstanding [intelligence] estimates would be requested.

"The Chairman decided that in the future CIA, instead of preparing a briefing paper, would present to the meeting a list of the significant developments of the week, leaving any interpretation to the IAC members.

"The FBI representative called attention to a report from his agency that a . . . country was considering the initiation of military action against Nasser. Most of the members had not received the report prior to the meeting and thus were not in a position to comment on it.

"Mr. Kent asked authorization from the IAC to set back the target date for the Estimate, 'British Position in the Middle East' until November 27th. This delay was accepted by the Committee." (Notes on IAC meeting, October 24; Department of State, INR Files: Lot 58 D 776)

370.   **Memorandum of a Conversation Between the President and the Secretary of State, White House, October 24, 1956, 11:30 a.m.** [1]

[Here follows discussion of unrelated subjects.]

2. I discussed the Suez situation and my concern at the lack of progress in resuming negotiations. I reported what I had learned about Hammarskjold's intentions to attempt to formulate a position and ask the Egyptians whether they accepted it.

We referred to Aldrich's cable (#2215) reporting Monckton's resignation because of disagreement with the "force" policy. [2]

We reviewed the prior suggestion I had made to the President that we might invite Eden and Mollet to come to Washington toward the end of November. We discussed whether or not to convey that invitation before the elections or immediately after. It was agreed that I would send a private message to Aldrich and Dillon inviting their comments. The President wanted it clearly understood that the invitation would not stand if in the meantime the British and the French engaged in military action against Egypt.

3. I reported to the President the developments in North Africa resulting from the French seizure of the Moroccan plane containing the Algerian leaders. I expressed great concern lest the British and the French commit suicide by getting deeply involved in colonial controversies in an attempt to impose their rule by force on the Middle East and Africa. The President indicated that he fully shared my concern in this respect.

[Here follows discussion of unrelated subjects.]

JFD

---

[1] Source: Eisenhower Library, Dulles Papers, Meetings with the President. Secret; Personal and Private. Drafted by Dulles.

[2] In telegram 2215, October 23, Aldrich reported that Walter Monckton had told him, in confidence, that Monckton had given up his position as British Minister of Defense not only because of physical exhaustion but also because he was convinced that the use of force in Suez would be a great blunder. Monckton also said, according to Aldrich, that Dulles was on the right track regarding this matter and that he, Monckton, could not remain as Minister of Defense and take the actions necessary if force should be used. (Department of State, Central Files, 974.7301/10–2456)

371.   **Telegram From the Department of State to the Embassy in the United Kingdom** [1]

Washington, October 24, 1956—5:04 p.m.

2950. Eyes only Aldrich and Dillon. President and I have been considering desirability of President inviting Eden and Mollet and their Foreign Ministers to come to this country for a tripartite discussion toward the end of November. Topics would presumably include Suez and Middle East matters and NATO problems which will be considered at December meeting, notably problem of strategy and forces and problem of development of NATO along non-military lines.

We should like your personal reactions to these points: (1) Do you favor the idea? (2) Do you believe government to which you are accredited will respond favorably? (3) Should intimation be privately given now that invitation will be forthcoming immediately after election assuming President reelected?

President has said invitation would presuppose there would be no forcible action taken against Egypt prior to the meeting as he would not want to invite them under conditions which might suggest we were joining in such action.

Please discuss this with no one.

Dulles

---

[1] Source: Department of State, Central Files, 033.4111/10–2456. Secret; Priority; No Distribution. Drafted by Dulles, cleared by Hoover, and approved by Dulles. Also sent Priority to Paris.

---

372.   **Editorial Note**

On October 24 in Amman, a tripartite military agreement was signed between the Hashemite Kingdom of Jordan, the Syrian Republic, and the Republic of Egypt. The announcement was made in a communiqué issued following the conclusion of military talks, which had been held in Amman among the Commanders in Chief of the Egyptian and Syrian Armies and the Chief of Staff of the Jordanian Army. According to the communiqué, the tripartite military agreement aimed "at unifying the fronts of the signatory countries and at concentrating their military efforts and coordinating their plans and exchanging aid amongst them plus reinforcing their potentialities for the joint defense of the Arab front under a unified command to repulse any attack launched at any of the three states, on the consideration that such an aggression would be an attack against them all." The agreement was to become effective as soon as it was signed. The text of the communiqué was transmitted to the Department of State in telegram 386 from Amman, October 26. (Department of State, Central Files, 786.5/10–2656)

---

373.   Editorial Note

According to several of the participants, on October 24 representatives of Great Britain, France, and Israel, who had been meeting secretly at Sèvres on the outskirts of Paris, signed a document which embodied the following understanding: Israeli forces were to invade the Sinai Peninsula on October 29 with the aim of reaching the Suez Canal Zone by the following day; Great Britain and France would then issue an ultimatum to both Israel and Egypt to withdraw 10 miles from the Canal Zone and accept a temporary Anglo-French occupation of the Zone; if Egypt rejected the ultimatum, Great Britain and France would begin military operations against Egyptian forces early in the morning of October 31. The document also provided for an Israeli occupation of the western shore of the Gulf of Aqaba and the islands of Tiran and Sanafir and contained a promise from the Government of Israel not to attack Jordan during the period of operations against Egypt. (The terms of the understanding are described in Christian Pineau, *Suez/1956* (Paris: Robert Laffont, 1976), pages 149–152, and Moshe Dayan, *Story of My Life* (New York: Morrow, 1976), pages 231–232.)

The Israeli Delegation, headed by Ben Gurion and including Moshe Dayan and Shimon Peres, had arrived in France and begun discussions with Prime Minister Mollet, Pineau, and Defense Minister Bourgès-Maunoury on October 22. That evening Lloyd met briefly with the others; the following evening (October 23) Pineau traveled to London where he discussed the matter directly with Eden and Lloyd. Back in France on October 24, after further discussions, the document was finally signed by Ben Gurion, Pineau, and Deputy Under Secretary of the British Foreign Office Patrick Dean, who attended the final discussions in Lloyd's place.

Dayan's *Story of My Life* (pages 211–234) provides a detailed account of the Sèvres meeting. Anthony Nutting in *No End to a Lesson* ((London: Constable, 1967), pages 101–105) reports what Selwyn Lloyd told him at the time about the meeting. Pineau's *Suez/1956* (pages 149–155) differs in some details from Dayan's and Nutting's accounts and from that of General Paul Ely (*Mémoires * * Suez . . . le 13 Mai* (Paris: Librairie Plon, 1969), pages 145–153); but all basically tell the same story. In his memoirs, Lloyd gives a similar description of the meeting at Sèvres but denies that what happened constituted collusion. According to Lloyd, at no time did British representatives request that Israel take military action; they "merely stated what would be our reactions if certain things happened." Also, while Pineau terms the document signed a "protocol", Lloyd maintains that it was simply "a record of the discussion on which the three delegations would report." (*Suez 1956, A Personal Account*, pages 186–188)

---

374. Report Prepared in the Executive Secretariat of the Department of State [1]

Summary No. 37   *Washington, October 25, 1956.*

SUMMARY OF DEVELOPMENTS IN SUEZ SITUATION

Hammarskjold Letter to Fawzi on Implementation of Cooperation [2]

Hammarskjold has given us and the British and French a letter which he intends to send Egyptian Foreign Minister Fawzi. In it the Secretary General sums up his understanding of the sense of the private talks which took place in New York and elaborates on the question of implementation of the principle of organized cooperation.

---

[1] Source: Eisenhower Library, Whitman File, International File. Top Secret; Eyes Only for Designated Recipient.

[2] On November 3, this letter was circulated to members of the Security Council as Annex I to a report by Hammarskjöld, entitled "Exchange of Correspondence between the Secretary-General and the Minister for Foreign Affairs of Egypt". (U.N. doc. S/37/28) The text of the letter was transmitted to the Department of State in telegram 396 from USUN, October 24. (Department of State, Central Files, 974.7301/ 10–2456) For text of the letter, see *United States Policy in the Middle East, September 1956–June 1957*, pp. 127–130.

The letter states that this cooperation obviously requires an organ on the Egyptian side, presumably the Canal authority, and a "representation" of the users which is recognized by the Canal authority and the Egyptian government. Provision should be made for joint meetings, with the users' representation entitled to raise all matters affecting the users' rights or interests but in such a way as not to interfere with the administrative functions of the operating organ. Arrangements should be made for fact-finding, reconciliation, recourse to appropriate juridical settlement of possible disputes, and guarantees for execution of the results of reconciliation or juridical settlement. Such fact-finding and reconciliation might be provided by a standing joint organ. In the case of unresolved differences, recourse should be possible to some standing local arbitration organ or to the ICJ, Security Council, or whatever UN organ might be established. The parties should recognize any award made by the arbitration organ as binding and undertake to carry them out in good faith. Any non-compliance should be registered by the arbitration organ, with both sides entitled to certain limited "police action" under certain circumstances, even without recourse to further juridical procedures.

The letter concludes that, if no objection in principle is seen to such arrangements as those described, it would appear from a legal and technical point of view, without raising political considerations, that the framework is "sufficiently wide to make a further exploration of a possible basis for negotiations . . . [3] worth trying."

Egyptian Views on Suez Negotiations

The British Ambassador in Cairo has informed Hare [4] that Fawzi told him Egypt wants to get down to direct negotiation on the Suez issue. Fawzi deplored British-French moves which he viewed as seemingly designed to impede progress. In this connection he cited the Security Council resolution which he thought was "unsportsmanlike" after prior agreement on the Six Principles. He felt that insistence on Egyptian submission of a detailed plan was like demanding the final draft of the treaty before beginning negotiations. The Egyptian government, Fawzi told the British Ambassador, continues to desire to act constructively and had accepted Hammarskjold's invitation to meet with the British and French at Geneva on October 29. Fawzi gave the British Ambassador the impression that Egypt is more interested in negotiations under Hammarskjold's auspices than in proceeding through Indian mediation. The British

---

[3] Ellipsis in the source text.
[4] Reported in telegram 1156 from Cairo, October 24, not printed. (Department of State, Central Files, 974.7301/10–2456)

Ambassador also told Hare that he had some reason to believe the Egyptians did in fact submit specific proposals to Hammarskjold in accepting the Geneva invitation.

[Here follows a report concerning the proposed staff for the Administrator of SCUA.]

Mollet Comments on US Policy [5]

In a speech last night at the official French farewell dinner for General Gruenther, Mollet placed his main emphasis on the importance of common global policies. Referring specifically to Suez, Mollet balanced his reference to French "bitterness" over certain hesitations and fluctuations of US policy with mention of the "immense importance" of the fact that ever since the first London conference the United States government "has been and remains in complete agreement with us as to the objectives to be attained."

Suez Transits

Consulate Port Said, reporting on the daily pattern of Canal traffic, states that one convoy each way transited the Canal on Sunday. The northbound convoy consisted of 22 vessels, including 11 tankers; 14 ships were in the southbound group. The total, therefore, was 36. There is no backlog.

(Summary closed 1:00 p.m., October 25, 1956)

---

[5] Reported in telegram 1903 from Paris, October 23, not printed. (*Ibid.*, 611.51/10–2356)

---

375.   Telegram From the Embassy in France to the Department of State [1]

Paris, October 25, 1956—5 p.m.

1956. Eyes only Secretary and Aldrich. Your 1471. [2] To answer first your question, I am certain that such an invitation would be welcomed by Mollet and by French parliamentary and public opin-

---

[1] Source: Department of State, Central Files, 684A.86/10–2556. Secret. Received at 3:42 p.m. Repeated to London. On October 26, Dulles forwarded a copy of telegram 1956 from Paris and telegram 2268 from London, *infra*, to President Eisenhower under cover of a note which reads in part: "I think that the points made by Dillon require careful appraisal". (Eisenhower Library, Whitman File, Dulles–Herter Series)

[2] Printed as telegram 2950 to London, Document 371.

ion. It would be generally looked on as concrete opportunity to discuss common problems on worldwide basis which is project dear to French and to Mollet personally.

In answer to question 3 I feel that it is immaterial whether Mollet informed in advance. French do not expect any new initiatives from United States until after election and accordingly are prepared to let relations with United States coast until then. Main advantage of prior intimation of invitation would be opportunity to sound out Mollet before invitation made public. I feel this should be done in any event. Danger is the always present possibility of an inadvertent leak to press. All in all, if project adopted I would be inclined to recommend informal approach to Mollet and Eden on November 8 followed by formal announcement as soon thereafter as could be coordinated.

Finally as to basic question of my views re idea, I feel that such a meeting could serve a most useful purpose provided it is reasonably successful. Present misunderstandings are serious and contain seeds of grave difficulties in future. Therefore every attempt to reach a common understanding is worth the effort. On the other hand a failure at such a meeting would have gravest consequences. To reach an acceptable area of understanding will undoubtedly require give and take on both sides. On United States side in particular if agreement is to be reached on a Suez policy which excludes war as instrument of policy, we must be prepared to be more forthcoming than heretofore regarding possibilities of economic aid to Western Europe in case Egypt bars passage through Canal. Exim Bank loans are not enough, there must be reasonable prospect of government aid to cover substantial share of extra costs entailed in use of cape route. Great advantage of such a conference would be opportunity of talking face to face with Mollet rather than with Pineau. Therefore provided we can enter talks with reasonably flexible position both on eventual use of economic sanctions including possible grant aid to cope with Suez question and on upcoming NATO problems, I would strongly favor such a meeting. If our objective, however, is limited to attempt to sell United States position to French and British without any possibility of compromise, I would doubt usefulness of exercise. I say this even though Mollet had deep admiration approaching veneration for President and would be deeply influenced by President's views. However, vital interests of France are at stake which would tend minimize effects of personal influence in persuading French agree to any program that they felt compromised these vital interests.

Meeting to be effective should permit working sessions on two consecutive days, followed by session on third day to approve communiqué.

In view precondition laid down in last paragraph reference telegram I am not certain French and United Kingdom would accept invitation but my guess is that they would, thus delaying any precipitate action which they might otherwise contemplate.

Dillon

376.   Telegram From the Embassy in the United Kingdom to the Department of State [1]

London, October 25, 1956—4 p.m.

2268. Eyes only Secretary from Ambassador. Paris eyes only for Dillon. Re Deptel 2950 [2] replying points enumerated second para:

(1) I heartily favor the idea.

(2) I believe HMG would respond favorably unless events should move so rapidly in Middle East that it would be impossible for Eden to leave London at time suggested. I make this qualification not because I have any information that HMG has decided to take forcible action against Egypt in near future but I have in mind generally explosive character of situation in that area.

(3) I believe intimation referred to, including presupposition that no forcible action would be taken against Egypt prior to meeting, should be given now. To do this would have obvious advantages because if invitation is encouraged by Eden we will know at once that no immediate use of force is contemplated and in any event Eden's reaction should throw further light on plans of British and French in immediate future. I would like to suggest that, if matter is to be broached privately now, it should be done by personal message from President to Eden; and that I be permitted to take message personally to Eden. I would thus be in a position to discuss situation with him if his immediate reaction should be unfavorable because of fear that his acceptance of an invitation on that condition now might tie his hands during the critical negotiations with Egypt which it is hoped will take place during the next few weeks. I do not believe that either Eden or the British Cabinet is so wedded to the possible immediate use of force in case negotiations regarding the Canal should break down in next few weeks as to be unwilling to accept the invitation on the basis suggested but it might require very careful presentation to persuade them to do so.

---

[1] Source: Department of State, Central Files, 641.74/10–2556. Secret; Priority. Received at 5:19 p.m. Repeated to Paris.

[2] Document 371.

It seems to me that it is clear that Eden and Mollet would wish to coordinate their action before replying to the invitation.

Aldrich

---

377.   Telegram From the Embassy in Egypt to the Department of State [1]

Cairo, October 25, 1956—2 p.m.

1166. Paid courtesy call on Foreign Minister Fawzi yesterday afternoon. Discussion centered entirely on Suez except for incidental reference to Algerian problem which Fawzi hoped would not interfere with progress Suez negotiations. He said might be maintained that Suez had political ramifications affecting various other problems but manifestly impossible solve all of them at one time; therefore must continue steadfast search for Suez solution.

Fawzi confirmed acceptance Hammarskjold invitation meet British and French later in month (Embtel 1156) [2] and said had been led to believe he might expect be informed replies of British and French by today.

Remainder of conversation devoted to lengthy discussion of demands being made by British and French for specific government of Egypt proposals. Fawzi maintained that this demand unreasonable since British and French already have ample material on which to negotiate if they really wish do so; if they persist in their demand it will be indication of bad faith and in that case there would be little use in resuming negotiations. In such event he would be most regretful but, if British and French wanted it that way, Egypt could face the prospect without being unduly perturbed but onus would not be on Egypt.

I said could see how Fawzi might have reached this conclusion if he was thinking only of negotiating position with British and French but this was question in which whole world now interested. Was Fawzi convinced that this position vis-à-vis world opinion would not be clarified if government of Egypt had something on record as specific as 18 nation proposals? As matters stand public, as

---

[1] Source: Department of State, Central Files, 974.7301/10–2556. Secret. Received at 5:23 p.m. Repeated to London, Paris, New Delhi, Amman, Beirut, Baghdad, Damascus, and Jidda.

[2] See footnote 4, Document 374.

distinct from private, record is somewhat out of balance and rightly or wrongly impression could be given that Egypt was not being forthcoming.

At first Fawzi remained completely adamant, maintaining that advancing formal and detailed proposals would be like beginning treaty negotiations by submitting draft treaty. Not only was this too much to ask but it could also affect negotiations adversely since various points thus presented could be seized on for public debate which might otherwise be quietly solved in private negotiations.

I then inquired whether, if Fawzi felt hitherto private record was so fully adequate as basis for negotiations, consideration might be given to making it public. At first, he was equally opposed to such an idea but as conversation continued he ended by saying that he would not want to make such a proposal himself but would probably not object if such suggestion was made by the British and French, although he doubted if it would help much. However if this idea were pursued, he thought it would be preferable to circulate government of Egypt proposals secretly to especially interested governments or to U.N. members as a whole, even though it was obvious that by so doing publicity would result. I made clear was talking purely personally and would not attempt make strong argument for this particular idea which was purely random thought which came to mind in exploring various possibilities. I felt however that some move by Egypt other than maintaining its present fixed position might be helpful.

Asked at end of conversation re status of Menon plan,[3] Fawzi shrugged shoulders and said Egypt always appreciated efforts of well-intentioned persons to be of assistance but Menon plan as such not under active consideration. However certain ideas in it might be found useful.

Hare

---

[3] For a description of the Menon plan, see Document 301.

378.   **Memorandum of Discussion at the 301st Meeting of the National Security Council, Washington, October 26, 1956, 9 a.m.** [1]

[Here follows a paragraph listing the participants at the meeting.]

Significant World Developments Affecting U.S. Security

[Here follows discussion of unrelated subjects.]

Secretary Dulles then adverted to the situation in Jordan, which he described as "very worrisome". There was grave danger that Jordan would presently disintegrate. If this happened, the result might be a war between the Israelis and the Arabs, not to mention wars between the Arab states themselves, notably Iraq and Egypt. Mr. Allen Dulles predicted that a coup was likely to take place in Syria. Admiral Radford commented that if King Hussein had really been assassinated, [2] there was very little doubt that the Iraqis would move into Jordan as quickly as possible. Moreover, the British may well have to move in additional forces in order to maintain their hold on their bases in Jordan. Finally, the Israelis will certainly wish to move to secure the west bank of the Jordan River. All in all, commented the President, we are going to have a donnybrook in this area.

Mr. Allen Dulles then expressed the hope that before this meeting ended he would have confirmation as to whether or not King Hussein had actually been assassinated. (At the end of the meeting Mr. Dulles stated that the rumors that the King had been murdered were without foundation.)

.   .   .   .

Dr. Flemming said it was his understanding that the British and French were still thinking of resorting to force in certain circumstances in order to solve the Suez Canal crisis. Secretary Dulles commented that they were indeed. Dr. Flemming then stated that if this were true, and in view of other developments in the Middle East, the Western powers may well lose use of the Suez Canal for a certain period of time.

---

[1] Source: Eisenhower Library, Whitman File, NSC Records. Top Secret. Prepared by Gleason on October 26. The time of the meeting is from the record of the President's Daily Appointments. (*Ibid.*)

[2] Allen Dulles began his briefing by mentioning, among other matters, that "rumors [were] flying around that the King of Jordan had been assassinated".

[Here follows discussion of unrelated subjects.]

S. Everett Gleason

---

379.   Telegram From the Embassy in Israel to the Department of State [1]

Tel Aviv, October 26, 1956—1 p.m.

415. Beginning yesterday morning and continuing until now (12 noon local time) there has been IDF call up on considerable scale of reservists and civilian vehicles in Tel Aviv and adjacent areas as far south as Rehovoth. To this moment operation has closely resembled in techniques and mobilization points expansion in Israel's arms strength which occurred at time of Nitzana action November last and Fedayeen operations this April.

Present movement has become widely known among local press people and public and there is good deal of speculation that "something big may happen". Report of special interest has been advice by family controller road transport to Embassy officer that week end trips should be cancelled and food supplies stocked. Reference was made to community of interests with French, a relationship which is being increasingly mentioned here in both public and private circles, with some references to Eilat and Strait of Tiran as possible scenes of actions (reference Embassy despatches 829, June 22, 1955 and 229, October 24, 1956). [2]

While impossible to know at this time whether present movement will shift from partial to complete mobilization or area of possible action, Embassy will attempt to check other important population centers with view to keeping Department informed.

Lawson

---

[1] Source: Department of State, Central Files, 674.84A/10–2656. Secret; Priority; Noforn. Received at 9:57 a.m. Repeated Priority to London and Paris.

[2] Neither printed. (*Ibid.*, 674A.84A/10–2255 and 674.84A/10–2456, respectively)

**380.   Report Prepared in the Executive Secretariat of the
Department of State** [1]

Summary No. 38   *Washington, October 26, 1956*

SUMMARY OF DEVELOPMENTS IN SUEZ SITUATION

[Here follows a summary of the Fawzi–Hare conversation reported in telegram 1166, Document 377.]

Black's Conversations with Egyptian Leaders

IBRD President Eugene Black has recounted to Under Secretary Hoover the details of his conversations with Egyptian Foreign Minister Fawzi in New York on October 11, and on October 13 with Fawzi and other Egyptian leaders including Ali Sabri, Nasser's political adviser, and Badawi, Chairman of the Egyptian Canal Authority. [2] Both meetings were at Fawzi's request. Black said he told Fawzi, and subsequently the others, that Egypt's nationalization of the Canal Company had undermined the confidence of the world community in Egypt. Consequently, it would be difficult, if not impossible, for Egypt to obtain funds from international sources for the development of the Canal. It seemed essential, therefore, that Egypt conclude an agreement with all of the countries and interests concerned with the Canal which would lead to restoration of such confidence. If an agreement were not reached, Black said, the USSR would be the only country to which Egypt could turn, and Egypt would become hopelessly entangled if it were to depend upon the USSR for financial assistance in developing the Canal or in maintaining its economy.

In a discussion of the question of the compensation which would eventually be paid to the old Suez Canal Company, and in response to Fawzi's question, Black said he would be glad to take part in discussions between Egyptian and Company representatives and even to arbitrate if desired. With regard to financing such compensation, Black said he thought the Bank might be helpful, but only after an overall agreement had been reached by all parties

---

[1] Source: Eisenhower Library, International File, Whitman File. Top Secret; Eyes Only for Designated Recipient.

[2] More detailed accounts of these conversations are in a memorandum of conversation by Wilkins, October 12, and a memorandum from Hoover to Rountree, October 23, neither printed. (Department of State, Central Files, 974.7301/10–1256 and 974.7301/10–2356, respectively)

to the present dispute and on condition that the Bank was invited to participate by all who might be affected.

[Here follows an unconfirmed report that the Soviet Union had offered financial aid to help Egypt develop and maintain the Suez Canal transit situation.]

(Summary closed Noon, October 26, 1956)

---

381.   Memorandum From the Director of the National Indications Center (Hitchcock) to the Intelligence Advisory Committee [1]

NIC #6–2237   *Washington, October 26, 1956.*

SUBJECT

Possibility of Israeli Raid on Egypt

1. Members of the Watch Committee have individually examined reports received since their last meeting concerning Israeli military and associated developments. They generally agree that the likelihood has increased of major Israeli reprisals, probably against Egypt in the near future. It is believed that the present Israeli mobilization, though on a large scale, is not a full mobilization, and therefore Israel does not intend that this action lead to general hostilities although it is preparing to meet the possibility of broader action.

2. Important developments which bear on the situation include:

a. Border incidents involving the killing of Israelis at El Auja on 21 October and a Fedayeen penetration into Israel in the Gaza area on 25 October.

b. Israel mobilization measures, including the requisitioning of engineer equipment and civilian vehicles and the call up of personnel to an extent which has seriously affected many industries and closed some. Two brigades have been brought up to full strength and forces in the Negev have been reinforced.

c. A heavy concentration of personnel and matériel in the Lydda-Ramle-Rehovoth area in the last two days, and continuing movements of troops, including elements of the 11th Armored

---

[1] Source: CIA Files. Top Secret. The National Indications Center was established to provide a central staff devoting full time to the problems faced by the Watch Committee. Additional information concerning the NIC is in CA–7918, May 14, 1955, in Department of State, Central Files, 101.2/5–1455.

Infantry Brigade, at least since 23 October in a southward direction from the Tel Aviv area.

d. An unconfirmed report that France may be planning actions in conjunction with Israel against Egypt.

For the Chairman:
James J. Hitchcock

---

382.   Editorial Note

During the afternoon of October 26, additional reports concerning the Israeli mobilization reached Washington. In telegrams CX–378, CX–381, and CX–383, the Army Attaché in Tel Aviv, Colonel Leo J. Query, reported to the Department of the Army that the Israeli call-up of personnel and matériel was continuing unabated and that most newly-mobilized troops were in bivouac south of Tel Aviv. Query described the mobilization as "very large scale", exceeding the extent of all previous Israeli mobilizations since the 1948–1949 war. The Attaché also reported that according to available sources, the French might be working with the Israelis, and he speculated that an Israeli move against the Straits of Tiran was a "good bet". ("Chronology of Significant Events Relating to the Current World Crisis," prepared by The Joint Chiefs of Staff Historical Section; JCS Files)

The Embassy in Tel Aviv reported in telegram 419, received in the Department of State at 6:44 p.m., October 26, that it had been able to verify the call-up of some reservists as far north as Haifa, including numerous villages and towns between there and Tel Aviv. Also, as of 8 p.m. Israeli time, the Ministry of Defense building and the army patrol stations, normally closed after sundown for the Sabbath, appeared in full operation. The Embassy also noted that in response to an Embassy query regarding the troop call-up, the Israeli Government had issued an informal reply mentioning the Egyptian-Syrian-Jordanian Unified Command and reported Iraqi troop movements. The Israeli Foreign Ministry also told the Embassy that in view of the foregoing, "Israel security authorities had decided a very partial mobilization was necessary." The Embassy commented that the Ministry's statement on the size of the mobilization appeared to be an understatement and that the Israeli public was apprehensive that events were moving toward actual hostilities. (Department of State, Central Files, 684A.86/10–2656)

383.   Memorandum of a Telephone Conversation Between the
Secretary of State in Washington and the Representative
at the United Nations (Lodge) in New York, October 26,
1956, 6:31 p.m. [1]

TELEPHONE CALL TO AMB. LODGE

The Sec. told re the Br. reaction to take the Hungary matter to
the GA, [2] and he told of the message he is sending out tonight. [3] The
Sec. said they could talk informally in the SC with the Russians.
The Sec. told of his sense of foreboding—Br., Fr. and Israel etc. It
looks bad all along the line. We don't know what the Br and Fr
agreed to in their last talks and the Sec. thinks they may be going in
to fight. The Sec. referred to Pineau's public statement they were
discussing with us and the Br re bringing the matter to the SC. [4] L.
said the Frenchman there [5] is outspoken that we should do something. L. mentioned the Latin American lunch he went to today and
it was full of it. L. thinks we will lose a good deal if we do nothing.
L. agreed we should do it in a constructive way. The Sec. said there
will be a meeting here at 9:30 [6] and then he will see the Pres. at 11.
He leaves at 12. He thinks we will reach some decision at 9:30 and
will then talk with the Pres. and let L. know right away. L. said
Hammarskjold asked him and the Br. and Fr. to meet at 10 re

---

[1] Source: Eisenhower Library, Dulles Papers, General Telephone Conversations.
Transcribed by Bernau.

[2] On October 23, anti-Soviet demonstrations in Budapest erupted in violence and
caused the Hungarian Government to invite the Soviet Union to send troops into
Hungary to restore order. The entry of Soviet forces on October 24, however, only
escalated the violence. Hungarian troops joined the rioters, and fighting in the streets
of Budapest turned into a general rebellion in areas outside the capital. On October
25, in telegram 2981 to London, approved by Dulles, the Department of State directed
the Embassy to consult immediately with the British Foreign Office concerning the
U.S. desire to seek Security Council action regarding the situation in Hungary. In
telegram 2290 from London, October 26, the Embassy reported the Foreign Office's
"preliminary view," subject to confirmation of the highest level, that the Hungary
item should be inscribed immediately on the U.N. General Assembly, not Security
Council, agenda and that debate could be deferred until the General Assembly
convened. Documentation concerning the Hungarian crisis is scheduled for publication
in volume xxv.

[3] Later that evening, Dulles directed Aldrich to advise Lloyd personally of Dulles'
concern and desire to focus immediate U.N. attention on the Hungarian situation.
(Telegram 3008 to London, October 26, is scheduled for publication *ibid.*)

[4] On October 25, Lucet discussed with Walmsley France's intention of filing a
complaint that day with the President of the Security Council entitled "Military
assistance by the Egyptian government to the rebels in Algeria". (Department of State,
Central Files, 330/10–2656)

[5] Presumably Cornut-Gentille.

[6] According to Dulles' Appointment Book, the 9:30 meeting on October 27 dealt
with Hungary. (Princeton University Library, Dulles Papers) No account of the
conversation has been found.

Palestine—complaint of Jordan etc. The Sec. told L. to tell Hammar-skjold in front of the others of our concern of this mobilization of Israel that is taking place. L. said he thought the Pres's statement [7] was good and with the reference to the UN Charter that is another reason to do something. They agreed re not waiting for the GA. The Sec. said he is sending a follow-up telegram tonight [8] and should have the score tomorrow a.m. The Sec. said if he couldn't call L., somebody would tomorrow. Can L. move on Sunday. L. said yes, and the Sec. indicated they might want him to then.

---

[7] Reference is to Eisenhower's statement of October 25 concerning the situation in Hungary. For text, see *Public Papers of the Presidents of the United States: Dwight D. Eisenhower, 1956*, pp. 270–271.

[8] Presumably telegram 3009 to London, *infra*.

---

384.   Telegram From the Department of State to the Embassy in the United Kingdom [1]

Washington, October 26, 1956—7:28 p.m.

3009. Eyes only Ambassador from Secretary. We are quite disturbed here over fact there is apparently a deliberate British purpose of keeping us completely in the dark as to their intentions with reference to Middle East matters generally and Egypt in partic-ular. We have had no high-level contacts on any of these matters with British Embassy for a week. We do not know their intentions with reference to resuming negotiations with Egyptians nor with reference to SCUA nor do we know what are understandings appar-ently arrived at with French. We have information of major Israeli preparations and suspect there may be French complicity with them and possibly UK complicity with various moves which they think it preferable to keep from us lest we indicate our disapproval.

Would appreciate promptest whether from your position you feel our concern is justified or whether it could be explained by other circumstances.

Dulles

---

[1] Source: Department of State, Central Files, 684A.86/10–2656. Top Secret; Niact. Drafted by Dulles, cleared by Rountree, and approved by Dulles.

385.   Telegram From the Embassy in the United Kingdom to the Department of State [1]

London, October 26, 1956—3 p.m.

2295. Eyes only for Secretary. At farewell dinner for Gruenther last night given by Eden, I was able discuss recent developments briefly with both Eden and Lloyd. Eden was in mellow, relaxed mood in contrast recent occasions on which I have seen him. He expressed view that Israel–Jordan situation and Egyptian involvement therein is of more fundamental importance even than Suez problem. On latter, Lloyd said there have been relatively few developments looking toward further negotiations between UK, France and Egypt, but understood that Hammarskjold is in process drafting letter to Fawzi in effort facilitate resumption negotiations. In response to question, Lloyd added still uncertain whether negotiations would take place Geneva October 29.

Specific information on developments connection such possible negotiations has been difficult to obtain owing largely, I think, to fact Lloyd and Eden have been essentially handling matter personally, but also due to detectable reticence government and officials to express opinions as to prospects. However, from various official sources we have learned that Hammarskjold has in fact drafted a letter which he proposes to send Fawzi and which purports to set down the measure of agreement reached between the UK, France and Egypt in talks at New York. He apparently has shown letter to UK Del New York but has not asked comments. It is not clear whether letter has yet been despatched to Fawzi. FonOff lower level view of text is that British would probably find it acceptable as basis for further negotiations, but they are extremely skeptical whether it clearly reflects Fawzi's statements, particularly in regard to machinery for the arbitration of disputes and "police" sanctions for compliance. They consequently doubt Egyptians will accept. Information re discussion when Pineau last came to London two days ago is particularly scarce. However, an official who should be in a position to know states Lloyd called Pineau here to attempt to persuade French to agree to further negotiations with the Egyptians without additional preliminary Egyptian clarifications. British apparently prepared proceed negotiations that basis if necessary, and were sufficiently optimistic that clarifications would be forthcoming, or negotiations could proceed without them, to retain hotel accommodations Geneva for 29.

---

[1] Source: Department of State, Central Files, 974.7301/10–2656. Top Secret. Received at 8:15 p.m.

We have also sought to get at bottom of British complaints over US role in Suez crisis. While public criticism has appreciably diminished in recent days with apparent realization among widespread serious elements that irresponsible outbursts endanger the fundamentally important US–UK relationship, efforts to emphasize to responsible officials the extent to which the US has gone in supporting Britain throughout the crisis at a difficult time and on an issue on which United States public opinion was largely unconcerned have been less than completely successful in top political official circles. I have been told, I believe reliably, that Lloyd still feels that the SCUA organization was originally conceived as an instrument of pressure on the Egyptians short of military action and that its development since its origin has been toward an instrument by which to compromise with Nasser on the basis of his continued control over the Canal with his prestige undiminished. Lloyd is further said to feel that this course is driving him into closer alliance with France and away to some extent from US, which he deplores. Among other things, he believes the French are politically inept and may be counted on to make major political blunders, such as the arrest of the five Algerian leaders.

I do not wish to over-emphasize the seriousness of this current British attitude, which I firmly believe to be a temporary manifestation largely resulting from the frustration into which Eden and Lloyd and the other members of the Cabinet, notably Macmillan, got themselves by their original reaction to the Suez seizure, and the letdown which inevitably follows. I think, however, that it does explain, though of course not justify, to a certain extent some of the brittle attitudes which are now being taken by the British, not only in relation to Suez but on such other matters as Cyprus, and in fact may be expected on anything affecting the British position in the eastern Mediterranean and the Middle East.

Aldrich

386.   Telegram From the Embassy in the United Kingdom to the Department of State [1]

London, October 27, 1956—noon.

2317. Eyes only for Secretary. Concern along line your telegram 3009 [2] has underlain my efforts obtain maximum available information re developments Middle East, SCUA and Egypt. Results of which reflected in my telegram 2295. [3] Same thought prompted my arranging private dinner with Lloyd tomorrow evening when I intend pursue these matters exhaustively. In conversation with him this morning he confirmed HMG's present attitude re Suez situation as reported my telegram 2295, adding that British have given Hammarskjold comments on his latest suggestion re negotiations and have emphasized that they desire definite Egyptian statement accepting SCUA. Possibly noteworthy as explanation absence recent developments at least re SCUA was Lloyd's remark that he has avoided pressing question payment Canal tolls pending further developments on negotiations with Egyptians which at the moment are primarily in the hands of Hammarskjold. I did not have opportunity today to discuss other matters referred to in reference telegram.

Aldrich

---

[1] Source: Department of State, Central Files, 684A.86/10–2756. Top Secret; Priority. Received at 9:58 a.m.

[2] Document 384.

[3] *Supra.*

---

387.   Memorandum of a Conference With the President, White House, Washington, October 27, 1956, 11 a.m. [1]

OTHERS PRESENT

Secretary Dulles   Colonel Goodpaster
Under Secretary Hoover
Deputy Assistant Secretary William
    Rountree

---

[1] Source: Eisenhower Library, Whitman File, Eisenhower Diaries. Top Secret. Drafted by Goodpaster.

[Here follows discussion of Hungary, scheduled for publication in volume XXV.]

Discussion next turned to the Middle East and Secretary Dulles referred to the partial mobilization by the Israelis, and the danger that they might make some substantial move. In response to a question by the President, Mr. Rountree suggested Jordan as the most probable direction. The Secretary next referred to indications of possible developments in Syria, and suggested that the Israelis might have information about this, and be planning to move against Jordan if anything were to occur in Syria.

Secretary Dulles then suggested to the President that the latter send a message to Premier Ben-Gurion. After discussion and certain amendments, relating primarily to the danger suggested by Mr. Hoover that tensions are so great that any armed action might set off great consequences, the President approved the message for dispatch, subject to any necessary editorial revision. [2]

Secretary Dulles handed the President an extract from a report in 1949 of the Foreign Relations Committee [3] indicating that U.S. ratification of the North Atlantic Treaty was not to be construed as endorsement of the colonial policies of other NATO countries.

The President wished the Secretary a good trip and a successful speech in Dallas. [4]

G

Colonel, CE, US Army

---

[2] *Infra.*

[3] Not attached to the source text. For text, see U.S. Congress, Senate, *Report of the Committee on Foreign Relations on Executive L, Eighty-First Congress, First Session, The North Atlantic Treaty* (Washington, 1949), p. 23.

[4] Dulles left Washington by air for Dallas at 11:59 a.m., October 27, and returned at 4:15 p.m., October 28. (Dulles' Appointment Book; Princeton University Library, Dulles Papers) For text of his address before the Dallas Council on World Affairs, see Department of State *Bulletin*, November 5, 1956, pp. 695–699.

388.   Message From President Eisenhower to Prime Minister Ben Gurion [1]

Washington, October 27, 1956.

DEAR MR. PRIME MINISTER: I received your message dated October 20. I have taken very careful note of the reasons you advance against the movement of Iraqi troops into Jordan which you had initially thought would be a constructive step. I am not sure that I agree with your present position but in any event and so far as I am informed there has been no entry of Iraqi troops into Jordan. I hope that you look upon the suspense of that movement as a contribution to peace in the area. I must frankly express my concern at reports of heavy mobilization on your side, a move which I fear will only increase the tension which you indicate you would like to see reduced.

These are days of great strain. Only statesmanship of a high order and self-restraint by all parties can assure that the tensions in the Middle East can be controlled and prevented from becoming a cause for a breach of the peace in that area and in others affected by the ramifications of those tensions.

I remain confident that only a peaceful and moderate approach will genuinely improve the situation and I renew the plea which was communicated to you through Secretary Dulles that there be no forcible initiative on the part of your Government which would endanger the peace and the growing friendship between our two countries.

Sincerely,

Dwight D. Eisenhower [2]

---

[1] Source: Department of State, Central Files, 684A.86/10–2756. Secret; Limited Distribution. Transmitted to Tel Aviv in Niact telegram 355, October 27, 12:25 p.m., with the instruction: "Please deliver urgently following message from President to Ben Gurion". Telegram 355, which is the source text, was drafted by Dulles and Rountree, approved in draft by Eisenhower and Dulles, and approved by Rountree who initialed for Dulles.

[2] Telegram 355 bears this typed signature.

389.   Telegram From the Department of State to the Embassy in Australia [1]

Washington, October 27, 1956—11:31 a.m.

136. Eyes only Ambassadors. Please communicate following to Menzies and Casey from Secretary personally.

"I assume you are following developments in Middle East particularly Suez. I am beginning to feel concerned lest this Suez matter may become involved on the one hand with French problems in North Africa, and on the other hand with Israel-Arab problems and that our Western European friends may become deeply involved on a broad anti-Arab front.

I am not myself in close touch with recent British-French thinking but in view of leading role which Australia has played, I feel it appropriate to express my concern to you." [2]

Dulles

---

[1] Source: Department of State, Central Files, 974.7301/10–2756. Secret; Niact. Drafted and approved by Dulles. Repeated to Ottawa.

[2] Telegram 207 from Canberra, October 28, reported the following response: "Delivered text Prime Minister afternoon 28th upon his return to Canberra. Menzies was gratified for Secretary's thoughtfulness in sending message. He had planned for some days send personal message to Secretary regarding Suez and he now hoped be able do so 29th. He remarked it was a pity timing of Hungarian problem interfered with work towards solution Suez. Assume message for Casey delivered London. He arrives Ottawa November 2." (*Ibid.*, 974.7301/10–2856)

---

390.   Telegram From the Department of State to the Embassy in Egypt [1]

Washington, October 27, 1956—5:31 p.m.

1282. Eyes only Chief of Mission, DLG, RLG, PLG. Reports [2]

---

[1] Source: Department of State, Central Files, 684A.86/10–2756. Top Secret; Niact. Drafted by Henderson and Rountree, cleared by Howe, and approved by Rountree who signed for Dulles. Also sent Niact to Amman and Damascus and repeated Niact to Tel Aviv, Beirut, Dhahran, Rome, Jerusalem, and Paris.

[2] In telegram 420, October 27, the Embassy in Tel Aviv reported that the Israeli call-up of reservists and civilian vehicles continued through the night and into the morning of October 27 and that the consensus was that Israeli partial mobilization had reached a point beyond that at any previous time. Moreover, according to a newspaper source, Israeli military censors were banning any press reference to these activities. The Embassy also noted that, while the previous day the Foreign Ministry

reaching Department re increased tensions in area focused primarily upon Jordanian situation lead us call matter your attention in context security American citizens. While we do not of course know intentions Government Israel, indications heavy mobilization point to possible military action of some nature perhaps within next few hours. We have FYI today dispatched message Ben Gurion urging great caution. While we hope this critical period will pass without serious incident you should be aware existing possibilities.

While we hope that our concern proves unjustified, we nevertheless feel you should be aware that situation disquieting. We therefore urge mission be on alert. All members should be immediately available to meet emergencies. We leave to your discretion what if any action be taken at this juncture in matter of affording protection US nationals. Department giving constant consideration evacuation question and will do utmost keep you informed whether existing Phase I should on basis information as it comes in be altered in direction making greater effort reduce Americans in addressee countries. It of course possible events might move so fast you may find it necessary take urgent action before messages from Department can reach you. In meantime Department relies on your judgment as to what you should do. You understand our problem. On one hand it would be unfortunate if untimely and hasty departures of US citizens apparently in state of alarm should make international situation in area more explosive than it is at present; on other hand there might be tragic developments if events should overtake us with result that large numbers US citizens would find themselves in war arena surrounded by fanatical and irresponsible mobs.

For period immediately ahead would appear greatest danger lies in Jordan in view unsettled situation generally and fact any Israeli action likely involve that country. Other estimates, however, indicate action planned against Egypt as reprisal recent incidents.

Cyprus being requested keep communication channels open on emergency basis. Tel Aviv, Jordan, Damascus, Cairo, Jerusalem and Beirut should assume twenty-four hour communications watch.

Dulles

---

had connected the partial mobilization with events in the east, Embassy observers were reporting principal troop movements in the south with the heaviest concentrations in the Rehovot and Negba areas. (*Ibid.*)

391.   Special Watch Report of the Intelligence Advisory Committee [1]

No. 325A   *Washington, October 28, 1956.*

The Intelligence Advisory Committee approves the following findings of its Watch Committee at a special meeting held this date to review the possibility of hostilities between Israel and the Arab countries:

1. The Watch Committee has examined new evidence of heavy Israeli mobilization on a scale which would permit Israel to:

a. occupy Jordan west of the Jordan River;

b. penetrate Syria as far as Damascus and occupy portions of this territory;

c. penetrate Egypt to the Suez Canal and hold parts of Sinai for a considerable time, depending on logistical limitations;

d. break the Egyptian blockade of the Gulf of Aqaba and keep the waterway open to Eilat;

e. gain air superiority over the Egyptian Air Force alone, or in combination with air forces of the other Arab States;

f. probably carry out any or all of the above, even in the face of the combined resistance of contiguous Arab States.

2. The motivations for such an Israeli mobilization were considered to be:

a. to launch a retaliatory raid on Egypt, prepared in case such a raid leads to broader fighting;

b. to launch a major but limited assault on Egypt or Jordan or both, before Arab forces pull ahead of Israel in military strength and while the USSR is preoccupied in Eastern Europe;

c. to prepare to take advantage of opportunities in the chaotic Jordanian political situation which is showing clear pro-Egyptian orientation;

d. to provide a diversionary threat against Egypt in order to afford greater freedom of action for France and the UK in the Suez situation and to relieve Egyptian pressures on France in North Africa.

---

[1] Source: CIA Files. Top Secret. The Watch Committee met in emergency session at noon on October 28. A copy of a two-paragraph memorandum entitled "Conclusions of the Watch Committee Meeting at 12:00 Noon Today", dated October 28, is in Department of State, INR Files: Lot 58 D 776, Middle East Crisis 1956 (Arab-Israeli Crisis). The first paragraph, which bears the marginal notation "Prepared for the Secretary", corresponds to the final paragraph of the Special Watch Report printed here. The second paragraph reads:

"Highly sensitive information indicates that the British have brought up their air strength on Cyprus in the last 48 hours to 63 Canberras (medium bombers), doubling previous strength. French transport aircraft to the number of 18 have arrived within the last 24 hours making a total of 21 and giving capability of airlifting 1500 men."

3. The scale of the Israeli mobilization and its damaging effects on the economy, together with Egyptian preoccupation in the Suez, Soviet preoccupation in Europe, French material support to Israel and the complicated inter-Arab rivalries in and over Jordan, particularly the growth in Egyptian influence in Jordan, all provide a favorable opportunity for a major attack. Past Egyptian provocations, the key role of Egypt in the Arab threat and UK involvement with Jordan indicate the attack will be launched against Egypt in the very near future, under the pretext of retaliation and exceeding past raids in strength. The scale of the mobilization indicates that Israel is prepared to meet or exploit such situations as may arise during such an attack.

---

392. Memorandum From the Director of the National Indications Center (Hitchcock) to the Intelligence Advisory Committee [1]

NIC #TS–6–372   *Washington, October 28, 1956.*

SUBJECT

Evidence Bearing On The Possibility Of An Israeli Attack On Egypt

The Watch Committee, in reaching its conclusions bearing on the possibility of an Israeli attack against Egypt (Special Watch Report No. 325A, 28 October 1956),[2] considered a number of recent reports, the most important of which are summarized below:

1. Intense Israeli military activity with very heavy call-ups of personnel and requisitioning of civilian vehicles and engineer construction equipment during the past few days. Mobilization of personnel is now estimated as 80 per cent of maximum with 170,000 active duty and there are indications that this mobilization will be a maximum one.

2. Large troop and matériel movements throughout Israel with maximum concentrations apparently in the southern and Rehovot areas as well as strong reinforcements of the Jordan border and Jerusalem areas.

3. Evidence of a state of alert in the Israeli Air Force although its reserves have not been mobilized in large numbers.

4. Israeli censoring of overseas telephone conversations.

---

[1] Source: CIA Files. Top Secret; Noforn.
[2] *Supra.*

5. Reports that the Israeli Defense Force has pressured Ben Gurion for a freer hand in determining the scale and direction of its military actions and the reported move of its headquarters out of Tel Aviv to an alternate operational headquarters.

6. Israel's announcement of its mobilization as justified by Egyptian commando operations, the new Egyptian-Syrian-Jordanian military agreement, the concentration of Iraqi forces on Jordan's east border and continued hostile Arab declarations against Israel.

7. Additional reports of close collaboration between the French and Israeli Governments, including the dispatch of Mystere aircraft, raising Israeli strength in this aircraft to 53–60.

8. The movement of 18 French air transports, of DC–6 size or larger, to Cyprus on 28 October, which with the available UK air lift of 21 aircraft, raises UK-French lift capabilities from Cyprus to 2500–3000 troops.

9. Arab actions against France including a complete general strike throughout Arab countries, in support of Algerian rebellion, and French riots and demonstrations resulting in the burning of the French Consulate in Jerusalem and attacks on the French Embassy in Damascus and the Consulate in Aleppo. French irritation at Egypt over the *Athos*, seized near Algeria with a cargo of Egyptian arms.

10. Evidence of closer collaboration among Syria, Jordan and Egypt in the recent military agreement among the three countries, placing the Jordanian forces under Egyptian command in the event of an Israeli attack and in the emergence of pro-Egyptian Jordanian personalities as a result of the Jordanian elections.

For the Chairman:
James J. Hitchcock

---

393.   Editorial Note

At 7 p.m. in Jerusalem (noon in Washington), the Israeli Cabinet issued a statement in which it confirmed that mobilization activities were in progress and explained that units were being moved to the Jordan border in view of recent threats that foreign troops might enter that country. The Cabinet indicated that the mobilization was also made necessary by Fedayeen activity which constituted a serious threat to Israeli security. (The text of the Israeli statement was transmitted to the Department of State in telegram 423, October 29; Department of State, Central Files, 684A.86/10–2956.)

Later on October 28, Ambassador Lawson reported from Tel Aviv that large-scale military action could be expected in the very near future, perhaps within the next 24 hours. According to Lawson, the country was apparently under almost complete mobilization with heavy equipment on the move and military check points established on roads from Jerusalem and in the south. The Ambassador reported that, because the Cabinet meeting had lasted all day, he had been unable to deliver President Eisenhower's letter of October 27 to Ben Gurion, but that he had an appointment scheduled for 8 p.m. with the Prime Minister. (Telegram 422, October 28; *ibid.*, 684A.86/10–2856)

---

394.   Message From President Eisenhower to Prime Minister Ben Gurion [1]

Washington, October 28, 1956.

DEAR MR. BEN GURION: Yesterday I forwarded to you a personal message expressing my grave concern regarding reports of mobilization in Israel and renewing my previous plea, which had been transmitted to you by the Secretary of State, that no forcible initiative be taken by Israel which would endanger peace in the Middle East.

This morning I have received additional reports which indicate that mobilization of Israel's armed forces is continuing and has become almost complete. This further message is prompted by the gravity of the situation as I see it.

Because of the wide repercussions which might result in the present high state of tension in the Middle East and because of the intentions which the United States expressed in the Tripartite Declaration of May 25, 1950, I have given instructions that this situation be discussed with the United Kingdom and France, which are parties to the Declaration, requesting them to exert all possible efforts to ameliorate the situation. I have also directed that my concern be communicated to other Middle Eastern countries, urgently requesting that they refrain from any action which could lead to hostilities.

Again, Mr. Prime Minister, I feel compelled to emphasize the dangers inherent in the present situation and to urge your Government to do nothing which would endanger the peace. [2]

---

[1] Source: Department of State, Central Files, 684A.86/10–2856. Secret. Transmitted Niact to Tel Aviv in telegram 357, October 28, 3:32 p.m., with the instruction: "Deliver urgently following message from President to Prime Minister Ben Gurion". The telegram, which is the source text, was drafted by Wilkins and Rountree, approved in draft by Eisenhower, and signed by Rountree for Dulles.

[2] Telegram 357 does not bear Eisenhower's signature.

395.   Statement Issued by the President [1]

Washington, October 28, 1956.

During the last several days I have received disturbing reports from the Middle East. These included information that Israel was making a heavy mobilization of its armed forces. These reports became so well authenticated that yesterday morning, after a meeting with the Secretary of State, I sent a personal message to the Prime Minister of Israel expressing my grave concern and renewing a previous recommendation that no forcible initiative be taken which would endanger the peace.

I have just received additional reports which indicate that the Israeli mobilization has continued and has become almost complete with consequent stoppage of many civil activities. The gravity of the situation is such that I am dispatching a further urgent message to Prime Minister Ben-Gurion.

I have given instructions that these developments be discussed with the United Kingdom and France which joined with the United States in the Tripartite Declaration of May 25, 1950 with respect to the maintenance of peace in the Middle East.

While we have not heard of such large-scale mobilization in countries neighboring Israel which would warrant such Israeli mobilization, I have also directed that my concern over the present situation be communicated to other Middle East states urgently requesting that they refrain from any action which could lead to hostilities.

The Security Council of the United Nations now has before it various aspects of the maintenance of peace in the Middle East.

I earnestly hope that none of the nations involved will take any action that will hinder the Council in its efforts to achieve a peaceful solution.

---

[1] Source: *Public Papers of the Presidents of the United States: Dwight D. Eisenhower, 1956*, pp. 275–276. Also printed in Department of State *Bulletin*, November 5, 1956, pp. 699–700; and *United States Policy in the Middle East, September 1956–June 1957*, pp. 134–135.

396.   Memorandum of a Conversation, Department of State, Washington, October 28, 1956, 4:30 p.m. [1]

SUBJECT

Middle East Situation

PARTICIPANTS

Ambassador Herve Alphand, France
Minister J. E. Coulson, Great Britain
Mr. R. W. Bailey, Counselor, Great Britain
Mr. Murphy, G
Mr. Rountree, NEA
Mr. Beam, EUR
Mr. Bennett, G

Mr. Murphy showed Ambassador Alphand and Minister Coulson [2] the President's statement [3] just released by the White House regarding the imminent danger of an outbreak of hostilities in the Middle East. He called attention to the references in the statement to the Tripartite responsibilities of the U.S., France and the UK.

In response to an inquiry from Ambassador Alphand, Mr. Murphy reviewed the reports of Israeli mobilization moves which have been received by this Government. He emphasized that the reports coming in from all sources point the same way massive mobilization during the last 24 hours about 80% completed, involving some 170,000 Israeli troops already called up, with the danger of a military move tonight. He explained that President Eisenhower had written to Prime Minister Ben Gurion two days ago [4] and said that this afternoon's statement, together with another message to Ben Gurion, [5] is in the nature of a supplemental appeal for restraint on the part of Israel. Mr. Murphy emphasized the President's hope that the British and French Prime Ministers would make a similar appeal

---

[1] Source: Department of State, Central Files, 684A.86/10–2856. Secret. Drafted by Bennett.

[2] On July 17, the British Government informed the United States that Ambassador Makins would be leaving his post in Washington to become the Permanent Secretary of the Treasury and that he would be replaced by Sir Harold Anthony Caccia, the Deputy Under Secretary of State in the British Foreign Office. On October 11, Makins left the United States by plane for London. Sir Harold Caccia embarked for the United States on November 1 and presented his credentials at the White House on November 9 (see Document 562). During the interim, John E. Coulson served as Chargé d'Affaires. (Letter from Dulles to Eisenhower, July 18; Eisenhower Library, Dulles Papers, White House Memoranda; memorandum from Elbrick to Hoover, October 10; Department of State, Central Files, 601.4111/10–1056)

[3] *Supra.*

[4] Reference is presumably to Eisenhower's letter to Ben Gurion, Document 388.

[5] Document 394.

and would do whatever they can in the way of using their influence to calm the situation.

Mr. Coulson said that the British Government had yesterday instructed its Ambassador in Tel Aviv to inquire of the Foreign Minister regarding reports of troop mobilization. He did not have any word as yet as to action which might have been taken by the Ambassador. Mr. Murphy inquired of Ambassador Alphand regarding reports of the movement of the *Jean Bart* and the *Georges Leygues* to the Eastern Mediterranean. The Ambassador said he had no reports of this; he went on to say that the French Navy was patrolling the Algerian coast but that he was not aware of any ship movements to the Eastern Mediterranean.

Mr. Coulson remarked that he assumed that Mr. Murphy's reference to consultation among the three powers was for the purpose of exerting a restraining influence. He asked in that connection whether the United States is sending additional naval vessels to the Eastern Mediterranean. Mr. Murphy replied that our purpose is to encourage restraint on the part of all parties involved and said that we are not sending any vessels to the Eastern Mediterranean.

Mr. Murphy emphasized that President Eisenhower takes a very serious view of this evolution of the situation in the Middle East. The President assumes that Paris and London will take a similarly serious view.

Mr. Rountree reviewed briefly the reports of disorders and demonstrations directed against the French on the Algerian question in Amman, Aleppo, and Jerusalem where the old French Consulate has reportedly been burned by mob action. He mentioned that there is some excitement in Damascus but said that the general strike in Egypt had been carried out without disorder. In answer to a question by Mr. Murphy, Ambassador Alphand said that things seem a bit calmer in Morocco. He said that changes in the government there have brought a concentration of Istiqlal forces in the Cabinet with Si Bekkai remaining as Prime Minister.

The group then reconvened in the Secretary's office.[6]

---

[6] See the memorandum of conversation, *infra.*

397.   Memorandum of a Conversation, Department of State, Washington, October 28, 1956, 4:49 p.m. [1]

SUBJECT

Reported Israeli Mobilization

PARTICIPANTS

The Secretary of State
Mr. Alphand, French Ambassador
Mr. J. E. Coulson, British Chargé
The Under Secretary of State
Mr. Murphy, G
Mr. Rountree, NEA
Mr. Beam, EUR

The Secretary saw the French Ambassador and the British Chargé after they had left Mr. Murphy's office.

The Secretary reiterated our great concern about the latest developments in Israel, referring to the President's appeal to Ben Gurion. He mentioned that the timing of the Israeli mobilization was very ominous. The Israelis might be thinking that a number of factors offered a favorable opportunity to start military action: the Suez dispute, the situation in Jordan and the American elections. They might be counting upon our reluctance to take strong measures during the last week of the elections; if so, they were miscalculating. The Secretary assumed the UK still stood by its obligations under the Jordan treaty.

The British Chargé said he was convinced this was the case and that his government had said so several times.

The French Ambassador and British Chargé reiterated that they had had no information from their governments regarding Israeli mobilization measures of a kind similar to that in possession of the US Government. Mr. Coulson mentioned that his government had however made an inquiry in Tel Aviv concerning reports of military preparations, expressing its concern.

The Secretary said Israel was claiming that developments in Jordan were forcing it to mobilize. He observed that the Negev however seemed far less subject to attack than recently.

---

[1] Source: Department of State, Central Files, 684A.86/10–2856. Confidential. Drafted by Beam. The time of the meeting is from Dulles' Appointment Book. (Princeton University Library, Dulles Papers) At 9:06 a.m., October 28, Dulles spoke with Hoover over the telephone from Dallas "re the Israeli situation". Hoover met Dulles on his arrival at the Miltary Air Transport Service terminal in Washington at 4:15 p.m., and they discussed the Israeli situation en route to the Department of State. Dulles spoke briefly with Hoover and Beam before the meeting with Alphand and Coulson. (Dulles' Appointment Book; ibid.)

The meeting ended with a brief exchange of information on latest events in Hungary.

---

398.   Memorandum of a Telephone Conversation Between the President and the Secretary of State, Washington, October 28, 1956, 5:38 p.m. [1]

Secy. Dulles.

In his office, discussion being held by Hoover, Murphy, Phleger & Rountree on question of evacuation. Substantial agreement reached that Dulles recommend we inaugurate the evacuation. [2]

President asked by what means?

Dulles replied probably use commercial means as far as possible, & military or naval craft as necessary. President thought of troop ships, but added that we probably have no good ones out there.

Mr. Dulles said President's statement earlier today gives a good cover now for doing this. If we don't do it after that statement, & then things go wrong, then people will think we are very remiss. President asked who they will take—Dulles said Syria, Israel, Jordan & Egypt. In first instance, would take them to Rome or Athens; at that time, they would have choice of coming home or going to some other post. There are about 350 in Jordan; considerably larger number in Egypt (about 3,000); & 2 or 3 thousand in Israel.

President asked if Dulles thought that, by starting this, would we exacerbate the situation?

Dulles replied that he does not think so. It may lead to some anti-American demonstrations; & if the British strike, it will lead to inference that we knew about it. But he thinks it will not basically make the situation more serious.

President said our statement today would take care of that one, because obviously we don't know anything about the British.

Mr. Dulles asked if President got the information about the build-up around Cyprus—30 to 63 in the last 48 hours; the other country's [3] transport had been increased from 3 to 21.

---

[1] Source: Eisenhower Library, Whitman File, Eisenhower Diaries. Prepared in the Office of the President. Another memorandum of this conversation by Bernau indicates that Dulles placed the call to the President. (*Ibid.*, Dulles Papers, White House Telephone Conversations)

[2] Reference is to the evacuation of American citizens from certain parts of the Middle East.

[3] Reference is to France.

President said he just cannot believe Britain would be dragged into this.

Mr. Dulles said 2 important French ships have been moved to the Mediterranean.

President said in sending this message,[4] we said we would ask both Britain & France to do something—have we taken any steps?

Mr. Dulles said he has just talked to French Ambassador & French [British] Chargé. They profess to know nothing about this at all. The Britisher said he had some information that they had acted to warn the Israeli against attacking Jordan. But, he said, their ignorance is almost a sign of guilty conscience, in his opinion.

President's thought is to wait till morning, to see if there's an attack. Asked when State proposed to issue this.[5]

Mr. Dulles said today; because if there is an attack, it would really be too late afterwards.

President does not see why it would be too late. An attack would not mean a city occupied; the rights of neutrals ought to be respected.

Secy. Dulles mentioned Joint Chiefs of Staff position.[6] Then President said okay, go ahead. Added that, of course, it will be a world-shocking thing. To which Dulles commented: "But not much more than your statement. I think that it will tend to reinforce your statement, perhaps. Of course the British & French have done this a long time ago. They have gotten all their people out."

The President said we probably can't expect to get any answer from Ben Gurion now.

---

[4] Reference is to Eisenhower's message to Ben Gurion, Document 394.

[5] Reference presumably is to the Department of State statement issued later that day (Press Release No. 563) indicating that "as a matter of prudence" measures were being instituted to reduce the number of Americans in several Middle Eastern countries. The statement noted that while a full scale evacuation was not contemplated, U.S. personnel not performing essential functions would be asked to leave until conditions improved and urged U.S. citizens to defer plans for visiting the area. It also emphasized that these measures "were of a precautionary nature" and expressed confidence that Middle Eastern governments would afford full protection to American lives and property in accordance with international law. For text, see Department of State *Bulletin*, November 5, 1956, p. 700, and *United States Policy in the Middle East, September 1956–June 1957*, p. 135.

At 6:04 p.m., October 28, the Department of State transmitted instructions to the Embassies in Amman, Cairo, Damascus, and Tel Aviv, and the Consulate General at Jerusalem telling them to begin immediately Phase Three evacuation procedures and reduce the number of U.S. citizens in their countries. All other Middle Eastern posts were to continue a 24-hour security watch. (Telegram 447 to Amman; October 28; Department of State, Central Files, October 28, 280.1122/10–2856)

[6] For a summary of the JCS position concerning evacuation, see telegram 1107, Document 325.

399.   Memorandum of a Conversation, Department of State, Washington, October 28, 1956, 5:57 p.m. [1]

SUBJECT

Reports of Mobilization in Israel

PARTICIPANTS

Mr. Abba Eban, Ambassador of Israel
Mr. Yohanan Meroz, First Secretary, Embassy of Israel

The Secretary
The Under Secretary
Mr. Robert Murphy, G
Mr. Herman Phleger, L
Mr. William M. Rountree, NEA
Mr. Fraser Wilkins, NE

The Secretary said that he asked Mr. Eban to call for the purpose of discussing reports we had been receiving regarding mobilization in Israel. The Secretary handed the Israeli Ambassador copies of the President's letters of October 27 (Tab A) and October 28 (Tab B), and a copy of the President's public statement of October 28 (Tab C). [2] The Secretary noted that the Department was also issuing a statement regarding the evacuation of the dependents of American Government personnel and of unessential American Government employes from Syria, Jordan, Egypt and Israel (Tab D). [3]

Mr. Eban took a few moments to read the letters and statement the Secretary handed him after which he said that if he had had a copy of the President's letter of October 27 before now he might have been in communication with his Government and might thus have been in a position to supply the Secretary with information on the question of mobilization. Mr. Eban said that Israel might be wrong but it had very good reason to fear that the Arab nations were concerting together in preparation for reprisal moves against Israel. As evidence of these preparations he cited the formation of a joint command by Egypt, Jordan and Syria, plans for the massive use of fedayeen activity, statements which have been made in Amman following the Jordan elections and the presence of Iraqi troops on the frontier between Iraq and Jordan. Mr. Eban thought that all of this evidence gave Israel a genuine feeling that overt aggression was being planned by the Arab nations. Israel felt that it was its

---

[1] Source: Department of State, Central Files, 784A.54/10–2856. Secret. Drafted by Wilkins on October 29. The time of the meeting is from Dulles' Appointment Book. (Princeton University Library, Dulles Papers)

[2] Tabs A, B, and C are printed as Documents 388, 394, and 395, respectively.

[3] Tab D is not printed. Regarding the statement, see footnote 5, *supra*.

elementary duty to be prepared. He said that some reserve battalions had been called up. If aggression was being planned by the Arab nations, mobilization in Israel might have the effect of stopping it. Mr. Eban also noted that a communiqué had been issued in Jerusalem today [4] which cited increasing tension between Israel and its Arab neighbors and the possibility of an attack by them on Israel. Mr. Eban summed up by saying that in other words the situation was extremely tense and some reserve units had been called up because Israel feared attacks might be made against it. He asked the Secretary if he had any reason to believe that such attacks would not be made.

The Secretary noted that Mr. Eban had referred to "some reserve units had been called up." The Secretary said that according to his information Israel was being totally mobilized. He added that he did not in any way question Israel's right to call up reserves. It seemed to the Secretary, however, that Mr. Eban had minimized the extent of mobilization in making his remarks. According to the Department's information Israel's mobilization was on a much vaster scale and included all of Israel's reserves. The Secretary continued that he, of course, did not know what the Government of Israel had in mind. Earlier Prime Minister Ben-Gurion had expressed concern regarding the possible movement of Iraqi troops into Jordan. Israel had described the move as dangerous. Since then Iraqi troops had not moved into Jordan. The Secretary said Israeli apprehensions might thus have been allayed by this development. Mr. Eban replied that the fact that Iraqi troops had not moved into Jordan had not allayed Israeli apprehensions. It was still possible for Iraqi troops to move because of their proximity to the Jordan frontier. He again recalled the statements made following the Jordan elections, the formation of the Egyptian-Syrian-Jordan joint command, and the possibility of increased fedayeen activities. The Secretary inquired whether Israel feared an attack from Jordan. Mr. Eban replied that Israel did and that, in the final analysis, the question was one whether Israel's intentions could be described as defensive or offensive. He added that all of his information indicated that Israeli mobilization was for defensive purposes.

The Secretary agreed it was a question of intent. He said he did not know what the Government of Israel had in mind and that he had to form his opinions and base his judgments on the facts as he saw them. The Secretary thought that at no previous time had Israel been as safe as it was today. The situation in Jordan had deteriorated with the growing weakness of the Government of Jordan. Iraqi troops had not moved into Jordan as had previously been planned.

---

[4] See Document 393.

Egypt was presently engaged in a dispute with Britain and France regarding the Suez Canal. For these reasons it was hard to see how Israel was endangered to such an extent as to require total mobilization. The Secretary thought, on the other hand, that Israel might calculate that this was the best moment in which Israel could move. The Secretary repeated that he was not informed regarding Israeli intentions and necessarily had to proceed on the basis of the facts in the situation as known to him. If Israeli intentions were defensive, every factor in the situation would seem to indicate that Israel should not be as concerned. On the other hand, if Israeli intentions were aggressive, Israel might calculate there were factors in the situation which would make it desirable for Israel to strike.

Mr. Eban commented that he had just returned to Washington and was not informed regarding developments in Israel. He recalled, however, that Egypt had been growing stronger militarily during the past year and stated that on the basis of the record Israel's fears were well-founded. He asked the Secretary if Ambassador Lawson had reported.

The Secretary said Ambassador Lawson had thus far not been able to speak with Prime Minister Ben-Gurion who had been tied up in Israeli Cabinet meetings. Ambassador Lawson had, however, telegraphed that he hoped to see Prime Minister Ben-Gurion late this afternoon. Ambassador Eban again noted that the Government of Israel had issued a communiqué today and that he would supply additional information to the Secretary as soon as possible, probably tomorrow. He hoped that the Department would let him know what Ambassador Lawson reported.

---

400.   Memorandum of a Telephone Conversation Between the President and the Secretary of State, Washington, October 28, 1956, 7 p.m. [1]

The President called about 7:00 p.m. to find out if anything significant had happened in my talk with the Israeli Ambassador. I told him that I had strongly expressed our concern and the difficulty we had in interpreting Israeli mobilization as purely defensive in view of the preoccupation of Egypt in other matters; the disintegra-

---

[1] Source: Eisenhower Library, Dulles Papers, White House Telephone Conversations. Drafted by Dulles.

tion of Jordan and the suspension of Iraqi troop movements into Jordan. I said that the Ambassador had merely reiterated his belief that the mobilization was "defensive".

The President said that he was concerned about his trip to Florida and was wondering whether to go or not. He said, however, that he assumed that we would have news before his scheduled departure at 8:30 a.m.[2] He asked as to whether or not there were any aggressive actions on the part of the Israelis.

I telephoned the President about 9 p.m. to tell him that I had checked on Israeli balances in New York and that there had been no recent significant withdrawals. I said I thought this was a good sign as the Israelis would doubtless fear that if they took an active aggression we would block their balances.

The President thanked me for this information.

JFD[3]

---

[2] October 29
[3] Macomber initialed for Dulles.

---

401.   Telegram From the Embassy in Israel to the Department of State[1]

Tel Aviv, October 28/29, 1956—midnight.

424. Reference: Department telegram 355.[2] I delivered President's message to Ben Gurion at his home in Tel Aviv at 8 p.m. He appeared tired and voice weak. He promised written reply, which he said he hoped I would cable, by morning, but he then responded orally to me using with elaboration self-exculpating explanation Foreign Ministry gave Embassy official Friday (Embtel 419)[3] he said:

While Iraq's interest in penetration of Jordan remained threat, it was greatly over-shadowed by new military alliance of Egypt, Jordan and Syria which tightened noose around Israel's neck. Almost immediately after Jordan elections, Hussein announced his determination to fight Israel. Now there was unified tripartite military command

---

[1] Source: Department of State, Central Files, 684A.86/10–2856. Secret; Niact. Received at 10:13 p.m., October 28.
[2] Telegram 355 transmitted Eisenhower's message to Ben Gurion, Document 388.
[3] See Document 382.

which "even child knows is not directed against US, Soviet or even Britain".

He continued: "We don't know from what point of ring around us we can expect attack if it is going to come. It may start from Syria where we have many settlements, or Jordan, or in south. We decided it was necessary to mobilize few battalions to face seven brigades which Syria has; put some on Jordan border; and few more in south. Mobilization is purely precautionary measure imposed on us by events. We shall be as happy as President if things remain quiet".

Against this encircling hostility, he repeated he had been obliged to call up "few more units". Such call up was conspicuous because unlike Arabs, who had large standing armies Israel had to rely on reserves. It had only tiny permanent establishment, maintained to manage military stores, camps and equipment and to receive and train new recruits. "We decided Friday and Saturday to mobilize few more units of our reserves. Then if we are attacked, they can hold line until rest are mobilized".

Developing his case of Israel being obliged to put itself in defensive posture from feeling of insecurity and frustration, he reviewed "disappointment" with SC decision on canal which he said had assured free transit to everyone but Israel. He declared Egyptian Cabinet member after Council meeting had specifically excluded Israel, and he said even "our good friend India" has declared that remedy for Israel lies in international court.

But even more important to Israel, he said, was Jordan and Egyptian blockade of Straits of Tiran which threatened Israel's very existence by choking flow of Israel manufactured goods to probably only real markets available to them in Asia and Africa.

In view of fact Ben Gurion spent so much time and effort in defense of his mobilization activity, I told him that my interpretation of President's letter was not that he objected so much to mobilization as such and for self defense but that he feared there might be elements and local developments not confined to self defense—that hostilities might come from such action.

He replied US would have no reason to worry if it succeeded in persuading other people to keep peace but "I am not sure you will succeed".

On question of safety US nationals, he avoided giving me unequivocal assurances, saying however, "I don't think there is any danger." We talked about air activity re my problem of women and children for whose safety as well as for all US nationals I had evacuation plan to invoke if necessary. He replied, "I cannot be certain but I think there is now sufficient means for aerial protection. We hope to intercept them before they come. We have good radar installations, but I cannot tell you with certainty that none would get through."

I raised question of Fedayeen as danger to US nationals. He admitted they were constant threat, although he said he did not think their activities would be directed against non-Jews.

Comment: Ben Gurion was in good spirits, despite degree or two of fever for which he had had medical attention today, and was very cordial to me. However, I felt he was deliberately minimizing extent of mobilization which still appears very large and is not to be dismissed in terms of "few battalions". He spoke, I felt, with considerable and deliberate caution and was not very effective in creating feeling of assurance there will be no hostilities. [4]

Lawson

---

[4] Early the next morning, the Embassy in Tel Aviv informed the Department that the President's message of October 28 to Ben Gurion had been delivered to the office of Ben Gurion's military aide at 5:35 a.m., October 29. (Telegram 426, October 29; Department of State, Central Files, 684A.86/10–2956)

---

402.   Editorial Note

During the morning of October 29, Secretary Dulles participated in a series of discussions concerning the Israeli mobilization. At 8 a.m., Dulles telephoned President Eisenhower. During their conversation on the Middle East, Secretary "said nothing had happened overnight with regard to the Israeli mobilization. President asked if Dulles had read cable from Lawson concerning his conversation with Ben Gurion [*supra*]. President said it was [of] interest; despite what seemed to be rationalizations on the part of Ben Gurion, Lawson felt definitely Ben Gurion was not talking frankly to him. The President said at least things on both fronts—Hungary and Israel—seemed a little better this morning than last evening. Dulles replied that at least 'we have gained 24 hours.' "

The two then discussed developments pertaining to aungary. President Eisenhower closed the conversation by saying that he was leaving immediately on a political trip to Miami, Jacksonville, and Richmond, but could be reached by the Secretary within a matter of minutes at any time during the day. (Memorandum prepared in the President's office; Eisenhower Library, Whitman File, Eisenhower Diaries)

At 9:15 a.m. during his briefing to the Secretary's staff, Armstrong noted that Israel's mobilization was approaching 100 percent. He also informed the meeting that, during a conversation with the United States Army Attaché, Colonel Query, the Foreign Liaison Officer of the Israeli Defense Forces, Major Dov Sinai, had alluded to the following developments: Israel was going to strike at Jordan and drive to the west bank of the Jordan River, Egypt would then enter the conflict, and Israel had come to a deal with Iraq according to which Iraq would occupy the rest of Jordan on the east bank. After Armstrong's briefing, Secretary Dulles noted that in dealing with the serious situation created by Israel's mobilization, the following areas of action were open to the United States: Israeli balances in the United States, U.S. aid to Israel, the United Nations, joint U.K.–French action in conjunction with the Tripartite Declaration, and President Eisenhower's promise to aid subjects of aggression. The staff then discussed the forthcoming Security Council debate on the Israel-Jordanian situation. Within this context, Secretary Dulles referred to his recent talk with Ambassador Eban and emphasized the importance of getting Eban to make a statement on Israeli mobilization during the course of the U.N. debate on the Jordanian situation. In conjunction with Dulles' latter statement, the Bureaus of International Organization Affairs and Near Eastern, South Asian, and African Affairs were asked to recommend whether and how Eban should be required to make such a statement. (Tentative Notes of the Secretary's Staff Meeting by Howe, October 29; Department of State, S/S Files: Lot 63 D 75)

After this meeting, Dulles told Lodge over the telephone that "tomorrow" the United States should call in Eban and demand a declaration of his government's intentions in going into total mobilization. (Memorandum of telephone conversation by Bernau, 9:44 a.m., October 29; Eisenhower Library, Dulles Papers, General Telephone Conversations)

403.   Telegram From the Department of State to the Embassy in France [1]

Washington, October 29, 1956—11:17 a.m.

1537. Eyes only Ambassador from Secretary. Bits of evidence are accumulating which indicate that French Government, perhaps with British knowledge, is concerting closely with Israelis to provoke action which would lead to Israeli war against Egypt with probable participation by French and British.

We have conclusive but highly secret evidence that French have supplied Israelis with more than double number Mystere-4 planes which was reported to NEACC.

There has within last few days been very large British-French air buildup in Cyprus. French are sending two of their principal naval units to Eastern Mediterranean.

There has been virtual total mobilization of Israeli military forces as to which French Ambassador yesterday said he was "uninformed."

There has in general been almost complete blackout of information from French and British with us regarding Middle East matters.

There are other items of information which cannot be reported here but which substantially round out picture.

It seems as though the action would take either or both of two forms—(1) an alleged "retaliatory" military movement by Israel which would quickly take over Jordan west of the river. Then when Egypt came to Jordan's assistance there would be an attack on Egypt; (2) an effort, as is reported, to put an Israeli ship through Suez Canal on assumption that if it is stopped that would then be occasion for British and French to act to enforce Treaty of 1888 and recent "principles" adopted by UN Security Council.

---

[1] Source: Department of State, Central Files, 684A.86/10–2956. Top Secret; Niact. Drafted by Dulles, cleared by Rountree, and approved by Dulles. Repeated to London eyes only for the Ambassador from the Secretary.

Prior to the drafting of this telegram, at 10:22 a.m., Dulles telephoned Allen Dulles. Their conversation went as follows:

"The Sec. said he is weighing the desirability of telling Dillon that there are a lot of pieces which were fitted into a pattern which suggest a high degree of cooperation between the French and the Israelis. To the Sec's mind the evidence is almost conclusive. Some of the evidence can't be told. AWD mentioned the buildup on Cyprus. AWD said that could be mentioned and the Sec. said the Mysteres could be too. AWD asked if the Sec. heard the report that there is a plan to force an Israeli ship through the Canal and use that as an excuse for force. That from the Air Attaché at Tel Aviv. AWD will be over at 4. AWD worried that a spark in the ME could give the Soviets a shield to do things they can't do now—he mentioned the clock might be turned back in Central Europe." (Eisenhower Library, Dulles Papers, General Telephone Conversations)

As you know, it is profound conviction of President and myself that if French and British allow themselves to be drawn into a general Arab war they will have started something they cannot finish and end result may very well be an intensive anti-Western sentiment throughout Middle East and Africa and intimacy with Soviet Union which will impair for long time indispensable relations of Europe with Middle East and Africa. Furthermore, the process will greatly weaken economies of France, Britain and Western Europe. Under circumstances it is unlikely US will come to aid of Britain and France as in case of First and Second World Wars where they were clearly victim of armed aggression.

We have no doubt that it may be calculated that Jewish influence here is such as to assure US sympathy with such operations as are outlined. However, if this is calculated we think it is a miscalculation.

This is for your background information with discretion for you to take, or to recommend to us that you be authorized to take any steps which might still avert what we believe to be very dangerous course of action. We must, however, bear in mind it is only matter of hours rather than days before situation may become irrevocable. [2]

Dulles

---

[2] The response to telegram 1537 was transmitted to the Department in telegram 2041 from Paris, October 29. Evidently drafted before news of the Israeli invasion reached Paris, telegram 2041 requested authorization to convey the next morning to Pineau a personal message from Dulles proposing a tripartite démarche to Israel and warning that the United States would be obliged to disassociate itself publicly from any support for offensive action. (Department of State, Central Files, 974.7301/10–2956)

---

404.   Telegram From the Embassy in France to the Department of State [1]

Paris, October 29, 1956—7 p.m.

2027. Re Deptel to London 3039, Paris 1533. [2] We discussed

---

[1] Source: Department of State, Central Files, 674.84A/10–2956. Secret; Niact. Received at 1:51 p.m. Repeated to London and Tel Aviv.

[2] This telegram, dated October 28, informed the Embassies in London and Paris that the Department had been discussing the Israeli mobilization with British and French representatives in Washington along the lines indicated in the statement issued by President Eisenhower on October 28. (Ibid., 674.84A/10–2856)

briefly with Daridan this afternoon tripartite conversations in Washington on Middle East. He said instructions not yet dispatched to Alphand but indicated line would be that French unwilling to discuss Israeli dispositions in isolation but happy to discuss grave situation throughout whole area. He then catalogued series of attacks on French institutions in several Arab countries during past few days and apprehension what is to follow. On other hand, he continued profess ignorance extent Israeli preparations and supposition they are defensive in intent.

Comment: It seems probable to us that French are making no effort restrain Israelis and that, whether or not they are privy to Israeli intentions, they would not be loath to see Israeli dispositions which might divert Arab attention from France, or perhaps even military action which would weaken Egypt and its allies. French are bound at this moment to look at developments in Middle East through spectacles increasingly bitter Franco-Arab hostility.

For this reason, despite probability French may not cooperate as we would wish in implementation 1950 declaration, we would consider it of greatest importance to remain in close consultation with them on this matter in order that their policy not diverge from ours any more than unavoidable minimum.

Dillon

---

405.   Telegram From the Embassy in the United Kingdom to the Department of State [1]

London, October 29, 1956—1 p.m.

2322. Reference: Embtel 2317 [2] and Deptel 3009. [3] In two and half hour private conversation with Lloyd last evening, at which Barbour and Beeley also present, we discussed Middle East, Suez, Algeria (reported separately) [4] and Cyprus (also reported separately.) [5] Re Middle East and Arab-Israel situation in particular, Lloyd

---

[1] Source: Department of State, Central Files, 684A.86/10–2956. Top Secret; Limited Distribution. Received at 2:06 p.m.

[2] Document 386.

[3] Document 384.

[4] In telegram 2321 from London, October 29, not printed. (Department of State, Central Files, 751S.00/10–2956)

[5] In telegram 2328 from London, October 29, not printed. (*Ibid.*, 747C.00/10–2956)

equally concerned with us over Israeli mobilization, and said with feeling, and I believe evident conviction, that major Israeli attack either on Jordan or Egypt at this time would put Britain in impossible situation. Although British also have reports Israeli troop movements south rather than east, Lloyd inclined believe Israeli attack more likely to be directed against Jordan than Egypt. While he noted that Israelis apparently have a recent Egyptian foray against Israel which they could use as pretext for reprisal, he unwilling believe Israelis would launch full scale attack Egypt despite temptation to do so, in present circumstances. He also said categorically his recent conversations with French give him no reason believe French are stimulating such an Israeli venture, although he has reports that Israelis may have received additional Mysteres in last few days. Lloyd's major concern is threat further large-scale attacks on Jordan which he feels might be decisive in the present state of Jordanian weakness. His apprehension extends to speculating that Jordan could be lost entirely in the near future, with disastrous repercussions in Iraq and consequently on the Baghdad pact. He said UK might even have to try to get out of its commitment to Jordan. Meanwhile, he also fears a coup in Libya, where his information indicates Egyptian penetration is so extensive as to make a coup possible at any time. Lloyd repeatedly emphasized the seriousness of the position in which Britain would find itself in the event of an all-out Israeli attack either on Jordan or on Egypt in the light of the UK-Jordan treaty and the Tripartite Declaration, and although he reiterated that he still would like to see something happen to Nasser, his concern over the consequences of Israeli initiative carried sufficient conviction for me to conclude that any UK complicity in such a move is unlikely. Similarly, I thought his doubts that French would find it in their interests to stimulate Israeli ventures at this time are genuine. This connection, we mentioned possibility French might be exploiting *Athos* arms case as pretext direct action against Egypt. Lloyd discounted that idea believing French motivated by desire strengthen case against General Assembly consideration of Algeria. He did note, however, that apparently virtually all French Cabinet except Pineau is more inclined toward direct action against Egypt than continuance of efforts find peaceful solution Canal problem through further negotiation.

Concerning Suez, discussion covered status and prospects resumption negotiations with Egyptians and SCUA with particular reference to payment Canal tolls. Lloyd confirmed information I have previously reported,[6] that Hammerskjold is now trying to get Egyptian concurrence in statement its position which will constitute

---

[6] Reference is presumably to telegram 2295, Document 385.

Egyptian proposal for implementation six principles agreed by Security Council and thus constitute basis for resumption negotiations. Lloyd is still optimistic that Egyptian action along that line will be forthcoming within the next few days and that consequently negotiations may be resumed promptly, possibly though not ideally behind the scenes in New York before and during the General Assembly. Lloyd intends proceed New York in advance of Assembly meeting. Lloyd gave fuller information re his last meeting with Pineau, which differs somewhat from reports obtained from other sources. He said he asked Pineau to come London to convince him generally of necessity proceeding with further negotiations toward peaceful settlement Suez situation. French Cabinet broadly reluctant pursue matter through negotiations, preferring invoke stronger measures presumably economic since military force not advocated this time. Lloyd, whose Cabinet colleagues are also not united behind desirability further negotiations but are prepared to give him reasonable period in which to seek negotiated solution, believes that he succeeded convincing Pineau negotiations should be pressed. He is not sure how Pineau will make out in persuading the French Cabinet, but believes they will concur if something is forthcoming from the Egyptians without too much delay.

On SCUA and Canal tolls, we went over carefully the communications which you and Lloyd have exchanged, ending with your message Deptel 2851.[7] I took line that on my reading of that message gap between US and HMG, regarding both concept of SCUA and the specific problem of Canal tolls, is less real than apparent, and that I in fact saw no divergence other than in relation to timing, which it should be possible to resolve. Lloyd concurred although he professed to be confused as to what you contemplated should be done in the interim period before a final settlement is arrived at with Egypt. I went over minutely in this connection the two paragraphs of your message, beginning "nevertheless I appreciate" and concluding "impounded SCUA pending such an arrangement". In my view, these paras were clear and not susceptible misunderstanding.

As a result this discussion, we reached a consensus of opinion on a five-step program which we all believe consistent with the positions of both sides and which Lloyd is prepared to support with his Cabinet colleagues. British will make available today a paper setting forth their understanding of this program, which I will transmit with comments immediately upon receipt.

Atmosphere of conversation was frank and Lloyd was forthcoming in his attitude. He is still smarting under public portrayal both in

---

[7] Dulles' message to Lloyd, Document 358.

US and UK press of US-UK divergences, particularly in view of close coordination which in fact took place on both sides at SC meeting in New York. However, he now seems less concerned with individual incidents which have contributed to this situation than with press campaign which has capitalized thereon to present distorted picture of the magnitude of such disagreement. [8]

Aldrich

---

[8] Later on October 29, the Embassy in London reported in telegram 2333 that, according to a Foreign Office official, the British Foreign Office did not understand the reason for the Israeli mobilization and had requested the British Ambassador in Tel Aviv to seek an explanation from Foreign Minister Meir. (Department of State, Central Files, 684A.86/10–2956)

United States Diplomacy and the Sinai and Suez Campaigns, October 29–November 6, 1956

THE ISRAELI INVASION OF SINAI AND THE ANGLO-FRENCH ULTIMATUM, OCTOBER 29–30

406. Memorandum of a Conversation, Department of State, Washington, October 29, 1956 [1]

SUBJECT

Tense Situation in the Near East and Israeli Mobilization

PARTICIPANTS

Ambassador Abba Eban, Embassy of Israel
Mr. Reuven Shiloah, Minister, Embassy of Israel
NEA—William M. Rountree
NE—Fraser Wilkins

Ambassador Eban called at his own request today. He thought it would be desirable to keep in touch daily during the present tense situation in the Near East. He said he had received a report of Prime Minister Ben Gurion's discussion of October 28 with Ambassador Lawson [2] which fully confirmed the sense of Ambassador Eban's own remarks to the Secretary on October 28 that the Israeli mobilization had been purely precautionary and protective. Ambassador Eban observed that, on the other hand, there were abundant signs in the Arab states of preparations for an attack on Israel. Three fedayeen units had been captured, which was clearly indicative of Arab aggression against Israel. The Egyptian Navy was moving toward Israeli waters. Egypt, Syria and Jordan had established a joint command. At a recent meeting decisions had been reached to intensify and concentrate fedayeen activities in Israel. Fedayeen activity was as much a method of warfare as would be an invasion by regular armed units; consequently, it was necessary for Israel to take precautions. Prime Minister Ben Gurion had said that he would be happy if peace and tranquillity could be preserved between Israel

---

[1] Source: Department of State, Central Files, 684A.86/10–2956. Confidential. Drafted by Wilkins on October 31.

[2] Summarized in telegram 424, Document 401.

and its Arab neighbors and that the United States need have no concern if it were able to restrain the Arab states.

Ambassador Eban and Mr. Shiloah emphasized their regret that Senator George reportedly stated on leaving a briefing session between the Secretary and several Congressmen that there was some doubt that the United States would be able to restrain Israel. Ambassador Eban categorically rejected the implication contained in the statement that Israel would attack. No danger arose from Israeli defensive measures. The American press was distorting the situation. It was saying that Israel was moving at this time because Jordan was weak, because the Soviet Union was busy in Eastern Europe and because Egypt was preoccupied with the British and French over Suez. Ambassador Eban urged that the Department take such steps as necessary to prevent such speculation by the American press. He hoped that the interpretations which he had today read in the press were not an accurate reflection of statements by Departmental spokesmen.

Ambassador Eban recalled the Secretary had told him on October 28 he believed Israel had never been safer than it now was. Ambassador Eban thought the United States' analysis and the Israeli analysis of the situation had never been further apart. The Government of Israel thought the danger was now greater than it had ever been. He asked if the Department had any specific information or any assurances from the Arab states on which the Secretary's remarks might have been based.

Ambassador Eban said the Government of Israel had been surprised to read in the press that the United States had renewed its economic aid program to Egypt. Israel believed that this would result in further inflation of Nasser's prestige and would strengthen his hegemony in the area. Ambassador Eban asked if the United States had now decided to assist Nasser.

Mr. Rountree said he appreciated Ambassador Eban's account of Prime Minister Ben Gurion's conversation with Ambassador Lawson. He wanted Ambassador Eban to know that the United States was deeply concerned and wished to stress that we could only look at the facts and not the intentions to evaluate the dangers inherent in the situation. It went without saying that the Government of Israel was entitled to take measures within Israel for its self defense. In the absence of evidence of attack by the Arab states, however, Israeli mobilization might understandably lead to apprehension in the Arab states. The President had expressed his deep concern to the Arab states as well as Israel. We had no knowledge of the intentions of the Arab states nor could we provide Israel with assurances it would not be attacked. We had, however, examined the general situation in the area and saw no reason for concern at this time in Egypt or in

Syria, although there was evidence of extreme tension in Jordan. There was no question in our minds that Israel could move defensively within Israel. The United States hoped both sides would take steps to preserve peace and tranquillity and viewed aggressive action by either side with equally deep concern.

Mr. Rountree said that he was unable to throw any light on the newspaper articles to which Ambassador Eban referred. At this time there was considerable interest in Middle Eastern developments. Speculation naturally resulted. He was certain, however, that no responsible officials in the Department of State would comment in a one-sided way. He had not been present when Senator George and other Congressmen had talked with the Secretary, but understood the Secretary had explained the situation in the Near East in perspective. Senator George's comment could not be taken as epitomizing the substance of the Secretary's remarks to the Congressmen on Egypt.

Mr. Rountree continued that the United States had never terminated its aid mission in Egypt. In 1955 a program for development assistance had been drawn up. Commitments and contracts had been entered into between the Government of Egypt and private suppliers. It had taken several years to produce and ship items thereunder. Penalty clauses affecting private contractors were attached to some of these contractual relations. We were following all shipments carefully. There were no new PL 480 programs, nor additional commitments for CARE. It could not be said as Ambassador Eban had indicated that the United States was taking steps to strengthen the Egyptian position or increase the prestige of Nasser. It was clear from an analysis of the facts that recent press accounts had been misleading.

Ambassador Eban and Mr. Shiloah also commented that press accounts of United States aid to Egypt were having an important political effect. Ambassador Eban said there had never been a case when Israel had urged the United States not to give economic aid to an Arab country. Israel had only asked that military aid not be given to Arab countries. If only CARE and PL 480 were involved, he would not have mentioned it today. He understood that present commitments to Egypt included locomotives, engines and similar items. If the United States permitted such items to go forward, the public would believe Egypt had come out on top in the Suez Canal question. Eban believed further evidence of Egyptian success could be found in reports of a Suez compromise. This compromise would not provide for the passage of Israeli shipments through the Suez Canal. The net result was a growing lack of confidence in the outcome of the Suez controversy.

Ambassador Eban and Mr. Shiloah returned to the question of Israeli mobilization and noted Prime Minister Ben Gurion had emphasized an important military difference between Israel and the Arab states. The Arab states had large standing armies whereas Israeli forces were small; consequently, any increase through calling up Israeli reserves would be conspicuous. Both Israeli representatives emphasized at some length the importance of renewed fedayeen activities. It was their view that fedayeen units should be regarded as similar to regular military units. Minister Shiloah said that although each fedayeen incident might seem small, they were now being conducted on such an intensive scale that they were tantamount to large-scale attacks. Ambassador Eban thought that Israel would have the right to protest against fedayeen activity under the UN Charter. He noted that the President had said on April 9, 1956 that the United States would assist a victim of aggression. It would be desirable, accordingly, to define aggression. It seemed to him that fedayeen activity could be described as aggressive and hoped that we would make this point to the Arab countries. At the present time the Arabs thought they could get away with fedayeen activity under the UN Charter in the sense that they had found a new way of fighting which could not be called aggression.

Minister Shiloah thought it would be beneficial if the Department could take steps to repair the public impression that Israel had become a trouble maker. He realized that the Department was not responsible for comments in the press but he thought we might find ways to correct through background press conferences.

Mr. Rountree said that it had never been the desire of the Department to present a lopsided account of an existing situation. At the present time the Near Eastern atmosphere was tense and highly charged. In making U.S. concern known, we had presented our views to the press, to the Congress and to other governments in a balanced objective manner.

Mr. Rountree reiterated that he did not challenge Israel's right to take action within Israel. He earnestly hoped there was no cause for concern as a result of Israeli mobilization. He noted that mobilizations were generally followed by military activity. He added that in so far as fedayeen activity was concerned there might be differences of opinion among various UN members as to whether it constituted aggression. He thought it important that there be maximum cooperation with the United Nations in the maintenance of peace and tranquillity between Israel and its Arab neighbors. Mr. Rountree referred to pending negotiations between Britain, France and Egypt and noted that they were suspended at the present moment. The United States continued to support the six principles on which agreement had been achieved in the Security Council and the proposal supported by the 18 powers in London. The United States had no thought of other settlements. There was also general agreement among the members of SCUA with regard to its basic objectives, although certain differences of views had appeared on some other points.

Mr. Wilkins, who was called from the meeting at this point, returned with press tickers reporting that Israeli forces had invaded Egypt and had taken up positions near the Suez Canal.[3] Mr. Rountree remarked that we had obviously been having an academic discussion. Ambassador Eban said he would be returning immediately to the Israeli Embassy where he hoped to receive further information.[4]

---

[3] Telegram 443, October 29, reported that the spokesman of the Israeli Army had made the following announcement: "Units of Israel defense forces have penetrated and attacked Fedayeen bases in the Kuntilla and Ras el Naqeb area and have taken up positions west of Nahel road junction towards the Suez Canal. This operation was necessitated by the continuous Egyptian military attacks on citizens and on Israel land and sea communications, the purpose of which was to cause destruction and to deprive the people of Israel of the possibility of peaceful existence." (Department of State, Central Files, 684A.86/10–2956) This telegram was received in the Department of State at 4:45 p.m. A statement issued that same day by the Israeli Foreign Ministry is printed in *United States Policy in the Middle East, September 1956–June 1957*, pp. 135–137.

[4] At 3:40 p.m. on October 29, Dulles telephoned Lodge in New York. Their conversation went as follows:

"The Sec. said the Israelis have moved into Egyptian territory. We don't know yet in what force or whether it is a raid from which they will retire etc. The Br. and Fr. are coming in and we will see if they will act in the UN calling upon the Israelis to withdraw. Partly it is to smoke them out to see where they stand. L. said the [Security Council] meeting tomorrow is on Palestine and the plan was for Hammarskjold to make a statement—stalling device to carry over until next week. L. thought of getting the Chinese to ask the purpose of the mobilization but they agreed it looks as if this overtakes it all. The Sec. said but you can't be sure although it increases the likelihood of a major war. Hammarskjold has a telegram (2) from Burns and they are on the wire. It confirms what the Sec. said earlier in the conv. L. said he cancelled the thing in LA. Wilkins got on and someone from the Mission read the telegrams." (Eisenhower Library, Dulles Papers, General Telephone Conversations) The texts of the two telegrams from Burns were transmitted to the Department in telegram 432 from USUN, October 29, not printed. (Department of State, Central Files, 684A.86/10–2956)

407.   Memorandum From the Secretary of the Joint Chiefs of Staff (Wentworth) to the Chairman of the Joint Chiefs of Staff (Radford) [1]

Washington, October 29, 1956.

SUBJECT

> JCS Actions with respect to the Middle East Situation agreed upon at JCS Meeting 29 October 1956 [2]

At their meeting on 29 October 1956 the Joint Chiefs of Staff agreed to take the following actions with respect to the Middle East situation:

1. *General.*

Dispatch a message to all unified commanders outlining the present situation, including the latest Watch Committee report, and informing them of actions being taken by the JCS.

2. *Army.*

a. Alert one regimental combat team in Europe for possible movement.

b. Alert one regimental combat team from the Continental United States for possible movement.

3. *Navy.*

a. Direct CINCNELM to establish command headquarters on the U.S.S. *Pocono* by 2 November 1956. (Defense and State clearance required.)

b. Order one hunter killer group [3] (consisting of one CVS, six DD, and two SS) from the west coast of Europe (Rotterdam) into the Mediterranean, to report to Commander, Sixth Fleet. (Defense and State clearance required.)

c. Cancel Sixth Fleet participation in NATO exercise "Beehive", and order carrier strike force to positions east and southeast of Cyprus and within six hours' sailing distance of Cyprus.

d. Cancel the amphibious exercise in the Atlantic and issue instructions to plan for loading out one Marine battalion landing team.

---

[1] Source: JCS Records, OCJCS 091 Palestine (Jun 56–Dec 56). Top Secret.

[2] According to the history prepared by the JCS Historical Office, this meeting was held shortly after the Israeli Government issued its communiqué concerning the invasion of Sinai. (See "The Suez Canal Crisis", pp. 19–20, Chapter X in *The Joint Chiefs of Staff and National Security, 1953–1956*; JCS Historical Office Files)

At 6:43 p.m. on October 29, Rountree telephoned Dulles and informed him of most of the measures described in this memorandum. Rountree told Dulles that they were decisions taken by the Navy and that he had learned of them from Herbert D. Riley of Admiral Boone's office. (Memorandum of telephone conversation by Bernau; Eisenhower Library, Dulles Papers, General Telephone Conversations)

[3] A naval unit equipped for anti-submarine warfare.

4. *Air Force.*

a. Alert one C–124 wing in the Continental United States for movement to the Middle East.

5. *Marine Corps.*

a. Alert one battalion landing team in the Continental United States for possible movement to the Middle East.

Wentworth

---

408. Telegram From the Embassy in Egypt to the Department of State [1]

Cairo, October 29, 1956—4 p.m.

1193. Have just returned from call on Nasser to deliver copy President's statement [2] and to express President's concern and request [to refrain] from any action which could lead to hostilities (Deptel 1289). [3]

Nasser was friendly and relaxed and said unable understand what all the turmoil was about. He had just taken vacation of four days and something seemed to have happened during that time of which he was completely unaware. President's statement had come as surprise. As far as border incidents concerned, he confirmed his efforts to keep them quiet and said he had recently sent message to King Hussein enjoining redoubled vigilance in stopping infiltration. Could it be that Israel really wanted war? If so, he could not see why. It is true that in monitoring Israeli radio a certain change in tone had been detected about five days ago but he had not attached any particular significance to it. What is it all about?

---

[1] Source: Department of State, Central Files, 684A.86/10–2956. Secret; Priority. Received at 4:51 p.m. Repeated to Amman, Damascus, Beirut, and Tel Aviv.

[2] Document 395.

[3] Telegram 1289 to Cairo, also sent to Amman, Damascus, and Beirut, October 28, instructed the Embassies to approach the host governments, express Eisenhower's concern over the situation in the Middle East, and request that the government refrain from any action that could lead to hostilities. (Department of State, Central Files, 684A.86/10–2856)

I then informed Nasser of our instructions to evacuate non-essential Americans and said I hoped GOE would facilitate our task (1) by arranging for rights, as required, for military transport planes and ships; (2) by expediting exit formalities and (3) by taking any measures which might be required to assure security. Nasser replied he was still at a loss to understand why such action on our part should be felt necessary but GOE would do all it could to be helpful and he specifically gave informal assurance on landing rights for planes and ships on understanding formal request be made. Regarding security, he said we could be assured of that regardless of what may happen. At my request he also designated the Minister of Interior as clearing house for evacuation problems.

Was unable see Fawzi this morning but have appointment do so this afternoon, when I shall go over much same ground and deliver formal note re landing rights.

Decision see Nasser taken due delay in Fawzi appointment and also in knowledge that action by Foreign Office usually slow unless specially stimulated. Also wished get first hand impression of Nasser's reaction who, if he was not genuinely puzzled, put on good act.

Hare

409.   Memorandum of a Conversation, Department of State, Washington, October 29, 1956, 4:50 p.m. [1]

SUBJECT

Applicability of the Tripartite Declaration to Present Situation in Near East

PARTICIPANTS

Mr. J.E. Coulson, Minister, British Embassy
Mr. Ronald W. Bailey, Counselor, British Embassy

Mr. Charles Lucet, Minister, French Embassy
Mr. Francois de Laboulaye, Counselor, French Embassy

The Secretary
The Under Secretary
C—Douglas MacArthur 2nd
NEA—William M. Rountree
EUR—Burke C. Elbrick
NE—Fraser Wilkins

The Secretary consulted late this afternoon with British Minister Coulson and French Minister Lucet on the question of the applicability of the Tripartite Declaration to the present situation in the Near East. The Secretary noted that each of the representatives of the three countries had suggested the consultations. [2] Mr. Coulson said that he welcomed them.

The Secretary said all three countries ought immediately to bring to the Security Council the question of the reported movement of Israeli forces into Egypt. He thought the psychological effect would be very good if action could be taken this evening. He handed Mr. Coulson and Mr. Lucet copies of a working group draft of a proposed Security Council Resolution calling for the cessation of hostilities (Tab A). The Secretary stressed that this was a working group draft which had been prepared approximately a year ago in the event of an emergency. He said that we were now thinking of

---

[1] Source: Department of State, Central Files, 684A.86/10–2956. Secret. Drafted by Wilkins on October 31. The time of the meeting is from Dulles' Appointment Book. (Princeton University Library, Dulles Papers)

[2] A memorandum for the files by Rockwell, dated October 29, indicates that Bailey of the British Embassy called during the afternoon to say that the British and French desired to see either Dulles or Rountree for further discussions on the Israeli mobilization. After consulting the Secretary's office, Rockwell informed Bailey that a 5 p.m. appointment had been made. Macomber subsequently called Rockwell and told him that the Secretary had moved the appointment to 4:30 p.m. and that he specifically desired to be assured that the ranking officers of the British and French Embassies would attend. Rockwell then informed Bailey of the new hour for the appointment and learned that French Minister Lucet would be attending and not the Ambassador. (*Ibid.*, 784A.54/10–2956)

moving along these lines. It was his belief that as parties to the Tripartite Declaration of 1950 the three powers should act quickly in order to have maximum effect in Israel and the Arab states.

Mr. Coulson said that he was without instructions. He had been planning on the basis of word from the British Foreign Office in London following his conversation with the Secretary on October 28 to discuss the applicability of the Tripartite Declaration to the general situation in the Near East. He said that as these instructions had been written prior to the Israeli move into Egypt they might be outdated. He wished, however, to note that London thought that for all practical purposes the Tripartite Declaration would be inoperative. The Egyptian authorities had said with specific reference to the Tripartite Declaration that it gave no rights to any of these powers. None of them had any right to station troops in Egypt. Mr. Coulson continued it was almost impossible for Great Britain under these circumstances to take military action against Israel. French Minister Lucet said that he shared British Minister Coulson's view regarding the impossibility of military action against Israel.

The Secretary replied that the United States was not in a position to take military action under its own constitutional procedures without reference to Congress. The Secretary said that at this stage we were thinking only in terms of action within the Security Council under the Tripartite Declaration. He observed that the United States contemplated some form of economic sanctions under the working draft of the proposed Security Council Resolution. The Secretary thought that a stoppage of United States Government aid might be useful in present circumstances. The Secretary made it clear, however, that this general question was still being discussed within the United States Government and that no final decision had been reached.

Mr. Coulson said there was a stronger case for action within the Security Council rather than outside it. Mr. Lucet said he had no instructions on this point.

Mr. Coulson continued that he thought it would be awkward to make reference to the Security Council this evening since instructions from London were lacking as was also the case with the French. Mr. Coulson suggested that the Secretary might make a statement indicating the possibility of reference to the Security Council tomorrow. The Secretary said he would make a statement to this effect.[3] Meanwhile, he would endeavor to get in touch with London. After the British and French received their instructions the proposed Resolution in the Security Council could be discussed and changed as desirable.

---

[3] See footnote 6, Document 411.

Tab A

Draft Security Council Resolution

The Security Council

Noting the report on the outbreak of hostilities between Israel and (the Arab state concerned);

Expressing its grave concern regarding the effect of this renewal of fighting upon the maintenance of international peace and security in the area;

1. *Determines* that a breach of the peace has occurred; (If possible, this paragraph would also identify the aggressor.)
2. *Calls for* the immediate cessation of hostilities;
3. *Calls upon* Israel immediately to withdraw its armed forces behind the established armistice lines;
4. *Calls upon* all Members to render prompt assistance to the United Nations in the execution of this resolution and to refrain from giving any military, economic or financial assistance to Israel.
5. *Requests* the Chief of Staff of the United Nations Truce Supervision Organization to keep the Security Council informed on the compliance given this resolution and to make whatever recommendations he deems appropriate respecting further action by the United Nations to assist in the implementation of this resolution.

---

410. Memorandum of a Conversation, Department of State, Washington, October 29, 1956 [1]

SUBJECT

  Israeli Military Move into Egypt

PARTICIPANTS

  Dr. Ahmed Hussein, Ambassador of Egypt
  Mr. William M. Rountree, NEA
  Mr. Stuart W. Rockwell, NE

Ambassador Hussein called at Mr. Rountree's request in connection with reports of a serious Israeli military move against Egypt. Mr. Rountree explained that the Secretary had wanted to see the

---

[1] Source: Department of State, Central Files, 684A.86/10–2956. Secret. Drafted by Rockwell on October 30.

Egyptian Ambassador personally but that he was at the moment meeting with the British Chargé and the French Minister. [2]

Mr. Rountree reviewed for the Ambassador the events of the past few days. He mentioned the reports we had been receiving of large-scale Israeli mobilization, the two messages sent to Prime Minister Ben-Gurion by the President urging restraint and warning against forceful Israeli initiative, the public statement issued by the White House along the same lines, and the decision of the United States to reduce the number of American personnel in certain Near Eastern states.

Mr. Rountree said that the Secretary desired the Ambassador to know that the United States viewed with deep concern the reported Israeli military move into Egypt. If the reports were confirmed, the United States contemplated the Security Council's being asked to take appropriate action. The situation was very serious, said Mr. Rountree, and he expressed the hope that the Government of Egypt would not take action which would jeopardize a clear-cut decision by the Security Council appropriate to the circumstances. It was important that there be time for the United Nations to take this appropriate action.

The Ambassador asked whether the Secretary had in mind anything beyond recourse to the Security Council. Mr. Rountree replied that this was the first step. Other steps would presumably be based upon the Security Council decision. In response to a further question from the Ambassador, Mr. Rountree said he believed that the Council might meet as early as tomorrow.

With reference to Mr. Rountree's statement concerning the need for Egypt to take no action which would jeopardize a clear-cut United Nations decision, Ambassador Hussein said Egypt's record was good. Despite large-scale provocations from Israel over the past year or so, Egypt had restrained itself. It was difficult to say what the Egyptian Government would do in these delicate circumstances. He assumed that the Secretary did not mean that Egypt should not defend itself. Mr. Rountree said that this was, of course, not the case. It was just that we thought that the United Nations should be at once seized of the matter and that nothing should jeopardize the chances of quick United Nations action.

The Egyptian Ambassador went on to say that Egypt did not think that Israel was a true entity. It was an artificial state created by the United Nations, or certain big powers. There were some, he continued, who thought that the big powers behind Israel had not really tried to restrain it. He was speaking frankly, he added. Mr. Rountree asked whether the Ambassador meant the United States,

---

[2] See *supra.*

and the Ambassador reiterated that he was speaking frankly. Mr. Rountree mentioned the steps he had already outlined which the United States had taken in an effort to stop the present Israeli action. The Ambassador asked whether Mr. Rountree thought that if the United States, United Kingdom and France really told Israel not to do something, that Israel would still go ahead and do it. Mr. Rountree referred to the 1950 Tripartite Declaration of the United Kingdom, United States and France, saying this had been reaffirmed many times. The Ambassador said that nonetheless the Egyptian people and Egyptian Government thought that not enough restraint had been placed upon Israel. Mr. Rountree replied that even so, the United States position opposing the use of force in the area had been made very clear. We had stressed that we would take action in and outside the United Nations to oppose aggression. The Secretary was at that moment discussing the matter with the British and the French.

Mr. Rountree terminated by reiterating the importance which the Secretary attached to this matter and the Secretary's desire that the Ambassador be urgently and personally informed of this. Ambassador Hussein thanked Mr. Rountree and took his departure.

---

411.   Memorandum of a Conference With the President, White House, Washington, October 29, 1956, 7:15 p.m. [1]

OTHERS PRESENT

    Secretary Dulles
    Under Secretary Hoover
    Secretary Wilson
    Admiral Radford
    Mr. Allen Dulles
    Governor Adams
    General Persons
    Mr. Hagerty (after first five minutes)
    Colonel Goodpaster

The meeting was called to discuss the situation arising out of the reports of Israeli invasion of the Sinai Peninsula. [2]

---

[1] Source: Eisenhower Library, Whitman File, Eisenhower Diaries. Top Secret. Drafted by Goodpaster.

[2] The Dulles Papers at the Eisenhower Library contain memoranda of several telephone conversations which preceded this meeting. At 5:45 p.m., Admiral Radford returned Dulles' call. According to Bernau's transcript, "Sec. asked him to be at the

Secretary Dulles referred to French actions in providing, apparently, a sizeable number of Mysteres to the Israelis in excess of agreed figures and without the notifications called for in US–UK–French agreements on arms to the Middle East. He also referred to a very large number of messages between Paris and Israel yesterday.

Several of those present reviewed the reports on Israeli movements to positions seventy-five miles within Egyptian territory, and—by air drop—to positions approximately twenty miles from Suez. There was next a review of intelligence reports regarding Egyptian force dispositions, particularly Egyptian forces in and near the Gaza strip.

The President asked whether the very first thing that Egypt should do should not be to counterattack and hold the Israeli forces in the desert where they would have difficulty maintaining themselves. Admiral Radford doubted the Egyptians could do this.

The President recalled that in 1950 and later we have said we would support the victim of aggressions in the Middle East. The question now is, how shall we do this. Admiral Radford said the 6th Fleet is in the area. The President asked if blockade would be effective. Admiral Radford said the affair will be "all over" in a few days; when the President challenged him on how it could be ended in that time, he said he meant that the Israelis would be to the Suez within two or three days. He thought Israel simply wants to seize the Sinai Peninsula.

Mr. Allen Dulles suggested that the Israelis might still be planning to withdraw—that the operations thus far have been in the nature of probing action. Admiral Radford thought that the operation has gone too far to pull back, and thought that the Israelis may attack Egyptian fields tonight. The President asked what Egyptian air forces would be doing at that time, and Admiral Radford said that their quality is not of the best, and they probably could not attack Israel in night operations. He thought that Israel is counting on the operations not running more than three days.

Secretary Dulles said the operation goes further than that. The Canal is likely to be disrupted, and pipe lines are likely to be

WH—via the back way about 6:30. R. said their assessment is it is going to get bigger as soon as daylight comes if not tonight. They don't think it can be stopped."

At 6 p.m. White House Press Secretary Hagerty telephoned Dulles from Richmond, Virginia, and said that he had been asked by Eisenhower to tell Dulles that the President's party would return to Washington as quickly as it could. Dulles then briefly reported to Hagerty on various developments of the day.

Twenty minutes later Eisenhower telephoned Dulles from Richmond and asked if Dulles wanted to see him. The Secretary answered yes and informed Eisenhower that he had asked Allen Dulles and Admiral Radford to attend the meeting. Eisenhower and Dulles then agreed that the meeting should begin at 7:15 that evening.

broken. In those circumstances British and French intervention must be foreseen. They appear to be ready for it, and may in fact have concerted their action with the Israelis. (At this point Mr. Hagerty joined the meeting.) Admiral Radford said that there are rumors that the British, French and Israelis have made a deal with Iraq to carve up Jordan.

Admiral Radford thought we are confronted with a question whether Egypt will ask for help from the Russians, or throw Nasser out and ask the British for help. He commented that Israel has obtained thirty to fifty Mysteres from France that we had not heard of—and perhaps more. Secretary Dulles recalled that the supply of these aircraft must have been in violation of our agreement whereby we were supposed to be notified.

Secretary Dulles said that in his opinion there is a basic issue that must be considered. The French and British may think that— whatever we may think of what they have done—we have to go along with them. The President asked what they would think if we were to go in to aid Egypt to fulfill our pledge. Secretary Wilson asked whether we are committed so tightly as this by our statement, and Secretary Dulles recalled that the Tri-Partite statement, and then the U.S. statement last April, called for exactly such action. Mr. Wilson said the Israelis must be figuring on French and British support, thinking that we are stymied at this pre-election period, and the USSR also because of difficulties in Eastern Europe.

The President queried whether Mr. Hagerty should not make a statement letting the information out that we are considering what steps we could take to support Egypt and redeem our pledge in this matter—including consideration of calling Congress back. Secretary Dulles recalled that Senator George today had referred to the possibility of calling Congress into session. The President thought that in these circumstances perhaps we cannot be bound by our traditional alliances, but must instead face the question how to make good on our pledge. He thought the UN might be the most valuable course to follow. Secretary Dulles pointed out that the USSR may beat us to the jump in the UN. He added that we have had no news from the British and French in nearly ten days. He suggested that we might plan to go to the UN, with the British and French if they wish to join us, but otherwise alone. He felt it imperative to get in ahead of the USSR.

The President said, in this matter, he does not care in the slightest whether he is re-elected or not. He feels we must make good on our word. He added that he did not really think the American people would throw him out in the midst of a situation like this, but if they did, so be it. Mr. Dulles said that one adverse result of this action may be a wave of anti-Semitism through the country, and general agreement was indicated.

The President next asked whether we should call Congress back into session, and specifically whether we could call them for the day following the election. He said that referral to the United Nations was not enough. We must take more definite action, since we are the only people the British and the French will listen to. Admiral Radford thought that we should take our action tonight, inasmuch as the situation may develop in a major way overnight.

Mr. Wilson asked what the Russians are likely to do in the circumstances (without any answer).

The President thought the British are calculating that we must go along with them (he thought they were not banking too heavily on our being tied up in the election, but are thinking in longer range terms.) He thought we should let them know at once of our position, telling them that we recognize that much is on their side in the dispute with the Egyptians, but that nothing justifies double-crossing us. He did not conceive that the United States would gain if we permitted it to be justly said that we are a nation without honor. Admiral Radford thought that this matter must be handled on the basis of principle, and the President agreed. Secretary Dulles said that tomorrow there may well be fighting along the Canal, with the pipe lines broken, and with the British and French moving in.

The President asked what the group thought of telling the British that we know the strain the French have been under and they may be playing us false—they have given extra Mysteres to Israel and there has been a sudden rise in their messages to and from Israel. We are, however, moved to help Egypt at once in order to honor our commitments. We know the French are already involved in war, which is being indirectly supported by the Egyptians, and all things are legitimate. If, however, the British get into this operation, they may open a deep rift between us. The President said we might indicate we are considering ways and means of redeeming our pledge to the Middle Eastern countries. If the British back the Israelis they may find us in opposition. He said he did not fancy helping Egypt in the present circumstances but he felt our word must be made good. Mr. Wilson again asked how clear cut our pledge is to the Middle Eastern countries, and the President recalled that we had told Israel quite recently that they did not need from us the arms they were seeking because of the assurance inherent in our pledge.

In discussion of the military situation of the two countries, including the deployment of their forces, Admiral Radford indicated Israel can take care of the Egyptian bombers, in all likelihood, with their fighters including the Mysteres.

Mr. Hoover pointed out that if we were to side with the French and British we would find the USSR lined up with Arabs and in fact with all of Africa. Admiral Radford said we must support principle in this case, and Mr. Hoover agreed. Secretary Dulles said that the Baghdad Pact ambassadors [3] were in seeing him today and pointed out that the United States is pledged to stop such aggression, and asked what we proposed to do.

The President thought it would be well to call Mr. Coulson, the British Chargé d'Affaires, in the absence of an ambassador and have him come to the White House right away. After discussion it was decided to have him come to the front gate, and Mr. Hoover called him to arrange this. Mr. Wilson recalled that Allen Dulles had said there is still a slight hope that the Israelis have sent probing forces into the desert and would back out. Admiral Radford said that the fact of the reported air drop showed that the Israelis were fully committed.

The President said he planned to say to Coulson that the French have moved fast and played a lone hand in this matter, that we propose to move as fast as we can in the United Nations, with our allies if possible, and if not then alone, and that we are going to do everything possible, even including a special session of Congress if necessary, to redeem our pledge.

Governor Adams suggested that if the situation deteriorates it might be desirable to convene the Congress before election. He saw considerable merit in putting Congress on notice to come in on a date certain. General Persons said that the purpose of the UN operation is to determine who is the aggressor and we should avoid prejudging this matter until the UN had acted. Mr. Allen Dulles reiterated that there is still a slight chance that this is a probing operation—he recognized that the chance may be very slight. The President repeated that he proposed for us to go before the United Nations, and say we are prepared to do all necessary to redeem our pledge.

Secretary Dulles said there has been a struggle between the French and ourselves to see who will have the British allied with them in the tense situations in the Middle East and North Africa. He thought there was still a bare chance to "unhook" the British from the French (who will be even more furious than they have been) and that it ought to be undertaken.

---

[3] At 6:05 p.m. Dulles, Rountree, and Burdett met with Ambassador Mohammed Ali of Pakistan, Ambassador Haydar Görk of Turkey, Ambassador Ali Amini of Iran, and Hashim Khalil, Counselor and Chargé d'Affaires of the Iraqi Embassy. A memorandum of the conversation by Burdett is in Department of State, Central Files, 684A.86/10–2956.

The President said that before Mr. Coulson came the group should go down to have their picture taken—he asked whether all present should not be in the picture, and there was agreement. Mr. Hagerty asked if there would be any statement, and the President thought that there might be one later. (Mr. Dulles was drafting a few notes as this discussion proceeded.) Admiral Radford said that Israel is too far committed to back out.

General Persons suggested the desirability of having a bi-partisan leadership meeting late this week. Others commented that our position must be very clear inasmuch as there would be a great deal of political activity in connection with any such meeting.

Mr. Wilson thought we should make clear tonight that we are going to the UN tomorrow, and the President recalled that Mr. Hagerty might state that we are considering whether to call a special session. Governor Adams suggested that the consideration be hinged on the developments in the next day or two.

I raised with the President and the group the question of the position of the Soviet Union in this matter, suggesting that consideration be given to the possibility that they might take radical action, and hence to what we might do to forestall this. The President asked what we could do, and others pointed out that the announcement of our plan to go to the UN, and of our general stand in the matter, might help in this. It was observed that we and the Russians might find ourselves on the same side in this matter.

At this point Mr. Coulson was brought in and the group went down to have pictures taken.[4] I stayed with Mr. Coulson. The President and Secretary Dulles returned in a few minutes. I was absent from their meeting for five minutes or so, and then joined it until Mr. Coulson left.[5]

I then returned to the meeting in the Red Room of those who had left the Oval Room, and Secretary Dulles joined this meeting shortly. A press release was drafted and reviewed with all those present by Mr. Hagerty and Secretary Dulles. The group dispersed and Mr. Hagerty returned to the West Wing to make an announcement to the press.[6]

---

[4] Copies of the AP wire photos are in the Eisenhower Library.

[5] See *infra*.

[6] The press release reads as follows:

"At the meeting the President recalled that the United States, under this and prior Administrations, has pledged itself to assist the victim of any aggression in the Middle East.

"We shall honor our pledge.

"The United States is in consultation with the British and French Governments, parties with us to the Tripartite Declaration of 1950, and the United States plans, as contemplated by that Declaration, that the situation shall be taken to the United Nations Security Council tomorrow morning.

Secretary Dulles said he would call Ambassador Lodge to put the matter before the UN at the opening of business tomorrow. After further discussion he said he would call Lodge tonight and ask that Lodge call Hammarskjold tonight in order that we may be "on record" first.

G

Colonel, CE, U S Army

"The question of whether and when the President will call a special session of the Congress will be decided in the light of the unfolding situation." (Department of State *Bulletin*, November 12, 1956, p. 749; *United States Policy in the Middle East, September 1956–June 1957*, p. 137)

---

412.   Memorandum of a Conference With the President, White House, Washington, October 29, 1956, 8:15 p.m. [1]

OTHERS PRESENT

    Secretary Dulles
    Mr. Coulson
    Colonel Goodpaster

I joined the meeting after it had been in progress for about five minutes. The President was saying that the prestige of the United States and the British is involved in the developments in the Middle East. He felt it was incumbent upon both of us to redeem our word about supporting any victim of aggression. Last spring, when we declined to give arms to Israel and to Egypt, we said that our word was enough. If we do not now fulfill our word Russia is likely to enter the situation in the Middle East. In his opinion, the United States and the United Kingdom must stand by what they said. In view of information that has reached us concerning Mysteres and the number of messages between Paris and Israel in the last few days, the President said he could only conclude that he did not understand what the French were doing. Mr. Coulson said he did not know about the messages. The President said that if he has to call Congress in order to redeem our pledge, he would do so. We will stick to our undertaking.

---

[1] Source: Eisenhower Library, Whitman File, Eisenhower Diaries. Top Secret. Drafted by Goodpaster.

Mr. Coulson asked if we would not first go to the Security Council and the President said we plan to get there the first thing in the morning—when the doors open—before the USSR gets there.

Secretary Dulles recalled that the Baghdad Pact ambassadors had seen him today, and had asked him what the U.S. is going to do to redeem its pledge. The President said that we had had a great chance to split the Arab world. Various of the countries were becoming uneasy at Egyptian developments. He does not know what Sir Anthony Eden is thinking at the present time, but he is certain that it is important that we stick together.

Mr. Coulson said it should be easy to agree in the Security Council. He recognized, however, that the French may be involved in this operation. The President said he could not understand why the French would conceal the movement of the Mysteres. He asked Mr. Coulson to communicate these ideas urgently to London and assure Selwyn Lloyd and Sir Anthony that we wished to be with them. He said he would not betray the good word of the United States, and he will call the Congress if necessary in order to redeem our pledge.

G
Colonel, CE, US Army

---

413.   **Editorial Note**

In New York on October 29, Lodge met with Dixon, Cornut-Gentille and Hammarskjöld at 4:30 p.m. to discuss the Israeli attack on Egypt. At the meeting, Hammarskjöld stated his belief that the only sensible move was to have an immediate meeting of the Security Council which would call upon Israeli troops to withdraw to their own boundaries. The Secretary-General noted press reports that Israel was occupying a position within Egyptian territory and commented that if this were true, it constituted aggression. He also showed to the others a report from the United Nations Truce Supervision Organization in Jerusalem indicating that the United Nations military observer in the El Auja area had under threat of force been expelled by Israeli authorities. The Secretary-General suggested that the Security Council should meet on October 30 at the latest whether or not the Egyptians filed a complaint. Lodge commented in his report to the Department of State that Dixon and

Cornut-Gentille reacted in a hesitant and lukewarm manner to Hammarskjöld's concern. Cornut-Gentille, according to Lodge, particularly showed great reluctance to take immediate steps to deal with the situation, and even argued with Hammarskjöld about the latter's interpretation that the Israeli action was more serious than usual. The British and French Representatives both stated that it would be impossible to obtain instructions before a morning meeting; and Dixon suggested that the matter be taken up during the afternoon meeting on October 30, which had been scheduled to discuss the Israeli-Jordanian situation. Hammarskjöld opposed this suggestion and pointed out that the United Nations must rob Egypt of any cause for counterattack. Lodge stated that the United States was prepared to meet that evening if the French and British agreed. The meeting then discussed a press statement to be issued by the President of the Security Council. The text to which they finally agreed indicated that the President of the Security Council had declared that the Israeli-Egyptian situation could be brought up at the Council meeting fixed for October 30. (During October 1956, the French Representative served as President of the Security Council.)

At 6 p.m. Hammarskjöld telephoned Lodge to inform him that Burns had agreed to issue immediately a request for a cease-fire on his own authority and that Israeli forces reportedly had penetrated 100 kilometers into Egypt without any response from Egypt. (Telegram 433 from USUN, October 29; Department of State, Central Files, 684A.86/10–2956)

Later that evening Hoover telephoned the Mission in New York and instructed it to seek an urgent meeting of the Security Council for the morning of October 30. When informed of the U.S. request, Hammarskjöld agreed to it at once, suggested that the meeting begin at 10 a.m. the following day, and assured the Americans that the U.S. item would have priority over any others. (Telegram 443 from USUN, October 30; *ibid.*, 684A.86/10–3056)

Lodge then informed Dixon of the U.S. request for a Security Council meeting and of the President's statement made earlier that day. Later, during a telephone conversation with Secretary Dulles, Lodge described his conversation with Dixon. According to Bernau's transcript, Lodge said that "it was one of the most disagreeable and unpleasant experiences that he had ever had. He said that Dixon until now had always been amiable but at this conference the mask fell off and he was virtually snarling. When Lodge spoke of living up to the Tripartite Declaration Dixon said, 'Don't be silly and moralistic. We have got to be practical.' Dixon said that the British would never go along with any move against Israel in the Security Council." (Memorandum of telephone conversation, October 29, 10 p.m.; Eisenhower Library, Dulles Papers, General Telephone Conversations)

According to Lodge's report to the Department of State, Dixon also said that he had heard that the Department of State intended to introduce a "fantastic" resolution, calling for economic sanctions if Israeli forces were not withdrawn. Dixon maintained that the United Kingdom would not have anything to do with it and "that he simply could not understand what the United States was thinking of." (Telegram 443 from USUN, October 30; Department of State, Central Files, 684A.86/10–3056)

Lodge then spoke with Hammarskjöld and Cornut-Gentille at the latter's apartment. The French Representative's immediate reaction was to object to not having been consulted while acknowledging that as President of the Security Council he would of course cooperate in arranging the meeting. French Deputy Representative Ordonneau, however, did make clear that France would not go along with the United States action. Following this meeting, Lodge forwarded to Hammarskjöld a letter requesting the meeting, which the Department of State had previously transmitted to Lodge. He then telephoned each member of the Security Council and explained the U.S. initiative in general terms. Lodge received a positive reception from the Representatives of Peru, Cuba, Iran, and China and a noncommital one from the Representatives of Yugoslavia, Belgium, and the Soviet Union. (Telegram 443 from USUN, October 30; *ibid.*)

The Department of State transmitted to USUN the text of a proposed letter from Lodge to the President of the Security Council in telegram 220, October 29. (*Ibid.*) For text of the final version of that letter, submitted to the President of the Security Council on October 30, see footnote 2, Document 423.

414.   Message From Prime Minister Ben Gurion to President Eisenhower [1]

Jerusalem, October 29, 1956.

DEAR MR. PRESIDENT: I thank you for your two messages transmitted to me by Ambassador Lawson, the first last night and the second early this morning. I wish to assure you, Mr. President, that my government and I are deeply grateful for your unremitting efforts over years, and particularly during the current year, to achieve a lessening of tension in the area and a peaceful settlement between Israel and her Arab neighbours. Under ceaseless provocation, boycott and siege we have prayed and continue to pray that your vision of regional co-operation and peace shall be realised. This hope has guided and will continue to guide our policy and action.

On reviewing the Middle Eastern scene during these past twelve months, I feel that you will agree that the obstacle to the fulfilment of our common aim is the attitude and activities of the Prime Minister of Egypt. Col. Nasser's expansionist policy has led to unprecedented tension in the area. The subversive operations of his political and military machine extend from the Atlantic Ocean to the Persian Gulf, demolishing the foundations of security and good will. In order to further his aim of establishing Egyptian domination throughout the area he has during this period acquired vast quantities of arms from Soviet sources which together with lesser quantities from Western sources, have converted the Egyptian army into a force of great magnitude by Middle Eastern standards.

Together with the undermining of security in other Arab countries he has created a ring of steel around the borders of Israel. On the night after the elections in Jordan his Commander in Chief visited Amman to establish a unified command of the armies of Syria, Jordan and Egypt under Egyptian control, the declared objective of which is to destroy Israel. As soon as there occurred a slight lessening of tension in the Suez dispute, with the conclusion of the Security Council deliberations, Col. Nasser's gangs renewed their incursions into Israel territory from Egypt and the Lebanon. Despite his formal acknowledgment of the Constantinople Convention on

---

[1] Source: Eisenhower Library, Whitman File, International File. The source text is a copy of the original letter signed by Ben Gurion which the Embassy in Tel Aviv sent in despatch 244, October 29. (Department of State, Central Files, 684A.86/ 10–2956) It was received in the Department of State on November 12 and forwarded to the White House on November 14.

The text of the letter was also transmitted to the Department of State in telegram 439, October 30. (*Ibid.*, 684A.86/10–3056) The copy in the Eisenhower Library was initialed by President Eisenhower. (Eisenhower Library, Whitman File, International File)

freedom of navigation for the ships of all nations through the Suez Canal—whose universality of application to include Israel was explicitly confirmed by the Security Council Resolution of 1 September 1951 and implicitly re-affirmed by the Security Council Resolution of 13 October 1956—spokesmen for the Government of Egypt have declared time and again that Israel shipping will not be permitted to pass through the Canal. This blockade is also extended to the Gulf of Akaba which is Israel's outlet to Africa and the Far East. The Egyptian Government bases these actions on the state of war which she insists in maintaining against Israel. The growing danger to the stability of the area in general and of Israel in particular as a result of Col. Nasser's manoeuvres has in the past few weeks been referred to by the heads of various western governments and is I believe widely recognised to-day by world opinion.

With Iraqi troops poised in great numbers on the Iraq–Jordan frontier, with the creation of the joint command of Egypt, Syria and Jordan, with the decisive increase of Egyptian influence in Jordan, and with the renewal of incursions into Israel territory by Egyptian gangs, my Government would be failing in its essential duty if it were not to take all necessary measures to ensure that the declared Arab aim of eliminating Israel by force should not come about. My Government has appealed to the people of Israel to combine alertness with calm. I feel confident that with your vast military experience you appreciate to the full the crucial danger in which we find ourselves.

Sincerely yours,

D. Ben-Gurion

---

415.   Telegram From the Joint Chiefs of Staff to Certain Specified and Unified Commanders [1]

Washington, October 29, 1956—9:38 p.m.

JCS 912463. From JCS. Exclusive for General Armstrong, Admiral Wright, General Harrison, General Partridge, General Gruenther,

---

[1] Source: JCS Records, CCS 381 EMMEA (11–19–47) Sec 47 RB. Top Secret; Operational Immediate; Noforn. The source text indicates that the message originated with Radford.

General Lemnitzer, Admiral Stump, Admiral Boone, General Lemay, General Fry pass to General Taylor, CSA.

1. The Senior Foreign Liaison Officer in Tel Aviv has reported that, "Israeli Defense Force units have penetrated and attacked Fedayeen bases in Kuntilla and Ras El Naqueb area and have taken up positions to the west of the Nahel Road junction, towards the Suez Canal." This action followed an accelerated Israeli matériel buildup lasting several weeks and an intensive mobilization substantially completed during past 12 days. This attack took place on night 29–30 October. Heavy IDF concentration has been reported Beersheba, possibly threatens direct route through El Auja to North Sinai where major Egyptian forces in Sinai located. No further information this action.

2. The Intelligence Advisory Committee has concluded that:

a. The scale and nature of the Israeli attack was sufficient to precipitate war with Egypt. Whether war results depends largely on the Egyptian reaction which is as yet unknown.

b. Franco-Israeli collaboration probably exists in connection with the Israeli move against Egypt with at least the tacit approval of the British. The British and French are prepared to and probably will intervene with force in the Middle East as opportunity occurs in connection with the Israeli-Egyptian action.

3. Strikes and violence in protest against French seizure of the Algerian rebel leaders [2] flared in most of the Arab world on 28 October. Further strikes and demonstrations have been called Algeria, Morocco, and Tunisia for 1 November, the anniversary of the Algerian Revolt. Large-scale intervention by French armed forces to protect French lives and property probable and could lead to France-Moroccan hostilities. Israeli attack in Egypt seems likely further inflame Arab world.

4. The Joint Chiefs of Staff consider that Israeli forces have gone so far as to leave little probability that they will now pull back. A serious consideration is the reaction of the USSR to this situation. The United States in concert with France and the UK is introducing the issue into the United Nations without delay.

5. Following United States actions being taken:

a. Sixth Fleet Carrier Strike Force and Amphibious Force directed proceed vicinity Cyprus.

b. Hunter-Killer Group and two submarines in Rotterdam directed proceed Eastern Mediterranean report COM Sixth Fleet.

---

[2] On October 22, the French Government seized a chartered airplane carrying five leaders of the Algerian rebellion enroute between Rabat and Tunis. The Algerians were arrested and incarcerated.

c. One RCT CINCEUR area, one RCT in ZI and one C–124 wing in ZI alerted for possible movement. [3]

---

[3] JCS 912773, sent on November 2 to the same Specified and Unified Commanders as JCS 912463, indicated that the Joint Chiefs had taken the following additional steps to improve overall military readiness: (1) moved the CINCNELM command to USS *Pocono* in the Mediterranean; (2) canceled the amphibious exercise in the Atlantic and issued instructions to plan for loading out one Marine battalion landing team; (3) authorized the loading of additional atomic weapons in CVAs *Forrestal* and *FDR* and placed them on short notice for possible movement; and (4) indicated intent to move U.S. Naval forces west of Crete as soon as evacuation of U.S. nationals was completed. (JCS Files)

---

416.   Telegram From the Embassy in the United Kingdom to the Department of State [1]

London, October 30, 1956—11 a.m.

2343. Eyes only for Secretary. Eyes only Ambassador. Lloyd asked to see me urgently this morning. He had four points he wished to make. Referring to conversations with Brit Chargé in Washington, he said US contemplates asking Security Council to declare Israel aggressor. He agrees to immediate SC consideration. However, his thinking is that Brit Govt would be in impossible situation politically here if they should have to take military action on the side of Egypt pursuant to a declaration of Israeli aggression. Along this line he tried to rationalize by calling Israeli action "a clear case of self-defense" on grounds that Egypt has denied Israeli access through the Canal and that Egyptian Fedayeen have for a long time been provoking the Israelis by commando forays into Israeli territory. Lloyd's second point was to inform me that Brit have obtained Israeli assurances that Jordan will not be attacked. He professed to have been particularly concerned on that score and to have made clear to the Israelis that if Jordan were attacked, the UK–Jordan Treaty would result in the UK immediately giving military assistance to Jordan. Thirdly, he expressed concern that the Brit now have some sterling 75 million worth of shipping in or near the Suez Canal, and he assumes that the Israeli military tactics will be to seize the Canal bridges to prevent Egyptian counter-action. Finally, he noted that Mollet and Pineau are coming to London this morning.

---

[1] Source: Department of State, Central Files, 974.7301/10–3056. Top Secret; Niact. Received at 8:59 a.m. Repeated to Paris.

I took strong issue with Lloyd's assessment of the Israeli justification for its attack, emphasizing that it seemed hardly explicable anywhere that an attack of this magnitude is justified by Egypt's barring Canal to Israeli ships, which has been going on for many years, and Egyptian Fedayeen raids, which in any case have been largely negligible in recent months. I left him under no doubt that it would be a serious mistake to calculate that Jewish influence in US is such as to assure US sympathy with such Israeli operations. I was surprised to find him take line that on contrary there is widespread anti-Semitism in the US, which I also obviously rejected. I also said that in any event it of overriding importance that UK support US Security Council action and that it would be manifestly disastrous for Brit position with other Arab countries if Brit should let present animosity toward Nasser dictate Brit taking a less forceful line with the Israelis than the US. With regard to the operation of the Tripartite Declaration, Lloyd stated Nasser in the past has said that he would not want UK assistance under that declaration, and Lloyd again repeated that military assistance to Egypt would be politically impossible in the UK at this time.

Lloyd then left for urgent Cabinet meeting. At my request he has agreed to see me again following the UK talks with Mollet and Pineau.

Aldrich

---

417.   **Telegram From the Embassy in France to the Department of State** [1]

Paris, October 30, 1956—1 p.m.

2055. Min saw Joxe this morning and inquired French position re United States draft SC resolution (Deptel 1557). [2] Joxe replied French Govt strongly opposes this draft and could not join in any resolution condemning Israel. He listed long series Egyptian provocations, including denial transit Canal to Israeli vessels, radio propaganda and commando raids within past few days, as full justification for Israeli "retaliation." He was unresponsive to points we made at

[1] Source: Department of State, Central Files, 684A.86/10–3056. Secret; Niact. Received at 8:59 a.m. Repeated Niact to USUN and to London.
[2] Telegram 1557 to Paris, October 29, contained the text of the draft Security Council resolution printed as Tab A to Document 409.

some length to effect that 1) while numerous provocations had occurred on both sides, none justified present act of war; 2) United States Government deeply concerned at probable repercussions Israeli action throughout Arab world both as to involvement other Arab states in hostilities and as to likely deterioration Western position throughout Moslem world; and 3) sure advantages to be gained by Soviets from this situation and possibility their indirect involvement if hostilities persist.

In response our query what alternative French had to our draft resolution, Joxe replied we must work toward cease-fire by appealing to both parties and condemning neither. He was unwilling to express a view as to whether Israelis would respond to an SC appeal for cease-fire.

We had impression Joxe was under instructions to tell US as little as possible at this time. He asked us however to call on him again late this afternoon after return Mollet and Pineau from London. We shall of course do so.

Ambassador [3] will be back in Paris tomorrow morning.

Dillon

---

[3] Dillon had been in southern France. During his absence the Embassy continued to sign his name to telegrams.

---

418.   Message From President Eisenhower to Prime Minister Eden [1]

Washington, October 30, 1956.

DEAR ANTHONY: I address you in this note not only as head of Her Majesty's Government but as my long time friend who has, with me, believed in and worked for real Anglo-American understanding.

Last night I invited Mr. Coulson, currently your Washington representative, to come to my house to talk over the worsening

---

[1] Source: Department of State, Central Files, 684A.86/10–3056. Top Secret. Transmitted in Niact telegram 3081 to London, October 30, 10:50 a.m., which is the source text, with the instruction: "Please deliver immediately following message from the President to Eden. Confirm time delivery.' Upon receipt of telegram 3081 at 4:30 p.m. London time, Aldrich telephoned Eden and learned that he was already speaking before the House of Commons. He arranged for the immediate delivery of this message to Eden at Commons. (*Ibid.*)

situation in the Mid East. I have no doubt that the gist of our conversation has already been communicated to you. But it seemed to me desirable that I should give you my impressions concerning certain phases of this whole affair that are disturbing me very much.

Without bothering here to discuss the military movements themselves and their possible grave consequences, I should like to ask your help in clearing up my understanding as to exactly what is happening between us and our European allies—especially between us, the French and yourselves.

We have learned that the French had provided Israel with a considerable amount of equipment, including airplanes, in excess of the amounts of which we were officially informed. This action was, as you know, in violation of agreements now existing between our three countries. We know also that this process has continued in other items of equipment.

Quite naturally we began watching with increased interest the affairs in the Eastern Mediterranean. Late last week we became convinced that the Israel mobilization was proceeding to a point where something more than mere defense was contemplated, and found the situation serious enough to send a precautionary note to Ben Gurion. On Sunday we repeated this note of caution and made a public statement of our actions, informing both you and the French of our concern. On that day we discovered that the volume of communication traffic between Paris and Tel Aviv jumped enormously; alerting us to the probability that France and Israel were concerting detailed plans of some kind.

When on Monday actual military moves began, we quickly decided that the matter had to go immediately to the United Nations, in view of our Agreement of May, 1950,[2] subscribed to by our three governments.

Last evening our Ambassador to the United Nations met with your Ambassador, Pierson Dixon, to request him to join us in presenting the case to the United Nations this morning. We were astonished to find that he was completely unsympathetic, stating frankly that his government would not agree to any action whatsoever to be taken against Israel. He further argued that the tri-partite statement of May, 1950, was ancient history and without current validity.

Without arguing the point as to whether or not the tri-partite statement is or should be outmoded, I feel very seriously that whenever any agreement or pact of this kind is in spirit renounced by one of its signatories, it is only fair that the other signatories should be notified. Since the United States has continued to look

---

[2] The Tripartite Declaration.

upon that statement as representing the policies and determination of our three governments, I have not only publicly announced several times that it represents our policy, but many of our actions in the Mid East have been based upon it. For example, we have in the past denied arms both to Egypt and to Israel on the ground that the 1950 statement was their surest guarantee of national security. We have had no thought of repudiating that statement and we have none now.

All of this development, with its possible consequences, including the possible involvement of you and the French in a general Arab war, seems to me to leave your government and ours in a very sad state of confusion, so far as any possibility of unified understanding and action are concerned. It is true that Egypt has not yet formally asked this government for aid. But the fact is that if the United Nations finds Israel to be an aggressor, Egypt could very well ask the Soviets for help—and then the Mid East fat would really be in the fire. It is this latter possibility that has led us to insist that the West must ask for a United Nations examination and possible intervention, for we may shortly find ourselves not only at odds concerning what we should do, but confronted with a de facto situation that would make all our present troubles look puny indeed.

Because of all these possibilities, it seems to me of first importance that the UK and the US quickly and clearly lay out their present views and intentions before each other, and that, come what may, we find some way of concerting our ideas and plans so that we may not, in any real crisis be powerless to act in concert because of misunderstanding of each other. I think it important that our two peoples, as well as the French, have this clear understanding of our common or several viewpoints.

With warm personal regard.

As ever

Ike E [3]

---

[3] Telegram 3081 bears this typed signature.

419.   Memorandum of a Conference With the President, White House, Washington, October 30, 1956, 10:06–10:55 a.m. [1]

OTHERS PRESENT

Secretary Dulles
Under Secretary Hoover
Mr. Herman Phleger
Governor Adams
Mr. Hagerty (for part of meeting)
Colonel Goodpaster

Mr. Dulles opened the meeting with a report that Ambassador Lodge had initially given notice last night to the President of the Security Council regarding our desire to inscribe an item on the Israeli attack. Inasmuch as the British had not had a chance to join in, and Mr. Coulson had indicated the British might wish to join us, Ambassador Lodge withdrew his request in an effort to enable Dixon to join. [2] Mr. Dulles indicated that, at the meeting at 11 this morning, we still hoped that the British would join with us, although if they did not we would submit the item alone.

The President asked if the French had been given the opportunity to join with us, and Secretary Dulles said that they had been given that opportunity yesterday. Neither yesterday nor this morning had they shown any evidence of desire to act rapidly on the matter. Mr. Dulles commented that according to radio reports Mollet has gone up to London today. He also pointed out that, with reference to our NATO partners, we may have to decide whether to go along with our partners who are colonial powers.

The President at this point read aloud a message which he had been drafting to Eden. At the close of this he read an INS report of imminent French and British landing which had just been received. The President suggested that Mr. Dulles take his draft message and edit it. The Secretary asked if it would not be possible to get it off

---

[1] Source: Eisenhower Library, Whitman File, Eisenhower Diaries. Top Secret. Drafted by Goodpaster. The time of the meeting is from the record of the President's Daily Appointments. (*Ibid.*)

[2] Prior to this meeting with Eisenhower, Dulles arranged for the withdrawal of the request during a series of telephone conversations with Coulson and Lodge. During the final conversation with Lodge, which began at 9:41 a.m., Dulles emphasized the importance of obtaining British cooperation with U.S. efforts. According to Bernau's transcript, the Secretary "said we are anxious to carry the Br—it is basic and goes to the heart of our relations all over the world and we have to give them a reasonable time." (*Ibid.*, Dulles Papers, General Telephone Conversations)

immediately, and he said the President revised it to their satisfaction and sent it to State for immediate dispatch. [3]

Mr. Phleger said that the British and French might take their action under the authority of the 1950 declaration, as a measure for protecting Egypt by establishing a "front" on the Canal area. The President pointed out that this action would have the French opposing the Israelis, whom they have supported in this action. Mr. Hoover said the thinking might be that the French and the British might simply take over the Canal, after which the Israelis could withdraw from the Canal area. The President asked if this action would not amount to repudiation by the French and British of their agreement with us in the 1950 Declaration and subsequent statements. Mr. Hoover said they might say it is not, but is simply an effort to achieve the purposes of the Declaration.

Mr. Dulles said he had talked to Secretary Humphrey regarding Israeli bank balances in the United States. [4] Initially Mr. Humphrey thought these could be held up informally today; after further study, however, he reported that they are widely scattered, the only concentration being in a single bank in New York, regarding which informal action did not seem practicable. Secretary Dulles said that if there were any attempt to stop the flow of charity money, a great outcry must be expected. The President asked whether such a flow could be permitted, however, if sanctions are imposed.

At this point Secretary Dulles took a call on the President's phone from Ambassador Lodge who reported that the British had suggested changing the title of the agenda item to "The Palestine Question," removing all reference to measures to bring to an end the operations of Israeli forces in Egypt. If this were done, they indicated they would join with us; otherwise they would not. The French had indicated they would not join with us at all. [5] The President suggested a wording which would avoid apparent prejudgment to the effect that the aggressor in the matter is Israel. Secretary Dulles then advised Ambassador Lodge to submit the item as revised, without British or French association.

Secretary Dulles next asked whether steps should be taken to keep American flagships out of the Suez Canal. The President

---

[3] *Supra*. A typed draft with handwritten changes is in Department of State, Presidential Correspondence: Lot 66 D 204, Eisenhower to Eden Correspondence 1955–1956 Vol I.

[4] Memoranda of these telephone conversations, which took place at 9:15 and 9:46 a.m., are in the Eisenhower Library, Dulles Papers, General Telephone Conversations.

[5] According to the memorandum of this telephone conversation Lodge also said that he thought that the French and British were both bluffing. Dulles disagreed with this statement and told Lodge that, according to information received, the British and French military units would have control of the Suez Canal by that afternoon. (*Ibid.*, Whitman File, Eisenhower Diaries)

thought the decision should be up to ship owners; he doubted whether the British and French, if they seize the Canal, would bar us. Mr. Dulles thought that the British and French might move in and operate the Canal, that Egypt would then attack them, and that U.S. ships would be damaged or sunk. The President thought U.S. ships would have to take their chances.

Mr. Dulles pointed to the danger of our being drawn into the hostilities as we were in World Wars I and II with the difference that this time it appears that the British and French might well be considered the aggressors in the eyes of the world, engaged in an anti-Arab, anti-Asian war.

The President said that in his judgment the French and the British do not have an adequate cause for war. Egyptian action in nationalizing the Canal was not enough to justify this. Mr. Dulles recalled that the British were practically in agreement with Egypt on a resolution of the Suez dispute at the recent UN meeting, but have been delaying any solution since then. He added that this is not a question of the Suez, but is really a question of Algeria for the French and position in the Persian Gulf for the British. He thought that the odds are high that the British may be evicted from Iraq, and that the pipelines may be blown up. He suggested that it may be necessary for us to make major adjustments in our oil situation soon.

The President said it may be that the British think they can settle the matter quickly, and thus have their oil supply continue without interruption. Unless they have reached some secret agreement with the Saudi-Arabians, however (such as possibly on Buraimi), there seems little chance that the flow of oil would continue. Mr. Hoover doubted that they could have reached an agreement regarding Buraimi.

Mr. Hoover added that the British and French may feel that they have forced us to a choice—between themselves and the Arabs. They may in fact have felt that they have forced us into a position where we must go against the Arabs. The President wondered if the hand of Churchill might not be behind this—inasmuch as this action is in the mid-Victorian style. If oil is cut off and American ships take the route around the Cape, the oil supplies to Western Europe will be greatly cut down. Mr. Hoover thought the British may be estimating that we would have no choice but to take extraordinary means to get oil to them.

Secretary Dulles said their thinking might be that they will confront us with a de facto situation, in which they might acknowledge that they have been rash but would say that the U.S. could not sit by and let them go under economically.

The President said he did not see much value in an unworthy and unreliable ally and that the necessity to support them might not be as great as they believed.

Secretary Dulles commented that he had been greatly worried for two or three years over our identification with countries pursuing colonial policies not compatible with our own. He has had several study groups working on this. Recently he made a statement on this matter which provoked violent comment by the French and the British. At this point the President was informed that a message from Sir Anthony Eden to him had been received by the British Embassy and would be sent over promptly. [6] The meeting adjourned until its arrival.

The meeting resumed in about fifteen minutes. The President, after reading Eden's message, commented that Eden says the attitude of Egypt over the past years has relieved the signatories of the three-power declaration from any obligation. The President commented further that the British case would be improved if the Egyptians had not simply nationalized the Canal, and then operated it effectively afterward.

The State Department group left at this point to work on the UN resolution needed this afternoon.

About twenty minutes later the Secretary called the President [7] to advise him of reports through the British Embassy here that Eden was announcing in Commons the landing of British and French forces in the Suez Canal area. The President commented that a "hands off" attitude by the United States might well be indicated. He thought that it would probably be necessary today to make clear publicly that we have not been, and are not now, associated with

---

[6] Document 421.

[7] The transcript of this conversation, which began at 11:37 a.m., reads as follows:
"The Sec. said Eden is on the air making a statement which presumably will announce their landings. The Pres. said because he sent an impatient message, he is acknowledging this one from Eden—something to the effect that apparently the difference is the way we regard the tripartite statement and since we have made no statement limiting ourselves he does not see how we can avoid fulfilling our word. The Sec. said the focus will be shifting. He said the Israelis will be out and back in a few hours. They have accomplished their mission and now the question is how to handle the British and French business. The Pres. said his offhand judgment is hands off—he does not think we should help them and let them stew in their own juice for a while. He does not see how we can go before our people and say they are our friends and we have to rescue them etc. etc. The Sec. thinks Eden will give the impression we have been kept informed. The Pres. said maybe that is the reason for his hurried telegram. He will send it over. The Sec. is not sure it is relevant because he thinks things will shift from the 1950 Declaration. The Pres. wants to get over to him that we are a government of honor and stick by what we say." (Eisenhower Library, Dulles Papers, White House Telephone Conversations.)

A memorandum of this conversation, prepared in the Office of the President, incorrectly indicates that the conversation began at 3:40 p.m. (*Ibid.*, Whitman File, Eisenhower Diaries)

the French and the British in their activities. He expressed concern over the possibility of Russian intervention on the side of Egypt, and thought that a blockade by the British (who have the forces to make it effective) might be the only way to prevent Russian entry into the area. He said he was not too sure now that Congress should be called into session that he had a great deal of question over any idea of asking Congress for $600 to $800 million to support oil deliveries and other economic aid to Britain and France when the full impact of their action begins to be felt.

G

Colonel, CE, US Army

---

420.   Editorial Note

At 4:45 p.m. in London (11:45 a.m. in Washington), Aldrich and Barbour were called to the British Foreign Office where at approximately 5 p.m. they were handed copies of ultimatums from the Governments of Great Britain and France to the Governments of Egypt and Israel, which had been delivered to Egypt and Israel at 4:30 p.m. Meanwhile, in a statement to the House of Commons, which began at 4:30 p.m., Prime Minister Eden reviewed the events preceding the outbreak of hostilities, noted that Great Britain had discussed the situation with the United States, and advised the Commons that unless hostilities could be stopped quickly, free passage through the Suez Canal would be jeopardized. Eden then informed the Commons that, in order to bring hostilities to a quick halt, the British and French Governments had addressed urgent communications to the Governments of Egypt and Israel, calling on both sides to stop all warlike action and withdraw their military forces to a distance of 10 miles from the Canal. Also, the Government of Egypt had been requested to agree that Anglo-French forces should move temporarily into key positions at Port Said, Ismailia, and Suez, in order to separate belligerents and guarantee freedom of transit through the Canal by ships of all nations. Eden explained that the Egyptian and Israeli Governments had been given 12 hours (until 6:30 a.m. Cairo time on October 31) to answer the communication; and that it had been made clear to them that, if at the expiration of that time, one or both had not undertaken to comply with these requirements, British and French forces would intervene in whatever strength might be necessary to secure compliance. (House of Commons, *Parliamentary Debates,* 5th series, volume 558, columns 1273–1275) The Embassy in London transmitted the text of Eden's statement and the texts of the Anglo-French notes to Israel and Egypt to the Department of State in telegrams 2357, 2359, and 2360, respectively, October 30, all in Department of State, Central Files, 674.84A/10–3056; see also telegram 2383 from London, October 31; *ibid.,* 674.84A/10–3156. The text of the Anglo-French ultimatum is printed in D.C. Watt (ed.), *Documents on the Suez Crisis* (London: Royal Institute of International Affairs, 1957), pages 85–86. A translation of Mollet's speech to the French Assembly made the same day, as well as the text of Eden's speech to Parliament are printed in *United States Policy in the Middle East, September 1956–June 1957*, pages 138–142.

---

421.   Message From Prime Minister Eden to President Eisenhower [1]

London, October 30, 1956.

I am sending you this hurried message to let you know at once how we regard the Israel-Egypt conflict.

We have never made any secret of our belief that justice entitled us to defend our vital interests against Nasser's designs. But we acted with you in summoning the London Conference, in despatching the abortive Menzies Mission and in seeking to establish S.C.U.A. As you know from our secret sources, the Russians regarded the Security Council proceedings as a victory for themselves and Egypt. Nevertheless we continued through the Secretary-General of the United Nations to seek a basis for the continuation of the negotiations.

Now this has happened. When we received news of the Israel mobilisation, we instructed our Ambassador in Tel Aviv to urge restraint. Soon afterwards he sought and obtained an assurance that Israel would not attack Jordan. This seems to me important, since it means that Israel will not enlarge the area of conflict or involve us in virtue of the Anglo-Jordan Treaty. In recent months we have

---

[1] Source: Eisenhower Library, Whitman File, International File. Top Secret. Delivered to the White House under cover of a note from Coulson to President Eisenhower which reads: "The Prime Minister has asked me to send you the enclosed message."

several times warned the Israel Government, both publicly and privately, that if they attacked Jordan we would honour our obligations. But we feel under no obligation to come to the aid of Egypt. Apart from the feelings of public opinion here, Nasser and his Press have relieved us of any such obligation by their attitude to the Tripartite Declaration.

Egypt has to a large extent brought this attack on herself by insisting that the state of war persists, by defying the Security Council and by declaring her intention to marshal the Arab States for the destruction of Israel. The latest example of Egyptian intentions is the announcement of a joint command between Egypt, Jordan and Syria.

We have earnestly deliberated what we should do in this serious situation. We cannot afford to see the Canal closed or to lose the shipping which is daily on passage through it. We have a responsibility for the people in these ships. We feel that decisive action should be taken at once to stop hostilities. We have agreed with you to go to the Security Council and instructions are being sent this moment. Experience shows that its procedure is unlikely to be either rapid or effective.

Selwyn saw Winthrop [2] this morning. We are meeting with the French later. I will send you a further message immediately after that meeting. [3]

---

[2] Winthrop W. Aldrich.
[3] Printed from an unsigned copy.

---

422.   Telegram From the Embassy in France to the Department of State [1]

Paris, October 30, 1956—4 p.m.

2059. While French remain uncommunicative as at present, we cannot obtain here solid information concerning their intentions. However report transmitted Embtel 2057 repeated London 355, [2]

---

[1] Source: Department of State, Central Files, 684A.86/10–3056. Top Secret; Niact; Limit Distribution. Received at 10:40 a.m. Repeated Niact to London.
[2] Telegram 2057 from Paris, October 30, reported that, according to a well-informed French journalist, the French Cabinet that morning had unanimously approved French military intervention in the Suez Canal Zone, provided that Great Britain also participated, and endorsed French use of the veto in the Security Council

though not confirmed, is entirely plausible. No effort is being made here to conceal that intensive military preparations are going forward in Mediterranean. Newspapers are full of reports concerning series high-level meetings at Defense Ministry, reinforcement troops in Cyprus and activities French fleet.

Our estimate is that, through current operation, French are continuing pursue objective they have had primarily in mind since onset Suez crisis, that is, overthrow or at least humiliation of Nasser. If this can be achieved by Israeli arms alone, French might refrain from overt intervention, though even in this case Franco-British occupation of Canal zone "to ensure free transit" would seem likely. Moreover, if Israelis should prove unable knock out Egyptians promptly or if in civil disorders French nationals in Egypt should be molested, French would be likely to intervene at once and on large scale.

Once French have intervened overtly with armed forces, they would not withdraw until their objective achieved. It would seem probable therefore that only hope of forestalling or limiting French action (unless we have already prevailed upon British to hold back) might be strongest and most solemn U.S. representations on highest level within next few hours.

Dillon

---

against any resolution condemnatory of Israel. Also, according to the source, three Cabinet Ministers expected that the landings might occur on October 31. The Embassy also noted that Pineau had left for London at 9:30 a.m. Paris time that morning and Mollet at 11:30 a.m. (*Ibid.*)

---

423.   Telegram From the Mission at the United Nations to the Department of State [1]

New York, October 30, 1956—4 p.m.

445. Re Palestine. We met with Dixon (UK) and Cornut-Gentille (France) this a.m. to invite them to co-sign our letter on

---

[1] Source: Department of State, Central Files, 684A./86/10–3056. Secret; Priority; Limited Distribution. Received at 4:39 p.m.

Israeli attack. [2] I told them President Eisenhower was most anxious to maintain tripartite cooperation on this problem.

Dixon replied that while UK was anxious work together with us on this matter, they were not a bit anxious emphasize tripartite approach publicly. Dixon said he could not possibly co-sign letter if it included last para indicating our objectives. I asked him if he could sign it without last para. Dixon said he would have to ask for instructions and there wasn't sufficient time. Summing up, he said he could not join in signing the letter at all because of public statements which had been made last night (referring obviously to news stories out of Washington) and which were not in accord with the objectives of HMG. He said he could make a statement before the Council saying "it seems to me right to have called the meeting" if the last para of our letter were dropped. He said he didn't want to be quoted as saying: "I agreed with them beforehand".

I asked if France would agree to my saying before the Council that meeting was called with their concurrence. They replied they could not. Cornut-Gentille said he couldn't agree because of long list of Egyptian attacks against Israelis. Cornut-Gentille said he had instructions to see me to say France does not want to be put in position of having to state publicly she was opposed to US stand. But he said if we proposed to condemn Israel in res, France could not go along with US. France, he said does not agree with our objectives.

Both Dixon and Cornut-Gentille were white-faced and hostile to any conciliatory suggestions. Their only contribution to the meeting amounted to proposals of dilatory tactics. I gave them every opportunity suggest alternatives including postponement of morn-

---

[2] The text of the letter which Lodge later forwarded to the President of the Security Council, reads as follows:

"The Government of the United States has received information to the effect that in violation of the General Armistice Agreement between Israel and Egypt, the armed forces of Israel have penetrated deeply into Egyptian territory. This military action commenced October 29, 1956 and is continuing in the Sinai area. The situation makes imperative an immediate meeting of the Security Council, charged as it is with the primary responsibility for the maintenance of international peace and security as well as responsibility for the observance of the Armistice Agreement.

"I have the honour, therefore, in behalf of my Government to request you to convene a meeting of the Security Council as soon as possible to consider 'The Palestine question: steps for the immediate cessation of the military action of Israel in Egypt.'" (U.N. doc. S/3706)

ing's meeting, but they declined on basis they had different objectives. [3]

Lodge

424.   Message From President Eisenhower to Prime Minister Eden [1]

Washington, October 30, 1956.

DEAR ANTHONY: This morning I sent you a long cable to say that we here felt very much in the dark as to your attitude and intentions with respect to the Mid East situation. I have just now received your cable on this subject for which I thank you very much. I shall be awaiting the further message to which you refer.

It seems obvious that your Government and ours hold somewhat different attitudes toward the Tripartite Declaration of 1950. Since we have never publicly announced any modification of the Declaration or any limitations upon its interpretation, we find it

[1] Source: Department of State, Central Files, 684A.86/10–3056. Top Secret. Transmitted to London in Niact telegram 3083, October 30, 12:09 p.m., which is the source text, with the instruction: "Following message from the President for immediate delivery to Eden. Confirm time of delivery." Aldrich received the message at 5:35 p.m. London time, and immediately forwarded it to Eden at the House of Commons. (Telegram 2363 from London, October 30; *ibid.*)

This message was sent from the White House to the Department of State under cover of a note from Eisenhower to Dulles which reads: "In view of the fact that one motivation of my earlier cable to Anthony was my astonishment that he should avoid giving us any needed information, I have put together the attached, which I request that you send off to him. If you should see any reason for revision, won't you please give me a ring?" The original of this note, initialed by Eisenhower, is in the Eisenhower Library, Dulles Papers, Misc. papers—U.K. (Suez Crisis). A copy, *ibid.*, Whitman File, Dulles–Herter Series, bears the marginal inscription: "sent 11:35".

difficult at this moment to see how we can violate our pledged word.

In any event, I shall earnestly and even anxiously watch the unfolding situation.

With warm regard.

As ever,

Ike E. [2]

---

[2] Telegram 3083 bears this typed signature.

---

425.   Memorandum of a Telephone Conversation Between the Secretary of State and Senator Walter F. George, Washington, October 30, 1956, 12:48 p.m. [1]

TELEPHONE CALL FROM SENATOR GEORGE

G. asked what the Sec. has heard this a.m. The Sec. said we have word from the Br that they say they have secured an agreement from the Israelis not to attack Jordan but apparently they are more or less conniving in an attack against Egypt and are using that as a prearranged pretext, I think, for a statement that unless the fighting stops within 12 hours they will move their forces into the Suez Canal area. They are calling upon both to withdraw to a zone which will leave the Canal free of either of their forces and that if they do not do that they will move in. The Egyptians are not going to move out and it is almost certain the Br and Fr are working in collusion with the Israelis in this matter. G. asked re a special session [2]—the Sec. said he does not think it necessary. G. hoped not. The Sec. said there is no occasion unless we were planning military action which we are not or unless we wanted to give massive aid and we don't plan to do that. The Pres. does not think there is need. G. asked re the UN, and the Sec. said it is before the UN now, G. said if they call on us then he guesses you might have to do something. The Sec. said yes—the res calls upon Israel to withdraw its forces and to abstain from any economic assistance to Israel so long as it is in violation of this res. This just means we suspend aid

---

[1] Source: Eisenhower Library, Dulles Papers, General Telephone Conversations. Transcribed by Bernau.

[2] Reference is to a special session of the Congress.

to Israel. The Sec. said it is all right for him to go home. The Sec. said we fought them off for 3 months against using force which they have been determined to do and now they are going ahead without us. The Sec. is afraid it will prove a disaster but they may prove they are right—the Sec. does not know.

---

426.   Memorandum of a Telephone Conversation Between the Secretary of State in Washington and Senator William F. Knowland in California, October 30, 1956, 1:02 p.m. [1]

TELEPHONE CALL FROM SENATOR KNOWLAND IN SACRAMENTO

K. asked re the ultimatum he sees on a ticker. Are we a party to it. The Sec. said he never heard of it before K. did. No intimation of it. K. is shocked and does not think the Congress or the American people . . . . [2] The Sec. said he does not know it is true but it seems to be. K. said it might indicate they put the Israelis up to it. The Sec. said the evidence is the Israelis were used as a decoy. K. is shocked. The Sec. said he had solemn assurances they would not— though they were private. K. praised the Sec. for the way he has handled himself. The Sec. said we have got the res in the UN. K. said that is safe as far as the people are concerned. He added the UN has an obligation on an occupation should it occur.

---

[1] Source: Eisenhower Library, Dulles Papers, General Telephone Conversations. Transcribed by Bernau.
[2] Ellipsis in the source text.

427.   Memorandum of a Telephone Conversation Between the President and the Secretary of State, Washington, October 30, 1956, 2:17 p.m. [1]

Secy. Dulles.

He will proceed on the UN matter at 3 o'clock today. Will have their resolution then. British & French have asked that action should be suspended until consideration could be given to the Eden proposals. But they propose to go ahead, & state that 2 items (Israeli invasion; & Suez Canal) should be kept separate & distinct.

Dulles said they gave a 12-hour ultimatum to Egypt that is about as crude & brutal as anything he has ever seen. He does not think there is much use in studying it. Said that of course by tomorrow they will be in.

The President asked, aren't they partially in now? Mr. Dulles did not know, but thinks not yet. They gave this 12-hour ultimatum apparently at noon.

President asked why they suggest waiting. Dulles said their reason is that Eden has made an important speech, & they want us to wait until we study it. The President just now received the ultimatum—so Mr. Dulles read his copy aloud. [2] The President agreed that it was pretty rough. Dulles said it is utterly unacceptable.

President thinks they would expect the Russians to be in on this. Asked where is Egypt going to turn?

Mr. Dulles said he did not know, but agreed with President on idea of the Russians. He again said he thinks we should push ahead on our resolution.

President wondered how the request came to us. Dulles replied that Dixon gave it to Lodge in N.Y.; & they also had message from the French Embassy here suggesting we defer action on our matter today. If we push it now, President asked, don't we tend to confuse these 2 issues? Dulles replied, no, on the contrary. One would be armistice between Egypt & Israel. The Suez Canal is still on our agenda, & should be taken up under the other agenda item.

President said it is all right with him that they go ahead—added that, after all, they haven't consulted with us on anything.

---

[1] Source: Eisenhower Library, Whitman File, Eisenhower Diaries. Prepared in the Office of the President. Another memorandum of this conversation, transcribed by Bernau in Dulles' office, is *ibid.*, Dulles Papers, White House Telephone Conversations.

[2] See Document 420.

428.   Memorandum From the Secretary of the Joint Chiefs of Staff (Wentworth) to the Chairman of the Joint Chiefs of Staff (Radford) [1]

Washington, October 30, 1956.

SUBJECT

> JCS Actions with respect to the Middle East Situation agreed upon at JCS Meeting 30 October 1956

At their meeting on 30 October 1956 the Joint Chiefs of Staff agreed to take the following actions with respect to the Middle East situation:

1. Send a memorandum to the Secretary of Defense requesting him to ask the State Department to secure the necessary authorization from the Government of Turkey to station a U.S. air task group at Adana, Turkey, in order to be prepared to assist in carrying out any directives which may be issued by the United Nations. [2]

2. Request representation from the Joint Chiefs of Staff of one general or flag officer (from JMEPC) on the Near East Watch Committee. The Chairman stated he would undertake with the State Department to secure this membership.

Wentworth

---

[1] Source: JCS Records, OCJCS 091 Palestine (Jun 56–Dec 56). Top Secret.

[2] In response to this memorandum, Secretary of Defense Wilson on October 30 sent a letter to Secretary Dulles requesting that the Department of State take action to acquire certain base rights requirements and overflight rights in order to move a substantial number of planes and accompanying Air Force personnel into the Middle East to help evacuate U.S. citizens. (Department of State, Central Files, 711.56300/10–3056) A supplemental memorandum on this subject from Radford to Wilson of November 1 was subsequently transmitted to Secretary Dulles by Assistant Secretary of Defense Gray on November 3. (*Ibid.*, 711.56300/11–356)

429.   Memorandum of a Telephone Conversation Between Secretary of State Dulles in Washington and External Affairs Secretary Pearson in Ottawa, October 30, 1956, 3 p.m. [1]

TELEPHONE CALL TO MIKE PEARSON IN OTTAWA

The Sec. said he is greatly concerned at these developments. All of his efforts have blown up. P. said he just talked with the High Comm in London. [2] The Sec. said the ultimatum is as brutal as anything he has seen. P said his impression is it is stupid. He does not see what they are going to make of it. He has been talking with the PM and told Roberts [3] we greeted it with dismay. The Sec. told of the message to Eden and Mollet. [4] He does not think it will do good—it has gone so far. The Sec. said we have been in complete ignorance. P said they did not know and hard to believe they have not been doing something as it happened so suddenly. The Sec. told how we had been blacked out re their activities for 10 days etc. etc. P. said none of their planes have gone forward nor will they. P. sent a message after talking with Merchant. He talked with Roberts and will get a telegram off though he does not know it will do good. He will be glad to do that as he shares the Sec's feeling on this act. The Sec. said just at the time the SU is falling in disarray and losing all credit, now we come along with action as bad or worse. P. agreed and said when the SC is meeting. P. said the movement has started and he has no illusion about it.

---

[1] Source: Eisenhower Library, Dulles Papers, General Telephone Conversations. Transcribed by Bernau.

[2] Norman Robertson.

[3] Reference is presumably to Robertson.

[4] *Infra.*

430.   Message From President Eisenhower to Prime Minister Eden and Prime Minister Mollet [1]

Washington, October 30, 1956.

DEAR MR. PRIME MINISTER: I have just learned from the press of the 12-hour ultimatum which you and the French (UK) Government have delivered to the Government of Egypt requiring, under threat of forceful intervention, the temporary occupation by Anglo-French forces of key positions at Port Said, Ismailla and Suez in the Suez Canal Zone. I feel [2] I must urgently express to you my deep concern at the prospect of this drastic action even at the very time when the matter is under consideration as it is today by the United Nations Security Council. It is my sincere belief that peaceful processes can and should prevail to secure a solution which will restore the armistice condition as between Israel and Egypt and also justly settle the controversy with Egypt about the Suez Canal.

Sincerely,

Dwight D. Eisenhower [3]

---

[1] Source: Eisenhower Library, Dulles Papers, Misc. Papers—U.K. (Suez Crisis). A note on the source text indicates that at 3:30 p.m., "Identical messages delivered by phone to Paris and London Embassies for Immediate telephonic delivery to Eden and Mollet."

[2] This sentence does not appear in two earlier drafts of this message in Department of State, Phleger Files: Lot 58 D 517, United Nations Aug.–Nov. 1956. Draft #1 contains the sentence: "It is my earnest plea that you should not take this drastic action." Draft #2 contains in its place the sentence: "I feel I must urge upon you what seems to me the great unwisdom of taking this drastic action even at the very time when the matter is under consideration as it is today by the United Nations Security Council." The change between draft #1 and #2 was made during a telephone conversation between Dulles and Eisenhower which began at 3 p.m. The transcript prepared in the President's Office records the conversation as follows:

"Dulles called the President with suggested text of message to be sent to British and French and made public here. It referred to the undesirability of the ultimatum of 12 hours they have issued.

"In one place it referred to an 'earnest request' that they do not issue it because of the matter being before the UN. The President asked that the sentence be made 'May I urge the unwisdom of taking this action at this time' . . . in other words to save ourselves, if we could, from a complete slap in the face . . . not to put it in the form of a prayer that would not be answered. Doesn't think it will make much difference either way. Doesn't think either country will pay any attention.

"President asked if all the State Department agreed on it. Dulles said yes. Then the President said, 'I think we almost have to (send the message). At least it establishes us before the Arab world as being no part of it (the invasion).'" Eisenhower Library, Whitman File, Eisenhower Diaries. (Ellipses are in the text of the quotation.)

The editor has been unable to determine who made the final change in the sentence before it was transmitted to Eden and Mollet.

[3] Printed from a copy that bears this typed signature

431.   Memorandum of a Conversation, Department of State, Washington, October 30, 1956, 3:28 p.m. [1]

SUBJECT

Israeli-Egyptian Conflict

PARTICIPANTS

The Secretary
Ambassador Hervé Alphand
Mr. Charles Lucet, Minister, French Embassy
William M. Rountree, NEA
C. Burke Elbrick, EUR

The Ambassador handed the Secretary a copy of the message from Prime Minister Mollet to President Eisenhower [2] regarding recent developments in the Israeli-Egyptian conflict. He said that it was the hope of the French Government that the United States would not press for the passage of a resolution in the Security Council until Israel and Egypt had answered the Anglo-French "appeal" for a cease fire. He said that the time limit for answering this appeal expires at 11:30 P.M. Washington time today.

The Secretary said that it was not clear to him why the Anglo-French action, which he could only characterize as a brutal ultimatum to Egypt, should cause a suspension of consideration in the Security Council. He could not agree to any such suspension. He pointed out that the ultimatum does not demand that the Israeli forces retire to their own frontier. If the British and French think that it is possible to reach an agreement on the basis of the ultimatum he felt that they were sadly mistaken. He went on to say that both the British and the French had deliberately kept the United States Government in the dark for the past two weeks, though we had reason to suspect what was going on. He felt he must say, frankly, that the French Ambassador had told him nothing about these plans. There was nothing personal in this criticism and the Secretary admitted the possibility that the Ambassador himself had not been informed. He felt that this was the blackest day which has occurred in many years in the relations between England and France and the United States. He asked how the former relationship of trust and confidence could possibly be restored in view of these developments.

---

[1] Source: Department of State, Central Files, 684A.86/10–3056. Confidential. Drafted by Elbrick. The time of the meeting is from Dulles' Appointment Book. (Princeton University Library, Dulles Papers)
[2] *Infra.*

The Ambassador said that Nasser's action in seizing the Suez Canal could not possibly be accepted by the French Government. He did not know whether there was any connection between the Suez crisis and the present intervention in Egypt but it was clear to him that the French Government had to take action to "stop" Nasser. The Secretary said he understood this attitude but that he could not understand why the French and the British employed a method which could destroy the United Nations and gravely impair relations with the United States. The Ambassador said that the North Atlantic Alliance is of the greatest importance to France. The Secretary said that France was making no effort to preserve it and that the action today by the French will be judged very harshly by the American people. He said it is a great tragedy, when the world stands shocked at Soviet brutality in Hungary, that the world should also be confronted by similar action on the part of the British and French in Egypt.

The Ambassador said that he felt that three power agreement is vital and that he wished to help in any way he could to reach such agreement. He asked whether the United States would table its resolution in the Security Council today, to which the Secretary replied in the affirmative. The Secretary said that the resolution calls, in essence, for Israeli forces to go back to Israel and not just ten miles from the Canal. He said the Security Council is due to reconvene at 4:00 P.M. today. [3]

---

[3] On November 1, in telegram 2124 from Paris, Dillon reported that, according to Pineau, the French Government had been very upset by Alphand's report of his interview with Dulles. Alphand informed his government that at one point in the conversation Dulles said that in his opinion there was no difference between Anglo-French intervention at Suez and the utilization of the Soviet army against the civilian population of Budapest. Alphand reported that he had gotten up to leave and that Dulles had then modified this statement. (Department of State, Central Files, 684A.86/11–356)

432.   Message From Prime Minister Mollet to President Eisenhower [1]

Paris, October 30, 1956.

The events unfolding in the Near East have not ceased seriously to concern the French Government, which deliberated on them again this morning. As a result of these discussions and conversations that I have just had with the Prime Minister in London, I wish to inform you of the conclusions which we have reached.

I understand, of course, the reasons that led the Government of the United States to bring before the Security Council the action just undertaken by Israel; in spite of certain appearances, it seems difficult, in my opinion, to consider it an act of aggression. From its beginnings, the State of Israel has constantly been the object of repeated provocations on the part of certain Arab States which have for some time been acting at the instigation of Egypt. Israel may therefore rightly consider herself in a state of self-defense.

These considerations led the French Government to judge it difficult at the present time to condemn Israel's action. The magnitude of its repercussions has, however, caused it to think that, on a temporary basis, immediate measures must be taken; it is important above all to put an end to the fighting.

It seems that the fighting is not yet on a large scale and that it is possible to arrest its course by acting without further delay. In agreement with the British Government we have decided to address to the Israeli Government and to the Egyptian Government a solemn appeal for them to end hostilities and for them both to withdraw their troops from the Suez Canal Zone. In order to guarantee that the cease-fire shall be effective, we are also asking to assume temporarily control of the key positions of the Canal. This demand is but too well justified by a long experience with failures to honor international agreements and with provocations by Arab States in the Near East. To mention only what touches us directly, I will point out that again yesterday the Embassy of France in Amman was stoned, while the French Consulate General in Jerusalem and French cultural institutions in Aleppo were set afire.

---

[1] Source: Eisenhower Library, Whitman File, International File. The source text is an official translation of the letter which Alphand handed to Dulles during their conversation which began at 3:28 p.m.; see *supra*. A covering note from Howe to Whitman, dated November 1, attached to the source text, indicates that the original of the letter from Mollet and an informal translation of it was transmitted to the White House on October 31.

I entertain the firm hope that the measures jointly decided on by the French and British Governments will receive your approval and that you will support them with your high authority.[2]

---

[2] Printed from an unsigned copy.

---

433.   Memorandum of Telephone Conversations Between the President and the Secretary of State, Washington, October 30, 1956, 3:40 and 3:50 p.m.[1]

TELEPHONE CALL FROM THE PRESIDENT

3:40 p.m.

The Pres. said he has a second message from Eden[2] with an explanation—he will send it over—he read the end of it. Here is something at last he is anxious for us to understand. The Pres. told Hagerty not to issue the paper[3] until the Sec. saw this. The Sec. said it has gone to London and Paris but we don't have to release it. The Pres. does not think it does any damage to let them have it but maybe instead of releasing it we should say we have sent a communication urging them to use the greatest caution etc. The Sec. said now they have done it they are going to try to get us to go along with them. The Pres. said they could have sent it yesterday. The Sec. said yesterday we might have tried to stop it. The Pres. said if we let it go along etc. etc. where do we get along with them against Communism. The Pres. does not want to be associated with them in the Arab world. They discussed handling it and the Sec. said he would call after reading it.[4]

---

[1] Source: Eisenhower Library, Dulles Papers, White House Telephone Conversations. Transcribed by Bernau. Another memorandum of this conversation, prepared in the Office of the President is *ibid.*, Whitman File, Eisenhower Diaries. It incorrectly indicates that this conversation began at 5:24 p.m.

[2] *Infra.*

[3] Reference is to Document 430. At 3:24 p.m. Hagerty called Dulles and told him that "the Pres. wanted it [the message] differently. H. will sit and wait till he hears re releasing it." (Eisenhower Library, Dulles Papers, White House Telephone Conversations)

[4] i.e., Eden's second message.

3:50 p.m.

The Sec. called and said he is not impressed by its sincerity. The Sec. thinks Hagerty should say it has been sent. The Pres. said he just told him to write such a statement. The Pres. will see the Sec. gets it. [5]

---

[5] Later that day the White House issued a statement indicating that upon learning of the ultimatum, President Eisenhower sent an urgent personal message to Eden and Mollet. It also noted the President's hope that the United Nations would be given full opportunity to settle the controversy through peaceful instead of forceful means and that the United States continued to believe that it was possible to secure by peaceful means a solution which would restore the armistice conditions between Egypt and Israel and achieve a just settlement of the Suez Canal controversy. (Department of State *Bulletin*, November 12, 1956, p. 749; *United States Policy in the Middle East, September 1956–June 1957*, p. 142)

---

434.   Message From Prime Minister Eden to President Eisenhower [1]

London, October 30, 1956.

I undertook this morning to send you a further message immediately after we had met Monsieur Mollet and Monsieur Pineau.

It may be that Israel could be accused of a technical aggression. On the other hand, for the reasons set forth in my earlier message, we think that Israel has a case for arguing that she is acting in self-defence under the ever increasing pressure of certain Arab States led by Egypt. Nevertheless we would not wish to support or even condone the action of Israel. We consider that, in view of the massive interests involved, the first thing to do is to take effective and decisive steps to halt the fighting.

We have had to act quickly for time is short, and since there appears to be very little fighting up to now, there is still a chance of preventing serious hostilities. Selwyn is giving a copy of the text of the Declaration to Winthrop. [2] I shall be announcing it this after-

---

[1] Source: Eisenhower Library, Whitman File. Top Secret. Delivered to the White House under cover of a note from Coulson to President Eisenhower which reads: "The Prime Minister has asked me to send you the enclosed message."

[2] The Embassy in London transmitted the texts of the messages to Israel and Egypt on October 30 in telegrams 2359 and 2360, respectively. (Department of State, Central Files, 674.84A/10–3056)

noon in the House of Commons at 4.30 p.m. This is absolutely necessary, since Parliament is sitting.

The purpose of the Declaration is to make similar requests upon each Party. First, that all hostilities by land and air should cease. Second, that the Canal Zone should be left free so that no fighting or incidents can take place there. But knowing what these people are, we felt it essential to have some kind of physical guarantees in order to secure the safety of the Canal.

We are asking for Port Said and Ismailia and Suez. As the Israelites appear to be very near to Suez, the requirement affects them as well as the Egyptians. We are emphasizing, of course, that this is to be a temporary measure pending a settlement of all these problems.

As I told you in my previous message, we entirely agree that this should go to the Security Council. But, as you know well, the Council cannot move quickly in a critical position and we have felt it right to act, as it were, as trustees to protect the general interest as well as to protect our own interests and nationals. You may say that we should wait until we are asked to move by the Security Council. But, of course, there could never be agreement on such a request.

Either side may refuse; in which case we shall take the necessary measures to enforce the Declaration.

Now you will wonder why apart from the Security Council we have acted so promptly. Of course, my first instinct would have been to ask you to associate yourself and your country with the Declaration. But I know the Constitutional and other difficulties in which you are placed. I think there is a chance that both sides will accept. In any case it would help this result very much if you found it possible to support what we have done, at least in general terms. We are well aware that no real settlement of Middle Eastern problems is possible except through the closest cooperation between our two countries. Our two Governments have tried with the best will in the world all sorts of public and private negotiations through the last two or three years and they have all failed. This seems an opportunity for a fresh start.

I can assure you that any action which we may have to take to follow up the Declaration is not part of a harking back to the old Colonial and occupational concepts. We are most anxious to avoid this impression. Nothing could have prevented this volcano from erupting somewhere. But when the dust settles there may well be a chance for our doing a really constructive piece of work together and thereby strengthening the weakest point in the line against Communism. [3]

---

[3] Printed from an unsigned copy.

435.   **Memorandum of a Conference With the President, White House, Washington, October 30, 1956, 4:25 p.m.** [1]

OTHERS PRESENT

> Dr. Arthur Flemming
> Colonel Goodpaster

Mr. Flemming said he would like to review briefly with the President the oil situation likely to result from the operations in the Suez area. [2] The President said he was inclined to think that those who began this operation should be left to work out their own oil problems—to boil in their own oil, so to speak. They would be needing oil from Venezuela, and around the Cape, and before long they would be short of dollars to finance these operations and would be calling for help. They may be planning to present us with a fait accompli, then expecting us to foot the bill. He said he is extremely angry with both the British and the French for taking this action unilaterally and in violation of agreed undertakings such as the Tri-Partite Declaration of 1950.

Dr. Flemming said he thought we should not help the British and the French in these circumstances unless they ration their consumption of oil. He said that the studies by his group indicate that we should have no problem for satisfying our own requirements. The President said he saw no reason for us to ration oil in that case.

The President said that by tomorrow he thinks we are likely to be getting requests for help. After discussion, he suggested that Dr. Flemming look into the possibility of fleet oilers (which does not incur dollar costs) to help meet the British shipping problem, if we

---

[1] Source: Eisenhower Library, Whitman File, Eisenhower Diaries. Top Secret. Drafted by Goodpaster on October 31. The time of the meeting is from the record of the President's Daily Appointments. (*Ibid.*)

[2] After consulting with Hoover earlier that morning, Flemming conferred with Assistant Secretary of the Interior Wormser and Hugh A. Stewart, Director, Office of Oil and Gas, Department of the Interior. These officials had told Flemming that the Plan of Action, developed for the U.S. Government by the Middle East Emergency Committee, could be put into effect at any time. It was agreed, however, that in line with the strategy of the current administration no indication of this fact should be given. It was also recognized that the turn of events set in motion by the Israeli invasion of Sinai altered many of the political and economic assumptions predominant at the time that the Plan of Action was developed in August. (Memorandum from Staff Secretary Joseph F. Vaughan, Office of Defense Mobilization, to Albert Toner at the White House, October 30; Eisenhower Library, White House Central Files)

should decide to do so. The British could pay us in pounds for the expenses incurred. [3]

G
Colonel, CE, U S Army

---

[3] Following this conversation, Sherman Adams telephoned Secretary Dulles. Their conversation went as follows: "The Governor said Flemming was there with him and also Goodpaster. Flemming thinks he needs a small operating group to take count of the stock from time to time on what happens to the Middle East oil situation. Adams said they would like to convene a group tomorrow composed of the Secretary, or his designee, Radford probably, Wilson, Robertson, Seaton, etc. Adams asked if the Secretary wanted to name Hoover. The Secretary said yes that Hoover knew the situation better than he did." (*Ibid.*, Dulles Papers, White House Telephone Conversations)

---

436.   Draft Message From President Eisenhower to Prime Minister Eden [1]

Washington, October 30, 1956.

DEAR ANTHONY: Thank you very much for your second explanatory cable which reached me shortly after I had dispatched one to you urging caution and moderation with full opportunity for the United Nations to do its best on this difficult problem.

I must say that it is hard for me to see any good final result emerging from a scheme that seems certain to antagonize the entire Moslem world. Indeed I have difficulty seeing any end whatsoever if all the Arabs should begin reacting somewhat as the North Africans have been operating against the French. Assuredly I hope, as I know you do, that we shall not witness any such spectacle as the Soviets

---

[1] Source: Eisenhower Library, Dulles Papers, White House Telephone Conversations. Top Secret; Personal and Private. Attached to a note from Whitman to Bernau which reads: "Here is the message the President just called Secretary Dulles about. He wants the Secretary to give it final approval before sending out."

At 4:54 p.m. on October 30 President Eisenhower telephoned Dulles and read to him the text of a draft letter responding to Eden's second message that had crossed Eisenhower's message earlier in the day. Dulles responded to the draft by noting, according to the White House transcript, "there is another thing, of course—the great tragedy just when the whole Soviet fabric is collapsing, now the British and French are going to be doing the same thing over again." Dulles suggested that the President add: "I am afraid we will be back in the same pasture as the Soviets in Hungary." Eisenhower agreed to "work it in" and said he would send the draft to Dulles for final editing. (*Ibid.*, Whitman File, Eisenhower Diaries; a separate memorandum of conversation by Bernau is *ibid.*, Dulles Papers, White House Telephone Conversations)

have on their hands in Hungary. However, I assume that you have your plan all worked out and that you foresee no such dreary and unending prospect stretching out ahead.

I think I faintly understand and certainly I deeply sympathize with you in the problem you have to solve. Now we must pray that everything comes out both justly and peacefully. [2]

With warm regard,

As ever

Ike [3]

---

[2] At 5:23 p.m. Dulles called the President and said he was looking the letter over and the last part is a bit too much assuming it is all going to happen. The Pres. agreed and said let us hold it until the a.m. (Note—a new letter will come over.)" (*Ibid.*)

A subsequent draft of this letter, dated October 31, is *ibid.*, Whitman File, International File. A marginal notation on that copy in Eisenhower's hand reads: "Do *not* send DE. Eden and I exchanged short cables last night, late. Be sure our file has copy of all incoming and outgoing message. DE"

[3] Printed from a copy that bears this typed signature.

---

437.   Memorandum of a Conversation, Department of State, Washington, October 30, 1956, 4:40 p.m. [1]

SUBJECT

Israeli-Egyptian Crisis

PARTICIPANTS

The Secretary
Mr. J. E. Coulson, Chargé d'Affaires, British Embassy
Mr. R. W. Bailey, Counselor, British Embassy
C. Burke Elbrick, EUR

The Secretary told Mr. Coulson that the President had despatched messages to Prime Minister Eden and to Prime Minister Mollet of France (copies of which were shown to Coulson) [2] and that public announcement of this fact was being made by the White House. [3] He expressed to Coulson his concern regarding latest developments and termed the ultimatum issued to Israel and Egypt a

---

[1] Source: Department of State, Central Files, 684A.86/10–3056. Confidential. Drafted by Elbrick. The time of the meeting is from Dulles' Appointment Book. (Princeton University Library, Dulles Papers)

[2] Document 430.

[3] See footnote 5, Document 433.

"brutal affair". He said that the President had received the message from Sir Anthony expressing the hope that the ultimatum would be accepted by the two countries but the Secretary felt that this was highly visionary. On the one hand, Egypt was called upon to surrender the Canal and a very large part of its territory and, on the other hand, Israel is allowed to keep the territory which it has occupied in the Sinai Peninsula.

The Secretary said that he did not know whether the Israeli action comes as a surprise to the United Kingdom but he felt that it had not been a surprise to the French. He felt that the build-up which had occurred in Cyprus must have had some reason and that the present plan which is being carried out by the British and French is too detailed not to have been concerted before the Israeli action. He felt that this action is a great tragedy both as it concerns our relations with France and England and as it concerns the world situation. The Soviet position in Eastern Europe is crumbling and the eyes of the world are focused on the evils of Communism in that area. The intended action in Egypt may well obliterate the success we have long awaited in Eastern Europe. The Secretary said that we had always urged peaceful solution for the Suez problem and had felt that in the recent action in the United Nations that agreement was within our grasp. He felt that the British Government had recently kept us deliberately in the dark about its plans.

Coulson said that he himself knew nothing about this situation, that he had had no instructions, but that it was extremely difficult for him to believe that the United Kingdom had had any part in urging the Israeli to attack Egypt. He could not agree that the action intended by the United Kingdom and France would "obliterate" the success of our policy in Eastern Europe. He felt that the Anglo-French action was quite different from the Soviet action in Hungary and that the main purpose of the Anglo-French ultimatum was to stop the fighting in Egypt. The Prime Minister, in the debate in the House of Commons, had stressed the fact that occupation of key points along the Canal would be "temporary". The British have no desire to keep British forces in Egypt any longer than is necessary to get an agreement between Israel and Egypt. The Secretary said this might take a "long, long time".

Coulson expressed his regret that this "awkward situation" should have arisen between us and expressed his fear that the press would play up this question of a divergence between the United States and the United Kingdom. He wondered if the Secretary could suggest any way of preventing this. The Secretary said that the only way to take care of this situation is for the British and French to stop the action they contemplate taking in Egypt.

438.   Memorandum of a Conversation Between the Egyptian Ambassador (Hussein) and the Assistant Secretary of State for Near Eastern, South Asian, and African Affairs (Rountree), Department of State, Washington, October 30, 1956 [1]

SUBJECT

Near Eastern Developments

Mr. Rountree said that he had asked the Egyptian Ambassador to come in because he thought it would be useful to continue their previous discussions during which he could explain developments as we saw them.

Mr. Rountree noted we had gone ahead in the Security Council and introduced an item on the Israeli invasion of Egypt. It called upon Israel to withdraw from Egypt. The British and French had already spoken in the Security Council and suggested that the adoption of a resolution be postponed. Ambassador Lodge had made clear that the United States was opposed to postponement; meanwhile, the debate was continuing.

Mr. Rountree said that he was sure he need not tell the Egyptian Ambassador how surprised we were to learn of the British and French requests to Israel and to Egypt. He emphasized the fact that we had only learned of these requests from press reports and that we as yet had no direct confirmation of them. Ambassador Hussein was visibly impressed by Mr. Rountree's statement.

Mr. Rountree continued that the President on learning of the issuance of the requests had addressed personal messages to Prime Minister Eden and Premier Mollet in which he requested both countries not to take the action contemplated. The President had authorized a press statement stating that these messages had been sent.

Mr. Rountree said he had spoken with Ambassador Hare in Cairo by telephone. Ambassador Hare told him he had just seen President Nasser who said he had declined the request of the British and French in their ultimatums. [2]

---

[1] Source: Department of State, Central Files, 684A.86/10–3056. Confidential. Drafted by Wilkins between November 1 and 5.

[2] According to Hare's report, Nasser said that Egypt would defend its soil against aggression from any source. A memorandum of the Hare–Rountree conversation by Rountree is *ibid.*, NEA Files: Lot 58 D 545, Egypt.

Late that evening in Cairo, the Egyptian Government broadcast Nasser's rejection of the Anglo-French ultimatum; a short time later in Israel, Foreign Minister Meir announced Israel's acceptance.

Ambassador Hussein said he understood that Prime Minister Eden had announced that even if Egypt accepted the British and French ultimatums and fighting stopped, the British planned to send token forces into Egypt. Mr. Rountree indicated we also had this report which in conjunction with other developments had caused us great concern.

Mr. Rountree said he had also spoken with Ambassador Hare about the evacuation of American citizens from Egypt. Although the Cairo Airport had been closed, we understood that it would be reopened at our request and that the Government of Egypt was prepared otherwise to cooperate in evacuating American citizens. On the basis of present information, however, the Ambassador doubted whether it was practical for planes to proceed to Cairo or for American citizens to move overland to Alexandria. Anything which the Government of Egypt could do to assist in evacuating American citizens would be deeply appreciated. In making this statement we did not wish in any way to imply that Egyptian cooperation had been lacking. Ambassador Hussein indicated he would do what he could.

Ambassador Hussein inquired what now would develop regarding the general situation. What steps did the United States plan to take? Mr. Rountree said that two developments were pending: 1) the United States' appeal to the Security Council on which we were unable to predict the result and 2) an appeal to the British and the French, to which there had as yet been no response. Ambassador Hussein commented that the Israelis were already marching towards Suez. As far as the British and the French were concerned, he did not understand their ultimatums. The Israelis, for example, were not yet within 10 miles of the Suez Canal; consequently, how could they withdraw to a point 10 miles from the Suez Canal? Ambassador Hussein thought the outlook very dark and believed that the Israelis, the British and the French had hatched a devious plot.

Mr. Rountree continued that two problems seemed to confront all of us: 1) The Israeli invasion of Egypt and 2) the question of the Suez Canal. Ambassador Lodge in addressing the Security Council had clearly separated these two problems. Regarding the Israeli invasion of Egypt, United States policy had the objective of obtaining Israeli withdrawal as quickly as possible as evidenced by steps the United States had taken in the Security Council. Regarding the question of the Suez Canal, the United States, realizing there were deep feelings among all of the parties, believed that there should be a solution which would be acceptable to all concerned regarding this matter which was now before the United Nations.

Ambassador Hussein pressed for information as to further United States steps on the Israeli invasion of Egypt. Mr. Rountree assured him that consideration was being given to this matter at the very highest level. We looked upon it as a very serious situation, but he was not in a position to say what new steps might be initiated until the results of action already taken were known. Ambassador Hussein hoped that these actions would be helpful. He thought the situation one in which none could win and all would lose.

439. Editorial Note

During the afternoon session of the Security Council, which convened at 4 p.m. on October 30, British Representative Dixon distributed the full text of Eden's statement made before the House of Commons earlier that day. After quoting extensively from the statement and reading the texts of the Anglo-French ultimatum to Israel and Egypt, the British Representative then noted that there was no action which the Security Council could constructively take which would contribute to the twin objectives of stopping the fighting and safeguarding free passage through the Suez Canal. He concluded, therefore, that nothing could be gained by pressing consideration of the United States draft resolution, which had been tabled before the body. Ambassador Lodge, in turn, proceeded to open discussion on the United States draft, the text of which reads as follows:

"The Security Council,

"Noting that the armed forces of Israel have penetrated deeply into Egyptian territory in violation of the armistice agreement between Egypt and Israel;

"Expressing its grave concern at this violation of the armistice agreement;

"1. *Calls upon* Israel immediately to withdraw its armed forces behind the established armistice lines;

"2. *Calls upon* all Members

"(a) to refrain from the use of force or threat of force in the area in any manner inconsistent with the Purposes of the United Nations;

"(b) to assist the United Nations in ensuring the integrity of the armistice agreements;

"(c) to refrain from giving any military, economic or financial assistance to Israel so long as it has not complied with this resolution;

"3. *Requests* the Secretary-General to keep the Security Council informed on compliance with this resolution and to make whatever recommendations he deems appropriate for the maintenance of international peace and security in the area by the implementation of this and prior resolutions." (U.N. doc. S/3710)

After some discussion, Lodge agreed to insert a new paragraph 1 to the draft, which reads: "Calls upon Israel and Egypt immediately to cease fire", and to renumber the remaining paragraphs. The draft resolution as a whole was then brought to a vote. The result was seven in favor (China, Cuba, Iran, Peru, the Soviet Union, the United States, and Yugoslavia), two against (France and the United Kingdom), and two abstentions (Australia and Belgium). As the two negative votes were cast by permanent members of the Security Council, the draft resolution failed of adoption. The Representative of the Soviet Union then proposed that the Council adopt as a resolution the preamble and the original article 1 of the U.S. draft, which called for Israeli withdrawal. The Soviet draft, however, failed of adoption, due again to the negative votes of France and the United Kingdom. The United States abstained from voting on this draft resolution. (U.N. doc. S/PV.749) For text of Lodge's remarks, made during the afternoon session, see Department of State *Bulletin*, November 12, 1956, pages 749–751.

At 9 p.m. that evening, the Security Council once again convened and agreed to include on its agenda a letter from the Government of Egypt requesting that the Security Council consider the Anglo-French act of aggression in sending Egypt an ultimatum. (U.N. doc. S/3712) After a 2-hour discussion, during which time another Soviet draft resolution (U.N. doc S/3713/Rev) was tabled and then vetoed by Great Britain and France, the Yugoslav Representative suggested that, as the Security Council had been rendered powerless by use of the veto, the members of the Council should consider the possibility of calling an emergency session of the General Assembly under the terms of General Assembly Resolution 377 (V), "Uniting for Peace." (U.N. doc. S/PV.750)

---

440.   Message From Prime Minister Eden to President Eisenhower [1]

London, October 30, 1956.

I have received your formal message, and I see that its substance has already been published. I realise that you wrote in this way in order to avoid encroaching upon the confidential nature of personal exchanges. But, in view of the publicity given to it, I shall be obliged in our Parliamentary discussions, which are to be resumed tomorrow, to comment on some of the points made in your letter in

---

[1] Source: Eisenhower Library, Whitman File, International File. Top Secret.

order to justify British policy and action. For this purpose, I think I must be free to make public the substance—though not, of course, the full text—of the two messages which I sent to you in the course of today. I am sure you will understand. [2]

---

[2] Printed from an unsigned copy A marginal notation by Eisenhower on the source text reads: "My answer was—'By all means use any part you see fit.' DE" At 10:52 p.m., October 30, Eisenhower's response to Eden was sent Niact to London in telegram 3103. (Department of State, Central Files, 641.74/10–3056)

In telegram 2400, October 31, Aldrich relayed a telephone message from Eden in which the Prime Minister said he had not used any quotations from the President's messages during the October 31 debate in the House of Commons. Eden also said that while he was planning to avoid using them on November 1, it might be necessary to do so because of increased pressure from the opposition. Eden also asked Aldrich to convey his appreciation for Eisenhower's consent to use such quotations. (Ibid., 684.86/10-3156)

---

441.   Editorial Note

In a memorandum to Ambassador Lawson on October 31, the Army Attaché in Tel Aviv, Colonel Query, gave the following account of a conversation which he had had that morning with Israeli Foreign Liaison Officer Major Sinai. Sinai told Query that "he [Sinai] had felt rather ashamed since his conversation with me in which he had intimated that Israel's military objective was primarily Jordan, since obviously that information was false and an attempt to delude me and divert my attention from the possibility of an attack on Egypt. He said he felt that his attempt had not succeeded." Major Sinai then proceeded to give Query a thorough briefing on Israel's plan of action and actual moves in the Sinai Peninsula. When during the briefing, Sinai referred to "French planes", Query inquired as to whether French pilots were involved. Sinai at first responded "I meant Mysteres" and when Query pressed the question, answered "No comment". Sinai then pressed Query to comment on why the United States had taken the position which it had in the United Nations; Query replied that he had not read the newspaper for days and therefore knew nothing of the event. Sinai then asked Query for his opinion as to what the attitude of the major powers would be concerning Israeli retention of the Sinai area. Query responded that as far as Great Britain and France were concerned the "so-called ultimatum seemed to answer the question". (Memorandum from Query to Lawson, "Briefing by Senior Foreign Liaison Officer", October 31; Department of State, Tel Aviv Embassy Files: Lot 65 F

51, 321.9 Israel–Egypt, July–Dec. 1956) Regarding Sinai's previous conversation with Query on October 28, see Document 402.

---

442.   Memorandum of a Telephone Conversation Between the Vice President in Detroit and the Secretary of State in Washington, October 31, 1956, 8:35 a.m. [1]

TELEPHONE CALL FROM THE VICE PRESIDENT IN DETROIT

N[ixon] just wanted a report. The Sec. said no report so far of any landings but the Sec. doubts that means they have called it off. UN action pretty much out the window. N. wants to hit it. The Sec. said he would not play up Israel particularly as he thinks they have been used. [2] N. asked what is wrong condemning the Br. and Fr.— the Sec. said nothing particularly if in moderation. The Sec. read from the ultimatum—they have not much to stand on. N. urged strongly against calling Congress back—the Sec. said they were not planning to. The Sec. said we will probably suspend our major economic aid plans to Israel as long as they are still in Egypt. N. said it is power politics etc. The Sec. said two things are important from the standpoint of history—it is the beginning of the collapse of the Soviet Empire—the second is the idea is out that we can be dragged along at the heels of Br and Fr in policies that are obsolete. This is a declaration of independence for the first time that they cannot count upon us to engage in policies of this sort. N. asked can it be said our policies are designed to protect the independence of small countries but is is also designed to keep American boys from being involved. The Sec. does not see any prospect of becoming involved. N. said the Pres. and the Sec. should get across we are being independent. N. said the papers there indicate we are to blame. The Sec. said he would emphasize the fact these associations have their ups and downs but to be healthy however a nation has to be free when basic principles are involved. It would have been catastrophic for the UN if we had not done it. However, we are of the same civilization— same beliefs etc.

---

[1] Source: Eisenhower Library, Dulles Papers, General Telephone Conversations. Transcribed by Bernau.

[2] Immediately prior to the 4 p.m. session of the Security Council on October 30, Dulles telephoned Lodge and told him, among other points, not to mention Israel too much in the discussion, as it had been made a "cat's paw". (Memorandum of telephone conversation, 3:56 p.m., October 30; ibid.)

The Sec. said he thinks the Pres. will cancel Philadelphia and will probably make a radio-TV talk tomorrow night. The Sec. does not know re Boston.

N. asked how the Sec. analyzed it politically, and the Sec. said N. is the expert. N. said we will lose some Israeli votes but they agreed they said there weren't many. N. said our policy is still one that has kept American boys out and at such a time you don't want a pipsqueak for Pres. The Sec. said how wonderful the Pres. has been—he has said throughout he wants to do what is right regardless of the election—he will not sacrifice foreign policy for political expediency.

---

443.   Tentative Notes of the Secretary's Staff Meeting, Department of State, Washington, October 31, 1956, 9:15 a.m. [1]

1. Murphy in the Chair.
[Here follows items 2–4.]
5. *Aid to French and UK*—Mr. Elbrick said that Defense is asking what we should do about military aid and, notably deliveries coming out of the pipeline, including whether there should be now raised a condition that such material not be used in the Middle East troubles. It was pointed out that there already is a condition that aid material cannot be used in aggression. The Secretary indicated that he saw no reason why pipeline deliveries could not be continued unchanged. He asked Mr. Elbrick to try and find out where the Israeli received the added group of Mysteres.
[Here follows item 6.]
7. *Suez—UN*—Mr. Wilcox indicated a growing sentiment to call the GA under the Uniting for Peace Resolution [2] which would require either 7 members of the Security Council or a majority of total members. He noted that the Asian-African Group and the Jugs were moving in this direction. The Secretary noted that if we seem to oppose we would appear insincere. He also thought that if it is probable that the GA would be called it is better to lead. He inclined toward Mr. Rountree's recommendation, however, that we should

---

[1] Source: Department of State, Secretary's Staff Meetings: Lot 63 D 75. Secret. Prepared by Howe.

[2] U.N. General Assembly Resolution 377 (V), which provided for emergency sessions of the General Assembly.

vote for but not initiate. Mr. Wilcox reported that the Egyptian resolution[3] put in last night will probably be discussed today and they may supplement it with a resolution. In this connection the Secretary noted that the UK-French ultimatum had not been published and he thought it was in our interest that they did become available to the press. The inaccuracy of the *New York Times* account of various information on this subject going to Ambassador Aldrich was also mentioned. Mr. Henderson reminded the Secretary that although Nasser is the object of aggression he is still a villain. Discussion followed on the legal basis on which the British and French have taken this action. The Secretary noted that under the 1954 treaty with Egypt[4] the UK is not justified to move in in response to action by the Israeli. On the other hand they could be justifying it, although he does not believe they have as yet, by the 1954 treaty on the basis that the nationalization of the Canal is a breach of the 1888 treaty which is a condition of the 1954 treaty.

8. *Eisenhower–Eden Correspondence*—The Secretary mentioned that the President had received from Eden last night a request to be free to use the correspondence which they had carried on during the day since there had been considerable public reference to it; and the President had acceded.

9. *Israel Aid*—Mr. Rountree noted that an early decision will be needed as to whether we will apply sanctions on Israel in the form of holding aid (pipeline) shipments. The Secretary asked Mr. Rountree to consider getting the Israeli Ambassador to declare more clearly the current Israeli purposes. The Secretary noted that the question of cutting off aid is a matter of degree and of abruptness because of the pipeline. The Secretary asked that a status report on our aid shipments should be requested of ICA and a comparable report on licensing.

10. *US Forces*—Mr. Rountree also indicated decision was needed on Secretary Wilson's letter on the disposition of US forces in the area.[5] Mr. MacArthur said that he and Mr. Rountree have a recommendation on this subject.

---

[3] Reference is to the letter from the Egyptian Foreign Minister to the President of the Security Council, dated October 30. (U.N. doc. S/3712) See Document 439.

[4] Anglo-Egyptian Agreement Regarding the Suez Canal Base, October 19, 1954.

[5] See footnote 2, Document 428. Later on October 31, Hoover telephoned Wilson and told him that Dulles believed that it would not be wise to appear to be moving combat military forces into the area. (Memorandum from Hoover to Dulles, October 31; *ibid.*)

444.   **Memorandum of a Telephone Conversation Between the Secretary of State in Washington and the Representative at the United Nations (Lodge) in New York, October 31, 1956, 10:50 a.m.** [1]

TELEPHONE CALL FROM AMB. LODGE

The Sec. returned the call, and congratulated L. on last night etc. etc.

L. said the acclaim the Sec's policy is receiving at the UN is something unprecedented and deeply gratifying. 21 Latin American nations are behind us as never before. He is sending it all in writing. The Sec. said it would be nice if L. sent a message or called the Pres. He was blue this a.m. L. will call. [2] L. read the statement Hammarskjold intends to make at 3 today. L. asked what he should say. The Sec. said he thinks we should give him a vote of confidence. Has there been criticism? L. said no but he said his study of the way nations start going to hell is when we don't speak and act when we should but then there comes a point when you have to speak out. The Sec. would be inclined to say as far as the US is concerned if there is a question of a vote of confidence in the Sec Gen we would strongly express that confidence.

The Sec. mentioned there would be decisions today—The Sec. thinks we should favor a special meeting of the GA—under the Uniting for Peace Resolution. L. said when and the Sec. said right away. We will talk about it today. L. thinks it is logical—you start it and have to go through with it. The Sec. said we have to exhaust all UN possibilities. This is not a decision but wanted L's reaction. There will be a big demand for it and it may happen at any rate. L. said the Indian Rep. [3] suggested the Pres. and Nehru call for it together. If you don't, you will have to say why. The Sec. thinks from a political standpoint it is important to keep it going. We will let you know. L. thinks the Russians would not agree to the res. but the Egyptians think they will. If you can get 7 votes you can always get a majority of the GA. L. said a note was just handed him and the USSR agrees. H. [4] said re SC action if the event of real warfare the res can be drawn in such a way they cannot use the veto. L. read

---

[1] Source: Eisenhower Library, Dulles Papers, General Telephone Conversations. Transcribed by Bernau.

[2] Lodge telephoned President Eisenhower at 11:45 a.m. and told him that there had never been such a tremendous acclaim for the President's policy. A memorandum of that conversation, prepared in the Office of the President, is *ibid.*, Whitman File, Eisenhower Diaries.

[3] Krishna Menon.

[4] Reference is presumably to Hammarskjöld.

Higgins' story. [5] Does the Sec. have proof they did it without our knowledge? The Sec. said the accumulation of facts is such but not proof for a court of law but there is not the slightest doubt in his mind. L. said the Asian-African group has gone on record for a special session. The Sec. said if you have it you may want to bring in the Hungarian thing. The Soviets would try to block that. L. said Lloyd wants to get together on the Hungarian thing.

---

[5] A story under Marguerite Higgins' byline in the *New York Herald Tribune* reported that Dulles had accused the British and French of cooperating with Israel to play "a giant international trick on the United States designed to lead to British and French reoccupation of the Suez Canal".

---

445. Memorandum of a Conversation, Secretary Dulles' Office, Department of State, Washington, October 31, 1956, 11:30 a.m. [1]

PRESENT WERE

    The Secretary
    The Under Secretary
    Mr. Murphy
    Mr. Phleger
    Mr. MacArthur
    Mr. McCardle
    Mr. Rountree
    Mr. Elbrick
    Mr. Wilcox
    Mr. Bowie
    Mr. Henderson
    Mr. Wilkins
    Mr. De Palma
    Mr. Macomber
    Mr. Greene

The Secretary said that Mr. Lodge reported to him that Mr. Hammarskjold had said he would rather like an expression of confidence from the Security Council and that if the Security Council were unhappy with his conduct he would resign. The Secretary said we can express our confidence in the Secretary-General if an appropriate occasion arises.

---

[1] Source: Department of State, Central Files, 330/10–3156. Secret. Drafted by Greene. The source text indicates this is an informal record of the meeting.

Mr. Wilcox propounded the questions of the Yugoslavian proposal for a Special Session of the General Assembly under the Uniting for Peace resolution; and the Egyptian letter to the President of the Security Council about the British-French ultimata. The Security Council would be meeting at 3:00 o'clock and Ambassador Lodge would need guidance.

Mr. Wilcox understood that the Egyptians would not press for consideration of their letter if the Uniting for Peace procedure were adopted.

The Secretary said he had discussed with the President [2] the matter of a Special Session under the Uniting for Peace resolution and that the President thought we should probably go along with the idea if the Security Council continued to be unable to act. While he thought it would be a mistake to finalize this at the meeting today, he thought that it would be difficult to stop the growing sentiment in the UN for a Special Session and that we should, therefore, remain in a position to use our considerable influence to guide the course of such a Session. He felt that while the General Assembly would be unlikely to deter the British and French from carrying out their military plans, action in the General Assembly might keep the hostilities from spreading. Moreover, we do not want the Russians to be able to run with the ball in a Special Session. Thus he thought the matter should be kept active in the Security Council, at least today, until it can be shown that the Security Council has really exhausted all courses available to it; this would amount to a stalling operation short of stultifying the sound position of moral principle which we have so far held.

Mr. Hoover came in to report that the British Admiralty has warned all shippers to keep away from the Suez Canal. This has led among other things to the oil people in Europe, including Britain, asking that the stand-by plans originally developed for the event that Egypt blocked the Canal now be put into effect. Among other consequences this means that the Western European countries who have a maximum oil reserve of 15 to 30 days will soon come to us for help and this will confront us with the problem of whether we want to help them, including the British and French, or hold off in hopes of deterring continuation of hostilities.

The Secretary said that we must notify American shippers of the British Admiralty warning and for safety's sake advise them to

---

[2] According to the record of the President's Daily Appointments, Dulles and Hagerty met with the President at the White House between 10:08 and 10:43 that morning. No account of this conversation has been found in Department of State files or the Eisenhower Library.

comply. Mr. Rountree said his people and the Navy could take care of this.

The meeting adjourned until 2:00 o'clock when it resumed consideration of the Security Council problem. It was noted that the British and French have asked us not to press in the Security Council for a Special Session of the GA, but would not object to such a Session being called by petition of the members. It was also noted that the Egyptians were understood to be willing, at least before Cairo was bombed, to forego Security Council action if the petition procedure would result in a Special Session. The Secretary said he would prefer that the matter not be discussed in the Security Council, but that the U.S. could subscribe to a petition.

JG

446.   Memorandum From the Director of the International Cooperation Administration (Hollister) to the Secretary of State [1]

Washington, October 31, 1956.

According to my understanding of the policy of the United States in connection with the invasion of Egypt by Israel armed forces, I have issued instructions to cease all aid to Israel at once. I have requested the Department of Commerce to refuse export licenses for any shipments financed by the International Cooperation Administration, and am notifying all banks with which we have financing arrangements for procurement for Israel to issue no more letters of credit. Where possible we will stop shipment of goods being procured outside the United States, although in some cases this is not in our control.

---

[1] Source: Department of State, Central Files, 611.84A/10–3156. Secret. A note attached to the source text from Macomber to Murphy reads in part: "In reading the memorandum, the Secretary expressed some surprise at the rapidity with which this action was being taken and wondered whether it had been done in consultation with the Department and if not, whether we in fact agree with the action."

Copies of Hollister's memorandum are in Washington National Records Center, ICA Director's File: FRC 61 A 32, Box 309, Israel. A note attached to one copy bears a handwritten notation by the Executive Secretary of ICA, John W. McDonald, Jr., indicating that Hollister's memorandum had been cancelled and that all copies circulated within ICA were to be recalled. Handwritten notes by McDonald of meetings held on October 30 and November 1 at ICA on this subject are also attached.

No transfers of funds to Israel accounts or releases of Israel currency will be made.

No more Israel trainees will be called up, although we will continue to support Israel trainees already in this country.

Let me call your attention to the fact that the Department of Agriculture has shipments scheduled for Israel under a PL 480 contract, and that the Department of Defense is currently shipping various military items. You will probably wish to request these departments to take action with respect to such shipments.

John B. Hollister

---

447.   **Memorandum of a Conversation, Secretary Dulles' Office, Department of State, Washington, October 31, 1956, 4 p.m.** [1]

PRESENT

The Secretary
The Under Secretary (later)
Mr. Murphy
Mr. Prochnow
Mr. MacArthur
Mr. Bowie
Mr. Kalijarvi
Mr. Wilkins
Mr. Burdett
Mr. Greene

SUBJECT

Sanctions Against Israel

The meeting discussed a memorandum to the Secretary from Mr. Rountree (attached). [2] Mr. Rountree suggested that there were three questions to be considered:

whether the U.S. should go ahead with measures against Israel in the absence of a Security Council resolution and in the presence of British and French armed attack on Egypt;

---

[1] Source: Department of State, Central Files, 786.56/10–3156. Secret. Drafted by Greene. The source text indicates this is an informal record of the meeting.

[2] Not attached to the source text. The memorandum, dated October 31 and entitled "Measures to be Taken Against Israel", is *ibid.*, 611.84A/10–3156. It contained a list of proposed measures to be taken against Israel.

whether measures should or could be considered against Britain and France; and

whether any measures against Israel would be practically effective in forcing the Israeli to desist and return behind the armistice lines.

The Secretary felt that the U.S. must do something and could act on the basis of the 1950 Tripartite Declaration, which provided that action could be taken within or without the United Nations. The Secretary wanted to know what would be involved in each proposed course of action, suggesting that the main purpose for the moment would be psychological, and did not want to take all the possible steps available to us now since this would not cause the withdrawal of the Israeli forces. On the other hand, taking some measures would disrupt their activities and show we mean business.

The Secretary also decided to send for the Israeli Ambassador and tell him we are considering economic measures and want to know his government's intentions.

Cancellation of aid

(a) Economic assistance and the delivery of goods to Israel should be suspended; current technical assistance projects may continue but no new projects should be initiated.

(b) Provision of surplus agricultural products should be suspended so far as practical without interfering with loading operations or shipments already underway.

(c) There is only $2000 left of the Ex-Im Bank loan, so that it does not matter whether withdrawals are suspended. The survey mission should, as indicated, continue to delay its departure.

(d) No new investment guarantees should be undertaken and we should not renege on investment guarantees already in force.

(e) No action need be taken on existing information media guarantees.

(f) (i) All shipments of military equipment should be suspended as practical, without interfering with operations too far advanced to be stopped.

(ii) All exchanges of military information should be suspended.

(iii) No new Israeli trainees should be accepted in service schools, but those already here, understood to number two, can remain.

Proclamation by the President [3]

Agreed not necessary.

---

[3] The Rountree memorandum advised that a Proclamation by the President declaring a state of national emergency was not desirable at that time.

Embargo on Shipments of Arms Munitions and Implements of War

Agreed that no export licenses will be issued for items on the munitions list and outstanding licenses will be suspended.

Export Licensing

Items on the positive list should not be licensed for export.

Embargo on Calls by U.S. Ships or Aircraft

Agreed no action at present.

Blocking Transfers of Funds [4]

The Secretary decided this should not be done yet but should be kept in reserve and the possibility used to persuade the Israeli to stop fighting.

Publicity

The Secretary agreed that an appropriate public statement should be prepared indicating that these measures are being taken in the context of the 1950 Tripartite Declaration and the President's statement of October 29 that we will honor our pledges and should make plain that we are suspending governmental assistance.

The Secretary also asked that Mr. Hollister's letter be answered by informing him of the conclusions of this meeting. [5]

Joseph N. Greene, Jr. [6]

---

[4] The Rountree memorandum recommended that the U.S. Treasury immediately issue an order blocking all Israeli funds in the United States, government as well as private, including transactions, and prohibiting all transfers of funds to Israel.

[5] The Department of State subsequently on November 1 transmitted a "Record of Decision", listing the eight decisions made at the meeting, to Goodpaster at the White House (Eisenhower Library, White House Central Files, Suez Canal Crisis) and to Hollister at ICA (Washington National Records Center, ICA Director's File: FRC 61 A 32, Box 309, Israel). A handwritten notation by Goodpaster on Howe's covering memorandum to Goodpaster indicates "Action changed—will await UN action." A handwritten notation on the copy in ICA Files indicates that the document was received in the Executive Secretariat of ICA at noon on November 1, and that it was cancelled by Hollister and Dulles at 2:30 p.m. on November 1.

[6] Printed from a copy that bears this typed signature.

448.   Memorandum of a Telephone Conversation Between the Israeli Ambassador (Eban) and the Special Assistant in the Bureau of Near Eastern, South Asian, and African Affairs (Burdett), Washington, October 31, 1956 [1]

SUBJECT

Israel

In accordance with the Secretary's instructions, [2] I telephoned Ambassador Eban in New York and spoke to him as follows: The Secretary is now considering economic limitations which we believe it is necessary to impose on Israel. Before making a final decision, the Secretary would like to know the Israel Government's intentions with respect to the withdrawal of its forces from Egyptian territory. If Ambassador Eban is in a position to give the Secretary any guidance regarding Israel's intentions, the Secretary would be glad to see the Ambassador right away. If the Ambassador is to see the Secretary tonight, it will have to be before 9 p.m.

Ambassador Eban replied that he had talked with his Prime Minister by telephone today in response to numerous private inquiries regarding Israel's intentions. He had also seen an "unofficial" telegram regarding Israel's intentions to the effect that: It is not the Prime Minister's intention to seize or hold Egyptian territory. The Prime Minister is prepared to propose to the Cabinet the withdrawal of Israel forces, but only if he receives certain reciprocal undertakings from Colonel Nasser through any source and commitments to refrain from hostile acts. I inquired whether the Ambassador could give the Secretary an "official" statement of Israel's position. He replied that he thought he would be able to do so and would very much like to see the Secretary tonight.

Subsequently Ambassador Eban telephoned again to say that he would be arriving in Washington by plane at 7:15 p.m. [3]

---

[1] Source: Department of State, Central Files, 684A.86/10–3156. Official Use Only. Drafted by Burdett.

[2] See the memorandum of conversation, *supra*.

[3] According to Dulles' Appointment Book, he did not meet with Eban until 2:08 p.m. on November 1. (Princeton University Library, Dulles Papers)

449.   Memorandum of a Conversation Between the Yugoslav Ambassador (Mates) and the Deputy Under Secretary of State for Political Affairs (Murphy), Department of State, Washington, October 31, 1956, 5 p.m. [1]

SUBJECT

1. Yugoslav Views on Middle East Crisis
2. Yugoslav Views on Polish and Hungarian Situation

Ambassador Mates, at his own request, called on Mr. Murphy at 5:00 PM today.

He stated that he was under instructions to inform us of his Government's attitude toward the Middle East crisis, to give us some of the reasoning behind its attitude, and to inquire with respect to our view on moving the issue to a special session of the General Assembly, and what position we would take there.

The Yugoslav Government was worried lest an accumulation of vetoes and consequent Council inaction would undermine the prestige and in general hamstring the United Nations. Without endeavoring to foresee what kind of recommendations would come out of a special session of the General Assembly and the specific position the Yugoslavs would take, the Yugoslav Government, nevertheless, felt that transfer of the issue to the larger body would provide an opportunity for private conversations and contribute to a cooling of feelings. He said that it would have been his Government's preference to have the special session called by petition of UN Members rather than Council action; but since the Soviet Delegation, and the Egyptians seemed to be poised with condemnatory resolutions to introduce, which would only invite further vetoes, his Government had decided upon the Security Council method of invoking the Uniting for Peace resolution. Ambassador Mates was obviously anxious to know whether the Yugoslav motion in the Council would have our support as he feared that if the motion failed to carry we might be even worse off than before. Mr. Murphy was able to assure him of this point, although we were not prepared ourselves to take the initiative.

The Yugoslav Ambassador also recounted in summary the two conversations that Brilej had had with Sobolev with respect to the motion to use the Uniting for Peace procedure. At first Sobolev was adamant, asserting that since the Soviet Union had opposed resolution 377 (V) in the first instance and consider it illegal, he, Sobolev had no freedom. Brilej reportedly was so insistent that Sobolev be

---

[1] Source: Department of State, Central Files, 684A.86/10–3156. Confidential. Drafted by Walmsley.

realistic and exercise his own judgment in a matter of this importance (Brilej appealed to the many other manifestations of increased
flexibility on the part of the Soviet Government in recent times) that
Sobolev "agreed" to take the matter under consideration. This was
yesterday.

This morning Sobolev notified Brilej that the Soviet Delegation
would be able to support convening a special session of the General
Assembly but said that if a special session is not called or failed of
approval, he had a resolution which he would, under instructions,
introduce in the Security Council. The "deal" seems to stem from
this set of circumstances.

As to the nature of our instructions to the US Delegation in case
a special session of the General Assembly is called, Mr. Murphy said
that the matter is under intense study.

[Here follows discussion of the Polish and Hungarian situation.]

---

450.   **Memorandum of a Telephone Conversation Between the
Secretary of State in Washington and the Representative
at the United Nations (Lodge) in New York, October 31,
1956, 5:13 p.m.** [1]

TELEPHONE CALL FROM AMB. LODGE

L. said they have a 30-minute recess. [2] The Russians agreed not
to put in their condemnation resolution on the understanding the
Yugoslavs would put theirs in for a special session of the GA. We
think there are 6 votes for one—the Chinese [3] will be the 7th but he
wants to call Taipei and we think we can get it. L. said the weight
of evidence is in favor of voting tonight. The Sec. asked when it [4]
would be held? L. said not determined—in a day or two. The Sec.
thinks tomorrow is premature. You have to get ready for these

---

[1] Source: Eisenhower Library, Dulles Papers, General Telephone Conversations.
Transcribed by Bernau.

[2] The Security Council convened at 3 p.m. that day to continue its discussion of
the Egyptian letter accusing Great Britain and France of an act of aggression. After
some discussion, Yugoslav Representative Brilej submitted a draft resolution which
called for an emergency special session of the General Assembly. The Security
Council then recessed for a half hour so that the members could examine the text.
(U.N. doc. S/PV.751)

[3] Chinese Representative Tingfu F. Tsiang.

[4] The emergency special session of the General Assembly.

things. L. asked re Friday. [5] The Sec. asked the view of the Br and Fr and L. said they want to put everything off—maybe to get their govts to change their policy. Both agreed that was ridiculous. L. said it is desirable to prevent the Russian res of condemnation. He doubts we can hold them until tomorrow. The Sec. asked if the Br and Fr know, and L. said yes and he has been able to make a little gratitude because they know he got them to withdraw. The Sec. asked if they will violently attack us if we vote and L. said he did not think so. D. [6] told him he would attack us if there were a res of condemnation. He is so emotional and . . . . Randolph Churchill is hanging around so the atmosphere is jumpy. The Sec. said to go ahead and vote for it but he would not have the meeting before Friday. L. said he just had a note handed to him that the Yugoslav said the USSR will insist if the Yugoslav res is not voted today on putting theirs in. L. will do. They discussed the Pres of the GA. The Sec. said if you have to elect one, Wan would probably be good as he is here. L. agreed. The Sec. said we have to think what we are going to do—we want to keep on top of it a bit. L. said in the GA the action on Israel can be considered so it takes some of the focus off the Br and Fr. The Sec. said he does not know how much we want to do it Friday. L. agreed. The Sec. said to gain as much time as he can. He thinks you need 24 hours' notice. L. will check. The Sec. said it will be chaos—there are 20 new members who don't know how you do things in the GA and a lot don't have reps there. [7]

---

[5] November 2.

[6] British Representative Dixon.

[7] After the Security Council meeting resumed, the British Representative moved that the Yugoslav draft resolution was out of order. The motion was defeated by a vote of six (including the United States) opposed, four in favor, and one abstention. The Yugoslav draft resolution was then brought to a vote and adopted, with seven (including the United States) in favor, two (Great Britain and France) opposed, and one abstention. (U.N. doc. S/PV.751)

451.   Telegram From the Embassy in Egypt to the Department
of State [1]

Cairo, October 31, 1956—6 p.m.

1240. Nasser asked me come see him today to say he had yesterday explained his determination to resist aggression (Embassy telegram 1226), [2] and now wished to have message delivered to President. Following is slightly edited text of rough oral English translation which he dictated from Arabic draft.

"The Anglo-French ultimatum regarding aggressive action against Egypt at a time when Egypt was defending itself against Israeli aggression has resulted in a very serious situation affecting the freedom of the Egyptian people and the United Nations Charter. Egypt decided to defend her sovereignty and territory against Anglo-French aggression in addition to defending her sovereignty and territory against Israeli aggression. The Egyptian Government has decided to ask for United States support against Anglo-French aggression."

Nasser asked what I thought would be reaction to message. I replied that, as he of course knew, the American Government had already made an exceptional effort in this matter in attempting to arrive at a just solution. In particular the President had intervened personally and, as long as hostilities remain averted, there was still hope that his efforts to promote a peaceful settlement would prevail. (Nasser had remarked that as of time of our conversation at 1:15 p.m. [3] there had been no reports of Anglo-French action despite fact no change in time expiration of ultimatum). We had thus gone far, and would doubtless continue to do what we could. Against this

---

[1] Source: Department of State, Central Files, 641.74/10–3156. Secret; Niact. Received at 11:25 p.m.

[2] In telegram 1226, October 31, Hare informed the Department that Nasser had summoned him the evening of October 30 to discuss the Anglo-French ultimatum. Nasser said that the British had been informed of Egypt's refusal to accept the ultimatum and that Egyptian territory would be defended against aggression. At the end of the conversation, Nasser was reminded by Fawzi, who was also present, that he had intended to send a message to President Eisenhower. According to Hare, Nasser had been unable to collect his thoughts and merely asked that the President be informed that Egypt was facing a threat of force and would defend itself. (*Ibid.*)

Nasser did send a message to Eisenhower that reached the Department of State at 9:30 a.m., October 31. It noted that Nasser intended to request U.S. assistance if Great Britain and France invaded Egypt, wished to know President Eisenhower's reaction, and did not intend for the present to request Soviet assistance. (Memorandum for the record by Higgs, October 31; Eisenhower Library, White House Central Files (Confidential File)). A marginal notation by Goodpaster on that document indicates that Eisenhower was informed of Nasser's message.

[3] Cairo time, October 31.

background what did Nasser have in mind in making this particular request for support.

Nasser replied that the kind of support would depend on the circumstances. Specifically it would mean military support in case of military aggression. Some people might have expected Egyptian Government to turn to USSR for such aid but GOE had thought matter over carefully and decided appeal to USG. He also hoped to refer publicly to this appeal in a speech he intended making so that Egyptian people could know what he had done. What was my reaction?

I observed that as far as military support concerned this would obviously be question which could only be answered by my government. However, I felt justified in expressing personal opinion that unable foresee possibility our going that far. Not only would this involve a policy decision of utmost gravity but would also require Congressional action. We had gone far, very far, but I just couldn't see our becoming embattled with old allies on this issue. Nasser indicated understanding.

Regarding publication I would think subject too sensitive for public airing. Nasser thereupon agreed not mention except by mutual agreement but insisted that if decided publish would first be done in Cairo or simultaneously in Cairo and Washington but not initially in Washington. He indicated strong desire publish and gave as reason possible deterrent effect it would have on British and French.

I then observed understood Nasser liked frankness and would venture ask frank question in hope it would be received in spirit intended.

Sometimes in field of foreign affairs questions are put more or less expecting negative answer and with object of clearing way for another line of action which otherwise might be regarded as objectionable. Specifically, it would seem tragic if, after our having done so much in this particular matter, we should be confronted with request going beyond our ability to comply and then have this taken as justification for turning to the Russians. All the good would be undone and only bitterness would remain.

At first Nasser seemed somewhat taken aback by this admittedly not too delicate approach but he quickly regained composure and said that Egyptian request was entirely sincere and had been reached after careful consideration and there had been no discussion of turning to Russians. In fact Egyptians had always depended on selves and this was first time foreign aid had been requested. Khrushchev had suggested furnishing volunteers but Egyptians had never replied either way.

As regards seriousness with which USG has worked on this problem, he fully recognized and appreciated but, if matter important to us it is life or death to Egypt. As far as Nasser himself concerned, will not surrender but neither will he run away.

In taking leave he said would be glad to have me come see him in any hour of day or night to receive reply.

Hare

452.   Editorial Note

During the early evening of October 31, British and French forces began their bombardment of Egyptian airfields in the vicinity of the Suez Canal Zone. Passage through the Suez Canal was effectively blocked the following day when the Egyptian ship *Akka* sank in the Canal near Lake Timsah. At the same time the Egyptian Government broke diplomatic relations with the British and French Governments.

Meanwhile, Israeli Defense Forces continued to advance in the central portion of the Sinai Peninsula and on November 1 began their movement in northern Sinai toward Al Arish. That same day the Egyptian Government recalled most of its forces from the Sinai Peninsula to defend the Canal Zone. Telegraphic reports concerning military developments related to the Suez Canal crisis are in Department of State, Central Files 684A.86.

453.   Telegram From the Embassy in France to the Department of State [1]

Paris, November 1, 1956—noon.

2120. Pineau sent for me this morning and gave me general background exposé of events leading up to initiation of hostilities and brief description of objectives of French and British Govern-

---

[1] Source: Department of State, Central Files, 651.74/11–156. Secret; Niact. Received at 7:11 a.m. Repeated to London and Niact to USUN.

ments. He fully admitted that operation was long planned Franco-British-Israeli affair. Details will follow in succeeding telegram. [2]

Pineau then expressed great concern about tonight's meeting of General Assembly. He said he fully expected and was prepared for a vote condemning Franco-British action but pointed out that resolution must be very carefully drafted so as not to give any possible excuse for a unilateral military intervention by the Soviet Union acting on behalf of United Nations. Such intervention could lead only to generalized world war or to complete occupation of Middle East by Soviet forces.

Pineau further said that primary reason for aerial bombardment of Egyptian air bases was to make it impossible for Soviet aircraft to fly into these bases from Soviet Union.

Finally, Pineau said that he hoped that General Assembly would consider Hungarian situation as well as Egyptian affair.

Dillon

---

[2] Telegram 2123, Document 459.

---

454.   Editorial Note

At 8:40 a.m. on November 1 Secretary Dulles telephoned President Eisenhower. Their conversation went as follows:

"The Sec. said we are going to have to make important decisions here today and don't know how much time we should spend at NSC. There is the question of our attitude toward the possible sanctions against the Israelis and the GA meets at 5. The Sec. would like time with the Pres. this a.m. NSC is mostly about the policy for satellite countries which the Sec. thinks is academic as the situation has pretty much taken care of itself. The Sec. will make a report on Suez and the Pres. said it would be a good thing to have a general discussion re the ME. The Pres. referred to what Lippmann said and the Sec. said he has not written anything favorable for 4 years and his facts are wrong. The Pres. also referred to what Stevenson said. The Pres. said we should not do anything that makes us look as if we are trying to get an excuse to pick on Israel. If we do anything against them, then we have to do something against Fr and Br. The Sec. referred to the statement re living up to the Tripartite Agreement. If we give aid to Israel when she is an aggressor it makes a mockery of everything. We have to have a position by 5." (Eisenhower Library, Dulles Papers, White House Telephone Conversations)

Another memorandum of this telephone conversation, prepared in the Office of the President, is *ibid.*, Whitman File, Eisenhower Diaries. The memorandum of discussion of the November 1 meeting of the National Security Council is *infra*. The syndicated column by Walter Lippman to which Eisenhower referred was entitled "Disaster in the Middle East" and appeared in the *Washington Post* on November 1.

---

455. Memorandum of Discussion at the 302d Meeting of the National Security Council, Washington, November 1, 1956, 9 a.m. [1]

[Here follows a paragraph listing the participants at the meeting.]

Upon entering the Cabinet Room from his office, the President informed the members of the Council that, except in so far as it was the subject of the DCI's intelligence briefing, he did not wish the Council to take up the situation in the Soviet satellites. Instead, he wished to concentrate on the Middle East.

1. Significant World Developments Affecting U.S. Security

[Here follows a briefing by Allen Dulles on the situation in Hungary.]

With respect to the hostilities in the Middle East, Mr. [Allen] Dulles stated that approval for the attacks on Egypt by the British and the French had so far come only from Australia and New Zealand. It was probable, moreover, that there was a wide split of opinion in Australia between Mr. Menzies and Mr. Casey.

Mr. Dulles indicated that he would not, as planned, cover military developments in the Near East, inasmuch as these would be covered by Admiral Radford. The President interrupted to say that he did not wish to go into the military situation at the present time. Instead, he wished to concentrate on the policy problem. Accordingly, Mr. Dulles concluded his briefing by stating that from reports received to date, the Israelis appeared to have gained a substantial victory over the Egyptians.

---

[1] Source: Eisenhower Library, Whitman File, NSC Records. Top Secret. Prepared by Gleason. The time of the meeting is from the record of the President's Daily Appointments. (*Ibid.*)

The National Security Council: [2]

Noted an oral briefing by the Director of Central Intelligence on the subject, with specific reference to the recent developments regarding Hungary and Poland, and the situation in the Near East.

2. *U.S. Policy With Respect to the Hostilities in the Near East* (NSC 5428, [3] as amended by NSC Action No. 1462 [4])

The President announced that he would start the discussion of this subject by asking the Secretary of State to bring the National Security Council up to date on diplomatic developments as the Secretary saw them.

Secretary Dulles observed that, following the meeting of the UN Security Council in New York some two weeks ago, it had been expected that negotiations among the British, French and Egyptians would be renewed in Geneva beginning October 29. This expectation had been based on an unofficial understanding reached at that meeting. Indeed, Selwyn Lloyd and Pineau had come very close to agreement with Egyptian Foreign Minister Fawzi on an acceptable settlement of the Suez problem. In fact, according to Selwyn Lloyd, an actual agreement on such a settlement would have been reached at that time had it not been for the stubbornness of Pineau, who dragged his feet in the early meetings of these three men.

In any event, after Selwyn Lloyd and Pineau returned home, they found sentiments in favor of resorting to force very strong in their governments. We had known all along that the French had been pushing strongly for a forceful solution of the Suez crisis. There had been no doubt of their attitude from the beginning. There were likewise elements in the British Government who wished to invoke force. These elements thought it best not to have Secretary Dulles around as they moved toward their objective. Accordingly, there was a blackout of communications between Washington on the one hand and London and Paris on the other, after Secretary Dulles' return to Washington. Secretary Dulles said he gradually became very concerned about this news blackout, and sent a cable to our Ambassadors in London and Paris last week expressing his concern. Subsequently, our Ambassadors had conversations in London and in Paris which were superficially reassuring. On the other hand, our fears became aggravated when it became clear that the French were working very close with the Israelis, as was shown, for example, in

---

[2] The paragraph that follows constitutes NSC Action No. 1626, approved by the President on November 6. (Department of State, S/S-NSC (Miscellaneous) Files: Lot 66 D 95, Records of Action by the National Security Council, 1956)

[3] For text, see *Foreign Relations*, 1952–1954, vol. IX, Part 1, p. 525.

[4] Taken at the 263d meeting of the National Security Council on October 27, 1955.

the heavy diplomatic traffic between Paris and Israel. This was followed by the Israeli mobilization and then by the Israeli strike.

Secretary Dulles indicated that we had thought that the Israeli attack might go against Jordan, since the Israelis are anxious to secure the territory up to the west bank of the Jordan River. Apparently, however, the British persuaded the Israelis not to strike at Jordan because to do so would involve the British in the invocation of the Anglo-Jordanian treaty. The result of British persuasion was, accordingly, an agreement that the Israelis would strike south at Egypt. This was a move which the British and French could use as a pretext to intervene to protect the Suez Canal.

When the Israelis commenced their attack, we promptly called in the British and French Ambassadors to see what their governments were going to do under the terms of the Tripartite Declaration of 1950. The British and French were evasive in their response. We said that we would honor our commitments under the Tripartite Declaration.

Coincidentally with the Israeli strike came the so-called ultimatum by Britain and France to Israel and Egypt. Evidently, said Secretary Dulles, this was not much of an ultimatum as far as Israel was concerned. They were only asked to keep ten miles back from the Canal itself. According to the terms of the ultimatum, even if the Canal were freed from the risk involved in the fighting, the British and French proposed to occupy the Canal Zone. All this Secretary Dulles described as a series of concerted moves among the British, French and Israelis, the French actually conducting the concerted planning and the British acquiescing. Moreover, the French had for some time been supplying the Israelis with far more military equipment than we knew anything about. They were thus violating an agreement among the three powers that each was to let the others know the extent of the assistance they were giving to Israel.

The whole matter is now before the United Nations in terms of a resolution introduced by the United States prior to the Anglo-French ultimatum. Among other things, this resolution called for the withdrawal of Israeli forces behind the armistice line, with no support to be given to Israel by the other nations, etc., etc. We have thought that the terms of this resolution continued to be appropriate even after the Anglo-French ultimatum had been served. The resolution, of course, was defeated by the British and French vetoes. The vote was seven to four, with two abstentions—Australia and Belgium. [5] These abstentions were significant.

---

[5] The U.S. draft resolution was brought to a vote at the 749th meeting of the Security Council on October 30. The result was seven in favor, two (Great Britain and France) opposed, and two abstentions. (U.N. doc. S/PV.749)

Under the Uniting for Peace Resolution, continued Secretary Dulles, a meeting of the General Assembly can be called in 24 hours if the UN Security Council is inhibited from action because of a veto. Such a meeting of the General Assembly has been called for five o'clock this afternoon in New York. We must be concerned with the U.S. position. Broadly speaking, this position, for at least the last three months, has been the position of avoiding resort to a solution by force. This has been a policy which has evoked greater international support for the United States than we have secured at any time in our history. Indeed, the whole world is looking to the United States for firm leadership in this critical situation.

Yesterday, at the meeting of the NATO Council, the United States duly made its report on the implication of these recent events so far as we were concerned. [6] On this occasion the British and the French said nothing. As far as can be ascertained from developments at this NATO Council meeting, the British have probably secured the support of the Netherlands for their action against Egypt. Apparently all the other members of the NATO Council are opposed to the Anglo-French action, though Portugal may yet line up on the British and French side thanks to its colonial preoccupations in India. They have not yet done so, and all of the other members expressed themselves as opposed to the use of force to reach a settlement. Moreover, the verdict of the rest of the world is altogether unanimous in the same sense. At this point, Mr. Allen Dulles interrupted to note the exception in the case of Australia and of New Zealand. Secretary Dulles replied that these were in a sense exceptions, but there was much unhappiness in Australia; and as for New Zealand, it was virtually a colony and almost invariably followed the lead of the United Kingdom.

Here Secretary Dulles paused to state that we were now squarely facing the problem of what the United States should do. He said that he had prepared yesterday and had with him at present a statement of what we proposed to do (presumably in carrying out our obligations under the Tripartite Declaration). [7] This statement proposed certain mild sanctions against Israel—namely, suspending some of our military and economic assistance programs. The sanctions would not touch such vital matters as the freezing of Israeli

---

[6] The text of the U.S. statement to be made at the October 31 meeting of the North Atlantic Council was transmitted to Paris in Topol 704, October 30. (Department of State, Central Files, 684A.86/10–3056) A report on the October 31 meeting is in Polto 960 from Paris, October 31, not printed. (*Ibid.*, 750.5/10–3156)

[7] No copy of the draft statement described here has been found in Department of State files or the Eisenhower Library. Dulles directed on October 31 that a public statement be prepared which would reflect the decisions made at the Department of State meeting held at 4 p.m. on October 31; see Document 447.

balances in the United States or suspending remittances from the United States to Israel. Pointing out that we still have a freeze on Egyptian balances in the United States, Secretary Dulles added that we must presently decide whether to keep these Egyptian balances frozen in the circumstances now existing.

Besides our action in implementation of the Tripartite Declaration, we also faced the question of what our position is to be in the United Nations. The great question is, do we reassert our leadership in the struggle against the use of force in this situation, admitting grave provocations on both sides? Certainly we must try to find ways and means to shorten the duration and limit the scope of the hostilities.

Secretary Dulles warned with emphasis that if we were not now prepared to assert our leadership in this cause, leadership would certainly be seized by the Soviet Union. But asserting our leadership would involve us in some very basic problems. For many years now the United States has been walking a tightrope between the effort to maintain our old and valued relations with our British and French allies on the one hand, and on the other trying to assure ourselves of the friendship and understanding of the newly independent countries who have escaped from colonialism. It seemed to Secretary Dulles that in view of the overwhelming Asian and African pressure upon us, we could not walk this tightrope much longer. Unless we now assert and maintain this leadership, all of these newly independent countries will turn from us to the USSR. We will be looked upon as forever tied to British and French colonialist policies. In short, the United States would survive or go down on the basis of the fate of colonialism if the United States supports the French and the British on the colonial issue. Win or lose, we will share the fate of Britain and France.

On this point, Secretary Dulles expressed his view that the British and French would not win. Indeed, recent events are close to marking the death knell for Great Britain and France. These countries have acted deliberately contrary to the clearest advice we could possibly give them. They have acted contrary both to principle and to what was expedient from the point of view of their own interests. Of course, we should not let ourselves be swayed by resentment at the treatment the British and French have given us, or do anything except what we decide is the right thing to do.

Summing up, Secretary Dulles stated that basically we had almost reached the point of deciding today whether we think the future lies with a policy of reasserting by force colonial control over the less developed nations, or whether we will oppose such a course of action by every appropriate means. Great Britain and France are, of course, our oldest and most trusted allies. If we became engaged in a war, these are the allies we would most surely depend upon for assistance. It is nothing less than tragic that at this very time, when we are on the point of winning an immense and long-hoped-for victory over Soviet colonialism in Eastern Europe, we should be forced to choose between following in the footsteps of Anglo-French colonialism in Asia and Africa, or splitting our course away from their course. Yet this decision must be made in a mere matter of hours—before five o'clock this afternoon.

The President broke the tension which followed Secretary Dulles' statement by saying that if anybody wanted to know how "political" this issue had become, this was shown by the telegram which the President had received last night from Governor Stevenson. It was sent from La Guardia Field at 7:25 p.m. Stevenson was writing the message even while the President was talking, [8] and he released the text of the message before he sent it to the President.

The President then said he wished to ask one question. Is the United States under the necessity of introducing the resolution in the UN General Assembly today, or could the Secretary-General, for example, introduce a resolution? Secretary Dulles replied that resolutions would either be introduced by the United States or by the Soviet Union. Indeed, any nation could introduce a resolution, and perhaps India would do so. Secretary Dulles added that he had had a long message from Prime Minister Nehru. He hadn't had a chance to read it as yet, but it was said to be cast in very general terms.

The President said that at any rate he thought it would be a complete mistake for this country to continue with any kind of aid to Israel, which was an aggressor. The President then interrupted himself and said that, on the other hand, Israel had not yet been branded as an aggressor, had it? Secretary Dulles answered that Israel had not yet been branded an aggressor by the UN. Nevertheless, at the very minimum we must do to the Israelis what the UN resolution called for. In illustration of this, Secretary Dulles read from the written statement to which he had referred earlier in the course of the meeting. This statement, as read, gave details as to what governmental aid by the United States to Israel would be suspended, including even such matters as shipments already in the pipeline, and the like. In concluding his reading of the statement, Secretary Dulles described these sanctions as very mild.

The President inquired whether it would not be wise to state plainly that the United States was party to a tripartite agreement made in good faith with two other nations. These other two nations have reneged on their commitment and deserted us. Accordingly this

<hr>

[8] The text of Stevenson's telegram to Eisenhower was printed in *The New York Times*, November 1, 1956.

statement must contain a review of exactly what we are going to do. The President then commented that since we had already made it clear that we would not involve ourselves in this war, what the Secretary of State proposed to say was generally correct, though the sanctions outlined in the statement seemed a little mild. The President inquired about the timing of the issuance of this statement. Secretary Dulles replied that if the President approved, he would issue this statement of mild sanctions today. He would then summon the Israeli Ambassador and inform him that these sanctions represented the minimum. This would threaten further steps by way of sanctions if the Israelis did not retreat to the armistice lines from which their military operations had commenced. He would, for example, threaten to suspend Israeli remittances from the United States to Israel.

Secretary Wilson inquired whether we could not wait for the United Nations to take action in this General Assembly before we undertook to do anything else. Secretary Dulles replied that it had been his intention to issue the statement he was discussing this morning.

At this point, Secretary Humphrey inquired whether our resolution could not simply demand that the United Nations determine who was the aggressor. Meanwhile we would withhold any further action of any kind until they made such a determination of the aggressor. The President replied that it seemed to him foolish for people who know as much as we do about what is going on, to continue to give, as a government, assistance to Israel. Secretary Humphrey then suggested that our best course of action might be to suspend all our government assistance to everyone concerned—Israel, Egypt, Britain and France.

The President replied that what we must now do is to agree among ourselves what the United States should do in the light of our statement. Secretary Humphrey countered with the view that until the United Nations actually identifies the aggressor, we should take no further action. After the identification is made, we could proceed to take appropriate action. Dr. Flemming pointed out that this still leaves us the question of the position we should take before the United Nations General Assembly. To this, Secretary Humphrey replied that we should take whatever position we think is right. Personally, he believed that the United Kingdom was the real aggressor, and Israel only a pawn.

The President led the discussion on a slightly different angle by stating that he had never realized that the Arab states had consistently afforded the UN inspectors access to their boundaries so that inspections could be consistently made. It was the Israelis who had refused similar inspection rights on their side of the boundaries.

Governor Stassen raised the question as to the merits of focusing the U.S. position in the United Nations on a simple cease-fire agreement. After all, our great objective is to prevent this war from spreading. A number of mistakes had already been made. The Soviets had made a grave error in putting arms in the hands of the Egyptians. Egyptian seizure of the Suez Canal was a grave error, in turn, and after all, the Suez Canal is an absolutely vital lifeline for the British.

The President answered Governor Stassen by pointing out that, in fact, transit through the Canal has increased rather than decreased since the Egyptians took over. Governor Stassen admitted that this was true, but emphasized that the British feel that they cannot possibly have an individual like Nasser holding their lifeline in his hands. In response to this argument, the President cited the six principles agreed on among the British, French and Egyptians, emphasizing in particular the principle that the Canal must be insulated from the politics of any nation. He accordingly could not agree, he said, with Governor Stassen. If the British would agree to negotiate a settlement, then the opinion of the whole world would be against Egypt.

Governor Stassen replied by expressing his agreement that the British had committed a terrible error. On the other hand, it was a vital friend who had committed this error, and our real enemy was the Soviet Union. One of the reasons for such strong sentiment in Britain was the British fear of the effect on the pound sterling of having the Canal in Nasser's hands. They were facing a genuine crisis. They had made a judgment that the future of Great Britain depended on getting the Canal into friendly hands again. The Soviet Union is still the great threat to the United States. We must accordingly approach the whole problem with a calm perspective. About all that we need to do now is to move toward the future; that is, in the direction first of a cease-fire, and then of a negotiated peace. Governor Stassen emphasized that he could not see how it would serve the interests of the United States to strike now at Britain and Israel.

With great warmth, Secretary Dulles said he was compelled to point out to Governor Stassen that it was the British and French who had just vetoed the proposal for a cease-fire. Of course, once they were thoroughly lodged in Egypt, they would be agreeable to accepting a cease-fire. Governor Stassen asked that even so, wasn't this kind of an acceptance of a cease-fire to our immediate advantage? Secretary Dulles replied with an emphatic negative, and added that what the British and French had done was nothing but the straight old-fashioned variety of colonialism of the most obvious sort. Even so, replied Governor Stassen, it seemed to him that the future of Great Britain and of France was still the most important consideration for the United States, and that all our efforts should now be directed toward a cease-fire.

At this juncture in the discussion, Secretary Humphrey called attention to the developing fissures in British public opinion. He said he referred not only to the split between the Conservative and the Labour Parties, but to differences of opinion among the Conservatives themselves. He was convinced, he said, that recent British action was primarily Eden's own creation.

Governor Stassen replied that if British public opinion was divided, so would American public opinion be divided if we go on with our plan against Britain, France and Israel. On the other hand, U.S. public opinion could readily be united under a course of action in which we avoided anything except the cease-fire. Governor Stassen turned to the President and went on to say that he might not succeed in gaining Congressional support for his long-term policies if U.S. action in the current crisis divided our people. We must keep the U.S. people united, and we would certainly not succeed in doing this if we split away from Britain and France and acted on the assumption, which Governor Stassen did not believe correct, that these two powers were going downhill.

The President responded to Governor Stassen by stating his emphatic belief that these powers were going downhill with the kind of policy that they were engaged at the moment in carrying out. How could we possibly support Britain and France if in doing so we lose the whole Arab world?

Secretary Wilson counseled that we must take a longer time to analyze this problem, and Secretary Humphrey repeated his suggestion that we defer action until the UN defines the aggressor. To these suggestions, Secretary Dulles responded that we would very soon find in the UN who is the aggressor if we permitted the Soviet Union to introduce its resolution. This resolution would certainly declare that Britain and France were the aggressors, and the Soviet resolution would win by acclamation. As a result, we lose our leadership to the Soviet Union.

Secretary Humphrey then asked Secretary Dulles what kind of U.S. resolution he really wanted. Secretary Dulles answered that he wanted a resolution which would call on the parties in the conflict to state the terms on which they would end hostilities and meantime pledge themselves to call off the hostilities. Secretary Humphrey said that if this was the case, what the Secretary wanted was in effect what we had all been talking about—a cease-fire. The President said that he likewise favored in general the idea of including the call for a cease-fire in the resolution. Secretary Dulles pointed out that unless the United States were to propose a resolution which was "moderate" in character, the Soviets would propose a resolution couched in very extreme terms. If we could not support such a Soviet resolution, we would be left in the backwash. Worse than that, Secretary Dulles predicted that the United Nations Organization would be unable to survive a failure to act on the great issues in the Near East.

Governor Stassen again put forward his suggestion that the resolution confine itself to calling for a cease-fire. With warmth, Secretary Dulles inquired of Governor Stassen how we could possibly do only this when the Israelis, the British, and the French were overrunning Egyptian territory.

The President inquired what the argument was really all about. Turning to Secretary Dulles, he said that the Secretary was asking for a mild U.S. resolution in the United Nations. The President said he couldn't agree more. Do we need to do anything beyond this? Secretary Dulles replied that he thought the best thing was for him to go back to the State Department and work in quiet on a draft.

Secretary Humphrey pointed out that we were all seeking some kind of delaying action in the United Nations before we proceeded to impose sanctions on anyone. Secretary Dulles insisted that his own list of sanctions constituted nothing more than a slap on the wrist to Israel. Nevertheless, this mild slap on the wrist might well avoid the necessity for more severe measures.

Governor Stassen again called for a resolution which sought only a cease-fire. The President, however, explained that we could scarcely call for a cease-fire and continue to send supplies and assistance to Israel. Secretary Wilson believed that we shouldn't make a goat out of Israel alone. Were we proposing to continue to send military supplies to Great Britain? The President replied that we would so continue to assist Britain in order that she might meet her NATO requirements. If the British actually diverted these supplies to other purposes, we would have to consider such an action to represent another case of "perfidious Albion".

(At this point, Secretary Dulles asked and was given the President's permission to leave the Cabinet Room to take a telephone call from Ambassador Lodge at the United Nations.) [9]

The President stated his firm belief that we should state clearly that we are going to suspend arms shipments to the whole Near Eastern region while the UN is considering this crisis. He then added that he could scarcely even imagine that the United States could abandon Britain and France. On the other hand, he believed that Secretary Dulles was correct in trying to devise some list of moderate sanctions. Secretary Wilson counseled that we stop everything

---

[9] No account of this conversation has been found in the Eisenhower Library.

while the President "took a look", but the President went on to say that he just knew that Secretary Dulles was right in trying to get from the United Nations something that was soft and reasonable. If he succeeded, we would avoid getting into a "runaway" situation. The President repeated this view when Secretary Dulles returned to the Cabinet Room. He counseled that we stop all arms shipments to the hostile areas at once, and that we decide later what we should do about "Hollister's stuff" (assistance programs under the aegis of the International Cooperation Administration). If the UN ended by branding Israel an aggressor, then assistance programs under the ICA would be stopped too. What the President said he really feared was the prospect of imposing a blockade against Israel.

Secretary Dulles turned to the President and warned that if he did not provide leadership at this point, the UN would be calling for a blockade likewise of Britain and France. It would not do for the United States to confine itself merely to calling for a cease-fire, with the Israeli forces running all over Egyptian territory.

Mr. Allen Dulles offered the suggestion that in the present circumstances of approaching military defeat, Nasser might well welcome a cease-fire in order to save his skin. Admiral Radford thought that this was unlikely, and added his further belief that the General Assembly would end by branding Britain, Israel and France as aggressors all.

Secretary Dulles pointed out that we have said to Prime Minister Eden that the kind of action which he had undertaken to carry out was nothing short of disastrous. Having nevertheless continued with his policy and action, do we, the United States, propose to go along with it? Governor Stassen argued that we must still try to save a friend from disaster, even though that friend had brought the disaster on himself.

Turning to the Secretary of State, the President suggested that the thing for him to do was to go now and see what he could draft up in the way of the mildest things we could do in an effort to block the introduction of a really mean and arbitrary resolution in the UN General Assembly. Secretary Dulles agreed, pointing out, however, that Ambassador Lodge had just informed him that if we did not come back to the UN with a resolution much along the lines of our earlier resolution, the Soviets would certainly introduce a very much more extreme resolution. Such an action on the part of the Soviets would plainly force the United States into one camp or the other. We would not be able to walk the tightrope after five o'clock this afternoon.

Secretary Humphrey asked whether we were not all clear in our minds that we cannot be on the side of the British and the French on this issue. The President said that at any rate we certainly couldn't be on their side unless he turned around completely from what he said in his statement last night (the 15-minute telecast from the White House). [10] On the other hand, the President stated with emphasis, we do not want the British and the French to be branded aggressors. Secretary Humphrey commented that we would want to do our best to extricate the British and the French from their error, but we didn't need to get into the error with them.

Coming back to the General Assembly meeting, said Dr. Flemming, are we in a position to get our resolution before the General Assembly earlier than the Soviets can get theirs? Secretary Dulles replied that we can do so if we move fast enough. He said he wanted to be quite clear: It is important that we suspend our economic assistance program to Israel at this time, though the fact of this suspension need not be made public. Both Secretary Humphrey and the Attorney General disagreed with the latter proposal, and expressed a preference for stopping arms shipments to the whole Near Eastern area. They believed that our action should cover the whole area and not be confined to a single country such as Israel.

Secretary Dulles, in response, pointed out that we had only yesterday been arguing in the UN Security Council in favor of suspending economic and financial assistance to the Israelis. Could we now abruptly change? Mr. Allen Dulles pointed out that if the British and the French were branded aggressors, would we not then have to apply sanctions against them as well as against Israel? This seemed to Mr. Dulles a very dangerous course of action.

The President added the further point that we would find plenty of Americans who think the Arabs are every bit as much aggressors as anyone else. In response to the President's point, Secretary Dulles stated that General Burns had been trying desperately to induce the Israelis to agree to inspection and patrol by members of the Armistice Commission. The Israelis had frustrated all his efforts. Governor Stassen admitted the truth of this statement, but pointed out that we could not fail to consider the state of mind of the Israelis in the face of so many provocations and fears. Secretary Dulles answered that one thing at least was clear: We do not approve of murder. We have simply got to refrain from resort to force in settling international disputes. Turning to Governor Stassen, he cited one of the Governor's own speeches, in which Governor Stassen had made this very point; and he again warned that if we

---

[10] At 7 p.m. in Washington, October 31, President Eisenhower reported to the nation over radio and television on developments in Eastern Europe and the Middle East. For text of the President's statement, see Department of State *Bulletin*, November 12, 1956, pp. 743–745; extracts pertaining to the Middle East are printed in *United States Policy in the Middle East, September 1956–June 1957*, pp. 148–151.

stand idly by in this great crisis the whole United Nations would go down the drain.

The President expressed agreement with Secretary Dulles' position, while Governor Stassen once again called for a cease-fire only. In some irritation, Secretary Dulles inquired whether Governor Stassen meant a cease-fire that would leave the aggressor in possession of his gains. Governor Stassen replied that, under the circumstances, the answer was yes, for which there seemed to be some support among other members of the National Security Council. Secretary Humphrey, in turn, called again for stopping all arms shipments to the whole Near Eastern area, without singling out the Israelis for special treatment.

Mr. Hollister raised the question of what supplies should be sent and what supplies should be held up for Arab states other than Egypt, while Governor Stassen outlined again his view of how we could best proceed in the UN General Assembly. He argued first for a resolution insisting on a cease-fire. This might be followed by a second resolution calling on Israel to bring back its forces within the armistice lines. This might be followed by a resolution looking to a settlement.

The President inquired whether we should not, as a precautionary measure, state that we are stopping all military, strategic, and governmental shipments from the United States to all nations involved in this mess at this time. In any event, he added, the Secretary of State must now be allowed to go off and put something down on paper. He could then come back and get together with the President and with other key members of the National Security Council.

After the Secretary of State had left the Cabinet Room, the President turned to the other members of the Council and said that of course no one in the whole world really expected us to break off our long alliance with Great Britain and France. We must not permit ourselves to be blinded by the thought that anything we are going to do will result in our fighting with Great Britain and France. Such a course of action is simply unthinkable, and no one can possibly believe that we will do it.

Mr. Allen Dulles served notice of an announcement that the British had sunk a ship in the Suez Canal, [11] which would probably block traffic in the Canal. Mr. Dulles said he believed that the ship in question had been filled with cement by the Egyptians for the express purpose of blocking the Canal.

---

[11] Reference is to the *Akka*; see Document 452.

The President then ended this phase of the discussion by calling on Admiral Radford to give the Council his report on the military situation in the area of hostilities.

Admiral Radford read his report, which gave a detailed appreciation of the military situation. (A copy of the substance of Admiral Radford's report is filed in the minutes of the meeting.) [12] When he had finished, Admiral Radford stated that the U.S. forces in the area had largely completed their first responsibility of effecting the evacuation of U.S. citizens from the area of hostilities. He pointed out that the Joint Chiefs of Staff were currently much concerned over the possibility of uprisings against Europeans in the several Arab states.

Dr. Flemming asked about the reports as to the likelihood of sabotage of the oil pipelines. Deputy Secretary of Defense Robertson inquired whether evacuation had been completed in Cairo. Admiral Radford replied that the evacuation of Americans from that city was not yet complete.

The President then asked Admiral Radford whether it was at all possible that the Russians could have "slipped" the Egyptians a half dozen atomic bombs. Admiral Radford replied that he doubted this, particularly in view of the manifest failure of the Egyptians to make effective use of the other weapons which the Russians had already provided them.

Secretary Wilson expressed a doubt as to the wisdom of keeping the Sixth Fleet in the area of hostilities once it had completed its task of assisting in the evacuation of Americans from the danger area. He said that the Defense Department needed guidance on this matter.

The President brought the meeting to a close by stating that we must go now and see what we can do about this business. His idea was to do what was decent and right, but still not condemn more furiously than we had to. Secretary Dulles was dead right in his view that if we did not do something to indicate some vigor in the way of asserting our leadership, the Soviets would take over the leadership from us. He had told Anthony Eden a week ago that if the British did what they are now doing and the Russians got into the Middle East, the fat would really be in the fire.

The National Security Council: [13]

a. Noted and discussed an oral report by the Secretary of State on the subject, particularly as regards appropriate U.S. action under

---

[12] Not found in Department of State files or the Eisenhower Library.

[13] Paragraphs a–c and the Note that follow constitute NSC Action No. 1627, approved by the President on November 6. (Department of State, S/S-NSC (Miscellaneous) Files: Lot 66 D 95, Records of Action by the National Security Council, 1956)

the Tripartite Declaration of May 1950; and the U.S. position in the meeting of the United Nations General Assembly scheduled later this date.

b. Noted the President's directive that the Secretary of State draft appropriate action papers in the light of the discussion at this meeting, for subsequent consideration by the President.

c. Noted and discussed an oral briefing by the Chairman, Joint Chiefs of Staff, on the military situation in the Near East.

Note: The action in b above, as approved by the President, subsequently transmitted to the Secretary of State for implementation.

[Here follows agenda item 3, "U.S. Policy Toward Developments in Poland and Hungary", which was deferred until a subsequent meeting.]

S. Everett Gleason

---

456.   **Memorandum of a Telephone Conversation Between the President and the Secretary of State, Washington, November 1, 1956, 11:05 a.m.** [1]

TELEPHONE CALL TO THE PRESIDENT

The Secretary read the attached draft [2] to the President and asked him what he thought of it. The President said certainly it was mild enough. The President added that he was trying to reduce the whole thing to writing. He thought we ought to get up to NY with

---

[1] Source: Eisenhower Library, Dulles Papers, White House Telephone Conversations. Transcribed by Asbjornson. Another memorandum of this conversation prepared in the Office of the President is *ibid.*, Whitman File, Eisenhower Diaries.

[2] Attached but not printed. Dated November 1, it is marked draft #2, bears no title, and indicates Dulles as the drafting officer. It reads as follows:

"Under the Tripartite Declaration of May 25, 1950, and the President's statement of April 9, 1956, the United States declared its deep interest in and its desire to promote the establishment and maintenance of peace and stability in the Middle East and its opposition to the use of force or threat of force between any of the states of the Middle East.

"On October 31 the President declared that it was the purpose of this Government to do all in its power to localize the fighting which has now broken out in the area and to end the conflict.

"As a provisional measure, the United States is suspending the shipment of goods of a military character and Governmental programs to the countries of the area of hostilities which in the judgment of this Government might prolong the hostilities. Appropriate agencies of the Government are being notified accordingly."

the draft of the resolution and have Cabot get as many people on it as possible. Then when it comes to a vote ours will prevail. He said the resolution had to be accompanied by such a statement. The President said that the first objective was a cease fire to keep the war from spreading. To develop the final resolution—that will represent the considered judgment of the United Nations. The President said we were not going to get a cease fire by merely telling everyone to stop fighting. You have to state your views and it has to be understood that a cease fire will require withdrawal to their own shores. The President said he saw nothing wrong with the statement at all.

The Secretary said that substantially the program he had indicated would be suspended. All this has been done in the case of Egypt already. It would suspend military shipments to Israel.

The President asked if the people here agreed with him on this. The Secretary said yes but they would like to go stronger. The Secretary said he would get to work on the resolution.

The Secretary then read the President #2120 from Paris.[3]

The Secretary said he may go up to NY for the meeting this afternoon. The President thought it a good idea. The President said he would send the Secretary up by plane if he wanted to go.

---

[3] Document 453.

---

457.   Memorandum of a Telephone Conversation Between the Secretary of State and the Secretary of Commerce (Weeks), Washington, November 1, 1956, 11:34 a.m.[1]

TELEPHONE CALL TO SEC. WEEKS

The Sec. said the Pres. has agreed we should suspend shipments of goods of a military character to countries engaged in hostilities— jeeps etc. but don't know definition. You are already suspending those for Egypt—W thinks so. The Sec. said he does not know his list but wish W. would think about it. Give the list the same kind of review as the Egyptian list—would not give publicity—this would cover Egypt and Israel. W. asked re letting it go to Br and Fr, and the Sec. said yes—we have not decided what to do about them. W.

---

[1] Source: Eisenhower Library, Dulles Papers, General Telephone Conversations. Transcribed by Bernau.

will get the list and see what is being done re Egypt. The Sec. thinks they are doing something more broadly for Egypt than you would have to do for Israel. W. wishes the Sec. would look at Br and Fr. The Sec. assured him we are. W. will report back. The precise paper says, and the Sec. read, the issuance of export licenses should be delayed for goods of a semi-military nature on the positive list. W. asked re Jordan and the Sec. said no—so far no hostilities involved there. The Sec. said we have other pressures for Br and Fr but we don't want it publicly announced at the moment.

---

458. Memorandum of a Telephone Conversation Between the Secretary of State and the Director of Central Intelligence (Dulles), Washington, November 1, 1956, 11:58 a.m. [1]

TELEPHONE CALL TO ALLEN DULLES

The Sec. asked if he gathered from what A[llen] said that he thinks Nasser may be toppling. Yes—he just had a pretty complete briefing on the military situation and thinks he is pretty well on the ropes. They think his air force will be knocked out by tonight. The Israeli troops are better. After the Sec. left [2] and the question came up and Radford and A. slightly differed. A. thinks Nasser might accept a cease-fire. He is up against overwhelming force. He does not think his military potential is very high and thinks he realizes it. The Sec. said no one thought they were going to win an old-fashioned war. The Sec. assumed the millitary collapse but wondered re Soviet infiltration, economics etc.—there is no question of the Arab world feeling. A. said that is not a good place for guerrilla warfare. There may be fighting in Cairo but he would imagine the Br would hold on the Canal. The Sec. assumed war would be carried on not primarily in Egypt but along the Persian Gulf and North Africa. A. said the area will be in flames but the military flames may not be so bright as they don't have much. The Sec. said there would be a strain on the Br and Fr and it will be economic and quickly— the oil problem will be acute pretty soon. A. would not take small measures against Israel—wait if you can. The Sec. said we are not

[1] Source: Eisenhower Library, Dulles Papers, General Telephone Conversations. Transcribed by Bernau.
[2] Reference is presumably to the Secretary leaving the 302d meeting of the NSC that morning; see Document 455.

making any statement but in fact are suspending shipment of arms of military stuff and economic assistance programs but not announcing sanctions against Israel. A. asked if the Sec. were going for a cease-fire or withdrawal in the UN Res. The Sec. said he does not know. A. thinks he [we] would more likely get a cease-fire. The Sec. said you can't get one which will be effective—a lot of underground business. A. said true but you are working for time, for where do we go from here, aren't you? A. said it would be difficult for a cease-fire in the Sinai peninsula. The Sec. asked does it mean anything? Then A. said yes—you only have hours and have to get something understandable to the people and not too complicated—simple and dramatic and then grapple with the difficulties later. A. is inclined to think Nasser might take it. They have not shown up well—not prepared. A. complimented the Sec. on his presentation.

---

459.   Telegram From the Embassy in France to the Department of State [1]

Paris, November 1, 1956—1 p.m.

2123. Following is description of events leading up to Suez hostilities given me by Pineau this morning. Pineau said that from the beginning French had considered the seizure of Suez Canal as a much more serious matter than did the United States. French looked upon this action as merely a step in Nasser's march toward domination of the whole of Middle East and North Africa. Therefore, French, as they explained at the time, felt that it was vitally necessary to take energetic action to cause prompt loss of face to Nasser. Pineau said that French were convinced if situation was allowed to drag time would work for Nasser and Soviet Union against the Western powers, including the United States. He said French were convinced that American influence throughout area had no possibility of withstanding the Soviet infiltrations backed as they were by Nasser. Pineau said that this obviously was a fundamental difference in the evaluation of the situation by France and Great Britain on one hand and by the United States on other hand. Pineau

[1] Source: Department of State, Central Files, 651.74/11–156. Secret; Priority. Received at 12:11 p.m. Repeated to USUN and London. The time of transmission on the source text (11 p.m.) is in error. According to the sequence of telegrams from Paris, telegram 2123 was evidently sent at 1 p.m.

then mentioned confidential démarche made to French by Sultan of Morocco and Bourguiba indicating that unless drastic action was taken against Nasser their position would be hopelessly compromised, and he said Great Britain had received similar information from Iraqi Government.

Pineau said that while French Government had been shocked and upset by casual attitude of Murphy on his arrival in London immediately after crisis, they had felt that Secretary had at that time understood seriousness of situation. Pineau said that he and French Government were well satisfied with results at first London conference and that on departure of Menzies mission for Cairo had really believed that it might be possible to avoid military action.

Pineau then said that divergence between United States and Franco-British policy first became acute after failure of Menzies mission when Secretary opposed an immediate recourse to United Nations Security Council, and instead suggested creation of Users Association. Pineau said that misunderstanding regarding fundamental purposes of Users Association was total. He said that French and British had originally considered that Secretary had suggested creation of this Association for purpose of bringing strong moral and economic pressure on Egypt as an alternative to military action. However, it rapidly became obvious that this was not the purpose of the United States. From the French point of view the Users Association as it emerged from second London conference, and in particular after it became apparent that United States was not prepared to use it as a means of denying Canal dues to Egypt, was a totally useless exercise. Pineau then discussed Security Council meeting which dealt with Suez and said that from French and British point of view the results had been inadequate as there was no indication that Egypt would agree to international administration of the Canal and therefore there had been no loss of prestige for Nasser.

Shortly after conclusion of Security Council meeting and after Pineau's return to Paris, Israelis approached the French and said that Israel had determined that she must act in self defense. Israelis told French that they had reached conclusion that United States had in effect decided to side with Nasser as against Israel and to allow the annihilation of Israel. The Israelis further said that in view of the rapid increase in Egyptian military capability due to the receipt of increasing quantities of Soviet arms, the fate of Israel would be sealed in a few months time. Matter was then taken up with United Kingdom Government and general agreement on present course of action was reached. Final decisions were taken during the course of Eden–Lloyd visit to Paris and decision was taken jointly by United Kingdom and French not to inform the United States. Both governments felt convinced that United States was in error regarding its evaluation of the danger of Nasser and considered that prior consultation with United States on this subject would serve no useful purpose.

I thanked Pineau for his frank exposé and said that there was one question I would like to ask which was not clear to me, and that was how the question of entry of Iraqi troops into Jordan figured in this affair. Pineau replied that discussions on that subject were primarily a smoke screen to divert attention from the decision to undertake a joint operation against Egypt.

I then asked Pineau what the objectives of the joint action were. Pineau replied the Israeli objective was the total destruction or capture of all Egyptian forces east of Suez and that Franco-British objective was the occupation of the Suez Canal zone. He emphatically denied any intention of extending the Franco-British occupation further into Egypt. I then asked Pineau what were French and British intentions regarding Nasser. He replied that this was a matter which would have to be left up to the Egyptian people and he said that French and British realized that they could not impose a government on Egypt. He said he hoped that the Egyptian people seeing the catastrophe which Nasser had prepared for them would themselves in due course act to get rid [of] him. In answer to a further question Pineau said that Israelis expected to complete their military operations in another two or three days and that French and British felt that occupation of Canal Zone could be completed in 8 to 10 days at a maximum. As to ultimate objectives, Pineau and French and British felt that a conference should be called whose membership should be very carefully thought out. The Soviet Union would obviously have to be a member, but care should be taken to limit the membership of disruptive nations. He felt that this conference might settle all the outstanding problems in the Middle East once and for all. He listed these problems as:

1. Arab-Israeli Peace Treaty.
2. Status of Suez Canal.
3. Future status of Jordan.

In terminating Pineau felt that he should tell me that French Government considered that while communications from President Eisenhower had been very measured and his television speech had contained nothing to which they could take exception, they had felt that public position taken by United States at United Nations and words used by United States delegate during debate there had been unnecessarily violent and had caused unnecessary damage to Franco-American relations. Pineau said that once this affair was settled he and French Government would devote all their energies to repairing breach in Atlantic alliance but they hoped that United States in meanwhile would exercise care and moderation in public utterances so as not to render this task more difficult. [2]

Dillon

---

[2] Rountree and Dulles discussed telegram 2123 during a telephone conversation on November 2: "Mr Rountree said he just read Dulles' telegram from Dillon, wherein Pineau has told him the whole unmitigated story, explaining the whole thing in cold facts. Dulles asked if the British are involved—Rountree said Oh, yes. Israelis approached them immediately after Security Council meeting in N.Y. (Israelis meeting held in Paris.) That is when they were firmed up—& that is when we knew they were firmed up. The Baghdad thing was a complete smoke-screen, just to divert attention. Mr. Dulles commented that it is all very interesting—Mr. Rountree added, particularly so in view of communications which came from the top level." (Memorandum of telephone conversation prepared in the Office of the President, 4:36 p.m., November 2; Eisenhower Library, Whitman File, Eisenhower Diaries)

---

460.   Draft Message From President Eisenhower to Prime Minister Eden [1]

Washington, November 1, 1956.

DEAR ANTHONY: I am sending you by mail a copy of a fifteen-minute talk I made to the American nation last evening. Its principal point with respect to Britain and France is that these two nations have long been our friends and, although in this particular instance we believe that they have made a serious error, we certainly shall do our best to sustain those friendships. I do not feel it necessary to provide to you any additional evidence of my own sincere desire to bring your nation and ours ever closer together.

If I may, in the circumstances, comment further on the unfolding situation, I should like to make some observations on possible eventualities involving the Soviets and submit a suggestion for your consideration concerning the Mid-East operations.

With respect to the first point, I have seen a press notice that Bulganin has dispatched to me a letter on the Mid-East difficulty. [2] It will probably be very tough. I think the first action we may expect from them is the introduction of a stringent Resolution before

---

[1] Source: Eisenhower Library, Whitman File, International File. During a telephone conversation with Hoover on November 2, President Eisenhower referred to a telegram which he had started but did not send to Eden. (Memorandum of telephone conversation, November 2, 11:16 a.m.; *ibid.*, Eisenhower Diaries) Presumably this draft message is the one to which Eisenhower referred.

[2] Document 505.

the General Assembly this afternoon. Possibly they will seek some kind of a Resolution that will commit the United Nations to call upon its members for forces with which to intervene in this affair. The reason I suspect something of this sort is because I could not imagine anything more embarrassing for your country. It is possible that even, unilaterally, the Russians may assert the right and attempt to send equipment and "volunteers" to Egypt. Of course this would not be possible if you are quickly successful in establishment of an effective blockade. [3]

With respect to my suggestion, I am, of course, ignorant of your minimum objectives and what you expect to do after you attain them. But I am struck by the emphasis you placed in your announcement, as well as in your message to me, on the word "temporary" in your occupation.

As of this moment, I have very sketchy information of actual military developments in Egypt and it appears that you and the French have not yet placed any land forces in the region. If, however, the very second you attain your minimum objectives with such forces, I think you could probably ease tension greatly by doing the following: one, instantly call for a cease fire in the area; two, clearly state the reasons why you entered the Canal Zone; three, announce your intention to resume negotiations concerning the operation of the Canal, on the basis of the 6 principles agreed by the United Nations; four, state your intention to evacuate as quickly as the Israelites return to their own national territory, and Egypt had [sic] announced her readiness to negotiate in good faith on the basis of the six principles. In this way I think the almost universal resentment now apparently [apparent] and the possibility of long drawn out, dreary guerilla operations would diminish.

This, of course, is gratuitous advice, but it springs from my very great desire to see the United Nations preserved, to keep in proper perspective before all of us the fact that the Soviet Communists are still the greatest menace of the free nations and to start restoring that feeling of confidence and trust between your nation and ours that I believe to be vital to the interests of a just world peace.

---

[3] At this point, it was intended presumably to add a paragraph identified as "insert", which is attached to the source text. The paragraph reads: "To forestall this, this Government hopes to take a position before the United Nations this afternoon that will be moderate in tone, but for which we might gain a sufficient support, before the meeting, to block any Soviet attempt of the kind I have described above. We would propose: (a) disapproval of forceful action in the settlement of this dispute; (b) an immediate cease fire; (c) a statement by each government of its intentions and objectives in the area and (d) the purpose of the United States to effect a return of all forces to their own borders at the earliest possible moment."

Just now I was notified that Nehru has dispatched to me a long communication. [4] What he will propose of course is anybody's guess, but it does illustrate how far-reaching may be the reverberations from an act that is intended to be fairly local. I have already had direct and indirect communications from a score of other nations. [5]

---

[4] The note from the Indian Embassy that transmitted Nehru's letter on November 1 is in the Eisenhower Library, Whitman File, International File. The signed original of the letter, dated October 31, which was forwarded to the White House on November 15, is *ibid*.

[5] Printed from an unsigned copy.

---

461.   Memorandum by the President [1]

Washington, November 1, 1956.

1. The first objective of the United Nations should be to achieve a cease-fire because this will:

(a) Keep the war from spreading.
(b) Give time to find out what each side is trying to gain.
(c) Develop a final resolution that will represent the considered judgment of the United Nations respecting past blame and future action.

2. The United States must lead because:

(a) While we want to do all the things in 1 above, we want to prevent immediate issuance by the United Nations of a harshly worded resolution that would put us in an acutely embarrassing position, either with France and Britain or with all the rest of the world.
(b) At all costs the Soviets must be prevented from seizing a mantle of world leadership through a false but convincing exhibition of concern for smaller nations. Since Africa and Asia almost unanimously hate one of the three nations Britain, France and Israel, the Soviets need only to propose severe and immediate punishment of these three to have the whole of two continents on their side; unless a good many of the United Nations nations are already committed to something more moderate that we might immediately formulate. We

---

[1] Source: Eisenhower Library, Dulles Papers, White House Memoranda. Attached to the source text is a note from Eisenhower to Dulles, dated November 1, which reads: "Just some simple thoughts that I have jotted down since our meeting this morning." Eisenhower initialed the note.

According to the record of President's Daily Appointments, Dulles met with Eisenhower at the White House from 12:50 to 1:27 p.m. on November 1. (*Ibid*.) No account of this conversation has been found in the Eisenhower Library.

should act speedily so as to have our forces in good order by 5:00 p.m. today.

(c) We provide the West's only hope that some vestige of real political and economic union can be preserved with the Moslem world, indeed, possibly also with India.

3. Unilateral actions now taken by the United States must *not* single out and condemn *any one nation*—but should serve to emphasize to the world our hope for a quick cease-fire to be followed by sane and deliberate action on the part of the United Nations, resulting, hopefully, in a solution to which all parties would adhere by each conceding something.

4. We should be expected, I think, to suspend governmental shipments, now, to countries in battle areas and be prepared to agree, in concert with others, to later additional action.

---

462.   Memorandum of a Conversation, Department of State, Washington, November 1, 1956, 2:08 p.m. [1]

SUBJECT

Question of Projects for Assistance to Israel, and Related Matters

PARTICIPANTS

Ambassador Abba Eban, Israeli Ambassador
Minister Shiloah, Embassy of Israel

The Secretary
NE—Fraser Wilkins

The Secretary said Ambassador Eban must have surmised recent developments had made it necessary for the United States to review projects for assistance to Israel and related matters. He asked Ambassador Eban if he had anything to say which would have a bearing on this question.

---

[1] Source: Department of State, Central Files, 684A.86/11–156. Confidential. Drafted by Wilkins on November 5. The time of the meeting is from Dulles' Appointment Book. (Princeton University Library, Dulles Papers)

Shortly before this meeting with Eban, Dulles told Attorney General Brownell over the telephone that he had decided against making a public announcement concerning the U.S. suspension of shipments to Israel. (Memorandum of telephone conversation by Bernau, November 1, 2:01 p.m.; Eisenhower Library, Dulles Papers, General Telephone Conversations)

Ambassador Eban replied he wished to make a personal observation that his remarks in the past had been based on his knowledge of Israeli policy. The Secretary responded that he had no personal feelings and that he relied upon what governments did rather than on their statements alone.

Ambassador Eban said he had just spoken to Prime Minister Ben Gurion. Ambassador Eban said there had been a complete collapse of Nasser's forces in the Sinai Peninsula. They were in headlong flight toward the Suez Canal and were leaving all of their military equipment behind them, including hundreds of Soviet tanks, guns and other Soviet matériel.

Ambassador Eban believed that with the fall of Nasser we were now standing at a crossroads of history which was equivalent to the collapse of other dictatorships in the past. The spread of Soviet Communism which had been the mainstay of Nasser's regime had also been checked. These developments in the Near East were equivalent to the defeat of Soviet Communism in Eastern Europe. The opportunity for peace among Near Eastern states which had been missed in 1948 was now possible in 1956. Ambassador Eban urged the United States to seize this opportunity.

Ambassador Eban continued that the Government of Israel appreciated the moral and economic assistance which it had received from the United States. He realized that during recent months there had been differences of judgment between Israel and the United States regarding developments in the Near East. He recalled the President's belief that in spite of differences in judgment between countries, they should endeavor to maintain their friendship. Ambassador Eban thought that the United States would act as Israel had if it had been confronted with the same type of threat on its frontiers and that Israel was entitled to take such steps as it considered necessary for its defense.

Ambassador Eban reiterated that Israel desired no territorial gain in Egypt and that Israel had only acted because of the mortal threat which Egypt presented. Prime Minister Ben Gurion wished him to say Israel believed the general armistice agreement should be restored. The Government of Israel would be prepared to undertake withdrawal from its present position in Egypt to the armistice line provided there were binding undertakings that threats to Israel's security would be removed, including fedayeen activity, and that Israel's maritime freedom would be respected, including passage of the Suez Canal. Prime Minister Ben Gurion also wished him to say that as Israel had become linked with two other friendly nations in its action it would be bound to take counsel with them on any proposal for the withdrawal of forces.

The Secretary said we should not limit our consideration to regrets about the past. He believed, however, that current developments had been a grave blow to the structure of peace and to the United Nations. It would not be possible just to wipe out events that have been taking place. We should not think only in terms of returning to the status quo ante but in terms of the precedent which might be set that any nation which is harassed could strike back with military force. Could we say that Pakistan could strike at India? If so, military anarchy would result. Mr. Shiloah intervened that Pakistan might find it necessary to strike if Indian leaders uttered threats against it. Had any Indian leader so spoken? The Secretary responded that public leaders of many countries were given to public statement but it was not what they said but the sum total of their actions that counted. The Secretary repeated that a return to the status quo ante was not enough and that we should adhere to the principles and purposes of the United Nations. Any immediate gain achieved through force would weigh lightly in the balance.

The Secretary and Ambassador Eban agreed that as they were both leaving for New York in a matter of minutes, they could continue their discussion there.

Ambassador Eban and Minister Shiloah later told Mr. Wilkins that Prime Minister Ben Gurion planned shortly, perhaps tonight, to make a statement during which he would stress the leading role which President Eisenhower had been playing in efforts towards a restoration of peace. Ambassador Eban hoped that the United States in considering steps which it might take with respect to countries engaged in hostilities in the Near East would not treat Israel any differently than it did any of the other countries. [2]

---

[2] Following this conversation, Dulles telephoned Allen Dulles at 2:26 p.m. Their conversation, as transcribed by Bernau, went as follows: "The Sec. said as a matter of intelligence, Eban came to see him and talked to Ben Gurion half an hour ago. The Egyptian forces had been completely defeated in the Gaza area—fleeing back and abandoning great quantities of Soviet equipment. He was in a very jubilant mood. . . . The Sec. said we probably will call for a cease-fire." (*Ibid.*) Secretary Dulles then departed for the Military Air Transport Service terminal and at 3 p.m. left for New York. (Chronology for November 1; Department of State, Conference Files: Lot 62 D 181, CF 803)

463.   **Memorandum for the Files of a Meeting Held in the Department of Agriculture, Washington, November 1, 1956** [1]

At 1:05 p.m., November 1, I was called by Mr. Kalijarvi of the State Department and informed that effective immediately all P.L. 480 aid to Israel was to be immediately discontinued, that cargoes now being loaded or afloat would not be stopped but that no further shipments should be made under existing contracts. I was further informed that no public statement should be made concerning this decision.

A conference of affected Department of Agriculture agency personnel and policy people was held immediately, the information transmitted and decisions made to inform contracting parties furnishing commodities under P.L. 480 agreements that no further effectuation of existing agreements would be carried out at this time.

At 2:30 p.m., November 1, Mr. Herbert Hoover, Jr., Under Secretary of State, called and said that no action should be taken of any kind at the moment, that we should continue to fulfill existing contracts under P.L. 480 agreements, that no new agreements should be negotiated in the Mediterranean area with particular reference to the area of conflict until the situation was further clarified. With respect to existing agreements, Mr. Hoover said we would be advised as to any changes as to their continued effectuation. By 2:35 p.m. I had informed Mr. Garrett, FAS, Mr. Lennartson, AMS, Mr. Berger, CSS, [2] that the decisions reached in conference following the

---

[1] Source: Department of Agriculture Records, Office of the Secretary, Commodities 5. Confidential. Drafted by Ervin L. Peterson, Assistant Secretary of Agriculture, on November 2.

[2] Respectively they were: Gwynn Garrett, Administrator of the Foreign Agricultural Service; Roy W. Lennartson, Deputy Administrator for Marketing Service, Agricultural Marketing Services; and Walter C. Berger, Associate Administrator, Commodity Stabilization Service.

1:05 p.m. information were to be ignored, that we would proceed on a normal basis until advice was received to the contrary.[3]

E. L. Peterson [4]

---

[3] On November 2, Hollister suggested to Hoover that either ICA or the State Department issue an official statement indicating, among other points, that there had been no formal cessation of U.S. aid programs in the Near East as a result of the recent hostilities, but that the evacuation of U.S. personnel in Egypt, Israel, and Jordan had automatically brought almost to a halt all technical assistance programs and had slowed down materially all development assistance activity. In a marginal notation on the document, Hoover advised that these points should be made verbally and that Lincoln White should use them for background. (Memorandum from Hollister to Hoover with attached draft statement, November 2; Department of State, Central Files, 780.5–MSP/11–256) On November 3, *The New York Times* and other newspapers reported that, according to Department of State spokesman Lincoln White, there had been no order to suspend economic aid to the area, although no new programs were going forward. The transcript of the Department of State press briefing for November 2 is in Department of State *Daily News Conferences*, 1956.

[4] Printed from a copy that bears this typed signature.

---

464.   Telegram From the Department of State to the Embassy in Egypt [1]

Washington, November 1, 1956—4:09 p.m.

1368. Embtel 1240.[2] You should orally acknowledge receipt of Nasser's message for President and say that President, Secretary and other USG officials are making every effort within framework of UN to bring about cease-fire and early withdrawal of forces in hostilities in Near East. US referred question Israeli action to Security Council. Proposed resolution was not adopted although seven Security Council members supported it. Last night President in television-radio report on Mideast crisis indicated our hope and intent that this matter would be brought before United Nations General Assembly. Meeting of GA was subsequently called for afternoon November 1. The Secretary is flying to New York for this meeting. US will continue to work in UN to resolve present grave threat to world peace.

Dulles

---

[1] Source: Department of State, Central Files, 684A.86/11–156. Secret; Niact. Drafted by Wilkins, cleared by Hoover, and approved by Dulles. Repeated to USUN.
[2] Document 451.

465.   Telegram From the Embassy in France to the Department of State [1]

Paris, November 1, 1956—1 p.m.

2121. Now that Franco-British military operation in Suez has definitely commenced, and despite manner in which their intentions and preparations were concealed from us, primary preoccupation this Embassy is naturally to limit insofar as possible damage to Atlantic Alliance, to narrow dangerous gap between France and United States and, to that end, to seek means by which divergent French and United States policies in Near East might possibly be brought to move along parallel and eventually converging lines.

Primary French objective is to overthrow or at least humiliate Nasser. We cannot conceive of French withdrawing from or limiting current operation until that objective has been substantially achieved, or has proved unattainable.

We have . . . felt it unwise for many sound reasons that military means be used. However, now they have been used, we would suppose it is in our interest they succeed and succeed rapidly. It is certainly preferable from overall Western viewpoint that they do so rather than that French and British fail or be involved in long drawn out guerrilla warfare. On this point our interest and theirs coincide.

It is also to our interest and theirs that conflict not spread. Once it starts spreading there is no telling where it would stop. Soviets have stressed this point. To extent United Kingdom and France can persuade Iraq and Jordan to keep out of war and perhaps can improve internal situation in Syria, to that extent chance of eliminating Nasser rapidly and of preventing conflict from spreading to ultimate advantage USSR will be enhanced. We could presumably play certain role along these lines in some Arab countries if we desired. This could be second coincidence United States–United Kingdom–French interests.

If we could hold the ring for a week or two, we might forestall some of more serious repercussions of armed conflict which we have foreseen. By that time presumably French and British will either have succeeded in their objective or have learned they cannot do so without prolonged and very costly campaign. By that time also we would expect almost universal pressure will have been exerted on French and British, inside and outside United Nations, to bring conflict to a close.

---

[1] Source: Department of State, Central Files, 684A.86/11–156. Top Secret; Priority; Limit Distribution. Received at 7:45 p.m. Repeated to London.

Our hope would therefore be that, while participating in United Nations action designed to bring about early cease-fire, we could (1) avoid taking individual lead in condemning French and British; (2) facilitate early and successful termination their operation by helping to prevent involvement other states; and (3) await, if operation not promptly successful, anticipated early effect on French and British both of military complications and world-wide political pressures.

We would feel that any purely United States attempt to force them to break off hostilities at this moment would be useless and would merely widen dangerous fissure in Atlantic Alliance, where two weeks from now either their objective will have been realized, or they will be in a far more chastened and amenable mood.

Dillon

---

466.   Telegram From the Embassy in France to the Department of State [1]

Paris, November 1, 1956—10 p.m.

2129. For Secretary and Lodge from Dillon. Most Urgent. Pineau called me during dinner and asked me to come to see him as soon as possible. On arrival I found him and Joxe together, both of them greatly disturbed.

Pineau said that they had just received intelligence information from sources in Syria that Soviet Union was planning military intervention through Syrian bases. Therefore, Pineau felt it was most urgent that some positive action be taken by U.N. General Assembly today to head off any such action by Soviets. Pineau suggested that General Assembly summon the Foreign Ministers of France, Great Britain, Israel, and Egypt to appear before it immediately. He said this would delay any action by Soviets for two or three days by which time he had good reason to hope the whole affair would be finished.

Pineau said latest reports indicated total collapse of Egyptian resistance to Israeli forces east of the Canal. He also said there were indications of unrest in Cairo and there was good chance that

---

[1] Source: Department of State, Central Files, 320.5780/11–156. Secret; Niact. Received at 5:04 p.m. Repeated to USUN. Attached to the source text is a copy of a memorandum from Howe to Goodpaster forwarding a copy of the telegram to the White House.

occupation of the Canal Zone could take place without any serious fighting or loss of life. Vital matter now was to prevent Soviets from turning present action into general war.

Pineau said that for obvious reasons France could not make such a proposal and he hoped that U.S. could do so or could arrange to have such a resolution introduced. [2] Pineau said he was prepared to leave immediately for New York. [3]

Dillon

---

[2] Alphand made a similar request to Murphy on November 1. (Memorandum of telephone conversation by Murphy, November 1; *ibid.*, 611.51/11–156)

[3] In Tedul 2 from USUN, November 1, Dulles commented regarding this telegram: "Admiral Radford strongly discounts credibility due (1) extreme difficulty of mounting effective intervention through limited base facilities available; (2) necessity for overflight of Turkey or Iran; and (3) exposure of bases to quick sneak bombing by Israelis. Allen Dulles, MacArthur and I concur. It appears to us that Pineau is desperately trying to stall for time." (*Ibid.*, 684A.86/11–156)

In response to telegram 2129, the Department of State on November 2 directed Dillon to "take matter up again on urgent basis with Pineau or Joxe requesting further details. Specifically what leads French to lend credence these reports? Can French give indication as to where and how such information obtained? Have they received any subsequent reports tending confirm this intelligence?" (Telegram 1656 to Paris; *ibid.*, 320.5780/11–156)

---

467.   Editorial Note

The first emergency session of the United Nations General Assembly convened at 5 p.m. on November 1 (its 562d plenary session), and the delegates proceeded to discuss the question considered by the United Nations Security Council during its two meetings (749 and 750) of October 30. After considerable discussion, Dulles introduced the text of a draft resolution, which reads as follows:

"The General Assembly,

"Noting the disregard on many occasions by parties to the Israel-Arab armistice agreements of 1949 of the terms of such agreements, and that the armed forces of Israel have penetrated deeply into Egyptian territory in violation of the General Armistice Agreement between Egypt and Israel of 24 February 1949,

"Noting that armed forces of France and the United Kingdom of Great Britain and Northern Ireland are conducting military operations against Egyptian territory,

"Noting that traffic through the Suez Canal is now interrupted to the serious prejudice of many nations,

"Expressing its grave concern over these developments,

"1. *Urges* as a matter of priority that all parties now involved in hostilities in the area agree to an immediate cease-fire and, as part thereof, halt the movement of military forces and arms into the area;

"2. *Urges* the parties to the armistice agreements promptly to withdraw all forces behind the armistice lines, to desist from raids across the armistice lines into neighbouring territory, and to observe scrupulously the provisions of the armistice agreements;

"3. *Recommends* that all Member States refrain from introducing military goods in the area of hostilities and in general refrain from any acts which would delay or prevent the implementation of the present resolution;

"4. *Urges* that, upon the cease-fire being effective, steps be taken to reopen the Suez Canal and restore secure freedom of navigation;

"5. *Requests* the Secretary-General to observe and report promptly on the compliance with the present resolution to the Security Council and to the General Assembly, for such further action as they may deem appropriate in accordance with the Charter;

"6. *Decides* to remain in emergency session pending compliance with the present resolution." (U.N. doc. A/3256)

The meeting then adjourned at 7:40 p.m. (U.N. doc. A/PV.561)

The General Assembly resumed its discussion at 9:50 p.m. that evening and after 5 hours of debate adopted the U.S. draft as General Assembly Resolution 997 (ES–I) by a vote of 64 in favor, 5 opposed, and 6 abstentions. During the discussion which followed, Lester Pearson explained that his government had abstained on the resolution, because it lacked two elements. Pearson noted that the resolution did not provide for any steps to be taken by the United Nations to bring a peace settlement to the area, and he affirmed his preference for a resolution which would have authorized the Secretary-General to begin making arrangements for a U.N. force of sufficient size to keep peace along the contested borders while a political settlement was being made. During his turn to speak, Secretary Dulles expressed his complete agreement with Pearson and added that the United States would be very happy if the Canadian Delegation would formulate and introduce a concrete proposal along the lines suggested by Pearson. After additional discussion, the plenary session adjourned at 4:20 a.m., November 2. (U.N. doc. A/PV.562) For text of Dulles' remarks made while submitting the draft resolution, see Department of State *Bulletin*, November 12, 1956, pages 751–755; or *United States Policy in the Middle East, September 1956–June 1957*, pages 151–157.

The procès-verbaux of this and other meetings of the first emergency special session of the General Assembly are printed in United Nations, *Official Records of the General Assembly, First Emergency Special Session, 1–10 November 1956, Plenary Meetings and Annexes*.

468.   Telegram From the Embassy in the United Kingdom to the Department of State [1]

London, November 2, 1956—2 p.m.

2455. Paris pass USRO. Beckett, Min Fuel & Power states:

1) Estimated UK stocks petrol products sufficient four weeks' needs with variations in stocks specific items.

2) Thought given need rationing, legal basis for which now established by order in Council, but introduction full rationing would require time-consuming organization, recruitment of staff, etc., so that UK plans try voluntary restraints consumption as first step. No estimate given re time element application consumption restraints but expected introduce shortly.

3) UK planning based upon close cooperation US. HMG therefore distressed at reports MEEC meeting and supply distribution subcomm scheduled Nov. 1 canceled at suggestion Dept State for stated reason meeting would serve no useful purpose pending clarification US policy. Also mentioned this connection report Justice Dept had withdrawn anti-trust immunity oil companies cooperate petrol problems arising out of disruption Middle East supply.

4) Beckett volunteered no connection between present events and previous UK urgency have OEEC oil committee adopt agreement mutual sharing shortages. He expects some OEEC Delegations will demand earlier meeting oil committee than presently scheduled Nov. 14. Would appreciate any background Dept can give on point three, with info to Paris for USRO.

Aldrich

---

[1] Source: Department of State, Central Files, 840.2553/11–256. Confidential. Received at 10:19 a.m. Repeated to Paris.

469.   Memorandum From the Under Secretary of State (Hoover) to the Secretary of State [1]

Washington, November 2, 1956.

The President called me at 12:20 p.m. today and said that he would like to meet with you when you got in from New York. [2]

He suggested, unless you have a better proposal, that we might put in another resolution calling for an Arbitration Commission to examine not only this specific outbreak but the entire Middle East situation. If the UN would want him to, the President would be willing to meet with Nehru, just the two of them, because he thought they came closer to commanding the respect of the world and it would make it difficult for the world to turn down our proposal. He would be willing to go anywhere for this meeting, Geneva, London, Greece, or anywhere else.

The President feels we are on the right track. Therefore, he is willing to do anything. He thinks we have got to keep up the momentum, and this would be very spectacular.

H.H. Jr.

---

[1] Source: Eisenhower Library, Dulles Papers, Meetings with the President. Secret; Eyes Only; Personal and Private.

[2] According to Dulles' Appointment Book, he returned by air from New York at approximately 2 p.m. (Princeton University Library, Dulles Papers) Earlier in the day, Hoover had discussed with President Eisenhower over the telephone possible responses to letters from the Indian, Libyan, and Ceylonese Governments on the Middle East situation. Memoranda of Hoover's three conversations with Eisenhower are in Eisenhower Library, Whitman File, Eisenhower Diaries.

470.   Memorandum of a Conference With the President, White House, Washington, November 2, 1956, 2:32–3:25 p.m. [1]

OTHERS PRESENT

Secretary Dulles
Secretary Hoover
Colonel Goodpaster (for part of meeting)

When I joined this meeting, the President was discussing the idea of a neutral strip around Israel, and explaining to the Secretary his thought of proportionate contributions to the width of the strip by the countries concerned—on the basis of their over-all land area.

The discussion next turned to the proposals that had been mentioned in New York that the President and Nehru might serve together to develop a solution to the Middle East dispute. Mr. Dulles spoke of the possibility of their serving as an elder statesmen "board of appeals"—he thought that they should not take responsibility for primary developmental action. He thought Britain and Israel will soon be coming to the United States for economic cooperation. There are several questions that must be considered in connection with the proposal. Does it build up Nehru too much? How strenuously would the Pakistanis object? Mr. Hoover commented that Nehru is likely to be offensive to the UK. The President said he thought Nehru was important to the UK economically. Mr. Hoover said he believed that India's trade was not as important as formerly but the President said he thought it was larger.

The President, referring to the plan for two committees, [2] said the key will be to find names which will bring maximum moral pressure on the participants. Mr. Dulles said there was good possibility that Mr. Pearson of Canada would suggest the Eisenhower-Nehru approach. The President thought it might be better to start out with the committees and to set up himself and Nehru later if

[1] Source: Eisenhower Library, Whitman File, Eisenhower Diaries. Secret. Drafted by Goodpaster on November 5. The time of the meeting is from the record of the President's Daily Appointments. (*Ibid.*)

[2] Later on November 2, the Department of State transmitted to the Mission at the United Nations the texts of two draft resolutions. The first, which dealt with the Arab-Israeli problem, called for the establishment of a five-nation committee which would prepare recommendations regarding the settlement of major problems outstanding between the Arab states and Israel with a view to establishing the conditions of permanent peace and stability in the area. This committee was to replace the current Palestine Conciliation Commission. The second draft resolution, which concerned the Suez Canal problem, called for the creation of a three-nation committee which would assume responsibility for the taking of measures for the immediate reopening of the Suez Canal as a secure waterway and for the preparation, adoption, and execution of a plan to operate and maintain the Canal and freedom of passage through it. (Telegrams 237 and 238 to USUN, November 2; Department of State, Central Files, 320/11–256)

needed. There was then further discussion of possible names for the committees, including Lange, Aranha [3] and Amini (on the assumption that Nehru would be "saved" for the higher group).

Mr. Dulles said we need to move quickly, keeping momentum and keeping out in front in the rapidly developing action. We should avoid any implications that we are simply going back to the situation that formerly existed in the area.

The President asked if there would be any point in having one or two others serve with Nehru and himself, and Secretary Dulles brought out that the Soviet Union might then press to serve. He added that the objection to Nehru might not be so great if someone other than the United States suggested his name.

The President asked whether the two committees could be handled separately, or whether the two questions were linked. Mr. Dulles thought that they could be kept reasonably separate, and the President indicated agreement to trying to set up the two committees.

Mr. Dulles said he would retain the idea of the President and Nehru serving if the suggestion could come from elsewhere. He thought it would be important for them not to take on the primary staff or detail responsibility.

Mr. Hoover suggested not getting into the matter too early because there is still bloodshed ahead. The President said the UN has ordered a cease-fire, but there must then immediately be machinery for straightening out the situation.

The President concluded by saying that if it were thought that he could be useful serving in this way, there should be no worry about preempting too much of his time.

G
Colonel, CE, U S Army

---

[3] Oswaldo Aranha, Brazilian Representative at the United Nations.

471.   **Memorandum of a Telephone Conversation Between the Secretary of State in Washington and the Representative at the United Nations (Lodge) in New York, November 2, 1956, 4:11 p.m.** [1]

TELEPHONE CALL TO AMB. LODGE

L. said he has the Br and Fr next door in a very emotional condition—they say there will be a bad impression at home if we are in a hurry to get them on the dock and drag in Russia. L. told them that was unjustified. The Sec. said they want the limelight off them and have the 3 of us go together. [2] The Sec. thinks it is a mockery for them to come in with bombs falling over Egypt and denounce the SU for perhaps doing something that is not quite as bad. L. agrees. The Sec. wants no part of it. L. is glad to hear that. The Sec. said no res this p.m.—discuss the situation and suggest it be useful to get a representative of the new Hungarian govt as quickly as possible and one is more or less en route and we should watch it carefully and have this fellow get here fast. L. does not think it possible for us to agree on a res. The Sec. said we don't have any hard info as to what is going on in Hungary—no doubt re Egypt. Keep it [3] on the agenda. L. will say we will be glad to attend the meeting—trying to get the rep here to get facts but impossible to take a stand on a res. The Sec. [4] said we may have to try to press for further action in the way of setting up a comm to deal with various aspects of it. GA resolutions tomorrow to work on different aspects—L. said then it means going ahead with Pearson's and the Sec's suggestions. The Sec. said the Pres. is anxious to have this done. L. said shall we ask for a meeting of the GA. The Sec. asked how much notice do you have to give and L. said 12 hours. Then he said any time because it is in session. The Sec. said to wait. The Canadians are working hard. Heeney is coming in. Then L. said Cordier said it may be necessary for a session in view of landings—they have a ticker they are taking place.

---

[1] Source: Eisenhower Library, Dulles Papers, General Telephone Conversations. Transcribed by Bernau.

[2] Reference is to Anglo-French efforts to obtain U.S. cooperation on the Hungary item in the U.N. Security Council.

[3] The Hungary item.

[4] At this point, the conversation evidently reverted to the topic of Suez.

472.   Telegram From the Embassy in Egypt to the Department
of State [1]

Cairo, November 2, 1956—3 p.m.

1279. New York for Secretary. Re Deptel 1368. [2] Delivered
President's message to Nasser this morning. He listened attentively
and took notes. Then asked I convey his appreciation to President
and also to say that, come what may, he and Egyptian people are
resolved to fight to end in order maintain their honor. He asked that
special mention be made of continuing heavy air attacks and report
they are now to be extended to radio stations as well as military
objectives.

Speaking then in a more personal vein he said he would adopt
technique of frankness which I had used in our last conversation
(Embtel 1240) [3] and admit that Egyptians had never really believed
us when we had indicated possibility that British and French might
embark on an independent policy which did not have our approval.
Now he recognized he had been wrong. Our action had been clear-
cut and doubt had been removed.

Turning to the military situation Nasser said he had been very
worried two days ago regarding Egyptian armor in Sinai which was
fighting without air cover. Furthermore whole aspect of hostilities
had been altered by Anglo-French intervention and it had therefore
been decided withdraw armor from Sinai as well as Egyptian forces
at Rafa, El Arish and El Agheila to west of canal in pursuance of
new plan of not defending canal but rather using canal as line of
defense. He had consequently been very relieved when large part of
armor got safely back across canal yesterday and some scattered
units arrived during night. However, small "suicide units" would
remain east of canal.

Regarding type of campaign he would fight, Nasser indicated it
would be a people's war; fighting town by town and house by
house. There would be no evacuations. For instance his own family
would remain in Cairo.

As to air activity, Nasser said his problem was shortage of pilots
and he had decided would be wasteful to commit them against
superior force. He preferred keep them in reserve for defense of
Egypt proper, i.e. Delta. As consequence Egyptian planes have been
kept on ground and heavy losses have been suffered.

---

[1] Source: Department of State, Central Files, 684A.86/11–256. Secret; Niact;
Limited Distribution. Received at 4:30 p.m. Repeated to USUN.
[2] Document 464.
[3] Document 451.

Queried on Egyptian force at Gaza, Nasser said had been instructed remain. [4] There had been some negotiations with Burns regarding situation and question of jurisdiction of Gaza strip had been raised. He now understood Israelis not pursuing idea of asserting jurisdiction, presumably for reason they did not wish assume responsibility for 300,000 refugees.

Nasser looked tired but he was calm, relaxed and friendly, and although I could well be mistaken, I for the first time gained impression of sincerity when he admitted he had been unduly suspicious our attitude.

Hare

---

[4] At dawn on November 2, Israeli forces began their march on Sharm al Sheikh and commenced operations to secure control of the Gaza Strip. By the following morning, Gaza had been secured. Sharm al Sheikh fell to Israeli forces on November 5. (Moshe Dayan, *Diary of the Sinai Campaign* (London: Weidenfeld and Nicolson, 1965), pp. 145, 153, 200–201)

---

473.   Memorandum of a Conversation, Department of State, Washington, November 2, 1956, 4:51 p.m. [1]

SUBJECT

General Assembly Action on Middle East Issue

PARTICIPANTS

The Secretary
Mr. Arnold Heeney, Canadian Ambassador
Mr. Saul Rae, Canadian Counselor
Mr. Phleger—L
Mr. Elbrick—EUR

Ambassador Heeney said that Foreign Minister Pearson was returning immediately from New York to Ottawa and that a Cabinet meeting was scheduled for tomorrow to consider the Middle East situation, with particular reference to the role that Canada might play in response to the suggestion made by the Secretary at the emergency General Assembly meeting. Prime Minister St. Laurent is expecting to address the nation by radio on Sunday when he will

---

[1] Source: Department of State, Central Files, 320.5774/11–256. Secret. Drafted by Elbrick. The time of the meeting is from Dulles' Appointment Book. (Princeton University Library, Dulles Papers)

explain the broad lines of the Canadian Government's thinking on this matter. The Canadian Government is at present thinking of another resolution to be presented to the General Assembly although St. Laurent will not refer to such a resolution in his broadcast.

The Secretary said that we had been studying this matter and had decided that it would be wise to introduce two separate resolutions in the Assembly, one concerning the Suez Canal and the other concerning the solution of the Palestine question. It seems essential to take action quickly before the Anglo-French military operations in Egypt precipitate matters to such an extent that a rash of resolutions calling for sanctions against the British and French are introduced.

Ambassador Heeney said that Pearson's objective is to help get the British and French "off the hook" but he wishes to be sure that the United States and the United Kingdom will agree to whatever proposal he may make. He said that Selwyn Lloyd's reaction to the general idea as presented to him by the Canadian High Commissioner in London seemed to be favorable. Pearson is thinking of providing for a United Nations police force, in the first instance, and a political settlement. He thought that both of these matters could be handled at a 24-nation conference, although his ideas about such a conference were still somewhat vague. His main objective is to restore as quickly as possible the US–UK alignment. With this in mind he thought a resolution might be prepared for circulation on Monday and for debate on Tuesday of next week.

The Secretary pointed out that there is a great danger that the situation may deteriorate rapidly. The United States controlled the situation in the General Assembly last night and if we had not done so the action taken by the General Assembly might have been much more severe in condemning the British and the French. We must direct our efforts to get people to think along constructive lines very quickly because if the Egyptian situation does deteriorate rapidly, the Russians may well move in and demand immediate sanctions. We hope to keep up the momentum generated last night in the General Assembly. We had always considered that a solution of the basic problems in the Middle East should be part of any program dealing with this question but we felt that the inclusion of such a program in the resolution presented to the General Assembly might have jeopardized its passage. We must now follow up on our action in the General Assembly. Ambassador Heeney said that he hoped that we could hold the matter in abeyance until Pearson could get some assurance from the British that his intervention has British approval. Pearson was thinking of a conference which would not only study the Suez problem but also the Arab-Israeli problem and the North African problem. The Secretary said he felt we should not mix the Canal problem with the others. We have already had a conference on the Suez Canal and we came very close to an agreement in the United Nations. The British and French felt, however, that something had to be done quickly to destroy Nasser and had not followed through on the proposal that they reach an agreement with the Egyptians because they felt that that would only serve to build up Nasser's prestige. Prior to that we had almost reached a solution and it seemed to us that it would only require a small committee to work out a solution now. We feel it would only be turning the clock back to have another conference on the Suez problem. If the Egyptian Army and Air Force are destroyed the British and French may feel they have done enough to prepare the way for a settlement of the Canal problem. If Egypt would support such an idea the Secretary felt there would be unanimous agreement in the General Assembly.

As for the Palestine problem, the question is whether the Arabs really want peace or not and they should be confronted with that problem. Certainly the only alternative is war since the situation cannot drag on much longer midway between war and peace. Our resolution on the Palestine question envisages the constitution of a committee which would take up all aspects of the problem. For example, we understand that the 300,000 Palestinian Arabs in the Gaza strip who are now cut off from Egypt will shortly be dying of starvation if aid does not reach them from outside.

The Ambassador referred again to the question of the constitution of a United Nations police force. The Secretary said that this raises many complications and that while such a force might ultimately be a good thing he did not think it possible to give effect to this idea in time to meet the present situation. The Ambassador said that he felt that General Burns' hand should be strengthened and the Secretary agreed, particularly since the Israeli had done nothing to facilitate his task so far.

The Secretary said that while we would welcome support from the Canadians on our two resolutions he wanted it clearly understood that we could not tie our hands in this matter and that we might possibly have to take urgent action tomorrow, depending on developments. We would, therefore, have to reserve complete liberty of action in sponsoring and presenting these resolutions.

474.   Editorial Note

On November 2, Egyptian Foreign Minister Fawzi informed Secretary-General Hammarskjöld that, except for one reservation, the Egyptian Government had accepted the framework, described by Hammarskjöld in his letter to Fawzi of October 24, for further exploring a possible basis of negotiation concerning the Suez Canal. On November 3, Hammarskjöld circulated to members of the Security Council a report entitled "Exchange of Correspondence between the Secretary-General and the Minister for Foreign Affairs of Egypt". Hammarskjöld's letter of October 24 is printed as Annex 1 to this report and Fawzi's letter of November 2 as Annex 2. (U.N. doc. S/3728) The text of this report was transmitted to the Department of State in telegram 470, November 2. (Department of State, Central Files, 974.7301/11–256) A summary of Hammarskjöld's letter of October 24 is in Document 374. The October 24 and November 2 letters are printed respectively in *United States Policy in the Middle East, September 1956–June 1957*, pages 127–130, 133.

Also on November 2, the Permanent Representative of Egypt delivered to the Secretary-General an aide-mémoire informing Hammarskjöld that the Egyptian Government accepted General Assembly Resolution 997 (ES–I), "on the condition of course that it could not implement the resolution in case attacking armies continue their aggression." (U.N. doc. A/3266) The text is printed in *United States Policy in the Middle East, September 1956–June 1957*, page 158.

---

475.   Letter From President Eisenhower to Swede Hazlett [1]

Washington, November 2, 1956.

DEAR SWEDE: [Here follows discussion of the Presidential election campaign and Republican politics; extracts are printed in Eisenhower, *Waging Peace*, page 85.]

The Mid East thing is a terrible mess. Ever since July twenty-sixth, when Nasser took over the Canal, I have argued for a

---

[1] Source: Eisenhower Library, Whitman File, Eisenhower Diaries. Personal. In *Mandate for Change* (p. 455), Eisenhower describes Captain Everett (Swede) Hazlett as a long-time friend and correspondent who had been raised in the same town as the President, attended the same high school, but had entered the U.S. Navy rather than the Army.

negotiated settlement. It does not seem to me that there is present in the case anything that justifies the action that Britain, France and Israel apparently concerted among themselves and have initiated.

The 1888 Treaty says nothing at all as to how the Canal is to be operated, although it did recognize the existence of the "Concession" dating, I believe, from 1868. I think, therefore, that no one could question the legal right of Egypt to nationalize the Canal *Company*. And what really became the apparent or legal bone of contention was, "Shall the world's users of the Canal, which is guaranteed as an international waterway in perpetuity, be privileged to use the Canal only on the sufferance of a single nation?" Even this, in my opinion, is not the real heart of the matter.

The real point is that Britain, France and Israel had come to believe—probably correctly—that Nasser was their worst enemy in the Mid East and that until he was removed or deflated, they would have no peace. I do not quarrel with the idea that there is justification for such fears, but I have insisted long and earnestly that you cannot resort to force in international relationships because of your fear of what might happen in the future. In short, I think the British and French seized upon a very poor vehicle to use in bringing Nasser to terms.

Of course, nothing in the region would be so difficult to solve except for the underlying cause of the unrest and dissension that exists there—that is, the Arab-Israel quarrel. This quarrel seems to have no limit either in intensity or in scope. Everybody in the Moslem and Jewish worlds is affected by it. It is so intense that the second any action is taken against one Arab state, by an outsider, all the other Arab and Moslem states seem to regard it as a Jewish plot and react violently. All this complicates the situation enormously.

As we began to uncover evidence that something was building up in Israel, we demanded pledges from Ben-Gurion that he would keep the peace. We realized that he might think he could take advantage of this country because of the approaching election and because of the importance that so many politicians in the past have attached to our Jewish vote. I gave strict orders to the State Department that they should inform Israel that we would handle our affairs exactly as though we didn't have a Jew in America. The welfare and best interests of our own country were to be the sole criteria on which we operated.

I think that France and Britain have made a terrible mistake. Because they had such a poor case, they have isolated themselves from the good opinion of the world and it will take them many years to recover. France was perfectly cold-blooded about the matter. She has a war on her hands in Algeria, and she was anxious to get someone else fighting the Arabs on her Eastern flank so she was ready to do anything to get England and Israel in that affair. But I think the other two countries have hurt themselves immeasurably and this is something of a sad blow because, quite naturally, Britain not only has been, but must be, our best friend in the world.

Only a star-gazer could tell how the whole thing is going to come out. But I can tell you one thing. The existence of this problem does not make sleeping any easier—not merely because of the things I recite above, but because of the opportunities that we have handed to the Russians. I don't know what the final action of the United Nations on this matter will be. We are struggling to get a simple cease-fire and, with it, compulsion on both sides to start negotiations regarding the Canal, withdrawal of troops, and even proper reparations. But the possibility that both sides will accept some compromise solution does not look very bright, and every day the hostilities continue the Soviets have an additional chance to embarrass the Western world beyond measure.

All these thoughts I communicated to Eden time and again. It was undoubtedly because of his knowledge of our bitter opposition to using force in the matter that when he finally decided to undertake the plan, he just went completely silent. Actually, the British had partially dispersed some of their concentrations in the Mid East and, while we knew the trouble was not over, we did think that, so far as Britain and France were concerned, there was some easing of the situation.

Just one more thought before I close this long letter. There is some reason to believe that the plan, when actually put into effect, was not well coordinated. It looks as if the Israeli mobilized pretty rapidly and apparently got ready to attack before the others were immediately ready to follow up, using the Israeli attack as an excuse to "protect" the Canal. In any event, British and French troops, so far as I know, have not yet landed in Egypt. Apparently there has been bombing of airfields, nothing else.

If you have any bright ideas for settling the dispute, I, of course, would be delighted to have them. From what I am told, Walter Lippman and the Alsops [2] have lots of ideas, but they are far from good—about what you would expect from your youngest grandchild.

Give my love to Ibby and the family.

As ever, [3]

---

[2] Syndicated columnists, Joseph and Stewart Alsop.
[3] Printed from an unsigned copy.

476.   Statement by Prime Minister Eden [1]

London, November 3, 1956.

The British and French Governments have given careful consideration to the resolution passed by the General Assembly on November 2. [2] They maintain their view that police action must be carried through urgently to stop the hostilities which are now threatening the Suez Canal, to prevent a resumption of those hostilities and to pave the way for a definitive settlement of the Arab-Israel war which threatens the legitimate interests of so many countries.

2. They would most willingly stop military action as soon as the following conditions could be satisfied.

(i) Both the Egyptian and the Israeli Governments agree to accept a United Nations force to keep the peace.

(ii) The United Nations decides to constitute and maintain such a force until an Arab-Israel peace settlement is reached and until satisfactory arrangements have been agreed in regard to the Suez Canal, both agreements to be guaranteed by the United Nations.

(iii) In the meantime until the U.N. force is constituted both combatants to accept forthwith limited detachments of Anglo-French troops to be stationed between the combatants.

---

[1] Source: Department of State, Central Files, 684A.86/11–356. A marginal notation on the source text indicates that the statement was handed to Murphy by Coulson at 10:15 a.m., November 3. Another notation indicates that "Eden made this statement in Commons at 7 a.m. E.S.T." The British Government quoted this statement in full in a letter to Hammarskjöld, dated November 3, which was circulated as U.N. doc. A/3269.

[2] For text, see Document 467.

477.   Memorandum of a Conference With the President, White House, Washington, November 3, 1956, 11:10 a.m. [1]

OTHERS PRESENT

> Secretary Hoover
> Mr. Phleger
> Mr. Rountree
> Mr. Hagerty
> Colonel Goodpaster

Mr. Hoover said he would like to review the situation, in view of the Secretary's incapacity. [2] The President said the first question was how the plan for the two committees (one for the Israeli-Arab question and one for the Suez question) was coming along. Mr. Hoover first commented on a message received from Eden [3] (which had been put on the tickers before it was received) and handed it to the President. It suggested having the UN take over the situation once French and British forces were installed in the Canal area, and we must be careful to avoid appearing in concert with them. (Eden said that he had furnished this proposal to Washington prior to his speech in Parliament.)

Mr. Hoover discussed the possibility of mob action arising in Cairo, as Army forces from the Sinai area reach the city. Mr. Rountree had talked by phone to Cairo and things seemed quiet at the moment.

The President said that the State Department spokesman yesterday, in announcing the suspension of shipments into the Middle East, had not handled the matter very well. [4] He could have mentioned that we have had requests from others in the area for shipments, and these too are being held up. He referred to an oral message from Nasser, [5] and suggested that we go back to Nasser cautioning him against mob action. Mr. Rountree said that we had sent back an oral message to Nasser already, and that he was very appreciative and said that for the first time he realized that the United States was not simply playing the British game in the area.

---

[1] Source: Eisenhower Library, Whitman File, Eisenhower Diaries. Secret. Drafted by Goodpaster. The time of the meeting is from the record of the President's Daily Appointments. (*Ibid.*)

[2] During the early morning of November 3, Dulles entered Walter Reed Hospital where he underwent surgery. He remained at Walter Reed until November 18.

[3] Reference is presumably to the text of Eden's statement delivered to the Department of State at 10:15 a.m. that morning, *supra.*

[4] For the transcript of Lincoln White's exchange with the press, see "Press and Radio News Conference, Friday, November 2, 1956," Department of State *Daily News Conferences*, 1956.

[5] Transmitted in telegram 1240, Document 451. The Department's oral response was transmitted in telegram 1368, Document 464.

Mr. Hoover said he is confronted with two problems at the moment. The first relates to the Hungarian resolution. The Security Council is meeting at 3 P.M. today to take up this matter. The Hungarians are asking for UN help, and the British and French want us to join them in a resolution on the matter. Mr. Phleger said Secretary Dulles did not want to join the British and French, and the President said that such a thought was almost absurd.

Mr. Hoover's second point related to the two Middle East resolutions. The situation has been complicated by Eden's statement. Mr. Phleger said there is now danger that Pearson, for Canada, will propose as the "sound action" of which he spoke in the UN meeting that a UN force simply take over from the British, French and Israeli forces in the Suez and Sinai areas. This is exactly what Eden is now suggesting in order to get himself off the hook.

The President said he understood the gist of the resolutions to be the formation of a Suez committee and an Israeli committee but said we must also indicate interim action, such as a neutral zone around Israel with depth of space contributed proportionately to [from] the areas of the countries concerned, and clearing the Canal and operating it.

Mr. Hagerty said we need an American position quickly, and need to announce it. Otherwise we will get ourselves mixed up in the proposals of others. The President agreed we should get in with our resolutions quickly, calling on all parties to open the Canal. The President said we should also bring out that there is no cause for the UK and the French to go into the Canal area—that the UN can put in the force and provide the select committees. It is important that we bring out that we are not waiting for or accepting the entry of the French and the British. In this way we would remove any need or basis for their landings. Mr. Phleger recalled that there should be a prompt call for the landings not to be made, and prompt withdrawal. (It was pointed out that the Egyptians would be happier to see a UN force enter the Canal area if the French and British were already there than if they were not.)

Mr. Hoover next referred to a message from Libya asking if the President's reply could be released and the President agreed that it could. [6]

The President asked whether it was thought he should get in touch with Eden, so as to keep the channel open, and there was

---

[6] The Embassy in Tripoli transmitted the message from Libyan Prime Minister Mustafa Ben Halim to President Eisenhower on November 1 in telegram 272. (Department of State, Central Files, 773.00/11–156) The Department of State transmitted President Eisenhower's response to Tripoli for delivery on November 2 in telegram 263. (Ibid., 780.00/11–256)

universal suggestion that he wait until after the resolutions had been submitted to the Secretary General.

G

Colonel, CE, US Army

---

478.   Memorandum of a Conversation, Department of State, Washington, November 3, 1956 [1]

SUBJECT

Visit of Group of Arab Ambassadors to Under Secretary

PARTICIPANTS

Dr. Moussa Al-Shabandar, Ambassador of Iraq
Dr. Victor A. Khouri, Ambassador of Lebanon
Sheikh Abdullah Al-Khayyal, Ambassador of Saudi Arabia
Dr. Mongi Slim, Ambassador of Tunisia
The Under Secretary
NEA—Mr. Rountree
O—Mr. Henderson
NE—Mr. Rockwell

The Under Secretary received the group of Arab Ambassadors, who had requested an appointment with him. He began by expressing his regret that the Secretary himself was not there. He had just been operated upon for what had been diagnosed as acute appendicitis and was resting as comfortably as could be expected under the circumstances.

The Lebanese Ambassador expressed the sympathy of the group for the Secretary in his illness. He added the deep thanks of the Arab World for the attitude of the United States Government in the current crisis. This, he said, was based on principles accepted by all peace-loving nations, as revealed by the overwhelming November 2 GA vote in favor of the United States resolution. Dr. Khouri added that if nations did not abide by the principles of the UN Charter, there was no hope for a better world. He also wished on behalf of the group to thank the President for the American position. Now that the GA resolution had been adopted, said Dr. Khouri, what steps did the United States Government contemplate taking next?

---

[1] Source: Department of State, Central Files, 601.8611/11–356. Secret. Drafted by Rockwell on November 5.

Mr. Hoover began by expressing appreciation for what the Lebanese Ambassador had said about the United States position. The United States believed in acting according to principle, although sometimes this was very difficult. The Ambassadors were aware of the special problems facing the United States in connection with the current crisis. The United States was at present devoting its principal efforts to bringing about a cessation of hostilities. At the same time, however, the United States was thinking of steps to resolve the basic problems which had brought the hostilities on. This afternoon the White House was announcing that the United States would introduce two new resolutions in the UN.[2] These had been fully discussed with the Secretary prior to his illness. The Under Secretary asked Mr. Rountree to describe the two resolutions.

Mr. Rountree said that these resolutions were the natural outcome of the GA resolution itself. We realize that this November 2 resolution did not embody a final solution of the problem. It was designed to establish an atmosphere of peace in which the basic problems could be dealt with. Of these there were two principal ones—to discover a new approach to the Arab-Israel problem, and a new approach to the Suez problem. The resolutions would show what mechanics we believed should be instituted to handle these problems. Once the basic November 2 resolution was adhered to, we had to get busy in resolving the basic issues which led to the outbreak of hostilities. The Lebanese Ambassador asked if Mr. Rountree meant that the United States envisaged a return to the status quo as the first necessary step. Mr. Rountree replied in the affirmative. Mr. Hoover commented that we should treat the basic disease in the area, not just the symptoms.

The Iraqi Ambassador asked what would happen if the parties to the hostilities did not obey the November 2 resolution. He said the Arab countries could not wait indefinitely. The whole Arab world was boiling. The Under Secretary replied that we did not know ourselves what was going to happen. We did not know whether British and French troops would actually invade Egypt. We were living minute by minute, and it was difficult to foresee the future. We did not know what the future plans of the French and the British and the Israelis were.

The Lebanese Ambassador repeated the question about what the United States would do if the November 2 resolution were not implemented. The Under Secretary said that we could not see all the way down that road now. Only events could tell. One thing was

---

[2] The statement is printed in Department of State *Bulletin*, November 12, 1956, p. 749.

certain—the decision rested with the UN. The United States was not going to enter the conflict unilaterally.

Mr. Henderson asked if the Arab Ambassadors had any suggestions as to what the United States should do. The Iraqi Ambassador said that the Arab States were not strong enough to stop the invasion, but that the UN could apply diplomatic and economic sanctions. There was danger of revolutions all over the Arab world. The Arab Governments were now restraining their populations, giving the United States time to bring about a just solution. If nothing was done, the Arab Governments would be in a terrible position. The United States was the world leader for peace, having now removed all possible claim by the USSR to that title. The United States position was never stronger. The Arabs wanted stronger United States action through the UN. They were ready to work with the United States and were waiting for the United States to follow up its first step.

The Lebanese Ambassador commented that the United States had saved the honor of the UN, but now must take stronger steps. Was there any tendency to strengthen the stated United States position against aggression? Mr. Hoover said that there were three ways to solve this problem—military, economic and moral. The moral way through the UN was the overriding one. The United States did not think that any country could long ignore the moral force of the overwhelming GA majority.

Mr. Rountree commented that in the procedure so far followed there had been avoided a situation in which it would be progressively more difficult for this moral force to be effective. Should the hostilities be enlarged, it would be much harder to apply moral pressures. All nations should refrain from expanding the conflict. The Under Secretary said that great self-restraint—especially by nations in the position of the Arab States—was necessary. He believed that the self-restraint that they were now exercising added to the moral pressure building up against the British, French and Israelis. The Lebanese Ambassador commented that restraint could come to an end if nothing happened.

Mr. Henderson stated that both in the UK and France, but especially in the UK, there were strong forces condemning the hostilities as much as the United States did. Public opinion in these countries was pressing increasingly hard for a halt in the hostilities. This public opinion would be strengthened by the new resolutions being tabled by the United States, since it would become apparent that progress was planned away from the previous sterile status quo. Both the Lebanese and Iraqi Ambassadors replied that they could not depend upon the slow process of public opinion.

Mr. Hoover said that we must keep moving through the UN so as not to lose momentum. Mr. Henderson expressed the hope that the Arab Governments would be successful in restraining their populations. The situation could become ten times worse if any additional NE countries became involved. The Iraqi Ambassador speculated that the Israelis would welcome such a development, so that they could grab the rest of Palestine. Mr. Henderson said that while he did not know what the Israeli Government might have in mind, no doubt the entry of additional Arab States in the hostilities would give Israeli extremists a pretext for seizing more territory. Israel could cause great damage to any Arab country which might intervene, and might overrun parts of the Arab world. The Under Secretary commented that the restraint so far exhibited by the Arabs had put Israel in a bad position, from the point of view of world opinion, with regard to the possibility of unprovoked aggression by Israel against other neighboring countries.

The Lebanese Ambassador called for strong pressure by the United States on the UK and France. Mr. Hoover said that the United States initiative in the UN and the profound difference on this problem with our two oldest allies revealed the pressure we had already put on the UK and France. Mr. Henderson added that if the United States were to apply military sanctions against the French and the British, an extremely explosive situation would be created. The world structure as it now existed might well be destroyed. He was sure the Ambassadors could appreciate this.

After thanking the Under Secretary for receiving them, the Arab Ambassadors took their leave. Before they left it was agreed that if they should be questioned regarding the meeting by the press they would say that they had come to express their deep concern over the NE crisis and to review developments with the Department of State.

479.   **Memorandum of a Conversation, Department of State, Washington, November 3, 1956, 6:15 p.m.** [1]

SUBJECT

General Assembly Consideration of the Middle East Situation

PARTICIPANTS

Mr. Heeney, Canadian Ambassador
Mr. Gray, Canadian Embassy
Mr. Murphy, G
Mr. Phleger, L
Mr. Elbrick, EUR
Mr. Bennett, G

Ambassador Heeney came in to present Canadian thinking regarding the introduction of a resolution on the Middle East crisis at tonight's special session of the General Assembly. He commented that the declaration made by Prime Minister Eden this morning could be perhaps described as a qualified acceptance for the Assembly's call for a cease-fire. At least it was not a flat "no" to the Assembly call. Canadian Foreign Minister Pearson did not think that Canada and the United States could support the British declaration as a solution, because such support would be sure to be considered to be collusion of the members of the UN. He felt, however, if some other resolution which included a concept of police action, if it could get sufficient support from the Afro-Asian group, would be all to the good. The Canadians are thinking of a resolution which would provide for the immediate appointment of a committee of five members to report within forty-eight hours on the composition of a UN police force to take over the situation at the Suez. Prior soundings would have to be taken, of course, and the resolution would only be adopted if there were an understanding with the British and French that their troop landings would be held up pending the committee's report. He suggested India, Brazil, Yugoslavia, and Sweden as four members for the committee. The fifth member might be Canada, if that were desired, or the United States, if it were willing; or some other power, such as Belgium or The Netherlands.

Mr. Murphy agreed on the importance of having a prior understanding with the British and French but inquired whether Egypt would also accept. Ambassador Heeney replied that he frankly did not know; but that Egypt was, in his opinion, already badly beaten up and might be presumed ready to accept such a solution. He

[1] Source: Department of State, Central Files, 320.5774/11–356. Confidential. Drafted by Bennett on November 4.

realized the value of exploring the matter with Egypt but wondered if there were time in view of the growing pressure at the Assembly by the Afro-Asians and others for a very strong condemnation of our oldest allies.

Mr. Phleger suggested that there should be added to the language of the resolution a statement to indicate that any measures proposed by the committee would be taken only with the consent of the parties concerned, i.e. Egypt, the United Kingdom, and France. Otherwise, without Egypt's approval it would just be a question of substituting the UN for the United Kingdom and France. From the Egyptian national point of view, that would be no less an aggression if it did not have Egypt's consent. He pointed out that what we want to arrange is a committee which will be able to achieve a cease-fire under UN auspices. Mr. Phleger suggested that for tactical reasons in getting the resolution adopted by the Assembly it would be better not to emphasize the police action concept. Ambassador Heeney then emphasized that the Canadian desire is to obtain a UN mechanism which will "hold the ring" as regards the Suez problem, and will prevent further deterioration in the situation. Such a step will be helpful in holding off the pressure building up for a strong condemnation of the UK and France, an action which would raise many problems for the United States as well as Canada.

Mr. Elbrick raised the question as to whether the UK and France would support such a resolution. Mr. Phleger thought they would, so long as the resolution made it clear that their consent was being requested. Mr. Murphy brought out that the type of resolution being discussed would fit in very well with the British declaration this morning.

Ambassador Heeney said that time was of the essence and that Foreign Minister Pearson was in New York with "pencil in the air." He will be having urgent conversations with other delegations to line up support. There was general agreement that India's support was fundamental, even though it might be hard to persuade the Indians to come along. Ambassador Heeney added that there was also the problem of arranging the landings to be held up, and Mr. Murphy commented that it would seem to him that a decision between landing with casualties or a twenty-four hour delay of troop action should be an easy one to make. Ambassador Heeney said that the Canadians have done nothing on the resolution with Paris; and there was general agreement that this was wise, if the British could be persuaded to come along and the French to follow.

480.   Memorandum of a Conversation, Department of State, Washington, November 3, 1956, 6:50 p.m. [1]

SUBJECT

Consideration of the Middle East and Hungarian Situations by the United Nations General Assembly

PARTICIPANTS

Ambassador Alphand, French Embassy
Minister Lucet, French Embassy
Mr. Murphy, G
Mr. Elbrick, EUR
Mr. Phillips, IO
Mr. Bennett, G

In considering the suggestion for a United Nations force to take over responsibilities in the Suez Canal, Ambassador Alphand expressed the opinion that his government would prefer to join in a proposal which would call for an international force in which could be incorporated the British and French troops now in the Suez area, similar to the inclusion of United States forces in Korea in the United Nations operation there. In response to a question from Mr. Murphy, the Ambassador acknowledged that Egyptian approval would be required for the entry of such an international force onto Egyptian territory, for otherwise the United Nations force would merely be replacing British and French troops.

Ambassador Alphand stated that he had been instructed to make clear to the Secretary-General of the UN that Egypt had voluntarily sunk obstructions in the Suez Canal. This had been a calculated action by Egypt and was not the result of British and French bombing as alleged by the Egyptians. He was instructed to point out to the Secretary-General that the Egyptian action constituted a violation of the 1888 Canal Convention.

[Here follows discussion of the situation in Hungary.]

Discussion then reverted to the Middle East. Mr. Phillips reviewed the two U.S. resolutions introduced by Ambassador Lodge. Ambassador Alphand said that he was certain that our resolution regarding the establishment of a UN commission would not be acceptable to his government. He had no instructions, but the French had always opposed this kind of committee activity. Mr. Phillips said that our aim had been to avoid outright condemnation of the British and French, and Mr. Murphy stressed the strong feeling in the Assembly and the probability of Asian-African resolutions con-

---

[1] Source: Department of State, Central Files, 320.5774/11–356. Confidential. Drafted by Bennett.

demning the British and French. Ambassador Alphand said that he had heard that India was trying to exercise moderation in that group. He commented that the U.S. resolution does not take into account the UK-French declaration made by Prime Minister Eden this morning.

Mr. Murphy replied that our resolution is by no means final. It is open to amendment. He understood that Canada is working on a resolution. He pointed out to Ambassador Alphand that the Assembly is a large body. The U.S. wishes to be in a position to still the probable clamor for sanctions against the British and French. We must use our ingenuity in order to induce moderation in that body, which neither we nor the French can control absolutely.

In response to an inquiry from Mr. Murphy, the Ambassador said that he had no information regarding the situation in Egypt beyond the fact that Egypt had blocked the Canal by sinking vessels and other equipment in the waterway.

---

481.   Memorandum for the Record by the Representative at the United Nations (Lodge), November 3, 1956 [1]

I telephoned the President at 7:00 p.m. He said that the two resolutions which we were sponsoring seemed to him the next step and provided a very definite method by which problems might be settled. They sought to attack the basic causes. He said it would be "a great tragedy" if the British and French got ashore.

The President is very anxious that someone get something to stall this landing operation off. The Canadians have a draft resolution which sets up a committee of 5.

The President, in order to stall this off and allow the negotiations to go on, wants to get the Secretary-General into the act, who could act more freely than a committee of 5 would.

Conditions:

That the Egyptians would be agreeable;

---

[1] Source: Department of State, USUN Files. Top Secret. Drafted by Lodge. The source text indicates that Lodge telephoned the contents of this memorandum to Hoover and Phleger at the Department of State.

That Lloyd and Eden will accept the proposal; and I am to see the Secretary-General, sell it to him, and then sell it to Pearson when he arrives. [2]

---

[2] Lester Pearson recalled in his memoirs that in response to comments which Secretary Dulles had made to Ambassador Heeney on November 2 (see Document 411) the Canadian Government decided to propose that the U.N. General Assembly create a Committee of Five to consider and report within 48 hours on the immediate establishment of an international "intervention force". The following day in New York, however, Lodge presented Pearson with a draft resolution prepared by the State Department, which Lodge felt would be acceptable to the Egyptians and consequently to the Afro-Asian group. Noting that the U.S. draft was simpler than the Canadian one, Pearson decided to adopt it with a few revisions and later that day presented the revised version to the General Assembly as a Canadian draft resolution. (*Mike, The Memoirs of the Right Honourable Lester B. Pearson*, Vol. II (New York: Quadrangle, 1973), pp. 249–251) No copy of the draft resolution which Lodge showed to Pearson has been found in Department of State files. The text of the Canadian draft resolution which provided for the involvement of the U.N. Secretary-General, is printed in Document 485.

---

482. Memorandum of a Telephone Conversation Between Secretary-General Hammarskjöld and the Deputy Representative at the United Nations Security Council (Barco), New York, November 3, 1956 [1]

SUBJECT

Suez—UN Intl Force in Egypt

At Mr. Lodge's request, I telephoned the SYG UN to tell him of the new developments. I told him we understood that Eden had already made a proposal for UN forces to take over in the Canal Zone. I said we had reason to believe that a resolution would be introduced to endorse this and which would set up something to carry it out. I said we felt that, for us to be a party to this, would appear that we were *particeps criminis* to the U.K.-French plan from the beginning, and that we could not believe that the UN or the Egyptians would agree to this kind of a solution forced upon them in this way.

Therefore, we would like to head this off by introducing our own resolution for which we would like to have priority. However I

---

[1] Source: Department of State, USUN Files, Unnumbered File, Suez Canal. Secret. Drafted by Barco. The source text does not indicate at what time the conversation took place; it may have been earlier in the day before the 7 p.m. Eisenhower–Lodge conversation, *supra*.

explained that I could not give him the text of our resolution as it was still being worked on in the Department, but it would not be the same type of resolution the British had in mind. I told Mr. Hammarskjold I would get our proposed resolution to him just as soon as it was possible—and he assured me that our resolution would have priority.

---

483.   Telegram From the Department of State to the Embassy in France [1]

Washington, November 3, 1956—7:41 p.m.

1684. Reference London's 2456 to Dept. [2] In response to press inquiries, Department spokesman said this afternoon: "The American Embassy in London has reminded the British Ministry of Defense of the provisions of the Mutual Defense Assistance agreement between the two countries with respect to military equipment provided by the United States to Great Britain under this agreement. It was pointed out that under these agreements such equipment is to be used only for the defense of the North Atlantic Treaty area. The importance of strict observance of these provisions was emphasized under the present circumstances. Similar representations are being made to the French Government. Other governments in the Middle Eastern area have been reminded that military equipment furnished by the US is for defensive purposes only."

---

[1] Source: Department of State, Central Files, 741.5–MSP/11–256. Confidential; Niact. Drafted by Jones (EUR/WE) and approved by Elbrick who signed for Dulles. Repeated Niact to London.

[2] Telegram 2465, November 2, reported that the Embassy had reminded the British Defense Ministry of provisions in the U.S. military assistance agreement with the United Kingdom to the effect that aircraft delivered to the British Government would be used only for defense of the NATO area and of the importance of strict observance of these provisions in connection with the Suez operation. (*Ibid.*)

French Minister was called in today and informed officially in above sense. He replied that he would promptly inform his government.[3]

Dulles

---

[3] Telegram 456 to Tel Aviv, November 3, instructed the Embassy to remind the Israeli Government as soon as possible that military supplies purchased under Mutual Security legislation should be used for purposes of internal security and legitimate self-defense only. (*Ibid.*, 784A.5–MSP/11–356) Telegram 501 from Tel Aviv, November 5, reported that the warning had been conveyed to an official of the Foreign Ministry who promised to relay it to Foreign Minister Meir. (*Idid.*, 784A.5–MSP/11–556)

---

484. Memorandum of a Telephone Conversation Between the Under Secretary of State (Hoover) in Washington and the Deputy Representative at the United Nations Security Council (Barco) in New York, November 3, 1956, 10:45 p.m.[1]

Mr. Hoover said that he thought we ought to press for the Canadian Resolution including, if it seemed right, a vote tonight. He indicated that we would seek to get support down here and subsequently reported, after Rountree had made a call to Ambassador Brosio,[2] that Brosio would get the Italians behind the effort right away.

In answer to an inquiry from Barco whether we should play a leading role in support of the Canadian Resolution, Mr. Hoover said yes.

Mr. Barco indicated that our two resolutions might have to be put a little aside if we were to get maximum effort on the Canadian Resolution. This seemed quite all right.

Mr. Barco discussed the Indian Resolution and particularly the passage calling for a report by SYG within 12 hours on the compliance with the GA cease fire. Although this tended to become confused with the Canadian Resolution, Lodge, according to Barco, thought they might be brought together, especially if the 12-hour compliance clause could be removed from the Indian Resolution and we might get the support of the backers of the Indian Resolution

---

[1] Source: Department of State, Central Files, 320/11–356. Drafted by Fisher Howe.

[2] Manlio Brosio, Italian Ambassador in the United States.

behind the Canadian. Mr. Hoover, after consultation with Mr. Rountree, agreed that if the two could be made inconsistent [*consistent*] and therefore complimentary [*complementary?*] this might be very useful.

Mr. Barco indicated that the SYG was all for the Canadian Resolution and will be pushing it.

Fisher Howe [3]

---

[3] Printed from a copy that bears this typed signature.

---

485.   Editorial Note

At the request of the Egyptian Government, the first emergency session of the General Assembly reconvened at 8 p.m. on November 3. Earlier that day the United States Delegation had circulated two draft resolutions as United Nations documents A/3272 and A/3273. Their texts read as follows:

Document A/3272

The General Assembly,

Recalling its resolution 194 (III) of 11 December 1948, by which the Assembly established the Palestine Conciliation Commission and laid down the functions of that Commission,

Noting that a final settlement of the questions outstanding between the Governments and authorities concerned with the problem of Palestine has not yet been achieved despite the efforts of the Palestine Conciliation Commission,

Noting the efforts of the Secretary-General undertaken under the Security Council resolutions of 4 April 1956 (S/3575) and 4 June 1956 (S/3605),

Recalling that the General Assembly, on 2 November 1956, adopted a resolution which noted the disregard on many occasions by parties to the Arab-Israel armistice agreements of 1949 of the terms of such agreements, and, inter alia, urged the parties to the armistice agreements promptly to withdraw all forces behind the armistice lines, to desist from raids across the armistice lines into neighbouring territory, and to observe scrupulously the provisions of the armistice agreements,

1. *Holds* that, in order to secure a just and lasting peace, it is necessary to remove the underlying causes of tension in the area and to achieve a final settlement between the parties to the general armistice agreements;

2. *Expresses its appreciation* to the Palestine Conciliation Commission, and discharges that Commission from the performance of further tasks;

3. *Establishes* a committee composed of —, —, —, —, —,

(a) To prepare recommendations, after consultation with the parties to the general armistice agreements of 1949, regarding a settlement of the major problems outstanding between the Arab States and Israel, with a view to establishing conditions of permanent peace and stability in the area;

(b) To submit its recommendations to the parties concerned and to the General Assembly, or to the Security Council as appropriate, and to submit reports to the General Assembly on the status of its assigned task;

4. *Requests* the Secretary-General, in cooperation with the committee, to continue his good offices with the parties;

5. *Requests* the Members of the United Nations to render all assistance to the Secretary-General and to the committee;

6. *Commends* the Secretary-General, the Chief of Staff and the members of the United Nations Truce Supervision Organization for their efforts to enforce the general armistice agreements, and urges the parties directly concerned to cooperate fully with the Chief of Staff and members of the Truce Supervision Organization in carrying out the tasks assigned or which may be assigned to them by the Security Council; and

7. *Urges* the parties directly concerned, as a matter of humanity, to lend all possible assistance in caring for and assuring the safety of the Arab refugees under the continuing care of the United Nations Relief and Works Agency for Palestine Refugees in the Near East, and recommends that Members consider and furnish what additional assistance may be required.

Document A/3273

The General Assembly,

Noting that the Security Council, on 13 October 1956, adopted the following resolution (S/3675):

"*The Security Council,*

"*Noting* the declarations made before it and the accounts of the development of the exploratory conversations on the Suez question given by the Secretary-General of the United Nations and the Foreign Ministers of Egypt, France and the United Kingdom,

"Agrees that any settlement of the Suez question should meet the following requirements:

"(1) There should be free and open transit through the Canal without discrimination, overt or covert—this covers both political and technical aspects;
"(2) The sovereignty of Egypt should be respected;
"(3) The operation of the Canal should be insulated from the politics of any country;
"(4) The manner of fixing tolls and charges should be decided by agreement between Egypt and the users;
"(5) A fair proportion of the dues should be allotted to development;
"(6) In case of disputes, unresolved affairs between the Suez Canal Company and the Egyptian Government should be settled by arbitration with suitable terms of reference and suitable provisions for the payment of sums founds to be due",

Noting the position taken by the Government of Egypt in document S/3728,

Recalling that the General Assembly, on 2 November 1956, adopted a resolution which, inter alia, noted that traffic through the Suez Canal was interrupted with serious prejudice to many nations, urged the parties to the hostilities in Egypt to agree to an immediate cease-fire and, as part thereof, to halt the movement of military forces into the area and urged that, upon the cease-fire being effected, steps be taken to reopen the Suez Canal and restore freedom of navigation,

Recognizing that the situation calls for a permanent solution consistent with the principles of justice and international law, the sovereignty of Egypt, and the rights of international users of the Suez Canal as guaranteed by the Convention of 1888,

1. *Establishes* a committee composed of —, —, and — to assume responsibility for:

(a) The taking of measures for the immediate reopening of the Suez Canal as a secure international waterway;
(b) The preparation of a plan, in consultation with Egypt, France and the United Kingdom, for operation and maintenance of the Suez Canal and freedom of passage through it in accordance with the Convention of 1888, and with the six requirements unanimously agreed to by the Security Council, with the concurrence of Egypt, on 13 October 1956;
(c) The adoption and putting into effect of such a plan;

2. *Requests* the committee to report to the General Assembly and to the Security Council as appropriate, and invites the committee to make recommendations as it deems useful to promote a just and permanent settlement of the Suez problem, consistent with the Purposes and Principles of the United Nations;

3. *Requests* the Members of the United Nations to render all appropriate assistance to the committee.

During the 563d meeting which began at 8 p.m. on November 3, two additional draft resolutions pertaining to the Middle East were tabled: a 19-power draft resolution sponsored by the Governments of Afghanistan, Burma, Ceylon, Ethiopia, India, Indonesia, Iran, Iraq, Jordan, Lebanon, Liberia, Libya, Nepal, Pakistan, Philippines, Saudi Arabia, Syria, Thailand and Yemen (U.N. doc. A/3275), and a draft resolution sponsored by the Government of Canada (U.N. doc. A/3276). Their texts read as follows:

Document A/3275 (Resolution 999 (ES–I))

The General Assembly,

Noting with regret that not all the parties concerned have yet agreed to comply with the provisions of its resolution of 2 November 1956,

Noting the special priority given in the resolution to an immediate cease-fire and as part thereof to the halting of the movement of military forces and arms into the area,

Noting further that the resolution urged the parties to the armistice agreements promptly to withdraw all forces behind the armistice lines, to desist from raids across the armistice lines into neighbouring territory, and to observe scrupulously the provisions of the armistice agreements,

1. *Reaffirms* its resolution of 2 November 1956 and once again calls upon the parties immediately to comply with the provisions of the said resolution;

2. *Authorizes* the Secretary-General immediately to arrange with the parties concerned for the implementation of the cease-fire and the halting of the movement of military forces and arms into the area and requests him to report compliance forthwith and, in any case, not later than twelve hours from the time of adoption of the present resolution;

3. *Requests* the Secretary-General, with the assistance of the Chief of Staff and the members of the United Nations Truce Supervision Organization, to obtain compliance of the withdrawal of all forces behind the armistice lines;

4. *Decides* to meet again immediately on receipt of the Secretary-General's report referred to in operative paragraph 2 of the present resolution.

Document A/3276 (Resolution 998 (ES–I))

The General Assembly,

Bearing in mind the urgent necessity of facilitating compliance with resolution 997 (ES–I) adopted by the General Assembly on 2 November 1956,

Requests, as a matter of priority, the Secretary-General to submit to it within forty-eight hours a plan for the setting up, with the consent of the nations concerned, of an emergency international United Nations Force to secure and supervise the cessation of hostilities in accordance with the terms of the aforementioned resolution.

Following the tabling of these resolutions, Lodge informed the Assembly that the United States "likes the Canadian draft resolution very much". Lodge then pointed out that the two U.S. draft resolutions dealt with long-range questions, which would require further study, and therefore the United States would not push them to a vote that evening. Instead, Lodge expressed his delegation's hope that the Canadian draft resolution be given priority and be acted upon promptly that evening. After additional discussion, the General Assembly adopted the Canadian draft resolution as Resolution 998 (ES–I) by a vote of 57 in favor, 0 opposed, and 19 abstentions, and the 19-power draft resolution as Resolution 999 (ES–I) by a vote of 59 in favor (including the United States), 5 opposed, and 12 abstentions. The meeting finally adjourned after 3 a.m. on November 4. (U.N. doc. A/PV.563) For text of Lodge's remarks during the 563d meeting, see Department of State *Bulletin*, November 19, 1956, pages 787–790.

---

486.   Telegram From the Embassy in Egypt to the Department of State [1]

Cairo, November 3, 1956—5 p.m.

1302. In conversation which followed . . . inquiry of Heikel as to, "What can be done to stop this thing?" Heikel said government willing "do anything" and cited following concessions which he

---

[1] Source: Department of State, Central Files, 684A.86/11–356. Secret; Niact; Limited Distribution. Received at 9:35 p.m.

thought (taking care point out speaking only for himself) government might make to end hostilities.

1. UN police force to guarantee Arab-Israeli border.

2. Establishment of UN body with full authority investigate and enforce solution to all outstanding problems in area, specifically including Palestine problem and charges that Egypt has been interfering with legitimate interests of Western Powers in the area.

3. US or UN forces (excluding British, French, Israeli or Egyptian) to occupy key points canal zone area to guarantee free transit canal (until provision 2 above implemented or US or UN wishes withdraw forces).

4. Egypt to agree abide by arms embargo applied freely all states in area (specifically GOE would stop receiving Soviet arms).

Comment: While, of course, Heikel has no official status, he is close confidant of Nasser and not unlikely in present deteriorating situation proposals along this line would be acceptable to Nasser (if not actually inspired by him), providing as they do for withdrawal Israeli forces and no occupation by British or French forces. More questionable would be his ability or willingness some future date make positive as distinct from passive attitude towards support UN settlement Palestine question as outlined point 2. Perhaps most significant feature this conversation not specific points but indication regime may be dispirited to point it prepared make substantial concessions.

Hare

---

487. Telegram From the Mission at the United Nations to the Department of State [1]

New York, November 3, 1956—11 p.m.

Delga 2. Re Suez. Guiringaud (France) showed me a telegram from Joxe, Director General of Foreign Office, the purport of which is as follows:

"The US res on Suez takes a solution to the Canal problem entirely out of our hands.

1. France is not a part of the proposed committee.

---

[1] Source: Department of State, Central Files, 974.7301/11–356. Secret; Priority; Limited Distribution. Received at 11:24 p.m.

2. France is placed on the same footing as Egypt, which is the guilty party.

3. Committee receives exorbitant powers notably as regards the reopening of the Canal.

4. International administration is for all practical purposes put to one side.["]

This is very serious for Franco-American relations, particularly at a time when the US is so much less demanding regarding the Hungary item than it is concerning situation in Middle East. Guiringaud urged me not to let this matter come to a vote."

Recommended action: that Dillon be instructed to explain to Joxe that he very seriously misunderstands res and that it does not contain the dangers to France which he evidently thinks that it does.

Lodge

---

488.   Telegram From the Embassy in Israel to the Department of State [1]

Tel Aviv, November 3/4, 1956—midnight.

485. I saw Foreign Minister Meir rather urgent request in Tel Aviv 9:15 tonight. She made following points:

1. Syria informed world it had sent note to United States [2] saying Syria about to discharge its responsibilities under Egyptian-Jordan-Syrian mutual defense pact. Accordingly Syria moving troops into Jordan. Since terms of Syria's note made public she thought it incumbent on United States to state its reaction publicly and disap-

---

[1] Source: Department of State, Central Files, 684A.86/11–356. Confidential; Niact. Received at 11:15 p.m., November 3. Repeated Niact to Damascus, Baghdad, Cairo, Beirut, Amman, Jerusalem, London, Rome, Paris, and USUN.

[2] On November 2, the Chargé of the Syrian Embassy in Washington, Dr. Mamun Hamui, handed to Deputy Assistant Secretary J. Lampton Berry a note, dated November 2, from the Syrian Government which reads as follows: "The Syrian Government has decided to implement, as of this moment, the joint Egyptian-Syrian defense pact. For this reason, the Syrian Armed Forces are put under the Egyptian-Syrian Joint Command, the Chief Commander of which is General Abdel Hakim Amer, Commander in Chief of the Egyptian Armed Forces. The Syrian Armed Forces are now taking orders from this Commander-in-Chief.

"Syria is now standing side by side with Egypt. Her full force, and all her resources are, from this moment on, devoted to their common cause."

Hamui told Berry that the note was an indication of action which the Government of Syria planned to take and was in Hamui's view "casus foederis". (Memorandum of conversation by Wilkins, November 2; *ibid.*, 674.831/11–256)

pointed United States had not promptly done so. Furthermore Iraqi troops also moving into Jordan.

2. She said Israel will not attack Jordan unless attacked. I then asked her point blank if in her view entry of Syrian and/or Iraqi troops into Jordan would be regarded technically as attack. I [She] did not give categorical reply but directed general comment toward implied threat contained in entry of troops into Jordan. She said she would be "very happy" if attack on Israel not intended. Syrian note declaring intention to implement Arab tripartite agreement which by its terms constituted Israel's destruction has ominous appearance taken in conjunction with reported movement of Syrian troops into Jordan. It equivalent of declaration Syria going to attack Israel. USG as recipient of Syria's note ought to insist on being informed what Syria has in mind and should publicly express its reaction.

I pointed out both United States and United Kingdom reportedly urged Arab States not take any action that might be regarded by Israel as act of aggression but I had no information on USG reaction to reported message from Syria.

Meir said radio broadcasts reported General Assembly meeting tonight and it might be appropriate place for United States to make its views known.

Returning to subject of Israel's reaction to Syrian-Iraqi troop movements I told her all day I had seen IDF tanks in considerable numbers moving south and east to Jordan-Syrian frontier. She refused to be drawn but replied, "We have no intention and no desire of doing anything at all to involve ourselves in Jordan border but if anything happens there we shall react and oppose it with all our might".

Meir, who said Cabinet met on this question this afternoon and would meet again tomorrow obviously wishes early answer re United States reaction reported Syrian note. She told me to call her as soon as I received reply no matter what hour tonight I have it.

Lawson

489.   Report by the Joint Middle East Planning Committee to the Joint Chiefs of Staff [1]

JCS 1887/298   *Washington, November 3, 1956.*

ANALYSIS OF POSSIBLE SOVIET COURSES OF ACTION IN THE MIDDLE EAST

The Problem

1. To examine possible Soviet courses of action during the current Middle East crisis.

Facts Bearing on the Problem

2. Military operations against Egypt by Israel, France, and the United Kingdom have created a situation which the USSR may attempt to exploit.

3. To date Soviet reaction to the current situation has been confined to diplomatic activity, particularly within the United Nations and including the 23 August statement of Khrushchev that, "Egypt, if attacked, will not stand alone".

Discussion

4. For Discussion, see Enclosure.

Conclusions

5. The study contained in the Enclosure represents an appropriate analysis of the possible Soviet courses of action during the current Middle East crisis.

6. Based on the assumption that the USSR will not risk a general war at this time, it is considered unlikely that they will take any military action which will significantly affect developments in the current Middle East crisis.

---

[1] Source: JCS Records, CCS 381 EMMEA (11–19–47) Sec. 47 RB. Top Secret. A cover sheet indicates that the Joint Strategic Plans Group and the Joint Intelligence Group were consulted in the preparation of the report.

On November 6, the Joint Intelligence Committee, which had been reviewing the study, concluded that Soviet air forces could be quickly and effectively employed in the Middle East, and the Soviet Union would probably undertake limited indirect military intervention by means of volunteer air crews and aircraft. (JCS 1887/300, November 6; *ibid.*) On November 8, JCS 1887/298, JCS 1887/300, and an unidentified "Army flimsy" of November 4 were referred to the Joint Middle East Planning Committee commissioned to undertake on a continuing basis the estimate of Soviet capabilities and possible courses of action in the Middle East. JCS 1887/298 was withdrawn from consideration on August 6, 1957. (NH of JCS 1887/298; *ibid.*)

Recommendations

7. It is recommended that the Joint Chiefs of Staff note the above conclusions.

8. No recommendation is made as to the distribution of this paper to commanders of unified or specified commands.

Enclosure

DISCUSSION

Analysis of Possible Soviet Courses of Action in the Middle East

1. *Introduction*

a. This study examines possible Soviet courses of action in the Middle East crisis.

b. It covers the current Soviet objectives in the Middle East, the possible courses of action based thereon, and examines the probability of implementation of the various courses of action in each country of the Middle East.

c. No courses of action are included which from the Soviet viewpoint would result in general war; this on the assumption that avoidance of general war is basic Soviet strategy at this time.

2. *Soviet Objectives*

a. The broad and primary Soviet objective is to eliminate Western influence in the area and substitute therefor Soviet influence throughout the entire Middle East. This would logically lead to Soviet domination of the area with ultimate subversion of individual governments into Soviet puppets.

b. Based on this broad objective, more immediate objectives might be stated as:

(1) To disrupt the NATO and Baghdad Pact Organization.

(2) To prolong and expand the conflict within the Middle East without overtly advocating same.

(3) Without being identified with the action, to disrupt the flow of Middle East oil and thus weaken the West economically and militarily, while at the same time adversely affecting the financial position of various Middle East countries.

3. *General.* The courses of action open to the USSR which are listed below are sensitive to the element of time which is of key importance to the USSR. It will attempt to prevent the United Kingdom, French, Israeli forces from the quick liquidation of Nasser, gaining control of the Suez Canal and the stabilization of the military situation to the advantage of the three allies. The USSR will

attempt actions which will enable Nasser to continue military opposition for as long as possible.

4. *Courses of Action.* The following courses of action are open to the USSR:

a. Direct military intervention.
b. Indirect military intervention (volunteers).
c. Strategic movements of Bloc troops on the periphery of the Bloc.
d. Attempt to broaden the conflict within the Middle East.
e. Reaffirm support of Nasser to include guarantees to replace lost matériel and damaged facilities and installations.

5. *Direct Military Intervention.* The Soviets are capable of direct military intervention, with ground, naval and air forces in the Middle East area. In view of the element of time, sufficient forces to affect the initial course of hostilities could not be introduced. Most important, however, the Soviets almost certainly estimate that direct military intervention would incur unacceptable risks of general war. The possibility that Soviet submarines under the guise of Egyptian nationality will be used against UK-French shipping and naval units in the Mediterranean cannot be ruled out.

6. *Indirect Intervention.* The USSR can introduce "volunteer" ground and air elements. However, as in paragraph 4 above, time would preclude introduction of sufficient ground volunteers to affect immediately the course of hostilities. Furthermore, in the Soviet view the introduction of significant numbers of "volunteer" ground troops would be likely to incur unacceptable risk of general war. In the case of "volunteer" air crews, even the addition of relatively small numbers would significantly improve Middle East air capability, providing combat aircraft and air facilities are available. It is possible, therefore, that small numbers of combat aircraft and crews may be flown into Middle East from the Bloc.

7. *Strategic Movement of Bloc Forces on the Soviet Bloc Periphery.* Soviet forces may engage in this type of operation with the objective of engendering fear of general war, thus increasing pressures worldwide to force withdrawal of UK-French-Israeli forces from Egypt.

8. *Broaden the Conflict Within the Middle East.* By use of propaganda, agents, and local Communist parties the Soviets can cause extensive anti-Western rioting, sabotage, and general disorder throughout the area, particularly at Western oil installations. To direct and assist in such operations the Soviets could introduce small numbers of professional agents and saboteurs. The Soviets also could attempt to encourage or engineer coups in Syria and Jordan with the object of establishing governments willing to attack Israel in order to broaden hostilities. Such attempts are considered likely.

9. *Reaffirm Support for Egypt to Include Guarantees to Replace Lost Matériel and Restore Damaged Installations*. This is a likely course of action aimed at precluding a quick surrender to UK-French-Israeli forces and to gain time for public opinion worldwide to crystallize in Egypt's favor and to allow the machinery of the UN to work on the side of Egypt. Additionally, the Soviet Union will probably break relations with Israel and move for that country's expulsion from the UN. They may seek or take advantage of any opportunity to have themselves appointed by the UN to restore order in the Middle East.

10. *Analysis of Soviet Actions With Respect to Middle East Countries.*

a. *Egypt*—In view of the time element, sufficient forces to affect the course of hostilities could not be introduced. This coupled with the resultant risk of general war, leads to the conclusion that direct Soviet military intervention will not occur. An exception, however, may lie in the use of Soviet submarines under guise of Egyptian nationality against UK-French shipping and naval units. Indirect intervention through the use of "volunteer" air crews and aircraft is possible. However, such action is limited by:

(1) UK-French control of the air.
(2) Destruction of air facilities in Egypt.
(3) Extreme ranges involved.
(4) Possibility of overflight difficulties.

It is likely that the USSR will reaffirm support for Egypt to include offers to replace lost material and repair damaged installations. This action would be aimed at precluding a quick surrender and allow time for the UN machinery and the pressure of world opinion to work favorably for Egypt. It would also provide an entry for additional Soviet technicians and propaganda into Egypt following the present crisis.

b. *Syria*—The Soviets may introduce volunteers and additional Soviet equipment into Syria. However, such action with the exception of air units would have no effect on the immediate situation in view of the time element involved. Lack of indigenous air facilities precludes introduction of significant numbers of Soviet aircraft. Additionally, it is likely that the Soviets will attempt to encourage or engineer a coup with the object of establishing a government more willing to attack Israel and thus broaden and prolong the conflict. Also, it is likely that propaganda will be intensified, and sabotage encouraged against oil lines traversing Syria. Three pipelines, of the five from the Kirkuk field, which carry 500,000 barrels per day, pass through Syria. (Western Europe is using approximately 2,000,000 barrels per day from the Middle East area.)

c. *Jordan*—Introduction of volunteers into Jordan is less likely than into Syria. Propaganda is likely to be intensified, and sabotage of pipelines encouraged. Two of the five Kirkuk oil field pipelines pass through Jordan. In addition, the Dhahran pipeline, which carries 300,000 barrels per day, traverses Jordan. Soviet inspired attempts to dethrone King Hussein will probably be intensified with the objective of solidifying the pro-Egyptian forces in the country.

d. *Lebanon*—The Government of Lebanon is more oriented to the West than is that of either Syria or Jordan and hence, there is less likelihood of Soviet action within that country. Western installations as well as the two pipelines that pass through Syria, and the Dhahran pipeline (Tapline) might be subject to sabotage.

e. *Iraq*—Action within Iraq would probably be limited to extensive anti-Western propaganda aimed at disrupting the Baghdad Pact. It is possible, but not probable, that the oil pipelines emanating from Kirkuk would be sabotaged within Iraq.

f. *Iran*—It is estimated that no Soviet activity will occur in Iran other than intensified anti-Western propaganda aimed at disrupting the Baghdad Pact, inasmuch as movement of Soviet forces into Iran would probably precipitate general war.

g. *Saudi Arabia*—It is estimated that Soviet activity in Saudi Arabia will be limited to intensified anti-Western propaganda, and encouragement of sabotage of oil pipelines and facilities. It is highly unlikely the Saudis would agree to any Soviet proposals for assistance.

h. *General*—Soviet forces may engage in strategic movement on the Soviet Bloc periphery with the objective of engendering fear of general war. This would be calculated to increase worldwide pressures for withdrawal of UK-French-Israeli forces from Egypt.

11. *Summary.* The following appear to be the likely courses of Soviet action:

a. Intensify anti-Western propaganda in all Middle East nations.
b. Provide Soviet volunteers, technicians and equipment to Syria and Egypt.
c. Encourage sabotage of oil pipelines and facilities.
d. Instigate the establishment of governments in Syria and Jordan more willing to attack Israel.
e. Reaffirm support for Egypt to include offers to replace lost material and repair damaged facilities.
f. Conduct strategic movement of large Soviet forces on the Soviet Bloc periphery.
g. Move for the expulsion of Israel from the United Nations.
h. Seek or take advantage of any opportunity to have themselves appointed by the United Nations to restore order in the Middle East.

490. Telegram From the Department of State to the Embassy in Israel [1]

Washington, November 4, 1956—4:32 a.m.

461. You should (Embtel 485) [2] orally inform Israeli ForMin along following preliminary lines on which we may have further comment:

We have no info at this time Syria intends attack Israel. Syria has from time to time told us that it intends to defend itself if attacked by Israel and has referred to Egyptian-Syrian defense pact. We strongly support UNGA res Nov 2 which calls for cease fire and withdrawal of troops as well as UNGA resolutions Nov 4 directing SYG re cease fire, halt of movement of mil forces and plan for emergency Intl UN Force. We cannot condone any steps which would lead to mil action. We assume ForMin in touch with Genl Burns and will be transmitting through him for Syria and for Jordan assurances of Israel's peaceful intent. We on our part would be happy to confirm to Syria and Jordan assurances which Israel sends through Genl Burns. We reiterate at this crucial hour, in spirit of President's and Secretary's earlier appeals, our hope that Israel will take no action which would further imperil situation and will avoid hostilities and will turn to UN, which is now meeting, to settle any difficulties between Israel and Syria and between Israel and Jordan.

FYI Your comments to ForMin should take into account fact Israel statement may be attempt to justify Israeli attack. [3]

Hoover

---

[1] Source: Department of State, Central Files, 684A.86/11–356. Confidential; Niact. Drafted by Wilkins, cleared with Rountree, and approved by Wilkins who signed for Hoover. Repeated Niact to Amman, Jerusalem, Damascus, and to Beirut, Cairo, Paris, London, and USUN.

[2] Document 488.

[3] Later that day Lawson reported that Foreign Minister Meir had complained that the United States was placing Israel and not Syria in the position of a defendant who was being told to behave itself. The United States, she maintained, should be seeking assurances of peaceful intent from Syria and Jordan, not Israel. Meir insisted: "We have no aggressive intentions. But if we are attacked, we will fight back. I am convinced that if Syria, Jordan and Iraq altogether attack us tonight we shall be able to cope with them in same manner as with Egypt. Point is we don't want to fight anybody." (Telegram 491 from Tel Aviv, November 4; Department of State, Central Files, 684A.86/11–956)

491.   Memorandum of a Conversation, Executive Office Building, Washington, November 4, 1956, 9:30 a.m. [1]

PRESENT

Dr. Flemming, ODM (Chairman)	General Persons
Secretary Wilson	Colonel Goodpaster
Acting Secretary Hoover	Mr. MacArthur
Admiral Radford	(2 from Interior) [2]
Governor Adams	

SUBJECT

Possible Activation of the Emergency Oil Committee

This meeting was called to discuss whether the US should take initiative in activating the emergency oil committee in New York in view of the situation resulting from the destruction of the pipelines [3] and the blocking of the Canal. After very considerable discussion of the pros and cons, the meeting concluded with the following agreements:

1. Nothing would be done today and no initiative would be taken.

2. The ODM would take the lead in getting an inventory of the stocks on hand and requirements of the smaller European countries, with a view to knowing what their demands were and estimating what hardships would be entailed. (This request was made by Governor Adams.)

3. Dr. Flemming, the chairman, said he would keep in touch with Mr. Hoover.

4. It was also fully agreed that nothing would be done until the committee had been called to consider this matter again. In other words, if anyone had any ideas, they would be submitted to Dr. Flemming and he would see to it that a meeting was called.

The main objection to taking initiative today was that since it would entail close cooperation with the British and French, our moral position might be impaired at a most critical moment and great damage done to our present position, particularly with the Asian and African countries. Furthermore, it was felt that one of the best cards we had to bring the British and French to take a constructive position was the way we handled the oil matter. If we rushed into cooperation with them, we would perhaps be giving

---

[1] Source: Department of State, Central Files, 840.04/11–456. Secret. Drafted by MacArthur.

[2] A marginal notation on another copy of this memorandum indicates that the two Interior Department officials were Secretary Seaton and Hugh Stewart. (*Ibid.*, Secretary's Memoranda of Conversation: Lot 64 D 199)

[3] On November 3, three IPC pumping stations in Syria, including the main one, were sabotaged. See vol. XIII, p. 594.

away a vital card. The chairman summed it up by saying he understood the consensus of the matter to be that we should play hard-to-get and let the initiative come from the European countries.

---

492.   Telegram From the Embassy in Egypt to the Department of State [1]

Cairo, November 4, 1956—3 p.m.

1314. . . . now informed as follows by Haikel:

(1) Four points mentioned Embtel 1302 [2] discussed with Nasser who has definitely assured he would accept.

(2) However in their efforts forestall British and French landings, GOE officials would welcome designation Sixth Fleet as only force capable timely action to act in capacity interim UN police force in Suez area.

(3) Great pleasure expressed at higher government levels as result UN action in GA, and especial praise regarding US role expressed to several . . . representatives so effusive in fact as to be almost embarrassing. In this connection Nasser said to have remarked "US has won area without firing a shot."

In conversation with another . . . representative Ali Sabry expressed himself along similar lines but specifically said Egypt would be prepared accept proposed two American resolutions.

Am reporting foregoing as what Nasser and his intimates are saying to us indirectly. What they will actually do if called upon to deliver may be another story. . . . Also to be recalled that drowning men grasp at straws.

Hare

---

[1] Source: Department of State, Central Files, 684A.86/11–456. Secret; Niact. Received at 12:16 p.m.

[2] Document 486.

493.   Memorandum of a Conference With the President, White House, Washington, November 4, 1956, 4 p.m. [1]

OTHERS PRESENT

> Under Secretary Hoover
> Mr. MacArthur
> Mr. Murphy
> Mr. Phleger
> Mr. Rountree
> Mr. Bowie
> Mr. Allen Dulles (for part of meeting)
> Mr. Hagerty
> Colonel Goodpaster

Mr. Hoover began by saying he would like to review to the President the latest development in the Hungarian situation, [2] including the plan to submit a resolution to the UN General Assembly in its meeting at 4:00 PM, and also the situation in the Middle East, including the progress being made by Hammarskjold.

[Here follows Phleger's review of the status of the Hungarian matter in the United Nations.]

With regard to Middle East developments, Mr. Phleger said the U.S. resolution had been presented, but not pressed to a vote, in order to enable action to be taken on resolutions submitted by Canada and India. [3] The first of these called for the Secretary General, within 48 hours, to develop a plan, in consultation with the parties concerned, to introduce a U.S. [U.N.] police force into the area. This was passed with a vote of 55 to 0, with 19 abstentions. The Indian resolution, also passed, called on the Secretary General to report in 12 (or 18?) [4] hours whether the cease-fire was being complied with. The vote on the resolution was 59 to 6, with 7 abstentions. [5]

Secretary Hoover reported that great progress was being made by Hammarskjold, who was trying to get at least a token force quickly, and forestall French-British invasion. The possibility of having the force composed of Canadian, Indian, Norwegian, and Colombian contributions was mentioned. It was expected that Hammarskjold would appoint General Burns of Canada as the chief of the force. Mr. Hoover also reported that Hammarskjold had sent a

---

[1] Source: Eisenhower Library, Whitman File, Eisenhower Diaries. Top Secret. Drafted by Goodpaster on November 5.

[2] On November 4, the Soviet Union launched a major assault on Hungary and crushed the rebellion.

[3] See Document 485.

[4] As on the source text. The resolution called upon the Secretary-General to report in 12 hours.

[5] The official vote count was 59–5 with 12 abstentions. (U.N. doc. A/PV.563)

message to the U.K. urging them not to move in with invasion forces. The President commented that if the U.K. would stop the invasion, they could then join in the resolutions on Hungary.

Secretary Hoover next discussed dangers that were appearing of an Israeli attack on Syria and Jordan, and reported discussions between Mrs. Meir and Ambassador Lawson. [6]

The President next considered a draft which Mr. Hoover handed him of a proposed letter to Bulganin. [7] The President redrafted the letter in order to offer a line of action to Bulganin by which he could reduce the shock and dismay the world has felt at Soviet actions in Hungary, rather than leaving the letter entirely denunciatory.

Finally, the group discussed a public statement that the President might make through Mr. Hagerty reporting the developments and actions of the day by the U.S. [8]

G
Colonel, CE, US Army

---

[6] See telegram 485, Document 488.

[7] Attached but not printed. The draft letter concerned the situation in Hungary.

[8] A memorandum by Greene, dated November 4, indicates that as a result of a White House decision in consultation with Hoover on November 4, "The President decided that no United States forces should participate in a United Nations force, but that United States military transport including airlift could be made available to get other national forces to Egypt under the United Nations resolution. Mr. Hoover informed Admiral Radford and Ambassador Lodge by telephone." A copy of this memorandum was sent to Rountree and is in Department of State, NEA/NE Files: Lot 58 D 398, The White House 1956.

---

494.   Telegram From the Mission at the United Nations to the Department of State [1]

New York, November 4, 1956—5 p.m.

Delga 4. For Hoover from Lodge. Re Palestine. I just met with Hammarskjold who gave me following report:

1. Cease Fire [2]

---

[1] Source: Department of State, Central Files, 320.5774/11–456. Secret; Niact. Received at 7:35 p.m.

[2] Early in the morning of November 4 Hammarskjöld received from the Permanent Representative of Israel an Aide-Mémoire, dated November 3, which affirmed that: "Israel agrees to an immediate cease-fire provided a similar answer is forthcom-

Hammarskjold said that he had received in three different forms (orally from Dixon–UK, by letter and by telegram from Selwyn Lloyd) that the UK Cabinet was considering urgently his appeal to them following last night's meeting for a cease fire. Hammarskjold regarded this as evidence that the door was open to their eventual acceptance. Lloyd asked that this message be circulated to the members of the GA. Hammarskjold felt that he should not do this at the present moment. SYG said that he had, as a result of his letter to the British and French, [3] made clear to them that the three conditions for a cease fire previously laid down by Eden [4] were out of the picture and that if they did not accept the UN cease fire proposal, they would be preventing cessation of hostilities between Israel and Egypt. Hammarskjold said that he felt that the British at least understood the predicament they were in. The time limit he had set for the cease fire (2000 hours GMT) would, however, be an hour before the French (Mollet and Pineau) would be arriving in London today for consultation. SYG said for practical reasons he had switched deadline from 2000 hours to 0500 GMT tomorrow which would be 12 midnight tonight NY time. What he intended to do instead of circulating British note about Cabinet meeting would be to put covering note on his cables to the parties saying that because of practical communications problems he had changed the deadline and circulated this. Hammarskjold said he expected, however, a reply from the British and French between 7 and 8 pm this evening. The GA would be in session at 8 pm and would have to act in light of the British-French reply.

2. UN Forces

Hammarskjold said his morning he had met with Pearson (Canada), Engen (Norway), Lall (India), and Urrutia (Colombia). [5] Engen

---

ing from Egypt." The Aide-Mémoire also maintained that repeated hostile acts on the part of the Egyptian Government over the years had made a fiction of the Israeli-Egyptian armistice agreement and that the only answer was the establishment of peace between Israel and Egypt by direct negotiations. (U.N. doc. A/3279)

[3] On November 4, in accordance with General Assembly Resolutions 997 (ES–I) and 999 (ES–I), Hammarskjöld sent cables to the Governments of Egypt, Israel, Great Britain, and France asking, among other points, that all the parties halt military actions in the area by 2000 GMT (8 p.m. London time), November 4. Hammarskjöld subsequently extended the deadline to 500 GMT (5 a.m. London time), November 5. Egypt promptly responded that it accepted Resolution 999 and was ready to halt all hostile military actions as requested, and took note that Israel was also being asked to withdraw its forces behind the armistice demarcation lines. ("Report of the Secretary-General on communications with the Governments of France, Egypt, Israel and the United Kingdom of Great Britain and Northern Ireland concerning implementation of General Assembly Resolutions 997 (ES–I) and 999 (ES–I) dated 2 and 4 November 1956," U.N. doc. A/3287. Hammarskjöld's cables and the Egyptian response are printed as annexes to the report.)

[4] See Eden's statement of November 3, Document 476.

[5] Colombian Representative to the General Assembly.

had agreed for Norway to furnish forces. Pearson had said that in principle they were in agreement and would furnish one battalion temporarily from Germany but this required final Cabinet decision. Urrutia said that one battalion would be made available at once if it could be transported. He did this on the authority of the President of Colombia. Lall's attitude was "very promising". Hammarskjold said that following this he planned to discuss the furnishing of troops with Denmark, Sweden, Brazil, Mexico, New Zealand, Iran and Ethiopia. He excluded Italy and Turkey for historical reasons and he did not like to ask Yugoslavs although he might mention possibility to them expecting refusal. He would exclude all permanent members of SC. He said that he believed that the UN today could reach a decision on the establishing of a UN command, and that the GA could appoint General Burns as head of the command.

He intended make full report on these developments to the GA and on the basis of this report hoped that a resolution would be introduced today to set up the command. Canada, Norway, India and Colombia strongly favored his making an immediate report along these lines. I told Hammarskjold we would be delighted have General Burns as commander.

3. US Participation

Hammarskjold said that if all went well, he would like to make final report at about 5 pm on Monday. In his final report, he would like to say that in view of special difficulties of getting forces immediately to the area, the US Government had expressed willingness to help with an airlift. He would like to go on and say if there were unavoidable delays in the availability of the forces from the countries furnishing them, the US would consider supplying a number of forces as a stop-gap and temporarily, until the others could arrive. He said he felt sure this would raise no difficulties with USSR, Arabs, UK and France because obviously the US had no intention of occupying bases in Arab world. (Egyptians have indicated to USUN officers that they had contemplated possibility of US forces exclusively coming in and on that basis had been favorable to UN force idea.) I told Hammarskjold US would attempt help with airlift but question of US forces as stop-gap would have to be determined at highest US Government level.

4. Pay and Equipment

Said that we contemplated that pay and equipment of the forces would be furnished by the countries whose forces were involved and that the UN would pay their maintenance of which we would, of course, pay one-third. Hammarskjold said that this seemed right and UN budgeting could be done on that basis.

[Here follows the verbatim text of a draft report by Hammarskjöld on the first stage of discussions on a U.N. command, which he planned to deliver that evening to the General Assembly. The final version of Hammarskjöld's report, entitled, "First report of the Secretary-General on the plan for an emergency international United Nations Force requested in resolution 998 (ES–I) adopted by the General Assembly on 4 November 1956" was later circulated as U.N. doc. A/3289.]

I raised with Hammarskjold the Israeli-Jordan situation and said that we were extremely alarmed over information that Israel was attempting provoke Jordan. I urged Hammarskjold to use all possible pressure on Israel. He agreed to do so.

Lodge

---

495.   Message From Prime Minister Eden to President Eisenhower [1]

London, November 4, 1956.

DEAR FRIEND: I am sending you a personal message to explain why, although we welcome the request to the Secretary-General contained in the Canadian resolution, we find it impossible to accept the Afro-Asian resolution. I send you this preliminary notice remembering the last occasion, when owing to cyphering delays my message failed to reach you before our announcement was made. [2]

Yours ever,

Anthony [3]

---

[1] Source: Eisenhower Library, Whitman File, International File. Secret.
[2] Reference is presumably to Eden's message to Eisenhower of October 30, Document 421.
[3] Printed from a copy that bears this typed signature.

---

496.   Editorial Note

During the 565th plenary meeting of the General Assembly (first emergency special session), which convened at 9:45 p.m. on

November 4, a draft resolution sponsored by Canada, Colombia, and Norway (U.N. doc. A/3290) was adopted shortly after midnight as Resolution 1000 (ES–I), by a vote of 57 in favor, 0 opposed, and 19 abstentions. This resolution, which the United States supported, established a United Nations Command for an emergency international force to secure and supervise the cessation of hostilities; appointed General Burns as Chief of Command and authorized him to recruit from the UNTSO observer corps a limited number of officers (with the exclusion of nationals of permanent Security Council members) and to undertake in consultation with the Secretary-General the recruitment from various member states (other than permanent members of the Security Council) the additional number of officers needed. For text of Resolution 1000 (ES–I), see Department of State *Bulletin*, November 19, 1956, pages 793–794; or *United States Policy in the Middle East, September 1956–June 1957*, pages 175–176.

---

497.   Telegram From the Mission at the United Nations to the Department of State [1]

New York, November 5, 1956—1 a.m.

Delga 7. For Hoover from Lodge. Re Palestine. Following telecon with Acting Secretary [2] I inquired immediately of SYG Hammarskjold how he envisaged UN command if (1) British and French had landed in Egypt before UN forces had arrived, and (2) if Egypt refused to accept presence of UN forces.

Hammarskjold said at once that in first place establishment of UN force was conditional upon coming into existence of all terms of GA resolution of 2 November, [3] calling for cease-fire, withdrawal of forces and halting of military movements.

He said it was clear that UN force could not be sent into Egypt without Egypt's agreement. He said we cannot as UN "occupy" Egyptian territory.

On the other hand, he did not feel that Israeli acceptance of UN forces in Egypt was necessary since UN forces would not be on Israeli territory.

---

[1] Source: Department of State, Central Files, 320.5780/11–556. Secret; Niact. Received at 1:18 a.m.

[2] No account of this conversation has been found in Department of State files.

[3] General Assembly Resolution 997 (ES–I). For text, see Document 467.

If, Hammarskjold said, UK-French forces landed in Egypt before UN command was even established, it would be an entirely new situation which would require new consideration. If UK-French forces landed after establishment of UN command but before arrival of UN forces, UN forces could not be introduced until UK and French forces had withdrawn. And it would be out of question for UN command and forces to provide UN umbrella for presence of UK and French forces.

Hammarskjold said, however, that it was desirable nevertheless even if UK and French forces landed before arrival of UN forces for UN command to have already been established. Problem then would be to get UK and French forces to withdraw and UN forces to take their place.

Lodge

498.   Telegram From the Mission at the United Nations to the Department of State [1]

New York, November 5, 1956—2 a.m.

Delga 8. For Hoover from Lodge. Re Palestine. As reported to Acting Secretary, shortly prior to vote tonight on Canadian, Norwegian, Colombian resolution establishing UN command, Pearson (Canada) informed me that he had just talked to Prime Minister St. Laurent. The Prime Minister had himself just talked to Eden by telephone in London. Eden said they appreciated Canadian good intentions but were going ahead with landings in Egypt. St. Laurent told Eden they could not expect help from Canada since they were not in agreement with UK. We communicated this immediately to Hammarskjold and agreed with him it was desirable press at once to vote on Canadian, Norwegian, Colombian resolution and move ahead as quickly as possible on getting Canadian troops from West Germany into Egypt before UK-French landings.

We succeeded in completing vote at 12:17 a.m., November 5, 1956.

After session I told Pearson that we would be ready to fly troops from Europe to area, that it was very desirable to get there

[1] Source: Department of State, Central Files, 320.5780/11–556. Secret; Niact. Received at 2:28 a.m.

immediately. He said that under Canadian constitutional practice this would require act of Canadian Parliament which would mean two day delay, unless Canadian Prime Minister decided to do it and then get approval of Parliament afterwards. He said that Prime Minister was thinking this over. I also told Hammarskjold that following telephone conversation with Acting Secretary US did not believe UN forces should go if Anglo-French forces were there already. Hammarskjold agreed (see my telegram Delga 7). [2]

Lodge

---

[2] *Supra.*

499. Message From Prime Minister Eden to President Eisenhower [1]

London, November 5, 1956.

DEAR FRIEND: It is a great grief to me that the events of the last
few days have placed such a strain on the relations between our two
countries. Of course I realise your feelings about the action which
we felt compelled to take at such short notice. But if you will refer
to my message of September 6 I think you will agree that what I
said then has already begun to be confirmed by events.

I have always felt, as I made very clear to Mr. Khrushchev, that
the Middle East was an issue over which, in the last resort, we
would have to fight.

I know that Foster thought we could have played this longer.
But I am convinced that, if we had allowed things to drift, everything would have gone from bad to worse. Nasser would have
become a kind of Moslem Mussolini and our friends in Iraq, Jordan,
Saudi Arabia and even Iran would gradually have been brought
down. His efforts would have spread westwards, and Libya and all
North Africa would have been brought under his control.

It may be that we might have obtained by negotiation a
settlement of the Canal question which gave us a part of what we
needed. But at best it would have taken a long time. Meanwhile
Nasser would have been taking the tricks all round the Middle East.
His last action in making a military command with Jordan and Syria
was bound to provoke the Israelis, and of course it did so. They felt
themselves imprisoned and naturally tried to break out. We were of
course relieved that they broke in the direction of Egypt rather than
of Jordan. But once they had moved, in whatever direction, there
was not a moment to be lost. We and the French were convinced
that we had to act at once to forestall a general conflagration
throughout the Middle East. And now that police action has been
started [2] it must be carried through. I am sure that this is the
moment to curb Nasser's ambitions. If we let it pass, all of us will
bitterly regret it. Here is our opportunity to secure an effective and

---

[1] Source: Eisenhower Library, Whitman File, International File. Secret. Delivered to
the White House under cover of a note from Coulson to Eisenhower which reads: "The
Prime Minister has asked me to give you the enclosed personal message."

[2] The airborne assault on the Canal Zone began at dawn on November 5, when
British and French paratroopers began landing in the environs of Port Said.

final settlement of the problems of the Middle East. If we draw back now, chaos will not be avoided. Everything will go up in flames in the Middle East. You will realise, with all your experience, that we cannot have a military vacuum while a United Nations force is being constituted and is being transported to the spot. This is why we feel we must go on to hold the position until we can hand over the responsibility to the United Nations. If a barrier can be established in this way between the Arabs and the Israelis we shall then be strongly placed to call on the Israelis to withdraw. This in its turn will reduce the threat to the Canal and restore it to the general use of the world. By this means, we shall have taken the first step towards re-establishing authority in this area for our generation.

It is no mere form of words to say that we would be happy to hand over to an international organisation as soon as we possibly can. As you can imagine, no one feels more strongly about this than Harold [3] who has to provide the money. We do not want occupation of Egypt, we could not afford it, and that is one of many other reasons why we got out of Suez two years ago.

I know how strongly you feel, as I do, the objections to the use of force, but this is not a situation which can be mended by words or resolution, it is indeed ironical that at this very moment, when we are being pilloried as aggressors, Russia is brutally re-occupying Hungary and threatening the whole of Eastern Europe, and no voice is raised in the United Nations in favour of intervention there. It may be that our two countries can take no practical action to redress that situation. But the Middle East is an area in which we could still take practical and effective action together.

I am sending you this message in the hope that you will at least understand the grievous decisions which we have had to make. I was deeply moved by your last message before our initial action, although I was not able to reply to it as I would have liked at the time.

After a few days you will be in a position to act with renewed authority. I beg you to believe that what we are doing now will in our view facilitate your action. I would most earnestly ask you to put the great weight of your authority behind the proposal which we are now making to the United Nations.

I believe as firmly as ever that the future of all of us depends on the closest Anglo-American cooperation. It has of course been a grief to me to have had to make a temporary breach into it which I cannot disguise, but I know that you are a man of big enough heart and vision to take up things again on the basis of facts. If you cannot approve, I would like you at least to understand the terrible

---

[3] Harold Macmillan.

decisions that we have had to make. I remember nothing like them since the days when we were comrades together in the war. History alone can judge whether we have made the right decision, but I do want to assure you that we have made it from a genuine sense of responsibility, not only to our country, but to all the world.

Yours ever,

Anthony [4]

---

[4] Printed from a copy that bears this typed signature.

---

500. Memorandum of a Conference With the President, White House, Washington, November 5, 1956, 10:20 a.m. [1]

OTHERS PRESENT

Vice President Nixon
Secretary Hoover
Mr. Phleger
Mr. Hagerty
Colonel Goodpaster

The President asked what were the differences between the "Afro-Asian" and "Canadian" plans regarding the Middle East made in the United Nations. [2] Mr. Phleger said that although they differ they are not inconsistent, and that both had been adopted. The reference was to the Indian and Canadian plans. Last night Hammarskjold reported that he had sent messages under the Indian plan to Britain and France, without reply as yet. He said the Norwegians, with support of others, had put in a follow-up resolution to establish a command which would exercise the police function in the Middle Eastern war areas. He understood that Canada, Colombia, Norway and India had agreed to put in forces. He said there was some indication that Eden now wants to join in with the other free nations to settle this matter. The President mentioned his two letters from Eden, [3] received during last night, and said he would try to

---

[1] Source: Eisenhower Library, Whitman File, Eisenhower Diaries. Top Secret. Drafted by Goodpaster.

[2] Reference is to General Assembly Resolutions 998 (ES–I) and 999 (ES–I), respectively. For texts, see Document 485.

[3] Document 495 and *supra*.

prepare a reply to Eden endeavoring to bring him into an acceptable position in this matter.

Mr. Hoover pointed out that our position is completely free with regard to the UN action now that the French and the British have in fact invaded. The President said he thought we should stick with the plan as developed thus far in spite of the UK and French landings.

Mr. Hoover reported that he had called Secretaries Robertson and Wilson with a request that military planning be started on how to move in the UN troops. The President indicated he was especially interested in getting the Colombians (and any other Latin Americans who might contribute) quickly into position.

Mr. Hoover showed the President a brief paper setting out the essentials of the policy we are following, [4] and the President said it looked excellent to him.

Mr. Hoover reported he had learned that Pearson had called Eden and told him that he has no support and will have none from Canada in this matter. Mr. Nixon said it was too bad that Bevan is allowed to make political capital out of supporting the same position we hold, since any swing to that school of thought would be tragic for us. Mr. Hoover said we must be careful not to appear to condone what the French and British have done. He reported information he had received to the effect that the British and French plan to make landings in Alexandria as well as the Canal zone. I mentioned the question of whether the French might be trying to widen and worsen the conflict for their own ends, which may now begin to depart from those of the British. The group indicated considerable concern over any possible landing in the Alexandria area, as drawing the British and French forces into a long struggle. The President said he would try to write up a message for Eden to try to influence him against any such action.

Mr. Hoover expressed his great concern over the situation in Syria, and the possibility of the USSR sending forces, volunteer or other, into Syria. The President said he understood the airfields in Syria were very poor. The President said that it will be very important to keep a close watch on the Syrian airfields and asked that Mr. Allen Dulles give special attention to this matter.

Mr. Hoover said that oil supplies from the Middle East are now largely cut off—only the tap line from Saudi Arabia remains in operation. The oil supply of NATO military forces in Western Europe may soon be endangered.

---

[4] Not attached to the source text and not found in Department of State files or the Eisenhower Library.

The President suggested we should put heavy tankers and oilers into use immediately, including all fleet oilers, and any used for non-military purposes should be on the basis of reasonable charges and rates. With regard to the oil problem faced by the French and the British, the President felt that the purposes of peace and stability would be served by not being too quick in attempting to render extraordinary assistance, and the Vice President reinforced this view. The President asked that ODM and Mr. Hoover work out arrangements for the Navy to help out in the over-all situation with its oilers.

[Here follows the remainder of the conversation pertaining predominantly to the Hungarian situation.]

---

501.   Memorandum for the Record by the Director of the Executive Secretariat (Howe) [1]

Washington, November 5, 1956.

The Acting Secretary and Mr. Phleger reported the following, following their conversation with the President at 10:15. (Colonel Goodpaster will forward official notes of the meeting.)

[Here follow items 1–6.]

7. *Press Guidance on UK–French landings*—Mr. Hoover reported that the statement originally drafted as a guidance to Linc White had been revised slightly and classified to Top Secret as a policy document. [2] It was not given to Mr. Hagerty for release. Apparently the President and Mr. Hoover believe that there is no immediate need for a statement on US attitude toward the UK-French invasion of the Suez although Mr. Hagerty believes there should be as much publicity as possible simply to keep the American people informed. (*Note:* Mr. Phleger suggested that a paraphrase could be prepared indicating that the step was not a surprise, and represents a further complication; but that a plan for a cease-fire was still underway at the UN.) Mr. Hoover undertook to prepare a guidance for Linc White which would be composed of a severe editing of the now approved policy statement.

[Here follow items 8 and 9.]

---

[1] Source: Department of State, Secretary's Memoranda of Conversation: Lot 64 D 199. Secret.

[2] Not found in Department of State files.

10. *Syria*—There was apparent discussion of the possibility that the Russians would take actions through and in Syria. The President had asked Mr. Hoover to request Mr. Allen Dulles to have his Agency keep a very close eye on this situation in Syria and elsewhere to indicate at the earliest moment such possible Soviet actions. (Mr. Hoover was to call Mr. Dulles.)

11. *UK-French Invasion*—Apparently there was some concern expressed that the UK-French activity was not a simple policy action or that the UK might not be able to control the French or may themselves wish to really clobber the Egyptians and not just get hold of the Canal.

---

502.   Draft Message From President Eisenhower to Prime Minister Eden [1]

Washington, November 5, 1956.

DEAR ANTHONY: I have both your cables. First off, let me assure you that you cannot possibly feel more saddened than I about the temporary but admittedly deep rift that has occurred in our thinking as respect of [*sic*] the Mid East situation. It cannot fail to have some harmful effect upon our joint efforts as we pursue the great objective of a peaceful world.

This morning I have news that your troops have begun landing. In a sense this creates a new problem, but I believe that the peace plans under development in the United Nations are sufficiently flexible so that this incident will not completely defeat them.

The big thing now is to prevent the situation from becoming more tense and difficult. It is possible that Nasser, knowing the United Nations is working on a peaceful solution might take the "cease fire" very seriously and temporarily accept the landings without opposition. Thus he would avoid actual military contact until he could see what might develop. It would appear that the basic objective of your own military action would be largely accomplished by the landings themselves, providing no serious fighting or disorder ensues. If no serious fighting came out, I think your

---

[1] Source: Eisenhower Library, Whitman File, International File. Top Secret. A marginal notation on the source text by Ann Whitman reads: "Pres. said events had gone too swiftly. letter was outdated. not to be sent."

position in the area and before world opinion would be tremendously eased.

One way in which serious disorders might be avoided would be keeping troops out of contact with any heavy concentrations of the civil population. In this way you would not get a great police function on your hands which you might not be able to drop easily.

If we could have for the next two or three days a period of relative calm while your troops did nothing but land, we might much more swiftly develop a solution that would be acceptable to both sides and to the world.

I have no doubt that you have thought over all these things most carefully and prayerfully, but I think at the same time that the French, in what has seemed to me to be a rather irrational approach to this whole matter, could be far less restrained and therefore make greater difficulties for all of us.

As you say, Harold's financial problem is going to be a serious one, and this itself I think would dictate a policy of the least possible provocation.

In the meantime, no matter what our differences in the approach to this problem, please remember that my personal regard and friendship for you, Harold, Winston [2] and so many others is unaffected. On top of this, I assure you I shall do all in my power to restore to their full strength our accustomed practices of cooperation just as quickly as it can be done.

New subject. Since dictating the above, I have been informed that the Soviets have made the move that from the first I feared would be their reaction. I am told that in Moscow they have released a statement to the effect that they are demanding that the United States join them in an immediate military move into the Mid East to stop the fighting. I understand that aside from making the proposal directly to us, they are placing it before the United Nations in the alleged hope that that body will give its sanction to this preposterous proposition.

I have not yet seen the text of the message so I cannot comment on it in detail.

With warm regard,

As ever,

Ike [3]

---

[2] Winston S. Churchill.

[3] Printed from a copy that bears this typed signature.

503.   Telegram From the Embassy in the Soviet Union to the Department of State [1]

Moscow, November 5, 1956—6 p.m.

1074. Shepilov this afternoon handed me a letter signed by Bulganin addressed to the President, suggesting in essence that US and Soviet Union should join its forces within the framework of the UN to bring about a halt to the aggression against Egypt. Shepilov, in handing me the communication, full translation of which will be in immediately following telegram, [2] stated that although the UN had shown activity the last week, the war still went on in Egypt and if the US and the Soviet Union could join together they could within the framework of the UN bring a halt to this aggression and restore peace in the Middle East.

I asked Mr. Shepilov what he meant by "within the framework of the UN", and he replied that any decisions would be taken within its framework and he had sent, as indicated in the letter, similar communications to Hammarskjold and the President Security Council. [3] I asked him if Soviet Government was seriously suggesting that the US should use armed force against England and France. He replied that was not being proposed and would not be necessary if the US and USSR would make plain their "determination" to see the fighting come to a halt in the Middle East. I told him I could not comment on so serious a matter but would send the proposal immediately to the President.

Although I did not raise with him question publication, in view recent background that question, since he has sent communications to UN I assume publication will take place very shortly.

Bohlen

---

[1] Source: Department of State, Central Files, 674.84A/11–556. Secret; Niact; Presidential Handling. Received at 12:28 p.m. A copy is in the Eisenhower Library, Whitman File, Dulles–Herter Series.

[2] For text of Bulganin's letter, see Document 505.

[3] See the editorial note, *infra*.

504.   Editorial Note

In a letter addressed to Secretary-General Hammarskjöld on November 5, Permanent Representative of the Soviet Union Sobolev asked that the text of a note dated November 4, from the Government of the Soviet Union to the Government of the United Kingdom (similar to one sent to France), be circulated as an official document of the first emergency special session of the U.N. General Assembly. In it, the Soviet Government affirmed that recent French and British actions in the Middle East constituted acts of aggression affecting the interests not only of Egypt, but of other states as well; and it warned that "the responsibility for all the possible consequences of those actions rests with the Governments of the United Kingdom and France." (U.N. doc. A/3298)

In a separate cable to the President of the Security Council on November 5, Soviet Foreign Minister Shepilov called for an immediate meeting of the Security Council to discuss "the non-compliance by the United Kingdom, France and Israel with the decision of the emergency special session of the General Assembly of the United Nations of 2 November 1956 and immediate steps to halt the aggression of the aforesaid States against Egypt." Shepilov's cable also included the text of a draft resolution, which provided, among other points, that it was essential for all member states, especially the United States and the Soviet Union, to give military and other assistance to the Egyptian Republic by sending naval and air forces, military units, volunteers, military instructors, and other forms of assistance, if Great Britain, France, and Israel failed to cease all military action against Egypt within 12 hours of the adoption of the resolution and withdraw their troops from Egyptian soil within 3 days. The letter also noted that the Soviet Government "for its part declares that it is ready to contribute to the cause of curbing the aggressors, of defending the victims of aggression, and of restoring peace, by sending to Egypt the air and naval forces necessary for the achievement of this purpose." (U.N. doc. S/3736)

The texts of the Soviet letter to the United Kingdom, dated November 4, and Shepilov's letter to the President of the Security Council, dated November 5, are printed in *United States Policy in the Middle East, September 1956–June 1957*, pages 169–171 and 178–180, respectively.

505.   Letter from Prime Minister Bulganin to President Eisenhower [1]

Moscow, November 5, 1956.

DEAR MR PRESIDENT: In alarming and responsible moment for cause general peace I appeal to you in name Soviet Govt.

Week has already passed since armed forces England, France and Israel, which is subservient to will external forces, attacked Egypt without any cause, causing death and destruction. Inhumane bombardments by English and French aviation of Egyptian aerodromes, ports, installations, cities, centers of population are taking place. Anglo-French troops have landed on Egyptian territory. From fire of occupiers have perished huge treasures created by work of Egyptian people, from day to day human sacrifices are increasing, before eyes whole world is unfolding aggressive war against Egypt, against Arab peoples, whose only fault consists of fact that they are defending their freedom and independence.

Situation in Egypt requires immediate and most decisive actions on part UN. If such actions are not undertaken, UN will lose in eyes of all mankind its prestige and will collapse.

Soviet Union and U.S. are permanent members of Security Council and are two great powers possessing all contemporary forms of armaments, including atom and hydrogen weapons. On US lies special responsibility to put stop to war and to restore peace and tranquility to area of Near and Middle East.

We are convinced that if Govts of USSR and USA firmly announce their will to guarantee peace and will condemn aggression then aggression will be terminated and there will be no war.

Mr. President, in these threatening hours when highest principles of morality, bases and objectives of UN are being subjected to an ordeal, Soviet Govt turns to Govt of U.S. with proposal for close cooperation to stop aggression and terminate further bloodshed.

U.S. has in area of Mediterranean Sea a strong naval fleet. Soviet Union also has strong naval fleet and powerful aviation. United and urgent use of these means on part of U.S. and Soviet Union in accordance with decision of UN would be reliable guarantee of termination of aggression against Egyptian people, against countries of Arab East.

---

[1] Source: Department of State, Central Files, 674.84A/11–556. Secret. Transmitted in telegram 1081 from Moscow, November 5, received at 2:03 p.m., which is the source text. A copy of telegram 1081 is in the Eisenhower Library, Whitman File, International File.

Soviet Govt appeals to Govt of U.S. to unite their efforts in UN for adopting decisive measures to terminate aggression.

Soviet Govt already has appealed to Security Council and extraordinary special session of General Assembly with appropriate proposals. [2]

Such joint steps of U.S. and Soviet Union would not threaten interests of England and France. Popular masses of England and France do not want war. Just as much as our peoples, they desire preservation peace. Also many other govts along with England and France are interested in immediate pacification and restoration of normal functioning Suez Canal disrupted by military actions. Aggression against Egypt was by no means undertaken for sake of freedom of shipping through Suez Canal which was guaranteed. Piratical war was unleashed for purpose of restoring colonial order in East which had been overthrown by peoples. If this war is not stopped, it is fraught with danger and can grow into third world war.

If Soviet Union and U.S.A. support victim of aggression, then other member-governments of UN will unite with them in these efforts. At same time authority UN will be increased to significant degree, peace will be restored and strengthened.

Soviet Govt is prepared to enter into immediate negotiations with Govt U.S. on practical execution of proposals presented above in order that effective actions in interests peace could be undertaken in nearest future.

In this tense moment of history when fate of all Arab East along with that fate of world is being decided, I await favorable answer from you.

Sincerely,

N. Bulganin [3]

---

[2] See the editorial note, *supra*.
[3] Telegram 1081 bears this typed signature.

506.   Telegram From the Embassy in the Soviet Union to the Department of State [1]

Moscow, November 5, 1956—8 p.m.

1083. It is hardly likely that Soviet Govt anticipates any possibility that their proposal for joint action bring fighting Middle East to halt would be accepted by the U.S. Govt, and therefore purpose behind this action should be sought elsewhere.

1. In large part, if not entirely, proposal is motivated by desire through spectacular proposal this nature to divert world attention from Soviet action Hungary and provide Soviet propaganda with additional question to agitate.

2. However, in extremely tense situation believe that it would be imprudent to dismiss this merely as an empty propaganda gesture.

3. Egyptian resistance has lasted now over a week and as indicated Embtel 1027 [2] possibility Soviet involvement would be related in part to duration Egyptian resistance.

4. Soviet Union in action against Hungary has cast aside any pretense to moral responsibility and this fact may increase willingness to risk more hazardous action in Middle East than would normally have been case.

5. I do not see Soviet Union deliberately starting World War III and reference to atomic and hydrogen weapons in communication may be merely designed to enhance dramatic effect of proposal, but some form of assistance to Egypt appears more likely than it did at initiation British and French action. As already reported Embtel 1060, [3] there was strong smell of some military deal in Syrian talks here, and threat to Iran is always present.

Not only because of Soviet proposal but rather in spite of it every consideration of wisdom would indicate speedy cease fire by British and French if this could be brought about without reference to Soviet proposal; if British and French could be induced to declare cease fire immediately this would undercut effect Soviet proposal

---

[1] Source: Department of State, Central Files, 674.84A/11–556. Secret; Niact; Presidential Handling. Received at 2:05 p.m. A copy is in the Eisenhower Library, Whitman File, Dulles–Herter Series.

[2] In telegram 1027, November 1, Bohlen advised the Department of State that a Soviet declaration on the Middle East, issued on October 31, was a profession of official non-involvement at this stage. Bohlen also noted, however, that should hostilities spread to other parts of the Middle East, including those close to the Soviet border, the possibility of Soviet action would increase. (Department of State, Central Files, 684A.86/11–156)

[3] Dated November 3, not printed. (*Ibid.*, 783.11/11–356) A Syrian delegation, headed by President Quwatli visited Moscow in early November.

and eliminate what element of real danger involved in Soviet attitude toward Middle East hostilities.

Bohlen

---

507.   Telegram From the Embassy in France to the Department of State [1]

Paris, November 5, 1956—4 p.m.

2184. I saw Joxe this morning and informed him regarding United States resolution on Suez in accordance with Department telegram 1688. [2] I told him that in my personal view, while I could see some points to which French might well object in resolution, [3] I did not feel that text of resolution as a whole seemed as bad as Joxe thought on Saturday night.

Joxe, who was calm but obviously suffering from lack of sleep, told me that French objection had been both a procedural one and an objection on substance of resolution. He said that French had been disturbed Saturday [4] morning when Lodge introduced in Security Council a resolution on Hungary without prior consultation with French. French had understood that there was solid agreement that measures regarding Hungary would only be taken after tripartite consultation, and they had been very much upset by United States unilateral action. They had felt that United States resolution was unduly soft and had wanted to submit strengthening amendments. However, French Delegation at United Nations recommended against such action so as not to air difference with Lodge over this subject in view of open differences on Suez problem.

French had understood that American United Nations Delegation was preparing some action for Saturday night which would have effect of heading off more drastic action which might have been presented by Arab-Asians or Soviets. They were however very much upset when they received word of our resolution on Suez.

---

[1] Source: Department of State, Central Files, 320.5780/11–556. Secret; Priority. Received at 2:05 p.m. Repeated to USUN.

[2] Telegram 1688 to Paris, November 4, instructed the Embassy that it might inform Joxe that the United States was not pressing for its two draft resolutions, submitted to the General Assembly on November 3. (*Ibid.*, 974.7301/11–356)

[3] Reference is to the U.S. draft resolution concerning the Suez Canal. Regarding French objections, see Delga 2, Document 487.

[4] November 3.

They felt that resolution gave a great deal too much authority to Committee of Three and result would depend entirely on who were chosen as members of this Committee. They particularly objected to the naming of French and United Kingdom along with Egypt as countries to be consulted. They felt that this in effect classified them with Egypt, a position which they obviously could never agree to. Joxe likened their position to that of a joint defendant at the bar. Finally, they felt that resolution in effect sounded the death knell of any plan for international administration of the Canal.

I told Joxe that I did not agree as far as international administration was concerned, and saw no reason why that might not be the best solution in accordance with the 6 principles adopted by Security Council October 13. Joxe agreed that this might be so but felt that if it was our intention to consider international administration it would be better to so indicate in the framework of resolution.

I then told Joxe that since the resolution had already been submitted and was before the General Assembly it would seem to me that if it was to be modified it would be very helpful if we could have French views promptly on possible specific modifications or alternatives, or at any rate could have a clear explanation of items to which they particularly objected. Joxe agreed that this was an excellent idea and said he would take matter up with Pineau as soon as Pineau arrived. Pineau is not expected at his office until about 2 o'clock this afternoon. Joxe said he would try and get in touch with me later this afternoon on this subject.

Dillon

508.   Memorandum of a Conversation, Department of State, Washington, November 5, 1956, 4 p.m. [1]

SUBJECT

> Landing Rights at Adana Base in Turkey
> UN Airlift to the Middle East

PARTICIPANTS

> Mr. Gordon Gray, Assistant Secretary of Defense (ISA)
> Admiral Radford, Chairman, Joint Chiefs of Staff
> Mr. Murphy, G
> Mr. MacArthur, C
> Mr. Wilkins, NEA
> Mr. Bennett, G

Mr. Gray and Admiral Radford came in to discuss the JCS desire for an approach to the Turkish government regarding landing rights at the Adana Base for use in the possible transit of troops to the Middle East. Admiral Radford stressed the strong feeling of the JCS that we must have authority for such use in the case of need. The approach to the Turks would not be a request for immediate deployment, but the JCS considers that we must have standby authority in order to be in a position to act quickly in case of need.

The request would cover two objectives. Authority would be requested on a contingent basis for:

1. The right to station Air Force units at the Adana Base, to be there for use in any operations which might be undertaken in connection with the situation in the Middle East. Admiral Radford assumed that we would approach the Turks on the basis that any operations we would undertake would be under a United Nations directive.

2. The right to fly . . . through Adana enroute to the base at Dhahran for protection of the oil installations there. Admiral Radford stressed that at present King Saud does not want production stopped and Americans are in high favor, but the JCS wants to be ready . . . .

In further discussion Admiral Radford stated that we now have a force of only 1200 at the Dhahran base, equipped only with small arms. We must be prepared to move in case something happens fast. In answer to Mr. Murphy's question as to how long the movement would take, the Admiral said that it might go on for some time if a follow-up air supply were necessary until we could get things in by surface vessel.

---

[1] Source: Department of State, Central Files, 711.56382/11–556. Top Secret. Drafted by Bennett.

The Admiral asked the Department's opinion as to the Turkish reaction to an approach of the kind he envisaged. Mr. Wilkins explained that the Turkish stand on recent Middle East developments is still unclear. Mr. MacArthur expressed the opinion that it would be difficult to get an advance, open-ended clearance such as Admiral Radford envisaged without telling the Turks of our plans. If we discussed our contingent planning with them, there might very well be a leak and, he was gravely concerned over an impression getting out at this time that the U.S. was planning military moves in the Middle East. Mr. Gray asked whether it would not be possible to have exploratory conversations with the Turks which would sound them out in a general way without having to go into future plans. Mr. Wilkins suggested that, in connection with our readiness to assist the contemplated UN force with an air lift, it might be possible to approach the Turks on the UN air lift and develop JCS needs simultaneously. Mr. Murphy thought Mr. Wilkins' idea had merit and went on to emphasize that U.S. stock in Saudi Arabia is very high at the present time.

Mr. MacArthur raised the question as to whether we would as a national decision decide to move troops into Dhahran in any event unless it were with the consent of the King of Saudi Arabia. Admiral Radford expressed the view that . . . we are going to have to take a decision within the next three or four days on supplying oil to Europe. When that decision is taken, assuming it will be affirmative, the U.S. will in the Admiral's view be tarred in Arab eyes with the same brush as the UK and France. Mr. Robert Anderson had told him today that the decision on oil could not be put off much longer. Mr. Murphy stated that Mr. Hoover is opposed to taking the decision just now, and he expressed the view that, by the same token, we should avoid putting the question of special use of the Adana base to the Turks at this time. Admiral Radford repeated that, if we take an affirmative decision on oil for Europe, opinion might move very fast in Saudi Arabia.

With respect to an air lift with the UN, Admiral Radford said that we had sufficient air lift in West Germany to take a Canadian force to the Suez Canal Zone and then follow up with transport of a Norwegian force. An alternative might be to take them to Suda Bay and carry them on from there by naval vessels. The Admiral said that the President would also like to make a gesture of moving the Colombian force, but he commented that it would be a very expensive proposition to move a battalion from Bogota by air. It was suggested that a token force might be moved from Colombia as well as from other countries, with the main body to follow by surface transport. Mr. Murphy mentioned reports that all the Scandinavian countries are coming forward with offers of troops for the UN force.

In connection with the cease-fire and entry of UN troops, Mr. MacArthur expressed the view that we can anticipate real trouble in getting the Israelis to pull their forces back, since it would mean their moving back across the Sinai Peninsula which they have so recently taken by force of arms.

---

509.   Memorandum of a Conference With the President, White House, Washington, November 5, 1956, 5 p.m. [1]

OTHERS PRESENT

> Governor Adams
> Secretary Hoover
> Mr. Phleger
> Mr. Hagerty
> Emmet Hughes
> Colonel Goodpaster

Mr. Hoover observed that the President had read the Bulganin note, and Bohlen's comment on it. [2] He handed the President a proposed statement to be issued by the White House on the matter. [3]

The President said that there should be a passage indicating that the United Nations, including the United States, would oppose any effort to violate the UN plan. In other words, we should give the Soviets a clear warning.

The President said his concern is that the Soviets, seeing their position and their policy failing so badly in the satellites, are ready to take any wild adventure. He thought it might be well to have a full-dress session of the NSC to examine the matter.

Mr. Phleger said the Soviets are making their offer to go in through the UN, and the President said our representative should say to the Arab States, "do you want the Soviets in the Middle East doing what they are now doing in Hungary?"

Mr. Hoover said the British and the French may be in a position from which they cannot pull back until Nasser is out. The question may well be "Eden or Nasser." He added that Nasser's position is wobbly at the moment. The President said this is something quite

---

[1] Source: Eisenhower Library, Whitman File, Eisenhower Diaries. Secret. Drafted by Goodpaster on November 7.

[2] Documents 505 and 506, respectively.

[3] Not found.

new since the British have always said their aim was to "deflate" Nasser. Mr. Hoover suggested for consideration the possibility that Hammarskjold tell Nasser he must resign. . . .

The President commented again how concerned he is over the possibility of Soviet armed intervention. He said the Soviets are scared and furious, and there is nothing more dangerous than a dictatorship in this state of mind. He referred to Hitler's last days in this connection.

The President, in following a suggestion, said he would like to send a message to Nehru to bring Nehru's weight to bear on the side of peace and a limitation of the hostilities. [4]

The President next reported that he intended for Governor Adams to send out on Wednesday a request for the Legislative Leaders to meet on Thursday or Friday. The group he had in mind would include the leaders on both sides, and the top men of both sides in the foreign affairs and military affairs committees.

The President then indicated, at the request of the State Department representatives, the general lines of the message he would like to send to Nehru.

G

Colonel, CE, U S Army

---

[4] Shortly after 1 a.m. on November 6, the Department of State transmitted to the Embassy in New Delhi for delivery the text of a message from President Eisenhower to Prime Minister Nehru dated November 5, which had been approved by Eisenhower at 11 p.m. The President also directed that the text of Bulganin's message to Eisenhower of November 5 and the White House statement made in reply be sent to Nehru. In his message to Nehru, Eisenhower affirmed the need "to exert the greatest possible restraint lest this situation radically deteriorate", and he expressed the hope that Nehru would add his "powerful voice to those counselling restraint with regard to this proposal for expanded military action." Eisenhower noted that "the United States has only one purpose in this matter—to support the United Nations in removing the threat to peace, and to restore peace and justice in the area," and he asked Nehru for any suggestions for additional action to assist in this situation. (Telegram 1176 to New Delhi, November 6; Department of State, Central Files, 684A.86/11-656)

510.   Memorandum From the Secretary of the Joint Chiefs of Staff (Wentworth) to the Chairman of the Joint Chiefs of Staff (Radford) [1]

Washington, November 5, 1956.

SUBJECT

> JCS Actions with respect to the Middle East Situation agreed upon at JCS Meeting on 5 November 1956

At their meeting on 5 November 1956 the Joint Chiefs of Staff agreed:

1. That the Chief of Staff, U.S. Air Force, would be prepared to provide airlift troops on the order of four or five battalions to the Middle East in the event that the United Nations established an international police force in the Suez Canal area.

2. That the Chief of Staff, U.S. Air Force, would ascertain from the Commander, Dhahran Airfield, whether the Arabian-American Oil Company (ARAMCO) is still loading tankers.

3. That all Chiefs of Services insure that the U.S. military personnel stationed with British and French units will not accompany those units into combat.

4. That all Chiefs of Services would make sure that foreign officers, particularly British and French, assigned to duty with U.S. headquarters or units are not in a position to obtain access to U.S. military or political plans.

5. That the Chief of Naval Operations would insure that U.S. naval forces in Suda Bay remain there for at least 48 hours more.

6. That the Chief of Naval Operations and the Chief of Staff, U.S. Air Force, take action to return C–124 aircraft from the Middle East to Germany upon completion of the evacuation of U.S. nationals.

7. That the Chief of Staff, Army, and the Chief of Naval Operations, finalize the arrangements for loading supplies and materials on a ship in the Far East and inform the Chairman, Joint Chiefs of Staff, as to what ship will be used for the purpose and provide him with a list of equipment to be loaded in order that he may discuss and clear the action with the Secretary of Defense.

8. That the Deputy Director, Logistics Plans, would attend the next meeting of the Petroleum Committee, headed by Mr. Flemming (ODM), and be prepared to present to the committee the military petroleum situation world-wide.

Wentworth

---

[1] Source: JCS Records, OCJCS 091 Palestine (Jun 56–Dec 56). Top Secret.

511.   Memorandum of a Conversation, Department of State, Washington, November 5, 1956, 6:15 p.m. [1]

SUBJECT

Soviet Maneuvers on the Middle East Situation; Franco-American
Relations

PARTICIPANTS

Ambassador Alphand of France
Minister Lucet, French Embassy
Mr. Murphy, G
Mr. Elbrick, EUR
Mr. Bennett, G

Ambassador Alphand said that since he had arrived at the Department he had been handed a news ticker regarding reported Soviet messages to Eden and Mollet in which the Soviet Union spoke of its "full determination" to settle the Middle East situation by force if necessary and raised the specter of attacks on Britain and France from a "stronger power", if they did not desist in their Suez action. [2] The Ambassador expressed concern over this news. Mr. Murphy commented that the Soviets were obviously trying to divert attention from their actions in Hungary through a propaganda move on the Middle East. He went on to say that this was evident also in the approach to the United States inviting us to join with the Soviet Union in intervening in the Middle East. All of these things taken together might mean that Soviet reactions and policy are developing in a spirit of recklessness with respect to the present situation.

Ambassador Alphand then declared in an accusing tone that all this could have been foreseen. He himself had foreseen the Soviet brutality in Hungary on last Saturday when he had encountered a certain optimism in the Department over talks between the Soviets

---

[1] Source: Department of State, Central Files, 974.7301/11–556. Secret. Drafted by Bennett.

[2] Between 9:45 and 10 p.m. Moscow time (2:45 to 3 p.m. Washington time) on November 5, the Soviet Home Service broadcast the texts of messages from Bulganin to Eden, Mollet, and Ben Gurion. The texts of these three messages are printed in *United States Policy in the Middle East, September 1956–June 1957*, pp. 183–188.

In his message to Eden, Bulganin asked: "In what position would Britain have found herself had she been attacked by more powerful states possessing all types of modern weapons of destruction?" In separate messages to Eden and Mollet, Bulganin informed these leaders of his proposal to the United States "to use, together with other members of the United Nations, naval and air forces in order to stop the war in Egypt and to curb aggression." He added the warning: "We are full of determination to crush the aggressor and reestablish peace in the East by using force." In his letter to Ben Gurion, Bulganin strongly condemned Israeli actions against Egypt, expressed the expectation that the Israeli Government would "come to its senses before it is too late," and informed Ben Gurion that the Soviet Ambassador in Israel was being recalled to Moscow.

and the Hungarians and the possibility of a withdrawal of Soviet troops from Hungary. He said that we must look at the situation with our eyes open and must realize that the Soviets have not changed. It will be a great mistake if we allow the Soviets to get away with their attempt to link their brutal actions in Hungary with the British and French action at Suez. Mr. Murphy responded that American eyes have been open for a number of months on this issue and that was why we had been so convinced that allied military action in the Middle East would precipitate a whole chain of events, not all of which could be foreseen or controlled. The Ambassador replied with some heat that he could not agree that the UK-French action and the Soviet behavior in Hungary are connected in any way. He stressed his long association with Soviet affairs and expressed his regrets over the way the American press has been linking the two situations. He implied that the press had been receiving official guidance in treating the two situations as linked together and said that he had been told by a "high source" that the press treatment had been inspired by the Administration. Mr. Murphy advised the Ambassador very emphatically that there was no truth in this information. There had been no such guidance to the press on the part of the U.S. Government. He said that it was undeniable, however, that many nations around the world do see the situation just that way and, unfortunately, do draw a connection between the two situations. Ambassador Alphand replied that he could not accept the "bad example" of the UK and France in the Middle East as parallel with the Soviet behavior in Hungary. Mr. Murphy reiterated that there is no desire or intention on the part of the U.S. Government to link the two situations but that it cannot be denied that the Soviet Union is exploiting the situation propaganda-wise. That is the problem—the allied action in Suez has made it possible for the Soviet Union to divert attention from its own misdeeds in Hungary. The Ambassador said he could not accept that interpretation. Mr. Murphy repeated that this government has never said the two situations were similar and said that he hoped the Ambassador would not make any such report to Paris. Mr. Elbrick pointed out to the Ambassador that the French and the Americans understand the difference between the two situations but unfortunately many other countries around the world do not understand the difference. Mr. Murphy emphasized that this was an important point, and we would want it clearly understood in Paris that the American Government had taken no such position. Later in the conversation the Ambassador again reverted to the alleged guidance to the press by the Administration, and Mr. Murphy once again repeated that there was nothing in the story. He went on to say that, if it would be of assistance to the Ambassador, we would be glad to clarify the matter with the correspondents. Mr. Murphy expressed regret that the Ambassador would give credence to such a story in view of his long familiarity with the American scene, and the Ambassador insisted that he had not given any credence to the story but had just reported what he had been told.

Mr. Murphy then said that he believed it was time to bring up a problem which is of great concern to this government. He referred to critical statements about the United States reported as being made by Foreign Minister Pineau. He said that one statement in particular regarding the activities of our Embassy in Cairo is unthinkable. [3] Mr. Murphy went on to say that Mr. Pineau's suspicions of the United States appear to be past belief. He stressed that intimate Franco-American relations are in fact a cornerstone of American foreign policy, and this government has been deeply concerned over attitudes taken by the French Foreign Minister. He told the Ambassador that we would appreciate anything he might do to create a better feeling in Paris and to restore the warmth of US-French relations. The Ambassador said that the fostering of good relations between our two countries is indeed his mission in this country, and he pledged himself to do everything in his power to improve the situation.

Ambassador Alphand said he would now like to turn to the subject matter which was the basis for his visit to the Department, namely, the messages today from the Soviet Government to the U.S., Britain and France and to the United Nations regarding intervention in the Middle East situation. Mr. Murphy said that with respect to Bulganin's message to President Eisenhower suggesting joint US-Soviet intervention in the Middle East, that matter was under discussion at the White House at this very moment, and he did not know what decision would be made regarding a reply. He referred to the discourtesy shown by the Soviets in publishing the message before we had even received it and said that, despite previous Soviet provocations of this nature, the President had decided not to make public his message of yesterday to Bulganin on Hungary. The obvious propaganda effort made by the Soviets with respect to today's Bulganin message, however, will provide an opportunity for the President to "lay it on the line" and make it emphatically clear

---

[3] In telegram 2186 from Paris, November 5, Dillon reported that, according to British Ambassador Jebb, Pineau believed that Nasser was prepared to resign on November 3 and that he only changed his mind after Ambassador Hare called on him and informed him of continued support of the U.S. Government and urged him not to resign. Dillon also reported that Pineau was apparently spreading this story throughout French Government circles in Paris. (Department of State, Central Files, 974.7301/11–556)

that we will not accept unilateral action in the Middle East outside the efforts being made by the UN to solve the problem.

Mr. Murphy also referred to Shepilov's message today to Secretary General Hammerskjold requesting an immediate meeting of the Security Council to consider the Suez action and suggesting that the UN call on the U.S. and the USSR to give arms and other aid to Egypt. Mr. Murphy said that we had not completed our analysis of this message but that it seems to indicate one of two things: (1) a diversionary action to take away attention from the situation in Hungary and (2) a real intention on the part of the Soviet Union to intervene in the Middle East. Our impression is that their action was motivated by the first alternative, but we cannot afford to exclude the possibility that it is the second. Ambassador Alphand pointed out that, if the Soviets should intervene directly against British and French troops, NATO obligations would come into play. Mr. Murphy suggested that the Soviets might choose to operate indirectly, say through Syria or through the use of Moslem volunteers to fight on the side of Egypt.

Ambassador Alphand stated that the latest news in his possession indicated that Egypt now denies having accepted a cease-fire as was reported earlier today. He called attention to another report he had received to the effect that 350 French marines have been taken prisoner by the Egyptians and will be paraded through the streets of Cairo. The Ambassador expressed grave concern over where such an action by Egypt might lead. Mr. Elbrick pointed out that our military information is to the fact that Egypt has accepted the UN call for a cease-fire. The Ambassador commented that this would, of course, be advantageous for Egypt and, in response to a question from Mr. Murphy, said that he had no information indicating a weakening on the part of Nasser. Mr. Murphy said that we had received a few reports which indicated some desire on the part of Nasser to work out a compromise and that made it all the more important to have a full understanding between ourselves and the French and the British at this time.

Ambassador Alphand said that the principal purpose of his call was to learn how we planned to handle the Shepilov communication to the UN; Mr. Murphy replied that we were still studying it. In that connection, he thought our action in the UN speaks for itself. He thought it could be anticipated that our action would continue along the lines already being followed.

In a further reversion to the importance of Franco-American understanding, Ambassador Alphand said that we would be trapped if we allowed the Soviets to divide us. In that connection he mentioned another rumor that he had heard that the U.S. was planning to take the leadership of the Bandung powers against "colonialism". Mr. Murphy commented that that was indeed a wild rumor and one without any basis whatsoever in fact. Ambassador Alphand went on to express the opinion that, even if the British-French action should succeed in Egypt in the next few days, it would not settle the Algerian question. He would still be recommending to Paris a more liberal policy on Algeria and in connection with other African problems.

Minister Lucet inquired regarding the position the U.S. would take at tonight's session of the General Assembly. [4] Mr. Murphy said that he had been busy with other matters and was uninformed as to late developments, but asked Mr. Bennett to look into the matter and telephone Mr. Lucet.

On departing, Ambassador Alphand mentioned the reported damage to oil pipelines in Syria and said to Mr. Murphy that he would want to have a talk in the near future about oil for Europe.

---

[4] The Security Council, not the General Assembly, met during the evening of November 5; see Document 514.

---

512.   White House News Release, Washington, November 5, 1956 [1]

The President has just received a letter from Chairman Bulganin which had been previously released to the press in Moscow. This letter—in an obvious attempt to divert world attention from the Hungarian tragedy—makes the unthinkable suggestion that the United States join with the Soviet Union in a bipartite employment of their military forces to stop the fighting in Egypt.

The Middle East question—in which there has been much provocation on all sides—is now before the United Nations. That world body has called for a cease-fire, a withdrawal of foreign armed forces and the entry of a United Nations force to stabilize the situation, pending a settlement. In this connection, it is to be regretted that the Soviet Union did not vote last night in favor of the organization of this United Nations force. All parties concerned, however, should accept these United Nations resolutions promptly and in good faith.

---

[1] Source: Department of State *Bulletin*, November 19, 1956, pp. 795–796. Delivered by Press Secretary Hagerty.

Neither Soviet nor any other military forces should now enter the Middle East area except under United Nations mandate. Any such action would be directly contrary to the present resolution of the United Nations which has called for the withdrawal of those foreign forces which are now in Egypt. The introduction of new forces under these circumstances would violate the United Nations Charter, and it would be the duty of all United Nations members, including the United States, to oppose any such effort.

While we are vitally concerned with the situation in Egypt, we are equally concerned with the situation in Hungary. There Soviet forces are at this very moment brutally repressing the human rights of the Hungarian people. Only last night the General Assembly in emergency session adopted a resolution calling on the Soviet Union to cease immediately its military operations against the Hungarian people and to withdraw its forces from that country. The Soviet Union voted against this resolution, just as it had vetoed an earlier resolution in the Security Council. The Soviet Union is, therefore, at this moment in defiance of a decision of the United Nations, taken to secure peace and justice in the world.

Under these circumstances, it is clear that the first and most important step that should be taken to ensure world peace and security is for the Soviet Union to observe the United Nations resolution to cease its military repression of the Hungarian people and withdraw its troops. Only then would it be seemly for the Soviet Union to suggest further steps that can be taken toward world peace.

Since Chairman Bulganin has already released his letter to the President, it is proper now to release a letter written by the President yesterday to the Chairman about the situation in Hungary.

[Here follows the text of Eisenhower's letter of November 4 to Bulganin concerning the situation in Hungary.]

513.   Telegram From the Department of State to the Office of the Permanent Representative to the North Atlantic Council [1]

Washington, November 5, 1956—7:52 p.m.

Topol 738. Paris for USRO and Emb.

1. Following guidance in view possibility request for action on oil through meeting Oil Committee OEEC and in view possibility question being raised either by British Chairman or Italian Vice Chairman.

2. We estimate oil shortages in Europe within month unless Suez Canal can be opened quickly which seems unlikely or unless coordinated action by international oil companies to prevent shortage undertaken soon. Coordinated action cannot prevent shortage if pipelines inoperative but can mitigate it.

3. We well aware adverse effects oil shortage throughout Europe on economic, political and social stability. However in view of US disagreement with UK and French action re Egypt we must not give appearance that we are now entering into special arrangements with UK and French to support their use of force against Egypt. Any such impression would undermine our position based upon fundamental principles and prevent us from exercising constructive influence with majority of free nations to limit damage done by UK–French resort to force. Therefore, we anxious avoid any action or consultation that gives impression of tripartite (US–UK–French) action. Would strongly prefer that such action as we take rest firmly on response to initiative countries which are prospective victims of consequences British-French action whether in a series of individual representations or through OEEC Oil Committee. US position least difficult if prime emphasis is on question relieving general European distress rather than offsetting shortages caused by British-French military effort. Have already received very general representations Sweden, Denmark, Portugal, Italy and note Norway remarks Polto 982 [2] suggesting US action to relieve potential shortages in Europe. Representation to date has been general expression of concern rather than specific request for action. Our replies have emphasized OEEC agreed principles resultant burden would be shared and countries

---

[1] Source: Department of State, Central Files, 840.2553/11–256. Confidential. Drafted by Moline (EUR/RA) and MacArthur; cleared by Rountree, Elbrick, Beckner (FSD), Timmons (EUR/RA), and in substance with Flemming; approved by Hoover. Repeated to London and Rome.

[2] Polto 982, November 2, contained an account of the private session of the North Atlantic Council held during the afternoon of November 2. (*Ibid.*, 740.5/11–256)

individually should not seek by their action cover own needs to detriment general position.

4. Have been somewhat surprised no request yet for OEEC Oil Committee attention this problem. Do not wish to stimulate it but foregoing is for guidance especially USRO, Paris and London Embassies on our desire keep emphasis on European as distinct from British-French aspects of problem. In any coordinated action which may later be taken we particularly desire that European effort be conducted within framework of principles approved in Oil Committee and particularly that there be the connection between London Advisory Committee and OEEC Oil Committee which was contemplated.

5. Do not approach British and French with foregoing and in response their approaches confine replies for time being to substance first two sentences para 3.

For Emb London: MEEC mentioned Embtel 2455 [3] was cancelled for reasons indicated. Not true Justice Dept has withdrawn anti-trust immunity.

Hoover

---

[3] Document 468.

---

514.   Editorial Note

On November 5, Hammarskjöld received responses from the Israeli, British, and French Governments to his messages of November 4 requesting a halt to military actions. Israel, in a letter dated November 4 (U.N. doc. A/3291), responded by asking certain clarifications concerning Egypt's intentions, while Great Britain and France, in their separate but identical (mutatis mutandi) responses of November 5 (U.N. docs. A/3293 and A/3294, respectively) conditioned their acceptance of a cease-fire upon an Egyptian and Israeli acceptance of the interposition of a United Nations force between belligerents. The Anglo-French replies noted that it was "necessary to interpose an international force to prevent the continuance of hostilities between Egypt and Israel, to secure the speedy withdrawal of Israel forces, to take the necessary measures to remove obstructions to traffic through the Suez Canal, and to promote a settlement of the problems of the area."

Later on November 5, Hammarskjöld received additional messages from the Egyptian and Israeli Governments. Egypt indicated (U.N. doc. A/3295) its acceptance of General Assembly Resolution 1000 (ES–I), which provided for the establishment of a United Nations force, while Israel made clear (U.N. doc. A/3279) that its previous request of November 4 for certain clarifications did not affect its undertaking for a cease-fire which it had sent to the General Assembly on November 3 (see footnote 2, Document 494). Subsequently, Hammarskjöld addressed an aide-mémoire to the Governments of France and the United Kingdom (U.N. doc. A/3310), in which he asked whether the decision of the General Assembly to establish a United Nations command met the condition which they had set forth for a cessation of hostilities. Shortly thereafter in New York, Israeli Representative Eban forwarded to the Secretary-General the text of a cable from the Israeli Government which reads: "6 November 01.46. Inform Secretary-General immediately that Israel agrees unconditionally to cease-fire. Since this morning, 5 November, all fighting has ceased between Israel and Egyptian forces on land, sea and air and full quiet prevails." (U.N. doc. A/3301)

Also on November 5, the Security Council met at 8 p.m. at the request of the Soviet Union, to consider the "noncompliance by the United Kingdom, France and Israel with the decision of the emergency special session of the General Assembly of the United Nations of 2 November 1956 and immediate steps to halt the aggression of the aforesaid States against Egypt." At this meeting, the Soviet Representative presented a draft resolution, the text of which had been sent by Shepilov to the President of the Security Council earlier that day. (U.N. doc. S/3736; a summary is in Document 504) The Security Council, however, decided against inscription of the Soviet item by a vote of 3 in favor of inscription, 4 opposed, with 4 abstentions. The United States voted against inscription. (U.N. doc. S/PV.755) For text of Lodge's remarks made during this session, see Department of State *Bulletin*, November 19, 1956, page 791.

515.   Telegram From the Embassy in France to the Department of State [1]

Paris, November 6, 1956—2 a.m.

2205. Pass immediately to Hoover and Lodge. I have just left Mollet and Pineau who were awaiting U.S. reply to Soviet notes. They have heard nothing from London. They say they are prepared to discuss cease fire which could take place in very near future. By morning the bulk of their forces will be ashore. I think they might accept cease fire effective by Tuesday night Suez time. However under no circumstances are they willing accept cease fire as a result of Soviet pressure.

Resolution in Security Council must be sponsored by U.S. or other non-Communist power to obtain their assent.

They are not prepared to withdraw their forces until an international force arrives on spot. They desire to be part of such international force and say they have on the spot all the necessary equipment to clear and reopen Canal to traffic which cannot be reassembled from elsewhere in less than a month or 6 weeks. They will not withdraw this equipment until Canal is functioning normally once again.

Mollet considering issuing statement at appropriate time reaffirming the temporary character their mission in Canal area and calling for free elections in Egypt so that freely elected representatives of Egyptian people can negotiate final settlement of Canal and Israeli problem.

Dillon

---

[1] Source: Department of State, Central Files, 684A.86/11–656. Secret; Niact. Received at 8:49 p.m., November 5. Also sent to USUN.

---

516.   Editorial Note

Harold Macmillan recalls in his memoirs that, in order to contain the serious loss of British financial reserves and thereby buttress the pound sterling, he had requested the International Monetary Fund to repay the British quota. According to Macmillan, his urgent call to New York was referred to Washington. It was only while the British Cabinet was sitting during the morning of November 6 that he received a reply that the United States Government would not agree to the technical procedure until Great Britain had agreed to a cease-fire. (*Riding the Storm, 1956–1959*, pages 163–164) No documentation concerning the British request or the American response has been found in Department of State files. Matters relating to the International Monetary Fund fell within the jurisdiction of the United States Treasury. The United States at a later date approved repayment of Great Britain's first two tranches. (Telegram 3914 to London, December 3; Department of State, Central Files, 398.13/ 12–356)

---

517.   Telegram From the Embassy in the United Kingdom to the Department of State [1]

London, November 6, 1956—10 a.m.

2510. For the Acting Secretary. Kirkpatrick telephoned me just now to convey an urgent message from Prime Minister, who wished us to know that HMG very much appreciated the position taken by US yesterday in the Security Council. HMG hoped that particularly since Soviet situation is currently obscure, we had no thought of urging British and French to leave Egypt before arrival UN police force. He said appears Soviets likely, if they have not already begun, to move air units into Syria. Situation fully under control at Port Said and going very well at Suez though still some resistance there. [2]

Aldrich

---

[1] Source: Department of State, Central Files, 684A.86/11–656. Secret; Niact. Received at 6:34 a.m. Repeated to Paris.

[2] At 6:44 a.m. that morning, the Department of State received from the Commander in Chief, U.S. Naval Forces, Eastern Atlantic and Mediterranean, Rear Echelon, Rear Admiral Walter J. Price, a telegram indicating that, according to the British Defense Ministry, British amphibious forces had landed at 060430Z (4:30 a.m. London time, November 6) at Port Said, Egypt. (Telegram 060726Z from CINCNELM Rear Echelon; *ibid.*, 684A.86/11–656)

518.   Memorandum of a Conference With the President, White House, Washington, November 6, 1956, 8:37 a.m. [1]

OTHERS PRESENT

> Mr. Allen Dulles
> Under Secretary Hoover
> Colonel Goodpaster
> Dr. Flemming (part of meeting)
> Governor Adams (part of meeting)

Mr. Dulles showed the President late intelligence indicating that the Soviets told the Egyptians that they will "do something" in the Middle East hostilities. Following discussion of the possibility of Soviet movement of Air Forces into Syria, the President asked Mr. Dulles to conduct high reconnaissance in this area, avoiding, however, any flights into Russia. Flights over Syria and Israel should be conducted.

Mr. Dulles and I reported developments as set forth in the intelligence summary and the State Department summary today. [2]

The President said our people should be alert. If the Soviets attack the French and British directly, we would be in war, and we would be justified in taking military action even if Congress were not in session. Mr. Dulles raised a question as to the status of Cyprus with respect to the NATO obligation. The President said that if reconnaissance discloses Soviet Air Forces on Syrian bases he would think that there would be reason for the British and French to destroy them. . . .

G
Colonel, CE, US Army

---

[1] Source: Eisenhower Library, Whitman File, Eisenhower Diaries. Top Secret. Drafted by Goodpaster. The time of the meeting is from the record of the President's Daily Appointments. (*Ibid.*)

[2] A memorandum by Armstrong, entitled "Summary of Intelligence Briefing, November 6, 1956" is in Department of State, INR Files: Lot 58 D 776, Middle East Crisis 1956 (Arab-Israeli Crisis). It contains a summary of developments pertaining to the Middle East and Hungary. The Department of State Daily Secret and Top Secret Summaries are *ibid.*: Lot 60 D 530.

519.   Telegram From the Embassy in the United Kingdom to the Department of State [1]

London, November 6, 1956—2 p.m.

2517. For Acting Secretary. Eden asked me to come to his office in the House at 12 o'clock today and handed me following message which he said he is planning to send to Hammarskjold today provided it is agreed to by French:

Begin verbatim text.

"HMG welcome the Secretary-General's communication of today's date [2] while agreeing that further clarification of certain points is necessary.

"If the Secretary-General can confirm that the Egypt and Israeli governments have accepted an unconditional cease-fire and that the international force to be set up will be competent to secure and supervise the attainment of the objectives set out in the operative paragraphs of the resolution passed by the General Assembly on November 2, HMG will agree to stop further military operations. The clearing of obstructions is not a military operation. The Franco-British forces are equipped to tackle this job and HMG propose that the technicians accompanying the force should begin the work at once. Pending the confirmation of the above HMG are ordering their forces to cease fire at (blank), unless they are attacked." *End verbatim text.*

Eden said that the last sentence would be included in the message and blank filled only if military events of today justified its inclusion. Eden stated that British and French troops had completed their occupation of Port Said and were proceeding down the road along the canal toward Ismailia but that Kirkpatrick had been in error when he said that they had actually reached Suez. Eden emphasized that everything was going extremely well. He reiterated the concern which Kirkpatrick has expressed to me this morning about Russians moving into Syria. Eden was extremely anxious that this message reach President immediately and said that if President wished to telephone him regarding it he would be available at any time. I asked Eden and Lloyd who was with him what their purposes were regarding actual withdrawal British and French forces

---

[1] Source: Department of State, Central Files, 320.5774/11–656. Top Secret; Niact; Presidential Handling. Received at 10:16 a.m.

[2] November 5; see Document 514.

from Egypt and they said that this message was not intended to cover anything except a cease-fire. [3]

Aldrich

---

[3] At 12:35 p.m. on November 6, the Department of State received telegram 2523 from London which reads as follows: "Confirming telephone conversation to Fisher Howe, Kirkpatrick informed Embassy at 1600 GMT [11 a.m. Washington time] that French have agreed to communication to Secretary-General that cease-fire hour referred to in last sentence thereof will be 2400 hours GMT [7 p.m. Washington time], that communication is consequently going forward now, and that Eden will make a statement in that connection in Commons at 1800 hours GMT." (Department of State, Central Files, 684A.86/11–656)

In addition to the cease-fire clause, the separate letters, sent by the British and French Governments to the Secretary-General on November 6 (respectively U.N. docs. A/3306 and 3307), included the proposal that British and French "technicians" accompanying the Franco-British force begin clearing the Suez Canal at once. The French note also contained a reminder that in the French letter to the Secretary-General of November 5 (U.N. doc. A/3294) had suggested an early meeting of the Security Council at the ministerial level to work out the conditions for a final cease-fire and a settlement of the problems of the Middle East.

---

520.   Telegram From the Embassy in the Soviet Union to the Department of State [1]

Moscow, November 6, 1956—3 p.m.

1091. Since dispatch Embtel 1083 [2] Soviet attitude as expressed in press, and in particular in communications to Eden and Mollet, becomes more ominous, and in the messages to Eden and Mollet comes as close to ultimatum as possible without so stating and fixing of time limit in proposed Soviet SC resolution is along same lines. While none of this can be accepted as conclusive evidence Soviet unilateral action if fighting in Egypt continues, Soviet Government, particularly in communications to Britain and France, are making it increasingly difficult for them to maintain complete inaction in event fighting continues and Egyptian Government and armed force are still capable of resistance.

I believe events here have gone beyond simple proposition of cover for Soviet action in Hungary. In fact, while it is obvious that Middle East provided psychological cover for Soviet action against

---

[1] Source: Department of State, Central Files, 674.84A/11–656. Secret; Priority; Presidential Handling. Received at 10:44 a.m. Repeated Priority to London and Paris.

[2] Document 506.

Hungary, Soviet decision in this regard may have been also, and perhaps more importantly, motivated by conviction that Middle East fighting might spread and that sooner or later Soviet Union would have to take some definite position. In such circumstances Soviet leaders, and military in particular, may have come to conclusion that under no circumstances could they lose their military position in Hungary no matter at what political or psychological cost. I shall be sending message later this morning giving joint opinion service attachés here as to military possibilities open to Soviet Union in regard to Middle East fighting. [3]

Key factor remains now of course of developments in regard to hostilities, and while Soviets have other irons in the fire I believe that they are primarily at this stage interested in seeing cessation hostilities. Soviet threat, I realize, has complicated situation but I still adhere to views expressed last paragraph reftel.

It is obviously important to convince Soviets that any military action on their part against Britain and France would encounter the armed opposition of the US. However, this warning would be very much more effective if it could be accompanied by some official communication from U.S. Government as to when all hostilities would cease against Egypt.

Bohlen

---

[3] In telegram 1093, November 6, Bohlen reported the following estimate, made by U.S. service attachés in Moscow, of Soviet capabilities to exert military influence on the Suez situation short of deliberate military operations: "(1) Clandestine movement of token volunteer forces by air or submarine, (2) overt movement by naval escorted shipping of volunteers and/or supplies, (3) Adriatic-based clandestine submarine action against Anglo-French forces under guise as Egyptians, (4) long-range submarine attack south of canal disguised as above, (5) overt naval visit to any Egyptian port threatened by Anglo-French action, (6) movement bomber and fighter aircraft to or through Syrian bases for employment by volunteer crews ignoring overflight considerations of Iran, Iraq, Turkey or Greece." Bohlen commented that this assessment was confined to operations in direct support of Egypt and did not include possible more serious actions which would involve world war, such as the bombing of Cyprus or direct Soviet military action. (Department of State, Central Files, 684A.86/11–656)

521.   Special National Intelligence Estimate [1]

SNIE 11–9–56   *Washington, November 6, 1956.*

SINO-SOVIET INTENTIONS IN THE SUEZ CRISIS [2]

The Estimate

1. The Soviet notes to Eden and Mollet constitute strong threats of military action against the UK, France, and Israel in connection with the Suez crisis. These threats are imprecise, however. They do not include a definite expression of Soviet intent to take unilateral military action; they still specifically call for UN action. Nevertheless, they are clearly intended to imply that the USSR may act alone.

2. There are several reasons for strong Soviet action in the Suez crisis:

a. to reassert the Soviet position as the champion of Egypt and of anticolonial countries generally;

b. to distract attention, both within and outside the Bloc, from the situation in Hungary;

c. to damage the interests and prestige of the UK and France and further divide and weaken the Western Alliances;

d. possibly, to re-establish the fear of the use of Soviet military force as a primary factor in world affairs.

3. We believe that our previous estimate that the USSR wishes to avoid general war continues to be valid.

4. It is our present estimate that the USSR:

---

[1] Source: Department of State, INR–NIE Files. Secret. According to a note on the cover sheet, "The following intelligence organizations participated in the preparation of this estimate: The Central Intelligence Agency and the intelligence organizations of the Departments of State, the Army, the Navy, the Air Force, and The Joint Staff." This estimate was concurred in by the Intelligence Advisory Committee on November 6. "Concurring were the Special Assistant, Intelligence, Department of State; the Assistant Chief of Staff, Intelligence, Department of the Army; the Director of Naval Intelligence; the Director of Intelligence, USAF; and the Deputy Director for Intelligence, The Joint Staff. The Atomic Energy Commission Representative to the IAC, and the Assistant Director, Federal Bureau of Investigation, abstained, the subject being outside of their jurisdiction."

[2] The minutes of the meeting of the Intelligence Advisory Committee for November 6 indicate that Allen Dulles made the following remarks concerning SNIE 11–9–56: "The DCI spoke of the developments since the approval of the report at 1:30 a.m. on November 6 and offered a revised draft of the first four paragraphs. He reported that the President had read the original draft that morning. The CIA revision was approved with some changes." The minutes also record that a CIA suggestion that SNIE 11–9–56 "be released to the British and Canadian governments was objected to by State on the grounds that the estimate might undercut the US position vis-à-vis the UK, and it was decided not to release the estimate." (*Ibid.*, INR Files: Lot 58 D 776) No copy of the original draft of SNIE 11–9–56 has been found in Department of State files.

a. will almost certainly not attack metropolitan UK or France—primarily because such an attack would make general war practically certain;

b. will probably not employ Soviet forces on a large scale in the Eastern Mediterranean—primarily because their capability to do so at an early date is inadequate, also because the risk of general war arising from such action would be very great;

c. may make small-scale attacks by air or submarine against UK and French forces in the Eastern Mediterranean—for the purpose of creating further pressures towards a UN settlement satisfactory to themselves, and showing themselves as the reliable champion of Egypt;

d. will continue to furnish military aid in the form of matériel, technicians, and logistics to Syria, and through Syria to the other Arab States, probably on an increased scale. They will probably send volunteers;

e. will at the least continue by threats to seek to create alarm in the West, in order to produce a UN settlement tolerable to the USSR.

5. With respect to the implied threat to the UK of using "rockets" (presumably guided missiles with nuclear warheads), the USSR is estimated to have the capability of delivering low yield atomic weapons by ballistic missiles with 800 nautical mile range which could reach the UK if launched from the Satellites. The 800 mile missile could reach major Israeli and Cypriot targets but not Egypt itself. Air-to-surface missiles, and probably submarine launched missiles with nuclear warheads are also within current Soviet capabilities and could pose a threat to all areas. We do not believe that the USSR would employ guided missiles with nuclear warheads in the Egyptian-Israeli conflict.

6. To attack Israel or Franco-British forces in the Eastern Mediterranean (except those on Cyprus) from present Bloc bases, the USSR would have to use aircraft of the Long-Range Air Force, or use IL–28 jet light bombers on missions involving no return to the Bloc. Establishment of bases for IL–28 bombers in Syria, Jordan, or Iraq is an alternative possibility, but would involve considerable problems of logistical support and defense of such bases, especially if they were used for sustained operations.

7. With respect to the Far East, we believe it possible, though it does not at present seem probable, that the Suez crisis might develop in such a way as to cause the Chinese Communists to take advantage of it by an attack on the British Crown Colony of Hong Kong.

8. This estimate is based on intelligence received up to 1100 hours EST, 6 November. In the fast developing situation our estimates of this situation must be kept under constant review. The flow of events will be drastically affected by day to day decision and action of the main participants, including in particular the USA,

and the estimate the Soviet Union reaches as to the probable course of action of the USA, and the UK and France.

---

522.   Special National Intelligence Estimate [1]

SNIE 30–6–56   *Washington, November 6, 1956.*

UK-FRENCH MILITARY INTENTIONS IN EGYPT

The Problem

To estimate whether the British and French intend to expand the area of ground operations beyond the immediate area of the Suez Canal.

The Estimate

1. We believe that the UK government probably did not intend, and does not now intend, to expand military action beyond the immediate area of the Suez Canal.

2. The French almost certainly wish to go further than the British but, being unable to act independently of the British, will follow the latter's policy.

3. The course of event might operate to change this intention— e.g., if UK and French forces along the canal are severely harassed by the Egyptians, and, possibly, the Sweetwater Canal is blocked. [2]

4. It seems to us more probable that events will act to restrict UK and French military operations to the Suez Canal area, and possibly to curtail them below present intentions. These events include: (a) the recent Soviet threat to use force, (b) the large and growing popular opposition in Britain to the entire venture, and (c)

---

[1] Source: Department of State, INR–NIE Files. Secret. According to a note on the cover sheet, "The following intelligence organizations participated in the preparation of this estimate: The Central Intelligence Agency and the intelligence organizations of the Departments of State, the Army, the Navy, the Air Force, and The Joint Staff." This estimate was concurred in by the Intelligence Advisory Committee on November 6. "Concurring were the Special Assistant, Intelligence, Department of State; the Assistant Chief of Staff, Intelligence, Department of the Army; the Director of Naval Intelligence; the Director of Intelligence, USAF; and the Deputy Director for Intelligence, The Joint Staff. The Atomic Energy Commission Representative on the IAC, and the Assistant Director, Federal Bureau of Investigation, abstained, the subject being outside of their jurisdiction."

[2] The Sweetwater Canal, which runs from the Nile River to Ismailia, is the source of fresh water for the entire canal area. [Footnote in the source text.]

the pressure of world opinion as shown both in the UN and elsewhere.[3]

---

[3] A memorandum by Charlton Ogburn (R/DRN), entitled "DRN Comments on ONE's Memorandum Entitled 'UK-French Military Intentions in Egypt'", takes exception to paragraph 4, concluding "that the British and French may very well be drawn into operations in the Delta regardless of their present preferences." (Department of State, INR Files: Lot 58 D 776, Middle East Crisis 1956 (Arab-Israeli Crisis))

---

523. Memorandum of a Conversation, Department of State, Washington, November 6, 1956 [1]

SUBJECT

Egyptian Request for Help of the United States

PARTICIPANTS

Dr. Ahmed Hussein, Ambassador of Egypt

The Acting Secretary
Mr. William M. Rountree, Assistant Secretary, NEA
Mr. Fraser Wilkins, Director, NE

The Egyptian Ambassador called at the Department today to present a note from the Government of Egypt in which it requested the help of the United States (Tab A). Prior to handing this note to the Acting Secretary, the Egyptian Ambassador had a preliminary discussion with Assistant Secretary Rountree.

On presenting the note to the Acting Secretary, Dr. Hussein said he had been instructed by his government to deliver it personally to the Acting Secretary. Mr. Hoover said he believed the fundamental problem today was whether the Government of Egypt would accept the establishment of a cease-fire under the resolutions of the General Assembly. The Ambassador replied he understood the Government of Egypt had already accepted the request for a cease-fire and the formation of a United Nations force but that the other parties had not yet responded. The Egyptian Ambassador also handed the Acting Secretary a copy of a statement which he had just received from Cairo regarding British bombing of Egypt (Tab B).[2] The Ambassador continued that according to radio reports British and

---

[1] Source: Department of State, Central Files, 684.86/11–656. Confidential. Drafted by Wilkins.

[2] Attached to the source text, but not printed.

French bombing of Cairo was continuing. He could not understand why this should be the case since Egypt had accepted a cease-fire. He also asked why Britain and France were continuing to send military forces into Egypt when Ambassador Lodge had indicated that the UN resolutions would prevent their introduction. He thought it was not honorable for two great powers to team up with one small power to attack a small country like Egypt. It would take years to repair the damage that had been done through British and French destruction. He hoped that the United States would come to Egypt's help.

The Acting Secretary said he understood the trials to which Egypt was now subjected. He knew that the Secretary-General of the United Nations was making every effort under UN resolutions to bring about a cease-fire and was hopeful it would soon be effected. He did not believe he could speculate beyond that point at this moment.

[Tab A]

Note From the Egyptian Ambassador (Hussein) to the Acting Secretary of State

Washington, November 6, 1956.

SIR: Acting on instructions from my Government I have the honour to communicate to the Government of the United States of America the following appeal by the Egyptian Government in the name of the people of Egypt:

"At this historic hour of decision when the best values of humanity's heritage are at stake and the human race is pushed back toward chaos and savagery, when France, Israel and the United Kingdom are launching a treacherous attack against Egypt and are defiantly bearing the standard of lawlessness and of shame, Egypt appeals for help by volunteers, arms or otherwise to all those who, all over the world, care still for the dignity of man and the rule of law in international relations.

"The people of Egypt are fighting a battle of survival and of honour. They are fighting it not only for themselves and their country but equally for the civilised world. As long as aggression continues against Egypt on her own territory and in defiance of the resolutions of the United Nations Egypt shall go on fighting in all determination and with every shred of its being against the forces of evil and in behalf of decency and a life worth living. She needs your help."

Please accept, Sir, the assurances of my highest consideration.

Ahmed Hussein

---

524.   Memorandum of a Conversation, Department of State, Washington, November 6, 1956[1]

SUBJECT

Message from the French Government to the President

PARTICIPANTS

The Acting Secretary of State	Mr. Hervé Alphand, French
Mr. Robert Murphy—G	Ambassador
Mr. C. Burke Elbrick—EUR	M. Charles Lucet, French Minister
Mr. William R. Tyler—WE	

The Acting Secretary received the French Ambassador who said that he was under instructions from his Government to see the President urgently in order to deliver a message to him. The Acting Secretary explained that the President was out of town,[2] but that he would be glad to convey to him any message which the French Ambassador might have for him. Ambassador Alphand expressed his thanks and proceeded to summarize the substance of his Government's message to the President as follows:

The French Government is greatly concerned by the threat in the letter from Bulganin to Eden and Mollet,[3] and cannot exclude the possibility of an attack by the Soviet Union against the UK and France. The French Government does not know what form this might take. However, the Ambassador said that his Government is in possession of intelligence reports from Central Europe of a concentration of Soviet divisions in Czechoslovakia, with a possible threat to Austria. The Ambassador was instructed to tell the U.S. Government of the importance the French Government attaches to

---

[1] Source: Department of State, Central Files, 751.5/11–656. Secret. Drafted by Tyler.

[2] On the morning of November 6, President and Mrs. Eisenhower drove to Gettysburg, Pennsylvania, to vote in the national elections. He returned by plane to Washington, arriving at the White House at 12:38 p.m. (Record of the President's Daily Appointments; Eisenhower Library)

[3] See footnote 2, Document 511.

the Soviet Union being warned in advance of the result of such a threat of attack, by the U.S. Government recalling the existence of the North Atlantic Treaty, and its commitment to resist any attack against its allies. Because of the gravity of this message, the Ambassador was instructed to deliver it personally to the President. The Ambassador subsequently made two further points: first, the reference to the Austrian situation was given only as an example, since the French Government is aware that Austria is outside the NATO area and guaranteed by the United States; and second, the French strongly agree with the view, often expressed by the Secretary of State, that miscalculation by a potential enemy can be avoided if a clear warning is given of the consequences of aggression. [4]

The Acting Secretary, in reply, said he fully recognized the importance of the French Government's message. He emphasized that the only way to get the situation back on the tracks was for the French and British Governments to accept unequivocally and unconditionally the UN resolution calling for a cease fire, with the withdrawal of forces, and the acceptance of a UN police force. The Ambassador suggested that this was a different matter, to which the Acting Secretary replied that on the contrary, the two were intimately related. He added that we had just heard unofficially that the French and British Governments had accepted the UN resolution. The French Ambassador said he was not informed of this, and then referred to the Swiss proposal for a meeting of the five heads of Government. The Acting Secretary said the U.S. Government appreciates the sincerity of the Swiss proposal but that it could not be

---

[4] A handwritten notation by Tyler on a typed "Memorandum from the Government of the French Republic to the President of the United States of America", reads: "This the only copy of the Nov. 6 message from Mollet to the President, which Ambassador Alphand handed me informally on Nov. 7, 1956." The text of the memorandum reads: "In view of the threat contained in the letter addressed by Marshal Bulganin to the governments of the United Kingdom and France, the French government does not exclude the possibility that an attack can be directed by the Soviet Union against both countries, in a way which it is obviously impossible to foresee.

"The French Government desires to bring to your attention highly reliable intelligence reports indicating troop movements in Central Europe and notably in Czechoslovakia, which constitutes a threat to Austria.

"It is essential that the United States government should make known in advance its attitude by confirming in a non-equivocal way that the provisions of the North Atlantic Treaty would apply immediately upon a Soviet attack directed against the allies of the United States." (Department of State, Presidential Correspondence: Lot 66 D 204, DeGaulle, Mollet, Gaillard 7/56 thru 1/61)

even considered before the UN resolution had been accepted and acted upon. [5]

525.   Transcript of a Telephone Conversation Between President Eisenhower in Washington and Prime Minister Eden in London, November 6, 1956, 12:55 p.m. [1]

The President called the Prime Minister of Great Britain.

The President: This is a very clear connection.

Eden: I can just hear you.

The President: First of all, I can't tell you how pleased we are that you found it possible to accept the cease-fire, [2] having landed.

Eden: We have taken a certain risk, but I think it is justified.

The President: Anthony, this is the way I feel about it. I have not ruminated over this particular situation at length. I am talking off the top of my head. You have got what you said you were going to get in that you have landed. It seems to me that from what—with regard to the cease-fire, and without going into any negotiations, I would go ahead with the cease-fire, not putting any conditions into the acceptance of the resolution and after cease-fire talking about the clearing of the Canal and so on.

Eden: We are going to cease firing tonight.

[1] Source: Eisenhower Library, Whitman File, Eisenhower Diaries. Prepared in the Office of the President. Another copy of the transcription is *ibid.*, ACW Diary. Eden described this conversation in *Full Circle*, p. 628.

[2] On November 6, the Governments of France and Great Britain informed Hammarskjöld that, pending clarifications concerning the U.N. command, their forces would cease fire at midnight GMT (2 a.m. Cairo time, November 7) unless attacked. (U.N. docs. A/3307 and A/3306, respectively)

The President: Could you not tell Hammarskjold that as far as the cease-fire arrangement is concerned, that that goes without condition.

Eden: We cease firing tonight at midnight provided we are not attacked.

The President: I see.

Eden: What you may call the long cease-fire, the cessation of hostilities, that is more complicated.

The President: Yes it is more complicated. Talking about the technical troops of yours.

Eden: They will cooperate with us in having a cease-fire tonight.

The President: If I may make a suggestion, I would offer them to Hammarskjold—but I would not insist that he take them.

Eden: It is always a bit of working out with the allies and everybody else to get this thing—with some difficulty.

The President: The point I want you to have in your mind is that the cease-fire tonight has nothing to do with technical troops. You cease anyway.

Eden: Unless attacked.

The President: The more permanent affair—we would like to know about the other thing.

Eden: I have got to go [to] my Parliament.

The President: Oh, all right.

Eden: In five minutes. Would you authorize me to say that you think this is helpful outside—

The President: You can say that I called to say how delighted I was you found it possible to cease fire tonight so that negotiations could start.

Eden: I am just getting it down—

The President: how delighted I was that you found it possible to direct a cease-fire tonight which will allow negotiations to proceed from there on.

Eden: Proceed—

The President: Yes. Wait a minute. Well, I will tell you what I am trying to get at. I don't want to give Egypt an opportunity to begin to quibble so that this thing can be drawn out for a week. After the cease-fire it seems like the little technical things of it would be settled very quickly, and when Hammarskjold comes along with his people you people ought to be able to withdraw very quickly. He is getting Canadian troops—lots of troops—together.

Eden: I hope you will be there. Are we all going to go out?

The President: What I want to do is this. I would like to see none of the great nations in it. I am afraid the Red boy is going to demand the lion's share. I would rather make it no troops from the big five. I would say, "Mr. Hammarskjold, we trust you. When we see you coming in with enough troops to take over, we go out."

Eden: That is not too easy unless they have good force, you know.

The President: I will tell you. If they have enough—and they attack, they attack the United Nations and its whole prestige and force—then everyone is in the thing. Then you are [not] alone.

Eden: May I think that one over.

The President: Now that we know connections are so good, you can call me anytime you please.

Eden: If I survive here tonight I will call you tomorrow. How are things going with you.

The President: We have given our whole thought to Hungary and the Middle East. I don't give a damn how the election goes. I guess it will be all right. [3]

Eden: How is Foster?

The President: Pretty good. He's making a pretty quick recovery.

Eden: Wonderful.

The President: All right. Thank you and go ahead with your meeting.

Eden: Thanks so much.

---

[3] Eisenhower was reelected President by an overwhelming margin.

---

526.   Telegram From the Embassy in Egypt to the Department of State [1]

Cairo, November 6, 1956—2 p.m.

1350. . . . this morning intimate Nasser advisers after clearing with President stated Egypt had not asked for Soviet help but could not . . . issue statement rejecting Soviet offer. However GOE requesting Hammarskjold act with utmost speed in dispatching UN force.

Advisers then pled for immediate dispatch Sixth Fleet as only hope forestall Soviets.

---

[1] Source: Department of State, Central Files, 661.74/11–656. Secret; Niact. Received at 1:26 p.m. Repeated Niact to London, Paris, and Moscow.

. . . Ali Sabri sent information that reports from Egyptian Ambassador Moscow and Kisselev here convince Sabri Soviets prepared go all the way in knowledge risking third world war.

Consider significant fact this message repeated and urgent request for Sixth Fleet intervention.

. . . ominous information received from Egyptian Embassy Moscow. . . .

Hare

---

527.   Message From President Eisenhower to Prime Minister Eden [1]

Washington, November 6, 1956.

DEAR ANTHONY: I was delighted at the opportunity to talk with you on the telephone and to hear that the U.K. will order a cease-fire this evening. On thinking over our talk I wish to emphasize my urgent view a) that the UN Resolution on cease-fire and entry of a UN force be accepted without condition so as not to give Egypt with Soviet backing an opportunity to quibble or start negotiations; items such as use technical troops to clear canal can be handled later; b) that it is vital no excuse be given for Soviet participation in UN force, therefore all big five should be excluded from force as UN proposes. Any attack on UN force would meet immediate reaction from all UN; c) I think immediate consummation UN plan of greatest importance otherwise there might be invitation to developments of greatest gravity.

Sincerely hope you find it possible to agree with these views and can so inform Hammarskjold before tonight's meeting.

---

[1] Source: Department of State, Central Files, 320.5774/11–656. Secret. Transmitted to London at 2:29 p.m. in telegram 3285, November 6, which is the source text, with the instruction: "Please deliver soonest following message from President to Eden. Confirm date and time delivery." Telegram 3285 indicates the message was drafted by Phleger, cleared by Eisenhower, and approved by Greene. A draft of the message, in an unidentified hand, bears changes by Eisenhower. (Eisenhower Library, Whitman File, International File). Telegram 2536 from London, November 7, reported delivery as of midnight November 6/7. (Department of State, Central Files, 711.11–EI/11–756)

Telegram 1708 to Paris, November 6, transmitted the text of a similar message for delivery to Mollet. (*Ibid.*, 320.5774/11–656)

Let me say again that I will be delighted to have you call me at any time. The telephone connection seemed very satisfactory. [2]

Warmest regard,

Ike E [3]

---

[2] Dillon informed Dulles of the impact which this message had on the French Government in a letter dated November 7. Dillon wrote: "Last night I had one of the strangest experiences of my whole career here in Paris when, shortly after midnight, I delivered the President's letter to Mollet asking him to agree that French forces would not be part of the international UN forces in Suez. For forty minutes I sat in Mollet's office taking part in a sort of informal French Cabinet meeting with Pineau and the Minister of the Interior.

"Mollet seemed to get the idea fairly easily, but I engaged in about a half hour argument back and forth with Pineau, who could see nothing good in the President's suggestion, while Mollet acted more or less as referee. Finally, I suggested that Mollet call up Eden to see what he felt about the matter. After a little persuasion Mollet agreed to do this, and when it was found that Eden's position agreed with Mollet's and the President's on this particular point, Pineau's opposition finally collapsed." (*Ibid.*, 110.11–DU/11–756)

[3] Telegram 3285 bears this typed signature.

---

528.   Telegram From the Embassy in Egypt to the Department of State [1]

Cairo, November 6, 1956—11 a.m.

1345. Following is my comment on Niact 1447. [2]

(1) I have not seen Nasser since Friday November 2 when I delivered President's reply to his message. There was no discussion at that time, nor had there been previously, of any question of Nasser's resignation. Only comment in Friday's discussion which might be considered as having indirect bearing on subject reference telegram was expression Nasser's intention not even evacuate his family.

(2) . . . contacts with government sources have revealed varying degrees despondency as situation progressed especially re destruction Egyptian Air Force but there has never been any intimation of

---

[1] Source: Department of State, Central Files, 774.11/11–656. Top Secret; Niact. Received at 4:56 p.m. Repeated to Paris.

[2] Telegram 1447 to Cairo, November 5, requested Hare's comments on the report (see footnote 3, Document 511) that Nasser intended to resign but changed his mind after being informed of continuing U.S. support. (Department of State, Central Files, 774.11/11–556)

intention Nasser or government to resign. On contrary attitude has been "if they want us, let them come and get us".

(3) I have constantly borne in mind throughout crisis necessity of separating questions of Anglo-French-Israeli attacks on Egypt and continuance of Nasser regime. My conversations have been confined exclusively to former and Nasser never attempted discuss latter.

(4) My reports to Department have been as complete and accurate as I could make them.

Hare

529.   Informal Summary of a Meeting Held in the Department of State, Washington, November 6, 1956, 5:45 p.m. [1]

PARTICIPANTS

 The Acting Secretary
 Mr. Hollister
 Mr. Murphy
 Mr. Henderson
 Mr. Prochnow
 Mr. Bowie
 Mr. MacArthur
 Mr. Hill
 Mr. Wilcox
 Mr. Elbrick
 Mr. Robertson
 Mr. Rountree
 Mr. Phleger
 Mr. Armstrong
 Mr. Greene
 Mr. Sohm

1. Mr. Hoover reported on the meeting at the White House at 12:30 (see separate memorandum), [2] noting that the JCS evaluation was that the Soviets could not immediately mount a major military operation in the Middle East.

2. Mr. Phleger discussed the situation in the UN in the light of the Secretary-General's press statement and his release of the British

---

[1] Source: Department of State, Central Files, 974.7301/11–656. Top Secret. Drafted by Greene.

[2] Not found in Department of State files or the Eisenhower Library. See footnote 1, Document 533.

letter on the cease-fire.[3] Discussion brought out general agreement that a simple cease-fire will be of no use unless accompanied by provision for withdrawal of British and French and Israeli forces from Egypt, probably to be negotiated over a period of a few days. Mr. Wilcox was to make sure that Ambassador Lodge knows our position in connection with handling the Secretary General's resolution and the Afro-Asian resolution expected to be discussed at the GA session scheduled for later in the evening.[4]

3. Mr. Wilcox was also to telephone Ambassador Lodge the Department's views of the 7 p.m. version of the Afro-Asian resolution, indicating that as an initial position we should try to get some clarifying amendments; in the end, to avoid an open break with the sponsor, we could vote for it as it stands if they would not agree to amend it.

4. The Acting Secretary reviewed some of the Defense Department plans[5] and noted that he had reminded Reuben Robertson that final decision on such questions as military leaves rested with the President. He also wished the Department to be in a position to evaluate quickly the results of the GA debate and be able to move, with Defense, as indicated by the results of the meeting. The Acting Secretary said he has asked Defense to have ready plans for providing the air lift and other support we have promised for a UN force and to have available an officer who could go to New York to be the single liaison channel between the SYG and the US military. Our military should deal only with the SYG and only after he has asked for assistance; our military should not deal with national delegations or governments.

5. The Acting Secretary noted that, in addition to a UN force, there may be a need for UN observers to oversee compliance with the resolutions which form the basis for stopping the hostilities.

6. Mr. Hill said that there would be a meeting at 9 a.m., November 7[6] to reach a final decision on a bipartisan Congressional meeting which is being tentatively scheduled for Friday.[7]

---

[3] In his press statement of November 5, Hammarskjöld summarized the developments described in Document 514. At the same time, he released the text of the first Israeli letter of November 5 and the British letter of November 5. Excerpts of his statement and the text of the letters were printed in *The New York Times*, November 6.

[4] On November 5, the Mission at the United Nations transmitted to the Department of State the "final text" of a resolution which certain Afro-Asian nations planned to introduce in the General Assembly. (Delga 13 from USUN; Department of State, Central Files, 320.5774/11–556) On November 6, the Mission transmitted a revised version of the same resolution. (Delga 17; *ibid.*, 320.5774/11–656) The General Assembly did not reconvene until November 7.

[5] See footnote 1, Document 533.

[6] No account of this meeting has been found in Department of State files.

[7] November 9.

7. Mr. Prochnow noted that the British, and possibly the French, economic situations are such that they may need help very quickly; in this connection the Treasury Department is opposed to a reported German plan for accelerating repayment of their post-war debt accounts to the British and others.

8. Mr. Elbrick had ready a proposed reply for the President of Switzerland on the latter's proposal for a Big Five meeting, but it was decided to let this matter wait a day or two before trying to reach a final position.

JG [8]

---

[8] Printed from a copy that bears these typed initials.

---

530.   Telegram From the Department of State to the Embassy in Egypt [1]

Washington, November 6, 1956—6:29 p.m.

1457. Embtel 1350. [2] You may in your discretion . . . convey message to Nasser along following lines:

For past five days UN with full US support has been making monumental effort achieve cease-fire, withdrawal of foreign forces now engaged in hostilities and formation UN force. Egypt's cooperation has been helpful. UK and France today accepted cease-fire and Israel has also agreed. Cease-fire established for 2 a.m. November 7 Cairo time. Meeting of UNGA scheduled this evening to complete arrangements for UN force which we expect will be sent to Egypt with greatest speed.

Egypt must recognize Soviet "offer" motivated by considerations other than attainment peace. As announced by President yesterday US has categorically rejected Soviet proposal for US–USSR military operation. Injection other foreign forces outside context UN action would be clear violation UN Charter and it would be the duty of all UN members including the US to oppose any such effort. There is no question that Egypt's interest and security can best be protected by looking to UN which is acting in most effective manner, and that Egypt should leave no doubt that it would not

---

[1] Source: Department of State, Central Files, 320.5780/11–856. Secret; Niact; Limited Distribution. Drafted by Rountree, cleared in substance by Phleger and Allen Dulles, and approved by Rountree.

[2] Document 526.

welcome unilateral Soviet intervention, consequences of which would be unpredictable. [3]

Hoover

[3] In telegram 1376 from Cairo, November 7, Ambassador Hare informed the Department that its intent was already being implemented and that he felt it inadvisable to seek a special interview with Nasser to reiterate the same ideas. Hare also advised the Department that it could expect Egyptian requests for economic or other types of assistance to restore losses suffered during the attacks of last week. Hare asked the Department for guidance on how to respond to these requests when they occurred. (Department of State, Central Files, 320.5780/11–756)

---

531. Telegram From the Embassy in France to the Department of State [1]

Paris, November 7, 1956—1 a.m.

2238. Re Deptel 1708. [2] Message reftel delivered by me to Mollet at 12:15 a.m. local 11:15 GMT. Pineau also present. Neither Mollet nor Pineau clear regarding desires of President in particular as to whether phrase "I sincerely hope that the UN proposal for the cease fire and the entry of UN troops are being accepted without conditions" was meant to include agreement to immediate evacuation of French-British forces and retreat of Israeli troops from Sinai area.

I suggested that Mollet call Eden for clarification which he did in my presence. Mollet reported Eden as saying that President only touched lightly on subject during their telephone conversation. Eden then said that it was impossible for French-British forces to withdraw until UN force arrives. He further said that UN force in British view could well be composed of elements from smaller countries as requested by UN proposal.

Mollet then ordered full Cabinet meeting to consider subject. It clear to me that he personally now prepared to accept UN force without French or British participation. Pineau in accord and this

[1] Source: Department of State, Central Files, 684A.86/11–656. Secret; Niact; Presidential Handling. Received at 8:35 p.m., November 6. A copy in the Eisenhower Library, Whitman File, International File bears the marginal notation by Goodpaster, "President informed".
[2] See footnote 1, Document 527.

will be French position if Cabinet approves which I consider probable.

French however will not withdraw forces until UN force in place and ready to function. French also wish U.S. to offer such arms as may be necessary to UN force. This also Eden's position as reported by Mollet after telephone conversation.

Pineau also said U.S. must guarantee UN force. I pointed out this guarantee already implicit in President's message which reasoning accepted by Mollet and eventually by Pineau.

I feel Mollet prepared give unequivocal favorable reply to President's message provided no withdrawal French forces implied prior arrival UN force. Pineau however has more complex attitude and was worrying whether unconditional acceptance might not imply commitment to use force to insure return Israeli troops within frontiers Israel.

I endeavored keep problem within simple bounds of Presidential message and felt that Mollet not sympathetic to Pineau complexities. Council of Ministers may however be influenced by Pineau to some extent. Therefore exact form message French will send Hammarskjold remains unpredictable.

Dillon

---

532.   Message From Prime Minister Mollet to President Eisenhower [1]

Paris, November 6, 1956.

The French Government accepts the principle of non-participation of the five permanent members of the United Nations in the international force established by the United Nations. However, the Anglo-French forces could not be withdrawn before the United Nations force has been constituted and is in a position to carry out its missions. Problems concerning the definition of its missions, the

---

[1] Source: Eisenhower Library, Whitman File, International File. Transmitted to USUN for Lodge in telegram 253, November 7, which is the source text. A memorandum for the files by Hagerty, which is attached to the source text, reads: "This message was phoned from the French Embassy after the French Ambassador presented the note to the President to William Tyler of the State Department. He called by telephone at 11:35 [p.m.] and read the English translation of the note. Secretary Hoover then presented it to the President who then called in the Vice President for a brief discussion."

disposition of the forces and the reopening of the Canal could be examined by the Security Council in the course of the session which it would be holding at the level of Ministers of Foreign Affairs.

I take the liberty of insisting that the United States should give to the forces which will be provided by the small and medium sized states, the material and moral help required to enable them to carry out the mission effectively.

Guy Mollet [2]

---

[2] Telegram 253 bears this typed signature.

---

533. Telegram From the Joint Chiefs of Staff to Certain Specified and Unified Commanders [1]

Washington, November 6, 1956—11:56 p.m.

JCS 912988. From JCS. Exclusive for General Armstrong, Admiral Wright, General Harrison, General Partridge, General Gruenther, General Lemnitzer, Admiral Stump, Admiral Boone, [2] General Lemay. Ref JCS 912901. [3] The JCS have directed the following actions to improve the state of readiness of United States forces in addition to

---

[1] Source: JCS Records, OCJCS 091 Palestine (Jun 56–Dec 56). Top Secret; Operational Immediate; Noforn. The source text indicates that the message originated with Admiral Radford.

During a White House meeting which began at 12:33 p.m. on November 6, the Joint Chiefs of Staff presented to President Eisenhower a series of recommendations to improve the U.S. military state of readiness. The record of the President's Daily Appointments at the Eisenhower Library lists the following participants: Eisenhower, Hoover, Nixon, General Nathan Twining, Admiral Arleigh Burke, General Williston Palmer, Allen Dulles, Radford, General Randolph M. Pate, Goodpaster, and 10 others. No memorandum of this meeting has been found at the Eisenhower Library, although Eisenhower gives a brief account of it in *Waging Peace* (p. 91). A memorandum listing the original recommendations agreed upon by the JCS during the morning of November 6 is attached to a memorandum from Wentworth to Radford of November 6 in JCS Records, OCJCS File 091 Palestine (Jun 56–Dec 56). The message printed here contains those recommendations approved by the President to be implemented immediately. The President did not approve a recommendation to improve the readiness of the Strategic Air Command and he deferred immediate action on a recommendation for all Services to recall all personnel from regular leave.

[2] Admiral Boone had established a temporary headquarters for the Eastern Atlantic and Mediterranean Fleet at Port Lyaute, Morocco.

[3] Not printed. The message to certain Unified and Specified Commanders directed that they exercise special vigilance in light of the recent Soviet notes. (JCS Files)

the actions listed in JCS 912463 [4] and JCS 912773. [5] Specific implementing orders will be issued through executive agents.

1. Continental Air Defense Command.

Assume status of "increased readiness" as defined in CONADR 55–3. [6]

2. Sixth Fleet.

Sail the USS *Forrestal*, the *Franklin D. Roosevelt*, one cruiser and three divisions of destroyers toward the Azores.

3. Atlantic and Pacific Fleets.

a. Send additional picket ships to DEW Line extensions.
b. Send additional antisubmarine warfare units to sea.
c. Prepare to reinforce the Seventh Fleet with 2 CVA's, 1 CA and 1 Desron.
d. Deploy submarines to reconnaissance stations.
e. Alert SOSUS.

4. Tactical Air Command.

Place all heavy troop carrier wings in the ZI on 12-hour alert and suspend training and routine support operations of these wings as directed.

5. The JCS consider that the above actions plus increased alertness on the part of intelligence personnel and general vigilance on the part of addressees and their subordinate commanders will satisfy readiness requirements at this time.

6. At the time this dispatch leaves Washington there is reasonable chance that U.N. action in obtaining a cease-fire in Egypt may reduce or eliminate the chances of overt Soviet military action which would enlarge hostilities. JCS expect that over-all knowledge of actions directed in paras 1 thru 4 will be limited in each command

---

[4] Document 415.

[5] See footnote 4, *ibid.*

[6] The JCS memorandum of November 6 noted that an improved state of readiness for CONAD would involve an increase in the number of interceptor aircraft on advanced state of alert; an increase from two aircraft on five-minute alert at each station to four aircraft, and a halt in training in all areas in which it interfered with increased readiness.

and that in carrying out specific actions commands will limit knowledge to those who need to know. It is probable that certain movements of preparatory action will become public knowledge. In such cases if queried answer that certain redeployments are being made to improve our defensive capabilities.

United States Efforts To Obtain a British, French, and Israeli Withdrawal From Occupied Territory, November 7–December 31, 1956

REFERRAL OF THE MIDDLE EAST ITEM TO THE U.N. GENERAL
ASSEMBLY; THE EUROPEAN OIL SUPPLY PROBLEM AND THE
ACTIVATION OF THE MIDDLE EAST EMERGENCY COMMITTEE'S PLAN;
ANGLO-FRENCH DECISION TO WITHDRAW FORCES FROM THE SUEZ
CANAL ZONE, NOVEMBER 7–DECEMBER 4

534.   Editorial Note

During an address to the Knesset on November 7, Prime Minister Ben Gurion rejected the proposals adopted by the General Assembly for the stationing of United Nations forces in Israel or in the areas occupied by Israel. He also declared the Israeli-Egyptian Armistice Agreement of 1949 to be "dead and buried", stated that the armistice lines had no more validity, and expressed Israel's hope for a peace treaty with Egypt. (Excerpts from Ben Gurion's address are printed in *United States Policy in the Middle East, September 1956–June 1957*, pages 199–204.)

That same day in New York, during the morning session of the General Assembly, Secretary-General Hammarskjöld called Ambassador Lodge aside and informed him that, according to a report from General Burns, the Government of Israel intended and might have already taken steps to force UNTSO observers from the Gaza area. Hammarskjöld told Lodge that if Israel persisted in this attitude he anticipated such a strong reaction from members of the United Nations that Israel might be expelled. Hammarskjöld then showed Lodge a copy of Ben Gurion's statement to the Knesset of November 7 and said that he intended immediately to register a protest with Ambassador Eban on this matter. Subsequently, Hammarskjöld informed Lodge that he had requested through Eban clarifications from Ben Gurion as to whether Israel would withdraw all its forces behind the armistice demarcation lines. Hammarskjöld also warned Eban that any actions taken against UNTSO observers would be reported to the General Assembly. (Reported in Delga 23 from USUN, November 7; Department of State, Central Files, 320.5780/11–756)

1038

535.   Message From Prime Minister Eden to President Eisenhower [1]

London, November 7, 1956.

DEAR FRIEND: Thank you so much for your message. [2] I am so grateful for the help which you are giving us.

I entirely understand the force of what you say. As regards your point (a) I do not think there need be any difficulty. In our reply to the Secretary General, we did not in fact make it a condition of our acceptance of the cease-fire and entry of a United Nations Force that the obstructions in the Canal should be cleared by our troops. This is however something which has got to be done most urgently in the interests of the world. We are on the spot and the only people who can do it quickly. We therefore think it right that we should be allowed to carry it through unhindered. I am personally inclined to agree with your point (b) namely that the Big Five should be excluded from the United Nations Force. This is however a matter on which there are very deep feelings here. I could not take a decision of such magnitude without consulting my colleagues and I will do so as soon as possible in the morning. I think that before we can take a decision we may want to know more about what the functions of the United Nations Force are to be.

I am asking our Representative at the United Nations to explain matters to Hammarskjold on the above lines. Do please believe that I am sincerely anxious that we should work together in all this. But these are matters of such importance for our country that I must ask for a little further time to consider them.

I too was delighted to hear your voice this evening. I hope that we can keep in close touch.

Yours ever,

Anthony [3]

---

[1] Source: Eisenhower Library, Whitman File, International File. Secret. Delivered to the White House under cover of a note from Coulson to President Eisenhower which reads: "The Prime Minister has asked me to give you the enclosed personal message."

[2] Document 527.

[3] Printed from a copy that bears this typed signature.

536.   Memorandum of a Telephone Conversation Between President Eisenhower in Washington and Prime Minister Eden in London, November 7, 1956, 8:43 a.m. [1]

At 8:43 (the morning after the election) the Prime Minister called the President. Colonel Schulz remained in the room (President took call in the Mansion). He reports as follows:

Apparently in accordance with a previous suggestion, the President said he would be delighted to have the Prime Minister and Mollet come to the United States, and asked the Prime Minister (because he was so close to Mollet) to call him and assure him that the meeting would not be complete without him. The President also said that an invitation would immediately be sent to Mollet (and the President later called Secretary Hoover to be sure that this was done). They are leaving tonight, meetings here Friday and Saturday. [2]

During the conversation the President said "after all, it is like a family spat."

The President thereupon called Hoover with gist of above.

About 9:10 Mr. Millard called from 10 Downing Street, to say that the Prime Minister had spoken to Mr. Mollet, who is fully in accord and delighted to come. Prime Minister assured him an invitation was on its way.

Mr. Selwyn Lloyd is accompanying the Prime Minister.

At first he said that the Prime Minister wanted to leave the publicity entirely in American hands and suggested a time of 1:00 p.m. our time of lease [*for release*]. 20 minutes later the Prime Minister's secretary Mr. Millard called back and said that the Prime Minister had talked to Mr. Mollet again and that Mr. Mollet, because of debate he was having in his Parliament, wanted to announce the matter at 5:00 French time, which would be 4:00 London and 11:00 here. That would be simultaneous announcement from the three capitals.

---

[1] Source: Eisenhower Library, Whitman File, Eisenhower Diaries. Prepared in the Office of the President.

[2] November 9 and 10.

537.   Telegram From the Embassy in France to the Department of State [1]

Paris, November 7, 1956—1 p.m.

2242. Crouy-Chanel gave us this morning rundown on French thinking re UNGA meeting this afternoon and French request for early SC meeting at ministerial level.

Crouy repeated several times very earnestly that French Govt considers cease-fire "extremely fragile." Soviets may still be encouraging Egyptians to resist and sending them assistance for this purpose. Recent distribution of arms to Cairo population may result in attacks on French or other Western nationals. French Govt is being strongly criticized by important elements public opinion for ceasing fire prematurely particularly while Nasser still in power.

Hence French Govt views with alarm GA debate marked by inflammatory speeches and provocative or unenforceable resolutions. Such demonstrations could create serious complications and lead to renewal and extension of hostilities. French very much hope we will cooperate with them in 1) directing GA efforts primarily to maintenance cease-fire, rather than immediate withdrawal of forces; 2) concentrating in hands of Secretary General responsibility for setting up international force; and 3) transferring to SC at earliest possible moment consideration of major outstanding problems, such as withdrawal of forces, reopening of Canal and establishment stable peace in Near East. French believe all of these can be much more successfully handled in restricted forum and under more flexible SC procedures.

Comment: As far as we can judge from this end, French arguments quoted above are sound and deserve our support. Possibility of violation cease-fire by Egyptians under Russian inspiration is of course obvious. Moreover Crouy is right in stating many important French elements (including probably most military) consider cease-fire premature, particularly in view Nasser's survival, and would be tempted to reopen hostilities if provoked in any way. It does seem of vital importance therefore that boat not be rocked any more than absolutely necessary and further public debate be limited to extent possible.

Dillon

---

[1] Source: Department of State, Central Files, 320.5780/11–756. Secret; Niact. Received at 8:46 a.m. Repeated Niact to USUN, Priority to London, and to Cairo. Fisher Howe forwarded a copy of this telegram to Hoover on November 7, under cover of a memorandum which summarized the subjects on which the French wished U.S. cooperation and which noted that Dillon supported cooperation. (*Ibid.*)

538.   Transcript of a Telephone Conversation Between President Eisenhower in Washington and Prime Minister Eden in London, November 7, 1956, 9:55 a.m. [1]

9:55 a.m.—Sir Anthony Eden.

President: I wanted to talk to you about your visit—so we can't have any misunderstanding & later regret it. As you know, we are committed to Hammarskjold's plan—& very definitely. If the purpose of the visit would be to concert ourselves in NATO & what we are going to do in the future, then we have nothing to fear. If we are going to discuss this plan & your people would find it necessary to disagree with us, then the resulting divided communiqué would be unfortunate.

Eden: We have meeting scheduled for 3 o'clock—trying to hammer out something for Hammarskjold. We will go along as far as we can on the lines you mentioned last night. I think we can pretty well agree to any scheme that will work—as long as we are in the dark . . . [2] But I don't want to come to talk about that.

President: I think that is very good. The only thing I didn't want for us to have to say we would discuss points that are up for discussion (before the UN).

Eden: I imagine they will discuss them long before I leave. I think at the worst we can always stay or make some declaration that we are in favor of any organization that will work. I don't want to block that any more than I can.

President: I don't want to put us in a false position. Then it is all right.

Eden: That isn't the thing in my mind at all.

President: Does Mollet understand that?

Eden: I never mentioned anything about the UNO to him. But I am sure he does understand it. I am taking Selwyn Lloyd who is going to the UN. He [3] speaks very good English. They might go along to UNO. That is all I said to him—never mentioned the business about the international force. I never referred to it at all.

Eden call of 9:55 (2)

President: Then I think my fears are groundless. But I was afraid we would get to talking about certain features & you would

---

[1] Source: Eisenhower Library, Whitman File, Eisenhower Diaries. Prepared in the Office of the President. A copy of this transcript and transcripts of other conversations between the White House and Eden's office which took place on November 7 are *ibid.*, ACW Diary.

[2] All ellipses in this document are in the source text.

[3] Presumably Mollet.

feel that you couldn't go along with the UN plan. If that were brought up at all—or any thought of it—then we would be in a bad spot, if we had to have a divided communiqué. But if we are going to talk about the future & about the Bear [4]—okay.

Eden: We have had two London undisguised observation planes (?). [5] Your people know it. Ask them. I think we ought to talk about what we should do with them. I think, on the kind of international force . . . as long as it works, I don't care what kind of international force we have.

President: I don't know exactly what the timing is.

Eden: The take-over (?) is perfectly all right. . . . about getting out.

President: do you want us to announce this at 11 o'clock?

Eden: Is that time all right with you?

(Agreed on 11 o'clock announcement.)

---

[4] Reference is to the Soviet Union.
[5] This question mark and the one below are in the source text.

---

539.   Memorandum for the Record by the President's Staff Secretary (Goodpaster) [1]

Washington, November 7, 1956.

On being informed by Mr. Hoover (who had been called by the President) that the President had received a call from Eden this morning [2] in which Eden asked for and obtained the President's agreement to his coming to Washington with Mollet tonight, Governor Adams and I met with the President to take up with him some questions that seemed to arise in connection with such a visit. The major point was the possible appearance that we were now concerting action in the Middle East independently of the UN action. The President said he had made clear that there could be no departure by the French and British from their agreement on cease-fire, and said that Eden had asked for the meeting because of the developing threat from Russia.

The President talked to Eden a second time, [3] indicating that the

---

[1] Source: Eisenhower Library, Whitman File, Eisenhower Diaries.
[2] See Document 536.
[3] See *supra*.

United States is committed to the Hammarskjold plan, and that he had considered the meeting's purpose to be to concert our positions in NATO and for the future. If, by any chance, Eden and Mollet were not in agreement, it would be very unfortunate to have a communiqué issued which would indicate we are in disagreement.

While the call was in progress, Mr. Hoover came into the President's office. When the call had ended he said we must be very careful not to give the impression that we are teaming with the British and French. He said he had talked to Secretary Dulles by phone, who said he was very much opposed to the visit at this time. I suggested to the President the desirability of letting Hammarskjold know about the visit, so he would not be thrown off balance in his efforts. Mr. Hoover said we would have to get out to the world that we have not changed our principles and our position. He said the Soviets have offered Egypt 250,000 volunteers (I left the meeting to call Allen Dulles for a check of this.) Mr. Hoover also said there is danger of a complete turn-about by the Arabs in this matter, placing themselves in opposition to Hammarskjold's efforts. The Russians are making great efforts to put themselves in the position of liberators.

Governor Adams asked the President whether he was still thinking of having the Congressional leaders in on Friday, and the President said he was. After further discussion the President decided to call Eden again and say that the timing of the visit was bad, and that it should be postponed. [4] In discussion it was suggested that he might refer to the dangers of throwing Hammarskjold—who is having a hard time getting the Egyptians and Israelis to unconditional agreement to cease fire—off balance, the possibility of having General Gruenther—who is known to have the complete confidence of the President—go up to London to see what the British view the Russian threat to be, etc.

Secretary Humphrey (who joined the meeting) said he appreciated how hard it was for the President to tell a man that he wouldn't talk to him, but thought that the timing question was overriding. The President said he had really looked forward to talking with Eden, and was quite disappointed. The President then called Eden who accepted what the President said, though with obvious disappointment.

---

[4] See *infra.*

I obtained at this point additional intelligence data which gave increased indications regarding the Russian threat, although nothing solid seemed to be involved.

G

Colonel, CE, US Army

---

540.   Transcript of a Telephone Conversation Between President Eisenhower in Washington and Prime Minister Eden in London, November 7, 1956, 10:27 a.m. [1]

10:27 a.m.—Sir Anthony Eden.

President: I am sorry to keep bothering you, but I have some problems. First, are we talking submarine cable & not on the air?

(Did not hear Eden's answer, if any.)

President: First of all, you have given us something on the military side I didn't know. First thing we should do—I have just had a partial Cabinet meeting on this thing, & they think our timing is very, very bad, & I am calling to tell you about it. First, we have got to get quickly in some way a coordinated military intelligence view. And what I could do is to ask Gruenther to come over to see you—and he could see your military people and could find out anything . . . [2] we could find out in a coordinated way just exactly what this thing is.

Next, although I had a landslide victory last night, we are not like you, and we have lost both Houses of Congress. Therefore I have to have the Senate and House leaders in right now. We have already issued invitation. They are to be here Friday and Saturday, and I have to be meeting with them. This is not so bad, you must remember, Anthony, because I have got to get them to back up whatever we agree to. My Congress won't be back in session until January 6.

And next, we ourselves have not made a study on the line you and I were discussing—and I don't want to repeat. We have to have the military in that even as seriously as we do the political side.

---

[1] Source: Eisenhower Library, Whitman File, Eisenhower Diaries. Prepared in the Office of the President.

[2] Ellipsis in the source text.

And then, finally, I find that the boys at the UN they are trying to put the pressure on now are Egypt and Israel. [sic] They are trying to put the squeeze on them. The general opinion is that any meeting until that gets done would exacerbate the situation, and they are going up in the air about that. As I told them, I am very anxious to talk to you and Mollet about our future. But I do believe, in view of what my people say, we will have to postpone it a little bit. I am sorry. We haven't said a word.

Eden: The only person I have told is Winthrop. [3]

President: I just don't see how we could do it now with so much on our plate—we just can't handle this at the same time. I am really sorry because, as I told you this morning, I *want* to talk to you.

Eden: I wouldn't think we would do anything to harm anyone.

President: No, I know it wouldn't harm anybody. What Egypt and Israel would draw from any announcement that we would make, might throw the fat in the UN.

Eden: We have called a cease-fire—a lot of problems arise out of that.

President: I am not talking about not meeting and talking with our friends. But I have had opposition about the timing.

Eden: What would you feel you would like on the time?

President: I will have to call you back—must have a full Cabinet meeting. I'm going out shortly to talk to Foster. Also must talk to State, Defense, ODM and others. I have had only a few of them in so far.

Eden: Will you be sending Mollet a message?

President: I think you had better call him.

Eden: He will speak in a half hour.

President: You'd better call him right away. [4]

Eden: Will I hear from you later tonight?

President: I will send you word later today.

---

[3] Reference is to Winthrop W. Aldrich.

[4] Pursuant to instructions, Tyler telephoned Prime Minister Mollet's office in Paris at approximately 11 a.m. on November 7 and spoke with a member of his Cabinet, Emile Noel. Tyler asked Noel to convey an urgent message from President Eisenhower and Acting Secretary Hoover to Prime Minister Mollet that Eisenhower had told Eden that the proposed visit by Eden and Mollet to Washington would require some consultation by the President within the U.S. Government and that certain preparations would have to be made. Consequently the visit should be postponed for a while. Noel said that Eden had already telephoned Mollet and told him of this. Tyler told Noel that it was most important that there be no publicity and Noel agreed. (Memorandum of telephone conversation by Tyler, November 7; Department of State, Presidential Correspondence: Lot 66 D 204, The Pres and Sec. exchanges of Corres. with De Gaulle, Mollet, Gaillard 7/56–1/61)

541.   Memorandum by the Director of the Executive Secretariat (Howe) [1]

Washington, November 7, 1956.

ACTING SECRETARY'S TALK WITH THE PRESIDENT

Wednesday Morning, November 7

Mr. Hoover reported to Messrs. Murphy, Phleger, Elbrick, MacArthur, Rountree, Sohm and Howe the discussions which he had with the President at the White House, in the car to and from the hospital and with the Secretary at the hospital. Part of this will be covered by notes taken by Mr. Macomber at the hospital. [2]

The President called Eden and postponed the meeting which had been arranged earlier in the day; the President felt that after the UK-French troops had left Egypt, which they were planning to do as soon as possible, it would be useful to get together; meanwhile the President would meet to check with Congressional leaders, etc. The President wanted to have a message sent very promptly to Eden confirming the telephone conversation and generally expressing the idea that, after thorough study on all factors in talking with his advisors, he had concluded that the meeting should be held as soon as possible without being misunderstood elsewhere in the world and that this would need to be after the troops had come out of Egypt. The message should point out that we are anxious not to give the Arabs any excuse to accept assistance, notably volunteers from the Russians.

(Mr. Hoover said that Eden had, in the phone conversation, put a great deal of emphasis on the Russian threat, on NATO involvement, etc.; he had, for instance, said that he (Eden) had information that two unmistakably Russian planes had attacked UK air facilities, presumably in the Suez area.)

Mr. Hoover said that the President had taken up with Eden, and this matter also should be included in the message of confirmation, that it was important to get a combined military and intelligence evaluation of Soviet capabilities, plans and intentions. (Mr. Hoover further reported the view of the President, although it was not clear whether this had been discussed with Eden, that Gruenther should be dispatched promptly to the UK to get their views and then come quickly back here to forestall having a sizeable UK group coming over here immediately. Goodpaster apparently took this Gruenther aspect in hand immediately. The President also thought that it might

---

[1] Source: Department of State, Central Files, 774/11–756. Secret.
[2] See *infra.*

be useful, presumably following the Gruenther discussions, to put together a US-UK combined staff to make a collective, and possibly continuing, military and intelligence evaluation of Russian capabilities, plans and intentions, although this joint group should by no means get itself into planning.)

Apparently the President has in mind that the meeting might take place, after withdrawal of all UK-French troops, possibly by the end of next week.

During the discussion with the President alone Secretary Humphrey joined and they discussed Eden's need and effort to get support in his serious, current troubles and that we could anticipate getting requests for oil and other support elements.

The President expressed the view that it was of critical importance that we get SYG to move ahead as rapidly as possible to get the peace force in position. (Mr. Wilcox was informed by S/S to reemphasize with Presidential backing the Acting Secretary's previous injunction on Lodge to put pressure in this direction on SYG.)

The President also felt there was a need now to get really tough with the Israelis if they were taking, as reported, the stand on non-withdrawal from Sinai. This should be done as much as possible through the UN but consideration should be given to cutting off remittances or even making contributions taxable. (Mr. Hoover asked Mr. Rountree to call in Eban and lay it on the line.)

Mr. Hoover also expressed concern, reflecting his meeting with the President, that through the UN we make every effort not only to prevent but to be sure to observe, any flow of volunteer personnel from the Orbit [3] into nearby Arab States, presumably by invitation.

H

---

[3] Reference is to the Soviet orbit.

542. Memorandum of a Conversation, Secretary Dulles' Room, Walter Reed Hospital, Washington, November 7, 1956, 11:10 a.m. [1]

PARTICIPANTS

The President
The Secretary of State
Mr. Hoover, Jr.

ALSO PRESENT

Mr. Macomber

The Secretary opened the conversation by congratulating the President on his victory. The President inquired concerning the Secretary's health, and this and the election results were briefly discussed.

The President then said that he had made a second telephone call to Prime Minister Eden suggesting that the Eden-Mollet trip to the United States be postponed. The President said that Eden, although quite disappointed, had agreed to the postponement. Eden was concerned about the Russians moving into the Middle East. The British realized that it is partly a propaganda effort but nevertheless they are scared. The President mentioned that Ambassador Bohlen also believed that this was largely a propaganda effort but at the same time felt we could not discount the possibility that the Russians would actually move into the area with force.

The President said that when Eden comes over here he wants to talk about "what the Bear will do and what we would do in the face of the Bear's acts." The President said he thought there was no point now in indulging in recriminations with the British, but rather that we should jointly consider what should be done in the face of the Russian threat.

The President pointed out, in this connection, that we have two problems at the moment: The first is that we have no military study of our own based on what we would do if the Russians do go into the Middle East. The second problem is that we have no coordinated intelligence estimate with the British. The President believed that we needed to get such an estimate which would take into account all the information which we and the British had. He also believed we should have the military study prepared as soon as possible.

---

[1] Source: Eisenhower Library, Dulles Papers, Meetings with the President. Top Secret. Drafted by Macomber.

The President said that it was now clear that he would definitely have a Democratic Congress. In view of this he thought that there was a need for a meeting with the Leaders before he met with Eden.

The Secretary said he thought the first thing to do now was to see that there was no hitch in the cease fire. He said also that it was extremely important to get the British and French troops out of Egypt as soon as possible. He said that if this is not done—at least within a week's time—the "fire will go on burning", and it may be impossible to put it out. In this connection it was reported that Mr. Hoover had instructed Ambassador Lodge to tell Hammarskjold to move with all possible speed in getting UN forces to Egypt so that an excuse could be provided for the British and French to get out. The Secretary inquired whether the United States could supply the transportation for the UN troops. The President replied in the affirmative.

The Secretary said it was very important that some Asian troops be included among the UN forces. The Secretary again stressed the importance of getting the UN troops in and the British and French out quickly—repeating that if this is delayed beyond a week the situation may be beyond repair.

The President said he thought we should begin to put pressure on Egypt and Israel. The Secretary agreed and thought that Eban should be called and told that the Israelis must get back to their Armistice line in compliance with the UN Resolution. He believed that Eban should be told that unless the Israelis complied with this Resolution, the United States would put an embargo on all funds going to Israel. The Secretary, having in mind the election results, stressed that this was the right moment to take this step with the Israelis. The President concurred that this was the appropriate moment, but indicated that he did not wish to threaten the Israelis until we had first learned whether the Israelis would be willing to comply without threats being applied.

The President asked if we embargo all remittances to Israel, did we not have to place the same embargo on everybody else involved in the Middle East crisis? The Secretary did not comment directly on this, but said he thought it would have a major effect on Israel if we made it clear that we were prepared to embargo all remittances if Israel did not comply with the UN Resolution. The Secretary suggested that Secretary Humphrey could also make all remittances to Israel taxable. It was agreed that this could probably be done by Treasury Department regulation and would have a profound effect on the Israeli Government.

Mr. Hoover said that he felt it was important to set up a complete isolation of the Middle East. Otherwise, he felt that when the British and French got out, the first thing the Egyptians would do, probably with Russian help, would be to repair their airfields.

The Secretary then asked about the status of our relations with Nasser. Mr. Hoover replied that they were not too good, that Nasser had renounced the cease fire until all foreign troops were off Egyptian soil. Mr. Hoover added, however, that at the moment there was a de facto cease fire in Egypt.

Next the question of how difficult a mechanical operation it would be to get the British and French out of Egypt was briefly discussed. It was agreed this would not be a particularly difficult operation to carry out.

The Secretary then said that the British and the French going into Egypt was "a crazy act". The President said yes, although it was somewhat more understandable if in fact the Russians were going to act in any case. The President added, however, that even if this were true, the British and French action was still ill-advised.

The President indicated that one of the reasons Eden wanted to come to Washington was that he needs to associate himself with some spectacular act at this time. The President referred to a British opinion poll which Mr. Hoover had mentioned to him. This showed British public opinion running strongly against the actions of the British Government in the Middle East.

The President next made the point that the important thing to remember in this present situation is that "the Bear is still the central enemy".

The Secretary then asked about the oil situation. The President said that at the moment there was just one pipeline operating, and we had intelligence that indicated that a recommendation had been made that this last line be knocked out. The President added that if this were done, then all the oil would have to come around the Cape of Good Hope. The Secretary said this would mean bringing Venezuelan oil in, and commented that once Venezuelan oil is out of the United States market, we would never get it completely back.

The Secretary then said that he wanted to make it clear to the President that he did not exclude the usefulness of a meeting between the President and Eden and Mollet. The President said that he understood this and recalled their discussions of this project before the Secretary's illness. The President said that he told Eden in his second telephone call that he would send him a cable this afternoon, indicating "how it looks from here" with regard to the visit. (At this moment a note was handed to the President indicating that Mollet had also agreed to the postponement of the meeting and had also agreed that there would be no publicity regarding the meeting at this time.)

The President said that Eden wanted to set a fixed date and was pushing for Wednesday of next week. The President thought that we should make the date of the meeting contingent on certain events taking place in advance. The Secretary agreed and suggested that first of all the meeting be contingent on the British and French having previously gotten their troops out of Egypt. The President said this could be put in the telegram that would be sent out this afternoon. The President said that he would ask the State Department to draft the telegram and would have it sent out to the Secretary before dispatching it. The Secretary said that he did not think this was necessary and that he did not want to slow things up. The President said that this would not slow it up.

The President then returned to the subject of a meeting with the Leaders. It was thought that such a meeting probably could not be set up before this coming Saturday.

The President then mentioned the fact that the present crisis in the Middle East, while it fell primarily in the domain of the State Department, also had many Defense Department implications. Because of this, the President said he had felt the need of a person who could coordinate the State and Defense efforts. He said that Governor Adams and Colonel Goodpaster were enormously overworked at this time and could not take on this added burden. The Secretary suggested Robert Anderson for this assignment. The President said that this had been his first choice, but he had some doubt as to whether Anderson could get away at this time. The Secretary suggested if Anderson was not available that Douglas MacArthur would be an excellent person. He was a first-class coordinator and in addition had a major responsibility in the Department for handling our liaison with the Defense Department. The President agreed that MacArthur would be excellent and he said he would take a look at this later in the day.

The Secretary then said that there was a danger that the Russians might really attempt to take advantage of the situation by coming to the aid of the Arabs. The President agreed and said he thought there was a danger of our "getting into the Arab doghouse" because of the opposition we would necessarily have to take to such Russian activity. The President added, however, that he had considerable confidence that the Arab leaders see the danger of the Russians coming into the situation supposedly in support of the Arab position.

.   .   .   .

The President then told the Secretary of his satisfaction at having a certain highly classified observation operation available to him at this time. [2] He felt that others had conducted operations with a similar objective, but these had been detected whereas our own had not been.

The conversation then closed with a discussion between the President and the Secretary regarding their medical experiences.

---

[2] Reference is presumably to the high altitude reconnaissance flights which President Eisenhower had directed to be flown over Syria and Israel on November 6.

---

543.   Editorial Note

During the 566th meeting of the General Assembly (First Emergency Special Session), which began at 10:30 a.m. on November 7, the delegates considered a report by the Secretary-General, circulated the previous day, which described the nature of the peacekeeping force to be established. According to the report, the force should be temporary, the length of its assignment being determined by the current needs of the situation; it should not influence the military or political balance in the area; and it could function only with the consent of the countries contributing troops and the countries on whose territory it was stationed. While a cease-fire was being established, the force would, with the consent of the Egyptian Government, enter Egyptian territory to help maintain the quiet during and after the withdrawal of non-Egyptian forces, and to secure compliance with other terms of the cease-fire resolution. (U.N. doc. A/3302)

While considering this report, Danish Representative Karl I. Eskelund tabled a draft resolution, in the name of the Governments of Argentina, Burma, Ceylon, Denmark, Ecuador, Ethiopia, and Sweden (U.N. doc. A/3308), which fully endorsed Hammarskjöld's report and declared it to be the will of the General Assembly to follow up and implement the proposals and suggestions made in the report. Shortly thereafter, Ceylonese Representative R.S.S. Gunewardene tabled an Afro-Asian or Nineteen-Power draft resolution, co-sponsored by the Governments of Afghanistan, Burma, Ceylon, Ethiopia, India, Indonesia, Iran, Iraq, Jordan, Lebanon, Liberia, Libya, Nepal, Pakistan, Philippines, Saudi Arabia, Syria, Thailand, and Yemen. (U.N. doc. A/3309) That draft resolution recalled and reaffirmed previous General Assembly resolutions relating to the Middle East crisis, once again called upon Israel to withdraw immediately all of its forces behind the Israeli-Egyptian armistice line, once again called upon the United Kingdom and France immediately to withdraw all their forces from Egyptian territory, and urged the Secretary-General to communicate the resolution to the parties concerned and to report on compliance with it. (U.N. doc. A/PV.566)

Discussion of these two draft resolutions continued at the 567th plenary meeting of the General Assembly, which convened at 3 p.m. that same day. After several changes were made in the text of the Seven-Power draft, it was adopted as Resolution 1001 (ES–I) by a vote of 64 in favor, 0 opposed, and 12 abstentions. The resolution as adopted provided for the establishment of an Advisory Committee composed of one representative from each of the following countries: Brazil, Canada, Ceylon, Colombia, India, Norway, and Pakistan, and chaired by the Secretary-General. The committee would "undertake the development of those aspects of the planning for the Force and its operation not already dealt with by the General Assembly and which do not fall within the area of the direct responsibility of the Chief of the Command". The Nineteen-Power draft was then adopted as Resolution 1002 (ES–I) by a vote of 65 in favor, 1 (Israel) opposed, and 10 abstentions. The United States voted in favor of both of these resolutions. (U.N. doc. A/PV.567) For text of Ambassador Lodge's remarks in the General Assembly on November 7, see Department of State *Bulletin*, November 19, 1956, pages 791–792.

---

544.   **Memorandum of a Telephone Conversation Between the French Ambassador (Alphand) and the Assistant Secretary of State for International Organization Affairs (Wilcox), Washington, November 7, 1956** [1]

SUBJECT

Middle East Situation

Ambassador Alphand called me this morning to say that he had heard Ambassador Lodge's speech in the General Assembly indicating that we intended to vote for the Afro-Asian resolution on the withdrawal of forces from Egyptian territory. He said he assumed this was our official position and inquired if his assumption were

---

[1] Source: Department of State, Central Files, 320.5780/11–756. Official Use Only. Drafted by Wilcox.

correct. I replied that it was and that it was my understanding that certain changes had been made in the resolution in accordance with the suggestions that we had made to the sponsors.

Ambassador Alphand then inquired about our interpretation of withdrawal. He pointed out that the phrase "immediate withdrawal" in the resolution suggested the possibility that French and British troops might be expected to withdraw from Egyptian territory prior to the entry of UN forces. I explained to him that our concept of the withdrawal was that the two things should be related—that the withdrawal of British and French troops would be properly phased and coordinated with the entry of UN forces. It was not our interpretation that the word "immediate" would result in the withdrawal of French and British troops in such fashion that a vacuum would be created before UN forces were ready to move in.

Ambassador Alphand then called attention to the French request to convene an urgent meeting of the Security Council in order to consider Middle Eastern problems and to complete the work which the GA had been doing. He said it was the French view that the GA has neither the power nor the responsibility to deal with many of the questions which now need to be settled. The general guide lines have been established by the GA and it was now time to settle the more specific problems that remain. He hoped therefore that we would be in a position to support the French move to convene the Security Council. I told the Ambassador that we had not had an opportunity yet to give the matter careful study and that I was therefore not in a position to comment on his request. I pointed out, however, that inasmuch as the matter had been referred by the Security Council to the GA that any attempt to move it back to the Security Council might meet with some opposition from the smaller states.

545.   Message From President Eisenhower to Prime Minister Eden [1]

Washington, November 7, 1956.

DEAR ANTHONY: I want you to know that I welcome the suggestion you made in our telephone conversation today regarding early consultation on many of our mutual problems, and that I agree we should meet at an early date. Now that the election is over, I find it most necessary to consult urgently the leaders of both Houses of the Congress. As you can understand, it will take some days to accomplish this. Furthermore, after a thorough study of all the factors and after talking to various branches of the government here, I feel that while such a meeting should take place quickly, we must be sure that its purpose and aims are not misunderstood in other countries. This would be the case if the UN Resolution had not yet been carried out.

I am heartened by the news that there is a cease-fire in Egypt and sincerely hope that the UN Force will promptly begin its work and that the Anglo-French Forces will be withdrawn from Egypt without delay. Once these things are done, the ground will be favorable for our meeting. I would hope that this would permit us to meet here by the end of next week. As I suggested by telephone I would hope that Al Gruenther might meet with you or your people shortly to get your evaluation of the matter you mentioned to me this morning.

With warm regard,

As ever,

Ike [2]

---

[1] Source: Department of State, Central Files, 684A.86/11–756. Secret. Transmitted to London in telegram 3318, November 7, 2:58 p.m, which is the source text, with the instruction: "Please deliver soonest following message from President to Eden. Confirm date and time delivery." Telegram 3318 also informed the Embassy that the Department would elaborate further on the Gruenther mission in a subsequent message. Telegram 2573 from London, November 7, reported that the message was delivered at 11:15 p.m. to Eden's secretary. (*Ibid.*, 711.11–EI/11–756)

A similar message was transmitted to Paris in telegram 1725, November 7, for delivery to Mollet. (*Ibid.*, 320.5774/11–756)

[2] Telegram 3318 bears this typed signature.

546. Informal Summary of a Meeting Held in Acting Secretary Hoover's Office, Department of State, Washington, November 7, 1956, 3:45 p.m. [1]

PARTICIPANTS

> The Acting Secretary
> Mr. Murphy
> Mr. Prochnow
> Mr. Phleger
> Mr. Rountree
> Mr. Greene

The Acting Secretary reiterated that the President and the Secretary wanted to be as firm as necessary with the Israeli in getting them to accept the cease-fire, including withdrawal from the Egyptian territory. The Acting Secretary thought our action in this respect could also gain us credit and influence with the Arabs. A letter from the President to Prime Minister Ben-Gurion was drafted, and additional talking points for use in delivering the letter to Ben-Gurion and a copy of the President's letter to be given to the Israeli Ambassador here were prepared. A statement for Mr. Hagerty's office was drafted and telephoned to the White House.

The consensus was that further action, such as withdrawing the administrative determination that grants tax exemption to contributions by American citizens to Israel, should, for the moment, await further progress on implementing UN resolutions, particularly the arrival of a UN force and the withdrawal of the British and French. It was felt that it would be more effective to urge the Israelis to get out of Egypt after the British and French had begun to withdraw.

It was also decided that Ambassador Hare should be instructed to urge Nasser in the strongest terms to accept Hammarskjold's proposal on the entry of the UN force.

JG [2]

---

[1] Source: Department of State, Central Files, 974.7301/11-756. Top Secret. Drafted by Greene.

[2] Printed from a copy that bears these typed initials.

547.   Telegram From the Mission at the United Nations to the Department of State [1]

New York, November 7, 1956—4 p.m.

Delga 21. Eyes only for Hoover from Lodge. Re Palestine—Suez. I met with SYG UN yesterday afternoon and informed him of President Eisenhower's conversations with Eden, Mollet, Nehru, [2] and St. Laurent. [3] I informed SYG the President had advised Eden not to equivocate or negotiate but to withdraw from Egypt. I told him the President had said if Eden attempted to negotiate, USSR would be right behind Egyptians stiffening them. I also said that in the President's telephone calls to Mollet, St. Laurent and Nehru, he had urged them to get 100 per cent behind the SYG, as he was.

I referred also to British-French reference to leaving their own technicians for clearing Canal, a proposal which US deplored.

SYG said he would take position he considered UK-French letter simply an offer of their technicians which he could accept or reject. He agreed completely with the President on necessity for complete and unequivocal withdrawal by British and French. He asked me to give the President, officially and personally, a message of his deep appreciation for the full support which the President and US had given throughout this entire undertaking.

SYG said he had telegraphed full text of his final report to UK and French at 3:00 am yesterday morning, and they had therefore had it when the Cabinet decision to agree to cease-fire and with- drawal of troops had been taken. There could be no question they had accepted on basis of principles expressed in his report, which included withdrawal of their forces.

I said question of time of withdrawal was as important as withdrawal itself, and as long as there were any UK or French personnel left, either military or technical, it would give USSR the excuse they wanted. SYG agreed with this. He said that as for clearing Canal, he was getting in touch with the Dutch and Danes

---

[1] Source: Department of State, Central Files, 974.7301/11–756. Secret; Priority. Received at 5:12 p.m.

[2] On November 6, Eisenhower had written Nehru to enlist his support for the U.N. cease-fire plan. In particular, Eisenhower had urged that Nehru use his influence with the British Government on behalf of the plan and that he accept the Secretary- General's invitation for India to furnish some part of the U.N. Emergency Force. The following day, Nehru informed Eisenhower that he had agreed in principle that India would participate in UNEF. Copies of these messages are in the Eisenhower Library, Whitman File, International File.

[3] Eisenhower spoke with Canadian Prime Minister St. Laurent on November 6. A transcript of this telephone conversation is *ibid.*, Eisenhower Diaries.

who had greatest number of experts available, and he hoped they would agree to provide such experts to him for clearing operation.

On question of US airlift, he was thinking of possibility of our taking two Colombian divisions, which Colombia had now offered, to Rome to have them in readiness to get them into Egypt when possible. This would be an ideal arrangement for first step, Hammarskjold thought.

I told SYG USAF in Germany could lift a battalion and could get its planes to field for lift quicker than Canadian battalion could get there. I said the time from Germany to Cairo would be 12 hours if Cairo fields are open. If US Air Force could not in first stages land in Cairo, we would take troops to Crete and the Navy could take them on from there.

I asked him to let us know at earliest possible moment of needs we would have to meet, the time, place, etc. Hammarskjold said he thought he would have to have Gen Burns here, and that Burns should go back with troops. This would, he felt, take 5 or 6 days, and he did not anticipate requesting us to get underway with airlift much before that time. He said he had asked Loutfi to obtain at once Egypt's acceptance of having SYG choose the force to come in. He had told Loutfi that a force composed of Indians, Scandinavians and Colombians would in his mind be the ideal composition.

SYG said he had not got to point of dealing with Israeli withdrawal, and thought that would be next big question, of course. He was sure Israelis would not agree until there had already gone into existence, on Egyptian soil, a UN force.

Hammarskjold said he was hoping avoid a meeting of GA last night in order give time for consolidating situation, although he recognized Asian-Africans might well insist upon meeting in view of doubt existing as to UK-French intentions on withdrawal.

Following my meeting with Hammarskjold, Cordier informed us that Egypt had requested meeting, supported by Asian-Africans, because of heavy fighting continuing at Port Said. It seemed unlikely it would have stopped by 7:00 pm, time for cease-fire to take effect.

He said Asian-Africans would put forward a resolution on withdrawal of forces, and SYG would arrange for a resolution to be introduced, probably by Sweden, Ecuador, Ceylon, Burma and some others, approving plan for a UN force as set forth in his final report yesterday morning. Cordier said SYG believed full support for his resolution would require support for a resolution on withdrawal.

I raised with Hammarskjold the question of meeting of SC at ministerial level as proposed by French and British. I questioned whether such meeting at this time would be helpful. Hammarskjold said emphatically he believed it would be unhelpful and should be avoided.

Following is Barco's report:

"After my telephone conversation with Secretary Hoover and Mr. Phleger, [4] I called immediately upon SYG. He had just arranged for last evening's meeting to be postponed until morning. I explained to him our concern that there be least possible delay in establishing UN force and getting it into Egypt. I said Secretary Hoover considered situation perilous and it was of utmost importance we act without any delay whatsoever. We were most hopeful that 4-5 day period for setting up force that he had mentioned could be substantially shortened, and that Gen Burns could set up his command in Egypt at once and that it would not be necessary for him return to New York.

"SYG said he fully appreciated our concern and was moving as fast as he possibly could. He would order Gen Burns to go at once to Cairo and establish his office. He could be there tomorrow. He did feel he needed Gen Burns here to supervise arrangements for sending in UN force and felt he could leave his Depty Chief of Staff (Col Ely) in Egypt and come on to New York.

"I told him it would be of great help for Gen Burns to go to Cairo at once. I then mentioned our anxiety there be no vacuum between time of departure of British-French forces and arrival of UN forces; that we believed UN forces should be in Egypt before British-French forces left.

"Hammarskjold said he had just not been able to get to point of thinking about staging of departure of UK-French forces and arrival of UN forces. He had been concentrating on getting cease-fire and agreement to withdrawal and establishment of a UN force. He understood our problem and would for this purpose need Gen Burns advice. He believed it would be possible to avoid a vacuum that anyone could take advantage of. He said that with Brit-French forces only in Port Said there was only a small area where this problem might arise, but even this he felt could be dealt with. He would keep us informed of developments.

"I also informed SYG of our views on Asian-African draft resolution on withdrawal. SYG agreed points which concerned Secretary Hoover and Mr. Phleger could be dealt with as he himself believed resolution needed further refinement.

"This morning I met with Ambassadors Entezam [5] and Abdoh (Iran) and Loutfi (Egypt) and explained objectionable features of Asian-African draft resolution which concerned US. I explained to them that a number of delegations would, I felt, share our doubts about these points and I thought Asian-African group would be able get greater support if they made changes we suggested. After considerable discussion they agreed on language which I considered close enough to our suggestions to meet objections. I told them that with these changes we would support resolution. They had not, however, had time for it to be circulated and during debate I suggested the Representative of Ceylon, who preceded Ambassador Lodge, should read text as amended to Assembly, in order that Mr. Lodge could

---

[4] No account of this conversation has been found in Department of State files.

[5] Head of the Iranian Delegation to the United Nations.

support it in his speech which immediately followed. This was what happened." (End of Barco report)

This morning, after talk with Hoover, [6] I spoke to SYG and, stressing our anxiety over Russian activities, urged his speedy action in getting international force into Egypt quickly. I said 4 or 5 days was much too long a delay. He said he would do his utmost. I also conveyed the President's words of praise to him and he was deeply appreciative.

Lodge

---

[6] No account of this conversation has been found in Department of State files.

---

548.   Message From Prime Minister Eden to President Eisenhower [1]

London, November 7, 1956.

DEAR FRIEND: When you told me of your pre-occupations with Congress during the next two days, I did not feel able to press my suggestion for an immediate meeting. I explained the position to Mollet, who readily accepted these reasons for postponement.

I do, however, hope that it will be possible for us to meet in the very near future. I should feel much more confidence about the decisions and actions which we shall have to take in the short term if we had first reached some common understanding about the attitude which we each intended to take towards a long-term settlement of the outstanding issues in the Middle East. I have for a long time felt that some at least of our troubles there derived from the lack of a clear understanding between our two countries, ever since the end of the war, on policy in the Middle East, and I doubt whether we shall ever be able to secure stability there unless we are working towards common objectives.

It may well be that even wider issues are now at stake. If the Soviets intend to seize this opportunity of intervening by giving substantial support to Nasser, they may create a situation which could lead to major war. Hitherto I have not thought it likely that

---

[1] Source: Eisenhower Library, Whitman File, International File. Top Secret. Delivered to the White House under cover of a note from Coulson to President Eisenhower which reads: "The Prime Minister has asked me to send you the enclosed message."

Russia would take this dangerous step. I have believed that it was anxious to avoid world war and that, although it would make all possible minor troubles, it would stick to the policy of making mischief by all means short of war. But the new men in the Kremlin may be less coldly calculating than their predecessors and, if so, they may be led into taking a step which may precipitate a really grave situation. The Swiss, as you know, have suggested another "Geneva" meeting. It may be that this would be worth considering.

On matters such as this it is difficult to come to considered conclusions by correspondence. I would feel much happier if we had been able to meet and talk them over soon. It was with these grave issues in mind that I suggested this morning that I might come out to Washington at once. I still hope that it may be possible for us to meet within the next few days, as soon as your immediate pre-occupations are over.

Yours ever,

Anthony [2]

---

[2] Printed from a copy that bears this typed signature.

---

549. Memorandum of a Telephone Conversation Between the President and the Acting Secretary of State, Washington, November 7, 1956, 5:30 p.m. [1]

Questioned whether he had consulted Secy. Dulles in the text of proposed message for Ben-Gurion—Mr. Hoover replied No.

The President's concern was on the phrase "Impair the friendship and cooperation between our two countries." The sentence was corrected to read "to impair the friendly cooperation . . ." [2]

---

[1] Source: Eisenhower Library, Whitman File, Eisenhower Diaries. Prepared in the Office of the President. The source text does not indicate who placed the call.

[2] All ellipses in this document are in the source text. The text of a "Suggested Letter" to Ben Gurion, which bears Eisenhower's handwritten corrections, is *ibid.*, International File. The original version of the sentence in question reads: "It would be a matter of the greatest regret to all my countrymen if Israeli policy on a matter of such vital concern to the world should in any way impair the friendship and cooperation between our two countries." For text of the message as sent to Ben Gurion, see *infra.*

Mr. Hoover asked if President had seen Ben-Gurion's statement. [3] The President said yes, & thinks it is terrible.

The Ambassador is coming to see Mr. Hoover at 6. Here, Mr. Hoover read to the President what he intends to say to him—which included 3 points about Israel, & her compliance with UN resolution. [4]

The President said he has no objection.

Mr. Hoover said they also have short Press Release. [5] They would like to get over to the Arabs . . . in order to make little change with them. Can't ignore them.

---

[3] Reference is to Ben Gurion's statement to the Knesset on November 7; see Document 534.
[4] See Document 551.
[5] Not further identified.

---

550. Message From President Eisenhower to Prime Minister Ben Gurion [1]

Washington, November 7, 1956.

DEAR MR. PRIME MINISTER: As you know, the General Assembly of the United Nations has arranged a cease-fire in Egypt to which Egypt, France, the United Kingdom and Israel have agreed. There is being dispatched to Egypt a United Nations force in accordance with pertinent resolutions of the General Assembly. That body has urged that all other foreign forces be withdrawn from Egyptian territory, and specifically, that Israeli forces be withdrawn to the General Armistice line. The resolution covering the cease-fire and withdrawal was introduced by the United States and received the overwhelming vote of the Assembly.

Statements attributed to your Government to the effect that Israel does not intend to withdraw from Egyptian territory, as

---

[1] Source: Department of State, Central Files, 674.84A/11–756. Confidential. Transmitted to Tel Aviv in telegram 482, November 7, 6:52 p.m., which is the source text, with the instruction: "Please deliver soonest following message from the President to Prime Minister Ben Gurion. Confirm date and time delivery." A copy of the message was handed to Shiloah during a meeting with Hoover at 6:15; see *infra.* The Israeli Embassy later informed the Department of State that as of 2 a.m., Washington time, the message had not yet been delivered to Ben Gurion. The Israeli Embassy subsequently cabled to Jerusalem the text of the message handed to Shiloah. (Memorandum of conversation by Blackiston, November 8, Department of State, Central Files, 684A.86/11–856)

requested by the United Nations, have been called to my attention. I must say frankly, Mr. Prime Minister, that the United States views these reports, if true, with deep concern. Any such decision by the Government of Israel would seriously undermine the urgent efforts being made by the United Nations to restore peace in the Middle East, and could not but bring about the condemnation of Israel as a violator of the principles as well as the directives of the United Nations.

It is our belief that as a matter of highest priority peace should be restored and foreign troops, except for United Nations forces, withdrawn from Egypt, after which new and energetic steps should be undertaken within the framework of the United Nations to solve the basic problems which have given rise to the present difficulty. The United States has tabled in the General Assembly two resolutions designed to accomplish the latter purposes, and hopes that they will be acted upon favorably as soon as the present emergency has been dealt with.

I need not assure you of the deep interest which the United States has in your country, nor recall the various elements of our policy of support to Israel in so many ways. It is in this context that I urge you to comply with the resolutions of the United Nations General Assembly dealing with the current crisis and to make your decision known immediately. It would be a matter of the greatest regret to all my countrymen if Israeli policy on a matter of such grave concern to the world should in any way impair the friendly cooperation between our two countries.

With best wishes,

Sincerely,

Dwight D Eisenhower [2]

---

[2] Telegram 482 bears this typed signature.

551.   Memorandum of a Conversation, Department of State, Washington, November 7, 1956, 6:15 p.m. [1]

SUBJECT

    Withdrawal of Israel Forces from Egyptian Territory

PARTICIPANTS

    Mr. Reuven Shiloah, Minister, Israel Chargé d'Affaires
    Mr. Yohanan Meroz, First Secretary, Israel Embassy
    The Acting Secretary
    NEA—Mr. William M. Rountree
    NE—Mr. Donald C. Bergus

The Acting Secretary received the Israel representatives at 6:15 p.m. The Acting Secretary stated that we had transmitted a message to the Israel Prime Minister from the President. He handed copies of the message to the Israel representatives for their information. [2]

The Acting Secretary said that he looked upon this as the most important meeting which he had had with representatives of Israel. A part of the world with which we were all concerned was in flames. He had discussed this matter with the Secretary, in the hospital, and the Secretary had added emphasis to what the Acting Secretary was about to say. The Acting Secretary wished to underline the gravity of the situation which the Free World faced today.

The Acting Secretary viewed the present situation in the Near East not only as it affected the various countries in the area, but as it affected world peace. There was evidence, of which the Israel representatives must be aware, that the Soviets were exploiting this situation in a manner which might bring major consequences of a disastrous nature particularly to the Near East but which could spread out. We felt that in such a situation Israel would be one of the first countries to be swallowed up. Right at this moment refusal by Israel to withdraw its troops as requested would lay it open to the charge that it was gravely endangering world peace and rendering it difficult or impossible for the United Nations to accomplish its purposes. The United Nations was the greatest hope, perhaps the only hope for area and world peace. The United States felt that the only way in which this matter could be approached was through the United Nations.

---

[1] Source: Department of State, Central Files, 674.84A/11–756. Confidential. Drafted by Bergus on November 8. A summary of the major points made by Hoover to Shiloah at this meeting was transmitted to Tel Aviv in telegram 255, November 7. (*Ibid.*, 684A.86/11–756)

[2] *Supra.*

The Acting Secretary feared that the failure of Israel to comply with the General Assembly resolutions and withdraw forces from Egyptian territory would place Israel in a position, in the eyes of the vast majority of United Nations members, of flouting world opinion. This was particularly so with respect to public opinion in the United States with an inevitable effect upon governmental and private aid so freely given heretofore by the United States. It was possible that in those circumstances a movement would develop for the suspension or expulsion of Israel from the United Nations.

It was virtually inevitable that if Israel should refuse to comply, a resolution would be proposed and adopted calling for strict sanctions against Israel.

In reply, Mr. Shiloah said he would not presume to anticipate his Prime Minister's reaction. He would convey the Acting Secretary's message with great faithfulness. There was no doubt in his mind as to the points made by the Acting Secretary and he was sure that there would be no doubt in his Government's mind.

Mr. Shiloah wished to ask one or two questions. The most important thing was what was intended after a withdrawal. In the Secretary's last talk with Mr. Eban, the Secretary had said that we could not return to the status quo ante. The Acting Secretary pointed out that the United States had introduced into the General Assembly a resolution calling for a commission of a group of people with the authority of the United Nations behind them charged to bring the Palestine problem to a solution. We would not wish to prejudice the studies of that Commission by comment at this time. The Commission might later ask for the views of the United States. We felt that the Palestine problem was inextricably in the United Nations and that we would have to work there.

Mr. Rountree said he wished to underline the Secretary's statement to Mr. Eban that we must find some way to solve these problems. We intended to pursue the two resolutions which we had placed before the United Nations. The first thing was to stop the fighting and bring about a withdrawal to the armistice lines. The peace of the world was endangered. Mr. Shiloah would recall the impression, and Mr. Rountree believed that it was the honest impression, which Mr. Eban and Mr. Shiloah had conveyed to Mr. Rountree on October 29 that Israel forces would not attack. That meeting had been interrupted with the news that Israel had moved into Egypt. Mr. Rountree referred to the assurances of the Israel Prime Minister that Israel did not seek territorial gains which had been conveyed to the Secretary on October 30. Therefore the Israel statements that they would not withdraw their forces came as a great shock to the United States. Withdrawal of Israel forces was perhaps the most important single element affecting the outcome of peace or war. Israel should conform with the overwhelming wishes of the United Nations.

Mr. Shiloah said he wished to comment. Mr. Eban had transmitted the message from the Israel Prime Minister to the Secretary with the full authority of the Israel Government. With regard to defensive precautions taken by the Israel forces, Mr. Shiloah thought that he could show the United States Government what it had discovered since its military operations in Sinai. This material proved that without the Israel military operation there would have been another one which would have occurred the same week involving all the Arab countries. Israel had in its possession genuine documents which implicated Lebanon, Syria, Jordan and Egypt. These had followed the signature of the Syria-Jordan-Egypt defense pact in Amman in October. [3] In this case there would not have been the existing relatively localized crisis but the whole area would be in flames. This was not an excuse or an argument. Mr. Shiloah referred to an earlier request for Mr. Eban to call on the Acting Secretary. The Acting Secretary pointed out that by the time the Israel request was received, plans had already been made to ask the Israel Ambassador to call to receive our expressions of concern.

The Acting Secretary indicated that he had a very pressing schedule in the next few days. He suggested that Mr. Eban make arrangements to call on Mr. Rountree.

---

[3] October 24. See Document 372.

---

552.   Circular Telegram From the Department of State to Certain Diplomatic Missions [1]

Washington, November 7, 1956—9:28 p.m.

372. FYI We have reports from USUN Soviets advising Arab States "hold out until Soviet volunteers arrive". Appears Soviets endeavoring impress upon Arabs that US will not insist that Israeli withdraw from Egyptian territory. It not clear whether Soviets will try place "volunteers" in Arab States even if cease-fire continues and UN forces dispatched to area. End FYI.

---

[1] Source: Department of State, Central Files, 684A.86/11–756. Secret; Niact. Drafted and approved by Rountree who signed for Hoover. Sent to Beirut, Cairo, Baghdad, Damascus, Amman, and Jidda. Repeated to Tel Aviv and USUN.

Suggest Chiefs of Mission Arab States approach Governments at highest level soonest to inform them that President today addressed message to PM Ben Gurion urging him act pursuant UN resolution with respect prompt withdrawal Israeli forces from Egyptian territory. US will continue to use its full influence obtain compliance UN resolutions relating Near East crisis. We firmly believe solution lies in UN action and injection of foreign forces outside context UN could gravely exacerbate present situation and do irreparable harm.

Hoover

553.   Memorandum of a Conversation, Secretary-General Hammarskjöld's Office, U.N. Secretariat Building, New York, November 7, 1956, 10 p.m. [1]

SUBJECT

Middle East Situation

PARTICIPANTS

UN Secretary-General, Mr. Dag Hammarskjold
Mr. Andrew W. Cordier, Exec. Assistant to the SYG
Mr. Ralph J. Bunche, Under Secretary
Ambassador Henry Cabot Lodge
Mr. James W. Barco, USDel
Mr. W. Park Armstrong, Jr. Special Assistant, Intelligence, Department of State

Mr. Armstrong opened the meeting by telling the Secretary General that the Acting Secretary of State and his immediate advisors on the Middle East situation were so convinced of the need for the greatest possible speed in introducing UN forces, even if token, into the Suez Canal area, that the Acting Secretary wished to convey to the SYG certain information bearing on this factor. Mr. Armstrong stated that he was authorized to disclose to the Secretary-General certain information from sources which the US Government regards as completely reliable and that he would request the SYG's treatment of the information on a confidential basis and as transmitted to him personally. Mr. Armstrong then proceeded

---

[1] Source: Department of State, INR Files: Lot 58 D 776, Middle East Crisis 1956 (Arab-Israeli Crisis). Secret. Drafted by Armstrong.

to brief the Secretary-General for approximately 15 minutes on the following points, going into detail in respect to each of them: [2]

1. The highly tentative and brittle character of the cease-fire and the remaining Egyptian military capabilities for attack or harassment.

2. Certain evidence of the conviction of the Egyptians that they will receive further Soviet support and assistance and the effect this may have on Egyptian willingness to violate the cease-fire or introduce further conditions.

3. The urgency of commencing operations to clear the Canal, the condition of its blockage, and the varying estimates of the time which would be required for clearance under optimum effort.

4. The Egyptian control of approximately two-thirds of the west bank of the Canal and the source and much of the length of the so-called "Sweet-Water Canal."

5. The highly explosive situation on the eastern border of Israel and the grave danger of provocation of that country by renewed and large-scale fedayeen activities.

6. Evidence of the intransigeance of the Israelis in respect to Sinai and the danger of this attitude hardening with the passage of time.

Mr. Armstrong then offered to answer any questions the SYG might have with respect to the foregoing points.

The Secretary General stated that he was impressed by some of the evidence presented to him which he had not known of before, and said that this would indeed argue for the utmost speed in carrying out the resolution which the GA had adopted earlier that evening. He said that he did not have any specific questions, but would like to point out what his present plans and rough time-table were.

The SYG stated that he had that evening sent a priority message to Cairo to raise with the Egyptian Government the acceptability of the nationalities which would compose the UN force. [3] He expected that he would get a prompt and probably favorable reply in regard to a first contingent composed of Canadians and Colombians. Assuming this, he had already sent General Burns and ten officers to Cairo to begin planning and to represent him with the Egyptian Government. He said that his current thinking was that the first units of a UN force could be gotten into motion and on the way by next Wednesday (November 14).

---

[2] Attached to the source text is an unsigned, undated memorandum entitled "Factors Which Render It Essential That United Nations Force Get to Egypt With the Least Possible Delay", which bears the handwritten marginal notation: "From Mr. Hoover's Office". The document lists, in different order, the six points that Armstrong enumerated for Hammarskjöld during this conversation.

[3] Text in Delga 27, November 7, not printed. (*Ibid.*, 320.5780/11–756)

At this point Ambassador Lodge interjected a question, asking if the SYG meant a week away. The SYG said "no," he meant three days away, and then, realizing that he had foreshortened the calendar, laughed and said that doing two days work in one as he had been recently had caused him to lose track of the days and that he really meant Saturday, November 10.

There followed some general discussion of transportation of units of various countries to Egypt (the SYG felt that it would not be psychologically helpful if US aircraft appeared in Egypt, and would prefer RCAF aircraft to handle the ferry leg from Italy to Egypt), necessary preparation of troop units for the climate and health conditions of the Canal Zone, etc. Mr. Armstrong suggested that these units which are most likely to be in the first wave should immediately start taking shots for the endemic diseases of the Canal Zone.

The conversation turned to the proffer of Czechoslovakian and Rumanian units for the UN force. The SYG indicated that he anticipated little difficulty in turning them down and said that he did not believe Egypt would press for their inclusion.

The meeting terminated at about 10:40 p.m.

---

554.   **Memorandum of Discussion at the 303d Meeting of the National Security Council, Washington, November 8, 1956, 9–11:25 a.m.** [1]

[Here follows a paragraph listing the participants at the meeting.]

1. European Oil Supply Position in View of Developments in the Near East

Upon taking his place at the table, the President informed the Council that the first item on the agenda was a discussion of the European oil supply position. Mr. Robert B. Anderson, former Deputy Secretary of Defense, would make a report to the Council, but wished to leave the meeting after this subject had been discussed.

---

[1] Source: Eisenhower Library, Whitman File, NSC Records. Prepared by Gleason on November 9. The time of the meeting is from the record of the President's Daily Appointments. (*Ibid.*) A talking paper prepared in the Bureau of Near Eastern, South Asian, and African Affairs and forwarded to Hoover by Rountree on November 7 for use at this meeting is in Department of State, Central Files, 684A.86/11–756.

Mr. Anderson stated that he would discuss three major aspects of the subject, beginning with an analysis of the precise oil supply situation as of today. He informed the Council that the Suez Canal was now thoroughly blocked by at least eight or nine ships which had been sunk in it. The Iraq pipeline had been sabotaged and three of its pumping stations destroyed. The Aramco tapline was still intact, but it was touch-and-go as to how long it would remain in operation. In the light of these developments, Mr. Anderson said that our first requirement will be for 350,000 barrels of oil a day to be delivered from the Gulf Coast to the East Coast of the United States. In addition, there will be a requirement of 450,000 barrels daily from Venezuela and from our Gulf Coast for Europe. Only approximately 700,000 barrels of oil a day can be generated from the Gulf Coast. With maximum use of all free world shipping, perhaps 800,000 barrels of oil can move each day from the Middle East around the Cape to Europe. Even if all these potentialities are realized, Europe would still be faced with a deficit of between 10 and 15% of its requirements. On the other hand, if we lost control of the Aramco tapline or fail to secure oil from the Middle East in the amounts mentioned above via the Cape route, the deficit in Europe would increase rapidly above the 10 to 15% level.

Mr. Anderson, who had been working with the oil companies, then informed the Council of the availability of crude and refined products in Europe at the present time. There was approximately two weeks' crude supply, and approximately a month to six weeks' supply of refined products on hand. The American oil companies estimate that it will take something between six months and a year to rehabilitate the Iraq petroleum company's pipeline, including the destroyed pumping stations. The British believe that this task can be accomplished sooner.

The second major aspect of Mr. Anderson's report concerned the dollar problem. If the European nations were to secure oil from the United States and Venezuela to make up the deficit, this will require the generation of dollars. Prices for crude oil are rising rapidly, but not as rapidly as prices for shipping oil in tankers.

Mr. Anderson then reminded the Council that some months ago the Middle East Emergency Committee of industry personnel had been set up under the Office of Defense Mobilization, to make plans for the control of shipment of oil from the Gulf Coast to Europe in the event of an interruption of normal Middle Eastern supplies. There were British and French counterparts to the Middle East Emergency Committee. Mr. Anderson added that the Organization for European Economic Cooperation (OEEC), composed of seventeen European countries, had recently met and made the following four recommendations to the seventeen member governments:

1. A recommendation for equitable sharing of shortages among the European countries.

2. A recommendation for the equitable distribution of such petroleum supplies as were on hand at a given time.

3. A recommendation that rationing machinery be set up in each of the member countries.

4. A recommendation that each country establish a petroleum advisory committee to advise each government on the relevant problems.

Mr. Anderson then informed the Council that differences of opinion existed among the heads of our American oil companies with respect to the best means of dealing with the present crisis. Many believed that the United States Government should not act in the matter of assisting to get oil to the European countries until the situation in the Suez Canal had been clarified. Others were concerned that U.S. Government participation in getting oil to Europe would be regarded by the Arab nations as tantamount to U.S. support for aggression against Egypt. To make matters worse, as of yesterday the Government of Saudi Arabia had prohibited the offloading of any ships with oil destined for the United Kingdom or for France. This government was also planning other measures with respect to Bahrein Island, which was under a British mandate. Accordingly, Mr. Anderson pointed out that if we now proceeded to implement the program developed by the Middle East Emergency Committee, such action would be regarded by the Arabs as U.S. participation in the aggression against them. While there was little doubt that we could get oil to Great Britain and France by the simple collaboration of the American oil companies without invoking the program outlined by the Middle East Emergency Committee, this course of action might invite difficulties under the existing anti-trust laws of the United States. In essence, said Mr. Anderson, this constituted the issue which the Council would have to consider.

The President first inquired whether any oil could be got from Sumatra or elsewhere in Indonesia. Mr. Anderson replied that some oil was produced from Sumatra, but most of the 350,000 barrels a day which landed on our Pacific Coast came from the Middle East.

The President then asked Mr. Anderson whether he could take any action to increase U.S. oil production for a period of six months, making it perfectly clear that there would be a cut-back after this interval. Or, asked the President, would the independent oil companies make a terrible fuss when the cut-back was instituted at the end of the six-months period? Mr. Anderson replied that this would be very difficult indeed to do, and suggested that it would be better for the oil companies, rather than the Government, to call for an increase in U.S. production.

The Vice President inquired how the oil companies were in a position to make a significant increase in oil production in as short a time as six months. Mr. Anderson replied that in point of fact the increase could be achieved very promptly. The President agreed, but wondered whether, if this were done and the price of oil rose, there wasn't danger that the stripper wells would come back into production. Mr. Anderson answered that in any event we could anticipate that the independent oil operators would charge that the Government always bailed out the big companies whenever they got into trouble. Moreover, he added, the independents would be airing this complaint at a time when the Congress would be in session.

The President suggested that what Mr. Anderson was looking for was some means by which to secure an increase promptly in U.S. oil production without at the same time getting the United States in a position, in the eyes of the Arab world, of bailing out the British and the French. Mr. Anderson agreed, and said that the real question was simply whether we invoke the program drawn up by the Middle East Emergency Committee or not. The President stated that as he saw it, just as soon as a cease-fire was achieved in Egypt the Arab states will all be eager to sell their oil again, since this was the main source of their revenues. The President then inquired whether anyone else around the Council table had any different ideas to contribute.

Secretary Wilson observed that no matter what happened there was bound to be an oil shortage of some months' duration in Western Europe. It was his suggestion that we set about ensuring increased production of oil in the United States without immediately disclosing what we propose to do to assist Great Britain and France.

Mr. Anderson prophesied that the rationing of petroleum may soon be required in Great Britain. Both the British and the French are extremely anxious to know what the United States proposes to do. If we do not inform them, the British and French may insist on holding on to every bit of oil available to them, and permit the shipment of none of this oil to other European nations to whom they normally would make such shipments. The President wondered whether it would not be possible to ensure the shipment of necessary oil to the neutral nations of Western Europe (excluding Great Britain and France) without arousing the wrath of the Arabs. Mr. Anderson replied that this would be very difficult because most of the other European nations do not have sufficient facilities to receive and store large amounts of petroleum at any one time.

Secretary Hoover commented that the Department of State had a very vital concern in this whole problem. In fact, hours and days are vital in getting this operation started. Even if we begin to increase U.S. oil production right now, it will still be very difficult to move that oil earlier than a period of fifteen to thirty days. Secretary Hoover predicted that there was going to be harsh rationing in Europe, which was bound to give rise to extreme anti-American feeling there on the ground that we will not seem to have done what is plainly in the vital interests of Western Europe.

The President interposed the observation that anything that succeeds in stopping the present hostilities in the Near East was very much in the vital interests of Great Britain and France. In reply, Secretary Hoover pointed out that the British and French have agreed to get out of Egypt as soon as the UN police force move in. Moreover, the United States is ready, as Ambassador Lodge had stated in the UN, to transport the UN police force to Egypt. Accordingly, it was absolutely crucial, in Secretary Hoover's opinion, to get the necessary increase in U.S. oil production. He then advocated use of the OEEC machinery just as soon as possible. Use of the OEEC machinery would, he believed, avoid the appearance that the United States was focusing attention on oil supplies solely for Britain and France. Furthermore, it should be possible for us to go to King Saud and promise him that none of his oil would go to France or Great Britain and that no British or French ships would go into his ports. In conclusion, Secretary Hoover again suggested that operations start immediately.

Dr. Flemming informed the Council that if the program devised by the Middle East Emergency Committee should now go into operation, it will operate under the approval of the Secretary of the Interior. Accordingly, the U.S. Government would be provided with an opportunity to control the schedules of shipments. We could, furthermore, use the OEEC machinery to guide us in making decisions as to the appropriate distribution of oil going to Europe.

Secretary Humphrey agreed with Dr. Flemming, but warned that we could not start this kind of operation without clearly indicating that the United States was right in the middle of it. Accordingly, Secretary Humphrey said, he was opposed to doing anything more than taking the steps which Mr. Anderson had earlier suggested. Mr. Anderson pointed out that the United States and Canada were, so to speak, associate members of OEEC. Any way you looked at it, he went on, there was bound to be a shortage of oil in Western Europe. The real question, therefore, was whether we prefer to let this shortage increase over a period of time, or immediately involve the United States Government in the problem by putting into action the program devised by the Middle East Emergency Committee.

The President reiterated his point that the vital problem now was to induce Egypt to agree to a cease-fire. To do this will be much more difficult if we presently announce that we are going to get oil to Great Britain and France. While this was very hard on the State Department, it was true just the same. Secretary Hoover replied that we had just sent a message to President Nasser through Dag Hammarskjöld last evening, a message which we do not believe Nasser is in a position to turn down. [2] Accordingly, we believe that we will have the Egyptian situation under control within the next 24 to 36 hours. In view of this, Secretary Hoover stated his belief that the program of the Middle East Emergency Committee should now be predicated on the likelihood of immediate success for the UN action.

Secretary Wilson took a different position, and recommended against any move involving the U.S. Government which would impair this Government's bargaining position at the present moment. Secretary Humphrey agreed with Secretary Wilson, who went on to state that the situation should be left alone for a little while. He warned that the British and French will soon be urging that the United States ration petroleum supplies as only fair if these countries have to resort to rationing. This would cause a lot of trouble for this Government.

Secretary Humphrey said he was sure that the committee of private oil industry people would secure greater efficiency in the matter of shipping oil. On the other hand, he believed that the most unfortunate aspect of this whole crisis was the clarity with which it pointed to a serious lack in the logistics system of the Western powers. It indicates to the Arabs what a singularly strong position they are in by virtue of their control of so much oil in the world. Accordingly, the United States would have to do what it could for Europe in the near future, but not at the present moment; that is, not until the British and French Governments have got back into a position of compliance with the directives of the United Nations.

The President pointed out that if we really get the Arabs sore at all of us, they could embargo all oil, which would ruin our present Middle East Emergency Committee plan which still counts on some 800,000 barrels of oil daily from Middle East sources. Mr. Anderson agreed, and said that furthermore, if the Arabs got sore enough, we could also lose what we are now getting from the Aramco tapline. Mr. Anderson thought it would not be amiss if the State Department talked to Ibn Saud and asked him to what countries he was willing that his oil be sent. After all, Saud is, in a certain sense, cutting off his nose to spite his face when he threatens to cut off oil presently going to Bahrein. The British and French get very little of

---

[2] Not found in Department of State files. During a conversation with Armstrong and Lodge on November 7, however, Hammarskjöld said that he had sent a message to Nasser; see *supra*.

their oil from Bahrein Island. Secretary Hoover commented that he had received another useful suggestion from Mr. Anderson, namely, that if our European friends come here to Washington in the next ten days, we should invite King Ibn Saud to visit us after their departure. The President expressed approval of this proposal, and pointed out philosophically that the way of the peacemaker is proverbially hard. For this reason he believed that the first thing to do is to try to avoid aggravating either side in the controversy any further. If all of this was an hour-by-hour proposition, the President believed we would be best advised to let our Middle East Emergency Committee study further action. With a smile, the President added that despite his stiff-necked Attorney General, he could give the industry members a certification that what they were planning and doing was in the interests of the national security. This might assist them with respect to any involvement with the anti-trust laws.

The President asked Secretary Humphrey if he had any objections to such a course of action. Secretary Humphrey replied in the affirmative, and said that he would prefer to see us do only what Mr. Anderson had earlier suggested, namely, to open up our coastwise shipment of oil to all foreign-flag vessels and to undertake to increase oil production in the Gulf area. For the time being, however, he would oppose programming oil shipments to Europe. The Emergency Committee's program could be got in readiness to move just as soon as the gong sounded and the British and French evidenced compliance with the orders of the United Nations.

Secretary Hoover stressed the matter of timing, and said our decision would have to be based primarily on a feel for public relations; that is, on when this Government believed it could move with due regard to Arab opinion on the one hand and the British and French viewpoint on the other.

Dr. Flemming stated that he would put the machinery into operation. He pointed out that foreign-flag tankers could then carry oil from the Gulf Coast to the East Coast. Thereafter, when the UN police force has been installed in Egypt, we will go on from this point to effectuate the program of the Middle East Emergency Committee. Dr. Flemming followed up his proposal with a statement of the crude oil inventory of the chief Western European nations.

Secretary Wilson warned that we must avoid thinking that we can deal with the Arabs as we would deal with businessmen. The Arabs are moved by emotion and not by the judgments of businessmen.

Secretary Humphrey pointed out, with respect to the money and dollar aspect of Mr. Anderson's earlier report, that the French have already come over here some three weeks ago and have arranged with the International Monetary Fund to pull out all their gold and dollars. They have already drawn on these to the limit. Overtures from the British suggest that they will presently follow the French example. To Secretary Humphrey it seemed clear that if the United Kingdom did not look out, it would bust itself to a point of bankruptcy and of no return.

The President remarked with a sigh that he wished we could have a complete history of this cabal in which the British and the French were involved. A step-by-step analysis of what they had done would be very illuminating. The President then severely criticized the conduct of British and French military operations against Egypt, pointing out that there was no excuse for the long delay in the landing of British and French troops in the Suez Canal area once they had made the decision to do so. . . .

Secretary Hoover commented that the Anglo-French cabal had not only "kidded" the United States; it had also kidded the nations of the British Commonwealth and, to some extent, the British public too. . . . The President agreed, and stated that this Government officially should keep out of the oil supply problem until we were assured that the cease-fire was in effect.

Mr. Anderson said that he felt compelled to state that it was difficult to encourage the oil companies to do their best, in view of their great anxiety about violation of the anti-trust laws if they followed a course that we suggested was in the national security interest. The President said with a smile that if the heads of these oil companies landed up in jail or had to pay a big fine, he would pardon them (laughter).

The Attorney General said that at the very least we owed it to these people to have a representative of the United States Government work with them. Mr. Anderson warned that he was not an official of the U.S. Government. To this the Attorney General replied that it would then be necessary to have a representative of the Department of the Interior work with the committee. We owed this, in all fairness, to the committee. The President said that this was OK with him, and asked that ODM or Interior make the necessary arrangements.

The National Security Council: [3]

a. Discussed the subject and possible U.S. actions related thereto, in the light of an oral report by Mr. Robert B. Anderson.

b. Noted the President's approval of the following courses of action:

---

[3] Paragraphs a–b and the Note that follow constitute NSC Action No. 1629, approved by the President on November 10. (Department of State, S/S–NSC (Miscellaneous) Files: Lot 66 D 95, Records of Action by the National Security Council, 1956)

(1) Authorize the movement of U.S. Gulf Coast oil to the U.S. East Coast in foreign-flag tankers.

(2) When a cease-fire has been arranged in Egypt and when the UN police force is functioning in Egypt, consider putting into operation the plan of action of the Middle East Emergency Committee.

Note: The action in b above, as approved by the President, subsequently transmitted to the Director, Office of Defense Mobilization, for appropriate implementation.

2. Significant World Developments Affecting U.S. Security

[Here follows a report by Allen Dulles on the situation in Hungary.]

Mr. [Allen] Dulles then moved on to the situation in Egypt. He described Nasser as still in control of the Egyptian Government. His prestige had been severely shaken four or five days ago as a result of the complete defeat of the Egyptians by the Israelis, but his prestige had now been considerably restored as a result of Soviet support. In any event, Egyptian disillusionment with Nasser was not likely to be strong enough to bring him down. Internal security in Egypt was still under Nasser's control and appeared to be reasonably good. His military situation was certainly poor, but not hopeless if, as is likely, he is planning now to wage a guerrilla war. Nasser has withdrawn Egyptian Army forces into the cities and towns where, of course, the British and French will be reluctant to attack because of inevitable civilian casualties. The Egyptian Air Force is practically gone, and virtually every airfield knocked out. Some Egyptian planes managed to escape to Saudi Arabia and perhaps to Syria. The Egyptian Navy was now negligible. Mr. Dulles then pointed out that, thanks to Soviet aid, Nasser might presently reverse his willingness to give the United States carte blanche to do what was necessary to save Egypt.

Mr. Dulles at this point turned to the military situation in the Suez Canal Zone. He indicated that Anglo-French control extended from Port Said as far down as Qantara. On the other hand, French reports that they had taken Ismailia were false. In the future we should take Anglo-French communiqués with a grain of salt. The Egyptians had done a pretty complete job of blocking the Suez Canal. After giving details, Mr. Dulles pointed out that the Egyptians had the capability of cutting the Sweet Water Canal. If they did, the whole area would be deprived of fresh water, and the task of the British and French would be made much more difficult.

Turning to the situation in the other Arab countries, Mr. Dulles indicated that the Government of Jordan was trying to keep out of hostilities, although Iraqi and Syrian troops were now deployed in

Jordan. Indeed, none of the Arab countries seemed particularly anxious to involve itself in a war with Israel. They talk big, but they have few military capabilities. Indeed, the Egyptian Government has already advised them that this is not the time to attack Israel, although Cairo has ordered sabotage operations from both Jordan and Syria.

Mr. Dulles warned that we must watch the situation in Syria with the utmost care, since this was the potential key to Soviet operations in the Near East if the USSR actually decided to intervene.

As for Iraq, it has so far only sent troops into Jordan. Nuri was in a most difficult position. He doesn't want to do very much, but he has to do something in order to keep public opinion in Iraq in line. Mr. Dulles went on to comment that the Israelis could readily use fedayeen activities on their borders as an excuse to strike at Jordan or Syria if they so desired. Destruction by sabotage of the Iraq petroleum company's pipeline had been very thorough. It might be possible to get some oil flowing through this pipeline again in three months, according to Aramco estimates. Full-scale restoration would be a much longer time. Moreover, further extensive sabotage operations have been ordered by Cairo. In view of this, we should watch the situation in Kuwait, because the British have tended to neglect adequate security measures in this important area. Admiral Radford commented that the British had now put troops in Kuwait and have shown an appropriate concern for the situation there.

Mr. Dulles then turned to the Soviet position, saying that the questions that we are all asking are how far will the Soviets go in this situation and what will they do? Mr. Dulles reminded the Council of Ambassador Bohlen's warning that the Soviet people had been thoroughly conditioned for any action which the Soviet Government may decide to take.

It was certainly clear that the Soviets are doing their utmost to stiffen the backs of the Arabs in order to prevent a psychological breakdown. In support of this statement Mr. Dulles summarized Foreign Minister Shepilov's recent activities. He added that the Soviet delegation in the United Nations had been urging the Arabs to hold out pending the arrival of Soviet volunteers to assist them. Indeed, both the Russians and the Chinese have made clear statements to the effect that some kind of volunteers will be sent. Mr. Dulles further noted that the language of recent Soviet statements was such as to pave the way for unilateral Soviet action if they chose to undertake it.

As to what the Soviets will do, as contrasted with what they say, this was a much more difficult question. It would certainly be hard for the Soviets to provide the Arab states with material and military aid. Accordingly, the CIA was inclined to think that for the time being the main Soviet emphasis would be on keeping the pot boiling. They hope that the cease-fire, if it occurs, will come unstuck. Nevertheless, the intelligence community by and large was adhering to its earlier estimate that the Soviet Union was not likely to take actions in the Middle East which they believed likely to induce general war. The real problem here was the possibility of chain reactions which might ultimately lead to general war without being so intended.

Mr. Dulles pointed out the great difficulty which the Soviets would encounter in an effort to get Soviet volunteers into Egypt. On the other hand, a good source has just informed us that the Soviets have asked Turkish permission to send five Soviet warships through the Straits.

After further speculation as to the various courses of action the USSR might follow, Mr. Dulles returned to his worries about the situation in Syria, where, he said, it would be easy for a coup to occur under Soviet auspices. It was possible that the Soviets would attempt to airlift paratroops as well as technicians into Syria despite the lack of airfield facilities in that country. Admiral Radford interrupted to state that one or two of the Syrian airfields were capable of servicing MIG aircraft.

Mr. Dulles concluded his comments on the Near East by again calling for a careful watch over Iran and Iraq. The Soviets might well try to frighten the Shah of Iran and to upset the Nuri regime in Iraq.

Admiral Radford said that he felt personally that the situation in the Near East as a whole was even worse than Mr. Dulles had suggested. He stated his belief that the Soviets were now in Syria and were absolutely determined to delay or prevent any solution of the crisis in the Near East. After all, he argued, the Soviets are perfectly well aware of the world oil situation and of the fact that sooner or later the United States will have to assist Europe, and that this will turn the Arabs against us. The presence of the Soviets in Syria seemed to be proved for Admiral Radford by the shooting down of an allied plane flying at an altitude of 45,000 feet. Such a feat would be impossible for the Syrian Air Force. Finally, Admiral Radford expressed his belief that the Russians were likely to encourage the Syrians to attack Israel. Moreover, the Russians may have much more air in Syria than we currently estimate.

While expressing agreement with Admiral Radford in general, the President commented that he just couldn't help believing that the Russians would play their game short of anything which would induce the United States to declare war on them. Furthermore, the President said, it remained wholly inexplicable to him that any state in the world, Syria included, would play with the Russians after witnessing what had happened in Hungary. It is for this reason, continued the President, that we must go on playing up the situation in Hungary to the absolute maximum, so the whole world will see and understand.

The Vice President agreed with the President's proposal, and said that in carrying it out we should not neglect Asia. Mr. Dulles indicated that the Free Europe Committee was already engaged in preparing a White Paper which would give the world all the facts about what had happened in Hungary from the beginning.

The President proceeded to quote from his most recent message from Nehru,[4] commenting that Nehru seemed to be falling for the Moscow line—buying their entire bill of goods.

The Vice President stated that the great message which we must get across to the rest of the world was that no state could afford to play in with the Soviet Union unless it wished to be taken over.

Governor Stassen expressed the thought that the Soviet request on Turkey to transit the Dardanelles might well presage a Soviet landing in Syria or Egypt. This was an especially grave matter and he therefore suggested the advisability of a UN embargo on the shipment of any further forces into any Near Eastern country by any other nation. Governor Stassen explained that he did not believe that the Soviets really intended to ship forces which would open an attack. What they really meant to do with these forces was to secure a foothold in Syria or elsewhere in the Near East from which they could never thereafter be dislodged.

Both Secretary Hoover and Admiral Radford inquired of Governor Stassen just how he imagined we could make such a UN embargo stick. Governor Stassen admitted that this might be difficult, but said at the very least we would put the Soviets in the position of violating a UN-instituted embargo.

Secretary Hoover changed the subject by stating that he would like to report to the Council in the first instance on some of the immediate things which this Government must do now, and thereafter certain other actions which were of intermediate-range character. As for the immediate steps, the first one was to get the United Nations police force established in Egypt. Secretary Hoover reviewed developments on this problem, and stated that they were satisfactory and were moving rapidly toward the objective.

Our second move was to get the UK and French forces out of Egypt. Here the State Department felt that it was significant to get even a token Anglo-French force moving out. This was the immediate objective.

---

[4] Not printed. (Eisenhower Library, Whitman File, International File)

The third move was to get Israeli forces moving back to the armistice line. Secretary Hoover reminded the President of the message which he had sent to Ben-Gurion last night,[5] and went on to say that he had had a very rough session with the Israelis at the State Department last night.[6] Although we had treated the Israelis very roughly, they had had no comeback.

Fourthly, there was the oil situation, which seemed to be under control and which Secretary Hoover said had been adequately covered by Mr. Anderson's earlier report.

Secretary Hoover covered this phase of his report to the Council with the prophecy that the Soviets would do everything in their power to prevent the achievement of a settlement in the Near East. On the other hand, if there were actually a Soviet attack on a UN police force stationed in Egypt, Secretary Hoover believed that such an attack would be tantamount to a Russian attack on the whole world. He paid warm tribute to the achievements of the Secretary General of the United Nations. Mr. Hammarskjöld, he said, had matured greatly in recent months. The only question seemed to be his physical endurance. He had had no sleep for three days. Secretary Hoover added that Mr. Hammarskjöld seemed without question to be on our side.

Describing the above as the immediate problems, Secretary Hoover then turned to problems which hereafter would soon be facing us. First of all, the UN police force was going into the Suez Canal Zone. . . . [7] The President suddenly interrupted to point out how rigid was Anglo-French thinking on the composition of the UN police force. In his conversation on the telephone with Anthony Eden, the British Prime Minister had expressed extreme reluctance to agree to the proposal that this police force would have no British or French troops as a component. When the President asked Sir Anthony how he proposed to exclude Soviet troops from the UN forces if he insisted on British and French components in the UN police force, Sir Anthony had indicated that this problem had not occurred to him, and that he would have to give it some thought. The President said he was absolutely astounded.

Secretary Hoover continued his remarks by pointing out that there would be no great problem for the UN police force to take over that portion of the Suez Canal Zone which was already in British and French hands. What, however, was to happen when the UN police force met the Egyptians in the area of the Canal Zone still under their control? There was no answer to Secretary Hoover's

---

[5] Document 550.
[6] See Document 551.
[7] Ellipsis in the source text.

question, although Mr. Allen Dulles suggested that the UN forces be stationed in Cairo rather than in the Canal Zone.

Secretary Hoover went on to his second emerging problem, namely, what kind of longer-range solution we would envisage for settling the Canal issue. Should we plan on a continuation and development of the instrumentality of the Suez Canal Users Association (SCUA)? Or, alternatively, should we put the whole question into the hands of the United Nations? Secretary Hoover indicated that he had asked Secretary Dulles to give as much attention as possible to this problem while he remained in the hospital.

Thirdly, continued Secretary Hoover, there was the whole problem of how we conteract the growing Soviet influence in many of these Arab states.

At this point the President interrupted Secretary Hoover to say that Admiral Strauss had just sent him a note stating that moving pictures had been taken of Soviet tanks killing Hungarians in the streets of Budapest. The President asked whether such movies should not immediately be disseminated through our Embassies all over the world. Mr. Streibert answered that the USIA was already engaged in doing precisely this, and was trying to get the story out just as fast as it could. The President said it would be a good idea to send one of the best reels to Nehru. The Vice President advised sending one to Sukarno in Indonesia.

Secretary Hoover continued his account by alluding to still another problem, namely, how we could focus the violent anti-Soviet feeling throughout Europe on the Middle East and on the Arab states. He concluded by reminding the President that these were only a few of the problems which were facing the United States.

The President commented that obviously the main thing now was to get the UN police force into Egypt and the British and French forces out of Egypt. This action would pull the rug out from under the Soviet psychological offensive. The President reverted likewise to his suggestion that the moving pictures of Soviet atrocities in Budapest be given the fullest possible exploitation. Secretary Hoover counseled that we not forget that the Soviets have been pounding away on the point that the whole affair in Hungary was caused by the interference of the United States Government generally and of the Central Intelligence Agency in particular. Mr. Allen Dulles replied that the line to take in this matter was simply to state that this was an insult to the Hungarians.

Secretary Humphrey stressed the need of getting oil to Europe in the near future. If this were not done, Europe would soon be on her knees. He also wondered whether it might not be necessary for the United States to move into various Arab countries in order to protect the oil wells. Admiral Radford commented that in any event we must be ready to do this if it proved necessary. The President said that it was ironical that all our plans on protecting the sources of oil had been predicated up to now on the desire of the Arabs to protect their wells from the Russians. Our plans for preserving the oil of the Middle East had never been drawn up in contemplation of the actual situation now facing us.

Governor Stassen stressed the necessity of providing real incentives to Nasser in order to induce him to work closely with the West. There should be a long-range settlement. We should see what we can do now to help get the high Aswan dam on the tracks. If we did not thus offer incentives to Nasser, he might very well decide to refuse the cease-fire and put his dependence on the Russians.

Secretary Hoover expressed disagreement with Governor Stassen's suggestion of incentives, expressing the view that Hammarskjöld was quite right in insisting that we will discuss nothing until the UN police force was installed in Egypt. The President commented that if Egypt fought a UN police force they would in effect be fighting the United Nations and the entire world. Governor Stassen indicated that he had not meant that the Egyptians would attack the UN police force; they would simply refuse to admit it to Egyptian territory. Secretary Hoover said that this was precisely the reason why our plans called for the phasing out of the Anglo-French troops only as the UN police forces were phased in. He expressed himself as very dubious as to the efficacy of the carrot principle in dealing with Nasser. After all, we had been trying this for the last couple of years, and the failure had been pretty complete. Governor Stassen still insisted that a combination of the carrot and the stick was the best way to deal with Nasser. Otherwise, he predicted that Nasser would certainly stall on the cease-fire agreement.

The President observed that there was another question on which he sought the Council's advice. How were we going to deal with the briefing of the Congressional leaders scheduled for tomorrow morning at nine o'clock in the White House? [8] We would certainly need Mr. Allen Dulles on the intelligence side. Admiral Radford should be prepared to talk about the military situation, and Secretary Hoover on what had been occurring on the UN side as well as what we are now trying to do. Arthur Flemming should be

---

[8] The memorandum of conversation for the bipartisan legislative meeting at the White House on November 9 is in the Eisenhower Library, Whitman File, Legislative Meetings. See footnote 3, Document 558. Prior to the meeting, the Department of State prepared remarks on the Hungarian and Suez situations for Hoover to make at the briefing. A copy of the memorandum, entitled "White House Congressional Presentation, November 9, 1956", is in Department of State, Central Files, 764.00/11–1356.

ready on the oil situation, and we should have the required maps and charts. The President described all the foregoing as constituting a briefing of the leaders on the situation. As to where we go from here, Secretary Hoover should be prepared to report on that. Above all, we should keep in mind, all of us who were involved in this briefing, that the real enemy of the United States is the Kremlin, not Cairo or Tel Aviv.

The Vice President expressed the hope that while we must deal with the Near East problem, we should also give the Congressional leaders a good stiff talk on Hungary. There has been too great a tendency to allow developments in the Near East to divert attention from Hungary. Let's assure that the Congressional leaders do not leave without a knowledge of what had really happened in Hungary. The Vice President thought this topic should come last in the briefing, and also suggested that the movies mentioned earlier should be shown to the Congressional leaders.

The President commented that the present Congressional leaders have been acting in a wholly admirable fashion.

The Attorney General warned the President that the Congressional leaders were very likely to ask him whether, in view of what had happened, the Government should not move now to exclude the Soviet Union from membership in the UN. The President replied that if he were asked this question he would say that we couldn't shoot from the hip, but state that this was certainly something to be considered.

The Vice President suggested that the briefing on the oil situation should be very short, perhaps no more than five minutes. This was a very complicated situation, which would involve domestic political considerations. Dr. Flemming pointed out that our present plans do not in any sense call for a rationing of gasoline. The Vice President said that he was glad to hear it, because if rationing was seriously discussed the result would be an inevitable rise in isolationist sentiment in the Congress and in the country.

Mr. Allen Dulles suggested that the Hungarian topic come first rather than last in the briefing of the leaders. The President and many other members of the Council thought this suggestion wise. The President went on to express the feeling that the Russians had jumped rapidly into the Near East situation not simply because the British and French had given them an opportunity, but because they have long hoped that somehow or other they could reach into the Middle East. Accordingly, we must be careful in briefing the Congressional leaders not to place all the blame for what had happened on Great Britain and France. Admiral Radford expressed warm agreement with the President's suggestion. It was unwise to blame overmuch the British and the French. We should instead put the

Near East situation in its true perspective, and indicate clearly ultimate Communist responsibility for what has occurred in the Near East.

Mr. Allen Dulles . . . indicated the possibility that the Soviets might presently intervene in the Middle East.

The . . . question moved Governor Stassen to suggest again his proposal for a UN embargo on all shipments to any Near Eastern state. The President, on the other hand, insisted that the immediate thing to do was to get the cease-fire and to get it as quickly as possible. If necessary, the next step could be a UN embargo of the whole Near Eastern area, so that nothing could be got in. Dr. Flemming asked if he could make an inquiry as to whether the President believed that enough was being done on the side of civilian defense in the light of the dangerous possibilities inherent in the present situation. For example, what about plans for relocating sensitive Government agencies? The President replied that this was certainly a period of tension, and it might be a good idea for the departments and agencies to go ahead with the perfecting of their relocation plans.

The National Security Council: [9]

a. Noted and discussed an oral briefing by the Director of Central Intelligence on the subject, with specific reference to developments in Hungary and world reaction thereto; the situation in Egypt and elsewhere in the Near East; and Soviet capabilities and intentions with regard to the Near East.

b. Noted and discussed an oral report by the Acting Secretary of State regarding current and possible future developments related to the situation in Egypt and the Near East generally.

S. Everett Gleason

---

[9] Paragraphs a–b that follow constitute NSC Action No. 1630, approved by the President on November 10. (Department of State, S/S–NSC (Miscellaneous) Files: Lot 66 D 95, Records of Action by the National Security Council, 1956)

555.   Memorandum for the Secretary of State's Special Assistant for Intelligence (Armstrong) [1]

Washington, November 8, 1956.

SUBJECT

Egyptian Proposal to Cooperate with U.S.

1. Muhammad Haykal in discussion with an Embassy official made the following points:

a. Yesterday the Soviets told Egyptian Chief of Cabinet Ali Sabri that they were prepared for World War III because the Soviet Union is an armed camp, surrounded by an inner ring of satellites and an outer ring of neutral states. The British aggression in Egypt was the first western attempt to break the outer ring, and the situation in Hungary is an attempt to break the inner ring. The Soviets cannot allow this to happen; therefore they are determined to help Egypt in their own self interest. Haykal said that neither President Jamal 'Abd-al-Nasr nor Ali Sabri believe this explanation, but feel it is a Soviet attempt to cash in on a situation already existing.

b. The Egyptian Government wants to know what United States policy is concerning the immediate removal of British and French troops and the withdrawal of Israel forces to the demarcation lines. (*Field Comment:* The Embassy official referred Haykal to U.S. sponsored UN resolutions on these subjects.)

c. The United States must not push Egypt too fast on the question of peace with Israel. No peace is possible until a United Nations Commission has come to the area and investigated the situation fully in concert with all interested parties.

d. 'Abd-al-Nasr is fully aware of the Soviet game in the area, realizes that he must make a choice, and has chosen the course of full cooperation with the United States.

.   .   .   .

---

[1] Source: Department of State, Central Files, 974.7301/11–856. Secret. Transmitted to the Department of State under cover of a memorandum from Gordon M. Stewart of the Central Intelligence Agency to Armstrong, November 8, which reads in part: "1. Attached is a message from Cairo reporting statements made by Muhammad Haykal . . . .

"2. It is requested that this report be brought to the immediate attention of the Secretary of State, Undersecretary Hoover, and Mr. Rountree." A handwritten notation on the covering memorandum indicates that Hoover saw the memorandum at the NSC meeting, presumably on November 8.

556.   Memorandum by the President [1]

Washington, November 8, 1956.

(1) Information, not yet official, indicates that both Israel and Egypt have now fully accepted the terms of the United Nations cease-fire plan, and that peaceful conditions should prevail soon in the Mid East.

(2) If the above hope is borne out by events of the next day or so, we should be promptly ready to take any kind of action that will minimize the effects of the recent difficulties and will exclude from the area Soviet influence.

(3) Measures to be taken under these elements, would be:

(a) Rapid restoration of pipe line and Canal operation. This might have to be done almost wholly by American technical groups, but I should think that we might also mobilize some people from Germany and Italy. This work should begin instantly.

(b) Push negotiations under the United Nations so as to prevent renewed outbreak of difficulty [*hostility?*].

(c) Provide to the area, wherever necessary, surplus foods, and so on, to prevent suffering.

(4) Simultaneously we must lay before the several governments information and proposals that will establish real peace in the area and, above all, to exclude Communist influence from making any headway therein. There are a number of things to do.

One of the first is to make certain that none of these governments fails to understand all the details and the full implications of the Soviet suppression of the Hungarian revolt. We should, I think, get all the proof that there is available, including moving pictures taken of the slaughter in Budapest.

We must make certain that every weak country understands what can be in store for it once it falls under the domination of the Soviets.

And beyond this, however, are the constructive things that we can do once these nations understand the truth of the immediately preceding paragraph.

For example, we can provide Egypt with an agreed-upon amount of arms—sufficient to maintain internal order and a reasonable defense of its borders, in return for an agreement that it will never accept any Soviet offer.

We should likewise provide training missions.

---

[1] Source: Eisenhower Library, Whitman File, Eisenhower Diaries. No drafting officer is indicated on the source text, but in *Waging Peace* (pp. 96–97), Eisenhower acknowledged authorship and quoted extensively from the memorandum.

We can make arrangements for starting the Aswan Dam on a basis where interest costs would be no higher than the money costs ourselves. This, of course, would be contingent upon Egypt negotiating faithfully on the Suez Canal matter and in accordance with the six principles laid down by the United Nations.

We could assist with technicians in the repair of damage done in Egypt in the late unpleasantness and could even make an economic loan to help out.

In Israel we could renew the compact (Eric Johnston plan) and take up again the 75 million dollar economic loan that they desire.

We could possibly translate the tripartite statement of May 1950 into a bilateral treaty with each of the countries in this area.

We could make some kind of arms agreement—particularly maintenance and training—with Israel of exactly the same type we could make with Egypt.

We could explore other means of assisting the Arab States of Iraq, Jordan, Saudi Arabia and Lebanon, and develop ways and means of strengthening our economic and friendly ties with each of these countries, either on a bilateral or group basis.

---

557.   Memorandum of a Conversation, Department of State, Washington, November 8, 1956, 10:45 a.m. [1]

SUBJECT

Proposal that Israel Prime Minister Visit the United States

PARTICIPANTS

Mr. Abba Eban, Ambassador of Israel
Mr. Reuven Shiloah, Minister, Israel Embassy
NEA—Mr. William M. Rountree
NE—Mr. Donald C. Bergus

There was a discussion of the transmission of the President's message of November 7 to the Israel Prime Minister. Mr. Shiloah stated that a copy of the text which he had transmitted at 2 a.m. Washington time on November 8 had arrived in Israel at 8 a.m. Washington time. [2]

---

[1] Source: Department of State, Central Files, 611.84A/11–856. Confidential. Drafted by Bergus on November 9. The time of the meeting is from a memorandum from Rountree to Hoover, November 8. (*Ibid.*, 784A.13/11–856)

[2] See Document 550 and footnote 1 thereto.

Mr. Eban said he had had two telephone conversations with Mr. Ben Gurion and was exchanging telegrams with him regarding the broad international context of recent developments. A profound process of reconsideration was going on within the Israel Government. Mr. Eban had talked to the Prime Minister in the early hours of the morning. Ben Gurion's concern was so great that he wished to come to the United States for discussions with the President and the United Nations Secretary-General. Mr. Eban asked if this could be arranged. He recommended that Mr. Ben Gurion be brought to the United States within the next day or two. The President's message had been a profound document, but more than documents were needed at this time. A suitable formula for Mr. Ben Gurion's visit could be worked out. It could be said that he was coming as head of the Israel Delegation to the United Nations. Mr. Ben Gurion would not set out on this journey, however, unless he was assured that the President would receive him for substantive discussion.

Apart from that, Mr. Eban was pressing his Government for a reply to the President's message. He thought the reply would be in the direction the United States wished but he did not know what degree of finality it would have.

Mr. Rountree indicated that he would take up this matter urgently with the highest levels of the Department. He was sure they would hope that Mr. Ben Gurion did not intend to await our views on his proposal to visit the United States before replying to the President's message. Mr. Eban confirmed that he was expecting a reply to the President's message within the next few hours.

Mr. Eban said that in yesterday's conversation in the Acting Secretary's office, Mr. Rountree had rightly referred to Mr. Ben Gurion's assurance, conveyed to the Secretary by Mr. Eban on November 1, that Israel would not hold on to any territory occupied as a result of present military operations. Mr. Eban confirmed that he had given this assurance and said that he had reminded the Prime Minister of it last night. It was still the Prime Minister's position that Israel would withdraw from the territory under conditions which would assure Israel's security and maritime freedom. A United Nations force at the Suez Canal might leave a vacuum in Sinai which fedayeen and other irresponsible elements could exploit to Israel's detriment. To leave a vacuum in Sinai would be irresponsible. The question of Israel's withdrawal involved not only what Israel did but how Israel did it.

Mr. Rountree pointed out that the United Nations had asked for immediate withdrawal unconditionally. We felt that failure to respond would endanger world peace. Mr. Eban mentioned remarks made in the General Assembly by Ambassador Lodge about a phased solution. Mr. Rountree pointed out that Mr. Lodge had spoken of phasing in terms of days, not in terms of a solution.

Mr. Eban stated that there were many aspects to be considered in an Israel withdrawal in favor of a United Nations force. Such questions as the place where the United Nations force is stationed, the effect on Israel's maritime communications, were not details but matters of cosmic importance. The questions as to how these things were done could make the difference between peace and war. It was such matters as these which the Israel Prime Minister wished to discuss.

Mr. Rountree agreed that the question of Israel's withdrawal was a decision of peace or war. Mr. Eban said that Israel would not live the next eight years in manner she had lived during the last eight. Mr. Rountree said that we agreed that the situation could not go on as it had. That was why the United States had put forward its two resolutions in the United Nations General Assembly. There was a profound feeling that the next and immediate step was the withdrawal of Israel forces. This was important not only in terms of the Near East but also in Western-Soviet relations and the relationship between the United States and Israel.

Mr. Rountree felt that before a definite response could be given to Mr. Ben Gurion's request to visit the United States, there should be an opportunity to consider his reply to the President's message. [3]

---

[3] In a memorandum to Hoover dated November 8, Rountree summarized the remarks made by Eban at this meeting and commented that the Israeli Ambassador had left the impression that Israel still intended to attach political conditions to a withdrawal. Rountree also noted:

"We believe that among the motives behind the Israel request [for Ben-Gurion to visit the United States] are: 1) stalling for time; 2) a desire in this dramatic way to give the rest of the world the impression that close collaboration between the United States and Israel continues. We believe the visit would be construed as bypassing the UN and would bring unfavorable reactions both among the Afro-Asian group and the NATO countries."

Rountree recommended to Hoover that the Department should await Ben Gurion's written reply to the President before answering Eban, and he advised that his current inclination was to inform Israel that the United States could not consider a meeting between Eisenhower and Ben Gurion until Israel had complied with U.N. resolutions. (Department of State, Central Files, 784A.13/11–856) A marginal notation on this document reads: "Approved by Acting Secy and the Pres on firm basis—'after compliance'."

558.   Memorandum of a Telephone Conversation Between the President and the Secretary of the Treasury (Humphrey), Washington, November 8, 1956, 3:15 p.m. [1]

The President called Secretary Humphrey and said that this morning he had called to talk about spending [2]—and now he has just figured a way we can save a lot. He referred to the Mid East. If settlement is gone through with, as now seems hopeful, we have got to move in to try to repair damage and to secure the area against the Russians; we have got to help these arrangements through bilateral treaties and be prepared to spend some money in the ultimate hope of reducing our defense budget. Can gain much through friendships and close ties with peoples of these countries.

President said he wanted something constructive to talk to the leaders of Congress about tomorrow. Wants Humphrey's approval of modest amounts. I will go back in the Aswan Dam, but I want these people to see we will deal with them. Willing to give 75 million loan to Egypt [Israel].

We want to demonstrate that we will be friends with them. [3]

The Secretary agreed, and thought that private capital could do much to help their developments.

---

[1] Source: Eisenhower Library, Whitman File, Eisenhower Diaries. Prepared in the Office of the President.

[2] The memorandum of this telephone conversation, which took place at 12:43 p.m., is not printed. (Ibid.)

[3] Eisenhower made the following remarks concerning economic assistance to the Middle East during a bipartisan legislative meeting held on November 9: "The President spoke strongly on the great importance of the Middle East in the cold war and his conviction that the United States has to step up its efforts to assist the cause of freedom in that area. He felt that the United States could start with some advantage now that the pitfall of Russian assistance is evident, hence our efforts might be more successful in the future than in the past. He thought our efforts ought to be concentrated to a greater degree on helping these nations strengthen their economies, by which it would be possible to prevent growth of sympathies for Russia and perhaps win back those already sympathetic." (Memorandum of discussion by Minnich, November 9; ibid., Legislative Meetings)

559.   **Memorandum of a Conversation, Department of State, Washington, November 8, 1956** [1]

SUBJECT

Withdrawal of Israel Troops from Egypt

PARTICIPANTS

The Acting Secretary
Mr. Abba Eban, Ambassador of Israel
Mr. Reuven Shiloah, Minister, Israel Embassy
NEA—Mr. William M. Rountree
NE—Mr. Donald C. Bergus

Mr. Eban handed the Acting Secretary copies of Mr. Ben Gurion's reply to the President's message (attached). [2] A similar message had gone forward to the United Nations Secretary General who had expressed satisfaction. [3] The Secretary General wished to discuss arrangements with Mr. Eban on November 9.

The Acting Secretary asked if the Israel Prime Minister were agreeing to withdraw behind the armistice line. Mr. Eban said he was not authorized to interpret the Prime Minister's message but that he could say he was instructed to take up these arrangements with the Secretary General. The Acting Secretary inquired concerning Gaza. Mr. Eban said that Israel did not want vacuums created in the area and for this reason he had been told to begin discussions with the Secretary General on this point as well as other arrangements. Israel's response to the call for withdrawal had been similar to that of the British and French. The Secretary General had said that Israel's response would enable him to act.

Mr. Eban said that the Israel Government had been concerned over reports of Soviet activities in the area, including the concentration of weapons in Syria and Egypt and the inspiration of fedayeen activities. He pointed to the recent upsurge of fedayeen activity from Syria and Jordan. Israel had asked the Secretary General to express to Soviet representatives Israel's fears on this point. The Acting Secretary pointed out that the United States had thought for a number of months that these developments might take place.

Mr. Eban said Israel felt that the reassertion of Western unity in the Near East was one of the best things that could happen. The Soviet Union was probably telling the Arabs that the Soviet inter-

---

[1] Source: Department of State, Central Files, 674.84A/11–856. Confidential. Drafted by Bergus on November 9.
[2] *Infra.*
[3] U.N. doc. A/3320.

vention had had its effect. This would raise Soviet prestige to new heights.

Mr. Eban said that Israel took very seriously the promise of the President's letter [4] that there would be no going back to the status quo ante. This was very urgent with respect to Egypt. The Egypt-Israel armistice agreement was in ruins, the others remained. We would lack statesmanship if we did not seize this opportunity. As for the draft resolutions submitted by the United States, Israel had some suggestions which Mr. Eban would be presenting to Ambassador Lodge. Israel felt that the resolution should put responsibility on the parties to negotiate.

The Acting Secretary pointed out that our draft resolution created a Commission with very broad powers and responsibilities.

Mr. Eban referred to Mr. Ben Gurion's desire to visit the United States. Mr. Ben Gurion felt that Israel and the United States should be drawing closer together. Once the ceasefire and withdrawal had been implemented there would be a great opportunity. Mr. Ben Gurion would still like to come and discuss these matters with President Eisenhower. Mr. Ben Gurion had not been to the United States since the President assumed office.

The Acting Secretary said he did not know the President's plans for the next few weeks and that he was unable to answer for him. Israel's action in withdrawing its forces would be taken with the great feeling that all were gratified that Israel was complying with the General Assembly's request.

Mr. Eban referred to the third paragraph of the Prime Minister's message. While these were not conditions they were very important matters requiring United Nations action. This was Israel's policy.

A discussion was held at the conclusion of the meeting concerning the release of the President's letter and the Prime Minister's reply. Mr. Eban was sure that the full text of both communications would be read by the Prime Minister in a speech which he had probably already started to give in Israel. Accordingly, it was agreed that the White House would release both texts at 7 p.m. on November 8. [5]

---

[4] Document 550.

[5] For texts of both letters, see Department of State *Bulletin*, November 19, 1956, pp. 797–798. Copies are also in Department of State, Central Files, 674.84A/11–856.

560.   Message From Prime Minister Ben Gurion to President Eisenhower [1]

Jerusalem, November 8, 1956.

DEAR MR. PRESIDENT: I have only this afternoon received your message [2] which was delayed in transmission owing to a breakdown in communications between the Department of State and the United States Embassy in Tel Aviv.

Your statement that a United Nations force is being dispatched to Egypt in accordance with pertinent resolutions of the General Assembly is welcomed by us. We have never planned to annex the Sinai Desert. In view of the United Nations Resolutions regarding the withdrawal of foreign troops from Egypt and the creation of an international force, we will, upon conclusion of satisfactory arrangements with the United Nations in connection with this international force entering the Suez Canal area, willingly withdraw our forces.

Although an important part of our aim has been achieved by the destruction, as a result of the Sinai operation, of Fedayeen gangs and of the bases from which they were planned and directed, we must repeat our urgent request to the United Nations to call upon Egypt, which has consistently maintained that it is in a state of war with Israel, to renounce this position, to abandon its policy of boycott and blockade, to cease the incursions into Israel territory of murder gangs and, in accordance with its obligations under the United Nations Charter to live at peace with member states, to enter into direct peace negotiations with Israel.

On behalf of my government I wish to express to you our gratification at your reference to the deep interest of the United States in Israel and its policy of support for our country. I know these words of friendship stem from the depths of your heart and I wish to assure you that you will always find Israel ready to make

[1] Source: Eisenhower Library, Whitman File, International File. Eban handed the text of this message to Hoover during their conversation on November 8; see *supra.*
[2] Document 550.

its noble contribution [3] at the side of the United States in its efforts to strengthen justice and peace in the world. [4]

With best wishes,

Sincerely yours,

David Ben-Gurion [5]

---

[3] In a letter dated February 5, 1957, First Secretary of the Israeli Embassy Yohanan Meroz informed Bergus that the words "noble contribution" should be corrected to read "humble contribution," the error being evidently due to a garbled transmission. Meroz noted that the incorrect version had been published in the Department of State *Bulletin*. (Department of State, Central Files, 684A.86/2–557)

[4] On November 9, President Eisenhower replied to Ben Gurion as follows: "I appreciate your message of yesterday informing me that you will withdraw your forces from Egypt. This decision will be warmly welcomed not only by the United States but by all of the nations which are striving to restore peace and security for all nations in the Middle East. It will contribute greatly to a situation in which a peaceful solution may be attained." The text was transmitted for delivery to Tel Aviv on 11:20 a.m., November 9, in telegram 494. (*Ibid.*, 674.84A.11–956) A copy of this message, with handwritten changes by Eisenhower, is in the Eisenhower Library, Whitman File, International File.

[5] Printed from a copy that bears this typed signature.

---

561.   Telegram From the Embassy in Egypt to the Department of State [1]

Cairo, November 8, 1956—3 p.m.

1406. Took advantage call on Nasser re UN Force (Embtel 1404) [2] also to discuss Soviet moves in line Deptel 1457 and circ 372. [3] Nasser replied "you need not worry about that" and then repeated familiar theme that Egypt had had long struggle to get rid of foreign domination and did not intend repeat that experience.

---

[1] Source: Department of State, Central Files, 320.5780.11–856. Received at 1:38 a.m., November 10. A marginal notation by Goodpaster on a copy in the Eisenhower Library, Whitman File, Dulles–Herter Series reads: "Noted by President 12 Nov. 56".

[2] In telegram 1404 from Cairo, November 8, Hare reported that Nasser was still considering Hammarskjöld's message of November 7 which had asked whether Egypt would object to the participation of Canadian, Colombian, Danish, Finnish, Norwegian, and Swedish troops in the force to be stationed on Egyptian territory. Nasser told Hare that he would be meeting with his advisers on the subject and raised the question of public impact, if "Her Majesty's British troops were replaced by Her Majesty's Canadians". Hare stressed to Nasser the importance of an immediate and favorable response to Hammarskjöld. (Department of State, Central Files, 320.5780/11–856; the text of Hammarskjöld's November 7 message is in Delga 24 from USUN, November 7; *ibid.*, 320.5780/11–756)

[3] Documents 530 and 552, respectively.

Added "I don't trust any big power." Laughed when I mentioned Soviet proposal to join with USG in ousting British and French by force. Did not however give impression of feeling anything especially involved except expediency.

Nasser then launched into discussion of events last 10 days. Said although air force hit very hard army still in good fighting trim. Most important, however, was morale Egyptian people which was higher than ever before and unity of Arabs which stronger than before. British and French on other hand had gained nothing except loss prestige and increased hatred of Arabs which made impossible their maintaining position in area, and prospect of severe economic strain in France and Britain when impact of canal closing becomes felt. He professed be unable understand why British and French had embarked on such a senseless venture.

The asserted collapse of prestige of Britain and France in area led Nasser to oft-repeated conclusion that if tie with West was to be maintained it would have to be with US, which would however be handicapped to extent that it might be bound by British and French or Israeli ties. However a United States steering an independent course should have no special difficulty in reaching an understanding with Egypt and other Arab states.

In conversation Nasser referred to destruction in Port Said in lurid terms of a city ¾ destroyed by fire, terrorized population, 10,000 refugees, etc. Difficult conclude whether he more or less believed or accounting for effect. [4]

Hare

---

[4] In telegram 1419 from Cairo, November 9, Hare verified that photographs of Port Said showed extreme damage and many grim human details. (Department of State, Central Files, 684A.86/11–956)

562.   Memorandum of a Conference With the President, White House, Washington, November 9, 1956, 8:45 a.m. [1]

OTHERS PRESENT

> Sir Anthony Caccia
> John Simmons
> Colonel Goodpaster

The meeting was held for Ambassador Caccia to present his credentials to the President. I joined the meeting after it had been in progress about five minutes. The President was referring to the measures presently under way in the United Nations for the resolution of the Middle East crisis, and said that once those had been agreed, and forces removed, the next stage is to keep the Russians out.

The President said that just because Britain and the United States had had a sharp difference over the attack on Egypt, there was no thought that we would not keep our friendship over the long term. As indicative of the reason why we opposed the British and French action in the Middle East so strongly, he cited a letter he had received from a member of the Hungarian Government, which has now been liquidated, to the effect that it was only the attack on Egypt by Israel, Britain and France that led the Soviets to seek to reimpose their domination of Hungary by force. The President referred to the great difficulties in developing an understanding of the Soviet action in the proper light. He referred to a letter from "someone in the Far East" who had told him that the Soviets had had to go back in order to restore order. People in the Far East had indicated that, to them, colonialism is not colonialism unless it is a matter of white domination over colored people. Ambassador Caccia commented that as long as such domination is over immediately adjoining areas, rather than across the water, it is all right. The President said that it seemed as though, when he points out the murders that are being committed in Hungary, some of the Far Eastern leaders just shrug them off.

Ambassador Caccia said Eden sent every good wish and hoped it would be possible for him to get together with the President on the broadest possible front. The President reverted to his bafflement that the Russians, as cruel and brutal as they are, can get away with murder, domination, etc. However, if we breach the smallest courtesy, the whole world is aflame. The only explanation he could give himself is that the West has been so successful in achieving high

---

[1] Source: Eisenhower Library, Whitman File, Eisenhower Diaries. Secret. Drafted by Goodpaster.

standards of life that there is an unconscious jealousy on the part of the others.

Ambassador Caccia said the Prime Minister hoped that the United States would not forget its other two resolutions on the Middle East situation. The President said there was no thought of that, and that such would be tragic indeed. He felt that, if we get this matter settled, he would do a little to keep the area from being touched by the Soviets—specifically he would spend a lot of money to raise the standards of life of the people of the area.

. . . The President said it is necessary to think beyond a single battle such as the Suez seizure, to the campaign as a whole. We must have world opinion with us in the Middle East if we are to bring about acceptable conditions in that area.

Ambassador Caccia asked whether the President had further actions in mind in the Middle East. The President referred to the two committees which will seek to achieve permanent solutions, and his intent to help raise living standards in that area. He would insist that acceptance of our help means that the countries must cut themselves off from affiliation with Russia.

In response to a question as to our plans concerning phased withdrawal of UK-French forces, and entry of UN forces, the President said that as soon as the international police force begins to enter, others must leave. From that time forward any attack on the UN forces would be an attack on the UN as a whole.

In closing the President said he would look forward to a productive association with Ambassador Caccia.

G

Colonel, CE, U S Army

563.   Telegram From the Department of State to the Embassy in Egypt [1]

Washington, November 10, 1956—2:11 p.m.

1520. For Ambassador. Embtels 1404, [2] 1418. [3] Department commends you for calm, reasonable tone you have taken in your recent conversations with Nasser relating to cease-fire, withdrawal of forces and question UN force.

We anticipate you will again probably be discussing these and other matters with Nasser from time to time in immediate future and suggest that if opportunity presents itself you weave in and emphasize following points:

1. US is trying strenuously to bring peace into area and to work out solutions based on justice and equity for all.

2. Nasser should complement our efforts by taking such actions as are within his power to stop activity of fedayeen whose continued actions would enlarge conflict in area.

3. Nasser might well give thought to developments in Hungary and note that what is happening there might well be indicative of fate for those in Egypt who accept assistance from Soviet Union.

Hoover

---

[1] Source: Department of State, Central Files, 320.5780/11–956. Secret. Drafted by Wilkins, approved by Hoover, and signed by Greene for Hoover.

[2] See footnote 2, Document 561.

[3] In telegram 1418 from Cairo, November 9, Hare reported that, during a conversation, Nasser had emphasized that the U.N. force must not remain along the Suez Canal after the Anglo-French withdrawal. Hare had emphasized to Nasser the importance of getting the UNEF matter settled affirmatively as soon as possible. (Department of State, Central Files, 320.5780/11–956)

564.   Memorandum From the Director of Central Intelligence (Dulles) to the Acting Secretary of State [1]

T.S. #158734   *Washington, November 10, 1956.*

1. We have been analyzing intelligence reports on developments in the Middle East (received to 1200 hours 10 November) and include in this memorandum the essence of our conclusions as to the situation that now confronts us in that area.

a. The withdrawal of British, French and Israeli forces from Egypt as contemplated would tend to leave a vacuum of power in that country. In fact, the only military forces will be the Egyptian Army of some 90,000 men with considerable equipment and some recovered aircraft. Opposed to this will be the UN force which will have high moral authority but will, I understand not be expected to engage in any military action.

b. Nasr remains in control of the Egyptian government and the remainder of its armed forces. He still exercises considerable influence over the military forces and sabotage units of Syria, Jordan and Saudi Arabia. Recent USSR diplomatic moves and threats together with the cease fires and the promised withdrawal of the invading forces have all tended to rebuild his shaken prestige and self-confidence. He is receiving secret encouragement and publicized promises of material aid from Moscow. As long as Nasr remains in power, he will endeavor to frustrate any UN moves (including a Suez Canal settlement) which he considers hostile to his ambitions if he is convinced the USSR will back him in such action and that there will be no effective counter action by the USA. Nasr is probably presently convinced that the US will prevent any renewed aggressive action against him by the UK, France or Israel; however his amenability to US influence will be directly proportional to his conviction as to our resolution to block any Soviet intervention in the area.

c. Syria is in a critical condition where a Communist coup might be pulled off particularly if Moscow is able to infiltrate hard core Soviet organizers plus a nucleus of a military force which would presumably be largely aircraft and air personnel. An overthrow of the Syrian government, and even possibly further Soviet pressures on the present government, could result in a Syrian invitation to Moscow to send troops into Syria ostensibly to protect Syria from Israel. This would lead to Syria's becoming a Soviet base of operations in the area in support of Egypt. Syria thus presents a second power vacuum into which the Soviet might move even more openly than in the case of Egypt and where there would be no UN force to

[1] Source: Eisenhower Library, Staff Secretary Records. Top Secret. Transmitted to the White House under cover of a note from Allen Dulles to Goodpaster, November 10, which reads: "I enclose a copy of a memorandum which I have just sent to Herb Hoover, Admiral Radford and Gordon Gray which I thought might interest you." The copy sent to Hoover is in Department of State, Central Files, 780.00/11–1056.

cover the situation. Jordan is equally vulnerable but geographically less attractive to the Soviet.

d. The Soviet notes to the US, Britain, France and Israel, the deep engagement of Soviet prestige in rescuing Nasr and the Arabs together with the promises of military assistance, indicate that it is likely that the Soviet will attempt a Syrian and possibly an Egyptian operation. The first would probably start as covert and become overt, if the Syrian government is subverted. The second would probably remain covert or under the guise of "volunteers", as long as possible.

·   ·   ·   ·   ·   ·   ·

Allen W. Dulles [2]

---

[2] Printed from a copy that bears this typed signature.

---

565.   Joint Proposal by the Departments of State and Defense [1]

Washington, November 10, 1956.

PROPOSED UNITED STATES CONTRIBUTION TO UNITED NATIONS INTERNATIONAL FORCE

1. The United States' non-reimbursable contribution to the establishment of the U.N. International Force will be as follows:

a) The U.S., upon call from the United Nations, will provide the initial air and surface lift for the forces designated to participate in the U.N. Force, currently estimated to be on the order of 3,500 to 5,000 troops. In providing this lift, commercial ships and planes may be chartered as necessary to supplement or in lieu of military lifts.

b) Nations with which the United States has bilateral agreements for military assistance will be granted authority by the United States to use equipment acquired through MDAP for the forces participating in this United Nations assignment.

---

[1] Source: Department of State, Central Files, 320.5780/11–1056. According to a handwritten notation, Hoover handcarried this document to the White House on November 10, together with the following covering note: "Enclosed for your approval is a joint proposal by the Departments of State and Defense regarding the United States contribution to the United Nations International Force authorized by the General Assembly November 6, 1956." The Department of State file copy of the document bears Eisenhower's signature and is dated 7:30 p.m., November 10. At 8:55 p.m., the Department of State transmitted the text to USUN in telegram 277 indicating that the President had approved the plan. (*Ibid.*)

2. It is anticipated that the United Nations Force will request logistic support as follows which the Department of Defense should be prepared to provide upon request by the Department of State:

Services:

(a) Personnel evacuation and hospitalization,
(b) Maintenance support,
(c) Transportation,
(d) Post exchange support.

Supply:

(a) Rations,
(b) Individual and organizational equipment,
(c) Spare parts,
(d) POL.

3. In regard to the non-reimbursable contribution indicated in par. 1, the Department of Defense will as necessary, seek supplemental appropriations to cover the cost involved. The cost of any logistic support covered in par. 2 above, furnished by the United States, will be reimbursed by the United Nations in accordance with provisions of the United Nations Participation Act and appropriate Executive Order and in accordance with arrangements agreed upon by the United Nations General Assembly.

4. No United States military personnel will enter nor will United States supporting facilities be established in the area under the supervision of the United Nations Force.

566.   Memorandum of a Conversation, Department of State, Washington, November 10, 1956 [1]

SUBJECT

General Discussion of Current Situation

PARTICIPANTS

Deputy Under Secretary Robert D. Murphy
Mr. Herve Alphand, French Ambassador
Mr. Charles Lucet, French Minister
Mr. F. de Laboulaye, Counselor, French Embassy
C. Burke Elbrick, EUR
W. R. Tyler, WE

The Ambassador called at his request. He referred to his conversation with the President on November 8 and said he had been much encouraged by the President's remarks on the need to do everything possible to strengthen the Western alliance. [2] The Ambassador said he had brought with him a reply from Prime Minister Mollet to the President's letter of November 7, which emphasized the belief on the part of the French Government that a meeting of the three Western Heads of Government should be held as soon as possible. [3]

---

[1] Source: Department of State, Central Files, 684A.86/11–1056. Secret. Drafted by Tyler.

[2] A memorandum of this conversation by Elbrick is *ibid.*, Presidential Memoranda of Conversations: Lot 66 D 149. According to the memorandum, Alphand told President Eisenhower that Soviet forces were massing in Eastern Europe and the French Government felt it would be helpful if Eisenhower could make it clear that the United States would stand with its allies, the United Kingdom and France, in the event of hostilities in Europe. In response, Eisenhower noted that two of his recent statements had been designed to express this position and that another such statement would not be timely. Prior to this meeting between Eisenhower and Alphand, Hoover had sent Eisenhower a memorandum which predicted Alphand's request and recommended that Eisenhower refuse to issue another statement. (*Ibid.*, Central Files, 611.51/11–856)

[3] Hoover handcarried Mollet's letter to the White House on November 10. A copy, under cover of a note from Howe to Goodpaster, is *ibid.*, 396.1/11–1056.

Regarding Eisenhower's message to Mollet, transmitted to Paris in telegram 1725, November 7, see Document 545 and footnote 1 thereto.

Mr. Murphy said that the President favored the idea of such a meeting, and fully recognized the importance of discussing matters of mutual interest, but that the problem was one of timing. It was most important, Mr. Murphy said, that nothing should be allowed to derogate or detract from the priority task of carrying out the UN resolution. To meet at this time would risk weakening the efforts of the UN, which should command the fullest support of us all, and be facilitated in every way. Ambassador Alphand agreed, but pointed out that the UN Resolution raised several extremely important questions which need answering and required immediate consultation first. As examples, he mentioned:

1) How long was the UN Force expected to stay? (The French feel that it should remain until peace with Egypt has been achieved and the Canal question settled.)
2) Where would it be stationed? (The French feel that Nasser's ideas on this seem to be contrary to what is desirable.)
3) When will the UK and French forces be expected to withdraw? (The French insist on phasing out as the UN force takes over, progressively, and are not disposed to withdraw simultaneously with the arrival of the UN force's first units.)
4) Will the area occupied by the UN force be entirely free of Egyptian forces?

The Ambassador stressed that the two major issues were: a) an Arab-Israeli peace settlement, and b) the settlement of the Suez Canal problem. The French Government, he said, is opposed to leaving these matters to the General Assembly. It feels strongly that they should be discussed and settled by the Security Council at the Foreign Ministers' level.

Mr. Murphy reminded the Ambassador that the Security Council was subject to a Soviet veto, and that, for example, its decision of 1951 on Israeli shipping, had never been observed or enforced. The Ambassador replied that it was a vicious circle: the three were expected to defer their meeting in order not to diminish the chances of execution of the UN resolution, but the chances of execution themselves depended on the three meeting first and agreeing on what had to be done. He insisted on the need for reestablishing Western solidarity and said that the Secretary General of the UN could not be expected to settle problems which required the assent of the three powers. Both these considerations argued, in the view of the French Government, for an early meeting of the three. The Ambassador added that he thought that the delay should not be greater than a fortnight or so, and Mr. Murphy said that about a fortnight might be considered to be a suitable lapse of time.

Mr. Murphy said we had looked at the situation carefully and had concluded that the Security Council held out little chance of making progress, and that the best hope seemed to be to refer the two resolutions, on Suez and Palestine, to the General Assembly when it meets for the first regular session on November 12th. The Ambassador objected that this meant that the resolutions would certainly be voted before the three could meet, and that this would thereby prejudge the course of action to be taken, which should, on the contrary, first be determined by agreement between the three.

At this point the Ambassador discussed the substance of Prime Minister Mollet's reply to the President and the justification for the French Government's belief that the general situation was increasingly menacing. It was agreed that the Soviet Union was striving to create the impression that it was very active in behalf of Egypt and the Arab world, and that it wanted people to believe that it was prepared to send in volunteers at once—both in order to exert pressure on the UK and France, and to maintain its pose of the champion of the Arab cause. It was, however, difficult to determine how much of this was political warfare, and how much it corresponded to reality. Mr. Murphy said there was, no doubt, an orchestration of Soviet efforts to create a sense of menace and terror. On the other hand, we had no evidence that the Soviet Union had in fact embarked on a course leading to imminent aggression. He said the Soviet Union was in the somewhat awkward position of having to give the Arabs the impression that it was living up to its inflated promises and declarations. At the same time, we don't really know what the Soviets have in mind, or what agreements they may have recently concluded with Syria.

The Ambassador mentioned the case of the super-tanker "Statue of Liberty" which was blocked in the Canal, and expressed his Government's fears that the Egyptians might be intending to scuttle it, now that its Dutch crew had been ordered off by Egypt. Mr. Murphy said we had received similar news, and that we entertained similar apprehensions.

In conclusion, the Ambassador referred to the French request that we should agree to represent French interests in Saudi Arabia. He said the matter was most urgent and important. Mr. Murphy said we had cabled our Ambassador in Saudi Arabia to find out what the situation was, and were expecting a reply at any moment. He added that we would notify the French of our answer as soon as we were in a position to do so. [4]

---

[4] On November 11, President Eisenhower sent the following response to Prime Minister Mollet:

"I thank you for your message of November 10. You may be sure that we are very much aware of the importance of the problems you mentioned, and I also hope that we shall be able to meet soon and have a full exchange of views. However, I feel that the most important thing now is to give full and undivided support to the execution of the UN program, including the introduction of the UN forces and the withdrawal of the Anglo-French forces. It is my view that nothing should be done which might hinder or slow up this urgent task. After it has been carried out successfully, we should then be able to consider arrangements for a meeting. I have sent a similar message to Prime Minister Eden."

The Department of State transmitted the text of the message for delivery to Paris in telegram 1784, November 11. (*Ibid.*, 320.5774/11–1156)

---

567.   Telegram From the Embassy in Israel to the Department of State [1]

Tel Aviv, November 11, 1956—3 a.m.

574. Re Embtel 573. [2] I saw Ben Gurion at his residence in Jerusalem this afternoon. He talked at such length that I again required heavy military escort for an after dark return to Tel Aviv.

He received me without any great warmth, I felt, and aside from his friendly opening comment of thanks for President's message (Deptel 494) [3] he spoke in serious and often sharp tones, raising his voice fit some emotion of occasion [*sic*]. The feeling and resentment I had expected last Thursday night when I repeated to him, as a supplement to President's letter of November 7, the serious comments made to Minister Shiloah by Acting Secretary Hoover (Deptel 483), [4] came forth with added emphasis today.

The Prime Minister launched at once [into] a spirited discussion of existing factors threatening peace in this area due primarily to the

---

[1] Source: Department of State, Central Files, 684A.86/11–1156. Secret; Priority. Received at 10:22 a.m.

[2] Telegram 573, November 10, reported that Eisenhower's November 9 message to Ben Gurion (see footnote 4, Document 560) had been delivered at 3:55 p.m., November 10. (Department of State, Central Files, 711.11–EI/11–1056)

[3] Telegram 494, November 9, transmitted the text of Eisenhower's November 9 message to Ben Gurion.

[4] Telegram 483, November 11, contained a summary of the points made by Hoover to Shiloah on November 7; see Document 551. (Department of State, Central Files, 684A.86/11–756)

Soviet penetration policies in Middle East as well as the effect of their recent oppressive action in Hungary on Arab thinking; prospect of Nasser's resurgence or at least survival with Soviet help; distinct possibility of Soviet use of Syria as a penetration instrument; and in general, encouragement given in these fields by the current United States Middle East policy including threats to Israel regarding withdrawal of troops.

Prefacing his remarks with statement, "speaking as a member of free world and not only as Prime Minister of Israel, I offer the following humble opinion." He then said in substance:

(1) US Government is making mistake if it believes that Soviets' brutal and oppressive acts in Hungary will create unfavorable impression among Arabs—on contrary, Arabs will admit Soviet is country which can act forcefully and promptly, even though ruthlessly, whereas United States uses words only. He said he had noted that Arabs, despite an obvious inconsistency in principle, voted in United Nations with Soviets on resolution demanding withdrawal of Soviet troops in Hungary. He expressed some surprise and regret over India's mild treatment of Soviet act as compared with India's denunciations of those forcefully opposing Nasser.

(2) The Middle East area is in immediate and critical danger from Soviet action. Soviets are now or soon will supply arms, material and other forms of military assistance to Egypt and Syria. In this connection there are two great dangers to peace in the area—Nasser and President of Syria Quwwatli. He said neither are communists but both have community of interest with Soviets in taking over entire area. Hussein will go same way and Nuri Said's days are numbered. Ben Gurion saw "the spector of entire Arab world, with African continent included later, under Soviet domination unless something is done soon to eliminate Nasser and Quwwatli".

He is confident there are many liberal elements in both Egypt and Syria who hate Nasser and Quwwatli but they are not getting encouragement from United States. He cited as an example premature surrender in Port Said by Egyptian commander who did so, in his opinion, because of his hatred for Nasser. Prime Minister terminated this part of his conversation with statement that, "if United States does not act, whole Middle East and Africa are in danger—and with that free world is in danger".

He said it was "an undeniable fact" that Nasser had opened Middle East and Africa to Soviet penetration and now Quwwatli was assisting him. He regretted to say it but United States had saved Nasser and continues to help him. Referring to his conversation with me last November (Embtel 515),[5] he said, "I told you then that Nasser would endanger Middle East and Africa. Unfortunately, I was

---

[5] Vol. XIV, p. 784.

right. Now it is a fact." He noted United States was the only big western power to oppose destruction of Nasser.

He then referred to Mister Hoover's strong words to Shiloah and seemed to be very much upset over threatening tone and actual threats contained therein. He felt these threats were unnecessary— that President's letter was enough. He asked whether Nasser had ever been so strongly threatened—had he ever been threatened with expulsion from UN, or application of economic sanctions, et cetera because he defied Security Council resolution? Will anyone now speak to Nasser re demands of UN Charter that he live at peace with fellow members—or re principle of freedom of transit of Suez if he should undertake to deny such freedom? Will anybody threaten him now that he has Soviets firmly behind him, and especially after United States has issued such strong threats to Israel regarding withdrawal of her troops from Sinai? He agreed with President there should be peace with justice but he wanted justice for Israel.

Regarding the realistic threat of Nasser to area and especially to Israel, he said he was asking USG if it would be just that Egyptian forces return to Sinai territory and again threaten frontier of Israel with Soviet arms. (Commented that incidentally Sinai was not originally Egyptian territory but had been passed on to Egypt by British who obtained it from Turks.) He said Egyptian threat to Israel had been proven to be far greater than anyone imagined. Equipment and supplies captured by Israel forces in Sinai were on enormous side. There was far more Russian equipment and quality was far better than anyone had predicted. Furthermore, he was impressed with fact that, despite starving masses in Egypt, war rations for Egyptian officers were much better than those enjoyed by Israeli officers.

He then commented on colonialism. He said he knew United States does not think highly of colonialism and although he was not taking sides with French or United Kingdom he must point out that their brand of colonialism is quite different than that of Soviets. UK and France had in fact relaxed their policies to considerable extent— India for example, and Morocco and Tunisia. On other hand Soviets had no intention of releasing any of their satellites in Europe. At moment they were brutally destroying Hungary. Ben Gurion said he was surprised United States had sided with Soviets against British and French "at the beginning".

With reference to his reply to President's letter Prime Minister said "he would fulfill what he had undertaken" but he felt it his bounden duty to warn United States of consequences of its present Middle East policy on the free world. He said he hoped I would report his remarks in spirit in which he gave them (his concern for free world and peace in this area).

At end he repeated his expressions of gratitude for President's kind words of thanks. He said comments he had just uttered would have been made other night when I delivered President's message but he did not want to couple them at that time with his reply. I noted his awareness of Soviet threat and felt confident his comments on all points raised would be read with interest by the Department.

Comment: I am inclined to believe Ben Gurion did not make his comment on Thursday night for a number of other reasons including: He had not fully felt the impact of our warnings, he was fully occupied with immediate problem of determining a policy, getting Cabinet approval, preparing broadcast and reply to President's letter; that he has in meantime received some indication of breadth of public disapproval as well as sharpness of opposition of non-government parties especially Herut. Although he obtained Cabinet approval he merely informed leaders of opposition parties, and Begin, most important Herut party member, at meeting of Foreign Affairs and Security Committee Friday criticized government for entirely too precipitous decision. Begin, who was in Sinai, had not participated on Thursday with Ben Gurion when he informed opposition parties.

Lawson

---

568.   **Message From President Eisenhower to Prime Minister Eden** [1]

Washington, November 11, 1956.

DEAR ANTHONY: I am in full agreement with the objectives set forth in your message of November 7 [2] which crossed mine of that same day. We have the problems you describe very much in mind and I, too, hope that we could meet in the near future. Meanwhile, I feel we must continue to push forward on the introduction of the UN Force and the withdrawal of Anglo-French forces, and that these things should be done with the utmost speed. We should then be in

---

[1] Source: Department of State, Central Files, 974.7301/11–1156. Top Secret. Transmitted to London in Priority telegram 3421, November 11, 1:53 p.m., which is the source text, with the instruction: "Please deliver soonest following message from President to Sir Anthony Eden. Confirm date and time delivery."

[2] Document 548.

a position to consider arranging a meeting. I have sent similar word to Prime Minister Mollet. [3]

My preliminary reports from Al Gruenther indicate that it would not seem necessary for him to come to London to see you. [4]

With warm regard.

As ever,

Ike [5]

---

[3] See footnote 4, Document 566.

[4] In a message to Goodpaster, dated November 8, Gruenther had described several difficulties arising from the proposal that he visit Eden in London to discuss the concerns which Eden had raised over the telephone with Eisenhower on November 7. Gruenther noted that his visit could not be hidden from the press, that his position as Commander of NATO forces placed him in a sensitive position, and that he would have to cancel dates with "important people" to make the trip. In a separate message to Goodpaster later on November 8, Gruenther reported that British Defense Minister Anthony Head had suggested that Marshal of the Royal Air Force, Sir William Dickson, visit Gruenther in Paris and that Gruenther could visit Eden later, if he still thought it to be necessary. Goodpaster subsequently reported to Gruenther on November 8 that President Eisenhower approved the arrangement. (Eisenhower Library, White House Central Files, Suez Canal Crisis)

[5] Telegram 3421 bears this typed signature.

---

569.   Message From President Eisenhower to Prime Minister Bulganin [1]

Washington, November 11, 1956.

I refer to your message to me of November 5. [2] The fighting in the Near East has now been brought to an end through the efforts of the United Nations, the body properly responsible for accomplishing this. It is essential that peace be totally restored to the area and that no action be taken which would in any way exacerbate the situation there.

With respect to your suggestion that the United States join with the Soviet Union in a bi-partite employment of their military forces to stop the fighting in Egypt, it is our view that neither Soviet nor any other military forces should now enter the Middle East area

---

[1] Source: Department of State, Central Files, 674.84A/11–1156. Secret. Transmitted to Moscow in Priority telegram 579, November 11, 11 p.m., which is the source text, with the instruction: "Please deliver soonest following message from President to Marshal Bulganin. Confirm date and time delivery."

[2] Document 505.

except under United Nations mandate. Any such action would be directly contrary to resolutions of the General Assembly of the United Nations which have called for the withdrawal of those foreign forces which are now in Egypt. The introduction of new forces under these circumstances would violate the United Nations Charter, and it would be the duty of all United Nations members, including the United States, to oppose any such effort.

It is difficult to reconcile your expressed concern for the principles of morality and the objectives of the United Nations with the action taken by Soviet military units against the people of Hungary. Your letter to me of November 7[3] concerning this tragic situation was deeply disappointing. Were the Soviet Government now able to comply with the Resolutions of the U.N. on the subject of Hungary, it would be a great and notable contribution to the cause of peace.

Dwight D. Eisenhower[4]

---

[3] Scheduled for publication in volume XXV.
[4] Telegram 579 bears this typed signature.

---

570.   Memorandum of a Conversation Between the President and the Secretary of State, Secretary Dulles' Room, Walter Reed Hospital, Washington, November 12, 1956, 11:30 a.m. [1]

ALSO PRESENT

Mr. Macomber

The President began the conversation by saying that Senator Green had called on him this morning and had said "all the right things". The Senator had indicated a strong desire to cooperate with the Administration and said further that he fully understood that it was the Executive Branch that had the responsibility for the conduct of our foreign relations. He had added that he not only understood this principle but heartily believed in it. The President had mentioned to Senator Green the Foreign Relations Committee hearings

---

[1] Source: Eisenhower Library, Dulles Papers, Meetings with the President. Top Secret. Drafted by Macomber.

this morning [2] and had asked the Senator to do what he could to prevent it becoming an occasion for partisan purposes. Senator Green had said he would do what he could, but pointed out that neither he nor anyone else could always handle a Senator who was seeking publicity.

In this connection the President said that he was sorry that the State Department had agreed to the hearings this morning. The Secretary also thought this had been unwise. The President believed the Senate Foreign Relations Committee and the House Foreign Affairs Committee made too heavy demands on the time of the State Department. He suggested that in the future when requests came for State Department officials to appear before the Committees that the former should take a firm line, indicating that they would appear for an hour and a half or some other set time and that after that time had elapsed they would have to leave for other appointments.

[Here follows discussion of unrelated subjects.]

The Secretary asked the President where we stood on the Big Three Meeting. The President replied that the situation stood as before, that no definite date had been set and it had been made clear to both the British and the French that there would be no meeting until all their troops had been taken out of Egypt. The President appeared to be thinking in terms of December 1 as a date when these meetings could begin. He said that this would have the advantage of allowing the Secretary to have a vacation in Key West before the meetings commenced.

The President talked briefly about his original invitation to Eden and Mollet to visit Washington. He said that he had made it very clear to Eden that the fact that we were willing to have such a meeting did not mean we would endorse what we have stood against. He had warned Eden therefore that there might be no communiqué or a split communiqué. The President told the Secretary that he thought this had averted any problem of seeming to endorse the British and French actions. He added, however, that the State Department had misgivings on this score and he had, as the Secretary knew, therefore postponed the meeting.

[Here follows discussion of unrelated subjects.]

---

[2] On November 12, Hoover, Allen Dulles, and Flemming testified in executive session before the Senate Foreign Relations Committee concerning U.S. policy, actions, and intelligence operations in regard to the Suez Canal crisis, the Arab-Israeli dispute, the European oil supply situation, and the Hungarian crisis. The transcript of their testimony is printed in *Executive Sessions of the Senate Foreign Relations Committee (Historical Series)*, Vol. VIII, *Eighty-Fourth Congress, Second Session 1956* (Washington, 1978), pp. 605–660.

Returning to the Suez crisis the President said he now believed that the British had not been in on the Israeli-French planning until the very last stages when they had no choice but to come into the operation. He had felt when the British originally denied collusion with the French and the Israelis that they were misleading us, but he had now come to the conclusion that they were telling the truth. One of the arguments the President cited to support this view was the long delay that took place between the time the British declared their intent to go into Egypt and the time they actually went in. He said that the British were meticulous military planners and he was sure that if they had been in on the scheme from the beginning that they would have seen to it that they were in a position to move into Egypt in a matter of hours after they declared their intention to do so.

The Secretary thought that the British having gone in should not have stopped until they had toppled Nasser. As it was they now had the worst of both possible worlds. They had received all the onus of making the move and at the same time had not accomplished their major purpose.

The President and the Secretary spoke again of the importance of getting UN police troops in Egypt as quickly as possible. The President said he did not see why they were assembling the troops at Naples. If he were running the operation he would move the troops in as they became available—in as small groups as fifty at a time if that were necessary. He felt the important thing was to get some UN troops moving in and some British and French troops started out.

The Secretary mentioned his wish to have the NATO meeting postponed until January. He felt that it would be very difficult to have a useful meeting in December, that it was necessary to let matters settle down before we could hope successfully to consider some of the problems currently confronting NATO. He said that it was going to be very difficult to make NATO an institution where all members increasingly took each other into their confidence so soon after the recent actions of the British and the French. The President agreed with the Secretary's observations and specifically agreed with the desirability of having the meeting postponed.

571.   Telegram From the Embassy in the United Kingdom to the Department of State [1]

London, November 12, 1956—3 p.m.

2648. For Acting Secretary from Ambassador. Following conversations with top level officials of HMG during past few days are all inter-related.

1. At evening reception Buckingham Palace November 8, Butler took me aside and said with great earnestness how deeply he deplored the existence of what he termed mutual misunderstandings of policy which had arisen between US and UK Governments. He quite evidently was greatly disturbed by the course followed by majority of Cabinet although he did not specifically so state. He said to me, "I have been meaning to come to see you for a long time to tell you that in my opinion you are the only man who is in a position to explain to your government in detail the various attitudes of the members of our government. Never has an Ambassador occupied a more important position than you do at the present moment." He went on to urge me to see Macmillan at the earliest opportunity.

2. On November 9 at Macmillan's request I saw him in the afternoon. He said he wished to get my advice as to whether he should ask Washington at once for permission to leave for Washington November 12 to see Humphrey and other Treasury officials about impact of current events in Near East on economic position of Great Britain with particular reference to dollar balances and oil imports. Having in mind that Department apparently wished to treat oil problem through OEEC rather than directly with Great Britain while British troops are still in Egypt, I advised Macmillan to wait until Eden had arranged to visit Washington and go with him at that time. Macmillan said he would follow that advice and asked me not to take the matter up with Washington at that time. Macmillan stated that he hoped that conditions for Washington's agreement to have Eden visit Washington could be fulfilled within the next week or fortnight. Macmillan further said that he regretted very much that he had had to give up post of Foreign Secretary because he was afraid that Selwyn Lloyd was "too young and inexperienced" for a position of such great responsibility under the present difficult circumstances.

---

[1] Source: Department of State, Central Files, 974.7301/11–1256. Top Secret; Priority; Presidential Handling—Limited Distribution. Received at 1:43 p.m. A copy of this telegram in the Eisenhower Library, Whitman File, Dulles–Herter Series is initialed by Eisenhower.

3. At Lord Mayor's banquet evening November 9 Eden asked me to talk with him privately and said that it was most urgent for him to have talk with President soon. As he expressed it, "the Bear is moving not only in the Middle East but in Eastern Europe and we must coordinate our plans concerning this situation." He also said that HMG had been forced to act in Egypt because of the impotence of UN and that a beginning must be made to strengthen that organization. In view of the messages which are being exchanged between Eden and President on Egypt I simply said that he knew as well as I what the President's attitude was about the timing of a conference between himself and the President.

4. Yesterday afternoon I visited Salisbury at Hatfield at his invitation and we had a private conversation of over an hour. He started by saying Macmillan had told him of his conversation with me and that he (Salisbury) agreed with my advice to Macmillan. He said that he and Macmillan had recommended that Lloyd should go to New York yesterday (which Lloyd did) to represent Great Britain at UNGA and that as soon as a conference had been arranged between Eden and French with the President in Washington, Lloyd should return to London and remain in London during that conference and Macmillan should accompany Eden to Washington.

Salisbury also said that additional information was accumulating regarding definite character and scope of conspiracy between Nasser and Russians to take over entire Middle East and its oil as soon as Nasser had established himself as head Arab world. Salisbury felt that fact Nasser had blocked Canal was highly significant. This act he said had not been necessary and was not in interest of Egypt but could only be explained as part of a plot to assist Russia by making it more difficult for Europe to defend itself or protect its interests in Middle East.

Eden, Macmillan and Salisbury have all stated to me that while they believe that some form of United Nations is the only hope of the world, they have lost faith in the efficacy of the United Nations Charter in its present form. The latter said, "I was one of the founders of the United Nations but I must confess that I now feel that it has become an instrument which prevents the big five powers from preserving the peace and invites aggression by small powers against each other." He said that he felt the Charter must be changed to set up some kind of an international force which could be available at short notice to prevent such aggression. Salisbury asked me to call the attention of the Department to the speech of Lord Coleraine on page 180 of Hansard for Thursday November 8 which he said contained very able discussion of the weakness of the United Nations Charter.

Comment: I believe that the thing which is at present disturbing the members of the British Cabinet more than anything else is that if Eden's visit to the President continues dependent on the moving in of an adequate United Nations force and the moving out of the troops of Great Britain and France, the visit may be indefinitely delayed because of Nasser's refusal to accept the United Nations force. They are deeply concerned about the possibility of a protracted negotiation between Nasser and United Nations over the entry of such a force.

Aldrich

572.   Telegram From the Embassy in France to the Department of State [1]

Paris, November 12, 1956—7 p.m.

2349. Re Deptel (Presidential Handling) 1784. [2] I delivered message reftel to Mollet at 3:30 p.m. local time, Monday. On reading it he said he could understand reasoning but felt that US decision was most unfortunate. After a few moments thought Mollet said that he would like to think out loud for a few minutes with the request that his thoughts be transmitted in detail and personally to the President. He talked for about 30 minutes and gave impression throughout of being discouraged and depressed.

Mollet said that in his view the supreme question of the moment was how to avoid a new Munich in the Middle East. The Arab problem as such was, in his view, greatly outweighed by the Soviet question. He felt that Soviet plans had been fully unmasked. It was now clear that if the Israeli operation had not taken place a joint Egyptian-Syrian-Jordanian attack on Israel, directed by Soviet officers and technicians, would have taken place at the latest during December or January. While Israel could have been expected to handle an Arab assault, who [it?] could not have withstood the impact of Soviet volunteers without outside help. Therefore, the result would have been either the annihilation of Israel or the

[1] Source: Department of State, Central Files, 684A.86/11–1256. Secret; Priority; Presidential Handling. Received at 5:54 p.m. A copy of this telegram in the Eisenhower Library, Whitman File, Dulles–Herter Series is initialed by Eisenhower.

[2] Telegram 1784, November 11, transmitted the text of Eisenhower's message to Mollet; see footnote 4, Document 566.

initiation of broad scale hostilities in the Middle East involving the Soviet Union, which would very likely have led to general war. Mollet said that there had been exaggerations regarding the Soviet equipment found in the Sinai Peninsula by the Israelis. But the extent and the extreme advanced design of the conventional armaments indicated clearly that they could only be for offensive operations. Also, no other interpretation could be put on fact that Soviets had delivered during past year 420 million dollars worth of military equipment to Egypt. Mollet considered that the placing of the Syrian and Jordanian armies under Egyptian command, and the trip of the Syrian President to Moscow were the final steps prior to a coordinated assault on Israel, which had now been forestalled by the Israeli operation.

Unfortunately, however, the end result of the operation had been a tremendous increase in Soviet prestige since the entire Arab world now considered the Soviet Union as their leader. He said it was clear that Nasser was now operating directly under Soviet orders and that this was particularly disturbing in relation to setting a date for a meeting between himself, Eden and the President. In effect the US position that such a meeting should not take place until after the UN force was fully installed and the French and British troops withdrawn gave the Soviets a kind of veto power over the holding of such a meeting. The Egyptians under Soviet guidance could be expected to place all sorts of obstacles in the way of the establishment of the international force in Egypt. This would further delay the meeting of the big three in Washington which was so needed to achieve overall unity.

Mollet cited, as an indication of the Soviets' rising influence in the Arab world, a broadcast made on Friday over the Moroccan state radio by an official of the Moroccan Ministry of Foreign Affairs in which it was stated on behalf of the Moroccan Govt that the Soviet Union was solely responsible for the defeat of the Anglo-French aggression in the Near East, and that now it was clear that the Arab peoples had only one power to whom they could look for effective friendship, namely the Soviet Union.

Mollet felt that effective strong action by the US was necessary in the Middle East very promptly if there was to be any possibility of offsetting a Soviet takeover. I asked Mollet what he had in mind and he said that what was needed was a clear cut indication that US would resist such a takeover. Action could take various forms. For instance, statement that US would oppose Soviet volunteers by force if necessary, or some form of guarantee for Israel, or US membership in Baghdad Pact. He said that he was prepared to reverse previous Quai d'Orsay policy regarding the BP and do everything possible to strengthen it, and especially to strengthen the present Iraqi Govt. He said he had cited these specific steps merely as examples which did not by any means exhaust the range of possibilities.

Mollet said the lack of close coordination of Western policy was sharply evident in the handling of the replies to the invitation of the Swiss Govt to a Five Power heads of govt meeting. He pointed out that Bulganin and Nehru had accepted the meeting which the President had rejected. [3] Meanwhile Eden had indicated willingness to accept such a meeting in principle, while he, Mollet, had not as yet replied. He said it was unthinkable that situation could arise where the US was the only power to refuse such a meeting and that we could be sure that his response would not put the US in such a position. However, he regretted that Eden's reaction had differed from US reaction.

Mollet then stated that the Swiss idea had originated with Mendes-France, who had sent one of his followers, a young deputy named Hernu, to Switzerland where he had sold the idea to the Swiss Govt. Mollet said that such a meeting at this date would only be a trap and would certainly be a direct repetition of the famous Munich conference. He said that this was all the more true since after the Indian actions in the UN on the Hungarian situation he could only conclude that basically Nehru was now opting for the Soviet side.

Finally, Mollet said he thought the President's first reaction in accepting the idea of an immediate meeting with himself and Eden had been the right reaction and that the advice of the State Dept experts that the meeting should be postponed was in error. Mollet then described his various telephone conversations with Eden which led him to the conclusion that the State Dept had persuaded the President to reverse his first judgment and to postpone the three power meeting. Mollet said he could only assume that US information on events on the Middle East was inaccurate in regard to the tremendous impact that the Soviet actions were having. He hoped that it would not be too late by the time a three power meeting was finally held. As I left he said that Munich had cost the world dearly in lives and he only hoped that the present situation would not lead to even more dire results within the next 3 to 5 years.

Comment: As it appears that high level meeting will not take place for some time, I feel it would be most helpful for me to receive in some detail US Govt's latest thinking on future developments in Middle East for transmittal to French. If I could be

---

[3] The Swiss invitation had been issued in the form of a letter from the President of Switzerland, Marckus Feldman, to the Heads of State of Great Britain, France, India, the Soviet Union, and the United States. For text of Feldman's letter of November 6 and Eisenhower's response of November 10, see Department of State *Bulletin*, November 26, 1956, p. 839.

instructed to deliver these thoughts direct to Mollet it would be most helpful. Pineau will undoubtedly press hard to get us thinking in New York. I do not have much confidence that Pineau would fully comprehend US position, much less report it accurately to Mollet. Therefore, I hope that I can be informed and directed to see Mollet both to offset such exaggerated and distorted reporting as may come from Pineau in next few days and to indicate US interest in problems now worrying Mollet.

Dillon

---

573. Memorandum From the Counselor of the Department of State (MacArthur) to the Acting Secretary of State [1]

Washington, November 13, 1956.

SUBJECT

Briefing of the President, 8:30 a.m., November 13, 1956

Colonel Goodpaster and I met with the President this morning pursuant to the new liaison arrangements. Following the intelligence briefing which Colonel Goodpaster gave, the President was briefed on pertinent items in the Top Secret summary. [2] In the subsequent discussion, the following points were of interest:

[Here follows discussion of unrelated subjects.]

4. The President commented on one of the items in the Department's daily Top Secret summary that Secretary General Hammarskjold did not want us to press ahead in the General Assembly on the Suez resolution until his return from Cairo next Sunday. [3] The President said he felt we should do what we could to meet the Secretary General's request and probably should not press the resolution itself in the Assembly until Hammarskjold's return.

---

[1] Source: Department of State, Central Files, 711.11–EI/11–1356. Secret; Limit Distribution. A marginal notation reads: "Secty saw 11/13/56. H.H.Jr."

[2] The Top Secret Daily Summaries are filed chronologically, *ibid.*, Daily Summaries: Lot 60 D 530.

[3] Hammarskjöld had requested that the United States postpone action on its draft resolution on the Suez Canal during a conversation with Lodge on November 12. Lodge reported on the contents of this conversation to the Department of State in Delga 68, November 12, and advised that it would be imprudent to go against Hammarskjöld's wishes on this matter. (*Ibid.*, Central Files, 320.5780/11–1256) Hammarskjöld visited Cairo between Friday, November 16, and Sunday, November 18.

5. The President also talked a bit about the Middle East problem and seemed particularly concerned about the situation in Syria, which he described as bad. . . . He then went on to say that in the past our position in the Middle East has been difficult because we have been faced with the dilemma of trying to act there in consonance with the UK and France. This placed us in a very difficult situation. Now, however, we have taken a separate position with respect to certain aspects of the Middle East problem from Britain and France. While this might have some disadvantages in terms of our alliance with the UK and France, on the other hand it had some good effects in terms of the Middle East. He said that we should be putting our best minds to work on the problem of what we might do, particularly with respect to Egypt, Saudi Arabia, and Syria, to keep them from gradually falling under Soviet domination. He had in mind, as he had mentioned in the Congressional briefing the other day, that we should be thinking about things we might be able to do to assist them in their economies. He said we must take the leadership in trying to save these countries and orient them toward the West, because the British and French have forfeited their position there and have no influence. I commented that as a result of the British and French action, their position in the Middle East had been totally destroyed for many years to come, if not permanently. Therefore, the only power which could really exercise a constructive influence in the Middle East was the US, and that the burden of trying to prevent Soviet penetration would fall very largely on us. The President said he agreed, and therefore we must, as he had earlier suggested, be thinking constructively and imaginatively about things we could do.

I assume that you will have S/S show appropriate paragraphs of this memorandum to appropriate Assistant Secretaries on a need-to-know basis.

DMacA

574.   Memorandum of a Telephone Conversation Between the President and the Acting Secretary of State, Washington, November 13, 1956, 11:56 a.m. [1]

[Here follows discussion of unrelated subjects.]

The President brought up the alarming messages from Britain [2] & France [3] about our not agreeing to meeting—all based on the theory that we are missing the point—that it is Russia that is moving in, with a much stronger & heavier transfer of power than we anticipated. Therefore if we don't agree to stopping it, we would antagonize the people who are going to win, the Arabs. To counteract that, the President thinks we ought, through our Embassies, to be talking to those governments in terms of the help we want to give as soon as satisfactory settlement is reached, economically, culturally, etc.

The President said we should study, as a matter of urgency, what we could & should do for Iraq, Jordan, Saudi Arabia, Libya, & even Egypt, "by holding out the carrot as well as the stick." He suggested Hoover discuss it briefly with Mr. Dulles—see how much we could put together now, & what could go into the program for the future. [4]

Secy. Hoover mentioned Selwyn Lloyd in N.Y., [5] & suppose he should want to come see the President. State's reaction is that it would be almost as bad as Eden coming.

The President agreed that it would be wrong, if he were coming for a long conference—but just as an old friend, it would be all right for him to call and pay his respects. The President hopes he will not make the request, because "why embarrass me when Anthony and I have been in direct communication?" The President will see him if he has to do so, but said that, if he came at all, he really should be seeing Dulles or Hoover.

The President concluded with, "I am very anxious to see the constructive side of what we are going to do out there."

---

[1] Source: Eisenhower Library, Whitman File, Eisenhower Diaries. Prepared in the Office of the President.

[2] See Document 571.

[3] See Document 572.

[4] Eisenhower's directive prompted Department of State officials over the following six weeks to prepare a series of papers dealing with the U.S. position in the Middle East, an effort which led to the formulation of what became known as the Eisenhower Doctrine. For documentation, see volume XII.

[5] Lloyd was in New York to attend the Eleventh Session of the General Assembly.

575.   Telegram From the Mission at the United Nations to the Department of State [1]

New York, November 14, 1956—noon.

Delga 87. For Hoover from Lodge. Re Palestine—Suez. Last night Selwyn Lloyd and Dixon had dinner with me. In course of long conversation Lloyd returned again and again to question of US position if UK-French forces did not leave Egypt. Lloyd said question was whether an "effective" UN force could take their place. He insisted they were anxious to leave, had not the means to stay for any length of time, and have never had any intention of reoccupying Canal Zone. If, however, they were to get out without being assured an effective" UN force was already there, the whole thing would be a mockery and the British Government could not last.

Lloyd said several times that US had "led the hunt" against the UK and France thus far and question was whether we would do so again if they stayed in Egypt. An effective force to take their place would have to be a great deal more than 3,000–4,000 troops made up of "Finns, Scandinavians and Colombians". It would have to be something closer to UK-French force which now numbered about 15,000 British and 3,000–4,000 French. Lloyd said they must not lose fruits of their action which were a settlement on the Suez Canal and a solution to Palestine question. The strong card they or Hammarskjold had to play against Nasser was UK force now in Port Said. The rest of Arab world, he said, was waiting to see whether UK would succeed. He said "you may feel we acted rashly, immorally and behind your backs, but UK had to do what it did. There was no alternative." Otherwise, he contended, a gradual process of shutting UK out of Middle East would have taken place over the next year or two, with first their losing Jordan, next Libya, then Iraq and finally Kuwait. They simply could not take this and would rather risk loss of all at once. Dixon said this was historical moment to act and historians like Toynbee would say so in future. Both Lloyd and Dixon contended their action was necessary to save West and unless they were supported now, all gains would be lost. Lloyd said, moreover, UK knew that an Egyptian attack on Israel was planned and would have taken place in five or six months. At same time he said UK had over-estimated Egyptian capabilities as recent action showed. (He had no reply when we said we had not been informed before on plan for Egyptian attack.) He also said Israel was com-

---

[1] Source: Department of State, Central Files, 684A.86/11–1456. Secret; Niact; Limited Distribution. Received at 12:32 p.m.

pletely justified in doing what it had done, and that the right was all on Israel's side.

Lloyd and Dixon both contended their action, if supported, would stop Soviet intervention in Middle East. Lloyd said their information had indicated Soviet penetration would have reached high point in five or six months and their action had stopped this. He discounted help USSR might be able give Egypt and Arab states now, and said even if there were 50,000 Soviet volunteers, UK force could take care of these. He clearly indicated he felt we were being bluffed by USSR and, if UK and France stood firm, USSR would back down and out of Middle East.

Lloyd and Dixon minimized their Charter obligations, saying it was monstrous to let small nations get away with aggression against them while accusing great powers of aggression when they acted in self defense. Lloyd said US had been guilty of aggression in Guatemala under Charter, but that we had been quite right in acting as we had there. Dixon said, in an aside, UK could not be held to so-called Charter principles they did not believe in. He felt question of force should have been argued out a month ago.

Towards end of conversation, we discussed question of clearing Canal and Lloyd said a large UK fleet was converging on Canal for that purpose and would reach there in a fortnight. He said he doubted there were any technicians who could handle clearing job as efficiently and quickly as UK experts. He said it could be done in half time if UK took it over. He was quite prepared to have UK clearance units under UN auspices, out of uniform and demilitarized. (He said clearance units were Royal Navy units with some few private contractors.) Lloyd felt he could work out clearance arrangements with Hammarskjold who, he felt, should be given task of negotiating Suez settlement rather than giving it to a committee as proposed in our resolution. He said Hammarskjold had been making progress in such negotiations prior Israeli action. In that connection he felt a committee probably was desirable for task of Palestine settlement. On latter point he had no specific thoughts as to a settlement except to say he believed Israel should announce its readiness resettle Gaza refugees, apparently assuming Israel would keep Gaza.

Close of conversation ended much as it began with Lloyd saying real problem was for UK to know where US stood if UK-French forces stayed in Egypt. He said flatly "we will not get out if we are not satisfied UN force is an effective one". Dixon said he did not believe that a phasing operation of withdrawal and replacement would work.

Lloyd made it clear that he was so determined to have a strong force in Egypt—either Anglo-French or a really strong international force—that he was quite willing to risk Soviet intervention. His attitude struck me as reckless and full of contradictions. It has made me more pessimistic about the British than anything that has happened in my service here.

Recommended action:

1. He may be going to Washington this weekend to see the Secretary. I recommend that either Dulles or Hoover tell him we are strongly behind the cease-fire and withdrawal and want the Anglo-French forces withdrawn on phased basis with the entry of the international force just as fast as possible.

2. If he does not go to Washington, I recommend that I be authorized to tell him this flatly here. He is in a dangerous state of mind which could touch off a war, and which, I understand, reflects Eden's view.

3. We should be prepared to face distinct possibility that British and French will not agree to get out because of their doubts that the UN force will be strong enough to suit them.

4. A further declaration of support by the President for the speedy unobstructed entry of the international force and the speedy withdrawal of the Anglo-French force would be a powerful help. If the President decided to make such a statement he might consider making it here—which would fortify the effect.

Lodge

---

576. Telegram From the Department of State to the Embassy in Egypt [1]

Washington, November 14, 1956—8:28 p.m.

1564. For Ambassador. During past few days Department has become increasingly concerned regarding rumors and reports of volunteers from Soviet Union for Egypt. It was clear Soviet Union was conducting psychological warfare of extensive character and there began appear indications Egypt might say they welcomed volunteers from Soviet Union in order strengthen their position vis-à-vis Britain, France and Israel. If this development should subsequently take place efforts which US has made and progress which UN has thus far achieved would be undermined.

---

[1] Source: Department of State, Central Files, 684A.86/11–1456. Secret; Niact. Drafted by Wilkins; cleared by Rountree and Walmsley and in substance by MacArthur and Phleger; approved by Howe; and signed by Rountree for Hoover. Repeated Priority to USUN, to London, Paris, and Moscow.

Department considered it desirable bring its analysis attention GOE to ascertain whether Egypt had requested Soviet volunteers and whether Soviet Union had agreed to supply them. Rountree had off-record conversation with Egyptian Chargé Niazi November 14 [2] in which he raised question of reports and inquired whether they were true.

Rountree recalled UNGA adopted Arab-Asian resolution on November 3 [3] to which Egypt subscribed which authorized SYG immediately to arrange with parties concerned for implementation cease-fire and halting of movement of military forces and arms into area and to report compliance forthwith and in any case not later than 12 hours from time of adoption of resolution. Rountree also recalled US resolution November 2 [4] recommended all members refrain from introducing military goods in area of hostilities and in general refrain from any acts which would delay or prevent implementation of resolution. SYG was requested to observe and promptly report on compliance with resolution.

Rountree said we assumed Egypt would wish all members of UN to live up to provisions of GA resolutions relating to hostilities in Egypt. Unless there was full compliance steps thus far taken by UN to effect cease-fire, formation of UN force and withdrawal of troops from Egypt might be adversely affected.

Rountree observed that Egypt's position in event breakdown of cease-fire, continued presence of foreign forces and introduction of new forces would be dangerous in extreme. It was our view that if Soviet volunteers proceeded to Egypt, such situation might exist and that world opinion would note this fact and world support for Egypt would diminish.

Egyptian Chargé indicated he would inquire of his Government and would be in touch with Department.

You are requested, following SYG Hammarskjold's arrival Cairo, to inform him substance Rountree's off-record confidential talk with Egyptian Chargé. We believe you should stress US efforts ascertain facts which if true would indicate new situation had developed. You may also express Department's view that Secretary General would have authority under GA resolutions, especially those of November 2 and 3, to investigate and report on introduction of military personnel and matériel into area. It seems to Department SYG would be entitled station representatives in seaports and at airports to determine whether resolutions were being complied with.

---

[2] No memorandum of this conversation has been found in Department of State files.

[3] Reference is to General Assembly Resolution 999 (ES–I); see Document 485.

[4] Reference is to General Assembly Resolution 997 (ES–I); see Document 467.

Department plans await response from Egypt Chargé and report of your own conversation with Hammarskjold with your evaluation before instructing you to approach Nasser re Soviet volunteers. However, if Nasser should independently raise with you, you may make observations similar to Rountree's to Egyptian Chargé.

Hoover

---

577.   **Memorandum of Discussion at the 304th Meeting of the National Security Council, Washington, November 15, 1956, 9–10:55 a.m.** [1]

[Here follows a paragraph listing the participants at the meeting.]

1. Significant World Developments Affecting U.S. Security

[Here follows a report by Allen Dulles concerning the situation in Eastern Europe.]

Turning to the situation in the Near East, Mr. Dulles pointed out that we were threatened with power vacuums both in Egypt and in Syria when the British, French and Israeli forces are withdrawn. There would remain in Egypt some 90,000 Egyptian troops well equipped with modern hardware. Nasser was obviously much encouraged by recent developments, as is well illustrated by the conditions he is seeking to place on the stationing of UN forces in Egypt. The degree of his amenability to U.S. pressure will largely depend on how sure he believes he can be that the United States is in a position to block British and French or Soviet moves. So far, added Mr. Dulles, he had no clear evidence that the USSR has sent any volunteers to Egypt.

[Here follow Dulles' comments on the situation in Syria and on the impact which recent events in the Near East and in Hungary had had upon Asia. Hoover then reported on several conclusions which the Department of State believed should be drawn from developments in the Near East and in Hungary. His first two conclusions dealt with the Hungarian situation.]

---

[1] Source: Eisenhower Library, Whitman File, NSC Records. Top Secret. Prepared by Gleason on November 16. The time of the meeting is from the record of the President's Daily Appointments. (*Ibid.*)

Secretary Hoover's third point concerned the Near East. He expressed the opinion that the Soviet volunteers operation was primarily designed to prove to the world that it was the Soviets who were forcing the British and French out of the Canal Zone, and that it was the Soviets who were the real champions of the Arab states. In point of fact, the State Department had no hard information that any volunteers were entering Egypt on any considerable scale. Nevertheless, Secretary Hoover pointed out, at the moment British and French prestige and power was at absolute rock bottom, both in the Middle East and in Asia. Thanks to the British and French operations, Secretary Hoover predicted that Nasser would emerge stronger in the end than he had been when he started.

Secretary Wilson commented that there were two good and sufficient reasons why British and French prestige and power was slipping so fast. The first reason was their decision to send military forces into the Canal Zone. The second reason was, once having taken this step, they failed to make the grade and carry through after their initial strike. The British and French move was a very bad one from a military point of view. To Secretary Wilson's two reasons for the collapse of British and French prestige, Secretary Hoover said he must add a third, namely, that British and French prestige was slipping rapidly in the Middle East even before the present crisis developed. He asked Mr. Allen Dulles whether he did not agree with this estimate of British and French prestige. Mr. Dulles replied that he would not give quite as high a rating to the position that Nasser would have at the end of the road as had Secretary Hoover, because of the complete defeat of the Egyptian Army by the Israelis and because of the miserable showing of the Egyptian Air Force. Admiral Radford agreed with Mr. Dulles' point, and said that in the hostilities between Egypt and Israel, every Egyptian who was able to had run away. Admiral Radford added that he failed to see why so much emphasis was placed on the misdeeds of the British, French and Israelis, and so little emphasis given to Nasser's long record of provocations.

The President said that he believed this distortion seemed perfectly natural in Arab eyes. Indeed, when one found Nehru apparently believing everything that Bulganin had said to him in explanation of Hungary, anything could happen. Bulganin's arguments had been completely specious, but his reasoning had apparently been accepted by Nehru. Secretary Wilson observed that Nehru was capable of rationalizing anything. The President added that Nehru, of course, would never be able to forget his experience in British jails. Admiral Radford said he believed that Nehru had done as much as any single individual to build Nasser up. In no sense could Nehru be described as a genuine neutral.

Returning to his report, Secretary Hoover pointed out that another immediate problem was shaping up in the Gaza Strip. In explanation, he read from a telegram from our Embassy in Beirut. [2] This telegram pointed out how serious conditions were in the Strip, with the Israelis having a difficult time holding down the Arab refugees in that area. There were already casualties, and the danger of a severe uprising. As a result, the Ambassador in Lebanon was suggesting that we should not urge the Israelis to move their forces out of the Gaza Strip until UN forces were able to get in.

Admiral Radford said that of course the UN forces would not be large enough to maintain order in the Gaza Strip. The President expressed himself as being at a loss to understand why anybody wanted the Gaza Strip, in view of the fact that there wasn't even any water in it.

At the conclusion of Secretary Hoover's report, Mr. Jackson indicated that Dr. Flemming would report briefly on the oil situation in Europe.

Dr. Flemming said that after last week's discussion of this problem in the National Security Council, he and Mr. Robert Anderson (former Deputy Secretary of Defense) had conferred at once with the presidents of the major oil companies. They had explained to these presidents our policies in this area, and the presidents had expressed themselves as in accord with our decisions. They favored at a later date pooling their shipping resources, which they regard as much more efficient than the individual action of each oil company, as was now the case.

Dr. Flemming added that in this discussion it had been agreed that the time had not yet come to put into operation the plans for supplying oil to Europe drawn up by the Middle East Emergency Committee. Nevertheless, Dr. Flemming recommended that the basic data on the oil situation available to the Committee should be brought up to date. There had been nothing new added in the last couple of weeks. This basic data, as to the problem of getting oil to Europe, could be obtained quietly and indirectly from the British and French through the agency of the Organization for European Economic Cooperation (OEEC). Once we have this additional basic data, Dr. Flemming indicated, we would be able to move very quickly when the time came to put the Middle East Emergency Committee plan into effect. It should also be possible to sound out the Saudi Arabians on their reaction to our effort to supply oil to Europe.

---

[2] Telegram 1200, November 13, not printed. (Department of State, Central Files, 684A.86/11–1356)

Secretary Hoover stated that it would be impossible for a few days to sound out the Saudi Arabian attitude, because King Saud was momentarily out of his country. Secretary Hoover then described a story printed in last night's Washington *Star*, alleging that the United States Government was actually withholding oil supplies from Great Britain and France in order to force them to comply with the decisions of the United Nations. This erroneous story, said Secretary Hoover, would have the most unfortunate effect when it became known in Europe, as it certainly would. The European nations would all descend on us to blame us for their shortages. For this reason, if for no other, this Government, said Secretary Hoover, has got to move into the European oil situation in a short time, not later than a day or two.

The President said that he had thought we had already determined to let Venezuelan oil go to Europe. Secretary Hoover replied that while this was so, the problem was the availability of tankers to get the Venezuelan oil to Europe, and that, of course, if the companies attempted to pool their ships, they would run afoul of the anti-trust law. The President made a jocular reference to his "stiff-necked" Attorney General, and after Secretary Hoover had insisted that we would have to organize the pooling of tankers along the lines suggested by the Middle East Emergency Committee plan, the President again offered to make a public statement which might help the oil companies by declaring that their pooling activities were the result of a serious emergency situation.

The Attorney General reassured the President that the Department of Justice already had a plan of action in this situation which could be put into effect as soon as the State Department told him to do so. Dr. Flemming confirmed this statement, and added that the Department of Justice was showing admirable cooperation. He explained that he was really not much worried about the legal angle. The President observed that we must certainly use every legal recourse to meet the situation. Above all, we want to increase the flow of oil from the Gulf Coast to our own East Coast, so that more Venezuelan oil can go directly to Europe. Dr. Flemming informed the President that this was already being done.

There then ensued a discussion of the problem of pooling tankers. Secretary Humphrey elucidated the dilemma. If the oil companies pooled their tankers and this fact became known, the Arabs could be expected to cut off further oil supplies. Accordingly, we might be worse off than as though there had been no pooling. Despite the gain in efficiency by pooling the tankers, Secretary Humphrey therefore opposed such a move at the present time. Dr. Flemming expressed the opinion that if the oil companies did pool their tankers, it would be impossible to disguise the fact that such a move had been suggested by the U.S. Government.

The President said it was his conclusion that it was best to go along with the recommendations made by Dr. Flemming earlier in the discussion, namely, to get the basic data available to the Middle East Emergency Committee up to date, and to find out what the Saudi Arabians would do if they were to learn that we proposed to ship oil to Europe under the terms of the Middle East Emergency Committee plan.

Admiral Radford pointed out that the Russians were already supplying oil to Egypt and were in general moving into the situation there. He warned that we may have to move ourselves very promptly, not only in Egypt but in Syria.

Dr. Flemming inquired whether the consensus of the Council could be summed up in the following terms: First, that we would proceed to bring our basic data for the Middle East Emergency Committee up to date; and second, ask the State Department to sound out the Saudi Arabians on their reaction to our plans, before any action is taken by us.

The discussion closed with a new expression of great anxiety over Britain's financial and economic situation from Secretary Humphrey.

The National Security Council: [3]

a. Noted and discussed an oral briefing by the Director of Central Intelligence on the subject, with specific reference to developments concerning Hungary and Poland; the situation in the Near East; the impact upon Asia of the foregoing events; and the situation in Korea.

b. Noted and discussed an oral report by the Acting Secretary of State regarding UN action on the Hungarian situation, and conclusions to be drawn as a result of recent events in the Near East.

c. Noted and discussed an oral report by the Director, Office of Defense Mobilization, on developments affecting the European oil supply position.

d. Noted the President's authorization to the Department of State:

> (1) To attempt to obtain recent data on the European oil supply position through the Organization for European Economic Cooperation (OEEC).
> (2) To explore discreetly probable reaction of Arab oil-producing states if the United States were to put into operation the plan of action of the Middle East Emergency Committee.

---

[3] Paragraphs a–d and the Note that follow constitute NSC Action No. 1632, approved by the President on November 19. (Department of State, S/S–NSC (Miscellaneous) Files: Lot 66 D 95, Records of Action by the National Security Council, 1956)

Note: The action in d above, as approved by the President, subsequently transmitted to the Secretary of State for appropriate implementation.

[Here follow agenda items 2–6.]

S. Everett Gleason

---

578.   Minutes of the Second Meeting of the Delegation to the General Assembly, Two Park Avenue, New York, November 15, 1956, 9:30 a.m. [1]

US/A/M(SR)51

[Here follows discussion of the agenda for the current General Assembly session and the situation in Hungary.]

Mr. Barco then took the floor. Since the Delegation was aware of the facts as carried in the papers, Mr. Barco confined his remarks to outlining the broad issues as we saw them. As of this morning, the Secretary General had reached agreement with France, the UK and Egypt, and the Secretary General would go in with the first contingent of the UN force, that is, with the Scandinavians and Colombians. [2] In his aide-mémoire the Secretary General had outlined the circumstances and terms of reference for the withdrawal and pointed up the U.N. Force's purpose—to deal with the problems referred to in the GA resolution. Both sides had accepted this interpretation. The aide-mémoire also said that the withdrawal was not contingent on the setting up of United Nations Forces. The UK and French reluctantly accepted this last condition.

Mr. Barco emphasized that *withdrawal* is the big question. The British-French-Israeli position is that they must judge whether the character of the UN force is sufficient. But did this mean that they wanted the UN force to be the same size as their own? Mr. Barco

---

[1] Source: Department of State, IO Files. Secret. Prepared on November 23. No drafting information is given on the source text.

[2] Lieutenant General Burns discussed the entry of the U.N. Force with Egyptian officials in Cairo between November 8 and 10 and again on November 12. (Burns, *Between Arab and Israeli* (New York: Ivan Obolensky, Inc., 1962), pp. 196–205) U.S. reports concerning these discussions and the simultaneous discussions between Hammarskjöld and Egyptian officials taking place in New York are in Department of State, Central File 320.5780. The first UNEF unit was flown to Abu Suweir, near Ismailia, on November 15.

pointed out that in the opinion of the British, French and Israelis, having such a force would be the greatest source of bargaining power. On the other hand, the Egyptians regarded the presence of the UN force in Egypt as being there with Egyptian permission. All other forces in the area were enemy occupation forces. The Egyptians, said Mr. Barco, would resist any UK-French flavor in the UN force. The UK and French had told the Secretary General they would agree to withdraw one battalion each. Mr. Barco emphasized that that information was only for those in the meeting and that it was Secret. Mr. Barco went on to reveal that the Israelis were saying that the United Nations forces should occupy the Sinai peninsula, and the islands in the Gulf of Aqaba. The issue as the Israelis saw it was whether the UN force could press the Arabs to a peace settlement. They had not disclosed their stand on the Gaza Strip and the only information we had was Ben Gurion's quotations in the press. Mr. Barco summed up the issues by asking whether the United Nations Force can satisfy all the parties that the force is doing what they want done. The UK and France considered the matter vital to their Middle East position. Was it possible for them to achieve their aims in this way.

[Here follows discussion of the United Nations role in regard to Hungary.]

Returning to the Palestine question, Mr. Lodge said that he had, in the last hour and a half, talked with the Secretary General, and with the British and French Delegations and found the positions of the latter extreme. They wanted UN Force to carry out all their objectives; they wanted the Egyptian consent on the dotted line— but that could not be done according to Mr. Lodge. The United Nations Force's mission was to prevent war in the area. If the UK and French point-of-view were carried to its logical end, the Egyptians would balk. Indeed these were "very anxious days", said Mr. Lodge.

[Here follows discussion of the sale of food to Hungary.]

Senator Humphrey then turned to corridor talk on the subject of the terms that Cairo had set down for the entry of the UN Force. The Senator was sympathetic with the UK-French view about the size of the force. Nasser was a threat and the Senator was not in favor of building up this "two-bit dictator". There would be less chance of Soviet action in the area if the United Nations Force were there in adequate strength. These were forces that only stopped shooting; they settled nothing. We must create conditions for negotiation. We should not make a fire department out of the UN Force. Its primary mission was to seal off the areas of hostility. The Senator had a question: "What are the UN Forces going to do? Are the UN Forces adequate to insist on a settlement?"

Mr. Barco interpolated that the Secretary General's intention was to carry out the General Assembly resolutions, namely that there would be no unilateral decision regarding the withdrawal of the UN Force. It would be a matter of negotiation at the time. The US attitude was that with the UN Force asking for consent to come in, we could not present this Force as equivalent to the UK-French Force in size. It would appear as an occupation force. Our approach was to get started on the UN Force and build it up. From now on the character of the force would be a matter of negotiation.

[Here follows discussion of the sale of food to the current Hungarian Government.]

Senator Knowland returned to the subject of the situation in the Middle East, agreeing that the UN should not let Nasser, on the one hand, or the British-French and Israelis turn this UN Force into its own creature. Senator Humphrey felt that the United Nations must not become an accomplice to an aggression. He did not believe that Nasser had been exactly "an eagle scout". Senator Humphrey made the point that he assumed that the reference to military goods in the UN resolution also included volunteers.

Mr. Lodge told the Delegation that it was the US approach to have the UN Force ease itself in, get itself established and build up its strength. Senator Humphrey thought it was important that we know where we were going, what our objective was. He would hate to think that we were going in just piece-meal. Mr. Lodge cited President Eisenhower's policy that we must find a basic settlement in the Middle East. The President from the very first day had emphasized that it would be tragic if we went through this upheaval only to find ourselves back where we were at the beginning. Mr. Lodge said that next Monday or Tuesday[3] he hoped we could go ahead with the two resolutions on Palestine and the Suez Canal. The Secretary General had asked us to hold off until he got back from Cairo.

The meeting adjourned at 10:15.

---

[3] November 20–21.

579.   Memorandum by the Director of Central Intelligence (Dulles) [1]

Washington, November 16, 1956.

Memorandum of Conversation at the French Embassy, 16 November 1956, with Monsieur Pineau, Minister of Foreign Affairs, the Ambassador, and Monsieur Daridan of the Quai d'Orsay.

After the usual amenities during which it turned out that both M. Pineau and I had attended the Ecole Alsacienne in Paris many years ago, M. Alphand, who had been on the phone when I arrived, joined us and started in immediately to discuss the U.N. resolution on which M. Pineau had been working with regard to the committee to deal with the Suez Canal question. M. Alphand said, (apparently after having talked with the State Department and possibly others) that it seemed desirable to add an additional "neutral" member to the committee to balance off the British and French representation so that it would include, in addition to the British and French and the U.N. Secretary General and an Egyptian delegate, one additional representative to be appointed by the Secretary General.

There was then some discussion as to whether such a resolution had any prospect of being accepted by the U.N., and M. Pineau seemed to have some optimism on the subject. He remarked that he felt that our original resolution would have caused great difficulty since the General Assembly would undoubtedly have got into a wrangle as to membership, and it therefore seemed necessary to clearly designate the membership initially. Pineau remarked that any committee which did not have British and French representation, as well as Egyptian, would not include the parties chiefly interested.

[Here follows discussion of the Syrian situation.]

M. Pineau then described the pressures which had been built up on France as a result of Nasr's Suez action, the feeling in France that after the negotiations both in London and in New York had resulted in a Russian veto and, in effect, futility, the French had reached the conclusion that we were not prepared to take any strong action against Nasr.

---

[1] Source: Department of State, Central Files, 974.7301/11–1756. Transmitted to the Department of State under cover of a note, dated November 17, from Dulles to Murphy which reads, in part: "I am sending a copy to Andy Goodpaster and if I get a chance this afternoon, I shall show it to Foster.

"If you think Herb [Hoover] would be interested please pass it on to him upon his return from New York."

A copy of this memorandum is in the Eisenhower Library, Staff Secretary Records.

After luncheon M. Pineau turned to me and said he wanted now to tell me in strict confidence what really had happened. On October 14 he had arrived back in Paris from New York after the U.N. meeting on the Suez Canal; on October 15, he was approached in Paris by Israeli representatives. They told him that Israel had definite proof that Egypt was preparing to move against them and that they could not wait much longer. They were therefore determined to attack Egypt; that they would do it alone if necessary but *do* it they would. On October 16, Eden had come over from London and the plan had been worked out among the three of them and that was that. He, in effect, apologized for not having kept us informed but said that under the circumstances it seemed to serve no useful purpose to do so. I remarked that he probably also was aware of the fact that if we had been advised we would have opposed the plan.

I asked M. Pineau whether he did not have any faith in working through the United Nations. He remarked that it seemed obvious that the United Nations had a double standard, that they acted vigorously against Britain and France in Egypt, whereas they had been impotent to do anything about the grievous Soviet aggression in Hungary; that an organization where Yemen and the United States had an equal voice tended to become a debating society and that the U.N. while it had possibly some capacity for decision after events had occurred, did not have any machinery for dealing with the gathering storm. They could only act, too late, after the storm had broken.

M. Pineau seemed to think that unless the Soviet Union was prepared to risk atomic warfare, or even initiate it, their power for overt intervention in the Middle East was limited, although he was apprehensive about the volunteer business. He and M. Daridan cited reports of large numbers of Soviet Moslem volunteers—he cited the number of 10,000—which might be ready to be transported to the troubled area of the Middle East. He recognized the logistic problem of getting them to Egypt and seemed to feel that Syria was a more likely danger spot than Egypt from the point of view of Communist infiltration and the use of volunteers.

He expressed great gratification at the speech of General Gruenther [2] which had been the one bright spot in recent events and had had great effect in Europe.

M. Alphand said that they were very disturbed at the report that the Secretary was seeing Mr. Martino but had declined to see

---

[2] Gruenther warned the Soviet Union of immediate retaliation in case of an attack on Western Europe. (Telegram 2371 from Paris, November 13; Department of State, Central Files, 711.551/11–1356)

M. Pineau. M. Pineau added that this put him in a very difficult situation. Either public opinion in France would reach the conclusion that M. Pineau had not desired to see the Secretary, or that the Secretary had refused to see him while seeing others, and either result would be equally bad. I said that I frankly did not know whether the Secretary was seeing Martino. M. Alphand assured me that such was the case according to information which he had just received.

Throughout the conversation which lasted about one and one-half hours, we found ourselves in agreement only on the following points:

The importance of Franco-American understanding; that the Communist menace was our greatest danger; that Syria was a potential weak point from the viewpoint of Communist penetration, and that Egypt and the Arab world could well dispense with the service of Nasr. There was some difference between us as to the degree of his rascality, and also as to the type of measures which were justifiable to effect a change. For example, when I suggested to Pineau that during the months following the seizure of the Canal, some progress was being made in undermining Nasr's popularity and position in Egypt, Pineau vigorously dissented and indicated that he never could have been shaken by peaceful measures of this nature.

I made it entirely clear to M. Pineau that I did not deal with policy questions but that my job, as he knew, was limited to pulling together intelligence for the policy makers.

---

580.   Message From President Eisenhower to King Saud [1]

Washington, November 16, 1956.

YOUR MAJESTY: I was pleased to receive Your Majesty's two

---

[1] Source: Department of State, Central Files, 684A.86/11–1656. Secret. Drafted in the Department of State by Newsom and forwarded to the White House under cover of a memorandum from Hoover to Eisenhower on November 16. It was approved by Goodpaster. (*Ibid.*, 320.5780/11–1656) The message was sent to Dhahran in Priority telegram 179, which is the source text, with the instruction: "Please deliver soonest following message from President to King Saud. Confirm date time delivery."

latest messages, through Prince Faisal and the Foreign Office on November 4,[2] and through our Ambassador on November 11.[3]

I am confident that you will continue to support measures such as those referred to in resolutions of the United Nations General Assembly which will restore peace to the area of hostilities. Beyond this, I sincerely hope that you may be able to encourage Egyptian cooperation to achieve solutions for some of the fundamental problems which gave rise to the current crisis.

I deeply appreciate the thanks which you have conveyed for the stand of the United States Government in the recent sessions of the General Assembly dealing with Near Eastern matters. I can assure you that the United States is trying strenuously to bring peace to the area and to work out solutions based on justice and equity for all. We will continue to use our influence to secure compliance with the United Nations resolutions and, thereafter, to encourage actions which will establish lasting peace and stability in the area.

We share with you the concern at the shadow cast, not only over the Near East, but over the whole world, by recent events. Our hearts are made heavy by the shadows cast by the ruthless suppression of the people of Hungary in their quest for freedom. I know that you will share our concern in this, as the events in Hungary may well be indicative of the fate of any who become dominated by the Soviet Union. We would hope that you will see your way clear to support us in our efforts in the United Nations to meet this crisis.

I have read Your Majesty's suggestion regarding Egypt. I share with you the deep regret at the suffering which may have been caused by these recent events. I am hopeful, however, that, when the United Nations forces enter and General Burns has had an opportunity to assess the situation, we may find that the damage was not as extensive or as great as was, at first, believed. Meanwhile, humanitarian agencies in this country and elsewhere are active in the provision of emergency relief.

I am pleased to have these opportunities to exchange views with Your Majesty. I hope that in the months ahead these exchanges may continue, and that perhaps at some stage we will have an opportunity to meet for a general review of problems of common interest.

---

[2] Not printed. (Transmitted in telegram 233 from Jidda, November 5; *ibid.*, 684A.86/11–1156) In the message Saud expressed special appreciation for the position taken by the United States in the Suez crisis.

[3] Not printed. (Transmitted in telegram 214 from Dhahran, November 11; *ibid.*) In the message Saud expressed appreciation for U.S. efforts to end Israeli-French-U.K. aggression against Egypt, condemned that aggression as a threat to the world, urged the President to work for the implementation of recent U.N. resolutions on the Middle East, and suggested that the United States use its influence to ensure that Egypt was compensated for the material losses suffered as a result of the fighting.

May God have you in his safe keeping.
Your sincere friend,

Dwight D. Eisenhower [4]

[4] Telegram 179 bears this typed signature.

---

581.   Memorandum of a Conversation, Department of State, Washington, November 17, 1956 [1]

SUBJECT

Call by French Ambassador on Mr. Murphy

PARTICIPANTS

Mr. Robert D. Murphy—G
Mr. William R. Tyler—WE
Mr. Herve Alphand, French Ambassador
Mr. Charles Lucet, French Minister
Mr. Francois de Laboulaye, French Counselor

The French Ambassador called at his request and gave an account of Mr. Pineau's unofficial visit to Washington on November 16th. He said that he had had talks with Mr. Allen Dulles and Admiral Radford. [2] (Mr. Pineau had told Admiral Radford that the Israeli forces had captured an extraordinarily large amount of Egyptian equipment of Soviet origin in the Sinai Peninsula, including 1500 vehicles of all kinds, this includes tanks). About 200 Egyptian planes had been destroyed. Mr. Pineau had told Admiral Radford that it was essential to prevent this "Soviet arsenal" from being reconstituted in Egypt and Syria, otherwise Israel would be condemned to undertaking preventative war.

[Here follows discussion of Syria, printed in volume XIII, page 605.]

Turning to Egypt, the Ambassador said that the question of the location, responsibilities, and duration of the UN force was a very serious matter. He said that there was a considerable difference between the UK and French interpretation of the UN resolution, and that of Egypt. He asked whether the United States supported the UK

---

[1] Source: Department of State, Central Files, 611.51/11–1756. Confidential. Drafted by Tyler.
[2] Radford's handwritten notes of the conversation are in Radford Papers, Memos for the Record, C–1.

and French interpretation. Mr. Murphy said that we did by and large, but that the most important thing was that nothing should be done which should detract from the chances of the United Nations bringing about a peaceful and satisfactory resolution. The Ambassador pressed the subject of what the United States would do, and whether we would continue to deal with Nasser. Mr. Murphy asked the Ambassador who else he thought there was to deal with in Egypt and whether the French had any alternative in mind. The Ambassador stated that Nasser is an unreliable and dangerous fanatic and that pressure must be exerted on him in order to obtain an acceptable solution to the present crisis.

The Ambassador said that the oil situation in France was extremely serious, and that failure to take measures to supply Western Europe with oil it needed in the coming months would precipitate grave social, political and economic repercussions. He asked whether the US approved of the role which the OEEC was playing with regard to oil, and Mr. Murphy said that we did.

The Ambassador said that Mr. Pineau had approved of the French proposed amendments to the US resolution on Suez. [3] The Ambassador said that he had talked with Mr. Phillips and he understood that the French proposals had been sent to New York. He understood that the preliminary reaction of the Department seemed to be that the proposed composition of the Committee might be taken by the Arabs as favoring the UK and France too much.

[Here follows discussion of the Soviet proposal for a summit conference on disarmament.]

---

[3] The Department of State transmitted the text of the three amendments, which it had received from the French Embassy in Washington, to the Mission in New York in telegram 315, November 16. One of the amendments provided that the Suez Committee, envisioned in the U.S. draft resolution, should be composed of one Egyptian representative, one French representative, one British representative, as well as one non-Egyptian person chosen by Egypt and a person who was neither French nor British, but had been chosen jointly by France and Great Britain. The Department advised the Mission that, before considering any changes in the draft resolution, it would want to consult with Hammarskjöld upon his return from Cairo and to await responses to inquiries being made by U.S. officials as to the availability of Pearson, Lange, and Lall to serve on the committee. (Department of State, Central Files, 974.7301/11–1656)

**582.   Memorandum of a Conversation Between the President
and the Secretary of State, Secretary Dulles' Room,
Walter Reed Hospital, Washington, November 17, 1956,
11 a.m.** [1]

ALSO PRESENT FOR PART OF THE MEETING

Mr. Macomber

[Here follow President Eisenhower's comments concerning a
recent conversation with the Greek Prime Minister.]

.   .   .   .

[Here follows discussion of the most recent letter from Bulganin
which concerned the Hungarian situation.]

The President told the Secretary that there were two things he
specifically wished to discuss with him at this time. First he said
that he had been giving a good deal of thought to what he should
say publicly in the nature of a deterrent to the Russians sending
"volunteers" into the Middle East. He said that he thought the best
thing he could do would be to make a statement to the effect that if
the Russians should do this he would immediately call a special
session of Congress. The President thought this was all he needed to
say. He believed the Russians knew enough of our Constitutional
procedures to be able to assess the great significance of such a move.
He felt it would be a strong warning without, at the same time,
committing us to any particular action. The Secretary thought this
would be a useful thing to do.

Secondly, the President wished to raise the question of bringing
oil into the Central Northern States from Canada. Senator Wiley had
called on the President and had urged that steps be taken to do this.
The President asked the Secretary whether he had given it any
thought. The Secretary replied that a great deal of thought had been
given to it in the Department, but he personally was not familiar
enough with the problem to discuss it at this time. He thought there
were some technical and legal difficulties involved.

[Here follows discussion of a personnel matter.]

The Secretary then told the President that he had been thinking
about what we should do about two committees—one to consider
the Suez situation and one to consider the Palestine situation. The
Secretary thought we should definitely go ahead with the Suez

---

[1] Source: Eisenhower Library, Dulles Papers, Meetings with the President. Top
Secret; Personal and Private. Drafted by Macomber. The time of the meeting is from
the record of the President's Daily Appointments. (*Ibid.*)

Committee. He was not so certain that this was the time to go ahead with the Palestine Committee. They discussed briefly who could serve on the Palestine Committee. It was thought that Bech, Fanfani and Spaak would be good, although Fanfani might be needed for the Suez Committee.

Next followed a brief discussion of United States foreign policy in the Middle East and Far East. During this the President remarked that it was essential to hold Japan, India and the Middle East.

The President then asked the Secretary for his thinking regarding "your personnel". At this point the undersigned left the room. (After the President had left, I asked the Secretary whether he wished to write a memorandum on this portion of the conversation. He said he did not wish to do so.) [2]

---

[2] Later that day at 4:57 p.m., Foreign Secretary Lloyd and Ambassador Caccia visited Dulles at Walter Reed Hospital. Hoover had already joined Dulles at 4:52 p.m. (Dulles Appointment Book; Princeton University Library, Dulles Papers) Lloyd subsequently recalled that Dulles greeted them "with a kind of twinkle in his eye" and said: "Selwyn, why did you stop? Why didn't you go through with it and get Nasser down?" (*Suez 1956, A Personal Account*, p. 219) No memorandum of the Dulles–Lloyd conversation has been found either in Department of State files or the Eisenhower Library.

---

583.   Telegram From the Embassy in the United Kingdom to the Department of State [1]

London, November 17, 1956—noon.

2782. For the Acting Secretary. Macmillan asked to see me yesterday afternoon. He said that the meetings of the OEEC in Paris have been very satisfactory and that he felt that if the oil committee in the United States should be reactivated immediately to cooperate with the oil committee of the OEEC it would not be necessary for Great Britain to make any special representations to the United States in connection with its problems regarding oil. Two things which are principally preoccupying him are 1) the question of obtaining the funds available to Great Britain in the IMF and 2) the possibility of borrowing from the Federal Reserve Bank on the American Securities owned by the British Treasury which he said amounted to approximately $900 million in market value. He as-

---

[1] Source: Department of State, Central Files, 841.2553/11–1756. Top Secret; Niact. Received at 8:39 a.m.

sumed he could borrow about ⅔ of the market value of these securities and if he got $600 million from this source and another $400 million or $500 million from the Monetary Fund it would be sufficient to tide Great Britain over the difficult period ahead. He thought that he could not go the United States alone himself in this connection because it would create lack of confidence in sterling if he should do so and he felt that it would be better for him to wait until Monday [2] before deciding exactly what he should do. At that time, Hammarskjold having returned from his mission to Nasser, it might be evident that the withdrawal of the British forces could begin pari passu with the introduction of the United Nations forces into Egypt, always presupposing that the UN forces would be so disposed in Egypt as to protect the canal and to assure that a satisfactory arrangement would be worked out for the future operation of the canal.

I am seeing Macmillan again Sunday afternoon. If the Department has any comments it would wish me to make at that time instructions will be appreciated. [3]

Aldrich

---

[2] November 19.

[3] The Department of State responded in telegram 3572, November 17, that it was not prepared to go beyond the information contained in circular telegram 411, *infra*, for Aldrich's November 18 meeting with Macmillan.

---

584.   Circular Telegram From the Department of State to Certain Diplomatic Missions [1]

Washington, November 17, 1956—2:47 p.m.

411. Following guidance relates to US actions and intentions regarding oil supply for Europe. It not for publication but may be used discreetly in response inquiries from senior officials various governments who have inquired or may inquire on these points. They also should be cautioned against publicity at this time. Principal purpose this information is to alleviate uneasiness based on

---

[1] Source: Department of State, Central Files, 840.04/11–1756. Confidential. Drafted by Moline; cleared by Flemming, Beckner, Elbrick, Timmons, and Rountree; and approved by Kalijarvi. Sent to Ankara, Athens, Bern, Bonn, Brussels, Copenhagen, Dublin, London, Luxembourg, Madrid, Paris, Reykjavik, Rome, Vienna, Oslo, Stockholm, The Hague, and Lisbon.

uncertainty re US intentions and remove any feeling US indifferent to European problem.

US Govt had established Middle East Emergency Committee (MEEC) of principal oil companies which had prepared plan of action for dealing cooperatively with problem oil supply to Europe in event of shortages created by closure of Suez Canal which seemed, in August and September, likely result from action by Egypt. Committee is still in existence and still authorized work together on oil problem. It has not been active, however, since British, French, Israeli action against Egypt. Its plan somewhat out of date but American companies now attempting correct deficiencies therein.

US Govt's decision initially to suspend committee work was due to desire appraise situation in light of new developments and different than anticipated cause for Canal closing. Decisions to date not to reactivate committee as yet have been based on two principal considerations:

1. We did not wish by action in MEEC, involving as it did British, French observers and requiring close cooperation with British, French industry committee in London, to give any impression of support British-French action against Egypt, especially as such impression would have seriously impaired our position in UN.

2. We wished avoid any impression which might have been created by starting committee that could have led Arab oil producing states either to sabotage additional facilities or impose additional restrictions on use of oil.

Both foregoing considerations and especially latter still seem valid though in lesser degree than week ago. We still do not wish upset by premature efforts at coordinating oil supply delicate negotiations regarding UN role in Egypt or give excuse for sabotaging Tapline in particular which would reduce the effectiveness of a coordinated effort to approximately same level as present uncoordinated effort.

Latter while less efficient than coordinated effort pooling same resources, facilities and shipping, nonetheless is important since all oil companies are doing utmost on individual basis maintain maximum supplies throughout the world.

We expect, assuming continued favorable development of situation in Egypt, to be able undertake coordinated supply effort soon involving cooperation through OEEC. This is not guarantee to do so. Still less is it attempt specify date for action. Nonetheless we seriously concerned with oil supply problems particularly in Europe which we following closely. Believe we have full appreciation possible consequences in economic, social, political, and military spheres if oil supplies to Europe should be markedly reduced and criticism we would face plus damage our objectives in Western Europe if, when we able to help, we should withhold the additional efficiency which a coordinated effort would introduce to improve Europe's oil supply.

Deeply interested your continuing appraisal of situation. Regret lack of earlier guidance. Will notify soonest any decision taken to activate coordination supply effort if, as now expected, this proves possible in near future.

Hoover

585. Memorandum From the Deputy Assistant Secretary of State for European Affairs (Elbrick) and the Assistant Secretary of State for Economic Affairs (Kalijarvi) to the Acting Secretary of State [1]

Washington, November 17, 1956.

SUBJECT

Impact of Oil Shortage Due to Middle East Situation on Our European NATO Allies

In recent days eight [2] West European governments have approached us, either here or abroad, or in some cases both, to express concern over the prospective oil shortage in Europe due to the

---

[1] Source: Department of State, Central Files, 840.04/11–1756. Confidential. Drafted by the Officer in Charge of United Kingdom and Ireland Affairs, William N. Dale; sent through Murphy to Hoover. Concurred in by Moline, John Wesley Jones (EUR/WE), and Rountree. A note attached to the source text, dated November 17, from Rountree to Murphy reads in part as follows: "I believe that NSC should be informed and I am inclined to think that we should be prepared to take substantive action with respect to the oil problem within the next few days. Any such action should deal with the oil problem of the Free World as a whole, and not just Western Europe. I assume that before proceeding with this substantive action we will have replies from the several missions to which the Department's telegram of November 16 was directed. In that telegram we asked for the estimates of the missions to Arab States as to whether coordinated supply efforts involving the United States, United Kingdom, Dutch and French companies could be taken in present circumstances without serious risk that such action would bring about a significant reduction in oil availabilities in the Persian Gulf and Eastern Mediterranean." Reference is to telegram 351 to Jidda, November 16, also sent to Kuwait, Baghdad, and Tehran; *ibid.*, 840.04/11–1656. A typed notation on Rountree's note by Bowie, dated November 20, reads: "I concur on same basis as Mr. Rountree."

[2] Italy, Ireland, Norway, Sweden, Denmark, Portugal, United Kingdom, and the Netherlands. [Footnote in the source text.]

Middle East situation and to ask about activating the London Oil Emergency Advisory Committee, or some other agency for cooperating with Western Europe in meeting this problem. Failure on our part to do this in the very near future can expose us to serious risks. In the first place, there are a number of NATO countries, sure to suffer from the prospective oil shortage, which regard themselves as innocent bystanders as far as intervention in Suez is concerned. The Danes, for instance, who by and large disapproved of the Anglo-French intervention in Suez, decidedly do not feel that they should suffer because of our unwillingness to restore cooperation with Western Europe. We rely on many of these countries to maintain our NATO alliance, even though in some cases they have not been as stable supporters of the West as we should like. If we show ourselves unresponsive to their needs, it is questionable whether we could count indefinitely upon their unreserved cooperation with respect to Western defense and NATO.

Scandinavian countries which have very insufficient and inferior coal resources of their own depend heavily on oil for power for industrial purposes as well as for transportation. They are exceedingly vulnerable to any prolonged interruption of their oil supply and there are already signs that some of them are becoming desperate in their efforts to find solutions to the anticipated shortage. That the largest share of the Middle East oil goes to Britain and France does not affect the fact that these smaller sovereign states share a critical dependence on oil and may be expected to react violently if they believe that the United States is dragging its heels in helping them to solve this problem.

So far as Britain is concerned, we appreciate that the appearance of cooperation might have an adverse effect among Arab oil producing states and those through which pipelines run. We must, however, sooner or later face the fact that since British coal production has been relatively inflexible in recent years, British industry, too, has come to depend increasingly on oil. If its supply is too much curtailed, production costs will rise and production volume fall which would affect adversely British exports. This, in turn, would further reduce its gold and dollar reserves which have already declined to $2.16 billion, just $169 million above the assumed danger line of $2 billion. A financial crisis in Britain now could scarcely serve our long-term interests and would certainly weaken that country's contribution to NATO defense forces.

It appears certain that, at the very least, a 20% shortage in oil will develop in Western Europe this winter and this will tend to make people particularly sensitive to any suggestions that the United States, which appears to them invulnerable to this crisis and hence not disposed to make sacrifices, did not act quickly to help alleviate their situation. We should also recognize the disillusionment in the value of the North Atlantic Alliance which would follow an apparent failure on our part to support the economies of our Western European allies. In addition to this psychological factor, we shall have to contend with the virtual certainty that military stocks in Europe will be drawn down with adverse effects on NATO's readiness to withstand attack, if we do not assist.

Recommendation:

It is recommended that you bring to the attention of the National Security Council or other appropriate forum the possible serious consequences of further delay in permitting the United States Government to cooperate with Western European nations in meeting the threatened oil shortage. [3]

---

[3] A note attached to the source text, dated November 23, from Hoover's Special Assistant, Earl D. Sohm, to Murphy's Special Assistant, Richard Finn, reads: "Mr. Murphy left this with Mr. Hoover. Mr. Hoover read last night, but made no comment. Suggest you return to Mr. Murphy. Sorry I can't be more helpful."

Another note attached to the source text, dated November 24, by Finn reads: "Mr. Hoover saw this but apparently did not act on it. Earl Sohm returned it to G. The best thing I think would be for you to take it up with Mr. Hoover if you think action required. Otherwise we can return it to EUR."

---

586.   Telegram From the Department of State to the Consulate General at Dhahran [1]

Washington, November 18, 1956—3:09 p.m.

182. For Ambassador Wadsworth. Rapid development oil supply crisis particularly in Western Europe necessitates implementation without delay emergency plans which call for US oil company collaboration with European counterparts in arrangements for meeting requirements in light closure Suez Canal and IPC pipeline. As you know one factor in our reluctance thus far to act this regard has been desire avoid implication to Arab producing countries that US seeking bail British and French out dilemma created by their action in Egypt. Important that decision to proceed be placed in its proper context so that Saudi reaction will not impair success of our effort.

---

[1] Source: Department of State, Central Files, 840.04/11–1856. Secret; Niact. Drafted by Rountree, approved by Hoover, and signed by Rountree for Hoover. Repeated Niact to Jidda.

Suggest you discuss matter with King Saud urgently along following lines:

Closure Suez Canal and rupture IPC pipelines has created oil supply problem throughout Western Europe and Arab-Asian areas which will require special measures primarily among international oil companies. In implementing these special measures US has much in mind extreme desirability minimizing effect of present situation on Saudi Arabia's supply position and thus Saudi Arabia's income. This objective can be accomplished best by coordinated efforts among international companies upon whom falls responsibility for shipping and marketing facilities. We therefore plan encourage US companies participate in such coordinated approach, working insofar as Europe concerned with Organization for European Economic Cooperation (OEEC) in which seventeen Western European users are represented. This arrangement will have effect of "pooling" oil deliveries to Western Europe with OEEC assuming responsibility for allocations among participating countries of Europe's share.

Similarly, shipments from all sources to Asian and African countries now faced with oil shortages and which are not in OEEC will be augmented by a coordinated effort among supplying companies.

Plan does not require any affirmative action on part Saudi Arabian Government. It reflects most practical means of meeting present situation and does not connote change in policy or permanent arrangement. In consonance our continuing desire exchange information of mutual interest, we wish King Saud to be fully informed in advance re these efforts which we confident he will support. We repeat it our earnest hope that present problem can be overcome with least possible adverse effect upon interests of SAG which will continue be uppermost in our minds.

You might take opportunity impress upon Saud that SAG interests deeply involved in continued operation of Tapline.

Report reaction urgently.

Hoover

587.   **Telegram From the Department of State to the Embassy in Egypt** [1]

Washington, November 18, 1956—4 p.m.

1615. Egyptian Ambassador Hussein accompanied special Nasser emissary Mustafa Amin [2] during call today on Murphy and Rountree. [3] Amin said Nasser asked him convey to President following views. Nasser has given Soviets no promise re base rights in Egypt and has not responded to repeated Soviet urging have Egypt request Soviet volunteers. He had made personal and direct request for aid in connection with attack on Egypt only to US. He had refrained from public announcement this effect in deference Ambassador Hare and for fear embarrassing US Government. His only other request was generalized public appeal. Realizing Soviets trying take advantage his present difficult position, Nasser has urged Arab chiefs of state, through Amin during recent Beirut meeting, give credit for successful Egyptian defense firstly to Egyptian people and Arab bloc and secondly to UN. Nasser does not believe Soviet Ambassador Kisselev assurance USSR willing wage war on behalf Egypt. Nasser does not want Egypt become second Korea or excuse for third world war.

Nasser says sooner British and French withdraw the better for US-Egyptian relations. Amin believes Nasser suspicious British and French may stay "longer than they should" and mere presence Canadian troops dressed like British and speaking English might arouse incidents among uninformed Egyptians. Amin said he had word yesterday that Nasser believed salvage operation in Canal should be under UN not UK-France auspices and held UN forces should be exclusively on Israel-Egypt frontier.

Murphy said Nasser's apparent hesitation on these and related points had been basis for deep US Government concern in recent days. Murphy and Rountree gave reasons why objections raised by Nasser appeared easily negotiable and urged Amin employ whatever influence he had dissuade Nasser from reluctance facilitate prompt establishment effective UN force in Egypt. Egypt first to gain from such action. Although Department not fully informed re outcome Hammarskjold–Nasser talks, preliminary reports not encouraging.

---

[1] Source: Department of State, Central Files, 684A 86/11–1856. Secret; Priority. Drafted by Hoffacker (NEA/NE) and Rountree and approved by Rountree who signed for Hoover. Also sent Priority to USUN, to London, Paris, and Moscow.

[2] An Egyptian newspaper publisher and confidant of Nasser.

[3] The memorandum of this conversation by Hoffacker, November 18, is not printed. (Department of State, Central Files, 684A.86/11–1856)

Amin seemed agree objections re Canadian troops might disappear with proposed modification uniforms and added GOE appreciated helpful role Canada had played in UN.[4] It was pointed out to Amin Egypt should recognize unusual safeguards and benefit dealing with UN, which above suspicion re appreciation Egyptian rights and sovereignty.

Egyptians raised again matter possible release at least some GOE frozen assets in US for purchase pharmaceuticals, and mentioned general question US freezing of funds. Department representatives replied matter of pharmaceuticals would be studied, but pointed out that frozen funds only one element of total problem solution to which would have to be by stages beginning with implementation present UN resolutions. Said meeting with President would be taken under consideration. Matter was left that another meeting of group would follow report by Hammarskjold on his visit to Cairo.

Hoover

---

[4] The Canadian Government proposed sending troops known as "The Queen's Own Rifles", who wore what was essentially a British uniform with U.N. badges. See Pearson, *Mike: The Memoirs of the Right Honourable Lester B. Pearson, Vol. 2, 1948–1957*, pp. 261 ff.

---

588.   Telegram From the Embassy in the United Kingdom to the Department of State[1]

London, November 19, 1956—1 p.m.

2791. From Ambassador to Acting Secretary. For President and Secretary. In accordance with arrangement referred to in mytel 2782[2] Macmillan spent hour and a half with me at Embassy residence late yesterday afternoon.

Macmillan said that it was evident that British Government may be faced within next few days with the terrible dilemma of either (a) withdrawing from Egypt, having accomplished nothing but to have brought about the entry into Egypt of a completely inadequate token force of troops representing the UN, whose only function is to police

---

[1] Source: Department of State, Central Files, 974.7301/11–1956. Top Secret; Niact; Presidential Handling. Received at 9:12 a.m. A copy is in the Eisenhower Library, Whitman File, Dulles–Herter Series.

[2] Document 583.

the border between Israel and Egypt, without having secured the free operation of the Canal or even being in a position to clear it, or (b) renewing hostilities in Egypt and taking over the entire Canal in order to remove the obstructions which have been placed there by Nasser and to insure its free operation and to avoid the complete economic collapse of Europe within the next few months. The danger of course in the minds of the British Cabinet of adopting the first alternative is that loss of prestige and humiliation would be so great that the govt must fall, while the second alternative would obviously involve the risk of bringing in the Russians and resulting in a third world war.

Macmillan said that faced with this desperate choice some members of the Cabinet would undoubtedly be willing to take the risk of the second alternative and go down fighting, but he said that he and Salisbury believed that if through a message from the President to Eden or in some other manner British Government could be assured that the United States Government intends to pursue a policy of obtaining through action of the United Nations the immediate clearance of obstructions from the Canal and its operation by an international agency in accordance with the principles developed at the first London conference on Suez a majority of the Cabinet would choose the first of these alternatives and would not only withdraw the British forces but also bring pressure on the French to withdraw their forces from Egypt at once. It would not be contemplated that the assurances to which I have just referred would be in the form of any agreement nor would they be made public.

I believe that the situation which is causing Macmillan and Salisbury to think along the lines I have just indicated is the realization of the desperate financial position in which they will find themselves at the end of the year unless by that time they are working in the closest possible cooperation with the US in both the economic and political fields. Macmillan indicated yesterday that the month of November may show a loss of 200 or 300 millions of dollar balances and he is of course faced at the end of the year with the payment of something like $180 million of the annual payment on the British debt to the US and Canada. If in order to meet these payments he has not been able to draw on the Monetary Fund and borrow on his securities from the Federal Reserve Bank as outlined in reference telegram he fears that there may be a real panic regarding sterling. Perhaps the above is only another way of saying that the British Cabinet is beginning to realize what a terrible mistake has been made and appreciate the fact that the only thing which can save them is the immediate and intimate cooperation with the US through the agency of the United Nations. Whether or not the government would fall under these conditions is anyone's guess, but I believe that leaders such as Macmillan and Salisbury feel that if they can make their colleagues understand that the ultimate support of the US has not been lost the government still could count on the votes of a sufficient number of Conservative back benchers to insure a majority for the government in favor of withdrawal from Egypt in state to [spite of] the fact that no satisfactory arrangement had yet been entered into with Nasser regarding the Canal. To put it in its simplest form I would say that the British Cabinet is prepared to withdraw from Egypt now and leave to the UN the settlement of the problems involved in the relations between Israel and the Arab world and the problems relating to the operation of the Canal provided that the tremendous moral influence and power of the President will be continuously brought to bear on the UN to insure through the UN the ultimate solution of these terrible problems in accordance with justice and international law.

It is interesting to note that in his talk with me last Friday [4] Macmillan in discussing the possibility of his seeing Secretary [omission in the source text] the immediate future said to me that perhaps he, Macmillan, could go to Washington as "Eden's deputy" as Eden himself might not be well enough to come. He said that Eden was very tired and should have a rest before he engaged in a conference as important as a top level Tripartite Conference would be at the present time. I cannot help wondering whether this might not be a hint that some sort of movement is on foot in the Cabinet to replace Eden. I have no reason other than the conversations which I am now reporting to reach any such conclusion, but I feel that perhaps I should raise the question.

It is perhaps interesting to note also in connection with the above that, as Secretary knows, both Macmillan and Salisbury have been among the most bellicose members of the Cabinet during entire Suez crisis.

Should appreciate if Secretary would transmit to Humphrey financial information contained this message.

Aldrich

---

[4] November 16.

589. Memorandum of a Conference With the President, White House, Washington, November 19, 1956, 11:07–11:37 a.m. [1]

OTHERS PRESENT

> Secretary Hoover
> Colonel Goodpaster

[Here follows discussion of unrelated subjects.]

Mr. Hoover said he was inclined to feel that there has been some improvement in the general situation in the last day or two, although nothing marked as yet. He referred to indications of difficulties within the Soviet ruling group, and also to recent exchanges between ourselves and the Arab countries, including instructions to Wadsworth to give King Saud our thinking regarding the developing oil situation. [2] The President reiterated strongly his feeling that we should be trying to build up Saud as an element of strength and stability in the Middle East.

Mr. Hoover reported that pressure is being generated by the British for large UN forces to go into Egypt. They evidently feel they need this action as a means of saving face regarding their own withdrawal from Port Said. Mr. Hoover said, in his opinion, we must back up Hammarskjold regarding UN insistence that the British and French withdraw very strongly. The President said that when the UN forces go into the area, so long as they are of reasonable size—enough to prevent brigandage—the whole UN prestige is pledged, and the question of exact numbers is not too important.

Mr. Hoover referred finally to reports that are being received of tensions within the British Government and Cabinet at the present time.

G
Colonel, CE, U S Army

---

[1] Source: Eisenhower Library, Whitman File, Eisenhower Diaries. Secret. Drafted by Goodpaster. The time of the meeting is from the record of the President's Daily Appointments. (*Ibid.*)

[2] Telegram 182, Document 586.

590.   Telegram From the Mission at the United Nations to the Department of State [1]

New York, November 19, 1956—6 p.m.

Delga 127. For Hoover from Lodge. Re Palestine—Suez. In discussion Phleger and I had with SYG Hammarskjold this a.m. on his return from Egypt, Hammarskjold made following points: [2]

1. Report to GA [3] would include series aide-mémoires which he had developed with Fawzi in course of talks in which Hammarskjold, Nasser, Fawzi, and Ali Sabry participated. One of these discussions with Nasser lasted 7 hours. SYG said that at three different times he threatened to walk out and take UN troops out of Egypt.

First aide-mémoire represented an agreement on basis for arrival and duration of stay of UNEF. SYG said he felt he could agree on this, since it was based on resolutions GA had already passed. As to other questions, he felt would have to put his aide-mémoires before GA for acceptance. He intended circulate aide-mémoires tomorrow, Tuesday, after giving Fawzi opportunity see their final form.

Aide-mémoire on basis for arrival of UNEF would relate to question duration of stay and consent of Egypt. Background of this was that Nasser took position if UNEF were now or at any time regarded as an enforcement measure against Egypt, Egypt would have to ask it to leave. SYG did not regard UNEF as an enforcement measure as far as Egypt concerned and in this connection accepted thesis that Egypt's consent to forces' presence in Egypt required, and hence Egypt's consent to continuance forces in Egypt required. UK and France on the other hand did regard UNEF as enforcement measure against Egypt. It was in light this that questions of duration and functions had to be viewed as well as question Canadian participation. Hammarskjold said Egyptians regarded UK as their principal adversary and spoke little about French. They felt British were consolidating position Port Said and had only one motive, which was to get upper hand with respect Canal. Thus Nasser felt that if Egypt were to take Canadian troops now, this would distort

---

[1] Source: Department of State, Central Files, 684A.86/11–1956. Secret; Priority; Limited Distribution. Received at 7:20 p.m.

[2] An unsigned memorandum, dated November 19, which lists the points made by Hammarskjöld during this conversation is *ibid.*, 320/11–1956. The memorandum indicates that the conversation took place at 9 a.m. in Hammarskjöld's office in New York and that Cordier and Barco were also present.

[3] Hammarskjöld's report, entitled "Report of the Secretary-General on basic points for the presence and functioning in Egypt of the United Nations Emergency Force", was circulated to members of the General Assembly on November 20. (U.N. doc. A/3375)

Egyptian popular view of UNEF which at moment regarded UNEF as helpful to Egypt. Canadian troops coming in, according to Nasser, would appear to Egyptian public as according with British view UNEF as enforcement measure against Egypt, and Egyptian attitude toward UNEF would go wrong from beginning. Hammarskjold said participation Canadian troops still open and in his opinion they could be used later along armistice lines, but not in Canal Zone. Nasser took position UNEF would have no function Port Said after withdrawal non-Egyptian forces.

It had been agreed Egyptians should request UN assistance in clearing Canal, and SYG's understanding with Egyptians was that UN would clear Canal "in cooperation with Egypt". He felt this logically followed from fact UNEF was in Egypt with Egypt's consent. He did not believe UNEF could, therefore, undertake clearance of Canal on its own as an enforcement measure, as British contended, any more than that UK and France could stay for that purpose. (The UK and French in their own public statements had said they had intervened to separate the opposing forces of Egypt and Israel.) Hammarskjold pointed out he had stated this to Pearson (Canada) who had said that it was a fair position. SYG believed his position would be supported overwhelmingly by GA and by countries contributing forces. SYG said UK had in mind obtaining settlement on Suez Canal better than the one they had in hand when military action began. He believed this was unrealistic and impossible achieve, and certainly that UNEF could not be used this purpose.

2. Hammarskjold said would circulate aide-mémoire (to be approved by GA) on clearing Canal. [4] In aide-mémoire he would take position that clearance work could begin immediately upon withdrawal non-Egyptian forces. Formula would be that Egyptians requested UN to undertake clearance. Hammarskjold said he expected Danish and Dutch clearance teams would explore possibility obtaining assistance from sub-contractors which might include British experts and equipment. (On this point Fawzi said would not ask Egyptian intelligence to find out where Danes and Dutch got their assistance.) Hammarskjold said he had taken position with Fawzi that as clearance teams begin work, they would be bound to ask for protection, and he would request Egypt agree to have UNEF police clearance action. This would, in his opinion, be accepted by Egypt and would keep UNEF in Canal Zone on that basis.

---

[4] On November 20, Hammarskjöld circulated to members of the General Assembly a "Report of the Secretary-General on the clearing of the Suez Canal." (U.N. doc. A/3376)

3. Hammarskjold said that he had asked Egyptians if they still accepted SYG's formula as a basis for negotiations for settlement Canal question. The Egyptians had said they stood by that undertaking. Their only reservation was on automatic sanctions. Hammarskjold said that while Fawzi was willing to have negotiations on this basis, he was very touchy on timing. Hammarskjold said Nasser had said he could not allow Fawzi to sit down with Pineau, who he believed had tricked them before. SYG said he believed time to press for negotiations was when it was clear UK and French willing negotiate on basis other than London proposals. He regarded it as too late to talk about internationalization. Hammarskjold felt we should lie low for time being on our Suez resolution. He seemed somewhat reluctant but nevertheless willing to take on role of negotiating Suez settlement. He regarded the advisory committee on UNEF to be sufficiently broad in its terms reference to function as advisory committee for a Suez settlement, and in his report to GA would link advisory committee to question of negotiations. Hammarskjold said, however, it was impossible to discuss now with Egypt their attitude on Israeli shipping when Israel had not agreed to leave Gaza or the islands in Gulf of Aqaba.

4. Hammarskjold said that by middle of week a fortnight would have passed since passage of resolution calling for withdrawal forces, and he would have to report to GA on compliance. He proposed, therefore, to ask three parties today:

(a) whether they had withdrawn,
(b) what their plans were for withdrawal, and
(c) what their reasons were for not having withdrawn. A report on their answers would be made to GA in an aide-mémoire Wednesday.

5. On both Suez and Palestine resolutions, Hammarskjold felt we should be extremely careful as to timing and advised that we discuss both resolutions at length with Fawzi which I intend to do unless Department objects. In this connection, Hammarskjold said he had told Nasser that Egyptians should repeat their action of 1948 and themselves sit down with Israel and not wait for other Arabs. He said had pointed out to Nasser that Egypt was stronger politically and morally than had been though weaker militarily, and that this provided opportunities for Egypt to sit down with Israelis. Hammarskjold said he said this several times to Nasser who at no time said no.

6. Hammarskjold said he did not see any "evidence" Soviet activity in Cairo. He said Nasser had referred to fact that he had told the US he had not asked for "volunteers" and that this was true. Nasser had gone on to say, however, that for 10 days he had

been in a very difficult position. If UN did not act, he knew he could get assistance, but if he asked for such assistance, he knew also that he would be letting, as Hammarskjold put it, "all hell break loose". Once UN was acting, he had something to rely on. He appreciated quick, energetic action by UNGA.

7. In summing up, Hammarskjold said he was not optimistic, rather the contrary. We were now facing new risks that British and French would not get out of Port Said, and everything centered around situation there. He said Nasser had requested that UN forces proceed Port Said even if British and French had not yet left because he recognized that with UN forces there, British and French could not undertake new action. Hammarskjold considered stationing UNEF forces Port Said and British and French withdrawal key to situation. Everything else followed from that.

Hammarskjold thinking in terms of GA consideration his various reports by end this week, and is hopeful that progress will be made on Port Said situation before then. Without British and French withdrawal from Port Said, he fears rioting, beginning in Port Said and spreading, which would provide UK with excuse for further intervention. It is at this point he fears Soviet intervention through Syria and Jordan. He also recognizes possibility Israeli action against Jordan and Syria and consequential Soviet intervention.

Recommended action: (1) that we coordinate action on our two resolutions with SYG and do not press either unless we are definitely sure of 2/3 vote;

(2) That I be authorized to see Fawzi and get his views because obviously he is key figure in our ability get 2/3 vote.

Lodge

591.   Memorandum of a Conversation, Department of State, Washington, November 19, 1956 [1]

SUBJECT

Israel

PARTICIPANTS

Mr. Abba Eban, Ambassador of Israel
Mr. Zev Argaman, Minister, Embassy of Israel
G—Mr. Robert Murphy
NE—Mr. Donald C. Bergus

Mr. Eban referred to the wish of the Israel Foreign Minister to pay a courtesy call on the Acting Secretary. He noted that the Acting Secretary had been unable to receive her on November 16 or 20. [2] He stated that Mrs. Meir would be available to visit Washington at the end of this week or the beginning of next and that she would be remaining in the United States until the middle of December.

The Israel Delegation in New York had had many discussions with Western European Foreign Ministers and their representatives. Israel was encouraged by their feeling on Nasserism. Israel felt it essential that Western unity be restored. The longer the present situation continued, the worse it would become.

There had been much public discussion about justification for Israel's action. Everything which Israel had discovered since that action demonstrated its value. Great arms stocks had been discovered in Sinai and Gaza, weapons of the most modern categories had been found, orders to Egyptian troops indicating that their ultimate mission was to destroy Israel had come to hand. A supply of very deadly poison, presumably for use in Israel wells, had been found in Gaza. Interrogation of prisoners had revealed not only Soviet philosophies but also Nazi doctrines. There had been copies of "Mein Kampf" in Arabic everywhere which probably reflected the efforts of Nasser's Nazi German aides. The Egyptian order of battle had been offensive. Had Israel sustained an assault later, world opinion might have been more favorable, but the military risk would have been much greater. Israel had been justified in what it had done.

---

[1] Source: Department of State, Central Files, 684A.86/11–1956. Secret. Drafted by Bergus on November 26.

[2] Hoover had disapproved a memorandum dated November 15 from Rountree, which had recommended that Hoover receive Meir for 15 minutes at his convenience. A note, dated November 19, attached to that memorandum indicates that the recommendation was disapproved "in view of our action regarding Lloyd and Pineau visits" and because of Hoover's heavy schedule. (*Ibid.*, NEA/NE Files: Lot 58 D 398, Memos to the Secretary thru S/S June–Dec)

Mr. Murphy asked how far Israel had intended to go in Egypt. Mr. Eban replied that Israel's objective had been not territory but security. Mr. Eban admitted that the question would be debated in history for a long time, that Israel was distressed at the divergence between the United States and Israel; but felt that the issue now at hand was a solution to the problem. Israel felt that a great mistake had been made by a majority of the members of the United Nations when it faced an eclipse of Nasserism, when his military power was broken and Arab solidarity had been shown to be a myth. There were echoes of Israel's views in the Arab states and strong feelings along these lines in Western Europe. The United Nations had put Nasser back on his feet. This might have been a case where the end would have justified the means.

Mr. Murphy pointed out that among other things there had been a tactical problem in the United Nations. Had there been no United States resolution there might well have been a USSR resolution on the subject. The other statements made by Mr. Eban raised the whole issue of "preventive war" as a justifiable course of international conduct.

Mr. Eban wondered how far we could go in relying on the United Nations as the only and exclusive guide. If the United States made this the only criterion, then the West was at a disadvantage. The United Nations could curb the use of force by free countries but not by the USSR and probably the Arabs. Therefore the USSR had a monopoly of force. The numerical composition of the General Assembly was such that it would not adopt a resolution opposed by the USSR, the Arabs and their Asian friends. Mr. Murphy stated that the General Assembly had passed a resolution on Hungary. The USSR had profited by Near Eastern developments. He mentioned Nehru's developing views on Hungary in response to Indian public opinion on the subject.

Mr. Eban said that the General Assembly would not uphold European, Commonwealth, Mediterranean, or Israel interests. The United Nations Charter had been used to defend the chief violator of the Charter. Mr. Argaman uttered the aphorism about he who comes into equity must come with clean hands. Mr. Murphy commented that as he understood the law both intent and act were factors in leading to a judgment. In this instance it appeared that the only action had been Israeli.

Mr. Eban said that the main problem now was the implementation of the cease-fire and withdrawal resolutions. All depended on the manner of implementation. If the United Nations entered the picture and Israel withdrew then Nasser returned to his previous positions, there would be a new explosion. It was possible to avoid this if implementation were carefully handled. Had Israel withdrawn from Sinai prematurely, the United Nations force would not now be in Egypt. Mr. Eban understood that the Security General was grateful for this.

Mr. Eban would begin his negotiations with the Secretary General on November 20. Israel was prepared to leave the Sinai Peninsula if the United Nations forces occupied keypoints preparatory to a UN-Egyptian agreement for demilitarization of the Peninsula without prejudice to Egyptian sovereignty. With respect to Tiran and the adjoining area, the Israel action had succeeded in opening an international waterway. Israel would pose three alternatives: either leave Israel in Tiran, leave the islands empty, or place a United Nations force there. The same principle applied to Gaza. Gaza could not be demilitarized but all Israel could say was that nothing would be less prudent than to bring Nasser back to Gaza.

There was a great debate going on in Israel with respect to the ultimate disposition of Gaza. The territory was too small to be attractive but the security aspects of the problem might well be overriding. Mr. Murphy asked if Israel wanted United Nations forces in Sinai. Mr. Eban replied yes, to be followed by demilitarization. Mr. Murphy said that it seemed to him that this proposal would have to be imposed on the Egyptians. Mr. Eban said that would depend on what the Egyptians wanted to gain from the present situation. Israel understood that if it asserted a claim to Gaza it would undertake a great responsibility. Israel had stated that it did not want the Egyptians to return. Israel thought that it wanted Gaza, certainly with its original population. The problem of the refugees there would have to be solved in terms of Israel and other capabilities to absorb them. Mr. Pearson of Canada and some Western European representatives had indicated understanding of Israel's position on Gaza.

Mr. Murphy inquired if Israel was in a position to give the facts concerning Soviet equipment captured. Mr. Eban said that Israel was writing a report on the subject and that he had told Mr. Allen Dulles that Israel would provide information. Israel had the idea that the USSR had been preparing to fight for the Canal. Returning to his forthcoming discussions with the Secretary General, Mr. Eban said that he felt Israel's desiderata could be negotiated within the terms of the UNGA resolutions. A fourth point was the Anglo-French position on the Suez Canal; the British and French were interested in what would come in their place.

Mr. Murphy said that we had been encouraged by the apparent willingness of Egypt to accept a United Nations force to occupy the Canal zone and clear the Canal. He hoped that this would give an opportunity to relax the blockade of the Canal.

Mr. Eban turned to the United Nations draft resolution of November 3 on Palestine.[3] He felt that the resolution should make room for the concept of a negotiated settlement. He admitted that negotiations might not be the only way to a settlement but felt that they should not be excluded. He wondered whether the resolution would be passed. The Arabs would oppose it, the USSR might, and then others in Asia and Africa would also oppose it. If it failed of passage then there would be a serious setback. The United States might have to amend this resolution to refer to previous UNGA resolutions. Mr. Eban indicated that this possibility would be distasteful to him.

Mr. Murphy said he had not seen the results of any canvass of United Nations delegations. There was tentatively some hope that the resolution could be passed. Some delegations would doubtless be influenced by developments in the area. Some momentum had to be initiated. Perhaps if the Suez resolution went through first then progress could be made on the Palestine resolution. The United States was not wedded to the present resolution, but felt that we must get away from the present fragile condition where fighting could resume. The problems posed by the Near East crisis were bigger than Nasser.

Mr. Eban said that views varied on statements made by the President and others as to possible United States reactions to Soviet moves in the area. Mr. Eban felt that we had created some uncertainty in the Russian mind. Mr. Murphy said that it was difficult to gage Moscow thinking because of certain indications of instability in the judgment of the men in power there.

Mr. Eban said that Israel would enter the Hungarian debate in the General Assembly. The Soviets could not be more abusive to Israel than they had already been. In the long run, the United States could not hope to compete with the USSR in winning Arab favor. Mr. Eban inquired if a policy had developed with respect to FY 1957 economic assistance to Israel. The Israelis had been informed by ICA that they were ready to proceed once the Department approved.

Mr. Murphy pointed out that current economic aid plans for the Near East were in suspense until we could see how the situation in the area developed. It was much in the mind of the President that if a long-term solution to Near East problems could be achieved that the United States would want to make an important contribution to such a solution.

Mr. Eban mentioned El Al Israel Airline's difficulty in obtaining United States export licenses for spare parts, and the cessation of

---

[3] Reference is to the U.S. draft resolution on Palestine tabled in the General Assembly on November 3; see Document 485.

USSR oil deliveries to Israel. He said that while the major problems affecting the area were important, he did not feel that pressures on Israel were a constructive way of achieving solutions.

---

592.   Editorial Note

At 8:25 p.m. in London (3:25 p.m. in Washington), Ambassador Aldrich telephoned President Eisenhower to inform him that the guess which he had made in telegram 2791 (Document 588) was correct and that he would be sending a full report of his most recent conversation with Macmillan (*infra*). Eisenhower at 3:35 p.m. then telephoned Hoover, who read to the President the complete text of telegram 2791 from London. According to the memorandum of this conversation, prepared in the Office of the President, "Hoover said it is very interesting, in that they are putting proposition up to us. They will either have to withdraw from Egypt, & have their Cabinet fall—or else they would have to renew hostilities, taking over entire Canal. Mr. Hoover's comment: Obviously things are very much in the making there. I think this is one time to sit tight, awaiting his further information."

At 3:45, Eisenhower telephoned Secretary Humphrey concerning Aldrich's report and noted that he and Humphrey had discussed the possibility of a change in the British Government at an earlier time. According to the memorandum of conversation, "The President told him that Amb. Aldrich says part of it is coming about—that there are a lot of conditions we cannot possibly meet. Will discuss it further tomorrow morning. Mr. Humphrey: 'I hate to have a man stick in there, & go to a vote of confidence & get licked.' " (Memorandum of conversations prepared in the Office of the President, November 19; Eisenhower Library, Whitman File, Eisenhower Diaries)

593.   Telegram From the Embassy in the United Kingdom to the Department of State [1]

London, November 19, 1956—10 p.m.

2814. To Acting Secretary from Ambassador. For President and Secretary. Macmillan came to residence tonight at his request. My telegram no 2791 [2] appears to have been correct in every detail. Eden has had physical breakdown and will have to go on vacation immediately, first for one week and then for another, and this will lead to his retirement. Government will be run by triumvirate of Butler, Macmillan and Salisbury. While Macmillan did not say so specifically, I gather that eventual setup will be Butler Prime Minister, Macmillan Foreign Secretary, Lloyd Chancellor of Exchequer, with Salisbury remaining Lord President of Council. Possibly Macmillan might be Prime Minister. First action after Eden's departure for reasons of health will be on withdrawal of British troops from Egypt. Macmillan said, "If you can give us a fig leaf to cover our nakedness I believe we can get a majority of the Cabinet to vote for such withdrawal without requiring conditions in connection with location of United Nations Forces and methods of re-opening and operating Canal, although younger members of the Cabinet will be strongly opposed."

Macmillan is desperately anxious to see the President at earliest possible opportunity and apparently consideration being given to appointment of Macmillan as Deputy Prime Minister during Eden's absence in order that such meeting might take place at once after withdrawal British troops.

Situation moving with great rapidity. Macmillan left me to see Eden and as he was leaving he asked me if I would be available to him at any minute, day or night. I replied that that was what I was here for and that I would deem it a great privilege if he would keep constantly in touch with me. Obviously, Macmillan asked me not to communicate all of this to anyone at this moment and I am therefore sending this message in utmost confidence.

Aldrich

---

[1] Source: Department of State, Central Files, 974.7301/11–1956. Top Secret; Niact. Received at 7:34 p.m. A copy in the Eisenhower Library, Whitman File, Dulles–Herter Series bears the handwritten notation: "Noted by President."
[2] Document 588.

594.   Telegram From the Embassy in Egypt to the Department of State [1]

Cairo, November 19, 1956—3 p.m.

1571. Deptel 1564 [2] instructing discuss volunteer question with Hammarskjold although serviced as missing only received 2145 yesterday following his departure. However, following action along general line reference telegram had already been taken.

(1) Recent discussions with Nasser on dealings with Soviets, including volunteers, reported Embassy telegrams 1491, 1512 and 1536. [3] Burden these messages was that only affirmative action taken by GOE was general appeal for volunteers; that Soviets had however made sweeping offers of assistance to Egypt, including volunteers; that no implementing action re volunteers had been taken because of GOE decision not to reply to Soviet offer; that GOE does not foresee changing this policy but cannot guarantee what it might do in future if hand forced.

(2) This attitude reflected yesterday in interview of Aly Sabry with American press in which reported to have said that, although Egypt had made general appeal for volunteers on November 6, it had delayed acceptances in order avoid increasing world tension. Sabry quoted as saying "at the moment we are counting on UN to solve this problem. But if hostilities start again we will accept help from anyone". To be noted that Sabry's observations related to demand that there should be no delay in British-French withdrawal, which might be seen as reason for his having taken stronger public position than did Nasser when speaking privately. However, should be emphasized that in both cases departure from present policy seen as possibility in event changed circumstances inimical to Egypt.

(3) Although then without instructions Embassy took liberty passing information referred to in paragraph 1 this telegram to Hammarskjold via Colonel Ely [4] on informal basis in order he might

---

[1] Source: Department of State, Central Files, 684A.86/11–1956. Secret; Received at 12:07 a.m., November 20. Repeated to London, Paris, Moscow, and USUN.

[2] Document 576.

[3] Dated November 14, November 15, and November 16, respectively, none printed. (All in Department of State, Central File 684A.86)

[4] Lieutenant Colonel David R. Ely of the Canadian Army was the UNTSO liaison officer at Cairo.

have for background in discussions with Nasser (Embassy telegram 1443). [5] He did not have occasion however discuss with him.

Hare

---

[5] The reference is evidently in error. Telegram 1443, November 11, concerns an unrelated subject. (Department of State, Central Files, 474.116/11–1156)

---

595.   Memorandum From the Counselor of the Department of State (MacArthur) to the Acting Secretary of State [1]

Washington, November 20, 1956.

MR. HOOVER: In the course of my 8:30 meeting at the White House this morning, the President brought up the question of the great undependability and unreliability of Nasser . . . .

The President said he thought the person to build up was King Saud, who was a great spiritual leader and keeper of the holy places, etc.

The President said he had in mind, and had mentioned to you yesterday, the possibility of Bob Anderson undertaking a trip to meet with Saud. Bob could point out that if the present situation continued, and if Nasser controlled the oil flow through the Canal and his influence on the Syrians, a situation could arise which could well be met by the West. For example, oil production in Texas could be doubled, there could be great increases in Venezuelan and Canadian production, and if we ever started on this course, we could be a competitor of Saudi Arabia for selling oil and it would be very difficult to cut back. In other words the Saudi Arabia economic future based on oil was being risked by Nasser's overweening ambitions, etc.

The President said he knew you were considering the feasibility and desirability of some such positive approach, and simply mentioned it to me because of his continuing interest in it.

DMacA

---

[1] Source: Department of State, Central Files, 774.11/11–2056. Top Secret.

596.   Memorandum of a Conference With the President, White House, Washington, November 20, 1956, 5:30 p.m. [1]

OTHERS PRESENT

> Secretary Humphrey
> Secretary Hoover
> Colonel Goodpaster

Mr. Humphrey referred to cables from the United Kingdom indicating the possibility of a Cabinet change, [2] and commented that, in his opinion, Butler would be the stronger of the two men being mentioned. The President said he has always thought most highly of Macmillan, who is a straight, fine man, and so far as he is concerned the outstanding one of the British he served with during the war.

Mr. Hoover showed the President a memorandum [3] that had been drafted in State concerning the next steps in the Suez matter affecting Britain. He and the President thought the United States might say that the day the British agree to start withdrawing at once, Under Secretary Burgess will be over to see how the financial and economic problems can be faced.

Mr. Humphrey said he had made a study of what could be done to help financially if we were to decide to do so. The French can, through taking out their money in the World Bank and borrowing the same amount in addition, obtain about $260 million. The UK can obtain $560 million by the same method. The Export-Import Bank could establish a credit of $600 million with which the British could pay for exports from the United States to Britain. He said the British should definitely not go to U.S. banks to try to obtain the $600 million they want. There is not that much free money, and their attempt would simply throw the financial community into disorder. He indicated that the other countries in Western Europe (except for Italy to which some help could be given), are in good shape dollar-wise.

Mr. Hoover said that Ambassador Brosio had been in to see him, and had asked for the oil coming through the Tapline for Italy. Mr. Hoover had told him he understood the OEEC was working on the basis of share and share alike, both as regards oil and dollar burden.

Mr. Humphrey said that the key point in his mind was that we *are* in position to supply the "fig leaf" which the British say they

---

[1] Source: Eisenhower Library, Whitman File, Eisenhower Diaries. Top Secret. Drafted by Goodpaster on November 21.

[2] See telegrams 2791 and 2814, Documents 588 and 593.

[3] Not printed. (Eisenhower Library, Whitman File, Dulles–Herter Series) Much of the contents of the memorandum were sent to London in telegram 3631, *infra.*

need to cover their nakedness in withdrawing from the Suez. We can furnish dollars to meet stringent needs, providing they start to get out of the Suez at once.

The President thought that if we have confirmed that such help on our part would be acceptable to the Saudi-Arabians and to the Egyptians, we could say publicly that we would help out as soon as the French and the British agree to start getting out of Suez at once. Mr. Humphrey thought we should simply indicate this in an informal way to the British now, rather than publicly. The President thought we should say to Saud that as soon as the British and French start getting out, we would like to know that he is agreeable to our trying to restore the situation (including restoring his European markets). Mr. Hoover said we had better wait for the start of the British and French out-movement. To approach Saud now may be too early. He said that the problem is now one of delicate timing, and the President and Mr. Humphrey strongly agreed.

The President thought that Mr. Hoover should tell Aldrich of the sequence that is shaping up in our mind, and suggested that he advise Butler or Macmillan to get on the phone with Humphrey or Hoover tomorrow, and that the latter tell what could be done if the United States so decides—and if the British and French promptly move to settle the Suez situation. Mr. Humphrey said we could say generally that we will be glad to supply the fig leaf and to support them financially.

The President said the sequence as he saw it was as follows: First, we are ready to talk about help as soon as the pre-condition (French and British initiation of withdrawal) is established; second, on knowing that the British and French forces will comply with a withdrawal undertaking at once, we would talk to the Arabs to obtain the removal of any objections they may have regarding the provision of oil to Western Europe; third, we will then talk the details of money assistance with the British.

Mr. Hoover questioned whether the British might not have another idea in mind when they speak of the "fig leaf." They might want us to take the responsibility for obtaining some satisfaction internationally which they can then offer as their reason for leaving the Canal. Mr. Humphrey thought that if they have the idea we are receptive to a request for help that is all they are looking for. The President said we can simply couch our statement along the lines "on the assumption stated by Macmillan (that is, that they will announce at once an immediate withdrawal) they can be assured of our sympathetic consultation and help." Also that Macmillan can meet with him on that assumption. There was discussion as to how this could be conveyed to the British, considering the unknown relationship as between Butler and Macmillan at the present time.

The President thought we could, through Aldrich, ask the Foreign Office to present the matter to the Government. The possibility of having Aldrich advise Macmillan and Butler together, privately, was also discussed. Mr. Humphrey thought we should try to find out from Aldrich whether he could meet with both without embarrassment. The President thought we could simply tell Aldrich we would assume that he could give the message to Butler and Macmillan. At this point the President put in a phone call for Aldrich. In further discussion, the President said we must keep the whole development on the basis of "their assumptions," not introducing conditions of our own. He saw merit in Burgess making the trip, and Mr. Hoover agreed.

The President and the others saw the possibility of some blessings in disguise coming to Britain out of this affair, in the form of impelling them to accept the common market. The President said that Bech of Luxemburg, for whom he has the highest regard of any European statesman, said that if the EDC had come into existence when planned he felt sure there would have been no Suez problem, and no European problem now.

At this point the President's phone call to Aldrich came through, and the President asked him if he could talk to Butler and Macmillan, (Aldrich apparently said he could) and mentioned the possibility of Burgess making a trip in the next day or two. [4]

After the phone call Mr. Humphrey said that we must talk to the Arabs soon, and tell them that we are putting great pressure on trying to get the troops out of Suez and we need their agreement to actions to bolster up Europe after this is done—a selling job needs to be done, in which we would point out that the effect of our action is to re-establish their oil markets. He also wondered whether we could not approach Nasser and tell him that he will not get value out of the Canal as long as it cannot be used in confidence. Great efforts will be made to circumvent its use. He must re-establish confidence, and this can only be done through some acceptable form of international control. He could then increase his tolls and improve his income. Mr. Hoover said that the Canal income will be taken up in paying off the Canal Company, and in widening and deepening it. He did not think Nasser could be relied upon in any way. He said in fact that before this attack occurred the other Arab leaders were

---

[4] In this conversation, which began at 6:15 p.m., Eisenhower instructed Aldrich to bring Butler and Macmillan together informally and to tell them that "we are interested and sympathetic, and, as soon as things happen that we anticipate, we can furnish 'a lot of fig leaves.' " Eisenhower also asked whether this approach would "be enough to get the boys moving?" Aldrich responded that he thought it would be. (Transcript of telephone conversation prepared in the Office of the President; Eisenhower Library, Whitman File, Eisenhower Diaries)

beginning to turn against him. The President recalled how he has stressed the importance of building up King Saud.

Mr. Hoover finally pointed out that if the British and French withdraw, Nasser must then come to an agreement with the UN, or the whole world would turn on him.

G
Colonel, CE, US Army

---

597.   Telegram From the Department of State to the Embassy in the United Kingdom [1]

Washington, November 20, 1956—8:35 p.m.

3631. Eyes only Ambassador from Acting Secretary. Re the President's telephone conversation with you this evening, he suggests you should see Macmillan and Butler together tomorrow, informing them we have sincere sympathy and understanding for UK financial difficulties and would like to be of assistance. However, if we undertook commitments before UK and French forces are withdrawn, we would be in the position of going back upon a matter of major principle, which we had no alternative but to adopt. We would also feel that there should be some hope of a prompt solution to the Suez Canal problem on basis of an agreement which is both reasonable and obtainable. The purpose of your talk with them tomorrow would not be to reach an agreement but primarily to let them know we are most sympathetic with their position which you have outlined in your wires. Obviously we consider the British our close friends and allies. (It is of utmost importance that substance of your talk with Macmillan and Butler be not divulged. Any leaks could have profoundly adverse effect on our ability to help and on outcome present delicate situation in the UN.)

FYI We also have in mind possibility of sending Randolph Burgess to London so you and he could have private talk with Macmillan and Butler (in view UK domestic political situation we believe you should see Macmillan and Butler together). Since Burgess visit could not be kept secret we would have to decide what could be said in response to queries as to purpose visit. Re tactics we

---

[1] Source: Department of State, Central Files, 841.10/11–2056. Top Secret; Niact. Drafted by MacArthur, revised by Hoover, and approved by Greene.

thought you might give informal dinner following which discussions could take place. This would give appearance of informal and partly social meeting and thus perhaps avoid creating impression in minds certain Arab-Asians notably Egyptians that we preparing give financial support to UK when they and French have not complied with UN Resolution re withdrawal of troops. It would be made clear to British in advance that purpose of visit is not conduct negotiations but to discuss difficult UK financial situation and ascertain in some detail their plans for meeting it.

You and Burgess would make clear while we have sympathy for UK financial plight, our ability assist dependent upon UK and French compliance with UN Resolution as well as nature and extent UK financial requirements. Similarly it would be pointed out our ability help Britain also dependent upon working out promptly solution to Suez Canal problem so oil on which their economy so heavily dependent can flow uninterruptedly on basis of agreement which is reasonably dependable and reasonably attainable. Would say we understand Lloyd has informed Hammarskjold UK would accept as basis for agreement memo which UN SYG gave Egyptian FonMin Fawzi and was accepted by him with one reservation. This important since it clear peaceful solution Suez Canal issue on basis Menzies proposal, rejected by Egypt, is not obtainable.

To summarize, you and Burgess would make clear while we sympathetic, our ability to aid depends in final analysis on constructive action by Britain re immediate problems with which they are faced. Therefore in addition to info you would hope obtain re their financial and economic plans and problems including exposure any pertinent financial and political commitments it also of greatest importance know their plans re compliance with UN Resolution and reaching settlement Suez Canal issue.

You and Burgess would say you and he will report all British say to Washington in light of which further discussions might be arranged to consider steps leading to realistic solution. Also at such time there would obviously be other matters we would wish discuss with UK.

Finally you and Burgess would say we proceeding on assumption UK has made no commitments to either French or Israelis re settlement Suez or Arab-Israel problems, but if this assumption not correct, we must know any such commitment before proceeding.

We would like your comments on above proposal, which should of course not be discussed with other than your Deputy Chief of Mission, and which would be dependent upon Macmillan's and Butler's reaction to your conversation. End FYI.

Hoover

598.   **Telegram From the Embassy in the United Kingdom to the Department of State** [1]

London, November 21, 1956—1 p.m.

2841. Eyes only to Acting Secretary from Ambassador for Secretary and President. I saw Butler and Macmillan together at the residence at 10 o'clock this morning. They were most grateful for the President's assurances of sympathy conveyed in his telephone conversation with me last night. They said that the government's policy concerning withdrawal of British troops from Egypt must be determined within the next two days and announcement thereof made in the House of Commons. Butler said that they have not yet received Hammarskjold's report and that naturally the substance of that report would have an important bearing on the consideration by the Cabinet of details of this policy. He further said, however, that he thought there was no reason to suppose that the decision of the Cabinet would not be to withdraw the British troops from Egypt and depend on the United Nations to bring about a solution of the controversies between Israel and Egypt and insure the early opening of the Canal and its operation under proper auspices. Macmillan emphatically concurred with this statement. Butler and Macmillan left me at 10:30 to go to a Cabinet meeting and they said that they would advise me as soon as possible conclusions which had been reached with regard to policy.

It was quite apparent that both Butler and Macmillan are still very anxious that Macmillan and possibly Butler also should see the President as soon as the situation has reached a point where this would be in accord with President's policy.

I did not of course discuss with them Dept's thinking on possible Burgess visit to London as set forth in Deptel 3631. [2] Their concern today was not with the financial problems facing them but with the political situation and the basic decision the Cabinet will have to make immediately in that connection. However, I did mention as indicative of the President's appreciation of the seriousness of the financial problem the possibility that Burgess might be sent to London for private talk if such a visit should prove desirable. My own feeling is that if British Cabinet makes correct decision within next two days it would be very much better for Butler and

---

[1] Source: Department of State, Central Files, 841.10/11–2156. Top Secret; Niact; Presidential Handling. Received at 10:34 a.m. A copy is in the Eisenhower Library, Whitman File, Dulles–Herter Series.

[2] *Supra.*

Macmillan or Macmillan alone to go to Washington immediately rather than have a junior minister come over here.

Aldrich

---

599.   Memorandum of a Telephone Conversation Between the President and the Secretary of the Treasury (Humphrey), Washington, November 21, 1956, 3:07 p.m. [1]

President called Secretary Humphrey. Apparently "fig leaves" did not mean merely financial help. It may have been something else that we have not even guessed. Humphrey said he had a hunch it was something else, as he thought had Hoover. Said something had come through on the ticker to indicate that the UN would undertake to close [clean] up the Canal. He questioned whether Burgess should go over to England now, said he thought the US had accomplished the purpose we wanted to accomplish—it looks to him as though it is up to the British to make the next move. He said if he were doing it alone, he would stick still now and wait until we hear further from them. The President said "that is correct." He said further that somewhere as between the British and ourselves there was a vagueness, not a frankness that he would like. We don't get the points cleared up that we would like. Humphrey agreed that the only way there would be frankness would be by a meeting. He said he thought "one of them" (Butler or Macmillan) ought to come over here.

President suggested an OEEC meeting, but Humphrey is afraid of OEEC trying to get in and decide where the money the United States will lend will go. He does not want another "Marshall Plan."

President said he made suggestion because of timing, does not want to lose everything we have gained. He repeated his conversation with the Prime Minister of Tunisia. [2] He said he was not going to fall under Nasser. . . .

Humphrey said we have got to keep working with the Arabs. We are on their side until these fellows get out. After they get out, we ought to be in the position of neutral friend of both that both can trust to try to work out a fair deal. The President agreed.

---

[1] Source: Eisenhower Library, Whitman File, Eisenhower Diaries. Prepared in the Office of the President.

[2] For the memorandum of this conversation, see vol. XVIII, p. 656.

Humphrey reported that Hoover talked to the Italian Ambassador and the Italian Ambassador repeated to the press everything he said.[3] He referred again to the fact he did not want OEEC to divvy up the money. He said we want to be generous, but at the same time watch our step and certainly make our own decisions.

---

[3] The story appeared in *The New York Times*, November 21.

---

600.   Telegram From the Department of State to the Embassy in the United Kingdom[1]

Washington, November 21, 1956—9 p.m.

3665. Eyes only Ambassador from Acting Secretary. Urtel 2814[2] was read with much interest and reviewed today at highest level. We do not believe meeting with Butler and Macmillan would be feasible until possibly week of December 3. We now have under active review probable time table of events in Europe and Middle East which may affect timing of meeting.[3] Would appreciate your comments and views.

We remain firm in our conviction that withdrawal of troops is of prime urgency and must be moving toward accomplishment before other important questions can be considered.

Foregoing for your background information only.

Hoover

---

[1] Source: Department of State, Central Files, 974.7301/11–1956. Top Secret; Priority. Drafted by Hoover and approved by Greene who signed for Hoover.
[2] Document 593.
[3] At 4 p.m., November 21, the President met with the National Security Council and other key government officials to discuss the Department of State's short-term and long-term plans in the Middle East. Documentation on the meeting and on development of the Eisenhower Doctrine is scheduled for publication in volume XII.

601.   Editorial Note

On November 21, the Government of Israel submitted to Secretary-General Hammarskjöld an aide-mémoire in which it affirmed that there had been withdrawal of Israeli forces for varying distances along the entire Egyptian front. The Israeli Government also reaffirmed the position conveyed to Hammarskjöld on November 8 that it would withdraw its forces from Egypt immediately upon the conclusion of satisfactory arrangements with the United Nations. The text of the aide-mémoire, which was sent to Hammarskjöld under cover of a letter by Eban, was circulated as Annex II to the Secretary-General's report of November 21 on compliance with General Assembly Resolutions 997 (ES–I) and 1002 (ES–I). (U.N. doc. A/3384)

602.   Telegram From the Embassy in the United Kingdom to the Department of State [1]

London, November 22, 1956—2 p.m.

2871. Eyes only to Acting Secretary from Ambassador for Secretary and President. Macmillan called me this morning to say that, while the position of Cabinet remains precarious, it has been decided that the British will remove one battalion from Egypt immediately and will continue withdrawal to completion as UN forces move in. Lloyd will make a statement to this effect in the UN tomorrow, adding that in taking this step British are assuming that the UN will (a) undertake and carry out the immediate clearance of the Canal and will proceed with the establishment through negotiation of arrangements for its free and dependable operation as an international waterway and (b) will endeavor bring about Arab-Israeli settlement. Macmillan said this decision was arrived at only after most serious deliberation and will inevitably arouse major opposition within the Conservative Party. Macmillan continued that it was even possible that the result of the decision might be that the government would lose its Conservative majority for this policy. In reply to my comment that after all he did not need a majority of the Conserva-

---

[1] Source: Department of State, Central Files, 684A.86/11–2256. Top Secret; Niact; Presidential Handling. Received at 11:51 a.m. A copy is in Eisenhower Library, Whitman File, Dulles–Herter Series.

tive Party to carry this policy through the House he replied that this would bring about the fall of the government. I then said that regardless of anything of that sort it was essential that the troops be withdrawn immediately, to which statement Macmillan assented. In the circumstances Macmillan urged that it would be extremely helpful and might even be controlling on the ability of the government to carry through with this policy for the US representative in the UN to give immediate approval of the reasonableness of the British position as stated by Lloyd. If Lodge does this it would head off possible extreme demands from other UN groups for immediate unconditional withdrawal which would be entirely unacceptable in Britain and complicate the British Government's position to the extent of dangerously jeopardizing their ability to maintain the policy of prompt and complete withdrawal. It would further be highly desirable that this US endorsement of this specific UK step be followed quickly by a more general statement by the President to the effect that the US is not prepared to abandon the Middle East to Communism and, through the United Nations, will continue to press for the solution of the Canal problem through some form of international operation of the Canal. Macmillan stressed the importance of statements by both Lodge and President. Manifestly he would wish the President's support to be in the strongest terms feasible but my impression is that the fact of the President's endorsement is more controlling than the substance.

Macmillan indicated British Cabinet changes which he has previously forecast will take place within the next few days.

Aldrich

---

603. Telegram From the Mission at the United Nations to the Department of State [1]

New York, November 22, 1956—11 p.m.

Delga 172. Re Palestine—Suez. I saw Lloyd at his request late this afternoon. In response his question as to where we stood (which was way he opened conversation), I told him I felt Hammarskjold's intention to employ Mr. McCloy, General Wheeler and General Clay

---

[1] Source: Department of State, Central Files, 684A.86/11–2256. Secret; Priority; Limited Distribution. Received at 12:29 a.m., November 23.

in operation of clearing Canal [2] was kind of development on which British could justify their immediate withdrawal. I made clear US regarded withdrawal as key element in present situation. Once it had begun remaining matters could proceed.

Lloyd responded most favorably to use of McCloy, Wheeler and Clay, expressing greatest confidence in their abilities effectively proceed in clearance operation. Lloyd then referred to his letter to Hammarskjold (Annex 3, document A/3384) [3] in which UK indicated decision withdraw at once an infantry battalion. He stressed UK withdrawal would proceed "as UN force becomes effective". He said he had agreed with Hammarskjold not to equate UK withdrawal to arrival UNEF on man for man basis. In fact UK battalion would leave Port Said and only company of UNEF would go in.

Lloyd said timing of withdrawal had to be considered as practical matter. This, he asserted, was fact and not excuse. He noted with pleasure Ceylon Prime Minister Bandaranaike had in General Assembly debate speech today, at Lloyd's request, made this very point.

In Lloyd's opinion exact details on withdrawal Anglo-French forces and stationing UNEF would have be worked out between General Burns and British General in command. He felt Burns himself would insist on this as only practical manner of proceeding. Lloyd referred in this connection to instability in Egypt, saying things "could go sour at any minute". For this reason Lloyd felt, and he believed Burns would agree, that command structure, support, etc., which would take some time, would have to be established and consequently all Anglo-French forces could not depart immediately.

Lloyd then referred to problem of clearing Canal. In British view, there were both long-range and immediate aspects this problem. As far as long-range aspects concerned, he was confident and most pleased with choice of McCloy, Wheeler and Clay, and in their ability proceed. He felt, however, it would take at least fortnight before their part in clearance operation would begin take hold. As Lloyd understood it McCloy and Wheeler would proceed to arrange

---

[2] On November 24, Hammarskjöld appointed a three-member team to handle the clearance of the Suez Canal. Lieutenant General Raymond A. Wheeler, formerly of the U.S. Army Engineer Corps, was to assist Hammarskjöld in organizing the technical aspects of the project. John J. McCloy, Chairman of the Board of the Chase Manhattan Bank, was to advise Hammarskjöld and Wheeler on financial problems. Alfred George Katzin, a Deputy Under Secretary in the U.N. Secretariat, was appointed to assist Hammarskjöld within the Secretariat. (*The New York Times*, November 25) General Lucius Clay evidently was not formally involved in the Canal clearance operation.

[3] "Report of the Secretary-General on compliance with General Assembly resolutions 997 (ES–I) and 1002 (ES–I)," November 21, U.N. doc. A/3384. Lloyd's letter to Hammarskjöld is dated November 21.

international consortium, negotiating contracts with salvage firms, and work out financial arrangements. All this would then have to come back to GA for approval. Given most speedy accomplishment these steps, he felt fortnight would be required.

In strongest terms, Lloyd objected to final paragraph SYG's report on arrangements for clearance Canal (document A/3376)[4] if it were taken at face value to mean all Anglo-French forces must be out before any clearance could begin. He felt it was "dangerous nonsense" to tie withdrawal as a precondition to beginning clearance. He said fortnight's loss of time could make all difference to smaller European countries. He said he felt Britain had sufficient reserves to withstand such delay and, therefore, he was arguing more in behalf other countries than for UK.

Lloyd said he had presented this argument to all members of Commonwealth and to members of SYG's advisory committee and they were generally sympathetic. Lloyd hoped build up considerable body opinion in GA on this point of view and felt he had made good start with Ceylon's reference to this this afternoon.

[Here follows discussion of technicalities related to the clearing of the Suez Canal.]

Lloyd concluded conversation by stressing importance UK Government attaches to clearing Canal forthwith. He said if Assembly refused authorize clearance operation to proceed on emergency basis, UK might have reconsider question of withdrawal. UK felt salvage operation should proceed "pari passu."

At same time withdrawals proceeding, Lloyd made strong plea for US to make public statement in GA supporting UK position on emergency nature of clearance and expressing confidence in UK announced intention withdrawal. He felt this most important in reestablishing Anglo-American solidarity and averting present anti-American trend in British public opinion.

Following is type of statement I would propose to incorporate into a speech on resolution containing SYG's report. This would be in response Lloyd's request and only if UK can give US indications actual withdrawal of UK battalion has begun:

"This looks like real progress. Let us hope that this foreshadows speedy compliance with the General Assembly resolution for withdrawal of all non-Egyptian troops. I have just been informed that the (blank) battalion has just stepped on board the (blank) at (blank) a.m. this morning heading for (blank)".

---

[4] "Report of the Secretary-General on the clearing of the Suez Canal," November 20.

Such a statement pleased UK and tends to commit them, without going beyond the facts. In telecon with Lodge Acting Secretary approved gist thereof. [5]

Lodge

---

[5] No account of this conversation has been found in Department of State files.

---

604.   Memorandum of a Conference With the President, White House, Washington, November 23, 1956, Noon [1]

OTHERS PRESENT

Secretary Hoover
Mr. MacArthur
Colonel Goodpaster

I joined the meeting a few minutes after it had begun. Mr. Hoover was saying that State's study indicated that it would not be possible to set a time table of precise dates. The President said he agreed, but what he was looking for was the sequential order in which certain conditions might be expected to develop or be created. Mr. Hoover said that they did believe that this could be prepared.

Mr. Hoover next reported to the President regarding U.S. action on two resolutions affecting the Suez. The first of these is being put in by the Secretary General, and we intend to support it. [2] The second is an Afro-Asian resolution, which tends to embarrass Brit-

---

[1] Source: Eisenhower Library, Whitman File, Eisenhower Diaries. Top Secret. Drafted by Goodpaster. According to the record of the President's Daily Appointments, this meeting actually began at 11:45 a.m., and Goodpaster joined it at 11:57 a.m.

[2] Reference is to the draft resolution, the text of which Hammarskjöld handed to Lodge in New York on November 22. Under its operative paragraphs, the draft resolution provided that the General Assembly would note with approval the aide-mémoire of November 17, which contained the understanding reached by the Secretary-General and the Egyptian Government concerning the basis for the presence and function of UNEF in Egypt (Annex to Secretary-General's report of November 20, U.N. doc. A/3376) and the actions taken thus far by Hammarskjöld in connection with arrangements for clearing the Suez Canal. The draft also provided that the General Assembly would authorize Hammarskjöld to proceed with the exploration and negotiation of agreements so that the clearing operations might speedily and effectively be undertaken. The text of this draft resolution was transmitted to the Department of State along with Hammarskjöld's request that the United States sponsor the resolution in Delga 164, November 22. (Department of State, Central Files, 320.5780/11–2256)

ain; on this we plan to abstain.[3] The President pointed out that, if the Secretary General's resolution carries, the second one is not necessary.

Mr. Hoover said that State is exerting all possible pressure to get the UN forces into the Suez. Hammarskjold is progressing slowly—now planning to take until about December 7th, and we are trying to accelerate the movement.

Mr. Hoover said he planned to have Ambassador Caccia in for a talk regarding the latter's query whether we were going to consult with the British.[4] He proposed to say that we have consulted steadily. On their side, they have maintained practically a blackout for the last five weeks, and have not consulted us in advance of decisions or actions. Mr. Hoover said he will ask if they intend to start consulting us now. The President said he should stress that we are avoiding anything that can be interpreted as abandoning the UN position.

Mr. Hoover said the oil situation is becoming very critical. European countries are feeling the pressure, and are putting pressure on us. Although the companies are doing a good job, efficiency is below what it could be with pooling. The psychological factor—the feeling of the Europeans as to whether we are supporting them or not—is assuming major importance. In his opinion we can only delay for another 24 hours or so. He said that we have sent background information to all of our embassies, giving special emphasis to elements of our policy as the different areas require. The President said he thought Mr. Hoover should tell Caccia that the first thing we must all give our attention to is helping out on oil. But in order to do that, we must stay 4-square with the UN, so Britain must take some preliminary actions. He was certain that we should tell King Saud as the British take certain actions we feel that we should take certain measures of support. He thought this should

---

[3] Reference is to a draft resolution cosponsored by 20 Afro-Asian nations, which was circulated to members of the General Assembly on November 22. (U.N. doc. A/ 3385) This draft resolution reiterated previous calls to Great Britain, France, and Israel to comply with U.N. resolutions requiring withdrawal from occupied territories. Delga 168, November 22, which transmitted the text of the draft resolution to the Department of State, also noted that according to Ramsbotham, the British Government would take it very hard if the United States supported this resolution, as Great Britain was carrying out its withdrawal in terms stated by the United States and Canada during previous debates, that is, phased withdrawal as soon as possible following the arrival and functioning of UNEF. (Department of State, Central Files, 684A.86/ 11–2256)

[4] During the evening of November 21, Ambassador Caccia had called on Hoover to deliver an oral message from Foreign Secretary Lloyd inquiring whether the United States was prepared to discuss Middle Eastern problems with the British at that time or whether the United States expected the British Government to make its own decisions for the area without consultation. (Telegram 3666 to London, November 21; ibid.)

be explained to all the Arab countries, excepting Egypt. Mr. Hoover referred to reports that Egypt had called on Saud to supply a quantity of oil, and to pay for it out of his own funds, and that Saud was doing so.

The President thought that we are in a period in which we can strengthen our bilateral arrangements with the various Arab countries, not being so bound as in the past by the Arab-Israel dispute. These might tend to bring Egypt into an appropriate role. He would be prepared to take some bold constructive action in this regard. Mr. Hoover said that Egypt has been caught instigating violence in Libya and Lebanon, and there was discussion of the possibility of inducing those countries to break off diplomatic relations with Egypt. [5]

[Here follows discussion of unrelated subjects.] [6]

G

Colonel, CE, US Army

---

[5] During the Acting Secretary's Staff Meeting that morning, the growing pressure on Lebanese President Camille Chamoun and the possibility of Egyptian involvement was discussed. (Tentative Notes by Greene, November 23; *ibid.*, Secretary's Staff Meetings: Lot 63 D 75)

[6] Additional documentation indicates that other developments took place at this meeting that are not recorded here. According to a handwritten notation on this memorandum, Hoover handed to Eisenhower during the meeting an unsigned memorandum, dated November 23, containing a brief discussion of Macmillan's suggestion that Lodge and Eisenhower make statements endorsing a position to be expressed in a forthcoming speech by Lloyd (see telegram 2871, Document 602). The memorandum, initialed by Eisenhower, recommended that the United States await Lloyd's statement before making a decision. (Eisenhower Library, Whitman File, International File)

Attached to the Department of State file copy of the memorandum printed here is a separate unsigned, undated memorandum entitled "Call on President" which contains a list of items which Hoover intended to raise with Eisenhower on November 23 and handwritten notations, presumably by Hoover, describing the President's reaction. In addition to several points recorded here, it notes that Eisenhower preferred that Macmillan alone, rather than Butler or the two together, should visit the United States and that the timing should be dependent upon a withdrawal of forces from Egypt, an agreement with the Secretary-General on the Canal, and the attitude of the Arabs (which would probably be satisfactory after withdrawal). Eisenhower also agreed that the French could come later if they wished and that once a favorable reply was received from King Saud (see telegram 182, Document 586), the United States could proceed immediately with the MEEC plan. (Department of State, Central Files, 684A.86/11–2356)

605.   Telegram From the Department of State to the Embassy in the United Kingdom [1]

Washington, November 23, 1956—7:51 p.m.

3702. Eyes only for Ambassador. Ref Deptel 3666. [2] Acting Secretary received Caccia today in response to latter's approach of November 21 on question of consultation with British on Middle Eastern problems. Hoover said he had been surprised by Lloyd's proposal that we now discuss these problems in view of "blackout" of information from British side over past five weeks. He said we had brought this situation to attention of British Government on several occasions to no effect and he inquired whether Caccia's approach of November 21 indicates fundamental change of view on part of British Government. If so we would of course welcome it. Hoover pointed out, however, that British must recognize much must be done if unqualified trust is once again to be established between our two countries.

Caccia said he could state flatly that British Government does desire reestablish close relationship which formerly existed and wishes to discuss urgently many problems of vital importance to UK. Acting Secretary replied that once full compliance with UN resolutions re Suez crisis is effected we will be in position to enter into full consultation on these matters. Caccia obviously not completely satisfied with this reply and pointed out British Government greatly concerned lest problems concerning UN force and withdrawal UK-French forces be solved in such a way as to ignore British position and hand Nasser complete victory. Hoover repeated US Government's conviction that introduction of UN force and phased withdrawal UK-French force should take place without delay and that once this is well under way we can enter into consultation with British on basic issues.

Hoover

---

[1] Source: Department of State, Central Files, 684A.86/11–2356. Top Secret; Priority. Drafted by Elbrick, cleared by Murphy, and approved by Elbrick who signed for Hoover.

[2] See footnote 4, *supra.*

606.   Telegram From the Mission at the United Nations to the Department of State [1]

New York, November 23, 1956—8 p.m.

Delga 178. Re Palestine—Suez. Pineau invited me to lunch at his apartment today. Present also were Alphand and Broustra. The tone was very different from last visit when he not only expressed no regrets for what had been done in the Near East, but also said he was sorry they had not gone further. Today it was evident they wanted to get out. He said as far as he was concerned he would be willing to let General Burns decide the question of timing of withdrawal of all Anglo-French forces. I said that it was a fine thing to have said it in private but what we need is something to be said in public. Would he be willing to say it in public? He said he would say it from the GA rostrum. (This could still be done by French, but Pineau himself departs for Paris tonight.)

I told Hammarskjold of this and he thought it extremely helpful.

Pineau and Alphand next talked to Lloyd and Dixon. Alphand told me later they were completely unsuccessful and that Lloyd had refused to change. [2] Alphand said Lloyd's entire preoccupation appeared to be with British domestic politics and the effect on Conservative Party fortunes of leaving the timing of the withdrawal of forces up to General Burns.

I then had a long talk with Lloyd, pointing out if he were to agree to this statement he was actually agreeing only to something that would happen in any event and which last night he had said privately to me was satisfactory. [3]

Lloyd replied by saying that he planned to vote no on the paragraph one of the Afro-Asian resolution which he called the "compulsory paragraph". He planned to vote for the other paragraphs and then to abstain on the resolution as a whole.

---

[1] Source: Department of State, Central Files, 684A.86/11–2356. Secret; Niact; Limited Distribution. Received at 9:19 p.m.

[2] At 10:30 a.m. on November 23, the Eleventh Session of the General Assembly began consideration of agenda item 66, "Question considered by the first emergency special session of the General Assembly from 1 to 10 November 1956". During this meeting, Lloyd had described the British position on withdrawal as follows: "It will take place as soon as possible, as the United Nations Force becomes effective and competent to discharge its functions." (U.N. doc. A/PV.591) The verbatim records of the meetings of the Eleventh Session (November 12, 1956–March 8, 1957) are printed in United Nations, *Official Records of the General Assembly, Eleventh Session, Plenary Meetings*, 2 vols.

[3] Reference is presumably to the conversation reported in Delga 172, Document 603.

He then gave vent to quite an explosion about being asked to give up the British right to decide on what terms they would get out. He said he would rather go down fighting than have these questions be decided by a "UN General". He felt sure that in England they would "go right through the roof" and he felt like going right through the roof himself.

He also said "those bloody French, first they put planes all over Israel and now they flatten out completely." He said he did not think we would reach a vote tonight on the Asian-African resolution and he would put the proposal to have General Burns make the decision on timing of withdrawals up to the Cabinet. He evidently did not relish doing so and did not expect them to agree.

In order maintain maximum pressure, I pointed out the Afro-Asian resolution merely reiterated principles we had stood for, thereby leaving him with impression we might vote for it. He said it would be very bad if we voted for it, but he was clearly engaged in making a demonstration to impress me.

Lloyd asked whether Egyptians would not make a concession concerning continuing present activities on clearance of Canal if British agreed to having General Burns decide timing of withdrawal. I said I doubted Egyptians would make such a verbal agreement in public but I felt sure when it came to actual operations, General Burns could run matters so that clearance would take place while troops were being withdrawn. In response to a question I said I based this on talks I had had with Egyptians which had led me to believe that the insistence that all troops must be withdrawn before any clearance was a talking point for publication and did not represent what they would accept when actual operations were under way.

Referring to Lodge–Murphy telecon [4] concerning effects of a vote by the US in favor of the Afro-Asian resolution on the Atlantic Pact, I would say from my talks with Pineau it would have no effect whatever and that while it would anger the British at the time, it would not by any means be enough to cause them to give up the Atlantic Pact.

The French have come up with a very good face-saver and the British have put themselves in the wrong by not accepting it. This makes clear that their basic motivation is their own political status at home. Lloyd admits Burns and Hammarskjold would operate the thing so that the clearance and withdrawal would take place pari passu yet he refused to accept this face-saving device which changes none of the basic realities.

---

[4] No account of this conversation has been found in Department of State files.

Afro-Asian feeling appears to be that British speech this morning took the position that it was up to the UN to measure up to British specifications before the British would withdraw. There is some justification for this view and there is also justification for the Afro-Asian contention that their resolution is very mild in view of the fact that it does not contain a specific condemnation and that it does not mention a date by which withdrawal should be complete.

1. Request Department make urgent representations in London and Paris urging them agree to make statement in GA that they will leave to General Burns decision on timing of withdrawals as Pineau has proposed. This must be done at once as matter will be decided tomorrow (Saturday) morning. On basis such statement, I believe question of withdrawals can be taken out of GA arena. British and French would recoup great deal of their position and provide practical basis for UNEF operation. Unless something like this is done, demand for complete and immediate Anglo-French withdrawal will grow and they will have to face issue of complying with or defying world opinion.

When Lloyd asked me Thursday night to make a statement about British progress towards withdrawal, I asked that I be given precise name of the British battalion which had been ordered to leave, the precise hour of its departure and the ship on which it was leaving. I said that, as fast as they furnished me evidence of progress, I would applaud that progress. Twenty-four hours have gone by and that information has not arrived. This point too might be conveyed to London.

2. Believe Department should realize that if we abstain on Asian-African resolution it may cause a distinct turn for the worse insofar as the withdrawal of troops is concerned. The whole question may thus get bogged down into a morass which will have consequences about which the best prediction that can be made now is that conditions will be even worse than they are now. Our abstention on this resolution will undoubtedly cause a slow-down in the present congealed snail's pace of withdrawal. This endangers the settlement of the Canal question, of the Palestine question and the avoidance of war. In view of what I have been able learn of the attitudes of the two Foreign Ministers, I feel tonight it is clearly more harmful to abstain than to vote in favor, unpleasant though this latter is.

3. A vital element is the opinion of the SYG who thinks an abstention by the US would imperil the whole withdrawal and would cause everyone to ask "has there been a change in American policy?" This might well require a public rectification by the President, because I do not believe a statement by me on the floor would cut any ice at all as far as political effect in the world is concerned

when compared with the effect of the vote. A rectification by the President, even though necessary, might conceivably do more harm to Anglo-American relations than the harm which would be done by my affirmative vote, which, I believe, would quickly pass. Knowing how keenly the President desires withdrawal and how wholeheartedly he wants to support the SYG, I feel the SYG's opinion is entitled to great weight.

Lodge

---

607.   Telegram From the Mission at the United Nations to the Department of State [1]

New York, November 23, 1956—8 p.m.

Delga 179. Re Palestine—Suez. Fawzi, Loutfi and Riad (Egypt) dined with me last night in my apartment. Fawzi seemed very relaxed, moderate, and not in any sense recriminatory.

Fawzi being ready talk business from start, I began by assuring him of US clear determination all non-Egyptian forces must withdraw from Egypt. At same time I reiterated our belief every effort must be made achieve long-range settlements of basic problems which led to present crisis.

From what Fawzi said in direct response my opening remarks, as well as everything he said throughout course of evening, it is perfectly clear, beyond any doubt, that until every British, French and Israel soldier has left Egyptian soil, it will be impossible for Egypt to go along with steps looking toward long-range settlement. It is equally clear that unless Egypt is ready to agree, no resolution of type we have in mind in GA can come close to ⅔ majority, and might well not get simple majority. But Fawzi gave every indication of being ready at appropriate time to deal in realistic way with basic causes of present difficulties and to agree to measures looking toward ultimate solution.

As timetable for tackling various issues in months to come, Fawzi set out following, which he described as admittedly "perfectionist": (1) withdrawal of all Anglo-French-Israeli forces; (2) clearance of Canal; (3) arrangements for settling status of Canal; (4)

---

[1] Source: Department of State, Central Files, 684A.86/11–2356. Secret; Priority; Limited Distribution. Received at 10:02 p.m.

Palestine settlement; and (5) perhaps contribution towards settlement of Algeria. When I indicated disapproval of holding up clearance until every last soldier was out, he smiled and said he stressed that with respect all these elements this was "perfectionist" timetable and he could accept something less than perfect. Even "two steps" away from perfect. At another stage in conversation, he said complete withdrawal Anglo-French forces must come before clearing began.

In connection with withdrawal, Fawzi referred to Asian-African draft resolution tabled last evening.[2] He regarded it principally as psychological lever. He said they and other Asian-Africans recognized it would be unrealistic to put any precise deadline in it, although Asian-African group was of a strong opinion it should take Anglo-French and Israeli forces no longer to withdraw than it had taken them to enter.

Fawzi knew of draft resolution Hammarskjold asked us and India to sponsor, endorsing Secretary General's reports concerning establishment of UNEF and arrangements for clearing Canal.[3] He appeared have no objection to it.

Fawzi expressed great interest in our ideas regarding methods achieving agreement on future status of Canal. He said there was no disagreement between us on substance, but he felt we must be extremely careful as to method to be adopted. He would not wish us to crystallize our views and foreclose others from expressing their opinions on it and perhaps contributing constructively to solution.

I assured Fawzi we had open mind as to precise method for reaching final agreement on status of Canal.

Fawzi felt use of "mediator" might be unrealistic since in difficult cases of this kind, mediator tends to get "squeezed out". At same time, he felt committee of negotiators might not be so effective if they served in their individual capacity, rather than as representatives of governments with full governmental backing. To return it to FonMins meetings would be to go backward. He pointed out there were numerous proposals extant concerning solution for Canal, mentioning Spanish suggestions, 18-power proposals, Egyptian and Indian proposals, among others. He made particular point of useful work done by Hammarskjold which had been designed culminate in meeting of three FonMins in Geneva on October 29. He referred to 6 points re Suez and SYG's paper elaborating these points. They provided real basis for further progress. Fawzi said Hammarskjold's work on this "might pop up again". He urged us adopt as motto "determination without impetuosity". He did not dissent to my rephrasing it as "making haste slowly".

---

[2] See footnote 3, Document 604.
[3] See footnote 2, *ibid.*

In connection with settlement Palestine question, Fawzi gave every impression of being reasonable. He stressed necessity preparing public opinion in such a step, pointing out that with Anglo-French-Israeli attack against Egypt most vividly in minds of Egyptians at this moment, time would have to elapse before this could be brought about. Phrasing it another way, Fawzi urged, in this case particularly, but as general rule as well, importance of "not doing the right thing at the wrong time". Fawzi said there must be a period of tranquility but that period need not be very long. He said that even in present period "responsible" men should and would take advantage of this time discuss confidentially ways and means proceeding to next public steps re settlement.

As Fawzi prepared to leave, he volunteered to give close thought to our two resolutions and to give us his preliminary comments on them within the next few days—as he put it—"as soon as tomorrow has become yesterday". He apparently attached considerable importance to anticipated activities of GA today on resolution renewing demands for withdrawal non-Egyptian forces.

Lodge

---

608. Circular Telegram From the Department of State to Certain Diplomatic Missions and Consular Offices [1]

Washington, November 23, 1956—8:27 p.m.

435. For Chiefs of Mission. Following for your info and guidance re US policy in current Near East crisis: Closure Suez Canal and severance IPC pipelines from Iraq to Mediterranean have brought about serious financial and economic problems in Western Europe and also in certain Afro-Asian countries. Impact of recent developments upon British position has been extremely great. Continuation this situation would seriously weaken those countries particularly in Western Europe whose strength is most important to common defense against Soviet menace. Among many reasons why US has exerted every effort bring about promptest possible settlement is our urgent desire reopen Canal and pipelines.

---

[1] Source: Department of State, Central Files, 684A.86/11–2656. Secret; Priority. Drafted by Rountree; cleared by Murphy, Bowie, Henderson, Phleger, Sebald, and Elbrick; and approved by Rountree who signed for Hoover. Sent to 53 posts in Africa, Asia, and Europe.

We have considered it unwise pending understanding re withdrawal UK and French forces to make any move which would indicate that we are giving extraordinary support to British and French while they fail comply UN resolutions; nor do we wish lose influence which our adherence to principle in this problem has engendered. Effect has been that we could not render maximum assistance to other friendly countries suffering results present situation, but have had to rely almost entirely on companies to do what they could to provide oil markets. Western European countries should not be penalized for acts for which they not responsible. They are now being subjected great hardships as winter approaches.

We hope decision soon will be made and announced by British and French that they are withdrawing from Egypt in full compliance UN resolutions. If such a commitment is given and such withdrawal progresses satisfactorily it should be possible for US to undertake special measures to meet oil crisis. When forces fully withdrawn we plan all-out effort this regard. Moreover, it inevitable that financial aid to several Western European countries, including UK, will be required in order avert major catastrophe affecting interest entire free world.

We aware probable effort seize US departure from its present "hands-off" policy to claim that assistance to UK and France demonstrates that we "rewarding" aggressors and claim US duplicity in purporting to oppose British and French military activity in Egypt. It is of utmost importance that we avoid to greatest possible extent harmful effects of any such claims. Efforts should begin at once to prepare Arab leaders for our next moves following satisfactory commitment and implementation UK-French withdrawals. Simultaneously, efforts should be made in Afro-Asian countries, oil exporting as well as oil importing, to obtain full support for such moves and to elicit pressures, based upon recognition vital interest which they have in matter, for undertaking energetic measures to reopen Canal and pipelines.

Means of accomplishing this objective will vary widely in addressee countries and Chiefs of Mission will have to act largely on basis of their judgment as to most effective approach. Careful thought and planning should be given by each Mission to assure maximum effectiveness. Major consideration should be to avoid statements which would give rise to suspicion of US reversal of policy regardless of compliance by UK, France and Israel with UN resolution. If Chief of Mission feels local circumstances such that no approach should be made at this time he should so report to Department.

In addressee Arab States it might be emphasized to top Government officials in advance of any announcement concerning US assistance that US has scrupulously avoided rendering assistance to British and French pending their compliance with UN resolutions. It has also given no assistance to Israel. No opportunity should be lost in playing up US peace role. US had endeavored in every feasible way to bring end to hostilities and effect departure of foreign forces from Egyptian territory. In order to avoid any hope or expectation on part of certain Arab States that US will continue this policy of denial assistance to our European Allies even after they withdraw forces, it might discreetly be said that our present policy will be continued until after commitment withdrawal in full compliance with UN resolutions. It should be made clear that our concern is not only for Western Europe but also for Afro-Asian countries which are directly affected by present situation. Effects upon them will increase greatly if situation should be prolonged.

It might be anticipated that questions will then be asked re our future intentions. It should be made clear that US attaches utmost importance to strength of Western European countries and to their continued capacity to contribute their substantial share to the security and the economic stability of the free world. Prolongation of adverse consequences of recent Near Eastern developments would seriously impair not only the interests of the European countries but those of all of us including Arab States. European and Afro-Asian consumers of Near Eastern oil and users of the Suez Canal should not be made indiscriminately to suffer for the action of the UK, France and Israel.

In oil producing countries of Saudi Arabia, Iraq and Iran special emphasis might be placed upon their obvious interest in moving the greatest quantity of Near Eastern oil and thus avoiding insofar as possible institution of any new supply patterns which would have not only short term but long term effect upon their oil income. Maximum effort should be made to play up their self interest and to demonstrate that the US is continuing to do everything possible to minimize financial impact upon them. It is of course necessary to include British and French companies in over-all supply effort since those companies control large portions of shipping and marketing facilities. British and French implementation UN resolutions would remove obstacles to US and other oil producing countries permitting them to play their essential repeat essential role in supplying oil to world markets.

While financial aid to Western European countries (particularly to UK and France) need not be mentioned specifically at this juncture approaches should take into account likelihood that such assistance will be forthcoming in near future after compliance with UN resolutions is assured. One point which might be used discreetly particularly by addressees in Arab States is that unnecessary prolongation of any policies by those countries seriously detrimental to economic interest of countries—particularly those which have no responsibility for the armed attacks on Egypt—relying upon Near Eastern oil or use of Suez Canal would inevitably create anti-Arab feeling which could jeopardize relations between Arab States and other free countries. Present world sympathies could rapidly shift and bring about new situation in which Arab States would have much to lose.

In implementing foregoing Wadsworth will of course relate to approach to Saud in accordance Deptel 182 to Dhahran, [2] results of which not yet known to Department.

Hoover

_____
[2] Document 586.

---

609.   Telegram From the Embassy in Israel to the Department of State [1]

Tel Aviv, November 23, 1956—11 p.m.

653. Foreign Ministry official informs Embassy that in conversation with Meir this week Hammarskjold replied to her question by stating UNEF's functions did not include assuring freedom of transit Suez. He had refused to be drawn into discussion of where this left Israel.

It apparent from reports from their people in New York, he said, that Nasser was dictating what elements General Assembly's November 2 resolution [2] Hammarskjold and UN should attempt to make effective. Hence Hammarskjold's declared intention to clear Canal physically for navigation while ignoring latter half of resolution's Article 4 which urges restoration of freedom of transit.

GOI seriously disturbed by apparent United States indifference to trends which would restore Nasser vis-à-vis Canal to status quo ante so that Canal users once again would be at mercy of his caprice.

Lawson

_____
[1] Source: Department of State, Central Files, 684A.86/11–2356. Confidential. Received at 6:36 a.m., November 24. Repeated to London, Paris, and USUN.
[2] Reference is to General Assembly Resolution 997 (ES–I); see Document 467.

610.   Telegram From the Department of State to the Embassy in Syria [1]

Washington, November 24, 1956—4:08 p.m.

973. Department has received convincing evidence Egyptian officials and groups under them have been responsible for certain terroristic acts and sabotage. Libya has publicly accused and expelled Egyptian Military Attaché for acts against Libyan security carried out by his private armed commandos. Lebanese security forces have during past few days discovered that Egyptian Military Attaché and Commercial Counselor unmistakably implicated in recent dynamitings Beirut buildings. Six Egyptian school teachers arrested Tyre in connection with local acts sabotage.

Lebanese Government appears undecided to what extent Egypt should officially be held accountable. American correspondents Beirut have not been permitted file true story Egyptian complicity Beirut dynamitings. According Lebanese Minister of Defense, Egyptian Ambassador who first heard story on BBC threatened President Chamoun Egypt would break relations with Lebanon if two attachés declared persona non grata.

We understand Egyptian Military Attaché Damascus has autonomous paramilitary organization which at present in collusion Syrian G–2 defies Syrian sovereignty and by its existence constitutes continued threat oil installations in Syria and neighboring Arab states as well as lives Syrian and other Arab personalities. Iraq has been aware of menace for some time and has kept Egyptians under surveillance reducing threat to minimum. Terrorists have not yet been active in Jordan or Saudi Arabia, but experience in Lebanon where they became activated only after government took position not desired by Egypt suggests potential threat all Arab states.

It is clear these Egyptian activities are actual threat to life and property in some Arab states and potential threat in others to those who may in future disagree with Egyptian policies. At same time, Egyptian activities have not apparently become public knowledge and there is tendency leaders not to face up to full implications Egyptian penetration. You are authorized at your discretion orally to inform high-level officials of governments to which you are accredited of substance these Egyptian activities. Your account should

---

[1] Source: Department of State, Central Files, 684A.86/11–2456. Secret. Drafted by Eagleton (NEA/NE), Wilkins, and Rockwell; cleared by Wilcox; and approved by Rountree who signed for Hoover. Also sent to Beirut, Baghdad, Jidda, Amman, Tripoli, and Khartoum, and repeated to Cairo.

contain only information which you consider it desirable impart based on your assessment of receptivity.

In addition following posts may in their discretion wish to make further suggestions as indicated below:

Beirut might suggest that if GOL desires bring facts into open may wish consider informing UN by letter to SYG re recent Egyptian activities in Lebanon. Subversive Syrian activities could also be mentioned.

Tripoli might suggest account of affair of Egyptian Military Attaché be circulated to other Arab Governments for their information.

Jidda may wish to inform King Saud in detail to provide graphic picture of what could happen in Saudi Arabia.

Amman may wish to stress way in which Egypt has also interfered in Jordan through radio broadcasts.

Hoover

---

611.   Editorial Note

At its 593d and 594th plenary meetings on November 24, the General Assembly debated and adopted by a vote of 63–5–10 the resolution sponsored by 20 Afro-Asian nations. (U.N. doc. A/3385/Rev.1) Under the operative paragraphs of this resolution, the General Assembly (1) noted with regret the limited compliance with withdrawal resolutions, (2) reiterated the call to France, Israel, and the United Kingdom to withdraw forthwith, and (3) requested the Secretary-General urgently to communicate the resolution to the parties concerned and to report to the General Assembly without delay. (Resolution 1120 (XI)) The United States voted for this resolution. Prior to the vote on the resolution as a whole, the United States had abstained on an amendment, tabled by the Belgian Government (U.N. doc. A/L. 215), which would have replaced operative paragraphs 1 and 2 of the 20-nation draft resolution with the following sentence:

"*Notes* that, according to the information received, one-third of the French forces has been withdrawn, the United Kingdom Government has decided to withdraw one infantry battalion immediately, and Israel has withdrawn a part of its troops, and considers that France, the United Kingdom and Israel should expedite the application of the resolutions of 2 and 7 November in the spirit in which they were adopted, particularly with regard to the functions vested in the United Nations forces." (U.N. doc. A/L.215)

The Belgian amendment was rejected by a vote of 37–23–18. The following day the Mission in New York suggested to the Department of State that it explain to Western European and Commonwealth countries that the United States had abstained on the Belgian amendment because it would have created the impression that the General Assembly was wavering in its determination that there must be an immediate withdrawal and that it was adopting the Anglo-French thesis that U.N. forces should take over the job which the French and British had begun. (Delga 186 from USUN, November 25; Department of State, Central Files, 684A.86/11–2556)

Also on November 24, the General Assembly approved a draft resolution sponsored by India, Canada, Colombia, Norway, the United States, and Yugoslavia. (U.N. doc. A/3386) According to the operative paragraphs of this resolution, the General Assembly noted with approval the contents of the Secretary-General's report on the presence and functioning of the UNEF in Egypt as well as the progress made by the Secretary-General in connection with arrangements for clearing the Canal and authorized the Secretary-General to proceed with the exploration of practical arrangements and negotiations of agreement so that the clearing operations might speedily and effectively be undertaken. (Resolution 1121 (XI)) The resolution was adopted by a vote of 65–0–9. (U.N. docs. A/PV. 593 and A/PV. 594)

For text of the remarks made by Ambassador Lodge at the 593d meeting, see Department of State *Bulletin*, December 10, 1956, pages 914–915.

612.   Memorandum of a Conference With the President, White House, Washington, November 25, 1956 [1]

OTHERS PRESENT

> Secretary Hoover
> Mr. MacArthur
> Mr. Hagerty
> Colonel Goodpaster

[Here follows discussion of unrelated subjects.]

Mr. Hoover and Mr. MacArthur said they have information that the French are now ready to accept a proposal to give to the UN the power to determine when their forces should leave the Canal zone. They added that we are now hoping to get the UK to do the same.

Mr. Hoover next discussed the critical situation and pressures developing regarding Europe's need for oil. He felt it was necessary to start the emergency committee in action very soon. The President recalled that we have held up this measure until the invading powers accepted immediate withdrawal of their troops. The President thought that, if the action is taken, there should be a careful statement bringing out that, with winter coming on, and in order to prevent widespread suffering in Europe, committees are being put into operation to see how fuel can be provided to relieve the situation. Mr. Hoover reaffirmed that he felt we should now go ahead with our actions on oil. [2]

Mr. Hoover said that, in his talks with Secretary Dulles, the latter had indicated that in the Middle East—Jordan, Syria, Iraq, etc.—he thought we must go the British and ask for an indication of their thinking as to what is now to be done. The President thought the British should say now that as soon as they have withdrawn from the Suez they are prepared to honor past commitments, participate in joint projects involving aid, etc. Mr. Hoover thought it might be necessary for us to approach the British and say that it looks as though they are "through" in the area, and ask if they want us to try to pick up their commitments. The President said we do not want to get in the position of automatically assuming a set of past patterns. He thought we should give the British every chance to

---

[1] Source: Eisenhower Library, Whitman File, Eisenhower Diaries. Secret. Drafted by Goodpaster on November 26. The record of the President's Daily Appointments does not contain an entry for this meeting. (*Ibid.*) A memorandum for the record, dated November 25, by MacArthur summarizes the items discussed at this meeting. (Department of State, Central Files, 711.11–EI/11–2556)

[2] According to MacArthur's memorandum, President Eisenhower and Hoover agreed that the Department of State should draw up a statement which would emphasize the European and world aspect of the oil situation rather than the aid that activation of the plan would provide to Great Britain and France.

work their way back into a position of influence and respect in the Middle East.

[Here follows discussion of unrelated subjects.]

G

Colonel, CE, U S Army

---

613.   Memorandum of a Conversation, Department of State, Washington, November 25, 1956 [1]

SUMMARY OF ACTIONS AND DECISIONS AT MEETING
WITH MR. HOOVER NOVEMBER 25, 1956

Present were Mr. Hoover, Mr. Murphy, Mr. MacArthur, Mr. Phleger, Mr. Elbrick, Mr. Rountree, Mr. Wilcox, Mr. Bowie, Mr. Beam, Mr. Greene, and Mr. Sohm.

1. *MEEC.*

The President has agreed that we cannot wait longer to set up the MEEC. This will be the principal responsibility of Dr. Flemming, in the Department Mr. Moline. Mr. Moline is to prepare for consideration at a meeting early Monday morning [2] with Mr. Hoover and Dr. Flemming necessary papers including a draft public statement. The latter should take account of our requirement for prior compliance by the British and French with UN resolutions, or at least a prior commitment on compliance, but should focus on the idea that we are acting to help all the other European countries which, through no fault of their own, have suffered as a result of the closing of the Suez Canal.

[Here follows discussion of the Hungarian refugee situation.]

3. *Middle East Resolutions.*

Mr. Wilcox is to elicit from USUN by Monday morning reports on what they are doing to keep each of the two US resolutions on

---

[1] Source: Department of State, Secretary's Memoranda of Conversation: Lot 64 D 199. Secret. No drafting information is given on the source text.

[2] November 26.

Suez and on a Palestine settlement alive and in the forefront at New York.

.   .   .   .

[Here follows discussion of unrelated subjects.]

---

614.   Telegram From the Embassy in the United Kingdom to the Department of State [1]

London, November 26, 1956—3 p.m.

2917. Eyes only for Acting Secretary. Have just seen Butler immediately before he went to a Cabinet meeting re Suez. He told me that he himself was perfectly calm and believed absolutely in the ultimate indestructability of good and close relations between the US and Great Britain because he believed with passionate intensity that such relations were absolutely essential to the survival of western civilization. He said, however, that the wave of anti-American feeling in Great Britain, caused by the action of the US on Saturday [2] in abstaining from voting for the Belgian amendment to the Afro-Asian resolution and the subsequent vote of the US Delegate in favor of the Afro-Asian resolution calling for the withdrawal forthwith of the British and French forces (in spite of the fact that it was clearly apparent that the withdrawal of such forces was already under way and when it was equally apparent from the resolution with regard to the clearance of the Canal that it was not intended that the British and French forces should be withdrawn except pari passu with the clearance of the Canal under the aegis of the UN) could not possibly be exaggerated. Butler said that he felt he should point out in all seriousness that he did not think it beyond the bounds of possibility that if the UN did not act with firmness to bring about immediate clearance of the Canal Great Britain would

---

[1] Source: Department of State, Central Files, 974.7301/11–2656. Top Secret; Niact; Presidential Handling. Received at 11:46 a.m.

[2] November 24. Regarding developments in the General Assembly on that day, see Document 611.

At the Acting Secretary's Staff Meeting that morning, Hoover noted that Aldrich had telephoned from London earlier that morning to emphasize the great concern in the United Kingdom over the U.S. vote in the General Assembly. Hoover asked the Bureau of European Affairs to consider steps to offset this unfavorable reaction. (Department of State, Secretary's Staff Meetings: Lot 63 D 75)

withdraw from the UN and the situation might even reach the point where the US would be asked to give up its bases in Great Britain. Butler did not mention the effect of such events on NATO.

On my way out from my interview with Butler I saw Salisbury who was deeply agitated and who said that if the story which appeared this morning in the *Daily Mail* regarding Egyptian brutality and especially regarding the action by Egyptian customs officials forcing British women to "strip completely in a little uncurtained room" were true, it would be extremely difficult to prevent the situation here from getting out of control.

I realize of course that is impossible to modify the action taken in the UN, but I feel that it is of extreme importance that the President should invite Butler and Macmillan to come to Washington for consultation at the earliest possible opportunity. I do not think that Butler could leave London at the present time, but Macmillan undoubtedly would come at once if invited. As Butler is planning to explain to Humphrey on telephone today Macmillan would not wish to appear to come as a suppliant for financial aid, but both Butler and Macmillan believe that early consultation is becoming vitally necessary. It is tragic to sit here in London and observe the rapidly changing attitude of the British public toward the US. I believe that it is not exaggerating in the slightest degree to say that we are rapidly reaching the point where we are thought of by the British public as enemies of Britain working against them with the Russians and the Arabs instead of as allies. I can think of no way in which this extremely dangerous trend of opinion can be halted except through an early invitation by the President to such conference as I have referred to above which invitation of course may be felt to be justified if British take action in UN along lines outlined in mytel 2915. [3]

Aldrich

---

[3] In telegram 2915, November 26, Aldrich reported that, according to Kirkpatrick, Lloyd had been authorized to tell Hammarskjöld that Great Britain was prepared to establish a definite schedule for troop withdrawal on the assumption that the United Nations would at the same time move ahead with Canal clearance using available equipment and that Hammarskjöld was in a position to obtain Egyptian agreement to an immediate clearance of the Canal. Lloyd's instructions, according to Kirkpatrick, envisaged that if Hammarskjöld could give this assurance, the British Government would make a public statement in the United Nations very shortly announcing the date for the completion of their evacuation. (*Ibid.*, Central Files, 974.7301/11-2656)

615.   Memorandum of a Conversation, Department of State, Washington, November 26, 1956 [1]

SUBJECT

Withdrawal of Israel Forces

PARTICIPANTS

Mr. Abba Eban, Ambassador of Israel
Mr. Reuven Shiloah, Minister, Embassy of Israel
NEA—Mr. Rountree
NE—Mr. Bergus

Mr. Eban reported that on the subject of the withdrawal of Israel troops from Egyptian territory, the Israelis had sent the UN Secretary General a letter on November 25 [2] repeating Israel's intention to withdraw subject to satisfactory arrangements being made. Israel suggested that it wished to discuss these arrangements immediately.

The Israelis had already spoken to the Secretary General informally. They had said that the practical problems created by Israel's withdrawal could be solved through the use of the United Nations Emergency Force.

The UNEF should be used at the entry to the Gulf of Aqaba to prevent a renewal of the maritime blockade there. This was an international waterway which Israel had succeeded in opening; it should not now be closed as a result of UN action.

With regard to Sinai, Israel wanted occupation of key points by the UNEF pending agreements between Egypt and the UN and Israel and the UN looking to the demilitarization of the Peninsula.

There had been troubles in Gaza but the situation looked better now. Tragic outbreaks had taken place on November 10 and 11. Municipal services had now been improved, and exports of citrus and dates from the Gaza strip were being facilitated. Regarding the long-term future of Gaza, Israel had been vague. The question for decision was whether the whole structure of the State of Israel, which had been based on a heavy Jewish majority, should be changed. On the other hand, Israel's absorption of Gaza and the assumption of responsibility for the people living there could be a large contribution to an ultimate settlement. Until this matter had been decided by the Israelis, Israel had no juridical aim in Gaza. For

---

[1] Source: Department of State, Central Files, 684A.86/11–2656. Secret. Drafted by Bergus on November 27.

[2] Reference is presumably to the letter from Meir to Hammarskjöld dated November 26 in "Exchange of letters between the Minister for Foreign Affairs of Israel and the Secretary-General", U.N. doc. A/3395.

the present, Israel would seek a non-Egyptian solution for Gaza which would leave open the possibility of eventual Israel sovereignty over the Strip.

The Secretary General thought that practical solutions to such problems as the Gulf of Aqaba could be reached if questions of sovereignty were not raised. Mr. Rountree inquired as to who, in Israel's view, was sovereign over the islands of Tiran and Sanafir. Mr. Eban replied that Israel understood they had been under Saudi Arab sovereignty, but that Egypt had occupied them, presumably with Saudi consent.

Mr. Eban continued that Mr. Hammarskjold wanted to know what UN member states thought about the problems of withdrawal. Mr. Eban urged that the U.S. give the Secretary General its views on these problems. The Israelis had approached Mr. Lodge on this question, but he had been uninstructed. The United States could not be an agnostic on these points.

Mr. Rountree indicated that these questions were occupying our attention. The U.S. position was that there should be a withdrawal of foreign troops from Egyptian territory and that UN influence should be directed to the prevention of the recurrence of the dangers in the Near East situation. Our views on the second of these points were not clearly defined and would depend on recommendations of the UNEF and the Secretary General.

Mr. Eban said that if Israel simply walked out of Egypt, a vacuum would be created which Egypt would have to fill. Mr. Lodge had talked of phasing. Mr. Rountree said that there was an obvious difficulty in defining a phased withdrawal. The British and French had talked of man for man replacement of their forces. Mr. Eban said that Israel's interest was in places rather than men.

Mr. Eban referred to the many economic possibilities of Aqaba as an alternative to the Suez Canal. Israel had decided to lay an oil pipeline from Eilat to Beersheba. Efforts to acquire the necessary pipe were currently underway.

Withdrawal created many problems. The Secretary General himself had insisted that Israel not leave a vacuum in Gaza. That is why Israel regretted peremptory UNGA resolutions calling for withdrawal which served only to delay discussions which would lead to withdrawal. Mr. Eban was surprised that the U.S. had voted for a resolution which stated that there had been no Israel withdrawal, when in fact substantial numbers of Israel troops had returned to Israel territory. Israel planned to publish its letter to the Secretary General. Mr. Rountree thought this might be a useful step.

616.   Telegram From the Consulate General at Dhahran to the Department of State [1]

Dhahran, November 26, 1956—5 p.m.

243. From Ambassador Wadsworth. Deptel 182 [2] and Contel 241. [3] My first presentation to King at formal audience November 23 was USG plan as outlined Department reference telegram for meeting world oil shortages. Knowing from earlier talk with Khalid that King had no intention modify SAG position re closing Bahrain pipeline, barring British and French tankers and prohibiting shipments to British and French areas (except India, Pakistan, Ceylon, Canada and South Africa) until after British-French forces had quit Egypt, I stressed assurance that in common interest we would keep Saudi interests uppermost in mind and minimize effects thereon of redistribution.

King and Counselors listened carefully. Only question was would plan be put into effect, with resulting easing British-French shortages, before British-French forces quit Egypt. I reiterated British-French dilemma was of their own creation and said it would seem clear their forces would have left Egypt before our redistribution plan could be brought into effect. This seemed to satisfy them.

King then said: "I have great confidence in USG and approve its plan for redistribution of oil, confident at same time USG will minimize loss which Saudi Arabia will sustain as result its implementation. We will welcome plan after withdrawal British-French forces in accordance UN resolutions, and thereafter it may be possible to restore relations with countries as before."

Davies and Ohliger [4] of Aramco tell me King vouchsafed similar statement to them November 25.

Carrigan

---

[1] Source: Department of State, Central Files, 880.2553/11–2656. Secret; Priority. Received at 4:11 p.m. Repeated to Jidda, London, and Paris.

[2] Document 586.

[3] Telegram 241, November 26, contained a brief overview of Wadsworth's visit to Riyadh, November 22–25, including a listing of conversations and the topics discussed. (Department of State, Central Files, 611.86A/11–2656)

[4] F.W. Ohliger, Vice President of Aramco.

617.   Telegram From the Department of State to the Embassy in the United Kingdom [1]

Washington, November 26, 1956—9:09 p.m.

3749. Eyes only Ambassador. Embtels 2910 [2] and 2917. [3] I agree it is in our best interest to reestablish consultation with British and French and hope it will prove possible do so. Basic requirement is concrete evidence of more substantial withdrawal British and French forces as build-up UNEF proceeds. At same time it is not necessary in our view that last UK-French soldier leave Egypt before consultation on Middle East problems be reestablished.

We appreciate British and French reluctance withdraw all forces without some assurances UN will follow through re (a) effectiveness UNEF (b) clearing Canal and maintaining its availability and (c) more permanent solution Suez and Palestine question. These problems and their interrelationship will be taken up by Phleger with SYG and Lodge in New York tomorrow and, in light his views, subsequently with British and French.

We will keep you advised.

Hoover

---

[1] Source: Department of State, Central Files, 684A.86/11–2656. Top Secret; Priority. Drafted by Lister and Elbrick, cleared by Hoover and Murphy, and approved by Elbrick who signed for Hoover.

[2] Telegram 2910, November 24, pointed out an inconsistency in telegram 3702 (Document 605) as to whether the United States intended to resume consultation with Great Britain after or during an Anglo-French withdrawal. (Department of State, Central Files, 684A.86/11–2456)

[3] Document 614.

618.   Memorandum of a Telephone Conversation Between the President in Augusta, Georgia, and the Secretary of State in Key West, Florida, November 27, 1956, 9:25 a.m. [1]

The President said he has a message from Pug Ismay which is very desperate in tone. [2] They have been the best of friends over the years—but now he is adopting the European conviction that we deserted our two friends in their hour of trial, and now won't even help them out with oil and gas, etc. Whereas, we are trying to time it properly so as to help them out permanently—which they don't seem to understand. Ismay says that the man who now seems to be kicked out will come back for sure; thinks they have done a terrible thing, and that NATO might be broken up.

Message from Britain says the boys are ready to go along with UN on assumption that cleaning up the Canal can proceed. The President thinks it is about time for us to try to make it clear that the second we know this, we can say that now we are going to make plans. Wadsworth had a talk with King Saud—and Saud seemed reassured when they gave him timing on troops being brought out.

Mr. Dulles mentioned George Humphrey's conversation yesterday with Rab Butler. [3] Dulles' feeling is that we will just have to give them those few days.

The President agrees on taking no action. But since we said the second they gave just an indication, we would resume our great effort. (Citing an example, from Dillon's message of transmittal:

---

[1] Source: Eisenhower Library, Whitman File, Eisenhower Diaries. Prepared in the Office of the President. Eisenhower took a working vacation in Augusta November 26–December 13. (Record of the President's Daily Appointments; *ibid.*) Dulles was in Key West November 18–December 2, convalescing after surgery. (Dulles' Appointment Book; Princeton University Library, Dulles Papers)

[2] Lord Ismay's message to Eisenhower consisted of oral remarks Ismay made to Dillon in Paris on November 25. Dillon transmitted Ismay's message in a telegram. (Eisenhower Library, Whitman File, Name Series, Lord Ismay, and Department of State, Central Files, 740.5/11–2756)

[3] No memorandum of this conversation has been found in Department of State files. Humphrey spoke to Eisenhower on the telephone at 9:30 a.m., November 26, and described his conversation with Butler as follows: "He [Butler] told a couple of encouraging things, and some suspicious. One encouraging thing: He was very grateful for picking up right where we left off. The principal thing he wanted was time. He said he has a difficult situation, and, if we could just not interfere with him—not have any more resolutions—he would appreciate it very much indeed. He wound up by saying we would hear from him as soon as he could get his affairs arranged." (Memorandum of telephone conversation; Eisenhower Library, Whitman File, Eisenhower Diaries)

Butler describes a telephone conversation with Humphrey which took place around the end of November in *The Art of the Possible, The Memoirs of Lord Butler* (Boston: Gambit Inc., 1972), p. 195.

service stations are refusing to fill American cars with gas; taxis are refusing to pick up Americans.)

Mr. Dulles said of course that is bad—but it is awfully hard to see how we can begin to use that oil to meet their needs before they have indicated that they would comply with the UN Resolution. The President said the public does not know this, and wondered if we shouldn't let it be known? Mr. Dulles thinks the public need not know, that a public statement might do more harm than good because it would look as though we were publicly subjecting them to pressure, which would be resented. He feels they would prefer to act under their own steam. The President's only thought was to say that we *understand* they are going to comply.

The President will reply to Ismay by saying simply that this is exactly what we are working on and to please sit tight. We are doing everything that is humanly possible. [4]

[Here follows discussion of Secretary Dulles' schedule.]

Mr. Dulles said we must make it clear that our position does not in any way mean we are trying to be friendly with the Arabs for the price of our British friendship. Once that principle is recognized, everything else falls into place.

This gave the President the idea that, while the Secretary could develop this subject in a press conference, he should perhaps say something on that order right now. He will get up a very short statement, which he will ask Jim Hagerty to phone back to Mr. Dulles for approval.

The President expressed concern about the kind of thing that is beginning to spread through documents: "might compel their withdrawal from the UN."

The Secretary said it was they who double-crossed us, and now are trying to put the blame on us. He said, "Nothing has been stronger and clearer than your letters to Eden."

---

[4] Eisenhower's message to Ismay, dated November 27, was transmitted through Dillon. Copies are in the Eisenhower Library, Whitman File, Name Series, Lord Ismay and in Department of State, Central Files, 740.5/11–2756. Subsequent correspondence between Eisenhower and Ismay on this matter is in the Eisenhower Library, White House Central Files, Suez Crisis.

619. Telegram From the Embassy in the United Kingdom to the Department of State [1]

London, November 27, 1956—5 p.m.

2948. Eyes only for Acting Secretary. I called Butler this morning in accordance with arrangements made to keep in touch daily and found him considerably encouraged by his talk yesterday with Humphrey. [2] I presume you have had Humphrey's version of that conversation, but you may be interested that Butler described his impression of it to me as indicating that as soon as the British can announce a definite date for complete withdrawal of forces from Egypt the US door will be open for urgent consideration of the various further problems which have arisen between us. In this connection Butler said that Lloyd will return to London tomorrow and will make a statement in the House of Commons Thursday along the lines given me yesterday by Kirkpatrick (first paragraph Embtel 2915). [3] He obviously hopes that this position will constitute the compliance with UN Resolutions which the US desires, although he did say that ultimate policy decisions cannot be finalized until Lloyd's return and report to Cabinet.

Incidentally, he told me that with particular reference to the US vote for the Afro-Asian resolution and abstention on the Belgian amendment, both of which actions still are principal causes of difficulty to him here, he had expressed hope to Humphrey that "there will be no more UN resolutions". He says Humphrey concurred.

Butler said he would call me tomorrow on any further developments. Meanwhile, I am seeing Macmillan later today at his request, on which conversation I will report separately.

Aldrich

---

[1] Source: Department of State, Central Files, 974.7301/11–2756. Top Secret; Priority. Received at 1:06 p.m.

[2] See footnote 3, *supra.*

[3] See footnote 3, Document 614.

620.   Telegram From the Mission at the United Nations to the Department of State [1]

New York, November 27, 1956—10 p.m.

Delga 201. Re Palestine/Suez. In meeting this morning between Hammarskjold and Phleger, the Secretary-General dealt with following points:

[Here follows an account of Hammarskjöld's remarks concerning the size of UNEF, the availability of forces, and the use of Canadians in UNEF.]

4. UNEF role in Canal clearance: Hammarskjold said nothing had happened to cast doubt on using UNEF for protecting Canal clearing operation but matter had not been brought any further than when he last reported.

5. Israeli attitude on withdrawal: Hammarskjold agreed that status quo ante with respect to freedom of transit in Canal and the occupation of islands in Gulf of Aqaba should not be reestablished but at same time it was a question of when was the best time and what was best manner to deal with these problems. He anticipated that Israelis would put conditions on their withdrawal under cover of satisfactory arrangements for functioning of UNEF. Hammarskjold said he had told Israelis that if this occurred, he would take matter to General Assembly. Hammarskjold agreed that UNEF should ultimately end up on Israel's borders.

6. Financing: Hammarskjold regarded ten-million-dollar fund voted by General Assembly [2] as enabling establishment of force, but he would expect to turn to regular procedures for financing rest of project. He said that in passing resolution yesterday, General Assembly had not necessarily agreed to financing force on basis of regular scale of contributions. He himself was thinking in terms of loan basis for financing rather than through regular contributions. He believed that some body, like Advisory Committee, should study and report on matter. He thought that Swiss offer to assume its airlift costs provided a very good precedent.

7. UK position on withdrawal: Hammarskjold said that he had seen Selwyn Lloyd on Sunday. Lloyd had stuck to his position that withdrawal should come at end of a four-week period for establishing UNEF with clearance of Canal to begin now. Lloyd said he

---

[1] Source: Department of State, Central Files, 320.5780/11–2756. Secret; Priority. Received at 10:49 p.m. An unsigned memorandum which lists the points made by Hammarskjöld during this conversation is *ibid.*, 320.5700/11–2756.

[2] Reference is to General Assembly Resolution 1122 (XI), adopted on November 26. The resolution authorized the Secretary-General to establish a UNEF special account with an initial amount of $10 million.

would give Hammarskjold a definite date on withdrawal when he was satisfied that arrangements for clearing operation were in order. Hammarskjold said Fawzi (Egypt) had told him that clearance operations could begin the day after withdrawals had been completed. Hammarskjold said he considered that Selwyn Lloyd had given clear indication that as soon as UNEF could be presented to world as going concern, British forces would withdraw. Hammarskjold felt next move would be for Lloyd to give Secretary General date on which withdrawal would be completed. In his talk with Fawzi on Sunday, Hammarskjold had asked Fawzi to obtain Egyptian government's agreement to hold up any action on British and French nationals in Egypt which Fawzi had undertaken to recommend to Egyptian Government.

8. SYG plan for linking withdrawal and clearance: Hammarskjold said that instead of working out an agreement under which UK and France would leave it to Secretary General to determine when UNEF was sufficiently established and withdrawal would be a phased operation in agreement with General Burns, he would prefer to deal with problem of withdrawal on basis of three announcements. These should be (1) that on a certain date UNEF will have reached a specified, sufficient strength; (2) that on a certain date UK and France will have withdrawn their troops; and (3) that on a certain date clearance of Canal would begin. He believed that while these three announcements should not be presented as one dependent on other, they would in fact have a connection in nature of things. He recognized that many people believed Egyptian position on clearing Canal was unreasonable, but as an executive of General Assembly he had to act in accordance with fact that General Assembly has given clear priority to withdrawal and there was as yet no reason why withdrawal should not take place.

9. Contractual arrangements for Canal clearance: Hammarskjold said that McCloy would enter into contracts for clearance operations to which Egypt's consent would not be required. He believed, however, that "heads of agreement" between Egypt and the UN should be established. UN would take responsibility for clearance project but he did not consider it feasible to ask Egypt to pay for it. He recognized that McCloy would have to obtain credit and UN would thus have to underwrite a loan. He was thinking of final payments coming from Canal tolls, but to try to get General Assembly to say that Egypt should pay would raise question of responsibility for present situation and this would lead to sterile debate and great difficulties.

10. Latest UK thinking on withdrawal: Phleger saw Secretary General again at 1 p.m. Secretary General said talk he had just had with Lloyd had provided some basis for encouragement but he felt

he could not reveal substance at this time. He said he would react as soon as possible to latest UK views and that meanwhile Lloyd would be consulting in London.

11. SYG views on Suez settlement: Phleger then pointed out present situation must not be permitted result in status quo ante and asked whether Secretary General believed Egypt now ready negotiate in good faith on Suez settlement.

Secretary General said he not discouraged by Fawzi's vague reply to his memo elaborating possible understanding on basis six principles,[3] although it is clear Egypt will not make a concrete proposal which other side could turn down. Secretary General believes he should continue try to get both sides to accept his elaboration of principles as basis for further talks. Once this is done, he believes Egypt will agree renew discussions, but timing is critical.

He stressed he must first bring about firm understanding on withdrawal of forces and beginning of Canal clearance. Once this achieved in "publicly-presentable" form, he will press on Suez negotiations. He plans set date for resumption these negotiations as soon as possible after withdrawal-clearing agreement obtained, but two questions must appear to be separate.

Phleger then asked whether pending US resolution on Suez would be useful in this regard. Secretary General said that advantage of our proposal was that it would regularize negotiations and perhaps add a new form of pressure. However, he still believed it would be preferable to maintain his role and to seek to have discussion resumed on basis of his memorandum. At some time it might be useful to have a resolution merely asking him to press on with his efforts toward a Suez settlement, but he was not at all sure about this.

Secretary General indicated that he could not hope to get Egyptian agreement now to resume these negotiations since Egypt fears United Kingdom and France would try to use presence of their forces as form of pressure. However, Secretary General is now convinced that while United Kingdom is still seeking to use presence of its forces as form of pressure to bring about an effective UN force and agreement on early clearance of Canal, United Kingdom is no longer seeking to use their forces as a means of bringing about Suez settlement along lines of their original ideas.

He also stated he did not believe Soviet Union would attempt involve itself as a party in negotiations for Suez settlement so long as US did not do so. He did fear that India might seek to become

---

[3] Reference is to Hammarskjöld's letter to Fawzi on October 24 and Fawzi's response on November 2. (Exchange of Correspondence Between the Secretary-General and the Minister for Foreign Affairs of Egypt, U.N. doc. S/3728)

involved through Menon but said that it was very clear to him that neither Fawzi nor Nasser wished to have Indians involved.

11. [*12.*] SYG views on Palestine settlement: Phleger pointed out there were disturbing indications that Nasser appears to be riding "new crest of influence". Nasser's activities in Syria, Libya, Lebanon and Ethiopia indicate that unless we obtain a Palestine settlement soon, Nasser may emerge as strong as ever. Secretary General said that there was no one he liked to deal with less than Nasser . . . . However, . . . Israeli action has forced us into position of appearing to support Egypt, he said, and we are still caught on that dilemma. He added "we must play Arabs down, but play them down by fair means."

Secretary General said there was now firm evidence of Nasser's unpopularity in much of Arab world and he felt this was card which could still be played. This, however, could only be done by US, and to do this US would have to utilize to full its new prestige in most of Arab states. He felt that US must work with stable elements in Arab world and use them to build up reaction against Nasser and in favor of an acceptable Palestine settlement.

Equally important he said was need to bring Israel to realization of need for moderation. Without Sharett, the Secretary General said, he has no channel to Israeli Government. Eban is only channel he can now use and he does not regard it as very satisfactory one.

Secretary General then commented in very general way about kind of Palestine settlement which should be sought, pointing out that refugee question would have to be handled rather separately and that any discussion of border changes would have to include some form of guarantees.

Phleger then asked Secretary General whether he thought that pending US resolution on Palestine should be kept in its present form or be made somewhat more specific. Secretary General said that it would not help to make it more specific and thought it would be dangerous to refer to past resolutions. As to timing for action on US-Palestine resolution, Secretary General said that he would have to have at least one week to nail down withdrawal-clearance problem. After that, and perhaps early during following week, it might be timely to bring up for discussion Palestine resolution. It would be a pity, he said, if nothing were done to stress UN interest in Palestine settlement before the Christmas recess. If we moved shortly after he has pinned down withdrawal-clearance matter, there would be time for adequate discussion of Palestine resolution before Christmas recess.

Secretary General also threw out name of Galo-Plaza, ex-President of Ecuador, as possible member of committee mentioned in

Palestine resolution. He did this after Phleger had noted that Lleras Camargo had been named for Hungarian investigating committee.

Secretary General also pointed out that Lleras would still be available for Palestine committee.

Lodge

---

621.   **Memorandum of a Telephone Conversation Between the Chairman of the Joint Chiefs of Staff (Radford) and the Counselor of the Department of State (MacArthur), Washington, November 29, 1956** [1]

Admiral Radford called me this morning to say that he was much disturbed about the Egyptian situation. He said he had read Ambassador Hare's recent messages of his talks with Nasser and the Egyptians, and he felt that Ambassador Hare was inclined to take the word of Nasser and his associates at face value. This was not realistic, since we had . . . information . . . which indicated that while Nasser talked one way to Hare, he was behaving in an entirely different way and was in general instructing his subordinates to do things which were very dangerous from our viewpoint.

Admiral Radford said he felt it was vital that arrangements be made for Ambassador Hare to see the same . . . reports which we received here. . . . he would be in a better position to evaluate what Nasser was really up to and would not be taken in by protestations of one kind when Nasser was acting in directly the opposite sense. . . .

I said I did not know what arrangements had been made for keeping Ambassador Hare up-to-date . . . , but I agreed it was important that he should know what we know. I said I would bring this to the attention of Mr. Hoover and Mr. Rountree. Admiral Radford said he was also disturbed because he did not think Ambassador Lodge had adequate knowledge . . . . At least this was the impression he had from some of the statements Ambassador Lodge had made.

Admiral Radford said he was desperately concerned about the situation in the Middle East and had called me because he wanted to

---

[1] Source: Department of State, Central Files, 774.00/11–2956. Top Secret; Limited Distribution. Drafted by MacArthur. Copies were sent to Hoover, Murphy, Rountree, and Armstrong.

get this off his chest. He said he personally felt the situation was going to bog down and disintegrate and that if it did so, the military had to be in a position to act if hostilities spread. The Department of State had opposed certain moves which Admiral Radford had proposed to strengthen our military posture in the Middle East. He was unhappy about this. He reiterated that he felt there would be no solution at the UN and that the situation would end up with Nasser in control and that Nasser would then start to do all kinds of things after the British and French withdrawal when there were no longer any strings on him.

I replied that we felt we must pursue these matters in the UN and that we were hopeful with respect to the withdrawal of British and French troops that some announcement might shortly come from London which would enable us to take constructive steps to be of assistance. Admiral Radford said he hoped I was right, but he had great forebodings about being able to work out anything in the UN since he thought the UN Secretary General had also been taken in by the Egyptians and the end result was going to be very bad.

The Admiral concluded by reiterating that he was so disturbed that he had called to get this off his chest, and I replied that I would of course bring his views to the attention of Mr. Hoover and Mr. Rountree.

---

622.   Telegram From the Embassy in the United Kingdom to the Department of State [1]

London, November 29, 1956—6 p.m.

3018. Eyes only for Acting Secretary from Ambassador. During my conversation with Butler referred to mytel 3004, [2] which took place immediately after a cabinet meeting, he stated that program which had been outlined by Kirkpatrick to me earlier (mytel 3006) [3]

---

[1] Source: Department of State, Central Files, 974.7301/11–2956. Top Secret; Niact. Received at 3:02 p.m.

[2] Telegram 3004, November 29, reported that Butler was hoping to reconcile as many as possible of the Conservative "rebel group" to the withdrawal policy to be announced on Monday, December 3. He felt that it would be helpful if the United States could announce implementation of the MEEC plan on November 29. (*Ibid.*, 880.2553/11–2956)

[3] Telegram 3006, November 28, reported that, according to Kirkpatrick, Lloyd would make a holding statement in Commons on November 29. Pineau would then come to London to coordinate French action with the British, and on December 3 the

had been adopted by the cabinet and that, subject to agreement by the French, final announcement of cabinet decision to withdraw from Egypt would be made Monday. Butler said that all of these matters covered by message which Caccia would deliver to you today. Butler stated that debate on the government's course of action would continue until Wednesday or Thursday of next week and that the final vote on the motion of censure would probably take place Thursday afternoon or evening. Butler said that it would be the greatest possible assistance to HMG and a great factor in healing US-UK relations if as soon as possible after the Foreign Secretary's policy statement on Monday afternoon the USG could (1) express satisfaction concerning HMG's intentions and policy, will [(2)?] put the full weight of the USG behind the Secretary General's plans to make the UN force an adequate and effective one, and (3) state (a) that the USG will give all assistance possible to see that the UN operation for clearing the Canal proceeds efficiently, (b) that USG desires to see a rapid conclusion of an agreement to give effect to the Security Council's October resolution setting forth the six principles of settlement, and (c) that USG intends to secure a permanent settlement of the basic problems of the Middle East area.

I am sure that Butler is right in his feeling that such a statement would not only be of great assistance to HMG in the debate next week but also a vital factor in improving the relations between the US and the UK. Assuming that the action of HMG is as satisfactory as has been forecast, I am firmly convinced that it would be greatly to the interest of the US for us to issue such a statement.

Aldrich

British Government would announce to Commons its definite intention to withdraw troops within 15 days. (*Ibid.*, 684A.86/11–2856)

623.   Telegram From the Department of State to the Consulate General at Dhahran [1]

Washington, November 29, 1956—8 p.m.

204. For Ambassador Wadsworth. Director Defense Mobilization planning issue in immediate future announcement summarized as follows:

Secretary of Interior will put into effect plan of action under which 15 US oil companies will coordinate efforts they have been making individually to solve oil supply problem created throughout the world by closure Suez Canal and severance some ME pipelines. Current transportation problem means reduction consumption and that output of oil cannot be maintained at normal levels in some producing areas such as ME. US desires cooperate as much as possible in lessening effects present situation in both consuming and producing countries. Contemplated coordination of industry efforts will ensure the most efficient use of available tankers for oil shipments. Even so there will remain substantial shortage in supply which cannot be overcome in some areas so long as Suez Canal remains closed and pipelines unrepaired. End summary.

You will note statement refers to coordination US company efforts and does not refer directly to UK–France. FYI However, in actual practice US companies would be working with foreign companies as they are to some extent at present time. End FYI.

Purpose Depcirtel 435 and Deptel 182 [2] was, of course, to prepare King Saud for such action. There is one point your conversation with King contained Dhahran's 243 [3] which indicates possible misunderstanding which you may wish urgently to clarify i.e., your statement that UK–French forces would have left Egypt before our redistribution plan could be brought into effect. [4] This connection, while implementation plan will follow assurance that UK and French forces will in fact withdraw, it was not contemplated that plan would be completely withheld pending full withdrawal. To do so would place undue heavy burden upon European and Asian consum-

---

[1] Source: Department of State, Central Files, 880.2553/11–2956. Secret; Niact. Drafted by Rountree and approved by McAuliffe. Repeated Niact to Jidda.

[2] Documents 608 and 586.

[3] Document 616.

[4] On November 28 in a letter to Hoover, Deputy Secretary of Defense Robertson expressed his concern over this aspect of Wadsworth's report of his conversation with King Saud, and recommended an approach to the King that would minimize the shock to him of any possible U.S. action. (Department of State, Central Files, 880.2553/11–2856) Hoover assured Robertson in a note dated November 29 that no action would be taken without the advice of the Cabinet Committee.

ers of oil and ME oil producing countries. Such punishment would do irreparable harm and would serve no useful purpose.

In further clarifying US position you should emphasize our concern for countries other than UK and France, pointing out that UK and France control adequate transportation facilities to meet their own petroleum requirements if they wished to do so at expense of other countries which UK and French interests have traditionally supplied.

In general our purpose re Saud is to inform him in advance of US actions of direct interest to him; to assure him that his interests are foremost in our minds; to demonstrate that actions which we propose are entirely consistent with our efforts to bring peace to the ME and withdrawal of foreign forces from Egypt; and to elicit his sympathetic attitude toward measures designed to meet critical needs of many countries throughout world who have no responsibility for recent ME developments. We attach utmost importance to his understanding our policies and motivations in matters of mutual concern.

You might find it possible discreetly to use fact that Soviets have offered large amounts of oil to various countries including France. This demonstrates not only Soviet duplicity but obvious Soviet effort to inject itself as supplier of oil as substitute for Saudi Arabia and other ME producing countries. [5]

Hoover

---

[5] According to the notes of the Secretary's Staff Meeting for November 30, the following comments were made concerning the instructions sent to Wadsworth in telegram 204: "After reading the actual cable on which this report was based Mr. Phleger said he believed we should make it quite clear that King Saud does not have veto rights over the extraction of oil from his country since legally by the terms of the concession the oil belongs to the US concessionaire for whatever purpose he intends to put it. He said he realized that an unfortunate precedent had already been created with respect to Israel, but that withholding oil in such countries as Sweden and Norway was very difficult; and that if enough of these precedents developed, they could prove detrimental to US security. Mr. Phleger also said that the US should not get itself in the public posture of using the control of oil to force the UK and French withdrawal from Egypt. He observed that withholding oil publicly might actually retard the withdrawal. Messrs. Murphy and Elbrick then advised of the ODM press release to be made at noon today." (*Ibid.*, Secretary's Staff Meetings: Lot 63 D 75)

624.   Circular Telegram From the Department of State to All Diplomatic Missions, Legations, and the Mission at the United Nations [1]

Washington, November 29, 1956—8:37 p.m.

451. Following is text press release to be issued 12 noon EST November 30 by Office Defense Mobilization. For your information and not for release elsewhere.

Begin verbatim text

The Director of ODM, after consultation with the Acting Secretary of State and with the approval of the President, today requested the Secretary of the Interior to authorize fifteen US oil companies to coordinate the efforts they have been making individually to assist in handling the oil supply problem resulting from the closing of the Suez Canal and some pipelines in the Middle East.

The present problem is essentially a transportation problem. The number of tankers available to carry oil is not sufficient to permit maintaining oil consumption at normal levels everywhere in the world. The shortage of tankers also means that, although the world supply of oil is adequate, under present conditions normal output cannot be shipped from the producing areas of the Middle East. The US desires to cooperate as fully as possible in lessening the effects of the present situation in both consuming and producing countries. The contemplated coordination of industry efforts will insure the most efficient use of tankers and the maximum availability of petroleum products, but there will remain, in all probability, some shortages in certain consuming areas which cannot be overcome as long as the Suez Canal remains closed and the pipelines are unrepaired. *End verbatim text.*

Anticipate release of foregoing (which will result in activation Middle East Emergency Committee) will bring considerable reduction in criticism US failure hitherto to activate Committee but will prompt many questions both technical and other regarding reasons for finally starting committee and likely effect of it.

While there will be effort on part press to interpret this 1) as result pressure other countries especially British and French; 2) and that delay in announcement represents effort on part US to put pressure on British, French to withdraw from Egypt we should not acknowledge either. Interpretative comment should be kept to mini-

---

[1] Source: Department of State, Central Files, 840.04/11–2956. Official Use Only. Sent Priority to all West European posts. Telegram 3837 to London, November 29, informed Aldrich: "In belief it may be helpful to Lloyd and Pineau in their discussion tomorrow re Suez request you inform Lloyd at earliest opportunity tomorrow morning that announcement contained in immediately following priority circular 451 re oil will be issued Washington 12 noon EST Nov. 30." (*Ibid.*)

mum in order de-emphasize as much as possible significance of release. Primary emphasis should be placed on:

1. Premature activation Committee would have jeopardized oil supplies and ability Committee work effectively.

2. Fact action taken is to minimize effect both on consumers and producers of oil throughout world who are affected by situation. Avoid any suggestion action represents support for British and French military action.

3. Basic problem is one of transportation and Committee will be concerned primarily with problem coordinating transport movements in order maximize oil deliveries.

4. Despite most energetic efforts at coordination oil movements normal Middle East suppliers and their customers particularly in Europe will experience reduction in output and supplies until normal channels are opened. FYI shortage in Europe may amount to as much as 20-25 percent. Shortages elsewhere probable but extent not yet clear. End FYI.

5. Delay in activating Committee has not significantly lessened deliveries due fact that last deliveries from Middle East just recently arrived and substantial flow oil from US Gulf already under way. Fourth week November this amounted over 300,000 bbls per day crude in contrast no oil first week November.

6. Start of Committee has no financial aid implications. While there will be additional dollar costs for alternative oil supplies countries should be able to meet these for a while from their own resources. Later problems this field will in any case be subject for governments not committee of oil companies.

7. It is anticipated that OEEC with the help of industry committees in Europe will determine European requirements and the basis for division of available oil supplies among its member countries.

Hoover

---

625.   Telegram From the Mission at the United Nations to the Department of State [1]

New York, November 29, 1956—9 p.m.

Delga 231. Re Palestine/Suez. Eban, Rafael and Kidron (Israel) called on me at their request. They came to inform me of conversation with SYG concerning expediting arrangements for "agreed with-

[1] Source: Department of State, Central Files, 684A.86/11–2956. Secret; Priority. Received at 10:43 p.m.

drawal". Eban said it was their aim to do everything possible to use UNEF to assure that UNEF, not Nasser, came into certain sensitive areas, and in order avoid Nasser's laying basis for future hostile activities against Israel. Eban had asked SYG what his plans were concerning phasing of withdrawal and functioning of UNEF.

1. First problem area was Gulf of Aqaba, islands at mouth, and strip on Peninsula overlooking them. By having UNEF take over in islands and mainland strip it would be possible for waterway to be kept open so long as UNEF remained. Eban asked SYG what chances were of getting agreement to have UNEF take over there, pending some arrangement to assure open waterway through Gulf of Aqaba. He said SYG felt something might later be worked out. Now it would not be possible, UNEF not now in sufficient strength to go there. Hence SYG favored accelerating Israeli withdrawal elsewhere and coming back to this later. Eban pointed out, in this connection, that Israel did not share UK view that there has to be numerical relationship between UNEF and Anglo-French forces. He also said Israel not concerned about evacuating two islands if UNEF can take over in strip dominating entrance to gulf. Eban said Hammarskjold took position that wherever UNEF went Egyptian forces were not to follow. Thus, if UNEF can take over at entrance to gulf, there will be no Egyptian forces, and consequently no firing upon Israeli shipping. Hammarskjold was reported to have told Eban that he would make a proposal regarding this area in last stages of withdrawal operation.

2. Situation in Gaza. Eban admitted that conditions there had been bad in first week Israeli occupation. He said present emphasis was now on civilian services, and that Israelis had linked up electricity and water in Gaza with supply lines from Israel. They were establishing "local based" civilian authority—using local Arabs. Eban said Hammarskjold had agreed, in view of complexities of Gaza situation, that it would be wise defer question withdrawal from Gaza to later stage also. He had urged Israelis to refrain from making statements concerning their long range ambitions re Gaza. He had pointed out there were very serious legal problems connected with status of Gaza.

3. Sinai. Eban said their aim was to get out of Sinai quickly. It was "bleak, hot and waterless"—"thoroughly unpleasant" to keep an army there and consequently understandable why Egyptians had not put up better fight. He said it was Israel's aim to avoid reconstruction of Soviet base in Sinai as well as underground depot. They favored ultimate establishment of buffer zone between Israel and Egypt. Hammarskjold had in mind establishing UNEF only in key positions in Sinai and having Egyptian and Israeli troops out completely. This was satisfactory to Eban.

Eban said Hammarskjold had in mind working on Sinai situation after Port Said had been completely taken care of. UNEF could then move into Sinai and, under Hammarskjold's theory, Egypt could not. UNEF would thus act as shield between two countries. This, however, raised in Eban's mind question of duration of UNEF. He feared that once Nasser was satisfied British and French forces completely withdrawn, he would turn upon UNEF to try to get them out. Eban strongly argued that control of duration of UNEF in Egypt must not be left in Nasser's hands, but was matter for UNGA to decide.

I interrupted at that point to ask whether Israel really feared Egyptian offensive capabilities. Eban answered: "Frankly no, as far as Egypt alone is concerned." What Israel does fear is Soviet role, particularly in developing Syrian situation.

Continuing, Eban reported Hammarskjold as stating, in view delicacy present situation, certain amount of "calculated ambiguity" had to be accepted. Over next several months while UNEF was functioning, there would be opportunity work out future arrangements.

Eban then came to specific request Hammarskjold made of them. He said Israel planned to take out equivalent of one more brigade shortly, leaving their forces in Sinai "very thin". Hammarskjold had requested that they announce "very soon" that there were no Israeli forces at all near Canal. Hammarskjold had in mind that, as soon as Port Said situation clarified, and Israeli forces were then considerable way back into Sinai from Canal, UNEF could be moved into area between Canal and westernmost Israeli positions. This plan of Hammarskjold's was linked to Canal clearance operation which could then begin in earnest. Eban said he had recommended to Foreign Office Israel agree to announcement requested.

Hammarskjold had also asked them not to say anything regarding nature of their discussions with him. All of above Eban wanted us to know confidentially.

Lodge

626.   Memorandum of Discussion at the 305th Meeting of the National Security Council, Washington, November 30, 1956 [1]

[Here follows a paragraph listing the participants at the meeting. Vice President Nixon presided over the meeting.]

1. Significant World Developments Affecting U.S. Security

[Here follows a report by Allen Dulles concerning the situation in Hungary.]

Mr. [Allen] Dulles then referred to the receipt of a series of dramatic cables from Great Britain and France, describing the acute rise of anti-Americanism in these two countries in recent days. In Great Britain this sentiment was largely confined to the ranks of the Conservative Party. Obviously, however, both Britain and France were in a highly psychopathic state which promised to become worse with the onset of cold weather. The British and French will naturally tend to blame the United States, rather than themselves, for the situation in which they will find themselves. Mr. Dulles thought that Premier Mollet's position was possibly threatened, except for the fact that no one seemed anxious at the moment to take over from him. Mendes-France was, of course, the most likely successor, but he will probably bide his time before trying to upset Mollet. The prospect of a French Government headed by Mendes-France could not be very appealing to the United States.

Feeling in most of the other NATO countries has been, up to now, strongly in favor of the policy of the United States. Of late, however, this approbation has been mixed with anxiety over the evident decline in Britain's prestige, which many of these people believe can not but impair the prestige of Western Europe as a whole. Mr. Dulles added the parenthetical thought that our recent strong statement in support of the Baghdad Pact [2] seems to have had a very salubrious effect.

[Here follows discussion of Syria; for text, see volume XIII, page 606.]

With respect to the situation in Egypt, Mr. Dulles pointed out that it was apparently the intention of the British to push their operations for clearing the Suez Canal at least as far as Qantara. In fact, they have already cleared the Canal for the use of small vessels

---

[1] Source: Eisenhower Library, Whitman File, NSC Records. Top Secret. Drafted by Gleason on November 30.

[2] For text of the statement, issued as a press release on November 29, see Department of State *Bulletin*, December 19, 1956, p. 918. Documentation on the Baghdad Pact is scheduled for publication in volume XII.

as far as this point. Meanwhile, Nasser was still playing both sides against the middle, to the considerable confusion of the Egyptian people. Outwardly, Nasser seems now to be playing down the threat of inviting in "volunteers" from the USSR. The economic situation in Egypt had deteriorated to a grave point, and Nasser has now gone far in his effort to drive out all Western and Jewish commercial interests. World reaction to these moves has been such that Nasser may well feel inclined to play them down, but he will nevertheless proceed less ostentatiously to get rid of the Jewish population of Egypt.

Nasser was still likewise negotiating for new arms from the Soviet bloc. There was very hard evidence on this point. On the other hand, his talks with the USSR in the political field have lately tended to be routine and general in character.

Mr. Dulles concluded his remarks on the situation in the Near East by a summary of the latest Special National Intelligence Estimate (SNIE 11–10–56, on "Soviet Actions in the Middle East", dated November 29, 1956; [3] copy filed in the minutes of the meeting).

As to the reports that the Soviet Union was prepared to supply oil from bloc sources for Europe, Mr. Dulles stated that the present indications were that the USSR is supplying approximately 90,000 barrels of oil a day to the free world. Of this total, some 50,000 barrels a day were going to Scandinavia, Finland and Iceland. The Soviet Union has indicated its willingness to supply in addition some 20,000 barrels a day to France—a rather surprising offer, in view of the existing situation. Mr. Dulles indicated that the Soviet bloc could supply considerably more crude oil to the free world if Western tankers were made available to haul the oil.

The National Security Council: [4]

Noted an oral briefing by the Director of Central Intelligence on the subject, with specific reference to the situation in Hungary; possible unrest in the USSR; the rise of anti-Americanism in Great Britain and France; and the situation in the Near East, including an estimate of Soviet objectives in that area.

2. Developments With Respect to the Near East Situation and Their Implications for U.S. Security (NSC Actions Nos. 1629, 1630 and 1632) [5]

Acting Secretary of State Hoover said he believed that the Council's focus of interest at the moment centered on the United

---

[3] Not printed here; scheduled for publication in volume XII.

[4] The following paragraph constitutes NSC Action No. 1638, approved by the President on December 5. (Department of State, S/S–NSC (Miscellaneous) Files: Lot 66 D 95, Records of Action by the National Security Council, 1956)

[5] Regarding NSC Action Nos. 1629 and 1630, see footnotes 3 and 9, Document 554. Regarding NSC Action No. 1632, see footnote 3, Document 577.

Kingdom and France. He did not believe that he could add anything to the report already made on Hungary by the Director of Central Intelligence.

Secretary Hoover stated that the current situation in London could best be grasped if he simply read portions of some of the private cables which he had received from Ambassador Aldrich. In general these cables pointed up the extreme disorganization of the British Government at the present time. As an example, Secretary Hoover then read from a cable from Ambassador Aldrich describing his appearance at No. 10 Downing Street just at the end of a meeting of the British Cabinet which decided on a withdrawal of British forces from the Suez Canal Zone. [6] The members of the Cabinet had expressed to Aldrich their very great fear that the Conservative Government would fall as a result of the decision to comply with the demands of the United Nations on the withdrawal of British forces. Nevertheless, the decision to do so was to be made public in a statement next Monday. Butler had expressed to Aldrich his great hope that, immediately after the British Cabinet statement on Monday, a strong U.S. statement of support would be issued. Secretary Hoover added that the State Department was currently engaged in drafting such a statement of support, but it was not yet possible to present it in its final form.

The situation in Paris was also extremely difficult. The French had abruptly changed their tactics in a fashion which it was difficult for us to understand. A few days ago the French were eagerly urging the British to agree to withdraw the allied forces from the Canal Zone; but now they have suddenly become very intractable in the opposite direction. As an illustration of the state of mind in Paris, Secretary Hoover read from a fairly lengthy and highly pessimistic cable sent by Ambassador Dillon just before he left Paris. [7] Secretary Hoover speculated that Ambassador Dillon might have been a little too alarmist in this message.

Secretary Hoover observed that Secretary Dulles, in his conversations on this matter, tended to feel that while it was unfortunate that the British and French seemed to be turning so bitterly against us, such an attitude was perfectly natural and logical. It was simply

---

[6] Reference is to telegram 3018, Document 622.

[7] Reference is presumably to telegram 2649, November 28, not printed. In this telegram, Dillon reported that the French reaction to France's deteriorating international position was one of frustration, humiliation, and rage and that the favorite scapegoats in France for recent adversities were the United Nations and the United States. Dillon warned that if the French were exposed to a substantial number of further "humiliations" over the coming months, they were capable of quitting the United Nations and NATO and retiring into a neutralist isolation from which they would hope to make separate deals with the Soviet Union. (Department of State, Central Files, 751.00/11–2856)

the result of complete and utter frustration. While this was regrettable, Secretary Dulles did not believe the development was alarming or that it foreshadowed any basic split between the United States on the one hand and Britain and France on the other. On the contrary, what was going on was essentially a violent family squabble, but not one which was likely to end in a divorce. Secretary Hoover commented that this view of Secretary Dulles was one which was apparently shared by practically everyone in the U.S. Government. He added further that the people of Great Britain were obviously very "rattled". This was not only true of British officials at home, but in Washington and in the United Nations, where all kinds of charges and accusations were constantly springing up. Evidence of the unsettled state of British officialdom was the approach of Kirkpatrick, the Permanent Under Secretary of the British Foreign Office, to Donald Cook, the representative of the *New York Herald Tribune* in London. In a conversation on Wednesday, Kirkpatrick had stated to Cook that the Conservative Government would almost certainly fall on Monday if it agreed to the UN demand for withdrawal, and that a general election in Great Britain would take place about the first of January. Other statements were made of an equally pessimistic and threatening nature. Secretary Hoover said that while he thought this might well be simply a means of trying to get U.S. support for the Conservative Government, Cook himself was so shaken by what Kirkpatrick had told him, that he had decided not to write for his newspaper the story based on this conversation.

Secretary Hoover went on to say that what we were witnessing at the present time was a very rare phenomenon for the United Kingdom. It was nothing less than a decision for complete reversal of a disastrous policy in the very middle of a crisis and without involving any change of the party at the head of the Government. If this reversal actually works, it will be a masterful stroke by Butler. Secretary Hoover asked Secretary Humphrey if he did not agree with this appraisal, and Secretary Humphrey said he did.

Secretary Hoover then pointed out that a delegation would be going to the NATO meeting in Paris which opened on December 10. Secretary Dulles has been preparing for this meeting, which will be perhaps the most important one ever held. He was hopeful that by this time the situation in the United Kingdom and in France would have been clarified if not actually resolved.

Turning to the Middle East, Secretary Hoover indicated that the immediate problems facing the United States in that area were three. First, to provide oil and financial support to the Western European states. This subject he said he would leave for later comment by Secretary Humphrey and Dr. Flemming. The second immediate problem was to get the Suez Canal cleared of its obstructions and the oil pipelines repaired. The third problem was to find ways and means, once the British and French have committed themselves to withdrawal from the Canal Zone, to support the Western position in the Middle East. Once our hands are freed by an Anglo-French withdrawal, we will be able to proceed to measures to this end which we have not been able to use up to now. We have a great many things in mind to propose when the time for action is at hand. For example, Ambassador Lodge has been considering several UN resolutions designed to deal with the serious threat in Syria. One such resolution calls for the admission of UN forces into Syria to oversee the restoration of the pipelines. There were also a variety of longer-term U.S. proposals which Secretary Hoover said he would not go into at this meeting. He then indicated that this was the substance of his report.

Secretary Wilson said it seemed clear enough to him that the time was at hand when somebody would have to tell Nasser to quit throwing his weight around. Particularly, we have got to insist that the Suez Canal be cleared of obstructions and opened up at once. Somehow or other we here do not seem to realize fully what is going to happen in Western Europe this winter.

Secretary Humphrey commented that the possibilities, for good and for evil, which could come out of the present situation were such that they could scarcely be exaggerated. The range was complete from great success to genuine disaster. In Britain, he pointed out, there was now going on a terrific fight between the two wings of the Conservative Party. It was touch-and-go whether the Victorians or the Moderns would end up in control of the Tory Party. If the Modern Conservative element did not win out over the old-fashioned element, the Conservative Government was likely to fall and we would be facing a meeting of the NATO Council in December under the shadow of a general election in England in January. What would happen to NATO under these circumstances was certainly impossible to predict. Thus anything that the United States can do to help the Conservatives through their difficulties and to work out an acceptable Middle East settlement, we certainly ought to be prepared to do. In short, the minute that the British Cabinet acts next Monday and states its compliance with the UN order to withdraw, this Government should be prepared to give Butler everything that he asks of us in the statement he makes on Monday. Similarly, we should make crystal clear our own attitude toward Nasser. We should make it plain that we will be just as tough with him, if he remains unreasonable, as we have been with the British and the French. He must be made aware that he is obliged, as were the British and the French, to comply fully with the terms of the UN Resolution. The UN Resolution prepares the groundwork for a fair settlement of the problems of the Middle East. To secure compliance with it we should be prepared to use our whips on both sides.

Secretary Hoover said that he had long felt that once the British and French had clearly made a commitment to withdraw from the Suez Canal Zone, the whole world could be expected to turn against Nasser if he did not change his tactics. Secretary Humphrey said that he was in 100% agreement with Secretary Hoover, and that he believed we should tolerate no monkey-business from Nasser once the British and French had complied with the UN Resolution.

Secretary Wilson warned that in all essentials the monkey was presently going to come off the back of the British and be put on our own back. It would be our job, in short—not the Anglo-French job—to compel Nasser to behave himself and to comply with the wishes of the United Nations.

The Vice President inquired whether this Government could not do anything to assist the Conservatives prior to Monday. He expressed himself as scared to death at the prospect of Nye Bevan in a position of power in a future British Government.

Dr. Flemming said that with respect to the oil situation most of the discussion in his Committee of late had turned upon the timing as to when to put the Middle East emergency plan into action. Messrs. Hoover, Humphrey, Admiral Radford, Governor Adams, himself, and others, had had a meeting late yesterday. [8] The result was a decision to recommend to the President that we announce at noon today that we were putting our emergency plan into action to get oil to Europe. Within 48 to 72 hours thereafter, Dr. Flemming predicted, we would begin to see considerable results from the pooling of resources and tankers by the oil companies. Great improvements in the shipping of oil to Europe would be visible a week or two thereafter. In fact, the oil companies believe that by thus pooling their resources, shipping efficiency will be increased some 25%. Dr. Flemming then provided the National Security Council with other details of the work of his Committee, including its work with the State Commissions, especially Louisiana and Texas. He concluded by stating that once the green light is given, much more oil will be made available to the Western European countries.

---

[8] Sherman Adams indicates in his memoirs that he attended, as a representative of President Eisenhower, several meetings dealing with the oil question in later November 1956. For Adams' account of the meetings which resulted in the decision presented to the NSC on November 30, see *Firsthand Report, The Story of the Eisenhower Administration* (New York: Harper & Brother, 1961), pp. 262–270. No accounts of these meetings have been found in Department of State files or the Eisenhower Library.

The Vice President inquired whether Dr. Flemming proposed to announce the implementation of the Middle East emergency plan at a press conference. Dr. Flemming replied that the announcement would be made through a press release to be made at noon today. Secretary Wilson asked to be cut in on the conference with the public relations people which would follow the press release. Secretary Hoover pointed out that only ODM and State were to comment on the contents of the press release. Dr. Flemming then summarized the statement which would be given out at 12 noon. [9]

Governor Adams broke in to state that the President had been talking with Secretary Dulles, and that Secretary Hoover would be asked to listen to a statement which it was proposed that the President would make. The Presidential statement would deal with the situation in the general context of the continued validity of our alliance with Great Britain and France. Accordingly, there may be this Presidential statement in addition to the statement issued by Dr. Flemming.

Secretary Hoover said that the proposal for the additional Presidential statement gave him some concern. At the very least, it was a calculated risk. A strong statement by the President on the alliance could be taken by the British and French as an indication that they need not get out of Egypt too quickly, and also might alienate the Arab world. Secretary Hoover said he believed that the President ought therefore to save his fire for the period after the British Cabinet made its announcement of withdrawal next Monday.

Secretary Humphrey commented that, as Admiral Radford had stated yesterday, we are all taking a risk on this statement to be issued by Dr. Flemming. If Dr. Flemming issues his statement at noon and the Arabs blow up the Tapline at six o'clock in the evening, we shall be in a terrible position. Indeed, the United States might find itself obliged to invade Syria in order to restore the sabotaged Tapline. Secretary Hoover replied that the United States was scarcely in a position to invade any Arab country in the light of the position that we had taken on the Anglo-French invasion of Egypt. Secretary Humphrey said that in any case he agreed with Secretary Hoover that the proposed Presidential statement should not be issued until after Monday. Governor Adams pointed out that the President's statement addressed itself not so much to the specific situation in the Suez Canal as it did to the general situation and the validity of the alliance. Actually, he added, he had not been in on the discussion of this statement between the President and the

---

[9] See circular telegram 451, Document 624.

Secretary of State, and had not seen the text. He said, however, that we would know what the text contained very shortly. [10]

Admiral Radford said he wished to give expression to his very great concern about the situation of Britain and France. The blocking of the Canal was a matter of the gravest import to these countries. While we did not actually know the precise extent to which the Canal had been damaged, we feel that it could probably be cleared a good deal faster than many of the current estimates. Unfortunately, as yet Nasser has not permitted anyone to survey the situation in the Canal as a whole. Accordingly, Admiral Radford recommended that if the President did make the proposed statement, he should add to it a statement that he was sending our top U.S. salvage men to survey the entire Suez Canal. Such a statement would have a very salutary effect, not only in Britain and France, but on Nasser himself. Essentially, the opening of the Canal is being blocked by the Russians. The Canal is the key to the situation both of Europe and of the Far East. A prompt move to open the Canal would have the support of the entire United Nations once the British and French were out. Accordingly, we should force Nasser to permit representatives of U.S. salvage concerns to survey the entire Canal.

Secretary Wilson said he would go even further than Admiral Radford. He believed that we could not permit Nasser to take a single additional negative position or action. We had been more than a little naive in our appraisal of Nasser and his objectives. Our position with respect to the British and the French had been "pure", but the time had now come when we must take over the burden of the British and the French in dealing with Nasser. Mr. Allen Dulles interrupted to warn that Nasser would be hard to deal with, and that if we pushed him he might threaten to turn to the Soviets. Secretary Wilson went on to say that, nevertheless, the time had come to take a strong position with Nasser and to force him to quit his obstructionist tactics. Admiral Radford added his conviction that Nasser was currently engaged in giving the United States and the West the "grand double-cross". He again called for forcing Nasser's hand, especially in the matter of the survey of the Canal by U.S. salvage teams.

Secretary Humphrey expressed his complete agreement with Admiral Radford on the behavior of Nasser and on the need for a prompt clearing of the Suez Canal. On the other hand, he pointed out, Hammarskjöld had just gotten together a survey group which was to survey the entire reaches of the Canal. This group was about to depart for Egypt, and everything depended on how it was

---

[10] The text of the White House statement, announcing activation of the MEEC plan, appeared in *The New York Times*, December 1.

received there. Thus, the fat was in the fire, and perhaps our best course was to try to proceed to have the Canal surveyed under the auspices of the UN group, at least until we are sure that Nasser will refuse entry of the Hammarskjöld survey group into the Canal Zone. Admiral Radford stated that officially, in any case, the United States must lend all possible weight to a survey by salvage teams and subsequently to the prompt reopening of the Canal. With this Secretary Humphrey expressed agreement, and Admiral Radford stated that Admiral Burke believed that with a vigorous program headed by U.S. experts, the Canal could be opened up to navigation in perhaps 60 days.

Secretary Wilson observed that if the British Government backed down and withdrew their forces from the Canal, as they seemed likely to do, we should realize how very difficult this decision had been for them and how handsomely they were trying to behave. Above all, we should be clear that it will then be up to us to take over and assert the position of the West vis-à-vis Nasser and the Soviets. Admiral Radford pointed out that some sort of U.S. official call for the prompt opening of the Canal would doubtless be of great assistance to the British when they made their statement of their decision to withdraw on Monday.

The Vice President then inquired as to the timetable of proposed actions by the British Government. Secretary Humphrey replied that the timetable now called for the Cabinet to make the public statement of the withdrawal on Monday next. This would be followed by a vote of confidence on a movement for censure on Wednesday in Parliament. The Vice President commented that we were thus essentially engaged in trying to shore up Butler. Secretary Humphrey said that this was the case.

Mr. Jackson reminded the Council that Secretary Hoover had omitted making any reference to the British financial problem in his report, on the assumption that Secretary Humphrey would deal with this matter. Perhaps the time had now come in the discussion to hear from Secretary Humphrey on this point.

Secretary Humphrey stated that in point of fact the financial aspects of Britain's problem were even more serious than her physical situation. The British reserves were falling very rapidly. Even some slight indication of a run on currency could spell disaster for Great Britain. We are prepared to handle the situation and to help them get themselves back in shape. We are certainly going to see them through. Secretary Wilson said that he was glad to hear this, but believed that it would be wiser for our help to be extended to the British through the World Bank and the International Monetary Fund, rather than directly. Secretary Humphrey assured Secretary Wilson that this was precisely what we were proposing to do.

The Vice President said that we had been talking a great deal about public statements by this Government. Should we not also give private assurances to the British Government as to our proposed financial assistance? Such assurances would help them through their difficult situation next Monday. Secretary Humphrey said that we had already given such assurances, and went on to state that the right people in the British Government know of our plans to assist them.

Admiral Radford again called for a public statement by the United States Government assuring that the Suez Canal would promptly be cleared and open to navigation. He believed that such a pronouncement would be of real assistance to the British in carrying through with their own statement on Monday. Secretary Humphrey said he had misgivings over this proposal, as he had earlier said. If we can just keep from rocking the boat and from getting ants in our pants over the next 48 hours, we can go all out in stating what we are going to do to get the Canal back into operation. He said he still had anxiety about making such statements prior to the British statement on Monday. The Vice President then countered with the possibility of a public statement offering Hammarskjöld U.S. salvage experts. To this, likewise, Secretary Humphrey expressed uncertainty. After all, he pointed out, we are merely talking about a matter of timing—a mere matter of 48 hours. If we can hold out for 48 hours more, and the British make their statement, we can then go ahead full steam with respect to the Canal. But meanwhile, if, under UN auspices, a move is on foot to prepare the opening of the Canal, we should not complicate the development by any additional suggestions or statements.

Assistant Secretary of State Bowie, who had replaced Acting Secretary Hoover as spokesman for the State Department, expressed his support for the views of Secretary Humphrey. He believed that an American announcement with respect to the clearing of the Canal, coming immediately after the British statement on Monday, would not only be the best way to bring pressure on Nasser, but would also be timely in reinforcing Butler's hand and keeping the Conservative rebels in check.

Governor Stassen said that he wished to give his full support to the main points made thus far in the discussion by Secretary Humphrey and Secretary Wilson as well. He was sure that we must provide quick support to Butler; that is, just as soon as the British Government issued its statement on Monday, we should be prepared to meet fully and quickly the requirements which Butler would levy upon us for our support and assistance. And, as Secretary Wilson had argued, we must follow this statement of support for Butler with strong and firm insistence that the Arab countries and Nasser behave themselves in a reasonable and constructive way. Governor Stassen then said that he had an additional point which he believed that he ought to make at this time. That is, we must be prepared to check any move by Nasser in turning toward the USSR. In order to prevent such a move, we must be ready to take the firmest possible kind of stand against Soviet intervention in either Egypt or Syria. We must say, as we had said in the matter of the Chinese Communist threat to the offshore islands, "You just can't move into this picture." If we did not issue as firm a warning to the Soviets now as we had issued to the Chinese Communists then, we would not end up with a livable world situation. Our vital interests were involved in the Middle East, and we should make this clear to the Soviet Union, which was, after all, the real aggressor in the existing situation.

Admiral Radford said that he couldn't agree more heartily with Governor Stassen's point, and said that we must indeed take a firm position vis-à-vis the USSR if the Soviets suggest the sending of troops to Syria or of large numbers of technicians to Egypt. Governor Stassen pointed out that the step he had in mind, with which Admiral Radford had agreed, should be accomplished under the auspices of the United Nations. In short, the United States should take a firm stand backing UN action with respect to Soviet intervention.

The Attorney General commented that the suggestion made by Governor Stassen seemed to him to call for a special session of Congress. Admiral Radford said that in his view the Congressional Resolution with respect to Formosa had actually prevented a war in the Far East. So, likewise, a Congressional Resolution conferring similar powers on the President to deal with the Soviets in the Middle East might have the similar result of preventing a world war.

Secretary Humphrey observed that we seemed to be looking a little too far ahead, perhaps, although he said he admitted that we might ultimately have to go "the whole way". Much depended on the events of the next few days.

Governor Stassen then expressed his agreement with Secretary Humphrey that if this Government did too much in support of the British prior to the Monday statement by the British Government, the result might be to make it harder for Butler to line up the Conservative Party behind the Monday statement of British withdrawal from the Suez Canal. On the other hand, as soon as the British statement was issued on Monday, this Government should be prepared to go all out to support Butler, so that he could be sure of winning his vote of confidence in Parliament on Wednesday. Mr. Bowie expressed his agreement that, once the British and the French had announced their departure decision, all possible heat should be turned on Nasser. This should be done not only by the United States and the Western powers, but by those Arab states who have had many private complaints against Nasser but who have been unable to express their hostility to Nasser because of the Anglo-French aggression against one of their number, Egypt.

Mr. Allen Dulles stated his general agreement with Mr. Bowie's point. He also expressed once again his extreme distrust of Nasser, and his conviction that we would need to mobilize all our resources to make the Egyptian dictator behave himself and to proceed with clearing the Canal.

The National Security Council: [11]

Discussed current and pending developments with respect to the Near East and their implications for U.S. security, in the light of:

> a. An oral report by the Acting Secretary of State on the current situation in the United Kingdom and France; and immediate problems with respect to the Near East situation, particularly the European oil supply position, the opening of the Suez Canal and the oil pipelines, and future measures in support of the Western position in the Near East.
>
> b. An oral report by the Director, Office of Defense Mobilization, on recent developments regarding the European oil supply position, and the method of putting into operation on this date the plan of action of the Middle East Emergency Committee.
>
> c. An oral report by the Secretary of the Treasury on the financial aspects of the European oil supply position.

S. Everett Gleason

---

[11] The following paragraphs constitute NSC Action No. 1639, approved by the President on December 5. (Department of State, S/S–NSC (Miscellaneous) Files: Lot 66 D 95, Records of Action by the National Security Council, 1956)

627.   Memorandum of a Telephone Conversation Between the Israeli Ambassador (Eban) in New York and the Assistant Secretary of State for Near Eastern, South Asian, and African Affairs (Rountree) in Washington, November 30, 1956 [1]

Ambassador Eban telephoned me from New York to say that he was seriously concerned over the implications which were being drawn from our statement on the Baghdad Pact, [2] which included a declaration that any threat to the members of the Pact would be viewed by the United States with the utmost gravity. The assumption was being made widely by members of the press and in the U.N. that this statement, having excluded any reference to Israel, connoted a different attitude with respect to that country.

On the other hand, the Ambassador said, Israel was being subjected to most alarming threats by several countries, particularly the Soviet Union. The Soviet threats included the very extinction of Israel. The U.S. had stated its policy regarding Israel on various occasions in the past, but Israel most earnestly desired a renewed statement in the context of the present situation which would leave no doubt regarding our attitude. He thought that "not many hours" could be allowed to elapse before such a statement was made. He was considering how this might be handled procedurally. He had thought of sending a formal communication to the Department asking for clarification of its position and attitude regarding the security of Israel. He was also considering taking the Soviet threat immediately to the Security Council, where the U.S. representative would have an opportunity to state the American position regarding Israel's security. However it was handled, he must insist that our attitude be made known publicly with the least possible delay.

I told the Ambassador that the statement which we had made yesterday was confined to the Baghdad Pact and its specific purpose was to set forth the U.S. attitude toward the Pact and its members. As he knew, the U.S. had been urged to join the Pact and a number of public statements had been made in this regard by members of the Pact. The statement did not intend nor could it be construed as intending to set forth the U.S. attitude toward the security of any countries which were not members of the Pact itself. The question of the U.S. attitude toward Israel was therefore an entirely separate matter. I would of course take the request under advisement but I could not comment further at this time.

---

[1] Source: Department of State, Central Files, 780.5/11–3056. Secret. Drafted by Rountree.

[2] See footnote 2, *supra*.

(*Note:* It should be noted in this connection that a primary objective of Israeli policy at the present time appears to be to elicit a statement of U.S. support for Israel; every conceivable pressure will be applied by the Israelis to obtain such a statement.[3] This is of course a matter with which we will have to deal with utmost caution, not because there is any doubt regarding our general support for the State of Israel but because we cannot permit ourselves to be maneuvered into a position of appearing to support Israel in the context of current situation which it has brought about for itself in Egypt. Mishandling of this matter could do irreparable damage to the whole American position in the current controversy and seriously diminish our effectiveness in dealing with the problem.)

---

[3] Also on November 30, Reuven Shiloah handed Rountree a note to Dulles from Eban requesting urgent public clarification of the U.S. Government attitude on the question of the preservation of Israeli independence against any possible aggression. (Memorandum of conversation by Rockwell, November 30; Department of State, Central Files, 684A.86/11–3056) On December 3, Eban wrote to Dulles concerning the Israeli request for a U.S. statement and attached a copy of the November 30 note. (*Ibid.*, 611.84A/12–356)

---

628.   Telegram From the Department of State to the Mission at the United Nations [1]

Washington, November 30, 1956—7:08 p.m.

384. Re Delga 176.[2] Re Palestine. You should inform Mrs. Meir that we believe Israel should comply with GA resolution and withdraw its forces from Egyptian territory and behind Armistice Line. In US view this should be accomplished without conditions and without delay. Questions such as blockade and build-up of Soviet arms while serious in themselves and requiring close attention should not affect Israel's compliance with UN resolution. In addition you may

---

[1] Source: Department of State, Central Files, 684A.86/11–2356. Confidential. Drafted by Gamon (IO/UNP), cleared by Rountree and Phleger, and approved by Wilcox who signed for Hoover.

[2] In Delga 176, Lodge reported that Meir and Eban had advised him that a complete Israeli withdrawal would only mean a renewal of the blockade and Israeli troops facing Egyptian troops on the old Armistice lines and a renewal of the build-up of Soviet war potential in the Sinai area. They said that if U.N. troops followed an Israeli withdrawal, that was another matter, but they had not received assurances from the United States that that was what was contemplated. Meir and Eban asked to be advised of the U.S. position. (*Ibid.*)

inform her we appreciate and will bear in mind concern of Israeli Government that Sinai, Tiran Straits islands, and Gaza not be permitted revert automatically to bases for Egyptian military action against Israel. You should make it clear to Mrs. Meir that US fully supports the position being taken by SYG regarding withdrawal of Israeli forces.

Memorandum Wilcox–Shiloah conversation Nov. 28 [3] touching on above being pouched.

Hoover

---

[3] Not printed. (*Ibid.*, 684A.86/11–2856)

---

629.   **Telegram From the Embassy in the United Kingdom to the Department of State** [1]

London, December 2, 1956—1 p.m.

3062. Lloyd called me to his residence late last evening. He said that as a result of their talks with the French Dixon is being instructed to inform Hammarskjold and Lodge that the following course of action has been agreed upon.

In his speech in Commons Monday [2] Lloyd will announce that British and French forces will be withdrawn from Suez "without delay". Withdrawal is premised on the fact that an adequate UN force is being built up, the UN is proceeding with the clearance of the Canal, and the Secretary General has undertaken to take steps to facilitate further negotiations looking toward the future operation of the Canal. He will not announce that British and French withdrawal will be accomplished by specified date but the intention is that the withdrawal will in fact be carried out in 15 days, i.e., by December 18. [3] The French objected to the announcement of a specific date on the grounds that such announcement might give an opportunity for the Egyptians and other Arab nations to arrange celebrations, demonstrations or other undesirable action immediately following such specific date. I argued that Soviets and Egyptians could exploit this imprecision but he said French are adamant. He added he himself

---

[1] Source: Department of State, Central Files, 684A.86/12–256. Secret; Priority. Repeated to Paris and USUN.
[2] December 3.
[3] The last Anglo-French forces left the Canal Zone on December 22.

feels it is desirable not to mention the date in order to keep the Soviets guessing. However, Hammarskjold and Lodge are being told that it will in fact be 15 days and Lloyd emphasized that the decision in this regard does not constitute stalling tactics. He hoped 15-day withdrawal period would remain confidential during Parliamentary debate but assumed it might not since it is already being speculated on freely in the press.

General Keightley is also being ordered to confer at once with General Burns with a view to Burns' taking over responsibility for law and order in Port Said as the British and French withdraw and assuring the safety of any British or French salvage equipment which may be left in the Canal. British are seriously concerned over possibilities of civil disorder when they withdraw.

Lloyd went on to discuss briefly the political effects internally of this decision. He said that the government may well fall as a result of it and that the government's ability to remain in power will depend on both the attitude of the Conservative back benchers and also the tactics adopted by the opposition. Lloyd professed to feel that decision to withdraw is correct in itself and that in fact the British have accomplished their primary purpose of terminating hostilities between Egyptians and Israelis and that their action has also resulted in the establishment of the UN force. He is consequently arguing with back benchers that withdrawal at this time is not a humiliation. He is, however, less than sanguine as to the result of his representations and feels strongly that the main determinant in their thinking will be the speed with which UN clearance of the Canal can be commenced. If UN clearance can actually begin within 4 or 5 days after his statement on Monday, i.e., before British and French withdrawal is completed, it will be very helpful and it would be of further material assistance if the UN can utilize some portion of the British and French salvage equipment even as little as one salvage vessel.

Lloyd also said that in addition to his speech in the House on Monday Macmillan will make an important economic and financial statement there Tuesday and it is still anticipated that the debate will conclude Thursday night.

Aldrich

630.   Telegram From the Embassy in Egypt to the Department of State [1]

Cairo, December 2, 1956—noon.

1752. In conversation with Nasser last night I again raised question treatment Jews (Embassy telegram 1663) [2] and noted that although reassuring public position taken by GOE and considerable improvement reported re attitude of responsible officials, Embassy continued receive reports of widespread pressure on Jews to leave and I made especial plea for stateless Jews who in most cases have roots only in Egypt. I also advanced arguments in Department telegram 1731. [3]

Nasser replied at loss understand why so much agitation. He had looked into matter and found that British and French Jews being asked leave not as Jews but as persons British and French nationality. Also some 250 stateless Jews were being expelled on individual cases as is but others allowed remain.

I said that quite frankly report given Nasser did not agree with information Embassy receiving from various sources. Also we were advised that there are number cases where no formal deportation order but pressures exerted which have same effect.

Nasser admitted there had been such cases but said now corrected and believed source of much misinformation this connection was head of Swiss unit in charge of British and French interests.

I then suggested that matter might be made clearer if correspondents allowed file stories entirely free of censorship. If this done GOE would probably see printed some things they would not like but stories would be more balanced than those emanating from foreign sources.

Nasser indicated he would take foregoing into consideration but I did not get impression of his feeling under impulsion to act vigorously. From this conversation was difficult decide whether Nasser not fully informed in what is admittedly highly complicated

---

[1] Source: Department of State, Central Files, 874.411/12–256. Secret. Received at 8 p.m. Repeated to London, Paris, Amman, Beirut, Baghdad, Damascus, and Jidda.

[2] Telegram 1663, November 26, reported that, according to a confidant of Nasser, the "highest levels" of the Egyptian Government had reviewed the status of British and French nationals and persons of Jewish origin and a clarification of policy would be issued later that day. (*Ibid.*, 641.74/11–2656)

[3] Telegram 1731, November 28, noted that the statement made by the Egyptian Government on November 26 had not relieved apprehension being fueled by stories in the U.S. press alleging the expulsion and mistreatment of Jews in Egypt. It instructed Hare, unless he strongly objected, to approach the Egyptian Government and point out the extremely serious effect on public opinion in the United States and elsewhere if Egypt carried out the repressive policies being reported. (*Ibid.*, 874.411/11–2756)

and confused matter or whether he understands and condones, or whether mixture both, which most likely.

In separate following telegram [4] Embassy has endeavored make factual analysis this subject although information still fragmentary and unreliable. Should also be emphasized that, unfortunate as have been developments affecting Jewish community in Egypt, action taken by GOE in respect Jews has been similar in spirit to that taken against British and French and little indication of anti-Semitism per se. However, dispassionate character of action does not of course constitute justification.

Hare

---

[4] Reference is to telegram 1777, December 3, not printed. (*Ibid.*, 874.411/12–356) In this telegram, the Embassy in Cairo noted that although official sanction had been given to the concept that all Jews regardless of nationality were identified with Israeli aggressors, other public statements by Egyptian officials had clearly rejected the policy of all-out anti-Jewish activities, and street violence (such as had occurred in 1947, 1948, 1949, and 1952) had been avoided. The Egyptian Government, however, clearly wished all non-Egyptian Jews to leave the country and had taken various official measures to achieve that end. (*Ibid.*)

---

631.   Telegram From the Embassy in Egypt to the Department of State [1]

Cairo, December 2, 1956—6 p.m.

1760. Re Deptels 1688 [2] and 1733. [3] In conversation with Nasser last night I raise question improper activity EG agents, especially MAs in neighboring Arab countries particularly Libya and Lebanon. Not unexpectedly, Nasser's reaction was evasive. He admitted MA in Libya had gotten out of line, especially following attack on Egypt,

---

[1] Source: Department of State, Central Files, 684A.86/12–256. Secret. Received at 9:46 a.m. Repeated to Damascus, Beirut, Baghdad, Jidda, Amman, Tripoli, and Khartoum.

[2] Printed as telegram 973, Document 610.

[3] In telegram 1733, November 28, the Department of State noted that, according to reports from the Embassy in Cairo, Nasser had publicly stated on November 21 that Egypt stood concretely for international law and that Nasser had pledged himself to the strict observance of all international law which currently existed. The Department suggested to Hare that he might at his discretion seek an opportunity to point out to Nasser that respect for international law would require the termination of subversive activities abroad, such as those of the Egyptian Military Attaché in Tripoli, the dynamitings in Beirut, and fedayeen terrorism. (Department of State, Central Files, 684A.86/11–2456)

and he (Nasser) had been too preoccupied with other matters to give matter necessary attention until it reached advanced state when steps taken correct. Re Lebanon he mentioned secret arrangements re arms (Embtel 1694)[4] but requested this not be mentioned to GOL since it could cause serious complications. When pressed re certain specific incidents not to be explained by alleged secret agreement Nasser was either non-committal or disclaimed knowledge specific details but I gained impression that facts adduced were not unfamiliar to him.

Hare

---

[4] In telegram 1694, November 27, Hare reported that, according to a confidant of Nasser, the arms and explosives which the Lebanese had found had been given to the fedayeen by the Egyptian Government at the suggestion of the Lebanese Government. (*Ibid.*, 684A.86/11–2756)

---

632.   Memorandum From the Regional Director of the Office of European Operations, International Cooperation Administration (Seager), to the Deputy Director for Operations, International Cooperation Administration (FitzGerald) [1]

Washington, December 3, 1956.

SUBJECT

Israel Programs

With a view to clarifying the status of our economic aid programs to Israel, we are setting forth a detailed description of the procedures currently being followed. These procedures have been formulated on the basis of our understanding of the policies and desires of the Director of this agency and the Department of State. We propose to continue these procedures until we are advised to the contrary.

There is to be no formal suspension of aid to Israel but every effort is to be made to slow down the implementation of our program until further policy guidance is received from the Department of State. In other words, we are to "drag our feet" but this

---

[1] Source: Washington National Records Center, ICA Director's File: FRC 61 A 32: Box 309, Israel. Secret. Cleared with Shaw, Bergus, and Oliver L. Troxel. A marginal notation on the source text by Hollister reads: "12/7/56 Noted".

should be done as inconspicuously as possible. More specifically, the procedures set forth below are to be followed.

1. There will, for the present, be no FY57 program approval. [2] Processing of the proposed program should, however, proceed normally to permit its prompt approval by the Director, if and when a policy decision is made that there is to be an FY57 program along past lines.

2. With respect to FY56 or prior year funds:

(a) No new procurement authorizations, project agreements or other obligating documents will be issued or entered into; on the other hand, no procurement authorizations already issued will be suspended, except that when extensions or amendments are requested, each case will be examined on an individual basis by the Regional Office and in consultation with the appropriate technical divisions and the Dept. of State.

(b) No new PIO's will be issued by USOM/Israel, letters of commitment will however, be issued by ICA/W against PIO's dated prior to October 29, 1956. PIO renewals or amendments will be examined on a case by case basis in consultation with the Dept. of State and the appropriate technical divisions.

(c) *Local Currency Programs*—No new local currency projects will be approved, and no additional counterpart funds will be released pending further notice.

(d) Procurement undertaken by the Israel Supply Mission will not be interfered with; GSA has, however, been instructed to suspend further procurement on outstanding PIO/C's.

(e) No shipments of goods or equipment will be stopped.

(f) No letters of commitment will be cancelled.

(g) No further participants will be called forward from Israel either for training in the U.S. or in third countries. Those trainees already in the U.S. or in third countries will continue their training until completed or until completed or until further notice.

(h) No new assignments or detail of technicians or employees will be made to USOM/Israel without the concurrence of the Regional Director.

(i) *Contractors*—ICA relations with contractors supplying technical services are currently under study. No new contractual obligations are to be entered, including those to whom letters of commitment have been issued, if this can be done without hardships to contractors involved.

(j) Supplies will continue to be made to voluntary agencies which provide relief to either Arabs in the Gaza strip or persons residing elsewhere, only after clearance with the Dept. of State on a case by case basis.

The above information is intended only as guidelines to appropriate officers of ICA/W and will not be discussed with non-U.S. Government and particularly not with representatives of the Israeli Embassy. In the event that the latter question officers of ICA/W

---

[2] D.A. and T.C. [Footnote in the source text.]

concerning the present status of the aid program to Israel, it is proposed to tell them in substance that:

As can be expected in view of the present situation, we are re-examining all our aid programs in the Near East. Delays must therefore be expected.
Current plans for the Near East are in suspense. The President has indicated a willingness to provide major support for a permanent solution of the problem, and we want to make certain that our aid contributes toward that solution. [3]

---

[3] Initials at the bottom of the source text appear to be those of FitzGerald.

---

633.   Telegram From the Embassy in the United Kingdom to the Department of State [1]

London, December 3, 1956—noon.

3070. Eyes only for the Acting Secretary. Pursuant to your telephone call last night [2] I immediately told Butler of the importance we attach to Lloyd's statement in Parliament today including a specific date by which British and French withdrawal will have been accomplished. I emphasized that in the absence of a public statement specifying that date, it is impossible for us to urge on the Egyptians that they agree to expedite clearance of the Canal. I also emphasized that public announcement of the date would be most important in determining the nature of any supporting statement the United States might make as the British have so urgently requested, and added in this connection that it is obviously also essential for us to have the text of Lloyd's speech at the earliest possible moment in order for US to consider the nature of any supporting statement that might be possible.

Finally, I suggested that if, as Lloyd had told me, the British expect the date to come out in the course of the debate, it would seem to be in the government's interest to volunteer it and get some credit for so doing rather than to have it forced out of them by Parliamentary pressure.

---

[1] Source: Department of State, Central Files, 741.13/12–356. Top Secret; Niact. Received at 8:44 a.m.

[2] No account of this conversation has been found in Department of State files or in the Eisenhower Library. Dulles had returned to Washington from Key West via Augusta, Georgia, on December 2. (Dulles' Appointment Book; Princeton University Library, Dulles Papers)

Butler promised to have the text of Lloyd's speech furnished us just as soon as it has been drafted and cleared by the Cabinet. With regard to public announcement of the date he said he understood our position but maintained that in addition to those objections by the French there were technical difficulties which caused the British military also to object. The military feel that it may be impossible to meet a two weeks deadline by a day or two, although it may on the other hand be possible to accomplish the withdrawal in a day or two less than two weeks.

Butler repeatedly stated that the assurances as to their firm intention to withdraw within two weeks which they have given to the Secretary General are regarded as satisfactory by him, and Butler reiterated that the British will in fact accomplish the withdrawal by December 18. [3]

Aldrich

---

[3] During the afternoon of December 3, London time, Foreign Secretary Lloyd told the House of Commons that the British Government was satisfied that Secretary-General Hammarskjöld would press forward with the task of clearing the Suez Canal, that work would begin as soon as technically possible, and that progress toward clearance would not depend on other considerations. Lloyd then noted that the French and British Governments had come to the conclusion that the withdrawal of their forces in the Port Said area could be carried out without delay and had instructed the Allied Commander in Chief General Sir Charles Keightly to seek agreement with U.N. Commander General Burns on a timetable for the complete withdrawal of Anglo-French forces, taking into account military and practical problems involved. (House of Commons, *Parliamentary Debates*, 5th series, vol. 561, cols. 879–885) A text of Lloyd's comments, as reported by the British press, was transmitted to the Department of State in telegram 3085 from London, December 3. (Department of State, Central Files, 684A.86/12–356) On December 3, the Embassy in Paris reported that at 5:10 p.m., Paris time, Pineau made a similar declaration in the French National Assembly. (Telegram 2754 from Paris; *ibid.*, 320.5780/12–356) The British and French Governments informed Secretary-General Hammarskjöld of their decision in separate notes verbales on December 3. (Note by the Secretary-General, December 3; U.N. doc. A/3415)

634.   Memorandum of a Telephone Conversation Between the President in Augusta, Georgia, and the Secretary of State in Washington, December 3, 1956, 1:30 p.m. [1]

Pursuant to prearrangement the President called me at 1:30. I said that the statements made by the British and the French with respect to their intention to withdraw their forces seemed to me to meet substantially the UN requirements which we had been backing. The only slippage over what we had expected was the fixing of a precise date or time period, but that I did not think this was necessarily essential since we knew in fact what their intentions were. The President said that on the basis of what he had read in the news ticker he thought that they had gone adequately to meet the requirements. I said that the State Department had prepared a statement indicating our satisfaction at the British statement and our hope that the UN would not proceed with reference to clearing the Canal, working out a permanent basis for Canal operation and dealing with the broader problems of the area. Also, George Humphrey was prepared [2] to give clearance to a statement which Macmillan planned to make tomorrow, indicating the availability to the UK of IMF gold withdrawals and Ex-Im Bank borrowing capacity. [3]

The President said that he thought we should proceed along both lines and feel that very satisfactory progress had been made. [4]

---

[1] Source: Eisenhower Library, Dulles Papers, General Telephone Conversations. Secret; Personal and Private. Drafted by Dulles.

[2] According to the memorandum of conversation by Bernau, the following telephone conversation between Humphrey and Dulles took place at 12:32 p.m.: "The Sec. said he thinks they [the British] go so far here that we have got to be prepared to go ahead on our side. H. said he does too." Humphrey "went on to say it is a wholehearted move to comply and we should take it at face value—we should use pressure to get work started on the Canal." (*Ibid.*)

[3] The following day, Macmillan informed the House of Commons that the U.S. Treasury would recommend to the U.S. Congress that it waive $143 million interest payment on a World War II loan, due on December 31. (Telegram 3119 from London, December 3; Department of State, Central Files, 841.10/12–456) For additional documentation, see *Current Economic Developments*, December 11, 1956, pp. 1–4.

[4] The source text is attached to a memorandum by Asbjornson of a telephone conversation between Dulles and Hoover, which began at 3:05 p.m. on December 3. Asbjornson's memorandum reads: "The Secretary telephoned Mr. Hoover in connection with the matter mentioned in the attached copy of memo of conversation with the President. The Secretary said that the President felt, on the basis of what he had read in the news ticker, that we should be very satisfied and should go right ahead. The Secretary thought there should be a Departmental statement. The Secretary said he had told the President we were giving out a statement along these lines and he approved of it. The Secretary suggested phoning the statement to Augusta so they would have it there before they saw it in the news ticker."

For text of the statement, released on December 3, see Department of State *Bulletin*, December 17, 1956, pp. 951–952.

635.   Memorandum of a Conversation, Department of State, Washington, December 3, 1956 [1]

SUBJECT

Israel

PARTICIPANTS

Mr. Abba Eban, Ambassador of Israel
Mr. Reuven Shiloah, Minister, Israel Embassy
NEA—Mr. Rountree
NE—Mr. Bergus

Mr. Eban reported that two things had been agreed upon with the United Nations Secretary General: Total withdrawal of Israel forces and an immediate Israel pull-back from the Suez Canal area. General Burns would shortly be in touch with the Israel command to discuss these matters.

This left a number of questions. One of these was Israel's right to use the Suez Canal. At present, the Canal was closed to the shipping of all nations without prejudice to any. There must be vigilance to ensure that when the Canal was cleared it would be open to all shipping on equal terms.

Israel had so much faith that passage through the Straits of Tiran would remain free that it had taken a number of steps such as informing world maritime powers that passage was now available to world commerce, improving the roads from Eilat to Aqaba, and commencing work on an emergency oil pipeline from Eilat to Beersheba. Israel and Egypt were the only two countries in the world which had both Mediterranean and Red Sea shorelines. It was essential that Europe have two lungs rather than one to breathe with in the future. The question of Tiran could be handled in the context of a United Nations force but the United Nations should not leave that area precipitately.

As for Sinai, Israel wished to prevent the re-establishment of Egyptian bases at El Arish, Abu Aweigila and Bir Gifgafa. These places should be centers of United Nations forces. This again raised questions as to the duration of the UNEF and the authority under which it would operate. These matters could not be left vague. Mr. Rountree said that he must confess that the matter was vague. As he understood it, the Secretary General had reported that he was proceeding on the assumption that the forces would remain in Egypt until their mission was completed. This decision would not be a unilateral one. Mr. Eban said that the Secretary General had told

---

[1] Source: Department of State, Central Files, 684A.86/12–356. Confidential. Drafted by Bergus on December 6.

him that this matter must be left vague for the time being. Mr. Shiloah expressed concern at the fact that the UNEF would contain Yugoslav and Indian troops. The attitudes of these two governments toward this question might be important.

Mr. Eban said that with respect to Gaza, Israel had accepted the Secretary General's advice to accept the status quo and to put forward no juridical or political claims. Israel was lying low as regarded public statements as to the future of Gaza. There had been an improvement in conditions in the strip and the municipal autonomy of Gaza had been strengthened. Meanwhile Israel was wondering about the impact which absorption of the strip and its inhabitants would have on Israel. Mr. Shiloah said that in this case Israel would strive to think on the same wavelength as the United States.

Mr. Eban pressed for an expression of U.S. views on these matters. Mr. Rountree pointed out that these questions were under active consideration.

Mr. Eban turned to the economic situation in Israel and said that Israel had suffered less as a result of events in Egypt than had other countries. Israel still needed assistance in a number of fields such as P.L. 480, FY 1957 technical and economic assistance, and the Export-Import Bank loan. He asked if discussions on these matters could be resumed. Mr. Rountree indicated that while the United States would like to recover the previous position, the present disposition was that the time had not yet come to do so. He hoped that there would be no delay but a little more time was required.

Mr. Eban inquired as to the factors which required time. He pointed out that the United States was trying to revive practical relations for other countries. Mr. Rountree said it was our desire and objective to do this for Israel. What we were doing for the British and French was really for the benefit of Europe as a whole. Britain and France had adequate sources of oil and a large number of tankers with which to supply their own needs if they wished to do so at the expense of other countries which their companies normally supplied. Among the countries which faced difficult situations were those who were suffering from the impact of recent events in Egypt but had not been in any way responsible for them. There were other measures with respect to Britain and France which the United States could take as soon as the British and French announced a firm intention to withdraw their forces from Egypt within a limited specified time.

Mr. Eban said that he had submitted a memorandum to the Secretary concerning Israel's need for oil.[2] While Israel did not require as much oil as European countries, the fact was that where Britain, for example, depended on oil for 35 percent of its energy requirements, Israel's energy requirements were entirely filled by oil. He had proposed that percentage of oil used for energy requirements be used as a criterion in allocating oil supplies among consumer nations.

Mr. Shiloah wondered if despite U.S. reluctance to proceed with economic assistance matters generally at this time, an exception might not be made for P.L. 480 transactions which were, after all, not aid but sales of surplus commodities. Mr. Rountree said it was felt that this was not the time to discuss new programs, projects, or sales agreements.

Mr. Eban passed on to the subject of Israel's request for a United States public statement of support and marshalled the arguments put forward by Mr. Shiloah on November 30.[3] Mr. Rountree indicated that the Israel note of November 30 together with Mr. Shiloah's remarks of the same day had been reported to the Secretary and that these matters were under consideration.

Mr. Eban said that he did not feel states which were members of the United Nations could rightfully refer to the possibility of the extinction of other member nations. He was thinking of introducing a general resolution into the United Nations General Assembly to this effect.

Mr. Eban said that Mrs. Meir would like to visit the Department of State this week and pay some calls. He understood how extremely busy the Secretary must be and would not press for a call on the Secretary himself. Mr. Rountree said that we would look into the matter.

Mr. Eban reported that Cairo radio had twice that morning announced that Fedayeen had been instructed to resume their activities in Israel.

---

[2] Eban had forwarded to Dulles a memorandum describing Israel's petroleum requirements on October 9. (*Ibid.*, 884A.2553/10–956) On December 5, Eban sent Dulles a letter which referred to the October 9 memorandum and noted that the Government of Israel welcomed the U.S. decision to activate the MEEC plan. Eban's December 5 letter also expressed the hope that the Committee would concern itself with the requirements of countries, like Israel, who were not members of the OEEC and that favorable consideration would be given to Israeli needs. (*Ibid.*, 884A.2553/12–556)

[3] See footnote 3, Document 627.

636.   Telegram From the Embassy in Israel to the Department of State [1]

Tel Aviv, December 3, 1956—5 p.m.

699. Prime Minister invited me to his Jerusalem residence Sunday afternoon for "little talk in informal atmosphere". Talk lasted hour and covered following: 1. Rhetorical questions as to US thinking on Israel's principal preoccupations in wake of withdrawal foreign forces from Egypt; 2. His conception Nasser's resurgence and probable moves henceforward; and 3. Probable development Soviet policy and actions in ME.

1. US views on principal Israel preoccupations: by way of introduction Ben Gurion emphasized influence President's letter [2] had in persuading him to agree to withdraw IDF from Sinai. He implied his alacrity in acquiescing entitled him to answers following questions:

How was freedom of navigation Suez to be guaranteed, once Canal is cleared, if Hammarskjold has agreed that Nasser can remove UNEF at will?

If Canal is not under protective control UNEF, what guarantee is there Nasser will not block it again, not only against Israel but physically block it if he is told to do so by Soviets or if he wishes to blackmail west?

For first time Israelis enjoying freedom of passage ships and aircraft over Aqaba. For time being this also means free passage for other countries seeking link between Asia and Europe as alternative to Suez.

What guarantees are there Israel can maintain this vital freedom if she withdraws her troops from area?

How is Nasser to be prevented from blocking it again if he wishes?

How can Israel be assured Sinai will not be used again as base for attack on Israel either by land or air?

What is to prevent Egypt from building up tremendous attack forces there again in implementation declarations she made only today to continue efforts to destroy Israel?

2. Nasser's resurgence: His portrayal of Nasser covered many points he had made in past but with following additions or new underscoring.

---

[1] Source: Department of State, Central Files, 674.84A/12–356. Secret; Priority. Received at 5:18 p.m., December 4. Repeated to Amman, Beirut, Cairo, Damascus, Paris, London, Rome, and Moscow.

[2] Reference is to Eisenhower's November 9 letter to Ben Gurion; see footnote 4, Document 560.

Despite Nasser's protestations of adherence to western democratic principles, his eagerly expressed desire for good relations with US, and his alleged refusal to accept Soviet domination, there has been no fundamental change in his ambitions, reliance on intrigues and machinations, or his basic attitudes towards US and west. He is working against west in Arab countries and establishing close associations with Soviets through Syria until such time as he can openly resume his partnership with Russia. Ben Gurion said he was very much afraid Nasser will be successful in convincing US and others who may have no conception of his mastery of deceit. He feared we did not understand Arab mind-difference between artistry of Arab lying and blatant crudeness of Communist lying which was transparent to anyone.

I expressed genuine doubt any country which had already experienced Nasser's unreliability would again be taken in. Ben Gurion replied he understood there were differences of opinion in Department as well as USUN as to how Nasser should be handled.

He said Nasser would move by phases, first insisting on British and French withdrawal from Egypt; then ousting UNEF, then demanding Israels' evacuation of Sinai and areas adjacent to Gulf of Aqaba, followed by campaign to win friends and obtain much needed economic assistance from US.

3. Probable development Soviet policy and actions in ME. Confirmation of substantial shipments of Soviet arms to Syria and persistent false accusations by both Syria and Russia of British, French and Israeli troop build-ups on Syrian border made him apprehensive Soviets had some definite aggressive plan affecting Israeli's security. Further evidence such intent was contained in Bulganin's letter attacking Israel, *Izvestia's* "very disturbing article" along same line (Moscow's 1345 to Department) [3] and reports he said he had from Israeli Legation in Moscow about Khrushchev's statements to diplomats that Israel could be wiped out with only few rockets sent from Russia. Ben Gurion said he was worried more by intent than threat because there were easier ways to accomplish same result. He said he did not take threat of Soviet "volunteers" seriously, having regarded it as hoax from very beginning. In his view it was part of cover for real plans of building-up military supplies in Syria utilizing it as ME base instead of Egypt for time being.

"Of course I have no knowledge how Soviets will operate but I believe one of their first moves would be to subject Israel to heavy bombing, small in terms of Soviet thinking but very large in Israel's". He returned several times to persistence of Soviet-Syrian

---

[3] Not printed. (Department of State, Central Files, 684A.86/11-2956)

accusations of Israel troop concentrations on Syrian border despite categorical denials by UN observers. He interpreted their repetition as indicating some plan of military action has been devised for future use by Soviets in conjunction with Syrians.

I expressed doubt as to his conclusions based as they were on two points mentioned. I referred to strong US statement against introducing "volunteers" into area, and pointed out we had taken lead in promoting UN resolutions against further introduction of arms to ME. I pointed up fact that after Soviet propaganda threatening to send volunteers to Egypt and Syria, Soviets had completely abandoned line. It seemed to me recent propaganda line on military build-up on Israel-Syrian border possessed even more of "war of nerves" flavor and might well fade out in due course. Furthermore, I said, I had not yet seen any evidence sizeable build-up Soviet supplies in Syria and specifically had seen nothing indicating that Soviet planes had been seen on Syria airfields. He admitted Israel had been unable to locate any such planes. In any event, he felt for moment at least, Soviets were definitely utilizing Syria as area penetration channel and that developments to date indicated serious threat to Israel's security.

Turning to our statement supporting integrity Baghdad Pact countries, he said Soviets would interpret statement's failure to mention Israel and Lebanon as expression of indifference to their fate. I argued such interpretation would be entirely unreasonable and illogical; and obviously contrary to any intent by US. Statement was addressed to specific and clearly defined area with no more reason Lebanon or Israel should have been included than any other country in ME. He admitted logic this view but said this would not change Soviet interpretation [garble] described Lebanon as small country courageous enough to defy Soviet-supported Nasser. This defiance brought about definite order from Nasser to his agents to assassinate President Chamoun at same time Egyptian agents were instructed to assassinate Nuri Said. Nasser might also try to incite Moslems against Lebanese Christians.

While assassinations and internal disturbances might suffice against Lebanon, strong military action would be required to wipe out Israel. "They know it would do no good to assassinate me as principle of democracy and freedom would continue here as long as there was an Israel". Accordingly he thought Soviets would depend on saturation bombing, immediately wiping out Israel's air bases and air force.

He said Syria was completely under domination of Nasser who, at this moment, was using Syria against US and west while his own cabinet and Egyptian press were instructed to appear friendly to US.

Quwwatly and Colonel Sarraj were directly under Nasser's order. To same extent he felt Nasser was directing Jordan's policies.

He concluded his conversation by saying if US was not willing make public statement warning Soviets against attack on Lebanon and Israel as it had in case of Baghdad Pact powers Secretary might call in Soviet Ambassador and make this point clear to him. I told him I would pass his questions and views to Department which would find them of interest although I could not assure him of specific replies in terms of US policy. As he knew our basic policy is to help in every way to settle Suez problem, settle Israel-Arab issues and bring peace to area and we meant peace with justice. Policy pertaining to each of his points might be under formulation and subject to future events and developments in which he had already agreed was very complex accumulation of factors. He had remarked that his comment was limited to viewpoint obtained within area and although he had long and close associations with regional problems he had said he could not undertake assess policies or recommendations involving other areas. Therefore he had indicated awareness that US had to consider many related factors of global nature. He agreed saying "never in history has so much depended on one power and I suspect one man. His decision will take courage". He repeated his confidence in President and his belief President's sincere desire to find just solution to area's difficult problems.

Comment

Ben Gurion was more composed and quiet than in some time. I feel his purpose was to put his thoughts on record and to justify his request answers to this questions: first, by virtue his cooperation with Hammarskjold who, he said, had requested him to withdraw IDF, so work could begin clearing Canal, and to allow international force to enter area vacated by IDF. Responsive to Hammarskjold's request he had instructed Dayan to move troops back some 30 miles from Canal [4] (I gathered Dayan was not too happy with suggestion); second, because US pressures were also in large part responsible for his decision to withdraw Israeli troops in first place. I had anticipated this argument as logical from tactical standpoint (Embtel 614). [5] However, while US pressure was certainly most powerful agent, fear

---

[4] On December 3, the Israeli Government informed Secretary-General Hammarskjöld that it was withdrawing its troops from the Suez Canal area, along the length of the Canal, to a distance of some 50 kilometers. (Report by the Secretary-General on compliance with General Assembly resolutions calling for withdrawal of troops and other measures, January 15, 1957; U.N. doc. A/3500)

[5] In telegram 614, November 16, Lawson reported that "all quarters" in Israel felt that the Israeli Government's decision to withdraw from Sinai had put the United States under an obligation to Israel and that there was some apprehension as to whether the U.S. Government felt this obligation. (Department of State, Central Files, 684A.86/11–1956)

of expulsion from UN and Israel's isolation were almost equally strong incentive factors.

While his comments coincide very nicely with line Eban and Golda Meir are now pushing, I believe him genuinely worried (1) over Nasser and his ability to deceive US and emerge victor, (2) that Israel may find itself facing same or even greater threats to her security than before Sinai campaign. Although he spent some time discussing them, I have impression he was less worried about Soviet-Syrian threat and US statement in support of Baghdad Pact countries' integrity which overlooked Israel (and Lebanon).

I doubt he expects definite replies to his questions but probably hopes for some general statement containing reassurance that these and other matters are in our minds as we study overall solutions for area. Obviously he would welcome any suggestion as we are prepared to make that our long term objectives if successful, would obviate most all fears he raised in his questions.[6]

Lawson

---

[6] On December 8, the Department of State responded to telegram 699 as follows: "Department approves comments you made to Ben Gurion. When you see him again you might thank him for sharing with us his estimate of present situation and his preoccupations concerning future. He can be sure that the various aspects of the basic NE problems are very much in our minds. Through UN and in other useful ways US is determined to assist in bringing about permanent settlement of Arab-Israel issue. We believe that road to such settlement will be less difficult if parties will offer full cooperation to UN in latter's efforts restore peace and stability to area. US will continue maintain its demonstrated interest in independence and territorial integrity of NE states." (Telegram 612 to Tel Aviv; *ibid.*, 684A.74/12–356)

U.S. RETROSPECTION ON THE ANGLO-FRENCH-ISRAELI COLLUSION; NATO SUMMIT MEETING AT PARIS; CONTINUED U.S. INTEREST IN GENERAL ASSEMBLY ACTION CONCERNING THE PALESTINE AND SUEZ QUESTIONS; AGREEMENT ON FINANCIAL ARRANGEMENTS FOR CLEARING THE SUEZ CANAL, DECEMBER 5–31

637. Memorandum From the Secretary of State's Special Assistant for Intelligence (Armstrong) to the Secretary of State [1]

Washington, December 5, 1956.

SUBJECT

Evidence of UK-French-Israeli Collusion and Deception in Connection with Attacks on Egypt

There is attached a copy of a study on the above subject which has been prepared with the cooperation of policy offices of the Department and certain senior officers. [2] The study has been reviewed by the Central Intelligence Agency . . . . A special intelligence supplement is also available separately. [3]

Because of the obvious sensitivity of the mere fact that the Department was making such a study, coordination with the military services has not, up to this point, been attempted, nor has the undertaking of such a study been made known to our missions abroad. Copies of the annexes will be made available only to those officers of the Department who would have had prior knowledge of their subject matter.

---

[1] Source: Department of State, S/P Files: Lot 66 D 487, Egypt. Secret; Sensitive.

[2] On November 27, Armstrong forwarded an earlier draft of the study to Hoover, Murphy, Henderson, MacArthur, Phleger, Rountree, Elbrick, Bowie, and Wilcox under cover of a memorandum indicating that while at Walter Reed Hospital, Dulles had expressed an interest in having an analysis prepared of the extent and interrelationship of Israeli, British, and French "collusion and deception" against the United States. In this memorandum, Armstrong had also requested each addressee, in the interest of completeness and accuracy, to examine the draft in light of his own experience and knowledge of the event. Documentation indicates that Rountree, Bowie, and Howe supplied Armstrong with comments and additional information, while MacArthur and Wilcox offered no comments. Elbrick, in a memorandum to Armstrong dated November 30, criticized the report for not taking adequate notice of various indications (such as statements made in Parliamentary debates and Eden's letter to Eisenhower of September 6) that the British were considering the use of force. Elbrick also asked that a sentence be added which would indicate that the French were encouraged by the United States to try to correct the arms imbalance between Israel and Egypt that reportedly existed at the time. (*Ibid.*, INR Files: Lot 58 D 776, Middle East Crisis 1956 (Arab-Israeli Crisis))

[3] Not found in Department of State files.

[Attachment]

RECORD OF EVENTS LEADING TO THE ISRAELI AND
ANGLO-FRENCH ATTACKS ON EGYPT IN LATE
OCTOBER 1956 [4]

I. General Approach

This report attempts to sift the available and relevant evidence
to ascertain the factors in the background to the Israeli attack on
Egypt (October 29) and to the Franco-British attack on Egypt
(October 31). The method employed is not strictly chronological,
since the treatment subsumes under several main themes a large
amount of material covering the period prior to July 26 and extending beyond the dates of the attacks. The report must be read as a
whole to understand the relations of the individual sections. The
documentation is necessarily selective, but it is fairly comprehensive
and representative. The chief conclusions of the analysis are contained in Section VI.

The report does not engage in an elaborate exegesis of the
meaning of the words "collusion" and "deception." It assumes that
the commonly accepted meaning of these words is understood and is
not likely to be obscured by the adduced evidence. The report does
seek to indicate degrees of collusion among the three major principals who acted against Egypt. In the end, the analysis supports the
view that collusion and deception did exist and that it was directed
not only against Egypt but also the US Government.

II. Israeli Fear of Egyptian Attack

Israeli fear of Arab attacks grew in intensity with the series of
Arab anti-Israeli actions and statements beginning with the conclusion of the Egyptian-Soviet arms deal in September 1955.

By March 1956 the Israelis had a fairly accurate idea of the size
and scope of the Soviet-Egyptian arms deal and were greatly
alarmed in particular by the quantities of Soviet aircraft passing into
Nasir's hands. (Memorandum of conversation, March 21, 1956, Se-

---

[4] According to the foreword to this study, "The following report is a coordinated
summary of information available to the Department of State in early December 1956.
It is based on materials in the Departmental files which have been received from
Officers in Washington and US Diplomatic Missions abroad, and on materials made
available by other intelligence services. Senior Departmental officials have had an
opportunity to review and contribute to the basic report. Appropriate suggestions for
changes have been incorporated. The Central Intelligence Agency has also reviewed it
in detail."

cret.) [5] By early May the Israelis had also learned of the 23 million dollar Syrian-Czech arms deal, completed in February 1956. (Memorandum of conversation, Paris, May 4, 1956, Secret.) [6]

The extreme vulnerability of Israel to air attack led the Israelis to put heavy pressure on the United States to approve the release to Israel of fighter aircraft from France, Italy, and Canada.

Israeli apprehension at Arab arming was increased by the growing influence of Nasir in Syria and Jordan, as evidenced by the conclusion of the Egyptian-Syrian and Egyptian-Saudi mutual defense pacts in October 1955. Israeli concern was heightened further by the quick growth of Egyptian influence in Jordan that culminated in the dismissal of General Glubb in March 1956. This was followed in April by a wave of fedayeen activity from both Egypt and Jordan. . . .

In a series of conversations between February and May 1956 with Departmental officials Israeli Ambassador Eban and Chief of Intelligence Shiloah reiterated the Israeli Government's conviction that Nasir intended to attack in June. (Memoranda of conversation dated May 5, April 8, and May 4, 1956, Secret.) [7] His ambition to gain hegemony over the Arab world was also repeatedly stressed. In a conversation with Department officials on March 21, Eban and Shiloah emphasized that the Israeli government would fall if its attempts to secure arms failed, and Eban stated that he possessed a letter from Prime Minister Ben Gurion to the President on this subject.

By June 1956 it seems clear that the Israeli Government had given up any hopes of relying on the UN to halt Arab raids into Israel. Hammarskjold's attempts to secure a cessation of border incidents had broken down. Israel evinced little disposition to cooperate with Hammarskjold's plans to stabilize the existing situation. Israeli relations with the UN were further complicated by the apparent mutual dislike existing between Ben Gurion and the Secretary-General.

Israel was also not convinced of the effectiveness of any measures which the United States might take to stop Arab attacks and by June had practically given up hope of obtaining aircraft through US auspices. (Memorandum of conversation, June 14, 1956, Confiden-

---

[5] Reference is to a memorandum of conversation among Eban, Assistant Secretary Allen, and others, not printed. (Department of State, Central Files, 784A.86/3–2156)

[6] Reference is to a memorandum of conversation among Shiloah, Rountree, and Burdett, not printed. (*Ibid.*, 784A.5622/5–456)

[7] The May 5 memorandum of conversation is printed in vol. XV, p. 614. The last two are not printed. (Department of State, Central Files, 674.85A/4–856 and 784A.5622/5–456, respectively)

tial.) [8] Hence the Israeli cabinet shift of June 17, in which Moshe Sharret was replaced by Ben Gurion's protege, Golda Meir, as Foreign Minister, undoubtedly represented a decision to break loose from a policy of cooperation with the US. It also represented a victory for the increasingly influential military and civilian elements who were demanding military action against Egypt before it was too late.

III. French Support of Israel

The veering of France toward Israel began well before Nasir's coup against the Suez Canal Company. Although France was one of the guarantors of the Tripartite Declaration of 1950 and was pledged to restrict the sale of arms to either the Arabs or Jews and to notify the NEACC concerning such sales, it observed the rising number and intensity of Arab-Israeli border clashes, the unfavorable results of the Czech arms deals with Egypt and Syria, and the evidence of Egyptian complicity in the Algerian rebellion. All these developments, particularly the last, seriously disturbed French policy-makers and persuaded them to re-evaluate French relations with Israel.

At least from mid-June, the French seemed disposed to encourage the military build-up of Israel. (See the memorandum of conversation, dated June 20, 1956, between the Italian Counselor of Embassy in Washington and officials of the Department.) [9] There is also some indication that the French believed that the US was not inclined to oppose a French effort to correct the arms imbalance as between Israel and Egypt. The Israelis themselves indicated on June 18 that they were receiving significant amounts of new weapons. (D–131, Tel Aviv, September 4, 1956, Secret.) [10] The French may even then have been the chief suppliers. The available evidence does not permit exact corroboration of the scale and kind of this traffic, but it appears reasonably certain that France and Israel were engaged early in arms dealings which contravened both the spirit and letter of the NEACC directives.

In August additional French Mystères not cleared through the NEACC appear to have arrived in Israel. Ben Gurion stated on August 31 that "there are some very great things now in motion, but the time has not yet come to speak of them publicly." It was also noted that the once urgent Israeli stress on the need for more arms in order to survive was gradually being abandoned, a probable

---

[8] Reference is to a memorandum of conversation among Eban, Murphy, and others, not printed. (*Ibid.*, 780.00/6–1456)

[9] For text, see vol. XV, p. 737.

[10] Not printed. (Department of State, Central Files, 784A.86/9–456) All documents referred to in this report with the prefix "D" are Department of State despatches.

indication that Israel was actually receiving arms satisfactorily, in quality and quantity.

. . . Two highly rated reports of early September . . . indicate that by this time close Franco-Israeli cooperation already existed regarding military plans against Nasir. . . . The tenor of these reports in September is further supported by the fact that Menahem Begin, leader of the ultra-rightist, expansionist, and activist Herut Party of Israel, visited Paris, September 9–24. He seems to have had an official status and the general backing of Ben Gurion. He was reported by the Israeli press to have established "bonds of friendship" with a number of high French civilian government officials. He is said to have assured members of the French Assembly that a Franco-British military operation against Egypt would be over within 24 hours if Israel joined in. Furthermore, Begin allegedly dismissed the possibility of military support to Egypt from either Egypt's Arab allies or the USSR. (*Jerusalem Post*, September 28, 1956.) A high official of the Quai d'Orsay (unidentified) is reported to have assured Begin that the UK would permit an attack on Egypt if Israel left Jordan alone. . . .

On September 27 Henri Roux, then Director of Near Eastern Affairs in the French Foreign Office, told the US Embassy that he had no knowledge of a decision to transfer 24 additional Mystère IV A's to Israel, although he knew Israel had been pressing for more Mystères and that the French Defense Ministry favored granting the request. Roux also disclaimed any knowledge of Begin's activities. (T–1488, Paris, September 28, 1956. Secret.) [11] . . . A UK source reported that on September 28 twenty French AMX tanks and an unknown number of French 75 mm guns arrived at Haifa on a French ship. (USARMA, CX–346, Tel Aviv, October 18, 1956, Secret.) [12]

.   .   .   .

Mme. Vered, Assistant Press Attaché of the Israeli Embassy in Paris, told an Embassy official that if the French had not sent the Israelis great quantities of arms in the past weeks the Israeli action

---

[11] Not printed. (*Ibid.*, 784A.56/9–2856) All documents referred in this report with the prefix "T" are Department of State telegrams.

[12] No copy of this report from the Army Attaché in Tel Aviv has been found in Department of State files. The Department of State did not systematically retain copies of intelligence reports received from military attachés abroad.

in the Sinai would have been impossible. (T–2133, Paris, November 2, 1956, Confidential.) [13]

.   .   .   .

By mid-October French expressions of sympathy with Israel were open and unreserved. A Foreign Office official, Jean Daridan, Director General of Political and Economic Affairs, in reaction to a UK warning to Israel not to attack Jordan, expressed the view that pro-Israeli sentiment in the French Assembly and among the public was so strong that the government would probably be obliged to stand behind Israel if hostilities should break out. (T–1761, Paris, October 15, 1956. Secret.) [14]

The French also expressed sympathy with Israeli fears concerning the movement of Iraqi troops into Jordan. They warned that the strong reaction of Israel should not be taken lightly. They also indicated that the movement of Iraqi troops into Jordan might presage an all-out British move to extend the Baghdad Pact to which the French were opposed. They hinted that the Iraqi move might have been prompted by the British to accomplish this purpose. This indication of French views concerning the British was given on October 18. (T–1917, Paris, October 18, 1956, Confidential.) [15] By that time the Anglo-French strategy against Egypt had been decided, the French concern about the British was later admitted to be "primarily a smoke-screen" to cover the real intent of the Anglo-French agreement.

On October 15 Ben Gurion had delivered a major foreign policy speech to the Knesset following a week-long cabinet meeting. He indicated that Israel was not so defenseless "as we were at the beginning of the year." The UN, he said, was helpless to stop Arab attacks or to force Nasir to let Israel through the Suez Canal. He stated Israel *has taken steps to strengthen its ties with several states* and that, while some of these measures have been extremely beneficial, he could not at this time give more details. He also intimated that Israel might soon be facing fateful decisions and events. This hint of possible pending action was not only consistent with French aid to Israel, but also with the almost agreed UK-French plan to act when Israel attacked Egypt.

Israeli fears were further heightened by the victory of the pro-Egyptian element in the Jordanian elections of October 21 and the ratification of the Egyptian-Jordanian-Syrian military pact a few

---

[13] Not printed. (Department of State, Central Files, 684A.86/11–256)

[14] Not printed. (*Ibid.*, 684A.85/10–1556)

[15] The reference is in error. It should be telegram 1817 from Paris, October 18, not printed. (*Ibid.*, 684A.85/10-1856)

days later. These events also increased apprehensions in London and Paris. French hostility toward Nasir was further aggravated by their seizure, about October 18, of the *Athos* which, they asserted, was carrying arms to the Algerian rebels from Egypt.

On October 22 the French Foreign Office advised that exports from France to Egypt of all categories which included trucks, jeeps, spare parts, and other quasi-military goods were suspended. Specific applications for radar and radio equipment were rejected. (T–1868, Paris, October 22, 1956, Secret.) [16]

.   .   .   .

About two weeks later, the Embassy in Paris reported (T–2125, November 1, 1956, Secret) [17] that the Air Attaché had reason to suspect that additional Mystères had been made available by France to Israel, by sale, loan, or the stationing of units in Israel. This was confirmed by a US service attaché report of October 30 that 20 Mystères with marking believed to be French were seen at Lydda and that 18 French jet pilots had arrived at the same Israeli airfield. (USARMA, CX–393, Tel Aviv, Joint Sitrep No. 2, October 30, 1956, Secret.) Subsequent reports indicate that French ground crews and technicians, in addition to pilots, arrived in Israel just prior to the attack on Egypt and that 2000 tons of jet fuel arrived in Haifa secretly from France on October 24. (Tel Aviv 641, November 21, 1956, Secret.) [18] There is no firm evidence, however, that French pilots actually participated in the Sinai offensive. . . .

IV. Increasing Estrangement of Israel, France, and the United Kingdom From the United States

The confused period between Nasir's nationalization of the Suez Canal Company on July 26, 1956 and the critical turning point in US relations with Israel, France, and the UK sometime in October passed through several phases.

The *first of these phases* was marked by a common Western sense of shock and disapproval consequent upon Nasir's action. From the outset, a sharp difference of opinion among the United Kingdom, France, and the United States was evident concerning the most appropriate method of dealing with Nasir. The British and French instinct was to use force, immediately and jointly, even though they were not militarily prepared to do so. This largely visceral impulse was an accurate reflection of British and French feelings at the time

---

[16] Not printed. (*Ibid.*, 474.518/10–2256)
[17] Not printed. (*Ibid.*, 784A.56/11–156)
[18] Not printed. (*Ibid.*, 684A.86/11–2156)

and, the evidence now confirms, of their ultimate intentions, if every other means failed to bring Nasir to "reason." Nevertheless, they were persuaded—practically "bludgeoned," in their eyes—into discussions of the Suez situation, which were agreed upon by the United States, France, and the United Kingdom on August 2. The first London conference on Suez resulted in the 18 Power agreement (August 23) as the basis of an approach to Egypt in the hope of securing Nasir's acceptance of some formula of international control and operation of the Canal. This phase ended with the failure of the Menzies Mission to Cairo (September 3–9) to obtain Nasir's compliance with the 18 Power agreement, which he had rejected, in effect, before the mission began its discussion with him.

The *second phase* was initiated by the US-UK-French agreement, even more reluctantly assented to by the British and French, to hold another conference in London on September 19 of the major users of the Canal to consider and approve the US-sponsored plan for a Suez Canal Users Association. The conference completed its work in three days and steps were then taken to carry out the plan, involving an immense amount of technical preparation and consultation among the three principal Western governments. Although the British and French governments accepted the SCUA principle and expressed a willingness to cooperate in its implementation, they do not appear ever to have regarded it with the optimism evinced by the United States. Simultaneous with attempts to put SCUA on a working basis, the UK and France had informed the UN Security Council (September 12) of the aggravation of the international situation by Egypt's rejection of the 18 Power agreement "which if allowed to continue would constitute a manifest danger to peace and security." Although they pressed their case in the Security Council on September 23 and subsequently, the original UK-French resolution against Egypt was shelved. On October 14, by a 9 to 2 vote, the Security Council approved the 18 Power proposals. Some progress was reported in private Anglo-French-Egyptian negotiations. Anglo-French reference of the Suez affair to the UN was mainly but by no means exclusively in the nature of "clearing the lines" against any moral or political odium attaching to the possibility of sterner UK-French measures against Nasir. Neither country had foresworn such measures and, in fact, [both?] since early August had repeatedly indicated they would use force as a last resort.

The *third phase* unfolded in the first two weeks of October when US-UK-French differences over SCUA came to a head, chiefly over the question of the payment of any dues to Egypt and the enforcement of SCUA authority in the face of a recalcitrant and defiant Nasir, now strongly backed by Soviet diplomacy. In this period effective communication among the three Western principals appears to be breaking down. Franco-Israeli and Anglo-French ties were becoming increasingly more intimate and exclusive. The United States was obviously not included within the developing scope of these understandings. In Israel, France, and the UK at official levels there was a decline in contacts and mutual confidence in dealings with US officials.

In all of these phases, especially the last two, the Anglo-French build-up of military strength in the Eastern Mediterranean continued with increasing emphasis on political and strategic cooperation. French units began to arrive in Cyprus on August 30 and were reenforced thereafter.

A brief review of the pertinent evidence for each country, Israel, France, and the United Kingdom, will make clearer the extent and the meaning of their growing estrangement from the United States.

1. *Israel*. The nature and scope of the Franco-Israeli tie-up, summarized above in II, indicate that Israel had no confidence in any negotiations with Nasir and had decided early to prepare for a "preventive" attack on Egypt. Israel took this decision knowing that it would alienate the US and the UN, both of which it regarded as unwilling or unable to assist it in containing Arab aggressions. In the Israeli view, the US appeared more interested in keeping the peace than in assuring "justice" for Israel. The UN was ineffectual, most Israelis believed, and the UN truce machinery had been discredited. Although Israel was concerned with free transit of the Suez Canal, it despaired of Egypt's allowing Israel to use it and had little faith in either UN or US interventions to make Egypt assent to Israeli use of the Canal. Given the siege-mentality of the Israelis and the Israeli belief that US desires to preserve a peaceful status quo in the Near East favored a policy of "appeasement" of Nasir, Israel shifted rapidly away from the US in basic policy aims and tactics. France supported this Israeli readjustment and largely made it possible by supplying Israel with aircraft and arms.

2. *France*. The French estrangement from the United States was cumulative but steady, punctuated by moods of professed cooperation in handling the Suez crisis and of black pessimism and disillusionment over the results. Fundamentally, the French attitude toward Nasir was one of unrelenting hostility and fear. The French never believed the West could do business with an "apprentice dictator," as Mollet called Nasir. He stressed early the serious dangers which existed in not reacting vigorously to Nasir's action and said, with Algeria uppermost in his thinking, that there was a real danger of a Moslem bloc extending from the Atlantic to the Pacific united against European nations and the United States if Nasir were not

checked. (T–532, Paris, July 31, 1956, Confidential.) [19] Subsequent events tended to harden this French view, behind which Mollet had a generally united country. He believed, as did Pineau, that from the beginning the seizure of the Canal was a much more serious matter than the US appeared to regard it. (T–2123, Paris, November 1, 1956, Secret, for Pineau's views.) [20]

Although the French leaders and public were inclined to accept the 18 Power agreement as a major achievement for the anti-Nasir forces, they did not try to conceal their dissatisfaction with the "inertia of the Western powers" and with an apparent US reserve concerning the use of strong measures against Nasir. The failure of the Menzies Mission, according to later testimony by both Mollet and Pineau, was a turning point in French thinking and greatly strengthened the pre-disposition to use force. Despite initial expressions of satisfaction that the SCUA proposals had had beneficial effects on Nasir, French dissatisfaction with the outcome of the SCUA conference developed quickly, reflecting "disillusionment and discouragement" and much criticism of the US. (T–1362, Paris, September 21, 1956, Confidential, and also T–1379, Paris, September 22, 1956, Secret, [21] where the French indicated to an Embassy official that they were determined to reserve their full "liberty of action" and not to cooperate in measures which they judged to be incompatible with the 18 Power agreement.)

The clandestine French broadcasts in Arabic, which began operations on July 28, contained repeated and violent attacks on the US from the time the Menzies Mission was formed (August 22) and on the Secretary's statement that in agreeing to receive the mission Nasir had contributed to the cause of peace. On August 29 the station introduced the theme that the US was trying to replace the UK and France in the Near East. Anti-American propaganda was absent between September 11 and 22 following the agreement to organize SCUA, but on September 22 after the second London conference and French charges that SCUA had been watered down, the station denounced US "treachery." Violent vituperation against the US continued thereafter, the main theme being that the US was seeking to replace France and the UK in the Arab world. (A clandestine British station, which began operating in late August or early September, attacked Nasir, but not the US.) Throughout the Suez crisis, according to public opinion polls, anti-Nasir and anti-US

---

[19] Not printed. (*Ibid.*, 974.7301/7–3156)

[20] Document 459.

[21] Neither printed. (Department of State, Central Files, 974.7301/9–2156 and 974.7301/9–2256, respectively)

French sentiment ran very high and the US tended increasingly to become the focus of bitter criticisms and attacks.

Although the French disposition to use force against Nasir varied with the circumstances, it appears to have been far more steady and strong over a long period than in the UK. Embassy Paris observed in early September that although some reservations existed in the French cabinet no one really opposed the use of force in certain circumstances. The final decision rested with three men— Coty, the President who opposed resort to force, and Premier Mollet and Defense Minister Bourgès-Manoury who favored its use. Coty could not veto substantive measures of the government. (T–1145, Paris, September 7, 1956, Secret.) [22]

Despite developing adverse French attitudes toward progress on a settlement of the Suez crisis, seven regional PAOs reported on September 19 that little enthusiasm existed in the country for the use of force and that its advocacy was largely limited to the Paris press and certain political elements. (T–1313, Paris, Confidential.) [23] Embassy Paris itself did not then believe force was likely. This consensus was shaken in the next few days by rapidly growing French criticism of the SCUA conference results and Nasir's negative attitude. Nasir's position was strengthened by the arrival on September 17 at Suez of 15 Soviet pilots to begin training for Canal operations.

Mollet made a major foreign policy speech on August 31 in which he stressed that "it will not be possible to resolve the Suez crisis by half measures, designed only to maintain the peace. We have to accept putting all our weight and force in support of what we believe to be the solution in conformity with the principles of justice and international law. On the eve of the debates of the Security Council it is not inappropriate to recall that the spirit of the UN Charter is not one of capitulation. The persistent search for a peaceful solution cannot signify the acceptance, but failing to act, of the accomplished fact." (T–1525, Paris, October 1, 1956, Confidential.) [24] Mollet's remarks considered in conjunction with the tightening Franco-Israeli connections, French preoccupation with the Algerian situation, and growing criticism of the US, have an ominous and prophetic ring.

3. *United Kingdom*. The alienation of the UK government from the US over Suez policy was gradual, reluctant, and divided. The chief British actors do not appear to have possessed the same unanimity and determination that seized the small core of French activists. For

---

[22] Not printed. (*Ibid.*, 974.7301/9–756)
[23] Not printed. (*Ibid.*, 974.7301/9–1956)
[24] Not printed. (*Ibid.*, 974.7301/10–156)

one reason, Eden despite his intense personal preoccupation with the Suez problem was up to a point both more responsive to and fearful of public opposition than Mollet. At first, the Labor Party appeared disposed to give Eden carte blanche in dealing with Egypt, although it subsequently denied that that had ever been its position. Given the disposition of the government and the temper of the country, Labor could not politically take the line that force might not have to be used in certain circumstances. During the summer, however, Labor persisted in its demand that the government refrain from any military course until it had exhausted every available diplomatic course, including an appeal to the UN. When Labor virtually forced Eden to carry his case to the UN in early September and the case in effect failed, Labor continued to oppose military action against Egypt by the UK and France.

Nevertheless, Eden was as determined as Mollet not to accept a situation of diplomatic drift and inaction which he apparently believed by early October had been largely confirmed by events. Eden had his way in the cabinet, not because it was internally united—there is reason to doubt that—but because under British parliamentary practice the cabinet must act as a unit or fall. None of his opponents within the cabinet was able to prevent Eden from adopting the course he decided upon. The custom of Cabinet unanimity aided Eden and weakened the anti-force moderates. Eden had never disavowed the use of force in certain circumstances, as he reminded Parliament as early as August 2 when Parliament recessed for the summer. He reiterated that position to a receptive Conservative Party audience at its annual conference in October. His estimate of Nasir . . . was in most essentials identical with that of the French.

Both British and French newspapers had given wide attention to President Eisenhower's comment during a press conference on September 11 that the US recognized the right of France and the UK to employ force in certain circumstances. The British press was far more scrupulous than the French, in reporting the President's remarks, to give due weight to his condition that the use of force could only be justified after all peaceful means to settle a conflict had been exhausted and that Egypt (in this instance) must clearly appear to be in the position of an aggressor. The French press lightly passed over these qualifications. In both the UK and France the remarks of the Secretary at his press conference on September 13 that the US would not be party to shooting its way through the Canal appeared to nullify the effect of the President's observations.

Eden, Lloyd, Pineau, and Mollet met in Paris on September 27 to conduct a broad survey of the British and French positions which events were forcing closer together. By this time, the French were in a fire-eating mood. The day before (September 26) Pineau had told the North Africa French Foreign Affairs Committee on Suez that the UK and France had "trumps in reserve" and would see how to use them. In the ensuing conversations the British seemed to have been a restraining influence. According to what British Ambassador Jebb told Ambassador Dillon (T–1488, Paris, September 27, 1956, Secret) [25] the use of force against Egypt was ruled out, unless Canal traffic was totally interrupted or there were serious riots or other similar actions in Egypt which would convince British public opinion of the necessity for military action. Deference to public opinion at home and abroad was still a lively concern of Eden. It troubled Pineau and Mollet less because they had a fairly united people behind a strong policy. The evidence that Nasir was aiding and abetting the rebels in Algeria tended to dissolve lines of party opposition to such a policy. Almost certainly, while the British were "restraining" the French, the latter were also extending the scope of their aid and understanding with the Israelis.

The first week of October did not open well for Anglo-American relations. The British, like the French, were disappointed by the unwillingness of the US to support a strongly worded UK-French resolution against Nasir in the Security Council and they believed that their case there had largely aborted because of US opposition. Then, Secretary Dulles' remarks on October 2 at a press conference concerning "colonialism" brought a sharp reaction from the British and French.

More important than this incident, an acute US-UK-French deadlock over the issue of payment of dues under the SCUA plan developed. The differences concerned matters of substance as well as procedure. The French took the position that the differences were absolute and irreconcilable. (T–1529, Paris, October 1, 1956, Secret, [26] for this view. It was really evident much earlier. See T–1408, Paris, September 24, 1956, Secret.) [27] The British insisted on October 8 that no dues be paid to the Egyptian government. This demand amounted to a reversal of a previously stated British and French willingness to accept the US offer to pay dues to SCUA (see T–1485, September 27, 1956, Secret) [28] not excluding some share of these payments to Egypt for expenses entailed in the upkeep and maintenance of the Canal.

The British and French desired the United States to use its maximum effort to persuade US-controlled shipping under foreign registry to abide by practices to be prescribed for shipping under US

---

[25] The reference is in error. It should be telegram 1485 from Paris, September 27; see footnote 4, Document 278.

[26] See footnote 7, Document 290.

[27] See footnote 5, Document 261.

[28] See footnote 4, Document 278.

registry. Apparently, neither the British nor the French were satisfied that the US had made this effort effectively or would make it. Nevertheless, the British position on the payment of dues issue at this date (October 8) and subsequently amounted to a deliberate misrepresentation of an earlier US-UK understanding on the payments problem. The inference is inescapable that the UK and France by early October had concluded that SCUA, as then developing, was an unworkable, undesirable, and unacceptable basis for dealing with Nasir and the Canal issue. They were inclined to blame the US for this situation, but it went much deeper than the immediate conflict over methods of payment of dues.

The British and French, it may again be noted, seemed not to have fully accepted the SCUA arrangements as more than a temporary US-sponsored device, despite their initial formal acceptance of its principles. They appeared not to believe in SCUA, except as a means of mobilizing world opinion against Egypt and of forcing Egypt, by other means, to acquiesce to the basic principles of the 18 Power Agreement. Although SCUA was admittedly not in itself a basis for negotiation and had no generally recognized negotiating powers, the British tended to think that this was the role the US was casting SCUA to perform. From being a provisional arrangement, as they viewed it, the British and French assumed that the US was coming to regard SCUA as a scheme of almost indefinite duration which in the circumstances might become permanent and would never succeed in bringing Nasir to terms.

The situation was not entirely redeemed, in British and French eyes, although it was improved, by Egyptian compliance with the Six Points voted by the UN on October 12. The UK and France regarded the Six Points as a step forward but as practically ineffective as a means of breaking what they had come to regard as an intolerable stalemate. Frustration and a desire to act together were reaching a point of extreme urgency in British and French thinking.

The period from October 8 to 15 was probably the critical one in US-UK-French relations. Mutual confidence fell off markedly at high working levels within the three governments. On the other hand, Anglo-French relations were marked by ostentatious professions of "solidarity" and a sharp upturn of criticism of the US in the pro-government British and French press.

In these circumstances it would probably be a mistake to view the British role in subsequent events as passive and merely acquiescent to stronger French demands for action on a military front. There is not much doubt that Eden and Lloyd never regarded themselves as being carried along by the French. They had weighty and independent reasons, as they viewed the Suez problem, for acting outside the channels of US-UK cooperation and against Egypt. The French set the mise-en-scène, but the British did not need to walk onto the stage unless they had wanted to do so. The fact is that Eden and Lloyd had determined to move on stage front and center, in company with the French. In some respects, the conjuncture of British and French interests in Suez and the Middle East generally was abnormal and artificial. Their interests were not identical, either historically or in the existing situation. They had more often been rivals than partners in this region. Their stakes differed in getting rid of Nasir, who happened to be the focus of their major difficulties and preoccupations. Both believed that their national prestige was deeply affronted by the act of nationalization and that Nasir must be "cut down to size." The British were primarily concerned with restoring the Canal to "secure" hands and with preventing the development of further political threats to their remaining positions in the Near East proper. The French held no positions of consequence in the Near East, and broadly speaking, had almost nothing to lose or reclaim. They had opposed the formation of the Baghdad Pact. French interest in establishing international control over the Canal was real enough, but their overriding concern was to scotch the Egyptian center of conspiracy which was making the subjection of the Algerian rebels a bloody and expensive business. In many ways, therefore, the Anglo-French entente, which was on the eve of momentous decisions, was a product of emergency crisis conditions rather than deep organic political ties and sympathies. British Conservatives had often spoken privately in disparagement of the French ability to govern themselves and others and did not regard highly the reliability of French policy in Europe. Eden appears to have had a rather dim view of Pineau, although he seems to have respected Mollet.

V. The British Join the Plan Against Egypt

Strictly guarded Anglo-French talks in Paris on October 16 sealed the agreement and the time-table of joint action by the two powers in the event of an Israeli attack on Egypt. The fact of this agreement is substantially corroborated by the statement made by Pineau to a high US official on November 16. Pineau said that when he arrived back in Paris from New York after the UN meeting on the Suez Canal (October 14), he was approached the next day by Israeli representatives. "They told him that Israel had definite proof that Egypt was preparing to move against them and that they could not wait much longer. They were therefore determined to attack Egypt; that they would do it alone if necessary but *do* it they would. On October 16, Eden had come over from London and the plan had been worked out among the three of them and that was that. He, in effect, apologized for not having kept us informed but said that under the circumstances it seemed to serve no useful purpose to do so." (Memorandum of Conversation, November 17, 1956, Secret.) [29]

This testimony is also supported by the report from Paris of a long conversation between Pineau and Ambassador Dillon on November 1. (T–2123, Paris, November 1, 1956, Secret.) [30] Pineau told Dillon substantially what he told the US official cited above, with a few additional points. The Israelis, Pineau said, told the French that they had reached the conclusion that the US had in effect decided to side with Nasir and to allow the annihilation of Israel. In view of the rapid increase of Egyptian military capability due to the receipt of increasing quantities of Soviet arms, the Israelis stated, the fate of Israel would be sealed in a few months time. Pineau then told Dillon that "the matter was taken up with the United Kingdom and general agreement on the present course of action was reached. The final decisions were taken during the course of the Eden–Lloyd visit to Paris and the decision was taken jointly by the UK and French *not* to inform the United States. Both governments felt convinced that the United States was in error regarding its evaluation of the danger of Nasir and considered prior consultation with the US on this subject would serve no useful purpose." Also on this occasion, in reply to a question of Dillon as to how the question of the entry of Iraqi troops into Jordan figured in this affair, Pineau said that "the discussions on that subject were primarily a smoke screen to divert attention from the decision to undertake a joint operation against Egypt."

Between October 16 and the launching of the Israeli attack on Egypt on October 29 effective communication among Washington, Paris, and London on Suez almost ceased. Working level contacts between NEA and the British and French Embassies in Washington virtually stopped. Pineau has since explained why (see above). No similar revelation of attitude or commitment is available from the British side. Both Ambassadors Aldrich and Dillon had indicated that their personal and official relations with high British and French officials on matters relating to the Middle East were not entirely satisfactory. Neither could put his finger at the time on the precise cause of the Anglo-French attitude of withdrawal. It is now apparent that they were being circumvented and misled by the Anglo-French collaborators. Both at home and abroad the extent and kind of Anglo-French commitment was a closely held secret. British and French Foreign Office officials, except for a very few, were kept in the dark. No British or French ambassador in the Near East or

---

[29] See the memorandum by Allen Dulles, Document 579.
[30] Document 459.

Washington appears to have been informed. The High Commissioners of the Commonwealth in London were not consulted or informed.

In retrospect, Pineau's long summary of the Suez situation
before the French Assembly on October 16 was more than a report
to the nation. It now seems to have reflected the culmination of an
agreement between the French and Israelis, many weeks in preparation, and between the French and the British, about to be concluded
that evening. Pineau placed great stress on the solidarity of the
British and French in all matters pertaining to the Near East and
Suez. He reminded the Assembly that "we still have considerable
trumps" and that "we are determined to carry out our solution."

British Minister of Defense, Sir Walter Monckton, resigned on
October 18, mainly on grounds of ill health. (T–2152, London,
October 19, 1956, Confidential.) [31] It had long been known that he
wished to be relieved of high governmental responsibilities because
of age and health. No satisfactory evidence is available that Monckton's action was influenced by his knowledge and disapproval of
possible Anglo-French armed intervention against Egypt. If he was
informed, he may have indicated that he would not be a party to it.
Some press speculation points to that possibility. His cooperation
would be crucial in such an event. His opposite number in Paris,
Bourgès-Maunoury, was obviously privy to the Anglo-French plan,
which accorded with his own predisposition. The timing of Monckton's resignation is therefore remarkably coincidental, at the very
least, with the Anglo-French talks in Paris on October 16, but it
proves nothing.

It is now certain that British willingness to join the French in
the plan to "exploit" an Israeli attack on Egypt came as a great relief
to the chief French actors in the developing plot. Long since, the
tone of French diplomacy had tended to assume an air of near
desperation arising from the realization that there was no *legal*
justification for the use of force against Egypt. A report prepared for
the French Foreign Affairs Committee by the Mendesist Radical
Lipkowski had indicated that legally Nasir's action in nationalizing
the Canal appeared within the limits of his authority under the right
of eminent domain. Lipkowski had further concluded that the entire
subject of the 1888 Treaty was also very arguable and it was far
from certain that France would have a tenable case at the International Court of Justice. The Lipkowski report, thorough and objective in tone, only added to the sense of French frustration. (T–1863,
Paris, October 22, 1956, Confidential.) [32]

---

[31] Not printed. (Department of State, Central Files, 741.13/10–1956)
[32] Not printed. (*Ibid.*, 974.7301/10–2256)

Almost certainly, Eden, Lloyd, and a considerable number of other ranking Conservatives shared this view. If legal action against Nasir was stopped, if Nasir was to be allowed to consolidate his grip on the Canal and strengthen his anti-British political position elsewhere in the Near East and if the negotiations along the line proposed by the US were to prove futile as both the British and French governments were convinced they would, then something must be done. Moreover, it is not incredible that the British and French decided to act because they feared that negotiations might succeed. One way or another, they were not prepared to accept the result. Selwyn Lloyd, the British Secretary of State for Foreign Affairs later explained to Ambassador Lodge the motivations behind this last ditch mentality that gripped the British and French governments. What these governments decided on October 16 was to take the law into their own hands.

VI. Concerted Deception of the United States

Considering the whole record of Franco-Israeli and Anglo-French planning that ended in the armed attacks against Egypt by these countries in late October, the following conclusions seem tenable—

1. France was largely instrumental in completing two main circles of collusion and deception, directed not only against Egypt but also against the United States. For a considerable time these circles merely intersected, but after mid-October they almost precisely overlapped and were nearly indistinguishable, at least as the French viewed them. It is important not to exaggerate the French role. They did not invent the Arab-Israeli conflict nor force the British to side with them. Israel was willing and so finally were the British. The French gave both the Israelis and the British a big push, at the right time and place.

2. France was engaged from an early period, probably June, in building up the military potential of Israel and thereby in encouraging Israel to attack Egypt, perhaps other Arab states. It is not material that this encouragement should have been a *French* idea, although it was subsequently claimed that it was. French aid coincided with mounting Israeli fears and a determination to move against Egypt when Israel was equipped to do so. France was made aware of the Israeli intention, approved it, and it was later accepted by the British as an integral part of the Anglo-French agreement to act.

3. In this respect, it is also not material whether the British knew of the Israeli intention far in advance. The British accepted a situation in which the Israelis were to play the part of deus ex

machina in the plot. They became accessories both before and after the fact. This amounted to constructive collusion on the British part. It is therefore disingenuous to believe that the British were unwitting tools of the French and Israeli principals and that they stumbled onto the scene at a late date without knowing what they were doing. Eden and Lloyd knew what they were getting themselves into, although they have not fully admitted it. Pineau has spoken for them and his evidence is conclusive.

4. On a pure technicality a case can be made for the fact that Anglo-Israeli collusion was not direct and immediate up to the very moment of the Israeli attack on Egypt. That, of course, is the position maintained by the UK. Although the French must have informed the British of the probable consequences of the Israeli mobilization initiated actively on October 25—Pineau made a hurried trip to London on October 24 [33]—the British were not necessarily "committed" by that knowledge, even after the British had reached their agreement with the French on October 16. But they were informed of the Franco-Israeli plan of action by October 18, probably two days earlier, . . . and were thus compromised by the knowledge of the Israeli intentions, because the French almost certainly knew of these intentions and undoubtedly told the British. The fiction that the French were acting in one way in relation to Israel and the British were acting in another quite different way in relation to the French is simply not supportable. The separate paths converged in Paris on October 16.

5. Although Pineau has admitted that the October 16 Eden–Mollet talks sealed the agreement of the UK to act with France when Israel attacked Egypt, one of the most interesting parts of this situation is that each of the other principals, Israel and the UK, has taken pains to assert that its role against Egypt was not a consequence of an inexorable chain of commitments. The Israeli Counselor of Embassy in Paris, Bendor, for example, told an Embassy officer that Israel acted independently of the UK and France, although he admitted that the latter "took advantage of the situation." His argument was that Israel had to act for various reasons, including the belief that an Egyptian attack was imminent. Once Egypt, the main target, was eliminated, he stated, Jordan was no problem, except that Israel would be concerned who grabbed it. (T–2228, Paris, November 6, 1956, Secret.) [34]

The British, on their side, have vehemently denied that because they acted with the French they can be assumed to have connived with the Israelis beforehand. Again, these ex post facto justifications

---

[33] Pineau visited London October 23; see Document 373.
[34] Not printed. (Ibid., 684A.86/11–656)

are almost meaningless, or at least very difficult to understand. The evidence is persuasive that the British did not connive directly with the Israelis, but is conclusive that the French did. The British agreed to go along with the French in certain contingencies, of which the Israeli action against Egypt was the operative one. The French knew the Israelis would move. The British knew that the French knew. It makes very little difference in the end whether the Israelis or the British said they acted independently. In the circumstances, neither acted independently and both knew that, too. The possibility cannot be excluded that the British and French reached an understanding that the British would refrain from direct contact with the Israelis. The three principals also agreed—all of them—to shut out the US from any knowledge of their actions after October 16, the French and Israelis long before that date.

6. Up to the moment of the Israeli attack on Egypt, however, Israeli, French and British officials denied to the US that the Israeli mobilization had any hostile intent. An Israeli statement to the Security Council as late as October 25 had affirmed that Israel would never start a war with its Arab neighbors. Of course, the war had never ended. Only an uneasy truce remained to be broken. On October 28 both Ben Gurion and a senior Israeli defense official reiterated the claim that Israel would not provoke a war and that the Israeli mobilization was purely defensive and precautionary. . . . This pretense was an obvious act of deception. The French understood it so, and probably the British.

7. Yet, Jean Daridan, French Foreign Office official, indicated on October 27 and again on October 29 that the Quai d'Orsay had no indication that Israel was contemplating any military action at that time. (T–2003, Paris, October 27, 1956, Secret.) [35] The assertion about the Quai d'Orsay may have been correct at Daridan's level. The Embassy commented two days later that "it seems probable to us that the French are making no effort to restrain the Israelis . . ." [36] (T–2097, Paris, October 29, 1956, Secret) [37]—a patent understatement of the facts. On October 29 Pierre Maillard, Deputy Director of Near Eastern Affairs in the French Foreign Office, also supported the Israeli claim concerning the defensive character of its mobilization, but the next evening he told an Embassy officer that, although he was not informed concerning current French government thinking (again, *he* may not have been informed, although it is hardly credible by this date), the "possibility of Franco-British armed intervention" should not be excluded. He also said France could not now support

---

[35] Not printed. (*Ibid.*, 674.84A/10–2756)
[36] Ellipsis in the source text.
[37] Reference is to telegram 2027, Document 404.

the Tripartite Agreement of 1950. (T–2076, Paris, October 30, 1956, Secret.) [38] Maillard expressed "regret" that the US and France took opposing positions on Suez and that in the last 24 hours a frank exchange of ideas had been impossible. Maillard's point of reference regarding the 1950 declaration is obviously to Egypt. Neither the UK nor France regarded the 1950 declaration as strictly invalid in its application to Israeli relations with Jordan, Lebanon, and Syria. At least, this appears true for the UK, it is less certain for France. Eden stated to the British House of Commons on October 30 that the position of Egypt was not the same as other countries, since Egypt had taken a stand that she would not accept the implications of the Tripartite Declaration. Much earlier, on September 13, Eden in the House of Commons had reaffirmed British obligations under this agreement. There is no doubt whatever that both France and the UK regarded the declaration as a "scrap of paper" as far as Egypt was concerned.

8. On the occasion of the ceremony connected with General Gruenther's farewell Premier Mollet, referring to Suez, had stated that France "intended to raise the lesson stemming from Suez developments (that is, the importance of Western unity) in the NAC as well as to discuss it directly with the US and the UK." (T–1903, Paris, October 23, 1956, Confidential.) [39] He also said on October 30 in a speech to the French Assembly that France and the UK have kept the US fully informed concerning "their preoccupations and their decisions (sic)". [40]

9. A ranking but unidentified British official disclaimed to a senior US official in London any knowledge that France might be prodding Israel to action against Egypt, but indicated that the French could support Israeli action without telling the UK. . . . Such statements were almost certainly calculated to deceive, but they again reflect a British desire to pretend that the conspiracy in which they were involved was really not of their choice, but upon which they had to put the best possible face. The statements are almost unbelievable. So, too, is the one on October 31, by William Clark, personal adviser to Eden, who denied any collusion between Israel and the UK. Clark resigned shortly thereafter. The point is, of course, that direct Anglo-Israeli collusion does not need to be assumed. Some British officials who denied such collusion probably spoke in good faith. They simply did not know the big picture; they had been shut out of it. Yet, the evidence is convincing that both Israel and the UK were involved in a *situation* of collusion from

---

[38] Not printed. (Department of State, Central Files, 651.74A/10–3056)
[39] See footnote 5, Document 374.
[40] As on the source text.

which neither could separate themselves. The French have not tried to do so.

[Tab A]

CIA ANNEX [41]

The conclusions expressed in Section VI of the basic paper can be summarized as follows:

The French, and through the French, the British had prior knowledge of an impending Israeli attack against Egypt, and by mid-October the British and French had decided to exploit this occasion by military action of their own against Egypt. Whether prior to mid-October the French knew of the Israeli intention of attacking Egypt, or whether they had encouraged the Israeli to do so, is not a decisive consideration in reaching this conclusion. It is likewise regarded as immaterial whether the British knew of the Israeli intention prior to mid-October. It is a subsidiary conclusion of the basic paper that the evidence is not persuasive that the British did in fact connive directly with Israel, but is conclusive that the French did, certainly to the extent of undertaking the military build-up of Israel.

The conversation between the Director of Central Intelligence and the French Foreign Minister, 16 November, quoted at length on Page 19 of the basic paper, [42] supports the view that the French and British on or about October 16 did reach an understanding regarding the operation which was based on Israeli action.

.   .   .   .

Although indications . . . give some insight into the developing state of mind of the British, they do not, of course, establish direct collusion with either the Israeli or the French prior to mid-October. At most they serve to indicate possible or probable courses of British action in the event that UK "estrangement" from the United States reached serious proportions, and indicate the degree of receptivity the British brought to the mid-October consultation with the French. In the days immediately following the mission to Washington of Patrick Dean and other British officials, i.e. during the Security Council meetings of 3–14 October, CIA representatives concluded that estrangement was becoming decidedly acute and so orally informed Department officials.

---

[41] Top Secret.
[42] See footnote 29 above.

Other special materials available strongly support the conclusion of direct French-Israeli consultation, particularly during the days immediately preceding the Israeli attack on Egypt. They do not, however, provide any material insight into British complicity.

.   .   .   .

638.   Telegram From the Mission at the United Nations to the Department of State [1]

New York, December 6, 1956—8 p.m.

Delga 276. Verbatim text. Re Palestine/Suez. Hammarskjold passed following note to Barco this morning:

"After further talks with the British, French and Egyptians, I advise definitely against trying to get a GA resolution on Canal settlement. A debate could only confuse an issue which is on the rails, as apparent from especially Selwyn Lloyd's Monday statement in Parliament."

Murray (Canada) [2] told us this morning Canadians felt it would not be wise to precipitate what could well turn out to be acrimonious debate in GA on Suez settlement. Furthermore, Canadians feel considerable interval should elapse before any action taken in GA looking toward final settlement of Palestine issue. They feel to push Arabs at this stage would defeat our purposes.

On Suez settlement, they felt most advisable leave handling of matter to SYG as continuation talks begun with UK-French and Egyptians in elaboration of six principles. As for Committee of 5 suggested in US draft res on Palestine, Murray felt it would be impossible for any group no matter how restricted to promote settlement. What was needed, in their view, was at most an "advisory committee" working with SYG similar to advisory group in UNEF. He said they were most impressed with effective way this latter group had proceeded and with way it permitted Hammarskjold utilize his talents to fullest in admittedly complex operation.

---

[1] Source: Department of State, Central Files, 684A.86/12–656. Confidential; Priority. Received at 8:28 p.m.

[2] Geoffrey S. Murray, First Secretary of the Canadian Permanent Mission at the United Nations.

Murray referred to forthcoming NATO meeting in Paris, stating Pearson anticipated useful discussions proceeding within and particularly outside NAC meeting.

Lodge feels SYG is on right track and that GA debate should not be allowed interfere. Recommend Secy plan, in his discussions with NATO Fon Mins, to take line that Suez settlement should be left in hands SYG working with immediately interested parties and that no debate ensue for present in GA.

Wadsworth

---

639.   Note From the Secretary of State to the Israeli Ambassador (Eban) [1]

Washington, December 7, 1956.

The Secretary of State presents his compliments to His Excellency the Ambassador of Israel and has the honor to refer to the Ambassador's note of November 30, 1956, requesting that the United States Government at this time make a public statement concerning its attitude toward Israel.

On a number of occasions during the past several years the United States Government has publicly made clear its position with regard to the security of the states in the Near East. These declarations have included statements to the effect that the United States would take action, within and outside the United Nations, to prevent any violation of the frontiers or armistice lines by the states of the area; that the United States would, within constitutional means,

---

[1] Source: Department of State, Central Files, 611.84A/11–3056. Drafted by Rountree in response to Eban's note of November 30 (see footnote 3, Document 627). Bergus handed the note to Meroz on the morning of December 7 during a meeting. At 8:17 p.m., December 7, the Department of State transmitted a summary of the note's contents to Kabul, Cairo, Paris, Tehran, Baghdad, Tel Aviv, Beirut, Moscow, Amman, Ankara, London, and USUN. (Circular telegram 477; Department of State, Central Files, 661.84A/12–756)

On December 5, while transmitting the text of the note for approval, Rountree had advised Secretary Dulles that Israel's primary motive appeared to be a desire to terminate its diplomatic isolation and, evidently, the Israelis were seeking to mobilize public opinion in the United States behind their request. Rountree recommended that the U.S. reply to Israel should be couched in such terms as to prevent its being publicly construed as a shift in U.S. policy toward the Near East crisis and that no new statement of policy toward Israel was required at the time. A marginal notation on Rountree's note indicates Dulles approved of the note's contents on December 7 and Hoover concurred. (*Ibid.*, 661.84A/11–3056)

oppose any aggression in the Near East and render assistance to the victim of aggression; and that United States foreign policy embraces the preservation of the independence of the State of Israel. There has been no change in the policy set forth in these statements, which reveal the concern of the United States Government for the independence and security of Israel and the other states in the area.

The November 29 statement of the United States Government to which the Ambassador of Israel alludes referred to the states concerned in their capacity as members of the Baghdad Pact. [2] Thus the inclusion of other states would not have been appropriate, and their exclusion can in no way be construed as indicating any particular attitude of the United States Government toward these states.

The United Nations has revealed its abiding interest in maintaining the integrity of states against aggression. In recent days the United Nations has taken effective action to preserve security in the Near East. The United States has provided strong support to the United Nations in this task, and will continue to do so.

In the light of the steps which the United States Government has taken to demonstrate its concern for the security of the states in the Near East, it is believed that the position of the United States on this point has been amply affirmed.

---

[2] Regarding the November 29 statement, see footnote 2, Document 626.

640.   Memorandum of a Conversation, Department of State, Washington, December 7, 1956 [1]

SUBJECT

> Israel

PARTICIPANTS

> Mrs. Golda Meir, Foreign Minister of Israel
> Mr. Abba Eban, Ambassador of Israel
> Mr. Reuven Shiloah, Minister, Israel Embassy
> The Under Secretary
> NEA—William M. Rountree
> NE—Donald C. Bergus

After an exchange of greetings, the Israel Foreign Minister said that the Israel Government, especially the Prime Minister, appreciated the messages from the President which spoke of the friendship between the two countries. The Israelis wanted all to know that they were looking forward to the resumption of matters which had been suspended. Among the problems which disturbed Israel was the security situation with respect to Syria. There were continuing false accusations of Israel troops poised to attack Syria. The USSR was helping to spread these false reports. Israel was very vulnerable to a Soviet attack via Syria. It was for this reason that Israel had desired that the United States make a public statement at this time of its attitude with respect to Israel.

There followed an exchange of comment on the situation in Syria and the degree of Soviet penetration there. Mr. Rountree summed up the United States position by stating that we were concerned at present trends in Syria but that our primary concern was not over the immediate potentialities. Mr. Eban indicated that he liked the Department's note to him of December 7 [2] but would like to see its contents made public so that the USSR and the Arab states might hear it. Even the Pakistanis were talking about the possibility of Israel's annihilation. Mrs. Meir expressed concern that the UNEF might be forced to leave the area before its mission was completed as a result of Egyptian pressure. She was apprehensive over the fact that Yugoslav and Indian units were participating in the UNEF between the Suez Canal and Israel.

The Under Secretary said that the immediate job was to get on with tasks set by the United Nations. The United States had confidence in the United Nations Secretary General and was giving

---

[1] Source: Department of State, Central Files, 684A.86/12–756. Confidential. Drafted by Bergus on December 10.

[2] *Supra.*

him its full support. As for the UNEF, the Secretary General had said that withdrawal of the force was not a unilateral matter to be determined by Egypt. An attack on United Nations troops would be an attack on the world.

---

641. Telegram From the Department of State to the Embassy in the United Kingdom [1]

Washington, December 8, 1956—1:43 p.m.

4056. Urtel 3171. [2] Department's views on role of SCUA as follows:

1. U.S. believes SCUA should be continued and will pay its share of SCUA expenses.

2. SCUA should have important role re future Canal regime which should be determined in connection with negotiations between UK, France, and Egypt under Hammarskjold's supervision based upon six principles set forth SC Resolution Oct 13. SCUA should not attempt unilaterally to take any of actions specified in Para X, A thru D, urtel. [3]

3. Undoubtedly, as consequence of negotiations on six principles, SCUA will require enlargement so that it will be organization capable of speaking for all users of Canal prepared to join it, and its functions will need to be altered from what they now are under declaration of Sept 22.

4. Since arrangements for clearing of Canal including financing being developed by UNSec Gen, believe unwise for SCUA to inject itself into problem.

---

[1] Source: Department of State, Central Files, 974.7301/12–656. Confidential. Drafted by Metzger; cleared by Shaw, Wilkins, Rockwell, Hoffacker, Rountree, and Lister; and signed by Rountree for Dulles.

[2] Telegram 3171 from London, December 6, reported on a meeting of a small group of SCUA Council members, during which Acting Chairman Stikker had circulated draft remarks intended for an informal Council dinner meeting. The Embassy requested the Department's comments on Stikker's draft and general guidance on the subject. (*Ibid.*)

[3] The points included a series of questions as to whether SCUA should either formally or informally contact Hammarskjöld to inform him of SCUA's existence and/or emphasize the importance of clearing the Suez Canal, consult on the problem of dredging the Canal, and discuss the costs involved and the problem of freedom of navigation; discuss internally whether Egypt should help bear the cost of clearance and whether SCUA would have a role in any reinvestment problem.

5. Agree Bartels comments regarding six points and eighteen-power proposals, penultimate paragraph urtel. [4]

6. Agree Barbour's comments injection dues problem unrealistic and likely prejudice negotiations this time.

Dulles

---

[4] Bartels thought that SCUA should not seek agreement from its members to the six points of the Security Council resolution or to Hammarskjöld's elaboration of them in his letter of October 24, as this might reopen discussion of the Eighteen-Power proposals which were outdated.

---

642.   Circular Telegram From the Department of State to the Mission at the United Nations [1]

Washington, December 8, 1956—5:51 p.m.

482. Re US resolution on Palestine. While Secretary did not have time yesterday explore fully this question, he stated his belief that US should seek have GA consider resolution on Arab-Israeli problem before Christmas recess. We note SYG statement in Delga 201 [2] that it is timely bring up discussion US Palestine resolution after arrangements made for withdrawal forces and clearance canal. We not certain whether SYG still holds to this view in light Delga 276. [3]

Now that substantial progress made by SYG to this end, Department requests GADel explore Palestine resolution on confidential basis with SYG in first instance and then UK, French and subsequently with select members of other delegations reporting to Department as matter progresses in event changes in position may be required.

---

[1] Source: Department of State, Central Files, 684A.86/12–856. Secret. Drafted by Sisco; cleared by Phleger, Meeker, Murphy, Rountree, and Nunley; and approved by Wilcox who signed for Dulles. Repeated to London, Paris, Cairo, Tel Aviv, Tripoli, Jidda, Amman, Beirut, Damascus, and Baghdad.

On December 6, Wilcox forwarded to Phleger, Rountree, and Elbrick a much longer draft of this telegram under cover of a memorandum that indicated that the draft had been the subject of considerable discussion at the working level and that Wilcox had asked Murphy to invite Phleger, Rountree, and Elbrick to a meeting in Murphy's office at 11:15 a.m. on December 7 to discuss the draft telegram. (*Ibid.*, NEA/IAI Files: Lot 70 D 229, Suez Problem) No account of the meeting has been found.

[2] Document 620.

[3] Document 638.

Following guidelines for GADel's use in consultations:

(1) Now that substantial progress made on withdrawals, deployment effective UNEF, and on practical arrangements for clearance canal, US believes GA must seek with equal vigor long-range settlements outstanding problems between Arabs and Israelis. US intends press hard for such settlements and to make every feasible effort to this end. FYI In view UK, French influence in Middle East has reached nadir, only US can provide free world leadership at this time. End FYI.

(2) US convinced early solution Arab-Israeli problem is prerequisite to political stability and economic and social progress in Middle East.

(3) US believes must look to some new approach to achieve basic settlement outstanding issues. While Palestine Conciliation Commission has made useful contribution since 1948, we are hopeful that new committee of Assembly can take fresh look at outstanding problems. US resolution envisages committee composed of five members which will prepare recommendations, after consultations with parties to the General Armistice Agreements, regarding settlement major problems outstanding between them. We believe this committee should submit its recommendations to parties concerned, to GA and if necessary and appropriate to SC. Objective is to achieve negotiated settlement agreeable to parties not a solution imposed on them.

(4) We do not believe it necessary for US resolution to refer to numerous past resolutions. In order to get fresh start emphasis should be on future rather than on past. Our desire not to include reference to numerous past resolutions, however, is without prejudice to position taken by parties in past.

(5) We are not now, of course, in position to say concretely what specific substantive recommendations committee may make after consultations with parties. Nevertheless in US view, following are principal issues: (a) refugee problems; (b) territorial problems, including lack of fixed boundaries between Israel and neighbors; (c) economic development projects such as Jordan waters; (d) security guarantees, including guarantees against incursions. US policy regarding above remains as defined by Secretary in August 26, 1955 statement.

Department pouching brief status report, for your guidance, regarding approaches made to Governments re specific individuals to serve as members of Palestine committee.

In event question raised regarding US plans on Suez resolution, GADel should indicate that in our view most fruitful approach at this time is for SYG promote quiet conversations between UK, France, and Egypt based on his elaboration of six basic principles adopted by SC on October 13. In connection these discussions, may be desirable at some stage submit resolution for GA consideration.

FYI Position Dept will take re substance Suez settlement will depend on course of negotiations between parties. End FYI.

Dulles

---

643.   **Memorandum of a Conversation, Ambassador Dillon's Residence, Paris, December 10, 1956, 9:45 a.m.** [1]

USDel/MC/1

PARTICIPANTS

United States	United Kingdom
The Secretary	Mr. Selwyn Lloyd
William Macomber	Dennis Laskey

SUBJECT

UK Concern over "Unconditional" Suez Withdrawal

After the usual amenities, Mr. Lloyd opened the conversation by saying that his Government had done an "extraordinary thing" in that it had agreed "because the U.S. demanded it" to come out unconditionally from Egypt. He added parenthetically that as the Secretary knew the sterling area also had a good deal to do with this decision.

He then said that the UK salvage fleet had to "up-hook" on Wednesday unless something was done about it. He said the fleet had to leave by Wednesday (or shortly thereafter) to maintain the evacuation schedule. The reason for the early departure was that the ships were rather unseaworthy and that a good deal of time had to be allowed for their transit. Mr. Lloyd said that the UK could not, as had been suggested, leave the ships behind and simply take out the crews. He thought it was ridiculous taking this equipment away when it could be extremely helpful in clearing the Canal. He said

---

[1] Source: Department of State, Conference Files: Lot 62 D 181, CF 814. Secret. Prepared by the U.S. Delegation to the North Atlantic Council Ministerial Meeting.

Dulles arrived in Paris on December 9 to attend the 18th Ministerial Meeting of the North Atlantic Council. (Dulles' Appointment Book; Princeton University Library, Dulles Papers) The U.S. representatives at this meeting, held December 11–14, were Dulles, Secretary Wilson, Secretary Humphrey, and Perkins. The complete list of the U.S. Delegation is printed in Department of State *Bulletin*, December 17, 1956, p. 951. The papers of the U.S. Delegation, including position papers, memoranda of conversations, copies of telegrams sent between Paris and the Department of State, and miscellaneous papers are in Department of State, Conference Files: Lot 62 D 181.

the UK would be willing to have the crews wear civilian clothes rather than their military uniforms. The UK would also agree to all guns being removed from the ships (he doubted there were any), have a UN flag fly on the ships and to have UN observers aboard the ships. He said that he had sent a message this morning to all of the Canal User Governments calling their attention to the imminent departure of these ships.

Mr. Lloyd next reported that Hammarskjold had told him that Fawzi's attitude with regard to the exchange of correspondence interpreting the six principles for settlement of the Suez Canal problem had stiffened.

Mr. Lloyd next discussed his concern over British assets in Egypt. Though no state of war had been declared against the British, the Egyptians had sequestrated all British assets in Egypt. The Secretary asked if the Egyptians justified this action as an offset to the damage which the British had done in bombing Port Said. Mr. Lloyd replied that the Egyptians had given no reasons for their action. He said that as a matter of fact certain Belgian assets had been sequestrated and also certain Egyptian assets as well. Mr. Lloyd said in this regard that the Egyptians appeared to be using the present situation in Egypt to act more and more like a Communist regime. Mr. Lloyd added that Egyptians were "turning out" all British civilians. He said that his Government did not expect to be able to do anything about this but they felt it essential that British property be looked after. Mr. Lloyd then raised again his great concern over the British withdrawal without first negotiating a settlement on the future of British assets. He conceded that the problem of these assets had inherent in it great legal complications. He said that what was needed at this time was an agreement with the Egyptian Government that these problems would be referred to some kind of arbitration procedure. He said at the same time he felt that there should be some indication of the future of the Canal before the British withdrew.

Mr. Lloyd said there was one exception to his statement that the British were withdrawing without obtaining any conditions from the Egyptian Government. There had been a rumor that the Egyptians were planning as soon as the British had withdrawn to declare war on the UK and having done this block passage of British ships through the Canal. Mr. Lloyd had raised this with Hammarskjold who in turn obtained a commitment from the Egyptian Government that it would not do this. Mr. Lloyd stressed that this was the only condition they had obtained in connection with the playing of the one card they had to play, i.e., their withdrawal from Egypt. He also said parenthetically at this point that withdrawal was the only card he thought Israel also had to play. Mr. Lloyd said that of course the

UK had "not quite played" that card. He then discussed briefly the delay that the French had asked for until after their debate in the assembly in the middle of this month. It was agreed that this delay would not cause serious difficulties, that it could be handled as an "administrative" delay. No announcement would be made at this time but one would be made shortly before the scheduled departure time indicating there would be a further delay of several days. It was felt that the Egyptians would not be unduly concerned as they would have already seen a great deal of British equipment move out of the country.

Mr. Lloyd next briefly discussed Egyptian casualties. He said that the UK's best estimate was that around 500 Egyptians had been wounded, that one to three hundred had been killed. He said that the majority of these casualties had taken place as a result of Egyptian violation of the cease-fire agreement. He said, however, Egypt would make extreme claims and we would be told there were 8,000 Egyptians dead "and that sort of thing".

Mr. Lloyd then said there was going to be an "awful row" in England when it was found that the UK had withdrawn without extracting any conditions from the Egyptian Government. He asked the Secretary "How do you think the UK should go about getting these conditions before their withdrawal?" Putting it another way he said, "How should the UK now do the things, which if they had not made an agreement with the UN, they would be doing for themselves?". Mr. Lloyd said that he had thought of asking Hammarskjold to go to Egypt to look into these matters on behalf of the British. His reasoning was that the UN had an obligation to look after these matters because of the British agreement with the UN and in lieu of the British doing it for themselves.

The Secretary prefaced his remarks by commenting on Mr. Lloyd's opening statement to the effect that the US "had told you to get out". The Secretary said he thought that was not an accurate way to describe what our position had been. He said the US thought that a good many of the ill consequences of the British-French action could be better taken care of by "your getting out than by your staying". The Secretary said that the US could not alleviate all the ill consequences resulting from this action but some things could be done. He mentioned as an example the US support of sterling which he said may run up as much as $100 million. He said that we would do all we can to expedite the reopening of the Canal.

The Secretary said that he believed the initial "revulsion" on the part of the American public against the British action was subsiding. He stressed that this revulsion had initially existed throughout the country with the possible exception of certain groups on the East Coast. (In this connection he counselled Mr. Lloyd against assuming that newspapers like the *New York Times* and the *New York Herald Tribune* fairly represented American opinion on this issue. He said that the great weight of opinion in the country was quite different from that which had been reflected in the two newspapers.) The Secretary said that he thought the stage was set for the rebuilding of close relations between our two countries together with such monetary assistance as we were able to give the UK in its present difficulties. He mentioned that Secretary Humphrey had said that the run on sterling had been checked in the last few days. In this connection the Secretary thought the thing to worry about was not the economic strain on a currency but rather psychological strain. He said that once it was known the US was prepared to lend money to the monetary fund on a substantial scale, the end result might be that we would not have to lend a particularly large amount. The fact that we were willing to lend this much money might in the end make it unnecessary actually to do so. The Secretary cautioned, however, that we were facing a budget squeeze in the US. One of the reasons for this was the ever increasing defense cost brought about by the great expense of modern weapons and equipment. As a result he told Mr. Lloyd that he would find that Secretary Humphrey was going to be "still tough" on fiscal assistance matters. The Secretary said we were facing a real problem but that we would do what we could to work it out. He said the President will personally concern himself with these matters when he gets back to Washington. He said the President will develop the general theme of the necessity of cooperating with the UK in his Inaugural address and in his message to Congress.

The Secretary then said he wanted to make the following point. He wanted Mr. Lloyd to know that the US did not act as it did because "we liked the Egyptians better than we did the British". Nothing, said the Secretary, could be more fantastic. He said the reason we acted as we did was that we were convinced that there would be little chance of establishing a world order or avoiding World War III if we acquiesced in the British action. The Secretary said that, as Mr. Lloyd probably knew, Syngman Rhee and Chang Kai-shek [2] had recently discussed a joint attack against the Chinese Mainland. The Secretary said that the interests which would dictate such an action by the Republic of Korea and the Republic of China were just as vital to them as were the interests to Britain and France which had led to the Suez invasion. He said that if the US did not adhere to a general position against the use of force in this type of thing we would never know where to draw the line.

---

[2] Respectively, the President of the Republic of Korea and the President of the Republic of China.

The Secretary went on to say that we have no confidence in Nasser. He said for a short time after the attack we had considerable influence with him and still had a certain waning influence but he assured Mr. Lloyd that we were under no illusions about our continued popularity and influence with the Egyptian dictator. He said, however, that we were prepared today to use our influence with Nasser and to put pressure on him to clear up the kind of matters Mr. Lloyd had raised. He again stressed our lack of any illusion that we would have any continued influence with Nasser. He said that our influence had begun to wane when Nasser realized that our actions were based on principle and not any love of Nasser. The Secretary said that before he left Washington he had indicated a desire to use our waning bank account of good will now while we had it.

The Secretary then discussed the future status of the Canal. He said that one of the two last acts he had taken before going to the operating table was to direct that a US resolution be introduced in the UN which would call for the establishment of a UN committee to deal with this matter. He said however that the thinking when he left Washington was that the resumption by Hammarskjold of his informal activities would be more effective than to pursue this problem by the formation of a UN committee. Hence, for the time being the US planned to leave its resolution in abeyance. The Secretary added, however, that as time went on it would be more and more difficult to reach a settlement. He asked for Mr. Lloyd's views on this.

Mr. Lloyd prefaced his answer by saying that he had made every effort in his public statements not to be critical of the US position during the Egyptian operation. He then reiterated the basic theme which had run through his earlier remarks. He said that he disagreed with the US position (making specific reference to Ambassador Lodge's statements at the UN) that the UK should withdraw from Egypt without extracting pre-conditions. He said if the British public finds that the UK has withdrawn from Egypt without clearance of the Canal and without agreements with regard to British assets which have been sequestrated "and looted" there will be a wave of indignation in the UK which will be a very "messy situation" and will undoubtedly lead to a new wave of anti-Americanism. He mentioned again the undesirability of having British salvage ships and equipment leaving on Wednesday. (At this point the Secretary asked what arrangements were being made for paying for the clearance of the Canal. Mr. Lloyd said that if the British had been allowed to do it they would have paid for it.)

Mr. Lloyd then asked, "Should not Hammarskjold go to Egypt?". He mentioned that Fawzi was leaving New York for Cairo tomorrow and indicated he thought Fawzi was a good influence. The Secretary said that he could not give a definite answer to this question without consulting his colleagues. He said that in general he agreed that the Egyptians should be pressed on the matters Mr. Lloyd had mentioned before the British withdrawal is complete. He said he realized this would be difficult to do because of the dilatory tactics of the Egyptians with which Mr. Lloyd was very familiar. Mr. Lloyd interposed to say that if the British troops left Egypt without any agreement on the release of the 500 UK canal base technicians now interned there, the British people would think their Government needed to have "its head examined". However, if an agreement were reached that allowed the interned technicians to walk out the day the last British troops went out, that would be satisfactory.

The Secretary returned to the subject of the British withdrawing without extracting preconditions. He asked Mr. Lloyd if the British Government had not already crossed that bridge. Mr. Lloyd said they had, that they had given their word to the US. The Secretary said not just to the US but to the UN. Mr. Lloyd said that he believed that the UK had been much more specific as to date in the assurance to the US. He believed that the assurance to the UN had been less specific. In any case, Mr. Lloyd said that the British were publicly committed to leaving and would do so. The only question was one of "administrative delay" while an attempt was made to get certain necessary guarantees. He said that even these administrative delays could not be accomplished without the US acquiescence. He said they had given their word to the US that they would get out and unless the US released them from this commitment, they could not do otherwise. The Secretary said that the US could not release the UK from this commitment as it was on this basis that we had laid our plans for future assistance to the UK. Also he said that the only way we had been able to obtain public support in the US for these plans was on the assumption that the UK would fulfill its commitment. If we released the UK from its commitment we would be guilty of a breach of faith with our own people.

On the other hand, the Secretary stressed that we would be willing to consider putting pressure on Nasser during the remaining period that the British troops would be in Egypt. To implement this,

Mr. Lloyd suggested a direct approach to Nasser by Ambassador Hare. [3]

[3] The remainder of Dulles' conversation with Lloyd on December 10 was recorded in another memorandum of conversation (USDel/MC/1/3). According to this memorandum, the following remarks relevant to the Suez Crisis were also made:

"At the end of Mr. Lloyd's call, and after the discussion of the Middle East had concluded, the Secretary said he wanted to express a general proposition. He said that generalities were always dangerous because of reservations which were often required when the problem departed from the general and became specific. However, as a generality he wished to state that the U.S. does not have the slightest compunction against using force to 'hold what we have got.' He said that he thought it was a very dangerous thing ever to indicate a wavering on that principle." (*Ibid.*, Conference Files: Lot 62 D 181, CF 814)

---

644.   Memorandum of a Conversation, Quai d'Orsay, Paris, December 10, 1956, 5–7 p.m. [1]

USDel/MC/5

PARTICIPANTS

United States	France
The Secretary	Foreign Minister Pineau
Ambassador Dillon	Mr. L. Joxe
Mr. C.B. Elbrick	Ambassador Alphand
Mr. R. Bowie	Mr. J. Daridan
Mr. W. R. Tyler	Mr. Crouy-Chanel
Mr. A. Berding	Mr. J. Roux

SUBJECT

General Discussion of Current Situation

[Here follows discussion of other subjects; see Document 647.]

THE PROBLEM OF NASSER

Mr. Pineau resumed the conversation by asking "Quid with regard to Nasser"? He said that his government was still resolutely against him.

The Secretary said that the US government had lost confidence in Nasser sometime ago. The action we had taken was not because

---

[1] Source: Department of State, Conference Files: Lot 62 D 181, CF 814. Secret. Prepared by the U.S. Delegation to the North Atlantic Council Ministerial Meeting. The Embassy in Paris transmitted a summary of this conversation to the Department of State in Secto 6, Document 647.

we love Nasser or wanted to keep him in power. We felt that if we did not stand up against the use of force to remedy such injustices as Nasser had committed, we would then have no valid argument against the use of force in other parts of the world, for example: Korea with Syngman Rhee, Chiang Kai-shek in Formosa. We also had to consider the possibility that there might one day be a government in Western Germany which would want to reunite Germany by force. There were some people who felt that Hungary should be liberated by force. We feel, said the Secretary, that we must stand by the UN charter under Article 1. There was a great danger, otherwise, that smaller wars might materialize in such a way as to lead to World War III. We do not want to defend Nasser, he said, but to support the principles of the Charter of the UN, and we do not want to argue either the merits or demerits of recent actions. He said that we had not acted because we preferred the Arabs to the UK and France. We have close traditional and sentimental ties with these last two countries, whereas we have no particular ties with the Arabs. . . . The Secretary went on to say that he did not feel that one could change foreign governments by direct action. To try to do so usually had the opposite effect. It tended to solidify the government in question and to rally support to it. We felt that political and economic pressures against Nasser would work. On the other hand, we believe that there are certain policies which will lead the Egyptian people to feel that Nasser is not a very good leader. There are Arab leaders, the Secretary said, outside of Egypt, who are jealous and afraid of Nasser. The Egyptian economy is in bad shape, and the US had taken economic measures immediately after the seizure of the Canal, such as halting our economic aid program, our agricultural aid program, and cutting off all tourists from the US. These measures had not been taken avowedly against Nasser, but on the ground that his policies were not such as to justify normal friendly relations with Egypt. The Secretary said we had encouraged Saudi Arabia in the direction of independence of Nasser's policies, and had given support to the Baghdad Pact and to Iraq. We think our policies will work, the Secretary said, but we do not think we can achieve our objections by directing our policies personally against Nasser. He said we can already see certain signs of disaffection in Egypt. We do not want to support Nasser, but we do not think it works to try to remove the head of any government. We say this, not because we like Nasser, he added, and recalled that he himself had said pretty strong things against Nasser publicly. However, it very rarely worked to try to force out a foreign government because this rallied support to it.

Mr. Pineau said that he had never asked the US government to choose between the Arabs and the West. He recalled that he had already mentioned the case of Nasser to the Secretary of State at the time of the bilateral talks in Washington in June, and had said that Nasser was a Soviet agent. On this point, said Mr. Pineau, he would speak very frankly and say that he regretted that the UK and France had not continued their military action for another two days so as to occupy the whole of the Canal. It was now a question either of building up Nasser or of letting him fall of his own weight, and he felt the second solution was the right one. The Secretary said he believed that the Arab countries and the Egyptian people themselves would take care of Nasser. It was the US view that if we go for Nasser and make him a symbol of martyrdom the Arabs will rally around him. The Secretary said that he believed that our policies will have the effect of discrediting Nasser, and that the Arabs will desert him, since they do not approve of his introducing Communism into the Middle East, but we should not make Nasser an open target. Mr. Pineau said that any loans should go first to the task of clearing the Canal, and that in any case no loan should be made to Nasser which he could use to buy arms from the Soviet Union. The Secretary observed that the US had no thought of extending a loan to Nasser.

ISRAEL

Mr. Pineau said that it was essential to give Israel a sense of security with regard to her neighbors, otherwise next time the situation might be worse still. He said that we must do away with the armistice regime and bring about a peace treaty. He said that he had already told Mr. Hammarskjold this. The Secretary recalled the proposals he had made on August 26, 1955, which had been supported by the UK and France, calling for a peace settlement, with defined boundaries for Israel guaranteed by the UN, and followed by the granting of loans and the development of the water resources of the region. The Secretary said that we had tried to get the Arab countries to make peace with Israel, but in vain. The possibility of achieving this was doubtless impaired by the fact that the Arab countries were already preparing to obtain arms from the Soviet Union. We were at that time unaware of the full scope of the arms negotiations with the USSR. The Secretary said that, looking back, we can now see that Egypt was striving to achieve a position of strength with regard to Israel. While it is true that Egyptian arms have now been captured in quantity by Israel, the situation has become greatly embittered by the Israeli action. The Secretary went on to say that it is important that a peace treaty be achieved, instead of an armistice. However, it is very difficult to extend guarantees to a country which does not have firm boundaries. He said that we had made a treaty with Korea, whereby we agreed to protect an Armistice line, but this was quite a different kind of line, with observer and a neutral strip of territory between the 2 parties. Mr. Pineau said that Israel was more worried by Soviet bombers in the hands of Egypt, than by the Egyptian army on the ground. The Secretary said that, in this sense, any real protection for Israel against planes is impossible. It was difficult enough for the US to figure out a way to protect itself from possible attacks by Soviet planes from 5,000 miles away; it was impossible for Israel to be effectively protected against planes from 5 miles away. He said that the bitterness of the Arabs against Israel would take a long time to die away. He thought that any Arab government now proposing the conclusion of a peace treaty with Israel would be overthrown, and that the situation was highly emotional. We had tried our best, but there was not much else we could do at this time. Mr. Pineau said that one form of reassurance to Israel would be to prevent the building of air forces in neighboring states. He said that Israel wanted to build a pipeline of 8 inches or perhaps even larger from Aqaba to Haifa, with private Western capital. He thought this would be a good idea. Mr. Pineau expressed himself in favor of introducing the US resolution on the Palestine question in the UN. The Secretary said he did not know whether we could get a ⅔ majority for it in the General Assembly because the Arabs were opposed to it. Mr. Pineau said he thought the Asian countries were less opposed to the Resolution than the Arabs were, and the Secretary agreed.

[Here follows discussion of other subjects; see Document 647.]

---

645.   Telegram From the Mission at the United Nations to the Department of State [1]

New York, December 10, 1956—8 p.m.

Delga 307. Paris for Secretary from Lodge. Re Palestine (Depcirtel 482). [2] This morning I called on Hammarskjold for discussion of planning on Palestine and Suez questions. I asked Hammarskjold his views on timing of further GA action and his estimate of best time to bring up two US resolutions for GA consideration. I told him of

---

[1] Source: Department of State, Central Files, 684A.86/12–1056. Secret; Niact. Received at 9:16 p.m. Also sent to Paris.
[2] Document 642.

Secretary's great interest in keeping momentum and asked his view on bringing up Palestine resolution before Christmas recess.

Hammarskjold said that he continued believe best approach to Suez question was to avoid further discussion in GA and reactivate negotiations between British, French and Egyptians on basis of Security Council's six principles. Existence of these negotiations would achieve purpose of our US resolution. He said Selwyn Lloyd was prepared enter these discussions promptly as was Fawzi but as yet French position was uncertain. He believed that these discussions could begin with withdrawal of British and French forces from Port Said and that since this was proceeding well, negotiations could begin very shortly. He intended in fact to begin making necessary arrangements for negotiations with parties at once. Hammarskjold said it was not only his own feeling that GA discussion was undesirable, but also feeling of parties themselves. He thought therefore that we should not proceed with our Suez resolution.

Hammarskjold said that Canal clearance operation was proceeding well although there had been difficulties over weekend about use of British ships and personnel. UK had taken position that it should be all or nothing. Either their total force of some 40 ships and some 2,000 civilians should be used or nothing. Hammarskjold said had taken position, on basis of political realities of situation, that he could not agree to this and his plan was to use only 6 of their salvage vessels. Cordier later told us only British personnel to remain on ships would be 3 on each for short time for training purposes and then ships would be operated entirely by Danish and Dutch personnel.

Re Palestine resolution, Hammarskjold was definitely opposed to raising Palestine question in Assembly before Christmas recess. He believed it could only produce bitter debate, harden positions, and make solution more difficult. This was particularly true in view of what he called "scorched earth" policy being taken by Israelis in Sinai Peninsula. He said Israel had systematically torn up the three roads running through Sinai Peninsula for a distance of 75 kilometers and had torn up as well 30 kilometers of the railroad. This was going to make it extremely difficult for UNEF to move into Sinai. Hammarskjold said General Burns had requested Israel to desist from their destruction of communications through Sinai and they had given unsatisfactory response. Result of this action by Israel, Hammarskjold feared, would be to further exacerbate Egyptian-Israeli relations.

I asked Hammarskjold if he did not think that a resolution which was basically procedural could be submitted with some chance of avoiding full scale debate. Hammarskjold said he doubted very much that this was possible. He felt previous resolutions would be brought up and debate would range over whole area of Arab-Israeli relations. He thought it might be easier to deal with procedural resolution in the SC at the appropriate time, but then only after more progress had been made on Suez settlement, including progress on Israeli freedom of transit. On latter point Hammarskjold thought Egyptians might agree to let ICJ decide Israeli rights as part of Suez settlement. Israeli contention that armistice agreement with Egypt was "dead letter" had been tactical error in his opinion and left Israeli rights to be determined in light of 1888 Convention, if Israel persisted in its attitude toward Armistice agreement.

Recommendation: I believe Near East crisis definitely impaired chances for successful negotiations on either Suez or Palestine and that in neither case would it be constructive at this time to engage in public diplomacy. Sharp focus private talks, on the other hand, are clearly desirable.

Paris telegram Secto 2 [3] just received. In addition to information contained in foregoing, further information re Canal clearance in immediately following telegram. [4]

Lodge

---

[3] In Secto 2 from Paris, December 10, Dulles reported that Lloyd had told him that day that the United Kingdom was not willing to permit its salvage vessels to remain without British crews. Dulles responded that he would undertake to obtain the latest information regarding the clearance operation. (Department of State, Central Files, 974.7301/12–1056) A memorandum of the December 10 conversation is printed as Document 643.

[4] In Delga 308, December 10, Lodge reported to the Department of State that Hammarskjöld had telephoned to convey his serious concern over insistence by the British that their crews remain with their vessels. Hammarskjöld warned that the British position would jeopardize everything that he had been doing and that otherwise arrangements for clearing the Canal were proceeding smoothly. The Secretary-General also informed Lodge that, according to what Lloyd had told the Swedish Ambassador in Paris, at a recent meeting of SCUA members an unnamed "American Ambassador" had taken the position that all SCUA members should urge upon their governments support for the use of British salvage vessels and personnel for clearing the Canal. (Department of State, Central Files, 684A.86/12–1056) Delga 308 was also sent to Paris.

646.   Telegram From the Mission at the United Nations to the Department of State [1]

New York, December 10, 1956—8 p.m.

524. For Hoover from Lodge. Fawzi (Egypt) asked to see me this afternoon. He expressed concern over implications of U.S. assistance now underway for Britain and France when there had been no similar show of interest in economic plight of Egypt. Fawzi said good will that had been created for U.S. in Egypt and Middle East by our recent actions was something which he very much hoped to preserve and build upon. While fully understanding need to assist Britain, France and Western Europe, whom he said he also wanted to see remain strong, there was bound to be unfavorable reaction in Egypt in view of failure U.S. or UN show any concern over conditions in Egypt. Fact was that however understandable to us and to him, we were now giving aid to the aggressors and giving no attention to the plight of country aggressed upon. Egypt had suffered severe damage in Port Said, in Alexandria, and to the Canal, and her airfields had been put out of commission. Egyptian economy was pretty well flattened out. Fawzi said he was not suggesting an aid program or anything that specific, but only that we should show concern and not allow our newly won position to be impaired by apparent lack of it.

In my letter of December 3 to Secretary, [2] I said: "It is generally agreed that some substantial program of economic assistance will be needed to rebuild the Middle East and advance our prestige in that area. There are clear signs that bilateral programs would not be welcome in certain countries of that area, whereas a multilateral UN program with U.S. participation would be very well received. There is the danger that in the absence of such UN action Soviet bilateral programs may attempt to fill the gap. For these reasons I feel that there must be a meeting of minds—and a decision—on this subject very soon."

I feel that careful consideration should be given to Fawzi's point and renew my recommendation above. I do not recommend this merely because it would be politically delicate for Egypt to accept aid from U.S., but chiefly because of the effect upon UK, Israel and other Arabs of a straight U.S.-Egypt aid agreement. What is necessary in the circumstances is a multilateral aid program under the aegis of the UN with appropriate controls through the IBRD.

---

[1] Source: Department of State, Central Files, 684A.86/12–1056. Confidential; Priority. Received at 9:52 p.m.

[2] Dated December 4. (*Ibid.*, 340/12–456) For text, see vol. IX, p. 399.

The best way for this to be put into effect would be for the President to recommend it in his State of the Union speech and to authorize me to announce here that he will do so. This would help greatly in furthering negotiations on a Palestine settlement. With an aid program underway, it would encourage progress in negotiations if only because failure to negotiate might lessen the chances of continuing aid.

Fawzi said that he expected call on Acting Secretary Hoover Wednesday or Thursday of this week when he would raise problem at that time. I recommend strongly he not be given negative answer.

Lodge

---

647.   Telegram From the Delegation at the North Atlantic Ministerial Meeting to the Department of State [1]

Paris, December 11, 1956—3 a.m.

Secto 6. Talk with Pineau Quai d'Orsay Monday, December 10, lasted two hours, interrupted only by ten minute absence Pineau in order cast vote National Assembly. Pineau expressed generally favorable opinion Wise Men report [2] except part relating functions Secretary General which he termed too broad and vague, needing sharper definition. Pleaded for need common policies applying "all four corners world" and including Near and Middle East and Africa. Secretary observed certain areas world such as Far East of which certain members NATO know nothing and in which have no responsibility. Said United States prepared discuss policy but could not undertake make its policies conform necessarily to views others.

Pineau announced desire discuss Middle East and North African topics at present NATO session under item general review. Enumerated fifteen points covering all aspects Middle East problem, and including North Africa and Algeria saying preferred hearing disagreeable things in NATO forum than in UN. Secretary observed would probably hear them in both. Pineau said favored frank discussions these matters even though could not achieve solution.

---

[1] Source: Department of State, Central Files, 786.00/12–1156. Secret; Limited Distribution. Received at 10:05 p.m., December 10. Repeated to USUN, London, and Cairo. For a memorandum of the conversation recorded here, see Document 644.

[2] Reference is to the report of a Committee of Three concerning non-military cooperation in NATO, presented to the Ministerial Meeting at Paris.

Pineau laid great stress importance clearing Canal criticizing Hammarskjold for not fulfilling promise that work would start as soon as time-table withdrawal made public.

Stressed importance usage French and British salvage equipment. Secretary agreed everything possible should be done press clearance and no difference views on this point at all. Said Gen. Wheeler Egypt now doing all he could expedite matter. Pineau in favor approach Hammarskjold urge him press for more speed. Pineau raised problem freedom navigation Canal, status French and UK citizens now Egypt, possibility trouble Port Said after withdrawal completed, and role UNEF. Discussion turned to manner further negotiations with Egypt and Pineau suggested United States Suez resolution might be amended to provide for enlarging membership committee to six (possibly Norway, Sweden, Ceylon) with Hammarskjold as chairman. Acknowledged, however, Egypt seemed opposed this procedure and French therefore inclined feel might revert Security Council procedure established in October calling for negotiation with Egypt under auspices Hammarskjold. Some discussion possible formula for financing clearing Canal and role SCUA as means controlling dues payments Nasser, if latter unwilling play fair. Pineau stressed importance preventing Egypt or Syria obtaining further arms from Soviet Union.

Pineau then discussed Nasser and reiterated strong hostility against him. Secretary gave lengthy explanation US position with regard Nasser government and stressed that while we do not love him or want to keep him in power we feel use of force and other strong pressures bound to be counter-productive and calculated strengthen rather than weaken him. Secretary said attempts change foreign governments by direct action apt to have opposite effect, but we believe certain policies will lead Egyptian people feel Nasser not good leader and other Arab states disposed be jealous and afraid of him.

Pineau then discussed Israel and need provide security by replacing armistice by peace treaty. Secretary recalled his proposal August 26, 1955 but pointed out present situation greatly embittered by Israeli military action so that very difficult now bring Arab countries toward acceptance idea peace treaty. Pineau said Israelis want build pipe line from Aqaba to Haifa and interested enlisting private western capital. Said he favored introducing United States resolution Palestine problem but Secretary said we don't know whether we could obtain two-thirds majority because of Arab opposition.

Pineau stated Lebanon interested becoming neutral country under UN auspices and base for permanent UN force in Middle East. Said this idea broached to French by Chamoun and that they had informed our Embassy Beirut. Pineau asked United States position Syria. Secretary answered we studying very intensively whole problem United States relationships Middle East area in which United States presence will have to be felt more than in past. United States considering various possibilities but no final conclusions yet reached.

Secretary solicited French views Algerian question. Pineau outlined military situation admitting continuing terrorism and claiming reinforcement Communist action. Outlined various political steps taken by French including agrarian reform and abolition municipal councils. Said French Government not willing consider solution granting independence but will propose at UNGA "new formula" leading to elections with international observers from countries where free elections are held. Pineau said could not commit United States Government position at this stage on basis inadequate specific information.

General atmosphere conversation relaxed and tone Pineau friendly avoiding irritating comments and clearly making conscious effort maintain pleasant atmosphere.

Dulles

---

648.   Telegram From the Delegation at the North Atlantic
         Council Ministerial Meeting to the Department of State [1]

Paris, December 11, 1956—5 p.m.

Secto 7. Reference: USUN 308; [2] Bonn Topol 2238; [3] Cairo 1844, [4] all to Department. Principal US concern is clearance of canal as quickly as possible in interest of all users and as only real way end current petroleum shortage. We understand reasons why British

---

[1] Source: Department of State, Central Files, 974.7301/12–1156. Secret; Niact. Received at 12:12 p.m. Repeated to London, Niact to Cairo, Bonn, and Niact to USUN.

[2] See footnote 4, Document 645.

[3] In Topol 2238, December 10, the Embassy in Bonn reported that the British Embassy had approached the German Foreign Office with a request that the German Federal Republic intervene with the Egyptian Government to permit British salvage operations pending a U.N. takeover. The Foreign Office requested to be informed of the U.S. position on the matter. (Department of State, Central Files, 684A.86/12–1056)

[4] Telegram 1844, December 10, reported that Hammarskjöld had authorized Wheeler to retain a certain number of French and British crew members on each salvage vessel for instructional purposes for a short period after which they would be replaced. (*Ibid.*, 974.7301/12–1056)

and French wish to see use of their salvage equipment or at least minimum portion and also reasons for Egyptian opposition. However, we believe US should be guided by what will bring about most expeditiously clearance of canal.

Under existing circumstances, SYG and General Wheeler in best position to judge what, if any, action by US or other users would assist in accomplishing objective. We not able to evaluate here whether British-French equipment actually needed or could be used effectively in manner described USUN 307 [5] to Department and Cairo reference telegram. Independent moves at this time by US or other users, uncoordinated with UN, could disturb present delicate situation.

Accordingly, unless Department has contrary views, if requested by General Wheeler or SYG, Ambassador Hare should make representation to Egyptian Government re use of any or all British-French salvage equipment but not otherwise. We hope UK and France will agree to use of their equipment in manner best calculated to expedite clearance.

If UN efforts fail to make progress quickly, and after receipt of full facts, we of course may wish to reconsider matter.

Other users (Bonn's Topol 2238) requesting US views may be informed along above lines. Lloyd has asked that US urge Egypt agree to use of British equipment.

Paragraph 2 of USUN 308 apparently refers to informal dinner meeting of SCUA given by Danish Ambassador in London not Paris. American Ambassador did not make statement attributed to him by Swedish Ambassador. [6]

Dulles

---

[5] Delga 307, Document 645.

[6] Aldrich's report of this meeting was transmitted to the Department of State in telegram 3208, December 8, not printed. (Department of State, Central Files, 974.7301/12–856)

649. Telegram From the Department of State to the Embassy in Egypt [1]

Washington, December 11, 1956—7:41 p.m.

1912. At early opportunity you should speak with Nasser along following lines:

April 9, 1956 statement issued on behalf of President declared that "US, in accordance with its responsibilities under UN Charter, will observe its commitments within Constitutional means to oppose any aggression in (NE) area . . . [2] US is likewise determined to support and assist any nation which might be subjected to such aggression."

On October 29 President, recalling that US had pledged itself to assist victim of any aggression in NE, said "we shall honor our pledge".

Events subsequent to outbreak of hostilities in NE have revealed effective manner in which US has lived up to this pledge. In doing so, US took actions which placed it in strong opposition to policies of its oldest friends, UK and France. US efforts to assist in bringing hostilities in Egypt to an end were made at heavy cost to US in terms of damage to traditional friendship with oldest allies at time when USSR, through its brutal policy in Hungary and its truculent public statements vaunting superiority of its military strength, once more left world in no doubt of its willingness to commit military aggression to serve its political ends. In light serious implications these circumstances GOE can have had no doubt of importance which US places upon preservation integrity NE states and maintenance peace in area.

US believes it has right now to ask what Egypt is prepared to do to promote area peace and strengthen area stability. Past Egyptian policies, especially re Suez Canal and fedayeen activities, had important responsibility for bringing on hostilities. It is unthinkable, in US view, that tensions in area be permitted to rise again. Rather, steps must be taken leading to solution of underlying problems. US expects GOE to demonstrate a constructive attitude in this regard, and to reveal due respect for principles of international law as stressed by Nasser in his November 21 speech. Specifically, following are kind of steps US desires see Egypt now take:

a) Offer full cooperation in urgent clearance of Canal;

---

[1] Source: Department of State, Central Files, 684A.86/12–1156. Secret. Drafted by Rockwell; cleared by Beam, Wilcox, and Sisco; and approved by Rountree who signed for Hoover. Repeated to Paris for the Secretary and to London.

[2] Ellipsis in the source text.

b) Offer full cooperation in renewal of negotiations on future Canal regime;

c) Place no obstacle in way of fulfillment by UN force of its responsibilities under GA resolution in Egypt;

d) Take effective measures to prevent fedayeen operations;

e) Cease operations by Egyptian agents in violation sovereignty and authority of neighboring states;

f) Move toward settlement of outstanding problems between Arab states and Israel.

In these and other ways GOE can make important contribution to strengthening of peace and stability NE. In view of its interest in security of area, recently so convincingly demonstrated, US believes it has right express friendly hope that GOE will take steps to bring about lessening of tensions. [3]

Hoover

---

[3] In telegram 1925 to Cairo, December 12, the Department of State added to these instructions as follows: "Following inadvertently omitted from list of steps US desires see Egypt now take in interests promotion area stability. Cessation of inflammatory radio attacks on neighboring states." (Department of State, Central Files 684A.86/12–1256)

---

650.   Message From the President to the Secretary of State [1]

Augusta, Georgia, December 12, 1956.

DEAR FOSTER: Thank you very much for your cable report that I received yesterday morning. [2] I am of course delighted that our friends seemed to accept our conviction that bilateral are preferable to tripartite talks and conferences.

---

[1] Source: Department of State, Central Files, 684A.86/12–1256. Secret. Transmitted to Paris in Niact Tedul 16, December 12, which is the source text. The message was drafted in Augusta, Georgia, where President Eisenhower was taking a working vacation. Goodpaster transmitted the text to the Department of State through the White House communications center with the instruction: "The President requests that Secretary Hoover look this message over, and if okay, send on to Secretary Dulles at once." A copy of the message is in Eisenhower Library, Whitman File, Dulles–Herter Series.

[2] Transmitted in Dulte 7, December 10, not printed. (Department of State, Central Files, 396.1–PA/12–1056) In his message, Dulles briefly reported that he had met with Lloyd and Pineau separately on December 10 (see Documents 643 and 644), that the meetings had been cordial, and "the strain has, I think, been ended". He noted that nothing of great significance emerged at either meeting.

I hope that our NATO friends will understand clearly that we have no intention of standing idly by to see the southern flank of NATO completely collapse through Communist penetration and success in the Middle East while we do nothing about it.

I am sure that they know that we regard Nasser as an evil influence. I think also we have made it abundantly clear that while we share in general the British and French opinions of Nasser, we insisted that they chose a bad time and incident on which to launch corrective measures.

Most important of all, I hope that our friends in Europe will see the necessity, as we see it, of beginning confidentially and on a staff level to develop policies and plans whereby the West can work together in making the Middle East secure from Communist penetration. I have no doubt that for some time to come we would have to be, at least in the public eye, the spearhead of any such movement. But it does seem that at long last we could get a pretty good general understanding among us as to what must be done and how we should go about doing it.

I continue to believe, as I think you do, that one of the measures that we must take is to build up an Arab rival of Nasser, and the natural choice would seem to be the man you and I have often talked about. If we could build him up as the individual to capture the imagination of the Arab World, Nasser would not last long.

A couple days ago I received a message signed by General Weygand and Marshal Juin, sent to me, [3] they said, on the basis of our former association as comrades-in-arms. I think the State Department will probably cable to you certain extracts from the letter. It may not be too important, but it does show at least one kind of thinking that is prevalent in Western Europe, especially in France.

New Subject. Yesterday Prime Minister St. Laurent stopped at Augusta to visit with me. While the visit was largely social, he had some ideas about the forthcoming visit of our Asiatic friend. [4] There was nothing particularly new in them, so I do not bother you here with their repetition. I shall probably see you Saturday.

---

[3] A translation of the Juin–Weygand joint letter to President Eisenhower of November 30 is in Department of State, Presidential Correspondence: Lot 66 D 204, DeGaulle, Mollet, Gaillard exchange of corres. with Pres/Sec/2/53/ thru 1/61. The letter conveyed Juin's and Weygand's concern over the effectiveness and future of the Atlantic Pact. Marshal Alphonse Pierre Juin was the Commander in Chief of Allied Forces in Central Europe. General Maxime Weygand (retired) was a former Commander in Chief of the French Army and Director-General of Algeria.

[4] Reference presumably is to the official visit to Washington of Indian Prime Minister Nehru December 16–20, 1956.

With very warmest regard and the hope that you are suffering no ill effects about going back to work so soon after your recent illness.

As Ever,

D.E. [5]

---

[5] Tedul 16 bears these typed initials.

---

651.   Telegram From the Secretary of State to the Department of State [1]

Paris, December 12, 1956—5 p.m.

Dulte 12. Eyes only Hoover and Lodge. Have considered Lodge's 524 [2] suggesting that economic aid for Middle East be contributed through multilateral UN program. While I do not exclude possibility some UN multilateral aid for area, my thinking at least when I left Washington was that after having considered various media for Middle East aid and in view of necessity of US making its presence felt in area to avoid vacuum, US should seek congressional authority for military and economic aid to area which would primarily be on bilateral basis in order to exert maximum influence upon policies of certain governments and so that we would have flexibility and maneuverability.

I would not exclude possibility of using some of this through Baghdad Pact or through UN but I doubt that political situation in area justifies exclusive or primary reliance on multilateral aid through UN. Whereas we would normally want to sterilize aid against political implacability in this particular situation we may not want to do so.

---

[1] Source: Department of State, Central Files, 811.0080/12–1256. Confidential. Received at 3:39 p.m. Repeated to USUN.

[2] Document 646. On December 11, the Department of State repeated telegram 524 from USUN to Dulles in Paris and transmitted Hoover's comments on it in Tedul 11. Hoover advised Dulles: "I believe in view of (a) our recent decision to conduct our Middle East foreign policy on a bilateral basis and to avoid multilateral commitments, and (b) the necessity, as never before, of having our economic policies working in full harmony with our political policies, any such proposal would be basically contrary to US security interests." Hoover also suggested that Dulles cable his views to Lodge before such a proposal was further advanced or suggest to Lodge that action await Dulles' return and further study and review. (Department of State, Central Files, 811.00/12–1156)

I trust therefore that there be no present commitment to use UN as primary channel. This would certainly be inappropriate for military aid and in many cases economic aid would need to be geared into and related to military aid.

Dulles

---

652.   Telegram From the Department of State to the Embassy in Egypt [1]

Washington, December 12, 1956—7:47 p.m.

1940. Embtels 1751,[2] 1808, 1830.[3] Circular 426 was general directive setting forth principles which will guide USG in its relationship with NE in light new circumstances prevailing in area. Within this framework specific US attitudes toward individual countries will be determined in light of local picture. Para 6 of Circular points out need for agreed acceptable basis for cooperation as well as requirement that trend of events in area offer reasonable prospects of success.

Feasibility of US efforts to cooperate with peoples of NE in promoting economic and social progress in area depends in important degree upon contributions by states in area to production of atmosphere favorable to success of such undertaking. In Egypt's case would be helpful if there were convincing evidence of determination to direct national resources to improving economic well-being of people. Also desirable would be constructive attitude re settlement Canal dispute and readiness make progress toward resolution Arab-

---

[1] Source: Department of State, Central Files, 684A.86/12–1256. Confidential. Drafted by Shaw and Rockwell and approved by Rountree who signed for Hoover. Repeated to Paris and London.

[2] In telegram 1751, December 1, Hare transmitted to the Department of State a summary of a conversation between the Embassy's Economic Counselor Robert Carr and the Assistant Under Secretary of the Egyptian Ministry of Finance Dr. Abdelmoneim El-Banna during which the latter requested the U.S. position concerning continued U.S. development assistance to Egypt and the unblocking of Egyptian dollar assets. Hare requested guidance from the Department as to whether the Embassy should respond to the Egyptian Government along the lines indicated in circular telegram 426, November 21 (scheduled for publication in volume XII) or whether there was a special directive in regard to Egypt which the Embassy should follow. (Department of State, Central Files, 874.131/12–156)

[3] Telegrams 1808, December 6, and 1830, December 8, informed the Department of State of Egyptian requests to obtain corn and wheat flour, respectively, under the P.L. 480 program. (*Ibid.*, 411.7441/12–656 and 411.7441/12–856)

Israel issue. Relaxation of tensions and strengthening of stability of area as result of steps taken by Egypt, Israel and other NE states would be example of helpful trend of events mentioned in para 6 of Circular 426.

Department has already requested Embassy outline to Nasser certain steps US would like see GOE take in interest improving regional atmosphere. (See Deptel 1912) [4]

Department concurs Banna's inquiry was of reconnoitering nature. GOE officials should be given no encouragement expect any change from US position on status aid for Egypt, which remains as set forth in Deptel 1283. [5] If matter US aid is raised at highest level it can then be discussed within context general US-Egyptian relations.

US position on unblocking Egyptian assets remains as described Deptel 1812. [6]

Rehabilitation of Port Said probably should be treated as special problem since it will be difficult separate it entirely from measures to rehabilitate Canal and place it in operation. Nonetheless GOE should not be encouraged raise subject US aid for this purpose.

Hoover

---

[4] Document 649.

[5] In telegram 1283 to Cairo, October 27, the Department of State advised that there were no shipments under development assistance programs for Egypt going forward or planned for the future except deliveries under the $40 million program committed prior to June 30, 1955. In addition, a limited technical cooperation program with Egypt was still going forward, but no new projects had been initiated under this program during recent months. (Department of State, Central Files, 774.56/10–2756)

[6] In telegram 1812 to Cairo, November 30, the Department of State among other points informed the Embassy in Cairo that the Treasury Department would not allow the use of blocked Egyptian dollars to pay for future oil products imports. (*Ibid.*, 611.74231/11–1956)

---

653.   Telegram From the Secretary of State to the Department of State [1]

Paris, December 14, 1956—1 a.m.

Dulte 16. Eyes only Acting Secretary and Rountree, information only Ambassador Cairo. Distribution to be made at Acting Secre-

---

[1] Source: Department of State, Central Files, 684A.86/12–1456. Secret; Priority. Drafted by MacArthur. Received at 6:56 a.m. Repeated to Cairo.

tary's discretion. I have had discussions with Selwyn Lloyd re rapid clearance of canal, importance of which cannot be over-exaggerated in terms of whole European economic situation. As result these conversations I had MacArthur put to Lloyd orally following proposition, on which I said we would use our maximum influence to gain acceptance if British Government concurred. This included our influence with Secretary General Hammarskjold and Nasser because we believed proposition was both reasonable and desirable in terms speeding clearing canal. Following is proposition:

1. We agreed six of UK-French salvage vessels presently working on clearance of canal north of armistice line could be most useful in rapid clearing of canal. We believed these were UK vessels.

2. These six vessels would fly UN flag. They would be operated by present captains and crews but captains and crews would be in non-military uniforms.

3. Guns and armaments these vessels would be rendered inoperable.

4. There would be handful UN personnel on each vessel. This would give further UN color to character of vessels while engaging in clearing operation, and in sense UN personnel would be observers. They would not engage in operation of vessels but could transmit general instructions from General Wheeler as to tasks vessels were to accomplish in canal.

5. Vessels would operate under General Wheeler's general direction in that they would carry out clearing tasks at various points in canal as directed by General Wheeler.

Lloyd said elements above proposition were not too dissimilar from what UK Government had already offered and said he accepted proposition in name of British Government.

He then asked whether six salvage vessels in question were those Wheeler had indicated he could use. We replied we could not answer specifically but would seek information this point. This however Lloyd said did not affect acceptance of proposal. He added that while he accepted proposal on basis six salvage vessels he wanted us to know he felt it was desirable to use entire UK-French salvage fleet. We replied we could not give him any encouragement on this. We also informed him we would let McCloy and our key people in Washington know of British acceptance this proposal and that while we would use our best influence to gain its acceptance, we could not of course guarantee it would be accepted.

Lloyd inquired when ships would be placed under UN control if above proposition accepted. We replied that in our view the sooner the better and if we could do this in next several days and before final British withdrawal, the better.

I believe important thing now is for us to use our maximum influence to gain acceptance of above proposal. Secretary Humphrey, who is fully informed, is telephoning McCloy this evening that message is being sent you on this problem and that we want him fully to support it with Hammarskjold. (Therefore important you get substance this message to McCloy.)

I will leave it to your discretion how to press Hammarskjold on this matter. I have in mind it might be useful for Phleger to go to New York tomorrow, and with Lodge, press above proposal on Hammarskjold. When we know Hammarskjold's reaction, on assumption he will be willing to press this strongly on Nasser, we should also be prepared have Hare urge Nasser to accept. (It also very important General Wheeler know our thinking and use all his influence with Egyptians to support this proposal).

I hope we are not crossing wires. If so, I leave decision to you.

Dulles

---

654.   Memorandum of a Conversation, Palais de Chaillot, Paris, December 14, 1956, 10 a.m. [1]

USDel/MC/12

PARTICIPANTS

United States	*France*
The Secretary	Foreign Minister Pineau
Ambassador Dillon	Mr. Joxe, Foreign Office
Mr. Elbrick	Ambassador Parodi
Mr. Tyler	

1. Mr. Pineau said that he had been informed by the Swiss that the Egyptian Government has been notifying French citizens in Egypt individually that they must leave the country by December 18. [2] The Egyptian Government has been careful not to publish any

---

[1] Source: Department of State, Conference Files: Lot 62 D 181, CF 828. Secret. Drafted by Tyler.

[2] On December 14 in Washington, French Minister Lucet called at the Department of State to emphasize French concern on this matter. U.S. officials assured Lucet that the United States had informed Nasser of U.S. concern about this situation and the treatment of Jews in Egypt. (Gadel 67 to USUN, December 14; *ibid.*, Central Files, 684A.86/12–1456) Also on December 14, USUN reported in Delga 347 that according to Andrew Cordier of the U.N. Secretariat, the Egyptian Government had assured U.N. officials in Egypt that further action against British and French nationals remaining in Egypt (approximately 13,000 people) was not contemplated, and consequently Hammarskjöld had advised Great Britain and France not to bring the matter before the General Assembly at this time. Cordier also maintained that facts available

decree of general expulsion, but the result is the same as if it had. Mr. Pineau said that about 3,600 French citizens had already left of their own accord or been forced out. (Subsequently, Mr. Pineau told Mr. Tyler that the number of French citizens affected would come to over 12,000.)

Mr. Pineau said his Government takes a very grave view of this matter. He said that the French Government has introduced a resolution in the UN GA [3] which will come up for debate on Saturday, December 15. The French Permanent Representative, Mr. Broustra, has had a talk with the Secretary General, who showed very great concern. At this point, Mr. Pineau read from a cable he had received from New York describing the fatigue and depression of Secretary General Hammarskjold at the news of this measure by the Egyptian Government. He seemed fully aware of its gravity and reportedly said that he personally had no reason to doubt Fawzi's good faith, but that this latest move was the result of Nasser's "primitive character" and of the unhealthy influences at work on him. Hammarskjold is also reported to have said he would not be surprised if Mr. Fawzi were to resign in the not-too-distant future. Mr. Pineau asked for US support in the vote on the resolution. The Secretary indicated that we would want to be helpful to the French in this matter. Mr. Pineau observed that unfortunately it was not certain that the French would be able to obtain a ⅔ majority.

2. Mr. Pineau said that General Wheeler had proposed that U.K. and French salvage ships be used in clearing of the Canal with Egyptian crews. Mr. Pineau said that this was out of the question. The Secretary said a telegram had been sent to the State Department and to Ambassador Lodge in New York to say that it seemed unreasonable not to use vessels with their customary crews. [4] Mr. Pineau said that the French would be glad to fly the UN flag on their salvage ships and that all that was necessary was to have a few UN troops on board each one. He said that the French government would even be willing to have a UN Captain for each ship, if this would help.

---

to the U.N. Secretariat did not substantiate rather lurid Israeli reports regarding the treatment of Jews in Egypt. (*Ibid.*)

On December 15, the Embassy in Cairo in telegram 1907 forwarded a Swiss Embassy report that while the Egyptian Government had not issued a formal general order to expel British and French nationals, the Egyptian Ministry of Interior in numerous cases had refused to extend exit visas beyond December 18 and had sent remaining nationals letters advising them to leave Egypt as soon as possible. (*Ibid.*, 684A.86/12–1556)

[3] The *Official Record* of the General Assembly records no such draft resolution. The General Assembly did not meet on Saturday, December 15.

[4] *Supra.*

3. Mr. Pineau said that Prime Minister Mollet had received a personal message from Mr. Ben Gurion and had asked Pineau to show it to him confidentially. (Mr. Pineau handed the text to the Secretary of State and asked to have it back later. It has been translated separately and the original was returned to Mr. Pineau.) [5]

4. Mr. Pineau said that a Soviet trade delegation had been in Paris for about the last six months negotiating a renewal of the Franco-Soviet commercial agreements. He said that the French are very desirous of concluding the agreement which involves the importation of anthracite, manganese, and chromium. He said that the Soviet Union wanted to place an order in France for equipment for television relay stations. Mr. Pineau said that this material is on the COCOM list of strategic items. He said that there was a COCOM rule that not more than 33% of any agreement should consist of strategic materials. He said that under the present negotiations, the Soviet television order would amount to about 40% of the total agreement. He hoped that the United States would not object to this, and added that the French had tried to increase the non-strategic percentage but had not been able to do so. The Secretary said that he was not familiar with this subject and that Mr. Pineau's request would be taken under consideration.

---

[5] Not printed. A copy of the English translation is attached to the source text. In his letter, among other points, Ben Gurion urged Mollet that he and Pineau convince Dulles that it was not too late to act to curb Nasser and to explain to Dulles the necessity of fulfilling Israeli requests concerning the U.N. forces.

---

655.   Memorandum of a Conversation, Palais de Chaillot, Paris, December 14, 1956 [1]

USDel/MC/6

PARTICIPANTS

United States	*United Kingdom*
The Secretary	Foreign Secretary Lloyd
Mr. MacArthur	Mr. Beeley, Foreign Office
Mr. Elbrick	Mr. Dennis Laskey, Foreign Office

---

[1] Source: Department of State, Conference Files: Lot 62 D 181, CF 828. Secret. Drafted by Elbrick.

Mr. Lloyd said there were several matters he would like to take up with the Secretary.

1. Expulsion of French and British nationals from Egypt.

Lloyd said the Swiss had informed the French and British that the Egyptian Government intended to expel all British and French nationals by December 18. The French had informed the British that they were introducing a resolution in the General Assembly today or tomorrow, and that the British had agreed to support the French on this resolution. Lloyd said, however, that the British had made this decision reluctantly and had pointed out to the French that a debate on this subject might easily lead to a general debate on the question of withdrawal. He had, therefore, suggested that the tactics to adopt in this case would be to avoid action on the resolution for the time being, hoping that Fawzi might be induced to say something helpful in the Assembly which would obviate the necessity for such a resolution. Lloyd said he realized that nothing could be done to prevent the expulsion of French and British nationals if the Egyptians were intent upon going through with it, although they would be entitled to be indemnified by Egypt. He said that Hammarskjold had reported that Fawzi is at loggerheads with Nasser and that there were reports that Fawzi might resign. In view of the news regarding intended expulsion of French and British nationals, of the question of expropriation of British and French property, and of the complications arising in connection with the clearance of the Canal, Lloyd felt that Hammarskjold should go to Cairo as quickly as possible. The Secretary pointed out that the resolution on Hungary envisaged a visit by Hammarskjold to Moscow, but he agreed with Lloyd that Hammarskjold could probably accomplish more in Cairo. Lloyd said he hoped we would support their position on this question of expulsion and on getting Hammarskjold to Cairo quickly. The Secretary indicated sympathy for the British problem but made no commitment.

The Secretary said he thought we should not try to disguise the fact that we are going to have a difficult time with Nasser before this is over. He felt we had taken the only possible course in connection with this affair and that bad consequences were unavoidable, but he thought the time had now come when we would have to bring strong pressures to bear on Nasser. Lloyd said he thought they saw the problem the same way. However, Lloyd was concerned that sufficient account and credit had not been given to the UK and France as a result of their withdrawal.

2. Syria.

Lloyd asked the Secretary whether the US has any influence with Syria. He said the Syrians were being "bloody" about the pipeline. He was much concerned about the effect of Syrian action on Iraq's economy, and particularly on the position of Nuri Said. The Secretary said we are fully alive to the unsatisfactory situation in Syria and we are exerting every effort to have the pipelines in Syria repaired. There is some hope that we can accomplish this as soon as the withdrawals are complete, in view of the fact that Syria is not only short of oil under present conditions, but also money.

[Here follows discussion of matters pertaining to Libya, Jordan, the communiqué to be issued by the NATO Ministerial Meeting, and the status of the Commonwealth battalion in Korea.]

7. SCUA.

Lloyd asked if the Secretary thought SCUA could still play a useful role. The Secretary replied in the affirmative and said he had seen Bartels, [2] who asked the same question. In working out a solution of the Suez problem, the Secretary thought there was a good chance of perfecting international cooperation through the Users Association, and he felt that the Association would play an essential role. He did not know, however, whether Nasser would agree, but he did feel it would be a great mistake to abandon the idea at this stage. He had told Bartels, who wanted to activate SCUA immediately, that he was not sure of the timing. Lloyd said he was glad to have the Secretary's views and that they both saw eye to eye on the future utility of SCUA. The ways and means of using it would, however, have to be considered further.

---

[2] Dulles spoke with Bartels at 12:30 p.m. at the Embassy Residence in Paris. A memorandum of that conversation (USDel/MC/7) is *ibid.*, CF 814.

656.   Memorandum of a Conversation, Department of State, Washington, December 14, 1956 [1]

SUBJECT

Review of Egyptian Situation with Foreign Minister Fawzi

PARTICIPANTS

Dr. Mahmud Fawzi, Foreign Minister of Egypt
Dr. Ahmed Hussein, Egyptian Ambassador
The Acting Secretary
G—Robert Murphy
NEA—William M. Rountree
NE—Maurice S. Rice

After an exchange of pleasantries, Dr. Fawzi spoke of the crisis in Hungary and agreed with the Acting Secretary that the aftermaths may be far reaching. He added that if Moscow continues in its present course, more walls around it may crumble. Dr. Fawzi then turned to the matter of the Soviet "volunteers" who had been reported as being prepared to aid Egypt during the recent hostilities. He said that Egypt had never asked for them. The present breathing spell, he stated, allows a chance for constructive work. He hoped there would be no more incidents which would further complicate the situation. He said that we must continue all efforts to bring about an atmosphere in the Near East and African area conducive to cooperation among nations, including the British and the French. In this connection, he hoped that some arrangement might be reached which would lead toward the recognition of the rights of the Algerians.

Suez:

Dr. Fawzi said that there is progress on the immediate task of clearing the Canal and expressed his satisfaction with the work of Lt. General Wheeler, who, according to Dr. Fawzi, had told Secretary General Hammarskjold that Egypt was cooperating with him. The Acting Secretary said that the problem of expediting the clearance of the Canal is of grave concern because millions of persons who had nothing to do with the Near East trouble are suffering as a conse-

[1] Source: Department of State, Central Files, 684A.86/12–1456. Secret. Drafted by Rice. Briefing papers prepared for this meeting include a memorandum from Murphy suggesting that a discussion of economic aid be linked with a discussion of how to solve the Arab-Israeli problem (*ibid.*, 684A.86/12–1356); three studies prepared in the Office of Intelligence and Research on Egyptian interference in the internal affairs of African and Middle Eastern states (*ibid.*, 670.74/12–1456); and a general briefing memorandum prepared in the Bureau of Near Eastern, South Asian, and African Affairs (*ibid.*, NEA Files: Lot 58 D 545, Egypt).

quence of it. Mr. Hoover added that Egypt would lose much good will if it insisted upon complete withdrawal of the British and French forces before allowing the salvage work to begin. He urged Egypt to take the initiative in starting the work and to permit the use of whatever equipment is available. Dr. Fawzi said General Wheeler had been allowed to start his survey of the Canal, despite initial opposition in Cairo, and to gather necessary equipment from any source. The survey should be completed at about the same time the withdrawal ends which, according to Dr. Fawzi, should be December 16 or 17. The Secretary General is fully informed and is satisfied with the progress, Dr. Fawzi added. Mr. Murphy asked about the use of British and French experts in the salvage operation. Dr. Fawzi said only three men would be permitted on each ship, on a temporary basis to train others in the use of the equipment. The Acting Secretary replied that owners of the equipment would not want persons unfamiliar with the equipment to use it. Dr. Fawzi evaded an answer and remarked that he was confident some arrangement would be reached.

The Palestine Dispute:

Dr. Fawzi expressed doubt that any progress could be made toward a solution of the Palestine issue at the present time, but indicated that after a period of study and consultation with other Arab leaders, Egypt might be willing to have a small group—perhaps even one man—outside the UN seek a basis for settlement. If this fails, however, the matter might go to the UN. He stressed his preference for an informal approach to the problem.

Aid for Egypt:

Dr. Fawzi then turned to the main point of his presentation: Egypt's concern over U.S. assistance to Britain and France, to the apparent exclusion of Egypt, the aggrieved, who had suffered severe losses and whose economy is damaged. He said that he could understand why the U.S. is helping her allies—and he believed the Arabs understood the reason. He said Egypt is not asking for aid, at least not at this juncture, but the situation creates a problem. How best can we deal with it, he asked? He indicated that Egypt might have to raise the matter in the General Assembly but, being aware of the acrimony that would result, he strongly preferred to handle the problem outside the UN. In reply, the Acting Secretary said U.S. assistance has wider implications than just aid to Britain, because of the dependence of a great part of the world on sterling trade and because the welfare of many people is involved. As for economic aid to the Near East, the Acting Secretary said the U.S. would evaluate the overall need of the area to determine how we can best help on the basis of expressed principles to bring about peace and stability. In reply to Dr. Fawzi's comment on U.S. blocking of Egypt's accounts, the Acting Secretary outlined how the action, arising from Egypt's nationalization of the Canal Company, had taken place and said the matter is of primary concern to the Treasury, which is studying it on a continuing basis.

Egyptian Activities in Other Countries:

The Acting Secretary then spoke in frank terms of our grave concern over the operations of Egyptian agents in the Near East. Incontestable information from our observers in the area tell of fedayeen raids in Israel, sabotage in Kuwait and hostile acts in Lebanon. The Acting Secretary said President Nasser and Dr. Fawzi might not be aware of these dangerous and inflammatory activities. He requested Dr. Fawzi to tell Nasser of our concern and to urge him to take remedial action. Dr. Fawzi, who listened attentively with no apparent sign of surprise, thanked the Acting Secretary for bringing the matter to his attention in such a frank and friendly manner and said he would ask Nasser to take action. He was grateful that the Acting Secretary had raised the point because, he said, such situations must be dealt with promptly and not allowed to grow and fester.

---

657.   Memorandum of a Conference With the President, White House, Washington, December 15, 1956, 2:28–4 p.m. [1]

OTHERS PRESENT

> Secretary Dulles
> Under Secretary Hoover
> Colonel Goodpaster

[Here follows discussion of other NATO-related subjects.]

He [Dulles] said that the biggest difficulty had been the desire of NATO countries to have U.S. policy made in the NATO Council. He had stressed that we stand ready to discuss policies—and prefer to do so earlier rather than later—but that we could not commit

---

[1] Source: Eisenhower Library, Whitman File, Eisenhower Diaries. Secret. Drafted by Goodpaster. The time of the meeting is from the record of the President's Daily Appointments. (*Ibid.*)

ourselves to anything of this kind. The President interjected that the others obviously could not either, for constitutional reasons.

Mr. Dulles said that the NATO countries had suggested a communiqué implying that all the countries, the U.S. included, had concerted a policy of handling the Middle East situation. When Mr. Dulles pointed out how such a statement would appear to world opinion and asked them to reconsider their proposal, they dropped this provision. The Secretary said it was difficult to find and to follow the narrow path between, on the one side, strengthening NATO, and, on the other, avoiding the appearance of "teaming up" and taking positions in the UN as a bloc.

[Here follows discussion of other NATO-related subjects.]

In further discussion concerning the Suez situation, Mr. Hoover said Hammarskjold's patience with the British and French is beginning to wear thin. Mr. Dulles said that their "take all or nothing" stand regarding their equipment for clearing the Canal had been unwise. He said that the British and French in Paris had told him they were giving up this stand (but Mr. Hoover thought they had not gotten this word through to Hammarskjold in New York).

Mr. Dulles suggested that we might be able to get Nehru to exert some pressure on Egypt in the direction of a decent permanent settlement of the Canal problem, prompt clearing of the Canal, and a settlement of the Israeli problem. Mr. Hoover said that the Arabs had been very clever in their dealing with Hammarskjold—much more so than the British, French and Israelis—with the result that they have frequently appeared to be in full concord with his efforts and objectives. Mr. Dulles said the problem of arranging for Israeli shipping through the Suez is going to be very difficult but thought it should be faced. The President commented that the Egyptians are likely to have a hard time backing away from the policy they have been following.

G

Colonel, CE, U.S. Army

658.   Telegram From the Mission at the United Nations to the Department of State [1]

New York, December 15/16, 1956—midnight.

Delga 358. 1. Suez Clearance; 2. French-British Nationals in Egypt. Early this evening Hammarskjold requested Barco call on him at his office. He said a very delicate situation had arisen which he wanted us to know fully. He did not request any action but simply wanted us have all information which he had.

On arrival SYG's office, Barco found Hammarskjold with Bunche, Cordier and Katzin. Hammarskjold appeared be in rather grim mood and spoke more deliberately than is his custom and with considerable show of discouragement. His comments follow:

1. Suez clearance. Hammarskjold said he had been informed earlier today by McCloy that there had apparently been agreement between the Secretary, Lloyd and Pineau in Paris to use British crews on six vessels to be retained by UN for clearance operation. McCloy also reported Black (president IBRD) had made démarche to this effect to Fawzi in Washington. Hammarskjold's manner and tone indicated considerable concern at this development which had occurred without consultation with him and when, as he said, he had just yesterday sent to Lloyd and US a full report on his position with respect use British crews. [2] He had been maintaining his position in interest of a prompt and successful clearance operation only to find contrary action vis-à-vis the Egyptians had been taken without his knowledge. Hammarskjold said he had, however, put as good a face on it as he could with Fawzi, who had indicated his willingness to recommend acceptance to Egyptian government on basis this was last compromise needed for British to save face. Number of British crew had been given to Fawzi as 90 and this figure had been referred to by Fawzi in his report to Cairo.

Next step, Hammarskjold said, in this "curious picture" was an ultimatum to him at 4 pm this afternoon by Dixon (UK) adding

---

[1] Source: Department of State, Central Files, 974.7301/12–1556. Secret; Priority. Received at 2:09 a.m., December 16.

[2] On December 14, Hammarskjöld provided the U.S. Mission in New York with a copy of a six-page memorandum which he had sent to Lloyd that day. The memorandum, written in the form of a General Assembly document, reaffirmed Hammarskjöld's position that only three British crew members per vessel would be allowed to remain as instructors. The text was forwarded to the Department of State in Delga 348, December 14. (*Ibid.*, 974.7301/12–1456) Delga 348 also noted that unless the United Kingdom agreed to Hammarskjöld's position on the use of non-British/French crews, the Secretary-General planned to issue the memorandum as a U.N. document. Also, Cordier had requested on behalf of Hammarskjöld that a copy of the memorandum be forwarded to Secretary Dulles.

additional conditions. Ultimatum was British would withdraw all their ships unless by 12 noon Monday New York time Egyptians agreed to retention British crews under following conditions for their protection:

"1. Armed UN sentries in each vessel authorized to open fire not only in their defense (which is said to be existing UN rule), but to resist any hostile action towards ships' crews;
"2. UN land forces to cover ships from one Canal bank;
"3. UN patrols to protect road convoy of stores, etc."

Dixon also said number of British crew was not 90, but 162. Hammarskjold said he had told Dixon he did not see how it was possible to have an answer by Monday noon and Dixon had replied he would try to have deadline extended 24 hours.

Hammarskjold said he would be seeing Fawzi tonight and as yet simply did not know what he could say which might be helpful in getting Egyptian agreement. He would have to report the latest figure on crews and conditions which meant, in effect, UNEF would have to extend itself along 100 miles of Canal. He feared answer from Egypt would probably be that no British crews would, in these circumstances, be permitted to be retained. Hammarskjold pointed out that in his original agreement with Egypt for UN to undertake clearance operation, formula had been that Egypt requested UN to undertake job. Fawzi's reference to "last compromise" to save British face made him fear new conditions would prove too much. Hammarskjold said as clearance operation by UN proceeded, protection measures British were now demanding would in fact have been worked out along similar lines. He feared British, by using method of ultimatum, were working up to point where they could say UN was not capable of doing the job if Egyptians now rejected their demands. British statement on their intention withdraw all ships if conditions not met by Monday noon implied sunken ships now being lifted would be dropped and it was mainly to avoid interrupting this operation that the six ships had been requested. Hammarskjold also said, throughout his discussions with British, there had been one shift after another in their position, always in direction of new conditions. He said attitudes being taken by British and French on the one hand, and Israelis on the other, had caused definite turn away from progress toward settlement larger issues.

. . . .

Hammarskjold said he no longer knew when E-day for withdrawal of British-French forces would be in these circumstances. He told Dixon during their discussion this afternoon, that if things went on as they had been, there would be another withdrawal, and that would be his own.

2. Treatment of British-French nationals in Egypt. Hammarskjold said Broustra (France) had also called on him today and had maintained French insistence on GA debate Monday afternoon on treatment their nationals in Egypt. Hammarskjold said he had pointed out they could not expect a debate limited to statement by British and French and reply by Fawzi. Debate would not end there, Israelis would have their say, and Arabs and others in GA would take the matter further. He expected there would be demand for new resolutions on withdrawals and probably war damages. Broustra had stated, however, French "were not concerned about the consequences." Broustra had admitted their demand for meeting Monday was because of debate in French Assembly on Tuesday. At same time that British were making an ultimatum on clearance operation and French were demanding debate in GA, both French and British had insisted on his going to Cairo immediately. French had said if he went today, they could then avoid debate in French Assembly. Hammarskjold said they were obviously trying to use him as a scapegoat while British based their request that he go to Cairo on the necessity of dealing with clearing problem. He had asked how they could expect him to go to Cairo on clearing problem when at same time they were demanding agreement by Monday noon, which was before he could get there. British had then referred to necessity seeking a "settlement." Hammarskjold said he had replied that settlement was more in their hands than in anyone else's at present time and, if he were to go anywhere for that purpose, it would be to London.

Broustra had returned later with request from Paris that SYG should announce he was going to Cairo to discuss treatment of British and French nationals in Egypt. Hammarskjold said he could certainly not make such an announcement on basis of what he now knew with respect to situation in Egypt of British-French nationals.

As to his actually going to Cairo, whatever reason the British and French might have for wanting him to do so, he had told them he would not go unless Fawzi thought it would be helpful.

Lodge

659.   Telegram From the Embassy in Egypt to the Department of State [1]

Cairo, December 16, 1956—8 p.m.

1926. Reference: Department Telegram 1912. [2] Talked with Nasser for three hours yesterday afternoon at government rest house at barrage outside Cairo where he has been in semi-seclusion past 10 days in order, he said, rest and formulate plans for future. I observed that in these circumstances my visit would seem well timed because it was of matters I desired speak under instructions from Washington and I thereupon presented substance reference telegram as instructed using original telegram to talk from in order to assure accuracy. Nasser listened attentively and took notes.

Taking his time and speaking deliberately and apparently thoughtfully Nasser said that he first desired make clear he shared our basic objective of assuring security and stability of area. Difficulty, based on experience past three years, had been in finding means. Said he had tried speak frankly with us in past but with indifferent success. However, would now try again and before answering specific questions raised in reference telegram wished give frank exposition of what in his mind. He then made following points:

(1) Most pressing need is to build up domestic economy of Egypt and raise living standard. This was in fact main objective in nationalizing Canal. Preoccupation with foreign affairs detracts from accomplishment essential domestic reform.

(2) Inclusion of Iraq in Baghdad Pact was, in view GOE, contrary to area security and stability. Also disturbed by activities of Turkey.

(3) Everything being done in Syria and Jordan is directed to avoidance outside domination. With such threats removed problem should not be difficult. Assertion re Communist activity in Syria is really effort to cover up Iraqi conspiracy dating back to early August of which GOE had been currently aware. Therefore, impossible assure area security and stability unless "other side", i.e. Iraq and Turkey, plays it square.

---

[1] Source: Department of State, Central Files, 674.00/12–1656. Secret; Priority. Received at 2:09 a.m., December 17. On December 18, Greene transmitted a copy of telegrams 1926, 1927 (see footnote 6 below), and 1946 (see footnote 7 below) to Goodpaster at the White House under cover of a note which reads: "The Secretary thought the President would be interested to read the attached telegrams if he has time." (Department of State, Central Files, 684A.86/12–1856) Copies of the three telegrams are in the Eisenhower Library, Whitman File, Dulles–Herter Series. Eisenhower initialed the first page of telegram 1926.

[2] Document 649.

(4) Nasser ready cooperate in taking steps toward solution area's problems but in order do so must have period of trust and confidence. Frankly, he had feeling in past that USG trying strengthen Israel and at same time keep Egypt weak; that we were working against Egypt in area and propagating untrue assertions, especially re supposed desire Egypt establish empire over the Arab States and allegation that Egypt now Soviet tool. Also we had not understood Egyptian misgivings re certain aspect of proposed US-GOE military assistance agreement which in Egyptian eyes would have constituted infringement on their sovereignty. When he had attempted explain these matters frankly, he had not been believed and had been accused of maneuvering. He could only repeat this not true and there is consequently need to lay foundation of confidence which in turn can lead to future conversations designed reach understanding.

In this connection, Nasser said position USG certainly greatly enhanced by recent events. For instance would frankly admit he had never thought USG would really attempt restrain Israel if it attacked Egypt. He had been surprised by our action and so also had been people. Similarly Egyptian eyes had been opened re usefulness of UN, and he repeated his misgivings when President Eisenhower had originally given assurance of American support through the UN and his (Nasser's) subsequent change of mind when such assistance had proved so effective. As consequence US position much better but, to use military term, he thought best policy for us follow now would be to consolidate our position.

(5) Reference arms purchase he said fully convinced he had taken right action in existing circumstances.

(6) Spoke at considerable length re cotton question, an unusual departure since he seldom mentions specific economic problems. To begin with said exaggerated reports being circulated re extent to which Egyptian cotton mortgaged for arms purchases. Thus payment in cotton this year only amounts to ten million Egyptian pounds which is obviously not amount to endanger Egyptian independence (Finance Minister Kaissouni told me same thing other day but avoided giving figure).

As regards trade with US, it of no major importance to GOE since imports from US greatly exceed exports and such cotton exports as being made are threatened by increasing production similar types in US.

Britain and France, however, had been important consumers Egyptian cotton but in 1953 they put on pressures by reducing cotton purchases, thus putting Egypt in difficult position, especially since it had been largely dependent on sterling bloc, including countries which had currencies tied to sterling, e.g. India and China.

As consequence Egypt forced resort to barter with Soviet bloc for which it had been greatly criticized but in reality there was alternative. Plan, however, had been to try limit apportionment cotton exports in principle to one third to Soviet bloc, one third to west and one third to Asia. However, after nationalization of Canal, situation made more difficult by freezing Egyptian assets. Difficult enough re American freezing but at least proceeds such rent transactions exempt whereas British and French freezing total. Thus cotton exports to Britain and France would have stopped completely except for assistance rendered by third countries acting as middle men and he specifically mentioned India, China, Germany (presumably West) and Italy.

Concluding discussion cotton, Nasser said must be realized Egypt cannot stockpile like we do but must sell currently since cotton main producer foreign exchange.

(7) Re Egyptian foreign policy it is basically one of non-alignment. This question had been debated by RCC at beginning and had been adopted on ground that any other policy would isolate government from people and probably result in popular movement to left. This was not a hostile policy but a defensive one.

(8) Re other Arab countries GOE does not give orders or exert pressure. Actually, action normally is initiated in other Arab countries as result of disagreement of people with their own political leadership and agreement with policies of Egypt. When this happens GOE feels it is appropriate to support as for example in case opposition of Jordanian people to Baghdad Pact when "we" offered assume responsibility for British subsidy. However, there is nothing covert about this policy; it is entirely straightforward.

Nasser added that only exception to his policy of letting initiative come from other Arab governments was Saudi Arabia. There he has type of relationship with King Saud where he feels he can exchange views freely without running danger of being misunderstood. Key to problem is that Saud is master in his own house whereas ideas advanced to other Arab governments inevitably become subject of contentious debate.

(9) There had been much commotion, especially emanating from Paris re the three circles of Egypt interest mentioned in his "philosophy of the revolution", i.e., Arab countries, Muslim world and Africa, to which he had subsequently added Asia. He had not been thinking in any sense in terms of hegemony but rather of strategy, to use military term, but meaning areas with which Egypt can work without encountering serious problems. For example, countries in these areas generally supported GOE when it nationalized Canal. Also he had found he could easily find common ground with Nehru

in discussing such matters as colonialism and non-alignment, although true they had differed on Israel.

(10) He had also mentioned Middle East oil in his book, but here again he had been talking in strategic terms; in terms of necessary cooperation with Western Europe, not domination by it; in terms of defense.

(11) Re Soviet Union, Egypt has no secret agreement with it and never even asked what it would do if Egypt were attacked for fear Soviets would impose conditions. Also there was [no?] consultation with Soviets before nationalization of Canal. There were, however, discussions at time of London conference.

Furthermore, there is no mutual policy with Soviets re Near East since Egypt desires maintain its complete independence of action. True that both opposed to Baghdad Pact but for different reasons.

(12) Although GOE in general policy agreement with Syria and Saudi Arabia they were not consulted re recognition Communist China nor purchase Soviet arms.

(13) Re supply Soviet arms to Syria, "Russians don't give arms free like you Americans do". Consequently, amount of arms Syria receiving related to Syrian financial capacity to pay. Re technicians, training, et cetera, Syria sent its trainees (air and tank) here for training by Egyptians trained in Czechoslovakia and Syrian planes also sent to Egypt for assembling by Egyptian and Soviet technicians. But before October 29 there were no Soviet technicians in Syria. He wished have this known because Turks had been putting out false information in that regard in order, he had been informed, to build up case for certain radar and anti-aircraft material which they wanted get from US.

As regards Sarraj [3] he is not a Communist but a Nationalist who may well have pro-Egyptian leanings.

(14) Concerning Jordan, new Prime Minister [4] is Nationalist who merely wants independence. Only three Communists in Parliament. Problem is that Jordan really dominated by Palestinians who violently anti-Israel and therefore put pressure on King Hussein to take same line.

(15) Re Israel, fact is that until 1955 Egypt was only country in Arab world where people were not particularly interested in Israeli problem. But today popular indifference has given way to hate and reason is Ben Gurion's policy from Gaza attack [5] to present. Re future he finds it difficult to see road ahead clearly. He had

---

[3] Lieutenant Colonel 'Abd al-Hamid Sarraj, chief of the military intelligence bureau in the Syrian Army.

[4] Sulayman Nabulsi, leader of the Jordanian National Socialist Party, whose government assumed power on October 29.

[5] Reference is to the Israeli attack of February 28, 1955.

discussed question with us [6] but he would now have to think over ideas he had previously expressed; situation more complicated. As he had previously told me present alternatives would seem to be continued tension, peace without a settlement, or settlement. He was inclined believe settlement now out of question but, as between continued tension and peace without settlement, he would be prepared cooperate to achieve latter. To try now for a settlement would only make things worse. Perhaps a few Arab politicians might speak to us more reassuringly but he could not do so in good faith. Who ever tried to force settlement now, even in UN, would, he believed, end up by losing out with both Arabs and Israelis. Recalling suggestion of meeting with Ben Gurion he also thought latter more interested in meeting than in bona fide effort reach agreement.

Furthermore, he did not see how Israeli problem can be settled unless related to settlement problems among Arabs themselves. Thus, as long as trouble with Iraq exists, Egypt could not take lead for fear of Iraqi exploitation and he mentioned in this connection recent anti-Israeli line of Nuri. Problem is one of fear of taking advantage. And surely neither Syria nor Lebanon could take lead despite what certain Lebanese might say confidentially.

Turning to specific points in reftel, Nasser made following comments:

(a) Cooperation in urgent clearance of Canal: He agreed and thought satisfactory progress being made. Only hitch brought to his attention had been statement by Gen. Wheeler that Ferdan Bridge had been destroyed by "explosives". Without specifiying exactly how bridge had been destroyed, said it was Egyptian position that all destruction or sinking of ships in Canal had been result of Anglo-French attack on ground of foreseeable application of principle of action and reaction. Consequently any finding of Egyptian responsibility was a political judgment which not proper for Wheeler to make. I told him Wheeler had mentioned matter to me and he had no such intent. I had no hesitance in giving assurance Wheeler only interested in getting job done which UN had given him.

Nasser also mentioned that for public relations reasons it was desirable avoid impression UN acting entirely on its own. Canal closed and obviously should be opened soonest but GOE would like have appear it is doing its share with UN assistance. Re salvage ships he said GOE had agreed to use of British and French ships but that it could not assume responsibility for security of British and French personnel. He put it in such way that I gathered he was not necessarily putting complete prohibition on use British and French

---

[6] Reported in telegram 1927, December 16, not printed. (Department of State, Central Files, 684A.86/12–1656)

crews but rather expressing general disapproval on security grounds. I thought it prefereable, however, not attempt probe matter further in knowledge this is subject delicate negotiate for which Hammarskjold responsible.

(b) Cooperation in renewed negotiations on future Canal regime: Nasser said this was one of main points he was now studying. SC resolution prescribing 6 points had foreseen peaceful solution which GOE had looked forward to furthering at proposed October 29 meeting. But peaceful concept destroyed by Anglo-French attack and now question how proceed. Could not foresee possibility direct negotiations with British and French. He mentioned had agreed generally on Indian plan but situation now changed.

I then inquired whether correct assume GOE prepared proceed on basis SC resolution and that only difficulty one of procedure. Nasser replied position in brief is GOE ready proceed on 6 points and convention of 1888 but not by direct negotiations with British and French. Meanwhile GOE prepared observe 1888 convention.

I then asked as personal suggestion if GOE might not find it possible relax prohibition on Israeli ships in connection with Suez settlement. It is really small matter from practical standpoint but looms large in public eye. Nasser replied doubtful if this feasible since in GOE view such relaxation regarded as part of Israeli problem as whole.

(c) Place no obstacle in way fulfillment by UN force of its responsibilities: Nasser said policy is to cooperate fully as long as force not used as instrument to further bonds of colonial power as demanded by Paris and London. In that case would not cooperate. However, wants to see UNEF successful since he sees inauguration of force as possible turning point in history and GOE wants make its contribution to its success. So far he had been impressed by correct way in which UNEF had been functioning.

(d) Measures to correct Fedayeen operations: Nasser observed should differentiate between three types of forces. First is army of Palestine under Egyptian and Arab officers which responsible for defense of Gaza Strip. Second force is Fedayeen who are regularly organized and paid force of commandos who are familiar with Palestine terrain and usually operate by night. Their function is to operate inside Israel as required because of difficulty in operating directly against Israel from outside by land or air. They are normally used in order to counter Israeli border attacks such as when they were called into action last August following an Israeli attack and when the Israelis then counter-attacked at Khan Younes. Similarly they were ordered into action after the Israeli attack on Gaza. The third type composed of unorganized Arab refugees who for past ten years have been involved in struggle with Israelis, are armed, often familiar with sabotage and operate on their own initiative with personal vengeance usually being motive. These irregulars are often confused with regulars Fedayeen, most of whom escaped to Israel or Jordan during recent hostilities.

I argued strongly for curtailment of such activity as step toward easing tension but I am not sure with how much effect.

(e) Operations by Egyptian agents in violation sovereignty and authority of neighboring states: This was only point in three-hour discussion on which Nasser was overtly evasive, remarking that this was matter we had discussed before and which would not seem to require further comment. I demurred, observing that this was point which we regarded as especially important and wished that understood. Furthermore, reports reaching us from all sides indicated problem was one of real magnitude, not just few isolated incidents. Nasser then went over familiar grounds re Libya and Lebanon and said as far as Kuwait oil sabotage concerned (which I had not mentioned) first he had heard of it was in papers although he understood being attributed to him. Realizing, of course, that Nasser could not actually admit to responsibility for clandestine operations, for which he might be responsible either directly or indirectly, I took tack of emphasizing that such activities obviously contrary to policy he supported for area security and stability and that furthermore his own reputation being prejudiced by personal attribution to him. Could not he therefore use his influence to stop? Again he was evasive, asserting difficult for him go to other Arab governments with list of criticism such as I was delivering to him. Only person with whom he could talk freely on such matters was King Saud.

(f) Settlement of outstanding problems between Arab states and Israel: This covered in paragraph 15 above. Only point which Nasser added when reaching this point in his notes was to protest against scorched earth actions of Israelis in Sinai which he maintained violation of cease fire.

(g) Cessation of inflammatory radio attacks on neighboring states: Nasser said he talked about this before in discussing clandestine stations operated by British and French. I said this not point but attacks on state in area. Nasser said not aware recent attacks in any area state except Iraq and that was by way of retaliation to Iraqis who had recently put in 200 kw station for purposes; this, he admitted, real propaganda war. I observed easy start a feud of this kind but difficult stop it since necessary find something to say each day more extreme than day before although things go from bad to worse. In fact, Nasser himself had said as much to me before when, talking of setting up stations to reply to clandestine British and French transmitters, he had indicated reluctance to do so for fear of not being able foresee where would end. Without replying to this,

Nasser noted that Turk radio had been launching venomous attacks on Egypt recently and that when Egyptian Chargé had sought protest Turkish Foreign Office he had not even been received. Similarly "Zafar", a Turkish Government paper had been conducting heavy anti-Egyptian campaign. GOE did not want have trouble with Turkey but Turks apparently felt differently and GOE had therefore decided retaliate in kind. I endeavored counsel moderation.

I regret burden Department with telegram of this length, especially since much of it repetitive of previous reports, but seemed desirable do so because Nasser was obviously in thoughtful mood and foregoing is present impromptu synthesis of problems confronting him which he is now endeavoring to rethink. Also, making allowances for sensitiveness of some of questions discussed and for deviousness of Nasser's thinking as well as his admittedly suspicious nature, his exposition believed to be just about as frank as we could expect and doubtless in his own view he felt going very far. In fact whole trend conversation, despite evasiveness on certain points, seemed indicate that in soulsearching which he is now going through importance of relationship with USG looms large. As consequence his attitude was no longer that of man on horse as when we last met but rather of one seeking to be understood even to extent at times of being actually deferential.

Incidentally, just as I was leaving Nasser said someone had recommended Washington's Farewell Address as being interesting reading. I observed that if I remembered correctly that was the one in which reference was made to no entangling alliances. Nasser laughed (not his chronic nervous giggle) and said "Yes, that is the one."

Distribution this telegram left to Department's discretion but suggested be treated as noforn since possible may lead to further and more important discussions which we would not wish prejudice. [7]

Hare

---

[7] In telegram 1946 from Cairo, December 18, Hare provided the Department with the following supplementary report concerning the evacuation of Port Said in his December 15 conversation with Nasser:

"Nasser said did not know who involved on Egyptian side and GOE unable assume responsibility or intervene effectively as long as denied access to city. Said GOE would like send in an official representative as well as police reinforcements and had made request of Burns to that effect three days before.

"I suggested that, irrespective of this jurisdictional difficulty, there must be means available GOE to get authoritative word to Port Said inhabitants preserve calm. Nasser said had endeavored use radio but was jammed. He would, however, look into further." (*Ibid.*, 684A.86/12–1856)

660.   Telegram From the Department of State to the Embassy in France [1]

Washington, December 18, 1956—7:44 p.m.

2333. Embtel 2932. [2] Following guidance keyed to points listed reftel.

1. Primary responsibility for clearance Canal rests with UN. SYG has established mechanism for handling and has arranged for salvage equipment be sent Egypt. General Wheeler, SYG's adviser on clearance operation now in Egypt. We understand he and SYG planning use UN salvage fleet plus certain number British and French units to clear Canal. We primarily interested in quickest opening of Canal and determination of equipment to be used should be made with this objective in view.

2. Role of UNEF in Egypt is to secure and supervise cessation of hostilities in accordance terms GA resolution November 2. After departure British and French forces Department envisages UNEF will continue move into Sinai as Israeli troops withdraw and will take stations on armistice lines. UNEF will presumably remain until objectives of GA achieved. GA should be authority to decide latter point.

3. We will continue support right of all nations including Israel to free and unfettered passage through Canal when latter cleared.

4. We believe negotiations between UK, France and Egypt, with assistance SYG, on basis 6 principles should be promptly resumed. We will not support solution less favorable than one based on these principles.

4a. Parties to negotiations should be as set forth above.

4b. We believe SCUA should have important role in connection with future Canal regime. This should be determined in context negotiations mentioned above.

4c. This problem under study in USG and firm position not yet reached. We are opposed to assessing damages to UK and France as suggested in some quarters.

5. US attitude toward economic relations Egypt set forth Deptel 2244 and Tosec 15. [3] Contents these telegrams should be revealed to French only on very general terms.

---

[1] Source: Department of State, Central Files, 684A.86/12–1356. Secret. Drafted by Rockwell; cleared by Sisco, Phleger, Looram (EUR/WE); and approved by Murphy who signed for Dulles. Repeated to Cairo, London, and USUN.

[2] In telegram 2932 from Paris, December 13, Dillon requested guidance on the 11 items discussed in telegram 2333. (*Ibid.*)

[3] Neither printed.

6. Problem arms purchases from USSR by NE states very difficult. We are considering methods of approach but no firm position reached.

7. Resolution set before GA by US on Palestine settlement shows how we believe this problem should be approached. Secretary's statement of August 26, 1956 remains basis US position on general settlement.

8. Status of Gaza and Aqaba matter for future determination in connection with advance UNEF into Sinai. We believe Israel forces should withdraw from these areas in compliance GA resolution of November 2 but islands should not be fortified and there should be free access into Gulf. Gaza should perhaps be UN responsibility.

9. Posture of Lebanon is matter to be determined by GOL. Lebanon of all NE states has assumed more reasonable attitude re basic NE problems. We agree Lebanon should be permitted acquire some additional defensive arms to strengthen its security. Creation of permanent UN force and stationing it in NE or anywhere else would require decision by GA. Present UNEF is emergency force set up only in connection recent NE hostilities. Question of possible permanent force in NE requires careful study and might be considered at subsequent stage after some of more immediate problems are dealt with.

10. Problem of Syria under study by USG. We believe unfavorable trend developments Syrian situation strengthened by tension and instability resulting from present crisis. Essential more normal atmosphere be urgently restored.

11. We believe US adherence to Baghdad Pact not at this time desirable. US issued statement November 29 reiterating its support for Pact and its interest in security Pact members. We studying other means strengthening US bilateral relationship with Pact countries.

Dulles

661.   Telegram From the Department of State to the Embassy in Egypt [1]

Washington, December 20, 1956—1:35 p.m.

2046. Personal for Ambassador from Secretary. The President and I have read with great interest the full report embodied in your cable 1926 of your talk with President Nasser. [2] You may in your discretion inform Nasser that Department takes satisfaction that he has spoken so fully and, we like to believe, so frankly with respect to the matter you raised with him.

You may also make the point that our objective must be to lift up the Middle East from the morass into which it has fallen as a result of the developments of the past year.

We believe that the bad turn of events can be dated from the active intervention of the Soviet Union in the area. We do not believe that there can be anything but increasing distress and misery unless this intervention is excluded for the future because the obvious purpose of the Soviet Union is to create trouble which will increase its opportunities to extend its influence in the area. If this were unopposed, the economies of Asia, the Middle East and Europe would be at the mercy of Soviet policies of aggrandizement.

It should be emphasized that when America through bilateral or multilateral arrangements provides help of any kind to another it does so without strings and seeking no special advantage or influence over others.

We hope that in your further talks with President Nasser he will indicate more concrete and positive contributions by Egypt to

---

[1] Source: Department of State, Central Files, 674.00/12–1656. Secret. Priority. Drafted by Dulles; cleared by Rountree; approved by Rountree; and signed by Howe for Dulles.

[2] In a letter to Dulles of December 19, Eisenhower indicated that he had read telegram 1926 (Document 659) and noted: "I think we should give the Ambassador something that he could convey to Nasser, even if nothing more than an expression of our great satisfaction (yours and mine) that Nasser has spoken so frankly and fully of the matter with which he is now concerned. My point is that the more we can encourage bilateral confidence and confidences, the better informed we should be as to the problems in the whole region." (Eisenhower Library, Whitman File, Dulles–Herter series)

Later on December 19, Dulles forwarded to Eisenhower the text of a draft telegram to Hare under cover of a note that reads: "I have attributed the views to the Department as I doubt it is wise at the present juncture to give Nasser the impression that he is in direct negotiation with you." (Department of State, Central Files, 780.00/12–1956) Eisenhower subsequently added the penultimate paragraph in the text of telegram 2046. (Memorandum of conversation with the President by Dulles, December 20; Eisenhower Library, Dulles Papers, Meetings with the President)

the reestablishment of confidence in the peaceful and progressive future of the Middle East.

Dulles

---

662.   **Telegram From the Mission at the United Nations to the Department of State** [1]

New York, December 21, 1956—8 p.m.

Delga 392. Re Palestine/Suez. Eban, Rafael and Kidron (Israel) called on me today to say because of SYG's dissatisfaction with Israel's previously planned rate of withdrawal from Sinai, [2] Israel has scrapped its previous schedule and now plans withdraw forces at rate which will see them completely out of Sinai west of El Arish by about first week in January. They plan inform SYG of this new schedule this afternoon.

Eban said this would leave a number of problems which they would also take up with SYG today:

1. Gulf of Aqaba. Israel believes UNEF forces must ensure freedom of navigation in the Gulf, possibly by stationing troops along shore and leaving them there until some more permanent form of guarantee can be worked out. They are also willing consider stationing a UN ship in Gulf if this could accomplish same purpose.

2. Gaza. [3] They understand SYG is not yet ready discuss his plans for Gaza strip.

3. Demilitarization of Sinai. Israel wants some assurance Egyptian forces are not permitted re-establish themselves in any strength behind UNEF lines and thereby recreate conditions which led to present situation. Eban said Israel believes SYG has power to decide what Egyptian forces will be permitted enter Sinai and where they will be stationed. Israel wants assurance UNEF forces will remain deployed in area east of El Arish so border areas will be entirely free of Egyptian forces. They also want be sure UNEF forces occupy key

---

[1] Source: Department of State, Central Files, 684A.86/12–2156. Confidential; Priority. Received at 8:23 p.m.

[2] On December 19, the Mission in New York reported that, according to a cable from General Burns to Hammarskjöld, Burns had "noted" but not accepted the Israeli statement that Israel would withdraw its forces from Sinai at the rate of 25 kilometers per week. Burns had accepted the Israeli statement only with regard to the positions to be reached during the first week. (Delga 377, December 19; *ibid.*, 320.5780/2–1956)

[3] On December 19, Ben Gurion told the Knesset: "In no event and in no manner will Israel agree to the return of the Egyptian invader" to the Gaza Strip. (Telegram 767 from Tel Aviv, December 20; *ibid.*, 674.84A/12–2056)

positions in Sinai west of El Arish, and that UNEF forces will remain long enough time for working out at least modus vivendi for border area, if not a peace settlement.

4. Fedayeen activities. Eban said Israel would also ask SYG use his authority under November 2 resolution [4] to prevent activation of Fedayeen units.

5. Suez Canal. Finally, Eban said when Suez Canal is reopened, it must be open to Israel ships.

Having accelerated their withdrawal, Eban said, Israel strongly hopes US will play active role in helping bring about above measures of security for Israel.

I said I was glad to hear news about accelerated withdrawal, and I would report Eban's views promptly to Washington where I was sure they would be given urgent and careful consideration.

Eban then asked about our plans for action on the two pending resolutions on Suez and Palestine settlements. Eban said that, at least as regards Suez settlement, it would seem the time has come for some action on this proposal. I told him while it seemed clear that the time has come for action on Suez settlement, and Egyptians seemed be inclined go along on this, we did not think it was yet time to press for Palestine settlement. I told him we were continuing to study question of timing on this resolution with a view to moving as soon as possible.

Lodge

---

[4] Reference is to General Assembly Resolution 997 (ES–I); see Document 467.

---

663.   **Telegram From the Embassy in Israel to the Department of State** [1]

Tel Aviv, December 23, 1956—2 p.m.

774. Called on Prime Minister at his Tel Aviv home at his request last night December 22. He immediately raised question of United States Suez-Sinai policy as it would affect Israel security after withdrawal military forces and said GOI wished very much coordinate [garble] with United States if possible. He requested earliest

---

[1] Source: Department of State, Central Files, 684A.86/12–2356. Confidential. Received at 8:18 p.m. Repeated to London, Paris, Beirut, Cairo, Amman, Damascus, and USUN.

some indication our thinking pointing out vital policy decision for Israel must be reached first few days January. By that time Israeli forces will have been withdrawn to El Arish thus freeing almost all of Sinai. (In response my direct question he said strip adjacent Gulf Aqaba not within area to be freed by that time. Apparently agreement withdrawal these limits telegraphed Hammarskjold Friday following latter's demand on Israel Thursday night in which those area and time limits designated by him.)

Reiterating early days January were vital days for Israel policy decision and stressing desire Israel "to coordinate its policy with United States policy if possible" he hoped he could be informed United States policy especially with regard:

1. Israel's free transit Suez.
2. Freedom Israel transit Gulf Aqaba re which he said "we can never again permit a position of blockage to return".
3. Possible reestablishment Egyptian military base in eastern Sinai and
4. Elimination Fedayeen attacks on Israel which now recurring from Jordan but under Egyptian orders.

In view grave security problems which must be considered in few days ahead he hoped for information permitting GOI coordination with United States policy. At this point he remarked "it is only when matters of life and death involved Israeli acts independently".

He implied now Hammarskjold definitely assured by Israel to point satisfying him and presumably United Nations, could not United States government give some indication (to Ben Gurion in strict confidence if necessary) of present direction United States policy as it specifically affects security assurances Israel considers so vital to formulation of its policy in early January.

He said Ambassador Eban would seek appointment with Secretary without delay and Ben Gurion hoped it would be possible discussion points raised might take place December 26 or 27.

Eban agreed transmit his interest and wishes. At same time I pointed out broad United States policy underlining our determination support United Nations. I then commented specifically along lines Deptel 612.[2] I also referred to occasions when United States officials had informed Mrs. Meir we thought Israel should withdraw behind armistice line and at same time assured her United States would continue bear in mind such security problems as he had mentioned (*Current Foreign Relations* summary December 5).[3] He re-

---

[2] See footnote 6, Document 636.

[3] *Current Foreign Relations* was a classified publication of the Department of State. (Master files are in Department of State, *Current Foreign Relations*: Lot 64 D 189) See also telegram 384, Document 628.

called these generalizations but thought it important he now know "how United States bearing them in mind".

Speaking of SYG's negotiations with Israel and Egypt he felt there were unequal pressures exerted on Israel and stronger pressures should be exerted on Egypt in accordance with United Nations resolution on cessation of hostilities especially with regard freedom of Suez for Israel and cessation fedayeen operations against Israel. He said although his November 8 decision to withdraw Israeli troops had unanimous approval of GOI cabinet opposition developing rapidly in government and outside by press and among public. This he thought based largely on increase in fedayeen operations and Egypt's insistence on maintaining state of war. Pressure on him to halt withdrawals very strong all week yet he had further extended them in accordance Hammarskjold's demand.

The conversation which lasted about half hour was pleasant, unemotional and not marked by strong threatening or emphatic tone or words. Ben Gurion in Tel Aviv few days because of recurrence his lumbago under colder Jerusalem weather. [4]

Lawson

---

[4] On December 23, Lawson transmitted to the Department of State the following supplementary report on his conversation with Ben Gurion: "During my talk with Ben Gurion he referred in strictest confidence to Eban's talks of December 5 and 12 with Hammarskjold. Purpose of reference seemed to be to underscore point Israel now meeting Hammarskjold's basic and agreed demands and that settlement problems withdrawal from Aqaba area remainder Sinai and Gaza expected to be left for later date but in meantime United States policy affecting basic security Israel and settlement Arab-Israel problem could proceed. Later Herzog of Foreign Office permitted me to have hasty glance at few passages of what he called copies verbatim record Eban–Hammarskjold talks believing Ambassador Lodge has access same. . . . " (Telegram 775 from Tel Aviv; Department of State, Central Files, 684A.86/12–2356)

664.   Memorandum From the Under Secretary of State (Hoover) to the Secretary of State [1]

Washington, December 24, 1956.

SUBJECT

Financing of UN Clearance of Suez Canal

As you know, Secretary Humphrey has been working closely with Mr. John McCloy, financial adviser to Secretary General Hammarskjold, on the problem of financing the clearance of the Suez Canal by the United Nations. Progress has now reached the point where rapid action can and should be taken.

Problem

A minimum of from $3 to $5 million will be needed by the UN on January 2, 1957, for preliminary payments to contractors engaged in clearance operations in Egypt. It is estimated that an additional $15 million will be required during the first quarter of 1957 to complete the initial phase of the work and to provide a clear channel through the canal to a depth of 25 feet.

A tentative estimate has been made by General Wheeler that $20 million more will be required for the second phase to restore the canal to its original usefulness, and to repair or replace shore installations which were damaged during the recent action. It is expected that the latter expenditures will be made during the second and third quarters of 1957. A total of about $40 million will therefore be required for the entire project.

The methods adopted for financing the initial $5 million will undoubtedly set the pattern for raising the additional funds that will be required as the work progresses. It is essential, therefore, that the financing be placed on a sound basis from the start. Inasmuch as other nations will expect the United States to provide an appreciable part of the funds, we have an excellent opportunity to guide future policy.

1. Source of Funds

While it is probable that the United States will have to put up a substantial proportion of the funds, it seems desirable that a maximum number of other nations participate with us in the operation.

---

[1] Source: Department of State, Central Files, 974.7301/12–2456. Secret. Drafted by Hoover; cleared by Murphy, Henderson (in draft), Rountree, Elbrick, Wilcox, Phleger (in draft), Hollister (in draft), and Overby.

Some consideration has been given to raising the funds through SCUA, having in mind that subscriptions should be proportionate to the use of the canal. Two practical objections are obvious, namely (a) the difficulty of determining fair quotas, inasmuch as the volume of tonnage does not necessarily indicate the relative beneficial use of the waterway, and (b) the lack of time for consultation before the first installment is required.

The simplest procedure would seem to be for (a) the SYG to call for voluntary contributions, and (b) the United States immediately to offer $4 million on condition that other nations, in the aggregate, will match our participation.

2. Nature of U.S. Contribution

The U.S. contribution could be either in the form of (a) an advance, or (b) in grant aid. While an outright gift might be regarded as a generous gesture on the part of the United States, and might minimize later arguments about repayment and responsibility for damage, nevertheless there appear to be overriding reasons in favor of an advance. These reasons are that (a) the canal is an economically sound enterprise and is able to generate ample funds, over a period of time, to provide for repayment, (b) wider international participation would be attained, (c) the United States and other users would be able to exert a maximum degree of leadership in subsequent negotiations, and (d) public and congressional support will be enhanced by placing the transaction on a repayment basis.

3. Method of Handling Funds

Assuming that the U.S. contribution would be in the form of an advance, ICA participation through Sec. 401 [2] would appear to offer the most rapid and straightforward means of making the funds available. ICA should therefore assume responsibility for the financial details of the transaction, under policy guidance from the Department of State, insofar as the U.S. participation is concerned.

It appears desirable that the International Bank (IBRD) act as the over-all fiscal agent for the Secretary General. Such an arrangement would have the following advantages: (a) confidence in the fiscal aspects of the operation will be increased; (b) the international character of the project will be enhanced; (c) negotiations for repayment of advances will be more effective if the IBRD represents all parties to the transaction than if each endeavored to negotiate independently; and (d) the IBRD will be the vehicle, in all probabili-

---

[2] Reference is to Section 401 of the Mutual Security Act of 1954. (68 Stat. 832) Section 401 authorized the creation of a Special Fund to be used when the President determined that such use was important to the security of the United States.

ty, for financing the compensation to the shareholders of the old canal company and for future major improvements to the waterway, and would therefore be the logical avenue through which to effect repayment of the advances.

4. Assurances from Egypt, United Kingdom and France

It would seem advisable that Egypt, U.K. and France should give assurances along the following lines prior to agreement for financing the rehabilitation of the canal:

(a) Full cooperation with the Secretary General in the work of clearance.

(b) Pursue rapidly the negotiation of an over-all agreement on the Suez Canal problem under U.N. auspices.

(c) Pending final agreement, the interim operation of the canal will be in accordance with the six points set forth by the Security Council.

(d) The final agreement will include provisions for repayment of advances for clearance.

We understand that the Secretary General prefers to obtain such assurances on his own initiative and that they will be included in his formal appeal to the United States for funds.

5. Additional Funds

While additional funds from the United States will undoubtedly be required, it does not appear desirable to make any advance commitments at this time. We should await the response of other nations to the appeal for funds, and should be in a position to exert maximum pressure for an equitable final settlement.

6. Procedure

It is our understanding, through Mr. McCloy, that the Secretary General will address a letter to the United States and other governments requesting contributions to cover the costs of clearance, and that this letter will cover the points outlined above. He would hope that the United States will not be in the position of stipulating conditions in making its contribution, in order to avoid haggling on the part of other contributors.

We expect to receive, informally and confidentially, a rough draft of the letter within the next few days. Upon arrival it will be urgently considered by all interested agencies. A tentative reply is now being prepared in the Legal Adviser's Office.

Recommendations [3]

It is recommended that the United States proceed immediately to make up to $5 million available to the Secretary General, on the understanding that the following conditions are complied with:

1. That a maximum number of other nations will participate on a matching basis.

2. That contributions will be on an advance or loan basis, and not by means of grant aid.

3. That ICA handle the financial details and provide the funds through Sec. 401, and that the Secretary General designate the IBRD as the fiscal agent for handling funds.

4. That the Secretary General will use his best efforts to obtain satisfactory assurances from Egypt, the United Kingdom and France of their intentions to (a) cooperate in clearance operations, (b) pursue negotiations rapidly for an over-all agreement, (c) operate the canal on an interim basis in accordance with the Security Council's six points, and (d) include provisions in the over-all agreement for repayment of the advances.

5. That the United States make no firm commitment for further contributions pending (a) response of other nations to the Secretary General's appeal for funds and (b) developments in the over-all Suez settlement. [4]

---

[3] A marginal notation on the source text by Greene, dated December 24 reads: "$5 million is firm figure—ICA being informed by S/S (per H. H., Jr.)." On December 26, Murphy informed Dulles that McCloy had received assurances from the heads of the Italian, Scandinavian, German, Netherlands, Australian, and Canadian Delegations at the United Nations that together their governments would more than match the amount of U.S. advance to begin work on clearing the Suez Canal. McCloy also reported that Hammarskjöld was sending out formal letters to all members of the United Nations urging contributions. (Memorandum from Murphy to Dulles; Department of State, Central Files, 974.7301/12–2656)

[4] Dulles initialed his approval of the recommendation at the bottom of the source text.

665.   Memorandum of a Telephone Conversation Between the Secretary of State in Washington and the Representative at the United Nations (Lodge) in New York, December 26, 1956, 5:15 p.m. [1]

TELEPHONE CALL TO AMB. LODGE

L. returned the call and the Sec. told him the handling of the Egyptian situation worried him. [2] Hammarskjold is the fellow who has the titular responsibility and the Sec. supposes he wants us to keep still unless he calls on us but the fact of the matter is the effective power behind this thing is the US. We are in a position to put some pressures on Nasser. We will take the blame if things go wrong. The Sec. is upset re Nasser not letting them clear the Canal until the last Israeli is out of the Sinai. [3] This he heard on the radio and read in the papers but does not know if it is true. The Sec.'s first reaction was to get hold of Hare and Hussein and raise hell. But then he can't do that in case it would cross wires with Hammarskjold. The Pres. is mad also. He said to get hold of the Egyptians and tell them if they don't do better the whole weight of the US will be against them. The Sec. wondered re having a talk with Hammarskjold and see if we can't help each other more. There are many problems and he doesn't know H.'s thinking but he won't get his problems solved unless we put our influence behind a solution. L. thinks he realizes that. L. said he could not have a better relationship with H. L. mentioned getting instructions and the Sec said it is not a question of instructions. If the Egyptians are getting balky then H. should call and say here is the problem what can we do. Maybe he thinks everything is going all right. We don't know. L. can easily find out. Are our pressures on the Egyptians as powerful

---

[1] Source: Eisenhower Library, Dulles Papers, General Telephone Conversation. Transcribed by Bernau.

[2] At the Secretary's Staff Meeting that morning, Dulles "expressed concern at the unsatisfactory state of our posture in regard to the future of the Suez Canal, noting that while we are the keystone of much of what is happening and will happen, including financing, and thus have greater responsibility, we seem to have very little authority and unsatisfactory, diffuse methods of asserting influence. He thought it would be a great diplomatic failure if the situation deteriorates to the point where US Forces have to go in to get and keep the Canal open. He speculated on the possibility of the US being appointed agent of the UN to deal with the matter, as in the Korean case, and on the desirability of his talking to Hammarskjold." (Tentative Notes; Department of State, Secretary's Staff Meetings: Lot 63 D 75)

[3] On December 25, a spokesman for Egypt's Suez Canal Authority publicly affirmed that there would be no work on clearing the waterway of obstructions until the last Israeli forces left. When asked if this meant leaving the Gaza Strip, the spokesman replied: "You can draw your own conclusions." (*The New York Times*, December 26, 1956)

as pressures on the Israelis. No. L. asked if we thought about how long to leave the Int's Force in there and is there a possibility legally to use that as pressure. Sec. would hope so. If N.[4] doesn't do what is asked, we should be able to use it. N. needs heavy pressure. L. said that is what he indirectly gets from Fawzi. They agreed N. does not do what F. recommends. L. asked if the Sec. would not contend the Force has to stay until there is a res to take it out. They agreed yes. L. will see H.[5] tonight and call in the a.m. and try to set a lunch up for Monday[6] for the three of them. The Sec. would like H. to know of our concern re what we hear—we want to help but sitting still because we assume he will let us know if he wants help. The Pres. is concerned. We are ready to cooperate but don't dare for fear we may be crossing him up. Yet we don't think things are going well. If there is anything he wants done now, have him let the Sec know.

---

[4] Reference is to Nasser.
[5] Reference is to Hammarskjöld.
[6] December 31.

---

666.   Memorandum for the Files by Richard F. Pedersen[1]

New York, December 27, 1956.

SUBJECT

Suez

Confirming Lodge–Dulles conversation December 27,[2] Ambassador Lodge met with the Secretary General at 9:00 a.m. on December 27 to discuss the latest problems in connection with the Suez Canal.

Ambassador Lodge told the Secretary General that the reports about Egypt not allowing clearance of the Canal until the Israelis were out of the Sinai had caused disturbances in high quarters in Washington. The Secretary General said that he had already taken

---

[1] Source: Department of State, Central Files, 974.7301/12–2756. Secret. Pederson was a member of the U.S. Delegation to the Thirteenth Session of the General Assembly and an Adviser on Political and Security Affairs with the Permanent U.S. Mission at the United Nations.

[2] The memorandum of this telephone conversation, which began at 9:45 a.m., December 27, is not printed. (Eisenhower Library, Dulles Papers, General Telephone Conversations)

this up with Fawzi. Fawzi had said that the whole connection between the two points was unknown to Egypt and had categorically denied there was any. The Secretary General thought that the Israelis had probably inspired the story. (Similar information given to Wadsworth by the Secretary General was telephoned to Walmsley (IO) on December 26.)

Lodge told Hammarskjold that the fundamental reason the British and Israelis were forced to withdraw from Egypt was United States economic pressure. He asked what we could do to continue to help the Secretary General in his efforts. He asked how the Secretary General was planning to continue from this point. He commented that a failure to solve the Suez situation would be serious for the United States but disastrous to the United Nations.

The Secretary General said that he understood this situation. At a certain stage pressure on Egypt from the United States would be helpful and welcome. However, he did not think that that stage had yet arrived. The Secretary General said that Fawzi had not so far backed down on any commitment he had made. The Secretary General had a fairly low opinion of Nasser, thought that he was unsteady and local in his viewpoint, but Nasser had not yet pulled the rug out from under Fawzi. The Egyptians had been sticky in a bureaucratic sense, on phraseology, paperwork, legalisms, etc., but not in a political sense. The Secretary General thought this reflected an underlying recognition of Egyptian interest in getting the canal going again. He observed that there had been no blocks or bureaucratic hindrances about the UN Force, which Egypt easily could have done.

On the Egyptian statement that it was no longer possible to negotiate directly with the UK and France on a canal settlement, Hammarskjold pointed to the word "directly" as a key word. The reason for the Egyptian statement was that Krishna Menon was arriving in Egypt tomorrow (December 28). The Secretary General said that while Menon was in New York he had tried to undermine the 6 principles of the Security Council and that the Egyptian statement had been made to counter this. The Secretary General knew that the Egyptians did not want to exclude the continuance of his efforts with the UK and France. Hammarskjold could foresee a situation where the user interest could be protected without the necessity of the direct participation of the foreign ministers of the UK and France. He noted that their interests could be represented by outstanding individuals, such as the Foreign Minister of Norway or others.

Hammarskjold said he wanted to tell Lodge some of his innermost thoughts on the long-range canal settlement, which he had not given to anybody. When the ball got rolling (by which he meant that, when the canal clearance was well under way and the Israeli troops were getting out of Egypt) toward the end of January, he intended to go to Cairo himself. He would need to know by that time clearly what the UK and France really wanted. This applied especially to the arbitration procedures which they had in mind. He felt that he could not push Egypt into an agreement until he was sure that the UK and France would also come to a firm understanding. About that time he thought that economic aid from the United States or pressure on Egypt might help in bringing about a settlement. He did not think that now was the time to do so.

The Secretary General also referred to the resolution on war damages which Egypt had presented on December 21.[3] Fawzi had told him that he had presented this as late as possible before the recess and in an inconspicuous manner. Fawzi had said that he did not want to push this resolution but that Egypt wanted an impartial settlement of the damages. Fawzi thought that the real settlement would be by negotiation and that such negotiations could lead to negotiations on wider issues (meaning negotiations on the Palestine problem).

On the evacuation of the Sinai, the Secretary General also observed that on December 19 the Israelis had agreed to an evacuation plan which would result in a phased withdrawal by mid-January. They had subsequently backed down from this agreement, and the Secretary General had threatened to put out a report on the issue. Yesterday (December 26) they had again agreed on the original plan and would be out by mid-January.

---

[3] See the editorial note, *infra*.

---

667. Editorial Note

On December 21, the Egyptian Delegation to the United Nations had submitted to the General Assembly a draft resolution (U.N. doc. A/3471) calling for an assessment of the damage caused Egypt by the military operations of Israel, France, and the United Kingdom, as a basis for the payment of compensation to Egypt. The text of this draft resolution was transmitted to the Department of State in Delga 391, December 21. (Department of State, Central Files, 684A.86/12–2156)

On the morning of December 21 the following discussion took place at the Secretary's Staff Meeting concerning the Egyptian action: "Mr. Phleger, with reference to reports that the Egyptians intend to open debate about the claims for damages arising from the blockade of the Suez Canal, said that we should move very cautiously and hold over the Egyptian Government's head the thought that the Egyptian Government itself is liable for all charges for clearance of the Canal and for damage claims arising out of blocking, which the Egyptians perpetrated. Mr. Henderson suggested that a fact finding commission under UN auspices would be a good way to establish responsibility for the blocking of the Canal and Mr. Rountree noted that the French have been thinking of a commission to go into this question as well as the matters of damages arising from the British-French attack and from the confiscation by the Egyptian Government of property of British and French nationals." (Tentative Notes; *ibid.*, Secretary's Staff Meetings: Lot 63 D 75)

---

668.   Telegram From the Department of State to the Embassy in Egypt [1]

Washington, December 28, 1956—6:46 p.m.

2114. Egyptian Delegation to UN has circulated resolution which would provide for assessment of damage caused Egypt by military operations by Israel, France and United Kingdom as basis compensation to Egypt. It is unclear at this point whether Egyptian Government intends to press for consideration of draft after General Assembly reconvenes on January 2.

You should approach GOE at level you deem appropriate in order ascertain intention Egyptian Government. You may make any following points as appropriate in light Egyptian response to our query:

1. Pressing Egyptian resolution unwise and untimely. It can only lead to fruitless and acrimonious debate. If GOE presses resolution re damages this will probably make it necessary for France, UK and Israel to raise counter claims against Egypt for damages they feel they have suffered as result of actions by Egyptian Government.

---

[1] Source: Department of State, Central Files, 274.00/12–2856. Limited Official Use. Drafted by Gamon (IO/UNP) and approved by Walmsley. Repeated to USUN, London, and Paris.

Charges and counter-charges will make considerably more difficult working out of many unresolved problems in the Middle East.

2. The United States Government would not support the resolution as tabled, and we believe considerable number Assembly members will share this view. Only resolution with any chance of passage would be one including, in addition to any Egyptian claims, a call for assessment of damages done by Egypt to other nations. These would probably include claims for damages arising from blocking of Canal, economic, and para-military action against Israel, sequestration of foreign properties in Egypt and treatment of minorities there, and reported activities of Egyptian agents in French North Africa, and elsewhere.

USUN: Please inform Secretary General of above approach.

Dulles

---

669.   **Telegram From the Department of State to the Embassy in Israel** [1]

Washington, December 28, 1956—8:09 p.m.

661. At earliest appropriate occasion please bring following to attention Prime Minister Ben Gurion, "under instructions":

USG seriously disturbed over statements by officials of Israel Government to effect that in their opinion recent events in Middle East have made Egyptian-Israeli General Armistice Agreement [2] invalid.

These statements indicate that Israel Government considers that either party to Agreement has right to determine unilaterally whether it must observe that Agreement or whether it may disregard it. USG cannot agree with this point of view which has dangerous implications for peace and stability of area.

Nowhere does Egyptian-Israeli Armistice Agreement envisage unilateral abrogation or amendment. On contrary, Article XII specifically provides that Agreement shall remain in force until peaceful settlement between Parties achieved. Only exception is that

---

[1] Source: Department of State, Central Files, 674.84A/12–2856. Confidential. Drafted by Gamon; cleared by Raymond, Rountree, and Murphy; and approved by Walmsley who signed for Dulles. Repeated to USUN, Cairo, Amman, and Damascus and pouched to Beirut, Paris, and London.

[2] The Egyptian-Israeli General Armistice Agreement was signed at Rhodes on February 24, 1949. The text is printed in United Nations, *Official Records of the Security Council, Fourth Year, Special Supplement No. 3.*

Parties may by mutual consent revise Agreement, or any of its provisions, other than Articles I and II. In absence of mutual agreement on revision, specific mechanism is provided for settlement of differences, through conference convoked by Secretary General in first instance, and in Security Council in second instance.

General Armistice Agreements were called for by Security Council and concluded under auspices of Acting Mediator pursuant to decision of Security Council. Security Council later expressed its satisfaction with agreements as important step toward establishment of permanent peace. Until Security Council decides otherwise, or until Parties by mutual consent decide to amend Agreements, world community, and especially Parties directly concerned, must base actions on assumption that all provisions of Agreements binding. Any contrary assumption is not in opinion USG, justified.

USG feels however that it is clearly in best interests of all signatories to General Armistice Agreements to uphold their integrity so as to facilitate transition toward Israel-Arab peace.

Dulles

---

670.   Memorandum From Phyllis D. Bernau to the Secretary of State [1]

Washington, December 28, 1956.

MR. SECRETARY: Mr. Dean called and said that at Eban's request he had breakfast with him and Mrs. Meir. They showed him a topographical map of the Canal and of Israel and primarily of the Gaza Strip and the Gulf of Aqaba. At the entrance to the Gulf of Aqaba where the Arabs used to fire on the Israeli boats coming up through there, they apparently have some soldiers there now and in an effort to keep the Gulf open they have advised Hammarskjold that they want to keep those people there until there has been some overall UN policy with respect to the relations between Egypt and Israel. They say if they were to—since ships cannot go through the Suez and since it is closed to everyone now—if they couldn't send ships through Aqaba they would be sunk. They have plans for building an 8-inch and subsequently a 30-inch pipeline starting at the Port where the Gulf of Aqaba touches on Israeli territory which

---

[1] Source: Eisenhower Library, Dulles Papers, General Telephone Conversations.

would carry oil from Iran and Kuwait up to Haifa. As AD [2] told you they tried to retain him on it and he said no—also told Lazard [3] no. Then they say on the Gaza Strip starting up on the northernmost part of that Strip immediately east of El Arish they want to stay there and either have the UN Force take over and make that a buffer state between Egypt and Israel or have some buffer state worked out in there or they want some system worked out so Egyptian troops won't be poking their guns at the border and shooting and sending Fedayeens over. They hope that somehow or other in connection with this overall settlement that formal legalisms of restoring the status quo ante would not be enforced so that they would have to withdraw from the Gaza Strip which would mean an entirely unacceptable situation, as it was before they attacked, would be brought back and they hope something constructive would be brought out of it and they would be permitted to occupy the Strip until the UN has been able to do something.

On the Gulf of Aqaba they hope to be able to work out some international concordat making it an international waterway which might be patrolled by international force because if they are forced to withdraw from the narrow strip they occupy at the tip of that peninsula northeast of the Cape of Mohammed, if the Egyptians were to come back there and fire on them, public opinion in Israel is such that they should shoot their way through the Gulf. AHD said he thought they had done enough shooting but if they were going to try to get this worked out they ought to work out their formal legal plans and try to get support for it and tell the Secretary what they had in mind—if they expect support on it the Secretary should not wake up some morning and find the shooting had taken place. This will take a tremendous amount of thought and study to work out an international agreement. They would have to educate people in the UN on it and it would need a lot of drafting and would have to be tied in with some kind of thinking that would be going on for the long-term settlement of the Suez and that otherwise Nasser might insist that he would not permit the clearing vessels to proceed in the Suez until they had gotten out of Sinai and the Strip and then they would find themselves arrayed against northwest Europe who would say if it weren't for Israel, they could get the Canal cleared. They might find themselves arrayed against the rest of the world and that should be avoided.

AHD thought it would be helpful for you to know this before your 4 p.m. meeting with Mrs. Meir.

---

[2] Reference is presumably to Arthur H. Dean.
[3] Reference is presumably to the Paris-based firm of Lazard Frères.

671.   Memorandum of a Conversation, Department of State, Washington, December 28, 1956, 4:05 p.m. [1]

SUBJECT

Israel

PARTICIPANTS

Mrs. Golda Meir, Israel Foreign Minister
Mr. Abba Eban, Ambassador of Israel
The Secretary
NEA—William M. Rountree
NE—Donald C. Bergus

After an exchange of greetings, Mrs. Meir said she wished to discuss the future. She regretted that there had been differences of opinion in the recent past but Israel had believed that it had been forced by circumstances and had had no alternative. She was happy that the Secretary had stated that the situation in the Near East could not be permitted to return to the status quo ante. Egypt had not complied with all of the provisions of the November 2 United Nations General Assembly resolution; there had been at least 21 fedayeen raids on Israel since December 2 and the Cairo radio openly boasted of them.

Israel would have evacuated more than half of Sinai by January 7. Israel was worried about what would happen in Sinai after its forces withdrew and hoped that there would be a wide strip occupied by the United Nations Emergency Force between Israel and Egyptian forces. In the negotiations on the Israel withdrawal, the United Nations Secretary General had suggested that the problems of Sharm al Sheikh and the islands of Tiran and Sanafir (positions commanding the entrance of the Gulf of Aqaba) and Gaza be left to the end. This meant that at some time after January 8 the Secretary General would wish to open negotiations on Israel withdrawal from these two areas. Israel did not wish to annex either Sharm al Sheikh or Gaza. Israel wanted assurance that the blockade of the Gulf of Aqaba would not be reinstated. The United Nations and the United States must oppose a blockade of an international waterway. Gaza presented a simpler problem in that it had never been Egyptian territory. Israel did not wish to annex the strip but insisted that it not be returned to Egyptian control. The presence of United Nations

---

[1] Source: Department of State, Central Files, 684A.86/12–2856. Confidential. Drafted by Bergus on December 29. The time of the meeting is from Dulles' Appointment Book. (Princeton University Library, Dulles Papers) A briefing memorandum, dated December 28, prepared by Rountree for Dulles is in Department of State, Central Files, 684A.86/12–2856.

forces in the strip would not solve the problem but would only provide a shield behind which fedayeen could operate. Israel could administer the Gaza strip until a permanent solution could be found. If a permanent solution involved Israel's taking over the strip, Israel would assume responsibility for the indigenous population of the strip and a share of the refugees there. Mrs. Meir hoped that the United States would suggest to the Secretary General that he not press for immediate Israel evacuation from Sharm al Sheikh and Gaza for a few weeks so that all concerned could work diligently for a permanent solution.

Mrs. Meir thought it important that the Israel position on these points be made clear so that the United States would not feel it had been taken by surprise. Israel public opinion would not permit Israel evacuation of these two areas in the absence of assurances that the blockade would not be reinstated and that Gaza would not be used as a base for fedayeen activity. Israel hoped to avoid a conflict with the Secretary General on these points which could lead to a General Assembly resolution calling for immediate evacuation which Israel would have to violate. Israel did not wish a conflict with the United States.

The Secretary made it clear that the recent United States misunderstandings with Britain, France, and Israel were not based on the fact that we had not been informed in advance but on our disapproval of the nature of the action taken by them. In the course of three months' consultation with the British and French we had conveyed fully our view that the United States would have to oppose a resort to force in Egypt or we would face virtual destruction of the United Nations with the resulting breakdown of world order and risk of World War III. We had not had an equal opportunity to express these views to Israel because we had not known that Israel contemplated forceful action.

Action had been taken through the United Nations which stopped the warlike activities before there had been disastrous consequences. The Secretary had stated publicly that there had to be processes remedying injustice as a counterpoise to the renunciation of force. The adequacy or inadequacy of those processes was not justification for the use of force; however all who wished to avoid force must see the injustices remedied. The Secretary thought we all knew that these processes of justice and accommodation did not work well in an emotionally charged atmosphere. The Israel action in Egypt did not make it easier for the United States to deal with problems where we agreed with Israel on the merits of the case.

The Secretary was perplexed as to now Israel regarded its long term future. The Secretary felt that it depended on amicable relations with Israel's Arab neighbors. If Israel remained surrounded by hostility there was no military strength which could protect it. Israel's principal outside support came from the United States. There were many American citizens who were loyal supporters of Israel. There were many others who disapproved of the course on which Israel seemed to have embarked. Despite the friendship and sympathy of this Administration for Israel, there was no feeling of close cooperation between the two countries. If there had been any Israel efforts to win Arab friendship, they had been ineffective. The United States had hoped that common long term policies could be worked out with Israel so that we could align ourselves effectively. We had not found them. Israel came forward with piecemeal suggestions which did not form a pattern which we could understand. Israel needed good relations with the Arabs to assure its future. What Israel had done in Egypt had deferred this possibility for perhaps a generation. The Secretary could not see where Israel's present course could bring about any solution to Israel's problems.

Mrs. Meir stressed the fact that close relations with the United States was a basic objective of Israel foreign policy, not only because of Israel's need for United States support but also because of the common ideals of the two countries. Israel sincerely believed that if peace in the Near East were dependent on Israel, there could have been peace at any time since 1948. The only condition which Israel required was that Israel exist. Efforts to reach peace in the Near East had failed only because Israel insisted on that point which the Arabs would not accept. The Secretary felt that the responsibility for the failure to reach peace lay mostly elsewhere but not wholly. Israel's retaliatory policies had prevented the establishment of better relations. Mrs. Meir said that since 1948 the number of Israelis killed and wounded by Arab incursion was the same proportionally as though 150,000 Americans had been killed and wounded by armed forays from Canada and Mexico. What would the United States have done in such a situation? The Secretary mentioned the possibilities for an improvement which could have arisen from the Secretary General's visit to the area and his efforts to carry out practical measures through the United Nations Truce Supervision Organization to strengthen security along the armistice lines. Mrs. Meir insisted that the armistice agreements had to be enforced as a whole, that the Arabs could not be permitted to select which provisions would be enforced. The Secretary felt that if the only basis for Arab hatred of Israel were Israel's existence, we would have seen a decline in such hatred in the nearly ten years since Israel came into being. Such had not been the case. There was more hatred now than in 1948. Mrs. Meir said this resulted from Nasser's use of the Arab-Israel issue as a means of carrying out his ambitions. She did not maintain that the Israelis were angels, but on this point Israel's conscience was clear. She could not agree that Israel had responsibility for the lack of peace in the Near East.

The Secretary concluded his general remarks by saying that it was of concern to us to learn about Israel's plans for its long range future in due course. With regard to the specifics which Mrs. Meir had mentioned, the United States was not in a position to come to agreements with Israel over matters being dealt with by the United Nations Secretary General. We were supporting him in his efforts to reopen the Suez Canal and to effect a withdrawal of troops. Mrs. Meir had presented Israel's case ably. With regard to Israel's use of the Suez Canal, we would stand by our previous position that Israel had the right to send its shipping through it. We believed that the entrance to the Gulf of Aqaba was an international waterway. Conditions for its use would have to be worked out with the Secretary General. We had no ideas regarding the problem of Gaza, which was quite complex. It was not Egyptian territory, neither was it encompassed by the Israel armistice line.

The Secretary would be seeing Mr. Hammarskjold in the course of the next few days. The topics mentioned by Mrs. Meir would in all probability be touched on in the course of that conversation.

Mr. Eban felt that the problem could be worked out in time but at least four or five days were needed. Both the Secretary General and Israel were flexible about Gaza. Neither could work well against the threat of another United Nations General Assembly resolution calling for immediate withdrawal.

As Mrs. Meir and the Ambassador left, the Secretary expressed the hope that there had been no misapprehension regarding our dedication to Israel and to the fact that there was no lack of close sympathy. The United States felt that Israel's future lay in a friendly Near East and that some of Israel's policies were not in line with this belief. [2]

---

[2] On December 30, Eban forwarded to Dulles a summary of Israel views concerning the Gulf of Aqaba, not printed. (*Ibid.*, 980.7301/12–3056)

Index

Abdoh, Djalal, 597, 674, 719, 1060
Abdulgani, Roeslan, 215, 267-269, 271
Aboul-Fetouh, Samy, 284, 305-306
Adams, Sherman, 833, 837, 851, 874*n*, 974, 1014, 1043-1044, 1223-1225
Adams, Ware, 582, 685
Aden, 384, 587
Afghanistan, 963, 1053
Africa (*see also* North Africa; *specific countries*), 334, 357, 640, 642, 1316
Soviet policy toward, 304, 568
Agriculture, U.S. Department of, 891, 928-929
Aklilou Abte Wold (Ato), 338, 537
Albert, Carl, 188
Aldrich, Winthrop W., 46*n*, 94, 98, 100*n*, 103*n*, 108-109, 112*n*, 119*n*, 204-205, 233, 518, 548
Israeli military intervention, 817-818, 846-847
Negotiations, 791, 793, 818-819
Oil supplies, 934, 1115, 1142-1143
Suez Canal Conference, 212, 516
Troop withdrawal, 1168*n*, 1174-1175, 1210-1211, 1232-1233, 1238-1239
U.S.-British relations, 671-673, 775, 781-782, 791, 819-820, 1046, 1115-1117, 1196-1197, 1204, 1211, 1264
Users' association proposal, 484-485, 496-497, 571, 623-624, 751-753
Alexander, Field Marshal, Earl (Hon. Sir Harold Rupert Leofric George), 62
Algeria (*see also* North Africa), 489
Ali, Mohammed, 837*n*
Allen, George, 38*n*, 50-52, 179*n*, 197
Allen, Leo, 188
Alpha Operation, 109

Alphand, Hervé, 414, 420-424, 455-458, 515, 576-577, 598-599, 647, 681, 1007, 1055
Israeli military intervention, 803-805, 867-868, 932*n*
Negotiations, 458, 955-956, 612-614, 1135, 1140
Soviet Union, 1003, 1005-1006, 1023-1024, 1139
Suez Canal dues, 424, 459-460, 574-575
Troop withdrawal, 1054-1055, 1105, 1182
U.N. Emergency Force, 955, 1139-1140
U.S.-French relations, 1003-1005, 1104-1107, 1136-1137
Users' association proposal, 456, 480-482, 507-508
Alsop, Joseph, 945
Alsop, Stewart, 945
Amer, Gen. Abdel Hakim, 311
Amin, Mustafa, 1149
Amini, Ali, 837*n*, 937
Amir Abdullah, 402
Anderson, Dillon, 148, 151-153, 154*n*, 166, 172, 188
Anderson, Robert (*see also* Anderson Mission *headings*), 136-138, 296-297, 310, 999, 1052, 1070-1077, 1129
Anderson Mission (Near East), 136
Anderson Mission (Saudi Arabia), 220, 230, 246-247, 273-276, 282-283, 287-296, 301-303, 340*n*
Anglo-Egyptian Suez Canal Zone Base Agreement, *1954. See under* Treaties.
Anglo-Iranian Oil Company, 180, 499
Anglo-Jordanian Treaty of Alliance, *1948. See under* Treaties.

Aqaba Gulf, 173, 180, 844, 1198-1199, 1205, 1216, 1244, 1325, 1327, 1339-1341

Arab-Israeli dispute (*see also* Israel: Western military aid to; Israeli military intervention; Jordan: Iraqi forces in; U.N. Emergency Force), 65, 108-109, 467-568, 659, 713, 723, 769, 1105, 1156

Armed attack, possible, 80-81, 87, 93, 266, 386-387, 519, 594, 977, 1079, 1123

British response, 620, 708, 722-725, 728-730

Egyptian position, 594

Israeli attack on Jordan, possible, 65, 591, 594-595, 614-615, 703, 722-726, 731, 750, 784, 973, 980, 1079

British position, 846, 856, 904

Israeli position, 137, 165, 180, 1067, 1158, 1250-1252

Soviet response, 723, 725, 731

Armistice, 398, 468, 583, 731, 769n, 908, 913, 1289, 1338-1339

Balance of power, 313-314, 519, 559-560, 594, 703, 723, 726, 824, 836, 920

Border incidents:

British position, 616n, 846

Egyptian-Israeli, 787, 832, 846-847

Israeli position, 22-23, 843-844, 1090, 1095, 1341-1343

Egyptian position, 832, 1317, 1319-1320

Fedayeen, 787, 846-847, 1319-1320

Israeli position, 800, 808-809, 821, 824, 1090, 1093, 1095, 1243, 1326

U.S. position, 813, 847, 1069, 1079, 1100

French position, 847

Jordanian-Israeli, 20-21, 603-604, 615n, 616n

Canadian position, 768

Israeli position, 563, 583, 608-609, 622, 733, 763, 1093, 1327-1328

U.S. position, 563, 583, 594, 604-605, 608, 614-615, 622, 628-629, 703, 722, 724-725, 730-732, 1079

Lebanese-Israeli, 843

Arab-Israeli dispute—Continued

Border incidents—Continued

Security Council meeting, possible, 23, 604, 769, 814

Soviet role, 1093

Syrian-Israeli, 1079, 1093

U.S. position, 93, 539, 1251, 1296n, 1309, 1343

British-French military intervention and, 65, 108-109

British position, 1174

Egyptian position, 141, 1318

French position, 42n, 1117-1118, 1286, 1292

Israeli position, 683, 728, 1343-1344

Neutral strip proposal, 936, 948

Palestinian refugees, 385, 628, 940, 942, 1124, 1129, 1216, 1237

Partition Plan, *1947*, 675, 683, 728-729

Saudi role, 89

Security Council appeal and, 336, 422

Soviet position, 225

Soviet role (*see also* Soviet intervention, possible), 88, 729, 1093, 1117-1118

Suez Canal issue and, 9n, 24, 36, 40, 42, 50-51, 87, 136n, 155, 179n, 266, 594

Tripartite Declaration, *1950*, 621, 723, 728-731, 764, 801-802, 817-818, 833

Troop withdrawal and, 1174

U.S. draft General Assembly resolutions on resolving, 936-937, 941-942, 947-951, 960-961, 1066, 1099, 1105-1106, 1141-1142, 1156, 1208-1209, 1276-1277, 1287-1289, 1323

Canadian position, 1271

Egyptian position, 964-965, 975, 1087, 1187, 1308

French position, 1105, 1287, 1292

Israeli position, 1094, 1161, 1326

U.S. position, 539, 594-595, 942, 944, 1286-1287, 1342-1343

Arab League, 168, 264, 296, 384

Arab Legion, 729

Arab nationalism (*see also* Arab states), 225, 266, 339, 390, 587

Arab states (*see also Arab subheadings under other subjects*; Oil supplies; *specific countries*):

Anti-Western propaganda, 605

Egyptian subversive activities in:

British position, 619

Arab states—Continued
  Egyptian subversive activities in—
    Continued
    Egyptian position, 587, 1235-1236,
      1314, 1316, 1320-1321
    U.S. position, 1191-1192, 1296, 1309
  Nasser leadership, 64, 82, 84, 87, 89,
    141, 154-155, 174, 189, 431-432,
    436, 642, 1101, 1128, 1208
    Arab position, 330-331, 384, 402,
      432, 1159, 1168-1169, 1208,
      1229, 1285-1296
    British position, 326, 402-404, 984
    French position, 326, 643
    Israeli position, 1159, 1251
    Security Council appeal and, 363-
      364, 431, 436
  Political situation, 951
  Soviet Union, relations with, 1286
    French position, 1118
    Israeli position, 1108-1109
  United States, relations with, 605-606,
    611, 663, 686, 914, 1180, 1208
    U.S. oil well protection, 200, 343,
      998, 1083-1084
Arabian American Oil Company
  (ARAMCO), 89-90, 246, 273n, 389,
  1002, 1071, 1075, 1079, 1200
Arad, Shimshon, 582
Aranha, Oswaldo, 937
Ardalan, Ali Qoli, 217, 529, 554, 597
Arends, Leslie C., 188
Argaman, Zev, 582-583, 1158
Argentina, 1053
Armour, Norman, Jr., 676n, 771n
Armstrong, Gen. Frank A., Jr., 844, 1035
Armstrong, W. Park, Jr., 300n, 338n,
  361n, 524-525, 559-560, 814, 1030,
  1068-1070, 1087, 1249
Artajo, Don Alberto Martin, 210, 259-
  261, 517-518, 537-538, 546-548, 555
Asbjornson, Mildred, 340n, 403n, 405n,
  418n, 430n, 472n, 639n, 916n, 1240n
Asia, 84, 640, 642, 1316
Aswan Dam:
  Soviet financing offers, 57, 81-82, 87-
    88, 587
  Suez Canal as financing source, 1, 55,
    57, 79, 82-83, 173, 189, 268, 418,
    570, 754
  U.S. financing, possible, 64-65, 173,
    1084, 1089, 1092
  U.S. refusal to finance, 1, 7, 55, 57, 79,
    82, 141, 269, 668 669

Aswan Dam—Continued
  U.S. refusal to finance—Continued
    French position, 40, 75
    U.S. public opinion, 196
Atomic energy, 180, 183, 397, 592
Atomic weapons, 915, 993, 995, 1019
Australia, 253, 261, 528, 553, 796, 882,
  902, 904-905, 1332n
  International canal system proposals,
    217, 482, 555, 617
  Suez Canal Conference, 97n, 104, 120,
    212, 516, 528-529, 532
Austria, 72-73, 1023-1024
Aziz, Abdul, 287
Azzam Pasha, Abdel Rahman, 220n, 347-
  349

Badawi, Helmi, 647, 666-667, 786
Baghdad Pact, 89, 91-92, 264, 384, 818,
  837, 840
  Egyptian position, 141, 587-588, 1314,
    1316-1317
  French position, 1118, 1263
  Israeli position, 1230, 1246
  Jordanian position, 1316
  Saudi position, 89
  Soviet position, 88, 969, 972, 1317
  U.S. position, 117, 142, 266, 1218,
    1230, 1246, 1273, 1285, 1298, 1323
Bahrein, 92, 587, 1072, 1075-1076, 1200
Bailey, Ronald W., 29n, 129, 146n, 322,
  803, 829-830, 875
Banat Yaqub, 609
Bandaranaike, S.W.R.D., 43, 1176
el-Banna, Abdelmoneim, 1299n
Barbour, Walworth, 30, 43-44, 75, 94n,
  203n, 340n, 416-417, 751, 817
  British-French military intervention,
    60-62, 204n, 346, 359 360
  Economic sanctions, 43, 45, 298-299,
    474
  London tripartite conversations, 119-
    124
  Suez Canal Conference, 128, 212, 516
  Suez Committee, 306-308, 312-313,
    316-317
Barco, James W., 706n, 707n, 714n, 717n,
  740, 957-960, 1060-1061, 1068,
  1132-1134
Bartels, Eyvind, 1276, 1306
Bartlett, Frederic, 645n
Beam, Jacob D., 339n, 344n, 803, 805,
  1195, 1295n
Beaulieu, Paul Leroy, 298

Bech, Joseph, 345, 1168
Beckett, John Angus, 934
Beckner, Earl R., 300n, 1009n, 1143n
Beeley, Harold, 533-534, 658, 714-715, 720, 817, 1304
Begin, Menahem, 1253
Belaunde, Victor A., 674
Belgium, 120n, 121, 515, 707, 842, 953
  Security Council discussion, 320-321, 336, 601, 638, 709-712
  Troop withdrawal, 882, 904, 1192-1193, 1196, 1204
Ben Gurion, David, 22-23, 165, 801, 1245-1247, 1252
  Eisenhower, correspondence with, 763, 795, 801, 843-844, 1063-1064, 1095-1096
  Israeli military intervention, 776, 811-813, 821-822, 843-844, 927, 1252-1254, 1268
  Jordan, Iraqi forces in, 615, 622, 630-632, 676n, 725-727, 763, 795
  Troop withdrawal, 1057, 1062-1063, 1090, 1095-1096, 1107-1110, 1244, 1325n, 1326-1328
  U.N. Emergency Force, 1038, 1304
  U.S.-Israeli relations, 23, 136-137, 1090-1091, 1094
Ben Halim, Mustafa, 948
Bennett, W. Tapley, 342, 749n, 803, 953, 955, 998, 1003
Berding, Andrew H., 212, 508n, 516, 658, 1284
Berger, Walter C., 928
Bergus, Donald C., 503, 562n, 614n, 686n, 722n, 1065, 1089, 1093, 1096n, 1158, 1198, 1236, 1241, 1274, 1341
  Jordan, 768-769
Bernau, Phyllis D., 46n, 131, 176n, 462, 487n, 494n, 563n, 613n, 639n, 674n, 745n, 770n, 833n, 851n, 861n, 862n, 863n, 865n, 870n, 884n, 887n, 896n, 917n, 918n, 927n, 938n, 1240n, 1333n, 1339-1340
Berry, J. Lampton, 395, 688n, 966n
Bevan, Aneurin, 656, 987, 1223
Bigart, Homer, 458, 463, 499
Birgi, Nuri, 219, 245, 535, 537-538
Black, Eugene, 786-787, 1311
Blackiston, Slator C., 50n, 178, 465, 467, 542n
Blanco, Carlos, 597
Bliss, Don C., 46n, 53, 212, 284, 300, 301n

Bloomfield, Lincoln P., 582
Boggs, Marion W., 165-176, 263
Bohlen, Charles E., 133, 149n, 156-160, 212, 237, 991, 995-996, 1016-1017, 1079
Boone, Adm. Walter F., 30, 38, 845, 1035
Border incidents. See under Arab-Israeli dispute.
Bourgès-Maunoury, Maurice, 177, 585, 76, 1259, 1265
Bowie, Robert R., 38n, 46n, 117n, 140n, 199n, 203n, 212, 509-510, 634n, 639n, 888, 891, 976, 1030, 1187n, 1195, 1227-1229, 1249n, 1284
Brazil, 686, 953, 979, 1054
Bridges, Styles, 188, 193, 195
Brilej, Josa, 895-896
British-French military intervention (see also British-French-Israeli agreement and British-French ultimatum under Israeli military intervention; Ceasefire; Troop withdrawal), 852n, 854, 900, 939, 984n
  Anglo-Egyptian agreement, 1954, as basis for, 641, 655, 750, 764, 886
  Arab-Israeli dispute and, 65, 108-109
  Arab nationalism and, 390
  Arab reactions to, possible, 63-65, 91-95, 96n, 99, 106, 357, 384-386, 418, 430-432, 435-436, 915, 950-952
  British position, 346, 526
  Saudi position, 273-274
  Belgian position, 649, 660, 710
  British and French civilian evacuation, 342, 350-351, 353, 358, 360, 377, 417, 475, 489
  British-French talks, 602
  British intentions, 10, 14, 30, 37, 40, 61-62, 109, 113, 171, 250, 328, 346, 402-403, 438, 473, 546, 641-642, 1255-1256
  British Labour Party position, 231-232, 234-235, 286, 314, 328, 474-475, 521-522, 671, 910, 1260
  British planning for, 5, 10, 14, 195-196, 204, 215-216, 234, 281, 285-286, 314, 327, 360, 581
  British public opinion, 65, 94, 108, 234-235, 250, 331, 346, 543, 591, 671, 903, 910, 951, 1020, 1051, 1260-1261
  Canadian position, 987
  Economic sanctions and, 462, 586, 755

British-French military intervention—
Continued
Egyptian position, 201-202, 878, 939
French intentions, 8, 76, 101-102, 110,
171, 327-328, 353-354, 358-359,
543, 624, 632-633, 641-642, 1255-
1256, 1259-1261
French military capabilities, 75, 210
French planning for, 8, 29, 37, 75, 177,
195, 350, 353, 857-858
French public opinion, 210, 328, 350n,
392n, 641, 903, 951
Indian position, 1108
Israeli participation, 53
Israeli position, 93
Joint Chiefs of Staff information
request, 279, 286
Military situation, 918-919, 939, 945,
987, 1013, 1015, 1078, 1097
Mobilization, 204, 215-216, 350-351,
374, 489, 711, 815, 1257
Cyprus, 350n, 353, 381, 467, 489,
595, 629, 642, 815, 876
Egyptian position, 310, 368
Israeli position, 467
Saudi position, 274, 288-290, 302,
349, 394n, 395
Watch Committee reports, 380-381,
544, 595-596, 629, 798n, 800
National Security Council discussion,
902-916
North Africa and, 47, 98, 101, 110,
183, 328, 396, 599, 632, 764, 853
North Atlantic Treaty Organization
and, 265, 345, 635n, 636, 868, 905,
1107, 1202, 1220n, 1221-1222
Pilots, 11-12, 25, 488-489
Renewed hostilities, possible, 1150-
1151, 1162
Secrecy, 15-16, 37, 68, 69n
Security Council appeal and:
British position, 313, 320-321, 328,
407, 521-522, 572
French position, 420, 423, 576, 585,
655
U.S. position, 323, 337, 342, 389,
412-422, 426, 430, 471, 527, 590,
618, 629, 633, 635, 643
Soviet influence in the Near East and,
80, 274, 334, 384, 386-387, 390-
391, 640, 816, 906, 915
Soviet intervention and, 1020
Soviet position, 159, 207, 489, 496

British-French military intervention—
Continued
Soviet responses, possible (see also
Soviet intervention, possible), 42,
80, 95, 387-388, 906, 968-972
General Assembly draft resolution,
896-897, 910-911, 913, 922-923
Saudi position, 274, 605
Special National Intelligence Estimates,
382-391, 524-528, 1020-1021
Suez Canal blockage as basis for, 39,
48, 233, 286, 404, 416-417, 490-
491, 527, 602, 764
Tripartite Declaration and, 873, 901
Tripartite heads of government
meeting and, 774-775
U.N. Emergency Force and, 947-948,
954, 956, 975, 982-983, 985, 987
U.N. position, 183, 976-977
United Nations, effects on, 911, 913-
914, 1342
U.S. ability to restrain, 68, 174, 527-
528, 858
U.S.-British relations and, 167, 389-
390, 393, 436, 884, 906-907, 930,
1098
U.S. committee proposal resolutions
and, 941
U.S.-French relations and, 167, 389-
390, 867, 884, 906-907, 921-922,
930, 1220-1221, 1224
U.S. oil aid to Western Europe and,
357, 546
U.S. participation, possible:
Arab reactions to, 389
British position, 24, 61, 98, 100n
Economic support (see also U.S. aid to
Western Europe under Oil
supplies), 186-187, 266, 510-511
French position, 76, 102, 655, 766
Joint Chiefs of Staff position, 21, 64,
67, 116-118, 151-152, 200, 264,
266-267, 279, 329
Military aid, 176-178, 187, 266
National Security Council discussion,
169, 174, 329-331
Secrecy, 152
Soviet response and, 98, 100n, 102,
133, 169, 174-175, 187, 509, 655
U.S. position, 11-12, 24-26, 37-39,
41n, 48, 69, 95, 96n, 102, 110,
195, 226, 389, 397, 816
U.S. public opinion, 98-100, 102

British-French military intervention—
Continued
  U.S. participation, possible—Continued
    U.S. political situation, 47, 585, 766-
      767, 770, 815
    U.S. position, 69-71, 149, 223, 334,
      396-398, 403-404, 439-440, 853,
      862, 873-875, 989-990
    U.S. public opinion, 98-100, 356, 436,
      635, 1280-1281
    U.S. public statements, 662, 684
    U.S. responses, 885, 901, 908-914, 918,
      922, 930-931, 988, 998-1000, 1021-
      1023, 1027-1028
    Users' association proposal and, 484-
      485, 489, 513, 520, 543, 756-757
    Watch Committee reports, 378-381,
      488-489, 543-544, 595-596, 629-
      630
    World public opinion, 189, 388-389,
      526, 543, 649, 1021
Brosio, Manlio, 959, 1166, 1173
Broustra, Vincent Paul, 1182, 1303, 1313
Brown, Winthrop G., 516
Brownell, Herbert, Jr., 1077, 1085, 1130,
  1228
Bulganin, Nikolai A., 156-160, 496, 619,
  694, 991, 993-994, 1000, 1001n,
  1003n, 1005, 1007, 1111, 1128
Bunche, Ralph J., 1068, 1311
Buraimi dispute, 291, 403-404, 853
Burdett, William C., Jr., 42n, 102n, 103n,
  112n, 119n, 212, 284, 513n, 516,
  536n, 837n, 891, 894
Burgess, W. Randolph, 30, 331, 1166,
  1168-1170
Burke, Adm. Arleigh A., 21, 28, 53, 62,
  64, 342, 749, 1035n
Burma, 92, 120, 963, 1053
Burns, Maj. Gen. Eedson L.M., 841, 913,
  942, 976, 979, 981, 1038, 1059-1060,
  1132n, 1176, 1233, 1325n
Butler, Richard A., 1115, 1163, 1166-
  1171, 1173, 1196-1197, 1202n, 1204,
  1210-1211, 1220-1221, 1227, 1238-
  1239
Byroade, Henry A., 55-58, 66, 105-107,
  133-135, 201-202, 296n, 299, 310-
  311, 334n, 417-418, 475
  Suez Canal Conference, 134, 14, 161-
    163, 201-202
  Suez Committee, 398-400, 446-447

Cabell, Lt. Gen. C.P., 391n, 539, 594,
  653-654, 703
Caccia, Sir Harold, 29-30, 37-38, 42n, 62,
  94, 100n, 103n, 112n, 115, 119n,
  129n, 203n, 1142n
  Suez Canal Conference, 120-121
  U.S.-British relations, 1098-1099, 1179,
    1181
Callender, Harold, 499
Camargo, Lleras, 1209
Canada, 43, 121, 1141, 1160, 1165, 1271,
  1332n
  Military sales to Israel, 504n, 559, 562-
    563, 608, 768, 865, 1251
  French position, 8-9
  U.S. military aid and, 23-24, 50-51,
    137, 181, 197-198, 467, 498-499
  U.S. position, 9n, 24-25, 181, 504-
    505, 563, 769
  U.N. Emergency Force, 933, 938, 940-
    942, 953-954, 976, 978-979, 982-
    983, 986, 1054, 1069, 1096n,
    1149-1150, 1154-1155, 1193
CARE, 54
Carnahan, A.S.J., 188
Carr, Robert, 1299n
Carre, Chester Morey, 300n
Carrigan, John W., 273-275, 282-283,
  1200
Casey, Richard G., 796, 902
CASU. See Users' association proposal.
Cease-fire (see also Troop withdrawal):
  Arab position, 949
  British position, 946, 978, 980, 1010-
    1011, 1015, 1025-1027, 1039
  Egyptian position, 964-965, 978n, 1006,
    1011, 1021-1022, 1051
  French position, 978, 1010-1012, 1041
  General Assembly Resolution 997
    (ES-I), 932-933, 946, 949, 981,
    1126, 1190
  General Assembly Resolution 999 (ES-I)
    (Indian), 959-960, 963, 976, 978n,
    980, 986, 1126
  General Assembly Resolution 1001
    (ES-I) (7-Power), 1053-1055
  Israeli position, 977n, 978n, 1010-1011,
    1190
  Soviet intervention and, 995-996, 1024,
    1028
  Tripartite heads of government
    meeting and, 1043-1044, 1046
  U.N. Emergency Force and, 946, 964-
    965, 981, 1012, 1026-1027

Cease-fire—Continued
  U.N. Emergency Force and—Continued
    British position, 946, 1010-1011,
      1013, 1015, 1039
    U.S. draft General Assembly
      resolutions, 907, 909-914, 916-917,
      919
    U.S. position, 919, 923-924, 931, 945,
      995-996, 1013, 1022, 1024-1028,
      1032-1033, 1074-1077
Central Intelligence Agency, 773, 1080,
  1083, 1249, 1270-1271
Ceylon, 43, 84, 92, 191, 607, 963, 1053-
  1054, 1060, 1176, 1292
  Suez Canal Conference, 97n, 104, 120,
    165, 212, 214, 244, 271, 326
Chaban-Delmas, Jacques Michel Pierre,
  753-757
Chamoun, Camille, 1180n, 1292
Charles-Roux, Francois, 647
Chauvel, Jean, 3, 13-15, 29-30, 42n, 100,
  103n, 112n, 119n, 205, 518
Chesney, George C., 188
Chile, 686
China, People's Republic of, 158, 1019,
  1079
China, Republic of, 321, 323, 842, 882,
  896
Chiperfield, Robert B., 188
Chipman, Norris B., 516, 536n
Choudhury, Hamidal Huq, 217n, 270
Churchill, Randolph, 897
Clark, William, 1269
Clay, Gen. Lucius, 1175, 1176n
Clements, Earle C., 188
COCOM, 1304
Colombia, 976, 978-979, 982, 986-987,
  1054, 1069, 1096n, 1193
Colombo Powers, 84
Comay, Michael S., 23
Commerce, U.S. Department of, 54, 694n
Committee of Five Powers. See Suez
  Committee.
Commonwealth, 4, 10-11, 15, 43, 92, 113,
  134
Compagnie Universelle du Canal
  Maritime de Suez. See Suez Canal
  Company.
Compton, Arthur A., 342
Congress, U.S.:
  Acts of:
    Agricultural Trade Development and
      Assistance Act (P.L. 480), 54,
      823, 891, 928, 1242-1243

Congress, U.S.—Continued
  Acts of—Continued
    Battle Act, 143
    Mutual Defense Assistance Control
      Act, 1951, 143
    Mutual Security Act, 1954, Sec. 401,
      1330, 1332
    "Trading With the Enemy Act," 574
  Oil supplies, 461, 463, 575, 578, 855,
    1085
  Presidential meetings, 189-196, 1001,
    1031, 1044-1045, 1047, 1050, 1052,
    1056, 1084-1086
  Senate Foreign Relations Committee,
    396-398, 588-592, 1112-1113
  Soviet intervention, possible, 1228
  State Department meetings, 396-398,
    588-592
  Suez Canal Conference participation,
    164, 188-189, 198
  U.S.-Egyptian relations, 835-937, 839,
    861, 884, 899
  U.S. military intervention, possible, 11-
    12, 41n, 47-49, 63, 69, 95, 152,
    169, 330, 356, 397
Connors, W. Bradley, 42n, 119n, 212, 516
Constantinople Convention, 1888. See
  under Treaties.
Cook, Charles D., 676n
Cook, Donald, 1221
Cooperative Association of Suez Canal
  Users (CASU). See Users' association
  proposal.
Copeland, Miles, 38n
Cordier, Andrew W., 1059, 1068, 1302n,
  1303n, 1311
Corea, Sir George Claude Stanley, 271
Corfu Channel Case, 180
Cornut-Gentille, Bernard, 571, 645n, 647,
  681, 715, 772, 789n, 840-842, 858-
  860
Cottman, J. Stewart, 212, 228n
Coty, M. René, 72
Coulson, Sir John E., 304n, 309, 374-375,
  448, 469, 476, 620-622
  Israeli military intervention, 803-805,
    829-830, 837-840, 875-876
  Security Council appeal, 319, 322-323,
    335-337, 411-413, 420-422, 438,
    560-562, 564-565, 658
  Suez Canal dues, 323-324, 413-415,
    422-424
Crosthwaite, Ponsonby Moore, 658
Crouy-Chanel, Etienne, 1041, 1284

Cuba, 323, 686, 717, 842, 882

Cunha, Paulo A.V., 271, 520, 536-537, 555

Cyprus, 91, 165, 388, 673, 792, 1014
British-French forces in, 350n, 353, 381, 467, 489, 595, 629, 642, 815, 876

Czechoslovakia, 72, 158, 1023, 1024n, 1070

Dale, William N., 1145n

Dardanelles, 274

Daridan, Jean Henri, 42n, 103n, 112n, 119n, 353-354, 358, 518, 551, 816-817, 1254, 1268, 1284

Davies, Fred, 273n, 1200

Dayan, Moshe, 776-777, 940n

De Palma, Samuel, 618n, 888

Dean, Arthur H., 498-500, 563n, 664-665, 1339-1340

Dean, Sir Patrick, 776

Defense, U.S. Department of, 54, 331, 628-629, 688-689, 694n, 891, 915, 1031, 1052, 1103

Dejean, Maurice, 149n

Denmark, 530-531, 553, 979, 1053, 1096
Oil supplies, 1009, 1145n, 1146
Suez Canal clearance, 1058-1059, 1155, 1288
Suez Canal Conference, 97n, 104, 212, 516, 530, 554, 602

Dillon, C. Douglas, 31-32, 100, 103n, 119n, 464, 518, 585-586, 634, 816-817, 847-848, 996-997, 1284
British-French military intervention, 74-77, 177, 210, 521-522, 756-757, 930-931, 1261
British-French-Israeli agreement, 900-901, 919-921, 1264
French position, 248, 353-354, 358-359, 462, 491-492, 624, 635, 654-655, 766-767, 857-858
Cease-fire, 1012, 1041
Economic sanctions, 567-568, 586
France:
Political situation, 551-552, 572
United States, relations with, 7-8, 74-75, 625, 755, 760-761, 775, 779-781, 868n, 921-922, 1005n, 1118-1120, 1220, 1264
Soviet intervention, possible, 1117-1118
Suez Canal Conference, 212, 233, 516
Suez Canal dues, 461, 753-756

Dillon, C. Douglas—Continued
Troop withdrawal, 1033-1034, 1041
U.N. Emergency Force, 1012, 1029n, 1033-1034
Users' association proposal, 490, 655-656, 756-757
Western European Union, 656

Disarmament, 150

Dixon, Sir Pierson, 676, 681, 714-716, 734n, 765, 770-772, 1123-1124, 1182, 1311-1312
Israeli military intervention, 840-842, 858-860, 881, 897
Security Council appeal, 408, 569, 571, 596-698, 647, 658

Duce, Terry, 246

Dulles, Allen W., 5, 38, 131-132, 166, 188, 745, 918-919, 1032n, 1035n, 1078, 1128, 1135
British-French military intervention, 63, 65-67, 79n, 815n, 902, 905, 912-914
Congressional meeting, 1084, 1113n
Egypt:
U.S. civilian evacuation, 67
U.S. policy toward, 1225, 1229
France, 1136-1137
Hungary, 1081, 1083, 1085
Israeli military intervention, 815n, 833-834, 837, 927n, 976
Oil supplies, 53, 65-66, 171, 173
Pilots, 7
Soviet Union, 79n, 932n, 987, 1014, 1018n, 1079-1080, 1086, 1101-1102, 1219
Suez Canal Company nationalization, legality of, 170, 174
Suez Canal Conference, 165
Syrian political situation, 784
United Kingdom, 1218
U.N. Emergency Force, 1027, 1083

Dulles, Janet, 734n

Dulles, John Foster, 131-132, 140n, 248, 451n, 618n, 745, 796
Anderson Mission, 301
Arab-Israeli dispute, 170, 182, 467-468, 591, 594, 614-616, 724-727, 730-733, 936-938, 1286, 1338-1339, 1342-1344
Border incidents, 603-605, 608-609, 614-616

Dulles, John Foster—Continued
Arab-Israeli dispute—Continued
U.S. draft General Assembly resolutions on resolving, 936-937, 941-942, 1141-1142, 1276-1277, 1287, 1292, 1323
Aswan Dam, 64-65, 173
British-French military intervention, 108-109, 171, 195-196, 281, 285-286, 327-328, 764, 1142n
British position, 545-546, 566, 581, 591
British public opinion, 231-232, 234-235, 314, 331
Eisenhower-Eden correspondence, 69n, 356n, 357n, 358n
French military capabilities, 210
Joint Chiefs of Staff information request, 279, 286
Soviet reactions, 391n
U.S. participation, 26, 39, 46-49, 98-99, 169, 174-177, 185-187, 330-331, 397
U.S. political situation, 766
U.S. position, 67-68, 100, 110-111, 167, 189, 194, 334, 396-397, 403-404, 430-431, 438-440, 884
U.S. responses, 901, 909-914, 917-918
Cease-fire, 831, 904, 907, 909-914, 916-917, 932-933, 1049-1051
Congressional meetings, 169, 188-196, 1112-1113
Eban, meetings with, 178-181, 465-469, 606-607, 608-610, 682-684, 727-733, 808-810, 925-927, 1341-1344
Economic sanctions, 66, 234, 276-278, 279n, 298, 300, 324, 449, 581
Egypt:
Economic situation, 547-548
France, relations with, 1303
Soviet Union, relations with, 506
U.S. civilian evacuation, 66-67, 331-332, 797, 806-807
U.S. policy toward, 192, 1282, 1284-1286, 1292, 1304-1305, 1324-1325
War damages resolution, 1337-1338
Eisenhower-Nehru meeting proposal, 935-937
Eisenhower statement, 315, 333-334, 340-341
France:
Political situation, 551

Dulles, John Foster—Continued
France—Continued
United States, relations with, 458-459, 462-463, 625-626, 632-637, 648-649, 656-657, 665, 762, 867-868, 884-885, 958-959, 1220-1221, 1261
Heads of government meeting, 764-765, 774-775, 1044, 1051-1052, 1113
Health of, 947n, 949
International canal use proposals, 100n, 105, 145, 208, 218, 226-229, 242-244, 254-256, 259-261, 665
Eighteen-Power proposal, 253-256, 267-269
International control, 114, 198-199, 237-240
Supervisory board, 199, 222-223, 232, 236
Israel:
United States, relations with, 609-610, 627-628, 1272-1273, 1343-1344
Western military aid to, 9n, 181, 467, 504, 563n, 608, 865
Israeli military intervention, 815-816, 825n, 863, 888-889, 902-904, 918, 922n, 1114, 1342
British-French ultimatum, 861-863, 865, 866n, 867, 870-871, 874n, 875-876, 886, 904
General Assembly, convening of, 885-887, 889-890, 896-897, 905, 929
Mobilization, 790, 794, 797, 805, 808-811, 813-816
Soviet responses, 932n
Tripartite discussions, 829-830
U.S. political situation, 885
U.S. responses, 834-840, 851-854, 861, 886, 890-893, 901, 905-908, 911, 913, 917-919, 925-927
Israeli shipping restrictions, 179n, 683, 1310, 1322, 1344
Jordan:
Iraqi troops in, 630-631, 722-723, 729-732
Political situation, 784
London tripartite meeting attendance, 10-11, 13, 15, 32, 35, 38-39, 63, 67-68, 72, 77
National Security Council, 148, 151-152, 154n, 325-327

Dulles, John Foster—Continued
NATO consultation, 309, 339-340, 344-345, 1309-1310
Near East, U.S. policy toward, 397, 1293, 1296, 1298-1299
Negotiations, 511-512, 519, 546-547, 626, 643-645, 650, 674, 702-703, 740, 742-743, 765, 770-771, 789-790, 1277-1278, 1282, 1322
  Nasser conference proposal, 458-459
  Negotiating body proposals, 612-614, 660
  U.S. draft General Assembly resolutions on resolving, 936-938, 941-942, 1141-1142
North Africa, 774
Oil supplies, 67, 180-181, 183, 189-190, 468-469, 610, 874n, 1306
  U.S. aid to Western Europe, 65, 172-173, 448-450, 462-463, 478-479, 481, 576, 853, 889, 1051, 1203
Operation Whiplash, 610-611
Panama Canal, 95, 163-164, 179, 191, 199
Pilots, 103-104, 115-116, 139, 482-483, 488, 508
Public statement, 506n
Soviet Union, 149-150, 163, 206-208, 221-227, 253-254, 391n, 506, 721, 932n
Suez Canal clearance, 1292-1294, 1300-1303, 1310, 1322, 1333-1334
Suez Canal Company nationalization:
  Arab positions, 605-606
  Legality of, 186
  Security Council appeal, 13, 49, 191-192, 194, 322-323, 335-338, 398, 406, 420, 540, 598-599
  British-French military intervention and, 286, 319, 328, 421-422, 425, 430, 471
  Letter proposal, 439, 455-456, 464, 466, 469-470
  Lodge draft resolution, 494, 495n
  Users' association proposal and, 411-414, 511-512, 517-518, 549, 553, 564-565, 590
  Security Council discussion, 576-577, 579-580, 627, 638, 649-650, 674-675, 692-693, 705-713, 721
  Arab-Israeli participation, 606-607, 658-659, 683
  Tripartite discussions, 639-645, 660, 681, 714-718

Dulles, John Foster—Continued
Suez Canal Company nationalization—Continued
  Tripartite discussions, 3-5, 13-16
Suez Canal Company reorganization proposal, 405, 418
Suez Canal Conference, 13, 49, 62-64, 104, 109, 112, 122-123, 145-146, 167-169, 189, 212, 280
  Chairmanship, 204-205, 209, 211, 213
  Participants, 30, 48-50, 94-97, 99, 104-105, 110, 113, 120-121, 144, 164, 179, 183, 209
  Procedure, 211, 213-214
  Progress of, 215-216, 218-219, 233-235, 245-246
  Reconvening of, 492-493, 505, 511-513, 516, 520, 528-532, 536-538, 544-545, 552-555
  Soviet participation, 149-150, 163, 206-208, 253-254
  Tripartite-Australian consultations, 216-218
Suez Canal dues, 103, 234, 324, 414-415, 423-424, 456-457, 459-461
Suez Committee, 216-217, 235, 267-273, 318, 327, 338-339, 419, 447n, 1258
  Membership, 237, 241, 249, 253, 256-257, 259, 261-262, 280, 284
Troop withdrawal, 1240, 1278-1284
U.N. Emergency Force, 938, 1114, 1322
United Kingdom:
  United States, relations with, 625-626, 632-637, 648-649, 656-657, 665, 762, 867-868, 884-885, 958-959, 1202-1203, 1220-1221, 1261, 1280-1281
  Heads of government meeting, 764-765, 774-775, 1044, 1051-1052, 1113
Users' association proposal, 351-352, 370-372, 392, 406, 440, 464, 555-556, 566-567, 678-680, 757-758, 1306
  Alternate oil sources and, 507, 575-576, 578-579, 589-590
  British-French public statement, 470-471, 472n, 476-478, 589
  Draft proposals, 533-534, 537
  Egypt, compensation for, 514
  Egyptian position, 491-492

Dulles, John Foster—Continued
  Users' association proposal—Continued
    Implementation strategy, 393, 441, 448-449, 456
    Mandatory participation, 513-514, 517
    Membership, 514-515
    Negotiations and, 1275-1276, 1322
    Organization, 470, 534
    Pakistani position, 573
    Security Council appeal and, 413-414
    Suez Canal Conference discussion, 544-545, 552-555
    Suez Canal dues and, 459, 470, 472, 478, 549-550, 574-575, 577-578, 584-585, 667, 720, 734-738, 744-745, 758-760
    Tripartite Foreign Ministers meeting, 487
    U.S.-French talks, 455-458
    U.S. public statements, 6n, 480-481, 589

Eagleton, William L., 1191n
Eban, Abba, 137, 179, 499-500, 822-823, 1208, 1341
  Arab-Israeli dispute, 608-609, 632, 682-684, 727-728, 731-732, 1161, 1326
  Dulles, John Foster, meetings with, 178-181, 465-469, 606-607, 608-610, 682-684, 727-733, 818-810, 925-927, 1341-1344
  Israeli military intervention, 808-810, 821-822, 824-825, 894, 925-927, 1158-1159
  Oil supplies, 52, 137, 179-180, 468-469, 499, 610, 1339-1340
  Security Council appeal, 465-466, 606-607, 658, 683
  Shipping restrictions, 51-52, 178-179, 466, 468, 683, 1326
  Troop withdrawal, 1089-1091, 1094-1095, 1159-1160, 1198-1199, 1215-1217, 1241-1242, 1325-1326, 1339-1340, 1344
  U.S.-Israeli relations, 50-51, 136-138, 197, 198n, 467-468, 664-665, 1090-1091, 1094, 1230-1231, 1272, 1274
    Economic aid, 51, 468, 498-499, 609, 682, 1161, 1242-1243

Eban, Abba—Continued
  Western military aid to Israel, 50-51, 467, 498, 562-563, 1230-1231, 1251, 1272-1274
Ecuador, 1053
Eden, Anthony (see also Heads of government meeting under United Kingdom: United States, relations with), 4-5, 9-11, 99, 113, 171, 1116
  Arab-Israeli dispute, 729, 791
  British-French military intervention, 10, 60-62, 204, 285-286, 545-546, 581, 602, 878, 982, 984-986, 1266-1267
  British public opinion, 234-235, 591, 910, 1260-1261
  Security Council appeal and, 312-313, 328
  U.S. participation, 24, 61, 98, 100n, 286
  Cease-fire, 946, 978, 1015-1016, 1025-1028
  Economic sanctions, 204, 234, 305, 474
  Eisenhower, correspondence and conversations with, 9-11, 304-305, 435-438, 848-850, 856-857, 860-861, 866, 871-872, 874-875, 882-883, 980, 984, 986, 989-990, 1025-1027, 1028-1029, 1039, 1040, 1042-1043, 1045-1046, 1056, 1061-1062, 1110-1111
  International canal system proposals, 218, 286, 312-313, 336, 472n, 476-477, 484, 486, 491, 772n
  Israeli military intervention, 848, 854-856, 860, 866, 870-872, 874, 1266-1267, 1269
  Political situation, 756, 1152, 1163
  Soviet Union, 304, 619, 1015
  Suez Canal dues, 234, 416-417
  Suez Committee, 235-237, 280n, 312
  U.N. Emergency Force, 946-947, 953, 985, 1015, 1027, 1039, 1082
Egypt (see also Arab-Israeli dispute; Arab states; Egypt and Egyptian subheadings under other subjects):
  Africa, relations with, 1316
  Anti-Western policy, 79, 82 84, 86-87, 100, 142, 189, 444, 1219
    Israeli position, 93
    Saudi position, 310, 395
  Asia, relations with, 1316
  British military aid to, 83, 143
  Economic development programs, 1314

Egypt—Continued
  Economic situation, 547-548, 579, 591,
    1219, 1285, 1290, 1315-1316
  Egypt-Syria-Saudi Arabia (ESS) Pact,
    592-593, 1251, 1254-1255
  Ethiopia, relations with, 541, 1208
  France, relations with, 900, 1254-1255,
    1302-1303, 1305, 1313, 1315-1316
  India, relations with, 593, 1316-1317
  Iraq, relations with, 106, 192, 401, 619,
    1191, 1318, 1320
  Jewish population in, 1219, 1234-1235,
    1302n, 1303n
  Jordan, relations with, 401, 605, 1101,
    1314
  Kuwait, relations with, 1309, 1320
  Lebanon, relations with, 605, 1180,
    1191-1192, 1208, 1235-1236, 1246,
    1309
  Libya, relations with, 87, 587, 619, 818,
    984, 1180, 1191-1192, 1208, 1235-
    1236
  Military capabilities, 75
  Neutrality, 1316
  Political situation, 1000-1001, 1029-
    1030, 1078, 1101, 1108, 1303, 1305
  Saudi Arabia, relations with (see also
    Egypt-Syria-Saudi Arabia (ESS)
    Pact above), 141, 246, 273, 311, 401,
    541, 591, 605, 619, 1101, 1192,
    1285, 1316-1317, 1320
  Soviet Union, relations with (see also
    Soviet intervention, possible):
    Aswan Dam, 57, 81-82, 87-88, 587
    British position, 618, 1116
    Egyptian position, 55, 587, 626n,
      695-696, 1096-1097, 1317
    French position, 74-75, 518-519, 642
    Israeli position, 42-43, 1107-1109,
      1245
    Military aid, 81, 88, 96, 489, 506,
      909, 915, 1051, 1078, 1101, 1219
    Egyptian position, 965, 1315
    French position, 1041, 1118, 1139
    Israeli position, 51, 843, 920, 1109,
      1250-1252
    Trade relations, 1316
    U.S. position, 74, 80-82, 87-88,
      141-142, 154-155, 264, 506,
      705, 1219, 1228, 1256
  Syria, relations with (see also Egypt-
    Syria-Saudi Arabia (ESS) Pact
    above), 141, 401, 587, 1101, 1314,
    1317

Egypt—Continued
  Syria-Jordan-Egypt tripartite military
    agreement, 775-776, 788, 800, 808-
    809, 811-812, 821, 843-844, 857,
    966-967, 973, 1067
  Turkey, relations with, 1314, 1321
  United Kingdom, relations with, 84,
    549, 581, 900, 1302-1303, 1305,
    1313, 1315-1316
    Anglo-Egyptian Suez Canal Zone
      Base Agreement, 1954, 18, 56,
      190, 204, 519, 641, 655, 711,
      750, 764, 886
  United States, relations with, 1084,
    1209
    Egyptian position, 310, 587-588, 668,
      1087, 1097, 1315
    Saudi position, 310
    U.S. civilian evacuation. See under Near
      East.
    U.S. economic aid to, 266, 548, 673,
      908, 929n, 1033n, 1089, 1290, 1300
    French position, 1286
    Israeli position, 822-823
    U.S. military aid to, 54, 143, 523-524,
      673, 908, 912-913, 917-918, 947,
      1021-1023, 1027-1028, 1088, 1315
    U.S. policy toward, 106-107, 140-143,
      1222-1223, 1225, 1227-1229, 1282,
      1284-1285, 1295-1296, 1305
    Egyptian position, 587, 1318-1321
    U.S.-British sanctions discussions,
      549, 581
    U.S. statements to Egypt, 1295-1296,
      1299-1300, 1307-1309, 1324-
      1325
  Western assets in, 66, 86, 1279, 1282
Egypt-Syria-Saudi Arabia (ESS) Pact,
    592-593, 1251, 1254-1255
Eisenhower, Dwight D., 6-7, 11, 26-27,
    39, 166, 174, 662-663, 684-686, 693
  Arab-Israeli dispute, 539, 594, 723-726,
    908, 936-937, 947, 1141-1142
  Ben Gurion, correspondence with, 763,
    795, 801, 843-844, 1063-1064,
    1095-1096
  British-French military intervention,
    62-65, 67-71, 74n, 110, 330, 334,
    356-358, 403-404, 566, 764, 943-
    945, 1260
    Arab reactions, 430-432, 435-436
    British political situation, 231, 314,
      331

Eisenhower, Dwight D.—Continued
British-French military intervention—
Continued
U.S. participation, 11-12, 25-26, 39,
46-47, 70
U.S. responses, 901, 910-914, 988
British political situation, 231, 314,
331, 1162, 1166
Cease-fire, 986, 1025-1029
Congressional meetings, 188-196,
1084-1086, 1112-1113
Eden, correspondence and
conversations with, 9-11, 304-305,
435-438, 848-850, 856-857, 860-
861, 866, 871-872, 874-875, 882-
883, 980, 984, 986, 989-990,
1025-1027, 1028-1029, 1039, 1040,
1042-1043, 1045-1046, 1056, 1061-
1062, 1110-1111
Egypt:
Soviet Union, relations with, 506,
915
United States, relations with, 1315,
1324n
France, 461n, 462-463, 625-626, 774,
1040, 1042-1049, 1051-1052, 1056,
1061, 1104n, 1107n, 1110-1111,
1113
Hungary, 976-977, 1008, 1083, 1128
Israel, U.S. economic aid to, 627-628
Israeli military intervention, 331, 843,
863, 866, 869-971, 874-875, 916-
917, 1114
Mobilization, 793-795, 801-802, 810-
811, 813
U.S. responses, 833-840, 848-855,
860-861, 901, 907-914, 925
Israeli shipping restrictions, 1310
Jordan, Iraqi forces in, 722-723, 763,
795
Near East:
Arbitration commission proposal,
935
Soviet role in, 194
U.S. civilian evacuation, 331-332,
806-807
U S. policy toward, 1088-1089, 1092,
1098-1099, 1121-1122, 1180,
1194-1195, 1296-1298
Negotiations, 626, 633, 1120, 1141-
1142
Suez Committee, 241-242, 418-419
Nehru correspondence, 258, 280, 502-
504, 685, 1001

Eisenhower, Dwight D.—Continued
Nehru meeting proposal, 935-937
North Africa, 774, 1293
Oil supplies, 67, 175, 191, 193, 662-
663, 1084, 1141
U.S. aid to Western Europe,171-173,
462-463, 873-874, 988, 1051,
1070, 1072-1077, 1130, 1153,
1179, 1203
Operation Whiplash, 611n
Panama Canal, 66, 163-164, 199
Public statements, 315, 333-334, 340-
341, 373, 446, 662
Saudi Arabia, 220, 294, 1137-1139,
1153, 1165, 1169
Soviet intervention, possible, 915, 922-
924, 989, 993-994, 1000-1001,
1007, 1049, 1052, 1080-1081,
1111-1112, 1141
Suez Canal:
Egyptian operation of, 432-433
International system proposals, 198-
199, 232-233, 236-237, 258, 280,
392, 502-504, 651-653
Suez Canal Company nationalization:
Economic sanctions, 27, 67
Legality of, 185-186
National Security Council discussion,
151-152, 154n
Security Council appeal, 334, 430,
580, 627, 648, 650-652, 661-663,
684
Security Council discussion, 692-693,
702, 721
Suez Canal Company reorganization
proposal, 405, 418
Suez Canal Conference, 77-78, 111n,
150n, 163-164, 188-189, 198, 210,
218, 245, 253, 261, 505, 520, 544
Troop withdrawal, 1050, 1057-1058,
1062-1064, 1095, 1096n, 1167,
1240
U.N. Emergency Force, 947-948, 956-
957, 1027-1028, 1034, 1039, 1042-
1043, 1082-1084, 1114, 1178-1179
United Kingdom, 461n, 462-463, 625-
626, 774, 1098-1099, 1104n, 1167-
1169, 1172, 1202-1203, 1240
Heads of government meeting, 1040,
1042-1049, 1051-1052, 1056,
1061, 1107n, 1110-1111, 1113
U.S. mobilization, 1035n
Users' association proposal, 392-393,
472n

Eisenhower Doctrine, 1122n
Elbrick, C. Burke, 38, 46n, 53, 129, 132,
    458, 476, 574, 577, 584n, 634n, 829,
    867, 875, 888, 940, 955, 958n, 1009n,
    1030, 1143n, 1181n, 1187n, 1201n,
    1267n, 1284, 1302, 1304
  Cease-fire, 1006
  France, 885, 1003-1004, 1047, 1104
  Israeli military intervention, 885, 1249n
  Oil supplies, 1145-1147, 1195
  Soviet intervention, possible, 1023
  Swiss heads of government meeting
    proposal, 1032
  U.N. Emergency Force, 953-954
Ely, David R., 1164
Ely, Gen. Paul, 777
Engen, Hans, 978-979
Entezam, Abdullah, 1060
Esso Shipping Company, 365
Ethiopia, 261, 307, 541, 553, 564, 642,
    963, 979, 1053, 1208
  Suez Canal Conference, 113, 120, 134,
    158, 165, 212, 244, 250-253, 325,
    516, 553
  Users' association proposal, 482, 535,
    537, 541, 545, 554, 616-617, 623,
    646
European Defense Community, 1168
Eveland, Wilbur, 273n
Eveland, William, 287
Export-Import Bank:
  Egypt, 143
  Israel, 23, 51, 181, 468, 498, 609, 627-
    628, 664, 682, 733, 892, 1242
  Western Europe, 479, 481, 568, 575,
    590, 737, 780, 1166

Fadden, Arthur, 280n
Faisal ibn al-Aziz ibn Abd al-Rahman al-
    Faisal al Saud, 274, 282-283, 287-
    294, 301
Fanfani, Amintore, 626
Faure, Maurice, 760-761
Fawzi, Mahmoud, 161-163, 200-202, 666,
    746, 786, 1154, 1185-1186, 1290-
    1291, 1303, 1305, 1308-1310
  Negotiations, 765-766, 778, 782-783,
    943, 1170, 1186, 1208
  Security Council discussion, 601, 638,
    674, 676-679, 689-692, 697-698,
    700, 706, 741, 748
  Suez Canal clearance, 1155, 1206,
    1307-1308, 1311, 1334-1335

Fedayeen. See under Arab-Israeli dispute:
    Border incidents.
Federal Bureau of Investigation, 773
Federal Reserve Bank, 1142, 1151
Feldman, Marckus, 1119n
Finland, 1096n
Finn, Richard B., 1147n
FitzGerald, Dennis A., 1236-1238
Fitzmaurice, Sir Gerald, 94, 112n, 119n,
    203n, 533-534, 714
Five-Nation Committee. See Suez
    Committee.
Flemming, Arthur S., 132, 784, 908, 913,
    1009n, 1014, 1084-1085, 1113n,
    1143n
  Oil supplies, 174-175, 685, 915
    U.S. aid to Western Europe, 171-172,
      873, 1074, 1076, 1129-1131,
      1195, 1223-1224
      Planning for, 53-54, 188-189, 192-
        193, 332, 449-450, 479, 974-
        975
Foreign Petroleum Supply Committee
    (FPSC), 53, 129-130, 171
Foster, Andrew B, 3-5, 212, 242n, 269n,
    516
Foster, Rockwood, 29-30, 35-41, 42n, 94n
France (see also North Africa; British-French,
    France, French, Tripartite, and Western
    subheadings under other subjects):
  Economic situation, 1032, 1076-1077
  Military capabilities, 75, 210
  Political situation, 551-552, 757n, 1218
  Saudi Arabia, relations with, 1106-
    1107
  Soviet Union, relations with, 76-77,
    496, 694, 1003, 1005, 1220n, 1304
  United Kingdom, relations with, 1257,
    1262-1263
  United States, relations with, 393, 634-
    637, 1119-1120, 1257-1259, 1262
    British-French military intervention
      and, 167, 389-390, 867, 884,
      906-907, 921-922, 930, 1220-
      1221, 1224
    French attacks on U.S. policy, 458-
      459, 461-463, 591, 617, 625,
      632-633, 641-642, 755, 761, 779,
      1003-1005, 1136-1137, 1258-
      1259

France—Continued
United States, relations with—
Continued
Heads of government meeting, 764-
765, 774-775, 779-781, 1040,
1042-1049, 1051-1052, 1056,
1061-1062, 1104-1107, 1110-
1111, 1113, 1118-1119, 1180n
U.S. economic aid to, 479, 481, 908,
1189
U.S. military aid to, 176-178, 187, 266,
885, 911, 914, 918, 958-959
Users' Association Executive Council,
646
Fritzlan, A. David, 630n
Fry, Maj. Gen. James C., 845
Fulbright, J. William, 588

Gaitskell, Hugh, 234-235, 286, 314, 328,
331, 474-475, 497
Gallman, Waldemar, Jr., 485, 599
Garrett, Gwynn, 928
Gaza Strip (see also Troop withdrawal),
1038, 1133
Jurisdiction:
British position, 1124
Israeli position, 940, 1160, 1198-
1199, 1216, 1242, 1325n, 1340-
1342
U.S. position, 1232, 1323, 1344
Palestinian refugees, 940, 942, 1124,
1129, 1216, 1237
General Services Administration, 1237
George, Walter F., 188, 416, 474, 490,
823, 835, 861-862, 1169n
Georges-Picot, Jacques, 674
German Democratic Republic, 72-73
Germany, Federal Republic of, 305, 531,
555, 1088, 1293n, 1332n
Suez Canal Conference, 72, 97n, 101,
104, 212, 214, 271, 516, 531
Ghaleb, Abdelhamid, 184
Gleason, S. Everett, 324-332, 594-595,
632-633, 701-714, 784-785, 902-916,
1070-1086, 1127-1131, 1218-1229
Glubb, Lt. Gen. Sir John Bagot, 620
Goodpaster, Brig. Gen. Andrew J., 5, 11,
26, 27, 62, 69n, 502n, 650, 652n, 793-
794, 833, 839, 851, 873, 893n, 947,
976, 986, 1000, 1098n, 1120, 1153,
1166, 1178n, 1194n, 1309
Eisenhower-Nehru meeting proposal,
936-937
Oil supplies, 974

Goodpaster, Brig. Gen. Andrew J.—
Continued
Soviet intervention, possible, 1014
Tripartite heads of government
meeting, 1043-1045
U.S. mobilization, 1035n
Gork, Haydar, 837n
Gray, Gordon, 53-54, 62, 132, 176-177,
185, 187-188, 199n, 212, 628-629,
953, 998-999
Greece, 120, 165, 309, 325, 464
Green, Theodore F., 188, 191-192, 1112-
1113
Greene, Joseph N., Jr., 888, 891-893,
1028n, 1030, 1057, 1100n, 1173n,
1195
Gruenther, Gen. Alfred M., 185, 187,
844, 1035, 1044-1045, 1047-1048,
1111, 1136-1137
Guatemala, 506, 1124
Guebre-Hiot, Balambaras, 541
de Guiringaud, Louis, 645n, 964-965

Hagerty, James C., 373, 833, 851, 870n,
889n, 947-948, 976, 986, 988, 1000,
1007n, 1194n
Haley, Sir William, 692
Halleck, Charles, 188, 191-192
Hallstein, Walter, 531
Hamilton, Tom, 742
Hammarskjöld, Dag, 840-842, 887-889,
1082, 1156-1157, 1190, 1302n, 1303,
1305, 1313
Arab-Israeli dispute, 164, 182, 398,
468, 1156, 1208-1209, 1251, 1288-
1289
British-French military intervention,
183, 977-978
Cease-fire, 986, 1010-1011, 1031
Negotiations, 740-743, 749, 770-774,
777-778, 791, 943, 1335-1336
Committee proposals, 1120, 1156,
1207-1208, 1271, 1288
Security Council appeal, 183, 376-377,
511-512
Security Council discussion, 676, 678-
680, 689-693, 696-698, 705-708,
712, 715, 717
Suez Canal clearance, 1058, 1155, 1177,
1205-1206, 1288, 1289n, 1311-
1312, 1333-1335
Troop withdrawal, 1038, 1058-1060,
1156-1157, 1182, 1199, 1205-1207,
1215-1217

Hammarskjöld, Dag—Continued
U.N. Emergency Force, 957-958, 976,
978-979, 981-983, 1059-1061,
1068-1070, 1132, 1154-1155, 1178-
1179, 1190, 1205
Hammarskjöld Mission, 22, 182
Hamui, Mamun, 966n
Hanes, John W., Jr., 212, 249n
Hansen, Hans Christian S., 530, 554
Hare, Raymond A., 27, 566n, 570, 782-
783, 827-828, 877-878, 898-900, 975,
1027-1030, 1033n, 1234-1235, 1299n
Arab states, Egyptian influence in,
586-587, 1235-1236, 1314, 1316,
1320-1321
Border incidents, 827, 1319-1320
Egyptian foreign policy, 1314-1318
Military situation, 939-940, 1097
Soviet intervention, possible, 1164-
1165
Suez Canal clearance, 1318-1319
U.N. Emergency Force, 964-965, 975,
1027, 1096n, 1100n, 1319
U.S.-Egyptian relations, 140n, 587-588,
1314-1321
Harlow, Bryce N., 188
Harrison, Lt. Gen. William K., Jr., 844,
1035
Haskey, D.S., 548, 658
Hay-Pauncefote Treaty, 19, 361-362
Hayter, Sir William Goodenough, 149n
Hazlett, Everett (Swede), 943
Heath, Donald B., 184-185
Heeney, Arnold D.P., 498, 768-769, 940-
942, 953-954
Heikel, Mohammed, 141, 964-965, 975
Henderson, Loy D., 303, 377, 475, 516,
688n, 796n, 949, 951-952, 796n, 1030,
1187n, 1329n, 1337
Economic sanctions, 298, 300
Israeli military intervention, 886, 888,
1249n
Suez Committee, 306-308, 338n, 366-
367, 392, 394, 398-400, 416, 419,
441-446, 511
British position, 308, 312-313, 316-
318
Participation in, 259, 276, 280, 284,
287
Users' association proposal, 369, 398-
399, 416, 487, 533, 535, 550
Herzog, Yaacov, 23
Hewitt, Warren E., 18-19
Higgins, Marguerite, 888

Hildreth, Horace A., 569-570, 572-573
Hill, Robert C., 588, 592, 1030-1031
Hitchcock, James J., 786-787, 799-800
Hoegh, Leif, 623
Hoffacker, Lewis, 1149n, 1275n
Hollister, John B., 53-54, 132, 890-891,
912, 914, 929n, 1030, 1329
Holmes, Julius C., 416, 474
Hong Kong, 1019
Hoover, Herbert, Jr., 46n, 131-132, 257n,
333, 366n, 369n, 598n, 618n, 692,
775n, 929n
Arab-Israeli dispute, 539, 559, 686-687,
722, 724, 727, 947-951, 959, 973,
977
Border incidents, 1100
British-French military intervention,
11-12, 24-26, 62, 79, 100n, 110,
350-351, 764, 837, 851-853, 949-
952, 988
British political situation, 1162, 1220-
1221
Cease-fire, 1021-1022, 1024-1025,
1032-1033, 1049-1051
Congressional meetings, 1084-1085,
11138n
Egypt:
Arab states, influence in, 1191-1192,
1309
U.S. civilian evacuation, 27, 66-67
U.S. policy toward, 1222-1223
Eisenhower-Nehru meeting proposal,
936-937
France, 1043-1044, 1047-1048, 1181,
1196n, 1201, 1220-1222
Hungary, 1083
International canal system proposals,
230, 393, 508, 653, 1168-1169
Israel:
Military capabilities, 653-654
United States, relations with, 928,
1094, 1158n, 1231-1232
Western military aid to, 25, 542,
562-563
Israeli military intervention, 110, 793,
805, 808, 829, 833, 888, 891, 1249n
Near East, U.S. policy toward, 686,
929n, 1122, 1194, 1222
Negotiations, 685, 947-951, 959
Oil supplies, 129-130, 592, 652, 874n
U.S. aid to Western Europe, 129-130,
873n, 889, 974, 987-988, 1009-
1010, 1073-1077, 1166, 1214-
1215, 1223-1224, 1308

Hoover, Herbert, Jr.—Continued
  Oil supplies—Continued
    U.S. aid to Western Europe—
      Continued
        Arab reactions, 1076, 1130, 1147-
          1148, 1179-1180, 1187-1190,
          1212-1213
        Troop withdrawal and, 1194-1195,
          1212-1213
    Pilots, 28, 592
    Saudi Arabia, 220, 230, 297n, 1153,
      1165, 1167
    Soviet intervention, possible, 79n, 989,
      1000, 1014, 1023-1025, 1030,
      1067-1068, 1081-1082, 1101, 1123-
      1125, 1128, 1149
    Suez Canal clearance, 1307-1308, 1310,
      1329-1332
  Suez Canal Company nationalization,
    3, 5-6, 38
    Economic sanctions, 27-28, 66-67,
      324, 1150, 1309
    NATO discussion, 26
    Security Council appeal, 322, 564,
      650-653, 661-662, 674, 701-703
    U.S. public statement, 6
  Suez Committee, 259
  Troop withdrawal, 1057, 1062-1063,
    1065-1068, 1082, 1093-1094, 1107,
    1109, 1194, 1201, 1231-1232
  United Kingdom, 1043-1044, 1047-
    1048, 1169-1170, 1173, 1181,
    1196n, 1201, 1220-1221
  U.N. Emergency Force, 947-948, 976,
    977n, 986-987, 1031, 1082, 1084,
    1129, 1149, 1178-1179, 1274-1275
  U.S. mobilization, 886n, 1035n
Hope, John, 623
Howe, Fisher, 71, 197n, 257n, 319n, 502n,
  796n, 885n, 959n, 988-989, 1047,
  1123n, 1249n, 1324n
Hughes, Emmet John, 1000
Humphrey, George M., 12, 63-68, 132,
  170, 627-628, 910-914, 1092, 1168-
  1169, 1223, 1225
  Israeli military intervention, 852, 908,
    911, 914
  Oil supplies, 53-54, 172-173, 478-479,
    1074-1077, 1083-1084, 1130, 1223-
    1224
  Suez Canal clearance, 1225-1227, 1301-
    1302, 1329
  United Kingdom:

Humphrey, George M.—Continued
  United Kingdom—Continued
    Economic situation, 1131, 1166-1168,
      1172-1173, 1226
    Political situation, 1162, 1221-1222,
      1226
    United States, relations with, 1044,
      1202n, 1204, 1226-1227, 1240
Humphrey, Hubert, 396-397, 1133-1134
Hungary, 938, 948
  Arab position, 1108
  Asian position, 1098
  British position, 985
  Egyptian position, 1307
  French position, 901, 996, 1003-1005,
    1136
  General Assembly discussion, 789, 888,
    901, 976-977, 1008, 1159
  Indian position, 1108, 1119, 1128, 1159
  Israeli position, 926, 1108-1109, 1161
  Soviet possible intervention in Near
    East and, 875-876, 995, 1003-1004,
    1006-1007, 1016-1018
  Suez Canal Conference, 72, 158
  U.S. position, 977, 1005, 1008, 1081,
    1083, 1085, 1088, 1098-1100, 1112
Hussaini, Jamal Bey, 274, 287
Hussein, Ahmad, 28n, 333-334, 491-492,
  695-697, 831-833, 877-879, 1021-
  1023, 1149-1150, 1307
Hussein, King, 417, 599, 615n, 620, 784

Iceland, 309, 345
India, 43, 92, 243-244, 388, 497, 593, 887,
  907, 953-954, 1108, 1118, 1316-1317
  Eisenhower-Nehru correspondence,
    258, 280, 502-504, 685
  General Assembly discussion, 954, 956,
    963, 1053
  Mediation proposals, 210, 645-646,
    662, 685, 693, 1310
    British position, 665
    Egyptian position, 593, 678, 697,
      778-779, 1208, 1319
    Negotiations, 191, 502n, 540-541, 663,
      1335
    Security Council discussion, 173, 596,
      607
  Soviet Union, relations with, 1081,
    1083, 1119
  Suez Canal Conference, 97n, 104, 120,
    168, 205, 212-214, 244-245, 326
  Suez Committee, 271, 288

India—Continued
   U.N. Emergency Force, 976, 978-979,
      986, 1054, 1058n, 1059, 1193,
      1242, 1274
Indonesia, 92, 267-268, 271-272, 963,
   1053, 1072, 1083
   Suez Canal Conference, 120-121, 163,
      165, 212, 214-215, 244, 326
Intelligence Advisory Committee, 524,
   528n, 773, 798-799, 845
Interior, U.S. Department of the, 53,
   694n, 1077
International Bank for Reconstruction
   and Development (IBRD), 368, 375,
   786-787, 1166, 1226, 1290, 1330-
   1332
International Chamber of Shipping, 40,
   46, 60, 73, 103
International Cooperation Administration
   (ICA), 54, 463, 886, 890, 912, 1330,
   1332
International Court of Justice, 36, 175,
   180n, 243, 394, 446, 592, 624, 680,
   778, 1289
International Monetary Fund (IMF), 493-
   494, 1012-1013, 1076-1077, 1142-
   1143, 1151, 1226
Iran (see also Eighteen-Power proposal
   under Suez Canal, international
   system proposals), 84, 90-92, 264,
   467, 642, 686, 842, 882, 963, 979,
   984, 1053
   Oil supplies, 529, 1189
   Security Council appeal, 323, 336-337
   Security Council discussion, 707, 716-
      717, 719
   Soviet Union, relations with, 201, 313,
      391n, 972, 995, 1080
   Suez Canal Conference, 113, 120, 212-
      213, 217, 219, 516
   Suez Committee, 261, 307, 441
   Users' association proposal, 482, 535,
      545, 554, 564, 617, 646
Iraq (see also Baghdad Pact), 89-92, 113,
   120, 264, 346, 485, 630, 930, 963,
   1053, 1189
   Arab-Israeli dispute, 675, 729
   Baghdad Pact, 141, 384, 1314
   Egypt, relations with, 106, 192, 401,
      619, 1191, 1318, 1320
   Israel, relations with, 621, 763
   Jordan, Iraqi forces in, 599-600, 769,
      922n, 1078-1079

Iraq—Continued
   Jordan, Iraqi forces in—Continued
      Armed attack, possible, 614-615,
         722, 973, 980
      British position, 616n, 620-622
      French position, 921, 1264
      Israeli position, 622, 631-632, 675-
         676, 683, 704, 708, 723, 727-728,
         731-732, 763, 800, 808-809, 811,
         844, 967
      U.S. position, 622, 630-632, 642, 659,
         683-684, 686-687, 703, 709, 729-
         732, 809
   Oil supplies, 155, 384, 853, 972, 1071,
      1079
   Political situation, 285, 385, 401-402,
      418, 641, 920, 984, 1080, 1108,
      1118, 1306
   Saudi Arabia, relations with, 143, 642
   Soviet Union, relations with, 972, 1019,
      1080
   Syria, relations with, 92, 386, 1314
   United Kingdom, relations with, 304,
      385, 853, 1123
   United States, relations with, 142, 686,
      1089, 1285
Iraq Petroleum Company (IPC), 90-92,
   384
Iraqi-Jordan Mutual Defense Treaty,
   1947, 630
Ireland, 1145n
Ismay, Lord of Worthington, 1202
Israel (see also Arab-Israeli dispute; Israeli
   military intervention; Israel and Israeli
   subheadings under other subjects)
   British military aid to, 42, 562
   Canadian military sales to, 504n, 559,
      562-563, 608, 768, 865, 1251
   French position, 8-9
   U.S. military aid and, 23-24, 50-51,
      137, 181, 197-198, 467, 498-499
   U.S. position, 9n, 24-25, 181, 504-
      505, 563, 769
   Economic situation, 1242
   France, relations with, 1252-1254
   French military aid to, 815, 834-836,
      840, 849, 904
   British position, 14
   French position, 8-9, 14, 31-32, 42,
      170, 543
   Israeli position, 137, 1251, 1253-1254
   U.S. military aid and, 197

Israel—Continued
  French military aid to—Continued
    U.S. position, 9n, 24-26, 31, 542-543,
      723, 733, 1249n, 1252-1253,
      1255, 1257
  Iraq, relations with, 621, 763
  Italian military aid to, 1251
  Military capabilities, 559-560, 653-654,
    703, 723, 726
  Political situation, 1110, 1251-1252,
    1328
  Shipping restrictions:
    Armistice and, 468
    Constantinople Convention and, 51-
      52, 683, 843-844, 1289
    Egyptian position, 1319
    French position, 422, 596-597, 847
    International canal system proposals
      and, 137-138
    Israeli military intervention and,
      1156
    Israeli position, 51-52, 93, 178-179,
      466, 732, 843-844, 1109, 1241,
      1244, 1326
    Security Council discussion of, 583,
      596-597, 607, 645n, 683, 727,
      812, 823
    Security Council resolution, 1951, 52,
      93, 178-179, 422, 607, 732, 844,
      1105, 1109
    Soviet position, 224
    U.N. Emergency Force and, 1190,
      1244
    U.S. position, 83, 222, 426-427, 847,
      1105, 1310, 1322, 1344
  Socony-Vacuum withdrawal from, 468
  Soviet Union, relations with, 88, 971,
    1003n, 1161-1162, 1230
  United Nations, relations with, 1251
  United States, relations with, 731,
    1090-1091, 1094, 1208, 1230-1231,
    1252, 1256-1257, 1272-1274, 1286-
    1287, 1327, 1343
  U.S. political situation, 498-500, 605,
    724-726, 816, 944
  U.S. economic aid to, 1160, 1236-1238,
    1242-1243
    Export-Import Bank loan, 468, 609-
      610, 627-628, 664, 682-683, 733,
      892, 1089, 1092
    Israeli position, 23, 51, 181, 498-
      499, 609, 664, 682, 1242

Israel—Continued
  U.S. economic aid to—Continued
    Israeli military intervention and, 830,
      861, 884, 886, 890-893, 905-908,
      913, 919, 928-929
  U.S. military aid to (see also Canadian
    military sales to above), 136-138,
    523-524, 610-611, 664-665, 959n,
    1089, 1251-1252
    Israeli military intervention and,
      891-893, 906-907, 912-913, 917-
      919, 947
  U.S. civilian evacuation, 812-813
  Western military aid to, 42, 91, 136-
    137, 264, 1251
Israeli military intervention (see also
  Cease-fire; Troop withdrawal), 825,
  900
  Arab responses, possible, 930, 952
  Border incidents and, 1095
  British-French-Israeli agreement, 776-
    777, 815-817, 834-837, 845, 849,
    861-862, 876, 887-888, 900-901,
    903-904, 919-921, 1114
    British position, 840
    Egyptian position, 832-833, 878
    French position, 1136, 1263-1264
    U.S. intelligence report, 1249-1271
  British-French ultimatum, 855-856,
    861-863, 865-871, 871-872, 875-
    877, 886, 904
    Egyptian response, 877, 898, 900
  Egyptian responses (see also Suez Canal:
    Egyptian obstruction of), 831-832,
    834, 877
  French position, 31, 847-848
  General Assembly, convening of (see
    also Cease-fire), 882, 885-887, 889,
    897, 905, 907, 929
    British position, 890, 897
    French position, 890, 897, 901
    Soviet position, 887, 895-897
  Indian position, 1108
  Israeli position, 110, 180, 883, 894,
    1158-1159
  Israeli public opinion, 1110
  Israeli shipping restrictions and, 1156
  Joint Chiefs of Staff position, 118,
    844-846
  Military situation, 902, 918-919, 926,
    927n, 931-932, 939-940
  Mobilization, 785, 788, 790, 794-795,
    797, 801-802, 809-811, 822-824
    British position, 817-818, 1268

Israeli military intervention—Continued
Mobilization—Continued
French position, 816-817, 1268
Israeli position, 800, 808-809, 811-813, 821-822, 824, 1268
Tripartite discussion, 801-805
Watch Committee reports, 787-788, 798-800
Oil supplies, effects on, 853, 918
Security Council discussion proposals:
British position, 830, 840-842, 846, 852, 857, 859-860, 863, 871-872, 877
Egyptian letter, 882, 886, 889
French position, 840-842, 851-852, 859-860, 863, 867, 869, 877
Soviet appeal, possible, 835
Soviet position, 842
U.S. position, 829-832, 835-841, 847, 849, 851, 860n, 862, 877-878, 889
Sinai Peninsula scorched-earth policy, 1288, 1320
Tripartite Declaration, 1950:
British position, 728, 731, 764, 818, 829-830, 841, 847, 849, 854, 857, 904
French position, 829-830, 904, 1268-1269
U.S. position, 621, 723, 729-730, 801-802, 817, 829-830, 833-836, 839-840, 849-850, 860-861, 892-893, 901, 904-908, 916n
Tripartite discussion, 801-805, 829-830
U.S. position, 80-81, 93, 143, 170, 331, 343, 386-387, 398, 630, 815-816, 902-916, 927, 1342
U.S. responses, possible (see also Security Council discussion proposals above), 814, 878-879, 929n
Blockade, 834, 912
Economic sanctions, 830, 842, 852, 861, 884, 886, 891-894, 901, 905-908, 911, 913, 925
Egypt, military aid to, 835-836, 839-840, 898-900, 1021-1023, 1027-1028
Israeli position, 925-927
Public statements, 892-893, 899, 908, 929, 947, 977
U.S. mobilization, 826-827, 845-846, 864, 886, 915, 998-1000

Israeli military intervention—Continued
U.S. responses, possible—Continued
U.S. political situation, 835-836, 847, 885
Italy, 29, 210, 529, 553, 572, 590, 1009, 1088, 1145n, 1166, 1332n
Suez Canal Conference, 97n, 120, 212, 214, 497, 516, 520
Users' association proposal, 497, 529, 555, 572, 602, 646

J.P. Morgan and Company, 14, 16
Jackson, C.D., 628, 701, 1226
Japan, 92, 553, 590, 616, 623, 646
Suez Canal Conference, 97n, 104, 212, 219, 516, 531, 535, 555
Javits, Jacob K., 500
Jebb, Sir Hubert Miles Gladwyn, 585, 602, 1261
Jenkins, Alfred L., 273n, 287
Johnson, Lyndon B., 12, 164, 169, 188, 190, 195
Johnston, Eric, 419, 609
Joint Chiefs of Staff, 12, 151-156
Arab-Israeli dispute, 313-314, 594-595, 750-751
British-French military intervention, 342-344, 749-750, 968-972
U.S. participation, 21, 64, 67, 116-118, 151-152, 200, 264, 266-267, 279, 286, 329
Israeli military intervention, 826-827, 844-846, 864, 968-972
Operation Whiplash, 523-524
Soviet intervention, possible, 845, 968-972, 1030
State-JCS meetings, 342-344, 749-751
U.N. Emergency Force, 999, 1002
U.S. civilian evacuation, 915
U.S. mobilization, 998-1000, 1035-1036
Joint Middle East Planning Committee, 968-972
Joint Strategic Plans Committee (JSPC), 21
Jones, Aubrey, 298
Jones, John Wesley, 958n, 1145n
Jordan (see also Arab-Israeli dispute; Arab states; Jordan and Jordanian subheadings under other subjects), 89, 485, 930, 963, 1053, 1317
Egypt, relations with, 401, 605, 1101, 1314

Jordan—Continued
Fragmentation, possible, 631-632, 676, 683, 704-705, 725, 728, 732, 784, 835
Iraqi forces in, 599-600, 769, 922n, 1078-1079
Armed attack, possible, 614-615, 722, 973, 980
British position, 616n, 620-622
French position, 921, 1264
Israeli position, 622, 631-632, 675-676, 683, 704, 708, 723, 727-728, 731-732, 763, 800, 808-809, 811, 844, 967
U.S. position, 622, 630-632, 642, 659, 683-684, 686-687, 703, 709, 729-732, 809
Oil supplies, 155, 169n, 384, 972
Political situation, 385, 387, 630, 642, 703-704, 722-725, 730, 768, 769n, 784
Egyptian influence, 87, 90, 401, 621, 729-730, 800, 844, 984, 1192, 1251
Egyptian position, 1317
Israeli position, 808-809, 844, 1108
Soviet influence, 729-730, 971-972
Soviet intervention and, 1019, 1102, 1157
Syria-Egypt-Jordan tripartite military agreement, 775-776, 788, 800, 808-809, 811-812, 821, 843-844, 857, 966-967, 973, 1067
Syrian forces in, 1078-1079
United Kingdom, relations with, 346, 385, 620-621, 750-751, 784, 1123
Anglo-Jordanian Treaty of Alliance, 1948, 620-621, 708, 722-725, 728-730, 733, 764, 768, 818, 846, 856, 904
United States, relations with, 143, 600, 929n, 1089
Jordan River Development Plan, 609, 1089
Joxe, Louis, 31-32, 358-359, 847-848, 931, 965-966, 996-997, 1284, 1302
Juin, Marshal Alphonse Pierre, 1297
Justice, U.S. Department of, 1130

Kalijarvi, Thorsten V., 891, 928, 1143n, 1145-1147
Katzin, Alfred George, 1176n, 1311
Keightley, Gen. Charles, 1233, 1239n
Kent, Sherman, 773

Khalil, Hashim, 837n
al-Khayyal, Sheikh Abdullah, 220n, 347, 949
Khouri, Victor A., 949-952
Khrushchev, Nikita S., 157
Kidron, Mordecai R., 1215, 1325
Kilmuir, David P., 3n
Kirk, Roger, 33, 38n, 53, 212, 652n
Kirkpatrick, Ivone, 250, 340n, 474, 1013, 1015, 1016n, 1197n, 1221
Kiselev, Yevgeniy, 134, 1028
Knowland, William F., 12, 164, 169, 188, 190-193, 196, 862, 1134
Kollek, Teddy, 614n
Kuwait, 83, 92, 108, 147, 285, 401, 1079, 1123, 1309, 1320

Laboulaye, François de, 420, 574, 829, 1104, 1139
Lall, Arthur S., 978-979
Lange, Halvard, 271, 520, 530, 534, 537, 555, 589, 937
Langer, William, 396-397, 588
Laskey, Denis, 1278, 1304
Latin America, 175, 335, 337, 389, 685-686, 887
Lawson, Edward B., 22-23, 1107-1110, 1244-1247, 1326-1328
Israeli mobilization, 785, 800-801, 811-813, 966-967
Jordan, Iraqi and Syrian forces in, 622, 631, 675-676, 708, 727, 729, 732, 966-967, 973n
Lay, James S., Jr., 116, 153
Lebanon (see also Arab-Israeli dispute; Arab states), 90-91, 296n, 346, 353, 385, 485, 609, 963, 972, 1053
Egypt, relations with, 605, 1180, 1191-1192, 1208, 1235-1236, 1246, 1309
Neutrality, 1292-1293, 1323
Oil supplies, 52, 155, 384, 972
United States, relations with, 143, 1089
Lemay, Gen. Curtis E., 845, 1035
Lemnitzer, Gen. Lyman L., 845, 1035
Lennartson, Roy W., 928
Lewis, Maj.-Gen. Millard, 524
Liberia, 574, 585, 619, 625, 754, 963, 1053
Libya, 87, 304, 346, 385, 388, 489, 963, 1053, 1122-1123
Egypt, relations with, 87, 587, 619, 818, 984, 1180, 1191-1192, 1208, 1235-1236
Political situation, 195, 418, 641, 818
Lippman, Walter, 901-902, 945

Lister, Ernest A., 339n, 1201n, 1275n
Lloyd, Selwyn, 13-16, 34, 38, 72-73,
    100n, 103, 729, 1279, 1282, 1304-
    1305
  British-French military intervention,
      14-16, 61, 94, 98, 279, 281, 320-
      321, 359, 648, 742, 1142n, 1260
    British-French-Israeli agreement,
        776-777, 1266-1267
    British public opinion, 234-235
    Planning for, 5, 204, 360
    Suez Canal Conference and, 113-114
  Cease-fire, 978, 1015-1016
  International canal system proposals, 5,
      15, 42, 218, 1170
  Israel, Western military aid to, 14, 42
  Israeli military intervention, 817-818,
      846-847
  Negotiations, 791, 818-819, 903
  Oil supplies, 1306
  Panama Canal, 95
  Pilots, 14, 103, 123
  Political situation, 1163, 1280, 1282
  Suez Canal clearance, 1175-1177, 1183,
      1197n, 1205-1206, 1278-1279,
      1301, 1334
  Suez Canal Company nationalization:
    Economic sanctions, 14, 43-45, 276-
        278, 298
    Security Council appeal, 319-321,
        336-337, 406-408, 420, 511-512,
        535, 549, 618
    Security Council discussion, 639-645,
        647-649, 658-659, 676, 689-692,
        696-697, 705-708, 714-718, 741,
        772n
  Suez Canal Conference, 60, 112-114,
      119-123, 203-205, 209, 213-214,
      216, 511-513, 540
    Participants, 42-43, 72-73, 94, 96-97,
        104, 113, 120-121, 179
  Suez Canal dues, 43-44, 60, 103, 123-
      124, 233, 409, 416
    Users' association proposal, 549-550,
        667, 691, 734, 738-741, 744-745,
        751-753, 757
  Suez Committee, 234, 269, 271-272,
      308, 360
  Troop withdrawal, 1123-1125, 1174-
      1177, 1182-1184, 1197n, 1205-
      1206, 1232-1233, 1238-1239,
      1278-1284
  U.N. Emergency Force, 1123-1125

Lloyd, Selwyn—Continued
  U.S.-British relations, 648-649, 656-
      657, 665, 740, 792, 819-820, 1040,
      1042, 1116, 1122, 1179n, 1282
  Users' association proposal, 409-410,
      476, 484-485, 487, 513-515, 533-
      535, 537-538, 555, 571, 616, 623,
      792, 1306
Lodge, Henry Cabot, Jr., 569, 639n, 689n,
    709
  Arab-Israeli dispute, 938, 1156-1157,
      1187, 1288-1289
  British-French military intervention,
      852n, 912
  British and French nationals in Egypt,
      1313
  Cease-fire, 959, 977-978
  Israeli military intervention, 825n, 839-
      842, 852, 858-860, 881, 887-888,
      896-897, 912
  NATO meeting, 1272
  Near East, U.N. economic aid to, 1290-
      1291
  Negotiations, 765-766, 770-773, 789-
      790, 1156, 1272, 1287-1288, 1335-
      1336
    U.S. draft General Assembly
        resolutions, 938, 965-966, 1156-
        1157, 1186, 1207-1208
  Soviet intervention, possible, 1156-
      1157
  Suez Canal clearance, 1058-1059, 1124,
      1155, 1175-1178, 1183, 1205-1206,
      1288, 1289n, 1311-1312, 1333-1335
  Security Council discussion, 494-495,
      569, 571-572, 596-598, 618, 647,
      658-659, 676-678, 681, 699-701,
      711, 714, 740, 742-743
  Syrian political situation, 1222
  Troop withdrawal, 1058-1061, 1123-
      1125, 1157, 1175-1178, 1182-1186,
      1199, 1205-1207, 1215-1216, 1231,
      1325-1326
  U.N. Emergency Force, 838, 956-957,
      964, 978-979, 981-983, 1059, 1068,
      1070, 1123-1125, 1133-1134, 1154-
      1155
  UNTSO observers, 1038
London Conference, 22-Power. See Suez
    Canal Conference.
London Oil Emergency Advisory
    Committee, 1146
Looram, Matthew J., Jr., 1322n
Loutfi, Omar, 1059-1060, 1185

Luce, Clare Booth, 572
Lucet, Charles, 420, 507, 574, 789n, 829-
    830, 867, 955, 1003, 1007, 1023,
    1104, 1139, 1302n
Ludlow, James M., 338n, 361n, 639n, 658,
    676n, 714
Luns, Joseph, 270, 530, 555

McAfee, William, 528
MacArthur, Douglas, II, 33, 46n, 280n,
    688n, 750, 829, 888, 891, 1009n,
    1123n, 1169n, 1178, 1300n, 1304
    British-French military intervention,
        279n, 1249n
    Egypt, 1209
    Israel, Canadian military sales to, 504-
        505
    Near East, U.S. policy toward, 1121,
        1210
    Negotiations, 1120
    Oil supplies, 974, 1195
    Saudi Arabia, 1165
    Security Council discussion, 658
    Soviet intervention, possible, 932n
    Suez Canal clearance, 1301
    Tripartite heads of government
        meeting, 1047
    Troop withdrawal, 1194
    U.N. Emergency Force, 976
    U.S. mobilization, 886, 998-1000, 1030,
        1052
McAuliffe, Eugene V., 132, 1212
McCardle, Carl W., 39n, 94, 103n, 112,
    119n, 199n, 203n, 212, 249-250, 508n,
    516, 566n, 639n, 734n, 888
McCloy, John J., 1175-1176, 1206, 1301-
    1302, 1329, 1331, 1332n
McDonald, John W., Jr., 890n
MacDonald, Thomas L., 219, 261n, 269
Macmillan, Harold M., 249, 520, 577-578
    British-French military intervention,
        60-62, 108-109, 171, 328-329, 521-
        522, 580-581, 591, 985, 990
    Oil supplies, 1115, 1142-1143
    Political situation, 1150-1152, 1163
    Troop withdrawal, 1174-1175
    U.S.-British relations, 1012-1013, 1115-
        1116, 1167-1168, 1171-1173, 1197,
        1240
Macomber, William B., 199n, 203n, 212,
    256n, 335n, 393n, 516, 639n, 658,
    714, 721n, 888, 890n, 1049, 1112n,
    1141n, 1278n
Maestrone, Frank E., 212

Maillard, Pierre, 1268-1269
Mak, Dayton S., 42n, 212, 511n
Makins, Sir Roger, 492-493, 579, 613-
    614, 803n
    Oil supplies, 32, 129-130, 449-451, 479
    Users' association proposal, 438-441,
        448-450, 469-473, 476-478, 483-
        484, 487-488, 577
Malik, Charles, 184-185
Mallory, Lester D., 615n
Mansfield, Mike, 164, 169-170, 396-397,
    567-568, 580, 588, 592
Manzini, Raimondo, 626n
de Margérie, C. Roland, 715
Marjolin, Robert, 298
Marshall, George C., 138
Marshall Plan, 168, 547
Martin, Joseph W., Jr., 12, 188
Martino, Gaetano, 210, 270, 345, 497,
    520, 529-530, 538, 555, 572, 1136-
    1137
Masoud, Mohamed, 273n, 394n
Mates, Leo, 895-896
Mathews, Elbert G., 300n
Maurer, Ely, 300n
Mayer, Daniel, 656
Meeker, Leonard C., 16-18, 1276n
Megee, Lt. Gen. Vernon E., 750
Meir, Golda, 675-676, 708, 966-967, 973,
    1158, 1190, 1231, 1252, 1274-1275,
    1339-1344
Mendès-France, Pierre, 1119, 1218
Menon, V.K. Krishna, 210, 242-244, 254-
    256, 271, 497, 540-541
    Negotiations, 395, 645-646, 662, 669-
        670, 674, 685, 693, 1208, 1335
    Suez Canal Conference, 164, 205, 209,
        272
Menzies, Robert G., 216-217, 233-234,
    796, 902
    Suez Committee, 235, 446-447
        Chairmanship, 256-257, 259, 272-
            273, 280, 307
        Negotiations, 305-306, 308, 316, 327,
            338, 339n, 367-368, 375-376,
            394, 399, 416, 441-445
Menzies Committee. See Suez Committee.
Merchant, Livingston T., 23-24
Meroz, Yohanan, 808, 1065, 1096n
Metzger, Stanley D., 212, 284, 516, 1275n
Mexico, 45, 172, 979

Middle East Emergency Committee (MEEC), 54n, 175, 192, 449, 873n, 974, 1071-1076, 1129-1131, 1144, 1180n, 1194-1195, 1210n, 1214-1215, 1223, 1243n
Middle East Policy Planning Group, 509-510
Middleton, Drew, 746
Millikin, Eugene D., 188
Minnich, L. Arthur, 188n
Mirza, Maj. Gen. Iskander, 572-573
Moline, Edwin G., 131, 212, 284, 516, 1009n, 1143n, 1145n, 1195
Mollet, Guy, 72, 74-77, 490, 572, 585-586, 617, 767, 1012, 1033-1034, 1218, 1257-1261
  Israeli military intervention, 776, 866, 869-870, 1267, 1269
  Soviet intervention, possible, 1024n, 1104, 1106, 1117-1118
  U.N. Emergency Force, 1012, 1029n, 1033-1035
  U.S.-French relations, 551, 764-765, 774-775, 779-781, 1040, 1042-1049, 1104, 1118-1119
Monckton, Walter, 774, 1265
Moore, Virgil L., 284
Morgan, Thomas E., 188
Morocco, 101, 388, 641, 643, 680, 804, 845, 920, 1118
Morris, Willie, 513n, 620, 622
Mossadeq, Mohammed, 107
Muntasser, Mahmud, 402
Murphy, Robert D., 94, 100, 108, 131-132, 139n, 144n, 688n, 1030, 1181n, 1187n, 1201n, 1276n, 1322n, 1329n, 1338n
  Arab-Israeli dispute, 750-751, 768-769, 1106, 1161
  British-French military intervention, 36, 60-62, 1249n
  France, 1003-1007, 1047, 1104-1107
  International canal system proposals, 43
  Israel:
    U.S. economic aid to, 1161
    Western military aid to, 42
  Israeli military intervention, 803-804, 808, 888, 891, 895-896, 976, 1159, 1249n
  Oil supplies, 1195
  Soviet intervention, possible, 1003-1006, 1023, 1160
  Suez Canal clearance, 1307-1308, 1332n

Murphy, Robert D.—Continued
  Suez Canal Company nationalization, 131-132
  Economic sanctions, 45
  NATO consultation, 309
  Security Council appeal, 342
  Tripartite discussions, 11, 12n, 30, 32, 34-36, 38, 42-45, 72-73, 103n, 112n, 119n
  Tripartite notes, 45-46, 58-60, 72-73
  Suez Canal Conference, 257-258
  Suez Canal dues, 28, 44
  Suez Committee, 259
  Troop withdrawal, 1057
  U.N. Emergency Force, 953-956, 1139-1140
  U.S. mobilization, 998-999
Murray, Geoffrey S., 1271-1272

Nabulsi, Sulayman, 1317
Nakkad, Naim, 273
Nasser, Gamal Abd'ul (see also Egypt and Egyptian subheadings under other subjects; Suez Canal Company nationalization), 1, 55-57, 133-135, 310-311, 333, 334n, 393-394, 415, 570, 592-593, 1149, 1234-1235, 1315-1316
  Arab estimations of, 330-331, 384, 397, 402, 1159, 1168-1169, 1208, 1229, 1285-1286
  Arab-Israeli dispute, 975, 1087, 1156, 1317-1320
  Arab states, Egyptian influence on, 1235-1236, 1314, 1316, 1320-1321
  British estimation of, 146-147, 304, 526, 580, 909, 944, 1260
  British-French military intervention, 939, 947
  French estimation of, 31, 761, 944, 1140, 1257-1258
  Israeli estimation of, 465, 843, 1108, 1244-1245, 1248, 1343
  Israeli military intervention, 827, 877, 898-900, 939
  Military situation, 939-940, 1097
  Negotiations, 626n, 975, 1208, 1319
  Suez Committee, 305-306, 311n, 367-368, 375-376, 393-394, 415-416, 442-446, 529, 593
  Political situation, 1000-1001, 1029-1030, 1305
  Soviet Union, 1087, 1096-1097, 1149, 1156-1157, 1164, 1316-1317

Nasser, Gamal Abd'ul—Continued
    Suez Canal clearance, 1318-1319
    U.N. Emergency Force, 975, 1100n,
        1149, 1154-1155, 1319
    U.S. civilian evacuation, 827-828
    U.S.-Egyptian relations, 310, 586-588,
        1097, 1314-1315, 1321
    U.S. estimation of, 64, 140-142, 167,
        192, 626, 886, 1084, 1133, 1165
    Users' association proposal, 491, 541,
        570, 593, 626n
National Indications Center, 787-788,
    799-800
National Petroleum Council, 694n
National Security Council, 148, 151-152,
    165-176, 325-327, 701-702, 1084-
    1086
    Actions:
        No. 1462, 903
        No. 1593, 175-176, 263, 325, 329n,
            509, 628
        No. 1597, 332
        No. 1619, 702-703
        No. 1621, 704
        No. 1626, 903
        No. 1627, 915-916
        No. 1629, 1077-1078, 1219
        No. 1630, 1086, 1219
        No. 1632, 1131-1132, 1219
        No. 1638, 1219
        No. 1639, 1229
    Documents, NSC 5428, 903
    Meetings:
        292d, Aug. 9, 1956, 165-176
        295th, Aug. 30, 1956, 324-332
        297th, Sept. 20, 1956, 539
        298th, Sept. 27, 1956, 594-595
        299th, Oct. 4, 1956, 632-634
        300th, Oct. 12, 1956, 701-704
        301st, Oct. 26, 1956, 784-785
        302d, Nov. 1, 1956, 902-916
        303d, Nov. 8, 1956, 1070-1086
        304th, Nov. 15, 1956, 1127-1132
        305th, Nov. 30, 1956, 1218-1219
Navy, U.S. Department of the, 988
Near East (see also Arab states; specific
    countries):
    British and French civilian evacuation
        and, 342, 350-351, 353, 358-360,
        377, 417, 475, 489
    Soviet influence in, 88-89, 194, 254,
        266, 924, 1083, 1092n, 1098-1099,
        1324

Near East—Continued
    Soviet influence in—Continued
        British-French military intervention
            and, 80, 274, 334, 386-387, 390-
            391, 640, 816, 906, 915
        British position, 304, 619
        French position, 568, 642, 919-920
        Hungarian revolt and, 1088
        Joint Chiefs of Staff position, 155,
            970
        Saudi position, 246, 311
    Soviet policy toward, 510, 969, 1323
    U.N. economic aid to, 1290-1291,
        1298-1299
    U.S. civilian evacuation, 27, 36, 46, 66-
        67, 351, 417-418, 475, 797, 806-
        807, 832
    Defense Department plans for, 331-
        332, 688-689, 864n
    Israeli position, 812-813
    Joint Chiefs of Staff position, 200,
        343, 915
    U.S. economic aid programs and,
        929n
    U.S.-Egyptian discussions, 827-828,
        878
    U.S. economic aid to, 1089, 1092, 1099,
        1121-1122, 1180
    U.S. military aid to, 911, 1299
    U.S. policy toward, 170, 397, 824, 835-
        836, 839-840, 1210, 1297
    U.S.-British consultation, 1191-1192,
        1194-1195, 1201
    Western bases in, 155, 265, 304
Near East Arms Coordinating Committee
    (NEACC), 8, 31, 543, 815, 1252
Near East war. See British-French military
    intervention; Cease-fire; Gaza Strip;
    Israeli military intervention;
    Negotiations; Soviet intervention,
    possible; Troop withdrawal; U.N.
    Emergency Force.
Negotiations (see also International canal
    system proposals; Security Council
    discussion under Suez Canal
    Company nationalization; Suez
    Committee)
    British position, 511-512, 672, 690,
        692, 696, 700, 706, 738, 752, 770,
        791, 793, 818-819
    British public opinion, 681, 715, 752
    Egyptian position, 593, 650, 670, 695-
        697, 741, 778, 782-783, 1186, 1319

Negotiations—Continued
Eighteen-Power proposal, 244-245, 250-253, 291-294, 303, 325
British position, 257, 409, 531, 641, 643
Egyptian position, 375-376, 529, 1256
Eisenhower statements, 315, 333-334, 340-341, 373, 446
French position, 490, 531, 567, 572, 624, 642-643, 655, 1258
Indian position, 254-256
Security Council appeal and, 420-421, 425-426, 519
Soviet position, 245, 270, 326-327
Spanish position, 252-253, 259-261
U.S. position, 268-269, 366-367, 512n, 640, 1170, 1276
Users' association proposal and, 409, 429, 490, 531
French position, 690, 692, 696-698, 700, 706, 715-716, 718, 741, 819
French public opinion, 681, 715, 1257
Geneva meeting proposal, 741-743, 747-749, 765-766, 769-770, 782, 791
Hammarskjöld mediation proposals, 509, 511-512, 519, 693, 1292
Indian mediation proposals, 210, 645-646, 662, 685, 693, 1310
British position, 665
Egyptian position, 593, 678, 697, 778-779, 1208, 1319
Italian proposal, 626
Mediation, 593, 626, 1186, 1335
Nasser proposals, 459, 485, 502n, 511, 527, 529-530, 541, 547, 553, 624, 670
French position, 459, 511
Soviet position, 527
Suez Canal Conference consideration, 493, 502-504, 511, 553
U.S. position, 458-459, 461, 488, 500-503, 509, 511, 512n
Saudi mission to Egypt, 296-297, 299-300, 303, 310-311, 347, 395
Security Council committee proposals, 509
British position, 511, 522, 579, 634, 644
French position, 511, 519, 599, 612-614, 635, 643
Soviet position, 649-650, 660

Negotiations—Continued
Six principles as basis of, 706, 712-713, 721, 962, 1271, 1275, 1335
British position, 715-716, 1211, 1262
Egyptian position, 748, 778, 943, 1156, 1207, 1262, 1279, 1319
French position, 716-718, 755, 1262
Hammarskjöld letter to Fawzi, 772, 774, 777-778, 791
U.N. position, 818-819, 742, 749-750, 1288
U.S. position, 716, 747, 773, 909, 923, 997, 1089, 1276-1277, 1322
Soviet participation, 670, 937, 1207
Suez Canal clearance and, 1331
U.N. position, 678-679, 740-742, 771-773, 1156, 1207, 1335-1336
U.S. conference proposal, 663
U.S. draft General Assembly resolutions, 935-938, 941-942, 947-951, 953, 956-958, 961-963, 1099, 1105-1106, 1120, 1141-1142, 1282
Egyptian position, 975, 1186
French position, 955, 965-966, 996-997, 1105, 1135, 1140, 1292
Hammarskjöld participation proposal, 956-957
U.N. position, 1156, 1207, 1271, 1288
U.S. position, 633, 651, 661-662, 674, 678, 770-771, 773, 789-790, 1278, 1296
Users' association role, 752-753, 1275-1276, 1322
Nehmer, Stanley, 300n
Nehru, Jawaharlal, 43, 164, 541, 907, 924, 935-937, 1058n, 1128n, 1316-1317
Eisenhower correspondence, 258, 280, 502, 685, 1001
Negotiations, 395, 497, 662
Nenni, Pietro, 656
Nepal, 963, 1053
Netherlands, 215, 305, 555, 602, 905, 953, 1145n
Suez Canal clearance, 1058-1059, 1155, 1288, 1332n
Suez Canal Conference, 97n, 212, 516, 530
New Zealand, 555, 617, 902, 905, 979
Suez Canal Conference, 97n, 104, 120, 212, 219, 221-222, 516, 532
Suez Committee, 261n, 262n, 267-270, 272, 284, 316

Newsom, David D., 273n, 287, 294n, 1137n
Niazi, Anwar, 746-748, 1126
Nigeria, 147
Nishi, Haruhiko, 531, 535, 553
Nixon, Richard M., 169-170, 175, 188, 194, 884-885, 986, 1035n, 1081, 1083, 1085, 1223, 1226-1227
  Oil supplies, 172, 988, 1073, 1224
Noel, Emile, 1046n
Noon, Malik Firoz Khan, 530-531, 535, 538, 550, 553-554, 569, 573
North Africa:
  Egyptian involvement, 87, 789n, 984, 1252, 1255, 1261, 1263
  Egyptian position, 1307
  French presence in:
    Arab demonstrations, 202, 800, 804, 817, 845, 869, 874
    French position, 1293
    U.S. position, 770-771, 774
  French-Soviet relations and, 76-77
  Saudi involvement, 89
  Suez Canal Company nationalization effects on, 31, 41, 74, 98, 101, 265, 393, 641-642, 754
    British-French military intervention and, 47, 98, 101, 110, 183, 328, 388, 396, 599, 632, 764, 853
  U.S. bases in, 155
North Atlantic Treaty Organization (NATO), 117, 260, 309, 339, 344, 775, 794, 911, 1146-1147, 1297
  British-French military intervention and, 265, 345, 635n, 636, 868, 905, 1197, 1202, 1220n, 1221-1222
  French participation, 75, 641, 656 757n, 761, 767
  Meetings, 339, 342, 344-345, 391-392, 1114, 1272, 1309-1310
    British position, 309, 324, 339, 340n
    French position, 1291
  Soviet intervention and, 1006, 1014, 1017, 1024, 1025n
  Soviet policy toward, 969
  Suez Canal Company nationalization and, 7, 13, 24, 26, 36, 39, 121, 264-265
Norway, 253, 545, 553, 589, 602, 617, 646, 1009, 1145n, 1292
  Suez Canal Conference, 4, 97n, 104, 212, 516, 520, 530, 537, 554
  U.N. Emergency Force, 976, 978-979, 982, 986, 1096n, 1193

Nunez-Portuondo, Emilio, 597
Nunley, William T., 1276n
Nutting, Anthony, 777
Nuwar, Maj. Gen. Ali Abu, 22

O'Connor, Roderic L., 396n, 588
Office of Defense Mobilization (ODM), 53-54, 663, 684, 974, 988, 1071, 1214, 1224
Ogburn, Charlton, Jr., 1021n
Ohliger, F.W., 1200
Oil supplies:
  Alternate sources (see also Economic sanctions under Suez Canal Company nationalization; U.S. aid to Western Europe below), 537
    British position, 546, 590
    French position, 103, 490, 496, 507, 568, 755
    Italian position, 497, 590
    U.S. position, 79n, 168, 180-181, 183, 274, 397, 404, 478-479, 492n, 514, 578
  Arab reliance on, 173, 180, 183, 191, 449, 1073, 1165, 1189
  Congressional meeting, 1085
  Disruption, possible (see also Suez Canal: Egyptian obstruction of):
    British position, 9, 28, 32, 67, 108, 168, 171, 190, 401-402, 546
    French position, 8, 168, 190
    Iraqi position, 168n, 169n
    Israeli position, 52, 179-180
    U.S. position, 6, 12, 65-67, 79, 86-87, 90-91, 148, 155, 167-168, 180, 265-266, 357, 389, 546, 834-835, 853, 918, 972
  Iraqi disruption, 1071, 1079
  Israeli pipeline and canal proposals, 52, 137, 172-173, 180, 468-469, 499, 1199, 1241, 1339-1340
    French position, 586, 610, 1287, 1292
  Saudi disruption, 1072, 1074-1075
  Soviet policy, 173, 969, 1131, 1213, 1219
  Syrian disruption, 148, 155, 168n, 169n, 384, 971, 974n, 1007, 1222, 1306
  Turkey pipeline proposals, 172, 437
  U.S. aid to Western Europe:
    Antitrust laws and, 1076-1077, 1130

Oil supplies—Continued
  U.S. aid to Western Europe—
    Continued
    Arab reactions, possible, 999, 1072-
      1073, 1075-1076, 1080, 1129-
      1131, 1144, 1146-1148, 1153,
      1165, 1179-1180, 1188-1190,
      1200, 1202, 1212-1213
    British-French funds, 457, 460-463,
      478-479, 481, 578, 589-590, 780,
      873-874, 1012-1013, 1076-1077,
      1142-1143
    British-French military intervention
      and, 357, 546
    British political situation, 1210n
    British position, 9, 32-33, 98, 129-
      130, 187, 414, 423-424, 449-450,
      853, 934, 1202
    Cease-fire and, 1074-1077
    Egyptian position, 1290, 1308
    French position, 187, 457, 460, 462-
      463, 575, 1140
    Israeli position, 1243n
    National Security Council
      discussions, 171-172, 1070-1078,
      1129-1131
    OEEC role, 934, 1009-1010, 1071-
      1072, 1074, 1115, 1129, 1140,
      1142, 1144, 1148, 1166, 1172,
      1215
    Planning for, 79n, 53-54, 129-131,
      175, 192-193, 449-450, 592, 652,
      662-663, 694, 1085, 1141, 1214-
      1215
    Security Council discussion, effects
      on, 663, 672-673, 684-685
    Suez Canal dues withdrawal and,
      414, 423-424, 459-460, 481, 578
    Troop withdrawal and, 1115, 1188-
      1189, 1194-1195, 1200, 1202-
      1203, 1212-1213
    U.S. announcement, 1214-1215,
      1223-1225
    U.S. oil well protection, 200, 343,
      998, 1083-1084
    U.S. position, 414, 423-424, 568, 575,
      578, 589-590, 737, 854, 873,
      974-975, 988, 1048, 1051, 1083,
      1143-1145, 1187
    U.S. public opinion, 63, 65
    Venezuelan oil, 171-172, 873, 1051,
      1071, 1130, 1165
    Western European position, 889,
      1074, 1130, 1145-1147, 1179

Oil supplies—Continued
  U.S. aid to Western Europe—
    Continued
    World economic repercussions, 223
Operation Alpha, 109
Operation Stockpile, 25, 182, 612
Operation Whiplash, 523-524, 610-611
Ordonneau, Pierre, 596-598, 715, 842
Organization for European Economic
  Cooperation (OEEC), 934, 1009-
  1010, 1071-1072, 1074, 1115, 1129,
  1140, 1142, 1144, 1148, 1166, 1172,
  1215
Organization of American States (OAS),
  663, 685-686
Overby, Andrew N., 53, 1329n
Oyevaar, Jan Johan, 617, 624

Page, Howard, 79n, 247
Pahlavi, Mohammed Reza Shah, 402
Pakistan (see also Eighteen-Power proposal
  under Suez Canal, international
  system proposals), 43, 45, 92, 191,
  253, 264, 530, 553, 607, 642, 963,
  1053-1054
  Political situation, 535, 642
  Suez Canal Conference, 97n, 104, 120,
    212-213, 217, 219, 505, 516, 535,
    538
  Users' association proposal, 545, 550,
    564, 569-570, 572-573, 590, 616,
    623, 646
Palestine Conciliation Commission, 936,
  960-961, 1277
Palestinian refugees, 385, 628
  Gaza Strip, 940, 942, 1124, 1129, 1216,
    1237
Palmer, Gen. Williston, 1035n
Panama (see also Panama Canal), 574-575,
  585, 607, 619, 625, 685, 754
Panama Canal, 135, 163-164, 179, 274,
  412
  Legal situation, 19, 49, 65, 95, 99, 190-
    192, 199
Parodi, Alexandre, 1302
Partridge, Gen. Earl E., 844, 1035
Pate, Gen. Randolph, 1035n
Pearson, Lester, 23, 345, 412, 467, 498,
  865, 987, 1155, 1160
  U.N. Emergency Force, 933, 948, 953-
    954, 957n, 978-979, 982-983
Peaslee, Amos J., 175
Pedersen, Richard F., 1334-1336
Peres, Shimon, 776

Perkins, George W., 309, 339n, 391-392
Persian Gulf, 66, 92, 155, 343, 384, 853
Persons, Maj. Gen. Wilton B., 185-186, 188, 833, 837-838, 974
Peru, 45, 323, 717, 842, 882
Peterson, E.L., 928-929
Petroleum Authority, 449
Philippines, 120, 1053
Phillips, Christopher H., 955
"The Philosophy of Revolution" (Nasser), 75, 141, 167
Phleger, Herman, 38, 46n, 103n, 112n, 119n, 131-132, 188, 199n, 508n, 510, 584n, 598n, 618n, 634n, 639n, 734n, 1028n, 1032n, 1123n, 1187n, 1231n, 1276n, 1322n, 1329n
    Arab-Israeli dispute, 940, 1208-1209
    British-French military intervention, 62, 947-948, 988, 1249n
    Cease-fire, 986, 1030-1031
    Egyptian war damages resolution, 1337
    International canal system proposals, 469, 476, 487, 533-534, 574, 577, 666-667, 720
    Israeli military intervention, 808, 851-852, 888, 1249n
    Negotiations, 650, 709, 940, 1207
    Oil supplies, 1195, 1213n
    Security Council discussion, 658, 678, 680-681, 705, 714
    Soviet intervention, possible, 1000
    Suez Canal Conference, 94, 203, 212, 233, 492, 516
    Suez Canal dues, 123, 574, 577
    Suez Committee, 259
    Tripartite heads of government meeting, 1047
    Troop withdrawal, 1057
    U.N. Emergency Force, 953-954, 976
Pilots:
    British-French military intervention and, 11-12, 25, 488-489
    British position, 235
    Egyptian-hired Soviet bloc pilots, 369, 482, 506, 508, 570, 642
    Egyptian control, 198-199, 222, 591
    French position, 394
    Required work, 1
        British position, 4, 14, 44-45
        French position, 8, 14-15, 44, 75, 462
    Tripartite position, 58-59
        U.S. position, 11-12, 25, 378
    Suez Canal dues and, 422

Pilots—Continued
    Users' association proposal, 352, 363-364, 371-372, 428, 434, 456, 482-485, 488-489, 508, 529
        British position, 450-451, 471-472
        Egyptian position, 399, 677
    Western withdrawal of, 394, 463
        British position, 103, 115, 484, 488
        Egyptian position, 202, 446, 490
        French position, 103, 115, 139n, 481-482, 485
        Saudi position, 289
        U.S. position, 11-12, 139, 377, 482-485, 488
Pineau, Christian, 7-8, 15, 30, 38n, 103, 123, 345, 464, 511, 1135, 1258, 1291
    Arab-Israeli dispute, 519, 1286-1287, 1292
    British-French military intervention, 100-102, 248, 462, 491-492, 648, 776-777, 900-901, 1260-1261
    British-French-Israeli agreement, 919-921, 1136, 1263-1265, 1267
    Cease-fire, 1012
    Egypt:
        France, relations with, 1302-1303
        Soviet Union, relations with, 519-520, 1139
        U.S. policy toward, 1284-1286
    International canal system proposals, 114, 218
    Israel, French military aid to, 8-9, 42
    Pilots, 44-45, 103, 115, 123, 485
    Security Council presidency, 597
    Soviet Union, 8, 496, 519-520, 931-932, 1136, 1139, 1304
    Suez Canal clearance, 1292, 1303
    Suez Canal Company nationalization:
        Economic sanctions, 44, 276-278, 298, 461, 567-568
        Security Council appeal, 420, 519, 531, 535, 585
        Security Council discussion, 601, 618, 639-645, 648-649, 676, 681, 689-692, 696-697, 706, 709-710, 714-718, 741, 772n
    Suez Canal Conference, 42, 72-73, 104, 112-113, 119-123, 205, 511-513, 567
    Suez Committee, 270, 272, 1258
    Troop withdrawal, 1033-1034, 1182
    U.N. Emergency Force, 1012, 1029n, 1034

Pineau, Christian—Continued
  U.S.-French relations, 921-922, 1005,
    1136-1137
  Users' association proposal, 476, 490,
    513-515, 531, 533-535
Plaza Lasso, Galo, 1208-1209
Poland, 72, 158
Popovic, Koca, 601, 618, 719
Portugal, 120n, 212, 516, 536, 555, 617,
    905, 1009, 1145n
Price, Walter J., 1013
Prochnow, Herbert V., 46n, 53, 577, 891,
    1030, 1032, 1057
Proctor, David, 38, 112n, 119n

Qatar, 83
Query, Col. Leo J., 788, 814, 883-884
al-Quwatli, Shukri, 592n, 995n, 1108

Radford, Adm. Arthur W., 174, 185-186,
    313-315, 342-343, 523-524, 594-595,
    784, 1084-1086, 1128-1129, 1209-
    1210, 1225-1226
  British-French military intervention,
    170-171, 195-196, 329-330, 750,
    912, 1079, 1128
  Israeli military intervention, 826, 834-
    838, 864, 912, 932n
  Oil supplies, 173, 175, 874n, 974, 1084,
    1223
  Soviet intervention, possible, 1080-
    1081, 1131, 1228
  U.S. civilian evacuation, 331, 915
  U.S. mobilization, 998-1000, 1035n
Rae, Saul S., 768, 940
Rafael, Gideon, 1215, 1325
Ramsbotham, Peter, 676n, 714
Rayburn, Sam, 12, 169, 188, 194-196
Raymond, John M., 338n, 361n, 369n,
    420, 424, 1338n
Reap, Joseph, 203n
Riad, Gen. Mahmoud, 1185
Rice, Maurice S., 338n, 1307
Rifa'i, Abdul Monem, 603-606
Ringwalt, Arthur R., 212, 269n, 516
Roberts, Randolph, 300n
Robertson, Norman, 865
Robertson, Reuben B., Jr., 62, 116, 610,
    874n, 915, 1031, 1212
Robertson, Walter S., 342, 1030
Rockwell, Stuart W., 144n, 374n, 480,
    566n, 614n, 831, 949, 1191n, 1275n,
    1295n, 1299n, 1322n
Romania, 72, 1070

Ross, Archibald David, 533
Rothschild, Robert, 709
Rountree, William M., 38, 46n, 48n, 53,
    71, 110, 132, 139n, 140n, 144n, 185n,
    199n, 203n, 216n, 279n, 281n, 318n,
    319n, 322n, 333, 338n, 339n, 344n,
    360, 369n, 455n, 469, 476, 480, 491n,
    492, 500n, 566n, 584n, 598n, 603,
    614n, 618n, 630n, 634n, 699n, 744n,
    790n, 796n, 815n, 837n, 947, 973n,
    1009n, 1030, 1032n, 1067n, 1143n,
    1147n, 1149n, 1187n, 1191n, 1212n,
    1231n, 1275n, 1276n, 1295n, 1299n,
    1307, 1324n, 1329n, 1338n, 1341
  Arab-Israeli dispute, 628, 632, 683-684,
    722, 724, 727, 950
  British-French military intervention,
    1021
  Egypt:
    United States, relations with, 668-
      669
    War damages resolution, 1337
  Israel:
    United States, relations with, 682-
      683, 1090-1091, 1094, 1230-
      1231, 1242-1243, 1272n
    Western military aid to, 197-198,
      504n, 542-543, 562-563, 653
  Israeli military intervention, 793, 803-
    805, 808, 821-825, 829, 831, 867,
    877-879, 885-886, 888-893, 922n,
    951, 976, 1249n
  Negotiations, 259, 412, 669-670, 674,
    748, 950
  Oil supplies, 1145n, 1195
  Pilots, 483-484, 508
  Soviet intervention, possible, 1123-
    1124, 1274
  Suez Canal Company nationalization:
    Economic sanctions, 347-349
    Security Council appeal, 335, 420,
      424, 438, 560, 562, 564
    Security Council discussion, 681,
      683, 695, 697, 705, 714, 750
  Suez Canal Conference, 204n, 212, 254,
    256
  Suez Canal dues, 414-415, 458, 746-
    747
  Troop withdrawal, 1057, 1065-1067,
    1089-1090, 1093-1094, 1198-1199
  United Kingdom, 762, 1047
  U.S. civilian evacuation, 688n
  Users' association proposal, 374-375,
    448, 507

Roux, Henri, 715, 1253, 1284
Rowan, Leslie, 38, 119n
Russell, Richard B., 38n, 110n, 140-143, 188, 190-191, 193, 196
Ryan, Robert J., 688n

Saad, Ahmad, 493 al-Sabri, Ali, 212, 601, 624, 668-670, 674, 786, 1028, 1087, 1154, 1164
Said, Gen. Nuri, 168n, 402, 418, 485, 599-600, 620-621, 630-631, 708
Said Pasha, Mohammed, 2
St. Laurent, Louis, 498, 940-941, 982-983, 1297
al-Salim al-Sahah, Shaik Abdullah, 147
Salisbury, 5th Marquess of (Robert Arthur James Gascoyne-Cecil), 100n, 328-329, 520-522, 591, 1116, 1151-1152, 1163, 1197
Salt, Barbara, 335, 411, 420, 560, 564, 600-601
Saltonstall, Leverett, 188, 194, 196
Sanafir Island, 1199, 1341
Sanger, Richard H., 20-21
Sarper, Selim, 675
Sarraj, Abd al-Hamid, 1317
Saud, King, 275, 294-295, 301, 402, 541, 592, 1137, 1165, 1179, 1316, 1320
    British-French military intervention, 273-275
    Negotiations, 296, 299, 394-395
    Suez Canal Company nationalization, 220, 273, 592
        Economic sanctions, 347, 349, 394n, 395
    U.S. oil aid to Western Europe, 1165, 1179, 1200
Saudi Arabia (see also Anderson Mission (Saudi Arabia); Arab states; Saudi and Saudi Arabia subheadings under other subjects), 89, 97n, 113, 120, 143, 274, 346, 468, 485, 593, 642, 97-¾2, 1106-1107
    Egypt, relations with, 141, 246, 273, 311, 401, 541, 591, 605, 619, 1101, 1180, 1192, 1285, 1316-1317, 1320
    Egypt-Syria-Saudi Arabia (ESS) Pact, 592-593, 1251, 1254-1255
    Oil supplies, 155, 169n, 200, 343, 384, 389, 972, 1072, 1074-1075
        U.S. aid to Western Europe, 1076, 1129, 1131, 1147-1148, 1153, 1165, 1179, 1189, 1200, 1202, 1212-1213

Saudi Arabia—Continued
    Political situation, 401-402, 541, 641, 984
    United Kingdom, relations with, 346, 853
    United States, relations with, 142, 686, 1089, 1137-1139, 1153, 1297
    Egyptian influence, 87, 89-90
Schulz, Col. Robert L., 1040
Seager, Cedric, 1236-1238
Seaton, Fred A., 53-54, 874n, 974n
Sebald, William J., 1187n
al-Shabandar, Moussa, 949-951
Sharett, Moshe, 138n, 1252
Sharm al-Sheikh, 1341-1342
Shaw, John F., 1236n, 1275n, 1299n
Shepilov, Dimitri T., 225, 270, 272, 519, 601, 618, 649-650, 660, 694, 710
    International canal system proposals, 203, 210-211, 221, 224-226, 237-240, 707
    Soviet-U.S. joint intervention proposal, 991-992, 1006
    Suez Canal Conference, 206-207, 209, 216, 223-224, 245-246
Sherwood, Robert K., 230n
Shiloah, Reuven, 51-52, 136, 178, 179n, 465, 499, 606, 682, 822-823, 1251
    Arab-Israeli dispute, 727, 731-733
    Israeli military intervention, 53, 110, 821-822, 824, 925, 927
    Troop withdrawal, 1065-1067, 1089, 1094, 1198, 1242
    U.S.-Israeli relations, 51, 498-500, 609-610, 1231n, 1243, 1274
Short, Dewey, 188, 192
Simmons, John F., 458, 1098
Sinai, Maj. Dov, 814, 883-884
Sinai Peninsula. See Israeli military intervention; Troop withdrawal; U.N. Emergency Force.
Sisco, Joseph J., 1295n, 1322n
Skean, Harold L., 556
Slim, Mongi, 949
Smith, H. Alexander, 164, 169, 188, 192, 194, 198n, 588
Snyder, Murray, 188
Sobolev, Arkadi Aleksandrovich, 896, 992
Socony-Vacuum, 468
Sohm, Earl D., 1030, 1047, 1147, 1195
South Africa, 43, 121

Soviet intervention, possible, 28, 381, 387-388, 837-838, 848, 855, 945, 1000-1001, 1045, 1106, 1228
Arab positions, 1052
British-French military intervention and, 1020
British position, 61, 98, 526, 544, 1013, 1047, 1061-1062
Bulganin notes, 993-994, 1003n, 1005, 1016, 1018, 1023, 1102
Cease-fire and, 995-996, 1024, 1028
Egypt, military aid to, 1044, 1067
British position, 1124
Egyptian position, 1096-1097, 1149, 1156-1157, 1164, 1219, 1307
French position, 1106, 1118, 1136
Israeli position, 1245
Soviet position, 992-994, 1006
U.S. position, 79n, 88, 96n, 99, 387, 863, 923, 1006, 1047-1048, 1052, 1079-1080, 1102, 1106, 1125-1128, 1141, 1246
Egyptian position, 201, 899, 1027-1028, 1087
French position, 8, 526, 544, 595, 901, 931-932, 1003, 1023-1024, 1136
Hungary, 1006-1007, 1016-1018
Iran and, 201, 313, 972, 995
Israeli position, 1107-1108, 1161, 1245-1247
Joint Chiefs of Staff position, 845, 968-972, 1030
Jordan and, 1019, 1102, 1157
National Security Council discussion, 1079-1081
Security Council appeal and, 850
Soviet position, 1097, 1087
Soviet-U.S. joint military intervention proposal, 990-996, 1000, 1003n, 1005-1007, 1032, 1111-1112
Special National Intelligence Estimate, 1018-1020
Syria and, 971, 987, 989, 995, 1013-1014, 1019, 1079-1080, 1101-1102, 1131, 1157, 1228
French position, 1106, 1117-1118, 1136
Israeli position, 1108, 1246, 1274
Tripartite heads of government meeting, 1043, 1045, 1047-1048
Troop withdrawal and, 1058, 1101-1102
U.N. Emergency Force and, 1028, 1061, 1083

Soviet intervention, possible—Continued
U.N. position, 1157
U.N. response, 1081, 1086, 1228
U.S.-British military evaluation, 1045, 1047-1048
U.S. civilian defense plans, 1086
U.S. mobilization, 998-1000, 1035-1036
U.S. NATO obligations and, 1006, 1014, 1017, 1024, 1025n
U.S. public statements, 1007-1008
U.S. support for British-French military intervention and, 98, 100n, 102, 133, 169, 174-175, 187, 509, 655
Soviet Union (see also Eighteen-Power proposal under Suez Canal, international system proposals; Soviet intervention, possible; Soviet and Soviet Union subheadings under other subjects), 225, 601, 638, 656, 972
France, relations with, 76-77, 496, 694, 1003, 1005, 1220n, 1304
Political situation, 1153
United Kingdom, relations with, 42, 496, 694, 1003, 1005
Spaak, Paul Henri, 320, 345, 412, 515, 601, 618, 649, 660, 674, 707, 709-712
Spain, 97n, 165, 212, 219, 516, 547
International canal system proposals, 210, 252-253, 259-261, 441-442, 458, 463
Users' association proposal, 505, 517, 537-538, 545, 555
Special National Intelligence Estimates:
SNIE 11-9-56, 1018-1020
SNIE 30-3-56, 78-93
SNIE 30-4-56, 382-391
SNIE 30-5-56, 524-528
SNIE 30-6-56, 1020-1021
Spender, Sir Percy, 511, 528-529, 532, 555
Standard Oil of New Jersey, 79n
Stassen, Harold E., 331, 909-911, 913-914, 1081, 1084, 1086, 1227-1228
Stelle, Charles C., 342
Stephens, Thomas E., 405
Stevenson, Adlai, 907
Stewart, Gordon M., 1087n
Stewart, Hugh A., 53n, 873n, 974n
Stikker, Dirk, 1275n
Strauss, Adm. Lewis L., 172
Streibert, Theodore C., 1083
Stump, Adm. Felix B., 845, 1035
Sudan, 45, 87, 120

Suez Canal (*see also* Pilots; Suez Canal headings and subheadings):
Clearance:
British-French participation, 1012, 1016*n*, 1026, 1028, 1058-1059, 1155, 1289*n*, 1292-1295, 1301-1303, 1310-1312, 1322
British position, 1015, 1016*n*, 1039, 1124, 1278-1279, 1288, 1289*n*, 1311-1312
Egyptian position, 1149, 1155, 1308, 1318-1319
French position, 1012, 1016*n*, 1292, 1303
British position, 1174, 1176-1177, 1183, 1197*n*, 1202, 1205-1206, 1218-1219, 1232-1233, 1239*n*, 1282
Egyptian position, 1185, 1186, 1206, 1307, 1318
Financing, 1275, 1282, 1329-1332
French position, 1012, 1016*n*, 1041, 1292, 1303
Troop withdrawal and, 1174-1177, 1183, 1185-1186, 1197*n*, 1202, 1205-1206, 1232-1233, 1239*n*, 1282-1284, 1308, 1333-1335
U.N. Emergency Force role, 1039, 1155, 1205, 1312
U.S. position, 1088, 1175-1176, 1183, 1222-1223, 1225-1227, 1229, 1283-1284, 1308, 1322, 1333-1335
Users' association proposal and, 1275, 1289*n*, 1330
Concession agreements, 2, 16, 47, 351-352, 361, 424, 451
Egyptian alleged obstruction of, 955-956, 1106, 1318, 1337
Egyptian operation (*see also* Israel: Shipping restrictions; Suez Canal, international system proposals), 1, 243, 648
As basis for military intervention, 28, 39, 106, 430, 433
British position, 10
Egyptian position, 56, 106, 134, 162, 184, 393-394, 442, 679
Legal situation and, 82
Political use, 83-86, 95, 134, 679
Israeli position, 1244
U.S. position, 186, 190, 222, 236, 292, 679, 909
Saudi position, 273, 302-303

Suez Canal—Continued
Egyptian operation—Continued
Soviet position, 224
Suez Committee study of, 307-308, 317
U.S. economic sanctions and, 143*n*, 510
U.S. position, 28, 39, 47, 79, 83, 95, 109, 185-186, 239, 404, 427, 432, 629
Future development financing, 83, 217-218, 647, 786, 1331
British position, 10
Egyptian position, 650, 666, 677
French position, 755
Income from, 65, 82-83, 194, 371, 570
Aswan Dam financing, 1, 55, 57, 79, 82-83, 173, 189, 268, 418, 570, 754
Physical maintenance (*see also* Clearance *above*), 352, 362-364, 371-372, 399, 428
Traffic control, 352, 362, 364, 371-372, 399, 428, 445, 591
Suez Canal, international system proposals (*see also* Egyptian operation *under* Suez Canal; Users' association proposal):
Arbitral commission, 229, 233, 252, 303, 445-446, 677, 679-680
Belgian proposal, 707
British position, 5, 10, 42, 71, 73, 104, 146, 218, 1175
Congressional-Presidential meeting, 190
Constantinople Convention as framework for, 58-59, 81, 85, 105, 109, 125, 168, 228-229, 250-251, 351-352, 361-363, 370, 374
Egyptian operation, 239, 292-294
British Labour Party position, 474-475
Egyptian position, 445, 669-670, 783
Indian proposal, 244, 268, 294, 326, 645-646, 665, 669-670, 674, 706, 783
Soviet position, 225, 238, 326, 660
Spanish proposal, 252-253, 259, 441-442, 458, 463
Egyptian position, 201, 393, 415, 445-446, 666-667, 676-680, 786
Eighteen-Power proposal, 244-245, 250-253, 291-294, 303, 325

Suez Canal, international system
    proposals—Continued
  Eighteen-Power proposal—Continued
    British position, 257, 409, 531, 641,
      643
    Egyptian position, 375-376, 529,
      1256
    Eisenhower statements, 315, 333-
      334, 340-341, 373, 446
    French position, 490, 531, 567, 572,
      624, 642-643, 655, 1258
    Indian position, 254-256
    Security Council appeal and, 420-
      421, 425-426, 519
    Soviet position, 245, 270, 326-327
    Spanish position, 252-253, 259-261
    U.S. position, 268-269, 366-367,
      512n, 640, 1170, 1276
    Users' association proposal and, 409,
      429, 490, 531
  Five-Power proposal. See Eighteen-
    Power proposal above.
  French position, 71, 218
  Future development financing, 10, 217-
    218, 650, 666, 786
  Indian position, 243-244, 646
  Indian proposal. See under Egyptian
    operation above.
  International control, 218, 1175
    Egyptian position, 106, 134, 184,
      333, 340, 375-376, 443-445, 677,
      695, 699
    French position, 101-102, 114, 624,
      920, 966, 997
    Soviet position, 238-240, 660, 707
    Tripartite notes, 45, 58-59, 145
    U.S.committee proposal and, 966,
      997
    U.S. position, 85, 95, 101, 105, 114,
      135, 163, 190, 240, 310-311, 640,
      651, 1168
  Israeli shipping restrictions and, 137-
    138
  Private operation, 651-653
  Sanctions for operation interference,
    218, 367, 679-680, 693
  Saudi position, 291-294, 303
  Soviet participation, 42, 71, 88-89
  Soviet position, 203, 210-211, 221,
    224-225, 238, 262
  Spanish proposal, 252-253, 259, 441-
    442, 458, 463
  Suez Canal Company, compensation
    for, 217, 251

Suez Canal, international system
    proposals—Continued
  Suez Canal dues, 198-199, 291, 303,
    393, 415, 445, 646, 666
  Supervisory board proposals, 190, 199,
    217, 222-223, 228-230, 232, 236,
    239, 241, 251, 294, 392
  Tripartite position, 43, 45, 58-59, 145,
    161n, 203n, 208, 211, 215, 243
  U.N. role, 43, 59, 183, 194, 221-223,
    243-244, 367, 679-680, 712
    British position, 15, 28, 37n
  U.S. position, 63, 85, 95-96, 101, 105,
    114, 170, 173-174, 198-199, 221,
    1168-1169
  U.S. press coverage, 651, 653
  U.S. proposal (see also Eighteen-Power
    proposal above), 227-229, 232, 238
Suez Canal Company (see also Economic
    sanctions under *T Suez Canal Company
    nationalization; Pilots; Suez Canal dues), 2-
    3, 16, 114, 165-166, 243, 405, 418,
    592
  Concession agreements, 2, 16, 47, 351-
    352, 361, 424, 451
  International canal system proposals
    and, 114, 217, 251, 534, 667, 680
Suez Canal Company nationalization:
  Arab positions, 79, 82-84, 89-91, 168-
    169, 174, 264, 605
  Asian reactions, 92
  Baghdad Pact, impact on, 266
  British condemnations of, 4, 37, 39, 83
  British-French draft Security Council
    resolution, 407-408, 412, 579, 600-
    601, 638-639, 691, 713-714, 1256,
    1261
    Egyptian position, 707
    French position, 576, 698, 716-718
    Soviet veto, 28, 312-313, 323, 328,
      376, 389, 427, 568, 583, 590,
      701, 715-719, 721
    British position, 521-522, 856
    Egyptian position, 696
    U.S. position, 425-427, 618, 635,
      651-653, 660, 710, 758
  British Labour Party position, 231-232
  British public statements, 5
  Commonwealth position, 43, 92
  Compensation, 366, 786-787, 1331
    British position, 10
    Egyptian announcement, 1, 6, 36
    Egyptian position, 55-57, 442
    Legal situation and, 16, 82

Suez Canal Company nationalization—
Continued
Compensation—Continued
Saudi position, 347-348
U.S. position, 65
Eastern European reactions, 84
Economic sanctions (*see also* Suez Canal
dues), 29, 79-80, 83, 320, 549, 581
Arab response, possible, 234
British-French military intervention
and, 462, 586, 755
British position, 14, 29*n*, 37-38, 43-
45, 204, 234, 278, 305, 323-324,
474, 641, 738-739, 744-745
Canal boycott proposals (*see also*
Alternate sources *and* U.S. aid to
Western Europe *under* Oil
supplies), 507, 568
British position, 44, 578
U.S. position, 434, 437, 439, 448-
449, 457, 472, 492*n*, 510, 578-
579
Egyptian position, 134, 310, 311*n*,
368, 1150, 1316
French position, 8, 14, 44, 417, 457,
462, 507, 568, 586
Saudi position, 289-290, 302, 311*n*,
347-349, 394*n*, 395
Soviet response, possible, 234
Tripartite discussions, 276-279, 298-
299
U.S. position, 14, 16-17, 27, 43*n*, 66-
68, 97, 143, 266, 300-301, 324,
395*n*, 434, 437, 439, 449, 509-
510, 673, 1285, 1300, 1309
Egyptian announcement, 1, 6, 57, 82,
669
Egyptian public opinion, 82, 106
France, impact on, 7-8, 14, 41, 83, 110,
189-190
Indian position, 593
Iraqi position, 91-92
Israeli position, 51, 93
Italian position, 29, 529
Joint Chiefs of Staff position, 151 156
Legality of, 157-158, 160*n*, 206, 243,
273, 302, 528-529
British position, 407, 531, 739
Egyptian position, 55-56, 82, 375,
442
French position, 424
U.S. position, 6, 13, 16-18, 39, 106,
109, 174, 185-186, 194, 208, 424,
944

Suez Canal Company nationalization—
Continued
NATO discussion proposals, 7, 13, 24,
26, 36, 121
NATO, impact on, 39, 264-265
Saudi position, 220, 273, 302, 592
Security Council appeal (*see also*
Security Council discussion *below*),
43, 182, 243, 335, 337, 376-377,
511, 529, 532, 538, 572
Arab-Israeli dispute and, 336, 422
Arab states, Nasser leadership of,
363-364, 431, 436
British-French letter proposal, 439-
440, 455-456, 464, 466, 469,
476-477, 481, 483, 557
British-French military intervention
and:
British position, 313, 320-321, 328,
407, 521-522, 572
French position, 420, 423, 576,
585, 655
U.S. position, 313, 323, 337, 342,
389, 421-422, 426, 430, 471,
527, 590, 618, 629, 633, 635,
643
British position, 4, 175, 312, 315,
319-321, 328, 336, 406-408, 412,
473-474, 532, 549, 560-562, 590
British public opinion, 406, 475, 590
Egyptian initiation, possible, 192,
413, 423, 432, 436, 439
Egyptian position, 134
Eighteen-Power proposal and, 420-
421, 425-426, 519
French position, 175, 406, 417, 420-
423, 561-562, 565, 599, 920
Israeli position, 465-466, 582-583
Pakistani position, 531
Soviet initiation, British opinion,
560, 564-565, 569, 640-641
Soviet intervention and, 850
Soviet position, 159
U.S.-British relations and, 633-635
U.S. position, 13, 25, 36, 49, 52, 175,
191-192, 194, 286, 312, 322-323,
335-338, 356, 370, 376, 397-398,
411-413, 419, 466, 476, 540, 599,
711
Users' association proposal and, 363,
371, 411-413, 513, 517-519, 530,
549, 564, 577, 590, 711
British position, 476, 481, 484,
535, 553, 640-641

Suez Canal Company nationalization—
Continued
Security Council appeal—Continued
Users' association proposal and, 363,
371, 411-413, 513, 517-519,—
Continued
French position, 476, 481, 507,
531, 535, 553
Suez Canal Conference discussion,
531-532, 536-538, 553
Security Council discussion (see also
British-French draft Security
Council resolution above;
Negotiations), 638, 674-675, 700-
701
Arab participation, 607, 645, 658-
659, 691, 700
British position, 596, 643, 645, 647,
658-659, 738, 1261
Egyptian item, 571, 576, 582
Egyptian position, 650, 695-697
Eisenhower participation, 626
French position, 576-577, 596, 601,
643, 645, 655, 658, 691
Israeli participation, 576, 583, 596,
598n, 606-607, 645, 658-659,
683, 691, 700, 727
Israeli shipping restrictions, 583,
596-597, 607, 645n, 683, 727,
812, 823
Joint Chiefs of Staff position, 749-
750
Lodge draft resolution, 494-495
Participants, 596, 601, 618, 638, 645,
658-659, 691
Arab positions, 645n
Procedure, 571-572, 576-577, 579-
582, 644-645, 647, 649-650, 652,
715
Tripartite consultations, 579, 601,
639-645, 647-649, 715-718
U.S.-Belgian discussion, 709-712
U.S. position, 576, 579-582, 598n,
645, 652, 658-659, 661-662, 683,
701-702
Soviet position, 157-158, 160n, 206,
264
Tripartite discussions, 3-5, 8, 10-11,
13-16, 29-30
Tripartite public statements, 15, 26-27,
40-41, 58-60, 63-64, 72-74, 104,
115, 126-127
Turkish reactions, 91

Suez Canal Company nationalization—
Continued
United Kingdom, impact on, 6, 83, 108,
110, 189-190
U.S. oil aid to Western Europe and,
663, 672-673, 684-685
U.S. position, 6, 17-18, 103-104, 111,
115-116, 123
U.S. press reports, 458-459, 461-463,
499-500, 651, 653
U.S. public statements, 6-7
Suez Canal Conferences, 128, 212-219,
221-229, 232-246, 248-262, 267-273,
276-281, 516, 520, 528-532, 536-538,
540, 552-555
Agenda, 203-204, 511-512
Asian countries coordination, 244-245
British position, 4, 65, 71, 73, 99, 104,
113, 147, 203-204, 213, 269, 1256
Chairmanship, 204-205, 207, 209, 211,
213
Congressional participation, 164, 188-
189, 198
Constantinople Convention signatories
participation, 4, 30, 41n, 46, 48, 59,
63, 69, 72-73, 94, 104, 120-121
U.S. position, 73, 81, 85, 101, 109
Eastern European participation, 72, 158
Egyptian participation, 43, 96-97, 121,
134, 161-163, 165, 188-189, 212,
537, 593
U.S. position, 41, 48-49, 63, 113
Egyptian position, 134, 161-162, 201-
202
French position, 41-42, 71, 104, 112-
113, 132, 217, 519, 567, 1256
French public opinion, 569, 572
Indonesian draft communiqué, 268-269
Invitation procedure, 40-41, 59-60, 73,
104, 112-113, 121-122, 163
Israeli participation, 179
Israeli position, 137
Israeli shipping restrictions, 179
Location, 4, 49, 104, 112-113, 124, 158,
207
Nasser proposal, discussion of, 493,
502-504, 511, 553
National Security Council discussion,
165-169, 325-327
Participants, 134
Approaches to, 132-133, 144-146,
149-150, 161-163
British position, 30, 40, 43, 46, 60,
73, 94, 96-97, 104, 113, 120, 122

Suez Canal Conferences—Continued
Participants—Continued
French position, 46, 60, 72, 104, 113, 214
Soviet position, 158, 207, 214
Tripartite position, 120-121
U.S. position, 4, 41, 46, 49, 59, 73, 101, 104, 111, 209, 505
Reconvening of, 244, 493, 495, 497, 1256
Rules of procedure, 96, 99, 124, 207, 211, 213-214, 269, 519
Saudi position, 282, 300-301
Soviet participation, 42, 71, 132, 163, 165
Approaches, 121, 132-133, 144-145, 149-150, 156-160
British position, 42-43, 71, 99, 104, 113, 132
Soviet position, 160n, 207
U.S. position, 41-43, 48, 71, 73, 80, 96
Soviet position, 157-158, 160n, 206-207, 213-214, 221, 445
Soviet role, 218-219, 253-254, 257, 304, 326, 355, 397, 649
Statements, 556-557
Timing, 49, 104, 111-112
British position, 60, 97, 99, 104, 112-113
Tripartite-Australian   consultations, 216-218
Tripartite statement of principles, 105, 119-120, 122-125, 203, 205, 216-217
U.S. position, 63, 69-70, 94-97, 101, 109, 183, 234
U.S. public statements, 506n
U.S.-Soviet discussions, 156-160, 206-209, 221-227, 238-240
Suez Canal dues:
Constantinople Convention provisions for, 28, 83, 173, 361-362
Egyptian position, 369
International canal system proposals, 198-199, 291, 303, 393, 415, 445, 646, 666
Users' association proposal, 361-362, 364, 371, 410, 414-415, 424, 428-429, 434, 437, 457
British position, 667, 691, 700, 706, 720, 738-739, 744-745, 752-753, 1261-1262

Suez Canal dues—Continued
Users' association proposal—Continued
Egyptian position, 570, 677, 679, 690-691
French position, 691, 749, 755-756, 1261-1262
Required payment, 513-514, 549-550, 574-575, 584-585, 634, 674, 735, 759
British position, 550, 602, 647, 674
French position, 568, 574-575, 602, 625, 647, 655-656, 754
U.S. position, 513-514, 535, 667, 693, 700, 706, 734-737, 744-745, 758-760, 920, 1261
Withholding proposals:
British position, 14, 29, 43-44, 60, 103, 124, 305, 409, 422-424
Egyptian canal blockage, possible:
British position, 233, 298, 414, 416-417, 764 French position, 496, 755
U.S. position, 28, 85, 130, 234, 446, 450, 456-457, 464, 470, 472, 478, 514, 574-575, 584, 591, 737, 755
French position, 44, 103, 123, 417, 456, 461
Negotiations and, 741-743
U.S. oil aid to Western Europe and, 414, 423-424, 459-460, 481, 578
U.S. position, 44, 68n, 103, 123-124, 194, 300
Users' association proposal:
British position, 531-532, 535, 549-550, 674, 741, 743, 920, 1261-1262
French position, 531, 743, 754-756, 920, 1261-1262
U.S. position, 550, 674, 920
Suez Committee:
Aide-mémoire, 441-442
Compensation, 366
Egyptian press campaign, 399, 416
Establishment of, 216-217
Australian position, 235
French proposal, 270-272
Indian position, 271, 288
Indonesian position, 267-268, 271-272
New Zealand proposal, 261n, 262n, 267-270, 272, 284, 316
Pakistani position, 530

Suez Committee—Continued
  Establishment of—Continued
    Soviet position, 270, 272, 501, 512*n*, 519
  Heads of Agreement, 307, 317, 338*n*, 339*n*
  Mandate of, 308, 316-318, 327, 338
  Membership, 237, 241, 250, 253, 259, 261-262, 276, 280
    British position, 235, 249, 256-257
  Menzies chairmanship, 256-257, 259, 272-273, 280
  Morale, 399, 419
  Negotiations, 284-285, 305-306, 367-368, 375-376, 392-394, 399-400, 416-417, 423*n*, 442-445, 1256
    British position, 308, 312, 316, 327, 360
    Egyptian position, 311*n*, 367-368
    French position, 308, 316, 327, 353, 1258
    U.S. position, 317-318, 338-339, 355-356, 369-370, 501, 503
  U.S. estimation, 306-307
  U.S. public statement, 458, 463
  U.S.-Saudi discussion, 287-288
  U.S. separate negotiations, 465
  Users' association proposal and, 399
Suhrawardy, Husayn, 550, 569-570, 573
Sukarno, Achmed, 267
Svendsen, Lars U., 603, 617
Sweden, 215, 222, 482, 519, 561, 617, 1009, 1145*n*, 1292
  Suez Canal Conference, 97*n*, 104, 212, 516, 532, 537, 554, 590
  Suez Committee, 253, 261, 307
  U.N. Emergency Force, 953, 979, 1053, 1096*n*
Sweetwater Canal, 1020, 1069, 1078
Switzerland, 1024-1025, 1205
Syd Neguib el-Rawi, 296*n*
Syria (*see also* Arab-Israeli dispute; Arab states), 296*n*, 485, 609, 963, 1053
  British and French civilians in, 353, 377, 417, 475
  Economic situation, 1306
  Egypt, relations with, 141, 401, 587, 1101, 1314, 1317
  Egypt-Syria-Saudi Arabia (ESS) Pact, 592-593, 1251, 1254-1255
  Iraq, relations with, 92, 386, 1314

Syria—Continued
  Jordan-Egypt-Syria tripartite military agreement, 775-776, 788, 800, 808-809, 811-812, 821, 843-844, 857, 966-967, 973, 1067
  Oil supplies, 52, 67, 90, 148, 155, 168*n*, 169*n*, 384, 971, 974*n*, 1007, 1222, 1306
  Political situation, 386-387, 642, 784, 930, 971, 1080, 1222, 1323
    Egyptian influence, 87, 90, 386, 401, 1101, 1191, 1208, 1246, 1251
    Egyptian position, 1317
    Israeli position, 1108, 1246
    Soviet possible intervention and, 971, 987, 989, 995, 1013-1014, 1019, 1079-1080, 1101-1102, 1131, 1157, 1228
    French position, 1106, 1117-1118, 1136
    Israeli position, 1108, 1246, 1274
  Soviet military aid to, 1245-1246, 1251-1252, 1317
  United Kingdom, relations with, 346

Tangier, 680
TAPLINE, 90, 389, 1148, 1166
Tappin, John L., 418
Taylor, Gen. Maxwell D., 21, 117-118, 154-156, 342, 749-750, 845
Thailand, 120, 963, 1053
Thomas, Charles Sparks, 7
Timmons, Benson E.L., 339*n*, 344*n*, 1009*n*, 1143*n*
Tiran, Straits of, 180, 610, 812, 1160, 1199, 1232, 1241, 1341
Treasury, U.S. Department of the, 694*n*, 1013, 1032, 1050, 1300*n*
Treaties:
  Anglo-Egyptian Suez Canal Zone Base Agreement, *1954*, 18, 56, 190, 204, 519, 641, 655, 711, 750, 764, 886
  Anglo-Jordanian Treaty of Alliance, *1948*, 620-621, 708, 722-725, 728-730, 733, 764, 768, 818, 846, 856, 904
  Constantinople Convention, *1888*, 2-3, 45
    British position, 4, 30, 73, 94, 104, 407, 886
    Egyptian position, 28, 56, 174, 190, 192, 244, 333, 375, 427, 442, 530, 1319
    French position, 72, 424, 955

Treaties—Continued
  Constantinople   Convention—
      Continued
    Indian position, 243-244
    International canal system proposals,
        58-59, 81, 85, 105, 109, 125,
        168, 228-229, 250-251
    Israeli shipping restrictions and, 51-
        52, 683, 843-844, 1289
    Non-discrimination, 515
    Panama Canal and, 65
    Soviet Union as signatory, 42, 99,
        159n
    Suez Canal Company nationalization
        and, 18, 243, 407, 424, 529, 886,
        944
    Suez Canal Conference and, 30, 41n,
        46, 48, 63, 69, 72-73, 81, 85, 94,
        104, 109
      Tripartite position, 4, 59, 120-121
    Suez Canal dues and, 28, 83, 173,
        361-362
    Supervision provisions, 646
    Update proposals, 226, 244
      Egyptian position, 134, 184
      Soviet position, 224-225
    U.S. position, 6, 36, 109
    Users' association proposal, 351-352,
        361-363, 370-371, 374, 377, 392,
        410-412, 451
    Warships provision, 27
    Western rights under, 18-19, 35, 415,
        427-429, 512
  Hay-Pauncefote Treaty, 19, 361-362
  Iraqi-Jordan Mutual Defense Treaty,
      1947, 630
Trevelyan, Sir Humphrey, 4, 778
Tripartite Declaration, 1950, 1089
  British-French military intervention,
      873, 901
  Israeli military intervention:
    British position, 728, 731, 764, 818,
        829-830, 841, 847, 849, 854, 857,
        904
    French position, 829-830, 904, 1268-
        1269
    U.S. position, 621, 723, 729-730,
        801-802, 817, 829-830, 834-836,
        839-840, 849-850, 860-861, 892-
        893, 901, 904-908, 916n
Troianovskii, Oleg A., 206n, 237
Troop withdrawal (see also Cease-fire):
  Arab-Israeli dispute and, 1174
  Border incidents and, 1090, 1341-1343

Troop withdrawal—Continued
  British assets in Egypt and, 1279, 1282
  British political situation and, 1150-
      1151, 1162-1163, 1174-1175, 1182,
      1210n, 1220-1221, 1233, 1280,
      1282
  British position, 980, 1171, 1174, 1183,
      1196, 1204, 1210-1211, 1233-1234,
      1238-1239, 1278-1280
  Egyptian position, 978n, 1051, 1149,
      1186
  Eisenhower letter to Ben Gurion, 1057,
      1062-1064, 1068, 1089-1090
  French position, 1041, 1054-1055, 1182,
      1194, 1220, 1232
  General Assembly discussion, 1041,
      1059
  General Assembly Resolution 997
      (ES-I), 932-933, 946, 949, 981,
      1126, 1190
  General Assembly Resolution 999
      (ES-I), 959-960, 963, 976, 980, 986,
      1126
  General Assembly Resolution 1002
      (ES-I) (Afro-Asian), 1031, 1053-1054,
      1060-1061
  General Assembly Resolution 1120 (XI)
      (Afro-Asian), 1178-1179, 1182-
      1186, 1192-1193, 1196, 1204
  Israel, U.S. economic sanctions against,
      1048, 1050, 1057
  Israeli political situation, 1328
  Israeli position, 1066, 1069, 1090-1091,
      1093-1095, 1107-1110, 1160, 1174,
      1190, 1199, 1244, 1247, 1325-1328,
      1336
  Negotiations and, 1288
  Security Council discussion, 1041
  Soviet intervention and, 1058, 1101-
      1102
  Suez Canal clearance and, 1174-1176,
      1185-1186, 1283-1284, 1308, 1333-
      1335
    British position, 1174, 1183, 1196,
        1197n, 1202, 1205-1206, 1232-
        1233, 1239n, 1282
    Egyptian position, 1185-1186, 1206
  Tripartite heads of government
      meeting and, 1052, 1056, 1110,
      1113, 1117-1118
  U.N. Emergency Force and, 981, 1069,
      1099, 1129, 1156, 1206

Troop withdrawal—Continued
  U.N. Emergency Force and—Continued
    British position, 1013, 1033, 1123-
      1125, 1132, 1143, 1176, 1206,
      1232
    Egyptian position, 1157
    French position, 1012, 1033-1034,
      1041, 1055, 1105, 1132
    Israeli position, 1059, 1095, 1159-
      1160, 1198, 1205, 1215-1217
    U.N. position, 981, 1156-1157
  United Kingdom, U.S. economic aid to,
    1166-1167, 1169-1170, 1179, 1280
  U.S.-British relations, 1181, 1196-1197,
    1201, 1204
  U.S. draft Security Council resolutions,
    831, 847, 860n, 863, 868
    British-French veto, 881-882, 904,
      909, 929
    Soviet position, 882, 887
  U.S. oil aid to Western Europe and,
    1115, 1188-1189, 1194-1195, 1200,
    1202-1203, 1212-1213
  U.S. position, 945, 1000, 1031, 1048,
    1050, 1055, 1065-1067, 1094, 1127,
    1177-1178, 1199, 1231, 1240
Troxel, Oliver L., 1236n
Trucial Coast States, 155
Tsiang, Tingfu F., 896
Tunisia, 101, 346, 388, 641, 643
Turkey (see also Baghdad Pact; Eighteen-
  Power proposal under Suez Canal,
  international system proposals), 91,
  864, 998-1000, 1080-1081, 1314,
  1317, 1321
  International canal system proposals,
    245, 535, 537, 545, 555, 602, 617,
    641
  Pipeline proposals, 172, 437
  Suez Canal Conference, 97n, 212, 219,
    516, 535, 538
Twining, Gen. Nathan F., 21, 264n, 749-
  750, 845
Tyler, William R., 212, 213n, 260, 507,
  508n, 516-517, 528n, 546, 639n, 658,
  709, 714, 1023, 1025n, 1046n, 1104,
  1139n, 1284, 1302n, 1303

U.N. Emergency Force:
  Arab-Israeli dispute and, 1133
  Arab positions, 1044
  British-French military intervention
    and, 947-948, 954, 956, 975, 982-
    983, 985, 987

U.N. Emergency Force—Continued
  British-French participation, 1028, 1059
    British position, 1039, 1082
    Egyptian position, 965, 1133
    French position, 955, 1012, 1029n,
      1033-1034
  British position, 946, 980, 1033-1034,
    1039, 1117, 1125, 1132-1133,
    1150-1151, 1153-1155
  Canadian position, 933, 938, 940-942,
    953-954
  Cease-fire and, 964-965, 981, 1012,
    1026-1027
    British position, 946, 1010-1011,
      1013, 1015, 1039
    Egyptian consent, necessity of, 954,
      981, 1117-1118, 1154
    Egyptian position, 964-965, 975, 979,
      1011, 1027, 1084, 1100n, 1127,
      1133, 1157, 1319, 1335
  Financing, 1205
  French position, 946, 955, 1010-1012,
    1033-1035, 1055, 1105, 1118,
    1132-1133, 1139-1140
  Gaza Strip, 1340
  General Assembly Resolutions:
    998 (ES-I) (Canadian), 957n, 959-960,
      964, 976, 980-981, 986
    1000 (ES-I), 980-981, 1011
    1001 (ES-I) (Seven-Power), 1053-1055
    1121 (XI), 1193
    1122 (XI) (Financing), 1205
  Indian position, 1058n
  Israeli participation, 965
  Israeli position, 1038, 1095, 1217, 1242,
    1244, 1274
  Israeli shipping restrictions and, 1190,
    1244
  Participants, 976, 978-979, 986, 999,
    1028, 1033-1034, 1039, 1050,
    1058n, 1242, 1274
  Egyptian position, 965, 1096n, 1149-
    1150, 1154-1155
  Security Council discussion, 1035
  Sinai Peninsula, 1160, 1216-1217, 1241,
    1288, 1322-1323, 1325-1326, 1341
  Soviet intervention and, 1028, 1061,
    1083
  Soviet participation, 971, 1028, 1082
  Soviet Security Council draft
    resolution, 1011, 1016
  Suez Canal clearance and, 1039, 1155,
    1205, 1312

U.N. Emergency Force—Continued
  Tripartite heads of government meeting and, 1042-1043, 1110, 1117-1118
  Troop withdrawal and, 981, 1069, 1099, 1129, 1156, 1206
    British position, 1013, 1123-1125, 1132, 1143, 1176, 1206, 1232
    Egyptian position, 1157
    French position, 1012, 1033-1034, 1041, 1055, 1105, 1132
    Israeli position, 1059, 1095, 1159-1160, 1198, 1205, 1215-1217
  U.N. observers, 1031
  U.S. participation, 965, 975, 977, 979, 1028, 1034, 1050, 1070, 1102-1103
  Joint Chiefs of Staff planning, 999, 1002, 1031, 1035-1036
  U.S. position, 942, 947-948, 958, 1048, 1068-1070, 1082-1083, 1114, 1134, 1178-1179, 1275, 1322, 1334
Unden, Osten, 215, 338, 532, 537, 554
United Kingdom (see also British-French military intervention; British, British-French, Tripartite, United Kingdom, U.S., British, and Western subheadings under other subjects):
  Anglo-Jordanian Treaty, 1948, 620-621, 708, 722-725, 728-730, 733, 764, 768, 818, 846, 856, 904
  Economic situation, 1032, 1077, 1131, 1146, 1151, 1166, 1226
  France, relations with, 1257, 1263
  Political situation, 756, 1150-1153, 1162-1163, 1166, 1171, 1174-1175, 1182, 1210n, 1220-1223, 1226-1228, 1233, 1260, 1280, 1282
  Soviet Union, relations with, 42, 496, 694, 1003, 1005
  United States, relations with, 625-626, 636-637, 648-649, 671-673, 762, 792, 1220-1222, 1224, 1259-1262
  British-French military intervention and, 167, 389-390, 393, 436, 884, 906-907, 930, 1098
  British political situation and, 1151-1152, 1226-1228
  British position, 656-657, 665, 740, 770-771, 819-120, 1115, 1181, 1202, 1204, 1211
  British public opinion, 633, 1202-1203, 1218, 1282
  Canadian position, 941

United Kingdom—Continued
  United States, relations with—Continued
    Heads of government meeting, 764-765, 774-776, 781-782, 1040, 1042-1049, 1051-1052, 1056, 1061-1062, 1104-1107, 1110-1111, 1113, 1115-1119, 1152, 1180n, 1197
    Israeli military intervention and, 836
    Security Council appeal and, 633-635
    Troop withdrawal and, 1181, 1196-1197, 1201, 1204
  U.S. economic aid to (see also U.S. aid to Western Europe under Oil supplies), 908, 1012-1013, 1166-1167, 1169-1173, 1179, 1189, 1226-1227, 1240, 1280-1281
  U.S. military aid to, 176-178, 187, 266, 885, 911, 914, 918, 958-959
United Nations (see also Hungary; U.N. Emergency Force; General Assembly, Security Council, and U.N. subheadings under other subjects):
  Arab-Israeli dispute, 769, 1105
  British position, 1116, 1124, 1197, 1203
  Egyptian position, 1315
  Egyptian war damages resolution, 1336-1338
  Eisenhower-Nehru meeting proposal, 935-937
  French position, 1136, 1220n
  General Assembly Resolutions:
    377 (V) ("Uniting for Peace"), 882, 885, 887, 889
    997 (ES-I), 932-933, 946, 949, 981, 1126, 1190
    998 (ES-I) (Canadian), 957n, 959-960, 964, 976, 980-981, 986
    999 (ES-I) (Indian), 959-960, 963, 976, 978n, 980, 986, 1126
    1000 (ES-I), 980-981, 1011
    1001 (ES-I) (Seven-Power), 1053-1055
    1121 (XI), 1193
    1122 (XI) (Financing), 1205
  Israeli position, 1159, 1257
  Security Council appeal. See under Suez Canal Company nationalization.
  Security Council discussion proposal, post-invasion, 1059, 1105-1106
  French position, 1016n, 1035, 1041, 1055, 1105

United Nations—Continued
Security Council presidency, 582, 597-598
Security Council resolution, *Sept. 1, 1951* (Israeli shipping restrictions), 52, 93, 178-179, 422, 607, 732, 844, 1105, 1109
U.S. draft General Assembly resolutions, 907, 909-914, 916-917, 919
U.N. Truce Supervisory Organization (UNTSO), 20, 840, 963, 981, 1031, 1038, 1343
Universal Company of the Suez Maritime Canal. *See* Suez Canal Company.
Urrutia, Francisco, 978-979
Users' association proposal (*see also* Suez Canal dues), 351-352, 361-365, 370-372, 428-430, 434, 437, 439, 451-455
Arab reactions, possible, 474
Asian participation, 478, 514
British-French military intervention and, 484-485, 489, 513, 520, 543, 756-757
British-French public statements, 460, 470-473, 476-477, 481, 486, 589
British position, 374-375, 398, 400-401, 406, 409-410, 438, 440, 469-470, 480-481, 538, 1256, 1262, 1306
British public opinion, 484, 496-497
Constantinople Convention as basis of, 351-352, 361-363, 370-371, 374, 377, 392, 410-412, 451
Draft proposals, 519, 533-535, 537-538
Egypt, compensation for, 454, 457, 471, 477, 513-514, 679, 759
British position, 734-735
Egyptian canal blockage, possible, 470, 472, 478, 481, 483, 514, 575, 578, 584, 591, 737, 742
Egyptian position, 541
French position, 490, 496, 507, 568, 755
Egyptian cooperation with, 677-679, 690-691, 699, 706-707, 712, 719, 747
Egyptian participation, 410, 429-430, 454, 457, 626n
Egyptian position, 399, 491-493, 520, 527, 541, 545, 593, 677, 679, 706
Eighteen-Power proposal and, 429, 490
British position, 409, 531
France, U.S. consultation with, 441, 448, 450, 455-456

Users' association proposal—Continued
French position, 456, 480-482, 490, 496, 507-508, 534, 572, 586, 1256, 1258, 1262
Funds, 534
Future development financing, 755
Implementation strategy, 363-365, 393, 399, 428-429, 441, 448-449, 456
British position, 375, 419, 470
Inaugural meeting, 571-572, 602, 616-617, 623, 646, 700, 744
Indian position, 497
Italian position, 497, 529
Membership criteria, 453, 470, 478, 482, 514-515, 552, 557, 623, 646
Negotiations and, 1275-1276, 1322
British position, 752-753
Organization, 453-454, 529, 534, 617, 624
British position, 470, 534, 602-603
Pakistani position, 550, 569-570, 572-573, 590, 616, 623
Participants, 535, 545, 554-555, 590, 602, 616, 623
Pilots, 352, 363-364, 371-372, 428, 434, 456, 482-485, 488-489, 508, 529
British position, 450-451, 471-472
Egyptian position, 399, 677
Purpose of:
British position, 736-739, 751, 792, 1262
Egyptian position, 746
French position, 920, 1262
U.S. position, 736-737, 744, 747, 751, 757-758, 769
Sanctions, 693
Scandinavian position, 497, 545
Security Council appeal and, 363, 371, 411-413, 513, 517-518, 530, 549, 564, 577, 590, 711
British position, 476, 481, 484, 535, 553, 640-641
French position, 476, 481, 507, 531, 535, 553
Suez Canal Conference discussion, 531-532, 536-538, 553
Shareholders compensation, 450, 760
Six principles and, 1276
Spanish position, 517, 537-538, 545, 555
Suez Canal clearance and, 1275, 1289n, 1330
Suez Canal Company and, 534

Users' association proposal—Continued
  Suez Canal Conference declaration, 557-558
  Suez Canal Conference discussion of, 504, 511-513, 529-532, 535-538, 544-545, 552-555, 557-558
  Suez Committee position, 416
  Tripartite Foreign Ministers meeting (*see also* Suez Canal Conferences), 478, 481, 487, 492-493, 513-515
  U.N. role, 352, 371, 677
  U.S.-Egyptian discussions, 566-567, 570
  U.S. position, 1306
  U.S. public statements, 479-481, 486, 496-497, 555-556, 589

Vallat, Francis A., 38, 42n, 103n, 119n
Valls Carreras, Aurelio, 546
Venezuela, 171-172, 686, 873, 1051, 1071, 1130
Vered, Mme., 1253-1254
Vimont, Jacques, 411, 480, 507
Vyshinsky, Andrey Y., 159
Von Brentano, Heinrich, 215, 271
Vorys, John M., 188, 191, 193-196

Wadsworth, George E., 246, 273n, 287, 289-291, 296-297, 299-300, 344n, 616, 1200, 1212, 1271-1272
Wainhouse, David W., 335, 618n
Walmsley, Walter N., Jr., 789n, 895n, 1125n, 1337n, 1338n
Warren, Avra M., 602
Watkinson, Harold, 112n, 298
Watch Committee, 378-381, 488-489, 526, 543-544, 595-596, 629-630, 798n, 800
Watson, Adam, 658, 714, 751
Waugh, Samuel C., 628n, 682-683, 733n
Webb, Clifton, 532, 555
Weeks, Sinclair, 53-54, 917-918
Wentworth, Brig. Gen. Richard D., 826-827, 864, 1002
West Bank, 631-632
Western Europe (*see also* U.S. aid to Western Europe *under* Oil supplies):
  Soviet Union, relations with, 656
  Union proposals, 636-637, 656, 673
Western European Union Council, 309
Weygand, Gen. Maxime, 1297
Wheeler, Lt. Gen. Raymond A., 1175-1176, 1292, 1294, 1301-1303, 1307-1308, 1318

Whiplash, Operation, 523-524, 610-611
White, Lincoln, 929n, 988
White, Gen. Thomas D., 342-344
Whitman, Ann, 69, 403n, 405n, 434, 874n, 989n
Wilcox, Francis O., 319n, 322, 335, 365, 369n, 411, 413, 420-421, 564, 574, 577, 582-583, 598n, 600, 612n, 614, 618n, 639n, 1191n, 1195-1196, 1231n, 1276n, 1295n, 1329n
  Israeli military intervention, 885-886, 888-889, 1030-1031, 1055, 1249n
  Security Council discussion, 658, 678, 680, 714
  Troop withdrawal, 1054-1055
  U.N. Emergency Force, 1048
Wiley, Alexander, 169, 188, 194
Wilkins, Fraser, 144n, 185n, 197n, 198n, 202n, 335, 338n, 347n, 361n, 411n, 420, 467n, 500n, 504, 511n, 560, 562, 566n, 606, 608, 678n, 686n, 877n, 929n, 973n, 1021, 1100n, 1123n, 1191n, 1275n
  Arab-Israeli dispute, 620-622, 727
  Israeli military intervention, 343, 808, 821, 825, 829, 888, 891, 925, 927
  Suez Canal dues, 746
  Suez Committee, 342
  U.S. mobilization, 998-999
Wilson, Charles E., 117, 153, 171-174, 313, 523, 1128
  Egypt, U.S. policy toward, 1223
  Israeli military intervention, 833, 836, 838, 908, 910-912
  Oil supplies, 172, 874n, 974, 1073, 1075-1076, 1222, 1224
  Suez Canal clearance, 1225-1226
  U.S. mobilization, 864n, 886, 915
Wilson, Evan M., 212, 516, 552n
Wolf, Joseph J., 339n
Wormser, Felix E., 53, 873n
Wormser, Olivier B., 298
Wright, Adm. Jerauld, 844, 1035

Yassin, Shaik Yusuf, 246, 274, 287, 289, 296-297, 299-300, 303, 310-311, 347, 395
Yemen, 89, 963, 1053
Young, George, 658
Yugoslavia, 158, 323, 601, 638, 707, 719, 842, 882, 889, 895-897
  U.N. Emergency Force, 953, 1193, 1242, 1274

Zionist Committee, 499